Human Resource Management

Second Edition

TB: To my grandfather, Franklin Bauer, who first exposed me to a love of higher education. Spending time in his office at the UC Berkeley planted the seeds of what was possible when it comes to pursuing a lifetime of teaching and service. In addition, my husband, Horst, sons Nicholas and Xander, and my mother, JoAnn, have brought love, joy, and support to my life and I am eternally grateful for them.

BE: To my grandmother, Zeliha Erdogan, who instilled in me the importance of education, and my parents, Fulda and Ilhan Erdogan, who enabled and supported all my educational pursuits. Finally, I am grateful to my husband, Emre, and son, Devin, whose love and support make life so much fun and enriching.

DC: To my parents, Jim and Leanne; my siblings, Sam and Emma; and my partner, Hannah.

DT: For Chip.

Sara Miller McCune founded SAGE Publishing in 1965 to support the dissemination of usable knowledge and educate a global community. SAGE publishes more than 1000 journals and over 600 new books each year, spanning a wide range of subject areas. Our growing selection of library products includes archives, data, case studies and video. SAGE remains majority owned by our founder and after her lifetime will become owned by a charitable trust that secures the company's continued independence.

Los Angeles | London | New Delhi | Singapore | Washington DC | Melbourne

Human Resource Management

People, Data, and Analytics

Second Edition

Talya Bauer

Portland State University

Berrin Erdogan

Portland State University

University of Exeter

David Caughlin

California Polytechnic State University, San Luis Obispo

Donald Truxillo

University of Limerick

FOR INFORMATION:

2455 Teller Road
Thousand Oaks, California 91320
E-mail: order@sagepub.com

1 Oliver's Yard
55 City Road
London, EC1Y 1SP
United Kingdom

Unit No 323-333, Third Floor, F-Block
International Trade Tower
Nehru Place, New Delhi – 110 019
India

18 Cross Street #10-10/11/12
China Square Central
Singapore 048423

Printed in the United States of America

Library of Congress Control Number: 2023031501

ISBN: 978-1-0718-7685-5 (paperback)

Acquisitions Editor: Lauren Gobell

Content Development Editor: Darcy Scelsi

Production Editor: Tracy Buyan

Copy Editor: Colleen Brennan

Typesetter: diacriTech

Cover Designer: Scott Van Atta

Marketing Manager: Jennifer Haldeman

This book is printed on acid-free paper.

24 25 26 27 28 10 9 8 7 6 5 4 3 2 1

BRIEF CONTENTS

Preface   xxiii

Acknowledgments   xxxv

About the Authors   xxxix

PART I HRM IN CONTEXT   1

Chapter 1   Introduction to Human Resource Management   3

Chapter 2   Strategic HRM, Data-Informed Decision Making, and HR Analytics   27

Chapter 3   Data Management and Human Resource Information Systems   59

Chapter 4   Diversity, Equity, and Inclusion (DEI), and Equal Employment Laws   95

Chapter 5   The Analysis and Design of Work   131

PART II MANAGING THE TALENT LIFE CYCLE   163

Chapter 6   Workforce Planning and Recruitment   165

Chapter 7   Selection Processes and Procedures   195

Chapter 8   Training, Development, and Careers   231

Chapter 9   Performance Management   269

Chapter 10   Managing Employee Separations and Retention   303

PART III REWARD SYSTEMS   333

Chapter 11   Developing a Pay Structure   335

Chapter 12   Rewarding Performance   367

Chapter 13   Managing Benefits   397

PART IV SPECIAL TOPICS IN HR   429

Chapter 14   Employee and Labor Relations   431

Chapter 15   Employee Safety, Well-Being, and Wellness   459

Chapter 16   Opportunities and Challenges in International HRM   491

Appendix: 2022 SHRM Body of Applied Skills and Knowledge (BASK)   519

Glossary   523

Endnotes   533

Index   585

DETAILED CONTENTS

Preface   xxiii

Acknowledgments   xxxv

About the Authors   xxxix

PART I   HRM IN CONTEXT   1

Chapter 1   Introduction to Human Resource Management   3

     Valuing Employees: The Case of Costco Wholesale   4

     Case Discussion Questions   5

     Introduction   6

     What Is Human Resource Management?   6

        HRM Decision Making in Action   8

        How Do You Know If You Are Making a Good Decision?   9

     Why HRM Matters   10

        People Matter   10

        Organizational Culture Matters   11

           Types of Organizational Culture   11

        How HRM Affects Organizational Culture   11

     The Changing Context of HRM   12

        Changing Demographics   13

        Pandemic Work Impacts   14

        Increasing Globalization   14

        Data and Processing   15

        Gig Economy   16

        Ethical and Corporate Social Responsibility Challenges   17

     HRM as a Profession   17

        Who Is Involved in HRM?   17

           Top Management Teams and HRM   18

           HR Managers and HRM   18

           Line Managers and HRM 18

        HR Practitioners and HR Careers   18

           HR Business Partners and HRM   19

           What Do Employers Look for in HR Applicants?   19

           Salary and Job Outlook   20

        HR Competencies   20

           Staying Up to Date: Evidence-Based Management   21

     Chapter Summary   23

     Key Terms   23

     HR Reasoning and Decision-Making Exercises   24

     Data and Analytics Exercise: Correlation Does Not Equal Causation   25

Chapter 2   Strategic HRM, Data-Informed Decision Making, and HR Analytics   27

     Data Analytics and Artificial Intelligence as HR Tools: The Case of Stanley Black & Decker   28

     Case Discussion Questions   29

     Introduction   30

Defining Strategy   30

   Strategy Formulation: Developing and Refining a Strategy   30

     Create a Mission, Vision, and Set of Values   32

     Analyze Internal and External Environments   33

     Pick a Strategy Type   33

     Define Specific Objectives to Satisfy Stakeholders   34

     Finalize Strategy   34

   Strategy Implementation: Bringing a Strategy to Life   34

   Contributing to Your Organization's Strategy   35

Strategic HRM: Linking Strategy With HRM   35

   The Origins of Strategic HRM   35

     Organizational Performance and the Balanced Scorecard   37

   Identifying Best Practices   37

   Systems Thinking: Considering the System and Context   38

     How Does a System of HR Practices Influence Organizational Outcomes?   39

Strategic HRM, Data-Informed Decision Making, and HR Analytics   40

   Defining HR Analytics   42

   Identifying HR Analytics Competencies   43

   Understanding the Levels of HR Analytics   44

HR Analytics and the Scientific Process   45

   Step 1: Identifying the Problem   45

   Step 2: Doing Background Research   46

   Step 3: Forming a Hypothesis   46

   Step 4: Testing the Hypothesis via Experimentation   47

     Qualitative Versus Quantitative Data   47

     Big Data Versus Little Data   48

     Data Collection and Measurement   49

   Step 5: Analyzing the Data   49

     Qualitative Data Analysis   49

     Quantitative Data Analysis   49

     Biases in Model Building, Testing, and Interpretation   50

   Step 6: Communicating the Results   50

Ensuring HR Analytics Success   52

Chapter Summary   52

Key Terms   53

HR Reasoning and Decision-Making Exercises   53

Data and Analytics Exercise: Describing Your Data   55

Chapter 3   Data Management and Human Resource Information Systems   **59**

Analytics-Driven Decisions: The Case of JetBlue   60

Case Discussion Questions   61

Introduction   61

Managing Data   62

   Enterprise Resource Planning Systems   62

   Human Resource Information Systems (HRIS)   63

Opportunities for Data Management and HRIS   64

   Track the Employee Life Cycle   64

   The Value of Automated, Employee-Centered HR Functionality   66

   Data Availability for Metrics and Analytics   66

     Data Quality   67

     Data Structure and Storage   67

   Data Visualizations   68

Challenges for Data Management and HRIS   71
   Cost   72
   Traditional HR Skill Sets   72
   Data Privacy Concerns   72
     Recognizability of an Individual's Data   73
     Social Security Numbers   74
   Data Security Concerns   74
     Approaches for Maintaining Data Security   75

Developing a Human Resource Information System   77
   Step 1: Initial Assessment   77
   Step 2: Assessing Organizational Needs and Project Parameters 77
   Step 3: Evaluating Available Platforms   78
   Step 4: Designing the System   78
   Step 5: Choosing a Vendor   79

Implementing a Human Resource Information System   79
   Managing Resistance to Change   80
   Organizational Culture and Realistic Timelines for Change   81
     Refreezing and Maintaining the New System   82

Getting Technical: Core Information System Concepts   83
   Database Management   83
     Table   84
     Key Variable   84
     Form   85
     Query   86
     Report   86
   System Users   87
     Other Users   87
   System Architectures   88
     Traditional Tiered Architectures   88
     Cloud-Based Architectures   88

Chapter Summary   89
Key Terms   89
HR Reasoning and Decision-Making Exercises   89
Data and Analytics Exercise: Data Cleaning   91

Chapter 4   Diversity, Equity, and Inclusion (DEI), and Equal Employment Laws   95

Diversity, Equity, and Inclusion as a Business Priority: The Case of Accenture   96
Case Discussion Questions   97
Introduction   97
The Importance of DEI   98
   Why Is Effective Management of Diversity Important?   98
   Why Is DEI Still Challenging to Achieve?   99
     Similarity-Attraction   100
     Stereotypes and Unconscious Biases   100
     Microaggressions   101
An Overview of Equal Employment Opportunity Laws   101
   Equal Pay Act of 1963 (EPA)   103
Title VII of the Civil Rights Act   104
   What Is Discrimination Under Title VII?   104
     Disparate Treatment   105
     Disparate Impact   106
   Manager's Toolbox: Avoiding Illegal Interview Questions and Employment Practices   107
   Title VII and Harassment   108

Title VII and Special Considerations Regarding Sex Discrimination 110
Title VII, Race, and Color 110
Title VII and Religion 111
Title VII and National Origin 112
Additional Antidiscrimination Acts and Protections 113
Laws Protecting Pregnant Employees 113
Age Discrimination in Employment Act of 1967 (ADEA) 114
Americans with Disabilities Act (ADA) of 1990 115
Creating Inclusive Environments for Neurodiversity 116
Genetic Information Nondiscrimination Act (GINA) of 2008 117
Lilly Ledbetter Fair Pay Act of 2009 118
Protections for LGBTQ+ Workers 118
Laws Protecting Military Personnel and Veterans 119
Diversity and Inclusion in the Age of HR Analytics 120
Should Companies Use Affirmative Action? 120
How to Comply With EEO Regulations 121
Internal Complaint Mechanisms 121
DEI Initiatives 122
Big Data as a Pathway to Increasing Diversity and Inclusion 123
Internal Audits 123
Pay Audits 124
Big Data and Legal Compliance 124
Chapter Summary 126
Key Terms 126
HR Reasoning and Decision-Making Exercises 126
Data and Analytics Exercise: Using the Chi-Square Test to Assess Disparate Impact 128

Chapter 5   The Analysis and Design of Work 131
Redesigning Work: Office, Remote Work, or Blended 132
Case Discussion Questions 133
Introduction 133
The Analysis of Work and Its Critical Role in HR Practice 134
Technical Terms Used in Job Analysis and Competency Modeling 135
Manager's Toolbox: Some Basics of Job Descriptions 136
What Are the Purposes of Job Analysis? 137
Seeing the Big Picture: Work Flow Analysis 139
Collecting Job Analysis Data 140
Logistical Issues in Job Analysis 140
Preparing SMEs for Job Analysis 141
Specific Job Analysis Methods and Approaches 141
Task–KSAO Analysis 142
Develop an Initial List of Tasks and KSAOs 142
Document the Criticality of Tasks and KSAOs 143
Demonstrate That the KSAOs Are Linked to Critical Tasks 145
Critical Incidents Technique 147
Position Analysis Questionnaire 148
Occupational Information Network (O*NET) 148
Competency Modeling 149
Designing Jobs to Enhance Motivation, Attitudes, Well-Being, and Performance 151
Job Design Considerations 152
How Effective Are Job Design Considerations for Predicting Employee Outcomes? 154
Job Crafting 154
Flexible Work Arrangements 155
Contingent Employees 155

Chapter Summary 156

Key Terms 156

HR Reasoning and Decision-Making Exercises 157

Data and Analytics Exercise: Evaluating Task–KSAO Analysis Data 159

PART II   MANAGING THE TALENT LIFE CYCLE   163

Chapter 6   Workforce Planning and Recruitment   165

Creating a College Recruitment Pipeline: The Case of PwC 166

Case Discussion Questions 167

Introduction 168

Understanding the Labor Landscape: Workforce Planning and Forecasting 168

Workforce Planning 169

Succession Planning and Leadership Development 170

Labor Market Conditions 170

Workforce Labor Shortages 170

Workforce Labor Surpluses 171

Talent Analysis 171

The Recruiting Process 172

Why Recruitment Matters 172

Recruitment Strategy 173

Recruitment Objectives 173

Strategy Development 173

Recruitment Activities 173

The Role of Recruiters in the Recruitment Process 173

Stages of Recruitment 174

Generating Applicants 175

Applicant Quantity and Quality 175

Realistic Job Previews 175

Recruitment Sources 176

Unadvertised Jobs 176

Internal Recruiting Sources 177

External Recruitment Sources 178

Company Websites 178

Internal Transfers and Promotions 178

Internal Job Boards 178

Alumni Employees 179

Employee Referrals 179

Search Firms 179

University Relationships 180

Internship Programs 180

External Job Boards 181

Social Networking Sites 182

Employment Agencies 182

Freelance Employees 183

Walk-Ins 183

Hiring From Competitors 183

Recruiting for Diversity 184

Gender Diversity 184

Racial Diversity 185

Age Diversity 185

Veterans 185

Differently Abled Individuals 186

A Broader View of Workforce Planning and Recruitment   187

    Recruitment Results: Evaluating Effectiveness and Metrics   187

        Manager's Toolbox: Common Recruitment Key Performance Indicator (KPI) Metrics   188

    Generating Applicants   188

    Maintaining Applicant Participation   188

    Job Acceptance   188

    After New Employee Organizational Entry   189

    Maintaining Applicant Interest and Participation   189

        Treatment During Recruitment   189

        Interviews   189

        Site Visits   190

    Influencing Job Choice   190

        Organizational Image, Brand, and Reputation   190

        Organizational Fit   191

        Job Features   191

        Alternative Offers   191

Chapter Summary   191

Key Terms   192

HR Reasoning and Decision-Making Exercises   192

Data and Analytics Exercise: The Transition Matrix and Evaluating Movement Into, Through, and Out of an Organization   193

Chapter 7   Selection Processes and Procedures   **195**

Overcoming Discrimination in AI-Assisted Hiring: The Data and Trust Alliance   196

Case Discussion Questions   197

Introduction   198

Setting the Stage for Selection: Job Analysis, Recruitment, and Legal Issues   198

    Job Analysis   198

    Using Recruitment to Enhance Hiring Decisions   199

    Legal and Ethical Issues in Hiring   199

Data-Driven Criteria for Choosing Selection Procedures: Reliability, Validity, and Utility   201

    Ensuring the Quality of Selection Measures: Reliability and Validity   201

        Reliability   201

        Validity   202

        Analytics: Showing the Importance of Validity in Hiring Decisions   204

        Do Organizations Have to Do Their Own Validity Research?   206

    Selection Utility   206

Strategically Choosing and Combining Selection Procedures   207

Selection Procedures   208

    Interviews   210

        Unstructured Interviews   210

        Structured Interviews   211

        Manager's Toolbox: Best Practices: How to Add More Interview Structure   212

    Personality Tests   213

        Five Factor Model (FFM) or the "Big Five"   213

    Integrity Tests   215

    Cognitive Ability Tests   216

    Work Samples, Situational Judgment Tests (SJTs), and Assessment Centers   217

        Work Samples   217

        Situational Judgment Tests (SJTs)   217

        Assessment Centers   218

    Biographical Data and Related Methods   219

        Training and Experience Forms   219

        Biodata   219

Résumés 219
Using Résumés for Job Applications 220
References and Background Checks 220
Physical Ability Tests 221

Current Issues in Selection 222

Applicant Reactions to Selection Methods and Procedures 223

Deployment of Selection Procedures 225

Chapter Summary 226

Key Terms 226

HR Reasoning and Decision-Making Exercises 226

Data and Analytics Exercise: Weighting Predictors via Regression 229

Chapter 8   Training, Development, and Careers   231

Training to Support the Nation's Workforce: The Case of Google 232

Case Discussion Questions 233

Introduction 233

The Importance of Training in Organizations 234

Training Needs Assessment 235
Organizational Analysis 236
Organizational Goals and Strategies 236
Organizational Culture 236
Organizational Resources 237
External Environment 238
Job Analysis 238
Person Analysis 240
Identifying KSAOs and Candidates for Development 240
Trainee Demographics 240
Developing Training Goals 241

Enhancing Learning 241
Trainee Characteristics 242
Organizational Context: Enhancing Transfer 244
Training Delivery Characteristics 245

Training Methods 246
On-the-Job Training 247
Lectures 247
Simulators 248
Programmed Instruction 248
eLearning 249
Behavioral Modeling Training 249
Training for Specific Purposes 250
Diversity Training 250
Training to Increase Team Effectiveness 250
Training for Managers and Leaders 251
Contemporary Workplace Training Methods 251
Onboarding New Employees 252
Effective Organizational Onboarding 252
Manager's Toolbox: What Can Managers Do to Maximize Onboarding Success? 254
Effective Newcomer Onboarding Behaviors 254

Evaluating the Effectiveness of Training Programs 255
Measures of Training Effectiveness 256
Analyzing the Effects of Training on Training Criteria 258

Career Development and Management   261

    Career Management Activities   261

    Career Movements   262

    Which Key Factors Can Affect Careers?   262

Chapter Summary   262

Key Terms   263

HR Reasoning and Decision-Making Exercises   263

Data and Analytics Exercise: Evaluating a Training Program   266

Chapter 9   Performance Management   **269**

Transforming Performance Management at AstraZeneca   270

Case Discussion Questions   271

Introduction   271

What Is Performance Management?   272

    Objectives of Performance Appraisals   272

      Giving Employees Feedback   272

      Development and Problem Solving   273

      Decision Making   273

      Data Analytics   273

      Legal Purposes   274

    Challenges of Conducting Fair and Objective Performance Appraisals 274

      Performance Appraisals as a Measurement Tool   275

      Performance Ratings as Motivated Action   275

    Characteristics of Effective Performance Appraisal Systems   275

      Strategic Alignment   276

      Perceived Fairness   276

      Accuracy   276

      Practicality   277

Design Features of Performance Management Systems   277

    Determining the Purposes and Desired Outcomes of Performance Appraisals 278

    Defining Performance   279

      Trait Appraisals   279

      Behavioral Appraisals   280

      Results-Based Appraisals   280

      Goal Setting   281

      Electronic Monitoring   281

    Choosing the Rating Method   282

      Absolute Ratings   282

      Relative Rankings   283

      Qualitative Assessment   285

    Choosing the Source of Performance Information   286

      Managers   286

      Coworkers   286

      Direct Reports   287

      Customers   287

      Self-Assessment   288

      360-Degree Feedback   288

    Choosing the Ratee   289

    Deciding How Closely to Link Performance Ratings to Compensation 289

Conducting Fair Performance Reviews   290

    Factors Leading to Rating Errors   290

      Impression Management   290

      Stereotypes and Bias   291

Liking   291
    Rater Motivation   292

Improving the Effectiveness of Performance Management   292
    Training Managers and Employees   293
    Increasing Rater Accountability   293
    Having Raters Keep Records of Employee Performance   293
    Auditing the System   294
    Teaching Managers How to Be Good Coaches and Build Trust 294
    Manager's Toolbox: Feedback Delivery Best Practices   295
    Developing a Feedback Culture   295
    Establishing Performance Improvement Plans (PIP)   296

Chapter Summary   296

Key Terms   297

HR Reasoning and Decision-Making Exercises   297

Data and Analytics Exercise: Using Predictive Analytics to Understand Performance   299

Chapter 10 Managing Employee Separations and Retention   **303**

Understanding Workplace Interactions to Increase Employee Retention: The Case of
Humanyze   304

Case Discussion Questions   305

Introduction   305

Voluntary Turnover   306
    Costs of Voluntary Turnover   306
    Causes of Voluntary Turnover   308

Managing Employee Retention   310
    Gain Upper-Management Support   310
    Ensure That Pay, Benefits, and Working Conditions Are Competitive   310
    Leverage Engagement and Attitude Surveys   310
    Utilize Exit Interviews   312
    Hire for Fit   312
    Structure Onboarding Experiences   313
    Invest in High-Commitment HR Practices   313
    Focus on Turnover Predictors   314
    Learn How to Cope With Turnover   315
    Managing Relations With Former Employees   315
    Manager's Toolbox: Retaining Top Talent   316
    Retirements   316

Involuntary Turnover   318
    Dismissals   318
        Costs of Dismissals   318
        When to Dismiss an Employee   319
        The Legal Side of Dismissals   320
        The Dismissal Interview   320
        Explaining the Decision to the Team   321
    Layoffs   322
        Costs of Layoffs   322
        Benefits of Job Security   324
        Deciding Layoff Criteria   325
        The Legal Side of Layoffs   325
        Delivering the Message   326
        Severance Pay   328
        Outplacement Assistance   329
        Managing Survivors   329

Chapter Summary | 329
Key Terms | 330
HR Reasoning and Decision-Making Exercises | 330
Data and Analytics Exercise: How High Is Your Turnover? | 332

PART III   REWARD SYSTEMS | **333**
Chapter 11 Developing a Pay Structure | **335**

Location-Based Pay Reductions for Remote Workers | 336
Case Discussion Questions | 337
Introduction | 337
Pay as a Reward | 338
  Reward Systems | 338
  Relational Returns | 338
  Total Compensation | 339
Fairness of Rewards | 339
  Equity Theory | 339
    Manager's Toolbox: Restoring Employees' Perceptions of Equity | 341
  Organizational Justice Theory | 341
Developing a Pay Structure | 342
  Ensuring Internal Equity | 343
    Job Structure | 343
    Job Evaluation | 343
  Ensuring External Equity | 346
    Labor and Product Markets | 346
    Market Strategies | 347
    Market Reviews | 347
    Match Job Descriptions | 349
    Apply Aging Factor | 350
    Apply Survey Weights | 350
  Integrating Internal Equity and External Equity | 351
    Market Pay Line | 351
    Pay Policy Line | 352
    Pay Grades | 353
  Ensuring Individual Equity | 354
  Ensuring Legal Compliance | 355
    Fair Labor Standards Act | 355
    Overtime | 355
    Minimum Wage | 356
    Hours Worked and Recordkeeping | 356
    Executive Order 11246 | 357
    National Labor Relations Act | 357
    Internal Revenue Code | 357
Person-Based Pay Structures | 357
Executive Pay | 358
Pay Administration | 359
  Pay Compression and Inversion | 359
  Adherence to Pay Policies | 359
  Pay Transparency and Pay Secrecy | 360
Chapter Summary | 362
Key Terms | 362
HR Reasoning and Decision-Making Exercises | 363
Data and Analytics Exercise: Evaluating Pay Compression | 365

Chapter 12 Rewarding Performance   367

Performance Bonuses: The Case of Wall Street Investment Bankers and Traders   368

Case Discussion Questions   369

Introduction   370

Pay as a Motivator   370
    Understanding Motivation   370
        Extrinsic Motivation   372
        Intrinsic Motivation   372
        Motivation and Performance   372

Theories of Motivation   372
    Reinforcement Theory   372
    Expectancy Theory   373
        Manager's Toolbox: Evaluating Pay-for-Performance Programs Using Expectancy Theory   374
    Goal-Setting Theory   375

Strategy and Pay for Performance   376

Pay-for-Performance Programs   376
    Individual Pay-for-Performance Programs   377
        Merit Pay   377
        Bonuses   379
        Spot Awards   379
        Individual Incentives   379
        Sales Commissions   381
    Group Pay-for-Performance Programs   382
        Team Rewards   382
        Gainsharing   382
        Profit Sharing   383
        Employee Stock Ownership Plans   384

Challenges and Opportunities in Rewarding Performance   385
    Performance Measurement   385
    Incentive and Sorting Effects   387
    Labor Costs   388
    Unintended Behavioral Consequences   389
        Organizational Citizenship Behaviors   389
        Unethical Behaviors   390
        Effort and Cooperation   390

Chapter Summary   391

Key Terms   391

HR Reasoning and Decision-Making Exercises   391

Data and Analytics Exercise: Evaluating Compensation   394

Chapter 13 Managing Benefits   397

Providing Mental Health Benefits to Workers   398

Case Discussion Questions   400

Introduction   400

Benefits as Rewards   400

Legally Required Benefits   400
    Social Security   401
        Retirement Income   402
        Survivor Benefits   403
        Disability Income   403
        Medicare   403

Workers' Compensation   403
Unemployment Insurance   403
Family and Medical Leave   404
Additional Health Care Requirements   405

Voluntary Benefits   405
Health Care Programs   406
Medical Plans   406
Traditional-Care Plans   407
Managed-Care Plans   407
Health Savings Options   408
Dental and Vision Plans   409
Manager's Toolbox: Health Care Terminology and Concepts   409
Disability Insurance Programs   411
Retirement Programs   412
Defined-Benefit Plans   413
Defined-Contribution Plans   413
Individual Retirement Plans   415
Life Insurance Programs   415
Wellness Programs   416
Work–Life Programs   416
Payment for Time Not Worked   416
Compensatory Time Off   418
Child and Elder Care   418
Flextime and Remote Work   418
College Savings Plans   419
Educational-Assistance Programs   419
Legal-Services and Identity-Theft Benefits   419
Perquisites and Other Benefits   419

Administering Benefits Programs   420
Flexible Benefits Plans   420
Taxes and Accounting   421
Discrimination   421
Selecting Benefits   422

Communicating Benefits Programs   423

Chapter Summary   424

Key Terms   424

HR Reasoning and Decision-Making Exercises   424

Data and Analytics Exercise: Evaluating Employees' Satisfaction With Benefits   426

PART IV   SPECIAL TOPICS IN HR   429
Chapter 14 Employee and Labor Relations   431

The First Amazon Plant to Unionize: The Case of the JFK8 Amazon Fulfillment Center   432

Case Discussion Questions   433

Introduction   433

Factors Influencing Employee Relations   434
Culture   434
Fair Treatment and Voice   434
Working Conditions   435
Employment Laws   436
Unions   436

Organizational Policies and Procedures   436
Employee Handbooks   436
Examples of Types of Organizational Policies   437

Legally Required Information   437
Code of Conduct   437
Leave Policy   437
Appearance   437
Social Media   438

The Labor Movement   438
Reasons Employees Unionize   439
Job Dissatisfaction   439
Working Conditions   439
Employee Disengagement   440
Why Do Some Organizations Resist Unionization?   440
Profit Concerns   441
Decreased Autonomy   441
Unions and Laws   441
Norris-LaGuardia Act (1932)   441
National Labor Relations (or Wagner) Act (1935)   442
Labor Management Relations Act (1947)   442
Labor–Management Reporting and Disclosure Act (LMRDA) (1959)   442
Right-to-Work Laws   443
Trends in Union Membership   443
Union Membership in the United States   444
Global Unionization   444
Union Formation and Dissolution   445
Steps to Forming a Union   445
Decertifying Unions   447

The Collective Bargaining Process   447
Conflict Management Approaches   448
Negotiation Phase and Collective Bargaining Content   448
Phase 1: Investigation   449
Phase 2: BATNA Determination   449
Phase 3: Presentation   449
Phase 4: Bargaining and Content of a Labor Agreement   450
Phase 5: Closure   450

Failure to Reach an Agreement   450
Alternative Dispute Resolution   451
Mediation   451
Fact Finders   451
Arbitration   451
Strikes and Work Stoppages   451
Disputes and Grievances   452
Step 1: Inform   453
Step 2: Evaluate   453
Step 3: Escalation   453
Step 4: External Resolution   453

Chapter Summary   454

Key Terms   454

HR Reasoning and Decision-Making Exercises   454

Data and Analytics Exercise: Using Opinion Survey Data to Gauge Employee Satisfaction   456

Chapter 15 Employee Safety, Well-Being, and Wellness   **459**

Well-Being in the Medical Profession   460

Case Discussion Questions   461

Introduction   462

The Role of HRM in Worker Safety and Health   462
  The Case for Employee Well-Being   462
  The Legal Backdrop: Government Agencies and Resources   463

Workplace Safety   464
  Workplace Safety Outcomes and Their Antecedents   464
    Other Antecedents of Workplace Safety   467
  OSHA Regulations and Compliance   469
  Ergonomics and Office Design   470
  Cybersecurity   472

Workplace Stress   473
  Challenge and Hindrance Stressors   475
  Work–Life Balance   475
  Ways for Organizations to Reduce Stress   476
    Determine the Sources of Employee Stress   476
    Eliminate the Root Causes of Employee Stress Before Looking for Fixes   476
    Training Programs   476
    Encourage and Allow for Employee Recovery Experiences   476
    Consider How to Redesign Work and Work Areas to Fit Employee Needs   477
    Support the "Corporate Athlete"   477

Employee Wellness Programs   477
  Benefits of Wellness Programs   478
  Types of Wellness Programs   479
  Employee Assistance Programs (EAPs)   480
  Best Practices for Implementing Wellness Programs and the Role of HRM   481
    Manager's Toolbox: Tips for Implementing an Effective Wellness Program   482

Workplace Interventions: Solutions to Address Specific Well-Being Issues   483
  Improving Work–Life Balance   484
  Enhancing Safety Through Improved Leadership and Communication   484
  Addressing the Needs of Specific Occupations   484

Total Worker Health®: An Integrated Approach to Worker Well-Being   484

Chapter Summary   485

Key Terms   486

HR Reasoning and Decision-Making Exercises   486

Data and Analytics Exercise: Investigating Employee Stress   488

Chapter 16 Opportunities and Challenges in International HRM   491

Managing a Remote Workforce Around the Globe: The Case of Remote.com   492

Case Discussion Questions   493

Introduction   494

Global Transfer of HR Practices   494

Important Considerations When Transferring HR Practices Across Borders   496
  Legal Context   496
  Unionization Rates   497
  Cultural Differences   497
  Causes and Forms of Internationalization   499

Managing HR Globally   500
  Recruitment and Selection   500
  Motivating, Rewarding, and Managing Employees   501
  Employee Separations   502
  Handling of Personal Data   503

Management of Expatriates   503
  Benefits and Downsides of Using Expatriates   504

Expatriate Adjustment   504
  Spouse Adjustment   505
  Language Ability   505
  Manager's Toolbox: Being Effective in Global Teams   506
  Cultural Distance   506
  Expatriate Personality   507
  Job Characteristics   507
  Support   507
Preparing Expatriates for Assignments   508
  Selecting Expatriates   508
  Cultural Training   509
  Relocation Assistance   509
  Compensation   509
  Risk Management   510
  Special Considerations Relating to Women and LGBTQ+ Employees as Expatriates   511
  Repatriation   511
Alternatives to Long-Term Relocation Assignments   512
  Digital Nomads   513
Chapter Summary   514
Key Terms   514
HR Reasoning and Decision-Making Exercises   514
Data and Analytics Exercise: Managing Expatriates Using Data   516

Appendix: 2022 SHRM Body of Applied Skills and Knowledge (BASK)   **519**

Glossary   **523**

Endnotes   **533**

Index   **585**

PREFACE

Welcome to *Human Resource Management: People, Data, and Analytics*, Second Edition. We set out to write this book because we believe that human resource management (HRM) has the potential to be an essential business partner in making data-informed decisions within organizations. This was true in the first edition and the potential for HRM has never been greater than it is today as the employment landscape changes due to financial, social, physical, and technological pressures. However, that potential will be realized only if business students are well versed in how people, data, and analytics work together as legs of a three-legged stool. If we focus on only one or two legs, the stool tips over. But when each part is understood and functioning, the results are stable and powerful. As you will read throughout this book, fluency in people, data, and analytics involves asking the right questions, gathering the right data to address questions, choosing appropriate analyses, and interpreting and communicating findings in a meaningful way. Moreover, recognizing and addressing ethical and legal challenges are critical for success. Today, organizations that are able to manage people, data, and analytics effectively are positioned to leverage HRM to inform and support organizational strategy.

Thus, a unique feature of this book is a focus on how HRM is rapidly evolving into a vibrant and data-rich field while also making sure that students are well versed in the basics of HRM. The demand for data and analytic skills is growing. For example, the 2022 glassdoor.com Best Jobs in America lists data scientist as number 3, HR manager as number 13, and corporate recruiter as number 17 and 2023 LinkedIn.com Jobs on the Rise list places HR analytics manager as number 2, diversity and inclusion manager as number 3, employee experience manager as number 4, and chief people officer as number 15. As a result, business students will be well served if they understand HRM regardless of their intended major or work setting. This book is designed to help students leverage the principles of *people, data*, and *analytics* to focus on *leveraging data to inform decisions in business in general and HRM specifically*. With ongoing changes in HRM, we have observed that many of today's leading organizations use a people, data, and analytics approach to design and implement HRM systems and procedures aimed at recruiting, selecting, training, managing, developing, rewarding, and retaining talented people. We incorporate this approach through the use of several features throughout the book as well as data-informed, hands-on student experiences in every chapter. At the same time, all the time-honored HRM concepts are covered in depth for students studying all business functions, including HRM.

OUR APPROACH

We teach in classrooms around the world. This book grew from our passion for helping students succeed both in the classroom and in the workplace as well as helping businesses be effective and fair. Each of us is passionate about bridging science and practice, and we bring that into our classrooms every day. We believe that an important way to bring this to life is through the use of hands-on practice and learning. The virtuous cycle of "learn–do–reflect" is one that allows students to see immediate relevance to what they are learning, become excited about it, and want to learn more. Employers report the power of students who engage with material in such meaningful ways.

When it came to developing a textbook with a people, data, and analytics focus geared to helping students of HRM master concepts and skills, we knew that designing experiences such as exercises that would support faculty and engage students in applying HRM concepts regardless of their major was essential. Therefore, we developed end-of-the chapter HR Reasoning and Decision-Making Exercises that put the student in the decision-maker role and present them with opportunities to practice making HR-related decisions while considering relevant HR concepts. In addition, we created Data and Analytics Exercises. These appear at the end of each chapter with Excel Extensions. These activities show students how to analyze data in order to make high-quality decisions. Finally, there are special features, including chapter-opening cases and Spotlights on Data and Analytics, Legal Issues, and Ethics.

Our goal was to write about critical concepts in an accessible, compelling, and informative manner. We did this through three key approaches to the content of this book.

1. **An approachable writing style.** We carefully consider student perspectives, and we believe it is important that we make material accessible and engaging. We understand that some students have little or no work experience, others have work experience not related to HR, while others do have HR-related experience. Our goal is to appeal to all of these perspectives. We also recognize that some of those reading this book are doing so as part of their coursework for a career in HR, while others are not. What matters to us is that we communicate the importance of HR-related decisions for everyone within organizations by equipping students with the tools to make high-quality decisions.

2. **Examples, examples, and more examples.** Throughout the book, you will find examples of different types of organizations, individuals in different positions and levels within organizations, and examples of effective and ineffective HR decisions. All of these examples help attune readers to considerations, approaches to decision making, and best practices and help them avoid the mistakes made by some organizations. The examples bring material to life, make the material relevant, and help students learn from the experiences of other organizations.

3. **Evidence-based practices.** Like many areas of business, people who work in HR have traditionally made decisions based on a "gut feeling." While intuition can be an effective and efficient way to make low-stakes, moment-to-moment decisions, critical, high-stakes decisions informed by evidence and systematic problem solving help avoid failure. Evidence comes in different forms and from different sources, and our book reflects this. First and foremost, we review scholarly research to inform recommended practices and to understand and explain human behavior at work. Second, we showcase ways in which organizations have systematically analyzed and evaluated their own data to inform high-stakes HR decision making. Third, we provide opportunities for students to practice applying different approaches to collect, analyze, and interpret data.

WHAT MAKES OUR BOOK UNIQUE

When we set out to write this book, it was important that we didn't write just "another" HRM textbook. Rather, we wanted to write a book that is modern, approachable, and effective at communicating the importance of HRM. In doing so, we believed it should describe the effective and evidence-based approaches to HRM. At the same time, we wanted to create a textbook that helps students understand the importance of people, data, and analytics for supporting the HRM functions within organizations. We are proud of the result. For example, this textbook is the first to include an entire chapter on data management and HR information systems (Chapter 3). This is an important feature given the pivotal space that data occupy in today's business landscape. We believe that upon reading this textbook, you will appreciate the importance of this innovation. We also highlight key trends in the people, data, and analytics space, such as the importance of online privacy for individuals and organizations or the increasing use of machine learning and artificial intelligence (AI) in every aspect of HRM, including recruitment, selection, talent management, and learning and development. While we see great potential in the integration of people, data, and analytics, we also feel that it is imperative for students to understand that just because something is possible using the most sophisticated analytic techniques does not mean it is ethical or even legal. Thus, one of our major goals is to highlight areas where the promise and the reality of people, data, and analytics have also produced challenges and ethical dilemmas for individuals and organizations alike.

We take a contemporary approach to HRM and its role in business regardless of one's formal position, title, or functional area. As HRM evolves, we are observing emerging pathways that are moving HRM beyond being simply transactional, toward becoming more transformational and strategic in nature. People are the life force of most organizations, and thus attracting, motivating, and retaining the best people is crucial for organizational success. HRM is uniquely positioned to inform the systems, policies, and practices organizations use to manage their people.

As we lay out in the next section, we accomplish this throughout the book via several approaches, including hands-on data and analytics exercises, spotlight features on data and analytics, as well as content, exercises, case studies, and spotlight features on legal and ethical issues throughout the book.

TEXTBOOK FEATURES

In-Chapter Features

Each chapter includes features that stand alone and that also align with the Society for Human Resource Management's (SHRM's) nine competencies (depicted in italics below):

Source: Reprinted from *SHRM Competency Model* with permission of the Society for Human Resource Management (SHRM). © SHRM. All rights reserved.

- A vivid **opening case** focusing on key business and HR practices as well as the implications of data-informed decisions appears in every chapter to help students engage in *consultation, business acumen,* and *DEI* within a variety of organizations. Examples of companies featured in chapter-opening cases include Costco, Stanley Black & Decker, JetBlue, Accenture, Credit Karma, PwC, Google, AstraZeneca, Humanyze, Morgan Stanley, NerdWallet, Amazon, and Remote.com. Our goal was to highlight small, medium, and large organizations in a variety of industries and settings.

- The **Spotlight on Data and Analytics** (*business acumen, analytical aptitude,* and *consultation*) is a major feature of our book. HRM has become more focused on data. This feature offers real-world examples of how companies have collected and analyzed HR data to inform decision making, as well as explanations of key data and analytics terms, concepts, and tools. This also includes the ethical use of data in organizations. Example topics include using artificial intelligence ethically, using analytics to inform a diversity initiative, gamification of personnel selection procedures, managing workers using algorithms, using sentiment analysis to understand employee engagement, evaluating pay-for-performance programs using data, using metrics to track employee grievances, and gathering data using wearable technology in the workplace.

- The **Spotlight on Ethics** (*ethical practice*) provides a focus on ethical issues central to HR and organizational decisions. The number and complexity of these issues has led to more sophisticated analytics. We address issues around data privacy and security for employees and applicants, the implementation of "ban-the-box" laws, the management of employee layoffs, and ethical issues in multinational corporations. By taking the time to dive more deeply into these topics, you will see examples of both ethical and unethical situations and approaches to dealing with the large variety of challenges within the organizational landscape.

- The **Spotlight on Legal Issues** (*ethical practice* and *business acumen*) recognizes that HRM is influenced and shaped by laws. Specifically, legal issues around civil rights legislation have shaped today's approach to diversity management and elevated job analysis from a "nice to have" activity to a foundational legal underpinning of HRM, recruitment, and selection. These legal issues will continue to shape the HRM landscape. Such legislation also has implications for how individuals are trained, developed, managed, and rewarded; the benefits they receive; and how their labor rights are managed and protected; as well as their occupational safety and health. And it is impossible to do work globally without understanding the laws of the countries within which one does business, an issue that is addressed in our chapter on global HRM. Examples of topics covered in this spotlight feature include the legal issues associated with the use of artificial intelligence for employment decisions, gig workers, reasonable accommodations for workers with disabilities, age discrimination, wrongful termination, tattoos in the workplace, and pay discrimination. In each chapter, we highlight important legal issues such as these.

- The **Spotlight on Global Issues** (*global mindset*) feature provides glimpses into HRM from an international perspective. In each chapter, we highlight the way the topic discussed in that chapter may need to be modified, changed, and adapted to business in a global context. This may include how a specific practice would work when doing business overseas and how a specific HR decision may need to be adapted to a context in which there is cultural diversity. When designing selection, rewards, benefits, and performance management systems, companies need to make modifications for the different locales in which the systems will be utilized. We are aware that our readers may end up working in organizations that do significant international business, have cultural diversity, or enjoy a global career spanning across national boundaries. Therefore, we include discussions of cross-cultural research as it relates to HR, as well as the implications of globalization on the way that work is done. Our author team brings significant international research and practice experience and is involved in international efforts professionally, which results in our culturally sensitive focus to HRM.

- **Decision-Making Exercises** for each chapter put the student in the role of a decision maker. Each exercise describes a scenario and asks the student to make a decision that is fair and ethical, fosters healthy employer–employee relationships, and is evidence based. These exercises require students to read and understand the material discussed in each chapter but then also weigh the pros and cons of different alternatives to arrive at a decision that meets the needs of all stakeholders. We find this approach useful in our own teaching, and therefore we included both a mini-case study and a decision-making exercise at the end of each chapter (*consultation* and *leadership & navigation*).

- **Data and Analytics Exercises** for each chapter are also included for instructors to assign as they choose. These end-of-chapter activities provide illustrations and applications of how data can be used to answer a question relevant to the chapter content. The feature in the textbook can also be paired with lifelike data available to instructors in the Excel Extensions should they be interested in having students analyze the data to answer the question. Done individually or in teams, this allows students to engage in *relationship management, leadership and navigation*, and *consultation* for organizational decision makers identified in the exercises. Example exercises cover techniques like describing data using descriptive statistics and data visualizations, using regression to understand performance, determining the amount of turnover using metrics, and evaluating a merit pay program using data visualizations (*analytical aptitude*).

- **Excel Extensions** for each chapter are included for instructors to assign as they choose. They offer hands-on opportunities for students to practice using data analytics in Microsoft Excel to inform decision making. These activities extend the Data and Analytics Exercises (*analytical aptitude* and *consultation*).

- **Summaries** and **Key Terms** serve to help students master the critical terminology with ease. Learning the vocabulary of HR is important to be able to communicate with other HR professionals more efficiently and to access the most up-to-date materials on a particular topic more easily.

Content and Organization

Part I: HRM in Context opens with an introduction of HRM and its relevance for all business segments (not just for those interested in HRM as a profession), how data and analytics allow for strategic decisions within HRM, an overview of the legal context and ethical issues around HRM and analytics, a discussion of HRM in the context of diversity, followed by coverage of job analysis and design as important tools for the remainder of HR practices.

Chapter 1, "Introduction to Human Resource Management," describes what HRM is; why it is foundational to business success; how it is changing due to larger changes and trends, such as changing demographics; the emergence of the gig economy, globalization, technology, and the availability of data; as well as ethical codes for HRM.

Chapter 2, "Strategic HRM, Data-Informed Decision Making, and HR Analytics," defines strategy, describes how strategic HRM has evolved and explains how HR analytics can be used to inform and support both HRM strategy and organizational strategy. It also examines the importance of the scientific process in HR analytics and explains how organizations can successfully leverage HR analytics.

Chapter 3, "Data Management and Human Resource Information Systems," describes key aspects of data management, opportunities and challenges for human resource information systems (HRIS), and keys to successful HRIS implementation. It also introduces the basics of information systems and technical aspects of developing an HRIS. All of this is critical to understanding how to address integrated questions utilizing a people, data, and analytics approach.

Chapter 4, "Diversity, Equity, and Inclusion (DEI), and Equal Employment Laws," describes the challenges and benefits of managing diversity effectively, presents an overview of equal employment opportunity laws, and identifies ways in which organizations may comply with the law and help create an inclusive workplace.

Chapter 5, "The Analysis and Design of Work," explains the importance of analyzing work for effective HR practice and introduces different types of job analysis and competency modeling practices. It also explains how to effectively design jobs to increase workers' motivation, performance, and well-being.

Part II: Managing the Talent Life Cycle covers the core employee life cycle functions of HRM (employee recruitment and selection, training, career development, performance management, and management of employee exit).

Chapter 6, "Workforce Planning and Recruitment," highlights the importance of workforce planning to maintain appropriate employment levels and understand and engage in effective recruitment practices. It also explains the role of internal and external recruitment sources, recruiting for diversity, maintaining applicant interest, and influencing ultimate job choice.

Chapter 7, "Selection Processes and Procedures," explains the key role of employee selection in organizational effectiveness, including the concepts of reliability and validity and how to enhance the financial value of hiring procedures. It also covers how to choose the most effective hiring procedures; newly emerging selection procedures and issues (e.g., the use of AI in selection); the role of HR analytics; legal, ethical, and global issues in selection; and how to enhance the job applicant's experience.

Chapter 8, "Training, Development, and Career," describes current best practices in the delivery of training in organizations. This includes conducting an effective training needs assessment, enhancing training effectiveness, key training methods and media available to employers, and how to evaluate training effectiveness. It also describes processes for effective career development and management.

Chapter 9, "Performance Management," differentiates between performance management and appraisal, introduces different ways of measuring performance, and explains how to give feedback to employees as well as how to create a feedback culture.

Chapter 10, "Managing Employee Separations and Retention," discusses the costs of voluntary and involuntary turnover in organizations, describes ways in which organizations can manage different types of turnover, and highlights best practices for managing employee separations in a way that is ethical, fair, and supportive of organizational objectives.

Part III: Reward Systems covers key areas of HRM policy including pay structures, pay-for-performance programs, and benefits.

Chapter 11, "Developing a Pay Structure," describes pay as a type of reward, discusses the importance of the fairness of rewards, and explains how to develop an equitable pay structure. It also describes person-based pay structures and challenges associated with compensating executives and examines the challenges and opportunities associated with pay administration.

Chapter 12, "Rewarding Performance," describes how pay can be used to motivate employees, discusses the importance of aligning organizational strategy with pay-for-performance programs, describes common pay-for-performance programs, and describes the challenges and opportunities organizations face when rewarding performance using pay.

Chapter 13, "Managing Benefits," examines employee benefits as a type of reward, reviewing legally required benefits associated with Social Security, workers' compensation, unemployment insurance, family and medical leave, and other required health care benefits. It discusses voluntary benefits associated with health care insurance, disability insurance, retirement insurance, life insurance, wellness and work–life programs, and perks. It also describes the ways in which benefits programs are administered and communicated.

Part IV: Special Topics in HR covers the topics of managing HRM in a unionized context, managing the health and safety of workers, and managing global HRM.

Chapter 14, "Employee and Labor Relations," explains what employee relations are and the factors that influence them, including culture, fair treatment, and working conditions. This chapter also outlines organizational policies and procedures, the labor movement, the collective bargaining process, and what happens if disputes are not resolved.

Chapter 15, "Employee Safety, Well-Being, and Wellness," describes the importance of employee well-being in organizations and the role of regulatory agencies. The chapter also describes the main safety outcomes measured by organizations, the concept of safety promotion, the variety of wellness programs and well-being interventions available to employers, mental health at work, and the role of an integrated Total Worker Health® approach to employee well-being.

Chapter 16, "Opportunities and Challenges in International HRM," explains the benefits and downsides of standardizing HR practices in a firm operating in multiple countries and discusses best practices in expatriate management and international mobility.

NEW TO THIS EDITION

- You will find new chapter-opening cases in this edition. You can find the first edition chapter-opening cases in the Instructor's Manual.

- The revised and expanded SHRM Body of Applied Skills and Knowledge (2022) has been integrated throughout the text with new associated figures, definitions, and examples.

- The Manager's Toolbox content has been integrated into discussions in the reading and is no longer a boxed feature within the text.

- Spotlights on Small and Medium-Sized Businesses are no longer boxed within the text but can be found in the Instructor's Materials.

Chapter 1

- New chapter-opening case on Costco

- Adjusted content areas for improved flow and comprehension. Introducing new heading levels and reorganization of content sections

- Updated content and trends overall

- Updated content and trends related to the Covid-19 pandemic

- Updated SHRM competency model (new and revised in 2022)

- Merged technology and data availability into access to data and processing power

- Added learning objective

- Updated flow of chapter organization

- Updated statistics throughout

- Updated references as relevant

- Updated figures as relevant

- Updated photos as relevant

- Updated examples throughout as relevant

Chapter 2

- New chapter-opening case on Stanley Black & Decker

- Updated discussion of organizational performance and the balanced scorecard

- Replaced Spotlight on Data & Analytics with new case on ethics of AI

- Replaced Spotlight on Legal Issues with one focused on bias and new regulation around AI in the United States of America

- Added artificial intelligence as a definition

- Updated flow of chapter organization

- Updated statistics throughout

- Updated references as relevant

- Updated figures as relevant

- Updated photos as relevant

- Updated examples throughout as relevant

Chapter 3

- New chapter-opening case on JetBlue

- Added latest research on reactions to technology

- Added discussion of the Great Resignation

- Added discussion of AI and machine learning

- Updated flow of chapter organization

- Updated statistics throughout

- Updated references as relevant

- Updated figures as relevant

- Updated photos as relevant

- Updated examples throughout as relevant

Chapter 4

- New chapter-opening case on Accenture

- Heavily revised chapter

- Fully revamped discussion on the importance of DEI for businesses, discussing the moral and business cases for diversity

- Added discussion of microaggression, the Pregnant Worker Fairness Act, neurodiversity, protections for veterans and active duty military personnel, bystander training

- Updated coverage of LGBTQ+ workers in light of recent supreme court decisions

- Added discussion of emerging laws relating to the use of AI

- Updated flow of chapter organization

- Updated statistics throughout

- Updated references as relevant

- Updated figures as relevant

- Updated photos as relevant

- Updated examples throughout as relevant

Chapter 5

- New chapter-opening case on redesigning work post-pandemic
- Updated SHRM competency model (new and revised in 2022)
- Updated Spotlight on Ethics
- Updated Spotlight on Global Issues
- Revamped and expanded upon discussion of job crafting
- Updated and expanded discussion of remote work
- Updated flow of chapter organization
- Updated statistics throughout
- Updated references as relevant
- Updated figures as relevant
- Updated photos as relevant
- Updated examples throughout as relevant

Chapter 6

- Updated chapter-opening case on PwC
- Added discussions related to the impact of the pandemic on the workforce and workforce conditions
- Added discussion of AI and machine learning
- Updated flow of chapter organization
- Updated statistics throughout
- Updated references as relevant
- Updated figures as relevant
- Updated photos as relevant
- Updated examples throughout as relevant

Chapter 7

- New chapter-opening case on The Data and Trust Alliance
- Added discussion of the impact of AI
- Added discussion of video interviews
- Current issues heavily updated, covering topics such as social media and DEI practices
- Updated flow of chapter organization
- Updated statistics throughout
- Updated references as relevant
- Updated figures as relevant
- Updated photos as relevant
- Updated examples throughout as relevant

Chapter 8

- New chapter-opening case on Google
- Added discussion of informal field-based learning
- Includes discussion of virtual reality–based training
- Expanded discussion of diversity training as well as issues related to sexual harassment
- Expanded discussion on career development and management
- Updated flow of chapter organization
- Updated statistics throughout
- Updated references as relevant
- Updated figures as relevant
- Updated photos as relevant
- Updated examples throughout as relevant

Chapter 9

- New chapter-opening case on AstraZeneca
- Added discussion of electronic monitoring, and management by algorithms
- Revamped discussion of stereotypes and bias pertaining to rater error
- Updated flow of chapter organization
- Updated statistics throughout
- Updated references as relevant
- Updated figures as relevant
- Updated photos as relevant
- Updated examples throughout as relevant

Chapter 10

- New chapter-opening case on Humanyze
- More currency in examples discussed, reflecting the Great Resignation and labor shortages
- Revamping of discussion of pay, benefits, and working conditions
- Updated flow of chapter organization
- Updated statistics throughout
- Updated references as relevant
- Updated figures as relevant
- Updated photos as relevant
- Updated examples throughout as relevant

Chapter 11

- New chapter-opening case on location-based pay reductions
- New Spotlight on Legal Issues on equal pay for men's and women's national soccer teams

- New Spotlight on Ethics on equitable pay
- Updated flow of chapter organization
- Updated statistics throughout
- Updated references as relevant
- Updated figures as relevant
- Updated photos as relevant
- Updated examples throughout as relevant

Chapter 12

- New chapter-opening case on performance bonuses
- Added new Spotlight on Legal Issues on pay transparency
- Updated flow of chapter organization
- Updated statistics throughout
- Updated references as relevant
- Updated figures as relevant
- Updated photos as relevant
- Updated examples throughout as relevant

Chapter 13

- New chapter-opening case on providing mental health benefits to workers
- Added discussion of unlimited paid time off
- Added discussion of mental health days
- Updated flow of chapter organization
- Updated statistics throughout
- Updated references as relevant
- Updated figures as relevant
- Updated photos as relevant
- Updated examples throughout as relevant

Chapter 14

- New chapter-opening case on Amazon
- Additional Key Terms added
- Updated non-right-to-work state list adding Michigan and Missouri
- Updated flow of chapter organization
- Updated statistics throughout
- Updated references as relevant
- Updated figures as relevant
- Updated photos as relevant
- Updated examples throughout as relevant

Chapter 15

- New chapter-opening case on medical doctor burnout
- Revamped discussion of stress and stressors
- Updated material throughout regarding latest developing research on stress
- Updated material related to interventions and on Total Worker Health®
- Updated government stats and similar stats throughout the chapter
- Added completely new section on mental health at work
- Add references to COVID and post-pandemic issues on health and stress throughout
- Updated flow of chapter organization
- Updated statistics throughout
- Updated references as relevant
- Updated figures as relevant
- Updated photos as relevant
- Updated examples throughout as relevant

Chapter 16

- New chapter-opening case on Remote.com
- Added the implications of GDPR for management of a global workforce
- Added Covid-19-related information on risk management
- New section on digital nomads and employer of record
- Updated flow of chapter organization
- Updated statistics throughout
- Updated references as relevant
- Updated figures as relevant
- Updated photos as relevant
- Updated examples throughout as relevant

ACKNOWLEDGMENTS

The authors would like to thank the following people who supported this book both personally and professionally. We offer our heartfelt thanks to Maggie Stanley, Associate Director, College Editorial who saw and shared in our vision to launch the project with Sage. We are also grateful to Lauren Gobell, our acquisitions editor, and Darcy Scelsi, our development editor, for their ongoing support to help us bring our vision to fruition in the second edition of this book. It was a pleasure to continue to work with you both. We would also like to thank our copy editor, Colleen Brennan, and our cover designer, Scott Van Atta. Tracy Buyan, our production editor, did a fantastic job bringing our book to life and keeping us on schedule throughout the process. We also send sincere thanks to Jennifer Haldeman, our product marketing manager, and Melissa Yokell, our product marketing specialist. They helped champion this textbook and communicate our people, data, and analytics HRM approach. This talented Sage team worked with us to develop compelling content and experiential exercises to help faculty teach the material and, more importantly, to help students learn to engage in HRM from a strategic and analytic perspective regardless of their position within the organization.

We give special thanks to Alex Alonso (SHRM-SCP, Chief Knowledge Officer) and Nancy Woolever (SHRM-SCP, VP, Certification) at SHRM for the invaluable resources they provide to individuals and organizations to engage in effective HR practices. As the world's largest and leading organization for human resources, SHRM provides thought leadership, certification, community, and advocacy for the effectiveness and practice of organizations and HR individuals and functions. Throughout this book, we drew upon SHRM's guidance and competencies to outline the key HR practices and approaches to cover across the 16 chapters of this book. Content for this textbook was mapped onto the new 2022 SHRM Body of Applied Skills and Knowledge (BASK) under the supervision of Nancy Woolever. This appears in the appendix as well as our online supplement.

No textbook acknowledgment is complete without recognizing the significant role that instructor feedback and reviews play in developing a vibrant, responsive, and useful book that helps faculty teach and helps students learn key concepts and develop their skills in applying what they learn. With this in mind, we offer special thanks to the following reviewers for their expertise, insights, questions, and suggestions throughout the development of each chapter of this book as well as the themes.

The authors and Sage would like to thank the following instructors who participated in reviews and market development for this book:

Reviewers of the Second Edition
Brian Bartel, Mid-State Technical College
Angela D. Boston, The University of North Texas Dallas
Hyeran Choi, Columbus State University
Benjamin Dean, the Citadel
Jane Haley, Longwood University
Greg Hardt, Xavier University
Choi Hyeran, Columbus State University
Eileen Kearney, Montgomery County Community College
Joel Koopman, Texas A&M University
Joyce LeMay, Bethel University
Laxmikant Manroop, Eastern Michigan University

Doreen Matthes, Kent State University
Kate McCombs, Tennessee Tech University
Alex Rubenstein, University of Central Florida
Tom See, CSUB

Reviewers of the First Edition
Susan Flannery Adams, Sonoma State University
Joann Adeogun, Point University
Devi Akella, Albany State University
Ron Alexandrowich, York University
Lisa M. Amoroso, Dominican University
Stephanie Bae, East Carolina University
Stacy Ball, Southwest Minnesota State University

Rimjhim Banerjee, Santa Fe College

Linda Barrenchea, University of Nevada, Reno

Robyn Berkley, Southern Illinois University, Edwardsville

Mike Bojanski, Methodist College

Emmanuele Bowles, Florida International University

Yvonne Brinson, Union University

Ronald Brownie, Northern State University

Otha Carlton Hawkins, Alamance Community College

Brian Cawley, Calvin College

Hyeran Choi, Columbus State University

Gwendolyn M. Combs, University of Nebraska Lincoln

Joseph Cooper, University of Toledo

Cody Cox, St. Mary's University

Stan Dale, University of LaVerne

Diana L. Deadrick, Old Dominion University

Caitlin A. Demsky, Oakland University

Karen Ehrhart, San Diego State University

Allison Ellis, California Polytechnic University, San Luis Obispo

John Fazio, Marieta College

Diane D. Galbraith, Slippery Rock University

Bruce Gillies, California Lutheran University

Deborah Good, University of Pittsburgh

Patricia Greer, University of Denver

Sheri Grotrian, Peru State College

Bruce L. Haller, Molloy College

Robert W. Halliman, Austin Peay State University

Robert Hanks, Portland State University

Jeffrey Hefel, Saint Mary's University of Minnesota

Heidi Helgren, Delta College

Terrill C. Herring, Lindenwood University

Michael W. Hill, University of Georgia

Kevin J. Hurt, Columbus State University

Patricia A. Ippoliti, Rutgers University

Sayeedul Islam, Farmingdale State College

Kathleen Jones, University of North Dakota

Jie Ke, Jackson State University

Chris Krull, Indiana University–Purdue University Indianapolis

Jeffrey D. Kudisch, University of Maryland College Park

Ann Langlois, Palm Beach Atlantic University

Julia Levashina, Kent State University

Waheeda Lillevik, The College of New Jersey

Kurt Loess, East Tennessee State University

Erin E. Makarius, University of Akron

Elizabeth Malatestinic, Indiana University

Gery Markova, Wichita State University

Lowell Matthews, Southern New Hampshire University

Randy McCamey, Tarleton State University

Jalane Meloun, Barry University

Ian Mercer, Auburn University

Mark S. Miller, Carthage College

Edwin Mourino, Rollins College

Steven Nichols, Metropolitan Community College

Lisa Nieman, Indiana Wesleyan University

Victor Oladapo, Webster University

Candice A. Osterfeld Ottobre, University of Akron

Deborah Powell, University of Guelph

Norma Raiff, Chatham University

Anushri Rawat, Eastern Michigan University

Kendra Reed, Loyola University of New Orleans

Kate Rowbotham, Queen's University

Lou L. Sabina, Stetson University

Terry J. Schindler, University of Indianapolis

Lewis Schlossinger, Fordham University

Tom See, California State University, Bakersfield

Joseph Simon, Casper College

Lauren Simon, University of Arkansas

Shamira Soren Malekar, City University of New York–Borough of Manhattan Community College

Alicia Stachowski, University of Wisconsin, Stout

Heather Staples, Texas A&M University

Steven Stovall, Southeast Missouri State University

Gary Stroud, Franklin University

Kyra Leigh Sutton, Rutgers University

Charmaine Tener, Thompson Rivers University

Neal F. Thomason, Columbus State University

Justice Tillman, Baruch College

Lee J. Tyner, University of Central Oklahoma

Stephen H. Wagner, Governor's State University

Carlotta S. Walker, Lansing Community
   College
Stacy Wassell, Frostburg State University
Brian D. Webster, Ball State University

Joseph R. Weintraub, Babson College
Don Wlodarski, Roosevelt University
Benjamin B. Yumol, Claflin University

Finally, we would like to offer special thanks to the thousands of students we have taught over the years. Each one of you has made us better teachers and scholars.
   Thank you!

ABOUT THE AUTHORS

Talya Bauer, PhD

Gerry & Marilyn Cameron Endowed Professor of Management

Talya Bauer earned her PhD in business with an emphasis in organizational behavior and human resources from Purdue University. She is an award-winning teacher, including being awarded the Innovation in Teaching Award from the HR Division of the Academy of Management. She teaches HR analytics, introduction to HRM, training and development, organizational behavior, and negotiations courses and has also been recognized by the Society for Industrial and Organizational Psychology (SIOP) with the Distinguished Teaching Award. She conducts research about HR and relationships at work. More specifically, she works in research areas across the employee life cycle, including recruitment and selection, new employee onboarding, and coworker and leader relationships. This work has resulted in dozens of journal publications, book chapters, and research grants, including from NSF and NIH. She has acted as a consultant for government, Fortune 1,000, and start-up organizations. She has been quoted and her work covered in the *New York Times, Harvard Business Review, Wall Street Journal, Fortune*, the *Washington Post, Business Week, Talent Management, USA Today*, as well as appearing on NPR's *All Things Considered*. Previously, she worked as a computer consultant and as a trainer in California, Idaho, Oregon, and Hong Kong. She has been a visiting professor in France, Italy, Spain, and at Google, Inc. Talya is involved in professional organizations and conferences at the national level, such as serving on the Human Resource Management Executive Committee of the Academy of Management and as SIOP president. She has received several Society for Human Resource Management (SHRM) research grants and authored SHRM's "Onboarding New Employees: Maximizing Success" and coauthored SHRM's "Applicant Reactions to Selection: HR's Best Practices" white papers. She is an associate editor for the *Journal of Applied Psychology*, the former editor of *Journal of Management*, and on the editorial boards for *Personnel Psychology, Journal of Management*, and *Industrial and Organizational Psychology: Perspectives on Science and Practices*. She has coauthored multiple textbooks, including *Organizational Behavior, Principles of Management*, and *Psychology and Work:Introduction to Industrial and Organizational Psychology*. She is a fellow of SIOP, APA, APS, and IAAP.

Berrin Erdogan, PhD

Express Employment Professionals Professor of Management

Berrin Erdogan completed her PhD in human resource management at the University of Illinois, Chicago, and her BS degree in business administration at Bogazici University, Istanbul, Turkey. Prior to her graduate studies, she worked as a corporate trainer at a private bank. She teaches human resource management, performance management and compensation, and global human resource management at undergraduate and graduate levels. Her research on the flow of people into and out of organizations focuses on applicant reactions to employee selection systems, newcomer onboarding, manager–employee relationships and skill utilization, and employee retention. Her studies have been conducted in a variety of industries, including manufacturing, clothing and food retail, banking, health care, education, and information technology in the United States, United Kingdom, Turkey, Spain, India, China, France, Germany, and Vietnam. Her more than 70 articles and book chapters have appeared in journals such as *Academy of Management Journal, Journal of Applied Psychology, Journal of Management, Personnel Psychology*, and *Human Resource Management*

and have been discussed in media outlets, including the *New York Times, Harvard Business Review, Wall Street Journal, BBC Capital*, and the *Oregonian*. In addition, she is coauthor of the textbooks *Organizational Behavior, Psychology and Work:Introduction to Industrial and Organizational Psychology*, and *Principles of Management*. Berrin served as an associate editor for *Personnel Psychology* and *European Journal of Work and Organizational Psychology* and is a former editor in chief of *Personnel Psychology*. She is a fellow of SIOP and APS. She has been a visiting scholar and has given invited talks at universities in Australia, Canada, Colombia, Greece, Singapore, Spain, Turkey, the United Kingdom, and the United States.

David Caughlin, PhD

Assistant Professor of Organizational Behavior

David Caughlin earned his master's degree in industrial and organizational psychology from Indiana University Purdue University–Indianapolis and his PhD in industrial/organizational psychology with concentrations in quantitative methodology and occupational health psychology from Portland State University. He is an assistant professor of organizational behavior at California Polytechnic State University, San Luis Obispo. He has taught undergraduate and graduate courses related to human resource management (HRM) and data analytics, such as introduction to HRM, reward systems and performance management, HR information systems, HR analytics, storytelling with data, organizational behavior, organizational psychology, practical statistical skills in psychology, and research methods in psychology. In his HR analytics courses, David teaches students how to use the programming languages like R to manage, analyze, and visualize HR data to improve high-stakes decision making; in the process, students build their data literacy and develop valuable critical thinking and reasoning skills. While working for the School of Business at Portland State University, David was recognized twice with the Teaching Innovation Award and twice with the "Extra Mile" Teaching Excellence Award. David conducts research on topics related to supervisor support, employee change, and occupational safety and health. He has worked with a variety of organizations in various industries on projects related to employee engagement, job analysis, selection, performance management, compensation, organizational culture, mistreatment prevention, and employee survey development. His research has been published in academic journals such as *Journal of Applied Psychology, Journal of Management, Human Resource Management, Journal of Business & Psychology*, and *Journal of Occupational Health Psychology*.

Donald Truxillo, PhD

Professor of Work and Employment Studies

Donald Truxillo earned his PhD from Louisiana State University. He is a professor at the Kemmy Business School, University of Limerick, Ireland, and Professor Emeritus at Portland State University. Previously, he worked in the areas of selection, employee development, and promotions in the public sector as an industrial psychologist and as a professor in the industrial/organizational psychology program at Portland State University. He studies the methods employers use to hire workers and the experiences of job applicants during recruitment and hiring. In addition, Donald examines issues related to workplace safety and health as well as age differences at work. He served as associate editor for the *Journal of Management* and is currently an associate editor at *Work, Aging and Retirement*. He is a member of nine editorial boards, including *Journal of Applied Psychology, Personnel Psychology*, and *Human Resource Management Review*. He is the author of more than 100 peer-reviewed journal articles and book chapters. Donald is the recipient of SIOP's 2017 Distinguished Teaching Contributions Award and a coauthor of the textbook *Psychology and Work:Introduction to Industrial and Organizational Psychology*. His research has been supported by the SHRM Foundation, the National Institute of Occupational Safety and Health (NIOSH), and the National Science Foundation (NSF), most recently to study privacy and security issues associated with online hiring. He has taught courses in human resource management, training and development, research methods, and industrial psychology. He has received three Fulbright grants to study abroad and has visited at universities in Italy, Portugal, Spain, Switzerland, Ireland, and Germany. Since 2010, he has been a member of the Doctoral Training Committee, Department of Psychological Science and Education, University of Trento, Italy. He is a fellow of SIOP, APA, APS, and IAAP.

HRM IN CONTEXT

1 INTRODUCTION TO HUMAN RESOURCE MANAGEMENT

VALUING EMPLOYEES: THE CASE OF COSTCO WHOLESALE[1]

Costco co-founder (and former CEO) James Sinegal is pictured in one of the company's stores in New York.

Photo by Pat Greenhouse/The Boston Globe via Getty Images

Costco opened in 1976 with one store in San Diego and grew from zero to $3 billion in sales within six years. It currently operates over 825 locations, boasts over 111 million membership-card holders, and has annual sales over $196 billion globally. This makes them the fifth largest retailer worldwide. It is not an overstatement to say that Costco transformed the retail world. It credits its success to three key qualities:

1. A commitment to quality

2. An entrepreneurial spirit

3. A strong employee focus

While it's one thing for the company to say it has "created a workplace culture that attracts positive, high-energy, talented employees," it's another to have others note such things. For example, "People matter here" was written by a Costco employee and posted to glassdoor.

com, a website that allows current and former employees to anonymously post kudos and critiques about companies. Costco is known as a desirable employer, in part, because of its strong human resource policies. For example, 50% of U.S.-based Costco employees earn more than $25 per hour (with a minimum of $16 per hour), compared to employees in other retail environments, where $10.50 is closer to the average hourly pay; and 65% higher than their biggest competitor, Sam's Club, which is owned by Walmart. Beyond that, Costco also covers 90% of health insurance expenses for both full-time and part-time employees, which is rare. Costco is also described as having a casual culture with strong job security, having managers who take employee development to heart, and providing many opportunities to learn and grow. Finally, the company is known to take its mission statement seriously and follow its Code of Conduct.

So, why does Costco make these huge investments in its nearly 300,000 people? James Sinegal, former CEO of Costco, is quoted as saying, "When employees are happy, they are your very best ambassadors." Although HR at Costco is not directly run by its CEO, you can imagine how such a strong set of values at the executive level influences all HR practices at Costco. Beyond Costco's stated appreciation of employees, Costco engages in many HR practices that indicate that the organization values its employees. For example, they promote from within. They encourage and listen to employee suggestions. They give managers authority to experiment with activities helpful to increasing sales and/or reducing costs (as long as the products are never marked up more than 15%). The effectiveness of such practices is among the reasons that Sinegal was named one of the 100 Most Influential People in Business Ethics. As a founder and CEO, he made a big profit for the company while putting people first, so it is hard to argue with his success. Although Costco pays considerably more than the industry average, including bonuses and other incentives, its revenues and stock price continue to grow. In fact, the value of Costco stock from 1985 until Sinegal's retirement in 2012 increased by 5,000%. It seems to be an investment that pays off well for the company. For example, estimates are that Costco employees generated twice the revenue of Sam's Club employees; their turnover rate is 5% after employees have worked at Costco for one year, which is extremely low for the retail industry; and their "shrinkage" (an indicator of employee theft) rate is one of the lowest in the industry.

A true test of a company's culture and HR practices rests on its ability to maintain its values even during changes in leadership. Costco has fared well on this dimension. The next CEO, W. Craig Jelinek, has continued this trend since taking over in 2012. Jelinek joined Costco in 1984 (the first club opened in 1983), so he was not a newcomer to the organization. Today, Costco is thriving, its stock price is at a record high, and Jelinek was named CEO of the Year by CNN.

CASE DISCUSSION QUESTIONS

1. Costco has grown a great deal since its founding in 1976. How do you think growth has influenced its HR practices beyond what is mentioned in this case? Please share specific insights.

2. James Sinegal, Costco co-founder, made a strong case for HR being foundational for organizational success. Do you agree with this position? Why or why not?

3. Why do you think James Sinegal kept his CEO salary at a modest level? Do you think this is a good decision in terms of HR? Does it matter that Craig Jelinek has not followed suit? Why or why not?

4. Do you consider Costco's policy of offering such high pay and employee benefits a waste of money or a wise investment? Why? Be prepared to defend your response.

INTRODUCTION

This textbook provides an introduction to the field of human resource management (HRM). This includes what HRM is, the evolving context and landscape of HRM, important best practices, and issues and controversies associated with HRM today. The first chapter of this book gives you an overview of what HRM is and why it is important. The world of HRM is changing in new and innovative ways. Much like the Industrial Revolution of the mid-1800s, where machines changed the way manufacturing work was done, we are currently in the midst of a *knowledge revolution*. Never before in history has it been easier to access information, connect globally, and manage a workforce remotely. We discuss the implications of this recent shift in this chapter, and it is integrated throughout the book. Chapter 2 specifically addresses how this knowledge revolution has created exciting opportunities for HRM to become invaluable within organizations in a variety of ways, including informing managers with best practices and data to aid decision making throughout the organization. As valued business partners, HRM specialists and generalists can span the range of activities from following procedures to creating and testing hypotheses regarding the most effective ways to manage employees. There is a lot to learn, so let us get started with addressing the basic question of what HRM is exactly, who is involved, and where HRM is located within organizations.

WHAT IS HUMAN RESOURCE MANAGEMENT?

LEARNING OBJECTIVE
1.1   Define human resource management (HRM).

Human resource management (HRM) is defined as the constellation of decisions and actions associated with managing individuals throughout the employee life cycle to maximize employee and organizational effectiveness. HRM relates to all aspects of organizational life.

HRM is prevalent in the world around us and is a subject you probably have experienced without knowing it. For example, if you have ever filled out a job application or been interviewed for a job, you have been exposed to a major function within HRM called *selection*. Even if you have never applied for a job, you have still interacted with thousands of people who have. Every teacher you have had in the classroom and every customer service interaction you have encountered was the result of HRM in some way or another: Teachers and customer service specialists are hired, trained, paid, and managed via their organization's HRM system. Interactions such as these may have given you some preconceived notions of what HRM is all about. This is a great thing because it means you can jump right in and start participating and discussing the material. But we suspect, as you progress through this book, you will also find yourself seeing the strategic value of HRM practices and why HRM is a key factor in organizational success regardless of the area of business you intend to focus on in your own career. That is why we set out to write this book.

HRM includes functions that range from analyzing and designing jobs; managing diversity and complying with local, national, and global employee laws; recruiting individuals to apply for jobs; selecting individuals to join organizations; training and developing people while they are employed; helping to manage their performance; rewarding and compensating employees for their performance while maintaining healthy labor relations and helping to keep them safe; as well as managing their exit, or departure, from the organization.

HRM is about making decisions about people. This decision-making process involves many questions that those within an organization must ask and answer. Over time, the answers may change as the

If you have ever applied for a job and had an interview, you have experienced HRM in action.

©iStock.com/dragana991

firm experiences growth or decline, external factors change, or the organizational culture evolves. For example, those involved in HRM need to address questions such as these:

- What type of employees do we need to hire?

- Where will we find the best and most diverse employees?

- How do we manage diversity to maximize its benefits and minimize group conflicts?

- How should we select the people who will join our company?

- How can we help them be safe and experience well-being at work?

- How should we motivate and reward employees to be effective, innovative, and loyal?

- What benefits would our employees find the most attractive?

- What training do our employees need, and how can we further develop them?

- How can we help to ensure employment relations between employees and managers remain healthy and include healthy feedback and voice from both sides?

- What can we do to ensure that employees engage in ethical decision making and behaviors?

- What do we need to do to remain competitive locally and globally?

- Why are employees leaving, and what can we learn from their exits?

All of these questions and more are part of managing the HRM system of decisions and actions associated with managing individuals throughout the employee life cycle (see Figure 1.1), from the hiring stage through the exit of an employee (due to voluntary or involuntary turnover) and everything in between.

FIGURE 1.1 ■ The Employee Life Cycle

HRM Decision Making in Action

Viewing HRM from a decision-making perspective has important implications for the success of employees and organizations. Let's take a look at how decision making with HRM systems can help overcome biases—types of favoritism or prejudice—that can be inherent in organizational decisions. Evidence indicates that individuals have biases, often unconscious, when engaging in decision making. Each of these biases represents a shortcut to making decisions. Based on years of experience, each of us has developed the ability to sort through copious amounts of information to arrive at decisions. Some are small, and we hardly ever give them a thought, but those can be dangerous decisions because biases such as availability, anchoring, or confirmation can influence the outcome unconsciously. Other choices, such as whether to hire one of three candidates, also have consequences.

For example, consider the availability bias, which is our tendency to rely more on information that is readily available to us, leading us to discount alternative information. To the degree that the information relating to the job candidates is subjective, such as when interviews are used, our past experiences will influence us to a greater degree, and bias can creep into the process. The bias might be subtle, such as your recollection that the last employee you hired from State University has done a great job. This might lead you to lean toward the one candidate on your short list from this same school. But is this a reasonable thing, given that State University graduates 8,000 students per year and the other two candidates graduated from schools from which your company has employed dozens of successful candidates? It probably is not. To avoid this as well as the other types of biases, take concrete steps, including recognizing that such biases exist; seeing the other side of your argument, including others in the decision making; assigning a devil's advocate (someone who challenges assumptions and ideas); and considering the consequences of an HRM decision. In other words, one of the functions of HRM is to design systems that prevent systemic biases from exerting undue influence over decision making, resulting in better decisions.

Anchoring bias, the tendency to rely too much on the first piece of information given, can be just as dangerous, as your decision can be influenced simply by the way others present information.

Overconfidence bias, the tendency to seek confirmation of one's own beliefs or expectations, can shortcut the exploration of a full range of options. All of these biases can hurt the quality of decisions made. A critical aspect of HRM is managing key aspects of decision making throughout the entire employee life cycle.

How Do You Know If You Are Making a Good Decision?

Making big decisions is not easy. Research shows that only about 50% of all decisions made within organizations are successful.[2] However, to help you understand whether a particular decision has the hallmarks of success, it makes sense to consider the following key characteristics. Doing so won't guarantee success, but it can help you develop more robust decision-making criteria that help to meet the needs of the entire organization rather than just solving a problem today that may create a larger problem tomorrow.

Ask yourself these questions:

- *Is this course of action legal? Is it ethical? Is it fair?* Legality is a good first step, but it is not enough. How would you feel if your course of action were shared on a major news outlet? If the answer is "not so great," that's an indication the course of action you are considering may be legal but may not be ethical or fair.

- *Is this decision based on evidence and data?* While decisions should not be made solely based on prior evidence and relevant data, they should consider both and try to leverage what is possible to know to rule out alternative courses of action.

- *Will pursuing this course of action help to make the organization healthier?* It is easy to make decisions and pursue courses of action in isolation from the larger organization. However, doing so can create problems. Stopping to consider whether you are doing something that is likely to help or hinder positive employee–employer relations is helpful in avoiding problems down the line.

- *Is this course of action time and resource efficient?* If the course of action you are considering is not time or resource efficient, it is not likely to be sustainable over time. This can lead to resource constraints, including employee energy and burnout as well as financial constraints.

- *Does this course of action take a systematic perspective and consider various stakeholders?* You might have all the information necessary to make a good decision. But you might not. And even if you do have the relevant information, including stakeholders in the decision-making process is a helpful way of securing acceptance of a decision. Thus, skipping this step will most likely lead to less effective decisions in the long run.

Another important implication for approaching HRM as a set of decision-making activities is to address the core issue of what makes a good decision. Figure 1.2 details the hallmarks of a good decision.

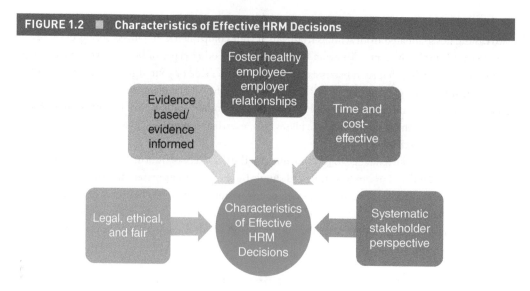

FIGURE 1.2 ■ Characteristics of Effective HRM Decisions

WHY HRM MATTERS

You might be taking this class because it is required at your school even if you are not an HRM major. Regardless of your major, HR is valuable for you and your career. Knowing about HR policies and practices is important because as a manager or future manager, you will be required to make employee-related decisions. You might be involved in recruiting and hiring employees, and in fact, you will be on the front line of the hiring process. You may play an important role in managing the performance of employees and allocating rewards. You may need to discipline employees or manage their exit. Your decisions, actions, and inactions will be used to assess compliance with the law. Therefore, much of the information included in this book is relevant as you build your managerial skills. For any HR practice to be implemented effectively, HR and line managers need to be partners. This involves each party understanding the rationale behind each practice, line managers remaining true to the spirit of the system in place and giving feedback to HR, and HR departments designing systems that meet the needs of line managers. Moreover, if you end up working in an area outside of HR, such as accounting or marketing, you will still be a consumer of the HR systems and services available at your organization. For example, your department may require a new training program, and thus, it will be essential to partner with the HR department to design and implement the new training program. As such, it is important to understand how HR systems and services work. In short, even if you don't have an interest in working in HR, learning about HRM will be a good investment of your time.

People Matter

It is well documented that the individuals who work within an organization matter when it comes to what an organization is like as a place to work and what it is able to do. Individuals influence its culture, informal rules, how hard employees work, how they should treat one another, how much risk employees should take, as well as what is considered acceptable in terms of performance and ethics. Influence happens through who is attracted to join the organization, who is selected to join the organization, and who decides to remain or leave the organization. This is called the A-S-A framework, standing for attraction-selection-attrition in organizations. In other words, organizations vary in terms of the human capital they have access to based on whom they attract, hire, and retain. *Human capital* refers to the collection of knowledge, skills, and abilities, as well as other characteristics (KSAOs) embodied in the organization's people. Human capital might refer to the KSAOs of a handful of people when a company is starting out to thousands of employees if the organization grows. Clearly, human capital needs change over time as well. When companies are starting out, they might not have a formal HRM department. However, as they grow, the decision to shift toward less outsourcing of HRM and more in-house HRM functions is a strategic HRM decision that must be made.

Richard Branson, founder of the Virgin Group, famously said, "Take care of your employees, and they'll take care of your business."[3] He argues that creating a great place to work involves a work climate where people are appreciated, engaged in their work, productive, and thriving rather than simply surviving. The numbers are dramatic in terms of the bottom line as organizations with engaged employees have 23% higher profitability, 18% higher productivity, and 43% lower turnover than organizations with less engaged employees. In fact, it is estimated to the global economy loses trillions each year due to low engagement.[4] Organizations increasingly understand that treating individuals isn't just about "being nice" to them; it's a win-win, as those employees who feel valued also tend to be more engaged and productive. Reading what employees say about the *Fortune* 100 Best Companies to Work For such as Costco, you start to notice a trend. They really value their people.[5] And we know that organizations that value their employees are more profitable than those that do not.[6]

If employing people who are valued, highly supported, and engaged at work promotes company success, why don't all organizations create such cultures? That is a great question. The answer is complex, but reasons include not understanding or believing the connection between organizational culture and success and not knowing how to create this connection.

Organizational Culture Matters

Organizational culture refers to shared, "taken-for-granted" assumptions that members of an organization have that affect the way they act, think, and perceive their environment.[7] Because of this, organizational culture influences how decisions are made within organizations, and it is also influenced by those decisions. For example, if being polite is highly valued within an organization, the approach taken when giving performance feedback would be much different than in an organization that values directness. During the Covid-19 pandemic, many organizations were challenged to maintain their organizational cultures as some individuals began working remotely and others faced physical and emotional challenges on the job. Such changes challenged established norms and ways of relating to one another at work. In fact, over 4.5 million Americans quit their jobs in November 2021.[8] This indicates how important cultures can be in creating a sense of stability within organizations.

Types of Organizational Culture

One popular typology of organizational cultures, called the competing values framework, characterizes them by their emphasis on collaboration, creating, controlling, or competing (see Figure 1.3).[9] In the competing values framework, clan cultures are collaboration oriented and are characterized by valuing cohesiveness, being people oriented, being team players, and empowering employees. Based on our understanding of Costco from the opening case, it appears to be consistent with a clan culture. Other examples of organizations that can be seen as having clan cultures are Southwest Airlines Company and SAS Institute. Adhocracy cultures focus on creating and emphasize being entrepreneurial, being flexible, taking risks, and being creative. Examples of adhocracy cultures are 3M, Google, and Facebook. Market cultures are characterized by competition and value being aggressive, competitive, and customer oriented. Examples of companies showing signs of a market culture are Amazon, Intel, and Netflix. Hierarchy cultures focus on controlling and value being efficient, timely, and consistent. Organizations such as Walmart and Boeing are examples of this type of culture.

How HRM Affects Organizational Culture

There is no one type of culture that leads to success and happy employees. The examples given for different cultures are all successful businesses in their industries. However, it is important to remember that there is a close connection between company culture and HR practices adopted, and in turn, the HR practices adopted will influence and shape the culture into the future. Company HR practices are often a reflection of company culture. For example, as an early adopter of gamified recruiting

FIGURE 1.3 ■ Types of Organizational Culture

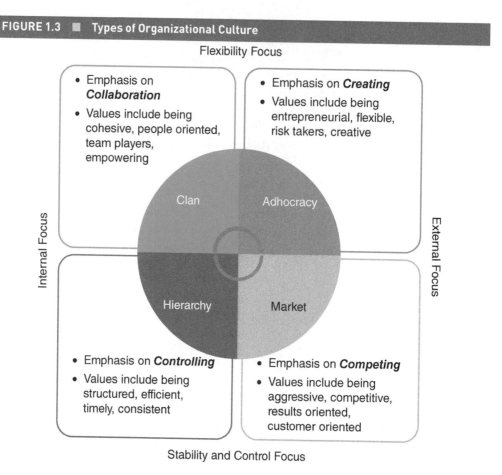

and selection processes, Marriott developed an online recruiting platform called "My Marriott Hotel." During this experience candidates manage different areas of the hotel's operations and lose or gain points for customer satisfaction and profitability. Such a recruitment tool reflects the company's values, such as being results and customer oriented.[10] You would not expect to see such a system in place in a company that emphasizes efficient and cost-effective hiring to fill specific positions.

Similarly, the HR practices in use will shape a company's culture. For example, imagine a company that adopts a performance review system that involves ranking employees on a bell curve and distributing rewards accordingly, such as Microsoft did for years. Requiring managers to compare employees with each other will shape the culture of the company toward a market culture, as survival in such a system will require competition among employees. Under new, more collaborative leadership, Microsoft shifted gears in 2013 and the culture has evolved since then.[11] Therefore, effective HR decisions will need to consider the implications of every decision for the culture the company has and the culture the company would like to have.

THE CHANGING CONTEXT OF HRM

LEARNING OBJECTIVE

1.3   Explain the developing role of analytics and technology's impact on the changing context of HRM.

Human resource management does not exist in a vacuum. Companies have gone from personnel departments exclusively using paper forms and tracking benefits to HR becoming a digitally transformed strategic partner in organizational decisions. Because of this, as the world and the fundamental characteristics of work continue to evolve, so must human resource management. This section outlines a number of these important changes in the contextual landscape that have major implications for HRM. These include changing demographics, pandemic work impacts, increased globalization, the availability of data and processing power, the emergence of the gig economy, and the ongoing and rising importance of ethics and corporate social responsibility (Figure 1.4).

FIGURE 1.4 ■ The Changing Context of HRM

Forces shaping human resource management continue to evolve.

©iStockphoto.com/PeopleImages; ©iStockphoto.com/ablokhin; ©iStockphoto.com/Blue Planet Studio; ©iStockphoto.com/NicoElNino; ©iStock-photo.com/designer491; ©iStockphoto.com/RapidEye

---

Changing Demographics

One of the largest impacts on HRM is that of the increasingly changing demographics of individuals in the United States and around the world. Changes include the aging population and increasing diversity. Given how prevalent this topic is, you are probably aware that the American workforce is aging. By 2030, 20% or more of those in the United States are projected to be aged 65 or older, which is more than double the percentage in 1970.[12] This represents a major shift in the working population, as nearly 73 million baby boomers (those born between 1946 and 1964) are expected to retire in the next 20 years, with only 46 million new workers from later generations joining the organizational ranks. The Covid-19 pandemic resulted in early retirements, with more than 3 million workers retiring early, further leading a shortage of qualified workers for many positions.[13]

Whereas the aging workforce is a key demographic shift, increasing diversity in the workplace is also an aspect of the changing demographic landscape, which has implications for HRM. For example, race is an area where we still see challenges with equal pay for equal work. Research finds that ethnic subgroups experience both an earnings gap and a glass ceiling. In 2021, for every dollar a male employee made, women made 92 cents. However, this also varies by industry, organizational level, and race. For example, Asian American women made almost as much as Asian American males did.[14] In 2022, a record number of Black Fortune 500 CEOs were leading six companies (Compass Inc., International Flavors and Fragrances, Lowe's, TIAA, Qurate Retail, and Walgreens).[15]

Such core changes in who is available to work has major implications for how to recruit, select, train, reward, and manage the workforce. Given that HRM is responsible for these functions, being aware of the changes as well as their associated challenges and opportunities is essential for organizations to remain competitive.

Pandemic Work Impacts

The first confirmed case of Covid-19 emerged in 2019, and the World Health Organization declared Covid-19 a pandemic in March 2020. The pandemic took a heavy toll on the world's citizens, claiming 6 million lives worldwide with nearly 1 million of those lost in the United States alone by 2022.[16] It also had profound effects on what work was needed, the workplace, and how work gets done. For some workers, it was possible (and often required) to shift to remote work. Gallup estimates that nearly 45% of employees in the United States worked remotely at least part of the time in 2021.[17] This allowed them great flexibility in terms of where they could live and afforded time savings from not commuting. It also allowed working parents an opportunity to be at home while their children were attending classes remotely. While the stress related to balancing such work–family challenges was acute for many, the case was made that remote work and remote workers can be effective.[18] And, it is unclear for many industries if remote work will ever go away. Indeed, employers such as Twitter, Facebook, and Shopify allow remote work. In fact, Shopify stated, "Office centricity is over."[19] Further, Gallup reports that of those workers who were able to work remotely, nearly 90% say they'd like to continue their ability to work at home post-pandemic. However, for other workers, especially frontline workers, the pandemic brought a great deal of additional stress in the form of unreasonable and sometimes violent customers, health and safety concerns, and long hours covering staffing shortages. Inequities among different types of work, as well as unfair and unpleasant work environments, led to what has been termed the "Great Resignation," where an average of 3.9 million U.S.-based workers quit their jobs in 2021.[20] While the reasons noted differ, there is no denying that the world of work has been altered post-Covid-19 pandemic. In the future, remote work, a focus on the employee experience, and the need to address work inequities will continue to be major issues for organizations and society as a whole.

Increasing Globalization

U.S.-based businesses recognize the importance of international business and international presence. India and China are the fastest growing economies, each of them being home to around 18% of the world's population. Major U.S. businesses have strategically placed themselves to benefit from a big portion of their revenues coming from overseas. For example, Intel receives 74%-82% of its revenue from overseas in 2021 and 2022.[21] And, several iconic "American," everyday brands are non–U.S. owned: Budweiser (Belgian-Brazilian-owned), 7-Eleven (Japanese-owned), Holiday Inn (UK-owned), and T-Mobile (German-owned). Globalization of business introduces a number of HRM challenges. Businesses recruit and hire employees from a more diverse pool of applicants given the realities of global mobility of potential employees. Businesses will need to consider the local laws and regulations in the different operations they run. It is also important to consider the role of cultural differences in the use of different HRM practices around the world. It is tempting to transport best practices developed in corporate headquarters, but such efforts, without sensitivity to the local culture, are often doomed to fail. As a result, in companies operating worldwide, effective HRM takes into account local differences in local laws and norms to create an effective global organization.

SPOTLIGHT ON GLOBAL ISSUES: LABOR LAWS DIVERGE GLOBALLY

A key aspect to global HRM success is to recognize that beyond cultural differences, different countries have fundamentally different approaches to work that may be instituted into labor laws. For example, France is a country known for having strong protections for workers. Within France, the workweek is limited to 35 hours, and employees have the "right to disconnect," or have the right to hours during which they are not required to check or answer e-mail. Further, in 2021, France unanimously voted for gender quotas for executive leadership. In Sweden, while legislation requires boards of directors to have at least 40% of board seats filled by women, it is strongly encouraged that they strive for gender balance. Another example is the General Data Protection Regulation (GDPR), which took effect in 2018 and mandates that the European Union's (EU's) 500 million citizens have specific data privacy rights and that companies with a presence in the EU must adhere to the rules or face stiff fines. These are just a few examples of how fundamental HRM policies may differ in terms of defining the workweek, contact outside of working hours, how data may be collected and reported, and the composition of governing entities. Thus, organizations interested in working on a global scale need to pay close attention to HRM and develop their own strategic plan for addressing both organizational and national rules, guidelines, and policies.[22]

Data and Processing

It may seem like everyone is talking about big data. We discuss this in greater detail in the next two chapters, but for now, it is helpful to know that *big data* refers to data that are large in volume, variety, and velocity. Technology has allowed for greater and greater computing power, and the Internet has generated so much data that during 2020, on average, 1.7MB of data was created every second by every person.[23] Every second, there are over 6,000 tweets, nearly 1,100 Instagram photos uploaded, over 2,000 Tumblr posts, 6,500 Skype calls, over 100,000 Google search queries, 94,000 YouTube videos viewed, and 3.1 million e-mails sent. Most recently, over 300 million Zoom meetings take place each day. These numbers continue to grow over time.[24] That's a lot of data. In addition, companies often gather annual opinion surveys, biometrics, as well as other employment data from millions of workers each year. As more and more transactions, communications, and shopping move online, more information is available each day. Thus, over 70% of business executives are investing, or plan to invest, in analytics related to big data, but most say they have not yet achieved what they called "broad, positive impact."[25]

In the past, vast amounts of data were actually a hindrance to analysis and could overwhelm those trying to see meta-trends. However, with rapidly evolving technology driving down the cost, processing power has become increasingly accessible. This increasing rate of processing power has accelerated technology's impact on HRM processes and procedures. As you will see throughout this book—and especially in Chapter 3—technology matters a great deal when it comes to HRM.

This book explicitly focuses on the importance of data in making effective HRM decisions. We offer examples and insights throughout the book as well as special features to help you become more familiar and more effective at thinking about and leveraging the availability of data and effectively utilizing processing power. Chapters 2 and 3 include much more depth on data and analytics. But for now, knowing that technology and big data are major trends that affect HRM throughout the world are the key points we want you to take away from this section.

SPOTLIGHT ON DATA AND ANALYTICS: DESCRIPTIVE, PREDICTIVE, AND PRESCRIPTIVE ANALYTICS

A survey of business leaders conducted by Deloitte found that concerns exist regarding the gap between the perceived need for data-driven approaches to HR and the existing skill base. Of the companies surveyed, 85% reported a belief that HR analytics is important, but just 42% reported a belief that their own organization is strong in this area.[26] A SHRM Foundation report on analytics found that two key skills are lacking: analytics skills and the ability to present findings in a convincing way to senior executives.[27] However, as more organizations such as Pfizer, Adidas, and Netflix continue to focus on analytics, we suspect that other organizations will continue to follow suit.

As you consider how analytics in general and HR analytics in particular may play a role in your future, keep in mind these different levels of analytics: *descriptive*, *predictive*, and *prescriptive* (Figure 1.5). *Descriptive analytics* is focused on understanding what has happened already—a "snapshot" of the past. Descriptive analytics might include describing an organization's prior monthly turnover rates. In contrast, *predictive analytics* is forward looking, as it focuses on predicting what is likely to happen given what is already known and evaluating the accuracy of those predictions. For example, an HR analyst might build a statistical model to identify the key drivers of employees' decisions to quit and then estimate the probabilities of specific employees quitting the organization based on their available data on those key drivers. Finally, *prescriptive analytics* extends predictive analytics by focusing on what actions should be taken in the future based on what is known and has been predicted. Prescriptive analytics might focus on what specific manager interventions should be used to retain those high-performing employees who were found to have higher probabilities of quitting.

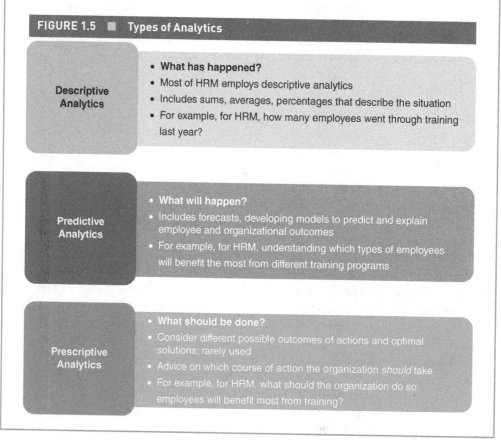

FIGURE 1.5   ■   Types of Analytics

Descriptive Analytics
- What has happened?
- Most of HRM employs descriptive analytics
- Includes sums, averages, percentages that describe the situation
- For example, for HRM, how many employees went through training last year?

Predictive Analytics
- What will happen?
- Includes forecasts, developing models to predict and explain employee and organizational outcomes
- For example, for HRM, understanding which types of employees will benefit the most from different training programs

Prescriptive Analytics
- What should be done?
- Consider different possible outcomes of actions and optimal solutions; rarely used
- Advice on which course of action the organization *should* take
- For example, for HRM, what should the organization do so employees will benefit most from training?

Gig Economy

A gig economy is characterized by the prevalence of temporary employment positions, and individuals are employed as independent workers rather than actual employees of an organization. A gig is defined as a single project or task that a worker is hired to do on demand. Think of Uber drivers or substitute teachers. In 2021, in the United States, an estimated 30 million gig workers were in this category.[28] Freelance employees note scheduling flexibility as a key reason for their attraction to freelance work. Other positives reported are variety and the ability to pursue one's interests. Reported downsides include inconsistency in pay and scheduling and the lack of benefits associated with this type of employment contract. As the U.S. Department of Labor noted about the gig economy, "These workers often get individual gigs using a website or mobile app that helps to match them with customers. Some gigs may be brief. . . . Others are much longer but still of limited duration, such as an 18-month database management project. When one gig is over, workers who earn a steady income this way must find another. And sometimes that means juggling multiple jobs at once."[29] Some occupations are more likely than others to employ contract workers. Arts and design, computer and information technology, construction and extraction, media and communications, as well as transportation and material moving are industry sectors at the top of the list for contract work. The implications of the emerging gig economy are vast. Because this class of employment is so relatively new, the legal environment has not yet kept up, and it remains an area that is unclear.

Ethical and Corporate Social Responsibility Challenges

Business ethics is a system of principles that govern how businesses operate, how decisions are made, and how people are treated. It includes the conduct of individual employees as well as the entire organization. These concepts should look familiar from our earlier discussion of the characteristics of effective HRM decision making. The concept of business ethics arose in the 1960s and 1970s in the United States as values shifted from strict loyalty to the organization to a stronger loyalty toward one's own guiding principles and ideals.[30] This manifested itself through environmental issues, increasing employee-versus-employer tension, human rights issues surrounding unfair and unsafe labor practices, and civil rights issues. Over time, additional issues surfaced, such as bribes and illegal contracting practices, deception in advertising, and lack of transparency in business transactions.

Concerns regarding business scandals such as financial mismanagement, increased corporate liability for personal damage, and fraud are pervasive. Scandals have led to several changes on the global stage, such as the United Nations Global Compact adopting a 10th principle against corruption. The Association of Advanced Collegiate Schools of Business (AACSB) includes ethics as part of an accredited business education, with a key provision on the importance of ethical decision making.[31] Given that HRM is defined as the constellation of decisions and actions associated with managing individuals throughout the employee life cycle, addressing ethical challenges and corporate social responsibility are key aspects of HRM. Thus, you will find a feature called *Spotlight on Ethics* in each chapter of this book. We encourage you to take the time to consider the ethical challenges you have and may encounter at work.

HRM AS A PROFESSION

LEARNING OBJECTIVE
1.4　Summarize the HRM profession.

Not every person reading this book plans to go into HRM as a profession. Nevertheless, understanding who is involved in HRM, the types of HR careers available, and what the core HRM competencies are should be helpful to all interested in business. We start with an overview of who is involved in HRM.

Who Is Involved in HRM?

The short answer to this question is everyone within an organization. This is because everyone is responsible for helping the organization be successful. However, some individuals, groups, and departments are more involved in HRM decision making and actions on a day-to-day basis than others. These include CEOs and the associated leadership team, HR managers, line managers, as well as HR specialists and generalists. In addition, other areas of the organization, such as information systems technology, play an important role in making sure the right people have the right information in place to make the most effective decisions possible. The marketing of products influences whether potential applicants know about and are attracted to the organization. The accounting and finance functions are critical to the fiscal health of an organization, and therefore, they also play an important role in keeping the organization's finances supporting human capital. They may be involved in compensation and benefits-related decisions as well. Each one of these departments also has managers who oversee it. Thus, it would be a missed opportunity to *only* focus on what happens within the Department of Human Resource Management within a firm.

Because this book is written with a special focus on best practices and functions of HRM, we focus primarily on the ways in which four important groups affect the culture and functioning of HRM within an organization. These include the top management leadership team, HR managers, and line managers as well as HR specialists and generalists.

Enrique Washington is an executive talent acquisition leader. He has recruited executives at sports organizations such as the ESPN, Portland Trail Blazers, video game maker Electronic Arts, and Nike. A key part of his job is advising hiring leaders on establishing role requirements to identify, assess, select, and integrate new executive leaders in alignment with their business goals.

Top Management Teams and HRM

The top members of the organizational team, such as the CEO, top management team, and/or owner of the organization, set the tone for HR and how much or how little human capital is valued. They also set the tone for how much HRM is valued as a strategic function to enhance the organization's effectiveness. The organization's chief human resource officer (CHRO) is also critical in this regard. Organizations often use executive recruiting functions within their organizations or hire external search firms to help them find the right talent at this level.

HR Managers and HRM

An HR manager is someone who oversees the personnel department or HR functions within a group. The degree to which an HR manager is passive versus proactive in terms of asking questions, gathering data, and helping to address the major challenges and opportunities of the organization can influence how effective HRM, and relatedly the organization, ultimately becomes. One of the other major functions of this individual is to partner with other managers across the organization. This is a critical coordination function. The HR manager might hold a variety of job titles such as HR manager/director, which is the most frequently advertised job position in HR.

Line Managers and HRM

Managers also play a critical role in making people decisions. For example, a hiring manager's opinion can be the difference between a person being hired, promoted, or fired. Managers also play a critical day-to-day role in managing workflows, helping support new employee development, and developing talent for greater responsibilities over time. Managers help to set the tone of a work group or department. Research shows that the climate managers set can influence the level of innovation, safe behaviors, and ethical behaviors within the group.[32] Most position announcements for HR manager require 3 to 5 years of HR-related experience to be considered for the job.

HR Practitioners and HR Careers

HR practitioners work on HR-related activities and regularly engage in HR-related strategic and process-related people or personnel decisions within the organization. They might be called HR manager, HR partner, or HR specialist. Each of these titles connotes different aspects of the HR practitioner's core job functions. The HR specialist attends to all aspects of one specific HRM function, such as recruitment, compensation, or training. An **HR generalist** spans the multiple HR functions. As you might imagine, the needs for specialists versus generalists is related to the size and scope of the HR function, as well as the industry the organization is in. The larger the organization is, the more likely it is to employ specialists. Thus, you might see job titles such as recruiter, compensation analyst, or HR analysts.

HR Business Partners and HRM

HR business partner (HRBP) is the second most frequently advertised job position in HR. An **HR business partner** is a more recent term and refers to someone who serves as a consultant to management on HR-related issues. As the Society for Human Resource Management notes, the "HRBP is responsible for aligning business objectives with employees and management in designated business units. . . . The successful HRBP will act as an employee champion and agent of change." The key aspect of HRBP is that their role is to anticipate HR-related needs, as well as being available to share advice and proactively address small problems before they become big ones.

What Do Employers Look for in HR Applicants?

The answer to this question depends on the level of the HR position in the organization, as well as the degree to which HR plays a strategic role within the organization. For example, an HR assistant position typically only requires a high school diploma. However, to move up in the organization, a college degree can make a big difference. An analysis of HR position announcements for jobs found that the top requested areas of college study included human resource management, business administration, psychology, and organizational development. Getting the first job and some HRM experience is only the first step. Those in HR need to stay up to date on the latest developments—especially as they relate to the ever-shifting legal environment.

There are organizations that exist in order to help HR practitioners stay informed of best practices and up to date on the latest trends that might affect HR. One such organization is the Society for Human Resource Management (SHRM). SHRM is the world's largest HRM professional society, representing over 300,000 members in more than 165 countries. Its headquarters are located in Alexandria, Virginia, and it has 575 affiliated local chapters throughout the United States, China, India, and the United Arab Emirates.[33] One of the key benefits of such professional organizations is that they have a wide view of what it takes to be effective in HRM. In fact, SHRM has spent a great deal of time and energy studying just that, as seen in the section on competencies.

Laura Fuentes, current chief HR officer for Hilton Worldwide held several roles across HR functions including Recruiting, Diversity, & Inclusion; People Analytics & Strategy; and Total Rewards.

Photo by Ben Hider/Getty Images for Concordia Summit

SPOTLIGHT ON ETHICS: HRM CODE OF ETHICS

Ethics is critically important to the effective practice of HRM. Ethical decisions and actions lead to greater trust and engagement within organizations and allow for all types of information to emerge, which is important for effective decision making. Given the importance of ethics to HRM, the Society for Human Resource Management (SHRM), which is the world's largest professional society for human resource management, developed a code of ethics. We encourage you to read this code of ethics whether you are an aspiring manager or HRM professional or one who is seasoned. The core principles noted are easily transferable to different organizational roles, and following them can help you avoid serious problems as you are faced with ethical dilemmas and decisions throughout your career. The six core principles described in the code provisions include the idea that professionals should engage in their work with a focus on professional responsibility, professional development, ethical leadership, fairness and justice, conflicts of interest, and use of information.

Questions

1. Describe a hypothetical scenario in which you would benefit from applying certain principles from the SHRM Code of Ethics.
2. Choose a business situation from the news or the HR literature where principles from the SHRM Code of Ethics could have made a difference. Specifically, what did the decision makers do right, or what could they have done better?

Salary and Job Outlook

The U.S. Bureau of Labor Statistics (see Table 1.1) reports that the median pay for an HR manager in 2021 was $126,230 per year, which is $60.09 per hour. Moving up to become an HR manager happens, on average, about 5 years after starting out. Overall, HRM is considered to have solid career prospects and to be an attractive job. For example, a 2022 survey by Glassdoor.com found that human resource manager was the 13th best job based on job projections, median base salary, and career opportunity ratings with high job satisfaction ratings of 4.3 out of 5.[34]

HRM Certifications The HR Certification Institute (HRCI) began offering certification in HR in 1976 and originally partnered with SHRM. However, SHRM now offers its own certification based on its HR competency model. Thus, the two major certifications in HRM are administered by SHRM (SHRM-CP and SHRM-SCP) and HRCI (SPHR and PHR). (We discuss what a competency model is later in this chapter and in greater depth in Chapter 5.)

One question that those interested in business and HRM practitioners alike ask is the value of HRM certifications. In an analysis of job postings for HRM, 42% noted a preference or requirement for certification. Further, some positions, such as HR business partner, were more likely than not to require certification, which indicates that certification may be beneficial in securing a job.[35] In addition, having a deeper knowledge of HRM should help the individual to master the HRM knowledge domain more fully and signals a deeper interest in HRM than noncertified individuals.

HR Competencies

You probably know what it means to be competent. A person who is competent is perceived to be able to perform specific functions reasonably well. A competency is a cluster of knowledge, skills, abilities, and other characteristics (KSAOs) necessary to be effective at one's job.[36]

SHRM developed its competency model based on 111 focus groups consisting of 1,200 participants and completed surveys from over 32,000 HR professionals (see Figure 1.6). Its goal was to create a model that is applicable to all HR professionals regardless of characteristics such as job function or career level, organization size, industry, or location. This was updated and expanded in 2022 based on extensive consideration. What emerged in 2022 was a set of core competencies. In addition, it identified technical competencies that reflect the knowledge specific to the HR profession and

TABLE 1.1 ■ HRM Careers by the Numbers	
HR Specialists	
Human resources specialists recruit, screen, interview, and place workers. They often handle other human resources work, such as those related to employee relations, compensation and benefits, and training.	
2021 Median Pay	$62,290 per year ($29.95 per hour)
Typical Entry-Level Education	Bachelor's degree
Work Experience in a Related Occupation	None
Number of Jobs, 2021	782,800
Job Outlook, 2021–2031	8% (faster than average)
Employment Change, 2021–2031	58,800 new jobs
HR Managers	
Human resources managers plan, direct, and coordinate the administrative functions of an organization. They oversee the recruiting, interviewing, and hiring of new staff; consult with top executives on strategic planning; and serve as a link between an organization's management and its employees.	
2021 Median Pay	$126,230 per year ($60.09 per hour)
Typical Entry-Level Education	Bachelor's degree
Work Experience in a Related Occupation	5+ years
Number of Jobs, 2021	174,200
Job Outlook, 2021–2031	8% (as fast as average)
Employment Change, 2021–2031	12,600 new jobs

Source: Bureau of Labor Statistics, U.S. Department of Labor (2021). Occupational employment and wages: https://www.bls.gov/ooh/management/human-resources-managers.htm; https://www.bls.gov/ooh/business-and-financial/human-resources-specialists.htm.

nine behavioral competencies that form three clusters of competencies with *interpersonal competencies*, including relationship management, communication, and global mindset; *business competencies*, including business acumen, consultation, and analytical aptitude; and *leadership competencies*, including leadership and navigation, ethical practice, and diversity, equity, and inclusion. As you will see throughout this book, we aligned our emphasis on people, data, and analytics in HRM to capture these competencies.

Staying Up to Date: Evidence-Based Management

We have seen how important learning the functions of HRM is. It is also important to stay abreast of changes in the field as they evolve by taking workshops and education courses (and continuing education) separately or as part of being certified. Another important way that managers, HRM practitioners, consultants, and researchers stay up to date on the latest findings and changes in the field is by learning about research findings conducted by others. In this way, practitioners can learn best practices to give their organization a competitive advantage by saving time by learning from others' mistakes and considering their successes.

Information regarding HRM comes from three main places. First, organizations often engage in benchmarking. Benchmarking refers to a measurement of the quality of an organization's practices in comparison with those of a peer organization. The best benchmarking follows the standards of good decision making and includes identifying the goal and parameters of the benchmarking, gathering data, analyzing data, and communicating the results. Benchmarking might occur within a specific

FIGURE 1.6 ■ SHRM Body of Applied Skills and Knowledge

A competency is a group of highly inter-related knowledge, skills, abilities, and other characteristics (KSAOs) that have been determined to relate to job success. The colored hexagons reflect HR knowledge, and the white hexagons are the identified HR skills and behaviors of the SHRM competency model.

industry sector or across functions such as HRM benchmarking. Benchmarking is often done at different levels as well, with Fortune 500 organizations often benchmarking against one another. For example, asking what the top 10 best companies in your industry do in terms of surveys with departing employees could be useful information if you are planning to make changes to your own exit process. One thing to keep in mind is that simply meeting benchmarks is not an advantage, but understanding them and moving beyond them can be.

Second, reports are written based on surveys and trends by HR organizations such as SHRM, the Conference Board, or the Association for Talent Development, and HR consulting firms such as PwC, Deloitte, SAP/SuccessFactors, and Aberdeen Group. These findings might be shared at industry conferences or in practitioner outlets such as *HR Focus, HR Magazine, Harvard Business Review, People Management, Workforce,* and *T+D* as well as via blogs or newsletters. These outlets may be reviewed but do not undergo the same scrutiny as peer-reviewed research articles.

Third, researchers within universities and in industry in the fields of HRM and industrial-organizational psychology (I-O) psychology generate new knowledge about best practices through their research streams. The findings are published in academic journals, which are peer reviewed by experts in that research area who evaluate the rigor of the studies and their contribution to the research and practice of HRM. Research findings are also presented at annual conferences such as the Academy of Management and Society for Industrial and Organizational Psychology.[37] Papers presented at these particular conferences are also peer reviewed but with less detailed peer review than for a journal, and attending sessions at conferences allows HRM practitioners and researchers to learn what some of the most current research is on a given topic. And of course, books on HRM topics are also important ways to stay up to date.

Given how important we feel evidence-based practice is, we include research findings throughout the book. When we can, we focus on key findings from meta-analyses in each chapter. Although we base much of this textbook on findings across many individual studies, a meta-analysis is unique in that it summarizes and synthesizes everything that researchers have found on a given topic up to that point using a statistical process. Another way to think about staying up to date is to follow the scientific process in gathering information within your own organization. Chapter 2 covers what this scientific process includes and how helpful it can be to HRM best practices.

SPOTLIGHT ON LEGAL ISSUES: U.S. EQUAL EMPLOYMENT OPPORTUNITY COMMISSION

The U.S. Equal Employment Opportunity Commission (EEOC) is the primary federal agency responsible for handling workplace discrimination claims. In 2021, the agency received over 67,448 individual filings.[38] In the United States, federal law prohibits discrimination in employment decisions based on protected characteristics. These laws are referred to as equal employment opportunity (EEO) laws. Most EEO laws pertaining to private, government, and state institutions are monitored and enforced by the EEOC, which is an independent federal agency. The EEOC ensures compliance with the law, in addition to providing outreach activities and preventing discrimination from occurring in the first place. EEO laws typically apply to organizations with 15 or more employees and cover business, private employers, government agencies, employment agencies, and labor unions and aim to prevent discrimination against employees, job applicants, and participants in training and apprenticeship programs. You will learn more about the laws that the EEOC covers in Chapter 4, but for now, the key point is to understand that this agency exists

CHAPTER SUMMARY

The case of Costco illustrates how HRM influences a company's success from its beginning as a start-up through years of expansion, including successes and setbacks. At this point, you know a great deal about what HRM is, why it matters, and different types of organizational cultures. We also covered an overview of six key aspects of the changing context of HRM, including changing demographics, the emergence of a gig economy, globalization, technology, availability of data, and ethical challenges and corporate social responsibility. The overview of HRM as a profession included understanding who is involved in HRM, different aspects of HRM careers, and HRM competencies. Finally, chapter Spotlights on global issues, data and analytics, ethics, and legal issues highlighted key points and examples.

KEY TERMS

Adhocracy culture
Anchoring bias
A-S-A framework
Availability bias
Benchmarking
Biases
Business ethics
Clan cultures
Competency
Hierarchy culture
HR business partner

HR generalist
HR specialist
Human resource management (HRM)
Magnitude
Market culture
Organizational culture
Overconfidence bias
Sign
Society for Human Resource Management (SHRM)
Spurious correlation

HR REASONING AND DECISION-MAKING EXERCISES

Mini-Case Analysis Exercise: Information Seeking as a New Employee

You have started work at a small company, Johnson Natural Shoes, which designs and produces children's shoes. The company has an innovative approach and uses all-natural materials. Its product has been increasing in demand in the few short years since it began. The company was founded by Shannon McKenzie. You found out about the position because you are friends with Shannon's daughter, who is an old friend of yours from high school. You were hired after you met with the founder, who remembered you from soccer games and birthday parties.

You do not have a job description or formal job title. But you are the only person in the organization with a degree in business, and Shannon McKenzie mentioned to you that you were hired in the hopes you could help the company manage its rapid growth. At this point, the company is on track to double in size this year compared with last year, when it only had 28 employees.

You notice from the first days on the job that employees enjoy collaborating and making decisions together, and you feel welcomed right away. You see great things in the company's future and want to help make Johnson Natural Shoes an international brand. You can't wait to start making a contribution.

Now it is your turn to decide how to help:

1. Given that you are still new to the company, how would you approach learning more about the company and its employees?

2. What are specific key questions you might want to ask employees about the company?

3. Based on your knowledge of business, what would you advise Shannon McKenzie to consider as HR priorities as the organization experiences high growth?

HR Decision Analysis Exercise: Unlimited Vacation?

In this chapter, we presented a lot of information regarding HRM and approaches to business in general. Given how many different things you have considered, we would like you to take some time to focus on some key aspects of making effective HRM decisions. Read on about some different HRM decisions that have been made.

Your company is considering giving everyone in the organization unlimited vacation time regardless of how long they have been with the company or how much they currently make. This is following the popularity of this approach at several major organizations such as Netflix, General Electric, and the Virgin Group. Your boss has asked you to take the perspective of wanting to ensure that HRM decisions are effective, and using Figure 1.7 as a guide, determine what questions should be asked to address how wise this policy change might be from a variety of angles.

Please generate questions and provide the rationale for them around each of the following characteristics. In other words, what questions do you need to have answered to determine if this is an effective HRM decision?

Legal, ethical, and fair

Evidence based/evidence informed

Fosters healthy employee–employer relationships

Time- and cost-effective

Takes a systematic stakeholder perspective

Considering your analysis, overall, is this an effective decision? Why or why not?

What, if anything, do you think should be taken into consideration to help make this decision most effective?

FIGURE 1.7 ■ Characteristics of Effective HRM Decisions

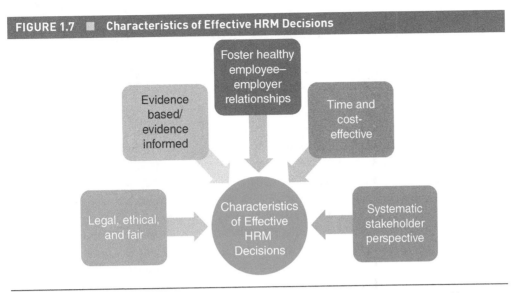

HR Decision-Making Exercise: The Changing Context of HRM

Making HRM decisions is often a group activity, as seldom does one person have all the required information, context, and expertise to tackle every HR issue. Working in a group, review the six trends we identified as impacting HRM today and into the future (changing demographics, the emerging gig economy, increasing globalization, technology, availability of data, and ethical and corporate social responsibility challenges).

1. Form your group.

2. Decide if there are additional trends your group believes might be as important or more important than these six.

3. As a group, decide which trend your group collectively feels is the *most* important factor that will influence HRM. It is as important to justify your answer in terms of your selection of the most important factor as it is to defend why the others are not seen as equally important.

DATA AND ANALYTICS EXERCISE: CORRELATION DOES NOT EQUAL CAUSATION

Given how important data and analytics are for understanding HRM, we wanted to give you an opportunity to explore a key concept in basic social science research. This is the fact that two things may be correlated but not necessarily causally. For example, if you notice a truck moving down the street with three people inside the truck pushing against the cab, you have enough basic physics knowledge to realize that the people are not causing the truck to move. But, their behavior is happening at the same time so it might seem logical to assume that they were making a difference because those two things are both happening at the same time. When it comes to understanding HRM, correlation is an important statistical tool, and it is utilized in different ways. A correlation coefficient is a number that conveys two important pieces of information: sign and magnitude. The sign (positive or negative) refers to the direction of a relationship, and the size of that relationship is its magnitude.

A correlation coefficient can range from –1.00 to +1.00 (i.e., its greatest possible magnitude is 1.00, and its sign can be either positive or negative). A correlation coefficient of –1.00 indicates that two variables are "perfectly" correlated and share a negative (inverse) relationship such that as scores on one variable get larger, scores on the other variable get smaller. Conversely, a correlation of +1.00 indicates that two variables are perfectly correlated and share a positive relationship such that as scores on one variable get larger, scores on the other variable also get larger. Specifically, the absolute value of a correlation coefficient indicates how strong the relationship is, where an absolute value of 1.00 indicates a perfect relationship and a value of 0.00 indicates no relationship. In HRM, we often describe the size of a correlation using qualitative descriptors. For instance, we might describe a correlation coefficient of 0.10 as *small*, 0.30 as *medium*, and 0.50 as *large*. Thus, a correlation coefficient provides a very efficient description of how much two variables are related in terms of the sign and magnitude of their relationship.

With all that said, remember that *correlation does not mean causation*. That is, two variables may covary with one another without being directly related. When a correlation is found between two variables that are not directly related, we refer to this as a spurious correlation, which may be the result of two variables that are not directly related but that share a common cause. For example, imagine that you find a large positive correlation (e.g., $r = .52$) between construction workers' self-reported annual consumption of ice cream and their level of self-reported job satisfaction. That is, as the amount of ice cream consumed by construction workers increases, their level of job satisfaction tends to increase as well. At first glance, we might look at this finding and conclude that ice cream consumption causes job satisfaction. Taking a closer look, we might think, "Well, this relationship doesn't make much sense given what we know about job satisfaction."

What, then, is a possible explanation for this potentially spurious correlation? The finding could be due to a third variable that causes both increases in ice cream consumption and increases in job satisfaction. Perhaps construction workers in this sample work in multiple locations around the United States. Accordingly, those who work in warmer climates consume more ice cream per year to cool off. In addition, those who work in warmer climates feel more satisfied with their job because they work outdoors in more pleasant temperatures. In this scenario, ice cream consumption does not cause job satisfaction, and job satisfaction does not cause ice cream consumption; rather, warmer climate is the common cause that leads to more ice cream consumption and higher job satisfaction, thereby resulting in the spurious correlation.

In sum, we should remain cautious when interpreting correlations and remind ourselves that *correlation does not equal causation*. To avoid making this mistake, we should evaluate each correlation coefficient through the lens of existing theory to make better decisions and draw more appropriate conclusions.

Excel Extension: Now You Try!

- On **edge.sagepub.com/bauer2e**, you will find an Excel tutorial that shows how to compute a correlation coefficient.

- Using Excel, answer the following questions:
  - What is the correlation between employee engagement and sales revenue?
  - Consider the sign and the magnitude of the correlation. How would you describe the nature of the relation between engagement and sales revenue to a manager who does not know what a correlation coefficient means?
  - What is the correlation between job satisfaction and customer satisfaction?

2 STRATEGIC HRM, DATA-INFORMED DECISION MAKING, AND HR ANALYTICS

DATA ANALYTICS AND ARTIFICIAL INTELLIGENCE AS HR TOOLS: THE CASE OF STANLEY BLACK & DECKER

©iStockphoto.com/njpPhoto

Known for manufacturing hand tools like power drills and wrenches, Stanley Black & Decker was founded in 1843 and today is a publicly traded Fortune 500 manufacturing company based in New Britain, Connecticut. The company owns a number of well-known brands, such as DeWalt, Black & Decker, Stanley, and Craftsman, with many of these brands' products sold in hardware stores. In 2021, the company ranked 41st on Fast Company's list of 100 Best Workplaces for Innovators.

Innovation at Stanley Black & Decker stems in part from its digital transformation strategy centered on human resource management. In recent years, Stanley Black & Decker has used data analytics and AI to support and enhance how it develops and manages its employees. Consistent with the company's "people plus technology" operations model, CEO Jim Loree assigned the company's new chief AI officer, Mukesh Dalal, to work within the HR function. Loree believes the purpose of AI and other digital transformation technologies is to support and enhance the organization's workforce. Both technology and people contribute to the company's ability to maintain a competitive advantage and to realize its strategic objectives.

In 2021, as part of a program to develop company-wide talent, the company announced new data-informed and technology-assisted programs. These include *StanleyConnex* for employee mentorship and *EI for Everyone* to develop employees' emotional intelligence. Around the same time and in partnership with DeepHow, Stanley Black & Decker launched its AI training platform they called Stephanie across 30 manufacturing sites. The Stephanie platform uses a three-step process to generate and deploy employee training content. First, using DeepHow's mobile application, individuals within the company record videos of expert employees performing actual job tasks and, in the process, capture the employees' workflow, knowledge, and skills. Second, using AI, Stephanie analyzes, indexes, and segments the video data to generate step-by-step training videos. Third, trainees use the resulting self-paced and searchable videos to learn important job-related tasks and workflows, and based on an algorithm, the tool recommends specific training videos to the employees who need them the most.

AI tools like Stephanie offer a number of potential benefits for employees, the HR department, and the organization. Employees can use cameras on their mobile devices to record training content, with no need for expensive video equipment and editing software. Thus, an organization can quickly assemble an internal library of video-based training modules. This enables a manufacturing company like Stanley Black & Decker to create new training content for rapidly changing jobs and products. It also allows them to capture the expertise of retiring and resigning employees who possess valuable knowledge and skills. To that end, Kevin Lemke, vice president of strategy for the Innovation Group, noted, "There is a tremendous opportunity to help our customers minimize the disruption caused by employee turnover" and that DeepHow's AI Stephanie tool provides a "knowledge transfer system for the skilled trades."

While AI tools like Stephanie offer promising solutions, organizations must also carefully identify and evaluate potential data-integrity, ethical, and legal challenges. When low-quality data are used as inputs, the AI tool will produce low-quality outputs (e.g., recommendations), a phenomenon often referred to as "garbage in, garbage out." For example, imagine a situation in which a number of training videos are created using the Stephanie AI application; however, instead of recording the workflows of employees with high expertise, employees with low expertise are recorded by mistake. The resulting video-based training might reduce employee performance. This example highlights the importance of human involvement and oversight when it comes to AI. In fact, some companies have announced new roles focused on using AI ethically and in ways that preserve human dignity. For example, some companies have established a chief ethical and humane officer.[1]

CASE DISCUSSION QUESTIONS

1. How has Stanley Black & Decker used data analytics and AI to support human resource management?

2. Could DeepHow's AI Stephanie tool be used for non-manufacturing jobs? If so, for what types of jobs would these tools be most appropriate or effective?

3. DeepHow's AI Stephanie tool is supposed to be used to record expert employees performing their work. How can an organization determine which employees are experts at their job?

4. Are there any other data-integrity, ethical, or legal challenges that organizations should consider when using AI tools for human resource management?

INTRODUCTION

As noted in the previous chapter, people matter for an organization's success. Jim Goodnight, CEO of SAS Institute Inc., is quoted as saying, "Ninety-five percent of my assets drive out the gate every evening. It's my job to maintain a work environment that keeps those people coming back every morning."[2] This chapter focuses on the role HR plays in managing people to achieve organizational success. This chapter explains how organizations combine strategy with HRM to achieve success and how HR professionals can make data-informed decisions that are accurate, fair, ethical, and legal—considerations that are becoming increasingly important as our society pushes forward into an era of big data and new technologies like artificial intelligence (AI).

DEFINING STRATEGY

LEARNING OBJECTIVES
2.1   Identify the steps for formulating and implementing a strategy.

Strategic human resource management is the process of aligning HR policies and practices with the objectives of the organization, including employee, operational, stakeholder, and financial outcomes. Central to strategic human resource management—and to strategic management in general—is the concept of a strategy. What is a strategy? Think of a strategy as a well-devised and thoughtful plan for achieving an objective.[3] A strategy is inherently future-oriented and is intended to provide a road map toward completion of an objective. Strategy reflects the way a unit, department, or organization coordinates activities to achieve planned objectives in both the short and long term.[4] In the opening case on Stanley Black & Decker, we learned how the company leverages data analytics and artificial intelligence to inform and support business strategies aimed at minimizing disruptions for customers when, for example, expert manufacturing employees and their "know-how" leave the company due to retirement. That is, strategy can be paired with data analytics and other digital-transformation technologies like artificial intelligence to make data-informed decisions, which improve the likelihood of achieving strategic objectives and sustaining a competitive advantage.

Some firms keep their strategies relatively private, while others, like Space Exploration Technologies Corp. (SpaceX), announce aspects of their strategy to the world. Based in Hawthorne, California, and ranked ninth on Fast Company's 2022 list of the World's Most Innovative Companies, SpaceX's mission is to "make humanity multiplanetary" by developing and launching fully reusable rockets and launch vehicles capable of traveling to the Moon, Mars, and beyond. In 2020, SpaceX took a big step toward realizing its strategy when it became the first private company to shuttle human beings to the international space station. The following year, the company successfully launched and then safely landed a vehicle called *Starship SN15*, a major milestone toward the goal of reusable rockets. With the help of its rockets, SpaceX also launches its Starlink high-speed Internet satellites into low orbit, and in 2022, Starlink satellites became critical and free communication tools for the people of Tonga after a volcanic eruption.[5]

SpaceX's employees are essential to realizing the company's strategic objectives and for achieving and maintaining a competitive advantage. To build a strong workforce, SpaceX leverages HRM as a strategic tool to design systems and procedures aimed at attracting, motivating, and retaining talented people. For example, Brian Bjelde, vice president of HR, has shared that, in addition to identifying talented, passionate, and driven job candidates, SpaceX selects candidates who value exploration and the company's mission. With competitors like Blue Origin, SpaceX must rely heavily on its human capital to outperform its competition.[6]

Strategy Formulation: Developing and Refining a Strategy

To realize their mission, organizations like SpaceX must both formulate and implement a strategy. Strategy formulation involves planning what to do to achieve organizational objectives—or in other words, the development or refinement of a strategy. In some organizations, the CEO and executive

In 2021, SpaceX achieved a major milestone in reusable rocketry when the company successfully launched and landed *Starship SN15*. Pictured here is SpaceX preparing *Starship SN15* for launch at Starbase Space Facility in Boca Chica, Texas.

©iStockphoto.com/ RoschetzkyIstockPhoto

team formulate the strategy in a top-down manner, whereas in other organizations, the strategy emerges from the pattern of many organizational decisions that are made over time. In some organizations, strategy formulation is the product of both top-down and bottom-up processes. Regardless of how a strategy originates, an organization's strategy is not set in stone. Rather, an organization should demonstrate flexibility by staying on top of dynamic changes in the internal and external environments and by re-envisioning and reformulating a strategy as needed. Strategy formulation often follows the steps depicted in Figure 2.1, which ultimately set the stage for strategy implementation. Figure 2.1

FIGURE 2.1 ■ Steps for Strategy Formulation

Formulating an organizational strategy requires identifying or developing the mission, vision, values, and strategy type; analyzing the internal and external environments; and defining objectives designed to satisfy stakeholders.

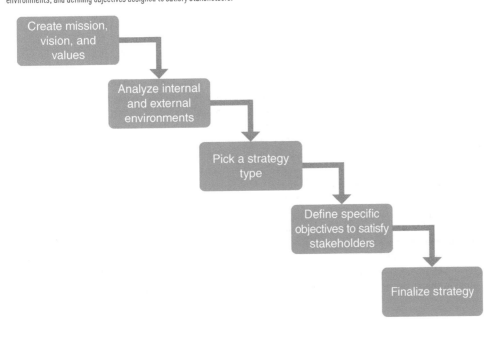

Create a Mission, Vision, and Set of Values

A **mission** describes a core need that an organization strives to fulfill and thus represents the organization's overarching purpose—or in other words, the organization's reason for existing. Recall that SpaceX's espoused mission is to "make humanity multiplanetary," and as you have probably observed, many organizations feature their mission statements prominently on their webpages. SpaceX is no exception. In addition to a mission, strategy formulation also involves stating a vision and articulating values. An organization's **vision** is an extension of the mission and describes what the organization will be, do, or look like at some point in the future. Creating a set of core **values** provides the organization with parameters and guidelines for decision making and bringing its vision to fruition.

SPOTLIGHT ON ETHICS: FIGHTING CLIMATE CHANGE WITH IMPOSSIBLE FOODS

©iStockphoto.com/ hapabapa

Stanford University professor Pat Brown founded Impossible Foods Inc. in 2011 with the mission to fight climate change by creating a more sustainable global food system. Recognizing the environmental impact of animal meat production, the company develops and produces plant-based substitutes for animal products like meat, fish, and dairy—sometimes referred to as "meatless meat." Impossible Foods scientists develop plant-based substitutes that mimic the taste and texture of common animal products while also mitigating the environmental impact of the production processes. Today, well-known food retailers and restaurants like Kroger, McDonald's, and Burger King sell Impossible Foods products like the now-famous Impossible Burger. The company's mission is also featured in its recruiting and selection materials, as the company seeks candidates whose values align with the mission of combating climate change.

Impossible Foods, however, is not immune from criticism. For example, John Mackey, CEO of Whole Foods, shared concerns that plant-based substitutes for animal products, like those produced by Impossible Foods, can be overly processed and thus unhealthy. In response, some food scientists and nutritionists have argued that high levels of processing do not necessarily imply a food is unhealthy or less healthy. Some evidence suggests that an Impossible Burger is probably about as healthy as its meat-based counterpart. Other critics point to a lack of transparency in the reporting of greenhouse emissions produced by Impossible Foods across all operations and supply chains. In the absence of such reporting transparency, some academic and third-party research has shown that plant-based substitutes result in considerably lower greenhouse gas emissions than meat-based products.

Despite its critics, Impossible Foods and its popularity continue to grow, with the company even considering an initial public offering (IPO) as of February 2022. Founder and CEO Pat Brown wants the public to have an opportunity to invest in the company in order to support the future of the planet by continuing to bring the company's strategic vision to life.[7]

Questions

1. How might the mission and ethical values of Impossible Foods influence its HRM policies?
2. As more companies begin making plant-based substitutes for animal products, what can Impossible Foods do to remain competitive while also living up to its mission and vision?

Analyze Internal and External Environments

An organization must look both internally and externally to understand how to bring its mission, vision, and values to life and to achieve a competitive advantage. That is, an organization must analyze the internal *strengths* and *weaknesses* that are under its control and the external *threats* and *opportunities* that are beyond its direct control—a process commonly referred to as a SWOT analysis.[8] When analyzing the internal environment, an organization comes up with a plan for how to leverage its strengths and improve on its weaknesses. When analyzing the external environment, an organization identifies opportunities and threats with respect to the state of its industry and competitors, as well as other external factors like the labor market, unemployment rate, and the general condition of the local, national, and/or global economies. Taken together, a SWOT analysis is a systematic and methodical decision-making tool used to formulate a *viable* strategy.

Taking a resource-based view during a SWOT analysis allows an organization to identify its strengths and weaknesses in terms of its physical, financial, organizational, and human resources and identify how these resources can be used to maximize opportunities and minimize threats in the external environment. According to the resource-based view, resources that are rare and inimitable are more valuable to an organization. A *rare* resource is scarce, and relatively few (if any) competitors have the resource. An *inimitable* resource is difficult (if not impossible) for competitors to reproduce, attain, or deploy. For example, reusable rockets are currently rare in the space industry, and SpaceX has found success building and launching the *Falcon 9* reusable rocket. Thus far, competitors have found it difficult to imitate SpaceX's reusable rocket program.[9] The process of identifying rare and inimitable internal resources provides a way of anticipating whether the organization, upon applying the strategy, will be able to achieve its objectives and sustain a competitive advantage.[10]

Pick a Strategy Type

After analyzing internal and external environments, an organization is ready to select a strategy type. A strategy type provides a general approach for how an organization will bring its mission, vision, and values to life, while at the same time leveraging its strengths and improving its weaknesses. Examples include the following[11]:

- *Differentiation*: The organization creates a product, service, or customer experience that is different from those provided by competitors, thus warranting a higher price or more attention from consumers.

- *Cost leadership*: The organization identifies ways to create a product or service at a lower cost compared with competitors. This can help the organization increase its margin or sell the product or service at a cheaper price than competitors.

- *Focus*: The organization uses differentiation or cost leadership but identifies a narrow consumer base to appeal to a specific product or service type that might not be produced or sold by competitors.

Ranked 40th on Fast Company's 2022 list of the World's Most Innovative Companies, Shopify's 2022 total revenue increased 21% compared to the prior year, reaching a full-year revenue of $5.6 billion. The company provides Internet infrastructure for commerce and exemplifies a differentiation strategy, which is reflected in the company's product. Shopify helps businesses reach customers through their own websites and through marketplaces like Facebook. At the same time, the company aims to give businesses the ability to retain their unique identities.[12]

Photo Illustration by Rafael Henrique/SOPA Images/LightRocket via Getty Images

Define Specific Objectives to Satisfy Stakeholders

Ultimately, an organization formulates a strategy to meet the needs of stakeholders and, above all, to be competitive. This means the strategic objectives should be designed to satisfy key stakeholders. Stakeholders include different groups that an organization must appeal to, such as

- customers,
- investors and shareholders,
- employees, and
- communities.

Finalize Strategy

Once an organization defines its mission, vision, and values; analyzes the internal and external environments; chooses a general strategy type; and defines its strategic objectives, it is ready to finalize the strategy. That is, the organization must create a clear plan before progressing to strategy implementation.

Strategy Implementation: Bringing a Strategy to Life

During strategy implementation, an organization follows through on its strategic plan. It is during this stage that an organization builds and leverages the capabilities of its human resources (which are often referred to as human capital at the organizational level of analysis), as human resources will ultimately play an important role in supporting the enactment of an organization's strategy. The following section discusses how to align an organization's HR policies and practices with its strategy and how a well-designed system of HR policies and practices can improve human capital capabilities within an organization and, ultimately, performance.

Contributing to Your Organization's Strategy

After the formulation stage, the strategy must be implemented, which requires the coordination and cooperation of employees and managers at all levels of the organization. As you might imagine, sometimes there are disconnects between an organization's official strategy and how managers interpret and implement that strategy. Managers who behave in their own self-interest—and not in the interest of the organization—can derail strategy implementation by delaying or reducing the quality of the implementation or even sabotaging the strategy! Here are some actions you can take as a manager to bring your organization's strategy to life.[13]

1. *Know what your organization's strategy is.* In a survey of employees from 20 major Australian corporations, only 29% of respondents were able to identify their company's strategy from a list of six choices.[14] Take the following steps to understand your organization's strategy:
    - Review the organization's mission statement, vision, and values.
    - Ask your manager to explain how you can contribute to strategic objectives.
    - Pay attention to formal communications from executives and upper management.
    - Stay on top of changes to your organization's strategy.

2. *Align your own goals with your organization's strategic objectives.* As a manager, it is important to align your self-interests with the interests of the organization, assuming the strategy aligns with your own personal ethics. Specifically, set goals that describe how you and your team can contribute to organizational objectives, such as decreasing turnover or increasing productivity.

3. *Communicate the strategy to your employees.* Explain the strategy to your employees, and engage them in activities that help them understand how they can contribute to the organization's strategic objectives. Remember, as a manager, you play an essential role in communicating company strategy to employees.

STRATEGIC HRM: LINKING STRATEGY WITH HRM

Recall that *strategic HRM* is the process of aligning HR policies and practices with the strategic objectives of the organization, including achieving employee, operational, stakeholder, and financial outcomes to achieve and sustain a competitive advantage. An important implication of strategic HRM is that HR practices and employees are company assets that add value and not merely costs.[15] If implemented in a systematic and data-informed manner, strategic HRM can help an organization realize its strategy and objectives through the deployment of its human resource capabilities.

The Origins of Strategic HRM

HRM activities have changed over the years. A growing number of organizations now focus on *strategic* HRM and using HR data to make better organizational decisions. Historically, the function was labeled *personnel management*, which carried with it the implication that employees were an organizational expense.[16] Personnel management professionals tended to focus mostly on transactional (e.g., recordkeeping, compliance) and employee relations activities. However, the amount of time spent on transactional activities has decreased over the past century as more processes have become automated, freeing up more time for transformational activities that help the organization leverage its human resources to achieve strategic objectives (see Figure 2.2). Today, it is common to hear the use of the terms *human resource management* and *people operations* instead of *personnel management*, as these terms emphasize the more strategic role that HR plays.

FIGURE 2.2 ■ Evolution of HRM Activities

The amount of time spent on transactional activities has decreased over the past century as more HR functions become technology-assisted, -augmented, and -automated. This leaves more time for activities designed to transform the organization by strategically deploying human resources.

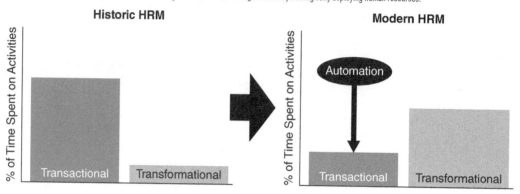

The focus on strategic HRM has also expanded the responsibilities of the HR function. According to Ulrich's model of strategic HRM, the HR function should play the roles of administrative expert, employee advocate, change agent, and business partner (see Figure 2.3). Specifically, HRM has retained foundational activities related to administrative and employee relations activities while introducing additional activities related to orchestrating change and serving as a business partner. Strategic HRM has expanded the influence of the HR function. Namely, the deployment of HR practices and human resource capabilities can be used to realize strategic change initiatives, such as mergers, acquisitions, reorganizations, and restructurings, as well as gain a "seat at the table" during key business decisions and influence strategy formulation and implementation. Though, with greater influence comes greater responsibility. The modern HR function now faces greater pressure to make impactful decisions and to link HR activities to organizational performance.

FIGURE 2.3 ■ Ulrich's Model of Strategic HRM

Ulrich's model indicates that HRM should provide administrative expertise, serve as an employee advocate, be an agent of change, and serve as a strategic business partner.

Source: Adapted from Ulrich, D. (1996). *Human resource champions: The next agenda for adding value and delivering results.* Cambridge, MA: Harvard Business School Press.

Organizational Performance and the Balanced Scorecard

Historically, organizational performance and strategy attainment were defined primarily in terms of financial indicators, such as return on assets, return on equity, and market return. Achieving financial outcomes is indeed a worthwhile and necessary objective, but other nonfinancial factors shed light on an organization's progress toward realizing strategic objectives. The introduction of the balanced scorecard was a game-changer in this regard because it made the case for considering both financial and operational factors when evaluating strategic progress and organizational performance.[17] As shown in Figure 2.4, the balanced scorecard is a strategic management support system that requires managers to "balance" different stakeholder needs, such as the needs of customers, investors and shareholders, employees, and the broader community. Specifically, this system directs managers' attention to four factors: financial, customer, internal processes, and innovation and learning. For each of those factors, managers identify specific goals that connect to the organization's overarching strategy, as well as develop measures (e.g., surveys) to track attainment of those goals. The balanced scorecard encourages managers to consider performance from both external perspectives (e.g., customer satisfaction) and internal perspectives (e.g., operational efficiency). An organization's HRM function can use a balanced scorecard to identify opportunities for aligning HR strategy with organizational strategy. For example, to help the organization achieve high external customer satisfaction, the HRM function might create a strategy aimed at acquiring, managing, and retaining talented individuals in customer-facing roles.

FIGURE 2.4 ■ Example of a Balanced Scorecard

The amount of time spent on transactional activities has decreased over the past century as more HR functions become technology-assisted, -augmented, and -automated. This leaves more time for activities designed to transform the organization by strategically deploying human resources.

Identifying Best Practices

Strategic HRM has roots in multiple disciplines, as it reflects the intersection of HRM and strategic management, and incorporates principles from other areas, such as industrial relations, economics, and organizational theory.[18] Together, these disciplines provide a basis for understanding how human resources can be deployed in the service of organizational strategic objectives. Some HR practices can be thought of as *universal best practices* because implementing them often leads to improved organizational performance, regardless of the organization. In HRM, evidence-based universal best practices include enhancing perceptions of job security among employees, promoting from within the organization, providing financial incentives linked to performance, offering training, and providing flexible work arrangements.[19]

Pfeffer's practices are examples of high-performance work practices that are instrumental for developing human capital capabilities across different contexts.[20]

1. *Create employment security* policies to encourage employee involvement and commitment.

2. *Selectively hire new employees* to create a highly qualified workforce that is a good fit.

3. *Organize employees into self-managed teams* to achieve higher-performing teams.

4. *Compensate employees based on performance* to attract, motivate, and retain talented employees.

5. *Train employees* to enhance the knowledge and skills necessary for high performance.

6. *Reduce status differences between employees* to leverage ideas, skills, and effort at all levels.

7. *Share information on strategy and performance* to motivate employees to contribute to the organization.

Such practices are often referred to as high-performance work practices.[21] Meta-analytic evidence indicates that certain well-designed individual HR practices generally have positive effects on organizational outcomes.[22]

Systems Thinking: Considering the System and Context

In addition to identifying universal best practices, such as high-performance work practices, it is important to consider how these practices and others fit into the broader HR system and organizational strategy. In other words, the effectiveness of some HR practices may be contingent on the context (e.g., industry, culture) and the configuration of other HR practices that are part of a larger system.[23] Thus, in addition to identifying universal best practices, we recommend taking a systems perspective, which means considering how all the pieces of the HR puzzle fit together, how HR fits within the broader organization, and how to address any misalignment in HR practices. When a system of HR practices is well designed and well integrated, certain synergies can emerge, such that the potential of the whole system may be greater than the sum of the system's individual parts.

Synergy between bundled HR practices, however, is not guaranteed. Without consideration of the organization's strategy and without taking a systems perspective, it is unlikely that a system of HR practices will reach its full potential. For instance, imagine a company in which teamwork is integral for achieving a strategic objective. Accordingly, this company devises a selection tool to identify job applicants who are likely to be team players and an onboarding program to train new employees to work effectively in teams. Now imagine the same company introduces a new compensation program that rewards only individual performance and not the performance of teams. Rather than interacting synergistically with the selection and training subsystems to improve team effectiveness, the compensation subsystem may thwart team effectiveness by focusing individuals' efforts on their own individual achievement, as opposed to the achievement of their team. In this hypothetical case, the whole might even be *less* than the sum of the parts when it comes to achieving the team-oriented strategic objective. Thus, to achieve desired organizational outcomes, it is important to develop HR practices with a strategic mindset and to focus on the entire system of HR practices as a whole and their potential configurations, as well as their interaction with the organization's culture and technology capabilities.

Research has shown that integrated systems of high-performance work practices outperform well-designed individual HR practices. Based on data from 968 organizations of various sizes and from a variety of industries, one study found that investing in an HR system can lead to valued organizational outcomes, such as lower turnover, higher productivity, and higher financial performance.[24] Offering additional support, a meta-analytic investigation of eight longitudinal studies showed that well-integrated systems of high-performance work practices lead to higher organizational performance than individual HR practices, which suggests that integrating different HR practices matters.[25] Further, the meta-analytic investigation showed that the relationship between HR practices and organizational performance was stronger among manufacturing firms compared with service firms, which lends support to the argument that the context matters from an industry standpoint too. Table 2.1 provides examples of other factors that have been found to influence the effectiveness of HR practices.

TABLE 2.1 ■ Factors Influencing the Effectiveness of HR Practices	
Factors	Description
Internal Environment	
Business Strategy	Although research findings have been mixed, some evidence indicates differentiation strategies enhance the effectiveness of HR systems in relation to certain organizational outcomes, such as reducing turnover.
Culture	Most evidence to date indicates that a positive and supportive organizational culture enhances the effectiveness of HR systems in relation to organizational outcomes.
Manager Characteristics	Research has shown that having more senior managers and managers with stronger HR backgrounds enhances the effectiveness of HR systems.
External Environment	
Industry Characteristics	The type of industry an organization operates within can influence the effectiveness of HR systems. For example, the positive effects of HR systems on organizational outcomes tend to be stronger in manufacturing industries (as opposed to service industries).

Source: Republished with permission of Academy of Management, from Jackson, S. E., Schuler, R. S., & Jiang, K. (2014). An aspirational framework for strategic human resource management. *Academy of Management Annals, 8,* 1–56; permission conveyed through Copyright Clearance Center, Inc.

How Does a System of HR Practices Influence Organizational Outcomes?

$$\textbf{Performance} = \textbf{Ability} \times \textbf{Motivation} \times \textbf{Opportunity}.$$

The **ability-motivation-opportunity model** proposes that a system of HR practices influences employee outcomes and, ultimately, operational and financial outcomes to the extent that the practices target three different elements: ability to perform, motivation to perform, and opportunity to perform. The first element—*ability* to perform—encapsulates employees' knowledge, skills, and abilities. In a sense, ability to perform can be thought as what an employee *can do* on the job. The second element—*motivation* to perform—refers to the work-related effort that employees exert toward goal completion and captures what employees *will do* on the job. That is, just because employees are able to perform the work does not necessarily mean they have the motivation to perform the work and vice versa. The third element—*opportunity* to perform—entails whether employees have the chance to perform on the job. Taken together, we can conceptualize employee performance as a function of their ability, motivation, and opportunity to perform. Thus, according to this model, if ability, motivation, or opportunity falls to zero, performance will be zero. We recommend using this conceptual formula to help you wrap your mind around how employees achieve high levels of performance in the workplace, as well as how different HR practices can be designed to target each of these three elements.[26]

SPOTLIGHT ON GLOBAL ISSUES: STRATEGIC INTERNATIONAL HRM

Today, many organizations, such as Amazon, Meta, and Marriott, span international boundaries. Consequently, these multinational companies operate across national and cultural contexts and conditions, with different laws, customs, and values. Strategic international HRM requires a nuanced and intentional approach to deploying human resources to achieve strategic objectives. To be successful in the international arena, scholars have argued that organizations must show flexibility in their HR practices to adapt to and fit with the different national environments. For example, in the Chinese national environment, organizations show higher performance when their HR practices emphasize the importance of complying with rules *and* encourage commitment to the organization. The flexible application of HR practices, however, is not without its challenges, as multinational corporations struggle with whether to integrate HR practices in a consistent manner via a global strategy or to tailor HR practices to fit the needs of each national context via an adaptive strategy.[27]

STRATEGIC HRM, DATA-INFORMED DECISION MAKING, AND HR ANALYTICS

We live in a world with ever-increasing amounts of data, technologies, and big decisions to make. We collect, analyze, and interpret data for many reasons but often with the goal of making better decisions—that is, decisions informed by evidence. For example, when Covid-19 brought the world to a standstill in early 2020, pharmaceutical companies developed and manufactured Covid-19 vaccines with unprecedented speed and efficacy. In the process, they demonstrated the importance of leveraging years of prior scientific research and technological advances and making decisions based on data collected using rigorous research designs like randomized clinical trials.[28] Further, technological advances in the form of artificial intelligence have made it easier for us to acquire, manage, analyze, and interpret data about ourselves and data about our organizations. As a society, we have grown more used to the idea of using data and technology to inform decision making. This has made its way into HR departments. In recent years, strategic HRM has expanded to place a greater emphasis on data-informed decisions, paving the way for HR analytics and technological advances like artificial intelligence.

At this point, you may be thinking, "Do I have to become an expert in data analysis if I work in HR?" The answer is no, but we do recommend that you improve your data literacy skills. Data literacy includes competence in mathematics and statistics, data analysis and visualization, and critical thinking and problem solving.[29]

Today, data-informed decision making is an important aspect of strategic HRM. Companies like Chevron have led the way when it comes to integrating advanced and strategically aligned data analytics into their HR function. The energy company launched a centralized HR analytics team, and from the beginning, the team made it clear that its mission was to "support Chevron's business strategies with better, faster workforce decisions informed by data." To do that, R. J. Milnor, the former head of talent analytics for Chevron, stated that "[HR] analytics is really about informing and supporting business strategy, and we do that through people data." With respect to workforce planning, the team built models to forecast future talent demand and supply 10 years in the future. These models identified key drivers of talent demand and supply for different geographic locations and provided estimates of future employee turnover with 85% accuracy.[30] Ultimately, informing HR decisions using data helps organizations to attract, motivate, and retain talented people. This can ultimately drive organizational outcomes, such as productivity and innovation, and reduce costs associated with turnover and counterproductive behaviors.

Using data to inform people decisions requires making a business case to organizational leaders by linking data to strategic organizational objectives. One way to garner support for HR analytics and data-informed decision making in general is to convince organizational leaders and HR professionals of the value of the scientific process. That is, organizational leaders and HR professionals must think like scientists when it comes to collecting, analyzing, and interpreting people data, but at the same time, they need business acumen to make a strong case for using science-based HR practices to improve the organization.[32] When using HR analytics in this way, an overarching goal should be to provide managers with actionable evidence-based practices that improve the management of people. In fact, recent research has linked the use of HR analytics to higher organizational performance, because HR analytics leads to better evidence-based management and managerial decision making, which in turn lead to higher organizational performance.[33]

Kenneth Chenault, who is a former chief executive at American Express and the current chairperson at General Catalyst, is the co-chairperson of a corporate group called the Data & Trust Alliance. The group developed a 55-question measure to evaluate algorithmic bias in AI-based recruitment and selection tools.[31]

Photo by Justin Sullivan/Getty Images

SPOTLIGHT ON DATA AND ANALYTICS: USING ARTIFICIAL INTELLIGENCE ETHICALLY TO ASSIST AND AUGMENT HUMAN RESOURCES

Advances in artificial intelligence (AI) and associated technologies have the potential to assist and augment many different aspects of an organization's human resources. As described in this chapter's opening case, Stanley Black & Decker partnered with DeepHow to deploy an AI training platform called Stephanie. Rather than automate the role of a training specialist, the AI assists the training function with collecting, indexing, and creating training materials for manufacturing jobs. In doing so, the AI supports HR by enhancing its ability to develop up-to-date training content for rapidly changing work and technology.

As another example, HR vendors are beginning to offer a recruiting platform with automated AI algorithms that score and classify applicants based on interviews. Because of inherent algorithmic complexities, the actions of AI platforms can seem mysterious to applicants, employees, and organizations alike. Scholar Jenna Burrell describes the following challenge when it comes to understanding AI algorithms: "When a computer learns and consequently builds its own representation of a classification decision, it does so without regard for human comprehension." Burrell goes on to say, "The workings of [AI] algorithms can escape full understanding and interpretation by humans, even for those with specialized training, even for computer scientists."[34]

The opacity of some AI algorithms has raised concerns about fairness and bias, leading to legal challenges and pushes for regulation. Governments have already been taking steps to address AI-related fairness and bias. For instance, the state of Illinois passed a law in 2019 requiring organizations to inform and explain to applicants how video-based interviews will be used and how the associated AI works. In addition, both the White House and the European Union have pushed for frameworks to guide the ethical development and application of AI.

Beyond legislation and regulation, some have encouraged the use of audits to ensure the ethical use of AI in HR. These audits would ideally involve collaboration between AI developers, HR subject matter experts, and psychologists. The purpose of audits is to uncover bias and fairness issues related to the algorithm itself as well as how people understand and perceive the algorithm. Experts have also encouraged the creation of "bias dashboards," which allow analysts to evaluate how a tool performs across groups of individuals from different protected classes. Recently, organizations like Humana, Nike, and Mastercard have joined a corporate group called the Data & Trust Alliance, which has created a system for detecting and evaluating algorithmic bias in AI-based tools. In 2022, the Society for Industrial and Organizational Psychology published a set of recommended guidelines for evaluating AI-based assessment tools. While AI presents many exciting opportunities for HR, the field must also recognize the potential for unintended consequences and the importance to develop and apply such technological advances ethically.[35]

Defining HR Analytics

Given its large focus on data and scientific decision making, HR analytics has been referred to as a "game changer."[36] Many would also argue that HR analytics has the potential to be HR's best friend. Collecting, analyzing, and interpreting people data can lead to valuable insights, and the emergence of HR as a strategic business partner has paved the way for HR analytics. Human resource (HR) analytics goes by different terms, such as people analytics, workforce analytics, human capital analytics, and talent analytics; it refers to the process of collecting, analyzing, and reporting people-related data for the purpose of improving decision making, achieving strategic objectives, and sustaining a competitive advantage. In other words, HR analytics is the systematic process of applying quantitative or qualitative methods to derive insights that shape and inform people-related business decisions and strategy. Thus, HR analytics is intended to provide data-informed decisions that improve decision making at all levels of an organization, including among frontline managers. In general, HR analytics can provide evidence supporting the links among HR systems, policies, and practices and employee, operational, stakeholder, and financial outcomes. Advanced HR analytics can even provide prescriptive recommendations for the future.

The growth of HR analytics signals that more and more organizations are beginning to understand the importance of making data-informed decisions to achieve a competitive advantage. To that end, after reviewing survey responses and panel discussions, the Society for Human Resource Management (SHRM) Foundation concluded in a report that leveraging HR analytics to achieve a competitive advantage is an important area of growth for HRM.[37] The report, however, concluded that talent shortages are on the rise and that HR must provide HR analytics to aid in strategic business decision making. The shortage of people who possess technical and data analytics skills extends well beyond those working in HR and has been reported by recruiters as one of the top challenges they face in finding qualified candidates for positions.[38]

Figure 2.5 displays growth in interest in HR analytics based on Google search term use. The value 100 represents the peak popularity for the search term, whereas the value 50 represents times in which this term had half the popularity. Data were queried from Google Trends for January 1, 2006, to January 1, 2023.

As shown in Figure 2.5, interest in HR analytics has been growing steadily since 2006, as indicated by the number of Google searches for the term "HR analytics." Numerous organizations, including Google, Meta, and Microsoft, have expanded their internal HRM function by adding an HR analytics team. Further, companies like ADP, Inc., Workday, and SAP SuccessFactors offer products and services for analyzing people data in addition to those related to data collection and storage. These changes reflect the findings from the 2018 Deloitte Global Human Capital Trends Report, which showed that 85% of surveyed companies rated HR analytics as "important" or "very "important" for their business, but less than half of the surveyed companies indicated they were "ready" or "very ready" for the HR analytics trend.[39] Thus, many organizations and HR departments are in need of individuals who possess knowledge and skills related to HR analytics.

FIGURE 2.5   ■   Growing Interest in HR Analytics

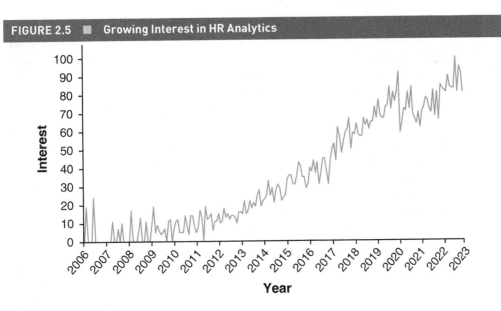

Identifying HR Analytics Competencies

Integrating HR analytics into the HRM function requires certain competencies that do not necessarily need to be held by a single individual. Ideally, HR analytics should be a team endeavor. Working as a team with diverse backgrounds and perspectives can facilitate sound judgments and good decision making, particularly when it comes to ethically or legally gray areas. While some HR analysts may have degrees in business or HRM, others may have backgrounds in industrial and organizational psychology, law, statistics, mathematics, data science, computer science, or information systems. Aside from educational differences among HR analysts, what matters most is that an HR analytics *team* is competent in the following seven areas: theory, business, data management, measurement, data analysis, employment law, and ethics (see Table 2.2).

TABLE 2.2   ■   The Seven Competencies of Effective HR Analytics Teams

Competency	Description
Theory	Knowledge of psychological and social scientific theory is critical because findings from people data should be interpreted through the lens of human behavior, cognition, and emotion.
Business	Business knowledge and skills ensure the activities of an HR analytics team are in the service of HR and organizational strategies and thus help the organization gain a competitive advantage.
Data Management	Data management knowledge and skills ensure that data are acquired, cleaned, manipulated, and stored in a way that facilitates subsequent analysis while maintaining data privacy and security.
Measurement	Measurement knowledge and skills provide a basis for developing sound HR metrics and measures that demonstrate sufficient reliability and validity.
Data Analysis	Knowledge and skills related to mathematics, statistics, and data analysis are critical, especially when it comes to identifying an appropriate analysis technique to address a given hypothesis or question.
Employment Law	Knowledge of employment law and HR legal issues separates an HR analytics team from a general business analytics team; teams lacking such knowledge might inadvertently violate laws when collecting data, analyze data that should not be analyzed, or use data in ways that may result in adverse consequences for protected groups.
Ethics	Knowledge of ethics helps the team navigate legally gray areas while also answering the question: "Just because we can, should we?"

Even if you have no desire to become an HR analyst but still wish to work in HR, developing data analysis skills is wise. A common complaint from data analysts is that managers do not understand or recognize the value of data analysis and data-informed findings. Conversely, a common complaint among managers is that data analysts fail to provide *understandable* answers to the questions that managers *actually* need answered. Both complaints lead to frustration, and it is not uncommon for a rift to emerge between data analysts and managers. In recognition of this communication issue, Tom Davenport, who is an independent senior advisor to Deloitte Analytics, wrote a blog post praising what he refers to as *light quants*.[40] Whereas a *heavy quant* would include the likes of a statistician, mathematician, or data scientist, a light quant is someone who knows enough about mathematics, statistics, and data analysis to communicate with a heavy quant and who knows enough about the business to communicate with a manager. Davenport contends that many organizations with an analytics function would benefit from hiring or training individuals who qualify as light quants, as such individuals can help managers pose better questions for heavy quants to answer and, in turn, translate the findings of heavy quants into words and ideas that are understood by managers. Davenport refers to these individuals as *analytical translators*. We agree with Davenport and argue that all HR students and professionals should develop their competence in mathematics, statistics, and data analysis, at least to the point where they are able to bridge the communication divide between so-called heavy quants and managers.

Understanding the Levels of HR Analytics

There are three levels of HR analytics and data analytics more generally: descriptive, predictive, and prescriptive. Descriptive analytics focuses on understanding what has happened already, providing a "snapshot" of the past. Often descriptive analytics involves operational reporting and includes summary statistics, such as sums, means, and percentages. For example, Kavitha Prabhakar, chief diversity, equity, and inclusion (DEI) leader at Deloitte US, and associates surveyed more than 1,500 U.S. workers to assess their trust in their organizations' DEI initiatives. Applying descriptive analytics, they found that 80% of workers trusted their organizations to reach their stated DEI goals but that 40% of workers would consider quitting their organizations if they couldn't trust their organizations' commitment to DEI.[41] Additional examples of descriptive analytics include commonly reported HR metrics, such as absence rate, turnover rate, cost per hire, and training return on investment. HR dashboards serve as decision-support tools and provide managers with summaries of key HR metrics and other descriptive analytics to help them understand their workforce. Descriptive analytics does not have to be complicated, and most involve simple arithmetic.

The next level of analytics is predictive analytics, which focuses on predicting what is likely to happen in the future given what is already known. True predictive analytics also involves validating and evaluating the accuracy of those predictions. Often, predictive analytics involves building statistical and computational models. What is a *model*? Broadly speaking, a model offers a parsimonious representation of reality or the way we think things work. By extension, statistical models are mathematical approximations of reality based on data sampled from an underlying population. A common type of statistical model used in predictive analytics is the regression model. In fact, there are many different types of regression models, which can be used as the basis of artificial intelligence and machine learning algorithms. Using regression, we can evaluate the extent to which scores on one or more predictor variables are associated with scores on a particular outcome variable. For instance, in the context of selection, we might estimate a model to test whether applicants' level of extraversion is associated with their future level of sales performance. We might then apply that model to future applicants' scores on extraversion to make predictions about their future sales performance scores. Note that we do not expect 100% accuracy in our predictive models, as human behavior is influenced by many factors that may not be captured in the regression model. However, we strive to forecast future events and outcomes with as much accuracy as we can. As described by a SHRM Foundation report, very few companies have reached the level of predictive analytics, as the vast majority relies on descriptive analytics and basic reporting for HRM.[42]

Finally, the most advanced form of analytics is prescriptive analytics, and at this point, relatively few companies effectively apply prescriptive analytics to HR-related decision making. Prescriptive analytics focuses on what actions should be taken in the future based on what is known and what is predicted to happen in the future. Prescriptive analytics is forward-looking, just like predictive analytics, but prescriptive

Dashboards act as decision-support tools. Some dashboards are interactive and allow managers to manipulate the data display, drill down into different teams and units, and conduct "what if" analyses.

©iStockphoto.com/NicoElNino

analytics builds upon predictive analytics by taking data-informed predictions and translating them into different decision alternatives and courses of action. An overarching goal of prescriptive analytics is to optimize decision making to ultimately achieve the best outcome that is aligned with organizational strategy.

HR ANALYTICS AND THE SCIENTIFIC PROCESS

LEARNING OBJECTIVES
2.4   Summarize the arguments for a scientific, ethical, and legally compliant approach to HR decision making.

Regardless of whether a company uses descriptive, predictive, or prescriptive analytics, we recommend you envision HR analytics—and data-informed decision making, in general—as a scientific endeavor. The scientific process offers a rigorous framework for guiding the way in which HR departments collect, analyze, and interpret data in service of HR and organizational strategies. In essence, the scientific process can be thought of as a rigorous and rational approach to problem solving and decision making and consists of the six steps shown in Figure 2.6. The goals of science are to describe, explain, determine the cause, or predict some phenomenon of interest, such as employee productivity and turnover.

Step 1: Identifying the Problem

Like any problem-solving approach, the first step of the scientific process is to identify and define the problem. That is, what specifically will you try to describe, predict, explain, or understand using analytics? Imagine your organization has been facing a retention issue, in which high-performing employees are leaving the organization voluntarily at a concerning rate. What's more, turnover is a major cost for your organization. In fact, some estimates suggest that recruiting, selecting, and training a replacement employee can cost an organization between 90% and 200% of the annual salary for each person who leaves the organization.[43] Given the cost of voluntary turnover and your organization's latest turnover rates (which represent a type of descriptive analytics), you might define voluntary turnover as a problem for which you wish to find a solution. Failure to solve the problem might impair the organization's ability to achieve strategic objectives due to insufficient human capital.

FIGURE 2.6 ■ Steps in the Scientific Process

The scientific process can be thought of as a rigorous approach to problem solving and decision making.

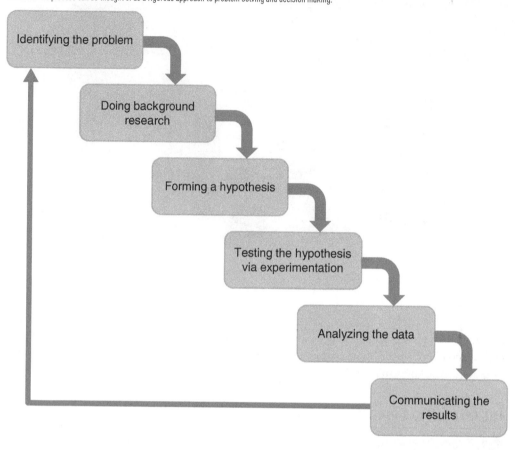

Step 2: Doing Background Research

It is unlikely that the problem you identified is entirely unique to your organization. For example, others who came before you have investigated the problem of voluntary turnover. Universities and other academic institutions employ organizational scholars and researchers who have investigated countless organizational problems. Thus, before starting from scratch, look to prior theory and research to help you understand the phenomenon you wish to investigate using the scientific process. If you were to look through scholarly journal articles for the phenomenon of voluntary turnover, for example, you would find thousands of articles on the topic. In doing so, you might come across a meta-analysis that shows job dissatisfaction, low work engagement, and poor leadership predict voluntary turnover.[44] Plus, you might find a theory that can help you wrap your mind around why turnover occurs. For instance, the *unfolding model of turnover* describes how sudden changes or "shocks" at work or at home might lead to thoughts of quitting.[45] For example, the Covid-19 pandemic was a global shock that led workers across industries to reevaluate their jobs and employers, motivating some to quit. From a practical standpoint, doing background research can save your HR department money, as you will spend less time and energy on trying to solve a problem for which others have already found a viable solution.

Step 3: Forming a Hypothesis

A hypothesis is simply a statement of what you believe or predict to be true. In other words, it is an educated guess based on the background research you performed. We recommend stating the hypothesis as an if/then statement. For example, based on your identification of the problem and background research, you might hypothesize: "If new employees perceive a low degree of job satisfaction, then they will be more likely to quit." As a suggestion, try to make your hypothesis as specific as possible by including conditional statements or qualifiers, such as "in this situation" or "for whom." For instance, you might revise your hypothesis to state: "If *new sales* employees perceive a low degree of job satisfaction *after 3 months on the job*, then they will be more likely to quit *by the end of their first year*." Remember, your hypothesis serves as a compass to guide you through the scientific process. For instance, a hypothesis informs what data you need to collect. In the turnover example, we would need to measure new sales employees' job satisfaction, as well as pull organizational turnover records for employees at one-year post hire.

Step 4: Testing the Hypothesis via Experimentation

A true experiment is one of the most rigorous designs you can use to test a hypothesis. For a true experiment, employees must be randomly assigned to either a treatment or control group. Under some circumstances it may be impractical or inappropriate to conduct a true experiment. For instance, imagine a scenario in which you developed a new training module aimed at increasing new sales employees' job satisfaction. Using a true experimental design, you could randomly assign half of new employees to a treatment group that receives the training and the other half to a control group that doesn't receive the training. At the end of the first year, you could evaluate whether fewer individuals quit when they received the job satisfaction training.

Although using a true experimental design could give you greater confidence that increasing sales employees' job satisfaction using training *causes* lower turnover, there are still practical and ethical concerns that should be considered. Namely, assuming the training increases job satisfaction and ultimately reduces the probability of voluntarily quitting, would it be ethical to withhold the new training from those in the control group? Given the potential consequences of not participating in the new onboarding module, you may argue that a true experimental design would not be ethical in this scenario. Instead, you might opt for another way of testing your hypothesis, even if it means you will be less confident that participating in the onboarding module is the reason behind reduced turnover. You might even conduct what are referred to as pre- or quasi-experiments, which lack a control condition or random assignment. Alternatively, you might opt for an observational design in which you survey employees or record their behavior through direct observation or archival organizational records. For example, to test our turnover hypothesis, we might administer a survey in which sales employees respond to a job satisfaction measure after 3 months on the job and then gather organizational turnover records 1 year later to assess whether each employee quit or stayed. Regardless of how a hypothesis is tested, it is important to consider the types of data that will be collected, as the type of data informs the type of analysis.

Qualitative Versus Quantitative Data

In general, there are two types of data: qualitative and quantitative (see Table 2.3). On the one hand, qualitative data are nonnumeric and include text or narrative data, such as interview transcripts or responses to open-ended survey questions. Additional examples of qualitative data include videos and photos. Qualitative data can be quite rich, providing important information about context and processes. Qualitative data, however, are analyzed differently than quantitative data. For instance, the transcripts from qualitative interviews could be thematically analyzed to uncover recurring themes. Qualitative data can also be used to uncover employee experiences that were not understood by the researcher. There are even software programs to facilitate this process, such as NVivo and ATLAS. ti. Sometimes HR analysts or artificial intelligence tools take qualitative data and transform them into quantitative data. As a simple example, an analyst might use sentiment analysis to determine the proportion of positive words relative to negative words that employees wrote when responding to an open-ended survey question. This process would, in effect, translate nonnumeric qualitative data to numeric quantitative data.

On the other hand, quantitative data are numeric and can be counted or measured in some way. Employee age is an example of a continuous quantitative variable, whereas employee voluntary turnover—when coded in binary as 0 = stayed and 1 = quit—is an example of a categorical quantitative variable. Statistical models can be estimated using quantitative data.

| TABLE 2.3 ■ Example of Qualitative vs. Quantitative Data | | |

This data table provides an example of a qualitative variable and a quantitative variable. The performance description variable is qualitative because the associated data are nonnumeric and text. The performance rating variable is quantitative because the data are numeric.

Employee ID	Performance Rating	Performance Description
9082625	2.65	Peter performed satisfactorily. He still struggles with his TPS reports and arrives late to work at least once a week. Nonetheless, he showed glimpses of potential from time to time.
9077854	4.99	Lisa's performance was exceptional this quarter. She went above and beyond on her grant proposals and showed great teamwork when she helped get a team member back up to speed who had been on maternity leave.

Big Data Versus Little Data

In addition to the qualitative vs. quantitative distinction, we can distinguish between big data and little data. The term *big data* has received a lot of attention in the popular press in recent years, and companies like Amazon, Meta, and Google have built enormous reputations and revenues from leveraging data to optimize business decision making. Amazon, for example, tracks huge volumes of consumer data and, using sophisticated algorithms, can predict what consumers will buy. In the realm of HRM, HR analysts have begun to use big data to make better people decisions.

But exactly what are big data? It turns out that the term *big data* means different things to different people. For some, big data simply mean a lot of data. For others, big data have to do with the structure of the data. For our purposes, big data refer to large (or massive) amounts of unstructured, messy, and/or quickly streaming data—sometimes from sources that we did not originally intend to use for analytical purposes (e.g., scraping résumé data). As shown in Figure 2.7, big data are also described in terms of four Vs: volume (amount of data), variety (different sources and forms of data), velocity (speed with which new data arrive), and veracity (trustworthiness of the data, data integrity, and certainty).[46] Together, these Vs provide an indication of the "bigness" and quality of big data.

| FIGURE 2.7 ■ Four Vs of Big Data | |

The complexity and size of big data can be described according to four characteristics: volume, variety, velocity, and veracity.

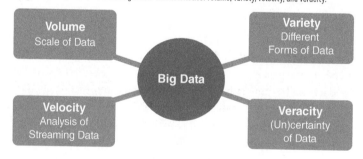

In contrast, little data are structured data that are gathered in smaller volumes, usually for previously planned purposes. Consider an analogy involving a water fountain and a fire hydrant to illustrate the distinction between little data and big data. Working with little data is like drinking from a water fountain; the water flow is steady, clean, slow, predictable, and easy to manage. Working with big data is like drinking from a fire hydrant spraying out untreated and unfiltered water; the water flow is voluminous, dirty, fast, largely unpredictable, and difficult to manage. Thus, working with big data requires a lot of up-front data management and restructuring, so much so that prepping big data for subsequent data analysis may require the expertise of a data scientist or data engineer.

Data Collection and Measurement

Regardless of how or where data are collected, sound measurement is key. Think carefully about what is being measured and how it is being measured and distinguish between two terms: concept and measure. A concept is a theoretical construct, and job performance is a prime example. Performance on a given job entails multiple different behaviors. For instance, a sales position requires the enactment of customer service behaviors. Different measures can be used to assess the concept of job performance for a sales position. For instance, an HR analyst might survey customers for feedback on their experiences working with specific salespeople. Or the analyst might observe and rate salespeople interacting with customers. That is, different measurement types and sources can be used to measure the same concept. Regardless of the measure type, an analyst's goal should be to measure the target concept consistently and accurately.

Step 5: Analyzing the Data

After testing your hypothesis through experimentation or observation, you are ready to analyze the data to formally test your hypothesis—that is, accept (confirm) or reject (disconfirm) the hypothesis. The way in which you analyze the data will differ based on whether you collected qualitative or quantitative data.

Qualitative Data Analysis

As mentioned previously, qualitative data can be analyzed using a variety of analytical tools; however, the notion of hypothesis testing for qualitative data analysis differs from that of quantitative data analysis. Qualitative data analysis often involves agreement between independent coders/analysts to determine whether a phenomenon exists and the processes underlying that phenomenon. A full discussion of qualitative data analysis is beyond the scope of this textbook, but nonetheless, we highly recommend that you learn more about qualitative data analysis tools and techniques, as qualitative data can be a rich source of data and can answer unique questions. In fact, if you are interested in learning more about qualitative data analysis applied to understanding people in a workplace, we recommend reading the article by Annika Wilhelmy and Tine Köhler found in this end note.[47]

Quantitative Data Analysis

A number of quantitative data analysis tools exist, and determining which one to use rests on a number of assumptions, including the type(s) of data you collected and your research design. For example, for categorical data analysis, statistical techniques like the chi-square test of independence may be appropriate. For designs in which the means of two or more continuous variables are compared, such as in a true or quasi-experimental design, a *t*-test or analysis of variance (ANOVA) may be appropriate. When testing the relation between two or more continuous variables, such as job satisfaction scores in relation to job performance scores, you might use analyses such as correlation or regression. Further, when you are modeling change over time, growth-modeling techniques can be applied, and when modeling the structure of social network interactions, social network analysis is appropriate. Our point is that there are many different types of statistical analyses, and part of the challenge being an HR analyst is determining which analysis is most appropriate given the data and the research design.

With the rise of big data, some HR analysts have begun to use artificial intelligence models and algorithms. The term *artificial intelligence* can mean many different things to different people, and what constitutes artificial intelligence is still a topic of discussion and debate. In HR analytics, however, artificial intelligence (AI) commonly refers to statistical or machine learning models that are highly complex, and AI can be used for both predictive and prescriptive analytics.[48] AI can be particularly useful when the goal is to identify patterns and make predictions using big data.

Interpreting results is the final stage of the data analysis process. Remember, data do not "speak"; they are interpreted or evaluated. That is, the act of interpretation, like other aspects of the scientific process, requires sound judgment and decision making. This also means that interpretation is susceptible to bias and error, which is addressed next.

SPOTLIGHT ON LEGAL ISSUES: BIAS, FAIRNESS, AND REGULATION OF ARTIFICIAL INTELLIGENCE

Advances in AI have improved organizations' ability to make accurate predictions about the future. For example, using AI-based recruitment and selection assessments, organizations have improved predictions regarding which applicants will excel on the job. AI tools can assist, augment, or automate key HR decision-making processes, which can free up time for HR analysts and other HR professionals to contribute to other transformational activities.

However, even when developers and analysts have the best intentions, AI-based assessments can result in biased, unfair, or discriminatory decisions. The inherently complex nature of many AI tools can render their internal workings a "black box" with little transparency, making some tools very difficult to fully understand and therefore challenging to defend. Further, bias can creep into an AI tool in different ways. For example, to improve prediction accuracy, AI tools are provided with training data that have (hopefully) been sampled from the target population (e.g., organizational employees). If the data used to train and build the AI are collected in a biased manner or reflect biases in the organization's systems or processes, the AI may perpetuate those biases in its recommendations or decisions.

Amazon uncovered this type of bias firsthand when an engineering team in Edinburgh, Scotland, began developing a recruitment AI. Their goal was to create an AI that could scour the Internet to find promising candidates. As a preliminary step, the team trained the AI using 10 years of the company's historical résumé data. Because the training data were collected over a 10-year-period in which Amazon overwhelmingly hired men, the AI began to favor résumés from men, ranking them as more promising candidates. Behind the scenes, the algorithm scored candidates lower if their résumés contained the word *women's* or the name of two specific all-women's colleges. Ultimately, Amazon executives stopped development of the AI and have since indicated that the tool was never used by the company's recruiters.

Amid growing concerns, calls have been made to regulate the development and application of AI in general and AI-based assessments specifically. In 2021, leaders from the White House Office of Science & Technology Policy called for an AI "bill of rights" that would describe the AI-related rights and freedoms of the public. Without added transparency and proper audits, Lander and Nelson argued that AI tools could negatively impact individuals' civil rights. That same year, the U.S. Equal Employment Opportunity Commission announced that it had launched an initiative on AI, with the goal of providing guidance to employers, employees, vendors, and applicants on how AI tools can be used in a fair and unbiased manner.[49]

Biases in Model Building, Testing, and Interpretation

We have hinted throughout this chapter that HR analytics involves many judgment calls and decisions. For instance, when building a regression model, the assumption is that you have included all necessary predictor variables to explain your outcome and no irrelevant predictor variables. This is a difficult assumption to meet, and it relies on the judgment and expertise of HR analysts to determine which variables to include and which to exclude in the model. Psychological and social-scientific theory can play a helpful role when determining which variables to measure and include in a model. At this point, we also reiterate a previous point that models are, by nature, a parsimonious approximation of reality—reality as perceived by humans. That is, models are inherently subjective. To that end, prominent data scientist and mathematician Cathy O'Neil reminds us of the subjective nature of models by stating, "Models are opinions embedded in mathematics."[50]

Step 6: Communicating the Results

The way you communicate the results of the scientific process depends largely on where you work and the company culture. In academia, communicating results takes the form of a formal research paper at a conference or publishing a paper in a peer-reviewed journal. In other types of organizations, it is common to communicate findings in internal presentations, technical reports, or white papers. Amazon, for example, is known for communicating findings in technical reports that are read silently during the first part of meetings. Many other companies rely on PowerPoint presentations in which written and oral descriptions of results are provided. In recent years, more value has been placed on creating easy-to-understand data visualizations. Data visualizations refer to pictorial and graphic representations of quantitative or qualitative data, which includes (but is not limited to) displays like bar charts, line charts, pie charts, and dashboards.[51]

Regardless of how you communicate the results, it is important to focus on the story you are telling. When storytelling with data, try to keep the story simple, be clear and concise, use repetition, and do not overburden the reader or viewer with too much information.[52] When possible, we recommend connecting the story to strategic objectives, a process referred to as *strategic storytelling*.[53] Finally, when deciding upon the specific results you wish to communicate, recognize the limitations of the data you collected and the study design you employed to test your hypothesis. In other words, take care not to overstate or exaggerate your findings. At the same time, do not understate your findings, either. See Figure 2.8 for examples of different data visualizations.

FIGURE 2.8 ■ Examples of Different Types of Data Visualizations

Data visualizations can take different forms, from simple text to bar graphs to geographic plots. Pick the visual that best represents the data and tells the most accurate story.

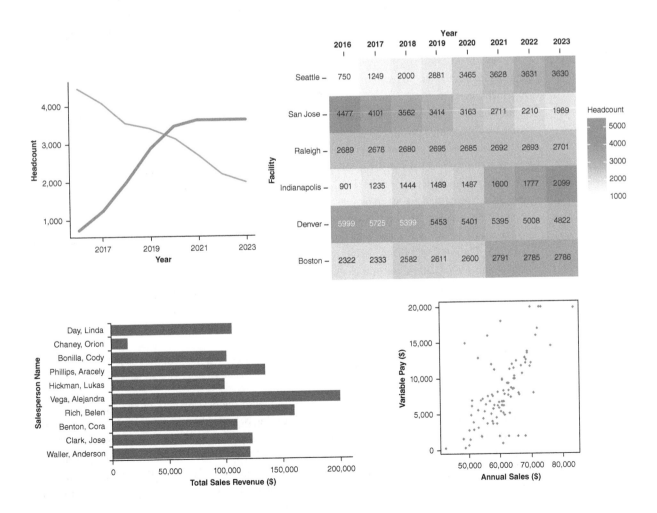

ENSURING HR ANALYTICS SUCCESS

2.5   Manage the components of a successful HR analytics function.

A sustainable HR analytics function requires considering several important issues. First, HR analytics should be integrated and embedded into HR and organizational strategies, and this requires taking a systems perspective of the organization and its various subsystems. Earlier in the chapter, we described how Chevron integrated its HR analytics team into the organization and created a community of practice to bring together those employees interested in analytics. HR analytics can become an integral part of the HR strategic business partnership by leveraging people data to inform and support people decisions and strategy. In other words, the HR analytics function can provide data-informed recommendations regarding the design and implementation of HR practices to facilitate the organization's achievement of strategic objectives.

Second, HR analytics should be integrated into the culture of HR and the organization. As we previously noted, many executives continue to make major decisions based on their gut instincts, or intuition. As such, developing an HR analytics function in some organizations may be difficult, especially if the culture does not ostensibly value data and data-informed decisions. By gaining manager support and creating a culture that supports evidence-based practices, the HR analytics function will have a better chance of implementing changes.

Third, and related to the second point, HR analytics must be paired with good change management, where change management refers to the "systematic process of applying knowledge, tools, and resources to transform the organization from one state of affairs to another."[54] People have a natural tendency to resist change, and thus, in addition to creating a culture supportive of data-informed decision making, a culture of continuous change should be cultivated as well.

Fourth, an HR analytics team must include the right people with the right mix of competencies. Earlier in the chapter, we recommended the following seven competencies: theory, business, data management, measurement, data analysis, employment law, and ethics. Deficiencies in any one of these competencies within a team may result in failure to contribute or, worse, may use HR analytics in ways that are illegal or unethical.

Finally, we cannot overstate the importance of ethics. Today, new information technologies make it easier than ever to collect, manage, and analyze potentially sensitive people and organizational data, and with these new technologies come new ethical responsibilities. For example, some platforms allow us to systematically scrape data about our employees from social media sites. Before doing so, however, we must pause and ask this question: "Just because we can, should we?" For example, just because we can scrape employees' social media data with ease and just because those data might be predictive of employee outcomes, should we do it? The same rigor that is applied to the scientific process should also be applied to decision making surrounding what data to use, how to use data, and whether to run certain analyses. Referring to the systems perspective once more is important because it reminds us of the interconnectedness between ourselves and other organizational entities. In other words, a systems perspective reminds us that one decision—ethical or not—can result in a large ripple effect through the organization system and beyond.

CHAPTER SUMMARY

HRM has evolved immensely over the past century, with the development of strategic HRM, data-informed decision making, and HR analytics. Leading organizations leverage their HR function to inform and support organizational strategy; to realize employee, operational, stakeholder, and financial outcomes; and to achieve a competitive advantage. Data-informed decision making in the form of HR analytics plays an important role in strategy realization. An effective HR analytics function can be leveraged to improve the quality of decisions we make by informing the way an organization collects, manages, analyzes, and interprets its people data.

KEY TERMS

Ability-motivation-opportunity model

Artificial intelligence (AI)

Balanced scorecard

Big data

Concept

Data visualizations

Data-informed decisions

Descriptive analytics

High-performance work practices

Human capital

Human resource (HR) analytics

Little data

Measure

Mission

Predictive analytics

Prescriptive analytics

Qualitative data

Quantitative data

Resource-based view

Scientific process

Stakeholders

Strategic human resource management

Strategy

Strategy formulation

Strategy implementation

Strategy type

SWOT analysis

Systems perspective

Values

Vision

HR REASONING AND DECISION-MAKING EXERCISES

Mini-Case Analysis Exercise: Organizational Culture and the Success of HR Analytics

Chapter 1 discussed the importance of organizational culture in relation to HRM. Specifically, the chapter reviewed a popular organizational culture typology called the competing values framework, which characterizes different culture types by their emphasis on either collaboration, creating, controlling, or competing. The culture types are as follows: clan, adhocracy, market, and hierarchy. Given what you learned in this chapter about HR analytics and data-informed people decisions, consider how the different culture types might influence an organization's acceptance of HR analytics.

Now, you decide:

1. For which organization culture type do you think HR analytics will best integrate? Is there an ideal culture type to support HR analytics? Why?

2. Which organization culture type will be least likely to accept HR analytics as a viable part of the organization's strategy? Why?

HR Decision Analysis Exercise: The Case of Gravity Payments

The CEO of Gravity Payments, Dan Price, made national headlines in 2015 when he announced that he would be increasing all employees' annual pay to $70,000 over the course of several years. Price had read a study showing that emotional well-being improved as income increased, up until about $75,000 a year, and he was inspired to raise his employees' pay with the hope that it would lift their emotional well-being. Reportedly, he moved very quickly when making this major decision. In the months that followed his compensation announcement, Price was both cheered and jeered. His supporters touted his inspirational message, while his critics argued it was all a publicity stunt and questioned his motives. In addition, not everyone within the company was happy with this decision. Within 3 months, two of his most-valued employees had quit, citing the fact that newer and less experienced employees would make the same amount of money. Some of his company's clients commended him, while other clients said he made their job harder because they feared they would have to justify the costs of services that might come with the pay increases.[55]

Six years later, in 2021, Dan Price reported that the company was thriving, having almost doubled its workforce and cut its turnover rate by half. After the company lost 55% of its business at the start of the Covid-19 pandemic, some employees voluntarily reduced their salaries to keep the company afloat. When business bounced back, the company repaid the employees who had voluntarily sacrificed their own pay.[56]

Now, answer the following questions regarding what you think about Price's HRM decision making in terms of the five characteristics of effective HRM decisions depicted in Figure 2.9.

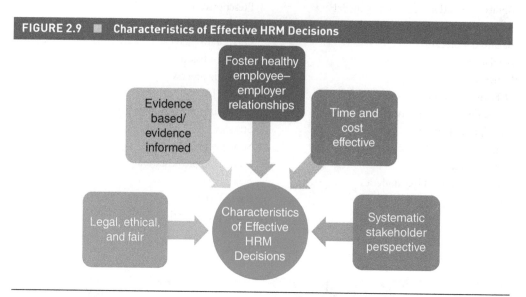

FIGURE 2.9 ■ Characteristics of Effective HRM Decisions

Be sure to include specific examples from the case or your own research to support your answers.

Was Dan Price's HRM decision legal, ethical, and fair?

Was it evidence based/evidence informed?

Did it foster healthy employee–employer relationships?

Was it time- and cost-effective?

Did it take a systematic stakeholder perspective?

Considering your analysis above, overall, do you think this was an effective decision? Why or why not?

What, if anything, do you think should be done differently or considered to help make this decision more effective?

HR Decision-Making Exercise: Building Your HR Analytics Team

HR analytics is an interdisciplinary field, and as a result, HR analytics teams are often composed of individuals from different disciplines, specializations, and degree programs. Critical areas of expertise in any HR analytics team include the following: theory, business, data management, measurement, data analysis, employment law, and ethics. For this exercise, work in a group to determine how you would recruit, select, and train members of an effective HR analytics team.

1. As a group, create a series of jobs for which you will ultimately recruit and select new employees. A given job may cover more than one area of expertise, and multiple jobs may overlap in terms of some areas of expertise.

2. For each job created in Step 1, identify the competencies and educational/professional experiences that are necessary for success.

3. Develop a brief recruitment and selection strategy for each job. In other words, where will you recruit individuals for these positions? Why? How and why will you select and hire individuals for these positions?

DATA AND ANALYTICS EXERCISE: DESCRIBING YOUR DATA

Summarizing people data using descriptive analytics can provide valuable insights into the state of your company. Although there are a number of common HR metrics such as turnover rate and yield ratio, often it is valuable to summarize basic demographic data, survey data, and performance data using descriptive statistics like frequency, percentage, mean, median, mode, and standard deviation. Part of the challenge is determining which descriptive statistic to use to describe a particular variable. Regarding quantitative variables, one can distinguish between categorical variables and continuous variables. Although variables can be described in even more specific terms, the categorical and continuous distinction is an important one.

A *categorical variable* consists of multiple levels, but these levels do not have a particular order or inherent numeric values. For example, race is typically operationalized as a categorical variable, where the levels of the race variable correspond to the different categories of race (e.g., Asian, Black, White), in no particular order. As another example, for reporting purposes, employee gender identity can be reported as a categorical variable with levels such as agender, man, woman, nonbinary, trans man, and trans woman. When we report categorical variables, we often use frequency or percentage to describe the data. For example, imagine that a company employs 230 women, 199 men, 8 nonbinary, and 4 trans women. We could describe gender identity using two frequencies: frequency of women (230), men (199), nonbinary (8), and trans women (4). Alternatively, we could describe each level of the gender variable as a percentage. For example, 52.2% of employees identify as women (52.2% = 230/(230 + 199 + 8 + 4) × 100), and 1.8% identify as nonbinary (1.8% = 8/(230 + 199 + 8 + 4) × 100). Data visualizations like the bar charts shown in Figures 2.10 and 2.11 facilitate the communication of such descriptive analytics findings.

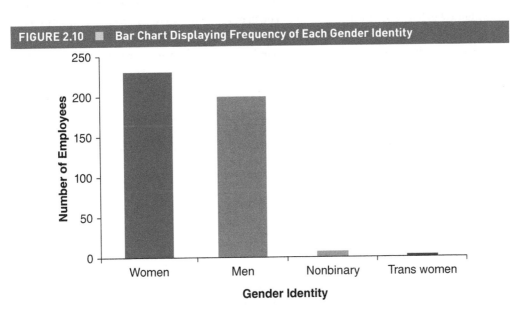

FIGURE 2.10 ■ Bar Chart Displaying Frequency of Each Gender Identity

A *continuous variable* consists of a continuum of numerically ordered values. A classic example is employee age when measured in years. Years can be ordered such that we can say someone who is 39 years is older than someone who is 38 years, and thus, one value is larger or higher than another value. Although many survey response scales technically represent what are referred to as ordinal variables, which are distinguishable from continuous variables, we often treat them like continuous variables for the purposes of data analysis. For instance, in an employee engagement survey, you might ask employees to respond to different survey items using a 5-point response scale ranging from *strongly disagree* (1) to *neither agree nor disagree* (3) to *strongly agree* (5).

To summarize employees' ages or their responses to the item "I am satisfied with my job," you could compute descriptive statistics of central tendency and/or dispersion. For example, you might find that

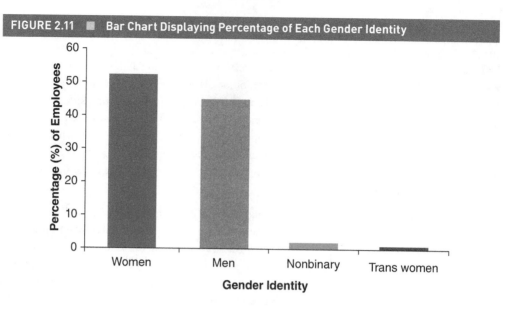

FIGURE 2.11 ■ Bar Chart Displaying Percentage of Each Gender Identity

the *mean* (average) employee age is 38.2 years with a *standard deviation* of 5.4 years. This means that the center of the distribution of employee ages is 38.2 years and that about two thirds of employees' ages fall within 5.4 years of 38.2 or, in other words, 32.8 to 43.6 years. Similarly, you might find that the mean response to the job satisfaction item is 3.0, which indicates that, on average, employees neither agree nor disagree with the statement: "I am satisfied with my job." A standard deviation of 1.2 for responses on that item, however, indicates that approximately two thirds of employees' responses fall within 1.2 points above and below the mean or, in other words, 1.8 to 4.2. Thus, in that example, a large proportion of employees' responses varied anywhere from slightly dissatisfied to slightly satisfied with their job. When creating a data visualization for a mean, there are many options; Figures 2.12 and 2.13 provide examples.

FIGURE 2.12   ■   Example of Data Visualization Used to Describe the Average Age of Employees

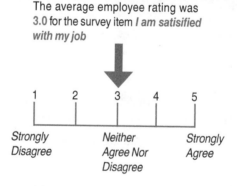

The average employee rating was 3.0 for the survey item *I am satisified with my job*

| 1 | 2 | 3 | 4 | 5 |

Strongly Disagree

Neither Agree Nor Disagree

Strongly Agree

FIGURE 2.13   ■   Example of Data Visualization Used to Describe the Average Employee Rating for a Survey Item

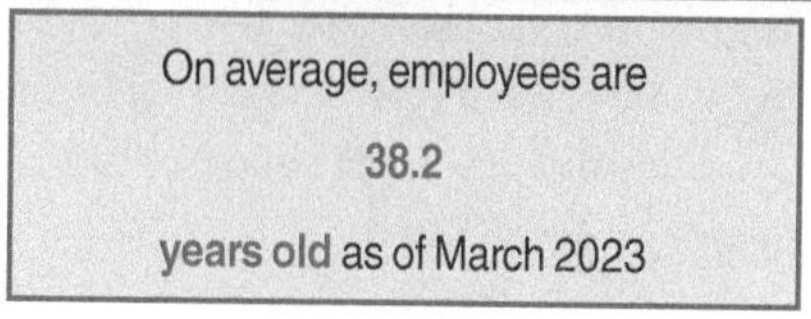

On average, employees are

38.2

years old as of March 2023

In summary, descriptive analytics includes basic summary statistics and the data visualizations used to communicate those summary statistics. Identifying the difference between categorical and continuous variables is the first step toward picking the right statistic to summarize your data.

Excel Extension: Now You Try!

- On **edge.sagepub.com/bauer2e**, you will find an Excel exercise on descriptive analytics. Specifically, you will compute basic descriptive and summary statistics for the following variables from a sample dataset: age, gender, race, engagement, and pay.

- First, you will classify each variable as either a categorical or continuous variable.

- Second, you will select and compute appropriate descriptive and summary statistics to describe the variables.

- Third, you will create a data visualization in Excel to help communicate your findings.

©iStockphoto.com/Galeanu Mihai

3 DATA MANAGEMENT AND HUMAN RESOURCE INFORMATION SYSTEMS

After reading and studying this chapter, you should be able to do the following:

3.1 Describe key aspects of data management.

3.2 Apply opportunities for data management and HRIS.

3.3 Identify and address challenges for data management and HRIS.

3.4 Describe basic technical aspects of developing an HRIS.

3.5 Address key points of the process of HRIS implementation.

3.6 Apply core information system concepts in HR management.

ANALYTICS-DRIVEN DECISIONS: THE CASE OF JETBLUE[1]

Photo by David Butow/Corbis via Getty Images

In one sense, airlines are simply commodities, as they move individuals from point A to point B. However, for anyone who has ever flown on a commercial airline, not all airlines are created equally. JetBlue Airways, a low-cost airline founded in 2000 at John F. Kennedy International Airport (JFK) in New York, carries more than 35 million customers a year to 100 cities in the United States, the Caribbean, and Latin America as well as flights from JFK to London's Heathrow Airport with an average of 925 daily flights. The airline regularly is named one of the best airlines to fly with in terms of customer satisfaction. For example, in 2021, JetBlue was named No. 1 domestic airline in the *Travel + Leisure* World's Best Awards, marking the third year in a row it received this honor.

The airline industry recognizes that customer satisfaction depends upon a number of key factors. One very salient factor related to employees' attitudes and behaviors is organizational culture. JetBlue is known for its unique organizational culture, focus on customers, and a fierce reliance on widely available and distributed data and analytics. JetBlue does many things in its quest to create a positive culture and to ensure crewmembers remain engaged and satisfied. For example, JetBlue created a "crewmember net promoter score," which regularly asks employees their willingness to recommend the company as a place to work. Net promoter scores are usually used to measure customer satisfaction, but JetBlue asks this question to all new hires on their hire dates, which means the company regularly tracks these data. Indeed, data and technology are the backbone of JetBlue's approach.

JetBlue prides itself on its integration and use of data and analytics, and JetBlue University includes a key section of its annual report highlighting data-informed improvements. To get to this point, JetBlue underwent an organizational redesign with a major focus on analytics and data-informed decision making. Examples of this redesign include the use of analytics to inform decisions, measure business impact, and improve performance. Their view is that analytics should lead to action.

Redesigns that incorporate analytics can be quite complicated to realize. Although JetBlue wished to engage in data-informed decision making across the organization, achieving this goal proved to be challenging due to the limitations of their data warehouse and transformation tools. As Ben Singleton, former director of Data Science & Analytics noted, "[These tools] were not designed for the explosion of data we've experienced." JetBlue needed to evolve and invest in more robust and capable systems to meet the demand of organizational data analysts and decision makers. One key change they made was to move from central ownership of data to shared collaboration. As Mr. Singleton put it, "The only way we can support JetBlue in becoming a data-driven organization is if more people can participate in the data transformation process. My data team can't scale fast enough to meet the needs of the company. We need to enable a distributed model of data management."

The system they created included five important features. First, it ensured compliance and security. Second, it enabled delivery of real-time data. Third, it allowed for catching and addressing data-quality issues before they impacted end users. Fourth, it implemented a workflow that was accessible for analysts. And fifth, it improved data transparency and documentation. It took three months for the data engineering team to migrate 26 data sources with over 1,000 model while adding 6,300 data quality tests. All of these features allow JetBlue crewmembers to do what they need to support customers and continue to thrive.

CASE DISCUSSION QUESTIONS

1. JetBlue underwent a great deal of change in a short period of time. How do you think the employees who were asked to make these changes reacted along the way?

2. Ben Singleton had five important features when considering JetBlue's major human resource information system (HRIS) project to redesign their data and analytics capabilities. Can you think of other important factors?

3. What role do you think HRIS plays in JetBlue's customer satisfaction success?

4. Do you think there are any downsides to having a HRIS in place? If so, what could be done to help mitigate those problems in the design and implementation phases?

Hear more about how JetBlue was transformed by putting data and analytics front and center in their day-to-day operations at https://www.youtube.com/watch?v=PoFpf_ylpfE.

INTRODUCTION

After reading Chapters 1 and 2 of this book, you can see that our approach to covering human resource management (HRM) is based on the concepts and developments you will need to understand now and in the future of the human resource (HR) field, organizations, business, and your own career. Among those concepts are the skills needed to make use of data to make sound HRM decisions. Effective

HRM requires that organizational members be knowledgeable about how data are managed, stored, retrieved, merged, analyzed, and reported to help with data-informed decision making. Even if they are not data analysts or experts in human resource information systems (HRIS), all employees should be familiar with issues around data management and HRIS. This is becoming more and more important as new technologies such as AI and machine learning are becoming more prevalent in the workplace. As illustrated in the opening chapter case of JetBlue, understanding these concepts will make you an effective consumer of data and its possibilities within your organization regardless of your position, functional area, or title.

MANAGING DATA

LEARNING OBJECTIVES
3.1 Describe key aspects of data management.

Recall from Chapter 1 that the availability of people data has increased dramatically with advances in technology and data-gathering tools. People data refers to data associated with various groups of individuals, such as employees and other stakeholders, who might be integral to an organization's success. As described in Chapter 2, HR analytics is an important approach to leveraging people data to make data-informed decisions that improve the flow of human capital into and through an organization. Because of this, strategic data management has become especially salient to HR professionals and HR analysts. As seen in the JetBlue case, HR has long since outgrown the days of employee records and data stored on paper and housed in filing cabinets. Before computer-based information systems became the norm, relatively small amounts of data were accessed with regularity, and merging data from different files was a cumbersome and time-consuming process. Today, with ever-accumulating amounts of people data and sometimes easier access to such data, we must think critically, ethically, and legally about how large volumes of data about individuals are stored and managed and how advances in information systems are used to facilitate this process. The human resource information system (HRIS) and electronic HRM (e-HRM) represent two closely related HRM data management topics that play an important role in that regard. In many organizations, HR information systems and e-HRM are integrated into a larger cross-functional data management system called an enterprise resource planning system—all of which can be broadly classified as information systems.

Enterprise Resource Planning Systems

An enterprise resource planning (ERP) system refers to integrated business-management software intended to coordinate and integrate processes and data across different functional areas of a company, such as accounting, sales, finance, operations, customer service, and HRM. For instance, an ERP might capture, track, and integrate data pertaining to payroll, inventory, production capacity, applicant tracking, and purchase orders, to name a few things. By integrating data cross-functionally, an ERP creates a robust data ecosystem, which enables organizational stakeholders to take a systems perspective when making important decisions. For example, imagine that customer service data residing within an ERP indicate that customer service representatives have been fielding increasingly more customer complaints having to do with faulty products. Using those data, a decision maker on the manufacturing floor might investigate where mistakes are being made in the production process. Ultimately, that decision maker might reach out to someone from the HR department with expertise in employee training to help design a new training program for manufacturing employees. Thus, a well-designed and well-integrated ERP has the potential to improve decision making across different functional areas, as the entire business can be viewed as an integrated system with separate yet related subsystems.

Like most technology, an ERP was originally a luxury of large companies. As computer processing speeds and data storage capabilities improved and came down in cost, introducing a robust ERP system became a reality for smaller and smaller companies. This has been great news for small and medium-sized businesses, as ERPs were historically extremely expensive, and now many HR needs can be met for smaller businesses using ERPs at prices that are affordable.

Human Resource Information Systems (HRIS)

You've probably heard a lot about AI and machine learning and the huge amounts of data associated with them. All that data needs to be available to be useful so it must be stored and readily accessible to be useful. Many organizations incorporate an HRIS within their broader ERP systems, such that HR processes and data are linked to and integrated with data from other business functions. An HRIS refers to a "system used to acquire, store, manipulate, analyze, retrieve, and distribute pertinent information about an organization's human resources,"[2] and the concept of HRIS can be nested within the broader concept of e-HRM. At its most basic, an HRIS is simply a system of the following: input → data management → output. Broadly speaking, e-HRM refers to Internet-based information systems and technology that span across organizational levels.[3]

An HRIS represents the confluence of HRM and information technology, and when coupled with strategic HRM, an HRIS offers a way to realize synergies between and across different HR practices. It can provide a wealth of readily available data to provide organizational decision makers with accurate and timely information.

Just like the broader ERP system, an organization can use its HRIS to integrate people data across different HR functions, such as recruitment, selection, training, performance management, compensation, and benefits. Moreover, an HRIS can be designed to automate transactional HR activities, such as benefits enrollment or applicant tracking. After World War II, the payroll function was one of the first to be automated using early computers and information systems. As computer technology advanced in the following decades, organizations began to integrate web- and cloud-based services into their HRIS.

An HRIS is a cost-saving tool, as it can reduce errors and increase efficiencies related to storing, accessing, and using data. For example, DHL, the largest international logistics company in the world, had employees apply for leave using physical forms that were then sent overseas to be processed, which was time-consuming and frustrating to employees who wanted to know the status of their leave requests in a timely manner. One of the results of the global pandemic is that it sped up the digital transformation of many organizations' HR functions. With so many employees working remotely, many things changed at a rapid pace. Seemingly overnight, selection interviews, onboarding, and meetings were all done via technology. An HRIS is a critical function to support these new data, HR functions, and platforms.

As seen in the opening case of JetBlue, the hallmarks of an advanced HRIS are consistency, accuracy, timely access to data, and integration. Rather than using a separate and insular information subsystem for each core HR function—such as selection, training, performance management, and retention—an advanced HRIS integrates people data across HR functions. When integrated into a company's ERP, the comprehensiveness of the data becomes even more robust. Further, allowing subsystems to "speak" with one another means that analysts can retrieve and merge data from multiple subsystem functions for subsequent analysis and reporting. Many vendors (e.g., ADP, Oracle, SAP, UKG, Workday) offer HRIS and ERP solutions, thereby facilitating data management and integration processes. Some vendors now integrate data analytics solutions into their data management platforms. Integrated analytics solutions reflect tremendous advances in computing power. At the click of a button, the software can run and generate off-the-shelf analyses and reports.

Vendors like ADP offer proprietary data analysis algorithms to predict important outcomes, such as employee retention. Because such algorithms are proprietary and thus considered intellectual property, the specific criteria used in the algorithmic models often remain locked in a "black box" where the contents are unknown. Still, HR professionals, and all organizational members, should do their due diligence to understand, to the best of their ability, what data are being used in such models and how to properly interpret output or results from such models.

OPPORTUNITIES FOR DATA MANAGEMENT AND HRIS

LEARNING OBJECTIVES

3.2   Apply opportunities for data management and HRIS.

When it comes to data management and HRIS, there are a number of challenges and opportunities. Figure 3.1 illustrates several of these when it comes to developing, implementing, and maintaining an HRIS. Opportunities exist in the form of being able to track the employee throughout their employment life cycles, automating HR functionality for employees, allowing data to be available for HR analytics, and storing and merging employee attitude surveys and other sources of people data over time. Sometimes it's important to be realistic about your organization's data maturity and what data are actually available. For example, when Dan Hilbert arrived as manager of Employment Services at Valero Energy, he wasn't quite sure what he wanted or needed to do. He found that basic data needed for HR operations and programs were not available. Worse yet, he also found that none of the company's systems were able to acquire data. To address this deficiency, he created a small team tasked with collecting HR data, with the goals of learning more about the organization's data needs and creating a foundation to build upon. Through this process, the team arrived at some important insights. Namely, all of the company's refinery managers were getting close to retirement age, and there was no program in place to find and train their successors. Being aware of the looming challenge allowed Valero to put a plan in place and saved the refineries millions.[4] Critical people decisions such as what skills are needed, who to hire, what training employees need, how they are performing, and how to develop leaders and make succession plans are all facilitated by having real-time data to help inform those decisions.

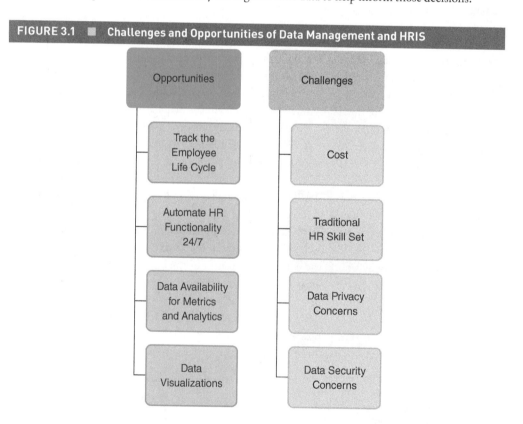

FIGURE 3.1 ■ Challenges and Opportunities of Data Management and HRIS

Track the Employee Life Cycle

Recall that HRM is *the constellation of decisions and actions associated with managing individuals through the employee life cycle to maximize employee and organizational effectiveness in attaining goals*. This includes a range of functions such as analyzing and designing jobs; managing diversity and complying with local, national, and global employee laws; recruiting individuals to apply for jobs; selecting individuals to join organizations; training and developing people while they are employed; helping to manage their performance; rewarding and compensating employee performance while maintaining healthy labor relations and helping to keep them safe; and managing their exit from the organization (see Figure 3.2).

FIGURE 3.2   ■   HRM as a Linking Pin for Critical People Decisions

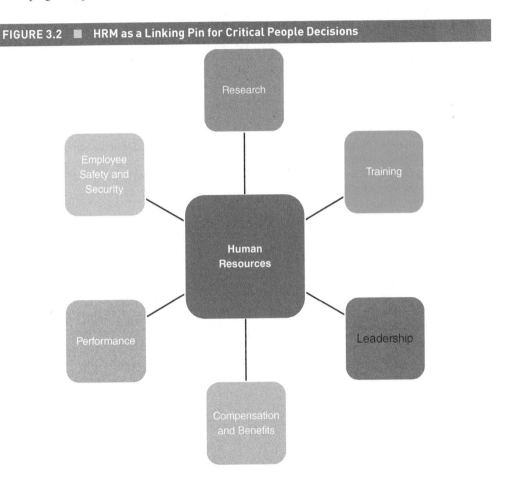

Thus, a major opportunity for an organization is to manage the valuable resources that are data in a manner that helps the organization not only describe its employees and predict their future movements throughout the organization but also prescribe what the ideal state of HR will be in the future. Effective data management and HRIS are critical to realizing this potential. One study of HR executives and managers working in diverse countries, including Argentina, Brazil, China, India, Latvia, and Slovakia, found the presence of a global HRIS was related to higher staff retention of global IT service providers in emerging markets. This was especially helpful in decreasing turnover for employees assigned to other countries, as the support of a global HRIS for scheduling and training were cited as helpful for new employees and their managers alike.[5] It is clear "the effective management of human resources in a firm to gain a competitive advantage requires *timely and accurate information* on current employees and potential employees in the labor market."[6]

SPOTLIGHT ON DATA AND ANALYTICS: KNOWING CAN BE POWERFUL

HR analytics has many uses, and companies have started leveraging data collected during and after hiring employees to predict and manage retention. Companies can link a wide variety of information at their disposal to employee turnover and determine the strongest drivers of turnover. Identifying employees at risk of turnover may then be used to develop targeted interventions for those employees. For example, the telecommunications company Sprint found employees who have not signed up for the company's retirement program are at risk of leaving shortly after being hired. In addition to identifying predictors of turnover, many companies examine low work engagement and job satisfaction as early and lagged indicators of turnover. This means conducting regular surveys and tracking results and metrics over time will be helpful.

Simply tracking satisfaction and engagement data may not achieve the goal of reducing employee turnover: The company will need to intervene using these data. The food service company Sysco tracks satisfaction ratings of its delivery associates and intervenes when satisfaction drops below a certain point. Using this methodology, the company was able to increase its retention rate from 65% to 85%.

It is also possible to identify the specific employees who are at risk for turnover for intervention purposes. At Credit Suisse, once employees with high turnover risk were identified, internal recruiters called employees to notify them about internal openings. This method allowed the firm to retain employees who might have left the company otherwise. Preemptive intervention is often a better strategy than providing a counteroffer to an employee who gets a job offer.

We recognize that not all organizations have the same data and analytics capabilities at any given point in time. However, there are metrics that any organization can, and should, gather, track, and review. These include turnover rates, average time to fill positions, HR-to-employee ratio, career path ratios, revenue per employee, and employee net promoter score.[7]

The Value of Automated, Employee-Centered HR Functionality

Chapters 1 and 2 point out the trend in HRM is moving away from processing paperwork and more transactional interactions toward more strategic work. We have discussed the benefits of this approach in terms of time and cost savings as HR becomes more efficient. However, it also means better customer service for employees. Rather than waiting for HR to process paperwork, answer questions, or implement changes, employees now have access to their HR systems 24 hours a day, 7 days a week. Some questions are escalated to HR professionals, but many of their more routine questions can be answered anytime and anywhere. Research shows the perceived ease of use and perceived usefulness of an HRIS are related to higher job satisfaction and lower turnover intentions.[8] Thus, moving toward automated, employee-centered HR functionality meets two goals. First, it enables employees to access information more quickly and to verify the accuracy of the data, as they can view and detect inaccuracies more readily, which helps them feel more satisfied with their jobs. Second, because HR data are increasingly accessible via the web or the cloud, data from across the organization can be retrieved and merged with greater ease, enabling timely and efficient analysis of the data for HR decision making.

Abbott Labs is a global health care technology provider that uses data analytics to counteract the Great Resignation. During the pandemic, it was critical that Abbott was successful in manufacturing and distributing reliable Covid-19 tests. The maker of BinaxNOW, Panbio, and ID NOW rapid tests was able to distribute more than 1.4 billion tests while facing challenging working conditions such as long hours, stress, and being short-staffed. They were also facing the general HR challenge of the Great Resignation and global labor shortages. In their quest to attract and retain employees, Abbott underwent a *digital transformation* of their HR system and started using a suite of 300 data elements, including text analytics to identify and address employee concerns before they led to resignations. As Mary Moreland, Abbott's executive vice president of HR said, "This lets us hone in and listen to our people to understand what is it that's driving that potential hot spot and how [to] address it. . . . What do they need, and what can we do to provide those needs so that they stay with the company." Abbott's goal was to use predictive analytics to find and address problems before they were able to derail the company's mission.[9]

Data Availability for Metrics and Analytics

The theme of technology has played a revolutionary role in the evolution of HRM. To make data-informed people decisions, data must be accessible. As experts state, "Data are the lifeblood of an organization."[10] As the Society for Human Resource Management (SHRM) notes, trends such as the

Photo Illustration by Rafael Henrique/SOPA Images/LightRocket via Getty Images

growth of social networking and the rise in data analytics and dashboards have fundamentally changed what HR needs.[11] Another HR expert, John Sullivan, shares his thoughts about the importance of HR metrics: "I have found the largest single difference between a great HR department and an average one is the use of metrics . . . bar none, there is nothing you can do to improve yours and your department's performance that succeeds the impact of using metrics."[12]

Having a clear data management plan and having an effective HRIS in place are critical aspects to HR analytics success, and an HRIS update, upgrade, or re-envisioning is a great opportunity to fix problems and set up the organization for success for becoming more deeply data informed when making people decisions. These are important considerations in avoiding huge problems and generating solutions while there is time to plan.

Data Quality

An important point to remember when thinking about metrics and analytics is the importance of gathering high-quality data, which starts with sound measurement. Recall from Chapter 2 that a *measure* is a tool or method used to gather data about a concept. Without sound measurement, we cannot state with any confidence whether we consistently or accurately measured a concept. With poor measurement techniques, we become susceptible to low-quality (e.g., unreliable) data—also known as "garbage data." When garbage data are collected, it does not matter how we analyze the data, as the findings and interpretations will be of low quality (e.g., invalid)—also known as "garbage findings." This phenomenon is referred to as "garbage in, garbage out," or GIGO (see Figure 3.3).

Data Structure and Storage

Databases are designed to store structured data, and a common approach to adding structure to data is to use tables. A table's rows represent distinct entities (e.g., individual employees), and its columns represent unique fields or variables that characterize the entities (e.g., employee start date, address, job title). Databases and data warehouses were designed to deal with such data. However, with the rise of semistructured and unstructured data, new forms of storage are needed. Thus, data lakes are a solution that many organizations are turning to, because unlike a data warehouse, a data lake stores a vast amount of raw data in its native format. Technology companies are meeting demand for data

FIGURE 3.3   ■   Garbage In, Garbage Out (GIGO) Phenomenon

An illustration of the "garbage in, garbage out" (GIGO) phenomenon. Analysts must collect high-quality data through sound measurement to ensure that subsequent analysis yields meaningful findings and interpretations. If poor data are used, useful conclusions cannot be drawn, regardless of how big the sample or how sophisticated the analytics.

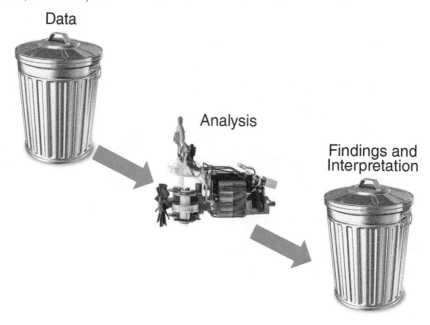

Data

Analysis

Findings and Interpretation

lakes, such as with Microsoft's Azure and offerings by Amazon Web Services and IBM Analytics. Some platforms allow users to use the open-source software framework called Apache Hadoop, which helps users process vast amounts of data across clustered computers. There are pros and cons to each storage approach, but at this point, consider what types of data you might have access to now and in the future, and plan data storage options accordingly and with the future in mind.

Data Visualizations

Although HRIS, HR metrics, and HR analytics are critical for making data-informed people decisions, effective data visualizations and storytelling with data can help facilitate the interpretation and communication of the findings. Today, HR professionals and managers use data visualizations to understand, predict, explain, and communicate their human capital challenges and opportunities based on available data. Data visualizations are useful tools for telling a compelling story about HR data.

Part of telling an effective story with data is knowing how to drill down to and communicate the most important findings. In other words, analyzing data can be quite complex, and thus, a good storyteller understands how to craft a straightforward, simple, and comprehensible narrative. Doing so requires striking a careful balance between engaging the audience and remaining faithful to the analytical findings derived from the data. As the saying goes, "A picture is worth a thousand words." Effective data visualizations play an important role when interpreting and communicating data and data-analytic findings in a succinct way. In fact, research even shows the way in which data are presented visually has an effect on how data are interpreted and which decisions are ultimately made. For example, adjusting the axis scaling of a scatterplot, as shown in Figure 3.4, can give the impression that two variables are more strongly correlated than they actually are, as the figure on the right seems to show a stronger pattern than the one on the left.[13] As such, it is important to be cognizant of the ways in which data visualization displays can be unintentionally or intentionally manipulated to affect the interpretations of different audiences. This means that choosing how to display data should be coupled with careful consideration of the ethical implications.

FIGURE 3.4 ■ Data Visualization With Scatterplots

The way in which data are presented using data visualizations can affect how the users interpret the data. Both scatterplots depict the same data; however, the *x*- and *y*-axis scaling for the scatterplot on the right is much larger, resulting in what appears to be a stronger relationship between Annual Sales and Variable Pay.

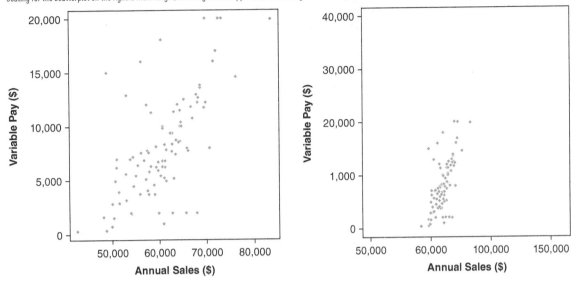

How does one begin to think through how to create the most effective data visualizations? Following work by experts on storytelling and data visualizations,[14] keep the following six points in mind when creating data visualizations:

1. *Understand the context.* When crafting a story, there are many ways to approach it; however, there are three key questions to ask at the highest level when thinking about storytelling. First, *what* do you want your audience to know after you are done? Second, *how* do you want them to feel? Finally, *what*, exactly, do you want them to do based on exposure to your presentation or report? In addition, it is important to determine the context, understand who your audience is, and determine the tone you want to take with them. For example, are you presenting in an informative, exploratory, or urgent way? It can be helpful to "boil down" your goal into a concise 2-minute story. If that is compelling, the presentation or written document stands a better chance of being clear and concise.

2. *Choose an appropriate visual display.* Regarding data visualizations, there are many kinds of elements for displaying data to choose from, including simple text, tables, bar graphs, line graphs, scatterplots, heat maps, and geographic charts. Certain display types are appropriate for communicating certain types of data or for communicating different messages. For example, if there are a few key numbers that make a powerful statement, simple text might have the most impact. Alternatively, if you are interested in sharing a table full of numbers but want to emphasize patterns in the numbers, a heat map, as presented in Figure 3.5, can be effective. Consider using one color for positive numbers and another for negative numbers. The key is to match your goals to an appropriate display.

In addition, there are several tools that can help you generate data visualization, ranging from simple Microsoft Excel visuals to SmartArt within the Microsoft Word program. There are also more sophisticated tools such as Tableau Software, Microsoft Power BI, and open-source software and programming language called R. The tools available for creating data visualizations will continue to evolve, but understanding the basic principles behind effective data visualizations continues to be an important skill for managers and HR professionals alike.

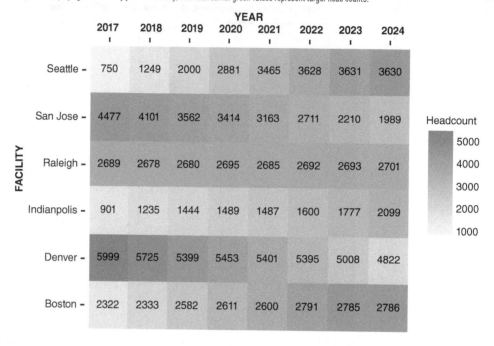

FIGURE 3.5 ■ Heat Map

Heat map table displaying headcount by year and facility, such that darker green values represent larger head counts.

3. *Keep things simple.* By removing clutter and focusing on your main points in the most efficient and succinct manner, you make it easier for your audience to focus because you are minimizing the energy they need to process the new information. In other words, you are decreasing their cognitive load. If anything in your visual is unnecessary, eliminate it! An example of this is to avoid gridlines, borders, and unnecessary shading on graphs. As you see in Figure 3.6, the graph on the left looks fine, but the one on the right is simpler and clearer and communicates the trend more clearly.

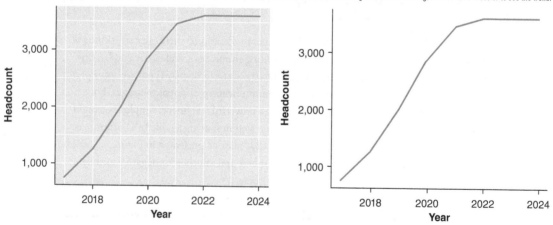

FIGURE 3.6 ■ Headcount Data Over Time

Two line graphs displaying the same headcount data over time. The graph on the right has less clutter in terms of gridlines and shading, which makes it easier to see the trend.

4. *Focus attention where you want it.* You can do this by using color and shading strategically. The use of color and bolding of lines and figures can help people see trends more quickly and accurately. Thus, as you can see in Figure 3.7, effective emphasis using color and shading is a factor to consider when it comes to data visualizations. However, please keep in mind that when it comes to color, less is more. Use it sparingly.

FIGURE 3.7 ■ Headcount Data for Two Facilities

Line graph displaying headcount over time for two facilities. Assuming the goal is to direct the audience's attention to the Seattle facility, the bold green line (contrasted with the thin blue line) signals importance.

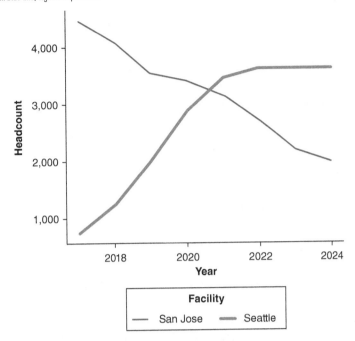

5. *Think like a designer.* You may have heard the phrase "form follows function." It is an important phrase for designers, as it helps them focus their work. In our case, the function is what we want the audience to do with the data, and the form is the visualization created to communicate this. Designers also focus on making things visually appealing, or attractive, which is a goal of design thinking.

6. *Tell a persuasive story.* Research tells us that one of the most effective ways to persuade individuals is through storytelling. As Cole Nussbaumer Knaflic writes, "At a fundamental level, a story expresses how and why life changes. Stories start with balance. Then something happens—an event that throws things out of balance."[15] This dramatic tension can feature data as the event that throws things off. Now you know something new, or a key point you had not noticed has become salient. Stories have a beginning, a middle, and an end. Stories start by introducing the plot and building the context for the reader or audience. With the audience in mind, the introduction should address the "So what?" question and explain why they should care about the topic at hand. The middle describes what could be possible, given more context and detail, and allows you to discuss potential solutions for the issues raised. The end should focus on a specific call to action so the audience truly understands what it is expected to do after hearing your story.

These six points can help guide the generation of data visualizations. However, the availability of data in the first place rests on the quality of your organization's HRIS and your ability to gather and merge the data necessary to tell your story.

CHALLENGES FOR DATA MANAGEMENT AND HRIS

LEARNING OBJECTIVES

3.3   Identify and address challenges for data management and HRIS.

Although there are a great number of potential opportunities for data management and HRIS, challenges also exist. Being aware of them can help organizations proactively assess needs and manage potential threats to successful implementation. The challenges include cost, the lack of analytics skills in traditional HR skill sets, and privacy concerns.

Cost

Typical HRIS costs include time, money, and/or opportunities. With respect to budgeting time, it is important to think about the skill sets available within your organization versus hiring a consultant to help implement a project. The cost of an HRIS varies by organization, their needs, and the sales force of the software vendor. Note that a request for proposal (RFP) is a key part of the HRIS vendor selection process. Of course, another way to think about costs is to more fully consider the potentially large cost savings due to system automation. Such cost reductions might include time entry and attendance tracking, benefits administration, recruiting, training, payroll, and performance management, to name a few. For large organizations, conducting a formal return-on-investment (ROI) analysis is a good idea when dealing with projects this large. For smaller organizations, it may simply be a matter of finding a package or platform that meets their needs into the foreseeable future.

Traditional HR Skill Sets

Unfortunately, due to a number of reasons, often HRIS projects stop short of their potential to enjoy greater efficiency and reduced costs. As organizations hire and train more and more individuals with critical thinking skills, data management skills, and data analytics skills, we anticipate that the HR departments will begin to collect and store more higher-quality data in their HRIS and will apply not only descriptive analytics but more sophisticated predictive and prescriptive analytics to inform and support decisions that impact the strategic objectives. In general, we expect HR to become more scientific.

Josh Bersin of Deloitte has found that it generally takes an organization between 5 and 8 years to put all the necessary pieces together in order to become a data-driven culture using data to inform decisions about people. This includes having the right people, processes, and infrastructure (such as hardware and software) in place. This is an important challenge, and as noted by *Forbes* columnist Vorhauser-Smith, "You can have access to the right data but without the right people to analyze it and—more importantly—act on it, what good is it?"[16] Indeed, 80% of surveyed HR directors who were relatively early adopters of HRIS reported that the HRIS improved their levels of information usefulness and information sharing. Fully 90% felt that an HRIS added value. Plus, the HRIS is quickly becoming a critical part of developing countries and their strategic HR successes.[17] When asked about how they felt about AI at work, respondents noted that they were afraid (25%), distressed (26%), apprehensive (44%), but also excited (74%), content (75%), and optimistic (80%).[18] Aligning the attitudes and skill sets of those in HRM with the new realities of data and analytics is necessary to realize the full potential for HRM via HRIS. This is especially important because we know that HRIS expertise is one of the major factors related to HRIS success across companies in industry sectors.[19]

Data Privacy Concerns

With great amounts of data comes great responsibility. Because the HRIS is a repository for personal data, safeguarding data and maintaining data privacy and security are foundational. To begin, data privacy refers to individuals' control over the collection, storage, access, reporting, and use of their personal data.[20] Research shows that when individuals can choose the types of HR systems they use, they report lower privacy concerns and higher satisfaction with the system. They are especially sensitive to medical data, which may be used for insurance purposes, for example, to be available to those within the organization who make decisions regarding their careers, such as managers.[21] In accordance with the Fair Labor Standards Act of 1938 and other legislation, U.S. companies are required to maintain basic employee data, such as name, Social Security number, address, pay, and hours worked. Understandably, many employees would prefer their personal data remain private, especially their pay or Social Security numbers. Employees grow concerned about their company's HRIS and data privacy when

- coworkers and supervisors are able to access employee data;

- employee data are used in employment and administrative decisions, as opposed to just HR planning purposes; and

- employees are unable to access and verify the accuracy of their own data.

Thus, an effective HRIS must guard against unauthorized access and disclosure of employees' personal data yet also allow employees to verify the accuracy of their own data. The rise of social media and scraping tools has turned the Internet into an enormous repository of data, where scraping and crawling tools include programs designed to scour and pull data from websites and other electronic sources in a systematic manner. In fact, a survey by SHRM revealed that over 80% of surveyed organizations recruited applicants using social media websites.[22] A 2021 study by CareerArc reported that fully 92% of employers did.[23]

SPOTLIGHT ON LEGAL ISSUES: SCRAPING DATA CAN LEAD TO BIG LEGAL TROUBLE

Back in 2010, a software engineer in Colorado named Pete Warden developed and deployed a program designed to "crawl" publicly available Facebook pages. In no time, he had gathered data from 500 million Facebook pages from 220 million Facebook users. The data gathered were identifiable, as they included names, locations, friends, and interests. In the interest of research, Mr. Warden created an anonymized version of the dataset and offered it to others to use.

However, this was not the end of his story. As Mr. Warden is quoted as saying, "Big data? Cheap. Lawyers? Not so much." Thus, in order to try to avoid legal problems with Facebook, he deleted all copies of his dataset and never made it public. Data scraped or crawled (automatically extracted using computer software programs) from websites are subject to three major legal claims against their collection, including copyright infringement, the Computer Fraud and Abuse Act, and terms-of-use violations, among others. Subsequent data privacy issues emerged when Cambridge Analytica gathered data from Facebook users. These breaches of trust led Facebook to rethink which data are gathered and how much control users have over what is shared about them. Subsequent rulings have muddied the waters, and it is unclear how data scraping will be treated, from a legal perspective, in the future. A safe option is to avoid relying on data scraped from the Internet unless you are sure it is legal to do so.[24]

Recognizability of an Individual's Data

The extent to which individual employee records can be recognized is largely dependent on how the data were collected in the first place. There are three terms to describe data in terms of recognizability: anonymous, confidential, and personally identifiable data. Anonymous data refers to those pieces of information that cannot be linked to any information that might link those responses to an individual, thereby disclosing the individual's identity. To be truly anonymous, data should be gathered without IP addresses, GPS coordinates, e-mail addresses, and demographic questions—all of which can be used to narrow down the respondent. Confidential data refers to data for which individuals' identities are known due to the linking of a name or code but are not generally disclosed or reported. This type of data is useful when dealing with sensitive issues such as salary, complaints, opinion survey responses, or exit interviews. In such cases, only those who need to know whose data they are have access to that information. Personally identifiable data refers to data that are readily linked to specific individuals.

The surprising thing with data recognizability is understanding how seemingly anonymous data, such as a query into a search engine, can give enough unique information to track that person down. For example, an IP address is a unique online identifier that may be tracked when a form is filled out or an online survey is taken. Although not 100% accurate, IP addresses can be used to identify a person or pinpoint their location, especially over a period of time as individuals travel to the same places (e.g., from their homes to work and back).

SPOTLIGHT ON ETHICS: EMPLOYEE MONITORING AND DATA PRIVACY

With the shift by many to remote work, concerns regarding employee monitoring have increased. The American Management Association found employees are frequently monitored, and monitoring can lead to outcomes ranging from warnings to firing employees. Fully 66% of employers monitor Internet connections, and 45% report tracking content, keystrokes, and time spent at a keyboard. However, some studies show that electronic performance does not necessarily lead to higher performance, but it does increase stress.

Beyond this routine time and content tracking, some organizations are gathering data to address employee health and engagement. For example, with the goal of improving employee well-being for partnering organizations, Virgin Pulse provides employees with wearable devices and applications to track their sleep, stress, activity level, and other personal data. Companies like Virgin Pulse tout their commitment to data privacy, security, and compliance, thereby implying that employee data will not be shared in an unauthorized manner.

However, if an organization decided to provide employees with wearable devices instead of working through a third-party vendor like Virgin Pulse, this could pose an ethical dilemma under certain circumstances. Namely, without proper data privacy and compliance restrictions in place, the data could be used in ways that would compromise individuals' privacy and other personal rights. Although providing employees with trackable devices is perhaps not illegal, HR professionals may run dangerously close to committing discrimination under the Americans with Disabilities Act (ADA) if they use these data to make employment decisions. Poor or irregular sleep, for example, does not necessarily constitute a disability according to the ADA, but it could be an indicator of various physical diseases or psychiatric disorders, which are protected as disabilities under the ADA. Further, even if deemed legal, using employee health data in this manner could be construed as unethical, particularly if the data are used in a way that deviates from their intended use.[25]

Questions

1. Is it fair to monitor employees using technology? What types of monitoring do you think are acceptable? Please explain your position.
2. Do you think the use of monitoring devices should be optional for employees? How would you ensure that employees who opted out of using the device would not be penalized for nonparticipation?

Social Security Numbers

One particularly sensitive issue is the safeguarding of Social Security numbers.[26] The Federal Trade Commission estimates that more than 9 million Americans have their identities stolen each year, and because Social Security numbers are such valuable targets to identity thieves, steps must be taken to ensure their safekeeping. Such steps include keeping all Social Security number information in secured locations (both virtually and physically) and allowing access from authorized-access computer stations. Only individuals with legitimate business reasons should have access. Any documents released should be destroyed by shredding, and all state and federal laws should be followed regarding the collection, storage, and destruction of Social Security numbers.

Data Security Concerns

Like data privacy, data security is a primary concern of both employees and managers. Data security refers to protective measures taken to prevent unauthorized access to employee data and to preserve the confidentiality and integrity of the data.[27] Cybersecurity can be thought of as data security applied to information accessible through the Internet. Data security can be threatened by a number of entities and for a variety of reasons. While data hacks, attacks, and viruses are real threats, human error is a huge risk when it comes to data security. An information system can have the most sophisticated password protection and security features, but an unintentional human error could still wreak havoc. Imagine a scenario in which you are logged into your company's HRIS while working on a company laptop in a coffee shop. You hear the barista announce your coffee order is ready and step away from your laptop for a moment, forgetting to log out. After picking up your order, you walk back to your table, and to your astonishment, your laptop is gone! An innocent human error and lapse of judgment on your part has put employees' personal data at risk. Unfortunately, human error is inevitable, but we can do our best to prevent these errors by training managers and employees on data security and providing rules and guidelines for protecting people data.

Approaches for Maintaining Data Security

There are several common approaches for ensuring data security. Some are technological, including requiring strong passwords, training users, using two-step authentication, and applying blockchain technology. Other approaches have to do with proper training of the users of data.

Technological Security Measures Increasingly complex passwords are something that we are all familiar with as we are creating and maintaining online accounts. As we now realize that human error is a large factor in many data breaches, it is important to realize that one of the ways these problems manifest themselves is via lack of password security, such as passwords being written down near computers, remembered by computers, or shared with others. In addition, as computing power increases, it becomes easier for computer programs to be able to decode passwords. It might be surprising to know that Mark Zuckerberg, founder of Facebook, has had his Pinterest, LinkedIn, and Twitter accounts hacked.[28] Although many websites allow only a few attempts before locking out users, it is still advisable to select strong passwords, not to reuse the same password across multiple accounts, and to change your passwords to important sources of information frequently.

An extra layer of security can be had in the form of two-step authentication (also known as multifactor authentication), an additional piece of information that only the user knows. For example, Apple computer, iPhone, or iPad users may be familiar with this authentication process when any new device is seeking to access Apple ID information. Of course, two-step authentication works well when you are in possession of your devices, but if a thief has access to both and they are not sufficiently password protected, that can be a bigger problem.

Manager's Toolbox: Tips for Creating Strong Passwords Some of the tips for creating strong passwords are obvious, such as not writing down the password anywhere physically near your computer. However, other tips are not so obvious. The following are some key considerations when dealing with password management, including creating passwords:

- *Long.* The longer the better, with 8 or more characters currently recommended.

- *Contain numbers, letters, and symbols.* There are only 26 letters in the English alphabet and 10 numbers on most keyboards. Mixing them up and using symbols helps to create more powerful passwords, which are exponentially more challenging to decode.

- *Include both upper- and lowercase letters.* Using both uppercase and lowercase letters allows for more options for the user and makes it tougher for hackers to crack your password.

- *Unique.* Some of the most common passwords include 123456, 123456789, qwerty, qwerty123, 111111, password, iloveyou, and admin. It is estimated that 10% of people have used at least one of the worst (because they are commonly known) passwords on this list, with nearly 3% using 123456 alone.

- *Generated randomly.* There are random password generators available online. Although they make remembering passwords more challenging, they are more secure than using actual words. Using a password manager such as LastPass can help with that part, but such a treasure trove of information can be a highly attractive target for hackers, and even that company, LastPass, has been hacked.

©iStockphoto.com/designer491

Blockchain Technology has and will continue to shape the way HR is managed and implemented in many ways. Blockchain is poised to disrupt the current practice of HR. Blockchain is "a distributed incorruptible digital technology infrastructure which maintains a fully encoded database that serves as a ledger where all transactions are recorded and stored."[29] It has also been more simply described as an approach that "provides a decentralized and secure ledger that gives participating parties a way of validating the information related to a secure transaction."[30] Because it is more secure than other technology available today, it has the potential to be used in compensation, background checks, recruiting, and other HR functions in ways that we can only imagine at this point (and other ways that likely we cannot yet imagine). Although blockchain is relatively new and will continue to evolve rapidly in terms of its applications to business broadly and HR specifically, it is important to include it in our discussion of potential data security tools. Maintaining data security is especially important given there were 1,862 data breaches in 2021. Identity theft rose 68% between 2020 and 2021.[31]

User Training One of the major entry points for data security breaches is human error. It is the number-one cause of data breaches (having a role in 52% of data breaches), especially for small and medium-sized businesses.[32] Thus, it makes sense to consider training as an essential part of a data security program. Training might include awareness of key security issues, ethics and compliance when dealing with sensitive data, and security training for new employees or those moving to more information-sensitive positions within the company. There are several steps to consider when training employees, starting with a needs assessment aligned with the desired outcomes of the training. Many organizations have developed such training programs and offer them to organizations not wishing to develop programs themselves. The key is to make sure the right employees are taking the training and engaging in safe data management behaviors.

SPOTLIGHT ON GLOBAL ISSUES: THE GENERAL DATA PROTECTION REGULATION (GDPR)

The General Data Protection Regulation (GDPR) is a regulation in European Union (EU) law regarding data protection and privacy that went into effect in 2018. Any organization working globally should be aware of GDPR and understand its rules and implications. Essentially, the law states the EU's nearly 500 million citizens have the "right to be forgotten." This means companies that continue to collect and store data will face major fines and penalties of up to 4% of their annual worldwide revenue or 20 million euros (whichever one is the larger amount).[33] This is a major consideration for multinational companies, as this far-reaching law states that companies need to provide a "reasonable level" of protection for employees' personal data, but it does not explicitly define what reasonable protection is exactly.

Companies affected are those that have

- a presence in an EU country, or no presence in the EU but process data of EU residents; and
- more than 250 employees or fewer than 250 employees but whose data processing impacts the rights and freedoms of data subjects more than occasionally or includes sensitive data.

Companies such Amazon, British Airways, Facebook, Google, H&M, Marriott, and WhatsApp have all paid millions in fines for violating the GDPR.[34]

DEVELOPING A HUMAN RESOURCE INFORMATION SYSTEM

LEARNING OBJECTIVES

3.4   Describe basic technical aspects of developing an HRIS.

As you have seen so far in this chapter, a complex and comprehensive HRIS can be a costly and time-consuming undertaking for an organization. Before deciding whether to do so and how, organizations are well advised to systematically work through a step-by-step process for evaluating the needs and feasibility of implementing an HRIS (see Figure 3.8).[35] After that, it is important to outline the features needed in such a system, to select a vendor, and to engage in activities designed to control costs.

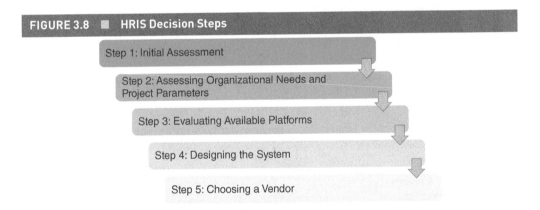

FIGURE 3.8 ■ HRIS Decision Steps

Step 1: Initial Assessment

Step 2: Assessing Organizational Needs and Project Parameters

Step 3: Evaluating Available Platforms

Step 4: Designing the System

Step 5: Choosing a Vendor

Step 1: Initial Assessment

In the initial assessment phase, a key question is whether the selection process is best led by internal HR individuals or whether engaging the services of an HRIS consultant to help with the process makes the most sense given time, experience, and cost factors. For example, if there seems to be a strong need for a new HRIS but the HR staff does not have a great deal of time or expertise in this area, it probably makes sense to bring in a consultant to help facilitate the process. During this phase, it is important to gain buy-in from management and key stakeholders by including them in the conversation; failure to do so may result in hurdles later in the development and implementation process, as ultimately management and certain stakeholders may be gatekeepers to key resources.

Step 2: Assessing Organizational Needs and Project Parameters

The next major activity is assessing organizational needs. The goal is to develop a system that meets all the current organizational needs as well as having room to expand in the future. Every organization will have a different set of needs, but all share some common goals with an HRIS, including the need to have a system that allows them to gather, organize, and securely maintain employee data. Another key factor to consider in the needs assessment phase is various ways to handle the merging and joining of data from different databases. Finally, research consistently finds that understanding users' individual needs is a critical component of success when developing a new HRIS.[36]

The system also must allow for the generation of standardized compliance and strategic HR reports such as EEO, VETS-100, new hires, and turnover. Beyond that, the goal of this step is to determine the needed features of a potential system versus the wanted features of the system. After identifying a list of minimum requirements and additional "wish list" items, assessing project parameters comes next, including budgetary, technological, and time constraints.

Step 3: Evaluating Available Platforms

Many systems allow for optional HR-relevant modules to be added, such as compensation, benefits, onboarding, and performance management modules. However, the needs of the specific organization's HR functions and strategy will determine the specific configuration. One thing to keep in mind is the need for system integration. It is one thing to "have" the data, and as many organizations find out, it is a very different thing to access, retrieve, and merge such data.

Having standalone modules within HR that do not have the capability to link data with other organizational systems is not optimal. Once the first two steps are completed, it is imperative to evaluate all available platforms against the established needs of the HRIS.

Step 4: Designing the System

Being as explicit and honest about these at this stage allows organizations to focus on features that are both feasible and desirable. These will lead directly into the design of the HRIS.

Two related but distinct factors are important to consider. These are logical design and physical design. On the one hand, logical design refers to the translation of business requirements into improved business processes.[37] For example, HR might identify all of the steps in the recruitment process, as well as the types of data that will be exchanged and stored. Often data flow diagrams, such as the one pictured in Figure 3.9, are used to depict the old and/or new business processes. As the name implies, data flow diagrams show how data flow from one entity to the next, as well as how the data are processed.

FIGURE 3.9 ■ Data Flow Diagram Excerpt

This excerpt from a data flow diagram depicts the logical design of a performance management system.

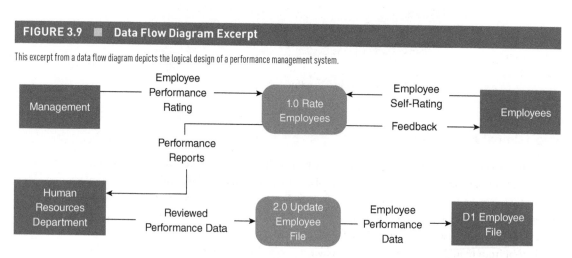

On the other hand, physical design refers to determining the most effective way to translate business processes into the software and hardware solutions that make those processes a reality. For example, information technology experts might take the logical design of a recruitment system designed by HR and determine the software and hardware needed to bring the system to life and to integrate with other existing systems. As a general rule, the logical design (including process and data requirements) should precede the physical design (including both the associated hardware and software), as sometimes the logical design will reveal that the current physical design is actually fine and, thus, just the process needs to be changed.

Step 5: Choosing a Vendor

The first step in choosing a vendor is creating a list of what you want the HRIS to be able to accomplish. This list is included in a request for proposal (RFP), which is sent to several potential vendors. When writing an RFP, important considerations include the price and the configuration of the plan. For example, does the organization seek to purchase and install the hardware and software on internal machines staffed by internal staff? Or is the organization interested in software as a service so a subscription to software makes sense and employees access the software via the Internet? There are, of course, pros and cons to either approach, so it is important to be clear regarding which of these options is desirable and viable when sending out the RFP. Small to medium-sized companies find the software-as-a-service option to be particularly attractive, as software can be accessed via web browsers without having to install it on local computers and other devices, such as tablets and smartphones. Easy access to HR systems and information paves the way for useful employee self-service functions such as benefits enrollment, tax information, and updating employee contact information, as well as more sophisticated functions such as access to onboarding materials, training and development programs, and performance management systems.

Identifying references is also important when considering different vendors. As the SHRM toolkit on designing and managing an HRIS notes, any reputable developer or reseller should provide references from current clients of similar size with comparable business processes.[38]

SHRM recommends that HR professionals ask vendors' references questions like these:

- How has the system improved HR functions?

- What modules are you using?

- Has the system met your expectations? If not, what is it missing?

- Are end users satisfied with the system?

- Has the system been expanded or upgraded since the original purchase? If so, how did the upgrade affect customizations and other features?

- How has the vendor responded to any problems?

- What do you like best about the system? What do you like least?

- Has the system provided the expected ROI? Why or why not?

- What was the implementation experience like? Did the vendor deliver on budget and on schedule?

After reviewing the different proposals that the organization receives and checking with vendor references, the selection committee should invite two or three vendors to give a demonstration of the HRIS platform to stakeholders within the organization. Finally, taking into consideration all of the available information, one vendor should be selected and a contract finalized. Among others, key points to consider in the contract are pricing, technical and maintenance support, and upgrades.

IMPLEMENTING A HUMAN RESOURCE INFORMATION SYSTEM

LEARNING OBJECTIVES
3.5   Address key points of the process of HRIS implementation.

We have walked through the points to consider when designing and choosing a package. Next comes implementation. Although an HRIS has the potential to transform organizations, and we covered several examples of HRIS successes, researchers note, "The available evidence suggests that in the vast majority of cases information technology (IT)–enabled HRIS have not helped produce a wholesale transformation of the HR function away from routine processing and compliance and towards the strategic business partner role that many were expecting."[39] Many of the challenges that get in the way of the potential benefits of HRIS are encountered during the implementation phase. Luckily, when it comes to implementing and maintaining an HRIS, there are some key points to consider in helping to ensure a successful project launch and ongoing implementation.

Managing Resistance to Change

Implementing a major HRIS or changing the way data are gathered, stored, and retrieved can be a major change within an organization, and it can be challenging to handle effectively. This has become increasingly apparent as AI and machine learning has become more and more prevalent with the introduction of access to ChatGTP and Bard. It is important to remember that it is not only about the software and hardware; it is also about the individuals whose work lives will be impacted by the change in procedures, job descriptions, and access to information. Thus, it is an organizational change process that must be managed, and such processes are, at their heart, people management challenges as well as opportunities. When it comes to changes to an HRIS, three specific groups are most likely impacted: those working in HR, who may have their work practices fundamentally altered; managers, who may have more access to information than ever before, which increases expectations of them; and employees, who may be asked to engage in more self-service HR activities than in the past. It is understandable that such behaviors might trigger concerns for organizational members.[40] In addition, we discuss other factors related to successful and unsuccessful change management attempts beyond understanding resistance to change.

"What if we don't change at all ...
and something magical just happens?"

©iStock.com/andrewgenn

People react to change in a variety of ways, ranging from active resistance to enthusiastic support, as depicted in Figure 3.10. Given that a survey of 1,400 executives found that 82% see the pace of change in their organizations increasing and that a SHRM survey found that resistance to change is one of the top two reasons change efforts fail, it is not surprising that overcoming resistance to changes such as a new HRIS is an important part of the process.[41] Some individuals may also experience ambivalence to change, which is an opportunity to move them toward a positive attitude.[42] The closer to support that you can get individuals, the more likely the change implementation will be successful. Whereas compliance is more helpful than passive or active resistance, the lack of enthusiasm can lead to short-lived gains, especially in the face of potential challenges or set-backs during implementation. Avon learned this the hard way when employees left in "meaningful numbers" following a challenging multiyear software overhaul project that was initially rolled out in Canada. Given the challenges during implementation, Avon opted to halt use of the new system and not to roll it out to the rest of the organization.[43] Thus, part of effective change management is knowing when to change course, as Avon did.

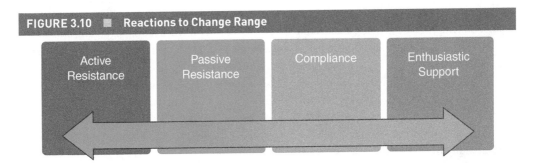

FIGURE 3.10 ■ Reactions to Change Range

Active Resistance   Passive Resistance   Compliance   Enthusiastic Support

Effective managers learn to overcome resistance to change. That doesn't mean that changes always go exactly as planned or as the manager wants, but it does mean they actively take steps to ensure a positive outcome. You might have a great idea, but people around you might not seem convinced, and/or they might express resistance. How do you make change happen?

We recommend that you

- recognize individuals may react negatively to change and plan accordingly,
- anticipate resistance and find ways to deal with it,
- listen to naysayers,
- show commitment and present a positive attitude toward the change,
- involve people in the process,
- ensure top management is visible and supportive,
- remind management and others that change is a process and successful change takes time,
- present data to your audience,
- appeal to your audience's ideals,
- reinforce change with incentives,
- communicate with employees and management,
- understand the reasons for resistance, and
- alter your approach if necessary.[44]

Organizational Culture and Realistic Timelines for Change

Part of understanding what is or is not a realistic timeline relates to understanding the organizational culture.[45] Is the culture one that embraces risk taking, or is the culture more conservative when it comes to change? Cultures vary in terms of how much they embrace collaborating, creating, controlling, or competing. Because *clan cultures* are collaboration oriented and are characterized by valuing being cohesive, people oriented, team players, and empowering employees, when implementing change and setting timelines, consider doing so after involving all affected internal stakeholders in the decision-making process. For *adhocracy cultures*, which focus on creating and emphasize being entrepreneurial and flexible, taking risks, and being creative, aggressive timelines may be feasible and even encouraged.

For *market cultures*, which are characterized by competition and value being aggressive, competitive, and customer oriented, changes in the ways things are done can be challenging if they take more time. Although the long-term payoff may exist, the time urgency within market cultures can make time one of the most salient concerns of employees. *Hierarchy cultures* focus on controlling and value being efficient and timely, and consistent strategies that emphasize the efficiency of HRIS changes may offset concerns regarding the short-term challenges during the transition and training period.

Organizations also differ in their appetite for new technologies such as AI and machine learning. For example, in a study by SAP/SuccessFactors, they discovered that not all organizations are ready to embrace intelligent technologies. They found that there are three maturity levels of organizations ranging from proactive implementation (34% of organizations surveyed) to non-active adoption (44% of organizations surveyed).[46]

In the end, it is important to keep in mind that successful implementation of HRIS or any ERP depends on creating and utilizing realistic timelines regarding how long each step will take and when a complete switchover can be undertaken. An example of an ERP failure occurred when a few years after starting a transition to a new ERP, Hershey's was unable to fulfill $100 million worth of Kiss and Jolly Rancher candy orders due to a failed ERP transition. Part of the reason for this failure has been attributed to its attempt to set tight timelines without sufficiently changing them when things went wrong.[47]

Refreezing and Maintaining the New System

When approaching a major change such as a new HRIS, consider simple heuristics to help you understand the key steps to follow during implementation. A simple model of organizational change was developed by Kurt Lewin in the 1940s, and many people continue to find it useful even today. It involves three steps: unfreezing the current system and checking to see that individuals are ready for change, enacting the change, and refreezing the new system in place so that it becomes the permanent replacement for the way things used to be done. Each phase is depicted in Figure 3.11 and features a unique set of opportunities and challenges. Much has been written about change management, and students interested in learning more about how to effectively enact and manage change are encouraged to read material covered in other courses such as "Organizational Behavior" or "Organizational Development."

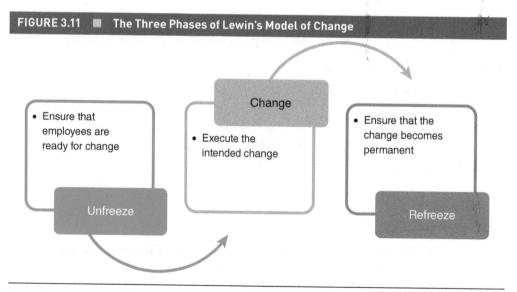

FIGURE 3.11   The Three Phases of Lewin's Model of Change

Source: Based on Lewin, K. (1946). Action research and minority problems. *Journal of Social Issues, 2,* 34–46.

Effective change managers are able to avoid the key reasons for systems failures by making sure sufficient and effective leadership is present, planning is well executed, change management best practices are followed, effective communication is present throughout the HRIS exploration and implementation process, and employees have sufficient training and support for the new systems.[48] Researchers have also identified five key areas for effective change champions to focus on during a change management process.[49] These are

- creating the case for change,

- creating structural change,

- engaging others in the process and building commitment,

- implementing and sustaining change, and

- facilitating and developing capability.

Following an effective unfreezing and subsequent change process, the next steps are to refreeze and maintain the change, which, in this case, means to solidify and stabilize the desired employee attitudes and behaviors in relation to the HRIS. During the refreeze and maintenance phases, organizations should consider several key questions: What will be needed to keep the new HRIS working effectively? How often will the effectiveness of the new HRIS be evaluated? When will updates be considered, and how will they be implemented? Who trains users on the new HRIS and associated changes, updates, and upgrades? Thinking through these questions initially as part of the process of HRIS feasibility helps avoid unpleasant surprises down the line. Research finds that employee attitudes and behaviors are affected by leadership before, during, and after an organizational change, which means that management involvement in the change process from start to finish is critical.[50]

GETTING TECHNICAL: CORE INFORMATION SYSTEM CONCEPTS

LEARNING OBJECTIVES
3.6   Apply core information system concepts in HR management.

It is clear that data and how they are gathered, stored, and retrieved are critical to the ability of those within organizations to engage in effective analytics. Now that we have delved into the intricacies of designing and implementing an HRIS, we define some core concepts and terms that are integral for understanding what a generic information system is and how it operates. Specifically, in the following sections, we describe concepts associated with databases, users, and architectures.

Database Management

In simple terms, a database refers to a collection of organized data, its structure designed to facilitate the realization of business processes. A database management system (DBMS) refers to the software used to manage and maintain a database or multiple databases. For example, today's organizations commonly use applicant tracking systems—a type of DBMS—to collect, manage, analyze, and evaluate applicant data and the various processes associated with recruitment and selection efforts that might necessitate the flow of applicant data from one data store (or collection) to another and through different processes. Organizations commonly design their information systems around what is referred to as a relational database; however, it is becoming increasingly common for organizations to store data in an unstructured manner as well.

A relational database is a specific type of database in which different subsets or collections of data are integrated through pieces of information residing within the data themselves. This avoids the need to include duplicate data in multiple locations within the database. Thus, data stored in different parts of the relational database can be linked through common identification number fields. For example, if a relational database contains a table filled with employee performance evaluation data and a table filled with compensation data, data from the two tables can be merged if a common field, such as one containing employee identification numbers, is present in both tables.

The software used to manage and maintain a relational database is referred to as a relational database management system (relational DBMS). Because different data sources can be linked in a relational DBMS, data are more readily shared by users from different functional areas and geographic locations.

Table

A table is a database object used to store data about cases (i.e., entities) and to add structure to the data. Often, a table takes the form of a matrix in which each column represents a different characteristic (or attribute) of cases and each row represents a unique case (or entity; see Table 3.1). In the absence of a table, data would be left unstructured, adding challenges regarding manipulating, managing, and analyzing the data. Each column in a table that represents a unique characteristic is referred to as a field or variable, and each case in a table is a record. For example, in a table containing employee personal data, one field might include the employees' names, and another field might include the employees' home phone numbers—both of which are characteristics of the employees. In this scenario, each row represents a unique employee record, such that by reading across a single row in a table, one can see the characteristics of the employee, as defined by the fields.

TABLE 3.1 ■ An Example of a Table Containing Employee Data			
	EmployeeID	EmployeeName	Gender
1	RDEA120	Waller, Anderson	Male
2	RDEA122	Clark, Jose	Male
3	RDEA123	Benton, Cora	Female
4	RDEA124	Rich, Belen	Female
5	RDEA125	Vega, Alejandra	Female
6	RDEA126	Hickman, Lukas	Male
7	RDEA127	Phillips, Aracely	Female
8	RDEA128	Bonilla, Cody	Male
9	RDEA129	Chaney, Orion	Male
10	RDEA121	Day, Linda	Female

Key Variable

A relational database is composed of two or more tables, which are "connected" via a key variable. A key variable—sometimes referred to as a *linking variable*—provides the information necessary to construct the relationships between tables. For example, in many HRIS, a unique identifier is given to each employee (e.g., employee identification number). As shown in Figure 3.12, the employee identification number serves as a key variable between the employee personal information table and the sales table. Note how a unique employee identification number is associated with each record (i.e., employee) in the employee personal information table but that employee identification numbers appear multiple times in the sales table. As described earlier in the chapter, relational databases reduce data redundancies by limiting the amount of repetition of identical data. Key variables are, consequently, used to connect tables so as to avoid data redundancies, which contribute to the process of database normalization.

FIGURE 3.12 ■ An Example of a Key Variable Linking Tables Containing Employee Data and Customer Invoice Data, Respectively

	EmployeeID	EmployeeName	Gender
1	RDEA120	Waller, Anderson	Male
2	RDEA122	Clark, Jose	Male
3	RDEA123	Benton, Cora	Female
4	RDEA124	Rich, Belen	Female
5	RDEA125	Vega, Alejandra	Female
6	RDEA126	Hickman, Lukas	Male
7	RDEA127	Phillips, Aracely	Female
8	RDEA128	Bonilla, Cody	Male
9	RDEA129	Chaney, Orion	Male
10	RDEA121	Day, Linda	Female

	InvoiceNumber	CustomerName	SaleTotal	EmployeeID
1	281	Reese, Kaylyn	153	RDEA120
2	367	Bantham, Karli	182	RDEA122
3	281	Weaver, Zoe	182	RDEA123
4	393	Hanna, Dana	419	RDEA120
5	348	Gill, Cory	493	RDEA123
6	403	Little, Brent	279	RDEA123
7	379	Ruiz, Grayson	671	RDEA123
8	243	Scott, Alana	232	RDEA128
9	431	Deleon, Skyler	547	RDEA129
10	359	Jimenez, Audrey	627	RDEA121
11	285	Lindsey, Nicholas	514	RDEA122
12	239	Olsen, Alexis	237	RDEA120
13	396	Bowman, Alessandro	54	RDEA122
14	349	Fuentes, Neeraj	226	RDEA123
15	331	Love, Izabelle	595	RDEA124
16	323	Meyer, Angeline	201	RDEA125
17	431	Mathews, Tristan	372	RDEA126
18	375	Atkins, Julie	106	RDEA127
19	321	Cohen, Leonard	150	RDEA128
20	345	Harper, June	627	RDEA129
21	231	Freeman, Courtney	284	RDEA121
22	285	Nicholson, Jack	461	RDEA121
23	261	David, Maria	516	RDEA121
24	384	McDaniel, Dereon	459	RDEA121

Form

A form is a database object that provides a user interface with which to enter, edit, and/or display data contained within a database. A well-designed form can facilitate the manner in which users interact with the database. Figure 3.13 shows an example of a form used for data entry, which, in this case, is used to enter applicant data from a paper application. To reduce the occurrence of data-entry errors, the form closely resembles the actual paper application. Often, these forms are directly connected to the data housed within the database, enabling users to update database objects (e.g., tables, queries) directly.

FIGURE 3.13 ■ Example of a Form

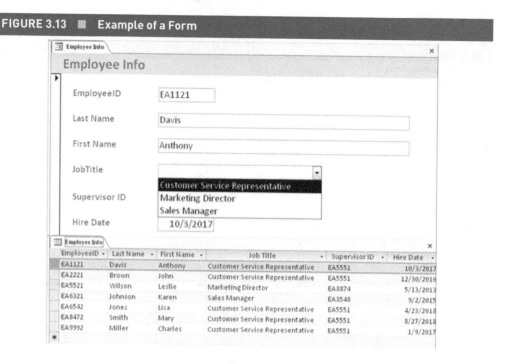

Query

As the name implies, a query is a question that is posed to a database. Such questions can be used to perform a number of different actions. For example, a common use of queries is to retrieve certain segments or subsets of data from one or more tables within the database. A query can also be used to display and/or sort data, create new tables, manipulate data, or even perform a specified calculation. Queries come in handy when users find themselves posing the same question over and over again to the database. For example, if a manager wants to know how much sales revenue each member of her sales team generates each quarter, a query can be created that conducts the same actions, even when the data in the database are updated or changed. Commonly, structured query language (SQL) is used by organizations to manage, maintain, and generate queries using their DBMS. Figure 3.14 provides an example of SQL script.

FIGURE 3.14 ■ An Example of a Simple Query to Compute Average of Quantitative Data From a Column in a Table Using SQL

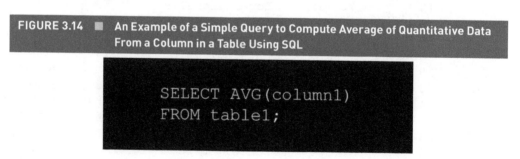

Report

A report is a database object that is used to organize, summarize, format, and present data residing in the database. The data used in a report can come from tables or queries. Like queries, reports are useful because they can be used to perform the same actions every time they are applied, even when the underlying data have been updated or changed. Recall the example used in the context of queries. The manager wants to go a step further than using the query to determine how much sales revenue each member of her sales team generated in the past quarter. Accordingly, the manager creates a report to summarize and format the total sales revenue data for each salesperson. Specifically, she creates a nicely formatted horizontal bar chart in which salespersons' names appear on the y-axis, and total sales revenue appears on the x-axis (see Figure 3.15).

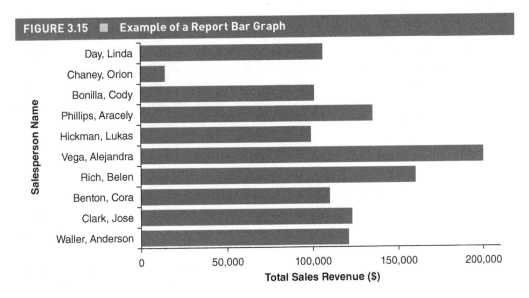

FIGURE 3.15   ■   Example of a Report Bar Graph

System Users

Different groups of individuals both within and outside of an organization may have reason to access and use an HRIS. As such, an HRIS should be designed with different system users in mind, as different system users often have different motivations or responsibilities when accessing an HRIS, and thus, user experience should be considered. Employees constitute a primary HRIS user group, as they need to access data within the system for entry, verification, analysis, and reporting purposes.

Even among employees, however, motivations or responsibilities when accessing the system may differ based on their roles. First, all employees need to interact with the HRIS for the purposes of viewing, changing, or verifying their own personal data. Many organizations allow employees to select their benefits during an open-enrollment period by accessing benefits self-service web portals. In this way, employees have direct control over their data in the HRIS instead of relying on a face-to-face meeting with a benefits administrator to select benefits. Second, some employees need to enter data into the HRIS for other users. Managers may be required to enter the performance appraisal ratings for each of their employees directly into the HRIS. Third, other employees play a more active role in updating the HRIS itself and/or analyzing and reporting data contained within the HRIS. For example, information technology employees are often responsible for implementing system design changes and fixing technology-related issues with the HRIS. In addition, HR analysts may analyze the existing HRIS data or collect new data for the purposes of finding answers to important HR-related questions. Finally, employees with managerial responsibilities may need to access actual employee data, but in many cases, they access data that are reported in aggregate about groups or units of employees. For example, CEOs may wish to know which organizational units have the highest turnover rates, and by accessing a dashboard with preconfigured yet customizable analytic findings, they can analyze turnover rates by organizational unit.

Other Users

In addition to an organization's employees, other users outside of the organization often need access to the HRIS. First, it is increasingly common for organizations to allow (potential) job applicants to enter their personal information, such as a résumé and applicant blank data, into the HRIS, often via an applicant tracking system. The system often allows applicants to log into the system at their convenience to check the status of their applications. Second, many organizations outsource some of their HR activities to third-party partners, and thus, some data need to be shared with these partners. For example, some organizations outsource their payroll functions to outside vendors; as a result, such vendors will need access to up-to-date compensation and benefits data for employees. Of course, sharing data with outside partners (or even internally with employee system users) may pose some data privacy and security risks.

System Architectures

System architectures for HRIS and other information systems have evolved since the advent of modern computing, and advancements in information technology are responsible for this evolution. For many decades, information systems were based on what are often called traditional tiered architectures, but in the past decade, there has been a rapid shift toward cloud-based architectures, especially as data transfer speeds and storage space have increased.

Traditional Tiered Architectures

In the mid-20th century, computers were the size of rooms and were so expensive that relatively few organizations had access to computers for information-system purposes. Nonetheless, some organizations devised systems so a few users could directly interface with a computer mainframe, which meant that all databases and applications lived on the mainframe. These were called single-tier or one-tier architectures.

When personal computers were introduced, came down in price, and gained popularity during the 1970s and 1980s, client–server architectures (sometimes called two-tier architectures) were introduced. Specifically, many of the simpler functions with fewer processing demands were decentralized to personal computers that system users directly accessed via a user interface client, and the databases and applications lived on a server, thereby creating two tiers—one for the personal computers and one for the server. The next evolution in system architectures occurred when the server containing databases and applications was split into two separate servers so more processing-intensive activities could be handled by a dedicated applications server.

Finally, with the advent of the Internet and expansion of its use, speed, and capabilities came what is referred to as N-tier architectures. (The "N" serves as a placeholder for any number that is four or greater.) By leveraging the Internet, N-tier architectures used the database and application servers of three-tier architectures but added web servers. Users no longer needed to download the user interface client onto personal computers because the user interface client was accessible via web servers. That is, through their personal computers, system users could log onto a web portal, which was hosted by web servers, to access and interface with the system. By introducing web servers, more and more devices, such as cell phones, could be used to access the system.

Cloud-Based Architectures

Today, we can access our music, movies, and software programs through the "cloud," or Internet-based databases and applications that are hosted remotely (from the perspective of the user). Cloud computing has revolutionized how we access information, as we can log on and interact with information through multiple devices and multiple locations, as long as there is a reliable Internet connection available. Cloud computing also has important implications for HRIS via cloud-based architectures, which allow organizational system users to access and interact with the HRIS in much the same way we access music and movies. In effect, cloud-based architectures move the database, application, and web servers of an N-tier architecture to the cloud. In this way, organizations do not need to house and manage their own servers; instead, their server needs are outsourced to a third-party entity that the organization partners with.

A common application of cloud-based architectures is **software as a service (SaaS)**, arrangements through which software and hardware associated with databases and applications are maintained and controlled by a third-party entity. An advantage of SaaS is that an organization can purchase access to databases and applications on a subscription basis, which means that the organization does not need to update DBMS software and hardware, as such responsibilities are taken care of by the SaaS provider. A potential disadvantage of SaaS and other cloud-computing architectures is that the organization relies on the cloud-computing provider to manage data security. Most providers take data security very seriously and put many safeguards and protections in place; however, using a provider along with other companies may increase the desirability for hackers to access the data.

CHAPTER SUMMARY

Managing data is important to HR because all organizations need to be able to make decisions about people, and data-informed decisions can be more effective. HR information systems, or HRIS, provide both opportunities and challenges. Opportunities include the ability to track employees through their employment life cycles, employee-centered HR functionality, data availability for metrics and analytics, and the ability to create effective data visualizations. Challenges to consider include cost, the HR skill set, data privacy concerns, and data security concerns. In developing an HRIS, an organization conducts a needs assessment, creates a design, and considers choosing a vendor. When an HRIS is implemented, the organization undergoes a process of change that culminates in refreezing; the HRIS must also be maintained over time. Core information system concepts include the management of databases and users, understanding of HRIS architecture, and relational database concepts.

KEY TERMS

Anonymous data

Blockchain

Change

Confidential data

Cybersecurity

Data flow diagrams

Data lake

Data privacy

Data security

Database

Database management system (DBMS)

e-HRM

Enterprise resource planning (ERP)

Field (variable)

Form

Human resource information system (HRIS)

Key variable

Logical design

People data

Personally identifiable data

Physical design

Query

Record

Refreezing

Relational database

Relational database management system (relational DBMS)

Report

Scraping and crawling tools

Software as a service (SaaS)

Storytelling with data

Table

Two-step authentication (multifactor authentication)

Unfreezing

HR REASONING AND DECISION-MAKING EXERCISES

Mini-Case Analysis Exercise: Determining Whether to Continue HRIS Consulting

The Monday morning meeting is just starting. The room is full of individuals from the HR team. As the newest member and best trained on statistics and HR analytics, you are looked to by staff to help them frame questions, conduct research to answer the questions, and help walk them through the implications.

John Bettle, a senior HR manager within your division, walks in. He starts the meeting off with several scenarios that the team has been asked to address. As the new HR analytics guru in your group, you've been asked to address key questions.

The organization has been spending a lot of money bringing in HRIS consultants and experts to help with understanding the HRIS needs of the organization. The vice president (VP) of HR, Raja Sutton, has asked John to let him know if he thinks the investment in time and money is worth it. John's gut tells him it is, but he's not sure how best to make the business case for this. Given the request came from "up high," John is asking for your help in how to address it.

Now, decide what you would do. Share your approach to how the team might best respond to this request from the VP of HR.

1. What specifically would you tell John to say to justify the continued investment in understanding the organization's HRIS needs?

2. Be specific, and outline your recommendations for John, being sure to include key points from this chapter.

HR Decision Analysis Exercise: Issues With Addressing a Skills Gap

Your new CEO recently went to a technology conference. On returning, she shared her excitement about artificial intelligence (AI), big data, and analytics and their roles in the future of management. She mandated that the HR department create proposals for a new and improved HRIS to make sure the company stays current on these technology trends.

However, you are concerned that you may not have the right people with the right skills within the HR area, as most of them earned their college degrees many years ago. When you mention this to your manager, he says, "Well, maybe we need to retrain our current employees, or maybe we need to replace them with new talent that has the skills we need." How might you react to the suggestion to move forward in replacing current employees with those with better technology skills?

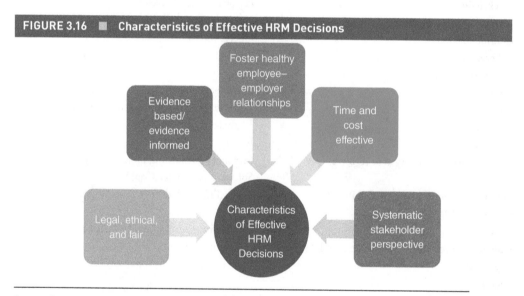

FIGURE 3.16 ■   Characteristics of Effective HRM Decisions

Source: Reprinted from *SHRM Competency Model* with permission of the Society for Human Resource Management. © SHRM. All rights reserved.

Please provide the rationale for your answer to each of the questions below.

Is this suggestion legal, ethical, and fair?

Is it evidence based/evidence informed?

Does it foster healthy employee–employer relationships?

Is it time- and cost-effective?

Does it take a systematic stakeholder perspective?

Considering your analysis above, overall, do you think this would be an effective decision? Why or why not?

What, if anything, do you think should be done differently or considered to help make this decision more effective?

HR Decision-Making Exercise: Organizational Attractiveness Audit

You work on a team with four other members of the customer service team at C-Zone, an auto-parts wholesaler. Your company has around 2,000 employees nationally. The company has low job acceptance rates of only 30%, which you suspect is too low, but since you do not work in HR, you have never mentioned anything about this. However, for a long time, you have believed the high customer service turnover (75% each year) and low acceptance rates of jobs offered are related. Thus, it may be time for your team to think about what might be done about this. Your company recently implemented a new HRIS, which now makes it possible to get data on employees on request. You decide it is time for your five-person leadership team to start doing a little investigation.

1. Develop a plan to examine why employees are hesitant to join the organization and always seem to be leaving. How can you assess why employees turn down job offers? How might you assess why employees are leaving? After you choose your method of measurement (i.e., focus groups, survey, interviews), develop an instrument, including the questions to be included. How would you analyze the data to identify the top reasons for employee departures?

2. Let's assume you found out the top three reasons for low job acceptance to your company are as follows:
   a. Management is very authoritarian and not supportive of employees. When potential applicants read the comments on Glassdoor.com, it scares them off.
   b. Compensation is below average compared with other similar organizations.
   c. Employees feel they are working all the time with little downtime. This is especially true in the call center when calls can be stressful and plentiful at peak times.

3. What would be your proposed action plan to deal with these issues? Be specific, and make sure your recommendations focus on recruitment, selection, training, compensation, and any other stages of the employment cycle.

DATA AND ANALYTICS EXERCISE: DATA CLEANING

One of the overarching goals of any HRIS is to provide users with accurate data. Further, the integrity of the data directly influences the integrity of the insights gleaned from the data, or in other words: garbage in, garbage out. Unfortunately, the data that reside within an HRIS are not always what we would hope or expect for. There are a number of reasons for this, but one of the most common reasons is human error.

Imagine that your HRIS is built around a relational database consisting of a number of different tables. In one of the tables, you store basic employee information, such as employee ID, employee name, job level, location, and department.

Here is an excerpt of the table:

Employee ID	Employee Name	Job Level	Location	Department
EA44312	Kim, Yeongjin	1	beaverton	Customer Service
EB58521	Dowsett, Jane	3	Hillsboro	
EA64533	Henderson, Lynn	4	Hillsboro	
EA89575	Mitchell, Terrance	1	Hillsboro	Customer Service
ET58748	Smith, John	1	Beaverton	Customer Service
ET96461	Martinez, David	4	Beavertn	Marketing
EB11248	Liu, Patricia	11	Beaverton	Customer Service

First, take a close look at the Location field. Do you notice anything? Note how the Beaverton location is spelled with a capital "B" for three of the cases and how it is spelled without the "o" for one case. Most likely, this difference in spelling was the result of an error during data entry. Errors like this might not seem like such a big deal, but down the road, they can lead to issues when it comes to merging and analyzing the data. Namely, many software programs such as Microsoft Access Excel will treat the two different versions of the word *Beaverton* (i.e., Beaverton, Beavertn) location as two distinct categories. That is, instead of treating the Location field as a categorical variable with two levels (i.e., Beaverton, Hillsboro), the Location field will be treated as a categorical variable with the following three levels: Beaverton, Beavertn, and Hillsboro. If you were to create a PivotTable in Excel to determine the frequency (i.e., counts) of employees who work at each location, you would end up with the following frequency table (Figure 3.17):

FIGURE 3.17 ■

Row Labels ▼	Count of Location
Beavertn	1
Beaverton	3
Hillsboro	3
Grand Total	**7**

Note how the frequency table correctly indicates that three employees work at the Hillsboro location but incorrectly indicates that three employees work at the Beaverton location and one employee works at the Beavertn location.

Second, take a close look at the rest of the table. Did you notice the missing data? Specifically, Jane Dowsett and Lynn Henderson are missing the names of the departments in which they work. More than likely these two employees work in a department that has a name. As such, it is important that these missing data are found and the table is updated.

Third, in this organization, there are only seven job levels, where a 1 corresponds to entry-level jobs and a 7 corresponds to executive jobs. Now take a look at the Job Level field. Note how Patricia Liu has a job level of 11, which is clearly beyond the 1–7 range. This might mean that someone accidentally entered 1 twice by mistake, resulting in 11. Again, a simple Excel PivotTable can be used to create a frequency table that displays how many employees fall into each job level. The frequency table here (Figure 3.18) shows in the left column that one of the job levels is 11, which is not correct.

FIGURE 3.18 ■

Row Labels ▼	Count of Job Level
1	3
3	1
4	2
11	1
Grand Total	**7**

The best course of action is to prevent these errors in the first place. For instance, you can design tables with data validation rules that allow only predetermined values to be entered into cells (e.g., Beaverton, Hillsboro). Alternatively, in the context of a relational database, you can create a form that facilitates data entry by requiring data to be entered into certain fields and allowing only certain fields to be completed using drop-down menus with provided options.

If, however, you still find yourself with "dirty" data, you will need to clean the data prior to analysis. Fortunately, Excel and other programs offer several tools that can facilitate the data-cleaning process, such as the PivotTable tool that was highlighted in the example.

Excel Extension: Now You Try!

- On **edge.sagepub.com/bauer2e**, you will find an Excel exercise on data cleaning.

- First, you will learn how to use the filter feature to identify potential data integrity issues.

- Second, you will learn how to use the PivotTable tool to construct frequency tables that can be used to identify potential data integrity issues.

- Third, you will practice applying these tools and interpreting and communicating your findings.

4

DIVERSITY, EQUITY, AND INCLUSION (DEI), AND EQUAL EMPLOYMENT LAWS

LEARNING OBJECTIVES

After reading and studying this chapter, you should be able to do the following:

4.1 Describe the challenges and benefits of diversity, equity, and inclusion (DEI) in the workplace.

4.2 Identify major U.S. laws pertaining to equal employment opportunity relating how they apply to various kinds of employment decisions.

4.3 Discuss the impact of Title VII of the Civil Rights Act.

4.4 Identify additional antidiscrimination acts and protections in the workplace.

4.5 Recommend ways in which organizations can maintain legal compliance and address key analytical, legal, ethical, and global issues associated with diversity, equity, and inclusion in HRM.

DIVERSITY, EQUITY, AND INCLUSION AS A BUSINESS PRIORITY: THE CASE OF ACCENTURE[1]

Julie Sweet, CEO of Accenture, sees top management commitment as the first step to building a diverse and inclusive culture.

Mark Kauzlarich/Bloomberg via Getty Images

With over 700,000 employees based in 200 cities in 49 countries, and serving clients in more than 120 countries, Accenture is a leading professional services company. As a company whose mission is to deliver on "the promise of technology and human ingenuity," creating an inclusive culture where employees with diverse characteristics are hired, supported, and are enabled to bring their best selves to work is a key priority. Accenture remains a leader in this area and was recognized as the number-one company in the United States for diversity by DiversityInc in 2022. The company is a winner of similar accolades, such as being the highest scoring company on Bloomberg Gender Equality Index and placing number 6 in the Fortune 100 Best Companies to Work For list.

Many companies made public statements about the importance of diversity and inclusion following societal events including the #MeToo movement, the killing of George Floyd, and the resulting widespread nationwide protests. However, real change remains elusive for many companies. Therefore, examining companies that seem to defy trends is worthwhile and can be informative. What exactly does Accenture do to build a diverse and inclusive workplace?

The company's CEO Julie Sweet outlines a three-step process to achieve measurable results: First, she outlines the importance of the belief that diversity is an important part of business success. Second is goal setting. For example, in 2017, the company announced that they were aiming to reach gender parity by 2023. Similarly, in 2020, they published a goal of increasing their representation of Black employees from 9% to 12%, and Hispanic employees from 9.5% to 13%. Finally, the third step is accountability. The top 500 leaders at Accenture are evaluated based on a scorecard, including metrics of employee engagement, talent retention, and diversity goals. In other words, she describes their approach to diversity management as one of ensuring top management commitment, measuring diversity outcomes, and treating it as one of the key business goals.

The company seems to be on track with respect to its stated diversity goals since publishing comprehensive statistics about their U.S. workforce in 2016. For example, in 2021, women represented 46% of their workforce and 32% of executive leadership. They improved the representation of African American and Black employees by 3.9%, and Hispanic American and Latinx employees by 4.3%.

Setting ambitious goals, tracking progress, and keeping leaders accountable is a process that is supported by numerous initiatives to reach goal achievement. For example, local demographics are often a barrier to diversity efforts: If a company is not located in a geographically diverse area, it is much harder to attract employees of different backgrounds. To tackle this, the company prioritized growing its office locations in diverse urban areas. Realizing that recruitment practices could serve as roadblocks, the company diversified the colleges and universities from which it recruits. It also built an apprenticeship program to fill positions where a college degree may not be needed, offering different pathways to employees with diverse backgrounds. Finally, the company has a vibrant community of employee resource groups, supporting employees with different religions, sexual orientation and gender identity, veteran status, and disabilities.

CASE DISCUSSION QUESTIONS

1. What do you think is the role of publicly set goals for developing a diverse, equitable, and inclusive workplace?

2. Many companies point to a pipeline problem, or the lack of suitable candidates, as a barrier to diversity efforts. How is Accenture tackling this problem? What else do you think the company can do that is not mentioned in the case?

3. What are the benefits of building an inclusive culture that is the responsibility of all leaders instead of just human resources (HR)?

4. What is the role of employee resource groups in facilitating an inclusive culture? How would you ensure they are effective?

INTRODUCTION

Having a diverse workforce and creating a culture of inclusion are good for business. By hiring, retaining, and supporting a diverse workforce, companies have the potential to achieve better business results such as a more satisfied and committed workforce with lower levels of turnover, while also minimizing the chances of costly lawsuits.

In this chapter, we first present the importance of managing diversity and explore why it still remains challenging to achieve a truly diverse workplace. Then we explore the legal landscape with regard to diversity in the United States, describing the most important laws and court decisions that HR managers need to be familiar with. Finally, we describe some best practices in managing diversity that organizations are advised to follow.

THE IMPORTANCE OF DEI

LEARNING OBJECTIVES
4.1   Describe the challenges and benefits of diversity, equity, and inclusion (DEI) in the workplace.

Diversity, equity, and inclusion (DEI) represents policies and programs that promote representation and fair treatment of employees from different backgrounds. As a collective characteristic, **diversity** refers to compositional differences among people within a work unit, which may lead them to perceive others as similar to them or different from them.[2] As society becomes more diverse, organizations are following suit, as the following statistics indicate. In 2022, women constituted 47% of the workforce in the United States. White employees were 77%, Hispanic or Latino 18.5%, Black or African American 12.6%, and Asian workers 6.7% of the labor force.[3] How organizations hire, manage, and retain a diverse workforce has implications for organizational effectiveness. There is a rich legal landscape that organizations need to be familiar with when managing their employees.

Why Is Effective Management of Diversity Important?

Due to societal trends such as increasing labor participation of historically excluded groups, an aging workforce, and greater prevalence of migrant workers, the workforce is increasingly diverse. Increasing diversity introduces management challenges for individuals and organizations, because of the persistence of stereotypes and prejudice, people having a tendency to prefer in-group members, and communication challenges and conflict.[5] At the same time, diversity's potential is unlocked when diversity is accompanied by equity and inclusion. **Equity** refers to ensuring that organizational policies and practices are impartial and fair. **Inclusion** refers to treatment of individuals of all backgrounds with dignity and respect, including them in decision making, and valuing them for who they are and what they bring to the group or organization. Inclusiveness allows individuals to be themselves. Everyone is valued not only for their performance but also as human beings. Employees have input in decision making, and everyone's ideas are heard. Research shows that having an inclusive climate is associated with higher levels of job satisfaction, organizational commitment, and work engagement, lower levels of employee withdrawal, and higher levels of individual and organizational performance. These effects are particularly strong in diverse organizations.[6]

There are many studies that show a "business case" for diversity. While we cover this research in this section, note that it is also important to understand the "moral case" for diversity. Removing barriers to inclusion is simply the right thing to do. Fair and respectful

The CEO of Lowe's, Marvin Ellison, made it a priority to diversify the company by investing in programs such as supporting employee education through tuition support and offering advancement opportunities through succession planning.[4]

Jared Siskin/Contributor

treatment, having equal access to jobs and organizational opportunities, working in an environment free from harassment and disrespect are important and should be accessible to everyone. There is emerging evidence that making a business case for diversity actually undermines the sense of belonging for under-represented groups by implying that their presence in the organization is a means to an end.[7]

Lack of diversity is detrimental to innovation. When people with different life experiences and viewpoints come together and share information, disclose their viewpoints, and make an effort to integrate them, they arrive at more innovative decisions. As a result, diversity and innovation are related such that the more diversity that exists within a group, the more innovative it tends to be.[8] Consider product design. Today, many products target a diverse set of customers. Yet when a product design team is homogeneous, members typically consider only their own experiences with the product and neglect to consider unique challenges users dissimilar to them may experience. As a case in point, facial recognition software led to the false arrest of a Black man in front of his family and being held in custody for over 30 hours. According to a 2019 study, the technology is up to 100 times more likely to misidentify Black and Asian faces as opposed to white faces.[9]

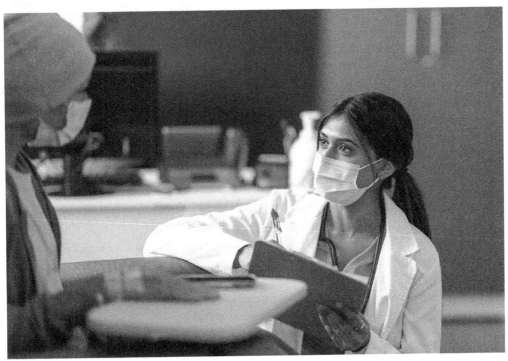

Most medical research does not use representative samples in drug trials. Women, people of color, Indigenous people, older adults, pregnant individuals, and those with disabilities are underrepresented, resulting in health inequities.[10]

©iStockphoto.com/FatCamera

Diversity also has effects on firm reputation and performance. Diversity at the highest levels of a company signals that the firm understands and appreciates the value of diversity and gives power to a diverse group of individuals. Therefore, it has benefits for how the firm operates and how it is perceived in the external community. For example, a study of racial diversity in U.S. law firms showed that racial diversity was positively associated with firm financial performance.[11] However, in 2022, only 1.2% of Fortune 500 companies had Black CEOs, 4% had Latino CEOs, and 7.7% were Asian. Further, 10% of Fortune 500 CEOs were women.[12]

Why Is DEI Still Challenging to Achieve?

Even though diversity, equity, and inclusion are important for organizations, there are barriers. Prejudices and biases continue to exist, and they may serve as barriers to hiring and retaining a diverse workforce. At the same time, the systemic absence of diversity in many industries and job categories is hard to explain solely through racism, sexism, ageism, or other forms of discrimination. Many of the challenges reflect simple human tendencies, which make it extremely difficult to eradicate them. In many cases, being aware of them is a useful first step, but instead of trying to change human nature, organizations are starting to design systems that recognize these biases exist and seek to prevent them from affecting HR decisions in the first place.

Similarity-Attraction

Perhaps the biggest challenge to having a diverse workforce and creating an inclusive work environment is the tendency of individuals to prefer others who are similar to them. Researchers name this tendency the similarity-attraction hypothesis. People tend to establish trust more quickly, show willingness to cooperate, and experience smoother communication with others who are similar to them. Similarity may not always refer to demographic characteristics such as sex, race, age, or nationality. It may also mean similarity in education level or functional background (e.g., marketing, finance, or HR major). For example, in an experimental study, participants played the role of a hiring manager and evaluated information on a simulated job applicant, including the applicant's social media page. The social media page contained a great deal of information, including the applicant's political affiliation. Participants rated the job applicant as more similar to themselves when they had the same political affiliation, which predicted liking of the applicant, and led to the perception that the candidate would be a stronger performer and better organizational citizen. As in this example, individual preference for similar others could be a barrier to hiring employees who are different from the existing employee pool. For example, consciously or unconsciously, a hiring manager who is white may feel greater affinity for another white job applicant who is also of a similar age and went to the same college. Similarly, in a firm where Asian and male employees are more prevalent, non-Asian and female employees may experience greater difficulty getting hired.[13]

Stereotypes and Unconscious Biases

Stereotypes may cause problems during and after hiring. Stereotypes are simplified and generalized assumptions about a particular group. These assumptions may be implicit or explicit. In other words, you may or may not be aware you have these stereotypes, and often they live in your subconscious. For example, if you believe younger people are more technologically savvy, and you are aware this is a perception you have, then this is an example of an explicit stereotype. However, if you don't consciously think that, and yet you are taken aback when you interact with a tech-savvy older person, then you may have an implicit, or unconscious, bias about how age affects technical acumen. Unconscious (or implicit) bias refers to stereotypes individuals hold that reside beyond their conscious awareness. To explore your own potential implicit biases, try the implicit association test developed by Harvard University researchers (https://implicit.harvard.edu/implicit/takeatest.html). Discrimination, or the actual biased decisions (e.g., a hiring decision) about individuals based on their group, is at least partly a result of stereotyping.

Implicit or explicit, stereotypes and biases could serve as barriers to diversity, equity, and inclusion, and both seem to play a role in decisions.[14] In the hiring process, an older applicant interviewing for a job at a technology firm may simply seem "wrong" for the company culture because the employee does not look like the typical technology worker. After being hired, stereotypes may result in differential treatment. After having a baby, an employee may be put on the "mommy track," with managers withholding challenging and developmental assignments with the assumption that the employee would no longer be interested in them. Using assumptions and generalizations when making decisions about specific individuals leads to unfair and potentially illegal decisions. And yet, particularly when they are a form of implicit bias, these tendencies are a challenge to eliminate. By definition, implicit biases are unconscious, and therefore a person may have difficulty identifying and eliminating them.

Confronting one's own biases and becoming more aware of how hidden biases affect organizational decision making is an essential first step in dealing with them. For this reason, unconscious bias training is common. Sephora, a personal care and beauty products retailer, surveyed 4,000 shoppers, and found that 40% of their shoppers had been a victim of racial bias in retail settings. This led the company to train all new hires on unconscious biases. Microsoft's unconscious bias training gives everyday examples of how unconscious bias operates, such as a woman employee repeatedly being interrupted in a meeting. Training highlights how common unconscious bias is, and what types of behaviors it may result in, so that participants can recognize it. Participants are also taught that although common, these behaviors are harmful and should be avoided. Finally, participants are taught how to question their assumptions and change their behaviors.[15]

Organizations are also designing structures and systems that aim to prevent unconscious biases from affecting decision making. One of the successful methods for dealing with lack of diversity in national orchestras has been to conduct auditions behind a screen, which has resulted in the admission of more female musicians to national orchestras even though they constituted only 5% of orchestra members in the 1970s. In another example, research conducted using research proposals to spend time on the Hubble Space Telescope showed that proposals received from women scientists fared better when gender identifying data were anonymized. Where possible, removing data identifying gender, race, age, and other protected characteristics may be an effective way of guarding against unconscious bias.[16]

Microaggressions

Discrimination experienced in the workplace is not always severe and may not rise to the level of illegal discrimination. Instead, often it may take the form of microaggressions, or subtle snubs, slights, and insults targeting marginalized populations, women, and other historically excluded groups. These may include examples such as questioning a woman's (but not a man's) credentials when they answer a call for a doctor in a flight, asking someone "where are they really from," calling someone who is sharing their experience with discrimination "overly sensitive," or claiming that someone got their position due to affirmative action.[17]

When experienced repeatedly over time, microaggressions are associated with negative psychological and medical outcomes, particularly among Black and Hispanic individuals. Given their harmful effects for individual health and well-being, addressing microaggressions remains a challenge for diversity, equity, and inclusion efforts. Training programs showing how to recognize and confront microaggressions is one of the ways in which companies deal with microaggressions.[18]

AN OVERVIEW OF EQUAL EMPLOYMENT OPPORTUNITY LAWS

LEARNING OBJECTIVES

4.2 Identify major U.S. laws pertaining to equal employment opportunity relating how they apply to various kinds of employment decisions.

Effective management of diversity, equity, and inclusion goes beyond simply complying with the law, but legal compliance is an essential first step. An important reason for understanding the legal side of diversity and inclusion is to limit the organization's legal liability. Discrimination lawsuits are costly in terms of legal fees and penalties and in terms of their costs to firm reputation. Although this chapter is not intended to give legal advice, it aims to create awareness of the basic federal laws and regulations that HR professionals need to be familiar with. When seeking specific legal advice, contact a lawyer.

There are two key factors that make diversity-related legal issues complicated. First, the legal landscape is dynamic and constantly changing. New federal and Supreme Court decisions set precedents that affect how the laws are interpreted in future cases. Therefore, HR professionals need to continually keep up with new developments in the legal field. Second, this book covers only federal laws relating to diversity. States and municipalities have their own laws, which offer additional protections to employees or place additional restrictions on businesses. Further, presidential executive orders, which carry the force of law, may be applicable to HR issues. HR professionals and managers need to understand their legal obligations by becoming intimately familiar with the federal, state, and local laws affecting diversity management.

In the United States, federal law prohibits discrimination in employment decisions based on protected characteristics. These laws are referred to as equal employment opportunity (EEO) laws. Most EEO laws pertaining to private, government, and state institutions are monitored and enforced by the Equal Employment Opportunity Commission (EEOC), an independent federal agency that ensures compliance with the law and provides outreach activities designed to prevent discrimination from occurring in the first place. In addition to the EEOC, the Office of Federal Contract Compliance Programs (OFCCP), a division of the Department of Labor, monitors EEO compliance of federal contractors.[19]

Most EEO laws apply to organizations with 15 or more employees. EEO laws cover business, private employers, government agencies, employment agencies, and labor unions. Religious institutions, such as churches and church-affiliated schools, and employees performing religious duties are often exempted (ministerial exception).[20] EEO laws aim to prevent discrimination against employees, job applicants, and participants in training and apprenticeship programs. Note that independent contractors, because they are not employees, are not covered. Whether an individual is considered an independent contractor or an employee is complicated; the more control an employer exercises on an individual in how the job is done, the more likely it is for that person to be an employee for the purposes of these laws.[21] This section reviews the major EEO laws, including the Equal Pay Act (1963), Title VII of the Civil Rights Act (1964 and 1991), laws pertaining to the protection of pregnant workers, Age Discrimination in Employment Act (ADEA, 1967), Americans with Disabilities Act (ADA, 1990), and Genetic Information Nondiscrimination Act (GINA, 2008).

Excluding the Equal Pay Act, EEO laws require applicants or employees to file a complaint with EEOC as the first step. In other words, even though illegal discrimination may have occurred, individuals do not have the ability to file a lawsuit without filing a charge with EEOC first.[22] Before filing a charge, individuals need to make sure they are actually protected by a specific EEO law. The laws also require employees or job applicants to file their complaint within a specific number of days following the discriminatory incident. Once a charge is filed, EEOC investigates claims of discrimination and seeks to help parties reach a settlement. Further, EEOC is authorized to file lawsuits in cases where there is evidence of bias. If EEOC finds evidence of discrimination but decides not to pursue a lawsuit, it issues a "right to sue" letter, allowing the individual to file a lawsuit on their own.[23] Figure 4.1 shows the number of EEOC claims for various types of discrimination in 1 year. Figure 4.2 provides an overview of the process from EEOC's perspective.

FIGURE 4.1 ■ EEOC Claim Statistics

Race discrimination, disability discrimination, and retaliation claims dominated the complaints reported to EEOC in 2022.

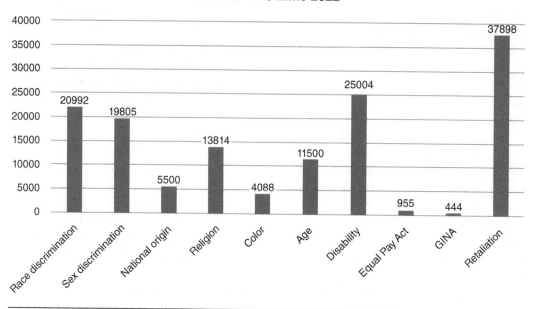

Number of Claims 2022

Source: EEOC. (2023). *Charge statistics (charges filed with EEOC) FY 1997 through FY 2022.* https://www.eeoc.gov/data/charge-statistics-charges-filed-eeoc-fy-1997-through-fy-2022

FIGURE 4.2 ■ EEOC Complaint Process

The EEOC complaint process begins when an individual files a complaint and ends with a settlement, a lawsuit, or a "right to sue" letter.

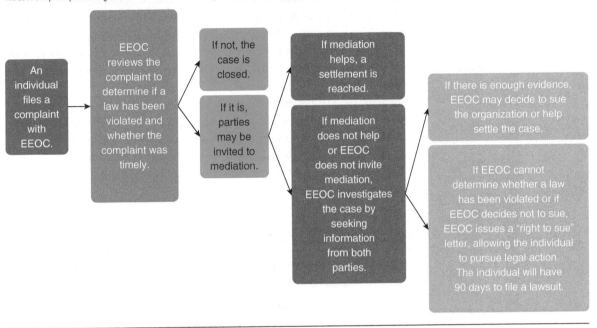

Source: EEOC. (2023). *What you can expect after you file a charge.* https://www.eeoc.gov/employees/process.cfm

EEO laws apply to all aspects of the employment relationship. Specifically, employers are prohibited from engaging in discrimination in hiring, promotion, training, job assignments, compensation, discipline, termination, and any other aspect of the employment relationship. To avoid discrimination, organizations are advised to collect only information necessary for them to assess employees' fit for the job and base employment decisions on job-related criteria. EEO laws also deem it illegal to **retaliate** against an employee who complains about discrimination or files a discrimination claim. Similarly, it is illegal to retaliate against those otherwise involved in a discrimination claim, such as acting as a witness. Retaliation may include actions such as reducing pay, terminating, transferring the employee to a less desirable position, threatening the employee, or giving the employee a lower performance evaluation. As shown in Figure 4.1, retaliation represents the most frequent source of complaints at EEOC. Training supervisors about what constitutes retaliation is important because untrained supervisors are a key cause of retaliation claims against organizations.[24]

Equal Pay Act of 1963 (EPA)

Pay equity between men and women remains a concern, with women being paid an average of 83 cents for every dollar men made in 2020.[25] Reasons for this gap include segregation of sexes across different occupations with different pay averages, résumé gaps due to child-rearing responsibilities, or sex discrimination. One piece of legislation aimed at closing the gap is the Equal Pay Act of 1963. This law applies to "employers engaged in commerce or production of goods," which means virtually all businesses. According to this law, in cases in which employees perform similar jobs requiring similar skills and under similar conditions, employees cannot be paid differently based on their sex. In order to make a claim, the employee would need to show that

   a. they and an employee of the other sex are working in the same place, doing equal work, *and*

   b. they are paid differently for the same work.

As a defense, the employer would need to show there is a reason other than sex for the pay difference, such as seniority, merit, or quality or quantity of production. Note that the individual does not need to prove the organization acted intentionally when paying sexes differently; rather, simply show-ing that the difference exists is sufficient. The law covers all aspects of employee compensation and rewards, including salaries, benefits, commissions, stock options, and allowances. Even though job titles may be different, if the job is essentially the same, then the pay of men and women is expected to be the same. As a case in point, a large auto dealership ended up paying $62,500 to settle a pay discrimi-nation lawsuit brought against them. The dealership was paying a female dispatcher less than a male dispatcher even though they were performing equal work. (The company fired the employee when she complained, which added a retaliation claim to the case.)[26]

When making pay decisions, HR professionals and managers need to consider the existing pay distribution and ensure that there is internal and individual equity; that is, pay differences among indi-viduals reflect differences in jobs or actual differences in performance. Further, if decision makers real-ize there is unfairness in the pay structure, they need to correct the situation. This correction can only occur by increasing the pay of the lower paid person. Reducing the pay of the highly paid individual is another violation of the law.[27]

TITLE VII OF THE CIVIL RIGHTS ACT

LEARNING OBJECTIVES

4.3   Discuss the impact of Title VII of the Civil Rights Act.

Title VII is the most comprehensive federal legislation relating to equal employment opportunities. The law, which applies to all employers with 15 or more employees, including state and government institutions, prohibits employment decisions based on sex, race, color, national origin, and religion. The law prohibits both intentional discrimination based on these protected characteristics and seem-ingly neutral decision criteria that have a discriminatory effect on different groups. The law includes harassment as part of discriminatory practices and prohibits retaliation against those who complain about discrimination, file a complaint, or are otherwise involved in facilitating a discrimination claim. Title VII applies to all groups equally. Discriminating against majority or historically privileged groups such as white or male employees is sometimes referred to as reverse discrimination. This is a contro-versial term because it implies that discrimination can only occur when a marginalized member is the victim. This is in fact, incorrect, and the term *discrimination* includes all acts of discrimination regard-less of the identity of the victim.

Title VII was originally passed in 1964 and then amended in 1991. The amendment allowed the plaintiff (the person or party bringing the case to court) to seek compensatory and punitive damages in addition to equitable relief. Equitable relief refers to payments made to a plaintiff to bring them back to the position they would have had if they were not discriminated against. This includes back pay and getting one's job back. Compensatory damages refer to providing financial relief to the complainant for damages incurred, such as mental and emotional stress suffered because of discrimination. Punitive damages are awarded if it is demonstrated that the company had engaged in reckless discrimination and failed to act in good faith. The 1991 amendment also introduced upper limits to compensatory and punitive damages. For example, if the employer has between 15 and 100 employees, the amount of damages a person may recover is limited to $50,000. At the same time, a group of individuals who have similar claims may sue as a group, creating a class action lawsuit. In these cases, the limits apply to a single person, and a class action suit may include large numbers of individuals, leading to significant costs for businesses.[28]

What Is Discrimination Under Title VII?

Title VII prohibits two basic types of discrimination: Disparate treatment and disparate (or adverse) impact. Disparate treatment refers to treating different groups of applicants or employees differently because of their race, color, religion, sex, or national origin. For example, if an organization requires a background check, it should be done for all employees regardless of employee race, sex, religion, or national origin. Using different tests, questions, and/or hiring and promotion procedures for different groups are examples of disparate treatment. Further, hiring or refusing to hire employees into a particular position based on these protected characteristics (such as giving preference to men for warehouse positions or giving preference to women for sales jobs in a store) is also illegal. Disparate impact involves using seemingly neutral criteria that has a discriminatory effect on a protected group. For example, a workplace policy prohibiting head coverings may seem neutral on the surface, but it is likely to have a disparate impact on Muslim, Sikh, and Orthodox Jewish employees.

Disparate Treatment

Despite the decades that have passed after the passage of Title VII in 1964, disparate treatment discrimination still occurs and continues to be costly to businesses. As a case in point, in 2022, Glow Networks in Texas was ordered to pay $70 million to 10 plaintiffs, 9 of whom were Black. The company had discriminated against the employees in promotions and layoffs, and retaliated against them.[29]

Here is how a disparate treatment case is handled: Imagine that an applicant applies for a job at a retail store. She wears a hijab, a veil traditionally worn by Muslim women. She is qualified for the job. The interviewer asks several questions about her need to wear this particular clothing and her religion in general. After the interview, the applicant learns that she did not get the job. Instead, the company hires someone who has less experience in retail. The applicant would have prima facie evidence (at first glance, or preliminary evidence) that discrimination may have happened because

  a. the person applied for a job for which she was qualified;

  b. she was rejected despite being qualified, and someone with similar or less qualifications was hired; or

  c. there is circumstantial evidence indicating that religion, a protected characteristic, may have been a factor.

After prima facie evidence has been established, the burden of proof shifts to the employer. Now the employer will need to demonstrate there was a nondiscriminatory reason for the decision. For example, if the job candidate lacked critical skills or the person who was hired was chosen for a different and nondiscriminatory reason, such as a specific expertise, this would be the employer's defense. If there is strong evidence that religion was the reason for not hiring this applicant (e.g., e-mails come to light that display religious prejudice on the part of the hiring manager), then the employment decision would be deemed illegal.

If the employer can present a nondiscriminatory reason, the burden of proof once again shifts to the applicant. Now the applicant would need to show that the reason provided by the employer is a pretext, or an excuse and not the real reason. This can be shown if the employer's reason is factually incorrect or there is some evidence that it was not the true reason.

What Should Organizations Do to Proactively Defend Themselves Against Disparate Treatment Claims? In Title VII disparate treatment cases, the employer may present two kinds of defense. First, they may show there was a nondiscriminatory reason for the adverse action against the applicant or employee. To do that, employers would need to be aware of the law and must avoid using legally protected characteristics in their employment decisions. Additionally, they must keep careful records of all applicants following interviews and document all employment decisions to be able to defend them when necessary.

A second defense of the organization could be to show that the protected characteristic in this particular case is a bona fide occupational qualification (BFOQ), or an essential necessity of the job. BFOQ is a very narrow defense that claims that a characteristic is important for the business in question because of customer preferences; this type of defense typically fails. Instead, successful uses of the BFOQ defense involve customers' privacy concerns. As a case in point, Beth Israel Medical Center was able to successfully defend itself in a lawsuit brought by a male OB/GYN. The doctor claimed the hospital was discriminating against him because it was accommodating female patients who expressed a preference for female doctors. In this case, the court found gender to be a BFOQ due to patients' privacy concerns. However, a similar argument was not effective when a spa owned by Marriott International, Inc., wanted to accommodate male customers who desired a female massage therapist. In this case, the BFOQ defense failed when the case reached the federal district court. Although there are circumstances that may make a protected characteristic a BFOQ, these cases are narrow, and customer preferences (other than privacy concerns) are unlikely to be considered a BFOQ.[30]

Disparate Impact

Discrimination that involves discriminatory intent, the use of different criteria, asking additional questions, or indicating a preference for one sex, race, religion, and national origin are types of disparate treatment. However, according to Title VII, discrimination does not necessarily involve discriminatory intent. Instead, employers may sometimes use seemingly neutral criteria that have a discriminatory effect on a protected group. This type of discrimination is termed *disparate impact* (or adverse impact). In fact, a charge of disparate impact does not imply intention on the part of an employer (see Chapter 7). For example, organizations often use tests that may lead to greater hiring of one group than others. CSX Transportation used physical ability tests to be hired into various jobs. These tests had a disparate impact on female job candidates who were seeking to be employed as conductors, material handlers, and clerks. The company settled the case for $3.2 million and agreed to stop using the test, pay lost wages and benefits to women who were unable to obtain employment because of the tests, and conduct job analyses before using physical ability tests in future hiring.[31] Even though the test was seemingly neutral and administered to all applicants, it had different effects on male and female candidates. When a test has different effects on different groups, the company will need to demonstrate that there is a business necessity to use that specific test or that it is a valid predictor of performance (see Chapter 7). If there is no compelling reason, then its use may be illegal under Title VII. Note that disparate impact claims are different from disparate treatment in that the plaintiff may not claim compensatory and punitive damages. The payments made to complainants are limited to equitable relief, in addition to an order to the organization to stop using the discriminatory practice.

Disparate impact claims do not necessitate showing evidence that discrimination was intentional. In a claim involving disparate impact, prima facie evidence can be demonstrated by showing that the selection criterion or employment policy has a differential effect on different groups. This requires a statistical analysis to assess the effects of the selection criterion. In 1978, EEOC, the Department of Labor, and the Department of Justice adopted the Uniform Guidelines on Employee Selection Procedures, which outline how selection systems can be designed to comply with EEO laws. According to the Uniform Guidelines, a simple way of establishing whether disparate impact occurred is to use the 4/5ths (or 80%) rule. According to this rule, one group's selection ratio (the number hired vs. the number that applied for the job) may not be less than 80% of the majority group's ratio. For example, let's assume that selection ratio for male applicants in a physical ability test is 98%, whereas for women, it is 60%. The question is, is this gap large enough to show that women applicants were negatively affected? To answer this question, multiply 98% by 80%, which is 78.4%. Given that women applicants had a selection ratio of 60%, which is less than 78.4%, there is prima facie evidence that the test was discriminatory. Alternatively, divide 60% by 98%, which is 61%. Because this is smaller than 80%, there is *prima facie* evidence that disparate impact exists. The 4/5ths rule is criticized because it is prone to giving false positives (shows discrimination when none exists). Instead, organizations may use more rigorous statistical tests such as a chi-square test, particularly if they have a large sample. An example of how to conduct the chi-square test to establish prima facie evidence for disparate impact appears in the Data and Analytics Exercise for this chapter.

Once prima facie evidence is established, the burden of proof shifts to the employer. Now the employer needs to demonstrate that the test in question is job related and is consistent with business necessity. If the employer can prove that performance on this specific test is predictive of job performance and skills assessed on this test are essential to the safe and effective performance of the job (or that they are valid; see Chapter 7), then the employer will be able to continue its use of this process. However, if the person challenging the selection procedure can demonstrate that there are other, nondiscriminatory alternatives to the test in question, then the employer may need to abandon their use of this criterion. The Uniform Guidelines (http://uniformguidelines.com/uniformguidelines.html#20) include information regarding how to validate selection tests and ensure that they comply with Title VII. In other words, an organization may continue to use a specific test if its validity can be established. However, often organizations have difficulty defending themselves because the requirements of selection tests may not reflect the reality of the jobs. For example, in manual jobs, the physical agility or ability requirements expected of job applicants may be harsher than what the job actually entails, leading to the conclusion that the test unnecessarily discriminates. Even though a test or other hiring method may *seem* valid, the organization needs to be able to defend its use through actual data.

What Should Organizations Do to Proactively Defend Themselves Against Disparate Impact Claims? When it comes to disparate impact cases, the employer's defense is to establish that the test being used is job related and there is a business necessity. To establish job relatedness, organizations need to be ready to defend the validity of their tests (see Chapter 7). The cutoffs used in selection tests should be reasonable and aligned with normal expectations in the day-to-day performance of the job. The Uniform Guidelines on Employee Selection Procedures is an important source for HR professionals in charge of selecting tests and setting decision criteria used to screen out and make employment decisions about employees and applicants. Figure 4.3 summarizes the two processes for showing disparate treatment and disparate impact.

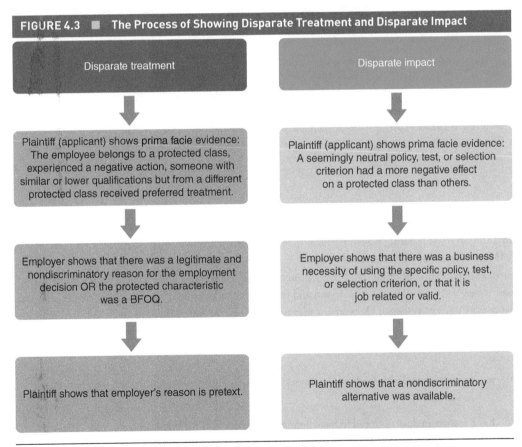

FIGURE 4.3 ■ The Process of Showing Disparate Treatment and Disparate Impact

Source: Based on information from https://www.eeoc.gov/policy/docs/factemployment_procedures.html

Manager's Toolbox: Avoiding Illegal Interview Questions and Employment Practices

Consider the interview questions and employment practices in Table 4.1 and why they may be potentially illegal.

TABLE 4.1 ■ Potentially Illegal Interview Questions and Employment Practices	
Are you married?	This question may violate state laws prohibiting marital status discrimination. If only asked to women, it may be an example of sex discrimination under Title VII. The organization may be trying to screen out female applicants who are likely to become pregnant, violating pregnancy-related discrimination laws. It is best to avoid asking this question during hiring.
How old are your children?	Again, if this is a question only asked to women, it would be an example of sex discrimination. Given its irrelevance to the hiring process and potential discriminatory effects, this question is best avoided.
You have an interesting accent. Where did you grow up?	This question could reveal the national origin of the applicant, which is a protected category.
Have you ever been arrested?	Statistically, Hispanic and Black men are more likely to have been arrested, and arrest record is not a reliable indicator of crime. Therefore, the use of this criterion could have disparate impact.
Using a thick accent as a reason not to hire	If the accent does not seriously interfere with one's performance at work, using someone's accent as a reason not to hire them may be discrimination based on national origin.
Using English-only rules	A policy forbidding the use of one language (e.g., no Spanish) would be illegal due to national origin discrimination. English-only rules may be legal as long as they are dictated by business necessity and job requirements. For this reason, implementing such rules during breaks will be suspect. If other languages are being used in a hostile way to harass others, English-only rules would be appropriate.
Using a language test as part of hiring	Even in cases in which communication in English is essential for the job, requiring language skills that go beyond what is needed during the regular performance of the job could be a violation of Title VII.
Do you have a disability that requires an accommodation? What impairments do you have?	Even with good intent, it is best to avoid this question. If the employee has a disability, the accommodation request should come from the employee. Learning about the applicant's disability in the prehire stage could result in liability. It is acceptable to ask whether the individual is able to perform the major functions of the job.

Title VII and Harassment

In addition to prohibiting discrimination based on disparate impact and disparate treatment, Title VII has prohibitions around harassment. Harassment involves unwelcome behaviors based on sex, race, religion, national origin, and other protected characteristics. Under Title VII, harassment that would be offensive to a reasonable person and that occurs on a frequent basis so that it creates a hostile work environment is illegal. Harassment may include name-calling; offensive jokes, pictures, or other explicit materials; and insults or mockery, among others. What is important to know about harassment is that

a. companies are liable for harassment perpetuated by supervisors, coworkers, nonemployees, and customers;

b. harassment does not need to have financial consequences for the employee; and

c. even individuals who are not the direct victims of harassment may have a legal claim if being part of a hostile work environment has been negatively affecting them.[32]

Sexual harassment, which includes unwanted advances and other harassment that is sexual in nature, is also prohibited. Title VII does not contain specific clauses about sexual harassment, but courts have treated sexual harassment as a type of sex-based harassment, and therefore Title VII applies to cases of sexual harassment. The victim of sexual harassment may be male or female, and the victim and the perpetrator do not need to be of opposite sexes. EEOC defines two forms of sexual harassment.

Quid pro quo harassment involves making employment decisions contingent on sexual favors. A manager hinting that a promotion or a raise depends on the employee providing a sexual favor or punishing an employee for refusing to fulfill a sexual request are examples of quid pro quo harassment. In other words, the use of sexual favors as a bargaining tool in employment decisions is prohibited. Alternatively, sexual harassment may be in the form of creating a **hostile work environment**, or conduct sexual in nature that contributes to an environment that a reasonable person would find offensive. Even though the #MeToo movement brought increasing awareness to this problem, sexual harassment remains pervasive. In a 2022 study, 50% of male and 55% of female employees reported having experienced sexual harassment. Importantly, remote workers reported experiencing greater levels of sexual harassment relative to in-person workers, as they often faced harassment over e-mail and text messages.[33]

Sexual harassment from customers is all too common in the restaurant industry. Research indicates that two structural reasons that contribute to this are financial dependence on customers due to tipping and "service with a smile" expectations.[34]

©iStockphoto.com/alvarez

What constitutes a hostile work environment? The following elements typically would need to be in place:

1. The plaintiff is a member of a protected class.

2. The plaintiff was subjected to harassment.

3. The plaintiff experienced harassment due to their protected class.

4. The conduct affected the employment of the plaintiff.

5. The employer knew about or should have known about the harassment and did nothing to protect the employee.

Because claims against organizations are more likely to be successful if the company had known and yet failed to act on the information, businesses should establish safeguards by training their managers and employees, ensuring there are clear and safe mechanisms for employees to voice complaints, and taking any such complaints seriously and resolving them promptly. Recall that retaliating against complainants or resolving the issue in a way that punishes the victim (such as transferring the victim to a less desirable job) are problematic and increase the company's liability. Research has shown that training that goes beyond simple instruction and incorporates elements such as practicing skills, perspective taking, and how to intervene as a bystander was more effective. Moreover, whether the training was in person or online did not make a difference in the outcomes.[35]

Title VII and Special Considerations Regarding Sex Discrimination

Title VII prohibits the use of one's sex in employment-related decisions. A simple way of thinking about this is that organizations may not classify jobs as "men's jobs" and "women's jobs" unless there is a strong reason to believe that sex is a BFOQ. Making assumptions about one's sex and using those stereotypes in employment decisions is also illegal. For example, an employer may not restrict jobs with physical demands to men with the assumption that men have greater physical endurance.

Both Title VII and the Equal Pay Act (EPA) provide protections, even though EPA is solely concerned with pay differentials, whereas Title VII is more comprehensive and includes all types of employment decisions. A plaintiff concerned about pay discrimination can technically utilize either or both laws, but there are important differences. When filing a claim based on EPA, plaintiffs are not required to go through EEOC. This means they can initiate a lawsuit themselves. Further, EPA applies to businesses of all sizes, but Title VII only applies to businesses with 15 or more employees. EPA claims may be filed within a longer period of time, and the prima facie evidence is simpler to establish. In this case, the plaintiff simply needs to show that a man and a woman, doing essentially the same work, are paid differently. In the case of Title VII, the plaintiff would need to show that the difference was motivated by differences in sex. Companies are often asked to run statistics such as linear regression analysis to show that there is a statistically significant pay difference between men and women. One main advantage of Title VII for plaintiffs is that it allows them to recover more money at the end of the lawsuit.[36]

Title VII, Race, and Color

Title VII prohibits discrimination in employment based on race or having policies and procedures that have a discriminatory impact on individuals of a particular race. Unfortunately, racism remains all too common, even in the face of national reckoning in the face of Black Lives Matter movement and heightened attention to systemic racism. Employers are legally required to provide a workplace free from racial harassment and discrimination. Being a target of discrimination and harassment has harmful consequences for the health, well-being, and productivity of employees. And yet, there are thousands of instances that rise to the level of formal complaints each year, not to mention more frequent and still harmful ones that do not rise to the level of legal action, or other illegal incidents where victims choose not to take action.

One type of racial discrimination is racial harassment. For example, Packaging Corporation of America Central California Corrugated LLC, a paper manufacturer in California, agreed to pay $385,000 to settle a lawsuit and take preventative measures. In the plant, coworkers and a supervisor routinely broadcast racial slurs over the radio system, two Black employees were taunted with graffiti and swastikas, and a shift leader drew a confederate flag and wrote down "long live the confederacy" on a workstation. The HR department took no action against the perpetrators. Companies are advised to have clear antiharassment policies and complaint mechanisms, train supervisors, and take prompt action when such conduct emerges.[37]

Restricting certain positions to a particular race is a violation of the law. For example, Edward Jones (the largest brokerage firm in the United States) agreed to settle a race discrimination case for $34 million. The company had disproportionately excluded Black and other nonwhite junior brokers from their GoodKnights program, which is a program where senior advisors assign some of the assets in their portfolios to junior advisors. Exclusion from the program meant lack of office space, support, and mentoring, and compensation differences. In other words, organizations are advised to examine their employment practices to ensure there are job-related and defensible reasons for decisions that lead to differences in pay, hiring, promotion, and advancement of employees of different races.[38] Finally, harassment based on one's race is illegal, and management is advised to take action immediately when informed of racial harassment.

Seemingly race-neutral policies such as definitions of work-appropriate hair may have uneven and unfair consequences. Many Black hair styles carry historical and emotional significance, and Title VII falls short of protecting individuals from discrimination based on their hair style. As of this writing, 20 states passed the CROWN Act, prohibiting discrimination based on hair style and texture.[39]

©iStockphoto.com/alvarez

Title VII and Religion

In addition to prohibiting discrimination in employment decisions based on religion, Title VII requires organizations to provide reasonable accommodation. Simple nondiscrimination is insufficient by itself, and in fact, uniform application of organizational rules with rigidity may be a cause for discrimination claims. Organizations are asked to make allowances for an employee for their religion unless doing so imposes an undue hardship on the employer. In other words, when the employer's dress code policy, work schedules, breaks, and time-off periods clash with employee religious needs, employers are expected to make a good-faith effort to accommodate them. This may involve making an exception for the employee with respect to the dress code or accommodating their schedule so they can take part in religious observances on a certain day of the week or time of year. For example, the City of Lansing in Michigan settled a religious discrimination claim for $50,000 in back pay and compensatory damages, and agreed to revise its religious accommodations policies. An employee who was a Seventh-day Adventist had informed her employer that she would not be able to work between sunset on Friday and sunset on Saturday because she observed Sabbath. Instead of accommodating her, the city terminated her employment. When handling requests to take the day off due to religious reasons, employers should allow employees to use their paid time off benefits, and if these are exhausted, allow them to take unpaid time off.[40]

The law defines a religion as one's sincerely held beliefs, which include both mainstream religions and those practiced by a small group or community. Title VII also protects individuals from being discriminated against because they have no religious beliefs. Finally, the expectation that the employee would need to be accommodated due to their religion may not be a reason to discriminate against an employee.

Companies may need to balance religious accommodation with their other antidiscriminatory policies. For example, two flight attendants were fired from Alaska Airlines for posting on the company intranet criticism of the company's support of federal legislation prohibiting discrimination based on sexual orientation and gender identity. The employees accused the company of religious discrimination, but the case was dismissed. It is important to underline that many people assume that the First Amendment allows individuals to speak their mind under all circumstances. This is a common misconception. Whereas the First Amendment prevents government intervention against free speech, companies can regulate employee speech, including online. While there are no hard and fast answers, companies have an obligation to offer religious accommodations while also ensuring that other rights of employees are also protected.[41]

Training managers is a key first step of legal compliance. An important issue is to avoid asking questions about religion during job interviews. Instead, focus should be on job characteristics and whether employees are able to perform the job. If it becomes clear that the employee needs a religious accommodation, the organization must consider whether a reasonable accommodation is possible. This is a high bar: If the employer chooses not to accommodate, it must show that accommodation would have been unsafe or extremely costly or would significantly affect other employees. Mere inconvenience for the employer is not a justifiable reason not to accommodate. If an HR manager observes or hears that someone is being harassed because of their religion (or due to other reasons), immediate action should be taken. The organization should outline and inform employees about communication channels they should use if they experience harassment.

Title VII and National Origin

Title VII has protections against national origin discrimination. Taking adverse action against someone due to their nationality or due to the nationality of someone they are related to (e.g., married to) is prohibited under this law. Harassment of others based on nationality is also prohibited. Seeking to hire U.S. citizens, unless necessitated by a government contract or other special reason, is prohibited, given that U.S. citizenship is not necessary to be legally employed in the United States. Discriminating based on accent is prohibited under Title VII, and instituting English-only rules, unless there is a business necessity such as safety of others, is a practice that should be used cautiously. It is also important for businesses to disregard nationality-related information in employment decisions.

SPOTLIGHT ON ETHICS: APPLICANTS WITH CRIMINAL HISTORY

Should an organization avoid hiring individuals with a criminal background? There is no federal law prohibiting discrimination against former incarcerated persons. Yet having blanket policies excluding those with criminal backgrounds has an ethical dimension. There are certainly legitimate reasons for not hiring someone with a criminal record, particularly when public health and safety are a concern. If the former incarcerated person commits a crime and harms a coworker or customer, the organization may be responsible for negligent hiring. At the same time, the rehabilitation of former incarcerated persons depends on finding employment. Depending on when the crime occurred and what it was, the risks to the business may be minimal. In some cases, individuals choose to plead guilty instead of fighting a conviction, which helps them avoid incarceration but results in a criminal record. Businesses such as Seattle-based Mod Pizza and Oregon-based Dave's Killer Bread are committed to giving those with criminal backgrounds a second chance, and they benefit from a qualified and highly motivated workforce. There is also a movement ("ban the box" or "fair chance hiring") for states and jurisdictions to pass laws banning the question "Have you been convicted of a crime?" on employment applications. These laws typically do not prevent companies from using criminal history as part of the hiring process, but they require the employer to wait until a job offer is made before a criminal background check is conducted; the offer may then be revoked if needed. There are no easy answers, but whether and how criminal records should be used in employment decisions is an ethical dilemma.[42]

Questions

1. As a manager, suppose you need to decide whether to hire a candidate with excellent qualifications for the position but with a felony conviction in their background. What factors would you take into consideration to decide whether to hire this candidate?
2. Think of a case, or find one in the literature, of a company that encountered legal trouble as a result of hiring an employee with a criminal record. What could have been done differently? What did the company do right?

ADDITIONAL ANTIDISCRIMINATION ACTS AND PROTECTIONS

Along with Title VII of the Civil Rights Act, additional acts and amendments have been put in place. These acts include, but are not limited to, the Pregnancy Discrimination Act of 1978, Age Discrimination in Employment Act of 1967, Americans with Disabilities Act of 1990, Genetic Information Nondiscrimination Act of 2008, and Lilly Ledbetter Fair Pay Act of 2009, along with additional protections for lesbian, gay, bisexual, transgender, questioning/queer, and other (LGBTQ+) workers. Although not discussed here, states and municipalities may have additional laws that protect employees.

Laws Protecting Pregnant Employees

The Pregnancy Discrimination Act (PDA) of 1978 law is an amendment of Title VII and prohibits employers from discriminating against employees due to a pregnancy or related conditions. An individual's pregnancy or assumptions about pregnant individuals may not be used in hiring decisions as long as the person is capable of performing the major functions of the job. Further, all employment-related decisions, including training, scheduling, benefits, and promotions, are protected. In cases in which the employee seeks leave, the employer may not treat a pregnancy-related leave any differently than leave granted to employees for other reasons. For example, the employer may not seek more evidence or information. Employers may not prevent an employee from returning to work following a pregnancy, and they may not assign them inferior work upon return.[43]

The PDA does not permit a paternalistic attitude in which businesses make assumptions about pregnant workers regarding their physical limitations or their ability to withstand particular work conditions. For example, in the Supreme Court case *UAW v. Johnson Controls* (1991), the company was challenged for its policy of excluding women who were of child-bearing age from certain jobs, with the rationale that they would become exposed to harmful levels of lead, harming their unborn children. This policy was found to violate the PDA.[44] Instead, businesses need to make efforts to protect all employees and inform employees about any risks but leave decisions regarding working arrangements to employees. Restricting pregnant employees or those who might get pregnant to specific positions, even with the belief that such restrictions protect the employee, is prohibited.

A second major legislation relating to pregnant workers is the Pregnant Workers Fairness Act (PWFA), which was signed into law in 2022. This law applies to businesses with 15 or more employees and requires employers to provide reasonable accommodations to employees due to pregnancy and childbirth. While PDA was a landmark law that prohibited discrimination, it did not explicitly require businesses to provide accommodations to employees due to pregnancy. PWFA corrects this situation by ensuring that businesses and employees engage in an interactive process to identify a suitable accommodation whenever possible.[45]

In addition to PDA and PWFA, there are other laws that pertain to pregnancy and related conditions. Pregnancy-related complications are protected under the Americans with Disabilities Act (ADA), which is discussed later in this chapter. The Family and Medical Leave Act (FMLA) covers leave employees are entitled to take, including for childbirth and adoptions. The Affordable Care Act (ACA) has provisions requiring some employers to accommodate the needs of new mothers by giving them sufficient break time to pump breast milk and a private space to do so. These legislative developments suggest that it would be helpful for employers to take a proactive approach toward pregnant employees to accommodate their needs and to ensure they do not experience discrimination.

The Pregnancy Discrimination Act protects employees during and after a pregnancy. Failing to give the employee the same or a similar job upon return to work may be a violation of the PDA.

©iStock.com/Yuri_Arcurs

Age Discrimination in Employment Act of 1967 (ADEA)

Stereotypes about older workers persist, despite accumulated evidence that these assumptions and stereotypes are simply wrong in the face of empirical evidence.[46] The Age Discrimination in Employment Act (ADEA) applies to employers with 20 or more workers and prohibits employers from discriminating against an applicant or employee due to their age. The ADEA protects only individuals 40 years of age or older and only applies in cases where old age is used as a rationale to exclude an individual from opportunities. When an older worker is preferred over a younger one, even when age is a factor used in decision making, the decision is not necessarily illegal under the ADEA. However, preferring a younger person to an older one is illegal, even when both are over the age of 40. In other words, if an organization favors a 50-year-old over a 60-year-old for a promotion and uses relative youth as a criterion, the decision would be illegal. Similar to other EEO laws, harassment due to one's age from managers, coworkers, or customers is also prohibited, and age-based comments and teasing that are frequent enough to create a hostile work environment are illegal.[47] While the law provides protections, age discrimination is challenging to prove. The Supreme Court decision of *Gross v. FBL Financial Services* in 2009 suggests that plaintiffs have the burden of proof that age was the key reason for the adverse employment decision. Simply showing that age was one of the factors leading to the adverse decision is not sufficient—the plaintiff needs to show that the employer would have acted differently if age was not a factor.[48] Interestingly, in a more recent Supreme Court case (*Babb v. Wilkie* in 2020), the Court adopted a more lenient standard for federal employees where age simply needs to be one of the motivating factors to prove discrimination.[49]

The ADEA becomes particularly relevant when discussing retirement issues with older workers. Forcing employees to retire by insisting on it or by eliminating their position will introduce the possibility that the decision is biased. Firing or demoting an employee close to a time of retirement discussions also opens the company up for liability.

One important first step to defend a business against ADEA claims is to avoid asking questions about the employee's age, which surprisingly still happens. Similarly, the organization should avoid using age or age-related stereotypes in employment-related decisions. Sometimes, job advertisements may create the perception that the company is looking for someone young, through the use of phrases such as "looking for digital natives," or describing the organization as "youthful company." Having a legitimate and nondiscriminatory reason for all business decisions and application of all HR decisions consistently across age groups is particularly important.[50]

To remain competitive in a tight labor market, Allegheny Health Network targeted nurses who had recently retired or had taken a career break. Flexible schedules and providing retraining to bring skills up to date were helpful in attracting these nurses.[51]

©iStockphoto.com/Dean Mitchell

Americans with Disabilities Act (ADA) of 1990

The ADA prohibits discrimination against individuals with disabilities who are able to perform the major functions of the job with or without accommodations. The act was amended in 2008 (Americans with Disabilities Act Amendment Act [ADAAA]). The act applies to organizations with 15 or more employees and defines a disability as a physical or mental impairment that affects one's major life activities. The ADAAA provides a list of major life activities in consideration of a disability and includes activities such as walking, reading, and communicating and major bodily functions such as functions of the immune system and respiratory, reproductive, and neurological functions. Having a history of a specific ailment and being perceived as disabled are two additional forms of protected disabilities. Impairments that are episodic are a disability if they limit major life activities when they are active. The ADAAA provides a list of conditions that are always considered a disability (e.g., HIV infection, cancer, bipolar disorder). There is also a list of conditions that are *not* considered a disability: pedophilia, compulsive gambling, voyeurism, and exhibitionism, among others.

For an ailment to be considered a disability eligible for ADA protection, it needs to limit major life activities. For example, in 2021, the U.S. federal government clarified that long Covid may be considered a disability, as it is associated with extreme fatigue, cognitive impairment, and other issues that affect day-to-day life.[52]

Each job has **essential functions** that every incumbent needs to perform, as well as **marginal functions** that can be assigned to others. Essential functions are core tasks that are expected of all incumbents and are important for effective and safe performance of the job. If the person is not capable of performing the essential functions even with accommodations, the employer is not required to hire or retain the individual. However, if the disability is preventing the person from performing the marginal functions, these functions may be reassigned to others, and the disability may not be a factor in decision making. Finally, the law uses the term *reasonable accommodations* to indicate that as long as accommodating the person does not cause undue hardship on the business, the employer is expected to provide accommodations. What is reasonable depends on the size and resources available to the business, indicating that employers are expected to make a good-faith effort in providing accommodations.

During the Covid-19 pandemic, many employees with disabilities were able to secure employment remotely and demonstrate that they were able to perform their jobs effectively by utilizing remote arrangements. There is reason to be optimistic that increasing prevalence of remote work will remove important barriers to the employment of workers with disabilities. To accommodate the individual, the organization needs to know about the specific disability and the need for an accommodation. Unless a disability is obvious, the request needs to originate from the employee, and once a request is made, the process of identifying a suitable accommodation needs to be interactive.[53] Employers are advised not to inquire whether the individual has a disability and to avoid asking medical questions as part of the hiring process. Among the accommodations that may be available to employees are remote work, particularly if it is available to other employees, and unpaid leave. Employees with disabilities are expected to be treated similarly to other employees seeking leave, and if evidence is requested for the reason for leave, such evidence should be sought from all employees seeking leave. Organizations are allowed to set maximum limits on how much leave employees are entitled to take, but they may need to make exceptions in the case of disability-related leave, as long as doing so does not create an undue hardship for the business. ADA compliance has few strict and specific rules other than making a genuine effort to consider the employee's request and provide accommodations within the organization's means.

ADA compliance requires careful planning. The organization would benefit from having updated job descriptions that clearly delineate essential job functions and marginal duties. Organizations should have job descriptions that reflect the actual job content as performed within the organization. Managers need to be trained in understanding what constitutes a disability. When a request for accommodation is received, it is essential for managers and HR to be open to ideas and work with the individual to arrive at solutions. Just because an accommodation is unusual is not a reason to dismiss it. The organization is not required to provide an extremely costly and burdensome accommodation, or even the first choice of the individual, but a good-faith effort is important. As with other EEO laws, organizations should ensure that employees are trained to be respectful to all colleagues, including those with disabilities.[54]

Creating Inclusive Environments for Neurodiversity

Neurodiversity refers to differences in the ways in which the brain functions. Conditions such as autism spectrum disorder (ASD), attention-deficit/hyperactivity disorder (ADHD), dyslexia, and Tourette's syndrome represent cognitive differences in how individuals process information. Those who process information in ways that are similar to the general population are considered to be neurotypical, whereas those whose cognitive functioning falls outside what is typical in the population are considered to be neurodivergent.

According to one estimate, 15% to 20% of the world population is neurodivergent. Providing workplace environments where these individuals are supported and thrive remains important and is a key part of creating inclusive environments. Neurodivergent individuals can bring unique skills to the workplace, including greater levels of pattern recognition, creativity, and diversity of thought. Neurodivergence is not necessarily a disability, but if it affects major life functions, it may be considered a disability as defined by ADA. If this is the case, organizations may be required to provide reasonable accommodations. Example accommodations may be noise-canceling headphones or utilizing apps to structure tasks and provide reminders for employees who have ADHD, or providing an environment that is free of harsh lights and following a specific schedule for an employee who has ASD. Many employees are neurodivergent but choose not to disclose their diagnosis because they worry about being stigmatized. It is important for companies to create an environment where individuals feel comfortable asking for the type of support they need to be effective and healthy in the workplace and where employees and employers can engage in a constructive dialogue to identify and implement the necessary accommodations.[55] Mastercard introduced a pilot program to hire more neurodiverse employees. Program elements include interviewing virtually over the course of a week instead of a single day, providing detailed instructions about the process, and allowing applicants choice in how to demonstrate particular skills.[56]

SPOTLIGHT ON GLOBAL ISSUES: EEO LAWS IN A GLOBAL CONTEXT

Each country approaches diversity and inclusion in its own way; some countries offer no protections, whereas others offer greater protections than are typically found in the United States. The EEO laws in this chapter apply to all businesses operating in the United States and its territories, regardless of where the business is headquartered. The EEO laws also cover U.S. citizens working in U.S.-based firms overseas. In the case of a multinational firm such as Microsoft or Facebook, all employees within the United States and all U.S. citizens working for foreign subsidiaries are covered, but citizens of the other countries in which these businesses are located are not covered. Further, when operating overseas, U.S.-based firms are permitted to violate EEO laws if compliance would lead to violating the laws of the country in which they operate.[57]

One interesting divergence between the United States and other countries is that many other countries use quotas as a way to ensure diversity of operations. For example, Germany, Norway, France, Spain, Italy, and other European countries have laws dictating that a specific percentage of board of director members be female. In China, public and private employers are required to hire individuals with disabilities as 1.5% of their workforce, and those failing to meet the quota are fined. When doing business overseas, organizations need to be aware of the EEO laws of the locales in which they operate, if any.[58]

Genetic Information Nondiscrimination Act (GINA) of 2008

The Genetic Information Nondiscrimination Act (GINA) of 2008 is a federal law that prohibits organizations from discriminating against applicants or employees in employment decisions (and in health insurance) based on genetic information. Genetic information is defined as the results of genetic tests, as well as family health history. This means that employers covered by GINA are prohibited from using an employee's family history and other genetic information when making decisions about them. It is also illegal for employers to require employees to submit their genetic information. The law covers organizations with 15 or more employees. It does not cover federal employees or members of the military, but each institution is covered by separate laws against genetic discrimination. In some instances, employers may obtain genetic information, such as through voluntary participation in a company's wellness program, but the employer needs to keep this information separate from employment decisions and protect information privacy. According to EEOC rules, employees may not offer employees incentives to disclose genetic information, with the exception of wellness programs. Genetic disclosures as part of wellness programs are regulated as well, with upper limits to how much incentive employers may provide to encourage participation in wellness programs and requirements to avoid discrimination based on this information.[59]

GINA is a recent law, and therefore complaints based on GINA are still rare but growing. GINA complaints usually result from requiring applicants or employees to submit data on their family history. In the first case that went to trial (*Lowe v. Atlas Logistics Group*, 2015), the transportation company wanted to find out the culprits of an employee wrongdoing by conducting genetic tests. The company narrowed the suspects to a small number of employees based on their schedules and asked employees to submit to a DNA test. Two employees (who were not found to be matches) later filed GINA complaints to EEOC. The lawsuit ended with the plaintiffs being awarded $2.225 million (later reduced to $300,000 per person).[60]

After this case, GINA violations have been based on requests for family medical information. In 2022, EEOC reached a settlement with Brandon Dermatology in Florida for a GINA violation. The medical practice was requiring employees to submit Covid-19 test results of their family members. The company could have legally asked employees to share whether they had come into contact with someone who was displaying symptoms of Covid-19, but requiring the submission of family health information was a GINA violation.[61]

Lilly Ledbetter Fair Pay Act of 2009

This law is an amendment to Title VII, ADEA, and ADA and specifically relates to pay discrimination cases. Prior to the passage of this law, a pay discrimination decision under these acts had to be filed within 180 days after discriminatory acts. This was highly impractical, because employees often do not become aware of discrimination until months or years after the fact. This was the situation for Lilly Ledbetter, who worked as a supervisor for Goodyear Tire until her retirement. Over time, her pay lagged behind that of her male peers, even those with less seniority. Ledbetter did not find out about the situation until she had worked there for 19 years, and therefore it was not possible for her to file a claim within 180 days. She filed a lawsuit, but the Supreme Court (*Ledbetter v. Goodyear Tire & Rubber Co.*, 2007) held that she should have filed the suit within 180 days. Under the Lilly Ledbetter Fair Pay Act (2009), the 180-day clock restarts with each paycheck, allowing employees to file a claim after they find out that discrimination occurred.[62]

Protections for LGBTQ+ Workers

Individuals may have gender identity or expression that differs from their biological sex, and they may be sexually or romantically attracted to the opposite sex, the same sex, both, or neither. In the United States, an estimated 20 million individuals identify as lesbian, gay, bisexual, transgender, questioning/queer, and other sexual identities. According to one estimate, half of LGBTQ+ adults have experienced workplace discrimination. Intersectionality matters, as these numbers are even higher for LGBTQ+ people of color and those with disabilities.

Ken Ohashi, CEO of Brooks Brothers, was named number 1 in the 2022 Top 100 LGBTQ+ executives. Under his leadership, the oldest fashion retailer in the United States partnered with organizations aiming to increase access to education among first-generation and underrepresented students and protect LGBTQ+ youth from bullying and harassment.[68]

Photo by Stefanie Keenan/Getty Images for Gold House

EEOC regards gender identity and sexual orientation as part of Title VII's sex discrimination clause, taking the view that Title VII provides protections to LGBTQ+ workers. In a 2020 decision, Supreme Court joined this interpretation in the *Bostock v. Clayton County, Georgia* decision. The court explained that sexual orientation discrimination by definition is a form of sex discrimination. If a company fires a man who is married to a man but does not fire a woman who is married to a man, this is a form of differential treatment of sexes. Similarly, if the employer fires an employee who is assigned male at birth but identifies as female and uses female pronouns, this is a form of sex discrimination because the employer would not fire an employee who is assigned female at birth and using female pronouns.[63]

Following the Supreme Court's decision, the EEOC issued guidance regarding the workplace treatment of LGBTQ+ employees. The guidelines state that it is unlawful to discriminate against someone in employment decisions due to sexual orientation and gender identity. It is also unlawful to create a hostile work environment based on sexual orientation and gender identity. Employers are not allowed to use actual or perceived customer preferences in assignment of LGBTQ+ employees and are not allowed to discriminate against them based on how they present themselves. Finally, employers are required to offer equal access to a bathroom consistent with the employee's gender identity if the employer offers sex-segregated bathrooms.[64] Despite advances toward equal protection of LGBTQ+ employees, the legal landscape remains fluid and there are efforts to curtail these rights. In 2022, a federal judge found EEOC guidelines unlawful and held that Title VII protections do not extend to the use of pronouns, dress, and equal access to bathrooms.[65]

Fear of disclosing one's gender identity and sexual orientation is associated with negative outcomes. For example, individuals who concealed their sexual and gender identity at work experienced diminished well-being.[66] Organizations are advised to be proactive with respect to adding protections for LGBTQ+ workers. Providing training for employees and managers, making allowances in the dress code for transitioning employees, using the correct names and pronouns, respecting confidentiality of employee plans to transition, and treating applicants and employees with dignity and respect regardless of their specific gender identity and sexual orientation are among the ways organizations may create an inclusive and respectful environment.[67]

Laws Protecting Military Personnel and Veterans

The Vietnam Era Veterans' Readjustment Assistance Act (VEVRAA) of 1974 prohibits discrimination against job applicants and employees based on their status as a veteran. The law is administered by the OFCCP and covers employers doing business with the federal government. The law also prohibits harassment and requires that the organization offer reasonable accommodations to veterans with disabilities. Federal contractors and subcontractors are required to have affirmative action programs in place to employ and advance veterans.

The Uniformed Services Employment and Reemployment Rights Act (USERRA) is administered by the U.S. Department of Labor. This law guarantees that active duty military personnel have the right to be reemployed when they return from military service or active training. Further, employees are entitled to military leave for service in the uniformed services, which includes serving in the reserves, in times of peace or war, regardless of whether the employee volunteered for military duty. This law applies to private as well as state and government employers, regardless of size.[69]

In 2021, there were 18.5 million veterans in the United States. Veterans have many skills that are in high demand in organizations, but they report transition to civilian life to be a challenge.[70]

SPOTLIGHT ON LEGAL ISSUES: GIG WORKERS

EEO laws cover applicants and employees, but they do not apply to independent contractors. Who is an employee? This issue is becoming less straightforward with the rise of the gig economy. Today, many individuals hold temporary positions and perform specific tasks. Technology vendors bring together those willing to perform tasks for others and consumers seeking to fill a need. For example, Uber and Lyft match travelers and those who are willing to drive. TaskRabbit and Bellhop allow consumers to hire someone for specific errands. These companies rely on the assumption that individuals performing the services are contractors and not employees. But are they?

The distinction between who is an employee and who is an independent contractor is a fine line, and it has little to do with the title assigned to the individual. The more control a company exercises over workers, the more likely those individuals are regarded as employees from a legal perspective. In 2018, the Supreme Court of California issued an A-B-C test to identify when a worker should be classified as an employee, which was defined as the employer not having direct control over how workers do their jobs, the work performed not being part of the employer's regular business activities, and the person normally works in their own business. In response, companies such as Uber, Lyft, DoorDash, and Instacart supported the passing of a California ballot measure (Proposition 22), which exempted gig workers from the state's classification law. Finally, in 2022, the U.S. Department of Labor announced proposed rules combating misclassification of employees.[71]

EEO laws apply to employees, but organizations need to understand the legal definition of *employee* to understand their legal obligations.[72]

DIVERSITY AND INCLUSION IN THE AGE OF HR ANALYTICS

LEARNING OBJECTIVES

4.5   Recommend ways in which organizations can maintain legal compliance and address key analytical, legal, ethical, and global issues associated with diversity, equity, and inclusion in HRM.

Up to this point, we have discussed the importance of diversity and inclusion and covered the legal terrain affecting diversity in the workplace. Now we address initiatives and methods companies are using in order to manage diversity effectively.

Should Companies Use Affirmative Action?

Affirmative action plans (AAPs) aim to increase hiring and labor participation of groups that suffered from past discrimination. Some companies are legally required to have AAPs. For example, under Executive Order 11246, businesses with at least 50 employees *and* government contracts exceeding $50,000 are legally required to develop AAPs for hiring women and people from marginalized communities. Federal contractors with more than $10,000 worth of business are required to have AAPs for hiring of workers with disabilities. Those with contracts exceeding $100,000 and having at least 50 employees also need to establish written AAPs for hiring veterans. Finally, courts may order a company to temporarily institute an AAP in order to rectify past discrimination. Employers are permitted to institute AAPs to rectify significant imbalances, but these need to be narrow in scope and temporary.[73]

Two myths about affirmative action in employment are that (a) affirmative action requires using quotas and (b) affirmative action permits or even requires hiring a less-qualified individual. Both are *false*. Simply hiring someone because they are from an underrepresented community, even though someone else is more qualified, is an example of illegal discrimination according to Title VII—regardless of whether the organization has an AAP in place. Further, race or sex quotas would violate Title

VII. Organizations may not have different selection criteria or different cutoff scores to encourage hiring of different groups of individuals.

The OFCCP provides guidelines and sample AAPs. Part of affirmative action is to conduct a workforce analysis to identify barriers to hiring marginalized persons, disabled workers, and women. When these roadblocks are identified, the organization is expected to take concrete steps. For example, a finding that Black and Hispanic employees have a high turnover rate may lead to the action plan that the organization will conduct exit interviews to assess reasons for their departure. The identification of disproportionately few female applicants for a position may result in an action plan in which the organization decides to contact vocational schools and women's community groups to recruit more female applicants for the position. A sample AAP is available from OFCCP's website (https://www.dol.gov/ofccp).

One challenge with AAPs is the potential for backlash on the part of nonrecipients of these programs and the potential for stigmatization of beneficiaries of affirmative action programs. Research suggests that beneficiaries of affirmative action programs experience stigma regarding their competence and likeability, which affects their effectiveness at work. Broadly publicizing qualifications of AAP targets is a useful method to counteract some of these effects.[74] The backlash against affirmative action and the association of AAPs with quotas and lowering the bar (even though both are actually illegal) has led to the relative unpopularity of affirmative action programs. Today, many businesses shy away from the term *AAP* and instead focus on diversity management and inclusion initiatives that aim to create more egalitarian workplaces. Further, AAPs that are monitored by the OFCCP are complex to create and evaluate. Therefore, organizations today typically adopt AAPs only when they are required to do so.[75]

How to Comply With EEO Regulations

The EEOC and OFCCP have specific expectations of businesses. At a minimum, there are precautions organizations need to adopt in order to remain on the right side of the law. These include the following:

- *Training decision makers* to understand their legal obligations are an essential first step in legal compliance.

- *Creating policies* around legally protected areas, such as family and disability-related leave, harassment, and nonretaliation.

- *Meeting documentation requirements set by the EEOC* is important. For example, all private employers covered by Title VII that also have 100 or more employees and federal contractors with 50 or more employees are required to annually file an EEO-1 report with the EEOC and OFCCP. This form requires the organization to count all full-time and part-time employees for each major job category and break them down by ethnicity, race, and sex.

Internal Complaint Mechanisms

Supreme Court decisions such as *Burlington Industries v. Ellerth* (1998) found that organizations are liable for unlawful harassment by supervisors. However, organizations may protect their employees and limit their legal liability by establishing internal complaint procedures and promptly investigating and taking action against discrimination and harassment.[76] As a result, establishing policies and procedures explaining what discrimination and harassment are and giving employees mechanisms through which they can file a complaint with HR may ensure that employees are protected in a timely fashion. This information should be included in the employee handbook and communicated to all employees clearly. Ignoring employee complaints and failing to take prompt action will increase the liability of the organization. Conversely, employees are expected to take advantage of these mechanisms when they believe that discrimination is occurring. Individuals who are victims of discrimination and harassment may have a stronger legal claim if they can demonstrate that they tried to take advantage of internal complaint procedures.

DEI Initiatives

Many organizations have diversity initiatives aimed at increasing inclusion. Having a DEI officer, having support for employee resource groups, and having mentoring programs that ensure that employees are matched to a mentor are among the methods in use in many companies to facilitate an inclusive culture. However, simply having policies and practices is no guarantee that the organization actually has built an inclusive culture. In fact, researchers observed that diversity initiatives have the potential to backfire, lead to negative spillover (such as increasing unfairness perceptions of nontargeted groups), or result in false progress (change in the metrics that create a sense of progress without real change).[77] Therefore, organizations should not assume that simply implementing diversity initiatives will work. A lot depends on how an initiative is introduced and implemented, how employees perceive the intent behind it, and whether the initiative is well designed. Instead, organizations should regard each initiative as one potential tool in their toolbox in the development of an inclusive culture.

To complicate the implementation of diversity initiatives, there is a political backlash against diversity initiatives, with the argument that it favors some demographic groups while putting others at disadvantage. As a case in point, the Texas governor sent a memo, in 2023 to state agencies and public universities, prohibiting the use of DEI policies.[78] We would like to underline that the goal of properly implemented DEI initiatives is to prevent favoring one group while putting others at disadvantage, rather than causing this very situation.

Employee resource groups are made up of employees who share the same interests and backgrounds. They provide support, offer career development opportunities, and remove barriers. In 2022, Yelp had resource groups for women in engineering, prior or current military, Black employees, Asian and Pacific Islanders, and parents, among many others.[79]

One of the popular initiatives in DEI is unconscious bias training.[80] As human beings, we all have implicit biases, and being aware of them and consciously making efforts to minimize their effects may lead to more inclusive workplaces. On a day-to-day basis, unconscious biases have implications for micro-inequities. If we feel closer to those of our own sex, we may be warmer, more helpful, or kinder toward them; perhaps smile at them more frequently; invite them out for lunch or coffee more often; or initiate conversations more often. If we have implicit biases that lead us to associate being a man with being a higher-potential employee, we may be more likely to give administrative and bureaucratic assignments to women while assigning more challenging ones to men. None of these actions are illegal or problematic if done once or twice, but when they constitute patterns of behavior, they affect how inclusive the workplace is.

While unconscious bias is important to identify and manage, there is increasing skepticism around the effectiveness of training programs aimed at rooting out unconscious biases. The most effective unconscious bias training is part of a systematic effort toward inclusiveness, gives participants tools to identify and combat biases, and presents opportunities to practice the learned skills.[81]

Bystander training has been identified as a more promising training form. In many instances, harassment and discrimination occur within full view of others. Many observers remain silent in the face of harassment because they do not know what to do, and they worry about confronting the offender. However, silence often implies acceptance and may encourage the harasser to continue their behavior. Bystander training teaches third parties to notice discriminatory and harassing behavior and offers them tools to stop inappropriate behavior before it rises to the level of unlawful actions.[82]

Diversity training (see Chapter 8) has been shown to be more likely to be effective if it is accompanied by other diversity initiatives and conducted over time.[83] In other words, a single diversity initiative is less likely to be effective compared to multiple initiatives, each of them supporting one another and conveying the message that inclusion matters. Further, as discussed in the opening case, goal setting, tracking diversity metrics, and sharing diversity data are regarded as more promising approaches.[84] In 2021, McDonald's tied diversity goals to executive compensation: With the new guidelines, 15% of the CEO's annual bonus was tied to meeting goals around increasing the share of women, Black, Asian, Hispanic, and other employees from marginalized communities in senior leadership.[85]

Big Data as a Pathway to Increasing Diversity and Inclusion

Organizations may leverage analytics as a pathway to build more diverse and inclusive organizations. There is often a great deal of data being collected in the natural course of business that pertain to diversity. All private employers with 100 or more employees and federal contractors with 50 or more employees must file a report with the EEOC (EEO-1) that breaks down their employees by sex, race, and job categories. Organizations can expand this data collection to include more categories and survey employees to allow them to express how they identify. Examining these data will give organizations an initial understanding of where they stand regarding the level of diversity that exists in their organization. Some organizations voluntarily release these data to improve accountability and to support their diversity efforts.[86]

Today's organizations can reach a diverse base of customers through targeted advertisements, as software companies like Google and social media firms like Facebook analyze data on consumer demographics and tailor advertisements to the audience. When organizations are able to purchase ad space to reach a more diverse applicant base, they diversify their recruitment pool.[87]

Organizations can use HR analytics to prevent biases from entering into the decision-making process. Selection tools such as GapJumpers and Unitive allow organizations to blind themselves to applicant demographic characteristics, socioeconomic background, and other factors that could be sources of bias.[88] GapJumpers uses software that acts like a blind audition for businesses. Applicants solve skill-based challenges, and their background information is hidden so that applicants are given a fair chance to demonstrate their skills.

Data analytics can also help with managing existing employees. Schneider Electric tracks metrics relating to diversity, equity, and inclusion, and uses it as a tool to help build an inclusive culture. The dashboard allows management to examine trends in the data, analyze departmental variation to spot where problems may arise, and explore projections based on historical trends.[89]

SPOTLIGHT ON DATA AND ANALYTICS: DIVERSITY INITIATIVE AT KIMBERLY-CLARK

In 2009, Kimberly-Clark, maker of products such as Huggies, Kleenex, and Kotex, came to the realization that although its customer base was 83% female, its leadership consisted mostly of men. Making diversity and inclusion a key initiative became an important business priority, and Kimberly-Clark tackled this question using data analytics. The analytics team analyzed data on which employees were promoted, derailed, and left the company and used the results to make specific changes.

One realization was that women were not applying for open internal positions unless they met most or all of the criteria, whereas men were more likely to apply if they met half the desired criteria. Some jobs required work experience that was unusual for women (e.g., mill experience), so the company moved to a comparable-experience approach rather than looking for narrow types of experience.

Despite the benefits of analytics, the company credits top management support as the key for the success of the initiative, which resulted in an 82% increase in women in high-level positions in 4 years, as well as helping create a more inclusive, creative, and innovative workplace. In 2023, Diversity First ranked the company number 5 among the top 50 companies for diversity.[90]

Internal Audits

Organizations can ensure compliance with EEO laws by conducting internal audits to identify problems and correct them proactively instead of risking a costly lawsuit. In particular, pay audits that examine gender differences in pay are often valuable in enabling the organization to take corrective action. At the federal level, the Equal Pay Act and Title VII provide protections against sex discrimination in pay. California passed a statewide Equal Pay Act in 2015, prohibiting sex differences in "substantially similar" work, and similar legislation in other states motivates employers to adopt a proactive approach.

Pay Audits

Pay audits can be used to rectify past mistakes and achieve equity within the firm. In 2015, the cloud-based software company Salesforce.com spent $3 million to tackle gender imbalance in pay. In cases in which pay differences were not explainable by factors such as job function, location, or level, adjustments were made for both men and women, which affected 6% of the workforce. A second global assessment in 2017 affected 11% of employees and again cost around $3 million. In its most recent audit, they found the need to adjust the pay of 8.5% of their global workforce, with 92% being due to gender and 8% due to race and ethnicity. To date, the company has spent over $22 million in an effort to rectify pay inequity.

CEO Marc Benioff sees addressing gender gaps in pay as only one piece of its push for diversity and inclusion. The company ensures that women are at least 30% of the attendees at every meeting, and the company's High Potential Leadership Program works to ensure fairness in advancement opportunities. HR leaders can access diversity statistics in real time, using a Tableau dashboard. The company redesigned its entire talent management process, with inclusion at its core.[91]

Even though it is straightforward to group jobs that are similar to each other and conduct a statistical difference test based on sex (or other protected characteristics), HR is strongly cautioned against conducting this analysis without top-management commitment and without legal counsel. The results of a pay audit are "discoverable" in and of themselves as part of legal proceedings. For example, if the pay audit reveals there were unexplainable differences between men and women, and if these differences are not corrected, the results of the audit become evidence for potential discrimination and increases the company's liability. Therefore, if the audit finds such differences, it is essential to promptly correct them, which will require resources and top-management commitment to the issue. Working with legal counsel during this audit to ensure that the audit findings are protected by attorney–client privilege is important. HR still plays a key role as part of diversity audits, ensuring that jobs are classified and grouped correctly and that reasons for pay differences across employees are well documented. HR should also ensure that initial pay offers and subsequent raises are based on justifiable criteria.[92] There may be many legitimate differences for observed pay differences, including number of years of experience, tenure within the organization, managerial responsibilities, cost-of-living differences, and having received merit pay based on clear criteria, among others. During the pay audit, these differences would be statistically controlled for and any unexplained differences identified.

Big Data and Legal Compliance

One of the key uses of predictive analytics is employee selection. Organizations may one day successfully eliminate human biases from their selection decisions by utilizing selection algorithms. Increasingly, companies are using artificial intelligence (AI) tools as part of recruitment and selection. Depending on how they are used, these tools may help organizations in helping increase diversity and inclusion. For example, LinkedIn Recruiter features "Diversity Nudges" that alert recruiters when the recruiter's keywords are resulting in a gender-imbalanced candidate pool and suggest different keywords to add to the search.[93]

As we discuss in Chapter 7, it is possible to statistically identify the profile of successful employees and hire employees that fit the profile of this "most likely to succeed" candidate. The idea to automate hiring using algorithms, or at least identify criteria that are most likely to predict desired outcomes using big samples, is appealing due to potential cost savings and the desire to make more objective selection decisions. HR technology vendors such as Cornerstone OnDemand provide software that helps companies use predictive analytics using publicly available information, test scores, and biometric data. There is research indicating that Facebook "likes" may reveal a person's IQ (e.g., liking the movie *The Godfather*, the music of Mozart, and, inexplicably, curly fries), and linguistic software may identify personality traits of applicants by analyzing the words they use (e.g., neurotic personalities are more likely to use words such as *awful* and *horrible*).[94] Software that aggregates high volumes of publicly available information about applicants may be used in an employee selection algorithm.

What are the legal consequences of these approaches? Data scientists and industrial/organizational psychologists caution that big data may not always be better data.[95] Essentially, these algorithms codify what success looked like in the past. Depending on how they were formulated, these algorithms may codify and perpetuate past systematic discrimination or potentially result in disparate impact. Certain metrics picked up by algorithms as predictive of performance may in fact be proxies for age, sex, race, or other protected categories. For example, suppose the algorithm discovers that those with a short commute to work are more likely to stay longer and be more effective at work and therefore recommends not hiring those with a long commute. This may make the selection pool less diverse due to the exclusion of some geographic areas if such areas differ in their level of diversity, which they often do. In other words, equating big data with more objective and unbiased data can be a mistake, and overreliance on historical data may result in biased decision making while also creating the illusion that the selection system is based on data and therefore must be unbiased.

There are currently many unknowns regarding how organizations may benefit from predictive data analytics while also ensuring compliance with EEO laws. Some localities are taking the lead about dealing with the use of AI in employment decisions. Illinois has the Artificial Intelligence Video Interview Act, which regulates the use of AI in analyzing video interviews. New York City passed a law that requires companies to conduct a bias audit before using AI technology in selection decisions.[96] Selection decisions based on big data may be challenged based on the disparate impact theory, and future court decisions are important to follow to understand best practices. Key issues include the following[97]:

- *Correlation does not equal causation.* What is included in the algorithm may be correlated with performance but may not be a cause of performance. For example, if performance evaluations are biased in favor of young men, factors identified as predictive of performance will be markers correlated with being young and male, but not because those factors lead to higher performance.

- *Publicly available information may be unevenly distributed.* When algorithms rely on scraping publicly available data, some groups may be underrepresented. For example, older workers may have a smaller digital footprint.

- *Algorithms are opaque.* A selection algorithm includes many metrics that change over time because of machine learning. There may be factors that result in disparate impact, but it is difficult for applicants to see how specific algorithms affect them, even if they know that they were screened out due to an algorithm. EEO laws apply to the use of software using predictive analytics, but it is unclear how compliance can be assured and how courts will treat them.

- *It is unclear how newer, complex algorithms should be validated.* The Uniform Guidelines require validating tests used to make selection decisions in order to ensure legal compliance. However, it is unclear how this may be done with more cutting-edge analytics developed in recent years. Since the early 20th century, selection systems have been validated by demonstrating that they predict performance using a simple statistical correlation or regression equation. Applying this logic, more complicated selection algorithms used today would be valid because they are statistically related to performance, and, in fact, this is why they are being used in selection. At the same time, some argue that this methodology is flawed for big data, given that relationships with performance may be spurious (i.e., two things may be correlated not because one causes the other but because both are related to something else). Further, the concept of statistical significance becomes less meaningful when the number of individuals included in the sample grows large, as virtually every relationship will be statistically significant by traditional standards. We encourage you to stay up to date regarding the most recent developments.

CHAPTER SUMMARY

Diversity has advantages for businesses, ranging from increased innovation to higher firm performance, but the benefits of diversity necessitate having an inclusive work environment. Diversity management has its challenges, particularly because individuals are more likely to be interpersonally attracted to similar others and because biases may serve as barriers to employment and advancement. There are numerous federal and state laws, executive orders, and local ordinances that aim to prevent discrimination based on sex, race, color, religion, national origin, age, disability status, pregnancy, and genetic information. Although HR analytics may be a crucial tool, the legal implications of big data in employee selection and talent management are still uncharted territory, which means HR professionals should pay attention to this rapidly evolving field.

KEY TERMS

Bona fide occupational qualification (BFOQ)
Bystander training
Class action lawsuit
Compensatory damages
Disparate (or adverse) impact
Disparate treatment
Diversity
Diversity, equity, and inclusion (DEI)
Equal Employment Opportunity Commission (EEOC)
Equitable relief
Equity
Essential functions
Executive orders
4/5ths (or 80%) rule
Harassment
Hostile work environment
Inclusion
Marginal functions

Neurodivergent
Neurodiversity
Neurotypical
Office of Federal Contract Compliance Programs (OFCCP)
Pretext
Prima facie evidence
Punitive damages
Quid pro quo harassment
Reasonable accommodation
Retaliate
Reverse discrimination
Sexual harassment
Similarity-attraction hypothesis
Stereotypes
Unconscious (or implicit) bias
Uniform Guidelines on Employee Selection Procedures

HR REASONING AND DECISION-MAKING EXERCISES

Mini-Case Analysis Exercise: Workplace Diversity Dilemmas

Imagine that you are working at a medium-sized business as an HR professional. You are faced with the following dilemmas. Decide how you would handle each issue in the short term and long term. What additional information would help you decide? What changes seem necessary to the company given these dilemmas, if any?

1. Your company's top salesperson, Jack Igers, used to date an administrative assistant in the finance department, Mary Adams. Now that the relationship has ended, it has come to your attention that Jack is harassing Mary. He frequently visits her at her office and repeatedly pressures her to go on a date with him and rekindle the relationship. She put in a written complaint to the HR department, and you are in charge of handling this situation. What will you do?

2. An applicant for your janitorial services is hearing impaired and is unable to speak. He was invited for a job interview. However, when contacted, the applicant informed management that he would need a sign language interpreter for the interview and that he could bring his sister as an interpreter. The hiring manager cancelled the job interview. What would you do?

3. An employee in your department sent you an e-mail stating that he examined the salaries of more than 100 employees working in the call center and found that male employees seemed to be paid more than female employees. What would you do?

HR Decision Analysis Exercise: Fair Algorithm?

Your organization just started conversations with a consulting firm. The firm is offering its platform for use in employee selection. In your discussions with the firm, it disclosed that its research-based algorithm assigns higher scores to applicants who

- drive a car with a manual transmission,

- have no gaps in their résumés, and

- have a history of staying at each job for at least 2 years.

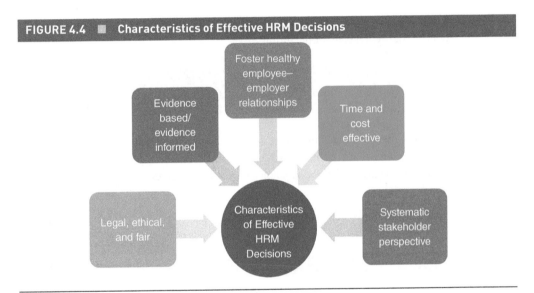

FIGURE 4.4 ■ Characteristics of Effective HRM Decisions

Should your organization use this selection system? Consider this decision using the following criteria.

Please provide the rationale for your answer to each of the questions below.

Is it legal, ethical, and fair?

Is it evidence based/evidence informed?

Does it foster healthy employee–employer relationships?

Is it time- and cost-effective?

Does it take a systematic stakeholder perspective?

Considering your analysis above, overall, do you think this was an effective decision? Why or why not?

What, if anything, do you think should be done differently or considered to help make this decision more effective?

HR Decision-Making Exercise: Assessing Disparate Impact

Recently, your organization advertised openings for sales associates. The selection process includes gathering and evaluating information on a personality test and an in-person interview.

Here is a breakdown of who applied and who was hired:

	Applied	Hired
Men	150	15
Women	90	15
White	100	10
Asian American	50	10
Black	30	5
Hispanic	60	5

1. Using the 4/5ths rule, do you have prima facie evidence that disparate impact may have occurred? Explain your rationale.

2. If there is prima facie evidence for disparate impact, what information can you use as defense? What would be your action plan for the future?

DATA AND ANALYTICS EXERCISE: USING THE CHI-SQUARE TEST TO ASSESS DISPARATE IMPACT

Given the downsides of the 4/5ths rule, including its high rate of false positives and its sensitivity to sampling errors, companies may rely on more sophisticated analyses. The 4/5ths rule is simply a "rule of thumb" adopted by the courts and is not based on a formal statistical test. An alternative method is the chi-square test.[98]

Consider the following example. Assume the use of a knowledge test resulted in the following distribution:

	Pass	Fail	Total
Men	70	90	160
Women	42	72	114
Total	112	162	274

These results indicate that if you disregard gender, 112 of 274 (40.9%) of all applicants passed the test, and 162 of 274 (59.1%) failed the test.

Now you need to calculate the distribution you would expect to see if gender plays no role. Without any systematic effects of gender, you would expect men and women to have the same pass and fail ratios. This is the *expected distribution*.

	Pass	Fail	Total
Men	65.4 (of 160 men, 40.9% should pass)	94.6 (of 160 men, 59.1% should fail)	160
Women	46.6 (of 114 women, 40.9% should pass)	67.4 (of 114 women, 59.1% should fail)	114
Total	112	162	274

Now you need to enter these data into Excel, as shown in the screenshot (Figure 4.5). Then insert the formula you see at the top into cell B12. The result is the "*p* value," which indicates whether the difference you observe between actual distribution and expected distribution is purely by chance, where a *p* value lower than .05 is considered statistically significant. The result has a *p* value of .25, which is not statistically significant (which indicates that there is no evidence of a gender effect on selection).

FIGURE 4.5 ■

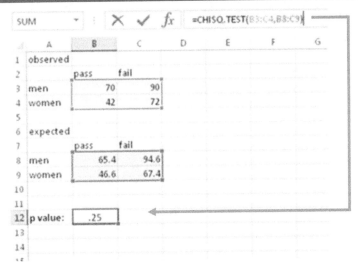

Excel Extension: Now You Try!

- On **edge.sagepub.com/bauer2e**, use the Excel worksheet and consider the following observed distribution of selection method performance for white and Black job candidates.

- Is there evidence of disparate impact according to your chi-square analysis?

- If so, for which job candidates: Black candidates or white candidates?

	Pass	Fail	Total
Black	66	140	206
White	50	64	114

THE ANALYSIS AND DESIGN OF WORK

LEARNING OBJECTIVES

After reading and studying this chapter, you should be able to do the following:

5.1 Describe the purposes of job analyses and competency models in organizations.

5.2 Demonstrate the use of different ways of collecting job analysis information.

5.3 Differentiate between job analysis and competency modeling, and evaluate the advantages of each approach.

5.4 Explain how job design can be used to increase employee motivation, job attitudes, and performance.

5.5 Describe how flexible work environments affect employee well-being.

REDESIGNING WORK: OFFICE, REMOTE WORK, OR BLENDED

©iStockphoto.com/SDI Productions

One of HR's key activities is the design of employees' work. Historically, one of the most basic assumptions about office jobs is that the work is generally done at an office controlled by the organization.

The Covid-19 pandemic, and associated health concerns with face-to-face interaction, challenged these assumptions. Supported by new technologies, around the world many organizations, whose work allowed it, switched to remote work seemingly overnight with many working from home or from anywhere. Employees learned to cope with not seeing their colleagues face-to-face and carving office spaces in their homes. Whereas remote work had been the exception before the pandemic, it became common for most office work, with online meetings becoming the norm within many organizations.

The adaptation to remote work was easier for some employees than for others. On the plus side, many employees enjoyed not having to spend time and money commuting, and they enjoyed the flexibility of spending more time with their families (or pets). On the other hand, some employees reported feeling disconnected from their colleagues, or found that it was hard to balance work and life responsibilities when these responsibilities were both going on in the same physical place. Either way, whether we like it or not, organizations and employees had to adapt when social distancing was required for public safety.

Many organizations expected that once the pandemic subsided, people would simply switch back to the old ways of working, that is, in a physical office. But that expectation has not happened as quickly as expected. Many employees were able to push back against their employers and maintain remote working arrangements, justifying its necessity given the possibility that new variants of the virus might appear.

In the hopes of returning to physical offices, many employers set deadlines for people to return to work while others simply closed their physical offices in favor of fully remote work. Some employers, such as Goldman Sachs and American Express, have succeeded in getting workers back to the office. But many employees have simply ignored those timelines or tried to push them further out. In mid-2022, surveys indicated that one third of workers wanted to continue to work from home. This issue is reflected in the fact that office vacancy rates in many U.S. cities have remained high.

One employer that has tried many approaches to deal with this issue is the personal finance company, Credit Karma. The company tried over much of 2022 to get their employees to return to work. But like many employers, their efforts were entirely successful. Many workers say they are more productive at home and note that many other organizations have gone to permanent flexibility in terms of location. Credit Karma's chief people officer, Colleen McCreary, has responded that employees can go to those competing organizations if they want that flexibility. Credit Karma also had to let some employees go because they were in locations where the company was not allowed to operate.

Whereas in 2022 many Credit Karma employees reported that they would prefer not to return to the office, some felt quite differently and said they would like to work in-office for at least a few days a week. They reported liking the personal relationships and deeper communication. Some writers have argued that these relationships at work are key to an employee's success. For example, it is not advantageous to stay invisible to a supervisor if one wants that supervisor's attention and support. It is also possible that as the job market changes in the favor of employers, employees will not be able to continue to work from home if their employer wants them at the office.[1]

CASE DISCUSSION QUESTIONS

1. One of the benefits of remote work is that it allows workers a good deal of autonomy and freedom to work where and when they want. How do you think this autonomy would affect employees' performance and well-being? How might this autonomy affect their commitment and willingness to stay with the company?

2. Some workers indicate they want to go back to the office, at least for a few days a week. What specific aspects of the design of a traditional office do you think are attractive to these workers?

3. Given many of the benefits of working from home, why do some employers like Credit Karma want to limit it?

4. What are some differences between people that might affect whether they prefer a traditional office design, blended work, or purely remote work?

5. How might you redesign remote work to gain the benefits of the traditional office?

INTRODUCTION

Organizations must understand how individual jobs help achieve organizational goals and how to design jobs to support employees. In this chapter, we describe the science and best practices regarding how to analyze jobs and work processes to ensure organizational success. We also discuss how the job is experienced by employees and why the employee experience is important to organizations.

THE ANALYSIS OF WORK AND ITS CRITICAL ROLE IN HR PRACTICE

LEARNING OBJECTIVE

5.1   Describe the purposes of job analyses and competency models in organizations.

For organizations to succeed, strategic goals at the highest levels must be translated down the organizational hierarchy into specific work processes. These processes must be further translated into the specific tasks and responsibilities of individual workers. In other words, employers must decide the work that needs to be done at the organizational level, what workers in different roles actually do, and the skills and abilities workers need.

This analysis of work and the employee characteristics needed to perform the work is called job analysis. Job analysis is an essential HR function that forms the basis for all other HR functions, including recruitment, selection, promotion and succession planning, performance management, training and development, and pay and rewards.[2] For example, consider the job of firefighter. When developing legally defensible procedures to recruit and hire people who fit this job (see Chapters 4, 6, and 7), the organization needs to understand the tasks firefighters perform and the skills and abilities needed to perform the tasks. In fact, city governments frequently conduct job analyses for their public safety jobs, such as firefighters and police officers, to develop hiring criteria and selection procedures.

At the federal level, the U.S. Office of Personnel Management, which provides HR support for the millions of federal employees in civil service jobs, offers detailed technical guidelines about how to conduct job analyses for developing selection procedures for these workers.[3] In the private sector, many corporations either conduct detailed job analyses or use the related process of competency modeling to better understand the different jobs in their companies and how they fit together to achieve organizational goals. For example, IBM has developed a competency model to document the core competencies of its professional employees worldwide.[4] In short, organizations recognize that an analysis of the work individual employees do provides significant advantages in terms of managing their human capital. Although you may or may not ever actually conduct a job analysis yourself, you have probably benefited from a job analysis, which helps determine selection procedures, pay, and promotion considerations.

It is commonplace for governments to maintain job analyses of their public safety jobs such as firefighter, a job that requires a number of specialized technical skills that are not familiar to members of the general public.

©iStockphoto.com/MaboHH

Technical Terms Used in Job Analysis and Competency Modeling

In this section we define some of the terms used in job analysis and competency modeling. First, tasks are the elements of a job analysis that are typically used to describe the job itself. They usually contain an action verb followed by an object and are clarified in terms of how the work is performed (e.g., under what conditions, using what equipment, and for what purpose). In the case of a barista's job, a task might be "Makes (action verb) espresso drinks (object) using espresso maker and other coffee equipment to serve customer needs (clarification of conditions, equipment, and purpose)." As another example, think about the job of a teacher and write one task statement: "_____ (action verb) _____ (object) _____ (clarification of conditions, equipment, and purpose)."

Second, knowledge, skills, abilities, and other characteristics (KSAOs) are used to describe the attributes workers need to carry out their work effectively. *Knowledge* is generally something a person learns from a book (e.g., knowledge of laws pertinent to the HR profession), a *skill* is something an employee can learn how to do (e.g., skill in the use of fire equipment), an *ability* is a relatively innate talent or aptitude (e.g., spatial relationships ability), and *other characteristics* refers to personality traits such as extraversion or integrity.

Third, the persons who provide information about the job are called subject matter experts (SMEs). In a job analysis, an SME is typically a job incumbent who performs the job as well as supervisors. Job incumbents and supervisors each give unique information about what the job involves.[5]

Over the past few decades, organizations have begun to use the related processes of competency modeling in addition to job analysis. Generally speaking, the goals of competency modeling are to understand what types of attributes and behaviors are required for a group of jobs, perhaps over an entire organization. (We will discuss competency modeling in greater detail later in the chapter.) The primary elements of a competency model are the employee competencies that are needed to perform the job, such as "competency in working with team members." For simplicity's sake, in this chapter, the term *job analysis* refers to either job analysis or competency modeling. Also, because work in the 21st century can change quickly—and organizations may not necessarily have a series of finite, stable "jobs"—the term *work analysis* may sometimes be used in place of the older term *job analysis*. Work analysis implies that, over time, an employee may need to perform a variety of evolving jobs within an organization.[6]

In addition, it is important to distinguish between the concept of a or job (job classification) in an organization versus a position. A job classification is a group of related duties within an organization, whereas a position is the duties that can be carried out by one person. For example, a city government may have the job classification of "police officer." There might be hundreds of individual police officers in that job classification, holding positions with titles such as "patrol officer" or "detective." Or a large, national drug store chain might employ individual pharmacists in thousands of positions across the country, but they would all be in the same job classification of "pharmacist."

It is also useful to distinguish between job analysis and the terms job descriptions and job specifications. In general, a job analysis results in a very detailed document that allows a person who is unfamiliar with the job to get a good idea of what the job involves in terms of tasks and required KSAOs. In fact, a detailed job analysis might list hundreds of tasks and dozens of KSAOs. In contrast, both job descriptions and job specifications are usually shorter documents than the full results of a job analysis, often a single page, although this can vary across different organizations. It can be useful to have a relatively short document like this to show job applicants and current employees what the job involves. Table 5.1 is a brief example of a job description and a job specification for a hypothetical administrative assistant position.

Job descriptions provide the title and purpose of the job, as well as a general overview of the essential tasks, duties, and responsibilities (i.e., observable actions) associated with the job. The material in job descriptions can be used in recruitment materials for attracting new employees, job ads, and postings so that applicants know what the job involves. Job descriptions are also given to employees so they understand their job.

In contrast to job descriptions, job specifications focus on the characteristics of an employee who does the job. They describe what the general requirements are for an employee doing the job, including the KSAOs and any physical or emotional requirements. Job specifications also include the qualifications a person needs to fill the job in terms of experience and education and thus are essential to consider when recruiting for and filling a position. Maintaining and documenting job descriptions and job specifications, in a format that is consistent across jobs within the organization, are essential tasks of HR departments.[7]

TABLE 5.1 ■ Sample Brief Job Description and Job Specifications for an Administrative Assistant

Administrative Assistant Job Specifications

Overview and Purpose

The purpose of the administrative assistant position is to provide support to other workers (e.g., managers) in carrying out their job tasks.

Duties

The administrative assistant carries out a range of duties in support of organizational functions, including scheduling meetings and appointments and answering phone calls. Includes providing assistance in preparing reports and developing and implementing filing systems. May also include taking notes and minutes.

Major Tasks and Responsibilities

- Plan and organize meetings, including developing a meeting agenda and taking notes and minutes as needed.

- Coordinate with others within and outside of the organization, including other administrative assistants, as needed.

- Make appointments for other staff within the business unit.

- Answer phone calls in support of the work unit.

- Develop filing systems for work unit and implement them.

- Order supplies as needed.

- Plan meetings and trips of office visitors, providing needed support.

- Develop office policies and procedures.

- Support simple bookkeeping functions within the unit, such as reimbursements and paying of vendors.

- *Job Requirements*

- Organizational skills

- Interpersonal skills necessary for working with coworkers and outside clients

- Ability to prioritize work

- Knowledge of basic office practices and procedures

- Basic knowledge of office equipment, including simple troubleshooting

- Oral and written communication skills

- Good attention to detail

Minimum Qualifications

- High school diploma (required); some college or college degree (desirable)

- Office experience, including at least 6 months working as an administrative assistant

- Demonstrated proficiency with typical office software

Manager's Toolbox: Some Basics of Job Descriptions

Writing and updating job descriptions are some of the most basic functions of an HR department, because these descriptions are used for a range of useful functions. For example, job descriptions are

- used to develop recruitment and job posting materials to attract job applicants and give them an idea about what the job involves;

- shared with job applicants during the selection process to provide a realistic preview of what a job actually entails; and

- provided to new and existing employees so they know what is expected of them and what criteria can be used to evaluate them.

One of the challenges in organizations is keeping job descriptions up to date, and this is especially true in dynamic business environments in which jobs change quickly. There are some ways that HR practitioners can keep an eye on this issue:

- One practice, especially in quickly changing industries and organizations, is to update job descriptions annually.

- Reviewing an employee's job description might be most useful during annual performance appraisal meetings between supervisors and employees. During these meetings, employees can inform their supervisor if the job has changed to an extent that would warrant an updated job description.

What Are the Purposes of Job Analysis?

Job analysis is often called the cornerstone of other HR functions. This is because it is essential to understand work processes and the human requirements for doing work to do other HR functions well. In short, good HR practice is based on a robust job analysis. Figure 5.1 shows the many HR functions that are dependent on a job analysis.

FIGURE 5.1 ■ Summary of the Relationship Between Job Analysis and Other HR Functions

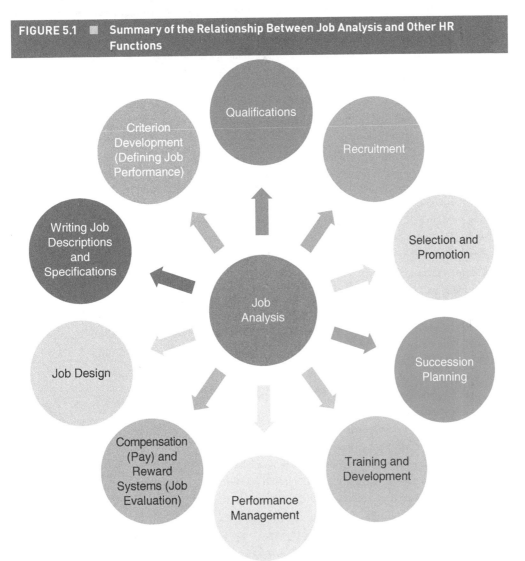

A job analysis is important for establishing the minimum qualifications the job requires, including education and experience. It is also used for recruitment, as it is necessary to understand the human requirements of a job prior to developing recruitment strategies and materials. For example, in hiring a software engineer, it is essential to understand the minimum qualifications of the job, such as the KSAOs and the amount of education and work experience needed (see Chapter 6). In addition, job analysis is necessary for developing selection procedures (see Chapter 7). This includes the basic requirements of the job (e.g., experience) and types of tests and assessments that should be used to determine a job applicant's fit with the job, including the KSAOs they should measure. U.S. employment law requires that selection procedures be based on a job analysis in order to be legally defensible.

SPOTLIGHT ON LEGAL ISSUES: JOB ANALYSIS AND LEGAL DEFENSIBILITY OF HR SYSTEMS

Because job analysis is often called a cornerstone of other HR functions, job analysis is key to their legal defensibility. This is perhaps best illustrated in the area of hiring.

For example, the U.S. federal government's *Uniform Guidelines on Employee Selection Procedures* (1978) state that with few exceptions, a job analysis is required to demonstrate the validity of selection procedures.[8] As we will see in Chapter 7, the validity of selection procedures is core to their legal defensibility. In other words, a valid selection procedure (i.e., one that predicts job performance well) needs to begin with a job analysis.

In addition, job analysis plays a critical role in implementation of the Americans with Disabilities Act (ADA, 1990). As noted in Chapter 4, a key aspect of complying with ADA is that employers identify essential functions of the job and include them in their job descriptions. An employer who makes a hiring decision based on requiring a nonessential function of the job or a marginal function that could be assigned to other workers could face legal challenges. The key is to carefully identify these essential job functions by means of a job analysis and to document them clearly in job descriptions following legally defensible procedures and guidelines.

An analysis of jobs and how they relate to each other is necessary for good succession planning. Succession planning (or succession management; see Chapter 6) involves taking stock of which employees are qualified to fill positions that are likely to be vacated soon. If no candidates are currently prepared to move into those positions, the best candidates can be given developmental experiences such as training and work assignments. For example, a medium-sized manufacturing company may realize that its plant manager will be retiring in 2 years. In preparation, the company can identify good candidates among current employees for taking on the plant manager's role. These candidates can then be trained or given appropriate work experiences so they can take on the plant manager's job when the current plant manager retires. In this example, a job analysis would identify which KSAOs are required for the plant manager's job; other jobs in the company that are similar to the job of plant manager; which employees are in those other jobs and thus could be good candidates for plant manager; and what additional KSAOs they would still need to take on the plant manager's job.

Job analysis is also necessary for developing the most effective training and development programs (see Chapter 8). Specifically, it is important to understand the KSAOs needed for a job when developing training and development programs, and it is a key part of conducting a training needs assessment. Job analysis is also needed in the development of performance standards to be used in performance management systems (see Chapter 9) to assess employees' current skill and performance levels.

Regarding employee compensation and pay, a job analysis is needed to set pay scales that are both fair to employees and are competitive with the current employment market (see Chapter 11). This type of job analysis involved in setting pay in organizations is called job evaluation (see Chapter 11). Further, job analysis is important for designing jobs that will motivate employees in their work (discussed later in this chapter). Job analyses are essential for writing job descriptions and job specifications. Finally, job analyses play a critical role in developing criterion measures—that is, the specific measures and metrics used to evaluate the effectiveness of HR systems, such as whether they are successfully hiring the best people and training them appropriately.[9]

Clearly, the role of job analysis is critical in organizations: A well-produced job analysis can provide a strong basis for the success of an HR system, while a poor (or nonexistent) job analysis can decrease the effectiveness of an HR system.

Seeing the Big Picture: Work Flow Analysis

Most of this chapter is focused on the analysis of jobs and individual positions. However, before moving into a discussion of analyzing individual jobs, it is important to step back and consider how work is accomplished at the organizational level. This broad, organization-level focus on work within the organization and within organizational units is known as **work flow analysis**. It is often useful to think of this process in reverse order: Begin with the desired final output; then enumerate the tasks necessary to create this output; and go on to identify the organizational resources, equipment, and human capital necessary to carry out these tasks. In this way, managers can think critically about organizational processes and how they might be carried out more effectively using fewer resources. Such an analysis might allow organizations to adjust to changes in the economic or technological environments. Work flow analysis can also provide guidance as to how to make jobs more motivating to workers, an issue we discuss later in this chapter.

As an example, managers in a restaurant might decide to analyze their operations. The restaurant's output is the production of food and drinks. They need to determine how they would measure this output, including measures of both the quantity and the quality of the output. From there they could decide what tasks need to be performed for producing this output, including tasks performed by the chef (e.g., preparing menus, cooking food) and those performed by others in the shop, such as the people operating the cash register (e.g., interacting effectively with customers, making change). From there they could determine the needed resources (e.g., chicken, lettuce, milk), equipment (e.g., oven, mixer, grill), and KSAOs (e.g., knowledge of recipes, skill at using equipment) that are needed to create the output. Note that work flow analysis is applied to different types of work, from the manufacturing of high-tech equipment to research and development work to large retailers. It should also be applied not only to individual workers but also to teams and other organizational subunits, as well as the organization as a whole, to better understand their functioning and improve their efficiency.

Although many organizations may skip this systematic analysis of their work, the use of increasingly sophisticated analytics techniques in organizations might change this. Specifically, an analysis of an organization's operations can facilitate the use of work flow analysis to increase efficiency. This might include the use of algorithms that assess how subtle changes in inputs can affect outputs, including the combined effects of inputs on work processes and outputs. In addition, online retailers such as Amazon and Walmart are constantly examining their work flow for ways to optimize them, as they must frequently adapt to ever-changing conditions, including supply, inventory, and delivery of goods.[10]

A challenge for work flow analysis is the use of reliable measures of both the quantity and quality of outputs. Moreover, the application of sophisticated analytics to work flow analysis may be used to mitigate some of the negative outcomes (e.g., worker displacement) associated with the increased automation of work processes.[11]

SPOTLIGHT ON DATA AND ANALYTICS: ANALYZING AND ADVANCING THE DATA SCIENCE PROFESSION

It can be difficult to develop a job analysis or competency model when the job or profession is new or changing. But professions need the guidance of a job analysis, even more so when the profession is changing rapidly. The job of data scientist within the field of data analytics and big data presents just such a challenge. Although data science as a field has been around for decades, the growth of AI and advanced analytics has created some confusion for HR departments. For example, what skills should they be seeking in candidates applying for data scientist jobs? And what types of skills will data scientists need to develop?

To address these issues, IBM has developed a competency model for the role of data scientist. Their model, originally developed in 2018, includes groups of competencies such as statistics, model building, data preparation, and leadership. It can be used as a basis for recruiting data scientists, setting job expectations for them once they are hired, and training them to meet future challenges in the field.[12]

COLLECTING JOB ANALYSIS DATA

LEARNING OBJECTIVE
5.2   Demonstrate the use of different ways of collecting job analysis information.

A number of methods may be used to collect job analysis data. First, *interviewing* subject matter experts (SMEs) is the most common method for collecting job analysis data; such interviews can be conducted individually or in small groups. The job analyst (typically an HR staff member) might discuss with SMEs (employees and supervisors) the job tasks they perform, the KSAOs needed to do the job, and critical job situations they might face. However, for more technical jobs, it may be necessary to *observe* people doing the work. For example, to understand the highly specialized equipment used by firefighters, it would probably be necessary for a job analyst to actually see how they use that equipment in their work. Similarly, it is common to do "ride-alongs" with law enforcement employees to gain a deeper understanding of the procedures they must follow.

For practical reasons, when there are large numbers of job incumbents and supervisors, it is common to conduct *surveys* of SMEs instead of interviews. Surveys can facilitate obtaining a representative sample for large organizations where there may be variations in the way the work is done across the organization. For example, if a large hospital's HR managers were analyzing the job of emergency room nurse, they might want to be sure to gain input from nurses who work on different shifts, as the types of emergencies nurses deal with—and thus the tasks they do and the KSAOs they need—might vary considerably depending on the time of day.

Note that software designed to help with the collection and processing of job analysis data is available from multiple vendors. In addition, new technologies are currently developing to help streamline the job analysis process, for both workers and employers. For example, a recent study shows that natural language processing of existing job descriptions and task statements can be used to generate KSAO ratings instead of extensive surveys and interviews with SMEs.[13]

Often it is not necessary to carry out a job analysis from scratch. Rather, if there is an existing job analysis in place, it may be possible to begin with that job analysis and simply update it. If not, existing job analysis materials are often available from professional organizations (e.g., a job analysis for engineers from an engineering professional association). In addition, a source of information about jobs is the O*NET, published by the U.S. Department of Labor and discussed later in this chapter. Note that existing job analysis sources such as these may not provide a complete job analysis in themselves, as they are not tailored to the specific job in the specific organization. However, these materials can provide a springboard to begin the job analysis process.[14]

Logistical Issues in Job Analysis

From an employee's perspective, a job analysis might be perceived as an organizational intervention: A person from HR shows up asking about your job in order to make decisions about important issues like hiring, promotion, training, and pay. Thus, the selection of which SMEs will participate in a job analysis is a major decision from an employee's perspective. SMEs should be chosen in such a way that they provide a representative sample of the employees in a particular job type. For example, if a chain of drugstores were developing the job analysis for a pharmacist, it might consider using a sample of

The American Society for Engineering Education has developed a competency model for engineering jobs. The model was developed to help educators and industry leaders develop training and standards for engineers.[15]

©iStockphoto.com/gorodenkoff

pharmacist SMEs that represent the different geographical store locations, as the pharmacist job might be different in different locations, such as dealing with different types of health conditions and customer questions.

Additionally, SME samples should be demographically representative in terms of characteristics such as gender and ethnicity. Not only might these lead to different results due to differences in the experience of work, but just as important is that the job analysis process be seen as fair by employees.[16] For example, if a city were doing a job analysis to develop a promotional procedure for the job of fire captain but only asked SMEs from certain ethnic groups to participate, employees would likely—and rightly—see the job analysis process as unfair.

Preparing SMEs for Job Analysis

An issue that often comes up when collecting job analysis information is preparing SMEs for the process, specifically, letting them know why the job analysis is being conducted. From an employee's perspective, a person showing up from HR wanting to discuss their job could be seen as anything from a nuisance to a threat; in the worst case, a worker may worry their job is being eliminated. For this reason, it is important to explain to employees why the analysis is being done—for example, that information is being collected to develop better hiring procedures and could directly affect who will be hired to be their future team members and colleagues. This not only allays employees' concerns but also increases their willingness to provide input into the process. It can also be helpful to let SMEs know in advance what types of questions they will be asked in a job analysis interview, such as the types of tasks they perform and what KSAOs are needed to do their job. In this way, employees will not have to think on their feet but will have had a chance to consider what their job involves.

SPECIFIC JOB ANALYSIS METHODS AND APPROACHES

LEARNING OBJECTIVE

5.3   Differentiate between job analysis and competency modeling, and evaluate the advantages of each approach.

As described earlier, there are a number of ways to collect job analysis data. In addition, there are a number of specific job analysis methods and frameworks. Each produces a slightly different job analysis product and is best for different organizational goals. Some methods provide detailed information about jobs and the KSAOs needed to do them (e.g., task–KSAO analysis) or critical job situations often faced by employees (critical incidents technique). Other methods are focused on providing general information about jobs (e.g., Position Analysis Questionnaire), and still others provide a broad organizing framework within which to classify and compare jobs (e.g., O*NET content model). Then there are approaches that focus on the competencies needed to do jobs within a profession or a larger organization, allowing for comparisons in what is required across different job levels or at different career stages (competency models). Each of these is described in the following sections; note that the goal is not to provide a complete list of job analysis methods, which can be found in other sources,[17] but rather to touch on some of the more commonly used examples.

Task–KSAO Analysis

Task–KSAO analysis is a job analysis approach focused on carefully defining the tasks that make up the job, as well as the KSAOs needed to do those tasks (see Figure 5.2). First, the job analyst determines the list of tasks that make up the job as well as the KSAOs that are needed to complete them. Second, the job analyst asks SMEs to document, often through a survey, that these tasks and KSAOs are critical to performing the job. Noncritical tasks and KSAOs are eliminated based on the analysis of these data. Third, the final list of KSAOs is reviewed by the SMEs to document that the KSAOs on the list really are needed to do the critical job tasks. Note that task–KSAO analysis is a detailed approach to job analysis, providing great detail about one or relatively few jobs. This detail involved in the analysis means it is a more difficult method to use to analyze many jobs at one time if the goal is to compare different jobs. However, it is a good method to use for certain situations, when trying to understand job details such as when developing job-specific technical training or when developing content valid selection procedures (see Chapter 7). We also refer the reader to other sources that provide more information about how to carry out a task–KSAO analysis.[18]

FIGURE 5.2 ■ The Steps in a Task–KSAO Analysis

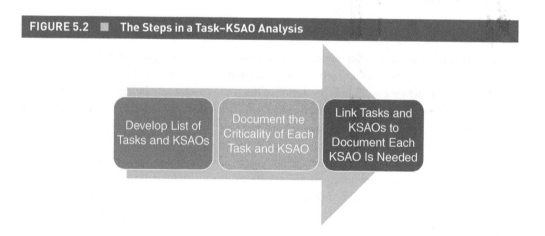

Develop an Initial List of Tasks and KSAOs

The first step of task–KSAO analysis is to develop a list of tasks that describe the job and the KSAOs that a person needs to do them. This is typically done based on a number of sources described earlier. The job analyst may observe workers doing the job, interview a sample of SMEs, and review existing job analysis materials such as O*NET descriptions and previous job analyses. Existing job analyses may come from past analyses done by the organization, analyses done by professional organizations, or even from other organizations. In fact, it is common in the public sector for organizations to share their job analysis materials with each other. For example, a city that is conducting a job analysis for the job of police officer might request job analyses from other cities where policing is done in a similar way.

Based on this information, the job analyst would then develop a list of job tasks, which are usually stated in terms of an action verb, an object of the verb, and a purpose and clarification of conditions and equipment. For example, Figure 5.3 shows that one task for the job of administrative assistant might be *contacts* (action verb) *client* (object) *to coordinate meetings using e-mail or telephone* (purpose and equipment). They would then develop a list of KSAOs based on their interviews and observations of SMEs and other research that would be needed to perform the task effectively. In the case of the administrative assistant task, some KSAOs might be "knowledge of how to use steamer/espresso maker" and "skill in assuring the proper consistency of frothed milk." Note that for most of the history of task analysis, the focus has been on observable tasks for physical jobs as those described. However, given the increased cognitive requirements of jobs, there has been a greater interest in cognitive task analysis, which focuses on mental tasks that may not be observable by others but could be described by an SME. For example, in addition to the task of "Uses computer and Internet to look up order status," a customer service representative's tasks might include "Determines best sources for looking up order status" or "Estimates time to delivery for a customer based on past experience."

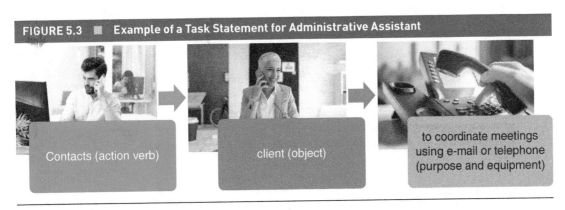

FIGURE 5.3   ■   Example of a Task Statement for Administrative Assistant

Contacts (action verb)

client (object)

to coordinate meetings using e-mail or telephone (purpose and equipment)

©iStock.com/BrianAJackson; ©iStock.com/vgajic; ©iStock.com/Szepy

Document the Criticality of Tasks and KSAOs

Once a list of tasks and KSAOs has been developed, a key step is to document that they are indeed critical to the job. For example, if a city government were conducting job analysis to develop a test for police officers, they may have come up with a list of 150 tasks that describe the job and 30 KSAOs needed to perform the job. It would be important to document that these tasks and KSAOs actually are critical to performance before basing a selection procedure on them. One approach would be to have a different group of SMEs review the tasks and KSAOs and ask them to eliminate or revise tasks and KSAOs they believe are not critical, for example, tasks that are unimportant or performed relatively infrequently.

A more in-depth analysis of the criticality of tasks and KSAOs occurs through a criticality survey, in which larger groups of SMEs rate each task and KSAO in terms of how critical or essential it is. Tables 5.2 and 5.3 show examples of task and KSAO criticality surveys for a hypothetical customer service job for a large retailer, in which SMEs would be asked to rate the importance of each task and KSAO.

Table 5.4 shows the results of the task criticality survey based on an administration of the surveys to 470 SMEs—specifically, 420 customer service specialists and 50 supervisors. As you can see, for most of the tasks and KSAOs, the mean (average) importance ratings are fairly high (between 4 and 5). The

TABLE 5.2 ■ Hypothetical Task Criticality Rating Form for a Customer Service Job	
Please rate each task on the following scale: 5 = Very important, 4 = Important, 3 = Moderately important, 2 = Slightly important, 1 = Not important	
Customer Service Specialist Tasks	**How important is this task for a customer service specialist?** (circle one)
1. Speaks with customers who are interested in new products.	1 2 3 4 5
2. Works to solve customer complaints.	1 2 3 4 5
3. Coordinates with supervisor to resolve customer problems.	1 2 3 4 5
4. Stays abreast of current sales and specials provided by the company by speaking with supervisor and coworkers and checking company website.	1 2 3 4 5
5. Uses telephone system to answer customer calls promptly.	1 2 3 4 5
6. Uses computer to look up customer orders.	1 2 3 4 5
. . .	
31. Cleans office kitchen area when it is their turn to do so.	1 2 3 4 5
32. Uses sit/stand desk correctly throughout the day to maintain own personal health.	1 2 3 4 5
33. Provides customers with refunds, as appropriate, if there is any problem with the product.	1 2 3 4 5

TABLE 5.3 ■ Hypothetical KSAO Rating Form for a Customer Service Job	
KSAO	**How important is this KSAO for a customer service specialist?** (circle one)
A. Interpersonal skills	1 2 3 4 5
B. Product knowledge	1 2 3 4 5
C. Keyboarding skills	1 2 3 4 5
. . .	
J. Decision-making skills	1 2 3 4 5
K. Knowledge of online order tracking system	1 2 3 4 5

standard deviation, which is a measure of the spread or dispersion of ratings (see Chapter 2), is low (under 1). However, this is not true for some tasks and KSAOs. As you can see in Table 5.4, Task 31, "Cleans office kitchen area when it is their turn to do so," has a mean of only 1.4, indicating that most SMEs thought it was not critical and it should probably be dropped. Task 32, "Uses sit/stand desk correctly throughout the day to maintain own personal health," has a fairly high mean, but it has a high standard deviation as well, suggesting there is disagreement among SMEs about the criticality of this task and it should perhaps be dropped or at least reconsidered. Similar analyses can be done for the KSAOs as well.

TABLE 5.4 ■ Means and Standard Deviations for the Task Importance Ratings for Customer Service Specialist, Obtained From 420 Customer Service Specialists and 50 Supervisors		
Customer Service Specialist Tasks	**Mean (1–5 scale)**	**Standard Deviation**
1. Speaks with customers who are interested in new products.	4.4	0.8
2. Works to solve customer complaints.	4.8	0.2
3. Coordinates with supervisor to resolve customer problems.	4.1	0.8
4. Stays abreast of current sales and specials provided by the company by speaking with supervisor and coworkers and checking company website.	4.0	0.9
5. Uses telephone system to answer customer calls promptly.	4.8	0.2
6. Uses computer to look up customer orders.	4.9	0.1
. . .		
31. Cleans office kitchen area when it is their turn to do so.	1.4	0.8
32. Uses sit/stand desk correctly throughout the day to maintain own personal health.	4.0	1.9
33. Provides customers with refunds, as appropriate, if there is any problem with the product.	4.4	0.9

Demonstrate That the KSAOs Are Linked to Critical Tasks

The final step of a task–KSAO analysis is to document that all the KSAOs are actually linked to critical tasks. This is an important step, as the KSAOs will be used as the basis for a number of HR functions, such as the development of training programs. This can be done through simply asking a panel of SMEs to document that all KSAOs are linked to tasks. However, for larger groups of SMEs, it is also possible to document that KSAOs are actually needed for important tasks through a linkage survey. Table 5.5 shows an example of a linkage survey, in which a sample of SMEs would be asked to indicate how important each of the KSAOs is to each job task. KSAOs that are not linked to any critical job tasks would be eliminated from the job analysis.

As noted earlier, task–KSAO analysis provides rich, detailed information about jobs. However, as you might guess, it can be a time-consuming process, and it may feel like a burden to SMEs who must complete lengthy surveys answering multiple questions about their jobs. For these reasons, there are a number of "best practices" from the research on how to reduce the load on SMEs and how to detect SMEs who are not taking the process seriously. These include

- providing incentives to SMEs who complete the surveys;
- breaking up task/KSAO surveys so that different groups of SMEs complete different parts of the survey; and
- introducing "carelessness" items on the survey—that is, items such as bogus tasks that can detect which SMEs are being careless while completing the survey so that their data can be eliminated.[19]

TABLE 5.5 ■ Task–KSAO Linkage Form for the Job of Customer Service Specialist

Using the following scale, please indicate how important each KSAO across the top is for performing each task in the left-hand column: 5 = Essential, 4 = Very important, 3 = Important, 2 = Moderately important, 1 = Not important

Customer Service Specialist Tasks	A. Interpersonal Skills	B. Product Knowledge	C. Keyboarding Skills	…	J. Decision-Making Skills	K. Knowledge of Online Tracking System
1. Speaks with customers who are interested in new products.	1 2 3 4 5	1 2 3 4 5	1 2 3 4 5		1 2 3 4 5	1 2 3 4 5
2. Works to solve customer complaints.	1 2 3 4 5	1 2 3 4 5	1 2 3 4 5		1 2 3 4 5	1 2 3 4 5
3. Coordinates with supervisor to resolve customer problems.	1 2 3 4 5	1 2 3 4 5	1 2 3 4 5		1 2 3 4 5	1 2 3 4 5
4. Stays abreast of current sales and specials provided by the company by speaking with supervisor and coworkers and checking company website.	1 2 3 4 5	1 2 3 4 5	1 2 3 4 5		1 2 3 4 5	1 2 3 4 5
5. Uses telephone system to answer customer calls promptly.	1 2 3 4 5	1 2 3 4 5	1 2 3 4 5		1 2 3 4 5	1 2 3 4 5
6. Uses computer to look up customer orders.	1 2 3 4 5	1 2 3 4 5	1 2 3 4 5		1 2 3 4 5	1 2 3 4 5
…						
31. Cleans office kitchen area when it is their turn to do so.	1 2 3 4 5	1 2 3 4 5	1 2 3 4 5		1 2 3 4 5	1 2 3 4 5

Using the following scale, please indicate how important each KSAO across the top is for performing each task in the left-hand column: 5 = Essential, 4 = Very important, 3 = Important, 2 = Moderately important, 1 = Not important				
32. Uses sit/stand desk correctly throughout the day to maintain own personal health.	1 2 3 4 5 1 2 3 4 5 1 2 3 4 5		1 2 3 4 5	1 2 3 4 5
33. Provides customers with refunds, as appropriate, if there is any problem with the product.	1 2 3 4 5 1 2 3 4 5 1 2 3 4 5		1 2 3 4 5	1 2 3 4 5

Critical Incidents Technique

The **critical incidents technique** involves asking SMEs to describe important situations they frequently encounter on the job. SMEs are then asked to generate examples of good and poor responses to these critical incidents. This might include responses they have seen other employees give or ways they themselves responded to a critical job situation very well or very poorly.[20] As an example, a customer service representative could report that a common critical incident they must face is an angry customer. A positive response might be to figure out what the customer is angry about and come up with solutions that work well both for the customer and the organization, whereas a negative response might be to become angry with the customer, which would only make matters worse. In Figure 5.4, we show some examples of critical incidents for the job of barista.

FIGURE 5.4 ■ Critical Incidents for the Job of Barista

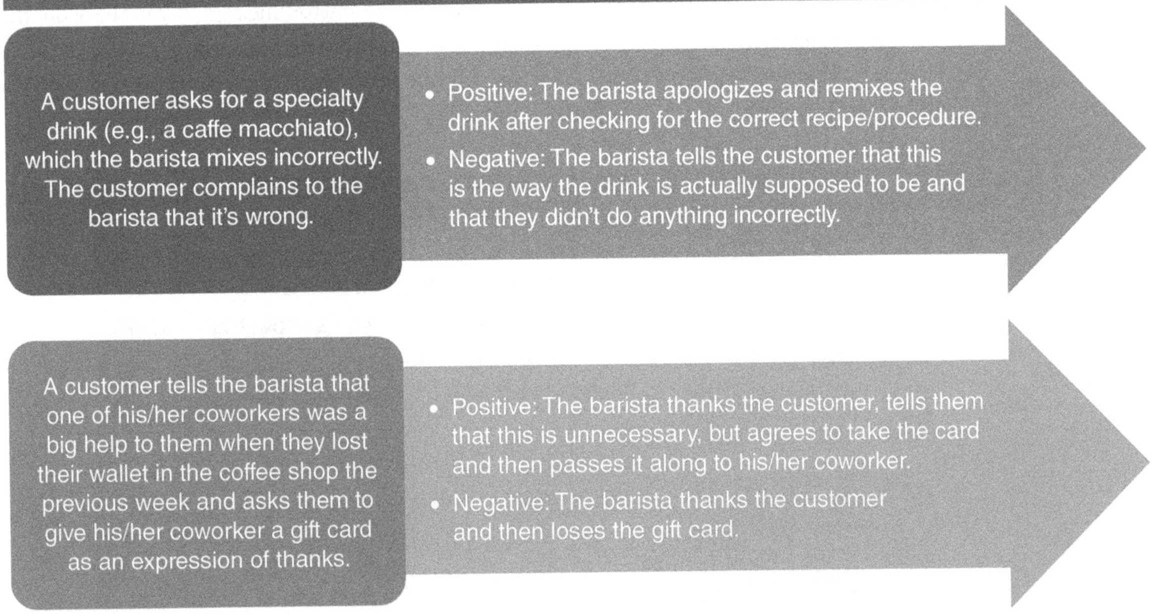

A customer asks for a specialty drink (e.g., a caffe macchiato), which the barista mixes incorrectly. The customer complains to the barista that it's wrong.

- Positive: The barista apologizes and remixes the drink after checking for the correct recipe/procedure.
- Negative: The barista tells the customer that this is the way the drink is actually supposed to be and that they didn't do anything incorrectly.

A customer tells the barista that one of his/her coworkers was a big help to them when they lost their wallet in the coffee shop the previous week and asks them to give his/her coworker a gift card as an expression of thanks.

- Positive: The barista thanks the customer, tells them that this is unnecessary, but agrees to take the card and then passes it along to his/her coworker.
- Negative: The barista thanks the customer and then loses the gift card.

The critical incidents technique may be used on its own or in conjunction with other job analysis methods. The technique provides rich information about frequently occurring, important work situations. It includes both positive and negative performance by employees, and it includes incidents that have actually happened on the job. This is valuable information for such purposes as developing job-related interview questions for hiring employees (Chapter 7), developing training content (Chapter 8), and developing performance management systems (Chapter 9).

Position Analysis Questionnaire

Unlike task–KSAO analysis and the critical incidents technique, each of which provides detailed information about jobs and are often built from scratch with direct input from SMEs, the Position Analysis Questionnaire (PAQ) takes a very different approach. The PAQ is an "off-the-shelf" job analysis survey consisting of 195 generic statements describing what characteristics a worker needs to possess.[21] For instance, in using the PAQ to conduct a job analysis, a job analyst might interview SMEs about their job, complete the PAQ survey based on the interviews, and then have the PAQ data scored online. Because the PAQ has been around since the 1960s, there is a substantial database, such that a detailed report can be generated about the job, giving recommendations for what types of selection procedures might be used for a job with this profile or what the pay should be relative to other jobs. The advantages of the PAQ are that it is far less labor intensive and thus less expensive than the task–KSAO analysis, and its generic items and rich database of jobs allow for comparisons across job types. On the other hand, it does not provide as rich detail as other job analysis methods. Also, because its items are written at a high reading level, it cannot simply be given to SMEs to complete, but it must be completed by a job analyst who has been trained in its use.[22]

Occupational Information Network (O*NET)

We have already mentioned the Occupational Information Network, or O*NET, published by the U.S. Department of Labor. O*NET is a handy source of job analysis data about a range of occupations, and it can provide a useful start to the job analysis process. However, it is important also to remember that O*NET provides a useful job analysis framework in itself. Figure 5.5 provides a summary of the O*NET framework, which includes elements used to describe what a worker needs to do a particular job (such as abilities, knowledge, skills, and work experience), as well as a job itself (such as tasks, general work activities, and labor market trends). The O*NET framework, because of its great depth, may even provide a framework for understanding the variety that can occur in jobs within an organization across different national contexts. The appendix to this chapter provides detailed information about O*NET including how the O*NET database is populated, and additional detail and documentation about O*NET can be found at the O*NET website (https://www.onetonline.org). If you check out the O*NET website and enter a job title, you will see the significant amount of data provided by the website. For instance, just type in *data scientist*—or any job title that may be of interest to you—to get an idea of the typical tasks and KSAOs that are part of the job.[23]

FIGURE 5.5 ■ The O*NET Job Analysis Framework

Elements That Are Used to Describe What a Worker Needs to Do the Job
- Worker Characteristics (such as abilities)
- Worker Requirements (such as knowledge and skills)
- Experience Requirements (such as work experience or certifications and licenses needed)

Elements Used to Describe the Work
- Occupational Requirements (such as work activities)
- Workforce Characteristics (such as current labor market trends)
- Occupation-Specific Information (such as tasks that are performed and tools that are used)

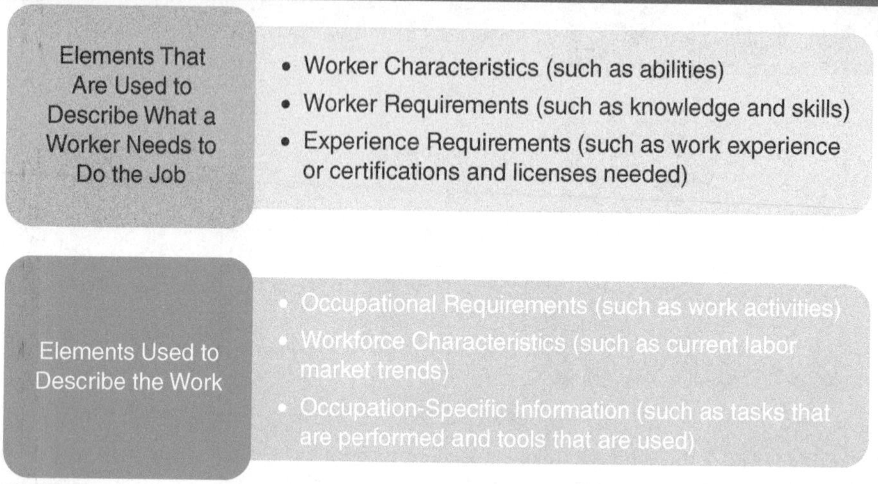

Source: Based on https://www.onetcenter.org/content.html.

Competency Modeling

Competency modeling began to emerge in the 1990s as an approach to analyzing jobs, and its use has increased steadily since then. The focus of competency modeling is similar to that of other job analysis methods in that it involves understanding what KSAOs are needed for doing a job and how these KSAOs—or competencies—are manifested on the job in terms of behaviors. However, competency modeling differs from traditional job analysis in several ways, and this is why competency models have grown in popularity. For example, the Society for Human Resource Management (SHRM) has taken a competency modeling approach to understanding HR jobs rather than using a traditional job analysis, as competency modeling offers a number of advantages.

Perhaps the biggest difference between competency modeling and most job analysis methods is the comprehensive nature of competency models. Competency models are usually broad enough that they can describe a range of jobs within an organization and do so across multiple levels of the organization. In that sense, competency modeling is beneficial to organizations wanting to understand similarities and differences across jobs. For this reason, SHRM chose to use a competency modeling approach to capture a range of HR job types as well as the different levels of experience required for different types of HR jobs: The breadth of the competency modeling approach allowed for that. IBM developed a competency model that allowed the company to organize the wide range of training needs of different jobs across a large, global organization. Other large organizations such as Boeing and Microsoft have also taken a competency modeling approach.[24] Competency models may also be beneficial for career development. That is because they can show the competencies needed at all job levels. This can help both organizations and employees see what competencies an employee may need to develop to advance their careers.[25] We will discuss careers in greater detail in Chapter 8.

Alexander Alonso, PhD, SHRM-SCP, is the chief knowledge officer for the Society for Human Resource Management (SHRM). He is responsible for SHRM's research activities, including the development of the SHRM competency model.

Courtesy of Alexander Alonso

Competency models also allow organizations to capture their goals and values and disseminate them across the organization.[26] For example, an organization that wanted to include a "Value for Diversity" across all of their jobs—and make sure that all employees realize the importance of this value for success in the organization—might include a "Value for Diversity" competency. As noted in the Spotlight on Ethics box, SHRM's competency model explicitly included the important behavior and skills of "Ethical Practice" in HR work because of its desire to articulate the importance of ethical behavior in HR work.

SPOTLIGHT ON ETHICS: DESIGNING ETHICS AND INTEGRITY INTO WORK

Throughout this book, we illustrate the importance of ethics and integrity to the practice of HR. Although ethical behavior is perhaps best modeled by company management, it is important to make ethical behavior an explicit part of the job analysis, competency model, and job description. In other words, the essential role of job analysis and competency modeling in other HR functions makes them critical to communicating the values of ethics and integrity to the organization's employees—and letting employees know that these are needed to get ahead in the organization. In this way, the value of ethical behavior will be echoed throughout the other HR functions, including recruitment, selection, training, and performance management.

There are a number of examples of how ethics can be incorporated into the job analysis or competency modeling process. For example, the O*NET framework published by the U.S. Department of Labor includes integrity as one of its work styles. SHRM's competency model incorporated ethical practice as one of its core competencies; these also include personal integrity, professional integrity, and being an ethical agent. Other professions have begun to focus on the development of ethical competency frameworks. For example, one ethically sensitive group of professions, health sciences, has begun to focus on in-depth training on research ethics. To do so effectively will require the development of ethics-based competency models, and that work is beginning. A competency model on health care research ethics might include knowledge of the policies, laws, and regulations related to health care research and the ability to describe complex research ethics in writing. Such explicit inclusion of employee ethics in describing job requirements should increase the odds of recruiting and hiring ethical workers, training them well, and rewarding ethical behavior.[27]

Questions

1. How would you define ethics and integrity? Do you see them as personal qualities? Can they also be characteristics of an organization? Of a specific profession?
2. Give some examples of events in the news involving ethics or integrity at the organizational level.

A review of the practice of competency modeling identified these and a number of other key differences between competency modeling and job analysis (see Table 5.6). For example, competency models are often directly related to organizational strategies: They identify differences in the ways that competencies are manifested across different job levels. Unlike traditional job analysis, which considers jobs as they are now, competency models often consider future job requirements—a critical factor in highly dynamic industries. In addition, the development of a competency model in an organization is often an organizational development intervention in itself. This is because it requires input from its members, particularly from the top, to identify the big picture of what an organization's members actually do and how that aligns with organizational goals across organizational levels. Plus, competency modeling is far more likely to catch the attention of executives than a traditional job analysis would, for many of the reasons described in Table 5.6. This possibility that competency modeling leads to greater executive buy-in and support is an important consideration: It means the process is more likely to be successful and the results will be used in strategic decision making.

TABLE 5.6 ■ Description of Competency Models and How They Differ From Job Analysis

1. Executives typically pay more attention to competency modeling than to job analysis.

2. Competency models often attempt to distinguish top performers from average performers.

3. Competency models frequently include descriptions of how the competencies change or progress with employee level.

4. Competency models are usually directly linked to business objectives and strategies.

5. Competency models are typically developed top down (start with executives) rather than bottom up (start with line employees).

6. Competency models may consider future job requirements either directly or indirectly.

7. Competency models may be presented in a manner that facilitates ease of use (e.g., organization-specific language, pictures, or schematics that facilitate memorableness).

8. Usually, a finite number of competencies are identified and applied across multiple functions or job families.

9. Competency models are frequently used actively to align the HR systems.

10. Competency models are often an organizational development intervention that seeks broad organizational change as opposed to a simple data collection effort.

Source: Republished with permission of John Wiley & Sons, from Campion, M. A., Fink, A. A., Ruggeberg, B. J., Carr, L., Phillips, G. M., & Odman, R. B. (2011). Doing competencies well: Best practices in competency modeling. *Personnel Psychology, 64,* 225–262; permission conveyed through Copyright Clearance Center, Inc.

Because competency models—like job analyses—are used as the basis for other HR functions, it is important that they be carefully developed in order to be both accurate and legally defensible. For example, because competency models are used to capture a wide range of jobs across the company, it may be tempting to write competencies that are so broad as to be relatively useless. Strong competency models should be legally defensible (e.g., if they will be used as the basis for personnel selection decisions), include the right level of detail for the particular organization, and stay current over time as the organization, teams, and individual jobs evolve. HR practitioners and researchers have developed best practices in competency modeling, and these should be reviewed prior to undertaking the development of competency models. These include using rigorous job analysis methods to develop competencies, thinking of future organizational needs while creating the model, and linking the model to organizational goals and objectives.[28]

SPOTLIGHT ON GLOBAL ISSUES: BUILDING GLOBAL COMPETENCIES

Given the increased globalization of work in the 21st century, it is not surprising that global issues are increasingly recognized in job analysis and competency modeling. For example, SHRM's competency model places a value on global knowledge with its Global Mindset competency.

In addition, organizations that operate in multinational environments need to develop competency models that are flexible enough to function in multiple national contexts. The challenge is to create a competency model that balances national and cultural differences. Such international competency models are starting to emerge. For example, in 2022 the World Health Organization (WHO) published a competency model to provide standards for its health care personnel who operate across multiple cultural contexts worldwide. This competency model includes dimensions such as Communication, Collaboration, and Evidence-Informed Practice. With continued globalization, competency models that encompass a range of countries and cultures will become more common in the coming years.[29]

DESIGNING JOBS TO ENHANCE MOTIVATION, ATTITUDES, WELL-BEING, AND PERFORMANCE

LEARNING OBJECTIVE
5.4   Explain how job design can be used to increase employee motivation, job attitudes, and performance.

So far, our focus has been on how to analyze jobs to understand (a) what a worker does on the job and (b) the worker characteristics needed to do the job and to define these as objectively as possible. Thus, the point of job analysis and competency modeling is to have a deep understanding of what the job involves to form the basis for developing HR functions such as selection, pay, or training, among others. However, it is also important to consider how jobs can be designed to better fit with human needs. Such an approach has many benefits, such as reducing worker stress. In addition, employers need to consider **job design** in terms of how jobs are *experienced* by workers, regardless of the objective characteristics of the work. Designing or redesigning jobs based on how workers perceive and experience their work (e.g., stressful, boring, meaningful) is also important; it can affect worker motivation, job attitudes, and job performance. In this section, we examine some of the ways to design jobs for workers and the job characteristics that have been shown to be important in redesigning jobs. In addition, Chapter 15 will discuss how designing the physical aspects of jobs, such as from an ergonomic perspective, can help improve worker safety and health.

Before discussing approaches to designing jobs to address human needs, describing a few key concepts is in order. First, the concept of job enlargement involves the addition of more responsibilities to a job so it is less boring and more motivating for workers. This might include adding some challenges that can make the job more interesting or allow workers to gain more skills. For example, having a worker take on a new project that is different from the ones they have taken on before could be a form of job enlargement. Second, job enrichment involves allowing workers to have greater decision-making power. For example, a team of workers in a high-tech manufacturing firm might be allowed to manage themselves rather than only being managed by the supervisor or team leader. Although both job enlargement and job enrichment are considered important for reducing boredom and improving employee motivation and performance, it is important to keep in mind that not all employees will do well with enriched or enlarged jobs: Some employees may prefer not to take on additional responsibilities, while others may not perform well with such responsibilities. Finally, job rotation includes rotating employees from one job to another, not only making their work less boring but also allowing them to learn new skills.[30]

Job Design Considerations

In the early 20th century, the scientific management approach (see Chapter 1) advocated for the simplification of jobs, such that a single worker would be required to do the same simple, repetitive task. Following this principle, jobs were often designed in ways that ignored issues such as worker boredom and social needs. The Hawthorne studies were the first major break from this approach. Their findings showed the value of designing work in a way that was motivating and supportive to workers, taking into account that social processes, group norms, and work variety all play in work performance.

The Tavistock Mining Institute Studies, conducted in England in the mid-20th century, were an early illustration of actively redesigning jobs for actual people, who can become bored and need social interaction. These studies found that a highly "logical" redesign of coal mining jobs during World War II—with, for example, a decreased emphasis on the intact teams that had previously functioned to make this uncomfortable and dangerous work less stressful—had resulted in serious decreases in productivity. It was at that time the importance of job design from the worker's perspective was first shown in stark relief.

Developed in the 1960s, Hackman and Oldham's job characteristics model (JCM) was the first complete model of job design, explaining which characteristics are the most important to increasing worker motivation and productivity. Most of the subsequent job design models are largely based on it. Figure 5.6 shows the basics of the JCM and the process involved. The model proposes that enhancing the characteristics of the job leads to improved psychological states, which leads to improved individual and organizational outcomes. Specifically, the characteristics of *skill variety* (applying a range of skills on the job), *task identity* (completing a complete piece of work on the jobs), and *task significance* (doing work that is important, e.g., work that affects others) lead to experienced meaningfulness of work; *autonomy* (freedom in how the work gets done) leads to experienced responsibility; and *feedback* (the degree to which the job gives feedback about performance) leads to knowledge of results. These three psychological states— meaningfulness, responsibility, and knowledge of results—all in turn lead to improved outcomes such as higher motivation and better performance.

Later models of job design take a slightly different approach from the JCM, with a focus on understanding how workers' experiences might affect outcomes such as stress. The job demands-control model (JDC) emphasizes that employees experience stress when there are high job demands and little control over their job. In a more elaborated version of the JDC, the job demands-resources model (JDR) (see Figure 5.7) emphasizes that job demands, such as workload and time pressure, can be counteracted by characteristics such as job control, participation, and supervisor support.[31] In fact, research suggests that providing factors like supervisor support can improve employee motivation and even health.

In the early 21st century, Morgeson and Humphrey developed a more comprehensive model of job design, which takes into account the dimensions from previous job design models (see Figure 5.8). The

FIGURE 5.6 ■ Hackman and Oldham's Job Characteristics Model

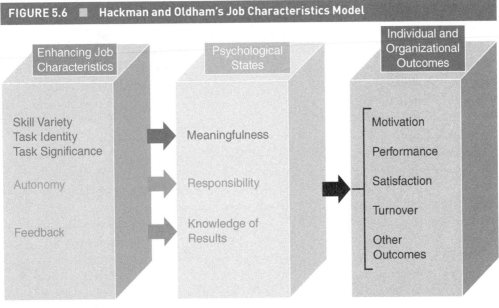

FIGURE 5.7 ■ The Job Demands-Resources Model (JDR)

Job Demands examples:

- Physical Workload
- Time Pressure
- Physical Environment
- Shift Work

Job Resources examples:

- Feedback
- Rewards
- Job Control
- Participation
- Job Security
- Supervisor Support

model includes 18 types of job characteristics falling into four broad categories: task characteristics, knowledge characteristics, social characteristics, and the work context (which includes physical aspects of the job). In other words, according to this model, there are a number of job characteristics that may be seen as "levers" available to organizational decision makers who want to enhance workers' jobs to increase motivation, satisfaction, and performance.[32]

FIGURE 5.8 ■ Morgeson and Humphrey's Comprehensive Job Design Model

Task Characteristics

- Autonomy
- Task Variety
- Task Significance
- Task Identity
- Feedback From the Job

Knowledge Characteristics

- Job Complexity
- Information Processing
- Problem Solving
- Skill Variety
- Specialization

Social Characteristics

- Social Support
- Interdependence
- Interaction Outside the Organization
- Feedback From Others

Work Context

- Ergonomics
- Physical Demands
- Work Conditions
- Equipment Use

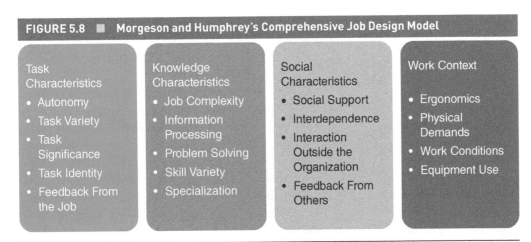

Source: Adapted from Morgeson, F. P., & Humphrey, S. E. (2006). The Work Design Questionnaire (WDQ): Developing and validating a comprehensive measure for assessing job design and the nature of work. *Journal of Applied Psychology*, 91, 1321–1399.

How Effective Are Job Design Considerations for Predicting Employee Outcomes?

Does improving the psychological characteristics of work actually pay off for organizations in terms of outcomes like job attitudes and performance? The research, as summarized in a large meta-analysis of 259 studies and more than 200,000 workers, suggests that it clearly does. For example, the experience of autonomy, task variety, and task significance among workers was positively related to increased job performance. Greater autonomy and task significance were negatively related to employee burnout. Increased support from coworkers was negatively related to intention to quit the job. Higher levels of most of the job characteristics were positively associated with greater job satisfaction.[33]

Interestingly, however, despite increases in the technological sophistication of work today, there continue to be many boring, repetitive, unenriched, and unmotivating jobs even in most developed economies.[34] Given the negative effects of such jobs, employers need to understand employees' experiences of their work. These experiences can be assessed through a range of methods, from sophisticated analytics to conversations and listening. Improving employees' experience of work through job redesign may provide a competitive edge for those organizations willing to make the investment.

Finally, it is important to know that some employees will value enriched jobs more than others; that is, enriching job characteristics may be beneficial to some employees but not to others. As one example, the age of the employee may determine which job characteristics employees want and need in their work. For instance, younger employees may especially need task variety, which allows them to gain the experience they need to advance in their careers. One study showed that increased autonomy led to increased job satisfaction and mental health of older construction workers compared to their younger counterparts. However, many other factors, such as the particular type of job and industry, likely play a role as well.[35]

Job Crafting

Most of the discussion in this section has been about how employees experience their work and what organizations can do to enhance this experience. In addition, workers themselves may redesign their own jobs to fit their needs and personalities, provided they stay within the guidelines of the organization. This process, known as **job crafting**, can lead to significant improvements in worker morale and performance.[36] For example, an employee may take on additional challenges in their job that make the job more fulfilling or help them get a skill they need to advance their career. You may have done some job crafting in your own work. Other employees may decide to job craft as they learn more efficient ways to do their job, or late-career employees may adapt their jobs to fit their changing needs.

In one early study of job crafting, researchers examined how cleaning crew workers in a hospital, a fairly low-skills job, experienced their work. In conducting interviews with these workers, the researchers found that some workers experienced their jobs to be rather boring and repetitive and without much meaning—just as you might expect. In contrast, other workers found their jobs to be quite meaningful. The difference was that these latter workers often performed tasks that were not in their original job descriptions, such as talking to patients. While the first group simply did their jobs as described, the latter group molded their jobs in ways that made their jobs more meaningful to them.[37] (You can see a short video describing this research here: https://youtu.be/C_igfnctYjA.)

Not surprisingly, the willingness and ability of workers to craft their jobs is associated with the personality characteristic of proactivity. This is because job crafting requires an active role on the part of workers.[38] A recent meta-analysis of more than 120 studies and 35,000 workers confirmed this, finding that more proactive and engaged employees reported more job crafting. In addition, job crafting seems to benefit the organization as well; for example, increasing challenging job demands among employees was found to be related to employee job performance.[39] Other studies have found that job crafting can lower employees' emotional exhaustion and improve safety behavior.[40] For job crafting to be successful, organizations need to give employees sufficient latitude to craft their jobs, and it is important to consider whether crafting by one employee might negatively affect other workers on their team.[41]

The willingness and ability to craft are not just a result of employee personality: Research suggests that job crafting is a skill that can be taught to employees. One recent study showed how training workers to craft their jobs around their personal strengths was especially useful to improving older workers' perceived fit with their jobs.[42] Crafting interventions may especially benefit some workers more than others, for example, workers with a high workload.[43] Research has also found that simple, low-intensity crafting interventions, such as just having workers reflect on their work, can be quite effective.[44]

FLEXIBLE WORK ARRANGEMENTS

LEARNING OBJECTIVE	
5.5	Describe how flexible work environments affect employee well-being.

There are other ways that organizations can design work to support employees. Many organizations offer flexible work arrangements to workers, with the goal of helping them to balance work and life needs. (We consider work–family issues in greater depth in Chapter 15.) One such work arrangement is flextime, in which workers can choose from a number of work schedules. For example, some workers in an organization may choose to work from 7:00 a.m. to 3:00 p.m., while others may choose to work from 9:00 a.m. to 5:00 p.m. Other examples include the possibility of working four 10-hour days each week. Some organizations allow workers to change their work schedules from day to day, while others require that workers choose a set time they are at work. Of course, many of these flexible work schedules are not suitable for all kinds of work. For example, medical personnel would need to ensure that hospitals are always sufficiently staffed.

Many organizations have now taken this idea of flexible work schedules a step further, implementing remote work. As discussed in the opening case, remote work (in the past sometimes called telecommuting) is a work arrangement in which an employee is not physically at an office or other location but instead works a substantial amount of time away from the office. For example, an employee might work from home and only come in to work 2 days per week (hybrid work), or they might work away from the office entirely. The idea is that such flexibility can allow workers to better manage their nonwork lives and save commuting time. This is the argument made by many workers who would like to continue to work remotely, as discussed in the opening case.

Although remote work and working from home were already on the rise, the Covid pandemic accelerated these changes. Whereas remote work had usually been done because a worker wanted it or requested it, many organizations mandated remote work during the pandemic.[45] This resulted in a different experience for different people (e.g., those with young children versus those without), with some people welcoming working from home and others finding it difficult. One study found those working from home during the pandemic experienced a number of challenges, including work and home activities interfering with each other and reduced communication with coworkers. Other workers reported procrastinating and feeling lonely. However, these negative effects were mitigated when workers had social support, job autonomy, and lower workload. The worker's self-discipline also made things easier.[46] Although the level of remote work has declined since the height of the pandemic, it remains at a much higher level than it had once been, with many workers less than willing to return to office work.[47]

One concern with remote work is that it can be hard to manage relationships at work, including the value of working face-to-face with collaborators for making real-time, data-based decisions. In fact, as noted in the opening case, while some companies (like Yelp and Airbnb) have gone completely remote or offer a completely remote option to employees, others are still trying to coax their employees to return to work or participate in some type of hybrid work (both in the office and at home.)[48] In short, although remote work has many advantages, it is not universally beneficial for all types of work. On the other hand, it can benefit certain employee groups.

Contingent Employees

Contingent employees are those who are hired for a limited, fixed term such as a short-term contract or a project consulting contract. The use of contingent employees has expanded, with some sources citing that 35% of U.S. workers hold contingent types of jobs.[49] The organizational benefits cited for the use of contingent workers include the flexibility of hiring workers with specific skills only when they are needed. In addition, organizations can deal with fluctuations in production, reduce the need for training (i.e., hiring employees who are already trained up on certain skills), and "try out" employees before making the commitment of hiring them permanently (temp-to-permanent).

The **gig economy** is a type of contingent work that links up workers with organizations, often using a digital platform. For instance, a company may need a team of programmers for a short-term project; it would not have the need to hire them permanently. Thus, it might hire a team of programmers from around the country or around the world to work on the project. Although the definition of gig work can vary, it is generally agreed that gig workers do not get salaries but work on a project basis and their work is temporary. There are different types of gig jobs in terms of how, where, and when the work is done.

Although there has been significant growth in contingent jobs, these work arrangements are not without their downsides to employees and to organizations. Gig-economy jobs have also been criticized because they leave workers vulnerable to job insecurity and wage theft. Contingent workers are also more likely than permanent workers to have lower pay, higher poverty rates, and decreased access to health insurance. Some types of gig jobs (e.g., ride-share workers) may be stressful for some people because their work is managed by an algorithm rather than a supervisor and involves constant ratings by customers. However, different workers may experience gig and temporary work differently. For example, a person who does gig work for extra money, someone who wants to gain needed work experience, and someone who is dependent on it for their main source of income may have very different experiences.

Some organizations argue that even the financial benefits of contingent workers are not completely clear and that hiring contingent workers does not necessarily lead to cost savings. For example, a simulation study on the cost-effectiveness of various contingent workforce strategies in organizations suggests that the use of workers from temporary agencies may be associated with decreased performance and increased turnover. In comparison, the use of independent contractors was more cost-effective, with the temp-to-permanent approach being the most cost-effective. In summary, it is important for organizations not to simply assume that the use of contingent workers is always cost-effective. Rather, they should carefully consider their particular circumstances, the different types of contingent work, as well as the advantages and disadvantages of using contingent workers for the workers themselves and for the organization. Further, with the expected growth in gig work in the coming years, research is needed on ways to assist workers in adapting to gig work.[50]

CHAPTER SUMMARY

Job analysis is the basis for most HR functions, including recruitment, selection, training, performance management, and pay. It is also used to develop job descriptions and job specifications. Methods used to collect job analysis data include interviews, observations, surveys, government data (the O*NET), and existing job analyses. Each of the various job analysis frameworks and approaches to analyzing work—such as task analysis, the critical incidents technique, and competency modeling—has its own unique advantages and disadvantages. Understanding how work is experienced from the employee's perspective in terms of motivation is also key to approaching the analysis and design of work as ways of increasing worker engagement, satisfaction, and performance. Flexible work arrangements such as flextime, remote work, and contingent work are increasingly common, although organizational decision makers should analyze their implementation carefully for their advantages and disadvantages.

KEY TERMS

Cognitive task analysis

Competency modeling

Contingent employees

Critical incidents technique

Criticality survey

Flextime

Gig economy

Job (Job classification)

Job analysis

Job characteristics model (JCM)

Job crafting

Job demands-control model (JDC)

Job demands-resources model (JDR)

Job descriptions

Job design

Job enlargement

Job enrichment

Job specifications

KSAOs

Linkage survey

Position

Remote work

Subject matter experts (SMEs)

Tasks

Work analysis

Work flow analysis

HR REASONING AND DECISION-MAKING EXERCISES

Mini-Case Analysis Exercise: Job Analysis and KSAO Ratings

The city of Jasper has conducted a job analysis of its firefighters. Specifically, the job being analyzed is a fire apparatus operator/driver (FAOD). FAODs are workers who, in addition to conducting direct firefighting activities, also drive the fire equipment and apparatus to the fire incident and have deep knowledge about operating the equipment.

Jasper has collected data from 35 FAODs and 10 of their supervisors, who served as subject matter experts (SMEs). The following table lists the means and standard deviations of the KSAO criticality ratings in terms of importance.

Means and Standard Deviations for the Criticality (Importance) Ratings of Each KSAO		
Fire Apparatus Operator/Driver (FAOD) KSAOs	**Mean (1–5 scale)**	**Standard Deviation**
A. Ability to work within a team	4.9	0.2
B. Mechanical ability	4.8	0.3
C. Upper body strength	4.5	0.3
D. Ability to read maps (both paper and online) and to memorize all city streets	3.8	1.2
E. Knowledge of fire equipment functions and capacity	4.8	0.1
F. Ability to supervise crew	3.2	1.3
G. Knowledge of fire-suppression principles related to residential buildings	3.6	1.1
H. Knowledge of fire-suppression principles related to commercial/high-rise buildings	4.8	.3
I. Critical thinking/decision making	4.7	.2

1. Based on your initial review of the mean criticality ratings for each KSAO, which KSAOs would you consider dropping from the job analysis? Explain why.

2. You know that a key role of this job is driving fire equipment (e.g., fire trucks) to the fire scene. But KSAO D has a fairly low mean and a high standard deviation. Why might this be? Rather than tossing out this KSAO, do you see any issue with the way the KSAO is currently written and how it might be edited?

3. You learn the city of Jasper collected most of the data for this job analysis from SMEs who are located in urban areas of the city rather than in the more suburban areas. Knowing this, would it affect any of your decisions about which KSAOs to remove from the job analysis? How might the city approach future data collections like this differently?

HR Decision Analysis Exercise: Strategic Issues in Choosing a Job Analysis Approach

You are currently working in the HR department of Sintra, Inc., a mid-sized health services provider, with approximately 500 health personnel (e.g., physicians, nurses) and more than 100 administrative staff. Sintra's focus is on providing urgent care in your state, with approximately 30 offices spread across urban, suburban, and rural areas.

Sintra is considering a change in the work flow of the services it provides; for example, it is toying with the idea of creating intact teams of health professionals to provide health services. As part of this work flow analysis, Sintra has examined its existing job analyses. For its health providers, there are essentially just two job descriptions, one for physician and one for nurse. However, Sintra's leadership realizes the need to do more specific, detailed job analyses for the individual specialty areas of its physicians and nurses so as to better understand what specific types of physicians and nurses do and thus to assemble the most effective teams. It is estimated that in reality, there are at least three specialty areas among the nurses and four among the physicians. This means that Sintra needs to plan to conduct at least seven job analyses to understand what its nurses and physicians actually do.

Not surprisingly, the nurses and physicians across Sintra are very interested in the results of these job analyses, as they will have a substantial effect on whom they work with and on the kind of care they are able to deliver to patients. They are dedicated to their jobs, and they want to be able to express their views about what they do on the job and how they can most effectively serve patients.

The vice president of HR, Margot Russy, has charged you with taking on the task of conducting these job analyses for these nurse and physician jobs. Consistent with what is described earlier, her goal is to develop a comprehensive competency model that will reflect the range of nurse and physician jobs in the company. She also sees the value of doing these job analyses well so as to assemble the best teams of health providers. However, she tells you that Sintra is under considerable financial pressure from its investors to do these job analyses as inexpensively as possible. Thus, she asks if you might simply use Sintra's largest clinic, located in the downtown of the major city in the state, to confirm the different job descriptions already in place and the interrelationships among the jobs. She also reasons this will allow the job analyses to happen quickly.

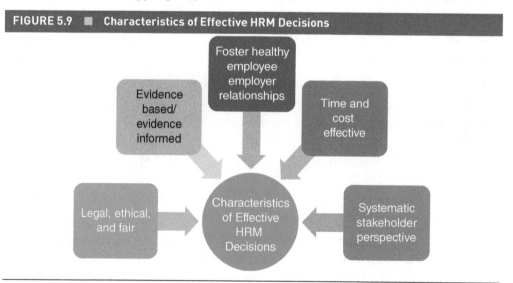

FIGURE 5.9 ■ Characteristics of Effective HRM Decisions

Please provide the rationale for your answer to each of the following questions.

Is the approach of the VP of human resources legal, ethical, and fair?

Is her approach evidence based/evidence informed?

Will her decision foster healthy employee–employer relationships?

Will her recommendations for how to approach these job analyses be time- and cost-effective?

Does she take a systematic stakeholder perspective?

Considering your analysis above, overall, what would be an effective decision? Why?

What, if anything, do you think should be done differently or considered to help make this decision more effective?

HR Decision-Making Exercise: Using O*NET

As discussed earlier in the chapter, O*NET was developed by the U.S. government to provide a general job analysis system to help employers to conduct their job and work analyses. Please go to the O*NET website at https://www.onetonline.org to answer the following questions.

1. Search for a job with which you are familiar. Were you able to find the job quickly, with the same job title you were using, or did O*NET use a slightly different job title? Or did it suggest multiple possible job titles? If so, why do you think this is?

2. Now look at the tasks, knowledge, skills, and abilities that O*NET notes as associated with that job. Do these match your impression of the job? Why might there be some differences between the job title you used and the job title in the O*NET database?

3. Sometimes no single O*NET job title captures the job for which you are searching. In your case, did it require piecing together the information from two or more jobs listed in the O*NET database to adequately describe the job you're looking for? If so, can you explain why this happened?

4. For most jobs you will search for, the O*NET job titles will not be a perfect fit for a particular job in a particular organization. More important, the content listed in the O*NET may not be a perfect match, either. Given these challenges, what do you see as the value to HR professionals using the O*NET when conducting job analyses?

DATA AND ANALYTICS EXERCISE: EVALUATING TASK–KSAO ANALYSIS DATA

When conducting a task–KSAO analysis, a list of tasks and KSAOs is generated for a particular job. To determine which tasks and KSAOs to retain, as well as which KSAOs are most important for performing each task, different questionnaires are administered to subject matter experts (SMEs), who rate the criticality (importance) of the tasks and KSAOs.

Two simple descriptive analytics—the *mean* and the *standard deviation (SD)*—can be used to determine which tasks and KSAOs are most critical, as well as the level of agreement of SMEs' ratings. First, a mean is a measure of central tendency. Assuming that ratings fall in a normal bell-shaped distribution, the mean represents the most central—or average—rating. In the context of a task–KSAO analysis, the mean rating for a particular task or KSAO represents its level of criticality. Thus, if a task or KSAO has a higher mean than another task or KSAO, it signifies it is more critical in the eyes of the SMEs. Second, a standard deviation is a measure of dispersion or variation. Assuming that ratings fall in a normal distribution, the SD represents how dispersed or spread out the ratings are around the mean. Thus, in the context of a task–KSAO analysis, a smaller SD indicates there is more agreement in SME ratings for a particular task or KSAO. Further, assuming a normal distribution of SME ratings, 68% of scores will fall between 1 SD below and above the mean rating, and 95% of scores fall within 2 SDs below and above the mean rating.

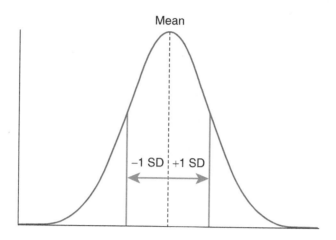

Excel software from Microsoft makes it easy to compute the mean and SD of a set of scores. To calculate the mean, use the =AVERAGE() function, and to calculate the SD, use the =STDEV.S() function. Within the parentheses of either function, simply enter the vector of scores for which you wish to calculate the mean or SD. For example, download the Excel spreadsheet containing subject matter expert (SME) data for task criticality ratings. Next, to calculate the mean and SD of the first task criticality ratings (i.e., 4, 3, 4, 4, 5, 2, 4, 5), you would enter the following in cells J2 and K2, respectively: =AVERAGE(B2:I2) and =STDEV.S(B2:I2). The mean is 3.88 and the SD is .99.

FIGURE 5.11 ■

Tasks	SME 1	SME 2	SME 3	SME 4	SME 5	SME 6	SME 7	SME 8	Mean	SD
1. Speaks with customers who are interested in new products.	4	3	4	4	5	2	4	5	3.88	.99
2. Works to solve customer complaints.	5	5	5	5	5	5	5	5		
3. Coordinates with supervisor to resolve customer problems.	4	4	5	4	4	4	5	4		
4. Stays abreast of current sales and specials provided by the company by checking company website.	2	1	3	4	2	2	5	1		
5. Uses telephone system to answer customer calls promptly.	3	3	4	3	4	3	4	4		
6. Uses computer to look up customer orders.	4	4	5	4	4	4	4	4		
7. Uses telephone system to notify customers about products received.	1	1	2	1	2	2	1	1		
8. Uses email system to notify customers about products received.	5	5	4	3	3	3	4	5		
9. Cleans office kitchen area when it is their turn to do so.	2	2	4	2	2	3	2	2		
10. Uses sit/stand desk correctly throughout the day to maintain own personal health.	4	3	4	4	4	5	3	4		
11. Provides customers with refunds, as appropriate, if there is any problem with the product.	1	1	1	1	1	1	1	1		

Excel Extension: Now You Try!

- Now, on **edge.sagepub.com/bauer2e**, using the same Excel spreadsheet, calculate the means and SDs for the remaining task criticality ratings. Once you have done so, respond to the following questions:
  - Which task had the highest mean? Which task had the lowest mean?
  - Which task had the highest SD? Which task had the lowest SD? What do these SDs indicate?

- Based on the means and SDs, which three tasks would you definitely retain? Which three tasks would you definitely remove? Why?

MANAGING THE
TALENT LIFE CYCLE

II

 # WORKFORCE PLANNING AND RECRUITMENT

CREATING A COLLEGE RECRUITMENT PIPELINE: THE CASE OF PWC[1]

©iStock.com/EyeOfPaul

PricewaterhouseCoopers (PwC) is one of the Big 4 accounting firms that, along with Deloitte, EY, and KPMG, handle 80% of auditing for all U.S. public companies. PwC provides tax, assurance, and advisory services to clients around the world and employs more than 328,000 people across 152 countries in hundreds of locations. In 2022, they provided services to 84% of the Global Fortune 500 companies. The work can be demanding. To ensure they have enough new employees each year, PwC recruits and hires regularly. For example, they hired 148,822 people in 2022. PwC focuses a great deal on its college relationships and recruiting from new college graduate programs. PwC has invested and continues to invest time, effort, and money toward these programs. Several of its recruitment activities are covered in this chapter. PwC hires thousands of employees each year via college campus recruiting programs and relationships and offers new college graduates $1,200 per year to help them pay off student debt. PwC has paid millions since launching its repayment benefit in 2016. Legally, firms are prohibited from asking about employees' personal debt, but nationally, a majority of college graduates have student loan debt of a little over $39,000 on average. Thus, this benefit has the potential to be highly attractive to college students weighing their options for employment after graduation.

PwC also offers Career*Advisor*, a website designed to help students assess their strengths and interests, maximize their resources to identify opportunities, prepare for the job search, and identify ways to present themselves to make the best impression. Career*Advisor* offers articles, videos, assessments, and tools to help students succeed in their new careers regardless of where they choose to go. It also introduced video interviewing to help busy students work around their schedules and classes. But PwC is also hoping that by offering innovative recruitment tools, its employment brand and reputation will be enhanced, which can help attract and hire the best candidates. Rod Adams, PwC's Talent Acquisition and Onboarding leader, noted that the use of video interviews helps to free up time during a site visit after an offer is made, creating a more enjoyable experience. In his words, "It becomes a sell visit instead of an interview. The benefit is candidate experience because [candidates] come into the office, they're not nervous because they already have an offer, and they can really just absorb our environment and what we have to offer them versus worrying about their interview."

Finally, one major source of new employees is internships that turn into job offers. According to PwC, 90% of its interns receive full-time job offers (compared to the U.S. average of 72%). To help students prepare for internships, PwC offers information regarding what students can expect including coaching and real-time development during internships. Its continued investment in its internship program has helped PwC earn the 8th spot on the 20 Most Prestigious Internships list for 2022, according to a survey by Vault.

Following are some job search tips from Alexa Merschel, a PwC recruiter, who has hired more than 500 people after reviewing 8,000 résumés and interviewing thousands of applicants:

- Keep your résumé short and up to date.
- Include volunteer experience.
- Include the name of the company to which you are applying in your résumé's "objective."
- Make sure your phone's voicemail greeting sounds professional.
- Create a profile on LinkedIn and make sure it is complete.
- Network widely.
- If interviewed, come prepared with stories illustrating your initiative and leadership skills, and be ready to answer specific questions about your accomplishments and leadership skills.

PwC is also working toward other strategic recruiting goals such as gamified training, which allows trainees to engage in work scenario role playing online. Further, PwC maintains a robust alumni network, which lets it cultivate future employees and stay in touch with former employees as potential clients and possible rehires.

CASE DISCUSSION QUESTIONS

1. Do you think PwC is offering the right mix of incentives to attract college graduates? Why or why not?

2. Are there other things PwC is not yet doing that you believe it should consider doing to attract college students and graduates?

3. Do you think the tips shared by Alexa Merschel, a PwC recruiter, would be helpful at other firms or in other industries? Why or why not?

4. PwC offers 90% of its interns full-time employment. What do you see as the pros and cons of this approach?

Read more about PwC's college student programs for recruitment for college freshmen, sophomores, juniors, seniors, and fifth-year students at http://www.pwc.com/us/en/careers/campus/programs-events.html

INTRODUCTION

This chapter discusses the basics of workforce planning and recruitment. Identifying, hiring, retaining, and supporting a strong workforce with the right qualifications is a key goal. In addition, by hiring employees diverse in terms of KSAOs (knowledge, skills, abilities, and other characteristics), gender, race, religion, age, sexual orientation, and physical abilities, employers can achieve better business results and, if done correctly, minimize the chances of costly lawsuits. As we learned in Chapter 4, having diverse employees and creating a culture of inclusion are good for business. Studying this chapter will give you the knowledge and tools to engage in effective recruitment.

UNDERSTANDING THE LABOR LANDSCAPE: WORKFORCE PLANNING AND FORECASTING

LEARNING OBJECTIVES
6.1   Describe workforce planning and its role in HR.

Chapter 2 discusses strategy and planning as important parts of effective human resource management (HRM). Workforce planning and forecasting are not exceptions to this. To survive in both good and tough times, organizations that successfully plan for future needs can navigate challenging times and avoid some of the labor-related surprises that are likely to occur over time (Figure 6.1). Engaging in the process of workforce planning can help eliminate surprises, smooth out business cycles, identify problems early, prevent problems, and take advantage of opportunities. Of course, no amount of planning can be 100% effective. However, as we will see in this chapter, planning and forecasting can help organizations avoid some obvious challenges out on the horizon. Plus, solving a talent problem that is years away from happening is much easier than trying to respond to one that is immediate as many organizations experienced during the global pandemic and subsequent Great Resignation. So what exactly is workforce planning, and how is it done?

FIGURE 6.1   ■   An Overview of Talent Flows and Staffing Processes

The recruitment process starts with building and planning and ends with a job offer being accepted. Understanding the potential labor pool is an important first step in the talent flow process.

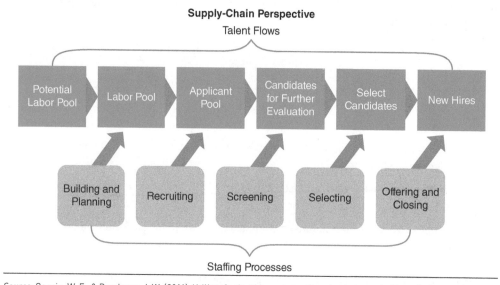

Source: Cascio, W. F., & Boudreau, J. W. (2011). Utility of selection systems: Supply-chain analysis applied to staffing decisions. In S. Zedeck (Ed.), *APA handbook of industrial and organizational psychology: Vol. 2. Selecting and developing members for the organization* (pp. 421–444). American Psychological Association.

Workforce Planning

Workforce planning refers to the process of determining what work needs to be done in both the short and the long term and coming up with a strategy regarding how those positions will be filled (Figure 6.2). Workforce planning is linked to strategic goals in many ways. For example, if the organization is considering entering a new industry sector, it will need to understand what skills are necessary to be successful in the new industry. For instance, when Future Mobility Corp (a Chinese start-up backed by Tencent Holdings) decided to enter the electric vehicle market, it needed new expertise. It decided to acquire expertise in this area by hiring the entire electric vehicle development team from BMW.[2] Whether this decision was effective remains to be seen, but it is an illustration of a strategic acquisition decision.

FIGURE 6.2 ■ Workforce Planning and Recruitment Process Steps

Each step of the planning process is important for long-term recruitment success.

Forecast → Set recruitment goals → Develop the recruitment process → Implement the recruitment process → Evaluate the recruitment process

This chapter is especially focused on the role of recruitment in workforce planning, and a key step in this process is forecasting. Forecasting refers to the act of determining estimates regarding what specific positions need to be filled and how to fill them. This analysis includes understanding internal and external talent supply and demand, labor costs, company growth rates, and revenue. The forecast can be as detailed or general as makes sense for the organization depending on how volatile or stable the organization, industry, or economy is at a given point in time. However, even positions that have historically been easy to fill can become challenging to fill over time as the workforce ages, unemployment rates decrease, or positions change in terms of how attractive they are to potential applicants.

The next step after engaging in a thorough forecast is to set recruitment-specific goals that are aligned with the organization's strategic plans. The overarching goal is to identify and attract qualified applicants while avoiding problems associated with labor shortages or surpluses. Many questions should be answered (Figure 6.3). For example, what skills are needed? How many of those skills exist already within the organization, and how many are new? What are the forecasted attrition rates during recruitment and selection as well as turnover rates, and how might they affect recruiting goals? The next step is to develop recruitment processes to achieve these goals. This is followed by implementation and, finally, evaluating the recruitment process for ways to improve it or alter it for the future.

FIGURE 6.3 ■ Sample Questions for Workforce Planning

Workforce planning requires asking and answering a lot of questions.

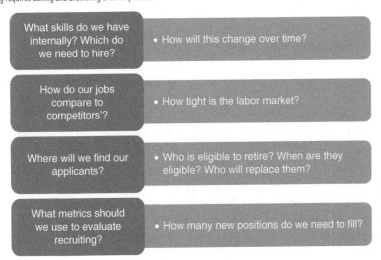

- What skills do we have internally? Which do we need to hire? • How will this change over time?
- How do our jobs compare to competitors'? • How tight is the labor market?
- Where will we find our applicants? • Who is eligible to retire? When are they eligible? Who will replace them?
- What metrics should we use to evaluate recruiting? • How many new positions do we need to fill?

Part II • Managing the Talent Life Cycle

Succession Planning and Leadership Development

Succession planning and leadership development are important parts of proactive and effective workforce management. Succession planning refers to the active forecasting of leadership needs and the strategies for filling them over time. Leadership development refers to the formal and informal opportunities for employees to expand their KSAOs. It is important to recognize that both recruitment and retention are tied to whether potential employees and existing employees perceive that there are developmental opportunities in the form of training and promotion. Thus, it is important to consider succession planning in terms of what KSAOs an employer will need, when they will need them, and how to develop employees so transitions in leadership occur smoothly. Doing so is part of effective workplace planning. At a minimum, organizations need replacement planning to identify a minimal plan of individuals to take over top leadership roles over time. Succession planning involves both the identification and training of individuals who might serve as replacements of top leaders within the organization. Finally, succession management refers to identifying and developing successors at all levels of the organization. Research shows that when it comes to technologies and HR functions, the use of analytics to support workforce and skill planning is an important area currently and it is expected to increase even more in the future.[3]

Labor Market Conditions

Labor market conditions refer to the number of jobs available compared to the number of individuals available with the required KSAOs to do those jobs. Earlier chapters referred to various Bureau of Labor Statistics (BLS) analyses, findings, and projections. The U.S. Department of Labor oversees the BLS, which is "the principal Federal agency responsible for measuring labor market activity, working conditions, and price changes in the economy. Its mission is to collect, analyze, and disseminate essential economic information to support public and private decision-making."[4] One of the important functions provided by this research arm of the Department of Labor is to help organizations understand labor market conditions, as this is a fundamental aspect of workforce planning and recruitment strategies.

Referring to the opening case, if a BLS report indicated that there are many qualified and interested applicants graduating from college every year without a lot of employment options, it would be less important for PwC to invest so heavily in its college relations and recruitment programs. However, if there is a lot of competition for a limited number of qualified graduates compared to the number PwC is seeking to employ, its college recruiting investment strategy makes sense.

Workforce Labor Shortages

Workforce characteristics may influence recruitment in various ways, including through labor shortages and surpluses. A workforce labor shortage refers to labor market conditions in which there are more jobs available than workers to fill them. When there is a labor shortage, there is a "tight labor market," with recruiters consistently reporting that finding skilled job candidates is harder. For example, organizations seeking to hire women in the computer sciences face serious recruiting efforts, as women accounted for only 20% of college graduates with this degree in 2022, down from 37% in 1984.[5]

A good example of this is projected within basic services fields. You may not reflect on all the steps the water you drink goes through before it comes out of your kitchen faucet. However, water treatment plant and system operators do. They monitor operating conditions, meters, and gauges, among several other things, at water treatment plants to make sure what you drink is safe. The job requires a high school diploma or equivalent and a license.

There is a need to replace retiring operators, with 10,800 new job openings expected by 2031. With that said, local and state governments around the United States are worried about whether they will be able to successfully fill water infrastructure positions, as a labor shortage is projected in this field. In fact, water treatment worker is one of the jobs most at risk in terms of not having enough qualified candidates, according to an employment report by the Conference Board. Websites seeking to attract applicants for the water treatment industry boast that such jobs require no college degree, offer good opportunities for advancement as well as great pay and benefits, are resistant to recessions, and provide the ability to benefit society.

Other basic services jobs also have challenges. For example, the electric power industry is plagued by staggering estimates of 30% to 40% of its entire 400,000-person workforce being eligible to retire. The nursing profession has similar issues, with job openings continuing to grow due to the aging population in the United States but new nurses not entering the profession quickly enough to keep up with demand. In 2022, the number of applications from younger generations dropped 49% from 2020 rates.[6]

Labor markets ebb and flow. In 2021, the Great Resignation saw 47 million workers quit their jobs. However, as noted by the U.S. Chamber of Commerce, it was more like the Great Reshuffle, with hiring rates outpacing quit rates since November 2022. It is important to keep in mind that although the overall employment rate is one indication of labor availability, there can be dramatic differences between jobs, industries, and even locations depending on the requirements of the jobs. For example, in 2022, durable goods manufacturing had a 50% labor shortage while professional and business services had a 70% shortage. Reports of police departments struggling to staff their ranks have led to signing bonuses and other ways to attract recruits.[7]

Workforce Labor Surpluses

Workforce labor surplus (slack) refers to labor market conditions in which there is more available labor than organizations need. Such a situation can result in high unemployment rates and make finding a job tough for individuals. This can be nationwide, or it can happen within specific regions or areas. For example, the logging industry was greatly curtailed in the Pacific Northwestern United States in the 1980s. Similarly, manufacturing jobs available have decreased in America's Midwestern states. Under such labor market conditions, the challenge becomes matching the skills needed to do the jobs with those in need of employment. Programs such as job retraining and educational reimbursements represent some ways that organizations, and at times the government, can seek to align skills in the local labor market more with local labor demands. Organizations facing a workforce labor surplus in their area or industry have an easier time finding employees to fill their positions. However, organizations must often compete for those with key skills.

Talent Analysis

A talent analysis refers to actively gathering data to determine potential talent gaps, or the difference between an organization's talent demand and its available talent supply (Figure 6.4). The talent supply, more often called a talent pool, is a group of individuals (employees or potential applicants) who possess the KSAOs to fill a particular role. As you can imagine, determining the needed KSAOs comes from job analysis information. Understanding the current and future talent needs is an important aspect of this analysis, as is understanding the current internal labor pool (those who already work for an organization) and future external labor pool (those who do not currently work

FIGURE 6.4 ■ Illustrating a Talent Analysis

By understanding potential talent gaps, organizations have a head start on managing them to avoid understaffing for key roles.

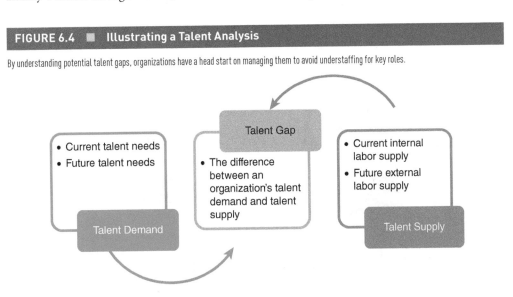

for an organization but who might be hired in the future). For example, Caesars Entertainment uses predictive workforce modeling techniques to predict and fill talent gaps before they develop. It considers several factors, such as business trends, associated workforce skill needs, internal workforce demographics such as skill populations, job levels, age and retirement eligibility, economic trends, and expected employee life cycles.[8]

One way that the talent pool can be increased is via immigrants to the United States. Data show that more than 28 million individuals who were born outside of the United States were legally employed here in 2021.[9] Thus, immigrants serve as a major talent supply if they possess skills that are in demand.

THE RECRUITING PROCESS

LEARNING OBJECTIVES
6.2   Identify what recruiting is and its key components.

Recruitment is the process of identifying and working to attract individuals interested in and capable of filling identified organizational roles. These individuals may be from either the external or internal labor markets. When it comes to recruitment, both quantity and quality matter. It is a mutual decision-making process on the part of both employers and individuals, with organizational representatives considering such factors as needs, costs, and timing and individuals considering factors such as their reactions to the recruitment process, location of the job, and organizational reputation.

Why Recruitment Matters

Effective recruitment is a critical aspect of organizational success. Reasons for this include innovation, firm performance, and organizational culture. Recruitment is one of the most impactful HR functions. As you may recall, HRM is defined as *the constellation of decisions and actions associated with managing individuals throughout the employee life cycle to maximize employee and organizational effectiveness in attaining goals.* Thus, recruitment is the start of the employee life cycle and the source of human capital within an organization, as illustrated in Figure 6.5.

FIGURE 6.5 ■   The Employee Life Cycle

The employee life cycle with an organization begins with recruitment. If an individual does not become part of the applicant pool, they will never join the organization.

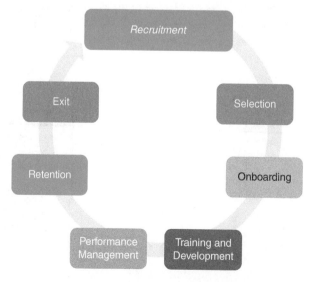

Recruitment Strategy

A recruitment strategy is the formalization of the recruitment process at a given organization. It includes recruitment objectives, strategy development, and recruitment activities, which may influence any of these factors.

Recruitment Objectives

Identifying recruitment objectives, or goals, at the start of the recruitment process sets the stage for the next steps. Objectives might include the number and qualifications and characteristics of applicants, time frame for recruitment, and how effective recruitment will be determined.

Strategy Development

There are many elements of a recruitment strategy, but overall, this is where needs are articulated, including whom to recruit, where to find them, how to reach them, who will interact with them, and what they will be offered to join the organization. Recruitment need refers to the results of the workforce planning process in terms of what KSAOs are needed within the organization as well as when they will be needed. Placement refers to two aspects of strategy development. First, where do we need the talent to be placed? Where in the organization are employees needed? Second, where will they be found? Will these be internal or external hires? Is the talent pool sufficient, or do steps need to be taken to develop the necessary talent?

Recruitment Activities

Recruitment activities include which methods will be used, what information about the job will be conveyed, and the details of the strategy developed in the previous step.[10] One opportunity to make recruitment more effective is to closely align the recruitment process to selection and onboarding. Many organizations focus so much time and attention on recruiting that they forget how important it is to have everyone on the same page regarding what the job entails, what is expected of new employees, and what they can expect when they enter the organization. Research shows that the more highly these are aligned, the more effectively new employees adjust to their jobs.[11]

The Role of Recruiters in the Recruitment Process

Recruiters are an important part of the recruitment process. In addition, a hiring manager is defined as the person who asked for the role to be filled and/or whom the new hire will be reporting to as their manager. Thus, recruiters and hiring managers are the gatekeepers of the hiring process and, in the best case, are working as partners during the recruitment process. The goal of the selection process is to obtain large pools of qualified applicants. However, recruiters and hiring managers can become inundated with large numbers of applications, overburdening hiring personnel with more applications than they can process. This can result in nonstrategic, suboptimal decision making as, in general, decisions made under tight timelines are more likely to result in little thought on the part of decision makers, and research has shown that placing increased information-processing burdens on decision makers allows biases to enter the decision-making process.

Further, recruitment decision makers need to feel confident that they can rely on the assessment solutions (e.g., employment tests, interviews) that they are using in the hiring process to help them find the best candidates possible. Thus, assessment solutions need to be valid predictors and legally defensible. In other words, recruiters need assessment systems that can provide large numbers of qualified applicants but that can effectively and efficiently determine who the best applicants are. Addressing these issues for recruiters will do much to increase the cost–benefit analysis of the hiring process.

Considering the role of recruiters is important to understanding organizational effectiveness at attracting talent. Overall, the job of recruiter is seen as a desirable one. Corporate recruiter has been listed as one of the 50 best jobs in the United States based on salary, job openings, job score, and job satisfaction ratings.[12] But recruiters are human, which means their effectiveness is subject to their strengths and weaknesses pertaining to their attitudes, decision making, and other behaviors. For example, have you ever wondered how the use of photos in social media affects the recruiting process?

Photos can send positive or negative signals to recruiters, 41% of whom say that seeing a picture of a job candidate before they meet in person influences their first impression.[13] Even more potentially damaging are photos focused on alcohol and a perception by a majority of recruiters that "oversharing" on social media sites counts against an applicant. Impressions do not end there. Researchers in Belgium studied the influence of attractive profile photos on Facebook and found that candidates with more attractive photos obtained 38% more job interview invitations than those with less attractive photos.[14] Recent recruiter surveys indicate that typos, drug use, body odor, and dressing too casually for interviews negatively impact hiring decisions.[15]

When it comes to interviews, factors that lead to favorable impressions include applicant enthusiasm, command of job requirements and skills, culture fit, and strong conversation skills.

©iStockphoto.com/fizkes

STAGES OF RECRUITMENT

LEARNING OBJECTIVES
6.3   Describe the three stages of recruitment and what takes place in them.

The stages of recruitment move through a **recruitment funnel** (see Figure 6.6) in which the number of participants gets smaller the further down the funnel the applicant goes. It is important to understand how critical this recruitment funnel is. This is because only those individuals who become applicants can ultimately be hired, and thus, the initial applicant yield ratio (how many ultimately hired compared to those who applied) is important. Thus, the goal is to get a large number of qualified applicants from which the employer can choose. Further, any applicants who remove themselves from the process cannot be selected, so keeping applicants' interest so they do not drop out is important. Thus, understanding this concept is helpful as we discuss the recruiting process.

At its most basic level, the idea behind the recruitment funnel is that the number of applicants needed at the start of the selection process is much larger than the ultimate number of hires made (see Figure 6.6). While every organization will identify its own ratios for success based on its workforce planning and actual number of hires per applicants, it is clear that as applicants move through the selection process and the best applicants are identified at each selection hurdle, fewer and fewer applicants are considered further. How wide or narrow the recruitment funnel is depends on the number of employees needed and the level of skills needed to perform the job. For example, when hiring a retail employee to help customers and ring up sales, there are often fewer requirements than when hiring a

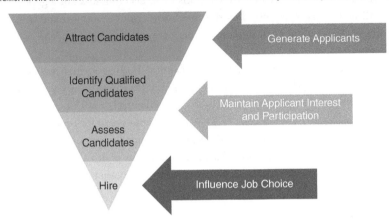

FIGURE 6.6 ■ The Recruitment Funnel in Relation to the Stages of Recruitment

The recruitment funnel narrows the number of candidates considered from the time of recruitment through hire, leaving the very best candidates to hire.

mechanic to fix cars. That is because retail employees can be more easily and quickly trained compared to mechanics, who take years to perfect their craft.

There are three fundamental stages of recruitment. The first is to identify and generate applicants, which is seen in Figure 6.6 in the first two parts of the recruitment funnel. The second stage focuses on maintaining applicant interest and participation as they continue through the assessment process. Thus, recruitment can really be thought of as a two-way process wherein the organization is trying both to assess and attract the best job applicants. Finally, the third stage is to influence job choice so that desired applicants are willing to accept offers made to them.

Generating Applicants

Generating applicants is an important first step to the recruitment process. It is one that has also garnered a great deal of well-deserved attention, as it represents a substantial investment of both time and money on the part of the recruiting organization. Generating applicants determines the talent pool that will be considered for positions within an organization. Following are some important considerations, starting with applicant quantity and quality.

Applicant Quantity and Quality

Although this chapter focuses on many aspects of recruitment, it is important to understand that there are two major goals within the first stage of the recruitment process. The first goal is quantity: Generating a sufficient number of applicants during the first stage of the recruitment process is important for several reasons, including that the effectiveness of the selection process depends upon having a large enough talent pool that has the skills needed to do the job and meets other strategic needs such as diversity and succession planning. We know that lower selection ratios—and thus how "choosy" the employer can be—are achieved by attracting large numbers of applicants. It is not clear, however, whether the relationship is causal. It may be that well-run and profitable organizations are more attractive than other organizations. Nonetheless, this does highlight the importance of having a sufficient number of applicants. The second goal is quality. Quality relates to applicants having the requisite skills needed as well as representing a diverse pool of applicants.

Realistic Job Previews

One important function of the recruitment process is to attract individuals to apply for jobs and be inclined to take a job if offered one. High turnover rates, however, can create recruitment challenges, as the organization needs to constantly recruit and hire new employees. Thus, an important consideration is to attract individuals to the job and organization while also being realistic enough that once they begin the job, they will not be disappointed and quit. One way in which organizations and researchers address these concerns is the realistic job preview (RJP), which offers potential applicants a realistic, and sometimes unappealing, view of the actual job.

For example, the Walt Disney Company shows job candidates a film depicting what it is like to work at Disney and outlines its employment policies and conditions. Some candidates self-select out of the recruitment process based on viewing this film, deciding it is not a good fit for them.[16] Research regarding RJPs has been mixed, with some studies finding support and others finding no appreciable differences between applicants who experience RJPs during recruitment and applicants who do not.[17]

One innovative example of an RJP is used by Zappos. It offers a financial incentive for new employees to quit after going through the training program, because it is only at that point that they can fully understand what the job would entail. Zappos effectively pays a new employee to quit if the employee doesn't feel they are a good fit. Specifically, Zappos paid for time invested in training, plus $4,000 if the person doesn't think it is the right position or company for them. About 2% to 3% of employees historically took the offer. Amazon adopted the policy after acquiring Zappos, but in 2022 they limited the payout to only those employees who graduated from their Career Choice Training program.[18]

When it comes to the labor market, it really depends on the industry and job sector one is in. For example, in 2023, while some industries such as the restaurant and service industries reported struggling to find employees, employees in the high-tech sector suffered from multiple layoffs with major companies such as Amazon, Google, Intel, and Meta all announcing reductions in the number of employees.

©iStockphoto.com/PixelsEffect

Recruitment Sources

Perhaps no single aspect of recruitment has received more time and attention than recruitment sources. Deciding exactly how to reach potential applicants is both a strategic and a financial decision. Recruitment sources can be divided into two main categories, passive recruitment and active recruitment (Figure 6.7).

Although research has been conducted around the globe in the hopes of identifying which recruitment sources are the most effective, what is effective for one organization may be less effective for another due to the differences in their recruitment strategies, brands, and industries. In addition, organizations may choose to focus on the recruitment of internal candidates, or they may look for talent outside of the organization. A SHRM survey found that 25% of organizations filled positions with current internal employees and 75% with external hires.[19] Table 6.1 summarizes some of the main types of recruitment sources used by organizations.

Unadvertised Jobs

Although the following sections outline both internal and external recruiting sources, another key recruitment source is word-of-mouth listings. Historically, about 50% of positions are filled via

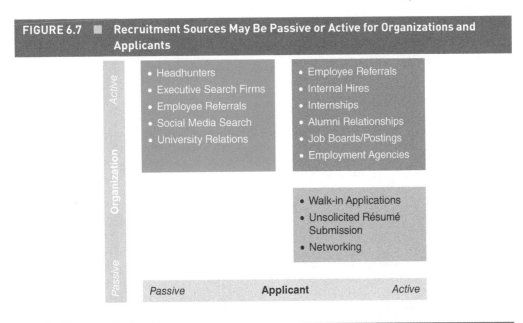

FIGURE 6.7 ■ Recruitment Sources May Be Passive or Active for Organizations and Applicants

TABLE 6.1 ■ General Recruitment Sources

Webpages
Unadvertised jobs
Job boards
Social networking sites

Internal sources
Internal transfers and promotions
Enlarge jobs for existing employees (e.g., longer hours, more responsibilities)
Alumni employees

External sources
Employee referrals
Search firms, agencies
University relations, internship programs
Freelance employees
Walk-ins
Competitors

informal channels and may never have been formally advertised or listed.[20] As a best practice, we recommend making a recruitment pool as large as possible; however, there may be times when informal channels yield unique talent acquisition opportunities for an organization. Thus, it is important to consider the pros and cons of hidden job listings and informal hiring, although very little research has been conducted in that regard. However, hiring those one knows can lead to lower diversity in terms of approaches and ideas, can be perceived by others as unfair, and might run afoul of federal guidelines, so reviewing recruitment processes regularly to ensure fairness in the process is important.

Internal Recruiting Sources

Succession planning is an important piece of workforce planning. Another benefit of recruiting for positions internally is that advancement and development opportunities can be attractive to current employees and, thus, help with retention. If you are able to redeploy talent throughout the organization rather than losing it, the organization is able to retain valuable organizational knowledge. However, estimates say that over 50% of job seekers overlook openings within their own companies.[21] Organizations such as SucceedSmart work to ensure that both internal and external job candidates are considered for positions by pairing technology with human expertise to ensure that the right candidates are considered for key positions within organizations.

SPOTLIGHT ON DATA AND ANALYTICS: RECRUITING AT CELANESE

Celanese is a Fortune 500 manufacturing company with over 7,500 employees across 42 countries. It has manufacturing and office locations in the United States, Europe, and Asia. Their recruitment needs are diverse as they hire nearly 1,000 new employees per year for positions ranging from plant-level operations to unique engineering and research and development positions. To attract the right applicants, the company decided it needed to change its approach to recruitment. In the past, it had traditionally recruited using an application that required a lot of information to be typed into online forms. To attract more digitally active candidates, the company was able to switch to maintaining the entire candidate life cycle from application through onboarding online. It was also able to customize these by region, including posting jobs in the local languages yet being able to have all data from around the world in a central location.

Because all the company's data are now housed within one system, the company is now able to create comparative metrics to help manage important functions such as efforts around diversity and hiring. In fact, the company was able to use these data to track where it was losing diverse candidates in the recruitment funnel. This helped generate insights to ensure that 93% of its hiring slates include diverse candidates (up from 77% in 2019).[22]

External Recruitment Sources

External recruitment refers to an employer's actions that are intended to bring a job opening to the attention of potential job candidates outside of the organization and, in turn, influence their intention to pursue the opportunity. A key aspect to external recruitment is to identify the most effective external recruitment sources. Types of sources include external services such as search firms, employment agencies, on-demand recruiting services, alumni employees, and military transition services, as well as job postings such as those in newspapers, on social media, and on career websites. In addition, as the opening case of PwC's college recruitment programs demonstrates, some organizations find that cultivating an employee pipeline to keep up with anticipated talent demands is useful. Thus, many attend college job fairs, work with college placement offices, and utilize internship programs. Another option is to consider non-U.S. citizens for hard-to-fill positions. This might include off-shoring or visa sponsorship issues. Each of these sources has potential benefits and drawbacks that should be considered as part of an organization's recruitment strategy.

Company Websites

For most organizations, their websites are a vital part of recruitment because it sends signals regarding what the organization is like and because it contains employment information. Public webpages may serve as recruitment sources for both internal and external applicants. Internal webpages, which are accessible only to current employees, are another important source.

Internal Transfers and Promotions

Organizations sometimes have challenges filling positions with internal candidates. To help address this problem, LinkedIn added a Learning Hub to its learning platform. While there, internal employees can see their employer's open jobs and work on setting goals and developing their own skills for potential job changes.[23] A key aspect of managing internal transfers and promotions is the use of an internal applicant tracking system (ATS), which offers a centralized way to house employee and applicant data in a single repository. This repository of data can then be linked with other HR information systems like that of retention and performance management to analyze the effectiveness of applicants from different recruitment sources, for example. It can also be used to track employee transfers and promotions over time. For a more detailed illustration of this, please see the Data and Analytics exercise at the end of this chapter.

Internal Job Boards

Internal job boards allow organizations to post available positions internally before the rest of the potential talent pool sees them. When internal candidates are given early consideration for positions, it can be good for morale and for mobility within the organization. In fact, some organizations invest a considerable amount to help existing employees find new opportunities within the organization because this may serve to help boost retention rates and retain top talent.

Alumni Employees

More and more organizations are considering rehiring former employees. This includes PwC, and this practice of employing "boomerang employees" who return to the organization is common in accounting and consulting firms. For National Basketball Association (NBA) players, for example, research revealed that for players who left a team and later returned, success was related to leaving on good terms initially, being successful while they were away, and the terms of their reemployment.[24] In general, research shows that rehires are less likely to quit and have an easier time onboarding back into the organization.[25] Following the Great Resignation has been the Great Regret, with up to 25% of those who quit their jobs expressing regret in doing so. This has led to more boomerang employees.[26] Organizations can cultivate effective alumni networks in several ways, including by creating a website with a directory of members, job boards, and information about networking events and professional development.[27] Microsoft traditionally has hired around 5% alumni employees each year. It launched the Microsoft Alumni Network in 1995, which currently has 48,000 members in 54 countries.[28]

Employee Referrals

An employee referral is a specific recruitment method that taps existing employees for potential applicant suggestions. Some firms, such as Google, pay existing employees a bonus for a successful referral. Other incentives might include a paid day off, gifts, or recognition at a staff meeting. Employers may give rewards immediately when referred employees are hired or after a set number of days of successful employment. They further work to ensure that current employees find the process pleasant by ensuring that referred individuals are contacted within 48 hours.[29] This can be an effective way to recruit, because existing employees understand the organizational culture and job demands and are in a good position to suggest potential candidates they feel would be successful.

To help ensure that referral programs are legal and do not result in unfair hiring practices, the Society for Human Resource Management (SHRM) recommends the following. SHRM also has an available online toolkit to help with designing referral programs.[30]

- *Reread legal recruitment guidelines.* This helps ensure you are not unintentionally creating a system that is inconsistent with existing laws.

- *Use a variety of recruiting methods when advertising job openings.* This will help keep the applicant pool more diverse.

- *Make employee referral programs open to the entire organization, not limiting them to specific employee groups, departments, or divisions.*

- *Evaluate all candidates—including employee-referred candidates—using the same qualification criteria.*

- *Conduct ongoing analyses of the workforce and the applicant pool to ensure the employee referral program is effective and is yielding the intended results.* Included in the analyses should be diversity categories, the quality of hire, and resulting tenure from referrals. If the program is not meeting its intended goals and is negatively affecting workforce diversity, you may need to reevaluate it.

Search Firms

Search firms are paid to find candidates and to help organizations fill roles. Executive search firms focus on the upper levels of an organization. Some organizations use search firms to fill all their positions. Others use them rarely. Some industries, such as higher education, tend to use search firms to generate candidates for key positions like university president, provost, or dean. Search firms can also be used to fill open positions quickly in areas in which the organization does not have an established recruitment process or brand. Regardless of who is responsible for the actual recruitment, it is imperative that positions are delineated so that job expectations and qualifications are clear and accurate. Not doing so can lead to higher levels of turnover and frustration for both those hired and organizations.

University Relationships

New college hires often originate from recruitment strategies aimed at leveraging university relationships such as targeting specific universities, attending university job fairs, and developing internship programs. Although in-person job fairs are prevalent, schools often host virtual job fairs so that a wider number of hiring organizations and students can attend at a lower cost. This is particularly important with the rise of remote work. Such relationships work for current students but can be effective for university alumni relations as well.

Internship Programs

Internships can be an important tool for both organizations and students. Research shows that students who have had internships almost double their chance of full-time job offers when they graduate.[31] This makes sense, as many interns are eventually offered full-time employment. Further, those who have had internships earn more than those who do not, have lower turnover, and are more likely to report that their college degrees helped prepare them for their careers.

Research shows organizations that want to hire interns tend to be more open to their creativity, which helps to attract interns who are interested in full-time jobs after graduation.[32] For organizations, interns are seen as an important and effective source of recruitment. And, as we saw with PwC, some organizations invest heavily in their internship programs. Table 6.2 lists some employers students are most interested in.

TABLE 6.2 ■ Which Organizations Are the Most Attractive to Business, Engineering, and IT Students?

Universum surveyed over 185,000 students to determine which employers they find most attractive. Here are the results for 2022:

1. Apple
2. Google
3. Microsoft
4. Amazon
5. L'Oréal Group
6. Deloitte
7. JPMorgan Chase & Company
8. Goldman Sachs
9. EY
10. KPMG

Source: World's most attractive employers 2022. https://poetsandquants.com/wp-content/uploads/sites/5/2022/11/WMAE_2022_report.pdf

Internships are also very successful recruitment tools for businesses. Resources for setting up internship programs can be found on the National Association of Colleges and Employers (NACE) website (https://www.naceweb.org/talent-acquisition/internships/15-best-practices-for-internship-programs/). Best practices include

- providing interns with meaningful work assignments,
- holding orientations,
- providing a handbook or relevant website for addressing rules and frequently asked questions, and
- conducting exit interviews at the end of the internship experience to learn how it went and ways to improve future internship experiences.

One thing to keep in mind is the legality of unpaid internships is questionable. Thus, it is important to be clear on the rules surrounding internships before launching a program.

Rosalind Brewer, CEO of Walgreens, started her career as an intern at a pharmaceutical company, which helped her get her first corporate job.

Paul Morigi/Stringer

External Job Boards

External job boards have made advertising jobs much easier than it was in the past. They have largely replaced the idea of placing help-wanted ads in the newspaper. Online job boards allow organizations to post for current and potential jobs, direct applicants where to apply, and provide specific information to help applicants narrow down potential positions via a number of search parameters such as location, job requirements, or pay. Types of job boards range from those with jobs in all categories such as Monster.com (one of the oldest job boards), Glassdoor.com, LinkedIn Job Search, Google for Jobs, ZipRecruiter, and Indeed.com to more specific job boards such as AllRetailJobs.com or www.truckerswanted.ca, the latter of which is specific to the trucking industry in North America and free for both drivers and companies to use. Globally, perhaps the largest job board is China's job51.com website, which reports having 81 million registered individuals, with 72 million résumés contained within its database.[33]

SPOTLIGHT ON ETHICS: APPLICANT INFORMATION PRIVACY

Job boards have become popular with organizations and job applicants. However, one major ethical concern has to do with information privacy. There are two considerations that seem especially important to consider.

First, who "owns" the data that applicants input into job board systems? Although online information privacy laws vary by country, with the European Union having stricter laws than the United States, the answer to this question is not clear. Imagine a scenario in which an online job board company tracks all your job application information and personal information and then sells this research about you. This is not as far-fetched as it sounds; there are documented accounts of job boards selling résumés and e-mail addresses.

A second concern is information security. Even if an organization does not plan to share your information with others, it is possible that cybercrime could lead to your information being stolen. For example, more than 1 million Monster.com subscribers had their information stolen. This is a serious concern, given how sensitive personal information such as Social Security numbers can be for identity theft. In response, Monster.com now allows users to make their résumés completely private so employers cannot search for you, but you can still search job listings and send out résumés and applications yourself.[34]

Questions

1. How would you discuss these ethical issues with the decision makers in your organization? Are there specific policies or practices you would recommend?
2. Beyond the issues described here, what other ethical questions might you ask about online job boards? Think of them from the perspective of the job applicant, the recruiting organization, the tech company that operates the board, and any other stakeholders.

Social Networking Sites

Each day, millions of people spend time on social media. These sites allow organizations to dramatically widen their reach when it comes to recruiting. Social networking sites such as Instagram, Twitter, Facebook, and Snapchat vary in the degree to which they have traditionally been considered recruitment sources. It is hard to ignore, however, the trend toward social networking sites being an important source for potential talent and networking. These sites are large and continue to add members. For example, LinkedIn reports having 810 million members.[35]

Using social media can help pinpoint specific skills and narrower needs. For example, PepsiCo shares job openings and responds to candidate questions on Twitter.[36] Nestlé holds virtual recruitment information sessions regularly. Marriott launched a promotional campaign to help staff 20,000 positions in its new hotels. Marriott found that videos featured on its website and a social game online allowing users to virtually manage their own restaurants as a way of exposing them to Marriott's coveted customer service principles were helpful.[37] Similarly, Domino's helped build positive brand awareness via the Domino's Pizza Mogul game, where users create and name their own ideas for pizzas with various toppings and for every item sold, they receive rewards.[38]

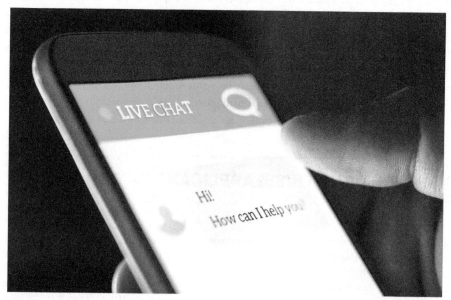

A recruitment chatbot is a virtual assistant powered by AI. Such chatbots can help answer questions, pre-screen applicants, and assist in scheduling interviews. Their use has been expanding and may be integrated via email, text, social media, and other messaging services.

©iStockphoto.com/Tero Vesalainen

Employment Agencies

Employment agencies vary a great deal in terms of the services they offer and roles they perform. For example, they might engage in roles such as information provider, matchmaker, or administrator. Employment agencies also provide employers with flexible workers. Staffing firms, also known as temporary employment agencies, can help organizations fulfill workforce needs and handle the administration of employees needed for only a short period of time. However, it is important to remember that those employers considering working with agencies should follow guidelines to ensure they work only with reputable firms, document any agreement with the agency with a written contract, and ensure the staffing agency controls all aspects of the working relationships such as setting hours, paying their employees, and complying with employment laws. Organizations should continue to work to make sure all employment decisions comply with all antidiscrimination and similar laws even for temporary workers hired by staffing firms.

Freelance Employees

The gig economy is growing every year. As more and more individuals are choosing freelance work as their primary form of employment or as side employment, gig workers have become a viable source for organizations to find desired skills. Although previous chapters describe the pros and cons associated with hiring freelance employees, it is becoming easier for employers to locate them using online marketplaces for work outsourcing. Sites such as Elance.com for business and engineering services, FlexJobs.com, Guru.com (which boasts millions of jobs and freelancers willing to do jobs), and GetAFreelancer.com help organizations locate the skills they need.

Walk-Ins

Traditionally, only a small number of new hires come from applicants applying in person at stores or facilities. With that said, depending upon the type of job, walk-ins may be an important form of recruitment source especially as restaurants and bars struggled with staffing during the global pandemic. The use of walk-ins as a recruitment source also depends a great deal on the industry. For example, in retail and hospitality sectors, walk-ins occur with greater frequency. Typically, individuals apply in person at local companies when seeking part-time work. The formula is simple: Organizations receptive to walk-ins should be prepared with job application forms. Depending on how strong the need is, some organizations give managers the freedom to interview prospective employees on the spot. One obvious and low-tech way to indicate that you are interested in walk-ins is to post a "help wanted" sign in the window of the business.

Hiring From Competitors

Another area of external sources of recruitment is other employers in the same industry and/or region. Competition among high-tech companies in the Silicon Valley has become so heated that pay and benefits have been driven up for new employees. This was a good situation for employees and job applicants but a costly one for companies. In 2017, the Walt Disney Company agreed to pay $100 million to end a "no-poaching" lawsuit, which claimed the company colluded with other animation studios in California to not hire each other's employees. In response to the suit, DreamWorks Animation paid $50 million and Blue Sky Studios paid $19 million to settle the case. In 2015, Apple, Google, Intel, and Adobe Systems Inc. paid $415 million in response to similar claims.[39]

SPOTLIGHT ON GLOBAL ISSUES: INTERNATIONAL HIRES

Global hires include employees who are able to secure company-sponsored H-1B visas. Organizations may employ non-U.S. employees by applying for and receiving H-1B visas. However, the number of such visas is determined by the government and varies from year to year. It is important to understand the laws associated with hiring non-U.S. workers within the United States. Websites such as the U.S. Department of Labor contain useful information (https://www.dol.gov/general/topic/hiring/foreign).

Offshoring refers to obtaining goods or services from a foreign supplier rather than from within the United States. A company may choose to offshore services to reduce costs or to improve an organization's focus on its core competencies. To avoid problems, organizations should align their strategies with decisions around offshoring. For example, offshoring call centers to a country with cheaper labor may save money, but if customers leave due to poor customer service, the organization may actually lose money. Years ago, when other organizations were outsourcing their call centers, JetBlue Airways made a strategic decision not to outsource its call centers. In contrast, some firms have effectively outsourced entire departments to other parts of the world.

RECRUITING FOR DIVERSITY

LEARNING OBJECTIVES
6.4 Explain the various aspects of diversity in recruiting.

Recruitment is covered by several laws designed to protect individuals from discrimination on the basis of their sex, race, age, or differential abilities. Laws such as Title VII of the Civil Rights Act, the Americans with Disabilities Act, and the Age Discrimination in Employment Act all serve to protect individuals. In addition to wanting to comply with legal requirements, organizations often also want to attract members of protected groups in order to leverage the positive aspects of having a more diverse workforce.[40]

One thing organizations can do to ensure stronger diversity within the organization is to treat their existing employees well and to invest in their career development once they are hired into the organization. If your organization does a reasonable job of attracting a diverse workforce but is not able to retain such individuals, it might be time to examine other factors such as the organization's culture and perceptions of how it is to work there from those on the front lines. It can also be illuminating to do an analysis of who is leaving to see if the numbers are equally distributed across different groups. For example, ride-sharing company Uber found out that ignoring such issues can lead to decreases in a diverse workforce as well as create a public relations problem, thereby affecting the bottom line.[41]

Gender Diversity

Some industries, such as the high-tech industry, have a challenging time recruiting and retaining women. There are many reasons for this. Research shows that women are less likely to engage in persistent job-search behaviors. This is consistent with findings regarding promotions within organizations such as Google, wherein it was found that women were less likely to put themselves up for promotions and less likely to persist if passed over the first time they applied.[42] Nevertheless, organizations can enact key activities to attract and retain women at all ranks of the organization, including the creation of a united front in which the message and behavior are clear regarding how women are to be treated within the organization. Other such activities include the spreading of a wide recruitment net, the development of a female-friendly benefits program, the serious treatment of sexual harassment and gender discrimination, and the placement of women in positions of power.[43]

Recruitment is a process in which unconscious biases of both applicants and organizational decision makers may play a role, limiting diversity. This is particularly challenging because it is unconscious, meaning that employers may not be aware of how their recruitment efforts are not attracting a wide range of applicants. Therefore, conscious effort may be needed to reverse the effects. Research has shown there are differences in how male- and female-dominated occupations advertise, with traditionally male-dominated occupations using words such as *competitive* and *dominant* in position descriptions. Textio is a Seattle-based start-up that develops software to get around this problem by analyzing the text of job postings to make postings attractive to a diverse pool of applicants.[44]

The recruitment of greater numbers of individuals for jobs with labor shortages such as nursing has led to the ongoing need for the recruitment of men as well as women. At this point, men represent only 12% of the 3.1 million nurses in the United States.[45] Thus, when it comes to gender diversity, the key is to give everyone access to the same positions for which they are qualified. It is important that applicants are able to pass key selection criteria such as the ability to lift a certain amount of weight or to drag heavy hoses in the case of firefighters if those tasks are job related. Diversity management is an ongoing process. These examples highlight the importance of considering diversity along a number of key dimensions.

Racial Diversity

Strategic ad placement can be an effective way to attract a more diverse applicant pool.[46] In addition to where ads are placed, the content of those ads may influence applicant attraction as well. Research found that Black or African American applicants were more attracted to organizations that emphasize a commitment to equal opportunity, access to training, and recruitment of applicants of color.[47] In addition, studies show that recruitment materials matter a great deal to applicants. For example, recruitment materials depicting employees of color have been found to attract Blacks or African Americans and Hispanic or Latinos without negatively affecting white applicants.[48] Further, when photos illustrated persons of color in supervisory roles, positive effects were even stronger.[49] An important consideration is to firmly align the recruitment message with the organizational reality. It makes no sense to recruit individuals with false promises of an organization that does not exist, because this results in an *un*realistic job preview. Further, doing so creates a costly situation for both individuals and organizations and can serve to undermine diversity recruitment and retention in the long run.

Age Diversity

Research shows there are few differences between the performance of older and younger workers. In fact, older workers are more likely to engage in organizational citizenship behaviors and have fewer unexcused absences.[50] In a study examining common age stereotypes, researchers found that across all available data, few of the older worker stereotypes are true: There was no evidence that older workers are less motivated, more resistant to change, less trusting, less healthy, or more vulnerable to work–family imbalance, although they may be less interested in training and career-development activities.[51] Additionally, given their extensive experience, older workers can be seen as bringing important human capital to an organization.[52] Thus, many companies are attracting more seasoned employees. For example, KinderCare Learning Centers, an organization that runs 1,500 child care locations across the United States, approached AARP (previously known as American Association of Retired Persons) in the hopes of recruiting older workers. And, major organizations such as Bank of America, Microsoft, and H&R Block have committed to AARP's pledge to hire more older workers.[53] Organizations would benefit from considering how the recruitment methods they utilize affect the diversity of their applicant pool. For example, the exclusive use of college recruiting programs may exclude older applicants and violate the Age Discrimination in Employment Act (ADEA). Similarly, using wording such as *new college graduate* and *digital native* may repel older applicants and may run afoul of the ADEA.[54] Further, recruiters play a key role, and they should be aware of their own biases against older applicants when making hiring decisions.

Older workers may be an important source of recruitment for organizations. During the Covid-19 pandemic, there was a surge in retirements, contributing to labor shortages. Pittsburgh-based Allegheny Health Network created a flexible schedule to entice retired nurses who were interested in working but not interested in going back to 8- or 12-hour shifts. The organization also offered job shadowing and retraining to help with reentry.[55]

Veterans

There are approximately 18 million military veterans in the United States.[56] Once service members leave active duty and enter the civilian job market, they represent another potential source of recruitment. Matching the KSAOs of military positions to civilian positions, however, can pose a challenge within civilian organizations, because the job titles, duties, and requirements may differ greatly. In fact, in a SHRM survey, 60% of respondents indicated they had experienced challenges related to the hiring of veterans for this very reason. Some companies see hiring veterans as an expression of goodwill.[57] Others see it as a win-win to close their talent gap.

For example, Raytheon Company hires thousands of engineers each year. As part of the U.S. Army's Partnership for Youth Success (PaYS) program, which connects new recruits with postservice jobs, Raytheon can hire qualified employees and get them security clearance, which is timely and can be expensive. Raytheon states, "Military professionals come to us with security clearances, and in many cases they've used our products, so they're familiar with the company and our processes. That's a big timesaver and cost-saver."[58]

The recruitment of veterans before and after they serve is an ongoing consideration for the military as well as civilian organizations. To recruit an additional 6,000 active-duty soldiers in 2017, the U.S. Army spent $300 million on bonuses and ads.[59]

©iStock.com/Steve Debenport

Several strategies for success when considering veterans as a recruitment source include

- understanding (and modifying as needed) beliefs about veterans,
- hiring and training knowledgeable decision makers to work on recruitment,
- increasing the organization's knowledge of military job-related tasks and KSAOs, and
- socializing veterans in the role requirements and norms of civilian organizations.

It is also important to consider retention when it comes to employing veterans. Work done as part of the SERVe (Study for Employment Retention of Veterans) grant funded by the Department of Defense found that supervisors can play a large role in retaining veterans by including emotional and instrumental support and engaging in role modeling creative work–family solution management.[60]

Differently Abled Individuals

The Americans with Disabilities Act (ADA) (1990) prohibits discrimination against a qualified applicant or employee with a disability. Determining who is qualified to perform the major functions of the job with or without accommodations is based on a job analysis. The ADA applies to organizations with 15 or more employees and defines a disability as a physical or mental impairment that affects one's major life functions. The key point to understand is that the ADA includes both applicants and employees, so it is in full force during recruitment efforts and, if requested, reasonable accommodations must be made in terms of all aspects of recruitment and selection. For example, an organization would need to make sure the recruitment methods it uses do not exclude applicants with disabilities as well as neurodiverse individuals.[61] If recruitment activities are conducted on a college campus or at a job fair, the location needs to be accessible. If online sources are used, it is important to ensure that applicants with visual and hearing impairments can complete the application process.

SPOTLIGHT ON LEGAL ISSUES: GENERAL GUIDELINES FOR RECRUITMENT

The information here should not be considered a substitute for legal advice. The application and impact of laws vary based on the specifics of the case, and laws may change over time. Thus, we encourage readers to seek out legal advice if unsure of the legality of specific programs or actions.

When it comes to recruitment, legal issues are an important consideration. As the EEOC's compliance manual says, "*Who* ultimately receives employment opportunities is highly dependent on how and where the employer looks for candidates." For instance, disparate racial impact occurs when a recruitment practice produces a significant difference in hiring for protected racial groups. It does not necessarily matter whether such differential impact is intentional—just that it occurred.

Here are some questions to ask about your recruiting practices to help avert or curtail potential problems. Ideally, you will be able to answer yes to the following:

- Do you have standardized recruiting practices?
- Have you ruled out that your recruiting practices indicate possible disparate impact?
- Can you provide evidence that each of your recruiting practices is consistent with business necessity and is job related?
- Are you casting a wide net in your recruiting sources by using a variety of sources accessible to everyone?
- Are recruiters and agencies you work with familiar with discrimination laws and how to comply with them?

A BROADER VIEW OF WORKFORCE PLANNING AND RECRUITMENT

LEARNING OBJECTIVES

6.5   Understand how to keep applicants interested in your organization.

Up to this point, this chapter has focused on various aspects of recruitment. Let's now consider some broader issues, including how to evaluate the effectiveness of recruitment efforts, how to keep applicants interested and motivated throughout the process, and how to choose the right job for the right applicant.

Recruitment Results: Evaluating Effectiveness and Metrics

When it comes to measuring the quality of their college hires, the energy corporation Chevron says it looks at ethnic and gender diversity, schools attended, campus interview assessment scores, total internships the employee has had, internships with Chevron, performance ratings, promotions, and turnover. As one of Chevron's recruiters says, "Being able to see what you're doing right and what needs attention is critical to the long-term health of your organization."[62] In their book *The Differentiated Workforce*, Brian Becker, Mark Huselid, and Richard Beatty suggest five principles when it comes to strategic workforce measures:

1. *Don't start with the measures.* While measures can be an important tool, they should not be the goal of strategic workforce planning and implementation.

2. *Don't rely on benchmarking.* By definition, benchmarking means matching what others do. Doing so will not generate competitive advantages to your organization.

3. *Don't expect measurement alone to fix problems.* While measurement can identify areas of strength and weakness in your recruitment processes, simply gathering the data is not enough to fix potential problems.

4. *Focus on the strategic impact of the workforce.* Not all individuals, teams, or divisions within an organization have the same impact on the organization's success on key goals. Focus on the places where it matters most.

5. *Measure both levels and relationships between workforce measures.* Some measures may go down when others go up. Understanding how they work together is important for getting a full picture of organizational functioning.

The key to implementing strategic recruitment is to think of these measures as a starting point rather than the goal. That is because such measures may serve to incentivize the wrong behaviors or mask important relationships with strategic implications. For example, time to hire and cost per hire are common metrics used in recruiting, and research shows a positive relationship between these metrics and firm performance. However, it is important to pay attention to the outcome of measuring behavior. For example, potential efforts to minimize measures might serve to encourage recruiters to engage in lowering how selective they are when choosing recruitment channels or actual applicants. A better idea would be to focus on other metrics such as the quality of hires. That could mask or create a problem. For example, if recruiters are given bonuses for hiring 20% of those who apply, they could increase their percentage by making offers to applicants with fewer alternatives. Although this could help them earn a bonus, it would hurt the organization overall because weaker employees are hired. All of these measures indicate the need for an effective tracking system to gather information. Adding new information such as new hire surveys is another way to tap into key metrics, such as new hire satisfaction levels. Similarly, the only way to address hiring manager satisfaction is to ask managers how they feel.

Manager's Toolbox: Common Recruitment Key Performance Indicator (KPI) Metrics

A variety of potential workforce metrics may be used to assess recruitment effectiveness. We list several of these metrics below within their recruitment stage.

Generating Applicants

- *Application completion rate percentage* (number of applicants who complete the application process/number of applicants who start the application process)

- *Qualified candidates* (those moving past the phone screen stage)

- *Source of hire* (tracking, surveys)

Maintaining Applicant Participation

- *Applicants per hire* (number of applicants hired/number of applicants who start the application process)

- *Candidate experience* (survey)

- *Time to hire* (number of days between when a person applies and accepts an offer)

- *Yield ratio* (number of applicants who move from one recruitment hurdle to the next)

Job Acceptance

- *Acceptance rate* (number of accepted offers/total number of offers)

- *Open vacancies versus positions filled*

- *Time to fill* (number of days a job is open)

After New Employee Organizational Entry

- *Cost per hire* ([internal costs + external costs]/number of hires)

- *Diversity* (qualitative and quantitative approaches)

- *Hiring manager satisfaction* (survey)

- *New hire satisfaction* (survey)

- *Performance* (track performance ratings)

- *Turnover/retention rate percentage* ([number of employees employed after 1 year/number of employees hired 1 year ago] × 100)

- *Quality of fill* refers to a combination of metrics, such as new employee satisfaction, performance, promotion, high potential ratings, and retention.

Maintaining Applicant Interest and Participation

A major consideration when it comes to the recruitment process and associated activities is maintaining applicant interest and participation.[63] If an applicant withdraws from the process or goes through the process without much enthusiasm for the organization and, ultimately, turns down a job offer, recruitment has not been effective. With this in mind, we cover some key factors related to the maintenance of applicant interest and participation.

Treatment During Recruitment

Research finds that recruiter behaviors (e.g., how personable, competent, and informative the recruiter is) matter. These behaviors are related to applicant perceptions of job attributes and how they feel about the organization and job, as well as the likelihood of accepting a job offer.[64] Timing and communication are fundamentally important factors when it comes to maintaining applicant interest and participation. Research shows that, overall, job applicants like to hear back quickly and have regular status updates. Not surprisingly, the *best* applicants have the most alternatives and are also the most likely to withdraw from the hiring process if they feel they are not being treated well.[65] Firms report greater success when they begin their recruiting process earlier. To help applicants understand where they stand in the recruitment process, Disney created a hiring dashboard through which applicants can track the status of their application.[66]

Interviews

There are two types of interviews to consider. The first is the informational interview, which is defined as the exchange of information with the goal of learning more about the organization and its industry. If you have ever had an informal discussion with a recruiter at a job fair or interviewed an organizational insider about their job, you have already been part of an informational interview. The purpose of such interviews is to begin the process of getting to know more about the organization and industry and potential career opportunities in general. Even though such interviews are informal, they may still serve to influence the reactions that applicants have to that organization. Imagine you are a supply and logistics student looking to find out more about the packaging and distribution industry. You reach out to three organizations, requesting an informational interview, but only one replies. You have a great time at the interview and learn a lot. Although you are not looking for a job right now, imagine if you would be more or less likely to pursue a job with the two companies that never got back to you versus the one that did.

The other type of interview is the selection interview, which is what we traditionally think of as a job interview; this type of interview is covered in detail in Chapter 7. Even though the selection interview puts the applicant "on the spot," it is also important to approach it as a two-way process. While the potential employee is being evaluated, this candidate is also gaining insights into what it would be like to work for the interviewing organization. And the organization is also still trying to attract the applicant to the job and the organization to increase the chances that the applicant accepts a potential offer. In these ways, selection interviews also serve a recruitment purpose.

Site Visits

One important part of the recruitment and selection process for both organizations and individuals is the site visit. On a site visit, the job applicant physically goes to the organization's location to meet with and be interviewed by its representatives. Site visits serve many important functions, including presenting a chance for applicants to meet key organizational members, compare their expectations to the realities encountered during the visit, and allow for them to have a more substantial set of interactions. Research shows that applicants report several benefits related to site visits, including opportunities to meet current employees, high-level organizational members, and those with similar backgrounds. In terms of site visit logistics, they report being positively influenced by being treated professionally, having a likeable site visit host, being housed in a quality hotel, and experiencing a well-orchestrated site visit.[67] With the rise in remote work, physical site visits have become less prevalent. This presents unique challenges that organizations must work to overcome. Companies like PwC and EY have begun using virtual reality (VR) technology to both assess job applicant skills and provide job applicants with tours of their facilities when they can't do so in person.[68]

Influencing Job Choice

As seen in the previous section on maintaining applicant interest and participation, poor treatment at any stage of the recruitment process can lead job applicants to withdraw. In addition, there are organizational and individual considerations that influence job choice (Figure 6.8).

FIGURE 6.8 ■ Job Choice Involves Weighing Features in Terms of Attractiveness

Many factors influence an individual's job choice as they weigh a number of pros and cons associated with a given job.

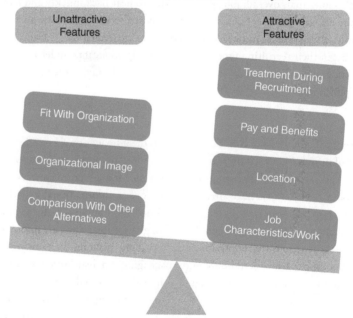

Organizational Image, Brand, and Reputation

NACE routinely surveys companies and finds that branding continues to be a key focus for university recruiting programs, and research supports the idea that organizational image affects applicants.[69] Slogans like "Work hard. Change the World," used at Amazon, help organizations signal important aspects of their culture. Being a well-regarded brand is a good problem to have, but it can make keeping up with the number of applications challenging. For example, Google receives millions of résumés each year. Worried that it might alienate its brand if it relied on algorithms to decide who makes the cut, Google modified its hiring process to ensure that human eyes look at every one of those millions of résumés.[70] And the importance of maintaining a company's brand is likely to continue. For example, the Conference Board surveyed CEOs and asked them to identify key challenges they anticipated in the coming years. At the top of the list was a need to use decision-making tools like data analytics to understand what is attractive about their brands and social media that reinforces a positive brand image.[71] Social media can also present opportunities and challenges for employment brands. The Twitter account of the Wendy's fast food chain got a great deal of attention based on online exchanges. In fact, the team who manages this account even has a publicist.[72] Research has shown that word-of-mouth opinions regarding the hiring process affect whether or not an applicant will choose a job.[73]

Organizational Fit

Research shows that applicants who highly identify with an organization are more likely to pursue jobs and to accept them if offered.[74] Organizational cultures vary a great deal, and they are not equally attractive to everyone. For example, someone attracted to a clan culture (e.g., Costco or Southwest Airlines) might be less attracted to a hierarchical culture (e.g., Walmart or Boeing). Research has found that specific values, such as an organization's social and environmental responsibility, are related to how attractive the company is to job applicants. Thus, organizational fit is another feature that job candidates consider when deciding whether to accept a job.[75]

Job Features

Pay and benefits are also important considerations for decision makers. For instance, when asked how important a significant increase in income or benefits was, 64% said "very important" in a Gallup survey. In fact, the importance of pay has risen from 41% saying very important in 2015 to it being the number-one factor in 2022. Other important aspects are greater work–life balance and better personal well-being, the ability to do what they do best, and greater stability and job security.[76] In addition to financial aspects of employment, the actual work that will be done and how it will be done (or job characteristics) also can serve to influence decision makers. In general, people tend to prefer work that affords them autonomy, is seen as meaningful, and allows them to receive feedback.

Alternative Offers

Finally, the process of individual decision making involves comparing potential alternatives. If a job candidate has multiple offers, they may simply decide that one offer is more attractive overall than another one. The best applicants tend to have the most job alternatives. Thus, organizations wanting to hire such individuals should consider putting their best offer forward as much as it can to attract these people.

CHAPTER SUMMARY

Understanding the labor landscape makes it possible to follow the steps in the workplace planning and forecasting process, including succession planning, leadership development, assessing labor market conditions, and talent analysis. Effective recruitment begins with setting objectives in order to develop a strategy. Its advantages for organizations range from increased hiring success to higher firm performance to the ability to attract a diverse set of applicants. Recruitment stages include generating applicants, assessing the quantity and quality of applicants, and accessing sources of recruitment—both internal and external. Hiring for diversity means attending to multiple kinds of diversity, including gender, race, age, veteran status, and differently abled individuals. In the process of recruitment, organizations need to comply with various laws and policies. Organizations strive to maintain applicant interest and participation so that the best applicants accept job offers. Global considerations also come into play in attracting talent. Measuring effective recruitment using metrics and analytics is also an important part of recruitment.

KEY TERMS

Applicant tracking system (ATS)

External recruitment

Forecasting

Hiring manager

Informational interview

Labor market conditions

Leadership development

Placement

Realistic job preview (RJP)

Recruitment

Recruitment funnel

Recruitment needs

Replacement planning

Site visit

Succession management

Succession planning

Talent analysis

Talent pool

Workforce labor shortages

Workforce labor surplus (or slack)

Workforce planning

HR REASONING AND DECISION-MAKING EXERCISES

Mini-Case Analysis Exercise: Employee Turnover Rate

You have been with your large high-tech organization for 3 years, having joined right after earning your college degree in business. You enjoy working in human resource management on the recruitment side of things. Lately, however, you have noticed that even though you are doing a good job at attracting applicants—you are able to keep them interested in the selection process and have established a strong acceptance rate among applicants—there is a problem. The turnover rate for employees within 18 months of being hired is 34%. Although that isn't the highest rate in the industry, it certainly is higher than you'd like to see, and it is higher than it used to be.

You have done some initial analyses and determined that part of the issue seems to be that recruiters tell potential employees things to attract them to the organization, but the reality once they join is quite different. Especially for top performers, other options at other organizations quickly become attractive.

You have spoken with your boss, the VP of HR, and she has authorized you to create a task force to investigate the issue further and develop a strategy to solve the root causes of the problem. She suspects that the turnover rate is a symptom of bigger problems rather than the main problem.

1. Whom do you think you need to involve in this decision? Why?

2. How should you begin to tackle this problem in terms of your approach and sources of information?

3. What data should you gather?

4. Are there experiments you might do to test potential causes and to identify different solutions?

HR Decision Analysis Exercise: Fairness of University Relations and Alumni Support

Imagine you are working as a college recruiter for your firm. As part of your job, you have a strong working relationship with the director of career services of one key university. The director's name is Les Sharp. Last week Les suggested that if your company was willing to donate to his university's fundraising campaign, he would be sure to channel the best students to interview with your organization before any other firms. It is tempting to consider this, because the competition for top talent from this school is fierce, and your company has been pressuring you to increase both the quantity and quality of interns and hires from this school. In fact, your job may depend on it.

Should you make this deal? Consider this decision using the established criteria.

Please provide the rationale for your answer to each of the following questions.

Is this deal legal, ethical, and fair?

Is this deal evidence based/evidence informed?

FIGURE 6.9 ■ Characteristics of Effective HRM Decisions

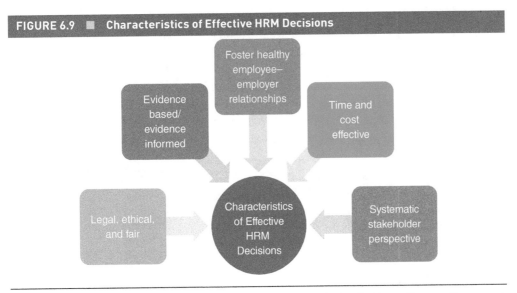

Does this deal foster healthy employee–employer relationships?

Is this deal time- and cost-effective?

Does this deal take a systematic stakeholder perspective?

Considering your analysis above, overall, was your decision effective? Why or why not?

What, if anything, do you think should be done differently or considered to help make this decision more effective?

HR Decision-Making Exercise: Recruitment and Beyond

Imagine you and a small team of two to five colleagues are working with a medium-sized retail company that is expanding internationally. Although the headquarters will remain in Columbus, Ohio, the firm is opening a second office in Japan. They want to know what your team recommends in terms of recruiting for this new 30-person office. Your team's job is to decide how to handle recruiting in the short term and the long term.

1. Should your company hire locally, hire expatriate employees, use a search firm, start developing a college recruiting program in Japan, or use a different recruiting approach? Explain the advantages and disadvantages of each of these approaches.

2. What additional information would help your team decide?

3. Where will your team begin its recruitment efforts?

DATA AND ANALYTICS EXERCISE: THE TRANSITION MATRIX AND EVALUATING MOVEMENT INTO, THROUGH, AND OUT OF AN ORGANIZATION

Understanding how employees move into, through, and out of different jobs in an organization is important for planning and staffing purposes. The transition matrix—also known as a Markov matrix—is a useful tool for examining such patterns of movement. As shown in what follows, a transition matrix communicates the number of employees or the proportion of employees who began in one job in one time period and who ended up in other jobs in the organization or even left the organization by another time period. First, take a look at the transition matrix with raw numbers, wherein the numbers represent employees. If read from left to right across a given row, the sum of the row values represents total number of employees who had a particular job title in the earlier time period. For example, a total of 15 (14 + 1) employees held the Research Scientist job title in 2021. Further, each row indicates where employees ended up in terms of their job titles at the later time period. For example, 14 out of the 15 Research Scientists from 2021 were still Research Scientists at 2024, and 1 out of 15 Research Scientists from 2021 exited the organization by 2024. Alternatively, if read from top to bottom by a given column, the sum of each overall column total represents how many employees held a given job title in 2024. For example, 20 (14 + 5 +1) employees held the job title of a Research Scientist in 2024. Further, 14 of those 20 individuals were also Research Scientists in 2021, 5 were Research Associates in 2021 but are now Research Scientists, and 1 was not in the organization in 2021 but is now a Research Scientist. Accordingly, a transition matrix comprised of raw numbers provides an indication of the number of employees who entered, moved within, and exited the organization, as well as which positions they held during their time in the organization.

Transition Matrix With Raw Numbers					
		2024			
		Research Scientist	Research Associate	Research Assistant	Not in Organization
2021	Research Scientist	14			1
	Research Associate	5	26		4
	Research Assistant		11	43	2
	Not in Organization	1	2	12	

Second, take a look at the transition matrix with proportions, wherein the values represent the proportion of employees from the earlier time period who hold various jobs at the later time period. The transition matrix with proportions is constructed to be read from left to right across a given row, as the sum of each row's proportions totals to 1.0. Further, each row indicates the proportion of employees from an earlier time period who ended up in the same or different jobs (or even out of the organization) by a later time period. For example, .93 (or 93%) of individuals who held the job title of Research Scientist in 2021 continued to hold the title of Research Scientist in 2024, whereas .07 (7%) of individuals who held the job title of Research Scientist in 2021 left the organization by 2024.

Transition Matrix With Proportions					
		2024			
		Research Scientist	Research Associate	Research Assistant	Not in Organization
2021	Research Scientist	.93			.07
	Research Associate	.14	.74		.10
	Research Assistant		.20	.77	.03
	Not in Organization	.06	.14	.80	

The transition matrix can be a useful descriptive analytics tool, as it can be used to describe the way in which employees have moved into, through, and out of the organization in the past. In addition, a transition matrix can serve as the basis for a predictive analytics tool called Markov chain analysis—an approach that can provide estimates for how employees will move into, through, and out of the organization in the future.

Excel Extension: Now You Try!

- On **edge.sagepub.com/bauer2e**, you will find an Excel spreadsheet containing the raw data for this exercise. You will complete this exercise using that Excel spreadsheet.

- Also on the textbook companion website, you will find a PDF tutorial document that explains step by step how to create a transition matrix with raw numbers and with proportions in Excel using the raw data.

©iStockphoto.com/Serp77

7 SELECTION PROCESSES AND PROCEDURES

OVERCOMING DISCRIMINATION IN AI-ASSISTED HIRING: THE DATA AND TRUST ALLIANCE

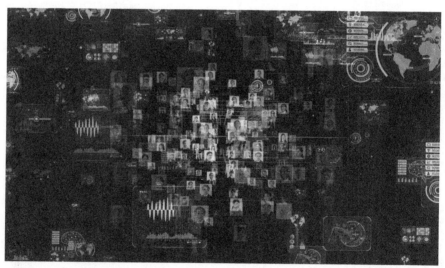

©iStockphoto.com/metamorworks

Over the past several years, the use of artificial intelligence (AI) in hiring has increased rapidly. AI can save time and costs by taking on a number of time-consuming tasks that were in the past done by HR employees. For example, AI can scan thousands of résumés to see which candidates may have the best fit for a given job. And increasingly, AI can be used to assess performance in a hiring interview, reducing the need for face-to-face interactions; this was particularly attractive to some organizations during the Covid-19 pandemic.

One of the early hopes of using AI in hiring was that it would lead to better hiring decisions. In addition, it was thought that AI would avoid human biases; that is, it would lead to more fair, less discriminatory hiring decisions than would be made by human decision makers. However, many employers and job applicants quickly realized this was not necessarily the case. In fact, the use of AI in hiring may actually result in discriminatory decisions.

How can a nonhuman algorithm be biased? There are several ways that bias can creep into an algorithm. Consider the fact that algorithms make decisions based on existing data. So, if existing datasets of job applicants include only men, the algorithm may not have a sufficient basis for good hiring decisions regarding women. As a second example, if past hiring decisions were biased in favor of or male candidates, the algorithm will use the existing data to replicate these decisions. In fact, AI may amplify these biased decisions from the past because of the large volume of decisions that AI typically makes!

These concerns have not gone unnoticed by government regulators. For example, in 2022, the White House released an AI Bill of Rights to guide employers. In addition, the Equal Employment Opportunity Commission (EEOC) released guidelines on the use of AI as it pertains to discrimination against people with disabilities. However, even stronger legal limits may be imposed by the European Union, which is on course to pass the Artificial Intelligence Act. This act covers how organizations can use AI in hiring, and it is expected to affect organizations worldwide.

Given the legal and ethical challenges of using AI to help with hiring decisions, organizations have been pressed to use AI more fairly. To do so, a group of businesses has created a consortium, the Data and Trust Alliance, to help employers use AI effectively and fairly. Developed in 2020, the alliance includes a wide range of industries, and its members include organizations such as Deloitte, General Motors, Meta, Nike, and Walmart. The alliance relies on the expertise of hundreds of experts from over 15 industries and from academia and government. It also includes input from vendors who sell AI expertise to companies.

Based on the assumption that AI is becoming part of organizational decision making and that employers need some standard guidelines for navigating AI-assisted HR decisions such as hiring, the Data and Trust Alliance provides support for employers in using AI ethically. These supports include their "Algorithmic Bias Safeguards for Workforce" to help HR employees in companies evaluate AI vendors. Vendors are evaluated on a number of criteria. To do this, the alliance provides a series of questions for employers to ask potential AI vendors. These questions ask vendors to explain how bias is minimized when developing the AI models to be used for HR decision making, how bias will be detected in the AI algorithm, and how bias will be monitored over time when the AI is actually being used to make decisions in the organization. The alliance can also help companies' HR personnel evaluate and compare vendor responses through a scorecard.

While these industry efforts are promising, there are similar efforts being taken by others. For example, the Responsible AI Institute is a nonprofit that is developing a separate system for certifying AI services. It also has the backing of several corporations and academic institutions.[1]

CASE DISCUSSION QUESTIONS

1. What do you see as the value of a consortium approach, such as the Data and Trust Alliance, for dealing with biased hiring decisions as opposed to individual organizations undertaking this on their own?

2. With the Data and Trust Alliance in place, do you see a continued role for government oversight and regulations? What about separate nonprofits like the Responsible AI Institute? Are there other ways you can think of to provide oversight in the use of AI to make unbiased hiring decisions?

3. Choose two of the organizations listed in the case. What types of hiring procedures would they use, and what types of bias would creep in as a result? Consider the characteristics of both the company and the industry.

4. What do you see as the advantages and disadvantages of decisions made by AI versus by human decision makers in terms of accuracy and the introduction of bias? In your view, which is more likely to lead to discriminatory decisions, and in what ways?

INTRODUCTION

People are arguably an organization's most precious resources. Luckily, we know how to choose the employees that best fit the job and the organization and how to do so in a fair, legally defensible way that aligns with an organization's strategy. This chapter reviews the science of employee selection, including data analytic techniques for enhancing the quality of hiring decisions. It also discusses the wide variety of selection procedures that are available to support hiring decisions and talent acquisition.

An underlying premise of this text is that the employees make the organization. One current trend is that fair hiring practices and a strong candidate experience are becoming ever more critical to hire the best talent.[2] Strong selection systems bring talented individuals into the organization, who in turn can help the organization realize strategic objectives.[3] Chapter 6 discusses how to recruit so that an employer can choose among the best job applicants. Let's say a company has 100 openings and is able to recruit 1,000 people to apply for that job. This would be a good problem to have. But then the next step is to address an important question: how to select the *best* 100 applicants and to do it in a way that is ethical and legal.

There are many choices when it comes to selection methods, including personality tests, background checks, and interviews. But how useful is each of these methods, and which are the best? What are the ethical and legal issues surrounding the use of these methods, and what legal issues need to be addressed? How are data involved in making effective hiring decisions? To answer that question, we begin by reviewing some issues from previous chapters—strategy, job analysis, recruitment, legal issues, and diversity—to tie each of these topics to their relevance in areas of personnel selection.

SETTING THE STAGE FOR SELECTION: JOB ANALYSIS, RECRUITMENT, AND LEGAL ISSUES

LEARNING OBJECTIVES

7.1   Explain how job analysis and legal issues apply to recruitment and selection.

By aligning employee selection with strategic objectives, an organization ensures that it will acquire the *right* talent to meet its unique needs and demands, which moves the organization in the right strategic direction. To achieve success, an organization requires selection systems that are aligned with organizational strategy. This is best considered in the use of effective recruitment strategies to attract the best talent (see Chapter 6) and identifying the needs of the job as it fits into the larger work unit and organization—all staying within legal and ethical guidelines.

Job Analysis

As noted in Chapter 5, job or work analysis and its cousin competency modeling involve the identification of the tasks that make up a job and the KSAOs (knowledge, skills, abilities, and other characteristics) that are required for the job. Job analysis is important for choosing selection procedures, because different selection procedures capture certain KSAOs more effectively. For instance, an integrity test—developed to assess applicant honesty—will generally be a better screener for honesty than will reviewing a résumé. To give a simple example, if a product-design job required engineering skills and teamwork, you would want to use hiring procedures that reflect these requirements. You might consider a personality test that reflects a person's abilities to work well as part of a team, and you might include engineering and teamwork questions in the job interview. Although this example shows that basing selection procedures on a job analysis are in many ways common sense, it is important to keep in mind that some sort of job analysis is also legally required for selection procedures, and it is also recommended by professional guidelines.[4] As shown in the opening case, the use of analytics to understand how job candidates' profiles fit their needs has taken off across industries. The trick is to do it fairly and accurately.

Using Recruitment to Enhance Hiring Decisions

Chapter 6 discussed recruitment as a way to increase the odds of hiring the best employees. (As a reminder, see the recruitment and selection funnel in Figure 7.1.) First, we want to increase the *size* of the applicant pool to increase the odds of selecting the best employees. For example, all things being equal, the ability to choose from among 10 job candidates will increase a company's odds of hiring the best person, as opposed to being able to choose from only one candidate. A second key goal of recruitment is to increase the number of *qualified* applicants. This is why it is so important during recruitment to focus on both getting a large number of people to apply *and* making sure they are the best qualified applicants.[5]

FIGURE 7.1   ■   The Recruitment and Selection Funnel

The recruitment and selection funnel decreases the number of candidates considered from the time of recruitment through hiring, leaving only the very best candidates to hire.

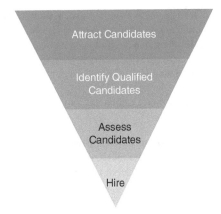

Legal and Ethical Issues in Hiring

Chapter 4 discussed the centrality of legal issues to HR decision making. Perhaps the area in which legal issues are most evident—and which has the most developed history in terms of laws and court cases—is selection. As a result of Title VII of the Civil Rights Act of 1964 and the subsequent court cases interpreting it (referred to as "case law"), a large body of laws and legal guidelines has developed to guide employers in choosing, developing, and using hiring procedures. To help employers make sense of this complex set of laws and court cases, the EEOC, Department of Justice, and Department of Labor developed the Uniform Guidelines on Employee Selection Procedures (1978). Although the Uniform Guidelines are not technically laws in themselves, they do summarize the laws up until that time and are typically treated by the courts as if they were law. As described in Chapter 4, the Uniform Guidelines provide substantial legal guidance to employers on the implementation of recruitment programs and the determination of whether a test has adverse impact against protected groups. This could be done by using the 4/5ths or 80% rule in terms of hiring ratios. We encourage you to review the material in Chapter 4 on adverse impact and how to calculate it, as it is a critical issue in understanding the implementation of selection procedures. In addition, the Uniform Guidelines set legal standards on a range of selection-related issues, such as establishing the validity of selection procedures, setting cutoff scores, promoting diversity in organizations, and monitoring the diversity of an employer's applicant flow and workforce. Note the Uniform Guidelines are now more than 40 years old, and there have been calls for them to be updated by taking into account more recent developments regarding the science of selection. Also, note that in addition to these laws and government guidelines, there are also professional guidelines on the development and administration of selection procedures, published by the Society for Industrial and Organizational Psychology.[6]

SPOTLIGHT ON LEGAL ISSUES: UNDERSTANDING REASONABLE ACCOMMODATION AS OUTLINED BY THE AMERICANS WITH DISABILITIES ACT (ADA) DURING SELECTION

Question. If an applicant has a disability and will need an accommodation for the job interview, does the Americans with Disabilities Act (ADA) require an employer to provide them with one?

Answer. Employers are required to provide "reasonable accommodation" (appropriate changes and adjustments) to enable applicants to be considered for a job opening. Reasonable accommodation may also be required to enable them to perform a job, gain access to the workplace, and enjoy the "benefits and privileges" of employment available to employees without disabilities. *An employer cannot refuse to consider an applicant because the person requires a reasonable accommodation to compete for or perform a job.*

Question. Can an employer refuse to provide an applicant with an accommodation because it is too difficult or too expensive?

Answer. An employer does not have to provide a specific accommodation if it would cause an "undue hardship" that would require significant difficulty or expense. However, an employer cannot refuse to provide an accommodation solely because it entails some costs, either financial or administrative. *If the requested accommodation causes an undue hardship, the employer still would be required to provide another accommodation that does not.*

Question. What are some examples of "reasonable accommodations" that may be needed during the hiring process?

Answer. Reasonable accommodation can take many forms. Accommodations that may be needed during the hiring process include (but are not limited to)
● providing written materials in accessible formats, such as large print, braille, or audiotape;
● providing readers or sign language interpreters;
● ensuring that recruitment, interviews, tests, and other components of the application process are held in accessible locations;
● providing or modifying equipment or devices; and
● adjusting or modifying application policies and procedures.

Question. Because of a learning disability, an applicant believes they need extra time to complete a written test. Does the ADA require an employer to modify the way a test is given to the applicant?

Answer. An employer may have to provide testing materials in alternative formats or make other adjustments to tests as an accommodation for such an applicant. The format and manner in which a test is given may pose problems for persons with impaired sensory, speaking, or manual skills, as well as for those with certain learning disabilities. For example, an applicant who is blind will not be able to read a written test but can take the test if it is provided in braille, the questions are audio recorded, or an automated text reader is provided. A hearing impaired person will not understand oral instructions, but these could be provided in a written format or through the use of a sign language interpreter. A 30-minute timed written test may pose a problem for a person whose learning disability requires additional time. Thus, *the ADA requires that employers give application tests in a format or manner that does not require use of an impaired skill unless the test is designed to measure that skill.*

Question. When does an applicant have to tell an employer that they need an accommodation for the hiring process?

Answer. It is best for applicants to *let an employer know as soon as they realize that they will need a reasonable accommodation* for some aspect of the hiring process. An employer needs advance notice to provide many accommodations, such as sign language interpreters, alternative formats for written documents, and adjusting the time allowed for taking a written test. An employer may also need advance notice to arrange an accessible location for a test or interview.

Question. How do applicants request a reasonable accommodation?

Answer. They must inform the employer that they need some sort of change or adjustment to the application/interviewing process because of their medical condition. They can make this request *orally or in writing*, or someone else might make a request for them (e.g., a family member, friend, health professional, or other representative, such as a job coach).

Source: Modified from material developed by the U.S. Equal Employment Opportunity Commission. (n.d.). *Job applicants and the Americans with Disabilities Act.* https://www.eeoc.gov/facts/jobapplicant.html

DATA-DRIVEN CRITERIA FOR CHOOSING SELECTION PROCEDURES: RELIABILITY, VALIDITY, AND UTILITY

LEARNING OBJECTIVES

7.2   Describe the concepts of reliability, validity, and selection utility and how they are demonstrated.

Selection procedures based on the "gut" impressions of hiring managers or their best judgment can be a legal liability for employers. Research shows this approach generally results in poor predictions of job performance.[7] In contrast, selection procedures based on systematic data collection and analysis results in more accurate, legal selection decisions. This requires attention to the reliability, validity, and utility (dollar value) of selection procedures.

Ensuring the Quality of Selection Measures: Reliability and Validity

Some selection procedures are better than others. There is a science—called **psychometrics**—used to estimate the quality of the measures used in personnel selection. Specifically, it is possible to examine how consistent or dependable a selection procedure is (called reliability) and how accurately its use results in predicting actual job performance (called validity; see Figure 7.2). Let's explore what reliability and validity mean and how they apply to HR selection.

FIGURE 7.2 ■ Reliability and Validity

Reliability
Consistency or dependability of measurement; a necessary condition for validity

Validity
The degree to which a test or other selection procedure measures what it is supposed to measure

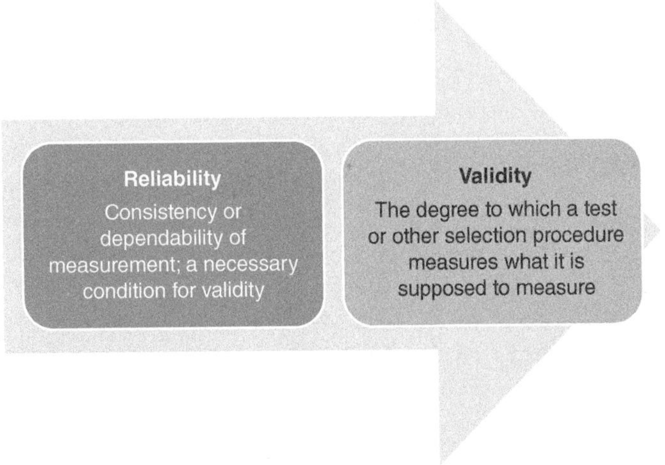

Reliability

Suppose you are trying to hire highly conscientious applicants. You give an applicant a personality test that measures conscientiousness, and it says they are highly conscientious. The applicant comes back in for an interview, and you give them the conscientiousness test again, and this time it says they are not very conscientious. This is a problem: The test cannot be measuring a stable personality dimension like conscientiousness if it is not measuring a person's conscientiousness consistently. That is the heart of what is meant by reliability, or the consistency of measurement. It is a necessary condition for validity. A test has to first measure something consistently and dependably before we can decide whether it is actually measuring the underlying dimension. The reliability of a test or measure is expressed as a correlation coefficient, on a scale of 0 to 1, with 0 indicating low reliability and 1 high reliability, although in reality few tests have a reliability of 1. Also, high reliability (approaching 1) suggests that a test has little measurement error.[8]

Validity

A key issue in the use of selection procedures is the concept of validity, or the degree to which a predictor actually measures what it is supposed to measure, such as an important individual difference variable that is related to job performance. In other words, whereas reliability relates to how consistently we measure something, validity relates to how accurately the test measures something, or predicts job performance. Note that although validity is a single concept, there are three common ways to show the validity of selection procedures: content validity, criterion-related validity, and construct validity. These are described in government guidelines such as the Uniform Guidelines on Employee Selection Procedures (see Chapter 4) as well as in professional guidelines (SIOP Principles).[9] Next, we discuss each of these.

Content Validity   Content validity is actually an approach to test development focused on sampling a domain such as the job. This is typically done via a job analysis and subject matter expert input. If you wanted to demonstrate that a selection procedure had good content validity, you would develop the test based on a job analysis and then have the test reviewed by subject matter experts (SMEs, generally job incumbents and supervisors). As an example, if HR staff at a local or regional bank wanted to develop a content-valid selection procedure for a bank teller's job, they might conduct a job analysis of the job and observe bank tellers doing their work. Then the HR staff would develop questions (perhaps for a written test and structured interview) based on the job analysis and observations. The HR staff might also have current bank tellers and their supervisors review the test questions to document that they reflect the job correctly. In showing content validity, there generally are no complex statistics involved; rather, the test's validity is shown by documenting that the test is based on a job analysis and that SMEs have judged the test content to reflect the content domain of the job.[10] For instance, the Biddle Consulting Group used a content validation approach for their CritiCall test used for hiring emergency dispatchers, which is available in different formats, including an online version (useful during the height of the pandemic). Specifically, they did a job analysis and had 66 SMEs rate the test on its relevance to the job.[11]

Criterion-Related Validity   The gold standard in selection research is to show that there is an empirical relationship (usually a statistically significant correlation) between a test and measures of job performance—using either a sample of current employees (concurrent validity) or job applicants (predictive validity). Showing this empirical relationship is called criterion-related validity, and this correlation between the test score and job performance is referred to as the validity coefficient. As an example, a company might give a test of emotional stability to 75 employees who work closely together on teams, finding that the test is correlated .29 with a measure of employees' job performance and that this correlation is statistically significant. In other words, it suggests that as an employee's emotional stability score goes up, their job performance is likely to go up. In the personnel selection context, that correlation would be considered evidence for the validity of the emotional stability test in predicting job performance. In the case of the CritiCall test for dispatchers described earlier, using a sample of 62 Florida Highway Patrol dispatchers and call-takers, it was found that CritiCall test scores were significantly correlated with job performance—evidence of the test's criterion-related validity.[12] Also, it is important to note that a test with a statistically significant negative correlation with job performance is good as well. For instance, if a test of conscientiousness was significantly correlated −.40 with aggressive behavior at work, it would be a useful predictor; it would suggest that people high in conscientiousness were less likely to be aggressive.

When conducting research to demonstrate a test's criterion-related validity, there are two main ways to approach it. Predictive validity involves administering the test to job applicants and then seeing how well the test scores correlate with their later job performance scores. For example, a clothing retailer might administer a test to its job applicants and then see whether those test scores are correlated to the actual sales numbers of hired applicants 1 year later. The second approach is through concurrent validity, which involves administering the test to current employees and showing that their test scores are correlated with their current job performance. In this case, the clothing retailer could ask current employees to take the test—assuring them that this is for research only and their test scores will not affect their jobs—and then correlate those test scores with job performance. If the correlation is statistically significant, it would suggest that the retailer is justified in using this test for making selection decisions. The CritiCall example is an example of a concurrent validation study. The concurrent approach is perhaps simpler and more straightforward, as it means the employer does not have to wait to see whether the test is valid. On the other hand, the samples of current employees used in concurrent validity studies may not provide the most accurate estimates of a test's validity among actual applicants: For example, current employees don't "act like" highly motivated job applicants in the actual testing situation. Still, both predictive and concurrent validity approaches provide evidence for whether the test is valid and should be used for making selection decisions.[13]

Construct Validity Construct validity involves the demonstration that a test actually measures a particular construct of interest, such as mechanical ability. This is typically shown through an accumulation of evidence about the test, including its pattern of relationships with other tests and measures that make sense from a theoretical or scientific point of view. For example, a test publisher might show that its test of conscientiousness has a pattern of correlations with other tests that makes logical sense: The test might show a high correlation with other tests of conscientiousness, a moderate correlation with tests of achievement orientation, and a relatively weak correlation with tests of verbal ability. On the other hand, if the conscientiousness test was found to correlate strongly with verbal ability, one might be concerned that it is not a clean measure of conscientiousness, since it also seems to be measuring verbal ability. In the hiring context, once a test's construct validity has been demonstrated, it might be used for hiring if that construct (in this case, conscientiousness) has been identified as important to the job through a job analysis.

Again, validity is best conceptualized as a single, unitary concept, not as consisting of three "types."[14] A test developed through a careful content validity approach should, theoretically, also show good criterion-related validity.[15] Content, criterion-related, and construct validity are three convenient ways of demonstrating the validity of measures. Table 7.1 summarizes different validity strategies, along with examples of each in an organizational context.

TABLE 7.1 ■ Summary of Different Validation Strategies for Personnel Selection Procedures		
Strategy for Demonstrating Validity	Definition	Example
Content Validity	Content validity involves developing a selection procedure such that it samples a particular domain. In the selection context, this is the job. Content validity thus involves developing the selection procedure based on a job analysis and with input from SMEs (e.g., incumbents) and documenting the process. It is often used when available sample sizes of employees and incumbents are too small to conduct empirical validation (criterion-related validity).	A city government needs to develop a knowledge test and simulation for selecting fire captains for promotion to the position of fire chief. It conducts a job analysis of the fire chief job and then develops the test and simulation with input from SMEs. SMEs also review the final test and simulation. The SMEs confirm that the two assessments sample the job and that the assessments measure knowledge and skills needed at the time the person is promoted. All processes are documented.

(Continued)

TABLE 7.1 ■ Summary of Different Validation Strategies for Personnel Selection Procedures (*Continued*)		
Strategy for Demonstrating Validity	**Definition**	**Example**
Criterion-Related Validity	An empirical relationship—most commonly a statistically significant correlation—between a selection procedure (e.g., test score) and job performance.	
Predictive design	Uses job applicants as the sample. Test scores obtained during the application process are correlated with later job performance (e.g., 6 months later).	A company wants to validate a mechanical ability test for hiring factory workers. It administers the test to a group of job applicants. Then, 1 year later, it correlates the mechanical ability test scores with job performance scores among those applicants that were actually hired. The company finds a statistically significant relationship ($r = .38$) between the mechanical ability test scores and job performance, which is evidence of validity, and suggests that the test can be used for future selection decisions.
Concurrent design	Uses current employees (incumbents) as the sample. Test scores obtained from incumbents are correlated with their current job performance.	A company wants to validate a mechanical ability test for hiring factory workers. It administers the test to a group of volunteer employees and then correlates the mechanical ability test scores with current job performance scores. The company finds a statistically significant relationship ($r = .35$) between the mechanical ability test scores and job performance, which is evidence of validity and suggests that the test can be used for future selection decisions.
Construct Validity	Accumulation of research evidence that the test or measure actually does measure the construct it purports to measure and does not measure unrelated constructs.	A test developer administers its new mechanical ability test to several groups, perhaps students as well as samples of employees obtained from its clients. It finds the test has a high correlation with existing tests of mechanical ability, a moderate correlation with tests of spatial relationships, and a low correlation with tests of extraversion and verbal ability. These patterns suggest the test is measuring mechanical ability and is not measuring unrelated constructs.

Analytics: Showing the Importance of Validity in Hiring Decisions

The validity of personnel selection procedures is one of the most important metrics used in HR decision making. Using valid predictors provides a competitive advantage to organizations because it is more likely to result in good hires. In contrast, organizations that decide simply to "go with their gut" rather than choosing the selection procedures with the best proven validity for choosing employees are losing out. (Consider also that gut decisions may lead to unfair or illegal hiring decisions.)

Figure 7.3 illustrates the importance of taking the time in organizations to research a test's validity. It shows a case of criterion-related validity—that is, the relationship between test score (on the *x*-axis) and job performance (on the *y*-axis) for jobs in a hypothetical company. We have marked where the passing score for the test is on the *x*-axis and where the break point is for employees who have acceptable performance and those with unacceptable performance on the *y*-axis. Based on a passing score on the test and the acceptable performance score, Figure 7.3 further breaks selection decisions down into accurate decisions (hits) and inaccurate decisions (misses). Hits include applicants who passed the test and turned out to be good employees (true positives), as well as applicants who failed the test and turned out to be unacceptable performers (true negatives). As you can see, the problem is the misses: These are the false positives, that is, employees who passed the test but turned out to be unacceptable performers, as well as false negatives, or employees who did not pass the test but who would have actually been good performers. Obviously, the goal in selection decision making is to increase the number of hits and avoid misses.

The importance of validity is seen in Figure 7.3. The first graph shows a case of moderate validity. Note the healthy number of hits but also some misses. The second graph shows what happens when validity drops to zero: The number of hits and misses is nearly identical, meaning that the test was essentially useless. The third graph shows what happens when validity is nearly perfect—that is, when there is a very high correlation between the test and job performance. In this figure, you can see that the distribution of scores includes almost entirely hits and almost no misses. Although near-perfect validity is something that is rarely achieved in the real world, the point is that carefully researching the best selection procedures and using those to make hiring decisions can have an enormous impact on the quality of hiring decisions and, more important, may help hiring managers avoid costly mistakes. In short, it is well worth the time and effort for HR decision makers to examine the validity of the selection procedures they are considering, including conducting in-house studies of predictors (especially in larger organizations). It is also important that organizations demand that test vendors show evidence of the reliability and validity of their selection procedures, including complete descriptions of the research that test publishers have done in similar industries and jobs.

The validity of a selection procedure directly impacts the number of correct hiring decisions. When validity is moderate, there are a number of hits but also some misses as well. When validity falls to zero, there are as many misses as hits—essentially random selection. But as validity gets higher, the relative number of misses declines drastically.

FIGURE 7.3 ■ The Importance of Predictor Validity to Accurate Selection Decisions

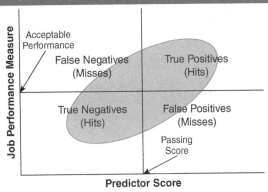

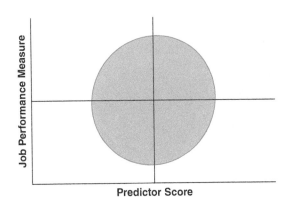

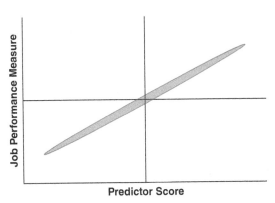

Do Organizations Have to Do Their Own Validity Research?

One question is whether organizations have to do their own research on selection procedures or whether they can rely on existing studies done by test publishers. This is at the heart of the concept of validity generalization, the assumption that selection procedures that have been validated for similar jobs in similar organizations can be assumed to be valid for new situations. As an example, let's say that the Vivace Company wants to use a selection procedure for hiring its online customer assistance agents. A test vendor approaches Vivace and points out that it has a situational judgment test (SJT) that it has used with other companies that employ online customer assistance agents and that the SJT has been found to have good predictive validity (i.e., it predicts the performance of customer assistance agents). Can Vivace confidently use this test for hiring its customer assistance agents? According to the theory of validity generalization, yes. This would especially be the case to the extent that the customer service jobs in these other companies are similar to Vivace's customer service jobs; this might be determined through a job analysis. Overall, the evidence supports the use of a validity generalization approach; however, legal guidelines also suggest that showing that the two jobs in consideration are actually similar is important and that employers should do their own local validation study (i.e., showing the test's validity for a job in their own organization) at some point if possible.[16]

Selection Utility

Utility is the degree to which selection procedures are worth the time and money to carry out (see Figure 7.4). One of the most important ways to increase selection utility is to be sure that selection procedures are valid. To the extent that selection procedures are good predictors of job performance, they are more worthwhile to use. Conversely, if selection procedures are not valid, it is not worth taking the time and money to use them.

FIGURE 7.4 ■ Factors That Can Affect the Utility (Dollar Value) of Using a Selection Procedure

A number of factors can affect the utility, or dollar value, of using a selection procedure.

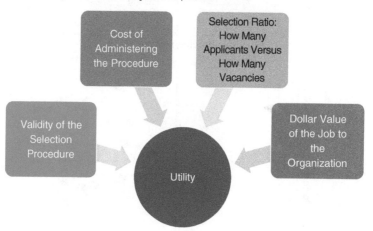

Second, the selection ratio, or the number of job vacancies relevant to the number of applicants, also affects the utility of selection procedures. Suppose you had two job vacancies and only two job applicants. It may not be worth the trouble to use any selection procedure other than to be sure the applicants were minimally qualified and not a risk to the organization, because you know that you will need to hire both of these applicants in order to fill the two vacancies. Rather, when there are more applicants relative to the number of vacancies, it is worth it to take the time and money to give a test—the utility of using a good selection system goes up. This again illustrates the importance of effective recruitment procedures to successful selection procedures.

Third is the cost of the selection procedure. All things being equal, there is greater utility in using a cheaper selection procedure than one that is more expensive. Finally, if the job is of high value to the organization, or if poor performance could seriously affect the organization (e.g., police officers for a municipality), the utility of using good selection procedures increases even further. For instance, a city government might decide that a valid test for emergency dispatchers has high utility because it fulfills a primary mission of the city and could even save lives. Recall the CritiCall test, which is used by public-sector organizations to hire emergency dispatchers and that was found in a study of the Florida Highway Patrol to predict the performance of dispatchers.[17]

STRATEGICALLY CHOOSING AND COMBINING SELECTION PROCEDURES

LEARNING OBJECTIVES
7.3   Demonstrate how to strategically choose and combine selection procedures.

Imagine that a company has researched the best selection procedures to predict customer service. Based on the job analysis and some background research, the company narrows it down to 10 possible tests to use in hiring customer service representatives. The company administers the 10 tests—which include three possible tests of conscientiousness—to 1,000 current employees (i.e., a concurrent validation study) and correlates the employees' test scores with employees' job performance, in this case, supervisor performance ratings. The company finds that all 10 tests have a significant correlation with the job performance measure. This means that all 10 tests are valid predictors of job performance—that is good news. But it also knows that administering 10 tests is not practical. It would take too much time, be costly, and perhaps annoy the job applicants.

Some further analysis of the data from the 1,000 current employees can help. Conceptually, the goal is to have selection procedures that are correlated with job performance but are not overly correlated with each other (redundant). Related to this last idea, selection procedures should complement each other. In other words, each selection procedure should uniquely predict some aspect of job performance. Figure 7.5 illustrates this issue conceptually using a Venn diagram, and Table 7.2 shows a correlation matrix that illustrates the situation statistically. Both the figure and the table show three valid tests (Personality Test A, Personality Test B, and a situational judgment test [SJT]) that are correlated with performance. In addition, the personality tests and the SJT complement each other in terms of prediction since the personality tests predict one aspect of job performance and the SJT predicts another aspect of performance. However, the two personality tests are highly correlated with each other (.92); they are redundant. In this case, it is best to use one of the personality tests but not both.

FIGURE 7.5 ■ Choosing Predictors That Are Correlated With Job Performance but Not Redundant With Each Other

When choosing among a group of predictors, it is best to choose predictors that are related to job performance. But you don't want the predictors to be too strongly related to each other. That would mean the predictors are redundant with each other. In this example, the three predictors—Test A, Test B, and the situational judgment test (SJT)—are all correlated with job performance. You can see in the diagram how they all overlap with job performance. That part is great. However, Test A and Test B overlap with each other; they are redundant. Thus, it is not necessary to use both Test A and Test B to predict job performance. Choose Test A *or* Test B, plus the SJT, to predict performance.

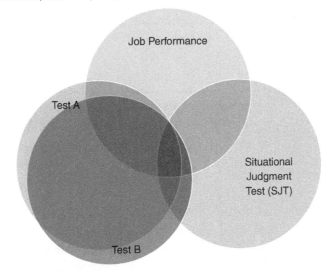

TABLE 7.2 ■ Hypothetical Correlations Among Three Tests and Job Performance				
	1	2	3	4
1. Conscientiousness A	-			
2. Conscientiousness B	.92	-		
3. Situational Judgment Test (SJT)	.19	.23	-	
4. Job Performance (Criterion)	.35	.37	.41	-

SPOTLIGHT ON GLOBAL ISSUES: DEPLOYING SELECTION SYSTEMS IN DIFFERENT COUNTRIES AND LANGUAGES

One question for multinational companies is whether to make personnel selection procedures consistent across the organization, regardless of the country. Such consistency in selecting employees, regardless of location, could enhance the consistency of the organization's culture worldwide. But it can be difficult to implement a one-size-fits-all approach to selection across national boundaries given differences in employment laws. Also, different predictors may work well in one country but not in another. For instance, a test of agreeableness may be a good predictor in one country but not in another due to cultural differences.

Another issue is that of translating an assessment from one language to another. This is typically done via a method known as translation and back-translation. As an example, an English test might be translated into Italian and then back-translated into English (see Figure 7.6). This back-translated English version would then be compared to the original English to help decide whether the Italian and English versions are basically equivalent.

Figure 7.6 is a specific example of the translation/back-translation process for an extraversion question, with the goal of creating an Italian item from the English. The final back-translated item is close enough to the original to suggest that the Italian item is an acceptable translation. Of course, the item would then need to be given to an Italian-speaking sample and the data analyzed (e.g., to assess its validity) to ensure that it actually is a good item.[18]

| FIGURE 7.6 ■ Back-Translation Example |

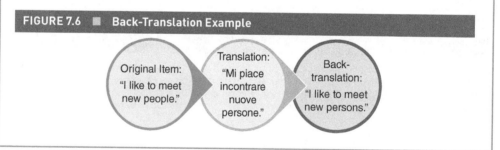

Original Item: "I like to meet new people." → Translation: "Mi piace incontrare nuove persone." → Back-translation: "I like to meet new persons."

SELECTION PROCEDURES

LEARNING OBJECTIVES

7.4 Identify the different selection procedures available for making hiring decisions and their advantages and disadvantages.

There is a wide range of selection procedures that are available to employers. Each of these selection procedures has advantages and disadvantages in terms of validity (how well it predicts job performance), utility (its cost), and its likelihood to cause adverse impact and thus affect the diversity of the organization. In this section, we describe the advantages and disadvantages of a wide range of selection procedures based on the research. We also will describe best practices for a number of these procedures so that organizations can get the best information from each. Keep in mind there is no best selection procedure for choosing applicants. Rather than considering one selection procedure (e.g., a personality test) for choosing applicants, selection procedures are best thought of as complementing each other. Thus, some combination of selection procedures is usually best. Websites such as Glassdoor.com allow individuals to share insights into the hiring process as well as specific interview questions. Of course, such anonymous information must be taken for what it is, but it can be worthwhile for candidates to research a company before interviewing with them. This discussion is not an exhaustive list of all selection procedures that are available but focuses on the ones that are most commonly used. Throughout this section, you will want to refer to the summary of selection procedures in Table 7.3.

TABLE 7.3 ■ A Summary of Selection Procedures, Their Validity, and Practical Considerations for Their Use			
Selection Procedure	Validity (average correlation with job performance)	Applicant Reactions[19] Most preferred = *** Preferred = ** Least Preferred = *	Practical Considerations for Using Them
Structured Interviews	Medium to Large (.44–.51)[20]	***	Behavioral interviews ("What have you done in the past?") may predict job performance slightly better than situational interviews ("What would you do in this situation?").[21]
Unstructured Interviews	Small to Medium (.19–.38)[22]	***	The ability of unstructured interviews to predict job performance may vary because of inconsistency across applicants and interviewer biases.
Personality Tests	Small (.11–.25)[23]	**	Although personality tests have been criticized for having low validity, they are low-cost assessments with low adverse impact. Validity can be enhanced by telling the applicant to think about how they are "at work" when responding.
Integrity Tests	Small to Medium (.26–.47)[24]	*	Solid predictors of counterproductive work behavior. Inexpensive, with fairly low adverse impact.
General Cognitive Ability	Medium to Large (.31–.51)[25]	**	One of the most consistently valid predictors of job performance. Low cost. However, they can have adverse impact against certain ethnic groups.
Specific Cognitive Abilities (e.g., clerical ability, mechanical ability)	Varies	**	Validity varies by the specific type of cognitive ability assessed. Certain cognitive ability tests may have adverse impact (e.g., mechanical ability and women).
Work Samples	Medium to Large (.33–.54)[26]	***	Work samples are highly correlated with job performance and preferred by applicants. Due to high administrative costs, work samples may be administered as a final hurdle to a smaller group of finalists rather than to all applicants.
Situational Judgment Tests (SJTs)	Small to Medium (.19–.43)[27]	***	Solid validity and appealing to applicants.
Assessment Centers	Small to Medium (.29–.45)[28]	***	Work samples are often used to assess manager candidates for promotion. Although they are expensive to administer, they may serve not only as a predictor of job performance but as a training and development tool as well.
Biographical Data	Small to Large (.22–.52)[29]	**	Practical method for predicting job performance for large numbers of applicants. Primary costs are in the initial research and development for a particular company or industry.

Note: Correlations between .10 and .29 are considered small compared to correlations between .30 and .49, which are considered medium, and those between .50 and above, which are considered large.

Interviews

The interview is the most commonly used selection procedure (see Figure 7.7). In fact, it is hard to imagine an employer not using some type of interview before hiring an employee. Due to the popularity of interviews and their long history, there is a large body of research examining the effectiveness of interviews in selection. There are also best practices for enhancing the validity of **selection interviews**. We focus on the two main types of selection interviews, unstructured and structured interviews, their validity, and how to use them most effectively to make hiring decisions.

FIGURE 7.7 ■ Percentage of Organizations Using Different Selection Methods to Hire for Individual Contributor Positions

A 2020 SHRM survey found that the structured interview was the most frequently used selection technique for nonmanagement/individual contributor positions.

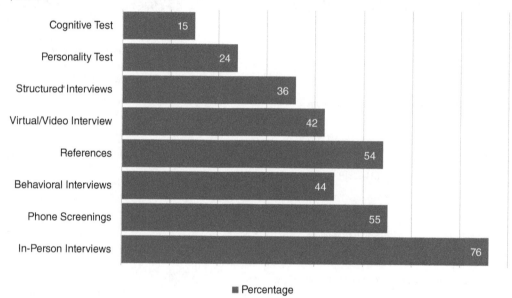

Source: Based on Society for Human Resource Management (2022). *SHRM Benchmarking Talent Access Report*. https://shrm.org/ResourcesAndTools/business-solutions/PublishingImages/Pages/benchmarking/Talent%20Access%20Report-TOTAL.pdf, with permission of the Society for Human Resource Management (SHRM). © SHRM 2022. All rights reserved.

Unstructured Interviews

The most common type of selection interview and the one that has been used for hiring employees through the ages is the **unstructured interview**. This is where the interviewer (e.g., a hiring manager or supervisor) has a conversation with the job applicant. There is no consistent set of questions for each applicant. In fact, different applicants are likely to be asked different questions, and the questions may not necessarily be job related. Not surprisingly—and despite the confidence that some interviewers have in their own ability to choose the best job applicant based on their instincts or "gut reactions"—the unstructured interview has relatively low validity in terms of predicting job performance. This is because the unstructured interview does not focus on job-related questions. Because different applicants may be asked different questions, it is hard to compare the responses of different applicants, and there is a definite risk of applicants being treated unfairly or introducing interviewer biases, even if they are unintentional or unconscious. For these reasons, the unstructured interview has largely fallen out of favor regarding selection, at least in terms of being the primary basis for hiring decisions.

Interviews are the most commonly used selection procedure, and there is a long history of research on how to make them most effective. Perhaps the most important finding of this research is that increasing the structure of the interview—such as asking all candidates the same job-related questions and having more than one interviewer—can significantly increase the validity of the interview in predicting job performance.

©iStockphoto.com/skynesher

That said, unstructured interviews are likely to continue to be part of most hiring decisions, and this is not necessarily a bad thing as long as they are used wisely. It is hard to imagine a situation in which a hiring manager or supervisor would not want to have the opportunity to have a casual conversation with a job applicant prior to hiring them. For an example of how this might work, once the most qualified job applicants are identified through other selection methods, a supervisor may then decide to interview the top candidates via an unstructured interview. Unstructured interviews may also be helpful to sell the applicant on the job, to give the applicant a realistic job preview (see Chapter 6), and to make an impression regarding the specific job and the organization.[30] Interviewers also give applicants an opportunity to ask questions about the organization, the job, and coworkers to help them decide if the job seems like a good fit. Although the research has shown that unstructured interviews have lower validity than structured interviews, unstructured interviews are not without their merits, including being a good way to assess interpersonal skills and some personality traits. In fact, it has been argued that unstructured interviews simply measure different characteristics than structured interviews, which are much more focused on job-related behaviors and skills.[31]

Structured Interviews

A different approach to interviewing would be to ask all job applicants the same, job-related questions. This approach, known as the structured interview, has been found to have good predictive validity in making hiring decisions (see Table 7.4). In fact, a recent meta-analysis found that the structured interview may be the most valid selection procedure available.[32]

There are two types of structured interviews: the situational interview and the behavioral interview. In the situational interview, job applicants are asked what they would do in a hypothetical work-related situation. For example, applicants for a supervisory role might be asked, "What *would you do* if you had an employee whose performance suddenly decreased? How would you handle the situation?"

In contrast, in the behavioral interview, applicants are asked how they handled a work-related situation in the past. For example, Google is a leader in the selection space, and behavioral interviews are part of its selection procedures.[33] For the supervisor position, applicants might be asked, "What *have you done* when you had an employee whose performance suddenly decreased? How did you handle the situation?"

TABLE 7.4 ■ Structured Interview Questions With Rating Scales

You and a coworker are collaborating on a project that is due in 10 days. You are beginning to fall behind because your coworker is not working quickly enough. How would you handle this?

Rating scale:

1—Candidate either ignores the issue completely or handles it in way that makes things worse (e.g., confronts the worker in a negative way).

2

3—Candidate recognizes the problem, but they develop a suboptimal solution, such as telling their boss.

4

5—Candidate develops a constructive solution, such as speaking with the worker to find out what may be wrong, what they may be doing to slow things down, or what they can do to help develop a solution.

Tell us about a time when you were dealing with a difficult customer. How did you handle the situation?

1—Candidate describes that they did something to make the situation worse, such as ignoring the customer or being rude.

2

3—Candidate chooses a suboptimal solution such as passing the customer on to their supervisor.

4

5—Candidate worked with the customer to figure out what the problem was and to come up with a mutually acceptable solution.

In other words, the situational interview asks what an applicant would do, whereas the behavioral interview asks an applicant what they have actually done in the past. Both situational and behavioral interview formats have good validity, and each approach could be appropriate depending on the particular circumstances. For instance, the situational interview might be more appropriate when job applicants have little work experience and thus cannot be expected to answer behavioral interview questions. Research has also suggested that these two types of structured interviews may be assessing slightly different things: The situational interview appears to measure cognitive ability and job knowledge, whereas the behavioral interview measures personality variables and (not surprisingly) job experience.[34]

Manager's Toolbox: Best Practices: How to Add More Interview Structure

The premise of the structured interview is that adding more structure helps increase the validity of the interview in making hiring decisions. "Structure" means asking the same questions of all interviewees. But what else is meant by "structure"? Here are a number of best practices identified in the research to make selection interviews more structured and thus more likely to lead to good hiring decisions.

1. *Develop job-related questions that are asked to all applicants.* This is one of the most important ways to increase interview validity. Consider what behaviors are performed on the job and what KSAOs are needed to perform them. These behaviors and skills can be derived from a job analysis or competency model. An examination of critical incidents faced by employees on the job can also help in the development of interview questions.

2. *Treat all interviewees consistently.* To the extent that all job candidates are interviewed under the same conditions—for example, in the same place and by the same interviewers—better information can be gained to compare job applicants.

3. *Train interviewers.* Train interviewers on how to interview applicants, and be sure that all interviewers use the same procedures when interviewing and evaluating job candidates. Note that interviews are susceptible to the same rating errors as performance appraisals (e.g., the halo error and contrast error, discussed in Chapter 9), and thus rating errors are often included as part of their training. They can also be trained in the use of rating scales so they are consistent in their ratings. Also, providing feedback to interviewers about how their ratings

compare to those of other interviewers can reduce rating differences between interviewers and improve interview reliability.

4. *Have more than one interviewer interview each applicant.* Where possible, have two or more people interview each job candidate to check for consistency in interviewers. This also allows interviewers to discuss their ratings of candidates and compare their observations.

5. *Have interviewers take notes.* This allows interviewers to check back as they compare different candidates, and it allows interviewers to compare their ratings with each other.

6. *Develop rating scales for each interview question.* Providing rating scales can be one of the most important ways to increase the validity of interviews. (See Table 7.3, which shows rating scale examples for structured interview questions.) Good rating scales also provide examples of poor, average, and excellent responses, so that interviewers have a consistent framework for rating job candidates and can compare their ratings with each other more effectively. Rating scales are typically developed with the assistance of SMEs. And if more than one interviewer is used (see Item 4), the ratings from each interviewer can be averaged together, and any differences among the interviewer ratings can be discussed.[35]

A current issue in the use of interviews in hiring is asynchronous video interviews (AVIs). In an AVI, the candidate responds to a series of questions (e.g., on their laptop or smart phone), and their responses are then recorded to be scored later either by a person or by an algorithm. Although some candidates may react negatively to AVIs because they lack the personal touch, AVIs allow the employer to process more candidates quickly and thus may be particularly useful early in the hiring process or when meeting in person is not possible (such as at the height of the pandemic). Research has found that candidates' reactions to AVIs may be improved by providing applicants with an explanation for using the AVI. In addition, given that AVIs are a new approach for most candidates, giving preparation time to candidates who are taking an AVI may lead to better AVI performance. However, because AVIs are a very new selection approach, more research is still needed on the validity of AVIs and how to use them most effectively in the hiring process.[36]

Finally, in recent years, the "group interview," in which multiple candidates are interviewed at one time, has seen increased use by organizations. Little empirical research on the validity of this approach has emerged in the literature, and we suggest caution in terms of having multiple interviewees compete within the same interview unless such competition is part of the job. At the same time, a recent study suggests that group interviews have acceptable applicant reactions except for applicants with certain personality traits (e.g., some introverts).[37]

Personality Tests

Since the early 1990s, there has been an interest in personality tests selection. Here we discuss the reasons for this interest among employers in using personality to hire workers.

Five Factor Model (FFM) or the "Big Five"

The interest in using personality tests in selection is partly due to a landmark meta-analysis, conducted in 1991 by Murray Barrick and Michael Mount, that examined the use of tests focused on the Five Factor Model (FFM)("Big Five") personality typology, which found that personality is related to a number of work performance dimensions. The Big Five is a typology of normal adult personality.

The five dimensions are best remembered by the acronym *OCEAN*. They are Openness to Experience, Conscientiousness, Extraversion, Agreeableness, and Neuroticism. Openness to Experience has to do with a person's inquisitiveness and willingness to learn new things and was found to be related to employees' performance in training programs. Conscientiousness includes traits such as dependability and achievement orientation and was found to relate to job performance across most jobs. Extraversion, which includes traits such as sociability, was related to jobs such as sales and management. Agreeableness is the degree to which the person is kind, sensitive, and pays attention to others' feelings. Finally, Neuroticism (or its opposite, emotional stability) relates to anxiety and worry.[38] Table 7.5 shows sample items for each of the Big Five dimensions. Numerous specific tests of the Big Five are available.[39]

TABLE 7.5 ■ Example of Big Five Items		
1–5 response scale, from "very inaccurate" to "very accurate"; the person would respond about how they perceive themselves to be.[40]		
Openness to Experience	**Conscientiousness**	**Extraversion**
Have a rich vocabulary.	Am always prepared.	Am the life of the party.
Have a vivid imagination.	Pay attention to details.	Feel comfortable around people.
Have excellent ideas.	Get chores done right away.	Start conversations.
Am quick to understand things.	Like order.	Talk to a lot of different people at parties.
Use difficult words.	Follow a schedule.	Don't mind being the center of attention.
Spend time reflecting on things.	Am exacting in my work.	
Am full of ideas.		
Agreeableness	**Neuroticism**	
Am interested in people.	Get stressed out easily.	
Sympathize with others' feelings.	Worry about things.	
Have a soft heart.	Am easily disturbed.	
Take time out for others.	Get upset easily.	
Feel others' emotions.	Change my mood a lot.	
Make people feel at ease.	Have frequent mood swings.	
	Get irritated easily.	
	Often feel blue.	

Interest in the use of personality inventories in selection has grown because most are relatively easy, quick, and inexpensive to administer, and they have generally been found to have lower adverse impact than other selection tests, such as cognitive ability tests (i.e., they are less likely to have a negative impact on an organization's diversity). However, their validity is not as high as some other selection procedures, such as structured interviews.[41] Further, note that for legal reasons, personality tests developed to make clinical diagnoses—that is, those not focused on normal adult personality—should not be used for hiring except under very specific, limited circumstances.

In addition, some worry about the possibility of applicants faking on personality inventories—that is, applicants not providing honest answers about how they are but providing the responses they believe an employer wants. However, some researchers suggest that personality tests are likely valid in spite of some faking activities on the part of applicants. Some researchers even suggest that faking behaviors can be positive: Applicants who infer what responses are expected of them may be demonstrating that they understand what would be required of them on the job. And other researchers say the term *faking* is actually a misnomer, and it may simply reflect an applicant's relatively normal—and benign—tendency to want to show themselves in the best light so they can get a job.[42]

Finally, it is important to know that the Big Five is only one approach to measuring job-related personality variables for use in selection. Other personality variables that have been found to be useful in selection include proactive personality; proactive people tend to recognize and act on opportunities at work. Research has shown, for instance, that proactive personality is a good predictor of performance of real estate agents, over and above conscientiousness and extraversion.[43] Another personality variable that has gained research attention as a selection procedure is adaptability, which has to do with a person's ability to adjust to new situations. Dimensions of adaptability include cultural, interpersonal, and learning adaptability.[44] Although the use of adaptability in selection research is still early, the interest in this personality variable for selection is expected to grow given the dynamic nature of work today. Finally, the dimension of honesty-humility (H-H), sometimes considered a "sixth" personality factor after the Big Five, is a tendency to be fair, honest, and cooperative with others. H-H is predictive of job performance; most notably, it is negatively correlated with counterproductive work behavior.[45]

Some personality variables can be useful for predicting job performance in certain specific jobs. For example, proactive personality has been shown to predict the job performance of real estate agents over and above conscientiousness and extraversion.

©iStockphoto.com/SDI Productions

Integrity Tests

At one time, employers used polygraph tests (lie detectors) to screen out job applicants who might steal or exhibit other types of counterproductive or antisocial behaviors while at work (e.g., using drugs at work, fighting with coworkers). However, because polygraph tests were found to have a high rate of false positives (i.e., people who were a low risk to the company but failed the test), the use of polygraph tests in selection was generally outlawed in the 1980s except for very limited circumstances, such as for certain job applicants in security service firms and pharmaceutical manufacturers.[46] Thus, employers now use self-report integrity tests to screen out applicants who are at risk of exhibiting negative behaviors on the job.

There are two main types of integrity tests: personality-based and overt integrity tests. Table 7.6 presents examples of each. Personality-based integrity tests are more subtle in their wording, such that the "correct answer" may not be obvious to test takers. Most personality-based integrity tests are considered to be a function of conscientiousness, neuroticism, and agreeableness, plus H-H.[47] Overt integrity tests, in contrast, ask the test taker to give their opinions about negative behaviors at work (e.g., theft), whether such behaviors are acceptable, and whether they have engaged in these behaviors themselves.

TABLE 7.6 ■ Examples of Overt and Personality-Based Integrity Test Items	
Overt Integrity Test Items	**Personality-Based (Covert) Integrity Test Items**
I have used illegal drugs at work.	It's OK to make some mistakes when you work quickly.
It's OK to hit a coworker if they yell at you.	You need to take risks sometimes if you want to get the job done.
I have stolen money from my employer.	I am always seeking excitement and thrills in my life.
If a coworker is rude to me, I would do something to their car.	I don't get along with other people because I always stand up for my rights.

At first glance, integrity tests might appear to be overly simplistic and easily faked. However, there have been a number of meta-analyses on integrity tests, and the findings are that these tests correlate .47

with negative work behaviors such as violence and theft.[48] Although there is still some difference of opinion among testing experts on just how valid these tests are for predicting performance, on balance, the research shows that integrity tests demonstrate sufficient validity, can pass legal muster, and provide value to employers trying to screen out job applicants who pose a risk to the organization and employees.[49] Also, integrity tests seem to have relatively low adverse impact, and they seem to be valid in a number of cultural settings.[50] Integrity tests are perhaps best considered in combination with other selection procedures such as cognitive ability tests and interviews, providing a screen for job applicants who are most likely to be difficult employees at work.

Cognitive Ability Tests

Cognitive ability tests have a long history in personnel selection, going back to the early 20th century. A cognitive ability test is an assessment of the ability to "perceive, process, evaluate, compare, create, understand, manipulate, or generally think about information and ideas."[51] On the positive side, cognitive ability tests may be one of the best predictors of job performance across a range of job types, with a correlation with job performance as high as .51[52] (although the magnitude of this correlation has recently been challenged[53]). Given their solid validity combined with their relatively low cost means they can have high utility.

On the negative side, cognitive ability tests are prone to lead to disparate impact, with the mean score of certain groups (e.g., Blacks, Hispanics) being significantly lower than the mean score of other groups (e.g., whites, Asians). (Note, of course, there is still substantial overlap between the scores of these different subgroups, even if there are differences in the *mean* score for each group.) Thus, many employers prefer to avoid the use of cognitive ability tests, both for reasons of diversity and for the possibility of legal challenges.[54] In fact, the increased interest in personality tests we discussed earlier may be partly due to the fact that personality tests have relatively low adverse impact compared to cognitive ability tests.

Employers use a few different types of cognitive ability tests. First are tests of general cognitive ability, sometimes referred to as "*g*" by psychologists. One theory as to why tests of general cognitive ability are such good predictors of job performance (a correlation of .51 according to some earlier meta-analyses) is that cognitive ability helps workers gain important job skills both during training and on the job. This may also explain why cognitive ability is thought to be such a good predictor for cognitively complex jobs.[55] One test of general cognitive ability that has a long history in personnel selection is the Wonderlic Personnel Test. The Wonderlic is a 50-item, 12-minute test that includes items such as math reasoning and verbal tasks. Available in many languages, the Wonderlic has amassed a large database, including norms—that is, the scores associated with different occupations.[56]

In addition, there are tests of specific cognitive abilities, such as tests of mechanical ability and clerical ability, which are designed for selection in specific job types. The adverse impact issue with these tests of specific cognitive abilities varies by the type of test. For example, tests of mechanical ability have been found to have some adverse impact against women.[57]

Finally, tests of emotional intelligence (EI) have gained attention as predictors of job performance. EI is defined as one's ability to recognize and appraise emotions in oneself and others and behave accordingly.[58] Some researchers define EI primarily in terms of being a personality variable, although other researchers describe it as a cognitive ability that is focused on social skills. Some tests of EI focus more on cognitive ability, whereas others focus more on personality traits. Given the interest in EI for making selection decisions, there have been numerous studies on EI, including meta-analyses, to better understand the role of EI in selection. Research has found that EI tests are better predictors of job performance when jobs are high in emotional labor. Further, research suggests that certain types of EI tests do not predict job performance over and above traditional tests like personality and cognitive ability; in other words, this research suggests the concept of EI is nothing new. Although more research is needed to understand definitively what different EI tests are actually measuring and their added value in selection decisions, some researchers point out that tests of EI may be a streamlined way for employers to predict job performance without using lengthy, time-consuming batteries of tests of personality and cognitive ability.[59]

SPOTLIGHT ON DATA AND ANALYTICS: GAMIFICATION OF PERSONNEL SELECTION PROCEDURES

Gamification, or the transformation of an ordinary activity into a game-like activity to increase engagement, motivation, and competition, is drawing increased interest in selection procedures. For example, conventional hiring procedures might require job applicants to take tests of cognitive ability or personality. In contrast, in gamified selection procedures, applicants might participate in a game activity to assess factors such as cognitive processing speed or risk tolerance. The idea is that such gamified assessments could attract job applicants who might not otherwise take conventional selection tests.

Some argue that gamified assessments offer other advantages such as longer, and thus more reliable, assessments. And because job applicants are engaged in the "flow" of a gamified assessment, they may be less likely to give dishonest or socially desirable responses. However, gamification of selection procedures is still fairly new, and more research is needed. For example, the validity of gamified assessments for predicting job performance relative to traditional selection tests has received relatively little scrutiny; a recent study found that a gamified assessment of cognitive ability may not be more valid than a traditional cognitive ability test.[60] Research does suggest that gamified assessments can positively affect an applicant's image of the organization and attraction to it, but this may be more the case for applicants with gaming experience. Certainly, employers considering the use of gamified assessments should conduct their own research to assess their value.[61]

Work Samples, Situational Judgment Tests (SJTs), and Assessment Centers

In this section, we describe three different "families" of selection procedures that directly sample a person's potential job performance and hence their fit for the job. These three selection procedures are work samples, situational judgment tests (SJTs), and assessment centers.

Work Samples

A work sample is a sample or example of the work produced by an applicant. Suppose an organization needs to hire a computer programmer. The company uses a cognitive test, an interview, and a review of applicants' work history to hire people. However, the hiring manager realizes that none of them directly samples what the person does on the job. To address this, the hiring manager decides to meet with each applicant and give them a short coding task to see how well they do. The hiring manager then has SMEs (current programmers) evaluate how well the applicants perform on the coding task.

As another example, JetBlue Airways used a job analysis to identify the key skills employees in its call center needed, and once it identified the desired KSAOs, it developed a call simulation test to use in the hiring process. With the use of this selection procedure, turnover decreased by 25%.[62]

Seeing how well an applicant performs the work tasks required on the job is the essence of a work sample. As you might guess, work samples have good validity. The research shows that they are correlated about .54 with work performance. In addition, they clearly have good content validity because they are an actual sample of the job. And applicants tend to like work samples, seeing them as very fair.[63] However, one drawback of work samples is that they are more expensive than other methods, usually requiring that one person at a time go through the assessment. Then applicants' performance on the work sample must usually be evaluated by trained SMEs. Given the cost of work samples—in terms of their individual administration and scoring—they are usually placed at the end of a series of cheaper selection hurdles. In a previous example, a company might decide to give cheaper tests and assessments to the original pool of qualified computer programmer applicants and then give interviews and work samples to the smaller group of top candidates.

Situational Judgment Tests (SJTs)

Because work samples are valid and attractive to applicants, HR researchers began to consider cheaper alternatives. This is where the concept of situational judgment tests (SJTs) comes into play. SJTs are sometimes referred to as "low-fidelity simulations." Specifically, SJTs capture some of the realism of work sample tests but in a format that can be used more easily with large numbers of applicants. An SJT might present the applicant with a scenario, in either paper or video format, and then ask the respondent to choose a series of alternatives. As an example of an SJT item, applicants for a retail job are given a scenario in which they are working with one customer to help them choose the best product when another customer interrupts them. They would then be asked how they would handle the situation. Note that while many SJTs use a written, multiple-choice format, others ask candidates to choose which video response seems most appropriate, and others use an open-ended format that must be scored later.[64] Additional examples of SJT items are given in Table 7.7. Because of their relatively low administration costs, SJTs have gained popularity. In fact, you may have taken an SJT when you applied for a job. In addition, they have solid validity, with correlations with job performance of .19 to .43. For instance, one SJT focused on medical school applicants' predicted work performance years later.[65]

TABLE 7.7 ■ Situational Judgment Test (SJT) Items for a Retail Clothing Job

You are helping a customer choose a tie. Another customer approaches you and interrupts your conversation. What would be the best thing to do?

a. Ignore the customer who interrupted you.

b. Tell the customer who interrupted you that you are busy and that he should not interrupt a conversation.

c. Kindly tell the second person that you would be glad to help him in a few minutes.

d. Explain to the first customer that you have given him all the time you can and you need to help others.

You have a friend who admires the clothing in the store where you work. She tells you that, although she doesn't have much money, she would really like to have a blouse from the store. Which of the following would be the best thing for you to do?

a. Tell your friend when there is a sale on the kind of blouse she likes.

b. Ask your boss if there are any extra blouses in the store so you can give one to your friend.

c. Take one of the blouses and give it to your friend.

A customer comes in to return a piece of clothing that is obviously defective. He is very angry about the failure of the item. Which of the following would be the best thing to do?

a. Tell the customer that this is not your fault personally, and so he should not be mean to you.

b. Tell the customer that you can replace the item and also give him a free gift card to make up for the inconvenience.

c. Try to calm down the customer by asking him to explain what happened and then work with him to find a solution.

Assessment Centers

Another type of work sample known as the assessment center was developed to assess management skills. Assessment centers were first pioneered in U.S. businesses in the 1960s at AT&T, and their popularity has grown over the years as a means of promoting people into management positions. An assessment center is not an actual place maintained by the company. Rather, center assessments are typically carried out over a series of days at a remote site provided by the organization, such as a hotel.

A common type of assessment center exercise is the role play, in which a candidate is asked to handle a situation with an actor or one of the assessors. For example, the candidate might be told that they will need to interact with an employee whose performance has declined in recent months, getting to the bottom of what the problem is and developing a solution. The actor would be trained to interact with the candidate in a way that reflects reality. Another common assessment center exercise is the in-basket or in-box, in which a candidate is told to provide responses to a series of e-mails they have received that morning. They would be asked to explain how they handled each e-mail. Generally, assessment center exercises are evaluated by at least two raters, typically expert managers or trained psychologists.

Not surprisingly, assessment centers are good predictors, correlating .37 to .45 with job performance and, by some recent estimates, more valid than tests of cognitive ability.[66] As with other work samples, they provide good content validity because they clearly sample the job domain. Not only can they be used to make promotion decisions, they are also good for training and development purposes, so that management candidates can see their strengths and weaknesses and determine where further development is needed. On the other hand, assessment centers are expensive, as they require the development of detailed, realistic materials and the use of teams of trained experts, often from outside of the organization, as assessors. For this reason, like work samples, assessment centers are typically not given to very large numbers of candidates but might be administered to smaller pools of finalists in the selection process.[67]

Biographical Data and Related Methods

In addition, employers can also collect useful data for screening job applicants from questions about their backgrounds.

Training and Experience Forms

Training and experience (T&E) forms ask applicants about their work-related education, training, and experience. Applicants' training and experience are then tabulated and scored based on an existing rubric determined through a job analysis and input from SMEs. In this sense, T&E forms can be seen as another flavor of structured résumés (see what follows), at least from the viewpoint of applicants. T&E forms have a long history in personnel selection, especially for government jobs. There is considerable variability in their validity in predicting job performance, ranging from a correlation between T&E scores and performance as low as .11 up to .45.[68]

Biodata

Employers can also use biographical data (biodata) as a predictor of job performance, with the assumption that past behavior—whether at work or perhaps even outside of work—is the best predictor of future behavior. For instance, a retail employer might be concerned that the high turnover rate for certain jobs is causing serious financial losses for the company. If they could get their employees to stay for at least 6 months, the costs invested in training them would be worthwhile. For this reason, they may ask applicants about how many jobs they have held in the past 3 years and then examine the relationship between the number of jobs a person has held and how long they remained on the job. Through this research, the company discovers that people who have held more than four jobs in the past 3 years are likely to quit in fewer than 6 months. In other words, employers find that this question allows them to determine which applicants are the best risk for staying with the organization.

In addition, biodata items could focus on nonwork experiences as predictors of work performance. As an early example of the use of biodata, in World War II, it was found that one item—whether an applicant for flight school played with model airplanes when growing up—was a good predictor of flight training performance. The idea was that an applicant who played with model airplanes was interested in flying and was thus a good bet for succeeding in flight school. Moving to recent times, a sports equipment retailer might find that people who participated in a range of different sports during their school years are the best at helping customers. This might be because these applicants are knowledgeable about a range of different sports and sports equipment, allowing them to help customers make good decisions in their purchases. Thus, employers can research a number of different types of background data that they suspect will predict job performance, choosing those that stand out as the best predictors in their research.[69] The key is for employers not to ask questions that might be unfair or have adverse impact, such as what part of town they live in. In addition, biodata items have solid validity, correlated about .35 with job performance.[70]

Résumés

Perhaps the most commonly used selection screening method is the résumé, in which job applicants describe their job-relevant education and work experience. The résumé is often used as a first-hurdle screening method, allowing a hiring manager, supervisor, HR recruiter, or (as in the opening case) an automated system to narrow down the applicant pool to a more manageable size. Given the ubiquitous nature of the résumé, one might think that it is well researched and has good validity. However, this is not necessarily the case. One of the biggest problems with résumés is that there is not a single format to use, in terms of the types of education and experience reported, the way the education and experience are described, or even the font used. Some applicants are better at putting together a résumé than others. For this reason, résumés from various applicants are difficult to compare, limiting their value as a screening device. In addition, because of the sheer volume of résumés received by organizations, as well as their length and the time needed to read them, they may overwhelm the recruiter due to time and cognitive overload. This may result in less-than-satisfactory decisions due to cognitive biases (often an issue with decisions made under time pressure) as recruiters may need to quickly sort through hundreds of résumés in a short period of time. Research has found that résumés can lead to conscious or unconscious discrimination by a screener.[71]

With these concerns, why do résumés remain popular? First is that résumés are now an expected, customary part of many job application processes. Second, some applicants may like the résumé. Applicants may perceive résumés as giving them a bit of control and an opportunity to show what they know, even if it is difficult for applicants to guess what it is that may strike the fancy of the recruiter.[72] The good news is that there is an increasing interest in using structured résumés, in which applicants must complete a résumé using a structure determined by the employer and based on a job analysis. Structured résumés can be easier for recruiters to scan.

Using Résumés for Job Applications

Despite the concerns we have raised about the résumé, it remains one of the most common selection tools. We have discussed employers' challenges of using résumés to screen job applicants (including bias that may be part of the résumé screening system, as discussed in the opening case), and that applicants have a generally positive reaction to the use of résumés in hiring. On the other hand, many applicants experience some frustration with this selection procedure, sending out dozens or even hundreds of résumés with little success and often with no response from employers.

What can applicants do to get better results from the submission of their résumés?

- First, as we noted in our opening case, résumés are often scanned by an algorithm before a person even sees them. For this reason, it is important that the résumé include important keywords that match the job ad. Also, stay away from nontraditional fonts like Comic Sans or complex formats (e.g., columns) that AI may have difficulty reading.

- Second, don't be shy about tailoring a résumé to a specific job application. Another way to think of this is to say that one résumé may not be sufficient for the range of jobs a person might apply to.

- Third, consider the importance of a meaningful cover letter—one that is not too generic or that simply repeats what is already in the résumé.[73]

References and Background Checks

Another screening device used by a number of employers involves gathering references from past employers, typically obtained through letters of reference. The idea behind references is that the best predictor of future behavior is past behavior, and knowing how a person behaved in previous employment situations can give some idea about their future behavior. Although the logic here is generally sound, obtaining accurate data about an applicant in this way is not without its challenges. First, applicants will, logically, tend to provide only the names of people who they know will give a positive recommendation. Second, many employers have policies that only allow them to say whether a person worked for them and will not provide an assessment of the quality of that person's work. These two factors alone limit the amount of good information that can typically be obtained through references. On the other hand, such references continue to be used by employers to screen out applicants who would be a high risk either to coworkers or to the company.[74]

Related to this, many employers, especially those hiring for high-security jobs (e.g., police officer, jobs working with children), may require some sort of background check (e.g., through legal databases) to ensure that the applicant is not a risk to others.[75] However, the use of criminal background checks is beginning to decline for many jobs and in certain U.S. states due to "ban the box" laws, described in Chapter 4. In addition, there is little research that shows that criminal record predicts job performance.[76] These laws continue to evolve and vary by state and municipality, but "ban the box" laws generally prohibit questions about past criminal convictions during the application process. In 2016, companies such as American Airlines, Starbucks, and Xerox were among many organizations pledging to voluntarily remove the box from their applications. In 2019, the federal Fair Chance Act went into effect to protect applicants for certain U.S. government jobs. Others are carrying this further; for example, the instant messaging company Slack worked with the Aspen Institute and Next Chapter (an organization focused on formerly incarcerated people in the workplace) to develop a playbook to support formerly incarcerated individuals after they are hired.[77] Note that employers might still do background checks, including asking about convictions after a job has been offered. Rather, the goal is to avoid disqualifying an otherwise qualified applicant at the outset of the selection process.[78]

Physical Ability Tests

Physical ability tests are used for hiring people for physically demanding jobs such as police officer. There are generally two approaches to physical ability testing. The first is like a standard work sample test, sampling the physical requirements. For example, a city might determine through a job analysis that a police officer's job requires them to run 50 yards in 8 seconds or to be able to climb a 6-foot fence. Thus, the physical ability test would include running 50 meters in 8 seconds or less and a portion that includes climbing a fence. The second approach to such physical ability tests is to determine the various types of strength required for the job (e.g., hand strength, arm strength) and to develop tests that measure these physical abilities. For example, hand strength might be measured by the ability to squeeze a hand grip 10 times within 15 seconds. One concern with these physical abilities tests is that they can have adverse impact against women, and employers need to ensure the ability measures are job related (e.g., based on a job analysis, correlated with job performance) to ensure their legal defensibility. For example, the City of Chicago was successfully sued, and required to pay millions of dollars, for including a test of strength that was not considered to be job related and had adverse impact against women.[79] In addition, some organizations provide information or even practice sessions for job applicants to reduce adverse impact; of course, all applicants (i.e., not just women) would need to be provided with the opportunity to participate in these practice sessions. Note that the use of physical requirements such as height has generally been discontinued as these may have adverse impact against some ethnic groups and against women, while not tapping into whether applicants can actually do the job.[80]

Physical ability tests are often used as part of the selection procedure for physically demanding jobs such as police officer or firefighter. Which physical abilities do you think are especially important for most law enforcement jobs or firefighting? Are tests for these physical abilities likely to have adverse impact?

©iStock.com/shaunl

CURRENT ISSUES IN SELECTION

<table>
<tr><td colspan="2">LEARNING OBJECTIVES</td></tr>
<tr><td>7.5</td><td>Recognize and explain key analytical, legal, ethical, and global issues associated with personnel selection.</td></tr>
</table>

Employers often use social media in the recruitment process. In addition, there is some interest in using social media information to make hiring decisions as well. However, because the research on this practice is a bit conflicting, we recommend caution. First, different applicants provide different types of information and different amounts of information on their social media; thus, comparing different applicants to make a hiring decision would not be fair. Second, research has shown that the information provided by social networking sites may not lead to good decisions. In one study, researchers found that recruiters' ratings of students' Facebook pages were not predictive of later work performance; they also found that decisions made on the basis of this information favored white and female applicants, suggesting that such decisions have systematic bias.[81] Another study found that information from personal social networking sites may give recruiters demographic data that are illegal to use for hiring decisions; this study also found recruiters' ratings of these sites did not predict performance.[82]

But it is also important to differentiate personal from professional social networking sites, as professional sites like LinkedIn may provide job-related information about a candidate.[83] One study showed recruiter ratings of LinkedIn pages can give good information about personality and cognitive ability, have low adverse impact, and can predict career success,[84] although the research on the accuracy of information gleaned from LinkedIn pages is not settled.[85] In short, more research is needed on the value of using social network information in selection. Of course, whether or not it is inadvisable for employers to make hiring decisions based on social networking sites, some may do so. Thus, we suggest that job applicants remain cautious about what they post about themselves on these sites.

As noted throughout this book, diversity and inclusion is a top issue in organizations today, and the topic continues to broaden. This includes the hiring of refugees as part of their integration into U.S. society. The nonprofit Tent Partnership for Refugees includes dozens of U.S. corporations (including Amazon, FedEx, Pepsi, and Marriott) that have committed to hiring and training thousands of refugees over the next 3 years.[86] As another example, the Employer Assistance and Resource Network on Disability Inclusion (EARN) works with employers to help them recruit and hire people with disabilities. They also assist with the hiring of neurodiverse employees, working with organizations such as Ford Motor Company, JPMorgan Chase, and Microsoft.[87]

In addition, there has been some interest among employers in using credit history as an applicant screening method. The assumption among some employers is that a poor credit history may be a sign of other problems such as low conscientiousness.[88] However, there are a number of reasons to caution against using credit histories in selection, and their use appears to be on the decline among employers. First, many people may have a poor credit score due to factors that are no fault of their own, such as being laid off from their job or having a health issue. Second, the relationship between credit scores, personality, and performance is not at all clear. For example, one study showed that a poor credit score is not associated with workplace deviance and that a good score is actually associated with poor agreeableness.[89] Third, there is also evidence that credit scores may show adverse impact. In short, credit scores cannot be assumed to predict job performance, and they may lead to adverse impact, such that they should not be used except when there is good reason to do so.

SPOTLIGHT ON ETHICS: KEEPING APPLICANT AND EMPLOYEE DATA SECURE

As we discussed throughout this book, applicant information privacy is a major ethical and legal issue faced by employers, and it is one that applicants are concerned about as well. We mentioned the issue of keeping applicant information secure—something that is more easily said than done due to the risks inherent in both human error and the ingenuity of cyber-criminals.

For example, in 2018, Huntsville Hospital in Alabama found that the private information of job applicants (including social security numbers) may have been breached due to a security issue with their recruitment platform. In 2021, Panasonic announced that hackers had gotten access to candidates' personal information. And in fall of 2022, the Five Guys burger chain found they had experienced a data breach involving job applicants' data. Often, the cause of such data breaches is simple human error—errors that result from behaviors that many of us engage in on a regular basis, such as using simple passwords and not logging out of sites after visiting them.

How does an employer protect applicant data? It is recommended that HR work closely with IT staff, set up communication channels among employees to share insights for protecting data security, conduct a risk assessment of where things might go wrong, and train employees in the basics of keeping data secure.[90]

Questions

1. What practices and cautions are you familiar with that would help keep personal data secure, for yourself or for others such as job applicants at your workplace or university?

2. Look up the Huntsville Hospital, Panasonic, or Five Guys data breach and read the details of what happened, how, and why. What could have been done differently? How did the employer respond once the breach happened?

APPLICANT REACTIONS TO SELECTION METHODS AND PROCEDURES

LEARNING OBJECTIVES
7.6 Describe the importance of applicant reactions to selection processes.

Although it is essential to consider the validity of selection procedures as well as their utility and effects on diversity, there is a growing realization that the job applicants' perspective, or **applicant reactions**, matters as well. Research has shown that how applicants perceive the hiring process, including how fairly they believe they were treated, can affect important outcomes such as their willingness to buy the company's products or even whether they accept a job offer.[91] In other words, organizations would do well to consider the **candidate experience** (the term for applicant reactions often used by employers) in developing their hiring procedures, and many now do so.

Many employers are concerned that a bad candidate experience could cause the best applicants to look for jobs elsewhere, and rightly so. Candidates may choose not to work for a company that treats them unfairly and disrespectfully during selection.[92] The British cable and mobile provider Virgin Media also realized that disgruntled candidates could be directly affecting their bottom line. Specifically, they found that a significant number of job candidates who had a negative interview experience (e.g., a rude interviewer) switched providers as a result, costing the company the equivalent of $5.4 million per year. To attack this problem head-on, Virgin put together an intensive program to train interviewers—a gold standard on how to treat applicants with respect. Part of the program includes inviting candidates to share their experiences as feedback to the interview team.[93]

An extensive body of research has examined what applicants want in a selection system. Applicants want to be treated fairly during hiring, and this perceived fairness in turn affects their attitudes and behaviors.[94] Applicants prefer selection methods that appear to be related to the job. As an example, applicants tend to prefer job interviews that ask clearly job-related questions rather than abstract questions with no obvious relationship to the job. In addition, applicants value feedback and communication from employers during the hiring process, and they also like methods that treat all applicants the same way. Finally, applicants want to be treated with respect: A cold or unfriendly person tells the applicant that cold relationships prevail in the organization. Interestingly, these characteristics of the selection situation that are valued by applicants seem to generalize across countries and cultures, having been found in North America, Europe, South America, and Asia.[95] A summary of some of the key factors that affect job applicants' perceptions is presented in Table 7.8.

TABLE 7.8 ■ Characteristics of Selection Systems That Have Been Found to Affect Applicant Perceptions and Behaviors	
Selection Procedure Characteristics	**Definition**
Job-Relatedness	The selection procedure is either obviously related to the job (e.g., a work sample), or the applicant understands that it is important to the job (e.g., a test of agreeableness and extraversion for a customer service job).
Opportunity to Perform	The selection procedure gives the applicants a feeling that they can "show what they know" or "show what they can do" relative to what is required for the job.
Interpersonal Treatment	The applicant is treated with respect by people from the organization. This might include respect in communications with the applicant, both written and in person, and letting the applicant know the final outcome (e.g., the employer lets the applicant know if they got the job rather than simply saying nothing).
Feedback Timeliness	Applicants are given the results of the application process in a timely manner.
Consistency	Applicants are all treated in a consistent manner.

Source: Bauer, T. N., McCarthy, J., Anderson, N., Truxillo, D. M., & Salgado, J. (2020). *What we know about the candidate experience: Research summary and best practices for applicant reactions.* SIOP White Paper series.

This all leads to the question regarding which selection procedures applicants prefer (see Figure 7.8). Not surprisingly, they tend to prefer procedures that are obviously job related, such as work samples, assessment centers, and job interviews; feel less positively toward more abstract selection procedures, such as résumés, biodata, personality tests, cognitive tests, and references; and feel least positively toward graphology (handwriting analysis), which is still used for selection in France, the use of personal contacts, and integrity tests, which may seem the least job related.[96] Note that one challenge for employers is that some of the methods most preferred by applicants are not always the most cost-effective to administer. For example, work samples are certainly valid predictors, but they can be quite expensive to administer and may be impractical for very large applicant pools. Research has also suggested that providing explanations to job applicants—for example, how a test that does not appear to be obviously job related actually has been carefully developed and researched to be quite valid—can help to alleviate applicant concerns.[97] The candidate experience is so important that the Talent Board, an organization that focuses on understanding the candidate experience, gives awards to organizations each year. In 2022, companies such as New York-Presbyterian Hospital, Walgreens, Foot Locker, and Intel were among the 50 winners recognized by the Talent Board.[98] In short, in addition to considering the validity, utility, and legality of selection procedures, employers should consider applicants' perceptions of these procedures.

FIGURE 7.8 ■ Selection Procedures Preferred by Job Applicants		
Most Preferred	Favorable Evaluation	Least Preferred
● Work Samples	● Résumés	● Honesty Tests
● Interviews	● Cognitive Tests	● Personal Contacts
	● References	● Graphology (handwriting analysis)
	● Biodata	
	● Personality Tests	

Sources: Anderson, N., Salgado, J. F., & Hülsheger, U. R. (2010). Applicant reactions in selection: Comprehensive meta-analysis into reaction generalization versus situational specificity. *International Journal of Selection and Assessment, 18,* 291–304; Hausknecht, J. P., Day, D. V., & Thomas, S. C. (2004). Applicant reactions to selection procedures: An updated model and meta-analysis. *Personnel Psychology, 57,* 639–683.

Although more research is needed on how applicants react to new technology such as AI-screened résumés and asynchronous video interviews, we do know some things. For example, although applicants may react negatively to automated résumé screening, some research shows these methods can also cause applicants to see the organization as more innovative. Applicant reactions may also be improved by providing an explanation to applicants for these new methods.[99]

Finally, one important finding is that the outcome an applicant gets (e.g., if they are given an interview or a job offer) is one of the biggest factors that affects applicant reactions. But of course, there will always be some applicants who don't get a job offer. What should an employer do for candidates that they cannot hire? The key is to treat applicants with dignity and respect; for example, explain to them that there were only so many openings. Some employers ask if the applicant would like to be considered for other positions in the future. Any feedback to applicants, whether verbal or written, should be considered from the applicant's point of view. And of course, let the applicant know their final outcome. Hearing no feedback at all from an employer gives a bad impression to an applicant.

DEPLOYMENT OF SELECTION PROCEDURES

Suppose an employer has decided to use a personality test, an integrity test, and a structured interview to hire its programmers. There are approximately 10 vacancies, and the company expects to have 100 strong applicants due to a successful recruitment effort. One simple approach would be to administer all of the selection procedures at one time. So an applicant might come into the organization and take the personality and integrity tests and then move on to the interview. However, there are some problems with this approach, primarily with the use of resources involved: Given that there are 100 applicants, interviewing all 100 of them, especially when there are only 10 vacancies, would not be very cost-effective in terms of using company resources and time. Instead, the company might decide to administer these selection procedures sequentially in what is called a multiple-hurdle approach (see Figure 7.9). Typically, the less expensive selection procedures—in this case the tests of personality and integrity—are put first. Those applicants who score sufficiently high on these two tests would then be put through the more costly structured interview.[100] You may have personal experience with this approach to selection, which is commonly used for hiring. Applicants might fill out an initial job application. Those that

---

FIGURE 7.9   ■   Example of the Multiple-Hurdle Selection Process

This is an example of a multiple-hurdle approach in which the least expensive selection procedures are put first with the full applicant pool, and the most expensive selection procedures are put last with fewer applicants to save on administration costs.

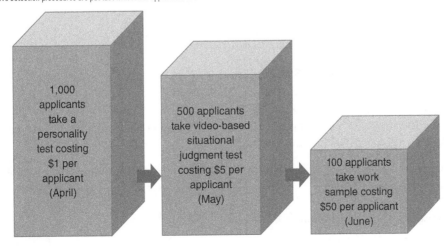

meet the minimum qualifications could take a test online, and the employer then would follow up with an interview if these initial tests suggest that the applicant is a good enough fit.

In this case, after passing an initial screening (e.g., a résumé check) to be sure they meet the minimum job qualifications, applicants are then given the tests (hurdles) in this order: the personality test ($1 per applicant), then the situational judgment test ($5 per applicant), and then the work sample ($50 per applicant). Only those who pass one hurdle are allowed to go on to the next hurdle. This saves money compared with giving all of the tests to all of the applicants.

It is important to note that the timeliness of decisions is important to applicants who would like to receive feedback quickly and who may also have other opportunities they are considering. Thus, making applicants wait too long between selection hurdles can give applicants a negative impression of the company and may cause employers to lose the best talent to other employers who are willing to move more quickly. In other words, using selection hurdles rather than administering all selection procedures at once makes a lot of practical sense, as long as the delays between hurdles are not too lengthy.

CHAPTER SUMMARY

Hiring the best talent provides an organization with a competitive advantage and is the main goal of selection. When choosing among personnel selection procedures, organizations should consider their validity, utility, and effects on diversity as well as legal issues. Understanding reliability, validity, and selection utility enables organizations to choose the best predictors for a given hiring situation. A range of selection procedures are available to organizations, and these should be compared in terms of their relative validity, practicality, and effects on workforce diversity. Practical issues such as the timing and sequencing of selection procedures to ensure cost-effectiveness need to be considered along with the candidate experience.

KEY TERMS

Applicant reactions

Assessment center

Behavioral interview

Biographical data (biodata)

Candidate experience

Cognitive ability test

Concurrent validity

Construct validity

Content validity

Criterion-related validity

Emotional intelligence (EI)

Five Factor Model (FFM)

Integrity test

Local validation

Multiple-hurdle approach

Predictive validity

Psychometrics

Reliability

Selection interview

Situational interview

Situational judgment tests (SJTs)

Structured interview

Unstructured interview

Utility

Validity

Validity coefficient

Validity generalization

Work sample

HR REASONING AND DECISION-MAKING EXERCISES

Mini-Case Analysis Exercise: Selection Systems for Hiring

You are working for a regional coffee chain, Al Bar. Currently the company has 900 employees, but it is expanding into several new urban areas, and moving forward, the CEO would like to be more systematic in the approach to hiring new baristas. Al Bar also needs a valid but practical and cost-effective approach given the large number of new hires expected in the coming years.

A glance at the O*Net database shows the following sorts of skills are typically required of baristas:

- Take orders from customers and give orders to coworkers for preparation.

- Prepare beverages such as espresso drinks, coffee, tea.

- Clean work area and equipment.

- Describe items on the menu to customers and suggest menu items that they might like.

- Take customer payments.

You have been asked to propose a new selection system for hiring baristas. Consider the following questions.

1. Which selection procedures would make the most sense for hiring baristas? Weigh each of your suggested selection procedures in terms of (a) validity, (b) enhancing workforce diversity, (c) utility, and (d) applicant reactions.

2. Once you have chosen your selection procedures, how would you deploy them? For example, in what order would you administer the selection procedures? Would you administer them in person or online (or some combination)? Explain why.

3. Assuming that you would use an interview at some point in the process, what would be some good interview questions? Would you use an unstructured interview, a behavioral interview, a situational interview, or some combination? Explain why.

4. Which selection procedures would you definitely not use for the barista job?

HR Decision Analysis Exercise: A New Approach to Hiring Employees?

You are working in the human resources department at Moderne Electronics, a leader in the field of electronic health care products. Recently, the CEO of Moderne has been interested in gamified personnel selection tests, including tests of personality and cognitive ability. As a result, the CEO has interviewed three companies that sell gamified tests and decided to sign a contract with one of these companies, Avanguardia Testing. Your CEO wants to use these gamified tests because "this is what today's applicants expect." Moreover, the salespeople at Avanguardia have told your CEO that the tests are good predictors of job performance and that Avanguardia has used big data algorithms to prove it. However, Avanguardia has not yet provided documentation to this effect.

Your boss, the vice president (VP) of HR, has questioned the switch to the new gamified system, partly because implementation of the new gamified tests will require a significant overhaul of the HR system, including thousands of hours of HR staff time. However, the VP of HR does admit that the tests provided by Avanguardia are attractive-looking and fun.

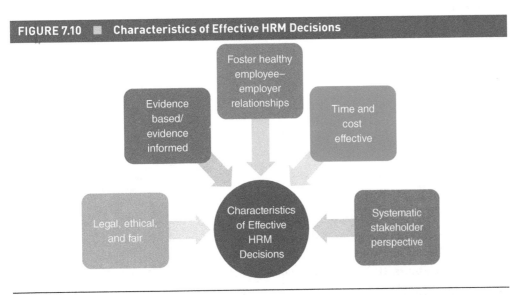

FIGURE 7.10 ■ Characteristics of Effective HRM Decisions

Please provide the rationale for your answer to each of the questions below.

Was the CEO's decision legal, ethical, and fair?

Was the CEO's decision evidence based/evidence informed?

Did the CEO's decision foster healthy employee–employer relationships?

Was the CEO's decision time- and cost-effective?

Did the CEO take a systematic stakeholder perspective?

Considering your analysis above, overall, do you think this was an effective decision? Why?

What, if anything, do you think should be done differently or considered to help make this decision more effective?

HR Decision-Making Exercise: Assessing the Validity of a New Test for Hiring Employees

A test vendor has approached the vice president (VP) of HR in your company with a new test of conscientiousness. The test vendor claims the new conscientiousness test is at least as valid as the old test that your company is currently using—plus the new test is half the price! As a result, the VP of HR has asked you to determine whether the company should use this new test of conscientiousness or stick with the old test. This is important, because having a valid test affects hiring decisions regarding hundreds of new employees. Plus, as you know, the test's validity is also important to the legal defensibility of the test.

You have been able to give the new conscientiousness test to 200 current employees on two occasions, 1 week apart. In addition, you have given these employees the old conscientiousness test, as well as tests of "achievement striving" and "verbal skills." Finally, you also have supervisor performance ratings on file for each employee regarding their organizational citizenship. In other words, you have a lot of what you need to begin to assess the validity of the new test of conscientiousness in terms of predicting job performance!

The correlations among these different tests and measures follow. Note that statistically significant relationships are indicated by an asterisk (*).

TABLE 7.9 ■ Correlations Among Tests and Measures	1	2	3	4	5	6
1. New Conscientiousness Test Time 1	-					
2. New Conscientiousness Test Time 2	.97*	-				
3. Old Conscientiousness Test	.92*	.90*	-			
4. Achievement Striving Test	.62*	.65*	.58*	-		
5. Verbal Skills Test	.11	.12	.12		-	
6. Job Performance: Supervisor Ratings of Organizational Citizenship	.35*	.33*	.32*	.25*	.15*	-

Take a few minutes to orient yourself to this correlation matrix. Note that most of the information you need is in the first column, which shows the pattern of correlations between the new conscientiousness test with other measures. Then, answer the following questions.

1. What do you think about its **construct validity** (i.e., its pattern of correlations with other tests)? Why?

2. What is the evidence for the **criterion-related validity** of the new conscientiousness test?

3. What do you think about the **content validity** of the new conscientiousness test? (*Hint*: Is the information needed to answer this question available in the table?) Explain.

4. Would you recommend using the new test or the old test of conscientiousness for hiring workers? Why or why not?

DATA AND ANALYTICS EXERCISE: WEIGHTING PREDICTORS VIA REGRESSION

As we described earlier, criterion-related validity of selection procedures can be shown through a statistically significant correlation between a test and a job outcome like performance. Going one step further, regression can show a predicted score on the outcome based on a test.

For example, if you had a dataset that allowed you to develop a regression equation (through a statistical program), you would get an equation in this form:

$Y = bx + a$

where Y is the predicted score on the outcome

X is the score a person obtained on the test

b is the weight of the test

and a is the constant or "y-intercept."

Let's say the specific equation you obtained from your dataset was as follows:

$Y = 3x + 1$

In this case, if a person obtained a 5 on the test, their predicted score on outcome would be 16. Note that this is not the score that all people with a 5 would get but is rather a *predicted* score or their most likely score.

Now let's go through an example where you have given three tests to a group of employees (concurrent design). The tests are proactivity, emotional intelligence, and situation judgment (SJT), all predicting customer service job performance.

You get the following results:

Correlations

		Proactivity	Emotional Intelligence	SJT	Customer Service
Proactivity	Pearson Correlation	1	.318**	.237**	.391**
	Sig. (2-tailed)		.000	.000	.000
	N	300	300	300	300
Emotional Intelligence	Pearson Correlation	.318**	1	.932**	.426**
	Sig. (2-tailed)	.000		.000	.000
	N	300	300	300	300
SJT	Pearson Correlation	.237**	.932**	1	.417**
	Sig. (2-tailed)	.000	.000		.000
	N	300	300	300	300
Customer Service	Pearson Correlation	.391**	.426**	.417**	1
	Sig. (2-tailed)	.000	.000	.000	
	N	300	300	300	300

** Correlation is significant at the 0.01 level (2-tailed).

All three tests have a significant correlation with customer service job performance. But the EI test and SJT are highly redundant, correlated .932. One of them should go.

Here is one way to settle this: You learn that the SJT costs $1 per person to administer, whereas the test of EI costs $10 per person. With thousands of applicants, you are concerned about the relative utility of the EI, and so you decide to drop it.

Now you have to decide how to weight the two remaining tests: proactivity and SJT. That would be found in the column listed as B.

	Coefficients	Std. Error	t Stat	p Value
Intercept	5.527	.539	10.249	.000
Proactivity	.385	.064	6.031	.000
SJT	.567	.085	6.714	.000

In this case, the weight of SJT is .567, and the weight of proactivity is .385. The constant is 5.527. So the equation then becomes:

Y (predicted customer service score) $= 5.527 + .567$ (SJT score) $+ .385$ (proactivity score)

Thus, if a person obtained a 10 on the SJT and a 10 on proactivity, their predicted customer service score would be

$Y = 5.527 + 5.670 + 3.850$

$Y = 15.047$

Excel Extension: Now You Try!

On **edge.sagepub.com/bauer2e**, in the Excel spreadsheet, run the requested regression models to get the regression weights.

©iStock.com/Blue Planet Studio

 **8** TRAINING, DEVELOPMENT, AND CAREERS

LEARNING OBJECTIVES

After reading and studying this chapter, you should be able to do the following:

8.1   State the importance of the role of training programs within organizations.

8.2   Describe the steps to a training needs assessment, including the purpose of each, and how they are used to develop training goals.

8.3   List the characteristics of the employee, the organizational context, and the training that can be leveraged to enhance training effectiveness.

8.4   Describe some of the most important training methods and media used by organizations and list their respective advantages and disadvantages.

8.5   Demonstrate the use of the major categories of criteria for assessing training effectiveness.

8.6   Analyze the factors associated with effective career development and management.

TRAINING TO SUPPORT THE NATION'S WORKFORCE: THE CASE OF GOOGLE

©iStockphoto/com/fizkes

A company's workforce is one of its greatest assets. Many companies invest in worker training to develop their employees and give themselves a competitive advantage. The same could be said about a country's workforce as well. Workers provide the value that drives a country's economy. We already know about the value of education for a country, but how can we scale up training to prepare a country's workforce for today's key jobs, to help compete in a global economy?

Google has recently taken on this challenge, addressing workforce training at a national level. In 2022, Google announced it would support three nonprofits with a $100 million fund: Merit America, Year Up, and Social Finance. Merit America focuses on technical training for people without bachelor's degrees. Year Up supports upward mobility for low-income workers aged 18 through 26. Social Finance sponsors student-friendly repayment plans.

Each of the organizations that Google chose to support has at least one thing in common: a proven track record of tangible success. This is not just success in terms of how many students complete their programs, but rather how many students actually get better-paying jobs after graduation. And Google is continuing to set a high standard for the program. While Google will provide some of the upfront training costs, the training organizations themselves will not get fully paid unless graduates land and stay in higher-paying jobs.

Students will be trained on technical skills such as data analytics and how to design a good user experience. But they will also learn critical skills for success like communication and teamwork. Students will also get help with child care as needed, career coaches, and developing an alumni network after graduation. Financial supports for students include zero interest on any loans they take, with no need to repay their loans until they have a job paying at least $40,000 per year. Finally, for most students, their payments will be $100/month and for no more than 5 years.

Google's goal is to increase wages by $1 billion for the planned 20,000 program graduates. Notably, an independent research firm will monitor the success of the programs over time and support the programs that provide the best results. In the end, Google hopes to provide a model for other organizations and to show the benefits of these types of training programs over typical government training programs.[1]

CASE DISCUSSION QUESTIONS

1. Google is clearly focused on supporting those training programs that succeed. In addition to the factors measured here, how might you define "success" for these kinds of training programs? How specifically would you measure the success of the program?

2. Can you think of how similar programs might be designed for training other types of skills besides technology skills? Describe what kind of job you would focus on, what types of skills would be needed by trainees, how you would train them, and how you would measure success.

3. As we will see in this chapter, the training context is critical to training's success. What contextual factors might help or hinder a trainee's success in these training programs? How has Google used the context in this case to improve the odds of a trainee succeeding?

4. What factors do you think drive Google's support for these training programs? Are they purely altruism and social responsibility, or is it some other factors?

INTRODUCTION

As we have stated in the preceding chapters, an organization's human capital is arguably its greatest asset. Developing employees through training may be one of the best investments an organization can make—if it is done well. Thus, it is important to implement best practices for training and developing employees in organizations throughout their careers.

This chapter describes the process for developing and implementing a training program and demonstrating its value to the organization. As shown in Figure 8.1, this process involves conducting a training needs assessment, addressing characteristics of the worker and the organization, choosing the appropriate training methods, and evaluating the program's effectiveness. Whether you are in charge of the training program or are a manager making decisions about whether to invest in training, this chapter provides the expertise you need to develop a training program or critically assess its value.

FIGURE 8.1 ■ The Process for Developing, Implementing, and Evaluating an Organizational Training Program

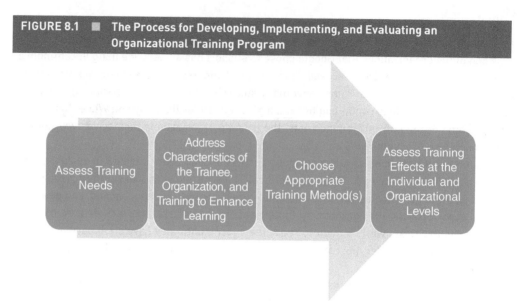

THE IMPORTANCE OF TRAINING IN ORGANIZATIONS

LEARNING OBJECTIVES
8.1   State the importance of the role of training programs within organizations.

For training to pay off, it is important that it address specific organizational needs, align with the organization's objectives, and fit the needs of employees. Additionally, the organizational decision makers should consider from the start how they will know whether the training worked.

These considerations are important given the sizable investment organizations make in training. As shown in Figure 8.2, U.S. companies spend thousands of dollars per employee each year on training programs.[2] (It is also noteworthy that training costs went down slightly in 2020, perhaps due to decreases in training-related travel during the pandemic.)[3]

FIGURE 8.2 ■ Corporate Training Expenditures in U.S. Organizations During 2020

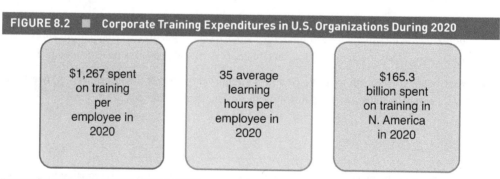

Source: Ho, M. (2021, December). What effect has the pandemic had on L&D? *TD: Talent Development, 75,* 24–29; https://www.statista.com/statistics/738412/size-of-the-workplace-training-market-north-america/

Most of you will be involved in organizational training and development activities at some point in your lives, at least as a participant. However, you may also need to decide about whether to undertake a training program for your employees or for your organization. The principles described in this chapter will help you to make more informed and effective decisions about training in your workplace, whether it is developing a training program in-house or choosing an effective training program delivered by an external vendor.

Given the large amounts of money organizations invest in training programs each year, helping you make better decisions about training is important. For example, much of the money organizations spend on training is paid to external vendors who specialize in various types of training. To promote their training programs, these vendors often cite examples of successes in other organizations. This is certainly a valid way for training vendors to show that their training can be effective. However, managers should ask whether the training would actually be beneficial to their own organization and industry: A training program that was successful among nurses may not work for construction workers. Just as important is to consider how training success was actually measured by vendors. For example, do vendors consider "success" simply to be trainee satisfaction, or can the vendor show that the training actually had an impact on measures of employee knowledge, skills, and performance? Does the vendor take a "one-size-fits-all" approach to training delivery, or do they understand your specific organization and industry and can they tailor the training to your employees' needs and your organizational culture? Can previous clients be contacted to get their experiences with the training program?

The potential payoff to organizations from training is substantial. Moreover, research shows workplace training can benefit not only the work organizations that provide it but also individual employees and even countries and societies.[4] In fact, although managers may observe that there is a skills gap between the general workforce and the available jobs, workers are often eager to gain more training to advance their skills—a win-win-win for employers, workers, and the economy.

TRAINING NEEDS ASSESSMENT

LEARNING OBJECTIVES
8.2   Describe the steps to a training needs assessment, including the purpose of each, and how they are used to develop training goals.

Training needs assessment is a systematic evaluation of the organization, the jobs, and the employees to determine where training is most needed and what type of training is needed. Training needs assessment is also a key part of developing clearly focused training goals that are aligned with organizational strategy and in understanding how to develop and implement the training program in ways that will have the greatest benefit to the organization.[5] Sophisticated analytics can also support training needs assessment by analyzing employee metrics (e.g., productivity), indicating where training is needed most.[6]

Today, HR functions face greater pressures for accountability. This is especially true of the training function because of the large amount of money that is spent on it. Still, although many organizations would be reluctant to invest in equipment without a good bit of analysis, many of these same organizations do not deeply analyze their training needs before investing in training. First, companies often assume that problems are due to a lack of training, but this is not always the case; as a result, they can end up spending resources on unneeded training. For example, a restaurant chain may believe its problem with decreasing sales is due to a skills gap among its servers and may decide to address the "problem" with training. In actuality, the problem may turn out not to be a training issue at all but something else (e.g., poor advertising). Second, even if top management in an organization correctly believes there are training needs among its employees, their training efforts need to be correctly focused. Using the restaurant chain again as an example, even if the company is correct that its servers need additional training, the servers' specific skills gap needs to be identified. It would not be useful to train the servers on customer service skills, when in fact the problem is that the servers do not know or understand the items on the menu well enough to advise customers. It would hardly be a good use of company resources to train employees on topics on which they are already proficient.

In short, before spending the capital needed to train employees, it is wise to get a better grasp on what the organization's training needs actually are through some sort of needs assessment process. In fact, conducting a training needs assessment may be the most important step in developing an effective training program. This process is typically conceptualized as having three components: organizational analysis, job analysis, and person analysis (see Figure 8.3).

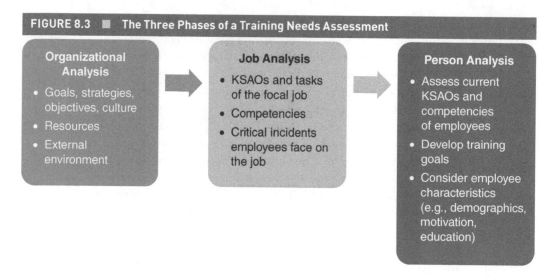

FIGURE 8.3 ■ The Three Phases of a Training Needs Assessment

Organizational Analysis

Organizational analysis involves a number of steps for getting to know the organization at a broader level so a training program can be developed to fit the organization. This includes issues such as

- understanding the company's *goals and strategies* so the goals of the training program are aligned with them;

- understanding the *organization's culture*, including the attitudes toward training among managers and employees;

- identifying the *resources* the organization can devote to training; and

- analyzing the organization's *external environment*.

Organizational Goals and Strategies

Understanding organizational goals and strategies is important for all organizational activities—including training programs. For example, if an organization's focus is to gain market share over the next 5 years, and the sales force and product development are considered key to increased market share, it may be worthwhile to consider training efforts focused on the sales force or on product development.

Organizational Culture

Similarly, understanding the company's culture—the shared beliefs that employees have about accepted behavioral norms—is key to implementing an effective training program. Although organizational decision makers may know that culture is important, the challenge becomes how to instill a strong, positive culture into the organization, starting with individual employees and teams. Research clearly demonstrates that supervisors and managers are key to communicating and supporting a positive culture. The research has also shown that organizational policies and practices play a significant role. For example, if a company's culture valued nonconfrontational, subtle interpersonal relationships, developing a training program focused on promoting an assertive, confrontational interpersonal style could be damaging. For example, Fresenius Medical Care North America (FMCNA) works to provide high-quality care to people with chronic conditions. In addition, their employees are encouraged to focus on giving emotional support to patients.[7] Imagine how counterproductive it would be for such a company to have training that encouraged workers to work as quickly as possible, rather than thinking through the purpose and result.

Although many organizations hire only skilled applicants, many hire with the plan to upskill employees later.

©iStockphoto.com/ katleho Seisa

Another issue that frequently comes up regarding culture is lack of support for training among managers and employees. If managers indicate relatively low support or value placed on training, or if the company has had failed training programs in the past, figuring out how to increase trainee motivation and support for training may be one of the most important challenges in designing the training program. In some cases, the culture may be so opposed to training that it is not a worthwhile investment at that moment. For example, supervisors who disagree with the type of training that is being offered to their employees may actually undermine training efforts, such that they tell employees not to perform the behaviors they learned in training. ("I know that's what you were taught in training, but that's not the way we actually do things here.") In this case, investment in training is unlikely to lead to transfer of skills to the job. One approach would be to get supervisors on board with the training early on. For example, an organization could get supervisors involved in the development of the training program as early as possible to get their input on how to increase the usefulness of the training. This would also help to gain their support for the training program once it is implemented.

Organizational Resources

It is also important to understand what resources the organization is able and willing to invest in the training program. This includes the organization's mindset regarding whether to invest in training at all and resources such as facilities and personnel. For example, some organizations may choose to focus on hiring the best talent ("buy" strategy). This strategy assumes that new hires will need little training. On the other hand, some employers may be willing to invest in training employees to align their skills with organizational needs ("develop" strategy). In addition, it is important to understand whether the company currently has employee subject matter experts (SMEs) who can act as trainers, or whether trainers will need to be brought in from the outside. For example, would a hospital be able to use current employees as trainers, requiring that these employees be trained themselves on how to be good trainers? Or would they be better off hiring professional trainers from outside of the hospital? Similarly, if the organization is considering the use of eLearning (discussed later in this chapter), do all employees have access to the computers or mobile devices that would be needed to train them? Or, if the training is best delivered by means of classroom training, are classroom facilities available? How many employees can be trained at one time? The issue of resources must be understood early on so the training can best be developed in a practical, scalable way, or the training may need to be limited to training for only certain employees on the most critical competencies.

External Environment

The organization's external environment should also be taken into account when developing the training program. This might involve various types of compliance training that is required for particular jobs, such as safety training or, during the pandemic, Covid-19 rules and restrictions.[8] In addition, the organization's external competition is an issue that can inform the development of a training program. For example, an organization's competitor may be providing certain key training to its employees on state-of-the-art technology. Should that be considered in this organization as well? In addition, laws and regulations, such as equal employment opportunity laws (see Chapter 4), can be important to consider when putting together a training program. This is especially true if access to or success in the training program can affect whether an employee is hired or allowed to remain in a job. For example, if firefighters must pass a certain type of annual training to keep their job, the training program would be having the same effect as a selection procedure. If so, issues related to disparate impact (e.g., Do different groups perform at different levels in the program?) need to be considered, and the training program would need to be legally defensible as job related.

SPOTLIGHT ON LEGAL ISSUES: TRAINING THROUGH THE LEGAL LENS: EQUAL ACCESS AND COMPLIANCE

Numerous legal issues are relevant to the training function in organizations. Broadly, these pertain to providing equal opportunity to employees via training programs and to an employer's obligation to provide many types of job-related training to employees and supervisors.

First, consider the Uniform Guidelines on Employee Selection Procedures (discussed in Chapters 4 and 7). Although training may not be a selection procedure per se, to the extent that a training program affects which employees are retained or promoted, the training program is part of selection decisions. For example, if success in a training program for new supervisors is necessary for an employee to keep a supervisory job, the training program is being used as a selection procedure. Thus, the organization needs to ensure that passing rates in the training program for different subgroups are equivalent, or it should be prepared to show the validity or job-relatedness of the training program in order to defend it. In addition, employees should have fair access to training programs that can provide opportunities for them to advance in their careers.

Second, many types of training programs are required by employers to remain compliant with current government guidelines and to avoid legal liability. Such compliance training is focused on regulations, laws, and policies related to employees' daily work. These might include providing supervisors with the skills training they need to be effective; safety training, particularly for workers in safety-sensitive jobs; and diversity and sexual harassment training to protect all employees and provide a safe work environment. If employees are not sufficiently trained, and if then their actions result in injury to themselves or others, the company may be held liable. In short, training programs should be examined with an eye to legal issues from their inception.[9]

Job Analysis

Once organizational analysis has been conducted, providing a better understanding of the organization and which jobs should be the focus of the training program based on the organization's goals and resources, the next step in a training needs assessment is to conduct a job analysis. A job analysis helps determine which KSAOs, tasks, and competencies are associated with a job, as well as the critical incidents that employees face on the job, in order to develop an effective training program. We have discussed the range of options for job analysis and competency modeling as well as the basics of how to do them in earlier chapters (e.g., interviews, surveys).

The task–KSAO approach is particularly well suited for the development of training, as it identifies the critical KSAOs, which will form the backbone of the training program. In addition, understanding which tasks are linked to the KSAOs—that is, how the KSAOs are actually demonstrated on the job in terms of behavior—provides rich material for the development of training content. For example, it would be important to know that a job requires the KSAO of "interpersonal skills." However, it would be even more useful to know which interpersonal skills are demonstrated on the job. For example, an administrative assistant might, as part of their coordination activities, focus on interacting with members of the team as well as the leaders of other work groups. In contrast, customer service agents for an airline would use their interpersonal skills to interact with customers. This key difference would determine what type of training content would be included for each of these different types of jobs: For the executive assistant, there might be role-plays focused on interacting with a difficult team member; for the airline customer service agent, the role-play might focus on dealing with an unhappy passenger. Relatedly, it would be good to know what critical incidents employees face on their jobs—such as dealing with a difficult team leader from a different group in the case of the administrative assistant—to understand how to develop the most appropriate training scenarios.

Both administrative assistants and airline customer service agents must deal with tricky interpersonal situations. These circumstances can be quite different in terms of whom the assistants and agents are dealing with, the levels of anger and anxiety involved in the interactions, and the mode of communication (e.g., in person, by phone, or by e-mail). What kind of interpersonal skills training content would you recommend for each type of job?

©iStockphoto.com/wundervisuals; ©iStockphoto.com/FS-Stock

Person Analysis

Once the critical competencies, KSAOs, and tasks of a job have been identified, it may seem there is enough information to develop a training program. However, there are still two broad questions that need to be answered:

1. Which specific KSAOs or competencies need to be developed, and for which employees?

2. Which characteristics of the employees (referred to as demographics) need to be considered in order to develop the most effective training program?

Identifying KSAOs and Candidates for Development

One approach an organization might take is to train employees on every KSAO that is required for the job. But this would assume employees are weak on all the KSAOs, which is unlikely to be the case. The more likely scenario is that employees are fine in terms of some KSAOs and weaker on others. It is also likely that some employees need training more than others do. Let's tease apart these two issues.

First, to train employees on KSAOs at which they are already proficient would obviously be a waste of resources. For that reason, organizations tend to focus on the skills they believe most employees need to improve. For example, a company that sells large-scale computer hardware may find that most of its salespeople are good at finding new customers, reaching out to existing customers, and making sales. Due to rapid advances and innovations in computer equipment, however, salespeople don't know what the various types of equipment can do, which limits their ability to match customer needs with the appropriate equipment. In this case, the training program could be fairly straightforward, such that it brings salespeople up to speed about the current product knowledge.

Second, it may be that only some employees need training, whereas others do not. Or it may be that some employees need training on some KSAOs, but other employees need training on different KSAOs. Using the sales example, the company may find that some salespeople need to be trained on the various computer products the company is currently selling, and others need to be trained on how to develop new client lists. The training program might therefore be tailored to address each of these different employee needs.

Note that a strategic decision regarding the training program is often whether all employees in a particular type of job should receive the same training or whether the training program should focus on individual employee needs. This decision is largely driven by balancing the difficulty of developing and delivering individualized employee training versus delivering a one-size-fits-all training program that sometimes trains employees on skills they already possess. There is no simple solution to this challenge. However, eLearning forms of training (discussed later in this chapter), which often allow employers (and employees) to choose from among thousands of possible training modules, to some extent facilitate the delivery of training customized to individual employee needs.

How are person analysis data obtained? Numerous methods are available to decision makers, and there is no one "correct" method. The options include examining objective production or sales data, customer survey data, performance appraisals, and survey of employees regarding their training needs. Person analysis data can also be collected by having employees take tests (particularly if the focus is on knowledge) or go through job performance simulations. The most appropriate method depends largely on which KSAOs are being assessed as well as the practicality and cost.

Trainee Demographics

Later in this chapter, we discuss how different employee characteristics can affect the delivery of training. At this point, however, it is important just to understand some basic employee demographics that might affect the type of training approach to be used. For example, employees' education level or age might affect the training methods the organization chooses to use. A group of employees with little exposure to computer technology may not be good candidates for an eLearning approach.

Developing Training Goals

Once the job analysis and person analysis data have been collected, an examination of the gap between the two can drive the development of training goals. In other words, the needs assessment will determine the gap between what the job requires and what KSAOs the trainees currently possess, and the goals of the training should be developed based upon this gap, as seen in Figure 8.4. For example, if the needs assessment showed that salespeople needed both technical and interpersonal skills, and that the sales force already had good interpersonal skills, the training could be focused primarily on technical skills.

FIGURE 8.4 ■ Developing Training Goals Based on the Gap Between Job Requirements and Current Employee Abilities

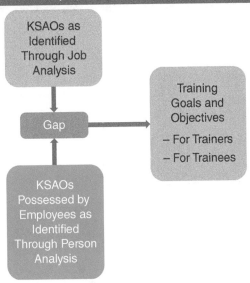

As much as possible, training goals should be expressed in specific, behavioral terms. For example, a weak training goal might be: "By the end of training, the employee can assemble equipment." In contrast, a stronger, more useful training goal would be: "By the end of training, an employee can assemble two pieces of equipment per hour." The latter goal is more useful for the final users of the training goals: training developers and trainees. Training developers will use the goals as the basis for their training programs. Trainees need to be given their training goals to help in their learning the material. (We will discuss the importance of goal setting for learning later in this chapter.)

In summary, investing in a training needs assessment can provide significant value for organizations, determining not only whether there is a need for training but also what type of training and for whom. In addition, it is important to remember that it is not always necessary to perform a training needs assessment with the exact steps and stages described here. In fact, many organizations approach the needs assessment process a bit differently. The key is to keep the goals of each of the stages of needs assessment in mind and to stay focused on organization, job, and persons as much as possible prior to designing a training program.[10]

ENHANCING LEARNING

LEARNING OBJECTIVES

8.3 List the characteristics of the employee, the organizational context, and the training that can be leveraged to enhance training effectiveness.

Once the training needs assessment is complete and the training goals are established, the next step is to consider ways to enhance learning. Learning can be defined as the acquisition of new knowledge, skills, behaviors, and attitudes and can occur either within or outside of the training context.[11] Effective training programs consider characteristics of the trainees, the organization, and the training delivery to enhance learning (see Figure 8.5). Understanding who the trainees are as well as the organization they will be working in helps to implement a training system that will be most effective. In addition, this will allow for consideration of how the training itself can be used to enhance training and transfer. The main idea here is that training is not a "one-size-fits-all" proposition, and consideration of the person and their context helps make the training more effective.[12]

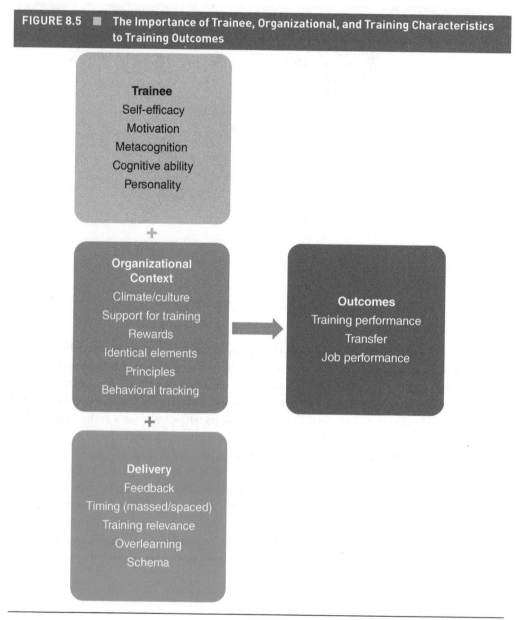

FIGURE 8.5 ■ The Importance of Trainee, Organizational, and Training Characteristics to Training Outcomes

Sources: Based on Chung, S., Zhan, Y., Noe, R. A., & Jiang, K. (2022). Is it time to update and expand training motivation theory? A meta-analytic review of training motivation research in the 21st century. *Journal of Applied Psychology, 107*(7), 1150–1179; Ford, J. K. (2020). *Learning in organizations: An evidence-based approach.* Routledge.

Trainee Characteristics

Various trainee characteristics may affect the success of a training program and should be taken into account to enhance the effectiveness of the training system. First, self-efficacy, or a person's belief that they can accomplish a task, is one of the most important predictors of training effectiveness. If a person does not believe they can master the material in a training course or that they can transfer their learned skills back to the job, they will not do as well in training. This is because people who don't feel they can master a particular skill will put less effort into accomplishing it. How can a training system address the possibility of low self-efficacy among some learners? One of the most effective approaches is to teach the material in small "bites" that allow people to feel a sense of mastery for specific aspects of a knowledge or skill.

Relatedly, trainee motivation is a significant predictor of training success. While you may be familiar with several theories of motivation, perhaps the most practical ones to consider for the training context are goal-setting theory and expectancy theory. Goal-setting theory states that setting specific, difficult yet achievable goals for people will lead to the highest performance. Performance can be further enhanced by adding rewards and providing feedback as to how well the person is achieving their goals. Goal setting should

- make the training goals specific but achievable,

- clearly communicate training goals to the learner, and

- provide feedback as to how well the goals are being achieved.

In sum, goal setting should provide clear guidance for enhancing trainee motivation and training performance. For example, if training factory workers on how to assemble products correctly, the goals of the training should be specific (e.g., "no more that 1% errors"), these goals should be communicated to the worker, and the workers should be told if they successfully achieved the training goals.

Further, goal accomplishment should be tied to rewards such as promotions, pay, or being able to do the job more effectively. Similarly, the expectancy theory of motivation suggests that if a person sees their efforts will lead to greater performance, and if they believe that performance will lead to an outcome they value, they will be more motivated. So in the training context, this might include showing trainees that if they try to do well in training it will lead to training success, and this success can lead to an outcome they value, such as better job performance.

A third factor related to training success is metacognitive skills. You may not have heard of metacognitive skills before, but you probably use these skills on a regular basis in your coursework. Metacognition is the person's ability to step back and assess their own performance—are they doing well in training? Are there some topics they find harder than others and that they need to brush up on? Some people are better at assessing their own performance than others, and this ability can have a serious effect on whether they learn. Consider two students, Carlos and Antonio, who both want As in a class. While Carlos is studying, he considers how well he is grasping the material, and he realizes he is at best at the C level. As a result, Carlos digs into the material to study even harder so he can achieve an A. On the other hand, Antonio, whose knowledge level is also currently in the C range, doesn't really assess his own level of expertise and assumes he is doing just fine by simply reading the chapters. Note the difference here: By being aware of his weaknesses, Carlos will address them with extra work and is more likely to earn an A in the class. In contrast, Antonio doesn't see his weaknesses and thus will be unlikely to do anything to address them. As a result, he is likely to get a C and be disappointed. In fact, the research suggests that poor performers are not only inaccurate in assessing their own skill levels but also tend to overestimate them.[13] How can the design of a training system address the fact that some people have poor metacognitive skills? As a solution, training can include giving learners frequent feedback about their actual performance levels and even remind them on occasion to step back and think about how well they are learning.

In addition, it is not surprising that both personality and *cognitive ability* (see Chapter 7) can affect a person's learning. For example, proactive personality, conscientiousness, openness to experience, and extraversion have all been shown to be related to training performance. And of course, cognitive ability is related to a person's learning speed. One way to address these personality and cognitive differences among learners is to devise training systems that allow people to proceed at their own pace. For example, a training program could be made up of three modules. More proficient learners could move through the three modules quickly, while less proficient learners could go more slowly.

Organizational Context: Enhancing Transfer

Perhaps one of the most important issues in training is **training transfer**, or whether the training results in changes in performance on the job.[14] The idea of transfer is core to the purpose of training in organizations—a training program may create increased knowledge among employees, but if performance is not affected, the training is not creating value for the organization.

There are a number of factors that can affect whether training results in transfer. First, what is the **training transfer climate** as expressed by supervisors—that is, is there support for training in the organization? For example, a bank may implement a training program that causes increased knowledge about how to interact with customers. In fact, the trainees may show strong improvement in their interpersonal skills while in the training environment. But when they return to work, the bank managers tell them the training is nonsense and there is no time to interact with customers in this way. In other words, despite the strength of the training, training knowledge and skills are unlikely to transfer due to an unsupportive climate. In fact, until the climate can be changed—and this usually starts by top management communicating and rewarding the desired climate and modeling the associated behaviors themselves—it may not be worth implementing the training. Relatedly, employees need to be rewarded for carrying out their trained behaviors.

In addition, training is more likely to transfer to the extent that there are **identical elements**, or that the training environment is like the work environment. For example, consider employee training focused on the use of a new software system. Company A gives its employees training on the system using computer equipment that is the same system employees use on the job. Company B simply gives a lecture describing the new software and how to use it. In this case, Company B's training approach is not much like the work environment and is not likely to lead to good results.

Mobile technology can be used to enhance the transfer of training. Behavioral tracking programs administered through mobile devices such as smartphones can help trainees set goals for performing trained behaviors on the job and send trainees daily reminders about performing trained behaviors back at work.[15]

©iStockphoto.com/putilich

Transfer through principles is when transfer is enhanced by training employees on the principles behind the content being taught. For example, consider a situation in which customer service workers are being trained on how to handle customer complaints. One company trains its employees on the issues involved—addressing customer complaints by balancing fairness and customer satisfaction, with the possibility of a small monetary concession from the company if the customer has a valid complaint or is a long-term customer. Company B, however, does not explain any such principles but only tells the trainees to apologize to customers if there is a complaint. Clearly, the employees in Company

A will be better able to handle a range of customer service complaints and also to handle them in a way that results in customer satisfaction.

Finally, transfer can be enhanced through a process called behavioral tracking, a process in which trainees keep track of their on-the-job behaviors and whether they are performing the behaviors they learned in training. Specifically, trainees might set goals for performing behaviors on the job and keep track of how often they perform the behaviors. The use of the behavioral tracking approach is facilitated using today's mobile technology. As an example, supervisors might go through a simple lecture about how to be supportive of their employees. Then they are asked to follow the behavioral tracking protocol for 3 weeks. Specifically, they are asked to set daily goals for performing supportive behaviors, and for 3 weeks they receive daily reminders on their smartphones asking them if they have shown support to their employees that day. As you can imagine, reminding trainees of their daily goals regarding applying training concepts on the job and asking them how well they have accomplished their goals can be a powerful tool in facilitating transfer.[16]

Training Delivery Characteristics

Different characteristics of the training program can be used to enhance learning and transfer, and some characteristics may be useful in particular situations. First, as mentioned earlier, providing feedback to learners as to their training performance can greatly enhance the effectiveness of training. For example, consider a situation in which you are completing several online training modules as part of learning your new job. If you were never told how successful you were in completing the modules, not only would that be very unsatisfying, it would not provide you with information to adjust your performance in order to do better in the training. As such, providing feedback can help learners understand how well they are mastering the training material and adjust their performance if necessary. Second, training relevance, or the degree to which trainees see the training as important to their jobs, can have a significant impact on the amount of effort they invest in the training. Third, providing trainees with a learning schema at the beginning of the training process can also enhance learning. A schema is an outline or framework to help learners organize the training material so they will better retain the material. For example, a retail employer wanting to train employees to work in a store could explain to them the different skills they will learn over the week—for example, how to interact with customers, how to handle money, how to handle customer returns—so that the learners know how to organize the material in their minds and thus retain the material more effectively. Often such a schema is given to learners in the form of a brief outline of the training material before training begins or in the form of a brief lecture. Clear training goals can also act as a schema to help employees organize the training content.

Two additional training delivery concepts can be considered for certain training situations. First, overlearning in training occurs when trainees repeatedly practice a particular behavior in the training situation so they can perform the behavior automatically without much cognitive effort.[17] Overlearning takes additional organizational resources—primarily the time of the trainer and trainees—and thus for practical reasons should not be used except under special circumstances. But overlearning can be very useful for training certain types of tasks, such as when the task is performed on the job infrequently or when it is performed under stressful conditions. For example, employees may rarely practice emergency safety procedures on the job, if at all, such that their knowledge of these procedures may decay. Moreover, emergency procedures are typically performed under stressful conditions—so much so that an employee might forget what to do when the emergency arises. By overlearning these emergency procedures during training through repeated drills, the employees will be more likely to handle the emergency situation if it arises.

Finally, the idea of massed learning versus spaced learning refers to whether the training occurs in one large chunk (massed) or through several sessions over time (spaced). Spaced learning is generally a more effective training method, as it allows learners to absorb the material, build self-efficacy incrementally, and even practice the newly learned skills on the job. However, many organizations opt for massed learning for practical reasons—it may be less expensive to deliver training in a large chunk rather than in small ones. For example, a New York company may hire a trainer to come in from Los Angeles and stay in New York overnight each time. The company could have the trainer come in once a week for 5 weeks (a spaced approach), or it could simply have one intensive session (a massed approach). Obviously, this massed approach would save money by reducing trainer travel expenses. Considering whether to use a massed or spaced approach to training has much to do with the type of training material and its suitability to massed training as well as cost.[18]

TRAINING METHODS

LEARNING OBJECTIVES
8.4   Describe some of the most important training methods and media used by organizations and list their respective advantages and disadvantages.

Training has been going on in organizations for more than 100 years. In that time, a number of common training methods have emerged, and there is some understanding of their general levels of effectiveness. As with many HR practices, there is no one best way to train employees. Rather, one should take into account a number of issues, such as the particular skill or ability that is being trained, how well the training method fits the characteristics of individual trainees and the organization (e.g., providing feedback, allowing people to work at their own pace), as well as practical issues such as cost. Further, it may be best to think about choosing the best combination of methods for training rather than one method. For example, rather than choosing between lectures and on-the-job training, an organization may choose to use a combination of both, interspersed together over weeks, to get the strongest effect at a reasonable cost.

In this section, we present an overview of some of the most common training methods, as well as their advantages and disadvantages. Keep in mind that the descriptions we provide here are broad and there is quite a bit of variability within each category of training method. For example, "lecture" may include a one-way video of a person talking, or it may be given to a class of 30 trainees with a lot of interaction and questions and answers. "eLearning" may include giving an online slide presentation to trainees, a sophisticated set of learning modules, or a simulation of a work situation. A summary of the advantages and disadvantages of these methods is provided in Table 8.1.

TABLE 8.1 ■ Summary of Advantages and Disadvantages of Different Training Methods		
Training Method	**Advantages**	**Disadvantages**
On-the-job training	• High potential for training to transfer back to workplace. • Can be useful in combination with other training methods.	• To be most effective, the trainer (current employee or supervisor) must be given proper support (e.g., training on how to be a good trainer; time to train newcomer).
Lectures	• Effective for getting knowledge/information to large numbers of people. • Excellent supplement to other training methods, e.g., as an introduction to or overview of other training. • Can provide learners with a schema for organizing their learning.	• May be boring or unengaging if not interactive. • Less useful on its own for teaching hands-on skills.
Simulators	• Can provide training of activities (e.g., piloting a plane) that would be dangerous to learn entirely on the job. • Can simulate rarely occurring but important situations for learners.	• Development of simulator equipment and materials can be very costly.

Training Method	Advantages	Disadvantages
Programmed instruction	<ul><li>Learners can proceed at their own pace.</li><li>Learners are given feedback as to whether or not they have mastered the material.</li><li>A good method in conjunction with other methods.</li></ul>	<ul><li>Up-front costs may be expensive, although they may pay off in the long run.</li><li>May lead to disengaged learners if good content/delivery is not used.</li><li>Some learners prefer to learn with a live trainer.</li></ul>
e-Learning	<ul><li>Flexible format in terms of when and where the learner takes the training.</li><li>Can provide training to large numbers of trainees.</li></ul>	<ul><li>May not be sufficient for certain skills (e.g., interpersonal skills) and may need to be supplemented with other training methods.</li><li>e-Learning that provides some guidance to learners will be more successful than letting learners completely guide their own training.</li><li>Should be tailored to individual and organizational needs.</li></ul>
Behavioral modeling training	<ul><li>Research shows that it is an effective learning method and the effects last over time.</li><li>Providing both positive and negative models to learners seems to improve transfer.</li></ul>	<ul><li>May be more useful for specific types of training (e.g., interpersonal skills).</li></ul>

On-the-Job Training

Perhaps the most commonly used training method is on-the-job training (OJT), in which a more senior employee works with a new employee to teach them how to perform the job tasks. OJT is a key component of most apprenticeship programs, wherein a person enters and learns a trade or profession (e.g., electrician). In fact, you may have experienced some form of OJT. In theory, OJT could be the most effective type of training: The training and transfer situation are the same, assuring a high potential for transfer. However, in practice, the advantages of OJT are often not maximized. Often the employee doing the training is not given much support. That is, the "trainer" employee often must continue doing their job, with the extra burden of training a new employee. Also, to do OJT well, the "trainer" employee should be given some training themselves on how best to do OJT, not just be told, "Go train this person." Still, mixed with other training methods such as lectures or online training, OJT can be a powerful training tool if done correctly.[19]

While most discussions of OJT focus on training new hires, current employees also continue to learn from their jobs, often informally. This informal field-based learning (IFBL), or when people decide to take part in learning on their jobs outside of a formal training context, might involve activities such as seeking new assignments, asking for feedback from others, or watching how other employees do their job. This issue has only been studied recently. But the little research to date is promising. For example, whether an employee undertakes IFBL is related to issues such as whether their job requires frequent updating, as well as whether the employee is promotion-focused. Given the potential payoffs both to employees and to organizations, we anticipate IFBL will gain more attention in the coming years.[20]

Lectures

Lectures are training events in which an expert speaks to a group of workers to explain and impart knowledge. Lectures have a bit of a bad reputation in terms of being boring and not very engaging. Although the lecture method does have its drawbacks, it also has its merits. Lectures can be great for getting information to a large number of people quickly. They can also be much more engaging and useful if they involve interaction between the lecturer and trainees, providing feedback for both the trainee (e.g., to see whether they understand the training content) and the trainer (e.g., to see whether trainees understand the material and in what ways the training may need to be adjusted). Lectures are also excellent supplements for other training methods. For example, a lecture, or a series of lectures interspersed with other training methods, allows learners to develop a schema for organizing the training content, and it allows learners to ask questions after trying to apply the trained skill. Further, despite lectures' negative reputation, meta-analytic research suggests they can provide significant value in terms of training many types of tasks and skills.[21]

Simulators

We know that OJT is a potentially effective training method. But it can be very dangerous to conduct OJT with certain types of jobs such as commercial airline pilots, for which simulation use is the norm. As just one example, at its Aircrew Training Center in Atlanta, Delta Airlines has 37 flight simulators reflecting nine different types of aircraft.[22] Simulations attempt to balance the limitations of OJT by providing a safe environment to train employees. In addition, simulators can allow the trainer to expose the trainee to some important but rarely occurring conditions. In the case of airline pilots, this might include dangerous although rare weather conditions that a pilot would need to be able to act on safely. The simulator experience is often followed up by a debriefing to discuss what happened during the training session. The drawback of many types of simulators, including pilot simulators, is their cost, and thus they are often only used for very specific types of jobs in which safety is paramount.[23]

Related to simulators, the advent of virtual reality has led to the adoption of virtual reality–based (VRB) training. Studies thus far are promising. A review of recent studies on VRB training among medical students and surgeons found that participants who participated in VRB training were able to complete procedures more quickly.[24] In fact, a recent study by PwC found that virtual reality–based training can even be used to reach "soft" skills such as resilience and leadership, and that participants can learn up to four times faster.[25] Although more research is needed, VRB training holds promise as a way of reducing training costs while improving training outcomes, especially if used in combination with other training methods.

Programmed Instruction

Programmed instruction involves presenting the learner with a set of learning modules or steps. After each module, the learner takes a quiz to demonstrate they have mastered the material. If they pass the quiz, they can go on to the next module. If not, they must repeat the module until they can demonstrate they have mastered the material. Despite its name and the fact that it is often administered via computer or online, programmed instruction derives its name from the fact that it is a "program of instruction." In fact, programmed instruction has been around since at least the middle of the 20th century, with modules and quizzes presented in paper form. You likely are familiar with programmed instruction in some form.

Programmed instruction provides numerous advantages from a learning perspective. It provides learners with needed feedback on whether they are mastering the material. It allows learners to go at their own pace. It may also be helpful for those with poor metacognitive skills to gauge whether they understand the training material. And once the up-front development costs are invested, programmed instruction can be cost-effective. In fact, programmed instruction is available from many vendors so organizations do not necessarily have to develop their own materials. In fact, many eLearning platforms take a programmed instruction approach. Programmed instruction may sometimes, however, lead to disengaged trainees, especially if the modules are little more than a series of PowerPoint slides. In other words, the learning is only as good as the programmed instruction content, and some learners much prefer to work with a live trainer. With that said, programmed instruction can be a great way to teach certain types of skills and can be used in conjunction with other training methods, freeing up a trainer's time to focus on training more complex skills that are best handled through face-to-face training.[26]

eLearning

eLearning, or training that is delivered through an online platform via computers or mobile devices, is growing exponentially as an industry that provides training to organizations. Although online and computer-based training have been around for years, as seen in Figure 8.6, investment in learning technology has grown substantially in the past few years, largely due to the pandemic. The flexibility and variety of eLearning means that companies have access to tens of thousands of eLearning modules, which can be tailored for specific skills within their particular industry. It also means that employees spread globally can have access to training that they may not have had in the past, and employers can even provide standardized training to their employees, regardless of location. eLearning has further come into its own during the recent Covid-19 pandemic. In 2020, 98% of employers were using virtual classrooms, and eLearning grew from 26% of learning in 2019 to 34% in 2020. Most employers say that Covid-19 was the main driver of those decisions.[27]

FIGURE 8.6 ■ Investment in Learning Technology

$18.66 billion invested in learning technology companies in 2019	$36.38 billion invested in learning technology companies in 2020

Source: https://www.prweb.com/releases/metaari_reports_massive_surge_in_global_edtech_investment_in_2020/prweb17643214.htm

At the same time, eLearning should not be seen as a panacea for all types of training. Rather, it should be seen as a training method that fits into a larger training system that includes multiple training methods.[28] Also, some research evidence points to the potential ineffectiveness of entirely learner-centered training in which learners decide their own training approach, as many learners may not choose the most appropriate learning exercises and learning options. This strongly relates to our earlier discussion about metacognitive skills. Instead, online learning approaches that provide guidance to learners may prove most effective, and the development of more sophisticated eLearning platforms should

help in this regard. As a positive point, a meta-analytic study showed that online training can be as effective as classroom training for teaching simple knowledge types of material, and it can be highly effective if it allows some learner control and provides feedback. In short, eLearning and other types of online systems hold promise for tailoring to individual workers' needs but are not the only solution for delivering training.[29]

eLearning platforms are sold by a number of online vendors, and the size of the course offerings is growing rapidly. One example is SAP's learning hub, which provides access to training 24 hours per day, 7 days per week.[30]

©iStockphoto.com/putilich

Behavioral Modeling Training

Behavioral modeling training (BMT) usually involves a trainee observing a person (model) performing a behavior (either live or in a video), practicing it, and then receiving feedback about their own performance. Grounded in Bandura's social learning theory, BMT is based on the idea that people can learn from observing others and then can practice that skill themselves and receive feedback about their own performance. BMT is often used to train interpersonal types of skills and is thus a popular type of training for supervisors, who need to develop strong skills for dealing with subordinates and providing them with feedback. Meta-analytic results show that BMT is a powerful training tool and its results last over time. Interestingly, BMT is more likely to result in good training transfer if learners are provided with both positive models (what to do) and negative models (what not to do).[31]

Training for Specific Purposes

Training employees on specific topics may be required in organizations. Examples may include mandatory training on sexual harassment or training specific to diversity and team effectiveness.

Diversity Training

Workplace diversity parallels increasing diversity within the U.S. population. It is also increasing due to growing numbers of work teams that comprise individuals from diverse cultural backgrounds working together remotely from around the world. One way that organizations seek to manage this diversity and even have it work in their favor is the introduction of diversity training. Although the question of how to conduct diversity training is far from settled, there are some conclusions to be drawn at this point. First, meta-analytic research suggests that diversity training does have an effect on affective (attitudes), cognitive (beliefs), and skill-based (behavioral) outcomes. Findings also showed that diversity training had stronger effects when spaced rather than massed (in this case, conducted face to face over time rather than in a single session). The researchers pointed out that more research is needed to understand how training can target unconscious processes (i.e., not focusing only on bias that participants are aware of), an approach that Google has taken in its gender diversity program. Others have noted that organizations will get better effects from diversity training if they frame it in positive terms to employees such as by making training voluntary, engaging employees, and increasing contact among workers from different backgrounds.[32] In addition, recent work has shown that diversity training may be more effective among people who have cross-race friendships and that additional training might be used to help people create these friendships.[33] Researchers have also indicated the need for more in-depth research on how to better understand the process involved in diversity training and better increase its impact. A recent review noted that the research on the specifics of how to implement diversity training in organizations is still lacking despite a strong interest in it by employers.[34] For example, we know how important needs assessment is for fitting any training program to the company and employees. But the needs assessment is often skipped in the implementation of diversity training, such that it is not tailored to the organization and employees.[35]

Sexual harassment (SH) training is related to diversity training yet distinguishable. Specifically, SH training is designed to change knowledge, skills, attitudes, or behaviors to prevent sexual harassment from occurring and help address it when it happens. Although SH training has been around for a while, it has recently gained attention as a result of the #MeToo movement. A recent meta-analysis suggested that organizational SH training works, with the strongest effects on knowledge, lesser effects on skills and attitudes, and weaker effects on transfer. As the authors note, while SH training appears to work, more research is needed to improve its effectiveness.[36]

Training to Increase Team Effectiveness

The workplace has become more oriented toward teamwork, and thus companies sometimes focus their training not only on individuals but on work teams as well. This could involve team members taking on each other's jobs or learning how to better communicate and coordinate among themselves. The research suggests that these team training approaches work. For example, a meta-analysis found that team training in health care settings, regardless of the training approach used (e.g., lecture, demonstration, practice), positively impacts important outcomes such as patient mortality. Another meta-analysis found that team training approaches focused on the task and those focused on interpersonal, "soft skills" training were both effective. Another study found that cross-training could help teams develop a shared "mental model"—or conceptualization—of their work, an important issue for team coordination.[37]

Training for Managers and Leaders

Many of the training methods described thus far can also be used to train managers. There are also additional options for training managers. These include role-plays, in which trainees act in managerial situations such as counseling a difficult subordinate; case studies, in which participants analyze a difficult business case; and games and simulations, in which teams challenge each other as if they were businesses in competition. In addition, assessment centers, which Chapter 7 discusses in terms of their use for selecting managers, can do double-duty as training and development exercises, providing managers with useful feedback about their strengths and weaknesses and giving advice for future development. In that same vein, executive coaching has grown in popularity as a way to provide individual advice and counseling to managers regarding their work and careers. In fact, it is also now possible to become certified as an executive coach. The research on the effectiveness of coaching is still scant, but researchers have pointed out that different types of coaches—such as trained psychologists versus those who have a management background—likely have different skill sets and can benefit managers in different ways. Managers' leadership skills and abilities can also be developed through the assignments they are given. For example, a member of the sales team might be given a series of supervisory and managerial assignments in different geographical locations as preparation for a middle management role. Finally, given the complexities of managing a culturally diverse workforce, particularly with the rise of multinational companies, there is an increasing need for managers to develop their global leadership skills.[38]

Cindy McCauley, PhD, is a senior fellow at the Center for Creative Leadership (CCL) in Greensboro, NC. During her 30 years at CCL, much of her work has focused on using leadership assessments and stretch assignments in the development of leaders. One of her projects helps groups improve their leadership processes by examining the critical outcomes of those processes: agreement on direction, aligned work, and mutual commitment to the group.[39]

SPOTLIGHT ON GLOBAL ISSUES: GLOBAL LEADERSHIP DEVELOPMENT

Being a leader can mean very different things around the world, and this determines the best ways to provide leadership training in different cultures. Consider the role of leaders in relation to their teams in different cultures. For example, individualistic cultures such as the United States tend to focus on individual goals, whereas more collectivist cultures might focus on how individuals' performance contributes to the performance of the group. Similarly, in hierarchical countries (e.g., India), it is assumed that a team has a leader with high decision-making authority. This contrasts with countries where much more authority is afforded to individual team members. In other words, being a good leader in one culture can be quite different from effective leadership in another.

What is particularly challenging in today's global business environment is that leaders may need to be effective in their own cultural environment as well as in cultural environments different from their own. Increasingly, leaders manage people from multiple cultural backgrounds. A person may need to be able to understand different cultural styles of leadership and adjust their own behavior accordingly. Thus, the development of such global leaders is a complex process, and it may vary from person to person depending on their background. Global organizations may need to be willing to provide such individualized development as coaching and individual experiences in multiple cultural contexts. Global organizations may also include intensive sessions in which participants learn more about managing themselves and others in multiple cultural contexts and honing their own abilities in terms of cultural perception.[40]

Contemporary Workplace Training Methods

A number of new types of training methods and approaches are emerging. The first of these is mindfulness training.[41] Mindfulness is a state in which a person allows themselves to be in the present moment and learns to notice things around them in a nonjudgmental way. Mindfulness is a topic of growing interest in organizations, especially its potential as a way of increasing employee well-being. Increased interest in mindfulness has led to the growing popularity of mindfulness training in organizations. Some results are promising in terms of affecting important outcomes, including reduced employee stress and better sleep.[42] According to one survey, 52% of large employers offer mindfulness training to their employees, and companies such as Google, Aetna, and Intel have found that mindfulness can decrease stress and increase focus and well-being.[43]

A second type of training that is gaining recent attention is gamification. Gamification might include training that is made into a game or simply competition among employees in terms of scores on their training performance (e.g., earning badges, test scores after training). The assumption among proponents of gamified training is that it can increase trainee motivation and engagement. Although interest in gamified training is increasing quickly, the published research on gamified training is very limited, and the results do not lend themselves to simple recommendations for implementing gamified training in organizations. For example, gamified training may work for some employees but not for others: Those with a lot of gaming experience (e.g., video games) may prefer gamified training, whereas others with relatively little gaming experience may prefer traditional training delivery. In short, although gamification of training may hold promise, more research is needed about how and when to implement it and for whom it is most effective when compared to traditional training methods.[44]

Another current training topic is microlearning, a type of eLearning that presents small bits of knowledge at a time. These short learnings (a few minutes each) keep the attention of the learner, plus they can give reminders about knowledge that might decay over time. While there is not a lot of research on microlearning at this point, its approach (e.g., maintaining learner attention) makes sense from what we know about effective learning.[45]

Onboarding New Employees

Onboarding (or organizational socialization) is the process of helping new employees adjust to their new organizations by imparting to them the knowledge, skills, behaviors, culture, and attitudes required to successfully function within the organization. When done right, onboarding can lead to positive outcomes for both organizations and individuals; these outcomes include better new employee role clarity, feelings of connectedness with coworkers, confidence in their new role, higher performance, better job attitudes, and higher retention.[46] While most employers think onboarding is important for retaining workers, 29% of employees say their experience was not a good one. This is important because of the role that such poor onboarding plays in turnover.[47] The goal of onboarding is to make sure new employees have the information, orientation, training, and support they need to be successful.

Both organizations and new employees contribute to the success of onboarding. Organizations and organizational insiders engage in activities that may help or hinder new employees in adjusting to the organization. Similarly, new employees can engage in several specific activities and behaviors that can either help or hinder their own adjustment to their new organizations. For instance, newcomers who are perceived to engage in more proactive behaviors may be given more attention by supervisors and have a better onboarding process.[48]

Effective Organizational Onboarding

Organizations can follow several onboarding best practices to set the stage for new employees' success. One way to think about how organizations can best direct their onboarding efforts is to focus on how to *welcome*, *inform*, and *guide* new employees.[49] Welcoming includes activities such as giving employees a welcome kit, giving them a personalized e-mail or call, having lunch with the new coworker, having the new employee meet their manager, providing the new employee with welcome gifts, or inviting them to a social activity or work meeting. For instance, research has found that having a workstation for the newcomer ready to go helped with newcomer adjustment.[50]

It is the informing portion of onboarding in which training comes into play. It is important for new employees to receive resources such as websites, internal discussion boards, materials, or orientations; on-the-job training; and additional training programs to help them learn what is expected of them and how to do their job well. The orientation program, a specific type of training designed to help welcome, inform, and guide new employees, is a great way to give new employees the information they need in a short amount of time. However, a key problem with orientation programs can be that they impart *too much* information all at once. Thus, it makes sense for organizations to think through what information is needed when. Zappos, for instance, spread the process of providing information to new employees over 5 weeks as newcomers attended an onboarding training course that focused on understanding the culture and values that make the company unique. This brings up a key point: The onboarding process should be more than just the new employee orientation program. Organizations such as Microsoft, NASA, and PwC think of onboarding as lasting 1 year and beyond (personal communication, T. N. Bauer, May 22, 2023).

Many different methods may be used during the informing phase of onboarding. For example, the Ritz-Carlton Hotel Company employs a systematic and innovative approach to employee orientation and training to aid retention. In the 2-day classroom orientation, employees spend time with management and dine in the hotel's finest restaurant. To show what great customer service looks like, the new employees receive handwritten welcome notes and their favorite snacks during the break. During these 2 days, they are introduced to the company's intensive service standards, team orientation, and its own language. New employees also complete 100 hours of additional training, and they are tested on service standards and are certified if they pass.[51] As another example, Bank of America onboards its new executives through a number of HRM activities tied to its onboarding plan (see Table 8.2). In addition, given the prevalence of remote work for many employees due to the Covid-19 pandemic, online onboarding for remote workers who may never meet their coworkers or supervisors in person is a particular challenge for organizations and for newcomers. Some recommendations for online onboarding are to do some "preboarding" (e.g., filling out paperwork) in advance of onboarding, get the whole team to help onboard the newcomer, keep the newcomer engaged with the group, and personalize the content to the newcomer when possible. The online onboarding should also be reviewed and revised as needed.[52]

TABLE 8.2 ■ Onboarding Tools Used at Bank of America		
Onboarding Tool	Why Is It Used?	When Is It Used?
Orientation Program	Includes information on the business, history, culture, and values of Bank of America	Held on the first day on the job
Written Onboarding Plan	Helps new executives organize and prioritize the onboarding process	Provided in the first week after entry
Leadership Tools	Helps new executives understand the leadership frameworks at Bank of America	Provided in the first week after entry
Key Stakeholder Meetings	Allow for important flows of information and for expectation setting	Must be done in the first 2 months
New Leader–Team Integration	Helps accelerate the development of relationships between the new executive and their team members	Occurs between 2 and 3 months after entry
New Peer Integration	Helps accelerate the development of relationships between the new executive and the rest of the executive team	Occurs between 2 and 3 months after entry
Key Stakeholder Check-in Meetings	Help diagnose potential problems, receive developmental feedback, and create solutions	Occur between 3 and 4 months after entry
Executive Networking Forums	Help new executives connect and network with other executives	Held quarterly
360-Degree Feedback	Helps new executives gauge how they are performing on key metrics as measured by those around them	Occurs after 6 months after entry

Sources: Bauer, T. N. (2011). *Onboarding new employees: Maximizing success.* SHRM Foundation's effective practice guidelines series. https://www.shrm.org/foundation/ourwork/initiatives/resources-from-past-initiatives/Documents/Onboarding%20 New%20Employees.pdf; Bauer, T. N., & Elder, E. (2006). *Onboarding newcomers into organizations.* Presentation at the Society for Human Resource Management annual conference, Washington, DC; Conger, J. A., & Fishel, B. (2007). Accelerating leadership performance at the top: Lessons from the Bank of America's executive on-boarding process. *Human Resource Management Review, 17,* 442–454.

Although large organizations may have the advantage of being able to invest more resources in developing onboarding programs, they face challenges as well due to their size. Specifically, larger organizations face two challenges: (1) determining how to scale their onboarding processes and (2) determining whether to create unique experiences in different business locations around the world. A key point is to survey new employees to understand how their onboarding process is going and to solicit ideas for how to improve upon it for future hires. In contrast, small and medium-sized organizations may actually have an advantage, as one-on-one onboarding can be very effective. The key for smaller organizations is to make sure that each new employee is able to get the information and support they need.

New employees who receive guidance from organizational insiders, such as their coworkers, managers, and mentors, are more successful than those who are left to find their own guidance. Thus, organizations may assign a "buddy" or peer to help a new employee with answers to questions, a tour of the facilities, and someone who checks in with the new employee on an ongoing basis. Other programs might include assigning mentors to newcomers. Yet another strategy organizations employ is to assign a single point of contact, starting with recruitment and hiring, and continuing until the new employee is fully adjusted. Research has consistently shown that organizational insiders are important for helping new employees adjust, so the extra effort to set up such relationships is worth it.[53]

Manager's Toolbox: What Can Managers Do to Maximize Onboarding Success?

- Make the first day on the job special.
- Implement formal orientation programs.
- Develop a written onboarding plan for every new employee.
- Consistently implement onboarding.
- Monitor and update onboarding programs over time.
- Use technology to help facilitate but not hinder the process.
- Engage organizational stakeholders in planning.
- Develop onboarding milestones and timelines.[54]

Effective Newcomer Onboarding Behaviors

Newcomers may feel overwhelmed during the adjustment process, but the good news is that much of their success is in their own hands. Engaging in proactive behaviors such as seeking feedback and information, socializing with coworkers, networking, seeking to build relationships with managers, and framing things positively to themselves all help newcomers adjust.[55] Research shows that newcomers who actively seek out information not only receive more of it but also get more ongoing attention from their managers.[56]

SPOTLIGHT ON ETHICS: THE TRAINING OF ETHICS IN ORGANIZATIONS

We discussed the fact that ethics have been integrated into SHRM's competency model as a key competency. It's not surprising, then, that many organizations have integrated the training of ethics into their training curricula. This might include training in more general ethical issues such as diversity training. Or it might be more specific to certain types of jobs, such as how to handle monetary transactions, gifts from clients, or conflicts of interest. There have been recent discussions into the ethical issues that are faced by those working in the high-tech industry and how what they do can affect millions of lives. (Critics say this sort of ethical training is not discussed enough within the industry, much less trained.) Still, other organizations do provide explicit training focused on ethics. For example, the National Institutes of Health (NIH) offers annual ethics training for its employees on understanding rules and issues such as those for gifts and financial conflicts of interest.[57]

EVALUATING THE EFFECTIVENESS OF TRAINING PROGRAMS

LEARNING OBJECTIVES

8.5 Demonstrate the use of the major categories of criteria for assessing training effectiveness.

Accountability for different organizational functions is becoming an increasingly normal part of organizational life. Likewise, there is considerable pressure for HR departments to demonstrate the effectiveness of training programs. Perhaps even more important, evaluating a training program can be helpful to understanding where the program may be falling short and thus in which ways the training program can be adjusted or improved to better meet an organization's needs.

However, evaluation of training is not something that takes place in all organizations. This is for a number of reasons. First, in some organizations, there is still the belief that training evaluation is not necessary or to simply believe that if the trainees said they liked it, the training must have been good enough. Second, even where there is an understanding that training evaluation is critical, some organizational decision makers may not want to undertake it for fear of finding that it did not work. Put differently, if you were the person who championed your company's new $100,000 eLearning platform, it could be a bit scary for you personally to find out that it didn't provide much demonstrable benefit to the organization. Relatedly, if the training is delivered by an external third party (e.g., a provider of an eLearning platform), they may have little motivation to look into the program's effectiveness or may simply rely on successes the program has had with previous clients as proof of the program's effectiveness.

Third, it is difficult to do a training evaluation well, and this in itself has its risks. As an example, let's say an organization did not have great measures of performance; in fact, they were a bit unreliable (see Chapter 7). In this case it would be very difficult to demonstrate the training program's effectiveness. Specifically, even if a program actually increased employee knowledge and performance, the use of poor (unreliable) measures to evaluate the program will make it look like the program did not work. And related to this, many training professionals do not have sufficient training in how to do training evaluations effectively.

Still, training evaluation is not an impossible undertaking, and organizations that do such evaluations and do them well can not only justify the use of organizational resources for training but also fine-tune how to improve their current program to make it even more effective. This section discusses the basics of how to evaluate an organizational training program. The primary goal is to describe how to conduct a robust training evaluation. The secondary goal is to provide information that helps managers who are not directly involved in the training function ask the right questions in order to better understand whether a training program is effective, and if not, whether it should be eliminated or adjusted to better support the achievement of organizational goals and objectives. The increasing use of sophisticated analytics in organizations provides many advantages for quickly getting metrics (e.g., learner satisfaction, time spent learning) about the success of a training program.[58] This can help decision makers adjust a training program as needed. In this section, we will first discuss the different categories of training outcome measures that can be used to determine the effectiveness of a training program, along with their strengths and weaknesses. Second, we will discuss some of the basics of how to analyze these training outcome measures to better understand how training is impacting employees and their performance.

Measures of Training Effectiveness

By far the dominant framework for classifying different measures of training effectiveness is the Kirkpatrick framework (see Figure 8.7). Kirkpatrick's model classifies training outcomes into four categories of training evaluation criteria: reactions, learning, behavior, and results. As Figure 8.7 suggests, the criteria can be conceptualized as existing on four levels, from the lowest and most basic (reactions) to the highest and most robust (results).

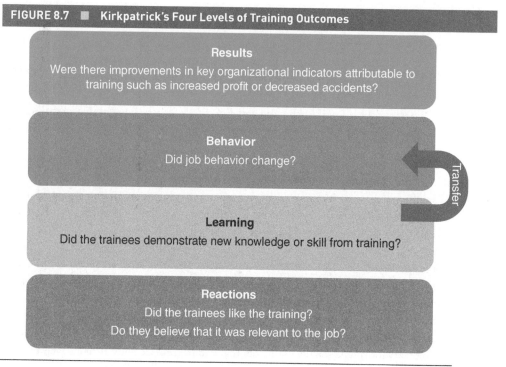

FIGURE 8.7 ■ Kirkpatrick's Four Levels of Training Outcomes

Results
Were there improvements in key organizational indicators attributable to training such as increased profit or decreased accidents?

Behavior
Did job behavior change?

Transfer

Learning
Did the trainees demonstrate new knowledge or skill from training?

Reactions
Did the trainees like the training?
Do they believe that it was relevant to the job?

Source: Kirkpatrick, D. L., & Kirkpatrick, J. D. (2006). *Evaluating training programs: The four levels.* Berrett-Kohler.

Reactions criteria have to do with assessing how trainees react to the training, namely, whether they liked it. For example, an organization may send a survey to trainees after they have completed the training program asking them whether they enjoyed the training, thought the training was interesting, or liked the trainer. An example with which you are probably quite familiar is course evaluations within the university, which ask at the end of the course what your perceptions of the course, the instructor, or the materials might be. One important point, of course, is that while training reactions can be important to training effectiveness, they do not necessarily indicate whether the training actually increased employee knowledge or, even more important, whether the training actually transferred to the workplace in terms of increased performance. Note that some types of training reactions—**training utility reactions**, or trainees' belief that the training was actually relevant and useful to their jobs—have been shown to be useful metrics for suggesting transfer. In other words, some types of training reactions may be more useful than others in indicating the effectiveness of training.[59]

The next level in the framework is **learning criteria**, or whether the trainee actually gained some sort of knowledge or skill while in training. For example, a company may train its employees on the use of a new software system to track the delivery of its product to customers. To evaluate the training, the company might give the employees a test at the end of the training in which the employees demonstrate they can use the software effectively. Note that this is a major step up from simply asking whether the trainees liked the training or thought it was effective.

Still, just because the trainees have gained knowledge or skill as the result of training does not in itself indicate the training is beneficial to the organization. For example, a company may provide training about safety practices on the job, and the employees may be able to pass a test about safe practices after participating in the training. But maybe the types of practices described in the training are not relevant to the employees' jobs. Or even if the safety rules are relevant, maybe the training will not transfer into actual safety behavior back at work because supervisors and the culture are not supportive of it. This is where the next level in Kirkpatrick's model, behavior, comes in. Behavior refers to actual behavior on the job, perhaps as measured by the supervisor. In this example of safety training, perhaps after training, employees may rate each other higher than they did before training in terms of actually following safety practices. This suggests the training actually transferred back to the job, resulting in improved safety performance.

To assess its training program, Bloomingdale's tracks its sales associates' knowledge acquisition, retention, and application. It can track this by employee and by store. Bloomingdale's can also analyze employee knowledge by individual knowledge categories and tie it back to employee behavior and results.[60]

©iStockphoto.com/Massimo Giachetti

The final and highest level of Kirkpatrick's training criteria is results criteria, or whether the training actually translates into improvements in organizational outcomes such as profits and performance. Using the safety example presented here, the company may be able to demonstrate that, because of the training program, accidents actually decreased company-wide, and there actually were decreases in employee injuries and medical claims as a result of injuries. These outcomes would thus reflect the ultimate goal of a safety program—reducing accidents, keeping employees from getting hurt, reducing costs. However, results criteria can often be the most difficult to tie back to training programs. For example, improvements in accidents, injuries, and medical claims could be attributed to many causes besides training.

It is important to make a few points about the Kirkpatrick framework. Its continued popularity for more than 50 years is largely attributable to its flexibility and intuitive appeal. These are important issues, but it is also important to note the model may gloss over certain outcomes that are important to organizations, such as attitude change (one of the primary outcomes of diversity training). Moreover, the model's flexibility is demonstrated in that many of the metrics available—including some of the newest analytics—can be classified into the Kirkpatrick framework. The additional types of training outcomes available to organizations today may not suggest the need to replace Kirkpatrick's model but simply to augment it, as illustrated in the experience of Xerox highlighted in the Spotlight on Data and Analytics box.

Finally, one of the most challenging aspects of developing a training evaluation approach in an organization is demonstrating that the training outcomes are actually tied back to business objectives—that is, to results criteria. The use of analytics in organizations can be particularly helpful in this regard, allowing decision makers and managers to see whether training is impacting training outcome measures (e.g., learning, behavior back on the job) and how these are impacting business outcomes. The key is to be able to measure these training outcomes accurately—not just quickly and cheaply—and in ways that can be meaningfully tied back to organizational outcomes. For example, an organization may implement a two-part training program, finding that although the training does increase employee skill levels and that this in turn leads to improved sales, it does not lead to increases in quality. Armed with this information, decision makers can determine how to tweak the program to provide better results. Thus, the linkage between training and organizational performance can be clearly illustrated in ways that can aid in organizational decision making.

SPOTLIGHT ON DATA AND ANALYTICS: HARNESSING ANALYTICS TO ENHANCE AND EVALUATE TRAINING

Analytics has been associated with the training function for decades, at least in the most progressive organizations. After all, Kirkpatrick first introduced his four categories of training outcomes for measuring training success back in the 1950s, and these measures have been adopted by organizations in the intervening years.

However, as with other areas of HR, the development of more high-tech analytics in recent years has led to significant opportunities for organizations to more effectively manage and evaluate their training functions. First, the measurement of training outcomes in organizations has become not only more sophisticated[61] but more easily accessible to organizational decision makers through useful summaries of the effectiveness of training on specific outcomes. As an example, Xerox evaluates its training efforts in terms of efficiency (e.g., number of trainees completing a training program; program cost), effectiveness (e.g., knowledge assessment scores), outcomes (e.g., whether the learner is engaging with the training program, such as website visits), and alignment (e.g., the training function's net promoter scores within the organization). These types of outcomes can help organizational managers, both within and outside of training, make more informed decisions about what people are learning and how training can be improved. A key here is to make these outcome measures relatively easy and affordable for the organization to collect. Elegant but overly expensive measures of training effectiveness may not be practical.

Similarly, automation resulting from the use of artificial intelligence (AI) in organizations may also lead to enhanced training functions. In the months after the delivery of a training program, AI can be used to follow up with learners to reinforce certain key learning points, or it can be used to survey learners to assess their knowledge retention. In short, AI may become a significant tool for enhancing human learning in organizations.[62]

Analyzing the Effects of Training on Training Criteria

Developing good measures of training effectiveness is the first step to training evaluation. The second step is tying these measures to the training program itself—in other words, gauging whether any change in the outcome can be attributed to the training program or to other factors. There is a robust science and deep literature on how to evaluate training data, but in this discussion, we provide only an overview of the key concepts. Let's explore a few different ways to conceptualize the effectiveness of a training program.[63]

1. *Is it always necessary to determine whether a performance outcome is attributable to a training program?* We tend to think of training evaluation as measuring change in an outcome that results from training. But in some limited circumstances this may not matter: The training will be delivered to employees no matter what, and all we really care about is whether performance is high enough after the training is done. An example here would be police training. It would be hard to think of a city that would decide not to train its new police recruits. And in evaluating the training, they would be more interested in whether the

recruits' performance is high enough to put them on the streets interacting with the public, not the fine points of whether the training created changes in the recruits' knowledge. Thus, in some circumstances, the main focus may be not whether the training caused change but whether performance after training was high enough for employees to be effective in their jobs.

2. *Assuming that there seemed to be change in the training outcomes, can we actually attribute it to training?* Consider the example of an organization that measured test scores prior to training in January and again after training in February. The results are shown in Figure 8.8. At first glance, it seems that the training worked—there was an increase in performance after training.

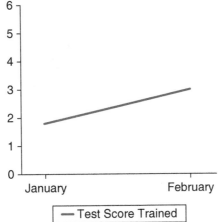

FIGURE 8.8 ■ Mean Trainee Test Performance Before and After Training

But now consider the information in Figure 8.9. Here it shows the same data plus a control group of employees who were not trained. As you can see in the figure, it looks like there was an improvement in the test scores regardless of whether the employees were trained. This may be due to a number of factors, such as normal maturation of employees as they get more job experience (the training wasn't necessary); the fact that employees simply learned the test and got better at it (the training may have worked, but we can't tell from these data); or the trained employees went back to their workplace and told their untrained colleagues about what they learned (the "control" group was actually trained by their trained coworkers). Note that this range of factors must be considered when attributing changes in measures to training.

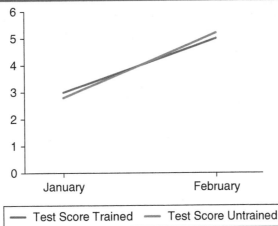

FIGURE 8.9 ■ Mean Test Performance of Trained and Untrained Employees Before and After Training

3. *What is happening during the learning process, and how should we change or adjust the training to address any problems identified?* One of the biggest benefits of training evaluation is that it helps organizations to determine how to adjust or reinforce employee learning to maximize the training's effectiveness. Figure 8.10 shows the results for employee training on emergency procedures. The training occurred between January and February. The good news is that employee knowledge actually increased after the training. But then the levels of employee knowledge seemed to decline—a classic case of "decay." This may be because emergency procedures (we hope) rarely need to be used on the job; for this reason, employees begin to forget the procedures. The organization might address this issue in a few ways, perhaps by overtraining (mentioned earlier in this chapter) or by providing "booster" training to employees—short bits of training simply to remind employees of what they have already learned. This additional information can allow decision makers to address any shortcomings in the training program.

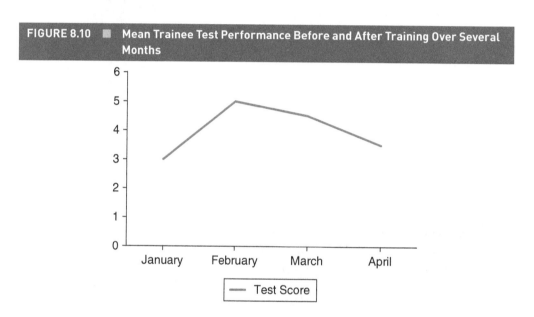

FIGURE 8.10 ■ Mean Trainee Test Performance Before and After Training Over Several Months

4. *Who are the end users of the training evaluation data? How can the results of the training evaluation be honed to fit their needs?* This last question can be illustrated with a simple example of whether to combine training measures into an average, or a composite, or to keep them separate (see Figure 8.11). In this case, the company is assessing training's effects on product knowledge, team process skills, and knowledge of company procedures. It has also averaged the three training outcomes into a composite. The composite shows an improvement post training, but it masks the effect that the knowledge of company procedures didn't really improve post training. When deciding whether to combine training outcomes, the most important thing is to keep in mind who is the consumer of the data. Perhaps a top manager may want to know only the bottom-line results regarding whether the training worked, in which case the composite gives a bottom-line answer, that is, whether the training worked. In fact, some managers may be more impressed with examples and stories about how the training improved performance. But if the goal is to fine-tune the training for the trainers to see where it could be improved, keeping the training outcomes separate would make the most sense.[64]

FIGURE 8.11 ■ Deciding Between the Use of Separate or Composite Measures of Training Outcomes

Do you average training outcome measures into a composite or keep them separate? Here we see that the average/composite line does show an increase after training, but the lines representing individual training outcomes show that some outcomes were more affected by the training than others.

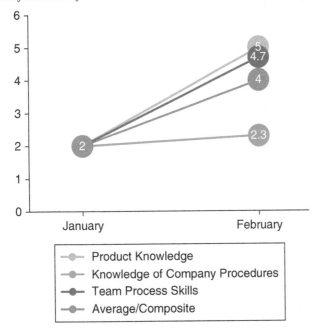

CAREER DEVELOPMENT AND MANAGEMENT

LEARNING OBJECTIVES
8.6   Analyze the factors associated with effective career development and management.

Another important aspect of development relates to one's career. Career management is the continual process of setting career-related goals and planning a route to achieve those goals. Understanding career management in the context of training and development is important because the needs of employees change over time. Note that measures of career success fall into two broad categories. Objective career success involves factors that can be observed by others or that can be measured in a standardized way (e.g., salary, promotion rate, job prestige), whereas subjective career success is whether individuals perceive that they are having meaningful career outcomes (e.g., career satisfaction).[65]

Career Management Activities

Three categories of career management activities within organizations are work performed, personal relationships, and education. First, work performed includes job rotation, which refers to employees who work on different assigned jobs within the same organization. Job rotation allows employees to develop a variety of skills and helps them to be more informed about various aspects of the business and to be exposed to different individuals, teams, and departments across the organization. At Raytheon, its multiyear job rotation program is a leadership development program that helps employees gain valuable leadership skills across a variety of settings within the organization.[66] In challenging (stretch) assignments, employees are given a task, project, or responsibility that is outside their current KSAOs.

Challenging assignments can be a useful development activity for employees being groomed for management positions. The key is not to stretch employees so far that they fail.

Second, personal relationships at work are important. Relationships with managers can help make or break an employee's career. In addition, other organizational members or even someone outside of the organization may be helpful in mentoring employees to achieve positive career outcomes. Research consistently shows that having a mentor can be helpful in terms of career outcomes such as compensation, promotions, and career satisfaction.[67] Coaching from a mentor can add value if done correctly. One study found that managers' coaching skills were related to their employees' sales performance.[68]

Third, employees may seek additional education to help them develop skills either at their own expense or via reimbursement from their organization. For example, several employers, such as Target and Amazon, provide tuition reimbursements for college degrees; while many employers have done this for years, it appears to have become more commonplace as employers try to attract the best talent post-pandemic.[69] Recently, the Home Depot Foundation partnered with the Home Builders Institute and 100 Black Men of America to increase the pool of Black workers in the architecture, engineering, and construction industries. The program includes skills training, internships, and certification and is being piloted in Atlanta, Philadelphia, and San Francisco.[70]

Career Movements

Sometimes an employee's career path is defined, and redefined, by promotions, transfers, and even demotions. A promotion, when an employee is given a greater amount of responsibility within their job, is often accompanied by a pay increase to compensate for the additional level of work. A transfer refers to an employee making a lateral move to part of the organization (domestic or international) without a major change in job duties, responsibilities, or compensation. Transfers can be helpful both for the organization (the better deployment of human capital) and to address employee needs.

Which Key Factors Can Affect Careers?

Both organizations and individuals play an important role in career management. For organizations, this means they should give employees the tools they need to develop their careers, foster a culture of learning, and train managers on how to support employees' careers. For individuals, career management strategies include seeking mentoring relationships, understanding your own strengths and weaknesses, setting career goals, and taking on challenging assignments.

Recently, research has begun to examine the concept of sustainable careers over time. This concept is important because people are now working over long periods of their lives within rapidly changing environments. Three categories of factors are thought to affect career sustainability. First are individual factors, which include a person both proactively looking ahead in their careers and reactively adapting to sudden changes (e.g., job loss). An individual also needs to be mindful of what really matters to them in their work and possess career competencies. A recent study found the career competencies of reflection (e.g., knowing your passions at work), communication (e.g., knowing who can help you with your career), and behavior (e.g., exploring the labor market) were related to early career workers' success and employability.[71]

Second, the person's context—including their organization, their work group, the labor market, and family needs—shapes their career. A third aspect of a sustainable career is recognizing that these individual and contextual issues can change over time. For example, an employee's work interests may change, or the labor market for the type of work they do may change, affecting the sustainability of their current career.[72]

CHAPTER SUMMARY

Organizations invest significant resources in training and development, and this investment can pay significant dividends in terms of increased performance at the individual and organizational levels. The best practices described in this chapter include conducting a training needs assessment, considering trainee and organizational characteristics when developing a training program, choosing the appropriate training methods for the situation, and measuring training outcomes that are tied to organizational objectives. When done well, training forms part of overall career development, which benefits both the employee and the organization.

KEY TERMS

Apprenticeship

Behavior/behavior criteria

Behavioral tracking

Career management

Case studies

Challenging (stretch) assignments

Compliance training

eLearning

Executive coaching

Feedback

Games and simulations

Gamification

Identical elements

Informal field-based learning (IFBL)

Informing

Job rotation

Learning criteria

Massed learning

Metacognitive skills

Mindfulness training

Needs assessment

Onboarding (organizational socialization)

On-the-job training (OJT)

Orientation program

Overlearning

Personality

Reactions criteria

Results criteria

Role-plays

Schema

Self-efficacy

Spaced learning

Trainee motivation

Training relevance

Training transfer

Training transfer climate

Training utility reactions

Transfer through principles

Welcoming

HR REASONING AND DECISION-MAKING EXERCISES

Mini-Case Analysis Exercise: Evaluating Training Programs

The Kehoe Company, which specializes in the sales of medical office software, has decided to invest in its sales force, specifically by providing training for its salespeople. The training includes live role-plays and online training about the products themselves.

To evaluate the program, the company assessed sales performance and product knowledge in the year before and the year after the training. The company was not able to randomly assign employees to training and control groups but instead compared employees in two regions, Atlanta and Houston, which were considered to be equivalent in terms of their performance and demographics. All metrics are on a 10-point scale.

Table 8.3 shows the results of the training evaluation for the two offices. The metric used to evaluate the training is a composite of sales numbers and a measure of employees' product knowledge.

TABLE 8.3	**Results of Training Evaluation**		
Office	Pre-Training Composite (Average) of Sales Performance and Product Knowledge	Post-Training Composite (Average) of Sales Performance and Product Knowledge	Sample Size
Atlanta (Trained)	8.4	9.2	449
Houston (Untrained/ Control)	8.5	8.7	398

1. Overall, based on these numbers, how effective would you say the training program is?

Next, the company decided to evaluate the effects of the training program on the two metrics separately. Table 8.4 shows a measure of average employee sales performance for the two offices pre- and post-training. Table 8.5 shows a measure of product knowledge for the two offices pre- and post-training.

TABLE 8.4 ■ Average Employee Sales Performance			
Office	Pre-Training Job Performance (Sales)	Post-Training Job Performance (Sales)	Sample Size
Atlanta (Trained)	8.0	9.4	452
Houston (Untrained/ Control)	8.5	8.6	398

TABLE 8.5 ■ Measure of Product Knowledge			
Office	Pre-Training Product Knowledge Test	Post-Training Product Knowledge Test	Sample Size
Atlanta (Trained)	8.8	8.9	449
Houston (Untrained/ Control)	8.5	8.8	403

2. Based on these numbers, what would you say is the effectiveness of the training program with regard to each of the training outcomes?

3. If the company wanted to adjust the training program, what would you recommend to it?

4. A colleague argues that sales numbers seem to be up as a result of the training program, so it doesn't matter whether employees showed an increase in product knowledge. What would be your response to that argument?

HR Decision Analysis Exercise: Are Training Needs Assessments Necessary?

You are currently working at Meran, Inc., a 2,000-employee provider of hardware and parts to the telecommunications industry. Recently, Meran has become aware of the desire for training and development among many of its employees. This awareness came as a result of requests from supervisors and employees both in product development and in manufacturing. In addition, top management has become acutely aware of the fact that Meran seems to provide fewer training opportunities than many of its industry competitors. In addition, the newest talent in the organization has voiced concern they had been promised significant career development during the recruitment process, including mentoring from more experienced managers.

The HR director, Yuxin Zheng, has tasked you with finding a training program or programs that would be most suitable for Meran's needs. This includes the employees at multiple levels and divisions in the organization, along with multiple skill levels.

Although there are multiple indications that the company could use some additional types of training, your inclination is to perform some type of needs assessment to confirm what these needs really are. However, Zheng does not want to do a training needs assessment, suggesting that the organization already knows what is needed. In addition, he is proposing the use of an eLearning vendor, as it would allow the company to deliver a range of content. He argues that eLearning would allow for the delivery of training on mobile devices, something that he believes the newer, younger employees would prefer over other types of training.

FIGURE 8.12 ■ Characteristics of Effective HRM Decisions

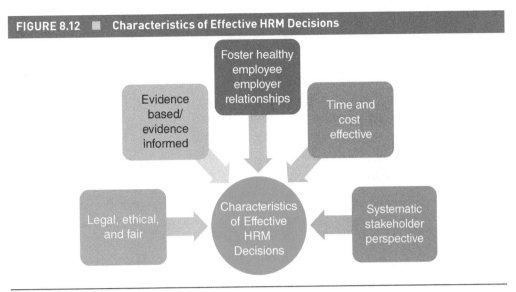

Source: Reprinted from *SHRM Competency Model* with permission of the Society for Human Resource Management. © SHRM. All rights reserved.

Please provide the rationale for your answer to each question.

Was Yuxin Zheng's approach legal, ethical, and fair?

Was his approach evidence based/evidence informed?

Does his decision foster healthy employee–employer relationships?

Are his recommendations for how to approach the choice of training programs time- and cost-effective?

Does he take a systematic stakeholder perspective?

Considering your analysis above, overall, what would be an effective decision? Why?

What, if anything, do you think should be done differently or considered to help make this decision more effective?

HR Decision-Making Exercise: Interpreting Training and Safety Knowledge Analytics

Table 8.6 shows the average knowledge of safety practices related to chemical leak emergencies at a chemical plant, based on a sample of 221 chemical plant employees.

The employees were given a knowledge test at the time they were hired. They were then given the test again at multiple time points after their original hire date. They were trained on safety procedures at 3 months post hire.

TABLE 8.6 ■ Knowledge of Safety Practices

Time of Hire/ Baseline Job Knowledge Test Score (out of 100)	1 month post hire	2 months post hire	3 months post hire Online Safety Training	4 months post hire	6 months post hire	9 months post hire	12 months post hire
55	60	64		88	80	76	74

The data presented here can be considered a *time-series quasi-experimental design* that can be used in evaluating the safety training program.

QUESTIONS

1. These data indicate a slight increase in the employees' mean performance on the emergency safety procedures knowledge test at baseline and for the first 2 months after they are hired (prior to the online safety training). What are some possible reasons for this effect?

2. There is a "bump" in the employees' performance on the knowledge test immediately after they are trained. However, their knowledge then begins to decline over the next several months. What are some possible reasons for this effect?

3. Why would employees' knowledge in this particular domain decline, even though they are on the job? Put differently, wouldn't their working on the job continue to maintain their knowledge of emergency safety procedures? Why or why not?

4. Safety is a top priority in companies such as this one. If you were a manager, what could you do to remedy this decline in knowledge level among employees post training?

DATA AND ANALYTICS EXERCISE: EVALUATING A TRAINING PROGRAM

Evaluation of training is important yet sometimes forgotten or ignored. But without thoughtful evaluation, a company might continue with a training program in which employees fail to demonstrate sufficient levels of proficiency on key training outcomes. If you recall, we can classify training outcomes using Kirkpatrick's four levels: (1) reactions, (2) learning, (3) behavior, and (4) results.

Different inferential statistical analyses, such as *t*-tests or analyses of variance (ANOVA), can be used to evaluate training programs, and the most appropriate analysis will depend upon the type of design used (e.g., posttest-only design with a control group). Before running inferential statistical analyses, however, it is useful to compute descriptive analytics (e.g., mean, standard deviation) and create charts to generate a basic understanding of how individuals performed on training outcomes.

On the one hand, a *mean* is a measure of central tendency. It is the average score. In the training context, we often examine the mean of trained or untrained groups on some outcome measure. On the other hand, a *standard deviation (SD)* represents how dispersed or spread out the scores are around the mean. Thus, a larger SD indicates there is more variation around the mean, whereas a smaller SD indicates there is less variation.

In a normal distribution, 68% of scores fall between 1 SD below and above the mean, and 95% of scores fall within 2 SDs below and above the mean. If higher scores on a training outcome indicate better performance, organizations typically want to see a high mean coupled with a small SD, which would suggest the average employee performed well and most employees performed at about the same level.

FIGURE 8.13 ■

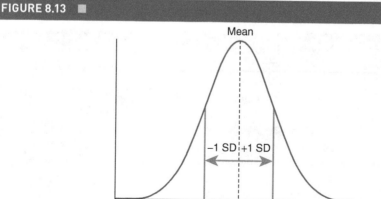

Fortunately, Excel makes it easy to compute the mean and SD of a set of scores. To calculate the mean, use the =AVERAGE() function, and to calculate the SD, use the =STDEV.S() function. Within the parentheses of either function, simply enter the vector of scores for which you wish to calculate the mean or SD. For example, to calculate the mean and SD for the set of training outcome scores (i.e., 7, 6, 4, 8, 6, 4) in the Excel sheet, you would enter the following in an empty cell: =AVERAGE(A2:A7) and =STDEV.S(A2:A7). Try this in Excel—you should get a mean of 5.83 and an SD of 1.60.

FIGURE 8.14 ■

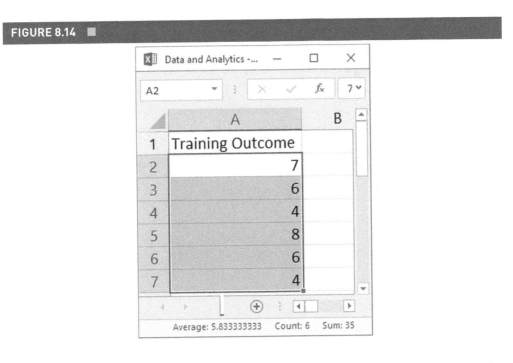

Now imagine that your company used a posttest-only with control group design to evaluate a safety training program. One group of trainees gets the new safety training program, and another group (control group) gets the old safety training program. The key training outcome is safety knowledge.

In this case, the big question is, *Did those in the new safety training program outperform those in the old safety training program?* Using an *independent-samples t-test*, we can assess whether two means are statistically different from one another. For example, if the *p*-value associated with the *t*-value we generate from the independent-samples *t*-test is less than the conventional cutoff .05, then we can conclude that the difference in means between the trainees in the new and old safety programs is significant.

Excel Extension: Now You Try!

- On **edge.sagepub.com/bauer2e**, you will find an Excel exercise on evaluating training programs.

- Using independent-samples *t*-tests, you will learn how to test different hypotheses and answer different questions based on training evaluation data.

©iStcokphoto.comNicoElNino

 PERFORMANCE MANAGEMENT

TRANSFORMING PERFORMANCE MANAGEMENT AT ASTRAZENECA[1]

©iStockphoto.com/chef2323@hotmail.co.uk kevin

AstraZeneca is a British–Swedish pharmaceutical company that makes drugs widely used in treatment of respiratory diseases including asthma, cardiovascular diseases, cancer, and chronic diseases. The company employed over 83,000 people worldwide in 2021, in roles ranging from lab technicians and scientists to sales employees. Headquartered in Cambridge, UK, with U.S. headquarters in Wilmington, Delaware, it is considered one of the top 10 pharmaceutical firms worldwide.

Despite a history going back to 1913, performance management has been a long-term struggle for the company. Historically, its annual performance review system was widely disliked by employees. A review of the employer review website Glassdoor highlights numerous employees unhappy with the company's review system prior to 2020, with complaints ranging from a forced ranking system requiring 10% to 15% of employees to be placed in the bottom category and resulting in loss of bonuses; not being given performance reviews; and being given reviews perceived to be arbitrary. The company's internal surveys confirmed these observations, with employees expressing dissatisfaction with the annual performance review system in place.

Taking action on the feedback, AstraZeneca engaged in a major overhaul of the performance management system during the Covid-19 pandemic. Instead of annual reviews, the company moved to a system that emphasizes a more forward-looking system focusing on setting goals and engaging with employees via frequent check-ins and quarterly meetings. A key piece of this change was to focus on employee development and coaching as opposed to looking into the past to evaluate employees. The new system utilizes regular coaching conversations with employees to bring managers and employees together to solve problems.

During this change, AstraZeneca offered numerous tools to managers to help them gain the skills that would be utilized under the new system. These tools included webinars, videos managers could watch on their own schedule, workshops, and calls with HR to help guide them. The company also utilized an AI-based simulation where managers were presented with different scenarios they could encounter so they could practice possible responses to a range of different performance incidents.

The combination of self-led tools with organized activities and providing managers with feedback about their progress was widely influential, resulting in 70% of managers reporting they felt more confident about holding meaningful coaching conversations with their employees and a 45% shift in employees reporting they held a growth mindset or they saw challenges and setbacks as learning opportunities. Attesting to the excitement around these changes, the company was the recipient of the 2022 Performance Management Award by *Personnel Today* magazine.

CASE DISCUSSION QUESTIONS

1. What are your thoughts about AstraZeneca's move from using annual reviews to frequent coaching conversations and quarterly meetings?

2. What is the importance of having flexibility in goals? What are the advantages and downsides of modifying goals after they are set?

3. What are the potential problems and concerns you could see under the new system? How might problems arise during the implementation of the new system?

4. What are the strengths of how AstraZeneca managed this transition? What else could they have done?

INTRODUCTION

Why is performance management important? The answer relates to a central concept of HR management: An organization's greatest asset is its people. Within organizations, employees need to know how well they are performing and how they can improve their performance so the organization's objectives can be fulfilled. In addition, companies often use performance as a criterion when making pay and promotion decisions. They need ways of measuring, capturing, and comparing performance levels of different employees. For all these purposes, companies need accurate performance measures.

For the past several decades, the annual review in which managers completed long evaluation forms rating employee performance on numerous dimensions was standard practice and a ritual in most large corporations around the world. Now, many of the same companies are questioning the need for an annual review, with Adobe, GE, and Microsoft appearing in headlines as they abandon their traditional performance review systems.

In this chapter, we discuss performance appraisals, or performance measurement, focusing on different methods and what purposes performance appraisal serves. Then we shift our focus to performance feedback and discuss how performance management systems may incorporate effective feedback delivery systems.

WHAT IS PERFORMANCE MANAGEMENT?

Performance management is the process of measuring, communicating, and managing employee performance in the workplace so that performance is aligned with organizational strategy. If we unpack this definition, it will be easier to see the critical components of a performance management system. First, performance management involves obtaining some form of measurement of employee performance, or **performance appraisal**. Performance appraisals may take a number of different forms, ranging from subjective assessments in which managers evaluate employee performance to quantitative metrics resulting from employee actions such as sales performance, accounts opened, and the time in which a transaction is completed. There are many uses for this information, ranging from distributing rewards to identifying high-potential employees, determining training needs, and terminating employees to validating selection systems. Second, performance management systems involve giving feedback to employees regarding where they stand. This is important to motivate employees, ensure that their behaviors are aligned with the organization's goals, and address performance gaps. Third, the ultimate goal behind performance measurement systems is the management of performance. When successful, performance management systems help with employee engagement, retention, and the achievement of organizational objectives.

In practice, organizations have traditionally treated performance management and once-a-year performance appraisals synonymously. Even today, most performance management consists of managers completing an annual evaluation form, rating the employee on several dimensions, and then communicating their rating to the employee in a performance review meeting. The problem with such systems is that feedback relegated to a once-a-year meeting has little hope of being useful to employees because it is too infrequent. Further, these ratings are often not regarded as fair or accurate because managers approach these ratings with multiple motives, such as rating generously to reward their team and increase loyalty. To many managers, these performance management systems and the resulting conversations feel forced and are perceived as a waste of time. To solve these problems, companies have started experimenting with different formats, whereas some larger employers abandoned formal, end-of-year assessment altogether in favor of more frequent informal feedback sessions.

Objectives of Performance Appraisals

Performance appraisal involves measuring employees' performance using predetermined criteria and sharing this information with employees. Following are at least five critical reasons why organizations are interested in measuring employee performance in the workplace. These include giving employees feedback, development and problem solving, decision making, data analytics, and legal purposes.

Giving Employees Feedback

One reason for conducting a formal performance assessment is to communicate to employees where they stand in the eyes of organizational decision makers. Individuals have their blind spots when it comes to their own performance. Knowing how they are perceived by managers, coworkers, or customers is useful for employees to develop their skills and find out through formal channels where they stand. The formal measurement of performance occurs annually, semiannually, or quarterly. Even if it happens several times a year, the formal performance review session has limitations as a medium for performance feedback. Because timeliness of feedback is so important, experts recommend supplementing these formal review sessions with regular **one-on-one meetings**, which are meetings managers have with their direct reports on a regular basis, usually weekly, to discuss performance goals, progress, and related issues. Still, regular formal performance reviews serve as tools to communicate to employees what they are doing well and what they can do better and to document their progress in their roles.

According to a Gallup poll, 19% of workers reported receiving feedback from their managers only once a year, suggesting there are some managers who use the periodic performance reviews as the only time they touch base with their employees.[2]

It is also important to note that simply providing feedback to employees is not a guarantee of performance improvements. In fact, a meta-analysis of the literature showed that about 33% of the time, feedback *reduced* performance instead of benefiting it.[3] Thus, performance management programs should ensure that feedback recipients are provided with training and tools to improve their performance rather than leaving it to chance.

Development and Problem Solving

Knowing where one stands with respect to performance criteria is a crucial step before taking corrective actions. An important objective of performance reviews is to identify employee strengths and deficiencies and develop ways to improve performance. This may take the form of employee training, providing additional coaching, taking corrective action in the form of putting the employee in a performance improvement plan (PIP, to be discussed later in this chapter), and supporting the employee in efforts to improve their performance. In other words, a key reason for conducting performance reviews is to take steps to improve future performance of the employee.

Decision Making

Organizations may want to make certain decisions using the performance metrics available to them. Performance ratings are the basis for many HR decisions, including pay raises, distribution of bonuses and other financial awards, promotions, and layoffs. For example, pay-for-performance is a commonly used model of employee compensation. The idea behind pay-for-performance is that when performance is rewarded, it will play a motivational role. In order to implement a pay-for-performance system, the company will need to have a reliable way of measuring employee performance. In other words, performance ratings are important inputs to these important decisions.

Data Analytics

The ability of a firm to harness the power of data analytics depends on the availability of high-quality data on critical outcomes of interest. Performance is one such outcome that companies are interested in predicting and managing. For example, companies may use performance ratings to decide whether the employee selection methods in place are valid. As discussed in Chapter 7, predictive and concurrent validity studies necessitate the availability of high-quality performance data.

For example, suppose a company is considering using a personality test as part of its selection system. It may administer the test to all applicants and hire without using the test scores. Then the company can examine the relationship between personality test scores and job performance metrics 6 months after hiring. A high correlation between the two would be good evidence for the predictive validity of the personality test in employee selection. Alternatively, the company may administer the test to existing employees and correlate test scores to job performance metrics. A high correlation would be evidence for the concurrent validity of the test. Demonstrating that selection procedures predict future performance is considered the gold standard of hire quality (see Chapter 7).

But this outcome will only be possible if the company has reliable performance data for its employees. Measuring and then mapping out the predictors of employee performance is an important area of opportunity for HR departments to add value using data analytics. Unfortunately, in many organizations, performance management systems do not cultivate high-quality, objective, and fair performance metrics that can be reliably used in data analytics efforts. The notable exception is when objective metrics such as call completion time, sales volume, or other productivity metrics are available. However, objective metrics have their own unique set of problems and may not necessarily be superior to more subjective evaluations. Performance management systems have the potential to produce data that can be predicted and managed using data analytic tools, but often the subjective and biased nature of these systems results in data that are not useful for analytics purposes—in other words, garbage in, garbage out.

SPOTLIGHT ON DATA AND ANALYTICS: THE RISE OF ALGORITHMIC MANAGEMENT

Performance data plays a role in management of employees. By measuring performance and giving employees feedback, management aims to shape employee behaviors to be more closely aligned with company strategy and departmental objectives. Taking this idea one step further, some businesses are automating the entire management of employees by developing algorithms that use performance metrics to make decisions about employees.

Being managed by an algorithm is particularly commonplace among gig workers. Ride share drivers are a case in point. Once they log in to the system, the platform keeps track of every move of Uber and Lyft drivers, including what percentage of rides they accept, customer ratings, and the locations they work in. The app oversees the daily work of drivers, offering bonuses and other incentives to encourage them to drive during busy periods and discouraging them from rejecting rides. The algorithm also highlights workers who are not meeting performance standards. For example, a driver might be deactivated when customer ratings fall below 4.6 out of 5. Unlike a traditional organization where workers know what metrics are being collected and how they are being used, gig workers typically lack the ability to appeal decisions, and there is little transparency over how performance metrics are being used. These conditions add to the stress employees experience. Even when performance metrics are widely available and accessible to companies, organizations need to consider implications on worker privacy, engagement, stress, morale, and well-being when utilizing these metrics.[4]

Legal Purposes

Performance metrics that are objective, accurate, and regularly collected are useful in defending organizations against costly lawsuits. Recall that Chapter 4 covered equal employment opportunity (EEO) laws that protect employee rights in organizations. Even though organizations have a great deal of freedom in how they manage their workforces, there are several *non*permissible decisions they may make, such as using sex, age, disability status, religion, or any number of other protected characteristics to make decisions about employees.

Imagine an organization that fires an employee due to poor performance. If an employee files a complaint against the organization, suggesting they firmly believe their religion was the reason for the firing decision, the organization's main line of defense is to show that the motivation for the firing decision was the employee's poor performance. This necessitates providing records and documentation of the employee's performance over time, and regularly conducted, objective, and systematic performance reviews will be helpful in making the organization's case.

An example like this makes it clear how the new trend in some large employers to abandon formal performance reviews introduces legal challenges. For example, the Equal Employment Opportunity Commission (EEOC) noted the absence of formal, regular, and consistent reviews in an organization may make it easier for the EEOC to defend a claim of bias. While moving toward more frequent reviews and check-ins is a positive development, companies need to maintain a systematic way of documenting performance of all employees and keeping these records for legal reasons.[5]

Challenges of Conducting Fair and Objective Performance Appraisals

Performance appraisals provide important information to organizations that can be used to make critical HR decisions. At the same time, this chapter began by pointing out that

The Covid-19 pandemic resulted in temporary changes in how companies used performance reviews. Facebook maintained the regular schedule of performance reviews during the early days of the pandemic but marked all employees as exceeding expectations to ensure that employees did not experience job insecurity during the pandemic-related closures.[6]

©iStockphoto.com/Sundry Photography

performance review systems are often disliked and regarded as unfair and that their accuracy and objectivity are often questioned. The challenge, then, is to design a system that is fair, relevant, and accurate.

Performance Appraisals as a Measurement Tool

The classical view of performance appraisals is that they are a measurement tool. This approach assumes that performance can be measured objectively, through the design of appropriate instruments. In fact, prior to the 1980s, most research into performance appraisals focused on examining the role of scale format in performance measurement in the hopes that it would make performance ratings more accurate. Once this approach proved unproductive, the focus shifted toward trying to understand how managers process the performance information they observe on a daily basis to form judgments about employees, with particular focus on the effects of prior expectations and memory on performance ratings. Scientists and practitioners experimented with different rating formats that would make it easier to eliminate unconscious biases from the review of performance. They also created systems and developed rater training programs that would increase managers' accuracy in observing, categorizing, and documenting performance information.[7]

Underlying all these efforts are the beliefs that performance appraisal is a measurement tool, raters have a desire to rate accurately, and if the right tools are designed, performance ratings will be objective and accurate. Decades of research in appraisals now show that this is a limited view of performance appraisals. It is true that some performance appraisal formats may increase the possibility of errors and bias. At the same time, it is naive to regard performance appraisals as simply a tool of measurement. In fact, managers seem to have multiple motives (in addition to just giving accurate ratings) when evaluating the performance of their employees, suggesting that simply examining performance appraisals from an information-processing perspective may be short-sighted. Further, researchers and practitioners began realizing that accuracy, although important, is not the *only* goal of performance measurement. Employee acceptance of the review is also a key goal, and acceptability of the feedback is essential for it to serve as a motivational tool.

Performance Ratings as Motivated Action

Today, there is greater recognition that performance rating accuracy and fairness are not achieved merely by presenting managers with the right tools to measure performance. Simply stated, managers are not always motivated to rate employee performance accurately. Instead, they may have competing motives, such as a desire to preserve their relationship with the employee, to send a strong signal to their employees regarding "who's boss," to ensure that employees are indebted to the manager, to avoid a potentially unpleasant confrontation in the name of preserving harmony, or to make themselves look good to upper management, among others. In other words, performance appraisals can be as much a political tool as a measurement tool. This means that HR departments need to understand that the effectiveness of a performance appraisal system in generating performance data and serving as a motivational tool depends not only on system design features but also on user buy-in and rater motivation to be fair and accurate. In other words, effective performance management is not an activity solely owned by HR, and it is important to consider the context in which ratings take place and ensure that the organization has a strong culture of feedback.

In reaction to such issues, companies such as Accenture and KPMG abandoned annual performance ratings altogether, moving toward systems that involve more frequent feedback and coaching. However, such moves will be effective only if managers and employees take feedback seriously, managers are motivated and able to provide such feedback, and employees are motivated to accept such feedback. If annual performance reviews are failing because managers feel uncomfortable having frank conversations with their employees or do not see much value in such conversations, replacing annual reviews with frequent check-ins will not achieve much unless those underlying problems are resolved.

Characteristics of Effective Performance Appraisal Systems

Performance appraisal systems, or the way performance is measured in organizations, are expected to meet certain criteria for effectiveness. As shown in Figure 9.1, these include alignment with organizational strategy, perceived fairness, accuracy, and practicality.

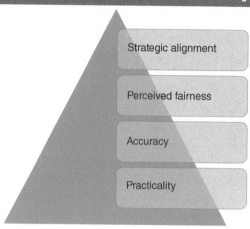

FIGURE 9.1   ■   Characteristics of an Effective Performance Management System

Strategic alignment

Perceived fairness

Accuracy

Practicality

Strategic Alignment

The most effective performance appraisal systems are aligned with corporate strategy. They motivate employees to demonstrate behaviors and actions that are consistent with the strategic direction of the organization. At ByteDance, the company known for its video-sharing platform TikTok, the company strategy is around innovation, and the performance management system supports the strategy. The company uses an "Objectives and Key Results (OKR)" system where goals flow from top to bottom, making sure that employee objectives are aligned with department and organizational goals. There is full transparency around the goals, and many goals require collaboration across teams.[8] In contrast, a company's performance management system may be encouraging behaviors that contradict the company strategy, as in the case of rewarding speed while having a strategy around service quality.

Perceived Fairness

The usefulness of a performance appraisal system as a tool in performance management depends on the degree to which it is perceived as fair. If employees do not perceive the system and their rating to be fair or feel they do not receive fair feedback, they are unlikely to be motivated to improve their performance. Therefore, fairness is a key criterion to determine the effectiveness of a performance appraisal system.[9]

Performance appraisals that give employees "due process" will protect employees' rights during the appraisal process and ensure that the resulting assessment is perceived as fair. Performance appraisal due process consists of three characteristics.[10] Adequate notice refers to the idea that employees should be evaluated using criteria and standards that were clearly communicated to the employee in advance. As a result, the measurement approach does not come as a surprise to the employee. Fair hearing involves a formal review meeting explaining to the employee why and how a particular rating was given. Allowing employees input in the evaluation process is also crucial to a fair hearing. When employees participate in the process and feel free to express their own opinions, fairness perceptions will be higher. Judgment based on evidence is the principle that performance standards are administered consistently across all employees, and the ratings are, to the degree possible, free from personal biases and prejudice. Research showed that performance appraisals that fit these criteria were associated with the most favorable user reactions to the system and evaluations of managers.[11]

Accuracy

Accuracy is a challenging goal to strive toward in performance ratings because it is difficult to measure. Outside of laboratory settings, it is often impossible to know whether performance ratings of managers are accurate, given that "true scores" are not known. Nevertheless, accurate measurement is a good goal to strive toward. Measures perceived as inaccurate are likely to be perceived as unfair.[12] Further, basing organizational decisions on inaccurate measures will be problematic. Accuracy has a lot to do with reliability and validity of ratings. As a reminder, reliability refers to the consistency of measurement. For example, given the same behaviors, different raters should evaluate the same person similarly (interrater reliability). Further, unless the individual's behavior has changed, the same rater who evaluates the individual on two different occasions should give very similar ratings (test–retest reliability). Validity involves using metrics that truly capture relevant dimensions of performance. For example, many business leaders judge employees based on the time spent at the office (or face time), and believe that employees who are out of sight are not working as hard. As Covid-19-related restrictions lifted, CEO Elon Musk demanded that all Tesla and SpaceX employees report to work, indicating his skepticism that remote work is as productive as in-person work. Many traditional managers subscribe to this belief. For example, one study conducted during the pandemic revealed that 38% of managers expressed skepticism regarding remote workers' ability to perform well and be effective.[13] When criteria used to judge performance is not perceived as accurate, employees will be frustrated and demoralized.[14]

Accuracy of measurement may be affected by unconscious biases (such as the case of a manager who rates an employee highly because the employee shares the manager's hobbies and they like each other) and intentional errors of raters (as in the case of a manager who rates an employee higher than warranted in order to avoid an unpleasant confrontation). Later, this chapter reviews factors contributing to rating errors and ways of minimizing their role in the performance evaluation process.

Practicality

An important aspect of an effective performance management system is its practicality. When the users of the system find it too time-consuming and burdensome, they are more likely to regard it as paperwork pushed on them by HR departments, and their motivation to embrace the system will be low. As a result, perceived practicality will affect how motivated managers are to rate employees accurately and how engaged employees and managers are with the system.

DESIGN FEATURES OF PERFORMANCE MANAGEMENT SYSTEMS

LEARNING OBJECTIVES
9.2 Compare the design features of different types of appraisals with respect to their benefits and downsides.

Performance management system design is a responsibility usually spearheaded by HR departments. There are a number of critical decisions to be made in the design stage, including

- determining the purposes and desired outcomes of the performance appraisals,
- defining performance,
- determining specific performance criteria,
- choosing the rating method,
- choosing the source of performance information, and
- deciding how closely performance ratings should be tied to compensation.

It is important to remember that system design features play a limited role in the eventual success of the performance management system. How the system is actually used by line managers and employees and the culture that supports performance and feedback remain more important to performance management system success. Therefore, any design effort must consider the user's perspective, and important decisions should be made with an eye toward securing user buy-in. For this purpose, securing top management commitment and gaining user buy-in through their involvement in the design stages are helpful steps to take. Top management sets the stage and helps to build a culture in which performance management is taken seriously and performance conversations occur regularly. As a result, top management is encouraged to display public support for performance management systems and model the expected behaviors. User involvement in system design is also useful because their perspective will help ensure the system design is tailored to account for user reactions, with the eventual result being greater commitment to use the system. As one critic noted in *HR Magazine* regarding the increasing use of smartphone apps to facilitate frequent solicitation and delivery of feedback: "Ultimately it will be up to managers to make new variations of performance management work. No software can provide feedback that human beings aren't willing to give."[15]

IBM has a history of involving employees in major initiatives. Its app-based performance review system, Checkpoint, was created with broad-based user involvement.[16]

©iStock.com/claudiodivizia

Determining the Purposes and Desired Outcomes of Performance Appraisals

Organizations may have different reasons for why they conduct performance appraisals as part of performance management. Some may be utilizing performance reviews for developmental purposes, which means they are primarily interested in providing employees periodical, formal feedback on their performances. Other organizations may utilize performance appraisals for administrative purposes, which means that performance appraisals are used to make decisions in the organization, such as assigning merit pay and bonuses, or determining which employees will be sent to remedial training and which will be promoted. Typically, organizations use one performance appraisal for multiple purposes. However, it is important to remember that different purposes may be addressed via different types of appraisals. For example, it is important for a system in which the goal is to assign bonuses and promotions to meaningfully differentiate between employees. This means the system will probably have to assign numerical ratings to employees. At the same time, it is important that the ratings assigned to each employee are different from each other so the organization can see who the highest performers are. In contrast, in an organization in which the primary goal is to give feedback to employees, what is more critical is to have data from multiple perspectives and to provide a lot of qualitative information about the employees' behaviors in different contexts. In such a context, assigning a numerical rating to employee performance may not be an activity that adds a lot of value and in fact may detract from the main purpose of the appraisal, which is to give feedback. These organizations may benefit from a narrative review with open-ended questions, in which the most relevant feedback may be provided to each employee.

Therefore, organizations may benefit from giving serious consideration to the seemingly easy question of what they will do with the performance appraisal results. If it is clear to the organization that bonuses and merit pay will be assigned via a different method (such as sales numbers, seniority, or quarterly bonuses tied to specific goal accomplishment), then the organization may design the system with an eye toward maximizing feedback as opposed to differentiating among employees and quantifying performance. The opposite would be true if the system is expected to be used for the validation of selection systems or the evaluation of training programs. In these cases, it is useful to tell managers that their ratings will be used for research purposes only. In other words, organizations should consider which aspects of the appraisal system add value to organizational goals instead of designing a generic performance appraisal system that theoretically serves multiple purposes but, in reality, shortchanges each of them.

Defining Performance

So, what is performance? For example, when evaluating the effectiveness of a retail employee, what should be the focus? Should we measure product knowledge and dependability? Should we capture how often the employee goes out of their way to help a customer find what they need? Or should we measure how often employees were late in the past month and the value of the merchandise they actually sold?

These examples describe three different approaches to measurement of performance: traits, behaviors, or results. Each approach has important strengths but also limitations. It is important to note that irrespective of whether traits, behaviors, or results are to be used in conceptualizing performance, the specific dimensions should come from a strong job analysis and the resulting job description. Further, the criteria and metrics used to assess performance should be directly aligned with corporate strategy. For example, focusing on short-term sales volume may be inconsistent with an organizational strategy that emphasizes customer loyalty and customer service, because employees may become overly concerned with increasing their sales volume while neglecting to take care of customers once the sale is made.

Trait Appraisals

Trait appraisals focus on measuring employees' different attributes, such as dependability, helpfulness, and product knowledge. These systems define performance as characteristics the employee has (rather than how they actually utilize or display these characteristics). The key advantage of traits is their simplicity of use. This approach does not necessitate identifying behaviors that constitute high performance, and therefore developing a trait-based appraisal is usually a simple and cost-effective process.

At the same time, trait appraisals have serious potential limitations that may serve to limit their usefulness. First, trait appraisals are associated with a greater number of rater errors and suffer more from lack of accuracy in ratings relative to behavioral appraisals. This is because they are quite vague— they require that the rater infer an employee trait rather than simply rating behaviors—and therefore are open to interpretation by raters. In fact, research shows that when trait appraisals are used, agreement between different raters, such as self and managers, tends to be much lower, suggesting poor reliability.[17] This is likely to lead to negative reactions toward the feedback received and to contribute to a sense of unfairness. Second, trait appraisals describe the person and not the behavior. Therefore, they increase the likelihood that any negative feedback will be regarded as an attack on the employee's personality, which tends to be stable, rather than an observation regarding behaviors, which can be changed more easily.

Behavioral Appraisals

Behavioral appraisals assess the frequency and quality with which employees demonstrate specific behaviors at work. For example, an organization that expects employees to approach customers about its extended warranty program may have a performance appraisal behavioral dimension related to how well the employee explains the warranty program to customers. A sales associate may be evaluated based on the frequency with which they make appropriate eye contact, smile, greet, and thank each customer. As you can see, these are specific, observable behaviors.

Behavioral appraisals are useful for feedback purposes, because delivering this assessment will make the employee aware of the types of behaviors employees are expected to demonstrate and point out gaps in performance. Behaviors are observable and are typically under the control of the employee. Therefore, they will give the employee the greatest amount of actionable feedback. At the same time, behavioral appraisals assume there is a set, predetermined way in which performance can be accomplished. In reality, it may not be possible to create a list of behaviors that capture high performance in all jobs, and in fact, the use of behaviors for employees who have a lot of expertise may alienate the employees and reduce their perceived autonomy. Therefore, using behaviors for new employees rather than more experienced employees may be meaningful. The use of behavioral appraisals may also be more appropriate when employees are expected to always display a specific set of behaviors, such as greeting customers, making product recommendations, and offering to open a store credit card.

Results-Based Appraisals

Results-based appraisals define performance in terms of the outcomes of a job. Sales figures, number of mistakes, number of reservations taken, number of new clients, customer satisfaction ratings, and minutes taken to complete a phone call may all be important metrics that describe an employee's performance. Results-based assessments of performance have important advantages over traits and behaviors. Their key advantage resides in their objectivity. Unlike behaviors and traits, results are naturally occurring outcomes of performance at work, and their measurement usually does not necessitate one person rating another. Therefore, these metrics are less subjective than other appraisal methods.

This does not necessarily mean that results-based metrics are superior to assessments such as behavioral ratings, but results-based assessments are less likely to result in charges of favoritism and subjectivity. It is also easy to see how an individual's performance serves organizational goals: When employee sales performance is high, we can assume the organization is benefiting from this.

At the same time, results-based assessments bring their own unique problems to performance measurement. To begin with, they are not always under the control of employees. For example, sales volume may depend on the territory assigned to the individual, quality of products, and availability of competition. If employees feel the metrics used to assess them are not under their control, they will develop a sense of helplessness and will not be motivated to put forth effort. Second, some important aspects of an employee's performance may not have easily measured metrics. Sales volume, for instance, is easier to track compared to quality of customer interactions. As a result, employees may develop a single-mindedness with respect to the aspects of their performance captured by metrics and neglect other important aspects of their performance such as helping coworkers and cooperation. In fact, pay-for-performance plans have been shown to be related to higher levels of helping behaviors when performance metrics were *subjective*. In other words, the use of objective metrics in measuring and rewarding employees may result in a single-minded focus on metrics that are being rewarded at the expense of other important behaviors that help create a positive workplace.[18]

Finally, metrics can be misleading. For example, the best doctors may have the highest patient mortality rates because the best physicians may attract patients who are in more critical condition. Similarly, the best salespeople may be assigned the more problematic customers because they are the only ones who can handle them. This means that simply looking at metrics may not provide an accurate picture of performance.

Goal Setting

An extension of results-based performance definitions is to engage in goal setting. Goal setting is one of the best methods available for increasing performance and therefore is a useful performance management tool.[19] Joint goal setting with one's manager at the beginning of a performance period, working toward a goal throughout the period, and assessing goal accomplishment at the end of the period are helpful methods for managing performance. Goal setting is a key part of **management by objectives (MBO)**, a management strategy in which organizational goals are translated into department goals, which in turn are converted into individual-level goals to ensure that individual and company goals and objectives are fully aligned. First, **key performance indicators (KPIs)** are defined at the company level. KPIs are measurable business metrics that are aligned with a company's strategy. These can be financial metrics, such as profit or cost; customer-related metrics, such as customer satisfaction; people metrics, such as turnover rate; or KPIs related to other strategic initiatives, such as organizational sustainability. Then these KPIs are translated into individual-level goals for employees, as discussed between the employee and the manager.

Goals that have the greatest motivational value are **SMART goals**:

- Specific,
- Measurable,
- Aggressive,
- Realistic, and
- Time-bound.

This means the most effective goals are quantifiable, difficult enough to motivate the employee although remaining reachable, relevant to the performance of the employee's job and aligned with corporate strategy, and accomplished within a specific period of time. A goal such as "increase the fee income from service contracts by 10% by December of the calendar year" is an example of a SMART goal. As long as employees have abilities to reach the goal and are committed to the goal, having SMART goals is associated with higher levels of performance.

Goal setting can be an effective way of measuring and managing performance, but it comes with caveats. Perhaps the biggest concern with respect to goal setting is the possibility of ethics violations, such as cutting corners or using ethically questionable means to meet the goal. For example, some studies show that when doctors are rewarded for better patient outcomes, they end up choosing healthier patients.[20] Further, goals narrow the focus of employees, leading to focusing on one or two dimensions of performance at the exclusion of others. Goals can also result in reduced motivation to learn new things and may lead to the creation of a culture of competition. All these downsides suggest that the use of SMART goals should be accompanied by careful monitoring and ensuring that *how* the goals are attained is not disregarded in the process.[21]

Electronic Monitoring

Companies are interested in measuring particular behaviors and outcomes, and technological advances can support that. But organizations should strike a balance between measuring important performance metrics via technology and creating a surveillance culture where employees feel their every move is recorded and managed. **Electronic monitoring** refers to using technology to observe, record, and analyze information that directly or indirectly relates to employees' job performance. With the rise of remote work, these technologies saw increased adoption. Many companies now use technology to take screenshots of workers' computers, logging workers' keystrokes and monitoring how often and how long employees take breaks. One survey of 2,000 organizations where employees work remotely indicated that 78% of the organizations were using monitoring software. They often used this technology without the knowledge of their employees and used this information as a performance metric.[22]

While technology is available to track a variety of behaviors, using these metrics as measures of performance is potentially problematic. Results from a meta-analysis show that such surveillance measures are related to higher levels of stress and strain. Further, these systems increase feelings of invasiveness and concerns around transparency, violating employee sense of privacy. Finally, there is little evidence that the use of these technologies actually improve performance metrics companies care about, such as quantity of output, accuracy, or performance complaints. Given the costs, and absence of demonstrated benefits, these systems may do real harm to organizational culture and employee morale.[23]

SPOTLIGHT ON ETHICS: A GOAL-SETTING SCANDAL AT WELLS FARGO

Goal setting is one of the most effective and promising ways to motivate employees and align individual effort with department and organizational strategy. At the same time, goal setting can have a serious side effect that suggests the organizations using this strategy should take steps to avoid harmful consequences. In an aggressive culture that emphasizes ends and disregards means, goal setting may be a tool that corrupts employees and harms the company reputation.

Wells Fargo's experience with goal setting offers a cautionary tale. The company made headlines with the revelation that it had opened hundreds of thousands of unauthorized accounts for its customers, leading to charging of fees for accounts customers did not realize they had. The company agreed to pay $185 million in fines; its CEO at the time, John Stumpf, resigned; and more than 5,000 employees were fired as a result.

The way goal setting was used at Wells Fargo illustrates some of the worst practices of goal setting and its consequences. Employees were required to reach impossible daily sales goals in order to keep their jobs. Managers did not seem to care *how* employees met the goals as long as they were met. In fact, in some cases managers encouraged employees to cheat, such as by opening up accounts for friends and family members or even opening accounts for customers without their knowledge, and apologizing afterward if the customer realized it. District managers pressured branches by discussing goal achievement four times a day. The company eventually replaced sales goals with a bonus structure emphasizing customer satisfaction.[24]

Questions

1. How would you advise your organization if top management proposed an aggressive goal-setting policy for employee performance? How might the organization reap the benefits of goal setting while avoiding negative consequences?
2. In your own work, how do you set goals for yourself and measure your progress in attaining them? What have you learned that might help you to gain more benefits from goal setting?

Choosing the Rating Method

Performance may be assessed using absolute ratings or relative rankings. Absolute ratings involve comparing employee behaviors or outcomes to performance criteria, whereas relative rankings involve comparing employees to each other. Both of these approaches involve quantifying performance in some way. In addition, some highly visible organizations have opted to abandon the tradition of assigning numbers to employee performance, switching to more qualitative approaches. Which approach to use should be motivated by the purpose of the performance assessment, but it is important to understand the strengths and limitations of each approach when making this decision. Figure 9.2 summarizes advantages and disadvantages inherent in each method.

Absolute Ratings

These systems involve a comparison of the employee's performance to predetermined criteria. These systems treat each performance score within a work group as independent of other employees' scores. In these systems, all employees can technically be rated as "exceptional," or all employees may be rated as "needs improvement." One employee's rating is not expected to influence ratings given to other

FIGURE 9.2 ■ Summary of Strengths and Limitations of Different Approaches to Performance Ratings

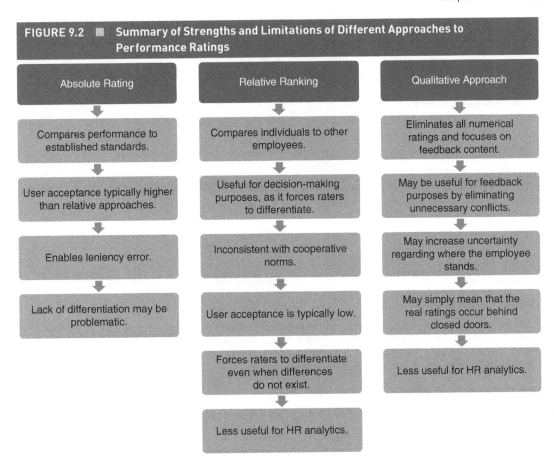

employees. The rater is expected to gather data about each employee's performance, compare performance to agreed-upon criteria, and then rate each employee. Systems that utilize absolute ratings may take the form of a graphic rating scale, behaviorally anchored rating scale (BARS), or behavioral observation scale (BOS). Figure 9.3 describes these different rating methods.

Relative Rankings

These systems involve comparison of each employee's performance to that of coworkers. Rankings may take the form of straight rankings, paired comparisons, or forced distribution. Straight rankings simply involve having the rater rank-order all employees from best to worst. Depending on the number of employees to be ranked, this could be a cumbersome process. Paired comparisons involve creating rankings by comparing two employees at a time until every unique pair of employees has been compared and then compiling the results; this approach can be thought of as a round-robin tournament involving employee performance comparisons. The frequency of endorsement of one employee over others determines the final ranking. Again, this could be mentally taxing for the rater if there is a large number of employees to be compared to each other. Finally, forced distribution, commonly known as "stack rankings," involves the rater placing a specific percentage of employees under the exceptional, adequate, and poor performer categories. The assumption behind ranking-based systems is that actual performance in organizations is normally distributed. Forced distribution was popularized by GE (but later abandoned by the firm, as well as by other early adopters such as Amazon and Microsoft). Today, it is often used behind the scenes when making important decisions such as workforce reduction. For example, in 2022, insiders reported that Google had asked managers to place at least 6% of all employees into the low performer category, leading some observers to suspect that the company was doing this to prepare for layoffs in the near future.[25]

When employees are ranked, the size of the differences in their performance will be disregarded. For example, the difference between B and C is much greater than the differences between C, D, E, and F.

FIGURE 9.3 ■ Descriptions of Different Absolute Rating Scale Formats

Graphic Rating Scale

Raters are presented with attributes and behavioral descriptions and are asked to rate the individual using an established scale.

Circle the number that describes the employee's

Quality of work

1	2	3	4	5
Unacceptable	Below Average	Average	Good	Exceptional

Quantity of work

1	2	3	4	5
Unacceptable	Below Average	Average	Good	Exceptional

Behaviorally Anchored Rating Scale (BARS)

Employee's behavior is measured on a scale that describes specific examples of behaviors that could occur for different levels of performance. These scales are developed following identification of critical incidents for high, moderate, and low performance levels. The purpose of the examples is to give all raters a common frame of reference and increase accuracy. These scales are useful as feedback tools, but could be challenging and costly to develop for all dimensions of performance.

Use the specific descriptions to rate the employee's customer service performance.

5 – Answers customer questions on the same day. Could be expected to investigate queries even when not directly within his/her line of responsibility.

3 – Answers customer questions respectfully and within a week.

1 – Treats customers with disrespect; customer inquiries are often ignored.

Behavioral Observation Scale (BOS)

The rater assesses the frequency with which the employee displays the behaviors in question.

	Never 1	Rarely 2	Often 3	Usually 4	Always 5
Answers customer queries within the same day.	1	2	3	4	5
Greets customers within 60 seconds of them entering the store.	1	2	3	4	5

Relative rankings have some limitations compared to absolute ratings. First, rankings are inconsistent with norms of cooperation, given that for some employees to be rated as exceptional, others will have to be rated as average or below average. In other words, performance is defined as if it were a zero-sum game in a work group. Second, recent evidence suggests that employee performance in organizations does not necessarily follow a normal distribution, violating a key assumption behind these systems. In fact, research shows that actual performance is distributed in such a way that a small percentage of employees show exceptional levels of success (superstars), whereas the remainder show performance that is below average.[26] As a result, trying to force employee performance into a bell-curve distribution seems problematic. Finally, managers and employees dislike these systems, given the necessity to differentiate between employees even when differences in performance are not large enough to be meaningful. For example, consider Figure 9.4, in which the size of the circles represents actual performance of each employee. When these employees are ranked, important information will be lost, such as the fact that the difference between A and B is actually smaller than that between B and C or that C, D, and E actually have very similar levels of performance or that both A and B are exceptional performers. The system will also force the rater to distinguish between C, D, and E even though their actual performances are so similar that the differences between them may be practically unimportant from the organization's perspective.

FIGURE 9.4 ■ Example of a Forced Distribution System

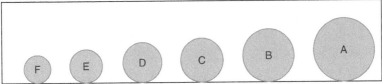

On a more positive note, though, these systems force the rater to differentiate among followers. Lack of differentiation in ratings even though there are real differences in performance can be a problem as serious as forced differentiation, and therefore using rankings may yield results that are more useful for decision-making purposes such as distributing bonuses, increasing pay according to merit, and making promotions.

Qualitative Assessment

Some performance assessments do not utilize quantitative ratings. Instead, these systems rely on qualitative assessment, or describing the areas of strengths and limitations for feedback purposes, without assigning a numerical rating to each employee. An example of this approach is the **critical incident method**, through which managers identify examples of exceptionally high and low incidents of performance and document them in narrative form.

In recent years, companies such as GE and Adobe have eliminated numerical ratings, replacing them with frequent check-ins and informal conversations. Such companies may choose not to quantify performance reviews because their primary purpose is developmental rather than administrative. In the absence of ratings, instead of getting overly focused on the rating they received or should have received, employees may more easily have a conversation around performance with their managers. For example, during the Covid-19 pandemic, the financial services company Synchrony asked managers to conduct check-in meetings instead of ratings and appraisals. Given the positive response to this change, the company decided to make this change permanent.[27]

Advances in machine learning may allow organizations to quantify narrative reviews. Research shows that managers' comments on employee performance often converge with managers' ratings and provide additional useful data. Using sentiment analysis, narrative comments may be converted into scores and tied to decision making. We are likely to see further advances in this area in the future.[28]

There is emerging evidence that eliminating ratings because employees do not like them and expecting that frequent feedback could replace them may be shortsighted. To begin with, the elimination of ratings may simply mean the company continues to rate employees behind closed doors but stops sharing ratings with employees. Employee performance will need to be evaluated somehow, even when assessments are not revealed to employees. When ratings are abandoned in

Even simple changes to performance management systems require careful planning: The U.S. Department of Agriculture (USDA) dropped its five-level performance rating system in favor of a two-level system (fully successful/unacceptable), necessitating changes to how bonuses are distributed, promotions are decided, and top performers are recognized.[29]

©iStockphoto.com/arcady_31

performance reviews, managers may still rate employees to determine pay raises and promotions, but the main change is that employees do not see or influence the ratings.[30]

A study by the consulting company Gartner indicated that when performance ratings were eliminated, performance dropped by around 4%. This was because managers struggled to explain pay decisions when there were no performance ratings, employees started doubting that performance was rewarded and recognized, and managers did not necessarily increase the frequency and amount of feedback provided to the employee.[31] These results indicate that having clear ratings of performance may be particularly desirable to high performers who are more attracted to organizations that recognize their contributions. Scientific research on the effects of the presence, absence, or elimination of ratings is lacking. Organizations are advised to consider the benefits they derive from ratings (if any) and the costs of not providing performance ratings (if any) before making this decision.

Choosing the Source of Performance Information

Who should provide information about employee performance? There are many possibilities. Due to the nature of their jobs and responsibility for employee performance, managers are typically the primary raters in performance appraisals and serve the role of a major coach and source of feedback for employees. Information from managers may be supplemented with feedback from coworkers, subordinates, customers, and self. Utilizing 360-degree feedback, or multiple-rater systems, presents employees with feedback from different stakeholders and has the potential to provide useful, rich information. At the same time, different sources have different limitations that need to be considered.

Managers

Because the role of a manager includes managing the performance of employees, managers are naturally involved in performance management. In industries such as manufacturing, the manager is the only rater during the annual or semiannual performance appraisal. Managers are often the most knowledgeable source in the assessment of employee performance, and they are in a position to collect more information if needed. They may provide higher-quality data to the performance assessment compared to other sources. For example, a meta-analytic study showed that the interrater reliability among different managers rating the same employee is typically higher than that among different coworkers rating the same employee.[32] Interestingly, this study showed that managers rated some dimensions of performance (productivity, quality) more reliably than other dimensions (interpersonal competence, communication competence), suggesting that supplementing manager ratings with those of coworkers for different dimensions of performance may add value.

Relying solely on a single manager as the rater could be problematic. In some contexts, managers may know little about the employee's performance. For example, this could occur if the employee is working in a field setting, when the manager is supervising a large number of employees and has limited interactions with each employee, or if the manager only recently started working with the employee. Although patrol officers are often supervised by a sergeant, they are often out on their own, and the sergeant has relatively little chance to observe their work behavior. Further, the nature of the relationship the manager has with the employee will affect the rating and the interactions during performance reviews, potentially resulting in skepticism among some employees that the appraisal process is biased. Adding multiple perspectives makes a lot of sense to ensure that ratings reflect diverse perspectives and capture the full picture of how the employee performs at work.

Coworkers

The involvement of coworkers in performance assessments introduces a rating source that potentially has more extended interactions with the focal employee. Because coworkers have the ability to rate certain aspects of performance (such as contributions to the team) more effectively, the introduction of coworkers as raters could increase perceived fairness of ratings. Given that work is increasingly performed in a team setting, coworkers are increasingly important stakeholders for employee performance, making their inclusion as a source of performance feedback natural. At the same time, coworker ratings have the potential to show bias toward the employee due to liking, similar to supervisor ratings.[33] As a result, companies often use these ratings for primarily developmental purposes rather than for reward or other administrative decisions. When coworker ratings are used, the best raters will be those who have frequent interaction with the person to be rated. A best practice is to have at least three coworkers provide ratings, and having responses shown in a form that preserves anonymity. Giving employees some say in which coworkers are selected can also be helpful.[34]

Netflix replaced their annual performance reviews with a system that relies on peer reviews. Employees identify behaviors that their coworkers should stop, start, and continue to do.[35]

©iStockphoto.com/Marvin Samuel Tolentino Pineda

Direct Reports

When the employee to be evaluated is a manager, the direct reports, or subordinates of the manager, are a relevant and important source of information. Feedback from the manager's direct reports could provide useful and actionable information and help the manager develop leadership skills. At the same time, anonymity of this feedback is essential to maintain the quality of subordinate feedback, as rating one's manager can be a threatening experience. In fact, research shows that when the source of subordinate feedback is known, raters (subordinates) have a tendency to inflate their assessments, resulting in distorted and unrealistic feedback.[36] This means that subordinates will be more useful as a source of feedback in large groups in which anonymity can plausibly be maintained. Further, similar to coworker ratings, feedback provided by subordinates shows more evidence of a leniency bias as a result of liking, compared to assessments managers provide for their employees.

Customers

Internal and external customers provide a unique perspective to performance measurement. Internal customers are users of an employee's output within the same firm, whereas external customers are outside the organization. Feedback collected from customers is relevant and often is one of the more important indicators of performance. Seeking feedback from customers also signals to customers that their opinions matter, which may contribute to organizational reputation and customer relationships. A primary challenge will be to gather these data, as often customers are reluctant or uninterested in giving feedback unless they have complaints. Further, customers have little accountability and motivation to provide fair feedback, and they have little training to do so. As a result, their ratings may suffer from biases. In fact, research has shown that customer satisfaction ratings suffer from bias against women and marginalized persons.[37]

Self-Assessment

Self-assessments have only moderate overlap with manager and coworker ratings. For example, a meta-analysis shows that self-ratings and manager ratings are correlated only .22, which is a significant but still modest correlation. This is perhaps not surprising, given that self-assessment may capture the person's intentions in addition to actual behaviors and outcomes observable to others. You may assume that self-assessments that are part of a performance appraisal system will be inflated. But research actually shows that rating inflation is more likely to occur if the information will be used for decision-making purposes (as opposed to developmental purposes), and the leniency of these appraisals was reduced when individuals were told that their appraisals would be verified through other methods. Further, self and manager ratings were less likely to diverge when behavioral as opposed to trait criteria were used and when employees were asked to evaluate themselves relative to others. Self-ratings seem to be most useful for developmental purposes, as a way of getting employees to think about their strengths and weaknesses and to have two-way dialogue during performance-related conversations, coaching sessions, and performance review meetings. Using self-assessments ensures that the employee is part of the conversation, has a chance to highlight their greatest contributions, and learns what their manager sees as their greatest strengths.[38]

Self-assessments are likely to be more useful if the criteria used for performance assessment are clear, objective, and unambiguous. For example, asking a student to evaluate their own "participation level" in class is likely to yield answers that may differ from the instructor's evaluation of the student, because students may define participation in class as attending the class, speaking up, coming to class prepared, discussing the class material with their peers in a small-group discussion, or any number of other ways. However, asking a student how often they spoke up in response to a question the instructor posed to the class is likely to yield answers more similar to what would be reported by the instructor or peers, because the question is more clearly defined and targeted. Similarly, asking employees to list their specific accomplishments within a period of time, tying ratings to a referent group (e.g., "compared to your coworkers"), may increase the usefulness of self-assessments and minimize disagreements between supervisor and employee ratings.

360-Degree Feedback

The 360-degree feedback approach is a method in which performance is evaluated from multiple perspectives all around the focal person, typically including manager, coworkers, and subordinates in the process. What we know about these different rating sources is that they each provide information that is not necessarily captured by the other. In other words, using multiple raters does not replicate information we already have; instead, different raters provide different perspectives on the same performance metrics. As a result, there is value in conducting 360-degree feedback in order to improve the quality of feedback available to the employee. At the same time, simply providing this feedback in raw form will not necessarily be useful for improving performance. In the most effective implementations of 360-degree feedback, managers are involved in the choice of raters and communicate with raters to reassure them about how the feedback will be used. The manager summarizes and provides context to the feedback while communicating it to the employee, and the system is used as part of an employee development system.[39]

SPOTLIGHT ON GLOBAL ISSUES: CULTURAL INFLUENCES ON PERFORMANCE MANAGEMENT

Performance management has the potential to be strongly shaped by the cultural context. For example, in a study of French multinational organizations that operate in the Middle East, researchers found that while Middle Eastern and North African subsidiaries adopted the same performance review system used in the headquarters out of obligation, there were extensive modifications and reinterpretations to the system during implementation. The interpersonal relationships between managers and employees and the paternalistic leadership style of leaders resulted in avoiding confrontation, not rating employees at low levels, and not conducting performance meetings. Managers also chose to give negative feedback more indirectly and implicitly.[40]

Companies are finding that their performance reviews work differently in their offices around the globe. In cases in which certain practices clash with local cultures, companies may choose to modify their global practices for particular local norms. For example, the French cosmetics company L'Oréal prides itself on its open culture in which employees feel free to confront each other. However, it quickly realized that open confrontation and criticism are frowned upon in its South American offices.[41]

Choosing the Ratee

So far, we have assumed that organizations are interested in measuring and managing individual performance. In reality, though, focusing on individual performance has a number of limitations. For example, with the increasing prevalence of teams in organizational settings, treating individual performance as if each individual performs independently may not exactly be realistic. Further, in many instances, individuals are expected to cooperate while performing their jobs. For example, a team of employees may make the sales, with input from each employee. Identifying which employee was responsible for making this sale may be challenging and may be inconsistent with the ultimate goal of cooperation.

Some organizations face the limitations of individual metrics by using team appraisals rather than individual-based measures. In these systems, goals and performance metrics may be at the team level. For example, banks often use "net promoter score" (a score that measures customers' likelihood to recommend the bank to others) to capture the performance of each branch. This is an important metric for banks, but it is unclear which employees have the most influence over a customer's likelihood to recommend the bank. Using team-based metrics may therefore focus employee attention on the unit's goals and encourage them to cooperate. In these organizations, individuals may receive team bonuses and team incentives depending either on team performance metrics or on whether their team meets specific targets. For example, Swiss banking software maker Avaloq utilizes a team-based review through which members evaluate the team's performance with respect to how well they worked together and whether the targets were reached.[42]

A challenge of team-based appraisals is the possibility of employees not pulling their weight because they are not individually accountable. To tackle this problem, the organization may assess the degree to which the individual supports the team and complements coworker efforts.

Deciding How Closely to Link Performance Ratings to Compensation

Pay for performance, particularly in the form of bonuses, has established effects on future performance.[43] Research shows that employees who feel they are treated fairly by the organization have stronger engagement and other positive job attitudes. Part of achieving fairness is ensuring that employees are rewarded and recognized in line with their contributions to the organization.[44] As Chapter 12 highlights, companies utilize different methods of tying pay to individual, team, or organizational performance, in the hopes that employee pay reflects different contributions employees make to the organization.

When performance metrics are objective and reflect results that naturally follow employee performance (such as sales volume), tying pay to performance is more straightforward and less subject to bias. One concern with more subjective assessments is that the knowledge that performance ratings will be tied to performance may affect the rating managers give employees. Such knowledge may result in inflated performance ratings so that more employees receive raises or deflated ratings because the organization has a limited merit pay or bonus budget. Unfortunately, both of these approaches to performance reviews can result in a disconnect between the actual performance of the employee and the rating given.

When performance appraisals are used to distribute bonuses and merit pay, it makes sense to conduct focal date reviews in which performance reviews take place on the same date for all employees. This way, the organization will find it easier to allocate its bonus or merit pay budget. One concern regarding focal date reviews is that all reviews within the company take place within the same short time period, resulting in a significant time investment for each manager supervising multiple employees. For instance, managers meeting individually with a large number of employees will incur a serious cognitive load as well as demands on their time.

An alternative to focal date reviews, particularly if evaluations will not be tied to compensation, is an anniversary review in which the employee is rated on the anniversary of their start date in the organization. This approach allows reviews to be spread out so the performance review period does not become a significant burden on employees and managers.

Of course, with any yearly review system, one risk is that managers will not remember how employees were performing at the beginning of the review period but simply rely on their memory of the employee's performance over the last few weeks or months. Thus, conducting yearly reviews, regardless of when they take place, needs to be coupled with frequent check-ins and coaching meetings between employees and managers to make sure that performance is actually managed throughout the year.

CONDUCTING FAIR PERFORMANCE REVIEWS

LEARNING OBJECTIVES
9.3   Identify best practices for making performance reviews fair and unbiased.

The focus so far has been on the design features of performance appraisals. Once the performance appraisal system is designed, implementation depends on the motivation and ability of raters to use the system in a fair and consistent manner. The rater is expected to work with the employees on a day-to-day basis, give regular feedback, and provide coaching and support throughout the evaluation period. When the time comes to give a performance review, the rater will have to look back on the employee's performance and provide an assessment. Although raters may have every intention of being fair and accurate, a number of errors can affect the rating process.

Factors Leading to Rating Errors

Performance assessment, particularly in jobs where quantitative metrics are not naturally available, requires raters to collect information about performance through observation and data gathering and then rate performance. Because this is a perceptual process, ratings often suffer from errors. Errors may include leniency error (the tendency of a rater to rate most employees highly), severity error (the tendency to rate most employees closer to the lower end of the scale), central tendency error (the tendency to rate almost all employees in the middle category), halo error (basing performance ratings on one or two performance dimensions, with one prominent dimension positively affecting how the employee is perceived on other dimensions), and horns error (the opposite of halo error; ratings on one dimension negatively influencing how the employee is perceived on other dimensions). Another issue in performance appraisals is the recency error, wherein a rater will focus on the most recent employee behaviors they have observed rather than focusing on the entire rating period. Manager awareness of factors that cause rating errors helps HR departments design training programs or other interventions for raters that will minimize the harmful effects of rater errors.

Impression Management

Employees are not passive recipients of performance ratings. In fact, they have the ability to influence the ratings managers give them through the careful use of impression management tactics. Impression management consists of behaviors individuals demonstrate to portray a specific image. Research shows that impression management tactics that are particularly effective in positively influencing performance ratings are supervisor-focused tactics, such as offering to do favors for the manager, complimenting the manager, and taking an interest in the manager's life. Impression management tactics that are more detrimental to performance ratings are self-focused, such as trying to show that one does a good job or working hard when performance is more visible to the manager. What differentiates these two types of impression management tactics is that supervisor-focused tactics positively shape the manager's belief that the employee is similar to the manager, whereas self-focused tactics negatively affect this perception. In other words, employees can influence the rating in ways that are different from working their hardest or increasing their performance.[45] It is easy to see that when managers fall prey to impression management tactics of employees who are perceived as poor performers by their coworkers, employees will likely question the validity of performance assessment and be concerned about favoritism.

Stereotypes and Bias

Performance ratings may be biased depending on the prejudices or stereotypes held by the rater. Stereotypes about women or men, younger or older workers, employees belonging to marginalized groups, employees who are pregnant, or employees who have disabilities have the potential to affect performance ratings and reviews, despite being illegal. For example, the software firm Textio examined 25,000 written performance evaluations. They uncovered signs of bias; for example, 88% of high-performing women but only 12% of high-performing men received personality-oriented feedback. Words such as *confident* and *ambitious* were used more often in describing men as opposed to women. There were race differences in the amount of written feedback received (an average of 100 words for white women versus 68 words for Black men). Younger workers were described as ambitious, whereas older workers were more likely to receive feedback on being responsible. These differences indicate that ratee characteristics may influence the rating and feedback received during the appraisal.[46]

SPOTLIGHT ON LEGAL ISSUES: AGE DISCRIMINATION LAWSUIT AT CBS AFFILIATE

Performance appraisals can play a critically important role in employment discrimination lawsuits. Sometimes they provide key evidence supporting the organization's argument that a decision taken against an employee was due to poor performance as opposed to illegal discrimination. At other times, the absence of a legally defensible performance review serves to support claims of discrimination. One example of the latter is the age discrimination case at KFMB-TV in San Diego, which is an affiliate of CBS.

A part-time assignment editor at the TV station claimed she was discriminated against based on her age. She based her claim on the fact that she was not selected for four internal positions she had applied to, and those who were selected for these positions were 30 years younger than she was. She also claimed she had received e-mails from the decision makers justifying their choice by stating a desire to infuse the newsroom with bold, innovative, and fresh thinking individuals. While the court dismissed the e-mail evidence as "inferential" and not direct evidence for ageism, the main piece of evidence in favor of the plaintiff ended up being the recent performance review the employee had received. Even though the company had claimed the new hires for this position were more qualified than the plaintiff, she was able to contradict this claim by showing the favorable performance reviews she had received recently. In the end, KFMB-TV chose to settle the case.

This case indicates the importance of ensuring accurate and non-biased performance ratings. In many companies performance ratings are inflated, but it is important to remember that those ratings are part of the employee's permanent record, and they may be used as indicators of how the company regarded the employee at the time.[47]

Liking

One other possible source of rating distortion is liking, or favorable attitudes toward the ratee. Liking an employee may result in unintentional biases such as giving the employee the benefit of the doubt for low performance or giving more credit for high performance. Alternatively, managers may knowingly distort their ratings when they like an employee in an effort to preserve the relationship quality. Even though it seems plausible that liking an employee should be a major source of bias in performance ratings, research supporting this argument is limited. In fact, there is some evidence that liking may be a function of the performance level of the employee. If this is the case, then liking would not be a biasing factor in performance assessments and in fact could be a good indicator of how well the employee is performing.[48] Further, research indicates that the role of liking in the performance review process is contingent on system characteristics. For example, liking seems to lead to inflated ratings when raters are coworkers or subordinates. Further, trait appraisal formats, as opposed to more results-based metrics or behavioral appraisals, are more strongly affected by liking.[49]

With the rise of hybrid work arrangements, companies need to guard against favoring in-person workers to remote workers and thereby creating a "zoom ceiling." Ensuring that accomplishments of remote workers are visible to managers and reflected in performance ratings remains a challenge.[50]

©iStockphoto.com/alvarez

Rater Motivation

Whether the rating actually reflects the employee's true performance level is also a function of how motivated the rater is to provide an accurate evaluation. Raters are thought to consider the advantages and downsides of rating the employee accurately versus inaccurately and how likely they are to get caught (or be called out for poor behavior). If the rater feels that giving the employee an inflated score is more advantageous and is likely to yield more positive outcomes for the rater, then the rating will be biased. This means that understanding why raters feel that inaccurate ratings are more beneficial will be helpful in counteracting this biasing factor. For example, rater discomfort with performance appraisals is known to yield overly positive ratings, presumably because raters are more highly motivated to avoid confrontation as opposed to providing high-quality feedback.[51] Retraining raters to alleviate discomfort helps increase rater motivation.

IMPROVING THE EFFECTIVENESS OF PERFORMANCE MANAGEMENT

LEARNING OBJECTIVES

9.4   Explain how to implement performance management for maximum effectiveness.

There are a number of ways in which companies can improve the effectiveness of their performance management systems. Much like other HR systems, it is important to frequently explore improvement opportunities and ensure that the system in place continues to meet organizational needs over time.

Training Managers and Employees

Even though performance management is a key part of managers' roles, skills involved in effective performance management are often lacking. For example, respondents in a survey of 600 people from different organizations noted that only half of them had a leader who led with compassion. Only 35% felt they had clarity on their career path within the organization. And only 35% noted that their organization had a program offering training to managers for coaching employees.[52]

Interestingly, research indicates that teaching raters about the different types of rating errors such as halo effect, leniency, and strictness does not lead to more accurate ratings, and in fact it reduces rater accuracy. As a result, rating error awareness training does not have much support with respect to its usefulness. However, a specific type of training, frame of reference (FOR) training, has benefits. FOR training involves having raters observe specific instances of performance through videotapes or vignettes and then telling them the "true score" and why raters should rate in a particular way so that different raters are on the same page and pay attention to similar aspects of performance. The purpose of this training is to ensure that all raters evaluating similar types of employees share a common conceptualization of performance. FOR training has been shown to reduce rating errors and increase accuracy.[53] Other types of training that could be useful include training managers in confronting performance problems and delivering positive and negative feedback. Such training is likely to increase rater confidence and motivation to provide high-quality feedback and therefore can yield significant improvements in the quality of feedback employees receive.

Increasing Rater Accountability

One assumption regarding performance appraisals is that keeping raters accountable for their ratings yields more accurate measurement. There is actually little research and empirical support for this argument. In fact, when raters are accountable to ratees (or when they know they will have to explain their ratings to the employee they are rating), they are more lenient.[54] Raters may also be accountable to their own superiors, but research shows no effects of this type of accountability on performance ratings.

Despite the lack of research on this topic, companies expect that increasing rater accountability may motivate raters to take the performance appraisals seriously and may curb the effects of rater favoritism. Organizations utilize three primary means to increase rater accountability. First, managers' effectiveness in giving feedback and conducting appraisals may be a performance dimension in their own evaluations. This approach would communicate the expectation that effective managers take performance reviews seriously. Second, the manager's supervisor may have to sign off on the appraisals, introducing accountability to a higher-level manager. Third, organizations including Google and Intel utilize calibration meetings, meetings in which groups of managers come together and discuss the ratings they will give their employees before ratings are finalized.[55] This approach makes managers accountable to each other by requiring them to justify their ratings and the distribution of their ratings to their peers. This method has its downsides, such as ratings being dependent on a manager's communication and negotiation abilities. Even though systematic information about the benefits of these methods is slow to emerge, it is important to know that these methods exist and are used with the hope that rater accountability improves ratee reactions to performance appraisals.

Having Raters Keep Records of Employee Performance

Rating performance periodically, even when it occurs regularly and frequently, such as on a quarterly basis, will require the rater to recall past performance for each employee reporting to them. As a result, raters would benefit from help in recalling performance information. Diary keeping, or keeping records of employee performance, is a method that has been shown to improve rating accuracy by enabling raters to recall specific information about their employees. Keeping a log of critical performance incidents could be helpful, even though managers may find it cumbersome. This method allows the manager to remember and recognize important milestones and provide feedback rich in detail.[56]

Auditing the System

One of the best practices of performance management is to periodically audit the system. An audit might reveal if raters are serious about evaluations, whether employees are satisfied with the quality of the feedback, and if they feel their efforts are fairly rewarded and recognized. Performance reviews may not always work the way they were intended. For example, the system may have low user acceptance. Managers' lack of skills in confronting performance problems may lead to unproductive conversations. In some instances, the performance review criteria may become outdated as jobs change and evolve. Auditing the system periodically will help uncover and address these and other problems. For example, a mid-sized law firm uncovered a number of biases in their ratings, including members of underrepresented groups having to prove themselves repeatedly, assumptions around mothers being less committed to work, and stereotyping. The company made changes to their system and provided workshops for raters to address these problems. To measure improvements, the company conducted another audit the following year and continued to make changes to combat the problem.[57]

Teaching Managers How to Be Good Coaches and Build Trust

A trust-based relationship between the manager and employee is essential to positive outcomes in relation to performance management.[58] Therefore, investing in a strong professional relationship with the employee and learning how to coach employees effectively are important. In companies that do the best job in performance management, managers serve as coaches to employees and give frequent feedback and support. Coaching is an important skill for a manager to have. Google's Project Oxygen, examining the behaviors that differentiated its more effective leaders from less effective ones, showed that coaching employees was among the eight differentiators. Coaches ask the right questions and model the right behaviors. They show employees how to complete difficult tasks, offer specific advice regarding how to tackle problems, and provide support.[59] As you can see, behaviors coaches perform are important for performance improvements.

Further, it is important to remember that the ongoing professional relationship between managers and employees and the trust that exists in this relationship provide the context in which feedback is delivered and performance is reviewed. As a result, thinking of performance reviews and feedback delivery in isolation from the relationship quality is a mistake. Unlike employee selection, in which job applicants are interacting with strangers and trying to make good first impressions, performance feedback is delivered to employees who have a history with the manager. Even though providing the right tools can help, in the absence of trust, feedback may not reach its potential and measurement may not be viewed as fair. For example, the same level of employee participation in the appraisal interview does not give employees the sense that they have voice in the process when trust in the manager is low.[60] This suggests that anything organizations can do to ensure that managers are trained in leading and that trust exists between management and employees should go a long way in improving the quality of performance management that takes place in the organization.

Pharmaceutical company Merck used a desktop simulation to teach managers how to be more effective coaches. Managers reacted to realistic scenarios and received feedback on their actions, improving the effectiveness of sales leadership teams.[61]

©iStockphoto.com/Sundry Photography

Manager's Toolbox: Feedback Delivery Best Practices

Feedback delivery is a skill that is useful to managers throughout their careers. Giving feedback allows a manager to recognize exemplary behaviors and confront performance that would benefit from improvement. Following are some best practices in feedback delivery that managers can apply in their organizations.[62]

- *Recognize contributions.* Many managers assume that feedback is delivered only when something is wrong. This may mean that high performance and "extra mile" contributions go unrecognized. It is important to recognize positive behaviors using specific language. You may consider describing what you saw, explaining why this was a good behavior to demonstrate, and thanking the employee for doing it.

- *Conduct regular one-on-one meetings.* These meetings are among the most helpful tools for ensuring you will give the employee regular feedback and have opportunities to coach and develop the employee. These can be easily conducted in person or remotely.

- *Be a role model for feedback.* Your direct reports and coworkers will feel more comfortable receiving feedback from you if you are someone who takes feedback seriously, seeks it frequently, and displays an openness to learn about your own blind spots.

- *Focus on actual behaviors or results, not personality.* When feedback targets an individual's personality, it may be perceived as unfair and taken personally. Instead, consider focusing on actual behaviors the employee may successfully change. For example, instead of "you seem low in energy," "you did not contribute any ideas in the past five meetings" is more behavioral and concrete and is less likely to put the employee on the defensive.

- *Use the "Start–Stop–Continue" model.* One way of structuring your feedback is to specify what the employee should start doing, stop doing, and continue doing. This framework ensures you will focus on both positive and negative behaviors.

Developing a Feedback Culture

A feedback culture is one in which employees and managers feel comfortable giving and receiving feedback. The characteristics of an organization that has a supportive feedback environment can be seen in Figure 9.5. Top management support, role modeling for feedback, and training managers to realize the importance of feedback as a tool for performance improvement are among the steps companies may take to help create a feedback culture. Organizations are realizing that annual or semiannual reviews are woefully inadequate to provide useful feedback to employees. As a result, many organizations are instituting ways that employees can quickly and easily seek feedback at the conclusion of a project, a big meeting, or product launch. For example, Starbucks and PwC introduced real-time feedback tools to ensure employees are receiving frequent and timely feedback from customers and coworkers.[63] It is

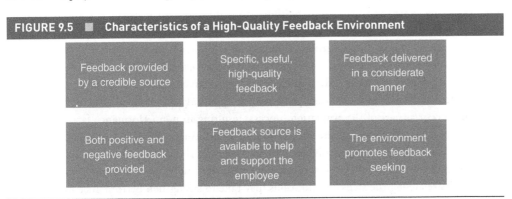

FIGURE 9.5 ■ Characteristics of a High-Quality Feedback Environment

Source: Steelman, L. A., Levy, P. E., & Snell, A. F. (2004). The Feedback Environment Scale: Construct definition, measurement, and validation. *Educational and Psychological Measurement, 64,* 165–184.

important to remember that such tools by themselves will not be useful unless there is a feedback culture in which employees feel comfortable and psychologically safe to seek and give feedback.

Establishing Performance Improvement Plans (PIP)

The beginning of this chapter notes that performance reviews also serve as a tool to document poor performance. In cases of employees whose performances do not meet established performance standards, tying performance reviews to a performance improvement plan (PIP) could make these systems more developmental. Performance improvement plans keep poor performers accountable and also give them a chance to improve. The plan starts with using specific language to document poor performance. Then a collaborative process is used to establish an action plan. Using SMART goals as part of the action plan ensures that it is clear whether the struggling employee meets the expectations at the end of the agreed-upon period. Having a third party such as HR or the manager's own supervisor review the plan would be helpful to ensure the plan is fair and free from tense emotions.

After a meeting between the manager and employee in which a plan is established, the manager and employee meet regularly to review improvements, and roadblocks are removed along the way. The PIP concludes when the employee's performance improves and reaches the established goals. If performance does not improve, actions such as transfer or termination may be taken.[64]

PIP is a tool to ensure that poor performers are given a fair chance to improve their performance. PIPs contribute to an overall sense of fairness in the organization and serve to protect the organization from costly lawsuits by showing that employees are treated fairly and given the benefit of the doubt. These plans emphasize the role management has to work with employees to improve performance rather than simply rating employees to make decisions about them.

A mechanical engineer working at NASA was placed on a PIP shortly after taking military leave (which is a legally protected activity). The presence of a PIP was not sufficient to protect NASA against claims of discrimination. NASA was asked to show that there was good reason to place the employee on a PIP in the first place.[65]

©iStockphoto.com/LaserLens

CHAPTER SUMMARY

Performance management takes the form of measuring and documenting employee performance. It provides useful feedback, documentation, and a metric that can be tied to rewards. Companies need to assess the validity and reliability of data collected and analyzed if it is to lead to good performance management practices. The traditional annual performance appraisal is too infrequent to be useful for daily feedback. Therefore, performance appraisals need to be combined with other feedback, such as one-on-one meetings or tools that allow employees to seek and receive feedback in shorter intervals. Performance appraisals may measure traits, behaviors, or results, and performance information may be derived from multiple sources, including managers, coworkers, subordinates, and customers. Because performance appraisals often involve subjectivity, many errors may occur as part of the evaluation process, resulting in nonperformance factors affecting performance ratings. Ultimately, the effectiveness of a performance management system depends on user acceptance. Therefore, involving users in designing the system, ensuring that managers and employees are trained in giving and receiving feedback, and helping develop a strong culture of feedback are among the steps organizations may take to strengthen performance management systems.

KEY TERMS

Adequate notice

Administrative purposes

Anniversary reviews

Calibration meeting

Central tendency error

Critical incident method

Developmental purposes

Diary keeping

Electronic monitoring

Fair hearing

Feedback culture

Focal date reviews

Forced distribution

Frame of reference (FOR) training

Halo error

Horns error

Judgment based on evidence

Key performance indicators (KPIs)

Leniency error

Management by objectives (MBO)

One-on-one meetings

Paired comparisons

Performance appraisal

Performance improvement plan (PIP)

Performance management

Recency error

Severity error

SMART goals

Straight rankings

Team appraisals

360-degree feedback

HR REASONING AND DECISION-MAKING EXERCISES

Mini-Case Analysis Exercise: Unfair Performance Reviews

You are the HR manager of a professional services firm with 300 employees. Your company utilizes annual performance reviews along with frequent check-in meetings throughout the year as part of performance management. Employees are evaluated on a number of questions assessing customer service quality and sales volume (results of a customer satisfaction survey and actual sales metrics, weighed at 60%) and demonstrating corporate values in day-to-day activities (mentoring others, driving change, and creativity, weighted at 40%).

The annual reviews have just been completed, and you hear from Orlando Nicholson, an employee who has been with the firm for 2 years. Orlando has a cordial but distant relationship with his manager. He asked for a meeting with you and revealed that he feels the most recent performance review he received is unfair. Orlando feels that his customer satisfaction scores are modest, but this is due to being assigned some of the most difficult clients the company has. In addition, the manager rated him as average in mentoring others, discounting the fact that he was heavily involved in the onboarding of two new employees 8 months ago. Orlando also feels that because he works remotely while his manager is usually at the office, he is at a disadvantage. In fact, there have been several times when he felt his contributions at meetings were overlooked and other people took credit for his ideas.

How would you handle this situation?

Outline:

1. What would you advise Orlando to do in this meeting?

2. What would you tell his manager, if anything?

3. Are there any systemic changes you can think of that may help prevent instances like these from happening in the future?

HR Decision Analysis Exercise: Should You Abandon Yearly Reviews?

You work for a large manufacturing organization with 8,000 employees. Your company has been struggling with having fair, accurate, and practical performance metrics. The performance review system consists of 360-degree feedback, semiannual reviews, and a combination of behaviors and results. You use end-of-year performance ratings to distribute performance bonuses. Managers are told to give employees feedback on a regular basis, but an employee opinion survey puts the average satisfaction with feedback quality at 3.2 on a 5-point scale.

Your company's CEO read in an airline magazine that many large companies are abandoning the use of annual appraisals. The article discussed real-time feedback tools that companies can acquire from various software vendors. These tools enable employees to seek and managers to give feedback regularly. The CEO also feels the end-of-year review should be abandoned, and managers may simply rank their employees to determine performance bonuses at the end of the year. The CEO's opinion is that having to justify their ratings to employees makes managers more lenient, costing the company a lot of money in bonus payments.

FIGURE 9.6 ■ Characteristics of Effective HRM Decisions

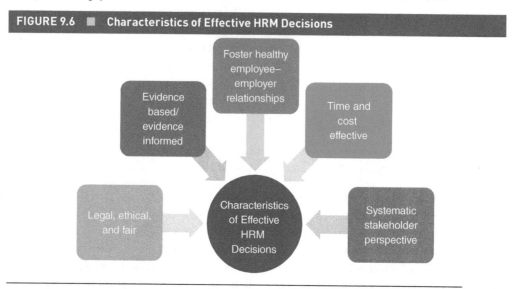

Should your organization switch to the system the CEO has read about? Consider this decision using the following criteria.

Please provide the rationale for your answer to each of the questions.

Is it legal, ethical, and fair?

Is it evidence based/evidence informed?

Does it foster healthy employee–employer relationships?

Is it time- and cost-effective?

Does it take a systematic stakeholder perspective?

Considering your analysis above, overall, do you think this would be an effective decision? Why or why not?

What, if anything, do you think should be done differently or considered to help make this decision more effective?

HR Decision-Making Exercise: Designing a Performance Management System

You are in the process of developing a performance review system for Grimard Groceries, a regional retail chain with 80 stores. The job description of hourly employees includes the following:

- Preparing sandwiches
- Baking bread and cookies

- Making sure that shelves and displays are organized and attractive

- Working at the cash register

- Assisting customers with their questions about merchandise

- Providing efficient service

- Helping customers during checkout

Employees are expected to be helpful, friendly, and fun. The company emphasizes good-quality customer service to build customer loyalty.

If you were designing a performance management system for this company, what would it look like? Assuming the company is interested in providing feedback to employees on a regular basis but also in tying pay to performance, propose a performance management system for the company. Please make sure your answer includes specific details such as the forms to be used and the criteria by which performance will be measured.

DATA AND ANALYTICS EXERCISE: USING PREDICTIVE ANALYTICS TO UNDERSTAND PERFORMANCE

In order to improve performance, it helps to understand what factors contribute to it. Organizations may use predictive analytics to find the answers to this question. For example, let's assume that managers just completed measurement of performance using the company's performance appraisal form.

Let's assume you have information on four criteria that could affect performance:
- Product knowledge (results of a test the employees took part in)

- Personality (a measure of employee extraversion)

- Time management skills (evaluated by each associate's manager)

- Cooperativeness (evaluated by team members)

Which of these metrics are in fact good predictors of performance ratings? This is important information for the organization. For example, if we find that product knowledge is an important predictor, we can increase investment in training on product knowledge. If extraversion is an important predictor, then we could select employees based on extraversion.

Employee	Product Knowledge	Extraversion	Time management	Cooperativeness	Performance Rating
1	3.75	2.33	2.67	4.67	4
2	3.4	3.8	4.4	2.5	2.5
3	3	2.33	4	4	4.33
4	4	4.67	4.33	4	4
5	4.8	3.75	3.33	3.4	3
6	3.5	2.67	4	4	4
7	4	2.6	3.5	4	4.6
8	5	5	5	2.67	2
9	4	4.6	5	2	2
10	3.4	2	2.3	4.3	4
11	4.5	2.5	4.4	3	4.5

Employee	Product Knowledge	Extraversion	Time management	Cooperativeness	Performance Rating
12	3.5	2.3	4.5	3.6	4.3
13	3.8	2.1	2.8	5	5
14	3.7	5	3.2	3.5	4.3
15	3.4	4.5	4.3	5	3.4
16	4.3	4.8	3.75	3.33	3.4
17	4.8	3.5	3.67	4	4
18	3.5	3.67	4	4	4
19	3.5	5	4.4	4	3.4
20	5	2.3	4.5	4.3	5

This is the dataset we will analyze. In order to understand which of the four potential predictors are related to performance ratings, you could use simple bivariate correlations. However, you have four predictors and one outcome. If you use correlations, you will look at each relationship in isolation. In reality, our four predictors may be correlated with each other. This means you may find that each of the four is correlated with performance ratings, but we would not know which ones are the best predictors once the others are accounted for.

For this reason, we will perform a regression analysis on these data. Note this is actually a very small sample size to perform this analysis, but let's do it for illustration purposes.

We will use the "Data Analysis" function of Excel. (You can perform these analyses very easily in the statistics software SPSS or using a regression calculator that may be found online as well.) Once you click on Data Analysis, you will be able to perform a regression analysis, as follows:

FIGURE 9.7 ■

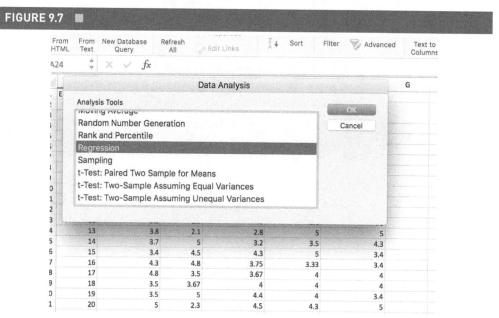

Now we will indicate the range of input. We marked the location of performance ratings under the Y range and the location of the other four variables under the X range. We included variable labels in the selection and then checked the "Labels" box to indicate that the selection includes variable names at the top.

FIGURE 9.8 ▪

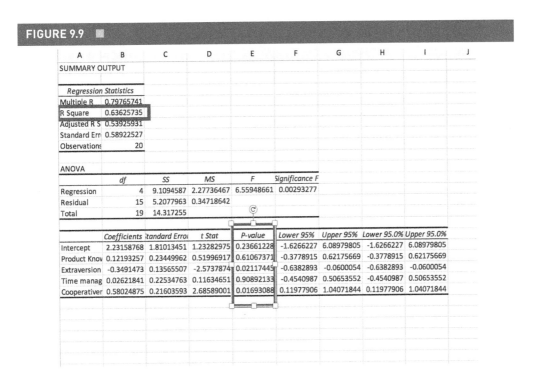

Once you hit OK, you will see a new sheet with the output:

FIGURE 9.9 ▪

	A	B	C	D	E	F	G	H	I	J
	SUMMARY OUTPUT									
	Regression Statistics									
	Multiple R	0.79765741								
	R Square	0.63625735								
	Adjusted R S	0.53925931								
	Standard Err	0.58922527								
	Observations	20								
	ANOVA									
		df	*SS*	*MS*	*F*	*Significance F*				
	Regression	4	9.1094587	2.27736467	6.55948661	0.00293277				
	Residual	15	5.2077963	0.34718642						
	Total	19	14.317255							
		Coefficients	*Standard Error*	*t Stat*	*P-value*	*Lower 95%*	*Upper 95%*	*Lower 95.0%*	*Upper 95.0%*	
	Intercept	2.23158768	1.81013451	1.23282975	0.23661228	-1.6266227	6.08979805	-1.6266227	6.08979805	
	Product Knov	0.12193257	0.23449962	0.51996917	0.61067371	-0.3778915	0.62175669	-0.3778915	0.62175669	
	Extraversion	-0.3491473	0.13565507	-2.5737874	0.02117445	-0.6382893	-0.0600054	-0.6382893	-0.0600054	
	Time manag	0.02621841	0.22534763	0.11634651	0.90892133	-0.4540987	0.50653552	-0.4540987	0.50653552	
	Cooperativer	0.58024875	0.21603593	2.68589001	0.01693088	0.11977906	1.04071844	0.11977906	1.04071844	

Now let's take a look at the sections we marked in blue boxes. R-square tells us the percentage variation in performance ratings that is being explained by the four variables in our model. An R-square of 64% means that the four variables explain 64% of the differences in performance ratings.

P values tell us about the statistical significance of each predictor. This is an indicator of the probability that the relationship you observe between each predictor and the outcome is actually not different from zero. High *p* values mean that there is a very good chance that any relation you observe is really due to chance. Small *p* values indicate that the chance of the observed relationship being zero is really small. In this output, the *p* values are smaller than .05 for extraversion and cooperativeness. In other words, these are the predictors to pay attention to.

Finally, take a look at the "coefficients" column for extraversion and cooperativeness. Do you see anything interesting here? The sign of the extraversion coefficient is negative. This means that extraversion is actually *negatively* related to performance ratings. Using these data, you would conclude that in this company, introverted employees are actually higher performers. In contrast, there seems to be a positive relationship between cooperativeness and performance ratings. These results would help you make decisions such as where to invest your selection and training budget and where not to.

Excel Extension: Now You Try!

On **edge.sagepub.com/bauer2e,** use the provided dataset and conduct a regression analysis to examine the relationship between four personality traits and job performance.

©iStockphoto.com/alphaspirit

10 MANAGING EMPLOYEE SEPARATIONS AND RETENTION

UNDERSTANDING WORKPLACE INTERACTIONS TO INCREASE EMPLOYEE RETENTION: THE CASE OF HUMANYZE

©iStockphoto.com/shironosov

Turnover is a fact of life in organizations. However, it became truly newsworthy in 2021 during the so-called Great Resignation where employees in the United States started leaving their jobs in record numbers. An average of 3.95 million workers quit their jobs each month in 2021, which is the highest number since Bureau of Labor Statistics started releasing these figures in 2000. These trends gave great visibility to an age-old problem of the importance of understanding and managing employee turnover.

Why do employees leave, and can businesses stem the tide? Advances in technology are increasing the types of data available to businesses. These data can be used to understand and preempt employee turnover. The Boston-based people analytics firm Humanyze is an example of using wearable technology to gain insights. Founded by doctoral students at Massachusetts Institute of Technology (MIT), the firm utilizes wearable smart work badges that include precision positioning technology and microphones to gather data on who talks to whom, when, how frequently, and how loudly, and even gathers data on how stressed the employee is during each interaction. The data can then be mapped onto other workplace metrics to understand the effects of communication patterns on employee satisfaction, productivity, and turnover.

Bank of America used Humanyze badges in its call centers to understand the effects of communication patterns on employees. By mapping communication patterns onto call logs, satisfaction surveys, and turnover, they found that employees who had the closest ties to others and those who regularly socialized with others had the greatest productivity and lowest turnover. The data also revealed that most of these interactions occurred during scheduled breaks. Armed with these data, the company modified the work schedules in underperforming branches, coordinating schedules of employees, and added a 15-minute shared coffee break to the day to give employees more opportunities to interact with each other. Within a year, the bank saw a 28% increase in their retention of employees.

The technology sometimes yields unexpected results. For example, for one client, Humanyze's analysis revealed that programmers who ate lunch at 12-person tables were more productive than those who sat at 4-person tables, presumably due to greater interaction opportunities available at longer tables. As wearable technology becomes more popular and advanced, as in smart watches and fitness trackers, the data generated by them provide fertile ground for generating new insights to important HR issues, including turnover.[1]

CASE DISCUSSION QUESTIONS

1. If you were developing such a model of employee turnover, what additional information would you want to collect so you could predict turnover?

2. What are the pros and cons of using wearables to predict turnover? What are some ethical concerns with this practice? How would the national culture or local laws affect their use?

3. What advice would you offer a company interested in using the technology described in the case? What type of resistance would you anticipate from employees? How would you address their concerns?

4. The Covid-19 pandemic resulted in widespread movement toward remote and hybrid workplaces. How would the lessons of this case be applicable for organizations where employees work remotely? What types of data would you want to collect in a remote workplace to understand predictors of turnover?

Ben Waber discusses the power of social networks in his book *People Analytics: How Social Sensing Technology Will Transform Business and What It Tells Us About the Future of Work* (FT Press Analytics, 2013).

INTRODUCTION

No employee will stay in an organization forever. Employees may decide to leave because they are unhappy with the job, have better alternatives, are retiring, are quitting the workforce to become a student or full-time caregiver, or are relocating. In other cases, organizations initiate the separation through either layoffs or dismissals. Understanding why employees leave is important for line managers and HR professionals. It is also important for them to know how to manage employee separations and retention to ensure the organization has the right talent to get work done.

Employee separations may take several different forms. Voluntary turnover is a departure initiated by an employee and is typically because of the availability of better alternatives or unhappiness with current work. Even though retirements are also voluntary, we discuss them separately because why people retire is distinct from other forms of voluntary separations. Involuntary turnover is a discharge initiated by the organization. This may take the form of a dismissal, or employment termination, because the worker failed to meet organizational expectations. Alternatively, involuntary turnover may be in the form of layoffs, which involve separation due to economic or strategic reasons. Such reasons can include technology-related productivity improvements necessitating fewer employees, downsizing, plant closing, outsourcing of work to a different organization, or offshoring of work to a different location, among others. In this chapter, we will consider each of these types of turnover separately.

VOLUNTARY TURNOVER

Voluntary turnover is a departure initiated by an employee and is typically because of the availability of better alternatives or unhappiness with current work. It occurs when employees quit their jobs. Quitting one's job may be regarded as the final stage of employee withdrawal at work. Employees, in fact, may withdraw from their jobs without quitting: Other forms of withdrawal include **tardiness**, or being late to work without giving advance notice, and **absenteeism**, or unscheduled absences from work. Even though tardiness and absenteeism may have many other causes, they may also be early warning signs that the employee will eventually leave. Research has shown that absenteeism is a much stronger correlate of actual turnover relative to tardiness, which has a modest link to turnover.[2] This means frequent absenteeism may be treated as an early indicator of eventual turnover much more reliably than frequent lateness to work.

Turnover rate is an important metric to be familiar with in order to manage turnover. You may calculate an organization's turnover rate using the following formula. This formula can be modified to calculate voluntary turnover (employee-initiated), involuntary turnover (employer-initiated), and overall turnover (employee + employer initiated). Simply adjust the numerator accordingly.

$$Turnover\ Rate = \frac{Number\ of\ departures\ during\ the\ year}{Average\ number\ of\ employees\ during\ the\ year} \times 100.$$

For example, if a company had 10 departures every month during the year and had an average of 1,000 employees during the year, its annual turnover rate would be 12% (10 × 12/1,000) × 100. Is a turnover rate of 12% high? This is not an easy question to answer, but it is important to consider the turnover rate within the context of industry averages and the unemployment rate. If other firms in the same industry are averaging 30%, our example company is doing well relative to competitors. Further, unemployment rate will suppress turnover rates: When the unemployment rate is high, employees may feel lucky to have a job and are more likely to stay put. As the unemployment rate shrinks, employees who are unhappy will start departing at a faster rate.

Another helpful formula helps calculate the retention rate. This is somewhat different from the turnover rate. This is because an organization may have a few positions for which it is difficult to hold on to employees, inflating the turnover rate. For example, let's assume a company has 10 employees. One leaves, and then the position is filled by four consecutive new hires who all quit during the year. Turnover rate for this company will be 5/10 × 100 = 50%. However, using the following formula,[3]

$$Retention\ Rate = \frac{Number\ of\ employees\ who\ stayed\ during\ the\ entire\ period}{Number\ of\ employees\ at\ the\ beginning\ of\ the\ period} \times 100.$$

in the same company, retention rate will be 9/10 × 100 = 90%. This indicates that 90% of the people who were with the company at the beginning of the year are still there at the end of the year. The 50% turnover rate interpreted within the context of a 90% retention rate indicates that some positions are more prone to turnover than others. Both metrics are useful, complement each other, and are helpful in spotting trends and identifying patterns.

Costs of Voluntary Turnover

In some cases, replacing an employee who leaves may cost three or four times the annual salary of the departing employee.[4] A meta-analysis has shown that voluntary turnover is negatively related to workforce productivity ($r = -.13$), with a particularly strong relationship in smaller businesses.[5] The Covid-19 pandemic, and the resulting period of Great Resignation when employees quit their jobs in large numbers, made the costs of turnover readily observable and a topic of much discussion, with alarmingly large gaps between supply and demand of employees in health care, retail, and hospitality industries.[6]

Voluntary turnover is problematic for company performance for three key reasons. First, when employees leave, there are direct costs involved in replacing, onboarding, and training the replacements. Second, when employees leave, the organization loses human capital, or the collective KSAOs that employees bring to the organization. Employees build expertise and organization-specific knowledge over time, and when employees quit, the company loses access to this expertise. Third, turnover involves the loss of "social capital," or interpersonal connections employees have developed with coworkers, managers, and clients. For example, a key client who enjoys interacting with a particular employee may take their business elsewhere when that employee leaves, whereas coworkers may find they no longer have someone to ask for information or advice on important matters. To make matters even worse, turnover is often contagious: An employee is more likely to leave when a close coworker, a manager, or a mentor leaves.[7]

Turnover is more harmful in some contexts than in others. For example, research has shown that in industries that require highly skilled professionals such as transportation and professional services, turnover has more negative effects on business outcomes relative to industries with more standardized business practices and fewer skill demands such as food services and retail. Similarly, business implications of managerial employees leaving are more negative relative to nonmanagerial employees leaving.[8] In general, when skilled and hard-to-replace employees leave, organizations will experience more negative consequences.

It is also important to recognize that not all turnover is harmful for organizations. You can imagine situations in which a particular employee's departure is a cause for relief and may be regarded as an opportunity to hire a better replacement. Researchers have proposed that every company has an optimum turnover rate at which the cost of turnover and costs associated with minimizing turnover are at their lowest. Still, even though the optimum level will vary by company, research shows that excessive turnover is problematic for company performance, and such negative effects on performance are stronger for small businesses, for younger firms, and in firms operating in tight labor markets.[9] In other words, many of the harmful effects of turnover may be hidden and become easier to observe over time.

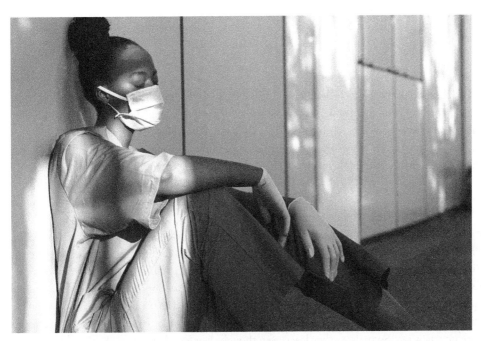

Feeling burned out, underpaid, and undervalued, nurses quit their jobs in large numbers following the emergence of Covid-19, with turnover rates increasing from 17% pre-pandemic to 20% to 30%. While some leave the profession altogether, others choose to serve as "travel nurse," taking short-term contracts that pay much better.[10]

©iStockphoto.com/insta_photos

Causes of Voluntary Turnover

Why do employees quit their jobs? Much of the turnover literature views voluntary turnover as a function of *desire to leave* and *ease of movement* (see Figure 10.1). According to this view, employees desire to leave when they are unhappy with different aspects of their jobs and when their jobs do not meet their needs. A meta-analysis showed that job satisfaction, organizational commitment, rewards offered beyond pay (such as benefits, career and growth opportunities, and training time), and a sense of fairness in the workplace are important correlates with turnover.[11] In a Pew Research Center study during the height of the Great Resignation, employees listed their pay being too low, lack of advancement opportunities, feelings of being disrespected at work, child care issues, and not having enough flexibility as the reasons that led them to change jobs.[12]

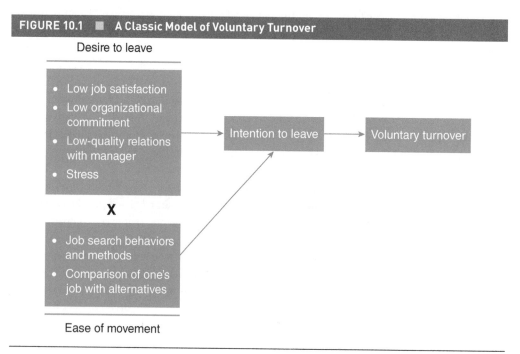

FIGURE 10.1 ■ A Classic Model of Voluntary Turnover

Desire to leave

- Low job satisfaction
- Low organizational commitment
- Low-quality relations with manager
- Stress

X

- Job search behaviors and methods
- Comparison of one's job with alternatives

Ease of movement

Intention to leave → Voluntary turnover

Source: Based on findings in Griffeth, R. W., Hom, P. W., & Gaertner, S. (2000). A meta-analysis of antecedents and correlates of employee turnover: Update, moderator tests, and research implications for the next millennium. *Journal of Management, 26*, 463–488.

On the ease-of-movement side, employees consider the job market, examine the availability of alternative jobs, and think about the likelihood of finding a job that is at least as good as their current job. You can think of ease-of-movement as employees having more leverage, or more opportunities to easily find an alternative. Even if they have no other alternatives lined up, assessing how the job market is doing, how quickly coworkers with similar qualifications found jobs, and how high the demand is for the employee's skills will give employees ideas about the ease of movement. The outcome of this decision-making process is voluntary turnover. Finally, social media platforms like LinkedIn have made it easier for employees and employers to find each other, providing employees with more information about the job market and the demand for certain skills.

Of course, this model does not summarize every possible quitting decision employees make. In fact, employees may leave even when they are happy at work. This could happen if the employee is relocating due to a spousal job change or quitting the workforce due to child care or for health reasons. In other words, happiness at work is not a guarantee for employee retention, and turnover decisions do not require a prior steady decline in happiness. Researchers identified an unfolding model of turnover to describe exceptions to the classic model.[13] This model recognizes that employees often leave without lining up a new job. Sometimes they leave even though they have happily worked in that firm for years. The model explains the turnover decision as a result of "shocks" to the system. The employee experiences a critical incident or change, which shakes them out of their status quo and gets them to consider turnover as an option. The shock could be at work (e.g., the company was acquired by a larger firm with a poor reputation), in one's career (e.g., receiving an unsolicited invitation to interview elsewhere), or at home (e.g., the employee finds out that they are going to be a parent, motivating them to reassess career goals). In some cases, the departure of a coworker or manager may be a shock in itself for those who stay.[14] Once a shock occurs, the employee may quit without lining up a new job, may start looking for a new job, or may decide that staying is better than leaving after all. The unfolding model suggests that shocks are more common predictors of turnover as opposed to simply feeling unhappy at work. The Covid-19 pandemic was an important shock for many employees. When faced with major disruptions in their personal and professional lives, many employees reassessed priorities and made job or career changes, including leaving the workforce, retiring, starting one's own business, or moving to a different industry.

Turnover literature also examines why people stay.[15] In fact, even when employees are interested in and motivated to leave, often they choose to stay. The job embeddedness model explains that employees stay because of their links to others and fit with the context at work and in their communities and how much they would have to sacrifice by leaving their work and communities, as illustrated in Table 10.1. According to this model, both on- and off-the-job embeddedness are negatively related to turnover. Note that the table lists only some examples of links, fits, and sacrifices. To illustrate, a high-level employee who worked for a highly reputable firm for a decade may find it challenging to leave due to high embeddedness. Changing jobs may mean relocation, which comes with forgoing one's current life, house, city, friendships, proximity to a beloved vacation spot, or any other number of off-the-job sacrifices along with leaving coworkers, managers, and social network at work. Leaving a highly reputable firm will also entail the sacrifice of how one is perceived due to organizational membership. For example, an employee who works for a well-known company such as Apple may receive respect and attention in their community as a result of being an Apple employee, which they would have to give up if they move to a firm that is less recognizable. As a result, even when unhappy at work, highly embedded employees may choose to stay. Interestingly, a meta-analysis showed that on-the-job embeddedness is more strongly and negatively related to turnover for employees in the public sector and in female-dominated samples, suggesting that the role played by embeddedness is situational.[16]

TABLE 10.1 ■ Job Embeddedness Model Explains Why Employees Stay		
	Work	**Community**
Links	● Relations with manager ● Relations with coworkers	● Membership in clubs and organizations ● Spouse's work ● Children's school and friends ● Friends, neighbors
Fit	● Fit with organizational values ● Fit with job	● Fit with community ● Fit with city
Losses (what must be forfeited when leaving the job)	● Ability to negotiate parts of job ● Nonportable benefits ● Job stability and security ● Social network ● Pride of organizational membership	● Short commute ● Familiarity with neighborhood

Source: Based on information contained in Mitchell, T. R., & Lee, T. W. (2001). The unfolding model of voluntary turnover and job embeddedness: Foundations for a comprehensive theory of attachment. *Research in Organizational Behavior, 23,* 189–246.

MANAGING EMPLOYEE RETENTION

Given that excessive voluntary turnover is problematic and related to undesirable outcomes, what can organizations do to retain their employees? Many factors play key roles in an organization's retention of employees, as we discuss in this section.

Gain Upper-Management Support

An important aspect of increasing employee retention is to have upper management care about the turnover rate. To make a case to receive management support for reducing turnover, HR will need to calculate the turnover rate, provide industry-level turnover rates for benchmarking purposes, and demonstrate the cost of turnover for the organization. For example, PGT Trucking recently calculated the cost of replacing a single driver is $9,500, excluding the impact such turnover could have on trucks and equipment. Using these figures in discussions around turnover and retention puts the problem in perspective and helps make a case to solve the problem.[17]

Ensure That Pay, Benefits, and Working Conditions Are Competitive

Employees are more likely to quit when they are unhappy with the company's offerings. Therefore, ensuring that pay, benefits, and working conditions are competitive is important. It is no surprise that workers often quit to get a job that pays better and provides better working conditions, more reasonable hours, and greater flexibility. In fact, National Economic Council deputy director Bharat Ramamurti noted the Great Resignation may be better described as the "great upgrade," as quitting was more widespread in lower paying industries. Further, comparing what the company currently offers to what it used to offer may not be an effective strategy. With the Covid-19 pandemic, some jobs such as those in retail and health care became more stressful, more physically exhausting, and more dangerous, with many employees feeling inadequately compensated for the emerging working conditions. In the resulting war for talent, businesses are experimenting with more effective compensation packages. As a case in point, Mechanical One, an Orlando-based air conditioning and plumbing company, announced that it would hold a drawing among employees who stay for a year. Two of these employees would get new houses, mortgage-free. To be eligible for the award, employees would have to take financial literacy classes the company pays for and also perform volunteer work at a nonprofit of their choice in addition to staying for a year.[18]

Leverage Engagement and Attitude Surveys

With the advent of predictive analytics, organizations have important tools at their disposal to predict with greater confidence which employees will stay and which ones will leave. One of the best predictors of voluntary turnover is reported intentions to leave. Asking questions about how much someone agrees with statements such as "I intend to leave my job in the next year" or "I intend to stay in this company for more than a year" is useful. Interestingly, though, turnover intentions only explain around 10% to 15% of variance in actual turnover. This is because turnover is a costly decision for employees, both financially and psychologically. Reporting turnover intentions is much easier than actually quitting, so many of those who report quit intentions may not take that step for some time. Employees who are less risk averse, who have more internal locus of control (i.e., who feel strong control over their own destiny), and who are low social monitors (i.e., who are less sensitive to social cues in their actions) will have a stronger relation between reported turnover intentions and actual turnover.[19] This means that the predictive models of turnover may be improved through consideration of individual personalities.

Yearly attitude and engagement surveys can be used to identify factors that share the strongest relation with actual turnover. Using these data, organizations may implement targeted interventions. Boston Consulting Group, a management consulting firm operating in 48 countries, observed that its mid-career, high-potential female employees had higher turnover than male employees at the same career stage. An examination of its employee engagement survey showed the female employees who ended up leaving sometime after responding to the survey responded with its lowest scores on items relating to mentoring and feedback received (as opposed to work–life balance or low career ambitions, which would have been the stereotypical explanations). Armed with this finding, the company instituted an Apprenticeship in Action program teaching managers how to build connections, give feedback, and provide high-quality coaching and mentoring. After the program implementation, attitudes toward feedback and mentoring improved across the board, and the gender differences in turnover rates in mid-career level disappeared.[20]

Companies may also utilize **pulse surveys,** which are short, frequent surveys. These surveys do not necessarily replace the rich and detailed information that can be obtained via annual surveys but could be used to predict and manage turnover and to even detect "shocks" like those discussed earlier in the chapter. In 2021, the U.S. federal government benefited from the results of their pulse survey of the federal workforce to understand employee sentiments regarding returning to work in the office. The results were helpful to show that employees had greater trust in their supervisors compared to their agency's leadership with respect to navigating the transition from remote work to office work. Further, the survey showed differences across agencies, with NASA and the National Science Foundation scoring on the high end, and the Veterans Administration and Department of Defense ending up at the low end.[21]

During the Great Resignation many companies saw their turnover rates increase. However, companies such as Southwest Airlines that had healthy, people-oriented cultures saw lower than average turnover.[22]

©iStockphoto.com/chanceb737

SPOTLIGHT ON DATA AND ANALYTICS: USING SENTIMENT ANALYSIS FOR ENGAGEMENT

A data analytics tool that will likely increase in utilization is sentiment analysis. This is the analysis of text and natural language to extract the mood of the conversation. Employers have access to employee speech and conversations in the form of e-mail exchanges, texts, and written feedback to open-ended questions in employee surveys. These exchanges are treasure troves of data, but it is impossible for one or more experts to sift through and analyze them manually. However, as technology that can conduct text analysis advances, organizations are increasingly capable of identifying the mood of their employees on an ongoing basis, noting changes, and intervening early.

For example, Trimble Transportation provides data-driven solutions to the trucking industry by utilizing metrics such as hours of service and data involving driver's behavior to predict driver turnover. Their algorithm also uses sentiment analysis, using the frequency and content of the text messages drivers send to their dispatchers as a predictor. A driver who sends a higher number of texts than normal may be experiencing problems. Complaints the driver sent to the dispatcher and the emotional tone of the words that are used can be combined with other available metrics to calculate the turnover risk for the driver. The system also puts the text message content into context. For example, if the negative messages from the driver started when the driver was dispatched to the same customer multiple times in a row, it would carry a higher weight for predicting turnover intentions. Even if the driver is not complaining about something specific, the system can detect changes in mood (e.g., a driver becoming more frustrated) to alert fleet managers. Through this system, companies can see changes in turnover risk for individual drivers and intervene. For example, they could avoid giving the driver an assignment that will make the problem worse, or they could have a conversation with the driver when the driver's sentiment begins to shift.

This technology is not perfect. Among other shortcomings, employees may perceive it as invasive. Companies can and do monitor these conversations, but structuring and formalizing this monitoring may create feelings of mistrust. Ultimately, these technologies exist, and they may be helpful in understanding how employees feel at a given time, but their usefulness will depend on how and for what purposes businesses use them.[23]

Utilize Exit Interviews

Companies may learn why a particular employee is leaving by conducting exit interviews with them relating to their departure. These interviews are opportunities to learn why employees are leaving and make changes in the organization to increase retention. For exit interviews to be useful, organizations need to conduct them regularly, analyze the data, and disseminate the data among decision makers who can enact changes. Many employees will be reluctant to share the reason for their departure, as they may worry that being honest will cost them a positive reference, or they simply may have little motivation to share their reasons. Companies may use exit interviews to understand which HR practices and departmental, managerial, and organizational factors contribute to departure and subsequently to make systematic changes. Experts recommend the following[24]:

- Exit interviews may be conducted by HR, but having a manager higher than the employee's own manager conduct the interviews has benefits, as that person will have power to make actual changes. The employee's own manager should not be present or conduct exit interviews, as the employee's manager often plays some role in employee reasons for leaving.

- It is beneficial to make exit interviews mandatory for some positions.

- Conducting the interview halfway between employee giving notice and actual departure will have benefits because the employee will not have mentally "checked out" yet. Alternatively, conducting the interview sometime after the employee leaves could be useful, as it allows the employee to give a less emotional and more reflective answer.

- The interview may be in person, via videoconferencing, or over the phone. All of these methods provide rich information, although in person or videoconferencing may be more helpful to build rapport.

- Information obtained in these interviews should be collated, analyzed, and shared among decision makers.

- When changes are made, it is useful to let other employees know the changes came about from exit interview information so employees see value in exit interviews—which could make them more forthcoming when they themselves leave.

- These interviews may be supplemented with stay interviews of employees who are not leaving. What is making them stay? Is the employee happy on the job and with their career? Having these conversations regularly with employees and making changes along the way may reduce the need for exit interviews in the first place.

Hire for Fit

Employees often leave because they are not a good fit with what the organization needs and provides. Therefore, hiring for skills, values, preferences, and personalities that will maximize happiness and engagement at work in the specific company is an essential tool for retention. Organizations can identify the traits, background, and experience factors that are best predictors of retention and performance and select employees based on those characteristics. Further, as Chapters 5 and 6 discuss, it is important to give employees a realistic job preview (RJP) to ensure that they can assess their own level of fit. Providing employees with information about their tasks, responsibilities, level of autonomy, job demands, and expected degree of change and stability are among the issues that would benefit from a realistic preview.[25] Organizations can improve retention using their recruitment and selection practices. Particularly with the move to remote work, hiring employees that fit with the company culture will become even more important. These remote employees will need to work with others without close supervision or opportunities for random interactions that may occur in a physical workplace.

Structure Onboarding Experiences

In a Qualtrics XM Institute survey, over half the respondents reported they would look for a job in the next 6 months. As you may recall from Chapter 8, successful onboarding can help increase the retention of the millions of new employees that will start working in new jobs. As discussed earlier, employees are less likely to quit when they are embedded into their jobs and communities. Conversely, newcomers will have the least embeddedness because they have not yet established fit or relationships and, thus, they do not need to sacrifice much when leaving the company. Onboarding teaches newcomers about the company culture, welcomes them to the organization, connects them to others, and sets them off to a good start. It is particularly important for these programs to dedicate time for team building and utilize technology for greater efficiency and consistency. These programs should also be easy to deliver remotely.[26]

Invest in High-Commitment HR Practices

HR practices and organizational policies that support employees' career development have been related to lower levels of turnover. This is because these practices show to employees that the organization cares about them; these practices also help create a sense of attachment to the organization. The availability of these employee supportive practices (such as developmental feedback and career workshops) was more important than whether the employees actually used them. Moreover, when these practices supported employees' career development, instead of focusing on short-term job performance, the practices were more effective.[27]

Interestingly, some HR practices that develop employee skills may create a high-quality relationship between the employee and the employer and could increase retention. However, they may also increase the ability of the employee to find an alternative job, potentially paving the way to voluntary turnover. Tuition reimbursement programs are a good example of this. Companies such as Target, Walmart, and Starbucks provide full or partial tuition reimbursement benefits. Others such as Disney offer preselected online degrees from specific institutions for free.[28] Though these programs contribute to retention during the employees' educational studies, their overall effects on retention are complicated. One study in a high-tech firm showed that when employees completed graduate degrees, they were more likely to leave, whereas obtaining an undergraduate degree or course enrollment without obtaining a degree did not contribute to turnover. Further, the turnover rate among those who earned graduate degrees but were promoted afterward was 56% less than those who benefited from tuition reimbursement but were not promoted. These findings show that simply investing in human capital may not generate high engagement and loyalty to the company; the organization will need to provide a job that is commensurate with the employee's newly acquired qualifications as well.[29]

Satisfying employees' advancement needs is an essential part of high-commitment HR practices. Today, organizations and employees have a more transactional relationship in which employers rarely promise long-term employment. As a result, the focus has shifted toward employability of the employee: Employees expect their current work to keep them employable over time. This means employees expect to gain skills and abilities that will help them find a job and be successful in their careers and do not necessarily define career success as advancement within a specific firm. In other words, the expectation is to keep one's skills current so that one can find employment as needed. Changing jobs frequently and moving across organizations are increasingly common.

This strategy seems to pay off for some employees. For example, a study of a large cohort of German professionals showed those who stayed within one firm over a period of 5 years had seen annual pay raises averaging 11%. Those who had worked for three or more firms during the same period had pay raises of 15% annually. Further, the promotion rates of job changers and job stayers were not different, suggesting that firms do not necessarily reward those who stay with frequent promotions. Because "job hopping" and job search are becoming more commonplace and a normal part of a person's career, organizations need to invest in the futures of their employees and, paradoxically, keep employees' skills marketable to other firms in order to retain them.[30]

Focus on Turnover Predictors

We know from research that important predictors of turnover include job satisfaction, work engagement, organizational commitment, manager–employee relationship quality, and stress. This means that by focusing on these factors, organizations may make progress in reducing turnover. **Job satisfaction** refers to employees' contentment with different facets of their work, including the work itself, supervision, pay, and advancement opportunities. **Work engagement** refers to feelings of emotional connection to work and a state of being in which employees bring their personal selves to work. Satisfaction and engagement are closely related, and both are related to turnover.[31]

What can organizations do to increase engagement, contribute to employee satisfaction, and build attachment to the workplace? Figure 10.2 outlines factors that are most strongly related to work engagement. Companies that are deliberate about designing jobs and working conditions that satisfy employee needs and desires will find it easier to attract and retain workers.

FIGURE 10.2 ■ Factors Associated With High Engagement

Job characteristics	Work context	Leadership
• Autonomy • Using various skills at work • Meaningful work • Feedback • Problem solving • Job complexity	• Social support • Low physical demands • Working conditions	• Transformational leadership • Manager–employee relationship quality

Source: Based on information contained in Christian, M. S., Garza, A. S., & Slaughter, J. E. (2011). Work engagement: A quantitative review and test of its relations with task and contextual performance. *Personnel Psychology, 64,* 89–136.

Stress is another reason employees quit their jobs. Difficulty balancing work with other obligations such as school, child care, and elder care responsibilities costs businesses in the form of turnover. Taking steps, such as introducing flexibility to schedules, allowing employees to work remotely as needed, and facilitating access to quality care facilities, are among the benefits organizations may provide that would reduce stress. Similarly, ensuring that each department is adequately staffed and employees are not working long hours is beneficial. As a case in point, LinkedIn created an initiative called LiftUp. LiftUp includes days where no meetings take place, provides management training to prevent employee burnout, and offers numerous mental health resources to employees. The company gave its entire workforce an extra paid week off in 2021 to allow them to rest and recharge.[32] In contrast, performing work in an understaffed department for extended periods of time will contribute to turnover because stressful working conditions erode engagement, which could encourage employees to seek jobs elsewhere.

Finally, building a trust-based relationship with employees is a key driver of employee retention. By recognizing employee contributions, ensuring that employee jobs provide sufficient challenge and meaning to employees along with providing development opportunities, eliminating unnecessary stressors, and providing social support, effective managers make a big difference in whether employees are attached to the organization or interested in leaving and how long they stay. A strong bond with one's manager is hard to leave behind, whereas poor management often drives employees to quit.

Learn How to Cope With Turnover

In industries in which turnover is chronically high, organizations will need to combine a turnover reduction strategy with a turnover management strategy. In other words, while taking the steps mentioned earlier to reduce turnover rate, businesses will also need to cope with the negative effects of expected turnover. In fact, research shows that when group norms promote the idea that turnover is threatening, turnover had more negative effects on group performance, suggesting that embracing norms around adaptivity could help businesses prevent the more harmful effects of turnover.[33] For example, the U.S. military deliberately limits the deployment of military personnel to war zones to 6 months or a year. This means, in some departments, there will be 100% turnover in a given office. These constraints are important to limit separations from family, exposure to dangerous work conditions, and long hours with no downtime. The military copes with this high planned turnover in individual offices by ensuring that jobs are standardized and simplified, the organizational structure is consistent across branches, and employees use the simplest technology that the majority of personnel will be familiar with.[34] In high-turnover businesses, each departing employee will take away organizational knowledge, so it is particularly important for organizations to make special efforts to ensure that knowledge is not compartmentalized and is accessible to everyone.

Managing Relations With Former Employees

It may be natural for managers to feel disappointment when a high-performing employee leaves. However, former employees may provide key benefits to organizations even after their departure. Many organizations are realizing the importance of leveraging the power of their alumni network. Chapter 6 points out that a company's alumni, or former employees, may be a source of referrals for future employees, may provide useful business intelligence, serve as brand ambassadors, and even become customers of the organization.[35] Some companies deliberately invest in alumni relations and stay in touch with them.

For example, McKinsey & Company provides a well-developed alumni network with a members-only website. It organizes events and gatherings for members and employs an alumni engagement person at each site. Being part of this exclusive alumni network is a selling point in McKinsey recruitment efforts for newcomers, and alumni bring significant business to McKinsey.

The amount of time and money invested in alumni networks will vary by industry and company strategy, but it is important to recognize that although turnover may conclude the employer and employee relationship, the two parties may still cross paths.

Sometimes former employees decide to come back to the organization, earning them the moniker boomerang employees. Even though some businesses refuse to hire former employees to encourage loyalty of current workers, those who choose to consider hiring them experience possible benefits. Hiring former employees requires less time investment, given the mutual experience. Onboarding takes less time for these employees. These employees can be more productive more quickly, given their familiarity with the company's products and services.[37]

Research shows that departing employees are more likely to come back if they left for personal reasons (e.g., relocation, family obligations), as opposed to leaving because they were unhappy with their work. Also, alumni are more likely to come back if they stayed away for a relatively short period of time, if they had chosen to stay in the same industry, or if they had a career break.[38] Finally, not all boomerang employees will have high performance when

Accenture is a company that invests in its alumni network. Registered alumni stay connected to the company and former colleagues, have access to job postings, and serve as brand ambassadors.[36]

©iStockphoto.com/JHVEPhoto

they return. A study conducted on National Basketball Association players is informative: Boomerang employees' performance after they return depended on their performance before departure and whether they stayed away long enough to acquire new skills, but not too long.[39] Further, boomerang managers showed similar performance to other newly hired or internally promoted managers in their first year. However, their performance did not improve as much as the performance of others over time, and their turnover rate was higher than that of other new managers.[40] In other words, organizations may want to follow a selective strategy for boomerang employees, considering their prior performance and the conditions under which they left, and also consider reaching out to employees they would be interested in rehiring in a proactive manner rather than waiting for some to come back on their own.

Manager's Toolbox: Retaining Top Talent

Every organization will have "star employees" whose voluntary turnover would constitute a major loss. How can an organization be proactive in retaining these employees? Top performers stay when they do meaningful work and have the opportunity to perform at their top level. To retain top talent, organizations may engage in the following targeted actions[41]:

- *Identify top performers.* The first step in retaining top performers is to know who they are. Performance reviews, or simply asking managers to identify top performers, could serve this purpose.

- *Track retention data for top performers.* Companies would benefit from calculating their top performer turnover rate. Although the company may have an incentive to tackle overall turnover, knowing how serious the issue of top talent retention is would be helpful to generate targeted interventions.

- *Be aware of their job attitudes.* The organization may break down the results of their engagement or attitude surveys by performance level to see what factors are systematic problems for high performers. In addition, having one-on-one conversations with them to understand their frustrations would be helpful.

- *Identify risk factors.* Organizations may use data analytics to identify factors most strongly related to voluntary departure of high-performing employees. Knowing the risk factors would allow the organization to identify employees who are at greater risk of leaving in the near future.

- *Rerecruit and reenergize.* Having "stay interviews" with these employees to find out why they stay and to give them reasons to stay are helpful tools. These meetings can be helpful in redefining their job to keep employees motivated and challenged. Further, the organization should make sure that over time, the employment conditions remain competitive with the market. For example, Netflix adjusts the salaries of high performers to the market periodically to ensure that employees find their current pay rate attractive and have little reason to consider the market for a pay raise.

- *Counteroffer or let them go?* No one, including high performers, will stay forever. Even though it is a great idea to be proactive in retaining them, there will be instances when the employee decides to leave. Should the organization present a counteroffer? Keeping an unhappy worker by paying them more may not make sense. If there is a way to reengage them and deal with problems that motivated them to leave, having that conversation could be helpful. Investing in the future of the employee sometimes may mean letting them go. Remember, they may want to come back some day or support the organization in other ways.

Retirements

Retirement is the process of ending one's work life. Retirements are normally a type of voluntary turnover (except in rare cases in which it is legally mandated), but it is worthwhile to consider them separately. Retirement is a type of work withdrawal where the employee chooses to finish working activities, replacing work with other life activities or perhaps to pursue a different career. When employees retire, the organization may experience some benefits in the form of the ability to hire lower-paid employees who may bring a fresh perspective to the job and organization. At the same time, retirement costs organizations in the form of lost expertise. As a result, organizations have an incentive to manage retirements, potentially creating programs to utilize retired employees and preventing retirement that is due to withdrawal from work. During the Covid-19 pandemic, retirements surged due to a combination of factors such as jobs losses, fears for one's health, having to take care of family members, and increases in the value of investments and real estate, contributing greatly to the Great Resignation trend.[42]

A review of the literature shows that retirement may be due to personal and work-related reasons. Financial considerations and health are among important personal reasons, with less healthy and more wealthy employees choosing to retire. Moreover, employees are more likely to retire when their spouses retire. Among work-related reasons, HR policies and practices, job characteristics, and whether the organization has an age-inclusive climate are among the factors related to retirement decision.[43]

The U.K. airline industry faced pilot shortages when twice the usual number of pilots chose early retirement during the Covid-19 pandemic and others changed careers, threatening the return of flights to pre-pandemic levels.[44]

©iStock.com/Christopher Ames

Organizations may continue to benefit from the skills and know-how of employees considering retirement by providing an "age-friendly workplace," allowing workers to switch to part-time roles, offering flexibility, ensuring that tasks still match employee capabilities, paying attention to workplace ergonomics, and building a workplace culture that supports age diversity. Many individuals find it difficult to leave the workforce altogether due to financial reasons and the desire to remain active and maintain social connections, so it may be possible to arrive at a solution that meets the needs of both parties. In fact, a study by the staffing firm Express Employment Professionals showed that 79% of respondents (ages between 57 and 75 years) said they preferred being semi-retired, with the primary reason mentioned being financial worries.[45] Many older workers are embracing bridge employment in the form of reducing one's hours or reducing job demands within the same or a different organization (and often reducing one's pay as well) instead of exiting the workforce. In the United States, bridge employment before full retirement is common, with around 60% choosing this option.[46]

Are there ways for organizations to encourage employees to retire? Because employees close to retirement are likely to be among the higher-paid workers due to their higher tenure, sometimes organizations see value in encouraging these workers to retire early. It is important to understand the legal implications of these moves. The organization may design an early retirement incentive plan (ERIP) for employees who meet particular criteria with respect to age, department, or position, offering them incentives such as continued health insurance coverage, severance pay (pay typically provided to dismissed employees), or access to pension benefits if they retire within a given window.

However, it is important to ensure that these programs remain voluntary, as forcing employees to retire is illegal under the Age Discrimination in Employment Act. Mandatory retirement due to age exists in only a small number of jobs such as law enforcement, commercial airline pilots, air traffic controllers, and judges in some states. Therefore, the organization needs to ensure there is no coercion involved in these programs (such as hinting that the employee will lose their job anyway, so it is to their advantage to accept the program).[47] In fact, questioning an employee about their retirement plans, asking whether they are planning to retire soon, or implying that at their age they should consider retirement could lead to an age-related discrimination lawsuit.

Organizations considering using early retirement programs are advised to seek legal counsel. Further, it is essential to conduct careful analyses before implementing such programs, because a larger number of employees than expected may take advantage of these programs, leaving the organization short staffed and with losses in critical expertise.

INVOLUNTARY TURNOVER

LEARNING OBJECTIVES
10.3   Indicate the costs of employee dismissals and layoffs to an organization.

Involuntary turnover is a discharge initiated by the organization. This may take the form of a dismissal, or employment termination, because the worker failed to meet organizational expectations. Alternatively, involuntary turnover may be in the form of layoffs, which involve separation due to economic or strategic reasons.

Dismissals

The employment relationship typically starts optimistically. However, sometime after organizational entry, it may become clear that an employee is a poor fit for the job. An employee's performance may fall short of expectations due to reasons such as poor person–job fit, poor work ethic, or behavioral problems. Therefore, the organization may decide to terminate the employment relationship.

Costs of Dismissals

Terminating a poorly performing or disruptive employee, while giving the organization a chance to hire a better replacement, comes with costs to the organization. Even in situations in which the problems are so egregious that it is obvious to everyone that the employee should be fired, there are risks to the organization. For example, the employee may say negative things about the company in person or online. The employee may sue the company for wrongful dismissal, which will cost time and energy to defend against even if the organization ultimately prevails. The terminated employee may engage in acts of sabotage or aggression. In some cases, the organization needs to continue to have a professional relationship with the dismissed employee; for example, a dismissed employee may be hired by a client organization and put in charge of the organization's account, essentially becoming a client to be pleased. All of these are not reasons to avoid dismissing an employee, but they indicate that a dismissal decision is not one that should be made in anger or impulsively. Developing fair procedures around how to dismiss employees, being systematic, treating employees consistently over time (and not being lenient to an offense that led to the termination of another employee), and making an effort to be respectful to the employee at every step of the process are helpful in minimizing these costs. In fact, research shows that when faced with a negative outcome, employees are most likely to retaliate when they are treated in a procedurally or interpersonally unfair manner.[48]

Although dismissals are costly, it is also important to remember that *not* dismissing some employees has its own costs, and in fact the organization may be considered guilty of negligence. For example, research shows that a "toxic worker" costs a team more than $12,000 by inducing their coworkers to leave.[49] Poor performers and disruptive workers may reduce morale and harm the ability of others to do their jobs. In fact, employees who harass, intimidate, or simply do not pull their weight may poison the group's atmosphere or cause other employees' performance to suffer.

When to Dismiss an Employee

When deciding whether to dismiss an employee for disruptive behavior or poor performance, there are a few questions to answer:

- *Did you investigate the root cause of performance deficiencies?* Is this a case of an employee mismatched with the current role but who could be valuable in a different role? Is this a previously good employee going through rough times? In some cases, the investigation may show that the solution is retraining or referring them to an employee assistance program (EAP). It is important to understand the root causes, because if the problem is the context, replacing the employee will not solve the problem.

- *Did you give the employee feedback and opportunities to improve?* Ideally, before you reach the termination decision, the employee should be given feedback and ample opportunities to improve. Having the employee perform at unacceptable levels without confronting the problem and then dismissing the employee for poor performance is unfair, as the employee may have thought that the current level of performance was satisfactory. Chapter 9 reviewed the basics of performance management, including performance improvement plans (PIPs). When feedback does not solve the problem, the employee may be placed on a PIP, with clear goals outlined for acceptable levels of performance.

- *Did you follow organizational procedures?* To ensure that termination decisions are systematic and fair, many organizations embrace a progressive discipline system. As shown in Figure 10.3, these systems aim to ensure that employees have a chance to correct their behavior and are given multiple chances. There may be some offenses that are cause for immediate termination, whereas others would follow the full spectrum of stages.

FIGURE 10.3 ■ Stages of Progressive Discipline

- Organizations are not required to have progressive discipline procedures unless there is a collective bargaining agreement in place that requires them. However, a formal discipline process ensures consistent treatment of all employees and provides legal defense in case of a lawsuit by ensuring that problematic behaviors have been documented and dealt with systematically.

- *Did you consider the timing of your decision?* Firing the employee at the wrong time may subject the company to a discrimination lawsuit or cause other difficulties. For example, terminating an employee shortly after the employee files a discrimination complaint will appear like retaliation, even when this is not the intent. (Note that firing an employee in retaliation for filing an EEOC complaint *is* illegal.)

The Legal Side of Dismissals

In the United States, with some exceptions, employment at will prevails, although it has been eroding in recent decades. This means that organizations have the right to terminate the employment of anyone at any time, and employees have the right to quit at any time. In fact, even though it is courteous, providing a 2-week notice before quitting is not a legal requirement given the at-will doctrine. Both the employee and the employer are free to initiate and terminate the relationship at any time.

At the same time, there are numerous exceptions to at-will employment, suggesting that from the organization's side, there are limits to when and why an employee may be dismissed. A dismissal that violates the law is termed wrongful dismissal. For example, employees who are covered by a *collective bargaining agreement* are subject to the contract negotiated between the union and the employer regarding when and how to terminate employment. There may also be an *employment contract* between the employer and employee with respect to terms and duration of employment and conditions for termination (such as one that may exist for teachers). If a contract is in place, the organization needs to follow it rather than assume that employment is at will. Sometimes, there may be an *implied contract* between the employee and the organization. For example, if the organization verbally mentioned that employees in this organization are not fired without a reason, this may constitute a legally binding verbal contract, an exception to employment at will. *Public policy exception* suggests the employee may not be fired in a way that violates public interest, such as firing an employee for performing jury duty or reporting illegal behavior of the organization. *Statutory exceptions* refer to myriad federal and state laws that prohibit discrimination based on specific actions or protected characteristics. Chapter 4 outlines many federal laws that protect employees, and these laws, along with other federal and state laws, are exceptions to at-will employment. Finally, some states endorse the principle of *covenant of good faith*. This means that in these states, it is illegal to dismiss the employee in a malicious way. An example of this is the dismissal of an employee to avoid paying them their earned sales commissions. All these exceptions suggest that in reality employment is rarely "at will," and organizations benefit from being familiar with state and federal laws that limit their ability to dismiss employees.[50]

When an employee is dismissed, there is the potential for a costly lawsuit if the employee suspects that the dismissal is unlawful. For example, imagine a situation in which a recovering alcoholic has been dismissed shortly after revealing past alcoholism, with the stated reason being tardiness to work. The company may be sued because alcoholism is a protected disability under the Americans with Disabilities Act as long as it does not adversely affect job performance. To protect itself from the lawsuit, the organization will need to show the real reason was tardiness. What is the organization's policy around tardiness? Was the employee given opportunities to improve? How were other employees with similar levels of tardiness treated? If the company has clear rules and procedures around tardiness and a progressive discipline policy, it will be easier to show the real reason was tardiness.

The Dismissal Interview

Experts agree there are right and wrong ways of conducting the termination interview. In the best-case scenario, the employee may still be unhappy with the outcome but will feel they were treated with dignity and respect. Following are some recommendations to facilitate a less negative interview.

- *Be there.* Ultimately, it is the responsibility of the dismissed employee's manager to communicate the news. A representative from HR may be a part of the dismissal meeting. However, the manager likely has more information about events leading up to the dismissal decision. Also, the manager is usually the person who made the decision. Instead of expecting HR to do the talking, it is reasonable to expect that HR play a supportive role.

- *Be straightforward.* Although thanking the employee for their contributions is a good idea, discussing how difficult this decision was for the manager or mentioning the strengths of the employee may appear patronizing. In fact, a study showed that even though mentioning positives of the employee seems to add to feelings of being respected, this positive effect actually reverses if the employee is then escorted out of the building, indicating that inconsistent treatment where actions and words clash is regarded as disrespectful.[51]

- *Do not lie.* Telling the employee their position is being eliminated to spare their feelings is sure to backfire when you are looking for a replacement. Such behavior erodes the company's credibility and is also likely to increase its legal exposure.

- *"It is not me, it is you."* When communicating difficult news, a natural tendency is to apologize, mention the employee's good qualities, and place the blame on the situation. Experts warn that this strategy is undesirable, may cause the employee to blame the organization, and may increase legal liability. Therefore, it is important to clarify that even though what happened is unfortunate, the blame solely rests on the actions or inactions of the dismissed employee. A quick summary of the steps that happened before you got to this point is warranted.[52]

- *Clarify the timeline.* This meeting is also a good opportunity to discuss what happens next. When is the employee's last day? Is the employee eligible for severance pay? (See more details later in this chapter.) What happens to unused vacation time and insurance?

Explaining the Decision to the Team

When an employee is dismissed, it is important to communicate the decision to the remaining employees. This is because employees try to make sense of organizational changes, including when a colleague is dismissed. There will be speculation about what happened. Employees will also wonder whether something similar could happen to them. As a result, it is important to reassure coworkers that the dismissed employee was treated with dignity and was given opportunities to improve, or simply provide a brief explanation of what happened. It is important to protect the privacy of the employee being dismissed but also to reassure the team that the decision was just. Firing an employee in an unfair manner may lead to loss of trust on the part of the dismissed employee's coworkers, and therefore the organization will need to provide an explanation to counteract the situation and reassure employees.

SPOTLIGHT ON LEGAL ISSUES: WRONGFUL TERMINATION LAWSUITS DURING COVID-19

The Covid-19 pandemic has been characterized by a large number of wrongful termination lawsuits against companies. Some examples include the following:

- During the early days of the pandemic, some companies refused to allow their employees to work remotely. Employees staying home because they were worried about catching or spreading the disease were forced to resign, or they lost their jobs because they were in violation of company policy.
- A manager working in a family-owned car dealership was fired because he complained the company was failing to protect its employees.
- An employee lost his job after he moved to a different country when his company's New York office closed and employees were asked to work from home. His doctor advised him to leave New York due to high levels of infection rates. The company approved his leaving New York but did not accommodate the move to a different country.
- Employers with a vaccine mandate fired employees who refused to get vaccinated when they decided that religious or medical objections could not be accommodated.

Organizations should ensure that termination decisions are not made lightly. Firing long-serving employees for a first offense, or for reasons that might seem frivolous, lends support to the argument that the decision is actually for a different, potentially illegal reason. Organizations can take several steps to stay on the right side of the law, such as the following:

- Being sure that employees are not terminated for illegal reasons (checking both federal and state laws).

- Ensuring that the organization establishes and follows consistent procedures for termination decisions.
- Having strong documentation of past performance. It is not permissible to go back and create a paper trail for past offenses. Instead, managers need to document problem behavior along the way, communicate with the employee, and ensure compliance.
- Carefully considering possible accommodations balancing individual rights and well-being of others.[53]

Layoffs

When organizations are faced with pressures to contain and reduce costs, reducing the number of employees is one method available to them. Layoffs refer to involuntary turnover of employees due to organizational restructuring, downsizing, or other strategic or economic reasons. Unlike dismissals, layoffs involve discharge of employees through no fault of their own. Some layoffs occur because of a desire to reduce payroll expenses in the short run. Others occur because the company may have strategically decided to switch focus, move out of a specific market or out of a particular line of work, or may have decided to offshore (i.e., move some aspects of production overseas to benefit from cost savings) or outsource production (i.e., instead of performing some operations inside the company, starting to purchase them from outside vendors). In each of these cases, the company decides that some positions, jobs, stores, or plants are no longer needed, resulting in layoff decisions.

Layoffs typically involve discharge of multiple employees, often reaching hundreds or even thousands. For example, in 1993, IBM laid off 60,000 employees in order to restructure the organization from one focused on mainframe computers to one focused on business solutions. More recently, in 2021, New Oriental Education in China laid off 60,000 employees when the Chinese government instituted a ban on for-profit tutoring of students from kindergarten to ninth grade.[54] Layoffs are painful for the employees being let go and their coworkers and managers, as well as families. As the numbers get larger, the effects may spread throughout the community in which the business is located, increasing the unemployment rate in the area and affecting housing and demand for the products of unrelated businesses.

Costs of Layoffs

The literature and the popular press treat layoffs as traumatizing events with good reason. The terminology used to describe these events often reflects this: Those directly affected by layoffs are sometimes termed "victims" of a layoff, whereas employees who escape the layoff are "survivors." Of course, this view is overly simplistic. In any layoff, there will be some employees who would prefer to be (and sometimes volunteer to be) among those who are being laid off; some employees may have been looking for an exit anyway, and the accompanying financial packages, such as generous severance pay, may seem an attractive way of leaving an organization they were not committed to. Alternatively, among those who are laid off, there will be some who look at it as a blessing in disguise: an opportunity to pursue a career, job, or life change they were hesitant to take while employed. At the same time, barring these exceptions, layoffs have numerous significant and negative effects and costs to employees, business outcomes, communities, customer relations, and the reputation of a business; thus, it is important to understand the direct and indirect implications of layoffs.

Layoffs negatively affect the psychological and physiological well-being of layoff victims, layoff survivors, and managers in charge of delivering the bad news.[55] When organizations engage in downsizing, it is often perceived as a violation of one's psychological contract with the organization. Employee justice perceptions, job involvement, loyalty, trust, creativity, and job performance suffer following downsizing.[56] In fact, research shows these effects are not limited to feelings of injustice and anger toward the organization they are leaving. Layoff victims experience lower levels of well-being, including dissatisfaction with their lives, stress, and lower-quality sleep.[57] Further, an individual's layoff history has been linked to voluntary turnover in jobs following the layoff. This is partially because employees are more likely to be underemployed or hold poor-quality jobs following layoffs but also because the psychological contract violation and trust violation following a layoff becomes part of an individual's personal history, preventing them from forming strong attachments to their next employer.[58] In other words, layoffs are traumatic in the sense that they erode trust in employers in general and lead to a pervading sense that organizations are not trustworthy.

Interestingly, whether layoffs ultimately improve organizational performance is controversial. Organizational downsizing is not always the result of a well-thought-out plan to benefit the organization. Sometimes it occurs through organizational mimicry when other firms in the industry downsize. Research shows that downsizing may result in some reductions in labor costs, but it also disrupts organizational relations, erodes the skill base of the organization, and harms the business, with several studies suggesting a negative relationship between downsizing and organizational performance. In cases in which studies identified positive effects on organizational performance, these were realized several years after downsizing, suggesting that any positive effects typically happen in the long term.[59]

Layoffs also have some direct financial costs. **Unemployment insurance** is payment made to unemployed individuals (see Chapter 13). Unemployment insurance is a federal program providing income continuation to employees who lost their jobs through no fault of their own. The program is administered by individual states, and therefore the amount and conditions vary by the state. Unemployment benefits are funded by a payroll tax, and the amount of this tax varies by an organization's experience with layoffs. In other words, this tax rate goes up as the organization lays off more employees and those employees end up drawing funds from the unemployment insurance. Also note that employees who are dismissed (as opposed to laid off) may also be eligible for unemployment insurance, but state laws vary about this, and in most cases employees who were dismissed due to misconduct are not eligible. In contrast, employees who leave voluntarily are never eligible for unemployment benefits.[60] To manage these costs, organizations may consider alternatives to layoffs such as retraining employees to utilize them elsewhere and speed up the process of finding a new job for laid-off employees through referrals, providing leads, and other forms of assistance in finding a new job.

SPOTLIGHT ON GLOBAL ISSUES: CULTURAL INFLUENCES ON EMPLOYEE SEPARATIONS

Historically, countries differed greatly in the long-term employment protections they provided to workers. This situation is changing, with layoffs becoming more prevalent around the world. Still, employment laws in various countries may provide greater worker protections, making it more difficult to dismiss or lay off employees. In fact, governments in European countries see job preservation as a key priority. For example, in the first nine months of 2020, 9.6 million employees lost their jobs in the United States, as opposed to 2.6 million people in the European Union (EU), even though the EU has a larger population. This is because EU countries utilized retention schemes where governments paid for parts of the costs of retaining employees on payrolls, whereas the U.S. government utilized unemployment payments and stimulus packages.[61]

When dismissing employees for cause, there are different procedures to be followed depending on the country or jurisdiction in which the dismissal takes place. For example, Italy passed new laws around layoffs in 2021. Companies with more than 250 employees are now required to give 90 days' notice when closing plants or engaging in layoffs involving more than 50 employees. The notice needs to be sent to unions, work councils, the Ministry of Labor, and other parties, explaining the reasons for the layoff. After the notice, the company is required to have a plan to mitigate the negative effects of layoffs, such as using layoff alternatives, including furloughs or turnover incentives, and providing training to laid-off employees.[62]

In the United States, severance pay is not a legal requirement, whereas in other countries, dismissed employees may be entitled to severance pay. For example in Ontario, Canada, employees with 5 or more years of service are entitled to severance pay if they are working for a business with a payroll exceeding $2.5 million.[63] As this example illustrates, terminating the employment of employees is much more challenging and costly in many locales outside the United States.

Overall, the negative effects of layoffs and the resulting feelings of job insecurity are contingent on the institutional context within a particular society and the social safety net and legal rights unemployed individuals have. Whether laying off workers or dismissing for cause, organizations operating in multiple countries are strongly advised to ensure that their employee separation procedures follow the local law.

Benefits of Job Security

Job insecurity, or the feeling and worry that individuals may suddenly lose their jobs, is an important stressor, with consequences for employee well-being and job attitudes. Although feelings of job insecurity may originate from individual factors such as personality and qualifications, having gone through layoffs and other adverse organizational changes in the past play an important role in generating feelings of job insecurity.[64]

Lincoln Electric, a manufacturer of welding products founded in 1895, follows a no-layoffs policy for its workforce of more than 10,000.[65]

©iStockphoto.com/Phonix_a

To avoid the negative consequences of layoffs and the resulting job insecurity, some organizations make a concerted effort to avoid layoffs. For example, San Antonio–based energy company NuStar follows a no-layoffs policy, which is one of the reasons it has been listed among the *Fortune* 100 Best Companies to Work For.[66] Companies that pursue zero-layoff policies aim to build long-term relations with their employees and seek alternative ways of managing their payroll expenses. Having such policies in place is likely to contribute to a sense of job security and help build attachment to the company, thereby improving employee engagement and retention.

HR can play a role in minimizing the need for layoffs through effective workforce planning. If an organization is in the habit of laying off employees regularly in response to seasonal fluctuations in demand and rehiring employees because key talent is lost after layoffs, these may be indications that this process is not being managed well. Instead, organizations may take a long-term view to layoffs by considering alternatives to layoffs and regarding layoffs as a last resort (see Table 10.2).

TABLE 10.2 ■ Alternatives to Layoffs	
Method	**Description**
Bonuses for productivity	Organizations may offer bonuses to employees who improve productivity or cut costs.
Reduced hours	The company may cut back on the hours of nonexempt employees or cut the number of work days along with the pay of exempt employees.
Furlough	Employees may be put on mandatory unpaid time off.

Method	Description
Unpaid time off	Employees may be offered unpaid time off for a period of time on a voluntary basis.
Seek ideas from employees	The organization may share information about the current financials of the company and seek ideas to save money.
Pay cut	The salaries or wages of some or all employees may be reduced.
Hiring freeze	The organization may cease hiring anyone for an extended period of time. Coupled with natural departures, this method results in a reduced headcount.
Job sharing	One full-time job may be divided between multiple part-time workers.
Offering early retirement	The organization may offer enticements to encourage employees to retire early.
Moving toward a contingent workforce	By utilizing temporary workers for jobs in which the demand for employees fluctuates, the organization may avoid seasonal layoffs.
Temporarily stopping production	The organization may stop production for a period of time and not pay employees for that period.
Retraining employees	Instead of laying off workers, the organization may invest in retraining and redeploying these employees.
Utilizing work-share programs	The organization may apply for state work-share programs to reduce work hours and pay of some employees, and employees receive unemployment insurance benefits while keeping their jobs.

Sources: Partially based on information contained in Anonymous. (2009, April). Maximize productivity, minimize layoffs. *HR Focus*, 10–15; Mirza, B. (2008, December 29). *Look at alternatives to layoffs.* SHRM. https://www.shrm.org/resourcesandtools/hr-topics/behavioral-competencies/leadership-and-navigation/pages/alternativestolayoffs.aspx.

Deciding Layoff Criteria

Organizations will decide how to handle layoffs depending on their needs. Some layoffs will involve entire departments or plants being shut down, whereas others may utilize reducing headcount in every department by a certain percentage. As long as the layoff criteria are not illegal (i.e., choosing employees based on their age, disability status, sex, or race), organizations are allowed to set the criteria to fit their business purposes. The organization may decide which skills are essential to retain and thus hold on to employees who have critical skills and let go of employees who have documented performance problems. Layoffs may be *seniority-based* and *performance-based*. When layoffs are based on seniority, the organization retains the most senior workers and lets go of the newer workers. Even though this may lead to the loss of newly acquired key talent, this method has the advantage of ease of implementation. Employees are simply let go based on their hire date, and the implementation is likely to be systematic. When performance is used as the layoff criterion, the organization will be able to retain higher performers. In practice, however, as reviewed in Chapter 9, any biases and subjectivity inherent in performance measurement systems will affect layoff decisions, which may lead to feelings of unfairness.

Regardless of the criteria used, organizations are advised to keep good records of what criteria were used to implement layoffs and to ensure the implementation is systematic. Further, it is important to conduct an adverse-impact analysis to identify the effects on diversity. In many organizations, women and marginalized workers may be clustered in staff functions and may have less tenure. Therefore, a seemingly neutral layoff criterion like seniority may wipe out one demographic group from the department. Understanding how different criteria will affect the level of diversity within the organization may motivate the organization to consider multiple criteria and to ensure the criteria being used are fair and defensible.[67]

The Legal Side of Layoffs

When an organization is planning a layoff, an important federal law to be familiar with is the Worker Adjustment and Retraining Notification (WARN) Act. This act covers employers with at least 100 full-time employees or employers with at least 100 part-time and full-time employees who work a combined total of 4,000 hours per week. Federal, state, and local government employees are *not* covered by this law. Further, when calculating the size of a business, employees who had been employed for fewer than 6 months in the past 12 months are excluded. Covered organizations who intend to do one of the following are required to provide 60-day written advance notice to employees:

a. close a plant or facility and therefore lay off at least 50 employees within a single site for a period of 6 months or more; or

b. conduct a mass layoff in which the organization lays off 50 to 499 employees within a single site within a 30-day period, and that number is at least 33% of the organization's workforce; or

c. the organization will lay off 500 or more employees within a 30-day period.

Even when a single layoff may not reach one of these thresholds, the organization may still be covered by the WARN Act if the organization lays off two or more groups of employees through which the total reaches one of these thresholds within a 90-day period. Further, in addition to laying off employees, if the organization is planning to reduce the hours of employees by more than 50% for 6 months, the WARN Act's notification requirements are triggered. For the purposes of this act, remote workers are considered to be part of their home base, or the unit from which they are assigned work.[68] If the organization fails to provide advance notice, the organization is responsible for back pay and benefits up to 60 days.

Some organizations choose not to provide written advance notice, instead opting to provide 60 days' pay and benefits in lieu of notice and lay off employees immediately. This is technically a violation of the WARN Act, but this approach means the organization has satisfied its WARN Act obligations by paying the penalty for violating the act.[69]

In addition to the federal WARN Act, state laws often extend the advance notice requirements for businesses engaged in layoffs. For example, states such as California, Illinois, New Hampshire, and New York have their own WARN Acts. In California, businesses with 75 or more employees (as opposed to the 100-employee threshold in the federal law) are covered. Further, the California law requires advanced notice for a layoff, plant closing, or relocation of 50 or more employees.[70]

The layoff decision needs to be compliant with the EEOC laws outlined in Chapter 4. When layoff criteria utilized by the organization intentionally or unintentionally discriminates against a protected group, the layoff decision may run afoul of the law. For this reason, as well as to maintain the fairness of the decisions, experts recommend that layoff decisions are based on objective criteria that can easily be verified, such as possessing multiple skills, seniority, and experience, as opposed to subjective criteria such as "attitude" or "initiative."[71]

Delivering the Message

Once the organization decides who the specific employees to be laid off are, it is important to deliver the news in a professional and compassionate manner. Layoffs often are emotionally charged and come as unexpected news to employees. Employees who learn about their impending layoff may feel anger and humiliation. Anything the organization may do to alleviate the negative consequences of layoffs (in the form of severance pay or outplacement assistance) and provide support to departing employees to help deal with the resulting uncertainty may result in better management of layoffs.

How the layoff victims are treated matters not only because fair treatment is the right thing to do but also because it affects the job attitudes, performance, and retention of layoff survivors. Poor treatment of layoff victims may harm the company's reputation. Social media and websites such as Glassdoor.com, where current and former employees leave comments about their treatment by a company, make it easier for tales of unfair treatment to spread to potential job applicants and clients.

It is also important to remember that delivering layoff news is stressful for managers, who may experience feelings such as guilt, worry about employees' reactions, anger at the organization's decision, and doubt regarding their self-image as an effective manager. Therefore, it is essential to train managers in delivering layoff news. Figure 10.4 shows the elements of an effective layoff communication training, which includes the components of *bad news delivery* and *procedural fairness*. In other words, managers need to be trained in how to structure the layoff interview to ensure the bad news is delivered in a professional way and to ensure the process teaches managers to be fair. Researchers showed in a series of two laboratory studies that a training program following this structure was successful in ensuring that layoff news was communicated in a fairer manner, and the negative emotions reported by managers delivering the news were lower when trained. Unfortunately, such training is not common because layoffs are a relatively infrequent event, but managers need to learn how to deliver bad news in general, particularly when it comes to layoff news.[72]

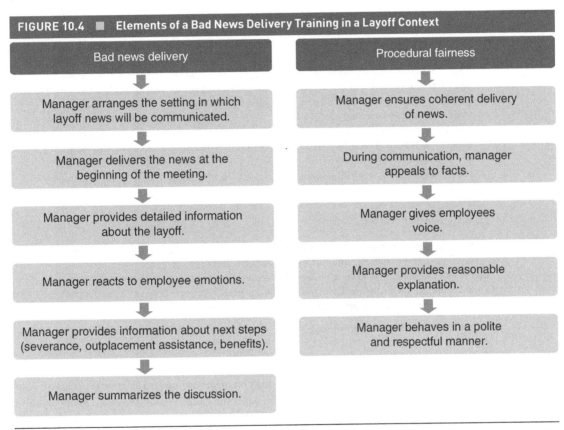

FIGURE 10.4 ■ Elements of a Bad News Delivery Training in a Layoff Context

Bad news delivery	Procedural fairness
Manager arranges the setting in which layoff news will be communicated.	Manager ensures coherent delivery of news.
Manager delivers the news at the beginning of the meeting.	During communication, manager appeals to facts.
Manager provides detailed information about the layoff.	Manager gives employees voice.
Manager reacts to employee emotions.	Manager provides reasonable explanation.
Manager provides information about next steps (severance, outplacement assistance, benefits).	Manager behaves in a polite and respectful manner.
Manager summarizes the discussion.	

Source: Based on information contained in Richter, M., König, C. J., Koppermann, C., & Schilling, M. (2016). Displaying fairness while delivering bad news: Testing the effectiveness of organizational bad news training in the layoff context. *Journal of Applied Psychology, 101,* 779–792.

SPOTLIGHT ON ETHICS: COMPASSIONATE DELIVERY OF LAYOFF NEWS

Even though not every layoff "victim" may feel like a victim, learning about one's impending layoff may be met with anger, humiliation, and a feeling that one is disposable. In some companies, the news is delivered in an unnecessarily careless and humiliating way. Here are some examples that miss the mark:

● *Escorted by security.* It is common for organizations to have security presence during mass layoffs or when retaliation and aggression are expected, but should escorting employees to the exit be routine practice? Organizations need to strike a balance between ensuring safety and showing compassion. A senior executive who was a long-time employee shared his experience: "I had to go down, grab some things quickly, and there was some security guards waiting. And then I got marched out of the building. And I thought that was so demeaning. . . . And the thing that I did find humiliating, I had to ring up and ask permission to come back and collect all my stuff."[73]

● *Learning about it last.* One employee reports his company was conducting layoff meetings while outgoing voicemails of departing employees were being changed. An employee's wife found out about the layoff of her husband from a voicemail message stating the employee no longer worked there.[74]

- *Mass announcements.* Companies sometimes find it cumbersome to conduct one-on-one meetings with employees to be laid off and resort to mass announcements. Although this method is efficient and legally permissible, employees often find it disrespectful and unfair. In 2021, the mortgage startup Better.com laid off 900 employees in a Zoom meeting, right before the holidays. Invitees joined the meeting assuming it was an end-of-year communication. Instead, they were told "If you're on this call, you are part of the unlucky group that is being laid off, and your employment here is terminated effective immediately." The meeting lasted only 3 minutes and caused outrage, affecting company's reputation.[75]

- *What's in the severance package?* Companies often offer severance packages that are intended to soften the blow, including extensions on health insurance, severance pay, and access to career services. In 2022, the maker of Internet-connected exercise equipment Peloton was criticized when their layoff announcement involving 2,800 employees also included complimentary memberships for 1 year. The announcement was considered to be insensitive, given the high cost of Peloton bikes and the assumption that the laid-off workers would still want to remain as customers.[76]

- *Can you come back and teach us what you do?* An employee who performed a task vital to the company's operations was laid off. A few days later, she received a call from HR. Apparently, no one had realized how important her job was to the operations until after she was laid off. Would she consider coming back for a few days and teaching what she did to someone still employed in the company?[77]

Questions

1. What reasons can you think of to explain why employers chose to use what can be perceived as insensitive layoff announcements like those described here?
2. Find an example in the news or in the HR literature of a layoff that was handled with respect and compassion for the workers. Were there any problems nevertheless? What did the company do right, and what could have been done better?

Severance Pay

Severance pay refers to payments made to departing employees during organizationally initiated turnover. Severance pay is not a federal legal requirement in the United States. However, many organizations choose to provide severance pay, and when severance pay is promised in an employee handbook or employment contract, it becomes a legally binding obligation. According to a study by Randstad RiseSmart, 64% of employers offered severance pay to employees who were let go. Many businesses offered severance pay to all workers, including contract workers, with the Covid-19 pandemic resulting in coverage of more categories of employees.[78]

Severance packages often include 1 or 2 weeks of pay for each year the employee has been employed by the organization. Further, they may include additional benefits, such as an extension of employee health insurance for a period of time. Even though severance may be provided for both dismissals and layoffs, organizations may choose not to provide severance when an employee is terminated for cause (such as stealing money, violating company policy, or willfully behaving in a way damaging to the company), whereas organizations with severance policies typically provide them to all laid-off employees.

Employers may want to provide a generous severance pay during layoffs in order to soften the blow and help out displaced workers. Even in the best-case scenario, employees may find themselves unemployed for several months, and providing a generous severance package helps employees deal with the financial stress that arises from the layoff decision. In addition to helping out the involuntarily displaced employee, severance packages play a protective role for organizations: Organizations usually provide severance pay in exchange for a waiver of one's right to sue the company for reasons of discrimination. In practice, signing a severance agreement and receiving severance payment do not automatically prevent an employee from suing for discrimination; the court may still decide the waiver is not valid. However, this waiver is usually valid if the departing employee signed it willingly and understood what it meant upon signing.[79] In other words, some companies are motivated to provide severance pay in order to potentially lower the likelihood of a lawsuit after the employee departs. This means the severance agreement should be prepared in consultation with legal expertise. Further, if you ever find yourself in the role of the departing employee, it is important for you to understand the terms and conditions of receiving severance pay and the legal rights you may be waiving in the process.

Outplacement Assistance

In addition to providing laid-off employees with severance pay, some organizations provide services that assist laid-off workers to find reemployment more quickly. Helping employees find new employment is part of showing concern for them. Outplacement services are typically provided by outside companies contracted by the organization. Ideally, the program will be individualized and tailored to the person. For example, key elements of these programs include working with a career coach who helps the person find a new job or make a career transition. Outplacement professionals may help laid-off employees identify how their skills match with the job market and help them use the latest technology or platforms to look for a job.[80]

Managing Survivors

An important aspect of managing layoffs is to have a plan for how the layoffs will be communicated to layoff survivors (i.e., employees who are not being laid off) and how these remaining employees will be reengaged and motivated. During layoffs, survivors will experience anxiety not only on behalf of the employees being laid off but also about what will happen next, who will take over the workload of employees who are departing, what changes the reduced workforce will have to face, and whether layoffs are expected to occur in the future. As a result, considering and managing survivor reactions to layoffs is crucial.

Because layoffs generate anxiety on the part of employees that the economic future of the company is uncertain and future layoffs are likely, the organization may end up losing critical talent it had no intention of laying off. When key talent unexpectedly leaves, the organization may find itself short-staffed and unable to meet its commitments. Even small-scale layoffs may increase voluntary turnover drastically. A study of 267 firms from multiple industries showed that layoffs targeting just 1% of the population were followed by an average of 31% increase in voluntary turnover.[81] Anxiety over the future of a company, a shaken sense of trust, and simply the change in how employees see a company (i.e., from a company providing stable employment to a "downsizer") are among the reasons survivors may leave an organization shortly after downsizing.

A strong communication plan may mitigate some of the negative effects of layoffs on survivors. For example, the use of active listening by management reduced feelings of insecurity in a company getting ready for layoffs.[82] Organizations have an incentive to clearly communicate the reasons and consequences of layoffs for the remaining workforce, as well as to provide the necessary reassurances if they are able. For example, if the layoffs were to be a one-time event and no other layoffs are expected or planned in the near future, communicating this information is beneficial. However, management needs to be honest: If layoffs are going to occur in the near future, providing reassurances may comfort employees in the short run but is bound to break trust when promises are not kept.

CHAPTER SUMMARY

Employee turnover may take the form of voluntary turnover such as quitting and retiring and involuntary turnover such as dismissals and layoffs. Because turnover is very costly to organizations in terms of time and effort as well as money, it is important for HR professionals to understand how to manage employee retention. Retention is influenced by many factors, including upper management's level of support for retention, the use of employee surveys and interviews, effective hiring and onboarding practices, investment in high-commitment HR practices, and attention to predictors of turnover. Although some forms of turnover may have benefits for organizations in the short and long term, organizations need to be deliberate in managing employee separations to ensure they have access to the talent they need in order to reach organizational goals. Effective HR practices may aid in turnover management, but ultimately managers play a key role in motivating employees to quit their jobs or retire, as well as how employee dismissals and layoffs are handled in the organization. Therefore, managing employee separation requires a true partnership between HR departments and line managers.

KEY TERMS

Absenteeism

Boomerang employees

Bridge employment

Dismissal

Employability

Employment at will

Involuntary turnover

Job embeddedness model

Job satisfaction

Layoffs

Progressive discipline

Pulse surveys

Severance pay

Stay interviews

Tardiness

Unemployment insurance

Unfolding model of turnover

Voluntary turnover

Work engagement

Wrongful dismissal

HR REASONING AND DECISION-MAKING EXERCISES

Mini-Case Analysis Exercise: Dismissing an Employee

You work for the HR department of a manufacturing firm. The company has 500 employees, a significant portion of whom have long tenure in the company.

Eric Jenkins, a department manager who was hired 2 years ago, contacted you, saying he is interested in dismissing Laura Harrison. Laura has been with the company for the past 25 years. He is concerned that Laura is not adapting well to the new technological changes that took place in the company over the past year. Plus, she is always debating every point with Eric, trying to argue that "this is not how we do things around here." Eric feels that Laura's knowledge of the business is stale, and she is displaying strong resistance to change and innovation. He also feels she is not respecting him because she is much older than he is. They have had performance conversations in the past, but Laura does not seem interested in improving. Eric gave Laura a 3 out of 5 (meets expectations) in her last performance review, which was about a year ago.

Your company is not unionized and does not have a formal discipline procedure.

QUESTIONS

1. What would you advise Eric to do? Should Eric dismiss Laura? Explain your rationale. What would be the consequences of dismissing and not dismissing Laura?

2. What additional information would be helpful to you in making your recommendation about this case?

3. Let's say you decided not to dismiss Laura in the short run. What would be your recommended action plan to solve this problem?

4. What type of procedures would be helpful to have in this company? Provide your recommendations for structural changes so that cases such as these are more easily resolved.

HR Decision Analysis Exercise: Hiring Bonus

You are a manager at a fast food company. Your location really struggled during the pandemic, with many employees quitting, leaving your location seriously understaffed. The current employees are unhappy, overworked, and feeling underappreciated. To ensure the staffing shortage is resolved and to reduce their workload, you thought of offering a $3,000 sign-on bonus for anyone who applies and stays for 4 months.

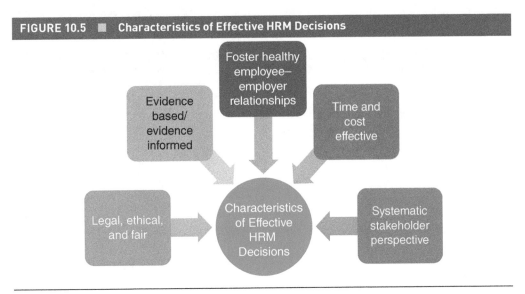
Please provide the rationale for your answer to each of the questions below.

Is your idea to offer a hiring bonus to new employees legal, ethical, and fair?

Is it evidence based/evidence informed?

Does it foster healthy employee–employer relationships?

Is it time- and cost-effective?

Does it take a systematic stakeholder perspective?

Considering your analysis above, overall, do you think this would be an effective decision? Why or why not?

What, if anything, do you think should be done differently or considered to help make this decision more effective?

HR Decision-Making Exercise: Creating a Retention Management System

You are working at Shek, Inc., an organization providing private and group surfing and scuba diving lessons, adventure tours, and rental services to tourists in Hawaii. Your company has around 200 employees consisting of instructors, sales, marketing, and office personnel. The company has an annual turnover rate of 80%, which you suspect is too high.

1. How would you assess why employees are leaving? After you choose your method of measurement (survey, interviews), develop questions to include in your instrument. How would you analyze the data to identify the top reasons for employee departures?

2. Let's assume you found out the top three reasons for turnover in this company are the following:
   a. Management is very authoritarian and not supportive of employees.
   b. Employee schedules vary a lot and often are announced with very short notice.
   c. Employees feel they are working all the time with little downtime.

What would be your proposed action plan to deal with these issues? Be specific, and make sure your recommendations focus on recruitment, selection, training, compensation, and any other stages of the employment cycle.

DATA AND ANALYTICS EXERCISE: HOW HIGH IS YOUR TURNOVER?

Shaffer Technologies is an educational software firm in the San Francisco area. This firm had the following number of departures and number of employees during the past calendar year:

Month	Number of departures	Number of employees
January	24	1070
February	88	1347
March	67	1213
April	29	1200
May	45	1422
June	77	1277
July	74	1286
August	18	1109
September	34	1272
October	14	1000
November	63	1263
December	72	1435

1. Calculate the annual overall turnover rate for this firm.

2. How would you decide whether this turnover rate is excessive for this firm? Explain the steps you would follow to make this decision.

3. Let's focus only on January. Assume that out of the 24 employees who are shown as departures, 2 left voluntarily, 9 of them are on FMLA leave, 5 of them were temporary agency workers who were let go, 2 retired, 4 were terminated for cause, and 2 were put on unpaid leave. What is the monthly turnover rate for January?

Excel Extension: Now You Try!

- On **edge.sagepub.com/bauer2e,** you will find an Excel exercise on turnover involving a different organization.

- First, you will calculate the turnover rate for different units in an organization.

- Second, you will make recommendations based on your findings.

REWARD SYSTEMS

PART

III

©iStockphoto.com/metamorworks

11 **DEVELOPING A PAY STRUCTURE**

LOCATION-BASED PAY REDUCTIONS FOR REMOTE WORKERS

With the goal of reducing the spread of Covid-19, at the outset of the pandemic, many organizations allowed large-scale remote work for the first time. Instead of attending an organization's physical location and interacting with colleagues face to face, workers interacted using e-mail, messaging applications, and videoconferencing platforms like Zoom and Microsoft Teams. Not only did remote work keep workers physically safer by limiting the spread of the virus, but it also benefitted some workers by, for example, reducing commuting time and expenses and facilitating their ability to navigate work and family challenges. Further, remote work enabled some workers to relocate to geographic areas with more affordable housing options while maintaining the same or similar level of pay, effectively increasing the value of their pay.

A report by the Working From Home Research Project estimated that immediately prior to the pandemic in March 2020, about 5% of the U.S. workforce worked remotely, but by June 2020 that number had skyrocketed to over 60%. Over the next couple of years, as many workers returned to face-to-face work, the percentage of those working remotely gradually declined and leveled off to around 30% by September 2022, with higher percentages of employer-planned remote work occurring in more densely populated areas like Brooklyn, New York, and Los Angeles, California. Still, despite overall decreases in remote work, nearly one third of U.S. workers still work remotely, a sizeable increase from pre-pandemic estimates.

Viewed initially by many organizations as a temporary public and workplace health solution, remote work continued, with some workers expressing a desire to continue working remotely indefinitely. With so many working remotely full time, organizations began considering how much full-time remote workers should be paid relative to those who worked a hybrid or full-time in-person schedule. For instance, according to a survey conducted by Payscale in 2021, 14% of organizations expressed plans to reduce wages for those who continued to work remotely. And that same year, well-known companies like Google began encouraging workers to return to its campuses for in-person work and proposed changes to pay policies for those who opted for permanent remote work. Specifically, Google proposed to reduce pay for those who continued to work remotely in locations with lower labor costs, whereas pay would remain the same for those who worked remotely in the same city as their home campus. Some estimates suggested that Google employees who worked remotely from locations with the lowest labor costs would see up to a 25% reduction in pay.

Pay plays a critical role in buying essential goods and services, like housing, food, and child care. Thus, it is perhaps not surprising that some remote Google workers were not pleased with the location-based pay reduction announcement, with some saying they wanted to leave the company. Research has shown that differences in pay may even lead to reductions in effort and performance for those who recognize they are paid less for performing the same work as coworkers. Finally, the gender pay gap may be worse for those who choose to work remotely from a different geographic location. This is because those who work remotely may be less likely to receive raises and promotions relative to those who work in the office, and research shows that women tend to provide disproportionately more child care and thus disproportionately choose to work remotely.[1]

Despite perks like campus bicycles and free food, some Google employees have chosen to work remotely.
© https://www.istockphoto.com/ SpVVK

CASE DISCUSSION QUESTIONS

1. Do you think location-based pay is fair for remote workers? Why or why not?

2. What are some potential unintended consequences of paying remote workers less than their hybrid and in-person counterparts?

3. Pay has been typically at least partly based on cost of living in the location. Do you think remote work is changing the role of cost of living as part of pay decisions? Why or why not?

4. Setting aside any potential differences in pay, do you think those who work remotely are as motivated as those who work in-person? Why or why not?

INTRODUCTION

When thinking about rewarding employees, pay is likely the first thing that comes to mind—and for good reason. Pay, which includes wages and salaries, often accounts for two thirds of a total compensation package's overall value. The remainder of a total compensation package may also include benefits such as health care and paid time off.[2] Managers and employees often view the role of pay differently. For managers, pay is often viewed as a major cost. For employees, pay often represents an outcome offered in exchange for work. This chapter focuses on how to develop an effective pay structure that addresses the concerns of both managers and employees.

PAY AS A REWARD

As a reward, pay receives a lot of attention—and rightfully so. Still, it is important to remember that pay is just one component of an organization's total compensation packages and reward systems. In other words, pay is one of many possible rewards employers may provide to employees. For example, in addition to pay, employers may reward employees with benefits, recognition, or status. Although pay was one of the top reasons U.S. workers quit a job in 2021, pay is not the only reason workers left their jobs. Other reasons for turnover included lack of advancement opportunities and feeling disrespected.[3] Further, research typically finds only a small correlation between employees' pay and their overall job satisfaction, meaning that employees who are paid more are only a little more satisfied with their jobs.[4] Why might this be the case? Like turnover, other factors contribute to employees' overall job satisfaction, such as interactions and relationships with coworkers and supervisors, characteristics and conditions of work, perceptions of the organization's HR practices and its corporate social responsibility, and even employees' ages, personalities, and personal interests.[5] With all that said, pay remains one of the most salient rewards for employees and, thus, will be the primary focus of this chapter. However, before focusing on pay, specifically, it is important to understand reward systems more broadly.

Reward Systems

A reward system refers to the policies, procedures, and practices used by an organization to determine the amount and types of returns individuals, teams, and the organization receive in exchange for their membership and contributions. That is, a reward system determines the types of returns people receive for working, such as pay, benefits, or recognition. On the one hand, a well-designed reward system attracts, motivates, and retains individuals who directly or indirectly can contribute to the development, sale, or provision of the organization's products or services. Moreover, an effective reward system integrates with other HR systems, aligns with an organization's strategic goals, distributes pay fairly, competes with the pay practices of other organizations, and follows federal, state, and local employment and labor laws.

On the other hand, a poorly designed reward system can create problems for an organization. First, even the most effective recruitment and selection processes could fail to attract qualified individuals if the rewards offered are not competitive with offers made by other organizations. Second, without a competitive rewards package, an organization may struggle to motivate existing employees to use and apply their KSAOs. Third, an organization may struggle to retain workers when other organizations offer more attractive reward packages or when workers are not rewarded fairly with respect to their contributions or position.

As we discuss next, we can distinguish between two categories of rewards: relational returns and total compensation.[6]

Relational Returns

Relational returns include nonmonetary incentives and rewards, such as new learning and developmental opportunities, enriched and challenging work, job security, and recognition. As a classic example, the job of a tenured university professor offers the promise of lifetime employment as well as the intellectual freedom to pursue developmental opportunities and challenging work. As another example, Google offered a "20% time" policy in which employees were encouraged to spend 20% of their time working on personal projects of their own choosing that had the potential to benefit the company. This served not only as an enriching activity for employees but also as a source of potentially valuable new products and services, such as Gmail and Google News.[7]

Total Compensation

Total compensation subsumes compensation and benefits, which are often referred to as direct pay and indirect pay, respectively. Compensation includes base pay and forms of variable pay (e.g., sales commission), and benefits include health, life, and disability insurance; retirement programs; and work–life balance programs. A 2023 report by the Bureau of Labor Statistics found that, on average, compensation accounted for 69% of total compensation costs for U.S. employers, whereas benefits accounted for the other 31%.[8]

FAIRNESS OF REWARDS

11.2   Describe how to develop internally, externally, and individually equitable and legally compliant pay structures.

An organization should strive for fair reward policies and practices. Specifically, employees should perceive (a) they are paid fairly relative to others both inside and outside of their organization and (b) pay decisions are made and communicated in a fair manner. To understand reward system fairness, two psychological theories offer useful frameworks: equity theory and organizational justice theory.

Equity Theory

Equity theory helps us understand how an individual's sense of fairness is influenced by others with whom they compare themselves. The theory posits that an individual's perception of fairness is driven by (a) the rewards they receive (e.g., amount of compensation) relative to how much they have contributed (e.g., effort, hours worked) and (b) how that ratio of rewards to contributions compares to some other individual's ratio of rewards to contributions.[9] The other individual in this scenario is known as the *referent other* or simply the *referent*. Example referents include coworkers, colleagues, or others who work in the same field. Equity theory includes the following propositions:

1. Individuals compare themselves to the referents (other people) based on their perceived ratio of rewards relative to contributions.

2. Individuals strive to maintain a state of perceived equity between themselves and referents. The greater the perceived inequity, the more tension individuals experience and the more motivated they become to adjust their rewards and contributions to improve the perceived equity of the situation.

In the context of equity theory, equality and equity are not one and the same. Rather, equality means that two individuals receive the *same* rewards regardless of their contributions to their job and organization. In contrast, equity means that two individuals may have different levels of rewards and contributions so long as their *ratios* of rewards to contributions are the same. If an individual receives the same reward as another individual but contributed more, then the reward allocation could be considered equal but not equitable. Interestingly, individuals typically prefer equitable rewards when comparing themselves to others at work as part of a formal employment relationship. However, they typically prefer equal rewards when comparing themselves to those with whom they share personal relationships, such as friends and family members.[10]

According to equity theory, individuals are sensitive to conditions of inequity, which can include under-reward and over-reward conditions, as shown in Figure 11.1. An individual who perceives they are being under-rewarded relative to another individual will be motivated to restore equity by increasing their rewards and/or reducing their contributions to adjust their ratio of rewards to contributions. For instance, they might be motivated to ask for a raise, reduce their effort at work, or both; or if the inequity cannot be addressed, they might choose to quit or even steal from the organization.[11] In contrast, an individual who perceives they are over-rewarded might be motivated to restore fairness by reducing their rewards and/or increasing their contributions. Or they may simply rationalize why they are over-rewarded compared to others. Not surprisingly, research has shown that individuals often do not, in fact, experience more tension when over-rewarded, and instead they tend to experience less tension in these situations.[12]

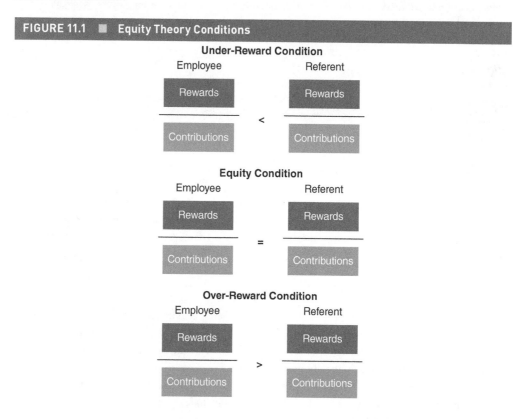

FIGURE 11.1 ■ Equity Theory Conditions

Under-Reward Condition

Employee — Referent

Rewards / Contributions < Rewards / Contributions

Equity Condition

Employee — Referent

Rewards / Contributions = Rewards / Contributions

Over-Reward Condition

Employee — Referent

Rewards / Contributions > Rewards / Contributions

    As an example of equity theory in action, consider the hypothetical case of Fatimah and Joanne, graduates of the same HR program who often confide in each other and share information about their jobs. Fatimah works as an external HR consultant for a for-profit consulting agency. Last year, Fatimah earned $75,000 in total compensation and worked on average 40 hours per week. Joanne also works as an external HR consultant but for a different for-profit consulting agency. Last year, Joanne also earned $75,000 in total compensation but, in contrast, worked on average 60 hours per week. Both Fatimah and Joanne began their current jobs at about the same time. All else being equal, do you think Joanne perceives under-reward inequity? To answer this question, let's consider their rewards relative to contributions. Both Fatimah and Joanne earned the same amount and thus received the same reward, but when it comes to their respective contributions, Joanne works on average 20 hours more per week. Thus, Fatimah's ratio of rewards to contributions ($75,000 to 40 hours/week) is more favorable than Joanne's ratio ($75,000 to 60 hours/week), which increases the likelihood that Joanne will perceive under-reward inequity. To reduce this inequity, Joanne may feel motivated to ask for a raise or to work fewer hours and apply less effort. Alternatively, Joanne might decide to completely remove herself from this inequitable situation by leaving the organization and seeking out an organization that will provide higher pay or fewer hours. Finally, as another possibility, Joanne may change her perceptions or choose a different referent. That is, Joanne may realize that she overlooked a reward that she receives but that Fatimah does not, such as more challenging work or greater autonomy. Or perhaps Joanne learns that Fatimah's job—although seemingly similar—is actually quite different in so many regards that Joanne switches her referent to another person who will serve as a better comparison.

    Research shows that individuals vary regarding their sensitivity to inequitable and equitable situations. The extent to which individuals are sensitive to equity is referred to as their level of equity sensitivity. There are three equity sensitivity orientations: entitlement, equity sensitive, and benevolent.[13]

Those with an entitlement orientation are more comfortable with over-reward inequity but less comfortable with under-reward inequity, and they tend to focus more on rewards than on their contributions. Those with an equity sensitive orientation prefer conditions of equity in which rewards are proportional to contributions. Those with a benevolent orientation are more comfortable with under-reward inequity but less comfortable with over-reward inequity, and they tend to focus more on their contributions than their rewards.

Equity theory, however, has received some criticism. Some have argued that people are concerned with the perceived fairness of their rewards relative to not only others but also the reward system as a whole.[14] That is, it is entirely possible that an individual perceives a state of equity between themselves and another person and yet perceives the overarching reward system as inequitable or unfair. Nevertheless, equity theory offers a way to understand how perceived fairness is based, in part, on how individuals perceive their rewards and contributions relative to others. Also, the theory centers on a person's perception. For this reason, if an employee approaches a manager about perceived inequity relative to another employee, the manager should first consider whether the employee's perceptions are accurate rather than accepting their perception at face value. This is because one way to restore equity might be to simply correct the employee regarding the details of their own rewards and contributions, or the rewards and contributions of the referent. Or perhaps the employee is comparing themselves to a person who is not an appropriate referent (e.g., perhaps a person in a different industry), in which case the manager can intervene by suggesting a more appropriate referent.

Manager's Toolbox: Restoring Employees' Perceptions of Equity

Managers can play an important role when it comes to their employees' perceptions of equity. Remember, the concept of equity is perceptual in nature, and people do not always have all the facts or entirely accurate information regarding their rewards and contributions relative to the rewards and contributions of others. Following are some steps managers can take to restore an employee's perception of equity.

1. **Choose the right referent.** If the employee is comparing themselves to an inappropriate referent, encourage the employee to select a more appropriate referent.

2. **Get the facts.** Verify whether the rewards and contributions information used by the employee are accurate.

3. **Restore equity.** Discuss how the employee can increase rewards, such as by asking for a raise or promotion, or fix the rewards if an error has been made.[15]

Organizational Justice Theory

Organizational justice theory stems from equity theory and similarly focuses on perceptions of fairness in the workplace. Organizational justice theory extends equity theory by positing that individuals' emotions, thoughts, and behaviors are influenced by the extent to which they perceive distributive, procedural, and interactional justice at work (see Table 11.1).[16] Considered in the context of reward systems, the theory provides a useful framework for understanding employee perceptions of existing

TABLE 11.1 ■ Three Types of Organizational Justice	
Distributive Justice	Perceived fairness of the allocation of an outcome or resource, which can include rewards, punishments, or other organizational consequences. Originates from equity theory and is sometimes referred to as *outcome fairness*.
Procedural Justice	Perceived fairness of the process used to determine how an outcome or resource is determined and doled out. Sometimes referred to as *process fairness*.
Interactional Justice	Perceived fairness of interpersonal treatment, such as with respect, consideration, dignity, and kindness, and of the manner and content of information provided, such as the explanation provided.

reward systems as well as for designing and implementing new reward systems. Further, organizational systems, policies, and practices that suffer from low organizational justice can result in negative consequences for the organization and its employees. For instance, lower organizational justice has been linked to employee health problems, stress, and absenteeism.[17]

The first type of justice is called distributive justice, which is an outgrowth of equity theory and is sometimes referred to as *outcome fairness*. Distributive justice refers to the perceived fairness or equity regarding the allocation of an outcome or resource, which can include rewards, punishments, or other organizational consequences.[18] Low distributive justice is associated with lower job satisfaction, lower organizational commitment, lower trust, and a greater likelihood of quitting.[19] Given this, care should be taken when distributing rewards to ensure employees perceive the outcome as fair.

The second type of justice is procedural justice, which is also called *process fairness*. Procedural justice has to do with employees' perceptions of fairness about the process used to determine *how* an outcome or resource is determined and distributed.[20] In the context of reward systems, we can apply the principles of procedural justice to understand how employees perceive the policies, procedures, and practices used to determine who is rewarded and how much they are rewarded. To achieve high perceptions of procedural justice among employees, processes should be designed and applied with the following considerations in mind: consistency, bias suppression, accuracy, correctability, representativeness, and ethicality.[21] Research has shown that employees who perceive lower levels of procedural justice tend to experience lower job satisfaction and organizational commitment along with lower trust and performance, as well as exhibit fewer helping behaviors and a greater desire to quit.[22]

The third type of justice is interactional justice. Interactional justice entails individuals' perceptions that they are treated well interpersonally—such as with respect, consideration, dignity, and kindness—as well as provided with an adequate explanation regarding the details of a particular process.[23] Research has shown that a lack of perceived interactional justice is associated with lower job satisfaction, organizational commitment, trust, and performance, as well as fewer helping behaviors and a greater desire to quit.[24]

Although organizations should strive to design and implement reward systems that are perceived as high in all three types of justice, sometimes it can be challenging to avoid low perceived distributive justice, as some outcomes may be particularly unlikeable. Fortunately, high procedural and interactional justice can buffer the negative effects of low distributive justice, and procedural justice becomes especially important in instances in which the distributed outcome is negative as opposed to positive.[25] Imagine that an employee is notified by his manager that he will not receive a year-end performance-based bonus, but the other members of the team will. Based on this information alone, the employee is likely to perceive low distributive justice. If, however, the manager delivered the bad news in a respectful manner and carefully explained the procedure used to determine who was eligible for the bonus, the employee may feel less upset about the negative outcome.

In sum, when it comes to reward systems, careful attention should be paid to distributing equitable rewards, developing and implementing fair processes, treating employees with respect and consideration when allocating rewards, and explaining and communicating the process in a fair and transparent manner.

DEVELOPING A PAY STRUCTURE

LEARNING OBJECTIVE

11.3   Describe the development of a pay structure.

A pay structure, which is one component of a reward system, refers to the way in which an organization applies pay rates and financial rewards to different jobs, skills, or competencies. When developing a pay structure, the associated policies should adhere to the aforementioned principles of equity and fairness. Steps should be taken to ensure individual employees are paid equitably with respect to other employees in the organization and with respect to employees at other organizations performing similar work. Further, a pay structure should abide by prevailing employment and labor laws. In sum, when developing and administering a pay structure, an organization should strive for the following goals: (a) internal equity, (b) external equity, (c) individual equity, and (d) legal compliance (see Figure 11.2).

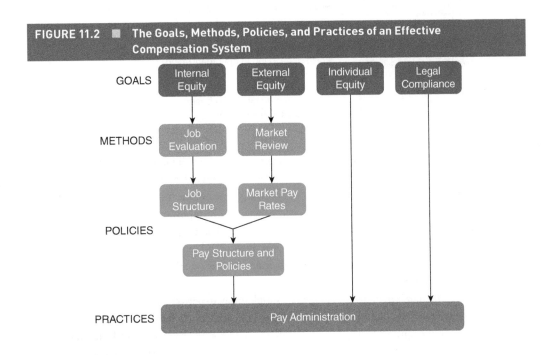

FIGURE 11.2   ■   The Goals, Methods, Policies, and Practices of an Effective Compensation System

Ensuring Internal Equity

Internal equity (sometimes called *internal alignment* or *internal consistency*) refers to the fairness of pay rates across jobs *within* an organization.[26] In other words, internal equity has to do with whether jobs of greater worth to an organization are compensated at higher levels.

Job Structure

Creating a fair job structure is an important step toward an internally equitable pay structure. A **job structure**—sometimes called a *job hierarchy*—refers to the ranking of jobs based on their respective worth. Once a job structure is in place, the organization can create a pay structure consisting of different pay levels, such that differentials between pay levels reflect the relative worth or value of different jobs to the organization. Ultimately, both the job structure and pay structure should be aligned with organizational strategy, such that those who work in jobs that contribute more (directly) to the organization's attainment of strategic objectives are paid at higher rates. In addition, internally equitable job and pay structures can motivate employees to seek promotions to jobs that provide more pay.

Job Evaluation

Job evaluation can be used to create a fair job structure. **Job evaluation** is a systematic process used to determine the relative worth of jobs within an organization. In a job evaluation, subject matter experts (SMEs) determine the relative worth of each job based on how much each job contributes (relatively speaking) to the organization's strategic objectives. However, before doing so, a rigorous, up-to-date job analysis should be conducted for all jobs that will be evaluated (see Chapter 5). The reason for this is that it is critical to identify the core tasks, KSAOs, and/or competencies associated with each job to systematically evaluate the relative worth of each job. In addition, a job analysis yields job descriptions and specifications that feed into the job evaluation and ultimately serve as the foundation of the job structure (as shown in Figure 11.3).

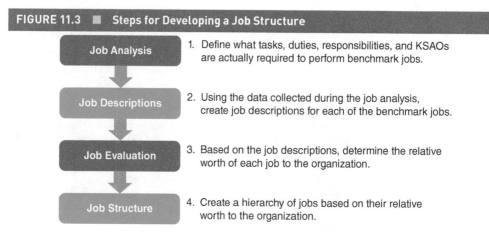

FIGURE 11.3 ■ Steps for Developing a Job Structure

Job Analysis → 1. Define what tasks, duties, responsibilities, and KSAOs are actually required to perform benchmark jobs.

Job Descriptions → 2. Using the data collected during the job analysis, create job descriptions for each of the benchmark jobs.

Job Evaluation → 3. Based on the job descriptions, determine the relative worth of each job to the organization.

Job Structure → 4. Create a hierarchy of jobs based on their relative worth to the organization.

An organization should take great care when determining who will be involved in the job evaluation and how decisions will be communicated to the rest of the organization. The job evaluation process requires many judgment calls, and thus employees may perceive the process as overly subjective or too political and therefore unfair. To alleviate such concerns, it is important to (a) select SMEs whom employees trust and (b) clearly communicate how the job evaluation process will unfold. Common SMEs include job incumbents, supervisors of job incumbents, and internal or external compensation experts. Prominent approaches for conducting a job evaluation include the ranking method, classification method, and point-factor method.

The ranking method is perhaps the fastest and simplest way to perform a job evaluation, especially when there is a relatively small number of jobs. A WorldatWork report revealed that 13% of surveyed organizations used the ranking method.[27] Although it is less rigorous than the point-factor and factor-comparison methods (which are discussed later), the ranking method captures the essence of what it means to order jobs by relative worth to create a job structure. In the ranking method, a team of SMEs evaluates the job descriptions and specifications for a selection of jobs and orders them in terms of their relative contribution to the organization's strategic objectives and mission. The ranking process results in a job structure. Despite its simplicity, the ranking method often lacks clear criteria for determining why and how jobs were ranked in a particular order, which can lead to (perceptions of) bias. As another limitation, the ranking method provides an ordering of jobs based on their relative worth but does not indicate how much more one job is worth relative to another.

The classification method differs from the ranking method in that discrete classification levels—each comprising one or more jobs—are developed in advance to cover different job types or levels within the organization. A written classification description is developed for each classification level, and based on its job description, each job is matched by SMEs to a classification level in which the classification description is most similar. Job descriptions, job specifications, and input from SMEs are used to develop each classification level and its classification description.

Like a job description, classification descriptions are developed for each classification level to describe the work content covered. Typically, each classification description includes specific criteria that provide guidance for determining which job belongs to a particular classification level. Although some jobs can be easily assigned to a classification level by comparing their respective descriptions, other jobs can be more challenging because they seem similar to two or more classification levels. Like the ranking method, the classification method does not necessarily indicate how much more valuable jobs in one classification level are compared to jobs in another classification level.[28]

The point-factor method is known for its rigor and relative objectivity.[29] A WorldatWork report found that 14% of surveyed organizations performed job evaluations using the point-factor method.[30] Like some other approaches, the point-factor method requires a team of SMEs, preferably including at least one person who is an internal or external compensation expert.

The point-factor method requires SMEs to identify compensable factors and to develop and apply scales and weights to the compensable factors. Compensable factors are the common dimensions by which jobs vary in terms of their worth to the organization. Examples of compensable factors include the levels of experience and education needed to do the job, the level of complexity inherent to the job, or even the level of danger and risk involved in performing the job. For instance, a job that requires an advanced degree and significant experience will pay more than an entry-level job requiring a high school degree, assuming education and experience are compensable factors. Compensable factors may also vary in terms of their relative worth to the organization. For example, imagine the following three compensable factors: experience, education, and complexity. Based on its value to an organization, complexity might be weighted more heavily (100) than experience (40) and education (60), as is the case in the example provided in Figure 11.4.

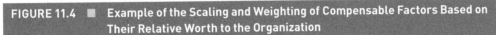

FIGURE 11.4 ■ Example of the Scaling and Weighting of Compensable Factors Based on Their Relative Worth to the Organization

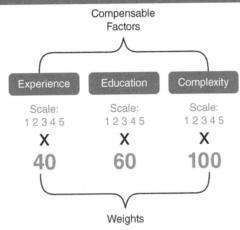

For a given job, the point-factor method earns its name by creating a specific point value for each compensable factor based on the extent to which the job embodies each compensable factor. This approach yields an overall point total for each job, such that the point total of one job can be compared to the point total of another job. This method results in a clear depiction of the relative worth of each job to the organization. Table 11.2 shows three benchmark jobs, where benchmark jobs are key jobs that are common across different·organizations. Job 1 has the lowest overall point total and Job 3 has the highest. Look at the columns associated with the three compensable factors of experience, education, and complexity, and note that each job's relative worth is based on the level of each compensable factor required for performing the job. After scaling and applying weights to benchmark Jobs 1, 2, and 3, the same scales and weights can be applied to compute the points for nonbenchmark jobs.

TABLE 11.2 ■ Example of Calculated Points for Benchmark Jobs Using the Point-Factor Method

Benchmark Jobs	Compensable Factors			Total
	Experience	Education	Complexity	
Job 1	200	60	200	460
Job 2	200	180	400	780
Job 3	200	300	500	1000

Off-the-shelf point-factor method platforms exist for purchase, and one of the most famous is the Korn Ferry job evaluation method, which was originally developed by the Hay Group before it was acquired by Korn Ferry. The job evaluation method is sometimes referred to as the Hay Plan or Hay System and can be implemented by the Job Evaluation Manager platform; it scores each job based on three compensable factors: Know How, Accountability, and Problem Solving.[31]

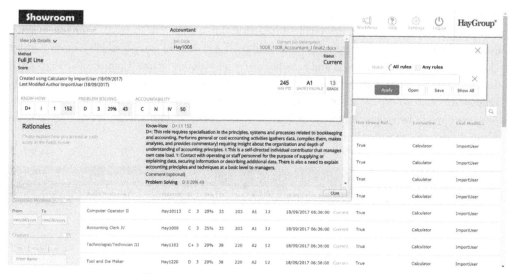

Example of the Korn Ferry Job Evaluation Manager point-factor method platform for the job of an accountant. The Job Evaluation Manager was originally developed by the Hay Group.

Ensuring External Equity

In addition to internal equity, organizations should also establish a pay structure that is high in external equity. External equity (also known as *external competitiveness*) refers to the extent to which the pay for a particular job is competitive and fair relative to the pay of the same or similar jobs at other organizations. In other words, external equity has to do with how well an organization compensates benchmark jobs compared to its competitor organizations.

In an ideal world, an organization would pay whatever it takes to attract, motivate, and retain top talent for each position. In reality, such an approach would quickly exceed an organization's compensation budget. For that reason, organizations should look to the external economic environment for guidance on how to pay people working in different jobs within the organization. Accordingly, compensation experts carefully consider the labor supply and labor demand for benchmark jobs and how much to pay those working benchmark jobs relative to competitors, which requires assessing the labor market and product market.

Labor and Product Markets

The labor market refers to the availability of talent outside of an organization, which can be viewed through the lens of talent supply and demand. Briefly, talent supply and demand are influenced by the unemployment rate, changes in technology, competition, shifts in populations, and various other factors. When talent supply exceeds talent demand, a talent surplus exists. Under talent surplus conditions, an organization will have more leeway when it comes to attracting and retaining talented individuals using pay, as employment opportunities for those in the labor pool are scarcer. Thus, employers may opt to pay employees less. Alternatively, when talent supply falls below talent demand, a talent shortage exists. Under talent shortage conditions, an organization may opt to pay more relative to competitors to ensure they attract talented individuals from the more competitive market.

In addition to the labor market, an organization must consider the product market, which refers to the final sale of products and services in the marketplace. If an organization pays its workers more than competitors pay their workers, it will likely have to charge more for the products or services it sells, and as a result, the organization may be less competitive in the marketplace. Selling fewer products or

As Covid-19 pandemic restrictions eased beginning in 2021, airline travel rebounded. Around the same time, Alaska Airlines lost pilots to retirement and to competitors, resulting in a shortage of pilots. In September 2022, the airline's management and the Air Line Pilots Association reached a contract deal to increase pay and improve relational returns like job security.[32]

services may result in reduced revenue and profit, which can ultimately limit the budget for acquiring and retaining talent through pay.

Market Strategies

By considering both the labor market and product market, an organization can create a better market strategy. An organization must decide whether to lead, match, or lag the market for a given job (see Figure 11.5). A lead-the-market strategy occurs when an organization pays individuals with a given job more than competitors pay for those with the same or similar job. (*More* is typically defined as being above the mean or median market pay rate for that job.) A match-the-market strategy involves paying individuals about the same as the average competitor. A lag-the-market strategy means paying individuals less than the average competitor. Often, organizations enact a mixed-market position, which means they choose to lead the market for some jobs and match or lag for others. So how do organizations determine whether they lead, match, or lag the market? The answer lies in market reviews.

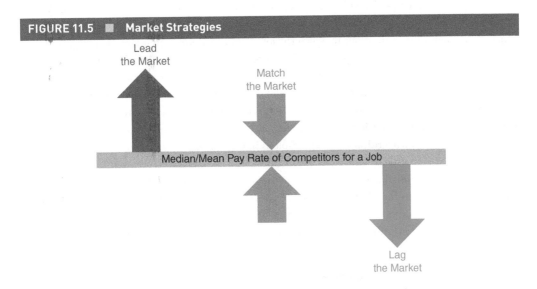

FIGURE 11.5 ■ Market Strategies

Market Reviews

A **market review** is the process of collecting pay data for benchmark jobs from other organizations. As described previously, a benchmark job refers to a key job that is common across organizations and has a similar job description across organizations. Examples of benchmark jobs include electrical engineer, psychiatrist, and customer service representative. Ultimately, the data collected by reviewing benchmark jobs can be combined with an organization's job structure data to create a pay structure that includes benchmark and nonbenchmark jobs alike.

Often, a market review is conducted with the help of a third-party survey company that collects pay data confidentially from employers or employees; sometimes these are referred to as *salary surveys* or *market surveys*. There are three primary sources of market review data:

- A *traditional survey* typically collects data from employers and is conducted by a government agency or professional organization. In some instances, access to survey data may be free. A traditional survey can provide important insights into the pay practices of other organizations, but sometimes it will lack the necessary level of specificity. For example, some traditional surveys report pay rates only at the national level, making it impossible to drill down to specific regions or organization types. In the United States, the Department of Labor provides wage and salary information through Bureau of Labor Statistics reports, which are publicly available. In addition, the Department of Labor sponsors the website CareerOneStop (careeronestop.org), which reports national- and state-level pay data for more than 900 benchmark jobs and links to O*NET (ONETonline.org). Other traditional surveys include those collected by WorldatWork, which charges a fee for accessing the survey results.

- A *customized survey* collects pay data from employers in a more targeted manner to achieve higher accuracy and specificity. It is often administered by an external compensation consulting firm or an internal compensation or HR team and can be designed to focus on pay in a specific job market where an organization is located (e.g., Silicon Valley). Further, depending on how dynamic the industry is, customized surveys may be conducted frequently to gather fresh data.

- A *web-based platform* typically collects data directly from employees via a website and offers up-to-date pay data, often for a fee.[33] Examples include Salary.com, Payscale.com, and SalaryExpert.com.

Regardless of the source, most market reviews yield important pay information regarding the mean or median pay level for a particular benchmark job as well as the 25th and 75th percentiles, as shown for the job of a certified nursing assistant in Table 11.3. Market review sources often collect and report information about the organizations to which the jobs belong. Information might include geographic location, industry, size, and type (e.g., for-profit, not-for-profit, private, public). This additional information allows market review users to drill down to pay information for benchmark jobs at a more granular level. For example, imagine a small critical outreach hospital with 25 beds located in a rural area. Now imagine a compensation analyst who wants to identify the market pay rate for the job of a registered nurse—a benchmark job. To obtain accurate pay information for registered nurses who work similar hospitals (i.e., small critical outreach hospitals in rural areas), the analyst identifies the median pay level just for those hospitals located in rural areas with 10 to 50 beds.

Using the pay information generated from market reviews, an organization can reasonably compare its own pay practices for benchmark jobs with the pay practices for the same or similar benchmark jobs from other organizations. In doing so, they can determine whether they are leading, meeting, or lagging the market. To ensure that market review survey data are accurate, it is important to match job descriptions, apply an aging factor, and apply survey weights, which we discuss next.

TABLE 11.3　■　Example of Market Review Data for the Job of a Certified Nursing Assistant

Descriptive Statistics (for Sample of Organizations)	Base Salary (Monthly)	Base Pay (Annual)	Variable Pay (Annual)	Total Cash Compensation (Annual)	Benefits (Annual)	Total Compensation (Annual)	Number of Organizations	Sample Size	Mean Weekly Hours
Mean	$2,833	$33,996	$0	$33,996	$5,456	$39,452	221	11,050	40
25th Percentile	$2,189	$26,268	$0	$26,268	$5,244	$31,512			
Median	$2,728	$32,736	$0	$32,736	$5,399	$38,135			
75th Percentile	$3,245	$38,940	$0	$38,940	$5,512	$44,452			

SPOTLIGHT ON DATA AND ANALYTICS: PAY AND HUMAN RESOURCE INFORMATION SYSTEMS

To design a competitive, externally equitable pay structure, an organization must obtain or access information about other organizations' pay practices. Traditionally, a consortium of organizations would subscribe to a third-party market survey and submit pay data confidentially, and in return, the organizations would receive a hard copy or an electronic copy of the survey results.

Today, some enterprise resource planning and HR information system vendors offer integrative solutions that reveal how well an organization is paying certain benchmark positions in relation to similar positions at other organizations. Both ADP and Payscale, for example, provide cloud-based software that facilitates the process by which organizations participate in market surveys, as well as off-the-shelf analytics and data visualizations for decision-making purposes.

Further, ADP leverages existing client pay information across different jobs to provide automated data analytics and visualizations, including information about pay equity related to race and sex. These advances place more pay information at the fingertips of key decision makers. Particularly in the case of pay equity data about protected groups (e.g., race, sex), however, organizations should think carefully about which employees are permitted to access pay equity data, and it is advisable that legal counsel be involved when analyzing any data that could reveal pay differences between protected groups.[34]

Match Job Descriptions

To conduct an effective market review, it is important to have up-to-date job descriptions available for benchmark jobs. Although market review sources often use similar job titles, sometimes the job descriptions vary across industries or between geographic areas. Alternatively, some jobs may have very different job titles but very similar job descriptions. As such, an accurate job description allows for the matching of an organization's benchmark job with the job description provided in a market review survey. Although this may sound like a straightforward process, the job descriptions included for market review surveys can vary from one sentence to a paragraph in length, making the matching process challenging.

As a result, subject matter expertise in the jobs at hand and critical thinking skills are often required when comparing job descriptions to determine if the pay information from a market review source is an appropriate match. As an illustration of this issue, consider Table 11.4, which provides the job descriptions for a licensed practical nurse from CareerOneStop.org and Salary.com. First, note how CareerOneStop.org provides alternative job titles (*licensed practical nurse* and *licensed vocational nurse*), whereas Salary.com provides just the job title of *licensed practical nurse*. Second, note how the job descriptions provided by these two market review sources are very different in length and level of detail. Now imagine that your company completed a recent job analysis for the job of a licensed practical nurse, which yielded a job description that is specific to your organization. The challenge becomes determining whether the benchmark job as defined by a particular market review source matches your own job description.

TABLE 11.4 ■ Job Descriptions From Two Market Review Sources for the Job of a Licensed Practical Nurse[35]		
Market Review Source	**CareerOneStop.org**	**Salary.com**
Job Title	**Licensed practical and licensed vocational nurses**	**Licensed practical nurse**
Job Description	"Care for ill, injured, or convalescing patients or persons with disabilities in hospitals, nursing homes, clinics, private homes, group homes, and similar institutions. May work under the supervision of a registered nurse. Licensing required."	"Administers nursing care under the supervision of a registered nurse or other medical supervisor. Provides basic medical care, including changing bandages, administering medication, and collecting specimens. Ensures the health, comfort, and safety of patients by assisting with bathing, feeding, and dressing. Monitors and reports changes in patient's condition to supervisor. Requires graduation from approved LPN educational program. Requires a state license to practice. Years of experience may be unspecified. Certification and/or licensing in the position's specialty is the main requirement."

Repeating the matching process for all benchmark jobs allows an organization to judge how competitive its pay practices are compared to competitors or other organizations in the industry. Table 11.5 shows a fictitious example of median monthly base pay rates pulled from three different market review surveys for benchmark jobs from the nursing job family.

TABLE 11.5 ■ Example of Market Review Data for the Nursing Job Family			
	Median Monthly Pay Rate		
Job Title	**Survey 1**	**Survey 2**	**Survey 3**
Certified Nursing Assistant (CNA)	$2,728	$2,216	$2,688
Licensed Practical Nurse (LPN)	$4,042	$3,674	$3,992
Registered Nurse (RN)	$6,078	$5,704	$5,947
Charge Nurse (CN)	$7,205	$6,845	$7,033
Nurse Practitioner (NP)	$8,928	$8,409	$8,771
Nursing Manager (NM)	$9,035	$8,722	$8,995
Nursing Director (ND)	$12,138	$10,038	$11,954

Apply Aging Factor

After matching job descriptions and pulling market pay rates for benchmark jobs, it is often wise to "age" the pay data because (a) they were collected at some point in the past and (b) decisions based on the pay data will be implemented in the future. Aging (of pay data) refers to a process whereby the analyst identifies when the pay data were originally collected and then weights the data based on the expected change in the market pay rates resulting from merit-based increases, cost-of-living adjustments, and other factors that affect pay. For example, imagine that the pay data from Survey 1 in Table 11.5 were collected 10 months ago, and your team decides to age the data to 1 month in the future when the pay structure is expected to be implemented. Your team uses the following process to calculate and apply the aging factor:

1. Using a merit budget factor from a survey vendor like WorldatWork, you determine the annual market movement rate is 2.5%.

2. Because the market movement rate represents an annual rate, you divide 2.5% by 12 to get a monthly rate of .002 (.025/12 = .002).

3. Because Survey 1 data were collected 10 months ago and you wish to forecast 1 month into the future, you will age the data by 11 months (10 + 1 = 11).

4. You multiply the monthly rate of .002 by 11 months to determine the aging factor for the 11-month period for which you are aging the data, and the resulting product is .022 or 2.2% (.002 × 11 = .022).

5. Given the market is forecasted to grow (and not decline), you add 1 to .022, which equals 1.022 (1 + .022 = 1.022), and this value reflects the aging factor.

6. Using the pay data for a licensed practical nurse from Survey 1 (Table 11.6), you apply the aging factor to the median monthly pay rate of $4,042. To do so, you multiply the aging factor by the median monthly pay rate, which yields $4,131 (1.022 × $4,042 = $4,131).

7. Finally, you apply the aging factor to each of the median monthly pay rates for the remaining benchmark jobs found in Table 11.6 and then repeat this process for pay rates from Survey 2 and Survey 3.

Apply Survey Weights

Often, it is a best practice to use more than one market review survey to help account for sampling error in any one survey. That is, it is unlikely that any one survey obtained perfectly accurate pay data for the entire population of relevant jobs; rather, each survey collects pay data for a sample of jobs from the underlying population, which inevitably leads to sampling error, as a sample is unlikely to perfectly represent the population. In some cases, an organization may choose to apply different weights to each survey source based on how many organizations were included in the sample or based on the relative rigor used by each survey source. Using market review data from Table 11.5 as an example, you might decide to weight Survey 1 at 50% due to its higher rigor and larger sample and weight both Survey 2 and Survey 3 at 25%. For the sake of explanation, let us assume the data presented in Table 11.5 have already been aged. Using this weighting scheme, you can compute the average median monthly pay rate for the job of a nurse practitioner in the following manner:

$$(\$8,928 \times .50) + (\$8,409 \times .25) + (\$8,771 \times .25) = \$8,759$$

As you can see, the median pay rate from Survey 1 carries more weight (50% or .50), which means it yields a larger contribution to the overall weighted average value of $8,759. Finally, in some instances, a sample-weighted average may be computed for each job from each market review source, assuming sample size is reported. This allows for the analyst to account for sampling error in a more direct manner. Finally, refer to Figure 11.6 for a summary of how to match job descriptions, apply the aging factor, and apply survey weights.

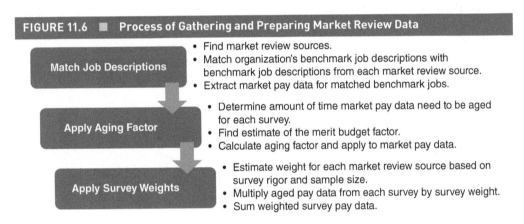

FIGURE 11.6 ■ Process of Gathering and Preparing Market Review Data

Match Job Descriptions
- Find market review sources.
- Match organization's benchmark job descriptions with benchmark job descriptions from each market review source.
- Extract market pay data for matched benchmark jobs.

Apply Aging Factor
- Determine amount of time market pay data need to be aged for each survey.
- Find estimate of the merit budget factor.
- Calculate aging factor and apply to market pay data.

Apply Survey Weights
- Estimate weight for each market review source based on survey rigor and sample size.
- Multiply aged pay data from each survey by survey weight.
- Sum weighted survey pay data.

Integrating Internal Equity and External Equity

So far, we have discussed internal equity and external equity separately. When integrated, internal equity and external equity can provide the foundation for an effective pay structure. By integrating the job structure data gathered from a job evaluation (internal equity) and the market pay data gathered from a market review (external equity), an organization can set the pay levels for all benchmark and nonbenchmark jobs.

There are different ways to integrate job evaluation and market review data. Compensation decision makers often place a greater emphasis on market review data as compared to job evaluation data; in other words, they tend to place more importance on external equity than internal equity. In fact, some organizations base their pay levels and pay structure directly on their competitors' pay levels and pay structures, a process that is referred to as market pricing.[36] Results from a 2019 WorldatWork report indicated that from 2012 to 2018, market pricing was the most dominant method for determining the relative worth of jobs. In fact, approximately 9 out of 10 surveyed organizations used market pricing during that time period.[37]

For a balanced approach, an organization can use the point-factor method of job evaluation combined with market review data to determine how much a single point is worth in dollars. This information can be used to establish a market pay line and a pay policy line for both benchmark and nonbenchmark jobs.

Market Pay Line

The market pay line reflects the relationship between the internal job structure of the organization for benchmark jobs, which is often represented in terms of job evaluation points, and the external pay practices of other organizations gathered from a market review. To create a market pay line, we can use regression analysis. For example, using the data from Table 11.5, we arrive at the following linear regression equation when estimating the relationship between job evaluation points and *actual* market review pay rates:

$$Monthly\ Base\ Pay\ (\$) = -8{,}988.99 + 19.71 \times Job\ Evaluation\ Points$$

In this equation, the Y-intercept (constant) is –8,988.99, and the slope (regression coefficient) is 19.71. The regression equation itself is a quantitative representation of the line-of-best-fit, and in this context, the line-of-best-fit represents the market pay line. Further, the *R*-squared value for the regression estimated equation is .98, which means that job evaluation points explain 98% of the variability in monthly base pay rates; in other words, the estimated market pay line closely fits the observed data. Employees would likely perceive such a pay structure to be high in both internal and external equity.

In Figure 11.7, the estimated market pay line is a solid black line; the jobs from the nursing job family and their respective job evaluation points are on the *x*-axis; the monthly base pay rates are on the *y*-axis; and the blue diamonds represent the observed data on which the market pay line was estimated. We can calculate the *predicted* market pay rates for each benchmark job in Table 11.5 by plugging their respective job evaluation points into the regression equation.

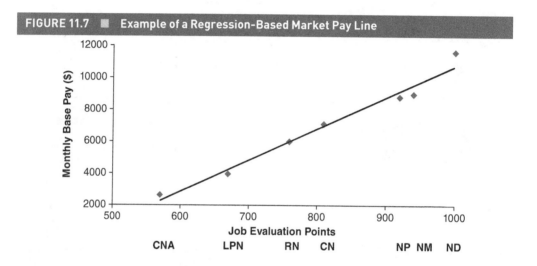

FIGURE 11.7 ■ Example of a Regression-Based Market Pay Line

Assuming job evaluation points have been calculated for nonbenchmark jobs, the same regression equation can be used to calculate the market pay rates for nonbenchmark jobs. If a nonbenchmark job such as a nurse anesthetist receives 920 job evaluation points, then that value can be entered into the regression equation to determine what a competitive monthly base pay would be. For the nurse anesthetist, this value is $9,144, which is calculated as follows:

$$\$9{,}144.21 = -8{,}988.99 + 19.71 \times 920$$

This process can be repeated for the remaining nonbenchmark jobs to calculate competitive market pay rates for all jobs in the job structure.

Pay Policy Line

Using the market pay line as a foundation, a **pay policy line** translates information about an organization's internal job structure and the external pay rates of competitors into actionable pay practices. To create a pay policy line, an organization specifies, depending upon its market strategy, whether it wants to pay above (lead), at (match), or below (lag) the market pay line for specific jobs or across all jobs. For instance, if the organization wishes to pay 5% over the market pay line across all jobs, the predicted market pay rates calculated from the market pay line regression equation are multiplied by 1.05 to realize the organization's strategy. For the nonbenchmark job of a nurse anesthetist, for which we determined that the predicted market pay rate is $9,144 per month, the 5% lead-the-market strategy results in a monthly pay rate of

$9,601 ($9,144 × 1.05 = $9,601), which is called the pay policy rate. In Table 11.6, the pay policy rates are presented along with the predicted market pay rates and pay strategy factor from which they were derived.

TABLE 11.6 ■ Job Evaluation Points, Actual Market Pay Rates, Predicted Market Pay Rates, and Pay Policy Line Pay Rates

Job Title	Job Evaluation Points	Actual Market Pay Rates	Predicted Market Pay Rates	Pay Strategy	Pay Policy Rates (Predicted Market Pay Rates × Pay Strategy)
Certified Nursing Assistant (CNA)	570	$2,590	$2,246	+5%	$2,358
Licensed Practical Nurse (LPN)	670	$3,938	$4,217	+5%	$4,428
Registered Nurse (RN)	760	$5,952	$5,991	+5%	$6,290
Charge Nurse (CN)	810	$7,072	$6,976	+5%	$7,325
Nurse Practitioner (NP)	920	$8,759	$9,144	+5%	$9,601
Nursing Manager (NM)	940	$8,947	$9,538	+5%	$10,015
Nursing Director (ND)	1000	$11,567	$10,721	+5%	$11,257

Pay Grades

A common practice is to establish pay grades based on the pay policy line. A **pay grade** represents a group of jobs with similar job evaluation point values that are then assigned common pay midpoint, minimum, and maximum values. Pay grades allow an organization to differentiate between employees holding the same job or similar jobs but who have different levels of performance, experience, or seniority. To create a pay grade, jobs with relatively similar job evaluation points are grouped together. For example, the nurse practitioner and nursing manager jobs received 920 and 940 job evaluation points, respectively (as shown in Table 11.6), and can be grouped together in a common pay grade. The pay policy rates for these two jobs are $9,601 and $10,015, respectively. To determine the pay grade midpoint, we might calculate the average of the two pay policy pay rates to arrive at $9,808:

$$\frac{\$9,601 + \$10,015}{2} = \$9,808$$

To establish the minimum and maximum values for the pay grade, market review data pertaining to the 25th and 75th percentiles for these two jobs can be used to set a floor and ceiling for the pay grade. Figure 11.8 shows five pay grades for the nursing job family, along with which jobs belong to which pay grade. Note how the pay policy line crosses the midpoint of each pay grade, as well as how different pay grades have different pay ranges, which reflects differences in their respective market-based minimum and maximum values.

Some organizations choose to use broadbanding instead of traditional pay grades. Broadbanding is the process of collapsing multiple pay grades into one large grade with a single minimum and maximum, resulting in fewer pay grades. Broadbanding may be used to complement delayering, the process by which the hierarchy in an organizational structure is reduced. Broadbanding can be advantageous in certain industries and circumstances because it allows for more flexibility in terms of how managers make pay decisions, given the broad range of jobs within a band. In addition, broadbanding allows employees to move more easily across different functional areas while remaining in a single band. Like any pay policy, the decision to implement a pay structure using broadbanding should be based on the organization's strategy.

FIGURE 11.8 ■ Example of Pay Grades Along a Pay Policy Line

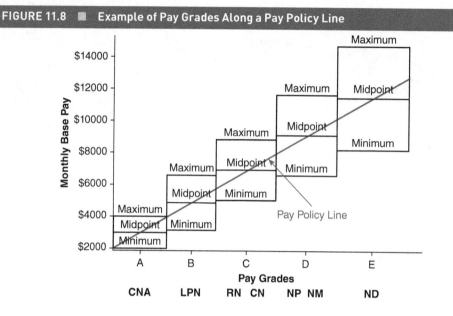

Ensuring Individual Equity

Once the pay structure and pay policies are in place, it is time to ensure that individual equity exists. Individual equity refers to the fairness of how pay is administered and distributed to individual employees working similar jobs within the same organization. For individual equity to exist, such differences in pay rates should be attributable to differences in performance, seniority, and/or experience, as opposed to other factors that are not job related (e.g., race, sex). Using the minimum and maximum values of a pay grade or broadband as upper and lower limits, compensation analysts and/or managers can determine how much to compensate each individual employee. Individual equity will be higher when higher performing, more senior, and more experienced employees in a given pay grade are compensated at a higher rate than lower performing, less senior, and less experienced employees in the same pay grade. To ensure individual equity, organizations should also consider freezing the pay of any employee who is paid more than the maximum rate of their pay grade, which is sometimes called "red circle rate." Conversely, organizations should consider increasing the pay of any employee who is paid less than the minimum rate of their pay grade, which is sometimes called "green circle rate."[38]

SPOTLIGHT ON GLOBAL ISSUES: EXPATRIATES' AND HOST COUNTRY NATIONALS' PAY

Expatriates, also known as international assignees, are individuals who leave their home country to take an assignment in another country or the host country. When considering an expatriate assignment location, individuals may expect higher pay in exchange for working in countries that they view less favorably.

In situations in which an expatriate takes an international assignment, they will likely work side by side with host country nationals who are paid differently. Understandably, concerns and conflicts can arise in situations in which two employees are performing seemingly the same job but are earning notably different incomes. Often, expatriates are paid using the *balance sheet approach*, in which the pay structure of expatriates is tied to that of their home countries, and additional pay in the form of allowances is provided to compensate for differences in living conditions and costs. The higher pay provided to expatriates can signal to host country nationals that the company values expatriates more, and this can lead to tension and perceptions of unfairness owing to an "us versus them" mindset, especially if the only identifiable difference between employees is their country of origin. Further, research has shown that, in general, the greater the difference in pay between expatriates and host country nationals, the greater the unfairness perceived by host country nationals.

Multinational companies should take steps to understand different host countries and to implement pay policies and practices that respond to host countries' cultural norms and values. Multinational companies can also set expectations for expatriates to contribute more in terms of professionalism, knowledge, and relationships with headquarters, thereby justifying their higher pay.[39]

Ensuring Legal Compliance

In addition to ensuring internal, external, and individual equity, a pay structure and the resulting pay policies, procedures, and practices should comply with federal, state, and local guidelines. In most cases, federal legislation is overseen and enforced by the Equal Employment Opportunity Commission (EEOC) or Office of Federal Contract Compliance Programs (OFCCP). Over the years, multiple pieces of congressional legislation and executive orders have shaped the pay landscape in the United States.

Fair Labor Standards Act

Enacted in 1938, the Fair Labor Standards Act (FLSA) introduced major provisions aimed at regulating overtime pay, minimum wage, hours worked, and recordkeeping. The FLSA covers nonexempt employees who work for organizations in which the annual gross volume of sales or business meets or exceeds $500,000 or those who are engaged in interstate commerce or in the production of goods for commerce. Hospitals, businesses providing nursing or medical services, schools, preschools, and government agencies are also covered by the law. Some exceptions to FLSA coverage include workers with disabilities, those who work in tipped employment, and student learners.[40]

An important component of the FLSA is the distinction between exempt and nonexempt employees. The term exempt refers to those employees who do not fall under the purview of the minimum wage and overtime provisions, whereas the term nonexempt refers to those employees who are directly affected by the provisions. As it currently stands, to be classified as exempt, an employee must typically meet all three of the following tests:

- earn $684 or more per week (which equals $35,568 per year),
- receive a salary or charge a fee (and not an hourly wage), and
- perform exempt job duties.[41]

Overtime

The overtime provision of the FLSA mandates that organizations pay at least 1.5 times a nonexempt worker's regular pay for time worked beyond 40 hours in a week.[42] Those workers classified as exempt are not eligible for overtime. Some cities and states have passed legislation to augment the federal minimum. For instance, California includes a provision in which nonexempt workers who work more than 12 hours in a single day must be compensated with 2 times their regular pay. Consider enacting the following actions when administering overtime pay.[43]

- At the time of hire, clearly state the overtime policy.
- In the employee handbook, clearly describe the overtime policy.
- For all employees who are eligible for overtime, ensure they are paid appropriately.
- Display an FLSA poster in the organization (e.g., in the break room) detailing the overtime provision and other provisions.

- At the very least, nonexempt employees are eligible for overtime at 1.5 times their regular pay should they work more than 40 hours in a week; however, be sure to check with your state and local legislation, as some states and cities offer more generous overtime provisions.

Minimum Wage

The minimum wage provision of the FLSA establishes an income floor, thereby providing some protection to workers in terms of unfair pay practices. Since 2009, the current federally mandated minimum wage has been $7.25/hour,[44] which some have argued has not kept pace with inflation and the general cost of living. In response, some attempts have been made to increase the minimum wage for certain populations of workers. For example, as of January 1, 2023, Executive Order 14026 increased the minimum wage for individuals working on federal contracts to $16.20/hour.[45] Further, although cities and states are not permitted to establish a minimum wage that falls below the federal level, some cities and states have passed legislation to increase the minimum wage. For example, as of July 1, 2023, the District of Columbia increased its minimum wage to $17.00/hour.[46]

Hours Worked and Recordkeeping

The FLSA also defines what constitutes hours worked for nonexempt employees as well as what information is required for recordkeeping purposes. Regarding hours worked, the FLSA defines a number of key concepts relevant for determining how hours are counted and tracked, such as waiting time, on-call time, rest and meal periods, and travel time.[47] As for recordkeeping, the FLSA requires that employers keep a record of nonexempt employees' names, addresses, birth dates (if younger than 19), sex, occupation, hours worked each day, regular hourly pay rate, overtime earnings, and other information relevant to pay.[48] It should be noted that many modern HR information systems facilitate the tracking of these data and that employers must retain these data for at least 3 years.

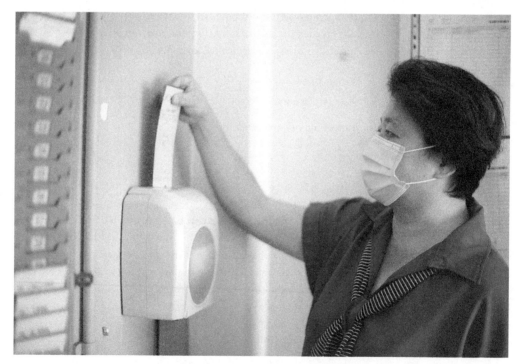

The Fair Labor Standards Act mandates that employers track nonexempt employees' hours worked, which often involves tracking when employees clock in and clock out of work. Accurate recordkeeping ensures that nonexempt employees are paid correctly and receive overtime pay if more than 40 hours per week are accrued. Newer technologies allow employers to perform time and attendance tracking using facial recognition and voice activation.

©iStockphoto.com/Alex Liew

Executive Order 11246

The issuing of Executive Order 11246 by President Lyndon B. Johnson in 1965 expanded the protections for different forms of employment discrimination (such as employee pay) to include employers with federal contracts or subcontracts in excess of $10,000.[49] The executive order reflected the federal government's increased focus on discrimination-related issues, including pay discrimination. In an effort to prevent pay discrimination by increasing pay transparency, in 2015, the OFCCP revised Executive Order 11246 to clarify that individuals (job applicants or employees) who discuss pay may not be discriminated against or discharged by a federal contractor.[50]

National Labor Relations Act

Enacted in 1935, the National Labor Relations Act (NLRA) includes a provision related to pay transparency. Specifically, Section 7 of the NLRA stipulates that employees protected under the act have a right to discuss pay as part of activities related to collective bargaining and protection, thereby providing an avenue through which employees may uncover pay discrimination.[51] In terms of coverage, most private-sector employees are protected under the NLRA. However, NLRA coverage specifically *excludes* public-sector employees, including individuals who work for federal, state, and local governments, as well as those employed as independent contractors or agricultural workers.

Internal Revenue Code

In addition to complying with antidiscrimination and fair-pay practices laws, employers and employees must also adhere to tax laws. The Internal Revenue Code of 1986 stipulates income and payroll tax regulations.[52] On one hand, taxpayers, which include individual employees and business entities, must pay income taxes, which are based on the amount of income or profits earned. On the other hand, employers must pay payroll taxes, which are based on how much employers pay their employees. Additional income and payroll taxes may be imposed by local and state governments.

SPOTLIGHT ON LEGAL ISSUES: EQUAL PAY FOR U.S. MEN'S AND WOMEN'S NATIONAL SOCCER TEAMS

The Equal Pay Act of 1963 and Title VII of the Civil Rights Act of 1964 prohibit pay discrimination based on sex. Differences in pay between men and women are permitted only if they are based on seniority, merit, quantity or quality of production, or some factor other than sex. When an organization is suspected of paying men and women at different rates for performing equal work, the Equal Employment Opportunity Commission (EEOC) can step in to investigate the employment practices and sue the organization in question.

In recent years, pay disparities between men's and women's professional sports have received increased scrutiny. The U.S. Women's National Soccer Team have been at the forefront of this issue, and in 2016, five players filed a formal complaint with the EEOC. The following year, the team agreed to a new pay structure, which included a 30% increase in base pay as well as higher incentives for winning games. Notably, this agreement did not result in pay equality between men and women players, but it did serve as an initial step toward closing the pay gap. Later, in February 2022, the women's team settled a pay discrimination lawsuit with the U.S. Soccer Federation for $24 million.

In September 2022, a new collective bargaining agreement with the U.S. Soccer Federation was signed by both men's and women's players. The new agreement established equal pay for men and women, which included identical financial terms (e.g., commercial revenue sharing), thereby concluding the U.S. Women's National Soccer Team's push for equal pay.[53]

PERSON-BASED PAY STRUCTURES

LEARNING OBJECTIVE

11.4 Identify basic principles underlying person-based pay structures.

The chapter's focus thus far has been on job-based pay structures, wherein pay rates are determined by the content of the job that a person occupies. In contrast, person-based pay structures emphasize individuals' unique competencies or skills when determining pay, such that a person who possesses a particular competency or skill receives additional pay.[54]

Person-based structures offer organizations greater agility when managing workflow, as those with certain competencies or skills are matched with appropriate tasks and paid accordingly. In doing so, organizations can avoid the rigidity of job-based structures in which employees are rewarded only for performing the tasks outlined in their job description, even if they possess competencies and skills that may contribute to task completion beyond their prescribed job. Further, job-based pay structures compensate employees who perform the same job relatively uniformly, even if some individuals lack proficiency in certain aspects of their job. Research has shown that person-based pay structures are linked to greater production quality and quantity, lower labor costs, greater individual skill change, and better attitudes.[55] However, compensating employees based on the skills or competencies they possess does not necessarily mean they are applying a particular skill or competency with regularity (or even at all). Thus, it is important to make sure employees actually apply the skills or competencies for which they are being rewarded.

EXECUTIVE PAY

LEARNING OBJECTIVE
11.5   Describe the philosophy and challenges of executive pay structures.

During the financial crisis of 2008, executive pay became a popular topic of conversation, as greater attention was paid to the often-large pay discrepancies between company CEOs and the average worker. This discrepancy between CEO pay and average worker pay is called pay dispersion, or a pay gap, and has direct implications for employees' perceptions of internal equity. In addition to costing companies a lot of money, large pay dispersions related to CEOs and other executive positions have been shown to have negative implications for short- and long-term company performance.[56] Yet over the years, the pay gap between CEOs and average workers has continued to rise in the United States, which led to the Dodd-Frank Wall Street Reform and Consumer Protection Act of 2010, which requires all publicly listed companies to report pay dispersion between the CEO and the average employee.[57]

Among the top 350 largest publicly owned U.S. firms by revenue in 2021, CEOs earned 399 times more than the average production or nonsupervisory worker.[58] In general, larger companies, companies with more board members, and companies with more independent board members tend to compensate their CEOs at higher rates.[59] Further, some companies weight market review data heavily when creating their executive compensation packages, which ensure high levels of external equity but not necessarily internal equity.[60] The reasons for such large pay dispersions also have to do with the fact that CEO pay has outpaced average-worker pay over the past 4 decades. After adjusting for inflation, CEO pay grew by 1,322% from 1978 to 2020, whereas typical worker pay grew by just 18.0% over that same time period.[61] This imbalance can be attributed, in part, to record-breaking company profits, resulting in corresponding gains in the stock market for publicly traded companies. Because CEOs often receive a sizeable proportion of their total compensation from stock options and other ownership programs, they stand to benefit tremendously from profit gains.

Regardless of which factors drive executive pay, employee perceptions of fairness play an important role. If executives are paid exorbitant sums compared to the average employee, employees and other stakeholders may perceive the system as unjust and internally inequitable. Some local governments have taken steps to address organizations with large pay gaps between their CEOs and employees. For example, in 2021, voters in San Francisco, California, passed Measure L, which, beginning in 2022, imposed a tax on organizations whose CEO pay is 100 times greater than the median pay of its employees.[62]

PAY ADMINISTRATION

LEARNING OBJECTIVE
11.6 Evaluate issues of pay administration such as compression and pay transparency.

Once a pay structure and policies have been designed, an organization must implement and administer them. When it comes to pay administration, there are multiple issues to consider. Here the chapter focuses on the following issues: pay compression and inversion, adherence to pay policies, and pay transparency and secrecy.

Pay Compression and Inversion

Pay compression and inversion can occur when a pay structure is based largely on market pay rates. Specifically, pay compression and inversion may occur when growth in the external market pay practices outpaces growth in an organization's internal pay practices. Pay compression and inversion are indicative of low individual equity.

On one hand, pay compression refers to one of two situations within a single organization: (a) a more recently hired employee with less experience earns nearly as much or the same as a more experienced, longer tenured employee in the same job or (b) an employee in a lower-level job earns nearly as much or the same as another employee in a higher-level job, the latter of whom might even be the supervisor of the employee performing the lower-level job.[63]

On the other hand, pay inversion is a more severe form of compression and occurs when a newer, less experienced employee in a given job earns (a) *more* than another, more experienced employee in the same job or (b) *more* than another employee in a higher-level job. As an illustration of pay inversion, consider the following scenario: Leilani was hired as a software engineer 3 years ago at an annual salary of $100,000/year, and since she was hired, Leilani has received exceptional performance reviews. Over the past 3 years, an external labor shortage emerged for software engineers, which resulted in organizations offering increasingly higher salaries to attract talented individuals. As a result, the organization hired Carlos, who has the same qualifications as Leilani except for fewer years of on-the-job experience, yet his starting salary was $120,000/year, which is an inversion of $20,000/year in favor of Carlos. Understandably, situations like these may negatively impact employees' perceptions of pay system fairness.

Adherence to Pay Policies

Evidence of pay compression and inversion may indicate that an organization is failing to adhere to its pay policies and pay structure. An HR metric called the compa-ratio can be a useful source of information when evaluating an organization's adherence to its pay policies. The compa-ratio reflects how much employees are actually paid for a given job or pay grade as compared to the espoused pay structure and policies; thus, the compa-ratio can be used to assess whether systematic compression or inversion is occurring.[64]

To calculate the compa-ratio, simply divide the average pay for employees in a given job or pay grade by the pay range or grade.

$$Compa\text{-}Ratio\ for\ a\ Group\ of\ Employees = \frac{Average\ Actual\ Pay\ of\ Employees}{Midpoint\ of\ Pay\ Range\ or\ Grade}$$

A compa-ratio value of 1.00 indicates that employees are paid, on average, at the midpoint of their pay range or grade, which reflects that pay practices generally adhere to pay policies. A compa-ratio value that is greater than 1.00 indicates that, on average, employees are paid more than the midpoint of their pay range or grade, which may indicate, for example, that competitive market pay rates are growing faster than expected, and thus the pay policies and pay structure need to be updated accordingly. Conversely, a compa-ratio value that is less than 1.00 indicates that, on average, employees are paid less than the midpoint of their pay range or grade, which indicates employees' pay may need to be upwardly adjusted to adhere to the pay policies, if the pay policy strategy of the organization is to match or lead the market.

A compa-ratio can also be calculated for individual employees by dividing the individual's pay by the midpoint of the pay range or grade to which they belong.

$$Compa\text{-}Ratio\ for\ One\ Employee = \frac{Actual\ Pay\ of\ Employee}{Midpoint\ of\ Pay\ Range\ or\ Grade}$$

Calculating the compa-ratios for individual employees can be a useful practice for detecting pay compression and inversion, especially when information about employee tenure is taken into consideration. For example, consider the scatterplot presented in Figure 11.9 in which individual employees' compa-ratios are plotted in relation to their tenure. Note that compa-ratio is on the *x*-axis, tenure is on the *y*-axis, and each circle represents a single employee. If the organization's policy is to pay longer tenured employees at higher rates than employees with shorter tenures, then the scatterplot reveals that the organization's actual pay practices depart dramatically from that espoused policy. In this example, employees with the shortest tenure tend to have the highest compa-ratios, which indicate that more recent newcomers to the organization earn notably higher wages than the midpoint of their pay range. The opposite appears to be true for employees with longer tenures in the organization. For these reasons, this scatterplot is illustrative of pay compression and inversion.

FIGURE 11.9 ■ Scatterplot of the Compa-Ratios and Years of Tenure for a Group of Employees

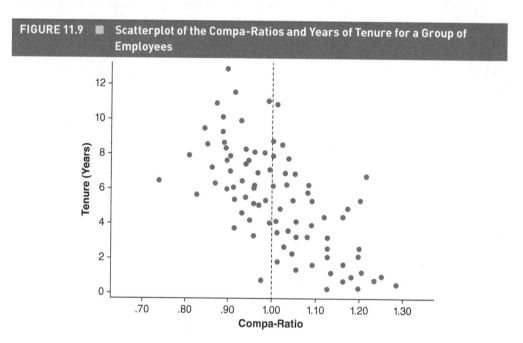

Pay Transparency and Pay Secrecy

Pay transparency and pay secrecy have emerged as important and controversial topics. Pay transparency refers to the extent to which an organization communicates pay information and the extent to which employees are permitted to discuss pay with each other; the term is sometimes called *pay openness*.[65] In contrast, pay secrecy refers to the extent to which an organization has policies and practices aimed at suppressing the communication and exchange of pay information. In practice, pay secrecy and transparency exist on either end of a continuum, and organization policies often fall somewhere in between the two extremes.[66]

On one hand, proponents of pay transparency argue that making pay information publicly available is an important step in reducing the gender and race/ethnicity earning gaps and in preventing discriminatory pay practices. A Pew Research Center report showed that in 2022 U.S. women earned $0.82 for every $1.00 that men earned, which has not improved much since 2002 when women earned $0.80 for every $1.00 men earned.[67] Regarding race/ethnicity, in the fourth quarter of 2022, African American/Black and Hispanic/Latino workers earned $0.81 and $0.75, respectively, for every $1.00 white workers earned, whereas white workers earned $0.74 for every $1.00 Asian workers earned.[68] Making pay data transparent can be used to highlight inequities, which is an important first step toward reducing pay gaps.

On the other hand, opponents of pay transparency argue that it may put the organization at risk by leading to dissatisfaction, lower productivity, and turnover. Some argue that public pay information may challenge workers' sense of worth and contribution to the organization; if they view themselves as top performers but learn they earn less than others, they may initiate thoughts of leaving the organization or decreasing performance. Further, open pay communication may encourage workers to engage in more frequent social comparisons with each other.[69]

In the United States, pay transparency is required for only certain groups of employees and employers, yet some organizations voluntarily and publicly communicate pay information. Section 7 of the National Labor Relations Act ensures that most private-sector employees have a right to discuss pay information, and this right extends to work-related discussions on social media (e.g., Facebook, Twitter, Glassdoor).[70] According to the U.S. Department of Labor, only about half of U.S. workers are allowed to discuss pay with coworkers in their respective organizations. In recent years, states like California, Colorado, and Washington have taken steps toward reducing earnings gaps by passing legislation that requires job postings to include pay range information.[71]

Although many organizations choose to keep pay information secret, some have taken steps to communicate earnings data across jobs and levels of the organization. For example, Whole Foods Market IP, LP, gained a reputation for pay transparency based on its 1986 initiative in which the company made wage information available to all employees.[72] As a recent example, in 2022, Google settled a class-action lawsuit alleging gender-based pay discrimination for $118 million. In addition to the monetary relief paid, which will be paid to approximately 15,500 women, Google has agreed to allow third-party experts evaluate its pay practices and make recommendations for improving pay equity.[73]

Research on the effects of pay transparency has yielded mixed findings. For example, communicating pay information may lead to envy of those who are paid more, but it may also lead to better performance, higher profits, and reduced gender-based pay inequity.[74] Thus, pay transparency may help reduce pay gaps between protected groups, but it may also lead to some negative consequences in the short term.

SPOTLIGHT ON ETHICS: EQUITABLE PAY STRUCTURE AT KACHKA

In many U.S. restaurants, tipping has long been an essential part of their pay structures for servers. Customarily, the customer decides how much to tip a server, with 20% of the cost of the meal being the expected standard for good service. Of course, the customer may decide to tip more or less than 20% based on the quality of service and other factors unrelated to the server's performance (e.g., food quality). Tipping is an inherently variable form of pay, as earning a tip depends in part on how many customers attend the restaurant and how much customers decide to tip. When a large proportion of a server's compensation comes in the form of tips, it may be difficult for the server to estimate how much compensation they will earn on a weekly basis; this may lead the server to feel financial strain and uncertainty. Some evidence also points to pay disparities that arise for tipped workers based on customer biases. For example, white workers have been found to earn more tips, on average, than workers from other racial and ethnic groups like Asian American, Black, and Latino workers.

Some restaurants have taken steps to build more equitable pay structures by adding a fixed service charge to each meal. In 2022, Kachka, a Russian restaurant located in Portland, Oregon, implemented a 22% service fee to all meals, which means customers no longer need to decide how much to tip for service. Further, the restaurant distributes the service fee to both front-of-house workers (e.g., servers) and back-of-house workers (e.g., cooks), which helps to reduce the pay disparities between those two sets of employees. In doing so, the restaurant increased the starting base wage for employees to $25 per hour and has taken additional steps to provide free health benefits and profit-sharing to employees. This initiative moved Kachka toward a more equitable pay structure for its service employees.[75]

Questions

1. Explain how this example relates to ethics, and describe your own reactions to the information contained in the case.
2. Can you think of any unintended consequences that might occur for restaurant employees when a restaurant eliminates tips in favor of a service fee?

CHAPTER SUMMARY

Pay, or compensation, represents one type of formal reward. A reward system encompasses relational returns (e.g., recognition, challenging work) and total compensation, where the latter includes compensation (e.g., base pay, variable pay) and benefits (e.g., health insurance, income protection). An effective pay structure requires fairness in the form of internal, external, and individual equity, as well as legal compliance. Regarding internal equity, a rigorous job evaluation ensures that jobs are internally aligned, such that jobs are structured hierarchically in terms of worth. As for external equity, using a thorough market review, an organization can look to the pay practices of other peer organizations to determine whether its pay practices are externally competitive. Integrating the principles of internal equity and external equity offers an opportunity to create an internally aligned and externally competitive pay structure. Once a pay structure and associated policies are in place, an organization should maintain individual equity, such that differences in pay for individual employees working similar jobs within an organization are attributable to differences in performance, seniority, and/or experience, as opposed to other job-unrelated factors. Executive pay represents another important equity consideration, as executive pay tends to be much higher than that of the average worker, which can be controversial. Above all, a pay structure and associated pay policies should adhere to prevailing employment and labor laws, and care should be taken to ensure that pay is administered properly and fairly.

KEY TERMS

Aging (of pay data)

Benchmark jobs

Benefits

Broadbanding

Classification method

Compa-ratio

Compensable factors

Compensation

Delayering

Distributive justice

Equity theory

Executive Order 11246

Exempt

External equity

Fair Labor Standards Act (FLSA)

Individual equity

Interactional justice
Internal equity
Internal Revenue Code
Job evaluation
Job structure
Labor market
Market pay line
Market pricing
Market review
National Labor Relations Act (NLRA)
Nonexempt
Organizational justice theory
Pay compression
Pay grade

Pay inversion
Pay policy line
Pay secrecy
Pay structure
Pay transparency
Person-based pay structures
Point-factor method
Procedural justice
Product market
Ranking method
Relational returns
Reward system
Total compensation

HR REASONING AND DECISION-MAKING EXERCISES

Mini-Case Analysis Exercise: Compensation Investigation

Karyn is the compensation analyst for a large manufacturing company with 20,000 employees. In her role, Karyn has administrative rights for both the compensation and employee personal information databases, which allow her to access employees' pay data as well as demographic information like their name, sex, race, and age. In fact, using employees' unique IDs, she has the ability to link employees' rewards data with their personal data.

Lately, Karyn has begun to wonder whether the employees of different sexes, races, and ages are paid similarly. Based on her data analytics training, she knows that t-test and correlation analyses would allow her to investigate whether systematic pay differences exist between protected groups in general and whether systematic pay differences exist for specific jobs and pay grades more specifically.

Karyn recently asked you if she can investigate if systematic pay differences exist. As Karyn's manager, you must decide whether you will grant Karyn permission to run the requested analyses. How would you handle this situation?

1. Do you have any concerns about allowing Karyn to run the requested analyses? Why or why not?

2. Is there any other person or entity you would like to involve in the decision-making process? If so, who?

3. What would you advise Karyn to do regarding the analyses?

HR Decision Analysis Exercise: Is Market Pricing the Way to Go?

Your company's current pay structure was developed using the point-factor method in conjunction with market review data. Following the lead of other companies in the industry, however, your CEO proposes that she would like to overhaul the current pay structure by using market pricing exclusively. Recall from this chapter that market pricing refers to the process of basing a pay structure (almost) entirely off of competitors' pay practices. The CEO declares the overhauled pay structure will do a better job at attracting and retaining top talent, as pay will match or exceed that of competitors.

You are the vice president of HR at the company, and the CEO values your opinion on HR-related topics and issues. The CEO has asked you to evaluate her proposal and provide her with feedback.

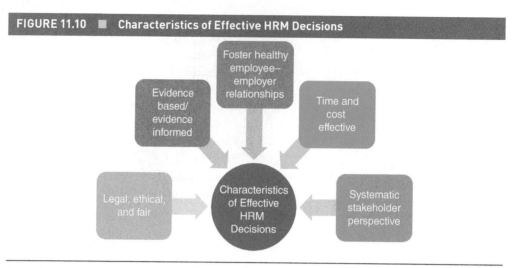

FIGURE 11.10 ■ Characteristics of Effective HRM Decisions

Should the organization overhaul the current pay structure using market pricing? Evaluate this decision using the following criteria.

Please provide the rationale for your answer to each of the following questions.

Is market pricing legal, ethical, and fair?

Is it evidence based/evidence informed?

Does it foster healthy employee–employer relationships?

Is it time- and cost-effective?

Does it take a systematic stakeholder perspective?

Considering your analysis above, overall, do you think this would be an effective decision? Why or why not?

What, if anything, do you think should be done differently or should be considered to help make this decision more effective?

HR Decision-Making Exercise: Conducting a Market Review

A video game company named Zenyah with 8,000 employees recently hired your consulting firm to develop a more externally equitable pay structure. Zenyah began as a start-up 10 years ago and has grown very rapidly ever since. Lately, the company has been having difficulty recruiting and selecting talented candidates for key software development, marketing, and sales jobs, which is likely due to the external labor shortage for individuals qualified for those jobs. As such, Zenyah has asked your consulting firm to conduct a market review for the following benchmark jobs:

- Computer programmer
- Systems software developer
- Applications software developer
- Market research analyst
- Marketing manager
- Advertising sales agent
- Advertising and promotions manager
- Sales representative

As part of the contract, Zenyah has requested that your consulting firm conduct new job analyses on the benchmark jobs, as it suspects that the job descriptions are out of date and inaccurate. As a starting point, you decide to use O*NET (ONETonline.org) to draft initial job description summaries that you can use to compare to the job description summaries that appear in the market review sources.

1. Using O*NET, write three- to five-sentence job description summaries for each benchmark job.

2. Using Salary.com and CareerOneStop.org as free market review sources, gather pay data for as many of the benchmark jobs as you can, and enter the data into a table. Be sure to match the job description summaries you created for Zenyah with the job description summaries in the market review sources to ensure you are making an appropriate comparison.

3. Imagine that the data in Salary.com and CareerOneStop.org were collected 1 month ago and need to be aged to 8 months from now. Use an annual aging factor of +3.5%.

4. Calculate the market-based pay midpoint for each of the benchmark jobs.

DATA AND ANALYTICS EXERCISE: EVALUATING PAY COMPRESSION

The compa-ratio can be a useful metric when investigating whether pay compression might be an issue for those employees who work the same job and thus belong to the same pay grade. For this exercise, you will calculate compa-ratios for individual employees using the following formula:

$$Compa\text{-}Ratio\ for\ One\ Employee = \frac{Actual\ Pay\ of\ Employee}{Midpoint\ of\ Pay\ Grade}.$$

For example, if an employee earns $42,000/year and the midpoint of the employee's pay grade is $40,000, then the compa-ratio will be equal to 1.05 ($42,000/$40,000 = 1.05). Because this compa-ratio value is greater than 1.00, it indicates the employee is paid more than the midpoint of the pay grade. If the compa-ratio had been less than 1.00, then it would have indicated the employee was paid less than the midpoint of the pay grade. Now let's imagine there are 100 total employees who work the same job, and we compute compa-ratios for each of them. In addition to each employee's compa-ratio, we also know the length of time (in years) the employee has worked in that position (i.e., tenure). Using the compa-ratio and tenure variables, we can construct a scatterplot to understand how these employees are compensated relative to their length of tenure.

The scatterplot indicates that employees with higher compa-ratios tend to have worked in the job more years. In other words, there does not appear to be evidence of pay compression, as individuals who

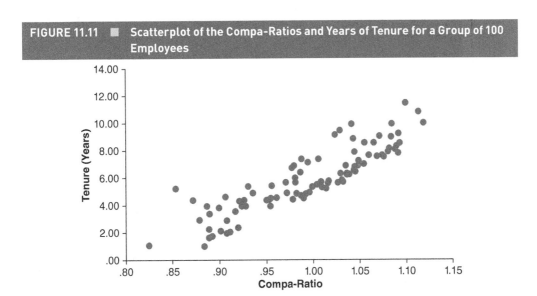

FIGURE 11.11 ■ **Scatterplot of the Compa-Ratios and Years of Tenure for a Group of 100 Employees**

have worked fewer years in the job tend to earn less pay relative to the midpoint than those who have worked more years.

Excel Extension: Now You Try!

- On **edge.sagepub.com/bauer2e**, you will find an Excel exercise on evaluating pay compression.

- First, you will compute the compa-ratios for groups of employees who work the same job.

- Second, you will construct a scatterplot to visualize the relationship between the compa-ratio and tenure variables.

- Third, you will evaluate whether there is evidence of pay compression.

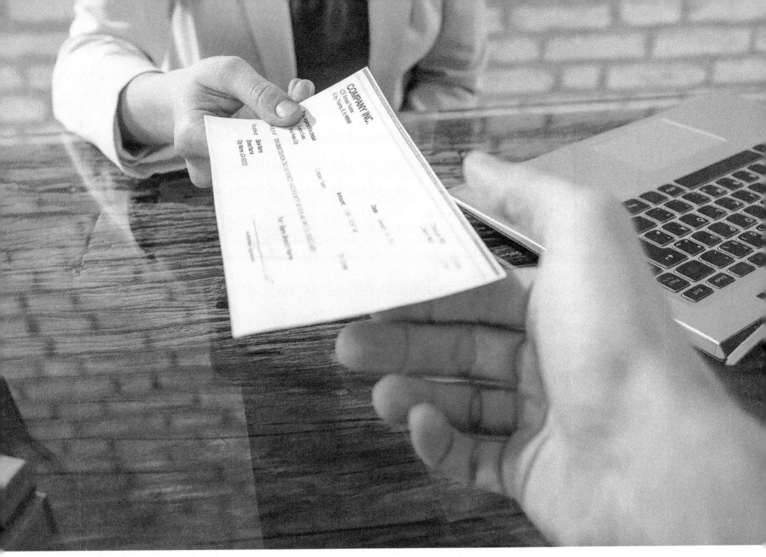

12 REWARDING PERFORMANCE

PERFORMANCE BONUSES: THE CASE OF WALL STREET INVESTMENT BANKERS AND TRADERS

©iStockphoto.com/Fabrice Cabaud

In the years following the 2008 financial crisis, large performance bonuses awarded to Wall Street investment bankers and traders have received increased attention. Some argue the size of these performance-based bonuses rewards risky and reckless behavior among bankers and traders, and the structure of these rewards encourages a focus on short-term as opposed to long-term gains. Others have argued that pay-outs of these large financial rewards ignore the broader economic environment, such as economic recessions or slowdowns.

As historical context, multiple major financial services institutions played a role in the collapse of the mortgage market that led, in part, to the 2008 financial crisis. For example, Goldman Sachs allegedly profited from misleading investors that its residential mortgage-backed securities were sound when they were, in fact, likely to fail. This led the organization to settle with the U.S. government for over $5 billion in 2016. Despite contributing to the financial crisis, major financial services institutions received bailout money from the U.S. government, as part of the Emergency Economic Stabilization Act of 2008, to prevent them from failing after their massive losses. Morgan Stanley, for instance, received $107 billion in economic relief from the federal government to prevent its collapse. And yet, in the year following the financial crisis, 428 of Morgan Stanley's bankers and traders received individual bonuses of $1 million or more. In fact, $577 million in bonuses was paid out across 101 of those same Morgan Stanley employees, highlighting how the organization distributed the bulk of its financial rewards to a relatively small number of employees.

Bonuses, like those paid to bankers and traders, are often tied to employees' performance. For instance, if a trader earns a larger amount of profit, then that trader will receive a larger bonus. In contrast, a trader who earns a smaller amount of profit will receive a smaller bonus or no bonus at all. Bonus pay and other forms of variable pay, however, are not the only types of financial compensation bankers and traders receive. Part of their total compensation package includes base pay, which is guaranteed so long as they remain employed at their respective financial institutions. In other words, their base pay is a reward for the content of the job itself as opposed to their performance on that job. Compared to the amount of variable pay they can potentially earn, bankers' and traders' base pay can be relatively small, particularly for those who are more senior and who perform at higher levels. By nature, however, variable pay is, well, variable and thus not a guaranteed form of pay. Instead, types of variable pay like bonuses and profit sharing are contingent on performance and thus must be re-earned over time as opposed to being built into base pay. When well-designed and aligned with the organization's strategic objectives, bonuses can motivate employees to reach higher levels of performance while also contributing to the organization's success.

At many Wall Street financial service institutions, the reward systems for bankers and traders offer high bonuses when individual performance levels are high (e.g., high profits) and low or zero bonuses when performance levels are low (e.g., low profits, losses). When bankers or traders lose money individually, they do not typically face a pay penalty other than not receiving a bonus; rather, they still receive their guaranteed base pay. Although they may face termination if their losses are too high, they are not required to pay back their losses to their organizations. Thus, the potential for large bonuses may encourage bankers and traders to make financially risky decisions and bets. After all, if they make large profits while engaging in risky and reckless behavior, they stand to gain considerable and possibly career-defining personal wealth. If they incur equally large losses while engaging in risky and reckless behavior, their penalty is relatively small in comparison: forgoing a performance bonus while still earning guaranteed base pay and possibly having to find a job at a different organization.

The financial rewards received by bankers and traders are not, however, always immune to economic uncertainty and slowdowns. For example, in 2022, as economic challenges associated with the Covid-19 pandemic continued and inflation increased, some Wall Street financial services institutions laid off workers, and on average, performance bonuses dropped by 26% compared to the previous year.[1]

CASE DISCUSSION QUESTIONS

1. In addition to base pay and bonuses, what other types of monetary rewards could Wall Street financial services institutions use to motivate employees to reach higher levels of performance on the job? What about nonmonetary rewards?

2. Can pay-for-performance programs like bonuses motivate employees to achieve higher performance while also minimizing risky or reckless behavior? How would such a system work?

3. How can financial services institutions design pay-for-performance programs (e.g., bonus programs) that align individual banker and trader behavior with the strategic objectives of the organization?

4. In your opinion, what is the right balance between the proportion of an employee's pay that comes from base pay (e.g., wage, salary) versus variable pay (e.g., bonus, profit sharing)?

To learn about the unfolding of the 2008 financial crisis, its aftermath, and Wall Street, watch the Frontline PBS documentary *Money, Power and Wall Street* (https://youtu.be/W-Q9AO p2FW8).

INTRODUCTION

Many employers use financial rewards to motivate employees to perform their job at a higher level and to attain key goals. Both traditional-pay programs and pay-for-performance programs can be integral parts of an organization's reward system. However, unlike traditional-pay programs, pay-for-performance programs compensate employees for the quantity and quality of the work they *actually* perform. Well-designed pay-for-performance programs help attract, motivate, and retain high-potential and high-performing individuals and can be used to reward individuals, teams and units, and the organization as a whole. In contrast, poorly designed pay-for-performance programs can lead to budgeting problems with labor costs and can motivate employees to behave in ways that are unethical and uncooperative. Nevertheless, an effective pay-for-performance program can support strategic objectives, when the program motivates behaviors that are strategically aligned.

PAY AS A MOTIVATOR

LEARNING OBJECTIVE
12.1   Describe the motivating potential of pay and other rewards.

A reward system comprises relational returns (e.g., recognition, job security), compensation (e.g., base pay, variable pay), and benefits (e.g., health insurance, work–life balance programs). With respect to compensation, we can distinguish between two types of programs: traditional-pay programs and pay-for-performance programs. In doing so, we can understand how pay can serve as a motivator for employees.

Traditional-pay programs reward employees based on the content of their job description, title, or level. They usually correspond to the relatively stable and fixed base pay component of individual employees' compensation package. Think of traditional-pay programs as being a wage or salary guarantee: In exchange for organizational membership and doing a particular job, employees receive a base pay amount that depends on the worth of the job they were hired to perform. As long as employees hold on to their jobs, they receive their base pay, regardless of how well they perform. Of course, employees who fail to perform at minimally acceptable levels and fail to do so consistently over time, even after progressive disciplinary action by the organization, will likely lose their base pay after being terminated.

In contrast, pay-for-performance programs, sometimes called *performance-contingent-pay programs*, reward employees for the behaviors they *actually* exhibit at work and for the results or goals they *actually* achieve. That is, pay is distributed as a reward for demonstrating a certain level of performance. Compared to traditional-pay programs, pay-for-performance programs are more strongly linked to on-the-job motivation. When financial incentives are attached to certain behaviors and goals, employees become motivated to align their behaviors with the objectives considered most critical for companywide success.[2] Pay-for-performance programs not only motivate individuals to perform at a higher level but also serve as a vehicle to attract high-potential applicants and to retain high-performing employees.[3] Later in the chapter, we cover pay-for-performance programs in more detail, but first it is important to understand what motivation entails.

Understanding Motivation

Employee motivation is an expected outcome of a well-designed pay-for-performance program. Motivation is a psychological force that propels an individual (or a group of individuals) to enact certain behaviors or to strive for a goal or result. Moreover, motivation consists of the following four components.

1. *Direction* refers to the behaviors, goals, or results on which an individual focuses attention.

2. *Form* refers to the types of behaviors an individual enacts or the types of goals and results an individual pursues.

3. *Effort* refers to the intensity with which an individual focuses on and/or enacts behaviors or pursues goals and results.

4. *Duration* refers to how long an individual persists in enacting certain behaviors or pursuing certain goals and results.

Thus, when conceptualizing pay as a motivator, we should consider how pay signals the desired direction and form of behavior and goal pursuit, and how pay encourages the amount of effort and duration that should be applied (see Figure 12.1).

FIGURE 12.1 ■ Effect of Pay on Enactment of Behavior and Pursuit of Goals

If deployed strategically and tied to particular behaviors or goals, pay can signal to employees the types of behaviors or goals they should spend their time and effort pursuing.

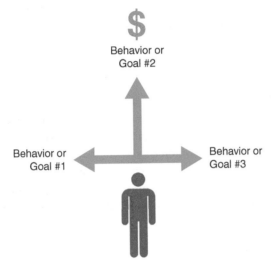

We can distinguish between two broad types of motivation: extrinsic and intrinsic (see Figure 12.2). Both are important for performance, but accumulated research indicates that they differ with respect to how they influence performance and what types of performance they influence.

FIGURE 12.2 ■ Intrinsic and Extrinsic Motivation

There are two types of motivation. Intrinsic motivation originates inside the individual, and extrinsic motivation originates outside of the individual. Both forms of motivation are important for goal attainment and performance.

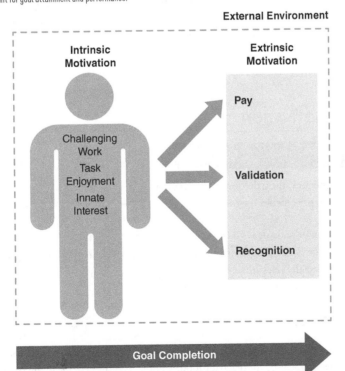

Extrinsic Motivation

Extrinsic motivation is a force that is external to an individual, and this force drives the individual to action.[4] Often, we use the term *extrinsic motivator* when referring to an external, environmental source of extrinsic motivation. The classic example of an extrinsic motivator is pay, particularly when pay is offered in exchange for performance. Other extrinsic motivators include nonmonetary awards and recognition such as praise or validation from a supervisor. With extrinsic motivators, individuals are not necessarily enacting certain behaviors or pursuing certain goals because they have the internal desire to do so, but rather because they receive some kind of compensation, reward, or award.

However, the extent to which a particular external, environmental force is motivating varies among individuals. For example, for some people, receiving pay may be perceived as very valuable and important and thus more extrinsically motivating. For others, pay may hold less value and importance and thus be less extrinsically motivating.

Intrinsic Motivation

Unlike extrinsic motivation, intrinsic motivation is an internal force that drives the individual to action because the action itself is perceived as meaningful, challenging, or enjoyable.[5] For example, in the workplace, some people might feel intrinsically motivated to write code for a software program because they simply enjoy the process of building something new and challenging. Intrinsic motivation would be low for an employee who finds writing code to be unpleasant and boring. For example, an individual who is promoted to a supervisory role may feel energized by the increased level of responsibility and control over how work is conducted and completed. The point is people vary in terms of what they consider to be intrinsically motivating.

Motivation and Performance

In general, higher motivation leads to higher performance, and both extrinsic and intrinsic motivation are important for performance. However, research indicates that they influence different aspects of performance. In a meta-analytic review of 183 studies on extrinsic and intrinsic motivation spanning 40 years, researchers found that extrinsic motivation is associated with the *quantity* of performance, or rather, *how much* an individual produces, completes, or provides in terms of products and services.[6] In contrast, intrinsic motivation is more strongly linked to the *quality* of performance, or rather, *how well* an individual produces, completes, or provides products and services. Interestingly, the researchers found that the positive association between intrinsic motivation and overall performance becomes even stronger when extrinsic motivation is present. That is, extrinsic motivation enhances the already beneficial effect of intrinsic motivation on performance. Thus, even though this chapter focuses mostly on extrinsic motivation (and specifically on pay), ultimately both forms of motivation are important for employee performance.

THEORIES OF MOTIVATION

LEARNING OBJECTIVE
12.2   Identify the prevailing theories of motivation and goal setting.

Theories of motivation provide us with frameworks for designing, explaining, and understanding the effects of pay-for-performance programs on behavior and goal attainment. Three prominent motivational theories are especially relevant to understanding how and why pay can motivate behavior: reinforcement theory, expectancy theory, and goal-setting theory.

Reinforcement Theory

Reinforcement theory provides a useful framework for understanding pay as an extrinsic motivator. This is especially true when pay is used for behavior modification, as is the case for many pay-for-performance

programs. Reinforcement theory is rooted in research on behaviorism and operant conditioning by Edward Thorndike, Ivan Pavlov, and B. F. Skinner, three influential social scientists from the early 20th century.[7] The theory proposes that environmental consequences, which include extrinsic motivators such as providing or withholding rewards and punishments, influence behavior. According to the theory, environmental consequences signal to individuals which behaviors they should continue or discontinue in the future.

The principles of reinforcement theory can be applied to encourage desired behaviors and dissuade undesired behaviors. If individuals receive a reward after enacting a desired behavior, then they will be more likely to perform that behavior again in the future. For example, if employees receive a bonus each time they make their end-of-quarter sales quota, then they will be more likely to strive to meet their sales quota in future quarters. On the other hand, if a punishment is given when individuals enact an undesired behavior, then they will be less likely to perform the behavior again in the future. For example, if employees receive a pay deduction each time they produce waste during the production process, then they will be less likely to produce waste in the future. Finally, if a reward is withheld when individuals enact an undesired behavior, then they will be less likely to perform the behavior again in the future.

In general, research has shown that to encourage a desired behavior, an environmental consequence, such as a reward or punishment, should be presented soon after the behavior is exhibited. If the environmental consequence is presented long after the behavior is enacted, the likelihood of an individual performing the desired behavior again in the future diminishes. The more quickly rewards are distributed (or withheld) after an employee demonstrates a behavior, the more likely the employee will continue to enact (or cease to enact) that target behavior again in the future.

It is worth noting that reinforcement theory does not directly help us understand *why* providing or withholding pay affects employees' motivation. Other theories, such as expectancy theory, help us answer those "why" questions.

Expectancy Theory

Expectancy theory proposes that motivation consists of three components: expectancy, instrumentality, and valence.[8]

As depicted in Figure 12.3, expectancy refers to an individual's perceived connection between their effort and their performance. An individual will perceive higher expectancy when they *expect* that exerting more effort will lead to higher performance. Imagine that your supervisor assigns you the following performance goal: *Sell 100 software licenses by the end of the month.* If you possess the knowledge of the software product and skills to sell it, then you will likely perceive that applying effort will help you accomplish the sales goal. You will feel more motivated because you perceive higher expectancy.

FIGURE 12.3 ■ Expectancy Theory

Expectancy theory proposes that motivation consists of three components: expectancy, instrumentality, and valence. Expectancy refers to the perception that effort will lead to performance, instrumentality refers to the perception that performance will lead to a reward, and valence refers to the perception that a reward is valuable.

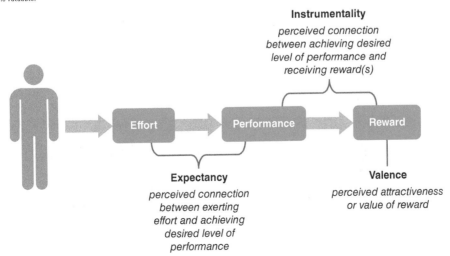

When administering group incentives, employees' perceptions of expectancy should be considered. Specifically, in situations in which a group as a whole is rewarded for its performance, individual group members may have a difficult time understanding how their efforts lead to higher group performance, particularly when there is a large number of group members. Thus, they may perceive low expectancy when there is not a clear line of sight between their effort and the performance of the group.

Instrumentality refers to an individual's perception that performing at a high enough level will lead to rewards. In other words, an individual will perceive more instrumentality when they perceive that performance is *instrumental* for earning rewards. As an example, if your organization tells you that selling 100 software licenses will result in a bonus, then you will perceive higher instrumentality (and thus higher motivation), especially if, in the past, you saw that similar performance was rewarded. Perceiving that a reward is directly tied to performance will heighten the degree to which you are motivated to earn that reward.

In the context of pay-for-performance programs, specifically, instrumentality often reflects the quality of the performance management and reward systems, as well as the degree to which they are integrated effectively. For instance, if performance is not tracked and measured accurately, then employees may perceive the rewards to be arbitrary or unpredictable. These can result in lower levels of perceived instrumentality and, thus, lower motivation.

Valence is the extent to which a person perceives a reward as attractive or important. It refers to the value an individual attaches to a reward. For example, you will likely perceive higher valence if the month-end reward for selling 100 software licenses is $1,000 as opposed to $5; consequently, you will be more motivated to apply effort toward demonstrating the level of performance necessary for attaining the reward when the reward itself is more highly valued. In general, the amount of pay for performance affects individuals' perceptions of valence, such that higher pay should be viewed as more attractive and more motivating.

Some have argued that expectancy, instrumentality, and valence share a multiplicative relationship, such that if one of the three falls to zero, then motivation falls to zero. For example, the theory proposes that an individual's motivation to attain a goal will drop if they perceive high valence and high expectancy but low instrumentality. The formula is as follows:

$$Motivation = Expectancy \times Instrumentality \times Valence$$

Manager's Toolbox: Evaluating Pay-for-Performance Programs Using Expectancy Theory

Without thoughtful communication and consideration of employee perceptions, a pay-for-performance program may fail to improve employee motivation and performance. Managers can apply expectancy theory to determine why the pay-for-performance program does not lead to higher motivation and performance.

1. *Expectancy.* If employees do not perceive a link between their effort and attaining a performance goal, then a manager should consider the following:
   - *Do employees have the requisite KSAOs necessary to meet the goal?* If not, the employees may need training.
   - *If a group pay-for-performance program is in place, do employees understand their role in the group and how they can contribute to the group's attainment of the goal?* If not, the manager should explain to employees how their efforts contribute to the group's success.

2. *Instrumentality.* If employees do not perceive a link between attaining a performance goal and receiving a reward, then the manager should consider the following:
   - *Do employees understand how the pay-for-performance program works?* If not, the manager should explain the program and, in particular, how rewards are determined and why they are distributed.

- *Is performance measured consistently, accurately, and fairly?* If not, the performance management system may need to be improved by enhancing the measurement tools, training users on how to use the measurement tools, or addressing office politics that influence the way performance is measured.
- *Is the reward distributed in a timely manner after the goal is attained?* If not, the manager should work to ensure that the reward is distributed soon after the goal is met.

3. *Valence.* If employees do not perceive the reward to be attractive or of value, then the manager should consider the following:

- *Is the size of the reward commensurate with the amount of effort and the level of performance it takes to earn the reward?* If not, the amount of the reward or the type of reward may need to be changed.
- *Do employees want a monetary reward?* If not, the manager should ask employees what nonmonetary rewards they might find valuable (e.g., praise, challenging work, flexible work schedule).

Goal-Setting Theory

Tying pay to specific performance goals can increase the motivating potential of a pay-for-performance program, as rewards signal the importance of goals and encourage the application of greater effort toward goal attainment. Indeed, the overarching objective of most pay-for-performance programs is to encourage employees to attain goals that are important to the organization. By integrating effective goal setting into a pay-for-performance program, an organization may be able to capitalize on increased extrinsic and intrinsic motivation, as pay can serve as an external, environmental motivator and challenging goals can stimulate a sense of innate enjoyment and fulfillment. Compared to fixed forms of pay (e.g., hourly pay), some evidence has shown that pay-for-performance programs, such as individual incentives and bonuses, can increase employees' commitment to goals.[9]

Originally introduced by Gary Latham and Edwin Locke, **goal-setting theory** offers a framework for understanding how and why certain goals lead to higher motivation and performance. Goal-setting theory has existed for more than half a century, and the tenets of the theory have been applied to work, educational, and sports settings. Over time, several best practices have emerged regarding the development of motivating goals. In most circumstances, individuals who strive for specific yet difficult (but not impossible) goals reach higher levels of performance than those who strive for do-your-best, easy, or abstract goals.[10]

The SMART acronym summarizes goal-setting best practices (see Table 12.1) and was introduced previously in Chapter 9. To review, SMART goals are specific, measurable, aggressive, realistic, and time-bound. The specific, measurable, and time-bound components of SMART reflect research findings that have shown specific goals often lead to higher motivation and performance than goals that are general or ambiguous. When pursuing a specific, measurable, and time-bound goal, an individual will have a better idea of

- the direction in which they should focus their effort and what form their effort and behavior should take (specific),
- how successful goal completion is defined and measured (measurable), and
- how much time is available to complete the goal (time-bound).

Further, the aggressive and realistic components of SMART reflect research findings that have shown individuals are more motivated by difficult goals than by easy goals. Difficult (aggressive) goals push the individual to apply greater effort—sometimes for greater durations of time—thereby opening the door for potentially higher levels of performance when compared to easy goals. Difficult goals can also inspire intrinsic motivation, particularly for people who revel in new challenges. Finally, goals should be attainable (realistic) and not excessively difficult or impossible. A goal should reflect an individual's KSAOs and not exceed an individual's capabilities given the timeline for completion. Goals

TABLE 12.1 ■ Crafting Goals With SMART	
Specific	Is your goal specific and well defined?
Measurable	Can you measure goal progress or completion?
Aggressive	Is your goal difficult and challenging?
Realistic	Do you have the right KSAOs to complete the goal?
Time-bound	Have you set a deadline for completing your goal?

that are too difficult or unattainable may be met with frustration and withdrawal, which ultimately may diminish motivation and performance.

Although goals can be specific to individuals, they can also be assigned to groups. If designed properly, team goals can improve team performance. By attaching pay or other rewards to a team's goal, an organization can signal that working together and interdependently is important. Research on goal-setting theory points to the importance of aligning team goals with the individual goals of specific team members.[11] Individual goals that lack alignment with team goals can lead to conflict and to individuals focusing more on their individual goals than the team goals. Thus, individual and team goals should operate as components of an integrated system.

STRATEGY AND PAY FOR PERFORMANCE

LEARNING OBJECTIVE

12.3 Explain how pay can be used strategically to motivate desired behavior.

A 2022 survey by Payscale found that 86% of organizations reported having or actively developing a formal compensation strategy, which was a 10% increase from 2021.[12] Further, survey results indicated that 51% of top-performing organizations (as compared to 39% of non-top-performing organizations) reported having a formal compensation strategy, and 48% of top-performing organizations (as compared to 33% of non-top-performing organizations) reported having a person or team dedicated solely to the compensation function. These statistics point to the strategic value of pay for an organization, as pay can be an instrumental force for motivating employees to attain strategic goals. Although having or developing a compensation strategy is a critical step in the process toward successfully implementing pay systems, an organization must also have a plan for disseminating and explaining the strategy to employees. Without careful communication, even the most thoughtfully developed strategy may go unnoticed or be misunderstood.

Regarding pay-for-performance programs, specifically, pay and other forms of rewards can be contingent upon meeting strategic performance objectives. Attaching financial incentives to the enactment of certain behaviors and fulfillment of certain goals can direct employees' attention to and align their behaviors with the objectives considered most critical for companywide success.[13] After all, pay is a finite resource within organizations, and thus distributing performance-contingent pay can signal the importance of pursuing some goals over others.

PAY-FOR-PERFORMANCE PROGRAMS

LEARNING OBJECTIVE

12.4 Describe common individual and group pay-for-performance programs.

Recall that pay-for-performance programs reward employees for the types of behaviors they exhibit at work and the goals they attain. Pay-for-performance programs can be designed to reward individuals or groups. In terms of time orientation, they can be attached to short- or long-term goals. This section addresses some of the more common types of pay-for-performance programs.

Individual Pay-for-Performance Programs

Pay-for-performance programs for rewarding individuals fall into two categories: merit pay and variable pay. Variable-pay programs may include bonuses, spot awards, and individual incentives. Both merit- and variable-pay programs can be used to reward individuals for demonstrating key behaviors or achieving certain goals or results; however, they operate differently in terms of how rewards are distributed and their potential effects on motivation and performance.

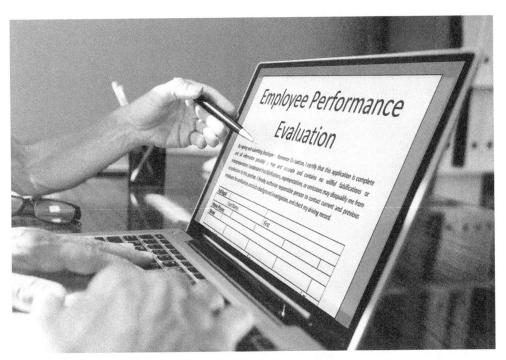

Merit-pay increases are often contingent upon the ratings an employee receives during a performance evaluation.

©iStockphoto.com/AndreyPopov

Merit Pay

Pay distributed to employees based on the ratings or feedback they receive on a performance evaluation measure is known as merit pay. By being integrated into an employee's base pay, merit pay results in the pay increase carrying forward to later pay periods. According to a Payscale survey, in 2021, nearly 80% of organizations reported using performance as a factor when determining increases in base pay, where other potential factors included external equity, internal equity, having in-demand skills, and inflation.[14] In many organizations, higher performance ratings result in larger merit-pay increases. For example, imagine an organization that uses a 4-point performance evaluation measure, where a rating of 4 indicates exceptional performance. Under a merit-pay program, an employee who receives a 4 rating would receive a larger pay increase than an employee who receives a 3 rating. In other cases, a fixed merit-pay increase is given for making a certain level of performance. For example, the organization might distribute the same merit-pay increase to anyone who receives a rating of 3 or 4.

Research shows that, in general, employees who receive merit-pay increases tend to show higher performance than those who do not receive merit-pay increases.[15] For example, results from a meta-analysis show that teachers in the United States who receive merit-pay increases tend to have students who achieve higher test scores when student test scores are used as an indicator of teacher performance.[16]

From the employer's perspective, merit-pay programs require thoughtful budgeting and management, because under these programs, pay increases are integrated into individuals' base pay. To create an effective merit-pay program, organizations should base pay-increase decisions on a well-designed performance evaluation measure and fair, unbiased performance ratings by supervisors. A merit-pay program depends upon close alignment between subjective performance evaluations and rewards, that is, an integration between performance management and reward systems.

SPOTLIGHT ON ETHICS: MERIT PAY FOR TEACHERS

Merit pay for teachers is a controversial issue, particularly in the United States. Supporters contend that merit pay motivates teachers to do a better job, thus leading to better outcomes for students in terms of academic achievement and eventual employment success. Critics, on the other hand, say the ways in which teacher performance is evaluated can lack transparency and may be beyond teachers' direct control.

Selecting key performance indicators for teachers can be particularly challenging. This is because teachers can be evaluated based on their own behavior or on the behavior of their students, and student behavior can be influenced by many factors other than the teachers' classroom performance. That is, teachers may be able to influence students' behavior, including their test scores, but students also arrive in a classroom with their own personal histories and unique circumstances that may affect how receptive and prepared to learn they are. Some critics argue that it can be unethical to base a substantial portion of teachers' take-home pay on their students' performance, particularly if performance is defined based on their students' success on standardized tests.

In the United States, the push for pay-for-performance programs for teachers gained traction in the 1980s and early 1990s. At about that time, a statistician named William Sanders began advising Tennessee lawmakers on a method for evaluating teachers based on the extent to which they improved their students' standardized test scores, referred to as the *value-added approach*. The value-added approach takes into account the historical trends in students' test scores, such as whether they improved, stayed the same, or declined, and determines whether a teacher improved their students' test scores more than would be expected given that history.

Critics argue that the value-added approach is unfair, as there are a number of factors outside of teachers' direct control that can affect their value-added scores. Moreover, some teachers teach subjects that do not have an associated standardized test, which can make it difficult to evaluate them in the same manner as their peers. Analytical software companies like SAS Institute have developed algorithms to calculate the value-added scores of teachers. Some teachers and administrators have complained that these algorithms are difficult for nonstatisticians to understand. Also, due to the often proprietary nature of the algorithms, there can be a lack of transparency when it comes to communicating how the value-added scores are computed. Supporters of the value-added approach point to evidence that students of high value-added teachers are more likely to attend college and to go on to earn higher salaries than other students.

Research has shown that incentivizing teachers with merit pay does not always lead to higher teacher motivation or better student outcomes. In fact, the empirical findings are mixed. Some evidence indicates that merit pay leads to higher student scores in math, science, and reading, whereas other evidence suggests that merit pay may have some effect on students' math scores but not on reading scores and that teachers do not find merit-pay programs to be motivating. As a way forward, some education reform advocates argue that rewarding teacher performance should not necessarily be thrown out; rather, the structure and organization of the schools themselves should also be taken into consideration when recognizing teacher performance.[17]

Questions

1. Given the risk that low-performing teachers may do a poor job of preparing their students for eventual career success, do you think it is ethical to pay teachers without taking into account their performance? Why or why not?
2. Do you think it is ethical to base teacher pay on key performance indicators that may be, to some extent, beyond teacher control? Why or why not? Give some examples to support your opinion.

Bonuses

Unlike merit pay, **bonuses** are a form of variable pay, which means they are not part of an individual's base pay. Instead, bonuses are given as a one-time payout in recognition of performance after the fact; they may be attached to a performance rating or to a completed goal. Bonuses can be given in recognition of individual performance, but they can also be given in recognition of team, unit, facility, or organizational performance. Because bonuses are not part of employees' base pay, they can be less expensive for the employer than distributing pay in the form of merit pay.[18] More and more organizations have begun to use variable-pay programs, such as bonuses, spot awards, and individual incentives. In 2022, 79% of organizations reported having some type of variable-pay programs, which was a 9% increase compared to 2021.[19] Of those organizations with variable-pay programs in 2021, about two thirds used some type of individual performance bonus program.

Spot Awards

Another type of after-the-fact recognition is **spot awards**, which are often reserved for exceptional levels of performance on a project or for exceptionally high overall job performance. As of 2022, nearly half of organizations surveyed by Payscale reported using spot awards and other similar programs to recognize employees.[20] Organizations vary with respect to the level of formality they apply to spot awards. Some organizations, such as the University of California, Berkeley, develop formal policies and procedures that describe the criteria for earning spot awards, eligibility guidelines, timing, and the amount of awards.[21] To support decision making around spot awards, companies like SAP SuccessFactors offer information system and technology solutions designed to facilitate the process of establishing guidelines and identifying potential spot award candidates (see Figure 12.4).[22]

FIGURE 12.4 ■ SAP SuccessFactors Spot Award Solution

Information system solutions, like this one created by SAP SuccessFactors, facilitate the process of determining and awarding various forms of variable pay such as spot awards.

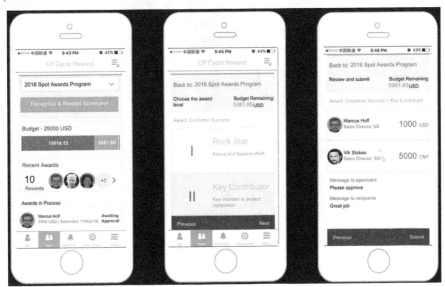

Individual Incentives

As a form of variable pay, **individual incentives** refer to the distribution of pay when an employee achieves a certain predetermined and objective level of performance. In general, they are nondiscretionary, which means managers do not have much say when it comes to who receives individual incentives and the amount of the rewards. Research has shown that individual incentive programs generally have a positive effect on performance outcomes.[23] Examples of individual incentives include piecework and standard-hour plans.

Piecework Plans In a piecework plan, employees are compensated based on their respective production levels. We can distinguish between two types of piecework plans: straight piecework plans and differential piecework plans. In a straight piecework plan, employee variable pay is based on the units they produce in a given time period, such that there is a direct correspondence between the amount of pay distributed and the number of units produced. For example, imagine that Fatimah works for a medical device company, and her main task is to assemble feeding tubes that will ultimately be used for patient care. A portion of her total compensation is variable and is distributed in accordance with a straight piecework plan. According to the plan, Fatimah earns \$0.25 for every feeding tube she assembles within a pay period. Thus, if she assembles 2,000 feeding tubes in a pay period, she will receive \$500 in variable pay (2,000 × \$0.25 = \$500).

In a differential piecework plan, employees are paid one rate for units produced below a particular standard in a given time period, and they are paid a higher rate for units produced above that standard. In some instances, a differential piecework plan may include more than one standard and thus three or more pay rates for units produced. The goal underlying differential piecework plans is to incentivize employees to strive for the highest levels of production. For example, imagine that Fatimah finds a new job at a different medical device company. Instead of a straight piecework plan, her new company distributes a portion of pay in accordance with a differential piecework plan. Under this plan, Fatimah earns \$0.25 for each of the first 1,500 feeding tubes she assembles within a pay period and \$0.30 for every additional feeding tube she assembles beyond 1,500. Thus, if Fatimah assembles 2,000 feeding tubes in a pay period at her new company, she will earn \$525 in variable pay (1,500 × \$0.25 + 500 × \$0.30 = \$525).

Piecework plans are common in industries where production levels are easily quantified and tracked, such as in manufacturing.

©iStockphoto.com/alvarez

Standard-Hour Plans In a standard-hour plan, employee pay is based on the completion of a particular task within a predetermined time period. These plans are often based on established hourly rates and expected completion times. Standard-hour plans are commonly used in service mechanic jobs. For instance, imagine that a bicycle shop determines that the services provided by bicycle mechanics are worth \$30 per hour. Different tasks require different amounts of time, such that fixing a flat tire might take the average mechanic 10 minutes, whereas building a wheel might take the average mechanic 1.5 hours. Based on historical data, the bicycle shop concludes that the average mechanic should be able to complete a bicycle overhaul (i.e., disassembling, cleaning, adjusting, and lubricating components) in 2 hours. Given the bicycle mechanics' hourly worth of \$30, each mechanic will earn \$60 for completing a bicycle overhaul ($30 × 2 hours = $60), regardless of whether the task takes the mechanic 1.5 hours or 2.5 hours. If the task is completed in 1.5 hours, the mechanic earns $60 in less time than expected, which frees up additional time to get started on other tasks and thus the potential to earn more money. Ambitious mechanics might find a standard-hour plan to be highly motivating; however, for these plans to work, it is important that the estimated completion times for common tasks be fair and reasonable. After all, if mechanics consistently take longer than the estimated task completion times, then they may perceive lost income potential, especially when making comparisons with other bicycle shops that offer a set hourly wage and no standard-hour plan.

Standard-hour plans are common for the job of a mechanic.

©iStockphoto.com/dragana991

Sales Commissions

Those who have worked in sales are likely familiar with sales commissions, which reward the sale of a product or service as opposed to the production of a product or provision of a service. Workers who sell products and services (such as cars, real estate, stocks, consumer packaged goods, medical devices, software, telecommunications, and insurance) are commonly paid in commissions or a combination of base pay plus commissions. Typically, the amount of a sales commission is based on the percentage of the revenue or profit associated with each sale, overall sales volume, or customer satisfaction.

How sales performance is quantified can have important consequences for the behaviors that a program incentivizes. For example, basing sales commissions entirely on sales volume or on the percentage of revenue or profit generated may motivate aggressive selling behavior, such that salespersons focus their attention and effort predominantly on making more sales in the short term, perhaps at the expense of cultivating quality relationships with customers and helping out with other aspects of the sales process, like processing customer returns. To motivate salespersons to build viable, long-term relationships with customers and to support other aspects of the sales process, an organization might also base sales commissions partly on customer satisfaction metrics. Establishing the right mix of metrics on which a sales commission program is based can help align the behavior of salespersons with the strategic goals of the organization.[24]

Perhaps unsurprisingly, research suggests that having upper limits on the total amount of commission salespersons can earn results in lower motivation and sales performance compared to when there are no such limits.[25] Further, it is important to note that the proportion of total compensation represented by a sales commission program should vary in accordance with organizational strategy.

Specifically, organizations that use a sales commissions program should consider how much salespersons' pay will be contingent upon sales performance versus base pay or other forms of variable pay.

Group Pay-for-Performance Programs

Many organizations distribute rewards for group performance. In fact, some argue that deploying pay-for-performance programs only at the individual level may discourage collaboration and effective teamwork.[26] The strategic deployment of group pay-for-performance programs—generically called *success-sharing* plans—can improve group performance under certain circumstances, and group performance can be used to motivate a team, unit, facility, or entire organization.[27]

Team Rewards

As with individual programs, an organization can use financial rewards to motivate teams to achieve goals and reach specified performance levels. For instance, an organization might provide a year-end bonus for the manufacturing team that reduces waste the most during the manufacturing process. Payscale reported that 20% of organizations surveyed in 2021 used some type of team reward.[28]

Meta-analytic evidence has shown that, indeed, team rewards can lead to higher performance, particularly when the team task is more complex.[29] That is, more complex and complicated tasks may require greater collaboration and integration among team members, and thus team pay-for-performance programs provide additional motivation to work together in order to attain a shared goal.

However, care must be taken to ensure team rewards align with any individual rewards that might already be in place. Without thoughtful alignment, employees' attention might be pulled in competing—or even conflicting—directions. Finally, the use of team rewards can have implications for unethical behavior. For example, when a team reward is at stake, team members have been found to be less likely to report another member of the team who is behaving unethically.[30]

Examples of team pay-for-performance programs exist across a wide variety of industries. In the professional sports industry, for example, organizations often reward teams for winning games, tournaments, series, or championships. In 2022, Major League Baseball rewarded each player on the Houston Astros team $516,347 for winning the World Series, and each player on the Philadelphia Phillies, which was the runner-up team, received $296,255. This team reward is funded each year by the playoff gate receipts, and in 2022, this pool of money reached a record $107.5 million.[31] Thus, beyond what individuals could receive in terms of their guaranteed base salary, Major League Baseball players also had opportunities to earn variable pay if their team reached and performed well in the playoffs. Interestingly, in other nonsports work contexts, some evidence has suggested that evenly distributing rewards to team members based on the team's overall performance may result in slower speeds but higher accuracy when it comes to the team's work, as compared to distributing rewards to team members based on their individual performance.[32]

As another example, in 2004, Google introduced its Founders' Awards, given to teams that made outstanding accomplishments on a project.[33] In the inaugural year, $12 million in stock was given to two project teams in recognition of their accomplishments. One of the award-winning teams created a process whereby Google users would be presented with advertisements that would be most relevant to them—an online experience that is ubiquitous today but was groundbreaking at the time. This team award served as a vehicle to motivate teams to continue pursuing excellence and maximize their contributions to the company. In addition to the financial reward, winning teams received accolades and recognition from their company and peers.

Gainsharing

Gainsharing is a type of group pay-for-performance program that rewards a group of employees—often a unit or facility—for achieving certain milestones. More than half of organizations use gainsharing as a way to reward groups of employees.[34] As the name implies, individual employees share in the success of the overall *gains* of their group, such as those related to productivity, quality, and customer service. Further, gainsharing programs can be implemented to improve individual employee involvement and participation in their group.[35] Research has shown that gainsharing can lead to higher productivity,[36] particularly when employees envision how their own actions contribute to the group's gains.

As an example, between 2006 and 2009, the Beth Israel Medical Center in New York City implemented a gainsharing program aimed at decreasing costs at the hospital level.[37] In total, 184 physicians participated in the gainsharing program, and through their involvement and participation, the 1,000-bed teaching hospital reduced costs by $25.1 million, while measures of patient care quality remained unchanged. Individual physicians shared in the hospital gains by receiving a portion of cost savings that was relative to their individual performance. In doing so, Beth Israel Medical Center managed to recognize individual contributions to hospital-level gains, thereby providing physicians with a clearer indication of how much they uniquely contributed to the hospital's success.

Although gainsharing programs are generally beneficial for employee performance, the effects may not be as consistent or as large as those of individual pay-for-performance programs.[38] Namely, group dynamics come into play, such that individuals may have a difficult time understanding the extent to which they are contributing to the group's success. In addition, some individuals might engage in social loafing, yet if their group still achieves the goal, these individuals will still receive the same reward as those who worked harder and contributed more to the group's success.

When designing and implementing gainsharing programs, legal and ethical considerations should be front and center in the decision-making process, just as in any other HR program. That is, organizations should ensure that gainsharing programs are implemented fairly and in accordance with relevant policies and procedures, and additional steps should be taken to explain gainsharing policies and procedures clearly.

Profit Sharing

As the name implies, **profit sharing** refers to pay-for-performance programs in which employees share in their organization's profits (e.g., return on assets). Profit-sharing rewards may be distributed as cash or placed in a retirement fund. Under profit-sharing programs, the organization shares profits with its employees when targets are met or exceeded. In many cases, organizations use a formula for determining how much each individual employee receives as part of the profit sharing; however, in other cases, the amount received by each employee may be at management's discretion.[39] In general, evidence suggests that organizations with profit-sharing programs tend to have higher productivity than comparable organizations that do not have such programs, and employees often have favorable attitudes toward these programs.[40] Further, a study of 912 employees from 45 organizations found that the positive effects of individual pay-for-performance programs on employees' perceptions of instrumentality were even stronger in organizations with an effective profit-sharing program.[41] (Recall from expectancy theory that instrumentality refers to perceptions that performance leads to rewards.) Because profit-sharing programs typically make rewards contingent upon the organization's success, employees may perceive less control over their ability to influence organizational profitability targets. Accordingly, employees may believe that profit-sharing programs carry more risk to their financial well-being than programs rewarding individual or team performance.

Telecommunications company Huawei Technologies uses a profit-sharing program to motivate its employees. In 2022, Huawei paid $9.65 billion in dividends to 131,507 current workers and to former workers who had retired.[42]

©iStockphoto.com/Panama7

SPOTLIGHT ON GLOBAL ISSUES: CULTURAL DIFFERENCES IN PAY-FOR-PERFORMANCE PROGRAMS

Pay-for-performance programs generally lead to beneficial employee and organizational outcomes. However, regarding employee preferences for different programs, research has shown that some differences exist between collectivistic and individualistic cultures, as delineated in the cultural dimensions proposed by researcher Gert Hofstede. In individualistic cultures (e.g., United States, United Kingdom), individuals tend to emphasize their own unique identity and focus more on their own outcomes. In comparison, employees in collectivistic cultures (e.g., China, Ecuador) tend to respond more favorably to team incentive programs and to perceive that they are procedurally fair. Further, those in collectivistic cultures are more likely to believe that their team can meet the team performance goals and, as a result, that their team will earn the reward. That is, individuals in collectivistic cultures often better understand how their individual contributions add to the team's collective performance and thus may be more motivated by team incentives when compared to those living in individualistic cultures. As an additional difference, employees in individualistic cultures tend to prefer performance-based individual incentives, whereas employees in collectivistic cultures tend to prefer rewards that are distributed equally to all members.

As a result, multinational corporations must consider how their pay-for-performance programs are designed and implemented in relation to the prevailing cultures in the locations where they have employees. This is particularly important if cultural differences in collectivism and individualism exist. They need to ask themselves what types of pay-for-performance programs are most effective in the cultures they operate within.[43]

Stock Options

Stock options are a type of group pay-for-performance program that makes employees partial owners of the organization. Such programs allow employees to purchase a certain number of stock shares at a fixed price in a given time frame. Stock options are a long-term incentive because an employee may begin exercising these options only after a vesting period. (A vesting period is the amount of time an employee must work for an employer before being able to own and exercise stock options.) Exercising stock options means that employees may sell their stock options at a price that is higher than the fixed price when they purchased the stocks originally, resulting in a financial gain. Some research has shown that organizations tend to have higher returns on assets when they have more managers who are eligible for stock options.[44]

However, if the company stock shares fail to exceed the original fixed price at which they were purchased, then the employee gains nothing. Thus, employees may perceive stock option programs as risky, and organizations may find it difficult to attract and retain high-performing employees if stock prices follow a downward trend. As a point of caution, corporate scandals and other outside forces that devalue shares may undermine employees' faith in stock option programs, given that employees often have little influence over such matters. For example, in 2022, Tesla's stock fell by more than 12% the day after it was announced that Tesla CEO Elon Musk had reached an agreement to buy Twitter.[45]

Employee Stock Ownership Plans

Like stock options, employee stock ownership plans (ESOPs) reward employees when company stock shares increase in value and can only be used after a vesting period. ESOPs are also a type of defined-contribution retirement plan. Under these plans, the organization provides employees with stock shares and places these shares in an account. Employees never actually have possession of the shares while employed at the organization; rather, the organization distributes the stock shares when an employee retires, dies, becomes disabled, or is fired by the organization. Some research has shown that ESOPs improve organizational performance, but the significant, positive effects of ESOPs on organizational performance tend to be relatively small.[46] Further, it is questionable how much ESOPs influence employees' motivation, as financial gains are often given out years in the future. ESOPs position employees as owners of their company, which may lead employees to feel more invested in their company and more motivated to participate in organizational decisions, especially when they are dissatisfied with the state of their company.[47] Some argue that the interests of the employees and company owners are more likely to align under ESOPs because employees begin to take on the added perspective of being company owners.

Publix Super Markets is a retail grocery and manufacturing company that uses an employee stock ownership plan (ESOP), which makes its employees part owners of the company. In 2022, the company ranked number 92 on Fortune 100 Best Companies to Work For.[48]

©iStockphoto.com/JHVEPhoto

CHALLENGES AND OPPORTUNITIES IN REWARDING PERFORMANCE

LEARNING OBJECTIVE
12.5 Assess common challenges and opportunities of pay-for-performance programs.

Like any HR system, developing and implementing pay-for-performance programs can be challenging yet can also provide opportunities for the organization. In particular, when it comes to rewarding performance, the following challenges and opportunities are important to consider: performance measurement, sorting effects, labor costs, and unintended behavioral consequences.

Performance Measurement

Effective pay-for-performance programs require sound performance measurement. Yet this is easier said than done, as performance on a particular job is often multifaceted and nuanced, making it challenging to measure reliably and accurately. Performance can be assessed using a variety of measures, including both subjective performance evaluations and objective performance indicators (e.g., sales volume). The quality of these measures, in terms of their reliability and validity, should not be treated as a foregone conclusion. Regardless of whether a performance measure is subjective or objective in nature, care should be taken to ensure that the measures used in a pay-for-performance program are well designed, relatively free of bias and judgment errors, and transparent and easy to understand. Ultimately, employee perceptions of fairness should be a primary focus when developing and implementing a performance measure, particularly when tied to administrative outcomes like pay increases.

Meta-analytic evidence has shown that subjective performance measures, such as those found in supervisor-rated performance evaluations, often suffer from lower-than-desired interrater reliability, which refers to a lack of consistency between raters in evaluating the same group of employees; however, supervisors tend to more reliably rate employees' overall level of performance as opposed to specific areas of performance (e.g., task vs. contextual performance).[49] In some instances, inconsistency between raters may be attributed to a contaminated or deficient measure. For example, imagine a performance evaluation measure designed for the job of an office manager in which supervisors are instructed to rate job incumbents using a 5-point scale along three behavioral dimensions: fiscal affairs management, staff management, and event management. If the behavioral dimension of event management is not relevant to the job but is still assessed, then the performance evaluation measure will suffer from contamination. If, on the other hand, a behavioral dimension called "office promotion" is relevant to the job but is not assessed, then the performance evaluation measure will suffer from deficiency.

Given concerns regarding contamination and deficiency, subjective performance evaluation measures should be designed or selected based on an up-to-date, rigorous job analysis, and supervisors should be trained on how to rate employees using the measures. Moreover, when designing or selecting objective measures of performance, efforts should be made to use only those measures that are relevant to how performance is conceptualized for the job in question so as to avoid contamination and deficiency.

SPOTLIGHT ON DATA AND ANALYTICS: USING DATA TO EVALUATE PAY-FOR-PERFORMANCE PROGRAMS

Some companies assume that pay-for-performance programs work no matter what. That is, if you offer employees a monetary incentive, employees will improve their performance. In actuality, pay-for-performance programs are susceptible to bias and decision-making errors when it comes to determining performance levels of employees. Performance indicators, metrics, and measures are subject to unreliability and inaccuracy such that employees' true levels of performance may not be adequately captured. This can become problematic in merit-based pay-for-performance programs in which pay increases are contingent upon performance evaluations. The presence of bias (e.g., favoritism) and decision errors (e.g., omission of key performance episodes when completing rating) during performance evaluations can result in strong performers who fail to receive a reward and weak performers who receive a reward.

Fortunately, companies can use data analytics to gain insights into the quality of their pay-for-performance programs. First and foremost, a correlation can be calculated between performance evaluation scores and the amount of pay received. If pay is supposed to be based entirely on performance, then one would expect a strong correlation between performance and pay. And if a small or negligible-sized correlation is found, then it likely indicates that pay decisions are being made based on factors other than performance. Should this be the case, companies can analyze whether protected group characteristics such as age, race, and gender, as well as other factors like tenure, leave history, or education, are associated with differences in performance and pay. Significant associations between these other characteristics and pay or performance might point to problems in the measurement of performance or in the distribution of pay.

Companies with pay-for-performance programs often have (or should have) data at their disposal to diagnose the extent to which the program actually bases pay on performance, as well as potential sources of bias and decision errors.

Bias, office politics, and other sources of error can also affect the quality of performance measures on which organizations base their pay-for-performance programs.[50] Yahoo Inc. found this out firsthand when a former employee sued the company for allegedly distorting and manipulating the performance evaluation rating system.[51] The lawsuit contended that Yahoo managers were required to sort employees into one of five different performance levels such that only a certain percentage of employees were allowed to be categorized into each level, resulting in some employees who were sorted into different performance levels even though they demonstrated the same or similar performance. The lawsuit alleges that Yahoo's system lacked transparency and relied on higher-level managers, who often had little contact with the employees in question, to provide input into the performance rankings. The allegations in this lawsuit highlight the importance of using performance measures that employees perceive as fair and are able to understand, particularly when such performance measures are used for administrative purposes like determining pay, promotions, or termination.

SPOTLIGHT ON LEGAL ISSUES: PAY TRANSPARENCY, PAY DISCRIMINATION, AND PAY-FOR-PERFORMANCE PROGRAMS

In recent years, pay transparency has been gaining momentum in the United States. So what exactly is pay transparency? If you recall from Chapter 11, pay transparency refers to the extent to which an organization communicates pay information and the extent to which employees are permitted to discuss pay with each other; the term is sometimes called pay openness. Those in support of greater pay transparency argue that more transparent pay structures and practices can increase fairness and reduce discriminatory pay-related practices, with the goal of reducing pay gaps between sex, racial, and other project groups.

As we have seen in Chapter 4, at the federal level, several pieces of landmark legislation prohibit discriminatory pay practices, including the Equal Pay Act of 1963 and Title VII of the Civil Rights Act of 1964. The Equal Pay Act stipulates that employers may not use sex as the basis for compensating employees differently, provided that employees of different sexes perform substantially similar duties. In other words, the legislation requires employees of different sexes receive equal pay for equal work. Employers that fail to abide by this law may face sex discrimination lawsuits. Similarly, Title VII of the Civil Rights Act protects employees from sex-based pay-related employment discrimination, but the act is also more expansive, as it projects employees from employment discrimination based on other protected characteristics like race, color, religion, and national origin. In the context of these acts, the Equal Employment Opportunity Commission (EEOC) interprets pay broadly, meaning that pay includes base pay, variable pay, and benefits. Thus, according to the EEOC, these acts also make it illegal for employers to discriminate against employees in terms of all forms of total compensation, which includes pay-for-performance programs like bonuses and profit sharing.

With the aim of increasing fairness and reducing pay discrimination, some states and cities have begun to introduce pay transparency laws, thereby mandating that pay information be made publicly available. For example, New York City passed a pay transparency law, as part of the New York City Human Rights Law, which went into effect on November 1, 2022. The law specifically requires employers with four or more employees or one or more domestic workers to include pay information in advertisements for all job, promotion, or promotion opportunities. Specifically, employers must include both the minimum and the maximum base salary or wage when posting advertisements. Notably, the law does not require employers to provide information about other forms of compensation, such as pay earned from pay-for-performance programs or the value of benefits offerings. On January 1, 2023, California enacted a pay transparency law that likewise requires only base salary or wage information to be shared in advertisements.

Although these new state and city laws take steps toward enhancing pay transparency and potentially reducing discriminatory pay structures and practices, they do not require that employers provide a complete view of compensation practices. By not requiring transparency related to pay-for-performance programs, specifically, a large proportion of pay information may be excluded from advertisements for certain jobs. For example, in sectors like asset management and private equity, some estimate that up to half of total compensation may be tied to bonuses. In such sectors, bonuses may be a major source of pay discrimination, especially when those bonuses are based on biased performance evaluation measures or metrics. Thus, requiring transparency for only base pay may limit the impact of such legislation on reducing discriminatory pay practices.[52]

Incentive and Sorting Effects

Thus far the chapter has focused primarily on the incentive effects of pay-for-performance programs. Incentive effects refer to the extent to which pay-for-performance programs motivate employees' on-the-job behavior and pursuit of goals. However, pay-for-performance programs may also have other effects on employee and nonemployee behavior. Empirical evidence has shown that individuals tend to gravitate to jobs with reward systems that fit their disposition, goals, and performance capabilities, and the associated processes of attraction, selection, and attrition are referred to collectively as sort- ing effects.[53] That is, individuals who view themselves as high performers or who are (or have been) high performers often prefer pay-for-performance programs, as they stand to gain when participat- ing in such programs.[54] In addition, to some extent, individuals who have a dispositional aversion to risk taking often avoid pay-for-performance programs and are less motivated by pay-for-performance incentives; in contrast, those who have a higher need for achievement and self-efficacy find pay-for- performance programs to be more attractive.[55]

Sorting can be understood by applying the attraction–selection–attrition (ASA) model, which proposes that organizational employees become more homogenous over time through the processes of attraction, selection, and attrition, resulting in a more uniform organizational culture (see Figure 12.5).[56] The process of attraction occurs when, through recruiting materials, image advertising, and word of mouth, potential employees learn the characteristics of an organization (e.g., values, required KSAOs) and ultimately base their attraction to the organization on their own perceived fit to the orga- nization. Meta-analytic evidence has shown that individuals who perceive a stronger fit between them- selves and an organization form a stronger sense of attraction to the organization, making it more likely that they will apply for a vacant position.[57] As such, individuals who believe they possess the required KSAOs and who value pay-for-performance programs (and believe they stand to benefit from them) will be more attracted to organizations with such programs.

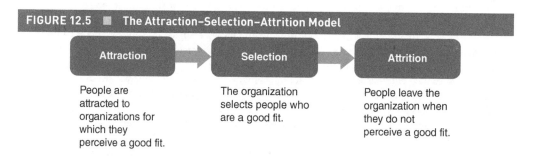

FIGURE 12.5 ■ The Attraction–Selection–Attrition Model

Attraction	Selection	Attrition
People are attracted to organizations for which they perceive a good fit.	The organization selects people who are a good fit.	People leave the organization when they do not perceive a good fit.

The attraction–selection–attrition model can be used to understand sorting effects. For exam- ple, people who prefer pay-for-performance programs and who are likely to reap the benefits of such programs prefer organizations with pay-for-performance programs. Thus, they are more likely to be attracted to an organization with a pay-for-performance program, more likely to be selected by an organization with a pay-for-performance program, and more likely to leave an organization that lacks a pay-for-performance program.

The process of selection occurs when an organization chooses those applicants with the KSAOs and values that are most similar to the KSAOs and values already possessed by current employees. An organization with a pay-for-performance program will be more likely to select applicants who have the required KSAOs and who value pay-for-performance programs.

The process of attrition occurs when, after some length of time, those employees who do not fit well into the organization ultimately leave the organization. This results in a more homogenous group of employees within the organization. With respect to pay-for-performance programs, individuals who possess KSAOs that enable high performance in an organization and whose values align with pay-for- performance programs will be more likely to stay in organizations with such programs.

Labor Costs

Labor costs should be monitored closely and forecasted accurately. In the United States, labor costs asso- ciated with pay-for-performance programs and other compensation programs account for 69% of an organization's total labor costs, and benefits programs account for the remaining 31% of labor costs.[58] Despite potential beneficial effects on employee motivation and performance, pay-for-performance programs make it hard to predict future labor costs, especially when the number of employees earning such rewards varies over time (see Figure 12.6). Because employees' performance levels fluctuate across time and can be influenced by forces in the external environment (e.g., ups and downs in the economy), the number of employees reaping rewards from pay-for-performance programs inevitably varies as well.

FIGURE 12.6 ■ Balancing Labor Costs When Pay-for-Performance Rewards Fluctuate

Managing labor costs within an organization can be challenging, especially when the number of employees earning pay-for-performance rewards fluctuates.

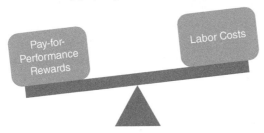

To plan for the anticipated labor costs associated with pay-for-performance programs, organizations can use statistical modeling and expert judgment. First, statistical modeling allows an organization to use prior evidence (e.g., performance, pay, and other factors potentially influencing performance and pay) to project how much money should be set aside to cover future labor costs. As a limitation, statistical modeling assumes that whatever happened in the past will continue to happen in a similar manner in the future. As such, in situations in which a historically rare or unexpected occurrence happens, statistical models may not provide accurate labor cost projections. Another limitation is that a statistical model contains uncertainty, making it unlikely to predict a future event perfectly. Statistical modeling is often a luxury available only to bigger companies with bigger workforces; smaller companies may not have enough employees to reliably and accurately estimate statistical models.

Second, expert judgment allows an organization to draw upon the subject-matter expertise of individuals who understand the industry, the employees, and the economic environment within which the organization operates. Expert judgment can augment the insights gleaned from statistical models, particularly in instances in which unexpected or unusual events occur that may have an impact on labor costs. For instance, imagine that an unexpected economic recession occurs. If an organization considers laying off employees, it should ask: What effect will layoffs have on remaining employees' performance? To answer a question like that, individuals can offer expert judgment based on their knowledge of pay-for-performance programs and human behavior to anticipate the extent to which a layoff will affect employee performance and ultimately the potential labor costs. Yet expert judgment has its limitations, as it is subject to any number of cognitive biases and judgment and decision-making errors. Thus, expert judgment is by no means a panacea when it comes to projecting future labor costs associated with a pay-for-performance program. Nonetheless, when used in tandem, statistical modeling and expert judgment can lead to more accurate labor cost forecasts.

Unintended Behavioral Consequences

Pay-for-performance programs can lead to unintended behavioral consequences, particularly when management fails to monitor employee behavior. The purpose of pay-for-performance programs is to motivate employees to enact behaviors to help realize the organization's strategic objectives. When unmonitored by management or poorly thought out, pay-for-performance programs may lead to such problems as employees demonstrating fewer organizational citizenship behaviors, more unethical behaviors, and, in the context of group pay-for-performance programs, less effort and cooperation.

Organizational Citizenship Behaviors

Some research has shown that pay-for-performance programs may motivate employees to enact core task behaviors and demotivate them to enact organizational citizenship behaviors, the latter of which include discretionary helping behaviors.[59] However, when performance is measured objectively using, for example, results-based metrics like sales volume, pay-for-performance programs may, at times, do such an effective job of focusing employees' attention on reaching goals related to the objective results-based metrics that some may ignore or forget to engage in extra-role, helping behaviors. In contrast, when performance is measured subjectively, such as by using supervisor-rated performance appraisals, pay-for-performance programs may lead employees to enact *more* helping behaviors.[60]

When employees' values are aligned with the values of the organization, the demotivating effect of pay-for-performance programs on organizational citizenship behaviors seems to disappear.[61] Thus, it is important to select and retain individuals who fit the organization's culture and values, particularly when pay-for-performance programs are used. Further, to encourage organizational citizenship behaviors, additional rewards can be made contingent upon enactment of organizational citizenship behaviors, and management can take an active role in encouraging employees to remember to help one another and the organization.

Unethical Behaviors

Another potential unintended consequence of pay-for-performance programs is unethical behavior. In general, when earning a reward is contingent on achievement of a certain level of performance, individuals may be more likely to enact behaviors that help them reach that level of performance, even if some (or all) of those behaviors are unethical (or just plain risky or reckless, as we learned in the opening case about Wall Street investment bankers and traders). Not surprisingly, research has shown that rewarding individuals for engaging in unethical behavior leads to even more unethical behavior.[62] However, pay-for-performance programs can unintentionally encourage unethical behavior.

Unethical behavior can also be costly for organizations. For example, as discussed in Chapter 9, in 2020 Wells Fargo paid $3.7 billion to settle claims that employees had opened millions of unauthorized or fake customer accounts. Four years earlier, the financial services company made headlines after it was revealed that employees opened and closed unauthorized bank accounts for customers. This is not only unethical and discourteous but also illegal. Employees engaged in this unethical behavior because they received financial incentives based on meeting their sales goals, which were contingent on how many customer accounts they opened. Thus, from a reinforcement theory perspective, the organization provided rewards in the form of additional pay when employees opened new accounts, thereby reinforcing the act of opening accounts. Perceiving the instrumentality of opening accounts and receiving rewards, some employees took advantage of the pay-for-performance program by opening accounts for customers without their knowledge or consent. Wells Fargo leadership was somewhat sluggish in its attempts to investigate the unethical behavior and allowed it to remain unchecked for some time. The company ultimately terminated thousands of employees who engaged in these unethical and illegal behaviors.[63]

Effort and Cooperation

Rewards targeted at team or group performance may not necessarily lead to more effort and cooperative behaviors.[64] Group pay-for-performance programs are often introduced to encourage collectives of employees to work more effectively and efficiently; the underlying logic is that individuals working together experience certain synergies that allow them to tackle large and complicated tasks. As this chapter describes, research has shown that group pay-for-performance programs (e.g., gainsharing, profit sharing) can lead to higher group performance; however, the degree to which the pay-for-performance program inspires group performance may depend upon the group's history, how the program is structured, and the degree to which the program is monitored.[65] Further, just because a reward is linked to group performance, groups will not necessarily cooperate well with other groups; rather, group rewards may inadvertently lead to competition between different groups, which may result in diminished information sharing between groups.[66]

When groups become too large or are left unmonitored, some members may engage in social loafing and free riding, wherein they apply less effort and thus fail to contribute their fair share.[67] In addition, in larger groups, individuals often find it challenging to understand how their own efforts contribute to the group's overall performance.[68] To reduce some of these unintended consequences, individual rewards can be used in combination with group rewards—as long as they are aligned—to encourage the engagement of *all* group members. Further, to avoid intergroup competition, organizations might consider adding a unit-, facility-, or organization-level pay-for-performance program (e.g., gainsharing, profit sharing) if one does not already exist. The addition of such a program may provide incentive for groups to work together (or at least avoid competing with one another) for the greater good of the organization.

CHAPTER SUMMARY

Unlike traditional-pay programs, pay-for-performance programs reward performance directly. That is, in pay-for-performance programs, if an employee meets performance standards or goals, the employee receives a reward. Pay is a classic example of an extrinsic motivator, as it represents an external environmental force that can affect an employee's effort. We can apply different theories, such as reinforcement theory, expectancy theory, and goal-setting theory, to understand and explain when and why different pay and pay-for-performance programs enhance motivation and performance. A variety of pay-for-performance programs exist; some reward individual performance, whereas others reward group performance. Individual pay-for-performance programs include merit pay, bonuses, spot awards, individual incentives, and sales commissions. Group pay-for-performance programs include team incentives, gainsharing, profit sharing, stock options, and employee stock ownership plans. Organizations face several challenges and opportunities when designing and implementing pay-for-performance programs. For instance, by deploying well-designed performance measures, organizations can maximize the effectiveness of their pay-for-performance programs, as well as ensure fairness and reduce bias. Further, forecasting labor costs for pay-for-performance programs can be challenging because many complex factors influence those costs. Finally, pay-for-performance programs can demotivate employees to exhibit helping behaviors and motivate them to exhibit negative behaviors, and organizations need to be vigilant against these types of unintended consequences.

KEY TERMS

Bonuses	Motivation
Differential piecework plan	Pay-for-performance programs
Employee stock ownership plan (ESOP)	Piecework plan
Expectancy	Profit sharing
Expectancy theory	Reinforcement theory
Extrinsic motivation	Sales commissions
Gainsharing	Sorting effects
Goal-setting theory	Spot awards
Incentive effects	Standard-hour plan
Individual incentives	Stock options
Instrumentality	Straight piecework plan
Intrinsic motivation	Traditional-pay programs
Merit pay	Valence

HR REASONING AND DECISION-MAKING EXERCISES

Mini-Case Analysis Exercise: Pay for Performance and Goal Setting

Several years ago, Xeon Manufacturing introduced a new pay-for-performance program. The program was designed to provide manufacturing workers with financial rewards for meeting individual goals related to waste reduction and units produced. Today, upper management is concerned that the pay-for-performance program has failed to motivate its manufacturing workers, as they have not observed discernible improvements in waste reduction and units produced. Interestingly, the manufacturing workers have communicated that the amount of financial rewards attached to goal completion is appropriate. Thus, the question remains, why aren't the manufacturing goals motivating?

Upper management has asked you to investigate why the pay-for-performance program is not, in fact, improving motivation and performance. You decide to use goal-setting theory (and the SMART goal acronym) to inform your investigation.

1. Based on goal-setting theory, what types of goals tend to lead to greater motivation and greater performance? Why?

2. Using goal-setting theory as a framework, if you were to interview current manufacturing employees about the motivating potential (or lack thereof) of the goals pertaining to waste reduction and units produced, what questions might you ask?

HR Decision Analysis Exercise: Aligning Individual and Team Rewards

For the past decade, your company has encouraged sales teams to work together in a cooperative and cohesive manner. This initiative is closely aligned with one of the company's core values: *"Together, we achieve more."* To motivate sales associates to cooperate with one another in their respective teams, at the end of each fiscal year, team managers evaluate their respective teams by rating them on a number of behavioral dimensions related to cooperation and cohesion. Teams that receive high marks on their evaluations receive year-end bonuses, and this bonus program accounts for 10% of compensation for those working as salespeople; the remaining 90% of compensation is distributed in the form of a base salary. Thus far, the company has found this pay-for-performance system to be quite effective, as team cooperation and cohesion have improved demonstrably.

Lately, your company has lost some of its top sales associates to competitors, and exit interviews revealed that some sales associates believed they were not recognized and rewarded for their unique, individual contributions to the organization—namely, their sales productivity. To address this issue, the company has decided to implement a new pay-for-performance program designed to reward individual sales associates for their sales productivity; specifically, the company plans to implement a sales commission program. This new variable-pay program constitutes 40% of their compensation, and the remaining 60% will be distributed in the form of a base salary (50%) and a team bonus based on manager ratings of team cooperation and cohesion (10%). Ultimately, the organization wants to incentivize team cooperation and cohesion as well as individual sales productivity in an effort to encourage collaboration and individual contributions.

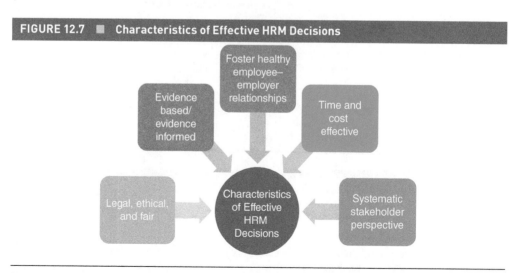

FIGURE 12.7 ■ Characteristics of Effective HRM Decisions

Source: Reprinted from SHRM Competency Model with permission of the Society for Human Resource Management. © SHRM. All rights reserved.

Consider the entire compensation package from a systems perspective. Do you have any concerns regarding the implementation of the new sales commission program? Do you think there will be any unintended consequences? Consider this decision using the following criteria.

Please provide the rationale for your answer to each of the questions below.

Is the compensation package legal, ethical, and fair?

Is it evidence based/evidence informed?

Does it foster healthy employee–employer relationships?

Is it time- and cost-effective?

Does it take a systematic stakeholder perspective?

Considering your analysis, overall, do you think this would be an effective decision? Why or why not?

What, if anything, do you think should be done differently or considered to help make this decision more effective?

HR Decision-Making Exercise: Applying Expectancy Theory to Understand Pay for Performance

Three years ago, a large clothing retailer called La Ropa de Moda developed and implemented a new pay-for-performance program targeted at sales associates. The relatively new program is a sales performance incentive fund (SPIF) that provides a bonus for selling certain items of clothing. La Ropa de Moda learned that one of its competitors used SPIFs to sell old inventory to great effect. Because La Ropa de Moda has been having issues selling clothes from prior seasons, the company decided to implement a similar program. Unfortunately, La Ropa de Moda has found that even when a SPIF is attached to certain items of clothing, much of the old inventory sits on sales floors across the company's many locations, and thus to date, the SPIF program has been largely ineffective when it comes to motivating employees to sell old inventory.

Sales associates' base hourly wage ranges from $17 to $22, and differences in hourly wage are attributable to years of experience in retail, seniority, and merit-based pay increases. SPIFs are attached to specific clothing items from prior seasons and range in value from $1 to $5. In addition to the SPIF program, sales associates receive a 7% commission on each article of clothing they sell. For example, if a sales associate sells a $100 pair of jeans, then the associate will earn a commission of $7. The average cost of an article of clothing in the store is $50, and on a typical 8-hour day, the average salesperson will sell $600 worth of clothing. The average salesperson works 33 hours per week.

On one hand, the base wage and commissions earned by sales associates each pay period are distributed in a biweekly paycheck. On the other hand, the annual SPIFs earned by a single sales associate are paid out in one year-end lump-sum bonus, so SPIFs are not included in the paycheck corresponding to the pay period in which they were earned.

Apply the principles of expectancy theory to understand why the pay-for-performance program at La Ropa de Moda is failing to motivate sales associates to sell old inventory.

1. Identify and discuss the core components and propositions of expectancy theory.

2. Based on the information provided, do you think that low perceived *expectancy* among sales associates explains the lack of motivation to sell old items with SPIFs attached? Why?

3. Discuss whether sales associates' perceptions of *instrumentality* explain the lack of motivation to sell items with SPIFs.

4. Discuss whether sales associates' perceptions of *valence* explain the lack of motivation to sell items with SPIFs.

DATA AND ANALYTICS EXERCISE: EVALUATING COMPENSATION

A reward system typically represents a major cost for an organization. As such, it is important to evaluate the system and its constituent components. One important metric is the *total compensation expense factor*. The metric is calculated to describe how much an organization spends on total compensation (i.e., compensation, benefits) for all employees relative to total operating expenses.

$$\text{Total Compensation Expense Factor} = \frac{\text{Compensation Expenses} + \text{Benefits Expenses}}{\text{Total Operating Expenses}}$$

For example, if the sum of compensation and benefits expenses across all employees for the year is $10.3 million and the total annual operating expenses for the company are $12.9 million, then the total compensation expense factor is .798 ($10.3 million / $12.9 million = .798). An organization can use this metric to benchmark (i.e., compare) its total compensation expenses with those of other organizations. Further, an organization can track this metric over time to identify trends or to budget for total compensation expenses in the future. Moreover, an organization may drill down to pay-for-performance program expenses (or other specific reward expenses) relative to total operating expenses by calculating the *pay-for-performance expense factor*.

$$\text{Pay-for-Performance Expense Factor} = \frac{\text{Pay-for-Performance Expenses}}{\text{Total Operating Expenses}}$$

For example, if the annual expenses associated with pay-for-performance program expenses are $1.2 million, and the total annual operating expenses for the company are $12.9 million, then the pay-for-performance expense factor is .093 ($1.2 million / $12.9 million = .093).

Another important metric is the *total compensation revenue factor*, which can be used to describe how much an organization spends on total compensation for all employees relative to the amount of revenue generated.

$$\text{Total Compensation Revenue Factor} = \frac{\text{Compensation Expenses} + \text{Benefits Expenses}}{\text{Total Revenue}}$$

For example, if the sum of compensation and benefits expenses across all employees for the year is $10.3 million and the total annual revenue for the company is $13.9 million, then the total compensation revenue factor is .741 ($10.3 million / $13.9 million = .741). Like the total compensation expense factor, the total compensation revenue factor can be benchmarked against those of other organizations and can be tracked over time for the purposes of trend identification and financial planning and budgeting. Further, an organization can drill down to pay-for-performance expenses (or other specific reward expenses) relative to total revenue by calculating the *pay-for-performance revenue factor*.

$$\text{Pay-for-Performance Revenue Factor} = \frac{\text{Pay-for-Performance Expenses}}{\text{Total Revenue}}$$

For example, if the annual expenses associated with pay-for-performance programs are $1.2 million, and the total annual revenue for the company is $13.9 million, then the pay-for-performance revenue factor is .086 ($1.2 million / $13.9 million = .086). In this context, the metric is useful for evaluating the extent to which increases in pay-for-performance program expenses are associated with corresponding increases in total revenue generated. For instance, if the pay-for-performance program expenses grew to $1.4 million the following year and total revenue stayed the same, then the metric would increase to .101 ($1.4 million / $13.9 million = .101). The shift from .086 to .101 from one year to the next might signal that the pay-for-performance programs need to be critically evaluated, as employees reaped greater rewards but did not generate more revenue.

Excel Extension: Now You Try!

- On **edge.sagepub.com/bauer2e**, you will find an Excel exercise on evaluating a reward system.

- First, compute the total compensation expense factors and total compensation revenue factors across 3 years.

- Second, compute the pay-for-performance expense factors and pay-for-performance revenue factors across the same 3 years.

- Third, identify and interpret any notable trends.

13 MANAGING BENEFITS

LEARNING OBJECTIVES

After reading and studying this chapter, you should be able to do the following:

13.1   Understand how benefits act as rewards and support organizational strategy.

13.2   Identify the different types of legally required benefits.

13.3   Describe the different types of voluntary benefits.

13.4   Assess the common challenges and opportunities associated with administering benefits programs.

13.5   Assess the common challenges and opportunities associated with communicating benefits programs.

PROVIDING MENTAL HEALTH BENEFITS TO WORKERS

©iStockphoto.com/PeopleImages

Each year, workers around the world experience mental health challenges, and these challenges have important implications for workers, organizations, and society at large. According to results from a 2023 Lyra Health survey of more than 2,500 U.S. workers, 86% experienced one or more mental health challenges during the prior year. In that same survey, 60% of respondents reported their mental health impacted their work, a finding corroborated by a meta-analysis that showed workers who experience poor mental health tend to demonstrate lower job performance. Globally, workers' poor mental health has profound consequences. In fact, the World Health Organization estimates that each year poor mental health (specifically, anxiety and depression) experienced by workers results in 12 billion lost working days and $1 trillion in lost productivity.

Despite the prevalence of mental health challenges and the associated human and financial costs, relatively few workers receive care to address those challenges. For instance, only one third of U.S. workers report they received some form of mental health care sometime during the prior year. Findings like these point to the opportunity and, some may argue, responsibility of employers to connect their workers with benefits aimed at improving their mental health.

Employers can offer a variety of mental health benefits for workers, including access to therapists, psychiatrists, coaches, health-promotion and self-care programs, and paid time off for mental health. Increasingly, employers offer digital mental health support, which can increase accessibility by enabling workers to access programs and resources via their smartphone. Ginger is an example of a digital mental health application that has merged with the meditation and mindfulness application called Headspace. The platform offers mental health services that workers may access via their smartphones. Well-known organizations like Kaiser Permanente, Cigna, Domino's, and Sephora have used Ginger to connect their workers to mental health care.

In recent years, it has become more commonplace for employers to offer paid time off for mental health. Some employers refer to this type of leave as mental health days or self-care days. To emphasize the importance of mental health days, some employers, such as the personal finance company NerdWallet, distinguish mental health and self-care days from other forms of paid time off (PTO) and sick time. NerdWallet's chief people officer Lynee Luque told the *Wall Street Journal*, "Mental health is the workplace crisis of our time" and went on to say, "We don't feel that taking care of mental health is something that should be lumped in with PTO or sick days." In addition to providing workers with unlimited PTO, 8 hours a quarter for volunteer work, and a 5-week sabbatical after working 5 years with the company, NerdWallet provides workers with 4 self-care days each year when they can focus on psychologically detaching from work as a means of improving their overall health. Psychological detachment refers to the process of workers mentally or physically distancing themselves from work outside of working hours. Research has shown that when workers psychologically detach from work, they tend to experience less fatigue and better sleep. Further, psychologically detaching from work helps workers reduce the negative effects of demanding jobs on their work engagement and health.

Offering mental health benefits like digital mental health support and mental health days, however, does not necessarily mean that workers will utilize them. Only about a quarter of employers report feeling satisfied with their workers' level of engagement in mental health benefits; yet, 84% feel it is important to reach a high level of worker engagement in such programs, according to a 2023 survey of 221 U.S. employers by the National Alliance of Healthcare Purchaser Coalitions. Thus, employers should develop a strategy for communicating mental health benefits offerings to workers and encouraging their utilization of such offerings.

Of course, offering benefits is not the only solution to addressing mental health. The World Health Organization recommends that employers support their workers' mental health by implementing organizational interventions intended to improve mental health and by training managers and workers. Regarding interventions, employers can, for example, redesign jobs to make them more engaging, meaningful, or safer and less boring, tedious, or stressful. In doing so, employers can take more of a preventative, as opposed to a reactive, approach to addressing employee mental health by making work and the work environment less stressful. On the other hand, training programs can teach managers how to recognize when workers are experiencing mental health challenges and how to connect them with available benefits and resources. Likewise, training programs can teach employees about available benefits and resources. To those ends, WTW's 2022 Best Practices in Health Care Survey of 455 U.S. employers revealed that 44% already provided manager training for mental health, and an additional 30% intended to begin offering such training over the following 2 years.

The mental health challenges faced by workers can have pronounced negative consequences, but fortunately employers can play an important role in offering a number of solutions, including benefits aimed to address poor mental health and promote thriving at work.[1]

CASE DISCUSSION QUESTIONS

1. What are the individual, organizational, and societal consequences of poor mental health?

2. Employers can offer access to therapists, psychiatrists, coaches, health-promotion and self-care programs, and paid time off for mental health. What are some other employee benefits that employers could offer to improve workers' mental health?

3. Given the positive effects of psychological detachment, how might an employer help workers psychologically detach from work during a designated self-care or mental health day? What can employers do to ensure workers psychologically detach on a regular basis?

4. What steps can an employer take to ensure that workers utilize available mental health benefits?

INTRODUCTION

Benefits are an important component of an organization's broader reward system and are an important part of an employee's total compensation package. In 2022, the U.S. Bureau of Labor Statistics reported that benefits, on average, accounted for 31% of organizations' total compensation costs.[2] While providing certain benefits is required by law, providing other benefits is voluntary. In many companies, HR plays a big role in administering and, sometimes, even selecting which benefits will be offered. In addition, HR professionals often play key roles in communicating what the benefit plan offering(s) entail(s), particularly if the organization will be contributing financially to employees' plans.

BENEFITS AS REWARDS

LEARNING OBJECTIVE

13.1   Understand how benefits act as rewards and support organizational strategy.

Benefits include programs, services, and perquisites (perks) related to health care, retirement, work–life balance, and income protection. In the United States, some benefits are legally required, whereas others are voluntary (see Figure 13.1). Like other rewards, employers may use voluntary benefits as tools to attract, motivate, and retain workers. For instance, when an employer offers benefits that appeal to a person's needs, that person may be more likely to apply to work for that organization and to remain at that organization if hired. Further, some retirement programs, such as profit-sharing and employee stock ownership programs, are contingent upon the company's performance, thereby motivating employees to focus on company goals and objectives. Similarly, paid time off and flexible work arrangements may be offered as incentives to motivate employees to reach performance goals.

It may come as no surprise that organizations can offer voluntary benefits strategically. When properly aligned with strategic objectives, benefits may help an organization achieve strategic objectives related to attracting, motivating, and retaining workers. In fact, employers that leverage benefits strategically to boost recruitment and retention efforts report higher organizational performance and higher-than-average recruitment and retention effectiveness.[3]

LEGALLY REQUIRED BENEFITS

LEARNING OBJECTIVE

13.2   Identify the different types of legally required benefits.

FIGURE 13.1 ■ Legally Required Versus Voluntary Benefits

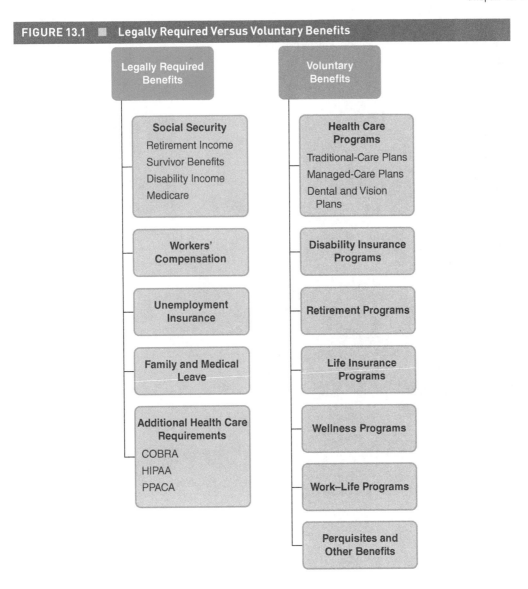

In the United States, some legally required benefits are called social insurance programs, as they address societal problems that many or all individuals face and provide a minimum income floor. Among civilian workers in the United States, legally required benefits account for, on average, 7% of employers' total benefits costs, and payroll tax contributions to such programs are a significant expense for most employees (as well as their employer).[4] This section describes the legally required benefits of Social Security, workers' compensation, unemployment insurance, and family and medical leave, as well as legally required health care programs.

In the United States, employers must provide certain legally required benefits, whereas employers may offer other voluntary benefits at their own discretion. With that said, some employers may face penalties for not offering certain voluntary benefits like health care programs (per the Affordable Care Act), making certain benefits effectively required for some employers.

Social Security

In 1935, the U.S. Congress passed the Social Security Act as part of the New Deal aimed at helping the United States recover from the Great Depression. As historical context, the Great Depression had left many Americans out of work and with few economic resources at their disposal. Today, the act provides economic security for those who are older, mothers and children, those with disabilities, those who are unemployed, and those whose family members have died. Together, these programs make up the bulk of what is called the old-age, survivors, disability, and health insurance (OASDHI) program, with Medicare accounting for the remainder of the program. Approximately 20% of Americans receive some type of Social Security benefit, which ensures they are provided with a minimum floor of income and supplements other sources of income. The Social Security Administration pays out over one trillion dollars in benefits annually.[5]

The U.S. Congress passed the Social Security Act of 1935, and President Franklin D. Roosevelt signed it into law.
Bettmann/Contributor

Social Security benefits are funded through a tax based on the amount of a worker's income (with a few exceptions). This tax is called the Federal Insurance Contributions Act (FICA) and is deducted from payroll. Both the employee and the employer contribute a set percentage of the employee's earnings to FICA. Self-employed individuals are responsible for paying both the employee and the employer tax.[6] FICA tax contributions fund current Social Security beneficiaries, with any remainder placed in trust funds, which will be drawn from at a later date.

The Social Security Administration uses a work credits system to determine whether an individual is eligible to draw upon certain Social Security benefits. Each person must earn a specified number of work credits to become eligible to receive benefits at different points in their life. These work credits accrue throughout a person's life based on the amount of income they generate working each year, and a person can earn up to four work credits per year. For example, in 2023, an individual earned one work credit for every additional $1,640 in annual income until four work credits were reached.[7] The amount of benefit an individual receives is dependent, in part, on the average income they earned during their life.

Retirement Income

Retirement income is one of the primary benefits provided through Social Security. To be eligible for Social Security retirement income, an individual must have earned 40 work credits during their life and apply for the benefit. At the earliest, an eligible individual can begin receiving benefits at 62 years but will receive a permanently reduced benefit, as 62 years is not considered full retirement age in the United States. The current full retirement age ranges from 66 to 67 years, and the exact age depends on an individual's year of birth. An individual may maximize the benefit amount by delaying receipt of benefits after reaching full retirement age.[8]

Survivor Benefits

If an individual who is eligible for Social Security benefits dies, some family members may be eligible to receive survivor benefits. For example, a surviving spouse can receive a one-time $255 payment and potentially recurring monthly benefits; under certain conditions, surviving children, parents, or even a divorced spouse may be eligible for monthly benefits as well.[9] Any monthly benefit received by a surviving family member will be contingent on the deceased person's average lifetime earnings as well as the age of the surviving family member(s) and their relationship to the deceased person.

Disability Income

Disability income was established to support those who develop or face a disability that inhibits their ability to participate in the workforce. Eligibility for disability income depends on an individual's current age, the age at which they first experienced the disability, and their accrued work credits. The disability benefit may also extend to a worker's spouse or child under certain circumstances. An individual will continue to receive disability income for the duration of their disability, and if they reach full retirement age, then they will shift over to receiving retirement benefits. The disability income benefit also provides incentives and assistance aimed at helping individuals transition back to the workforce.[10]

Medicare

As a Social Security benefit, Medicare is a government-funded health insurance program designed for those who are 65 years or older. In addition, Medicare is available for those who are under the age of 65 and have qualifying conditions (e.g., disabilities, specific medical conditions). Medicare is designed to cover some but not all health care costs.[11]

Workers' Compensation

One program funded entirely by the employer through payroll taxes is called workers' compensation. It typically provides medical coverage, including rehabilitation services and income replacement, for an individual who was injured or fell ill due to accidents or hazards at work.[12] In addition, workers' compensation programs often provide benefits to an individual's family members in the event the individual dies due to an injury or illness sustained from work. It is important to point out that such programs are not the same as Social Security disability insurance programs. Nearly all states mandate that employers offer workers' compensation programs to employees. Many private employers purchase workers' compensation coverage through insurance companies, whereas public employers provide coverage through government programs. The amount of payroll taxes an employer must contribute to workers' compensation programs varies by industry; industries with higher rates of injuries and illnesses typically contribute more.

Unemployment Insurance

The U.S. federal–state unemployment insurance program provides income replacement and job-search services to individuals who become unemployed through no fault of their own yet are still able to work and available for work, assuming they meet certain eligibility requirements. For example, as the Covid-19 pandemic unfolded, many workers found themselves out of a job, and unemployment insurance benefits helped many of these workers meet their basic needs while searching for new employment opportunities. The unemployment insurance program is funded through payroll taxes contributed by employers and is overseen and administered by the U.S. Department of Labor.[13] The Social Security Act incentivizes states to pass unemployment insurance laws by allowing employers to credit up to 90% of their state unemployment tax contributions to a federal unemployment tax.[14] The weekly benefit distributed to eligible individuals through unemployment insurance is a function of past income, with the amount of benefits received limited by certain minimums and maximums. During 2022, 4.4 million individuals were beneficiaries of the regular U.S. federal–state unemployment insurance program.[15]

Family and Medical Leave

The U.S. Family and Medical Leave Act (FMLA) was introduced in 1993 to protect employees' job security when they need to take unpaid leave due to certain family or medical issues (e.g., serious health issue, giving birth, adopting a child). Eligible employees may use up to 12 weeks of unpaid leave in a year, during which their job and health care benefits remain protected. A spouse or family member of a service member may use up to 26 weeks of FMLA in a year to care for the individual. Employees can take FMLA all at once or intermittently. In general, employees must provide supporting documentation to their employer at least 30 days prior to taking leave, and the employer must grant the leave request. FMLA covers virtually all public and private employers with 50 or more employees. To be eligible to take leave under FMLA, an employee must have worked at least 1,250 hours for their employer for at least 12 months, must have worked at an employer's location (e.g., campus, facility) that has at least 50 employees working within a 75-mile radius, and must face at least one of the following challenges:

- being unable to work due to a serious health issue;

- giving birth or caring for their own infant, including receiving treatment for pregnancy complications;

- adopting a child or placing a child in their own foster care; and/or

- providing care for an immediate family member who is experiencing a serious health issue.[16]

SPOTLIGHT ON GLOBAL ISSUES: PARENTAL LEAVE IN THE EUROPEAN UNION

Parental leave has the potential to benefit both children and parents. In fact, evidence from brain-imaging data suggests that parents who act as primary caregivers experience changes in the brain associated with empathy, and these benefits were found for both mothers and fathers. While unpaid parental leave has become relatively commonplace around the world, paid parental leave is rarer.

In the United States, the Federal Employees Paid Parental Leave Act makes federal government employees eligible for up to 12 weeks of paid parental leave after the birth or adoption of a child; however, offering paid parental leave is not a legal requirement for civilian employers. With that said, some state governments, such as California, New Jersey, and Rhode Island, offer some form of paid parental leave.

Outside of the United States, many developed nations, including members of the European Union (EU), offer paid parental leave; yet, there remain significant differences in policies for paid maternal leave (leave for mothers) compared with those for paid paternal leave (leave for fathers). For instance, employers in all EU countries must provide at least 14 weeks of maternity leave, with each country determining when maternity leave can be taken and for how much pay. In contrast, paternity leave remains unregulated by the EU.

Nevertheless, the majority of EU member countries do offer some form of paid paternity leave, although the amount compensated varies by country. As an example, on January 1, 2021, Spain introduced one of the most generous paternity leave policies of any EU country to date, with the paternity leave policy matching its maternity leave policy. Specifically, Spain provides 16 weeks of fully paid leave for new fathers. Unlike some EU countries, the leave is non-transferrable, which means that a father cannot transfer used leave to a partner.

As another example, Finland offers approximately 23 weeks (or 160 days) of dedicated paid leave for each parent, including the father (if applicable). If there are two parents, the parents can take only 18 days of leave concurrently. In terms of payment, Kela, Finland's Social Insurance Institution, typically provides each parent with a monetary allowance that is approximately 70% of the parent's income.

Other EU countries offer shorter paid paternity leave times but compensate fathers at 100% of their typical salary. Not surprisingly, some evidence indicates that fathers are more likely to take advantage of paternity leave in countries where they are compensated at a higher percentage of their overall income. Estonia, Italy, and Portugal are notable for making paternity leave mandatory. For instance, in Italy, the mandatory government-paid paternity leave lasts 10 work days.[17]

Additional Health Care Requirements

Many U.S. employers must abide by other important health care laws. For example, the Employee Retirement Income Security Act (ERISA) of 1974 and subsequent amendments established minimum standards for many private employers' health care plans and did so as a means of protecting employees.[18] (We discuss ERISA as it relates to retirement plans later in the chapter.) Two amendments to ERISA have implications for many employers and their health care coverage: the Consolidated Omnibus Budget Reconciliation Act (COBRA) and the Health Insurance Portability and Accountability Act (HIPAA).

The Consolidated Omnibus Budget Reconciliation Act (COBRA) of 1985 protects employees' (and their beneficiaries') health care coverage for a designated amount of time in the event of voluntary or involuntary job loss, work-hour reductions, or other major occurrence (e.g., death, divorce).[19] For example, imagine a worker who gets laid off, and amid the stress of hunting for a new job, they have to seek out new health insurance. COBRA can alleviate some anxiety in this situation, as the worker has an opportunity to continue their existing health insurance coverage while finding a new place to work. However, if eligible, the employee may have to pay for the entire cost of the plan and a 2% administrative fee.

COBRA protections apply to employers with 20 or more employees that offer group health insurance plans. It allows individuals to continue their health care coverage even after major job and life events. COBRA protection can last for a maximum of 36 months, and the specific length of coverage is dependent on the type of qualifying job or life event that the individual experienced.

The Health Insurance Portability and Accountability Act (HIPAA) of 1996 adds protections to the portability of employees' health care coverage as well as protections to ensure the privacy and security of employees' health care data.[20] Specifically, HIPAA put into place certain protections for preexisting health conditions, where previously a health insurer might exclude individuals with certain conditions (e.g., genetic predispositions) or a prior claim history. In addition, HIPAA protects individuals against discrimination in which they are targeted for their general health condition and/or specific illnesses or injuries.

The Patient Protection and Affordable Care Act (ACA) of 2010 offers rights and protections associated with access to health care coverage. (Some refer to the ACA as "Obamacare," as it was signed into law by President Barack Obama.) The act mandates that employers with more than 50 full-time employees provide affordable health care programs to at least 95% of their employees; failure to do so results in a financial penalty. As of 2023, the ACA provides a number of benefits and protections to individuals, including the following:

- Insurance providers are required to eliminate exclusions on the basis of preexisting conditions as well as other discriminatory practices.
- Tax credits are provided to individuals and their families, which they can use to purchase coverage through a government-operated marketplace.
- All marketplace plans (and many other plans) are required to cover preventive medical services.
- Children and other dependents are allowed to remain on their parents' insurance plan until they reach 26 years of age.
- Lifetime and certain annual benefits limits are eliminated.
- Employers must offer affordable health care plans to full-time employees or potentially pay a fee.[21]

VOLUNTARY BENEFITS

LEARNING OBJECTIVE

13.3 Describe the different types of voluntary benefits.

In addition to legally required benefits, many organizations voluntarily provide benefits to employees. Voluntary benefits can add value by helping to attract, motivate, and retain talent, particularly if competitor organizations are not offering the same benefits. Yet at the same time, many of these benefits have substantial financial costs for both the organization and its employees, leaving the organization to weigh the potential short- and long-term advantages of offering such benefits relative to the short- and long-term disadvantages of doing so. Some of the most common employer-sponsored voluntary benefits include health care, retirement, life insurance, and work–life programs. Table 13.1 describes the characteristics of three common funding structures for voluntary benefits.

TABLE 13.1 ■ Funding Structures for Voluntary Benefits[22]	
Group Insurance	• The employer issues an insurance policy, and the employees are insured under that policy as a voluntary benefit. • The employer is allowed to pay anywhere from none to all of the coverage costs associated with the voluntary benefit, often with the employees paying any remainder. • This is a less risky and burdensome funding structure for the employer in terms of financial risk because the insurer is responsible for administering most components of the policy and for bearing the risk that the benefits paid to those covered by the policy exceed original expectations. • It is commonly used for medical, dental, vision, life, and retirement insurance.
Self-Funding	• The employer is responsible for administering, bearing the risk of, and covering all costs associated with the voluntary benefit. • It is commonly used for paid time off, work–life programs, and wellness programs, as well as some perquisites.
Individual Insurance	• This is a voluntary benefit offered by the employer in which the employee bears all of the coverage costs associated with the benefit if the employee decides to participate in the benefit. • Examples include some executive benefits as well as some supplemental life insurance plans.

Health Care Programs

In general, health care programs provide employees with access to health care providers and services to prevent and treat medical, dental, and vision conditions.

Medical Plans

Medical plans provide health care and treatment opportunities for those who are plan members. For employer-sponsored medical plans, it is not unusual for employers to share the costs with employees, and in recent decades, employer and employee costs for medical plans have generally increased. For instance, according to a Kaiser Family Foundation report, U.S. premiums for single-coverage employer-sponsored medical plans increased 240% from 1999 to 2020. During 2022, workers, on average, contributed 17% of the premium for single coverage plans and 26% of the premium for family coverage plans as part of the cost-sharing mechanism.[23]

In 2022, a dramatic rise in inflation led many employers to consider how to pay for increased health care costs. Many employers had to decide whether to pass rising costs on to employees through increased premiums, deductibles, and/or co-payments, which can pose major financial challenges for employees. For example, raising deductibles may result in financial hardships for employees who are not prepared for the out-of-pocket expenses associated with major procedures or surgeries. With expectations that health care costs would continue to rise in 2023, surveyed employers generally did not plan to increase employees' costs by increasing premiums, deductibles, or co-payments, according to preliminary results from a 2022 national survey by Mercer.[24]

According to the results of a Society for Human Resource Management survey, the percentage of employers offering tele-medicine benefits increased from 73% in 2019 to 93% in 2022. This increase may be attributed, in part, to the Covid-19 pandemic and the need for socially distanced care.[25]

©iStockphoto.com/Yaroslav Olieinikov

It is not uncommon for employers to offer employees more than one medical plan from which to choose, each with different associated costs. Next we review some common types of medical plans as well as health savings options.

Traditional-Care Plans

Also called conventional-indemnity plans, traditional-care plans allow participants to select any provider of their choosing without affecting how they are reimbursed, and participants' expenses are reimbursed as they are incurred. Over the past century, true traditional-care plans have become increasingly rare, as more organizations opt for managed-care plans.

Managed-Care Plans

Designed to provide wide-ranging health care services to plan participants, managed-care plans are preferable to traditional plans when it comes to meeting cost-containment goals and managing the quality and use of services. A common theme among managed-care plans is that participants incur lower cost sharing when they use in-network providers and services. In-network refers to providers and services that are members of the managed-care plan, and out-of-network refers to providers that are not members.

Managed-care plans use a variety of provisions aimed at managing costs, quality, and utilization. For instance, some plans may have preadmission provisions, where plan participants must receive authorization or complete certain tests prior to being admitted to a hospital for nonemergency situations. And some plans may require participants to receive a second opinion after a provider recommends them for elective or nonemergency surgery, which is designed as a cost-saving mechanism. Table 13.2 describes some of the most common managed-care plans.

TABLE 13.2 ■ Common Managed-Care Plans and Health Savings Options	
Managed-Care Plans	**Characteristics**
Health Maintenance Organization (HMO)	*Definition:* a plan in which out-of-network, nonemergency services are not covered, and plan participants select an in-network primary care physician who acts as a gatekeeper for in-network specialists. <ul><li>Provides a comprehensive array of health care providers and services, ranging from generalists to specialists, as well as physical therapists and mental health providers.</li><li>Most require lower out-of-pocket costs for plan participants and sometimes even lack a deductible.</li><li>May not cover physician and specialist visits that are deemed out of network.</li></ul>
Preferred Provider Organization (PPO)	*Definition:* a plan in which participants incur lower cost sharing for in-network service providers, and seeing a primary care physician is not required prior to seeing a specialist. <ul><li>Unlike an HMO, PPO participants may see providers outside of their network; however, going out of network will result in higher cost sharing by participants.</li><li>Unlike an HMO, PPO participants are not typically required to select a primary care physician.</li></ul>
Exclusive Provider Organization (EPO)	*Definition:* a specific type of PPO in which participants are covered only when they seek services from in-network providers, except in the event of an emergency.
Point-of-Service (POS)	*Definition:* a plan that is essentially a hybrid between an HMO and a PPO. <ul><li>Like an HMO, participants must select an in-network primary care physician who typically serves as the gatekeeper for referrals to specialists.</li><li>Like a PPO, participants may go out of network to find service providers at higher cost sharing.</li><li>In some plans, visiting a primary care physician and receiving preventive services do not contribute to the deductible, which reduces the out-of-pocket costs for routine care and treatment.</li></ul>
High-Deductible Health Plan (HDHP)	*Definition:* a plan with a high deductible (and often higher out-of-pocket maximums than other plans). <ul><li>According to the Internal Revenue Service, as of 2022, a plan becomes an HDHP when the annual deductible meets or exceeds $1,400 for an individual or $2,800 for a family.[26]</li><li>Technically, an HDHP may be a special type of HMO, PPO, or POS that includes a high deductible.</li><li>Typically, an HDHP offers more affordable plan premiums than other plans and incentivizes participants to think carefully about which service providers they visit and which treatments they pursue.</li></ul>
Consumer-Driven Health Plan (CDHP)	*Definition:* an HDHP that is combined with a health reimbursement arrangement (HRA) or health savings account (HSA), resulting in certain tax advantages.[27]

Health Savings Options

In the United States, there are various health savings options. In Table 13.3, we review three that are recognized by the Internal Revenue Service: health flexible spending arrangement, health reimbursement arrangement, and health savings account. These programs offer tax advantages aimed at reducing overall out-of-pocket health care expenses for individuals. Each option differs with respect to eligibility requirements and specific savings stipulations.[28]

TABLE 13.3 ■ Common Health Savings Options	
Health Savings Options	**Characteristics**
Health Flexible Spending Arrangement (Health FSA)	*Definition:* an option that offers tax advantages for individuals who are enrolled in some employer-sponsored health care plans. ● Permits employees (and optionally employers) to set aside funds into an untaxed account, which means employees do not pay taxes on the money within a health FSA. ● Imposes certain limitations regarding how the funds can be used. For example, funds cannot be used to pay premiums but can be used to pay deductibles, co-payments, prescription medication, and medical equipment, as well as other qualified medical and dental expenses. ● With some exceptions, participants cannot roll the entirety of account funds forward to the subsequent year in the event they do not use all the funds.
Health Reimbursement Arrangement (HRA)	*Definition:* an option that allows an employer (and not the employee) to contribute unlimited funds to an account, such that the account reimburses the employee on a tax-free basis for qualified medical costs. ● For each coverage period, there is an upper limit on how much tax-free reimbursement a participant can apply toward qualified medical costs. ● At the end of the year, any remaining funds can be rolled forward to the subsequent year. ● Because the employer owns the HRA, the employer retains control of the funds should the employee leave the organization, so some view the HRA as an employee retention inducement.
Health Savings Account (HSA)	*Definition:* an option that permits participants to contribute a portion of pretax income to an account that can be used to pay for services. ● Contributed funds are not taxed. ● Funds can accumulate tax-deferred interest. ● At the end of the year, any remaining funds can be rolled forward to the subsequent year.[29]

Dental and Vision Plans

Insurance plans for dental care and eye care may be offered as a supplement to medical plans or as stand-alone plans. Dental and vision plans typically operate much like a medical plan in that there is a designated network of approved service providers, premiums, deductibles, co-insurance, and co-payments. Regarding dental plans specifically, many plans provide coverage for routine preventive and maintenance services like X-rays, cleanings, and fillings. Dental plans often differ with respect to what and how much a plan will cover when it comes to more costly procedures such as root canals or orthodontics.

Manager's Toolbox: Health Care Terminology and Concepts

Employees often ask their managers for help understanding their benefits. Health care programs involve numerous terms and concepts that a manager may need to define and explain.

- *Participant:* an individual who is enrolled in a plan during a coverage period, allowing them to have access to the plan benefits.

- *Cost sharing:* a reimbursement model in which a participant is reimbursed for qualified services and procedures at a specified rate, subject to certain exceptions and limitations.

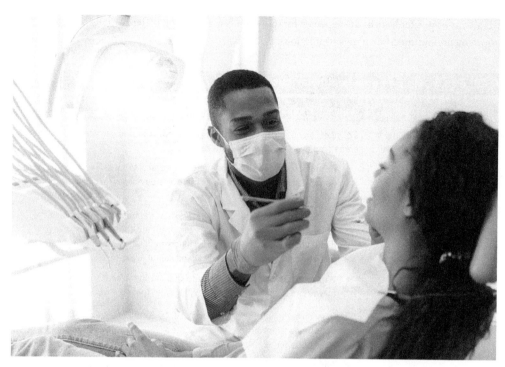

Many employers offer some type of dental plan, yet many plan participants do not know what their dental plan covers or how much they will be expected to pay out of pocket. As such, employers should communicate plan details and costs to help employees recognize the value of their benefit.

©iStockphoto com/Prostock-Studio

- *Premium:* a fee for a plan coverage period, which may be paid by any or all of the following entities: employer, employee, or union.

- *Deductible:* a set amount that a participant must pay during a coverage period for services rendered before the insurance provider begins contributing payments for expenses.

- *Co-insurance:* a cost sharing between the insurance provider and the participant, wherein the participant pays a percentage of expenses and the insurance reimburses the rest; typically comes into effect when a participant reaches the deductible for the coverage period (or if there was no deductible in the first place).

- *Co-payment (or co-pay):* a fee charged when a participant receives a particular service or visits a particular provider; may be as little as $5 for preventive care such as an annual physical.

- *Maximum out-of-pocket expense:* an upper limit for how much the participant will pay for a coverage period after reaching the deductible (if applicable); once reached, the insurance provider typically covers subsequent expenses.

- *Maximum plan limit:* an upper limit of how much an insurance provider will pay to cover a participant's expenses for a coverage period or during the participant's lifetime; the Patient Protection and Affordable Care Act prohibits annual and lifetime limits, except when applied to certain services that are not considered essential.

- *Primary care physician:* a physician who provides most routine and preventive services (known in the past as a general practitioner or family doctor) and who serves as the main contact for the participant; may also be a gatekeeper who must authorize referrals to specialists and nonemergency hospital visits; some medical plans require participants to select a primary care physician.

- *Specialist:* a health care provider who provides less-routine or highly specialized services, such as the services provided by a dermatologist, obstetrician-gynecologist, neurologist, oncologist, or cardiologist.

SPOTLIGHT ON ETHICS: MAKING CHANGES TO HEALTH INSURANCE PLANS

It is not unusual for employers to change health insurance plans. For example, an employer may switch to a plan with lower monthly premiums and a higher deductible or may switch from offering a preferred provider organization (PPO) to offering a health maintenance organization (HMO). Employers may make such changes to achieve cost savings over the previous plan, or they may do so in an attempt to improve employee coverage or benefits utilization. Many health insurance plans are inherently complex and nuanced, such that employers and employees alike may experience unintended positive or negative consequences when changes are made. Given this uncertainty, it is incumbent upon organizational decision makers, particularly benefits experts, to do their due diligence when determining what changes to make to a plan, which might include a benefits utilization analysis, survey, or cost-benefit analysis.

Consider an organization that originally used a three-tiered employer cost-sharing system, wherein employees who earned the least income were placed in the first income tier and employees who earned the most were placed in the third income tier. Employers in the lowest tier received the highest employer cost-sharing contributions to monthly insurance premiums, whereas those in the highest tier received the lowest. To refine the cost-sharing tier system, decision makers subsequently designed and implemented a five-tier system based on the same cost-sharing principle.

The decision makers in this scenario hoped that this refinement would make benefits administration fairer, as the additional tiers made the differentiations between employees of different incomes more nuanced. Unfortunately, there was an unintended consequence that adversely affected some of the most vulnerable employees. Specifically, some employees who were originally in the first tier subsequently moved to the second tier based on this change. This resulted in higher monthly premiums for those individuals, leaving them with lower take-home pay after the benefits were deducted from their paychecks. Some of these individuals ended up leaving the organization.

If the organization had applied data analytics to model the potential effects prior to making the decision to implement the new five-tiered system, they would likely have anticipated the negative impact on certain employees. This example illustrates why it is an organization's ethical responsibility to identify potential unintended consequences of changes to benefits. By leveraging the available data, an organization can avoid an unfortunate outcome.[30]

Questions

1. In your opinion, to what extent are employers ethically obligated to provide employer-sponsored health insurance for their workers? Give examples to support your answer.
2. In the scenario described, how might the company's HR administrators have intervened after the new five-tiered system was implemented to prevent employees from leaving due to reduced take-home pay?

Disability Insurance Programs

In addition to legally required workers' compensation and Social Security disability insurance, employers may also offer voluntary benefits in the form of short- and/or long-term disability insurance plans through private providers. Unlike workers' compensation, employees may be eligible to draw on disability insurance benefits even if their disability originated outside of work. Both short- and long-term disability insurance plans provide income protection to plan participants, and with the exception of some states, employers may voluntarily contribute fully or partially to employees' disability insurance.

Short-term disability insurance is a form of income protection for employees who temporarily become unable to work because of an illness or injury, whether sustained at work or during their personal time. In California, Hawaii, New Jersey, New York, Rhode Island, and the District of Columbia, employers (with some exceptions) are required to offer short-term disability insurance to employees working in those jurisdictions.[31] In most organizations, employees first draw upon accrued paid time off prior to accessing any short-term disability benefits covered through their plan. For the majority of short-term disability insurance plans, employees may receive their income protection benefit for 90 to 180 days, and the income protection benefit usually covers 60% to 75% of their base pay.[32] As long as the combined benefit received does not exceed 100% of base pay, employees may coordinate short-term disability insurance benefits with other programs, such as workers' compensation, if applicable.

Long-term disability insurance is similar to short-term disability insurance, except that it offers longer-term benefits that activate once short-term disability insurance benefits expire. Although long-term disability insurance also provides income protection benefits, the percentage of overall base pay is sometimes lower than the percentage afforded by short-term disability insurance benefits. Some plans stipulate a maximum time period for receiving income protection benefits, whereas other plans allow individuals to continue receiving the benefits through retirement. Like short-term disability insurance, those who draw income protection benefits from long-term disability insurance can coordinate their income protection benefits from other programs, as long as the combined benefit does not exceed 100% of their base pay.[33]

Retirement Programs

An employer may offer employees a variety of different retirement plans, which might include defined-benefit and defined-contribution plans, as well as plans designed to contribute to employees' individual retirement plans. In fact, a 2022 SHRM benefits report indicated that 94% of employers offered a traditional 401(k) plan to their employees, which is a type of retirement plan we will cover in more detail later on in this section.[34]

For many retirement plans, the U.S. federal government oversees voluntary retirement plans and provides protections for employees. The Employee Retirement Income Security Act (ERISA), mentioned earlier in this chapter, established minimum standards for many private-sector retirement plans (as well as health care plans) as protections for employees.[35]

Notably, ERISA does not cover plans maintained by government entities or religious institutions. Further, ERISA does not mandate that employers provide retirement plans for their employees; rather, ERISA requires private-sector employers with retirement plans to implement certain minimum plan standards. Under ERISA, employees participating in voluntary retirement plans have a right to

- access critical information regarding the retirement plan, such as how it is funded and what the specific characteristics of the plan entail;

- fair and time-efficient processes pertaining to benefit claims under such plans, such as those related to appeals and grievances;

- sue for issues related to benefits provision or fiduciary duty breaches.

If a retirement plan is terminated or fails, ERISA also protects employees' rights to certain benefits, which is accomplished using the Pension Benefit Guaranty Corporation (PBGC).[36] The PBGC is a U.S. government agency set up by Congress. It insures private-sector retirement plans, such that when a voluntary retirement plan is terminated or fails, PBGC steps in as trustee to ensure employees receive the benefits owed to them.[37] Consistent with ERISA, PBGC does not cover government- or religious-institution–maintained plans. Further, PBGC does not cover 401(k), profit-sharing, employee stock ownership, money-purchase, or health care plans. In sum, the U.S. government has put certain safeguards into effect to protect the retirement plans of private-sector workers.

Next, we distinguish between two types of retirement plans that are commonly offered: defined-benefit and defined-contribution retirement plans (see Figure 13.2).

FIGURE 13.2 ■ Two Types of Voluntary Retirement Programs

Defined-benefit plans and defined-contribution plans are the two types of voluntary retirement programs.

Defined-Benefit Plans
Retirement program in which the employer provides participating individuals with an established benefit to be paid out over a fixed time period

vs.

Defined-Contribution Plans
Retirement program that does *not* yield an established benefit for the employee and is instead based on employee and/or employer contributions

Defined-Benefit Plans

In a defined-benefit plan, the employer provides plan participants with a pre-established benefit to be paid out over a fixed time period. A defined-benefit plan is also known as a *traditional pension plan*. Sometimes a defined-benefit plan may stipulate an exact amount to be distributed, such as $3,000 per month at retirement. The funding for these plans sometimes differs between the public and private sectors. Often, both the employee and the employer are required to contribute to defined-benefit plans in public organizations, whereas in many cases, only the employer contributes to such plans in private organizations.[38] Compared to other retirement programs, defined-benefit plans allow employers to contribute more. Plus, by definition, defined-benefit plans offer predictable benefit amounts that can be accrued relatively quickly, which may be appealing to many employees, particularly those who have a discomfort for incurring risk.

Depending on the employer, defined-benefit plans may be paid out to employees on a fixed periodic basis or in a single lump sum. The amount of the pre-established, determinable benefit for each employee is typically calculated using an actuarial formula based on employee earnings, years of service, and age. For instance, some plans use an employee's age and/or pay over the 3 most recent years to determine the amount of the benefit. Although they are still offered by many companies, defined-benefit plans are becoming less common as more companies opt for defined-contribution plans. This trend may be partially attributable to the more costly and administratively complex nature of establishing and maintaining defined-benefit plans compared to defined-contribution plans and to U.S. financial accounting standards (e.g., Generally Accepted Accounting Principles), which treat defined-benefit plans as liabilities.[39]

A cash balance plan, sometimes referred to as a *guaranteed account plan*, is one type of defined-benefit plan. Under this type of plan, participants are provided with an account that is credited annually with a compensation credit and an interest credit. The compensation credit will often take the form of a percentage of the compensation an employee earns from the employer, and the interest credit refers to a guaranteed interest rate (either fixed or variable). Unlike other defined-benefit plans, under cash balance plans, the amount of the deposits to participants' accounts is not based on their age.[40]

Defined-Contribution Plans

Unlike a defined-benefit plan, a defined-contribution plan does not provide a pre-established, fixed benefit for the employee. Instead, a defined-contribution plan is built on employee and/or employer contributions to an investment fund and any investment gains or losses of that fund.[41] Typically, such plans permit certain contribution amounts from the employee or employer and enforce a maximum contribution amount for the year. Employee contributions are typically tax deferred. This means that the taxable income an employee contributes to a plan will not be taxed until a later date, often when the earnings are distributed during retirement. Because plan contributions are placed in an investment fund, employees take on investment risk. In fact, investment gains or losses can have a significant effect on the amount of earnings distributed upon retirement (or termination).[42] Common types of defined-contribution plans include 401(k), 403(b), profit-sharing, employee stock ownership, and money-purchase pension plans.

401(k) and 403(b) Plans. Both 401(k) and 403(b) plans are types of defined-contribution plans. Both typically allow employees to direct their own investments, and employees are often allowed to transport their plan balance to another employer's plan should they switch jobs.

An employee enrolled in a 401(k) plan makes contributions to an individual account in the form of deferred income. Depending upon the parameters of a particular plan, the employer may also be able to contribute to the employee's plan. In fact, some plans, such as safe harbor and SIMPLE 401(k) plans, *require* the employer to make plan contributions. According to a 2022 Society for Human Resource Management report, 83% of employers made contributions to traditional 401(k) plans and 76% made contributions to Roth 401(k) plans.[43] As long as employer contributions fall under section 404 of the IRS code, employers may deduct the contributions on their federal tax returns.[44] Some plans allow employees to make contributions on a before-tax basis, whereas other plans require employees to make contributions on an after-tax basis.[45] Further, some plans allow employees to withdraw benefits prior to retirement, such as in the event of personal hardship or loans. In 2022, an estimated 94% of surveyed employers offered a traditional 401(k), while 68% offered a Roth 401(k).[46]

Regarding vesting of 401(k) plans, employee and employer contributions operate differently. For employees, from the moment they defer income from their paycheck to their plan, they are considered 100% vested. This means employees have control over the entirety of the funds they contributed after they have fulfilled certain contractual terms of employment, such as working for the organization for a certain length of time; however, they may be subject to additional taxes if they withdraw prior to a specified age. Employer contributions, on the other hand, often vest on a graduated schedule, which means that employees may not be able to access the employer portion of their benefit until they have worked for that employer for a specified amount of time.[47]

Interestingly, when employers offer to match employee contributions, employees do not always take full advantage of such programs; however, a research study conducted by Google and academic researchers found that employees who received an extra "nudge" (i.e., additional information about the matching benefit) were more likely to increase their 401(k) contributions, resulting in greater retirement savings.[48]

A 403(b) plan is sometimes referred to as a *tax-sheltered annuity plan*. A 403(b) plan is very similar to a 401(k) plan, but a notable difference between the two is that 403(b) plans are reserved for public schools and universities, religious organizations, and certain tax-exempt organizations such as charities. Similar to a 401(k), the employee (and sometimes the employer) contributes to an individual account using deferred income. Typically, a 403(b) plan allows employee income to be deferred on a before-tax basis.[49]

Profit-Sharing Program. A profit-sharing program is one type of pay-for-performance program that can double as a retirement plan. Employees earn rewards by sharing in their organization's profits (e.g., return on assets), and rewards may be distributed as cash or placed in a retirement plan. Employers typically use a formula for determining how much each employee receives as part of the profit sharing. When designed for retirement, a profit-sharing program can be considered a type of defined-contribution plan and may even include a 401(k) option.[50] Under a profit-sharing program, employers are under no legal obligation to make certain levels of contributions or to contribute every year. Further, unlike a 401(k), true profit-sharing programs are based solely on employer contributions, and the moment that a profit-sharing program incorporates deferred income from employees, it becomes a 401(k) plan.[51] In terms of withdrawal, employee personal loans are permitted under a profit-sharing program. With that said, any withdrawal made when the employee is under age 59.5 years may be subject to an additional tax. Finally, stock bonus plans are similar to a profit-sharing program; however, under stock bonus plans, employers contribute stock as opposed to cash.

Employee Stock Ownership Plan (ESOP). Like profit-sharing programs, an employee stock ownership plan can double as a pay-for-performance program and a retirement program. Specifically, an employee stock ownership plan (ESOP) rewards employees when company stock shares increase in value and can be used only after a vesting period. As an employee benefit, ESOPs are defined by the U.S. Internal Revenue Service as a defined-contribution plan, wherein the bulk of contributions are invested in an employer's stock.[52] ESOPs are different from stock options and stock purchase plans in that ESOPs typically allow an organization's employees to own a substantially larger portion of the organization (and sometimes even own the organization outright). Further, only employees are eligible to participate in ESOPs, so when employees separate from their organization, they are required to cash out of their ESOPs.[53] Those who participate in ESOPs stand to benefit should their organization perform well throughout their tenure.

Money-Purchase Plan. In a money-purchase plan, employers simply contribute a specified amount to each plan participant's account. Compared to some of the other plans, these plans are relatively straightforward and simple to communicate to employees. The amount specified for each employee can be a percentage of annual compensation, and up to 25% of the amount of a participant's annual compensation can be contributed to their plan. Like other defined-contribution plans, contributions to money-purchase plans are invested into a fund. Consequently, the amount of an employee's fund at retirement will be a function of all employer contributions to the fund as well as the investment gains or losses of the fund over time.[54] For example, imagine that Juana's company contributes 8% of each employee's pay to a money-purchase plan. Because Juana earns $65,000 a year, her company will contribute $5,200 ($65,000 × 0.08 = $5,200) to her money-purchase plan at the end of the year. Over time, investment gains or losses will affect the fund value.

Individual Retirement Plans

Plans that allow individuals to make tax-deferred investments for retirement are called individual retirement plans or individual retirement arrangements (IRAs). Although individual retirement plans can be employer sponsored, they need not be. Any individual who earns income or is compensated, whether as an employee or through self-employment, may be eligible to contribute to an individual retirement plan, subject to some restrictions.[55] Individual retirement plans may be especially beneficial for those who are self-employed or lack access to employer-sponsored retirement plans.

Examples of individual retirement plans include traditional individual retirement accounts or annuities (traditional IRAs) and Roth IRAs, both of which offer tax advantages and impose restrictions on the overall amount of contributions made each year. Traditional IRAs and Roth IRAs do, however, differ in key ways, as shown in Table 13.4.

TABLE 13.4 ■ Traditional Versus Roth IRA	
Traditional IRA	**Roth IRA**
Does not allow individuals older than 70½ years old to contribute.	Does not allow individuals to contribute if their modified adjusted gross income is larger than specified amounts.
Individuals can deduct their contributions, but the tax deduction may be limited if they also participate in an employer retirement plan and earn an income above specified amounts.	Individuals cannot deduct their contributions.
Individuals must begin withdrawing or distributing minimum amounts the year after they turn 70½ years old.	Individuals are not required to take minimum distributions or withdrawals at any point as long as they are the original owner of the plan.
Withdrawals and distributions are taxable.	Withdrawals and distributions are not taxable, with some exceptions.

Source: U.S. Internal Revenue Service. (n.d.). *Traditional and Roth IRAs.* https://www.irs.gov/retirement-plans/traditional-and-roth-iras

Life Insurance Programs

As another common voluntary benefit, life insurance programs provide financial compensation for designated beneficiaries when the insured individual dies, and the compensation can be distributed in the form of a lump-sum payment.[56] According to a 2022 report by the U.S. Bureau of Labor Statistics, 60% of workers had access to life insurance programs, and of those employees, 98% enrolled in a program, suggesting that life insurance plans are popular benefits when offered.[57] Some employees enroll in plans in which the benefit is paid out as a fixed multiple of their annual earnings, whereas others enroll in plans in which the benefit is paid out as a flat dollar amount. Regardless of how the benefit is paid out, an employee should meet with those who are knowledgeable about the different benefits offered through the employer-sponsored life insurance program to ensure the employee selects the benefit that will be most appropriate for their family's financial needs in the event of the employee's death.

Wellness Programs

Wellness programs include those employer-sponsored or -provided initiatives aimed at promoting healthy behaviors, such as smoking cessation, weight management, and behavioral and lifestyle coaching programs. In 2022, 46% of surveyed employers rated wellness benefits as "very important" or "extremely important" benefits for employers to offer.[58] In fact, some employers even provide employees with incentives for participating in wellness programs. Accumulated evidence indicates that, in general, wellness programs work (and employers believe that they work), as they are associated with positive employee health and work outcomes, as well as organizational financial outcomes.[59] Chapter 15 provides additional information on wellness programs.

Some organizations offer smoking cessation as a wellness program.

©iStockphoto/solidcolours

Work–Life Programs

Work–life programs can help employees navigate the demands of their work and nonwork lives. Work demands have the potential to influence employees' personal lives, and nonwork demands from employees' personal lives have the potential to influence their work lives. Programs that help employees navigate the competing demands of their work and nonwork lives can be especially attractive and useful. For instance, employees benefit from programs that enable them to receive pay while taking time away from work due to sickness, travel, holidays, or other reasons. They also benefit from assistance with legal issues, caring for a family member, or pursuing educational opportunities. Research has shown that when employees perceive work–life programs as useful, they tend to engage in more helping behaviors at work as well as perceive that their organization supports them.[60]

Payment for Time Not Worked

Employees need time away from work for a variety of legitimate reasons, and many employers voluntarily provide payment for time not worked. At the federal level, the U.S. Fair Labor Standards Act of 1938 does not require employers to pay employees for time away from work due to sickness, vacations, holidays, or other circumstances.[61] However, some state and local laws do require payment for time not worked under certain circumstances. In the following paragraphs, we describe different types of payment for time not worked.

Paid Time Off (PTO). When an employer compensates employees for time away from work, it is most often under a **paid time off (PTO)** program. A Payscale survey found that 57% of employers offered PTO.[62] Approved reasons for using PTO often include vacation, holidays, non–work-related illness or injury, and personal days. In addition, some employers offer PTO for jury duty, military duty, or other unforeseen circumstances or absences. It is becoming more common for employers to treat PTO as an inclusive program in which there is little or no distinction regarding the reason an employee takes time away from work. In many organizations, employees accrue PTO based on the number of hours worked and years of service, and the PTO accumulates into a pool until the employee decides to use some or all of it. Some employers place restrictions on how PTO can be used, such as limiting how many PTO days can be used for vacation versus sickness, whereas other employers allow employees to use PTO as needed without a specific reason.[63]

Some employers offer unlimited PTO, which allows employees to take as much time away from work as they need as long as they meet performance expectations and, in many companies, if their supervisor approves the time off. The video-streaming company Netflix gained attention when it announced an unlimited PTO program in 2004, a benefit that Netflix continues to offer to this day.[64] In 2023, 13% of organizations surveyed by Payscale reportedly offered unlimited PTO, which was down 0.6% from 2022. Because accrued PTO is owed to employees, U.S. financial reporting standards require organizations to treat accrued PTO as a liability. Thus, when an organization adopts an unlimited PTO policy, it removes this liability, making the organization look more valuable from an accounting perspective.[65]

Introducing an unlimited PTO program may, however, lead to some administrative challenges. For example, the Family and Medical Leave Act (FMLA) protects qualified employees' jobs while they are on leave, whereas extended leave under PTO does not necessarily do so. Thus, ideally, employers and employees should distinguish FMLA leave from traditional PTO to ensure that an employee's job remains protected.[66]

Sick Time. When an employee takes time off from work due to a foreseen or unforeseen personal health issue or an immediate family member's health issue, it is referred to as **sick time** or **sick leave**. As an example, if an employee takes time away from work due to the flu, this could be considered sick time. Alternatively, if an employee takes a day off to care for a child who is having outpatient surgery, this could also be considered sick time. In many cases, sick time is accrued each year based on the cumulative time worked.

Holiday Pay. When employees take time off from work on a recognized federal, state, or local holiday, employers use **holiday pay** to compensate workers. Examples of recognized U.S. federal holidays include Martin Luther King Jr. Day, Juneteenth, Independence Day, and Thanksgiving Day.

Vacation Pay. Many employers provide **vacation pay**, which is compensation for taking time away from work for planned reasons, such as for relaxation or travel. Often, an employee must schedule vacation time in advance and receive approval from a supervisor. In many organizations, paid vacation time is accrued based on cumulative time worked per year. Because many employers' vacation pay policies allow employees to roll unused vacation time forward to subsequent years, it is not uncommon for employees to have unused vacation time when they leave an employer, and states vary regarding whether an employer is required to "pay out" any unused vacation time.[67]

Personal Leave. Often used as a catch-all for any foreseen or unforeseen time away from work, **personal leave** is a benefit employers use to supplement their vacation and sick time offerings. Employers may offer personal leave as paid or unpaid. Personal leave is distinguishable from leaves of absence covered under the Family Medical and Leave Act (FMLA) or the Uniformed Services Employment and Reemployment Rights Act.

Mental Health Days. According to a 2022 survey conducted by the Society for Human Resource Management, 20% of organizations offer paid mental health days that are separate from traditional sick time.[68] As described in the chapter's opening case on mental health benefits, employees can use mental health days to psychologically detach from work and focus on mental recovery from work. For instance, an employee might use a mental health day to spend time relaxing at home and disconnecting from work-related stressors.[69]

Compensatory Time Off

As described in Chapter 11, the U.S. Fair Labor Standards Act requires employers to classify employees as exempt or nonexempt from minimum wage and overtime provisions. When a nonexempt employee works overtime hours and receives paid time off rather than earning time-and-a-half pay for the extra hours worked, it is known as **compensatory time off** or, more commonly, **comp time**. In the United States, comp time is currently only permitted for employees who work in the public sector, although some HR professionals have encouraged the U.S. Congress to introduce legislation that would require private employers to offer comp time.[70] To illustrate how comp time works, consider the following scenario: A nonexempt public-sector employee works 48 hours in a week, and the employee applies the extra 8 hours (beyond 40 hours) to comp time, which enables the employee to take 8 hours of paid time off at a later time.

Child and Elder Care

Many workers require child or elder care when they are at work.[71] In fact, many workers find themselves caring and providing for children and parents simultaneously, a phenomenon referred to as the "sandwich generation," as adults are sandwiched between younger and older individuals in need of care. From a financial perspective, accessing or providing such care can be costly. For example, results from a 2022 Care.com survey revealed that half of parents applied more than 20% of their household income to cover child care costs.[72]

The Covid-19 pandemic has exacerbated the child care challenges faced by many employees and their employers. Prior to the pandemic, estimates showed that inadequate child care cost employers $13 billion per year and resulted in $37 billion per year in lost income for working parents due to missed work and other issues, and during the pandemic, 63% of parents reported difficulties finding child care.[73]

Employer-sponsored or -subsidized child and elder care can help workers cope with the challenges of balancing work and caring for loved ones. Some employers provide child care services on site. As an example, The Home Depot offers the Little Apron Academy at a location in Atlanta. This center provides affordable on-site child care and educational services for employees' children aged 6 weeks to 5 years.[74] In addition to providing low-cost services, the Little Apron Academy offers The Home Depot employees convenience, as they do not need to drop their child off at a separate location or rush across town if their child becomes ill. However, programs like the Little Apron Academy are relatively rare. Among family-friendly policies offered by U.S. employers, on-site child care is implemented with the lowest frequency, whereas PTO, flexible work hours, and remote working are implemented with the highest frequency.[75]

Even though child care services represent an immediate cost to the employer, they can achieve a net reduction in costs for the organization and improve employee outcomes. For instance, employers that offer on-site child care may be eligible for a tax credit.[76] Among other advantages, access to child care is associated with lower turnover.[77]

Flextime and Remote Work

Allocating time for family and nonwork responsibilities can be challenging for many workers. For example, workers are spending more time commuting to and from work, which may limit the time they have available for nonwork responsibilities. According to a 2019 report by the U.S. Census Bureau, workers spend on average 27.6 minutes on a one-way commute, which represents an increase of 2.6 minutes from 2006.[78]

To cope with such demands, many employees seek flexible work schedules and arrangements. Flextime and remote work (which is also called telecommuting) have emerged as two prominent forms of flexible work arrangements. Flextime occurs when an employer permits employees to adjust their work schedule to meet family and nonwork demands while also meeting their overall work-hours requirement.

In contrast, remote work occurs when an employee works from home or another remote location, such as from a library or a coffee shop or even another country. After the onset of the Covid-19 pandemic in late 2019/early 2020, many workers began working at home. In October 2022, an estimated 55% of individuals with jobs that could be performed remotely chose to work remotely all of the time; however, by March 2023, this percentage of individuals working remotely dropped to 35%, which is only up 7% from pre-pandemic estimates.[79]

Some employers, however, continue to embrace remote work. For example, Airbnb launched its Live and Work Anywhere policy in 2022. The policy allows most employees to work anywhere in their current country or work in one of 26 Airbnb offices around the world. Moreover, the policy permits employees to work remotely up to 90 days per year in over 170 countries.[80] Chapter 5 offers additional information on remote work.

College Savings Plans

To help employees save for future college expenses, employers can contribute to or offer college savings plans. One plan, called the 529 College Savings Plan (529 plan), even offers certain tax advantages.[81] Namely, many states allow for tax credit or deduction after payments have been made to a 529 plan. Further, the funds in a 529 plan can be invested, and federal taxes are not applied to investment gains. Finally, the funds from a 529 plan can be withdrawn for qualified higher-educational expenses without being subject to state or federal income taxes. Although individuals can open their own 529 plans, some employers administer 529 plans as a voluntary benefit; this enables employees to apply after-tax income directly to their plan.[82]

Educational-Assistance Programs

In addition to administering and/or contributing to college savings plans, employers can also offer direct financial assistance for educational expenses. An educational-assistance program refers to an employee benefit program wherein the employer provides financial assistance for employee educational expenses, which may come in the form of tuition assistance, payment toward qualified educational expenses, or employer-sponsored scholarship programs. Under certain circumstances, an employer can apply these financial contributions as a tax deduction, and under the American Taxpayer Relief Act of 2012, employees do not have to pay income tax on their employer's contributions if the contributions are $5,250 or less per year.[83] A growing number of employers are partnering with universities as part of their educational-assistance programs. For instance, Starbucks partnered with Arizona State University to offer full-tuition support toward a bachelor's degree for full- and part-time U.S. employees.[84]

Legal-Services and Identity-Theft Benefits

Legal services and identity theft can impose heavy demands on employees' time and finances. These demands not only disrupt their family and nonwork lives but also have the potential to disrupt their work lives. Common reasons for legal services include divorce, bankruptcy, lawsuits, wills or trusts, and traffic violations. Some employers sponsor legal services to help employees through legal difficulties and to support their physical presence and psychological focus at work. Like other voluntary benefits, legal services can be deducted from participants' paychecks. Alternatively, employers may also opt to provide a referral service, possibly through an employee-assistance program, wherein employees are referred to outside legal resources.[85] Finally, with identity theft on the rise, more individuals are facing the inconvenience and difficulties that come when identities are stolen.[86] As such, employers offer identity-theft benefits to help employees protect their personal information.

Perquisites and Other Benefits

Nonmonetary services or benefits that an employer provides to its employees are referred to as perquisites, or perks. Essentially, the term *perks* is a catch-all for any voluntary benefit that does not fit neatly into one of the classic programs previously covered in this chapter. Perks represent one more way that employers can differentiate themselves from their competitors. Typical examples of company perks include a designated parking space or an office with a view.

For several decades, many companies expanded their perks by introducing new types of benefits that set them apart from their competitors. Companies like Google were leading pioneers in the perks arena. Famously, Google provided employees with free food via small displays, kitchen areas, and dozens of cafeterias; in fact, to encourage healthy eating choices, Google offered smaller plates, places the healthiest free-food options closer to eye level and less-healthy options in places that are harder to see and reach.[87] Google also offered on-site hair salons, dry cleaning, and bike repair as conveniences, although employees paid for those.[88] Due to recent cost-cutting measures, as of 2023, Google has reduced or eliminated free massages, company-sponsored fitness classes, and stocked pantries, but it still provides access to free meals.[89]

Historically, companies in the high-tech industry were leaders in employee perks, including free meals. However, to cut costs, some companies like Google have eliminated or reduced some perks, such as free massages and company-sponsored fitness classes.[90]

©iStockphoto.com/_jure

ADMINISTERING BENEFITS PROGRAMS

> ### LEARNING OBJECTIVE
>
> **13.4**   Assess the common challenges and opportunities associated with administering benefits programs.

If benefits are selected and deployed in house, internal HR professionals must possess the knowledge and skills necessary to administer legally required and voluntary benefits programs. In fact, larger organizations often have a team of individuals who work as dedicated benefits specialists. Regardless of who administers benefits, HR information systems often play a critical role in gathering, storing, analyzing, and reporting the data. In this section, we describe the common challenges and opportunities associated with benefits administration.

Flexible Benefits Plans

Some employers choose to administer flexible benefits plans. As the name implies, employer-sponsored **flexible benefits plans** offer employees some degree of choice when it comes to the voluntary benefits they select and the benefits they can receive on a pretax basis. Employees typically make contributions to flexible benefits plans as paycheck deductions, and the employer also pays a portion of the costs. The plan might provide employees with credits, which they can use to purchase the benefits that best suit their needs. For example, using their allotted credits, employees might choose from various medical, life insurance, and retirement plans, and they may be entitled to cash out a portion of their unused credits. Flexible benefits plans provide employees with greater control over benefits selection while still offering consistent benefits choices across employees. In fact, adopting a flexible benefits plan may improve employees' satisfaction with their benefits.[91]

Flexible benefits plans go by other names, such as flex plans or cafeteria plans—the latter name communicates how these plans work: Employees may choose from a variety of benefit offerings as though they were walking through a cafeteria line and choosing from a variety of food options. These plans are also referred to as Section 125 plans, a label that references the applicable section of the U.S. Internal Revenue Code.[92] Section 125 permits flexible benefits plan participants to select two or more benefits, where at least one benefit is taxable and at least one benefit is qualified. Under Section 125, taxable benefits include cash payments that are taxed upon receipt. Qualified benefits include the following approved benefits that are received on a pretax basis (with certain limitations):

- employer-sponsored accident and health plans;
- group life insurance plans;
- child, elder, and other dependent care plans;
- adoption assistance programs; and
- health savings accounts (HSAs).

Different variations on flexible benefits plans exist, including modular plans, core-plus options plans, full-choice plans, and flexible spending accounts.

Taxes and Accounting

Different laws and taxes must be considered when administering benefits. Moreover, different benefits often have different sets of rules, regulations, reporting standards, and taxes. Accordingly, successful benefits administration entails partnering with individuals, departments, or consulting firms with expertise in taxes and accounting. A comprehensive review of all pertinent tax and accounting forms and statements (e.g., Statement of Financial Accounting Standards 106) is beyond the scope of this textbook. However, we encourage interested readers to review documentation provided by government and professional organizations, such as the Internal Revenue Service (www.irs.gov) and the Financial Accounting Standards Board (www.fasb.org).

Discrimination

As with other core HR functions, benefits should be administered fairly and consistently across employees and should not be administered in a manner that intentionally or unintentionally discriminates against different legally protected groups. Consistent with U.S. legislation (covered in Chapter 4), benefits administration should not discriminate on the basis of race, color, religion, sex, national origin, age, pregnancy and associated medical conditions, disability, or genetic information. This legislation includes Title VII of the Civil Rights Act of 1964, Age Discrimination in Employment Act of 1967, Pregnancy Discrimination Act of 1978, Americans with Disabilities Act of 1990, and Genetic Information Nondiscrimination Act of 2008. In addition, benefits should not discriminate in favor of highly compensated employees. For example, for a benefit to be classified as qualified, an employer must demonstrate that all employees, regardless of their compensation levels, have access to the benefit and are helped by the benefit in similar ways.

To be classified as a qualified benefit, voluntary benefits programs must meet certain guidelines, one of which relates to discrimination in favor of highly compensated employees. In the United States, qualified benefits plans offer several potential tax advantages for the employer and employee: (a) employer tax deduction, (b) employee pretax payroll contribution, and (c) tax-free investment returns. As such, to earn the "qualified" distinction, an employer must demonstrate that all employees, regardless of their compensation levels, have access to the benefit and are helped by the benefit in similar ways.

SPOTLIGHT ON LEGAL ISSUES: SAME-SEX MARRIAGE AND SPOUSAL BENEFITS

In June 2015, the U.S. Supreme Court ruled that the Constitution guarantees the right to same-sex marriage. In the years leading up to the Court's decision, 37 states and the District of Columbia had already ruled in favor of same-sex marriage. Nonetheless, this landmark case guaranteed the right to same-sex marriage and spousal benefits at the federal level and across all states, in the process becoming the law of the land. Two years prior, the Supreme Court voted to strike down a federal law that denied spousal benefits to married same-sex couples; however, the Social Security Administration continued to deny same-sex spousal benefits for some individuals in states where same-sex marriage was not yet recognized. As such, the subsequent 2015 ruling provided blanket protections across the 50 states and the District of Columbia, and in the case of the Social Security Administration, spousal Social Security benefits for married same-sex couples became guaranteed.[93]

Selecting Benefits

When selecting which voluntary benefits to offer, organizational decision makers should determine (a) the benefits employees want and (b) the benefits competitors offer. Regarding the first objective, a variety of data-gathering methods can be implemented, such as benchmarking, employee surveys, employee requests, focus groups, and union negotiations.[94] In particular, employee surveys represent a relatively efficient data-gathering method because a large number of surveys can be sent out quickly. High survey response rates from all departments or units can help ensure that employees' responses are representative of all employees in the organization. Although potentially less efficient than surveys, employee focus groups offer an opportunity to gather rich, in-depth information regarding the most sought-after benefits. Regarding the second objective, competitor benchmarking based on market reviews remains one of the best approaches for determining what benefits other organizations offer.

SPOTLIGHT ON DATA AND ANALYTICS: EVALUATING BENEFITS OFFERINGS

Offering voluntary benefits to employees has the potential to add value for both employees and the organization. Analytics can be used as a decision-making tool (a) to determine which voluntary benefits to offer and (b) to evaluate the extent to which employees utilize different voluntary benefits. In fact, data analysis may reveal differences between the benefits employees say they want and the benefits they actually use.

To determine if any new voluntary benefits should be offered, HR professionals should collect systematic data on employee needs and wants. One of the most efficient ways to collect data from a large number of employees across the organization is to use an employee survey, and the survey should include items (i.e., questions or prompts) aimed at measuring employees' attitudes and behaviors toward existing benefits and potential benefits offerings. For example, to gauge employees' overall level of satisfaction with current benefits offerings, you might ask employees to rate the extent to which they agree with the following survey item, using a 1-to-5 scale (1 = strongly disagree, 5 = strongly agree): "Overall, I am satisfied with the company's current employee benefits offerings."

To avoid disappointing employees, make sure that any potential benefits offerings mentioned in the survey are actually ones that the organization has the means to implement. Otherwise, if the employees overwhelmingly respond in favor of a particular benefit but the organization is unable to offer the benefit, the employees may feel disappointed and dissatisfied. In other words, be sure to manage employees' expectations.

After designing the survey, efforts should be made to collect survey responses from a representative sample of employees. Consider that, collectively, all employees in the organization constitute the employee population. To gather a representative sample of employees, steps must be taken to encourage responses from as many employees as possible and to ensure that employees from all functional areas and units respond to the survey. Once survey data collection has been completed, the demographic characteristics (e.g., age, gender, race, ethnicity, functional area) of the sample can be compared to the demographic characteristics of the entire employee population in the organization. Ideally, the demographic characteristics of the sample should be similar to the population. In doing so, HR professionals can ensure that any decisions made regarding benefits offerings are based on data that are representative of the entire organization. Finally, as a best practice, any time an organization collects data via employee surveys, the organization should report the aggregate findings back to the employees so that they know that their voices have been heard.

In addition to collecting data related to offering new voluntary benefits, the organization will need to determine which existing benefits offerings to change or eliminate. Data analytics can be used as a decision-support tool for evaluating benefits utilization. Using data that are perhaps already captured in the HR information system, an organization can analyze the number of employees enrolled in each benefit and the frequency with which employees access or use each benefit. In doing so, the organization can assess which benefits presumably reflect employees' needs and wants. Further, low utilization of a particular benefit may signal that the organization needs to better communicate the details of the benefit and/or its value. Finally, using statistical analyses like regression, HR professionals can investigate whether the enrollment in or use of certain benefits is associated with important employee and organizational outcomes such as turnover and performance.[95]

COMMUNICATING BENEFITS PROGRAMS

LEARNING OBJECTIVE

13.5 Assess the common challenges and opportunities associated with communicating benefits programs.

The importance of effectively communicating benefits programs to (prospective) employees cannot be overstated. This process includes communicating program details and the value of benefits. Some evidence has shown that employees' awareness of their benefits offerings can be enhanced by providing them with informational materials about available benefits and by meeting with employees to discuss the available benefits.[96] Findings from a SHRM survey indicated that HR professionals generally perceived face-to-face communication methods like one-on-one communications and orientations as being effective.[97] As for virtual communication methods, approximately one third of the surveyed HR professionals thought online benefits portals were effective.

In addition, HR professionals should make an effort to communicate the *value* of benefits programs. Employee benefits represent a major cost for employers, and employees tend to underestimate the amount their employer contributes to their benefits.[98] In fact, many individuals may be unaware of how much benefits are worth. Differences in benefits offerings may ultimately lead a job applicant to accept a job offer from one organization over another. Thus, it is advisable to provide job candidates with an accurate preview of what benefits will be available to them should they accept, as well as how much those benefits are worth. Current employees can view pay stubs, which include information about employee and employer contributions to legally required and voluntary benefits programs; however, the information is often presented in tabular form such that the relative cost sharing between the employer and employee may not "jump off the page" for employees; data visualizations can be effective tools for communicating the value of benefits. Finally, because HR managers may lack the time or expertise to conduct formal communication about benefits, they may benefit from partnering with public relations managers or firms to determine how and when to deliver benefits communications.[99]

CHAPTER SUMMARY

Benefits are part of the organization's broader rewards system, and like other rewards, strategic deployment and administration of benefits can have important implications for attracting, motivating, and retaining workers. In the United States, legally required benefits include Social Security benefits, workers' compensation, federal and state unemployment insurance, and certain health care benefits. Voluntary benefits are discretionary in nature; employers must think carefully and strategically to decide which benefits they will offer. They must also monitor the extent to which employees are utilizing already available benefits. Examples of voluntary benefits include various forms of medical, dental, vision, life, and retirement insurance, as well as wellness and work–life programs and perquisites. Finally, employers often encounter challenges and opportunities when administering and communicating benefits to employees.

KEY TERMS

Cash balance plan

Compensatory time off (comp time)

Consolidated Omnibus Budget Reconciliation Act (COBRA)

Defined-benefit plan

Defined-contribution plan

Educational-assistance program

Employee Retirement Income Security Act (ERISA)

Family and Medical Leave Act (FMLA)

Federal Insurance Contributions Act (FICA)

Flexible benefits plans

401(k) plan

403(b) plan

Health Insurance Portability and Accountability Act (HIPAA)

Holiday pay

Individual retirement plan : individual retirement arrangement (IRA)

Life insurance program

Long-term disability insurance

Managed-care plans

Money-purchase plan

Paid time off (PTO)

Patient Protection and Affordable Care Act (ACA)

Pension Benefit Guaranty Corporation (PBGC)

Perquisites (perks)

Personal leave

Profit-sharing program

Short-term disability insurance

Sick time (sick leave)

Social Security Act

Tax deferred

Traditional-care plans

Vacation pay

Workers' compensation

HR REASONING AND DECISION-MAKING EXERCISES

Mini-Case Analysis Exercise: Communicating the Value of Benefits

Trident Health System has been experiencing difficulties attracting and retaining registered nurses (RNs) at its central hospital. Based on data from follow-up surveys with former applicants and from exit interviews conducted with former employees who voluntarily left the organization, HR leaders have concluded that a large number of individuals have been lured to a local competitor called Advantage Health. In particular, a number of former applicants and employees have reported that their primary reason for leaving was because Advantage Health paid RNs higher hourly wages as well as higher night and weekend pay differentials.

The HR leadership at Trident Health System acknowledges that they pay RNs lower wages than Advantage Health. However, based on market review data, they have reason to believe that Trident Health System offers one of the most generous benefits packages of any similar-sized health care organization in the region. Specifically, they offer generous employer cost-sharing contributions to employee medical, dental, and vision plans, as well as on-site subsidized child care services and a free employee cafeteria. Despite their generous benefits package, HR leaders are concerned that perhaps they are not doing a good enough job communicating information about their benefits to job candidates and current employees. At this time, job candidates and current employees can access information about benefits via the company's benefits webpage, and current employees can also look at their benefits deductions presented in their biweekly pay stub.

1. What can Trident Health System do to improve how it communicates benefits to job candidates? What about current employees?

2. What methods would you recommend that Trident Health System use to communicate the value of its benefits offerings? Why?

3. What data collection method(s) can the HR leaders use to determine which benefits employees (a) say they want and (b) actually utilize?

HR Decision Analysis Exercise: Unintended Consequences?

For the past 12 years, your company has offered an employer-sponsored health maintenance organization (HMO) medical plan to employees and their dependents. After employer contributions are taken into account, employees contribute $38 per biweekly paycheck, on average, to pay for their plan premiums. The HMO does not have a deductible, and the annual out-of-pocket maximum is $1,250 for an individual and $2,500 for a family. The HMO does not cover out-of-network providers, procedures, or services.

Over the past few years, an increasing number of employees have come to your company's benefits specialists with complaints about the lack of out-of-network coverage. For instance, one employee conveyed a tragic story about how her husband, who was covered under her plan, chose not to see a nearby world-renowned oncologist for his cancer treatment because the oncologist was out of network; ultimately, he died from complications due to cancer. Based on your recommendation as the director of benefits, the company replaced the HMO with a preferred provider organization (PPO), with the goal of providing some financial relief for those receiving care from out-of-network providers. It is estimated that the average biweekly premium paid by employees is now $51, which is higher than the average premium for the old HMO. In addition, the annual out-of-pocket maximums are $1,500 for an individual and $3,000 for a family, both of which are higher than the out-of-pocket maximums for the HMO. Finally, the co-pays and co-insurance for the PPO are roughly the same as the HMO.

FIGURE 13.3 ■ Characteristics of Effective HRM Decisions

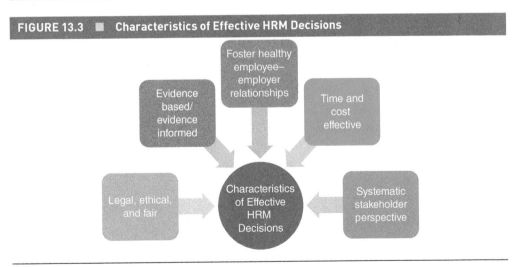

Do you have any concerns about switching to the PPO from the HMO? Do you think there will be any unintended consequences of switching to the PPO? Consider this decision using the following criteria.

Please provide the rationale for your answer to each of the questions below.

Is this decision legal, ethical, and fair?

Is it evidence based/evidence informed?

Does it foster healthy employee–employer relationships?

Is it time- and cost-effective?

Does it take a systematic stakeholder perspective?

Considering your analysis above, overall, do you think this would be an effective decision? Why or why not?

What, if anything, do you think should be done differently or considered to help make this decision more effective?

HR Decision-Making Exercise: Paid Parental Leave at Jembe Banks

Jembe Banks is a regional bank that is headquartered in Detroit, Michigan, and has branches throughout Michigan, Indiana, Wisconsin, and Illinois. The bank currently employs nearly 350 employees at its headquarters and more than 2,300 employees at its various branches.

Each year, the HR team at Jembe Banks conducts a benefits survey designed to measure employees' preferences and attitudes regarding different benefits, as well as which benefits they plan to enroll in during the next fiscal year. At the end of each year's survey, the HR team provides the following open-ended question: "Is there a benefit that you would like for Jembe to offer in the future? Explain why." After reviewing responses from last year's survey, the HR team discovered that 121 employees out of the 899 who completed the survey stated that they wanted Jembe to offer paid parental leave. Respond to and discuss the following questions:

1. Legally, does the company have to provide paid parental leave? Explain.

2. If the company decides to provide paid parental leave, how many weeks of paid leave should the company provide? Why?

3. Should the company provide the same amount of paid parental leave to mothers and fathers alike? Why or why not?

4. Should a mother and father who are both employed by Jembe be allowed to take their paid leave concurrently? Why or why not?

DATA AND ANALYTICS EXERCISE: EVALUATING EMPLOYEES' SATISFACTION WITH BENEFITS

Offering the right mix of benefits can be quite challenging. Employers want to manage costs while also providing benefits that attract, motivate, and retain potential and current employees, and employees want benefits that meet their needs. Even a company with the best assortment of benefits offerings can face problems if program details are not properly communicated and explained to employees. Employee surveys can be a powerful data collection tool when used to understand employees' attitudes toward benefits and how to improve benefits offerings.

Imagine an employee survey with items (e.g., questions) pertaining to the following attitudinal and behavioral concepts: overall benefits satisfaction, turnover intentions, and attendance at a benefits information session. Overall benefits satisfaction and turnover intentions are assessed with five-item measures, where employees rated each item using a 1 = strongly disagree and 5 = strongly agree response scale. An example item for overall benefits satisfaction is "I am satisfied with the company's current medical plan offerings." A sample item for turnover intentions is "I am considering leaving the organization in the next 6 months." A single item is used to assess attendance at a benefits information session, such that employees respond either "Yes, I attended" or "No, I did not attend."

In what follows, we include a sample of employee response data for illustration purposes, where each row contains a unique employee's data and each column contains employees' scores on each of the three attitudinal and behavioral concepts. To simplify things, the average of employees' responses (i.e., scores) on the five-item measures for overall benefits satisfaction and turnover intentions have already been computed.

Overall Benefits Satisfaction	Turnover Intentions	Attended a Benefits Information Session
3.78	2.87	Yes
4.60	1.91	Yes
3.19	2.14	Yes
4.12	1.90	Yes
3.88	2.90	Yes
3.84	1.64	Yes
4.68	1.63	Yes
3.46	3.29	Yes
3.26	2.45	Yes
4.52	2.07	Yes
2.06	2.98	No
2.84	2.97	No
3.63	3.01	No
3.36	3.17	No
3.64	3.45	No
2.84	4.09	No
2.71	3.40	No
2.84	3.14	No
2.86	2.83	No
2.93	2.66	No

Given these data, we will attempt to answer the following questions:

- Is there a negative correlation between overall benefits satisfaction and turnover intentions, such that employees with higher overall satisfaction with benefits offerings have fewer intentions to leave the company?

- Do employees who attended a benefits information session have higher overall satisfaction with their benefits than employees who did not?

To answer the first question, we can use simple linear regression, where overall benefits satisfaction is specified as the predictor variable and turnover intentions is specified as the outcome variable. Using Excel, we find the following:

	Coefficients	Standard Error	t Stat	p-value	Lower 95%	Upper 95%
Intercept	4.81	.61	7.89	.00	3.53	6.09
Overall Benefits Satisfaction	−.60	.17	−3.49	.00	−.97	−.24

The results indicate that the regression coefficient for overall benefits satisfaction in relation to turn-over intentions is –.60, which means that the association between the two variables is negative. Such an association means that for every 1-point increase in overall benefits satisfaction, we tend to see turn-over intentions drop by .60 points. The corresponding p value is less than the conventional two-tailed cutoff (alpha) value of .05, which means we can treat the regression coefficient of –.60 as being statistically significant. Together, these two pieces of information provide evidence that, indeed, employees with higher overall satisfaction with benefits offerings have fewer intentions to leave the company.

Regarding the second question, we can run an independent-samples t test using Excel to determine whether the average overall benefits satisfaction score for those who attend a benefits information session is significantly higher than the average overall benefits satisfaction score for those who did not attend a session.

	Yes	No
Mean	3.93	2.97
Variance	.29	.22
Observations	10	10
Pooled Variance	.26	
Hypothesized Mean Difference	0	
df	18	
t Stat	4.22	
p(T<=t) one-tail	.00	
t Critical one-tail	1.73	
p(T<=t) two-tail	.00	
t Critical two-tail	2.10	

The results indicate the t statistic that corresponds to the difference between the two means (averages) is 4.22, and the associated two-tailed p value is less than the conventional cutoff of .05. Based on this information, we have evidence that in fact there is a statistically significant difference between the average overall benefits satisfaction score for those who attended a benefits information session and the average overall benefits satisfaction score for those who did not attend a session. To determine whether those who attended the information session had a higher average, we can look at the mean scores. The mean for the group of employees who indicated "Yes, I attended" was 3.93, whereas the mean for those who indicated "No, I did not attend" was 2.97. Thus, we found support that indeed those who attended an information session tended to have higher satisfaction with the company's current benefits offerings.

Excel Extension: Now You Try!

- On **edge.sagepub.com/bauer2e**, you will find an Excel exercise that provides additional practice evaluating employees' satisfaction with benefits offerings.

- Using regression and independent-samples t tests, you will test different hypotheses and answer different questions based on employee survey data.

SPECIAL TOPICS IN HR

14 EMPLOYEE AND LABOR RELATIONS

LEARNING OBJECTIVES

After reading and studying this chapter, you should be able to do the following:

14.1 Define *employee relations* and *labor relations*, and identify key factors that influence them.

14.2 Compare different types of organizational policies and procedures.

14.3 Recognize the role that the labor movement plays globally.

14.4 Outline the collective bargaining process.

14.5 Evaluate the possible courses of action when negotiating parties fail to reach an agreement.

THE FIRST AMAZON PLANT TO UNIONIZE: THE CASE OF THE JFK8 AMAZON FULFILLMENT CENTER

Supporters of Amazon workers attempting to win a second union election at the LDJ5 Amazon Sort Center join a rally in support of the union on April 24, 2022, in Staten Island, New York. Chris Smalls successfully organized the JFK8 Amazon Fulfillment Center across the street, making it the first Amazon plant to unionize.

Photo by Andrew Lichtenstein/Corbis via Getty Images

Amazon is a multinational technology company. It was founded in the state of Washington in 1994 by Jeff Bezos as an online marketplace for books under the name of Cadabra, Inc., but the name was changed to Amazon by 1995. In the years that have followed, Amazon has expanded dramatically into new ventures beyond selling books. It is a worldwide company with headquarters in the state of Washington and Arlington, Virginia. And, it's big business. In fact, Amazon is the world's largest retailer outside of China and is currently the second largest private employer in the United States. In 2022, Amazon's revenue was nearly $514 billion.

From the start, Amazon prided itself as a customer-centric company with four guiding principles: customer obsession rather than competitor focus, passion for invention, commitment to operational excellence, and long-term thinking. Amazon is a major employer and boasts that it has created more U.S. jobs in the last decade than any other company. While Amazon was ranked 14th on the Forbes World's Best Employers list and pays relatively well (an average of $18 per hour), it is also known to demand a lot out of employees. In 2018, then Amazon chief Jess Bezos said, "We don't believe we need a union to be an intermediary between ourselves and our workers." However, when it comes to labor relations, it is predictable that when employees feel their needs are not being met, they tend to seek ways to change that. Unionization is one highly visible way to do it.

Amazon is an obvious candidate for unionization attempts given that it's a large employer with major operations in blue-collar occupations such as warehouse employees, fulfillment, and delivery. Unionization is something the company has fought against successfully for decades. However, in 2022, the company's first labor union in the United States formed in a warehouse on Staten Island where approximately 8,000 people are employed. The new union is called Amazon Labor Union at JFK8. Amazon lost its appeal to overturn the historic vote to form Amazon's first union. In the months that followed, two more union attempts failed. Given a number of economic factors, Amazon cut over 18,000 jobs in early 2023. What this all means for both unions and organizations such as Amazon remains unclear at this point. But what is clear is that unions are seeing more and more support in the United States, with over 70% of Americans currently supporting them when asked if they approve or disapprove of labor unions.[1]

CASE DISCUSSION QUESTIONS

1. Prior to reading this case, were you aware of whether or not Amazon had units that were unionized?

2. If you were a manager at Amazon, how would you react to a unionization attempt? Would your answer change if you were an employee?

3. What are your thoughts regarding the pros and cons of unions?

4. Do you agree or disagree with former Amazon CEO Jeff Bezos's statement regarding there being no need for a union as an intermediary between upper management and the organization's frontline workers? Explain your answer.

5. Do you think that the successful unionization attempt on Staten Island has positive or negative implications for employee relations? Explain your answer.

To hear more about unions in the United States, view this YouTube video: https://www.youtube.com/watch?v= pb-8pxjGcTg

INTRODUCTION

Much of employee relations is tied to an organization's HR policies and procedures. In addition, organizations must adhere to formal labor laws such as terms of employment and particularly labor laws relating to **labor unions** and collective bargaining, referred to as labor relations. Employee relations and labor relations are associated with a wide range of HRM topics you have already learned about in this book such as rewards, benefits, training, and job security.

This chapter explores the key components of both employee relations and labor relations from both historical and modern organizational perspectives. We begin by delving into the definition of employee relations and factors related to this concept. Then we shift the focus to organizational policies and procedures, employee rights and responsibilities, and grievance procedures, which are also aspects of employee and labor relations. We discuss the labor movement and issues associated with union formation, functioning, and dispute management. We then outline the collective bargaining process and the alternative methods of resolving negotiations when an agreement cannot be reached.

FACTORS INFLUENCING EMPLOYEE RELATIONS

Employee relations refers to the collective relationships between different employees as well as between
employees and management in an organization. The act of managing these relationships through
adherence to labor laws and relationships with unions and collective bargaining agreements is termed
labor relations. Many factors influence employee relations. If you have taken an organizational behavior or principles of management course, you are probably familiar with such factors, as entire chapters
are devoted to many of them; this textbook has touched on several of these issues as well. Here the
focus is on these five important factors that might influence employee relations: culture, fair treatment,
working conditions, employment laws, and unions (see Figure 14.1).

FIGURE 14.1 ■ Factors Influencing Employee Relations

Employee relations are influenced by several aspects of organizations, including those depicted here.

Culture

Culture is defined as the shared assumptions that members of an organization have, which affect how
they act, think, and perceive their environment. Therefore, the culture that evolves within an organization can exhibit a major positive or negative effect on employee relations. It is also important to keep in
mind that subcultures may also develop within organizations such that different groups may have different perceptions or experiences that influence their employee relations. One major factor that affects
culture and employee relations is how individuals are treated in terms of both procedures and outcomes. In fact, employment law experts argue that doing five things is important in avoiding lawsuits:
Create strong relationships with employees, handle employee issues quickly, document well, comply
with all laws, and have written policies and/or **employee handbooks** to help guide decisions.[2] Thus, the
next point we will cover is how fair (or unfair) treatment may affect employee relations.

Fair Treatment and Voice

Fair treatment is so important for employee relations that SHRM's Code of Ethics includes fairness
and justice. Specifically, it reads, "As human resource professionals, we are ethically responsible for
promoting and fostering fairness and justice for all employees and their organizations." This includes

cultivating an environment of inclusiveness, developing and administering policies that are fair and consistent, and respecting individuals. When individuals feel that they are not being treated fairly, they tend to have lower job attitudes, poorer performance and greater withdrawal behaviors, and a higher likelihood of joining a union.[3] Thus, organizations wishing to develop and maintain positive employee–employer relations should keep fairness in mind when interacting with employees and applicants, to gather feedback from employees regularly to see what issues and improvements might be addressed, and to keep fairness and justice in mind when making decisions that impact employees. Unfortunately, research shows that 34% of employees reported experiencing mistreatment, and 44% reported witnessing mistreatment of others at work. The financial cost of such unfair mistreatment is estimated to be between $691.70 billion and $1.97 trillion annually.[4]

Not complying with labor laws can be costly. For example, in 2021, Chipotle was sued by New York City for $151 million for what they say is 600,000 violations of workers' rights. Chipotle eventually settled the case out of court for over $20 million.

©iStockphoto.com/PierreDesrosiers

Working Conditions

When we refer to working conditions, there are many possible aspects of work that relate to employee relations. For example, rewards and benefits are aspects of work that are often reasons for employees to passively withdraw or actively look for employment elsewhere. Similarly, working in unsafe conditions can be a major concern and has been related to strained employee relations. In other instances, the actual workplace might be physically safe but create stress due to shift work, overtime, or a lack of flexibility in how or when work gets done. As the opening case on Amazon indicates, changes to benefits led to strained employment relations and union activity. Some companies such as Costco are known as leaders in their industry in terms of wages and benefits even in the low-margin world of groceries and retail. The company is known for promoting from within, like Craig Jelinek, a 3-year veteran who took over as CEO in 2012. In fact, 98% of store managers have been promoted from within stores. Costco also pays well, with an average of $24/hour versus $15/hour at Walmart, a store offering similar items, or the national average of around $11/hour for retail employees. Employees also receive full health benefits, a 401(k) retirement plan with stock options after 1 year, and generous vacation and family leave policies.[5]

Employment Laws

In the United States, employment laws are a major factor in the practice of HR. Understanding how they influence and regulate employee relations is important. Employment laws matter for the practice of HRM and for what employees expect in terms of employment relations with organizational members and the organization as a whole.

Unions

Finally, as we saw in the opening case and you will read in the pages that follow, the mere possibility of an organization's workforce joining a labor union (referred to as "unionization") may influence employee relations. However, once a union is in place, employee relations become formalized in specific and prescribed ways. Much of this chapter focuses on understanding the history of labor unions, trends in unionization, how unions are formed, and how they function. Also covered are organizational policies and procedures, which exist regardless of whether a union is in place. Keep in mind, however, that unions are tasked to bargain over policies as well, so at times, they are deeply involved in forming, informing, and monitoring organizational policies and procedures.

ORGANIZATIONAL POLICIES AND PROCEDURES

<table>
<tr><td>LEARNING OBJECTIVE</td></tr>
<tr><td>14.2   Compare different types of organizational policies and procedures.</td></tr>
</table>

Designing, implementing, and enforcing organizational policies and procedures are often managed by HR departments. When unions are in place, these policies are negotiated, as we will see in greater detail in the sections that follow. However, it is important to understand how organizational policies and procedures are communicated and what they typically entail regardless of how they came to be.

Employee Handbooks

Organizational policies and procedures outline the rules and expectations for both employees and employers. Although there are laws that require employers to inform their employees about their specific workplace rights, it is not a legal mandate to have an actual employee handbook. However, many organizations do create handbooks including such information because they are useful for employees and managers to understand what is expected of them. Some handbooks are long and read like legal documents. Others are short and written simply. However, it is critical that employees of all levels understand that handbooks are part of the HR compliance process, so what is written in the handbook provides an answer if disputes occur between managers and employees. Thus, it is important that what is included is accurate, consistently enforced, and understood by everyone within the organization. Not doing so can put organizations at risk should an employee complaint be filed.

Normally, new employees receive their handbooks as part of the onboarding process of orientation and compliance. Handbooks can make for pretty dry reading, and it might be tempting to skip reading it while trying to adjust to one's new job. Some companies such as The Motley Fool, which has appeared on Glassdoor.com's Best Places to Work list, have created fully interactive onboarding experiences, which include a video introduction from the CEO, as well as specific company policies and procedures, and a list of key terms for employees. When Zappos founder Tony Hsieh was running the company, the Zappos.com's employee handbook was written in a comic book style and featured a story of a grandmother explaining Zappos's culture, policies, and procedures.[6] Regardless of how entertaining the information is, all new employees should take the time to read and understand the handbook given what an important document it is as the basis for the employment relationship.

Examples of Types of Organizational Policies

Organizations vary in how many policies they include in their employee handbook depending on a number of factors, including the organization's industry, size, age, and culture, as well as state and local requirements. Rather than review all the potential policies that might be included, the focus is on five different types of policies that might be included: legally required information, code of conduct, leaves, appearance, and social media policies.

Legally Required Information

Although employee handbooks are not legally required, policies are often included in them because policies that must be addressed by law are important to outline and share with employees. These include worker's compensation policies, family medical leave policies, and EEOC nondiscrimination policies as required by the U.S. Department of Labor. Requirements change over time, so the suggestion to review the content shared with new employees is an ongoing task.

Code of Conduct

The code of conduct might include information about expectations for workplace behaviors, such as respect, confidentiality, and EEO compliance, and unacceptable behaviors, such as discrimination or sexual harassment. It is important that organizations communicate their expectations regarding what constitutes a *conflict of interest* that might unduly influence decisions or have the appearance of doing so. Such policies should include definitions of conflicts of interest and what to do if such conflicts exist. Some organizations include code-of-conduct training that all employees must complete. Often employees will be asked to sign that they have read, understand, and agree to the code of conduct.

Leave Policy

Beyond the Family Medical Leave Act considerations, some organizations prescribe and strictly enforce how sick days, personal days, and/or vacation days are to be taken. Other organizations, such as Zoom, LinkedIn, Oracle, and Netflix, have no limit on the amount of paid leave that can be taken.[7] Instead, they trust employees to behave responsibly and only take as much time as they need while keeping up with their responsibilities. Regardless of where a company is on this continuum, it is important to be clear about what the policy is and how employees should schedule days off to avoid confusion or resentment.

Appearance

There are many aspects of employee appearance that may or may not be outlined in an employee handbook. For example, dress codes, personal hygiene, facial hair, and body art and piercings may be addressed. Dress codes range from business formal, such as wearing a specific uniform, to casual. The type of dress code often depends on multiple factors, such as the type of industry the organization is in, the type of work an employee does, whether special dress or equipment is needed for safety (such as when working in construction sites), geography, and/or the organizational culture. Personal hygiene issues range from a safety requirement at work, such as a restaurant employee washing their hands before returning to work, to an uncomfortable topic such as body odor. Managers and employees need guidance in how to handle such matters with sensitivity, and SHRM reminds us that odors may be caused by many factors outside of an employee's control, such as a medical condition or a specific diet. Thus, such issues must be addressed appropriately to avoid violating the Americans with Disabilities Act or triggering other claims of discrimination.[8] Including guidelines on what is expected and whether perfumes and colognes are allowed in the workplace can be helpful for employees and those who work around them to deal with the issues professionally and discreetly. Overall, the thing to keep in mind is that as long as they do not discriminate on the basis of a protected class, organizations have the legal right to adopt whatever dress codes and grooming requirements they desire to fit their culture and/or promote a particular brand or look. However, the policies they choose to enact will most likely have an influence on employee relations.

SPOTLIGHT ON LEGAL ISSUES: TATTOOS IN THE WORKPLACE

In the United States, more than 29% of adults of all ages, and nearly 41% of Millennials specifically, have at least one tattoo.[9] In general, employers have the right to choose not to hire someone, or to fire them, for tattoos. An exception to this is when tattoos are due to religious reasons. In one case, Red Robin restaurant fired a server for having tattoos that were part of his religious practice. Red Robin lost its case for termination in court and paid the server $150,000.[10] However, this is relatively rare in terms of outcomes for such court cases, especially those dealing with personal-expression or freedom-of-speech arguments. Another way employers can get into trouble, however, is if they discriminate against some types of tattoos but not others. The key for organizations is to be consistent and fair in applying their dress code and grooming standards across all employees.

The First Amendment of the United States Constitution protects the rights of individuals to free speech, and this includes the display of tattoos. But that does not mean that employers in the private sector have to allow them. A survey found that 60% of HR professionals felt that visible tattoos would negatively impact an applicant's chances of securing employment, and 74% felt that way about facial piercings. It is not clear how these negative reactions may evolve over time given the growing number of individuals with tattoos in the United States. For example, 60% of working Americans say that the definition of what's considered "professional" changed during the pandemic.[11] Well-known organizations such as Disney, UPS, the U.S. Army, and Virgin Atlantic are examples of those relaxing visible tattoo restrictions in the workplace.[12] The key for organizations is to be consistent and fair in applying the dress code and grooming standards across all employees.

Social Media

Nordstrom is famous for having a handbook that fits on a 5 × 8 card. It includes the following:

> *Our number one goal is to provide outstanding customer service. Set both your personal and professional goals high. We have great confidence in your ability to achieve them, so our employee handbook is very simple. We have only one rule. . . . Our one rule: Use best judgment in all situations. There will be no additional rules.*

That, however, is not the end of Nordstrom's workplace policies. For example, Nordstrom's social media guidelines point to 10 guidelines as an offshoot of its original rule stating, "If you use social media accounts to connect and share about Nordstrom, we ask that you use good judgment and follow these additional guidelines."[13] Starbucks fired one employee in Indiana for posting a TikTok complaining about demanding customers, which the organization argued was a policy violation. Keep in mind that policies should follow employment laws like those related to the right of employees to discuss working conditions, as this is behavior protected by the National Labor Relations Board (NLRB) laws. For example, an ambulance company, American Medical Response of Connecticut, fired an employee for criticizing her supervisor on Facebook, and the NLRB filed a complaint that this violated workers' rights.[14] Organizations should clearly delineate their policies regarding social media both during and outside of work hours, as this has become an increasingly controversial issue.

THE LABOR MOVEMENT

LEARNING OBJECTIVE
14.3   Recognize the role that the labor movement plays globally.

The history of the labor movement and the growth of labor unions can be traced back to fundamental changes in the workplace. In the early 1900s, factories began to set up procedures to address concerns regarding employee wages and additional labor concerns. However, following the Great Depression in the 1930s and then World War II, a surge in union membership took place through the 1950s. Union membership has been on a steady decline in the United States in recent decades. Whereas the decision to organize or join a union is a personal one for each employee, there are some common reasons why employees pursue unionization in their workplaces. There are also various types of unions. We next turn our attention to some potential reasons why employees seek to unionize.

Reasons Employees Unionize

Employees unionize for a variety of reasons including job dissatisfaction, working conditions, and employee disengagement. We start with job dissatisfaction.

Job Dissatisfaction

Dissatisfaction with one's job is a major reason employees organize and join unions. This makes sense, because when an individual is unhappy about a situation at work, they may engage in a number of behaviors in response. Different reactions to job dissatisfaction are illustrated using the exit–voice–loyalty–neglect framework, which argues that employee behavioral reactions range in terms of how active workers are as well as how constructive they are. Behaviors directed toward withdrawing from the organization include employee lateness, absenteeism, and turnover and are termed *exit*. Active and constructive responses to dissatisfying working conditions include *voice*, through which employees attempt to improve conditions. *Neglect* and *loyalty* are passive and refer to allowing the conditions to worsen or hoping they will get better. Figure 14.2 illustrates these four possible reactions in terms of these factors. Attempts to organize and unionize represent one potential form of voice behavior. Indeed, in the first half of 2022, union election petitions (an early step in certifying a union) grew by 57%. One area of dissatisfaction for workers is the requirement to "upskill" for the needs of the future workplace.[15]

FIGURE 14.2 ■ Four Possible Reactions to Job Dissatisfaction

Employees may respond to dissatisfaction through exit, voice, neglect, or loyalty.

Working Conditions

So what specific things might employees be dissatisfied about? There are multiple reasons related to working conditions that may affect whether employees are motivated to organize or join a union. These include concerns regarding working conditions such as pay, benefits, safety, job security, hours, the working environment, and treatment. In other words, employees interested in voting for a union believe that the union will help them get more of the financial and nonfinancial working conditions they value.

The 40-hour workweek did not come into existence in the United States until 1937 with the passage of the Fair Labor Standards Act at the urging of unions, leading to the union slogan "Labor Unions: The folks who brought you the weekend."[16]

Underwood Archives/Getty Images

Although union membership has been declining, the inequality in hourly wages has been increasing, suggesting that unions do influence wages. In support of the argument that union workers enjoy greater levels of compensation, on average, union members earn more and enjoy better benefits (e.g., health insurance and retirement accounts) than their nonunionized counterparts across the United States within the same occupations.[17] For example, across all industries, union workers earn a median weekly pay rate of $1,216 versus $1,029 for nonunion workers in 2022.[18]

Employee Disengagement

How engaged employees are at work is also related to whether employees are interested in unionizing. Employees who reported not being engaged with their work also reported being more likely to vote yes to a union and to become union members.[19]

Employees who are disengaged or dissatisfied or feel unfairly treated can work with organizations toward improvement. But organizations need tools to do so. One such tool is the administration of an annual employee opinion survey to gauge employee attitudes and to identify problems and potential problems within the organization. Such surveys are big undertakings in terms of employee time to respond as well as the effort to create, administer, and analyze the results. Although large organizations such as Disney, Walmart, and Ford Motor Company already administer such surveys, more and more organizations are also beginning to administer smaller surveys more frequently (see Figure 14.3).

Why Do Some Organizations Resist Unionization?

Not all organizations resist unionization, but it is common for organizations to work to avoid it for a number of reasons, including profit concerns and decreased autonomy. We discuss each of these.

FIGURE 14.3 ■ Results of an Employee Engagement Pulse Survey

Qualtrics, a survey platform company, advocates for the benefits of pulse surveys, which are shorter and administered more frequently than annual opinion surveys. Such surveys allow organizations to track changes in responses month to month and quarter to quarter such as the results shown here.

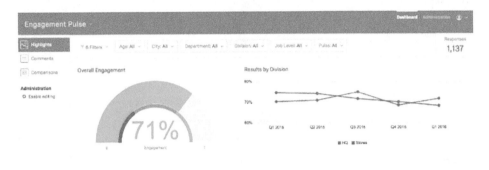

Source: Courtesy of Qualtrics. https://www.qualtrics.com/human-resources/employee-pulse-surveys/

Profit Concerns

It makes sense that organizations might be concerned that if they pay workers more in terms of wages or increase worker benefits and programs, they will become less profitable. However, that is only true if there are no financial benefits to workers being satisfied, such as stronger productivity or innovation. There is a great deal of debate regarding whether belonging to a union makes employees more or less satisfied overall. Similarly, it is not clear if organizations with unions are more or less profitable than their nonunionized counterparts, as it depends on a variety of factors. Even though the reality for a given organization within a given country or industry is unclear in terms of profit, it is clear that unions do decrease an organization's autonomy to make decisions that impact employees.

Decreased Autonomy

As you will see in the pages that follow, when an organization's workforce is unionized or has a union in place, it serves to decrease how much discretion the organization has to alter wages and benefits and to set policies that affect employees. Rather than having full autonomy to make changes as long as they are legal, organizations with union members must consider the contract in place. This can make them less able to respond quickly to changes in the market or to changing conditions. This can be a concern for organizations. In fact, it has been observed that the worse the market conditions are, the more likely executives of a firm are to choose union-avoidance strategies rather than union–labor cooperation strategies. Business and labor do not have to have an adversarial relationship. In countries such as Denmark, unions and employers work together closely, and Denmark is considered one of the easiest countries in the world in which to conduct business, as are Singapore and New Zealand.[20]

Unions and Laws

To really understand the context of labor movements, it is important to trace the series of laws associated with their growth and regulation from the 1930s through today. First and foremost, unions exist in a legal context. Thus, we will move to a discussion of the different laws that set the legal context for work and workers. While many laws relate to employees and unions, we will highlight some of the most important acts related to HR practices, starting with the Norris-LaGuardia Act.

Norris-LaGuardia Act (1932)

This act was a critical step toward changing national labor relations. It outlawed the ability of federal courts to stop union activities such as a picket or **strike**. It also outlawed agreements from employees to employers that they would not form or join a union. The passage of this act signaled a new era of support for unions and their activities. Although not a comprehensive act in itself, it is regarded as being important in laying the foundation of changing attitudes toward supporting labor movements in the United States.

National Labor Relations (or Wagner) Act (1935)

Building upon the legislative momentum of the Norris-LaGuardia Act, the National Labor Relations (or Wagner) Act regulated national labor relations by granting unions fundamental rights and powers. These included important provisions such as the right to collective bargaining and the definition of unfair labor practices, and it established penalties for companies that violated these rights. The act describes five key unfair labor practices that include the right to

self-organization, to form, join, or assist labor unions, to bargain collectively through representatives of their own choosing, and to engage in other concerted activities for the purpose of collective bargaining or other mutual aid or protection, and shall also have the right to refrain from any or all such activities.

These rights, however, do not extend to the railway or airline industries. Finally, the act established the National Labor Relations Board (NLRB). As an independent U.S. government agency, the NLRB is tasked with supervising union elections and is empowered to investigate suspected unfair labor practices. The NLRB consists of a five-person board, and general counsel is appointed by the president of the United States with Senate consent. According to the NLRB, in 2022, the NLRB handled nearly 20,500 unfair practice charges, and historically more than 90% of meritorious unfair labor practices are settled by agreement (by board settlement or mutual private agreement).[21] For example, the NLRB argued that the following provisions within T-Mobile's employee handbook violated the Wagner Act: maintaining a positive work environment, not arguing or fighting, failing to be respectful or to demonstrate appropriate teamwork, outlawing all photography and audio or video recording in the workplace, and barring access to electronic information by individuals not approved. The court ruled that these handbook items did not violate the act and that "a reasonable employee would be fully capable of engaging in debate over union activity or working conditions, even vigorous or heated debate, without inappropriately arguing or fighting, or failing to treat others with respect."[22]

Labor Management Relations Act (1947)

The Labor Management Relations Act (1947), also known as the Taft-Hartley Act, amended and limited the National Labor Relations Act in key ways. For example, it added additional unfair labor practices employees might engage in rather than limiting such unfair acts to companies. In essence, the act was designed to limit the power of unions and to limit the ability of labor to strike. Specifically, it prohibited jurisdictional strikes so that only unions directly related to the work of a targeted business could participate, prohibited unions and corporations from making independent expenditures for federal candidates, outlawed closed shops that required employers to hire only union members, allowed states to pass right-to-work laws, required unions and employers to give 80 days advance notice before striking, gave the president of the United States the power to stop strikes if they might create a national emergency, allowed employers to terminate supervisors for supporting union activity, and gave employers the right to oppose unions. Finally, the act gave federal court jurisdiction to enforce collective bargaining agreements. We will cover the details of such agreements later on in this chapter.

Labor–Management Reporting and Disclosure Act (LMRDA) (1959)

The Labor–Management Reporting and Disclosure Act (LMRDA) (1959), also known as the Landrum-Griffin Act, deals with the relationship between a union and its members by prescribing how unions are internally regulated. The act protects union funds and was established to promote union democracy and fair elections. It requires labor organizations to file annual financial reports and reports on labor relations practices and established standards for the election of union officers as well as a Bill of Rights for union members. The act is administered by the Office of Labor-Management Standards.[23]

Right-to-Work Laws

A highly political topic involves who is covered and required to financially participate in unionized settings. A shift in this has taken the form of state right-to-work laws (Figure 14.4). Such laws, if enacted, mean that no one within that state may be compelled to join a union or pay fees or union dues to obtain or keep their job. In states without this law, employees who benefit from union activities such as collective bargaining, even if they choose not to join it, may be compelled to pay their "fair share" of union dues. The Labor Relations Act (also known as the Taft-Hartley Act), section 14(b), grants the right of states to enact such laws. The first two states to enact this were Arkansas and Florida in 1944. Since that time, as of 2023, dozens of additional states had joined them. Missouri and Michigan bucked this trend by overturning the controversial right-to-work laws in their states. In 2018, the Supreme Court ruled that nonunion workers cannot be forced to pay fees to public-sector unions, which overturned a 40-year-old ruling that led to fair-share fees.

FIGURE 14.4 ■ Right-to-Work States

States shown in blue are right-to-work states where employees decide whether to join or financially support a union. States shown in green are non-right-to-work states and may require all employees within unionized organizations to pay union dues, whether or not they are union members.

Disclaimer: State laws, include employment laws, are in a constant state of flux. Always check the most recent edition of your state's laws to ensure compliance with the latest provisions.

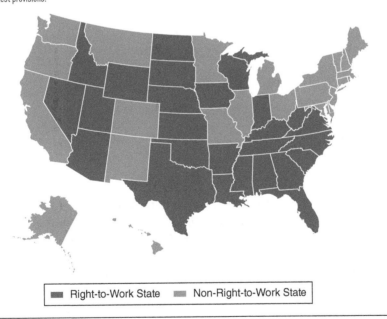

- Right-to-Work State
- Non-Right-to-Work State

Source: Based on information from National Right to Work Foundation, http://www.nrtw.org/right-to-work-states/

Trends in Union Membership

The Great Depression began in 1929 in the United States, and although unemployment was at record high levels, union membership grew by 300%. Unions had fewer than 3 million members in 1933 and more than 10 million by 1941. That trend has reversed itself in the past 35 years, and union membership has been on the decline in the United States, with 14.3 million workers belonging to a union in 2022, down from a high of 17.7 million workers in 1983.[24]

Union Membership in the United States

Union membership has decreased by nearly half since the 1980s, with 20% of all workers belonging to a union in 1983 and only 10.1% belonging to unions in 2022, according to the Bureau of Labor Statistics (Figure 14.5). Some of this is due to the changing nature of work. Unions tend to be highly concentrated within certain industries, such as transportation and utilities, construction, manufacturing, education and health services, wholesale and retail trade, and public-service employees. However, even in many of those industries, membership has been declining. It is interesting that unions are actually winning more workplace elections (i.e., elections that would allow them to form a union in their workplaces), with 72% of the elections conducted by the National Labor Relations Board in 2016 being successful. Additionally, 70% of adults generally support labor unions during this period of decline, but fewer elections are being held.[25]

FIGURE 14.5 ■ Union Membership, 1983–2022

This chart illustrates how union membership (as a percentage of employed workers in the United States) continued to decrease. We have seen a high of 20.1% in 1983 to a low of 10.1% in 2022.

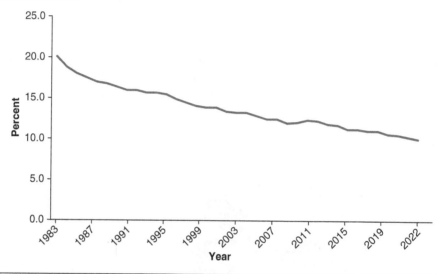

Source: Bureau of Labor Statistics. (2023). https://www.bls.gov/news.release/union2.nr0.htm

---

Global Unionization

The global landscape stands in sharp contrast with the trend in the United States. For example, over 92% of workers in Iceland belong to a union. Figure 14.6 indicates that the United States has a relatively low percentage of unionized workers compared with much of the industrialized world. For multinational corporations, which must deal with different labor laws and norms in different countries, it is important to understand the concept of *work councils*. These comprise elected employee representatives who work alongside management to help make decisions regarding working conditions. Work councils are mandated by law for organizations operating in EU countries if they exceed certain sizes.[26] In Norway, the Working Environment Act regulates key provisions for employment relationships: Employees work 37.5 hours per week; flexible hours are encouraged; employees get 5 weeks of holidays per year, with employees more than 60 years old getting an additional week of vacation; 43 weeks of paid parental leave are available for employees who have worked for at least 6 months; and employers have obligations to provide systematic training on health and safety issues.[27] It can be challenging for companies to navigate the different union rules and cultures, as they vary from country to country. For example, Amazon faced strong opposition in Germany from warehouse workers who wanted to organize toward a union. Whereas resistance to such activities might be common within the United States, in Germany it's virtually unheard of. In 2022, the German union called on Amazon workers to strike during Amazon's 2-day sale.[28]

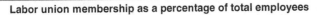

FIGURE 14.6   ■   Percentage of Eligible Workers With Labor Union Memberships (2020)

Labor union membership as a percentage of total employees

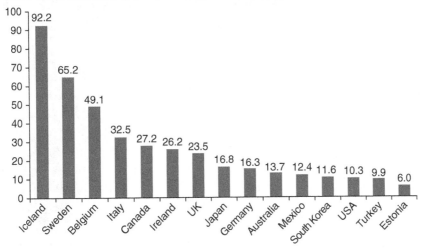

Source: OECD. (2020). https://www.oecd.org/about/members-and-partners/

SPOTLIGHT ON GLOBAL ISSUES: LABOR UNION MEMBERSHIP RATES VARY AROUND THE WORLD

A number of factors influence the percentage of employees who are represented by a union; these factors include history, politics, laws, and employment conditions. As you can see in Figure 14.6, global union membership as a percentage of total employees in several countries varies a great deal. For example, under 10% of employees belong to unions in Turkey versus over 92% in Iceland. The United States has relatively fewer union members as a percentage of total workers than countries such as Iceland, Sweden, Belgium, or Italy. However, it is also important to note that the 10.3% in the United States still represents a large number of individuals, as the United States has well over 334 million citizens versus the number of individuals in a smaller country such as Iceland, which has fewer than 350,000 citizens.

Union Formation and Dissolution

Even though union membership is in decline in the United States, it is still important to understand how unions are formed and dissolved, as the 14.3 million unionized workers in the United States is still a sizable number of individuals. Also, the potential for unionizing exists in most industries even if it is not traditionally a union industry. For example, digital news media has seen a surge of unionization, with 220 Huffington Post staffers joining the Writers Guild of America and East becoming the largest digital news company to become unionized.[29] Further, social media technology such as Unionbase by Larry Williams Jr. is making it easier than ever for workers to connect with unions.[30] Unfortunately, by 2023, many digital news outlets were laying off employees along with many organizations in many other industries.[31]

Steps to Forming a Union

The first step to the formation of a union is to conduct an organizing campaign. Formation is dependent on the union organizers getting at least 30% of the employees in the bargaining unit to sign an authorization card to prompt a union election. In order to secure those signatures, organizers normally need to have identified key issues that might motivate employees to want a union. This is because employees who are satisfied and feel they are treated fairly are less likely to join a union.

A statue by sculptor Rodin in Paris, France, is surrounded by piles of trash due to a 3-week garbage collectors' strike over changing labor conditions. The 2023 strike resulted in the accumulation of 10,000 metric tons of refuge. Such sanitation worker strikes help make a compelling case for the importance of those jobs.

©iStockphoto.com/Olivier DJIANN

If the union organizers are successful in gathering 30% to 50% of the required signatures, they can file an election petition and conduct a union election online or via paper ballots.[32] It is important for employers to understand what is possible to do as well as what is not possible to do during an organizing campaign (see Table 14.1).

TABLE 14.1 ■
During a union organizing campaign, employers and managers may not
● threaten employees with loss of jobs or benefits if they join or vote for a union,
● threaten to close the place of work if employees select a union to represent them,
● question employees about their thoughts about unions or union activities,
● promise benefits to employees to discourage their union support, or
● transfer, lay off, terminate, or assign employees more difficult work tasks, or punish employees for engaging in union activities or for filing an unfair labor practice charge.

Source: National Labor Relations Board. (2023). *Your rights during union organizing.* https://www.nlrb.gov/about-nlrb/rights-we-protect/the-law/employees/your-rights-during-union-organizing

Achieving more than 50% of signed authorization cards may lead to the union organizers requesting that the company voluntarily recognize the union. If the employer does, the National Labor Relations Board is asked to certify the union. If the employer does not recognize the union, things can become more complicated. If the union wins the election, officers are elected, and they or a designated team begin negotiations with the employer on their membership's behalf. The process, even after this point, is long. Research shows that it takes over 500 days to contract ratification.[33] Figure 14.7 summarizes the steps to forming a union.

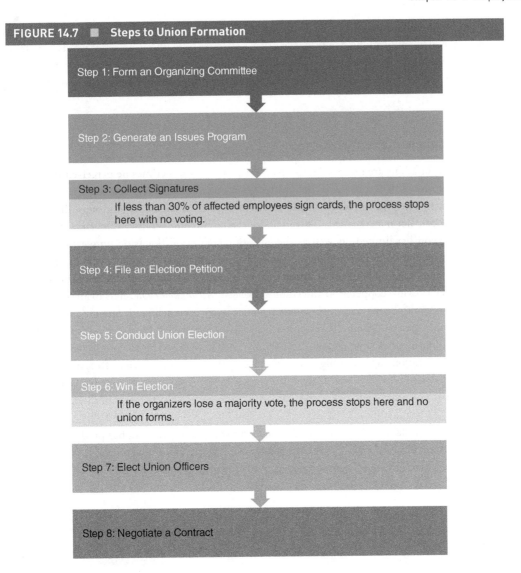

FIGURE 14.7 ■ Steps to Union Formation

Step 1: Form an Organizing Committee

Step 2: Generate an Issues Program

Step 3: Collect Signatures
If less than 30% of affected employees sign cards, the process stops here with no voting.

Step 4: File an Election Petition

Step 5: Conduct Union Election

Step 6: Win Election
If the organizers lose a majority vote, the process stops here and no union forms.

Step 7: Elect Union Officers

Step 8: Negotiate a Contract

Decertifying Unions

The Labor Management Relations Act (Taft-Hartley Act), discussed earlier in this chapter, laid out employees' rights to elect union leaders of their own choosing. In much the same way in which unions are formed, they can also be disbanded, or decertified. This may happen for a number of reasons, such as if employees do not think the union is doing a good job of representing them or if they prefer a different union. The process is parallel to union formation, with at least 30% of the workers in the bargaining unit needing to sign the petition to vote to decertify the union. However, the timing of union decertification is important. A decertification election may not take place when a contract is in place or within 1 year following a union's certification by the National Labor Relations Board.[34]

THE COLLECTIVE BARGAINING PROCESS

LEARNING OBJECTIVE
14.4   Outline the collective bargaining process.

If a union is in place, it is responsible for negotiating with the employer on behalf of its members. This is one of the major functions of a union. The final agreement addresses details outlining wages, hours, and working conditions for employees. The process of negotiating in good faith toward agreed terms on wages, hours, and working conditions is called collective bargaining. In other words, the union and employer engage in negotiations on behalf of the employees/union members. Engaging in effective negotiations includes having a conflict management approach, which we discuss in the following section.

Conflict Management Approaches

Although negotiations are not necessarily conflicts, they can sometimes be perceived that way or become that way. This is especially true in high-stakes negotiations between unions and management. Thus, it is helpful to recognize and understand that individuals and groups differ in their approach to conflict management. This includes the level of cooperation (focusing on both parties keeping conflict limited) as well as the level of competition (focusing on getting what they want) they engage in and their preferences for each approach. These approaches are summarized in Figure 14.8 and include avoidance, accommodation, compromise, competition, and collaboration. *Avoidance* refers to low cooperation and competitiveness. *Accommodation* refers to low competitiveness but high levels of cooperation. *Compromise* refers to an approach predominantly in the middle range of cooperative and competitive approaches. *Competition* refers to an approach that is low on cooperation but high on competition. And finally, *collaboration* refers to approaches that seek to find win-win solutions by being high on both cooperation and competition. Research shows that conflict and negotiation preferences may vary by national culture.[35] But generally, labor relations should be better when win-win collaboration strategies are sought because both parties will see their needs met at least partially. For example, in unionized manufacturing facilities, areas with more collaborative labor relations should have lower costs, less scrap, higher productivity, and a higher return on direct labor hours than those characterized as more adversarial. In a study of 356 HR managers and CEOs in Belgium, cooperative labor relations was related to positive workplace outcomes.[36]

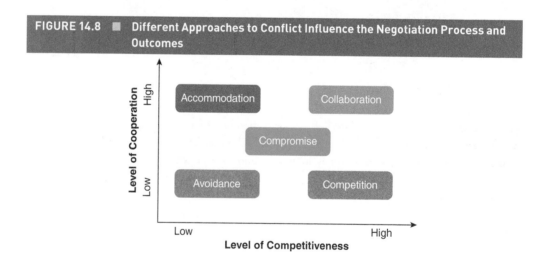

FIGURE 14.8 ■ Different Approaches to Conflict Influence the Negotiation Process and Outcomes

Negotiation Phase and Collective Bargaining Content

Negotiation is defined as the give-and-take process between two or more parties aimed toward reaching an agreement. Because collective bargaining is a form of formal negotiation, it helps to understand the five phases of the negotiation process. Different activities take place in each of the five phases of negotiation. These phases are the investigation, BATNA determination, presentation, bargaining, and closure (see Figure 14.9).

FIGURE 14.9 ■ The Five Phases of Negotiation

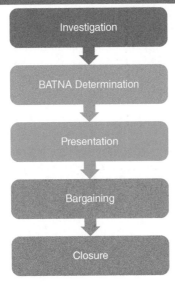

Phase 1: Investigation

In this first stage of the negotiation process, both sides gather information and investigate what the key issues are, identify the key goals that the team wishes to accomplish, review what data they have to support their positions, and determine what might have been done related to these issues in the past. Although this is a critical first step, not all negotiators spend enough time engaging in investigation at this phase, which can lead to suboptimal outcomes in the process. Research shows that the specific goals and interests being negotiated have an impact on how the negotiations are approached as well as the final negotiated outcome.[37]

Phase 2: BATNA Determination

BATNA stands for best alternative to a negotiated agreement.[38] While this second phase is important for any negotiator, it is especially important in a union negotiation process, because the alternatives can be quite costly to the organization, union, and employees, as well as to those who depend on the organization's work to be done in the case of a strike. Best practices for determining your BATNA include

- brainstorming a list of alternatives that you are willing to accept as a worst-case scenario,
- considering the modification of proposals to make them more attractive to both sides if necessary,
- going into the negotiation with back-up alternatives in case what you have planned to present does not work as well as you had planned,
- revising your BATNA over time as the negotiations progress, and
- keeping your BATNA private within your team.

After the investigation and BATNA phases are complete, it is time to formally prepare for the negotiation presentation.

Phase 3: Presentation

In the third phase of the negotiation process, all the information is summarized and presented in a manner that supports the negotiator's case. Both parties present their initial offers to one another.

Phase 4: Bargaining and Content of a Labor Agreement

In the bargaining phase, each party discusses their initial presentation of their offer. As part of this process, concessions are normally made. In other words, parties do not normally walk into collective bargaining negotiations expecting to get every single one of their demands met, as that is not realistic. Thus, having some idea of how to offer and accept concessions is helpful during bargaining.

Wages, hours worked, and benefits are three types of mandatory bargaining items established by the National Labor Relations Act. These items directly affect employees and may be bargained until an impasse takes place. It is also legal for employees to strike and for employers to lock out employees in the hopes of obtaining a mandatory item of bargaining. Permissive (or voluntary) bargaining items are not directly related to work. Examples include ground rules for negotiations and how unfair labor charges will be settled. Thus, both parties may agree to bargain over these; however, they are not required to, and they are not legally allowed to strike over permissive items. Finally, illegal bargaining items include closed-shop provisions or discrimination. Such items may not legally be entered into a collective bargaining agreement.

Phase 5: Closure

The final phase of the negotiation process is closure, in which both parties come to an agreement on the negotiated offers or if one party determines that the final offer is unacceptable. If an agreement is reached and signed by both parties, it becomes a written, legally enforceable contract for the specific period of time as negotiated (often 1 year). It includes details of working conditions, terms of employment, and procedures for dispute resolution. This may be known as a labor agreement, labor contract, or union agreement.

Getting to an agreement can be a major accomplishment.

©iStockphoto.com/Ridofranz

FAILURE TO REACH AN AGREEMENT

LEARNING OBJECTIVE

14.5   Evaluate the possible courses of action when negotiating parties fail to reach an agreement.

What happens if the parties fail to reach an agreement? The failure to reach an agreement may result in an impasse. An impasse may be resolved via mediation or arbitration, or it may result in a strike. Unfortunately, research shows that negotiators who fail to reach an agreement may become less willing to work together in the future, share information, or behave cooperatively. Thus, having negotiators with experience and confidence in their negotiating abilities can be effective in helping to buffer these negative effects of impasse. In addition, helping negotiators reach an agreement can be important for labor relations.

Alternative Dispute Resolution

When two parties fail to reach an agreement, alternative dispute resolution may be entered into either voluntarily or involuntarily. Alternative dispute resolution is defined as any method of resolving disputes that does not involve litigation. There are several different types of alternatives, including mediation, fact finders, and arbitration, which we discuss next.

Mediation

In mediation, the two parties are still in control of reaching a mutually acceptable agreement. The mediator is an impartial, third-party individual who helps the parties communicate more effectively and may be helpful in cases in which the ongoing relationship is important to preserve, such as in the case of collective bargaining. However, if one or both of the parties are unwilling to cooperate, mediation may not result in a resolution of the disputed contract terms.

Fact Finders

With fact finding, an impartial third party listens to the evidence and makes specific nonbinding recommendations to both parties. Fact finders gather and assess the information presented to them and also gather new information via investigation and consultation with experts. Their goal is to evaluate the facts of the case objectively to propose resolutions.

Arbitration

An arbitrator is an impartial third party who hears the facts of the case and then decides the outcome of the disputed contract terms. Arbitration may be *binding*, meaning that both parties agree to abide by the arbitrator's decision and not seek other options to resolve the dispute. A *nonbinding* resolution means parties may pursue a trial if they do not accept the recommended outcome.

Strikes and Work Stoppages

The history of HR was powerfully impacted when workers organized and began to demand better treatment. In fact, it was following a bitter strike in 1901 that the first human resource department was established by the National Cash Register Company. Thus, it is clear that the failure to reach an agreement can end in a strike or work stoppage (see Figure 14.10). A *strike* is defined as a type of work stoppage as the result of a concerted refusal of employees to work. The number of strikes in the United States has been decreasing since the 1940s. At the same time, in China, strikes are becoming increasingly common, with 2,726 strikes in 2015 compared to only 185 in 2011.[39] A violent revolt at the world's largest iPhone factory in China highlighted the challenges of the pandemic on factory workers around the world. In 2022 in the United States, there was a total of 23 work stoppages involving nearly 100,000 employees.[40] Another type of work stoppage is a *lockout*, defined by the Bureau of Labor Statistics as "a temporary withholding or denial of employment during a labor dispute in order to enforce terms of employment upon a group of employees."[41] Lockouts are initiated by the management of an organization.

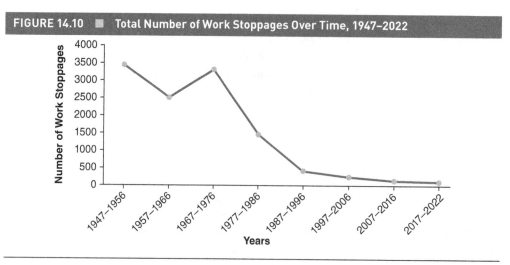

FIGURE 14.10 ■ Total Number of Work Stoppages Over Time, 1947–2022

Source: U.S. Bureau of Labor Statistics. (2023). https://www.bls.gov/wsp/

SPOTLIGHT ON ETHICS: WRITERS GUILD OF AMERICA STRIKES OVER TIME

A lot of money is made in the entertainment business, but it is not equally distributed. In November 2007, 12,000 screenwriters for film, TV, and radio represented by the Writers Guild of America went on strike over what they perceived as an unfair portion of profits made by studios on the shows compared to writers of those shows. The fundamental issues revolved around DVD residuals (a type of pay), new media such as Internet download and streaming videos (another issue of pay), and whether reality and animation shows should be covered by the Writers Guild. These writers worked for 397 entertainment companies including CBS, NBCUniversal, News Corp/Fox, Walt Disney Company, and Warner Bros., among others. They were joined by members of the Screen Actors Guild including actor Katherine Heigl, of the TV show *Grey's Anatomy* at the time. The strike went on for 100 days. It is estimated that the strike cost $2.1 to $3 billion and shut down more than 60 TV shows. The final agreement was ratified, with nearly 94% of members voting in favor. Over the years, The Writers Guild has engaged in four major strikes, including one in 1959 that lasted nearly 6 months and one in 1988 that lasted 155 days. The 2017 strike led Amazon, HBO, Warner Bros. TV, NBCUniversal, Disney, CBS Studios, and others to suspend deals in process due to the ongoing writers strike. In 2023, the writers strike called by the Writers Guild of America was joined by the actors union (the Screen Actors Guild—American Federation of Television and Radio Artists) to form the largest labor action since 1960 with tens of thousands of individuals striking, which includes not working or promoting any projects. The major issues driving the strike included the desire for changes in compensation to address rising costs from inflation, smaller residual payments due to changes in the consumption of media from streaming, and issues surrounding AI. Balancing the ethical implications of studio owners paying writers fairly versus the fiscal implications of strikes continues to be a challenging dilemma.[42]

Questions

1. What do you see as the ethical aspects of going on strike? Examine this question from the workers' point of view and from the employer's point of view.
2. Some categories of workers in the United States are legally prohibited from striking. What ethical grounds do you see for such laws?

Disputes and Grievances

As you might imagine, even with an accepted labor agreement or following a successfully completed strike, labor relations may remain strained, which may result in employees feeling unfairly treated.

Thus, unions are responsible for ensuring that the terms of the contract are followed. If a member feels that the agreement is being violated, they may file a grievance or a formal complaint. For example, if a unionized construction employee feels they have been required to perform practices that are unsafe and not in their job description, they may file a grievance against the company. How grievances are handled is normally specified in the labor agreement. Typically, the *grievance procedure* consists of four steps.

Step 1: Inform

The first step in a grievance procedure is normally to inform one's supervisor formally or informally. Often a grievance form must be completed.

Step 2: Evaluate

After the first step, three things may happen. First, it may be determined by the supervisor and the union representative that the grievance is not valid. If this occurs, the process ends. Second, the grievance may be resolved to the satisfaction of the employee. If so, the process stops at this step. Finally, if the grievance is not resolved to the employee's satisfaction, it moves to the next step.

Step 3: Escalation

In Step 3, the grievance is escalated to the next level in the organizational hierarchy. If the grievance is resolved at this level, the grievance process stops here. If this grievance is not resolved, the next step typically involves moving outside of the organization.

Step 4: External Resolution

In Step 4, an outside arbitrator may be called upon to help reach a resolution. And ultimately, if the grievance remains an ongoing concern, either the employee or the union may end up pursuing litigation. One reason that organizations have grievance procedures in place is to avoid such public resolutions of disputes within their organization.

SPOTLIGHT ON DATA AND ANALYTICS: TRACKING GRIEVANCE-RELATED METRICS

Organizations without unions often have grievance procedures in place to give employees a process to share concerns. Although not necessarily a common HR practice, it is recommended that organizations track metrics related to employee grievances. This becomes more and more important the larger the organization becomes because it is more challenging to know what employees are thinking as the number of employees grows. As data are gathered, summarized, and monitored, individuals within the organization can use these data to gain a better understanding of what is working in terms of employee relations and where there is room for improvement before small problems become large ones. Understanding the causes for grievances may require a combination of analytics in terms of numbers such as the following as well as qualitatively examining themes that emerge. To get started, recommended metrics include

- the number of grievances per month, quarter, and year by number of employees;
- a calculation of the cost of grievances, including the time spent by managers, HR, lawyers, and other organizational members to handle the complaints;
- a determination of the root cause of grievances so that corrections may be made;
- average time to close or complete the grievance and make a decision; and
- return on investment calculated as revenue or profit per employee before and after changes to employee grievance procedures.

As Missildine-Martin, formerly of Dovetail Software, says, "Data leads to insights; insights lead to action."[43]

CHAPTER SUMMARY

Employee relations can be influenced by many different factors such as culture, fair treatment, working conditions, employment laws, and unions. Employee relations are managed through organizational policies and procedures. The types of policies an employer has will set the tone for the employee experience in that organization. Businesses use employee handbooks to ensure that workers know what is expected of them, including code of conduct, rules or guidelines for appearance, and the use of social media. The labor movement can be a major issue in the workplace. Reasons employees may seek to organize or unionize include job dissatisfaction, working conditions, and employee disengagement. Conversely, employers may resist unions based on concerns about profit and loss of autonomy for the business. HR professionals need to know about types of unions, laws pertaining to labor relations, and procedures to form and dissolve a union. The collective bargaining process includes conflict management approaches, negotiation phases, and what alternatives are available if an agreement cannot be reached. Proactively managing employee relations in a way that helps keep employees satisfied is a key component to promoting and ensuring more positive employee–employer relations.

KEY TERMS

Alternative dispute resolution

Collective bargaining

Employee handbook

Employee relations

Impasse

Labor Management Relations Act (1947)

Labor–Management Reporting and Disclosure
    Act (LMRDA) (1959)

Labor relations

Labor union

National Labor Relations Act

National Labor Relations Board (NLRB)

Negotiation

Right-to-work laws

Strike

Unfair labor practices

HR REASONING AND DECISION-MAKING EXERCISES

Mini-Case Analysis Exercise: Growing Pains

You are a manager at a small firm with 85 employees. Not long ago, your firm had just 15 employees, and it felt like a big family more than a workplace. But as you've grown, the "family feeling" has dissipated. You just heard from your good friend Robert that employees are starting to complain about management not listening to them or caring about them. He has even heard some talk about interest in considering a union to make sure that they are heard.

Given the highly competitive market your firm competes in and how slim the profit margins are, you are worried that the potential move to a union would be devastating and result in people actually losing their jobs if the firm couldn't afford to give everyone raises and instead had to lay people off. When you talk to your boss, Kelvin, he says that you are 100% right. There is no way that the firm would survive becoming a union shop, and you must do everything you can to stop the employees from unionizing. You keep thinking back to your HRM course from 7 years ago and have a lingering concern that this may not be legal, but you aren't sure. You want to do what is best for the firm and the employees, but you aren't sure what that is.

How would you handle this situation?

1. What kind of actions are you legally able to take in this situation?

2. What would you tell your boss, Kelvin, if anything?

3. How common or unique do you think this situation is? In other words, how likely is it that dealing with this type of situation might happen to someone taking an HRM course at some point in their career? Please discuss your rationale.

4. Are there any systemic changes you could think of that might help prevent more concerns like these from happening in the future?

HR Decision Analysis Exercise: Online Surveillance?

You work for a large retail organization with more than 16,000 employees nationwide. Because so much of your business occurs during the months leading up to the winter holidays, historically you have hired a large number of seasonal workers who come on for 3 months and then are let go. In the 14 years you have been with the company, this has never been a big issue. However, you have noticed that the shrinkage (the unexplained loss of inventory) rates go up each holiday season and then back down again afterward. In other words, you see a big spike in theft during the same time that the seasonal workers are working in the stores.

After bringing this up at the next meeting at your company headquarters, the consensus is to begin monitoring all employees with cameras throughout the office, including in the restrooms. Kris, another team member at the meeting, voices concern that this may be an invasion of privacy, but the consensus in the room is that it is an important enough issue that doing whatever it takes to catch those stealing from the company is worth it in the long run. Although the investment in a new video monitoring system is large, you have been tasked with implementing and running the program for the entire organization nationally.

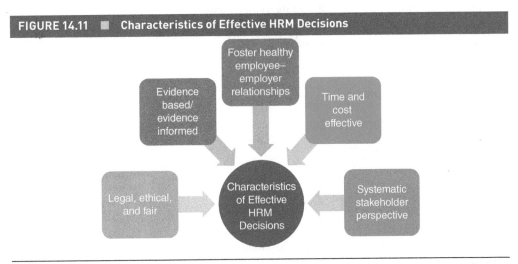

FIGURE 14.11 ■ Characteristics of Effective HRM Decisions

Should your organization switch to a system like this? Consider this decision using the following criteria.

Please provide the rationale for your answer to each of the questions below.

Is it legal, ethical, and fair?

Is it evidence based/evidence informed?

Does it foster healthy employee–employer relationships?

Is it time- and cost-effective?

Does it take a systematic stakeholder perspective?

Considering your analysis above, overall, do you think this would be an effective decision? Why or why not?

What, if anything, do you think should be done differently or considered to help make this decision more effective?

HR Decision-Making Exercise: A Tale of Two Training Programs

You are in the business of developing training and development materials and programs for work organizations. Your company is currently in the process of developing new training products. As someone who oversees a large 30-person team that develops, sells, and administers different workplace training programs, you have always made money each year, and how much profit you have to reinvest in developing new programs is directly tied to the number of trainings held each year. Your team recently came up with a new training program that is in big demand. Each of the sessions is selling out quickly, and you need to add more and more training days to meet demand. On the other hand, one of your other training products that helped build up the company and has been taught for the past 20 years is seeing decreasing demand. The two programs are very different. There are five individuals who are solely dedicated to the older program but only three to the new one. Unfortunately, the five employees working on the more established but less attractive training program can't teach the new ones, as they do not have the right expertise. Your company is small, and the trends are clear that demand is growing for the new program and dwindling for the older one. If the trend continues, pretty soon the company will be paying five employees to conduct fewer than one training per week, whereas the other three are giving three and four trainings per week. If you cancel the older program, you will have to let these five employees go. You don't see any way around these issues, but you want to let the group make recommendations.

Please answer the following questions. Be sure that your answer includes specific details such as what you think needs to be done and the goals you are trying to achieve.

- Given the current trends you have observed, what do you think your training team should recommend to address this growing problem?

- What do you think they will recommend?

- How might you guide them?

DATA AND ANALYTICS EXERCISE: USING OPINION SURVEY DATA TO GAUGE EMPLOYEE SATISFACTION

Gathering and analyzing opinion survey data from existing employees is a common practice for medium and large businesses. However, small businesses can also benefit from this activity. It doesn't have to be a long, time-intensive survey to help small businesses track how satisfied their employees are over time. Such data can also be helpful in understanding reactions to organizational changes because you have the data both before and after.

1. All of your employees have been filling out an anonymous survey every year they have been with your small but growing organization. In 2010, there were eight employees. Since 2010, you've been averaging hiring around three new employees each year but sometimes only one in a given year.

2. You want to analyze the data to see what trends are occurring in terms of their overall job satisfaction scores for each year, which range from 1 (completely dissatisfied) to 7 (completely satisfied). The data from those annual surveys appear in the following table:

	2015	2016	2017	2018	2019	2020	2021	2022	2023
1									5.1
2							6.2	5.9	5.0
3				4.5					

	2015	2016	2017	2018	2019	2020	2021	2022	2023
4	7.0	6.8	5.1	2.0					
5	5.9	5.8	5.8	5.6	5.7	5.9	5.6	5.8	5.9
6	6.3	6.2	6.5	5.9	6.1	6.6	6.3	6.3	5.8
7	6.4	6.6	6.7	4.1	5.1	5.5	6.2	5.8	5.1
8	4.0	4.0	4.0	4.0	4.0	4.0	4.0	4.0	4.0
9						6.2	5.9	5.0	5.0
10					5.0	5.0	5.0	5.0	5.0
11				7.0	6.8	6.6	6.0	5.3	5.0
12				5.0	5.0	5.0	5.0	5.0	5.0
13		6.0	6.0	3.8	5.0	5.2	5.1	5.6	5.4
14									7.0
15									6.8
16								7.0	7.0
17				4.0	5.2	5.2	5.4	5.5	5.5
18						4.0	3.8	3.6	3.0
19			7.0	6.2	6.8	6.0	6.1	6.4	6.0
20						6.6	6.0	5.3	5.0
21		6.0	6.0	5.0	6.0	6.0	6.0	6.0	6.0
22								6.3	6.4
23						5.4	5.3	5.5	5.7
24						5.4	5.3	5.5	5.7
25					1.0	1.0	1.0	1.0	1.0
26	7.0	7.0	7.0	7.0	7.0	7.0	7.0	7.0	7.0
27				5.5	4.9	5.1	5.4	5.5	5.5
28				4.0	5.2	5.1	5.5		
29			2.0	2.0	2.0	2.0	2.0	2.0	2.0
30							5.0	5.0	5.0
31				5.9	5.4	5.2	5.5	5.5	6.1
32				5.4	5.9	5.1	5.5	5.6	5.7
33			5.1	5.4	5.9	5.1	5.5	5.6	5.7
34				6.4	6.1	5.3	5.1	4.8	4.2
35	7.0	7.0	7.0	7.0	7.0	7.0	7.0	7.0	7.0
36									
37	5.3	5.6	5.3	5.4	5.9	5.1	5.5	5.6	5.7
38								5.3	5.7

1. Do you have any concerns about these data? Why or why not?

2. Is it truly anonymous? Explain your rationale.

3. What questions would you ask about these data?

4. What action would you take based on these data?

Excel Extension: Now You Try!

- On **edge.sagepub.com/bauer2e**, you will find an Excel exercise on evaluating employee survey data.

- First, you will learn how to create a heat map.

- Second, you will practice interpreting and communicating the results.

15 EMPLOYEE SAFETY, WELL-BEING, AND WELLNESS

WELL-BEING IN THE MEDICAL PROFESSION

©iStockphoto.com/puckons

Historically, one of the most attractive, high-status jobs has been that of medical doctor. This profession promised not only good pay but also a chance to make a meaningful difference in people's lives. The primary care physician is the doctor that most people deal with, the one they call first if they need medical help.

The past decade has seen dramatic increases in burnout among doctors of all kinds, but especially among primary care physicians. This trend has accelerated as a result of the Covid-19 pandemic. For example, physicians' satisfaction with their work dropped from 75% to 48%, with 51% of family physicians reporting they were burned out in 2022. Studies have shown that this burnout is related to a number of negative outcomes. For example, one meta-analysis showed that physician burnout is associated with doctors disengaging from their profession and quitting and that it may also lead to lower-quality patient care, including medical errors.

These trends have serious implications for the general public: Although there had been some predictions of primary care physician shortages before the pandemic, this has accelerated. Many older primary care physicians are deciding to retire early, and younger primary care physicians are simply quitting. There are also financial implications for health care in the United States: One study found that burnout-related turnover among primary care physicians led to $260 million in excess health care costs in the United States, concluding that addressing physician burnout may be a key way to reduce health care costs. The physician shortage issue is becoming so critical that members of Congress are working to develop ways to address it.

What are the reasons why primary care physicians burn out in the first place? A good bit of research has been done on this issue, and the reasons for physician burnout include the following:

- Excess paperwork
- Feeling undervalued
- Dealing with difficult patients
- Work–life balance issues
- Lack of autonomy and control over work
- Concerns over the ability to make a difference in patient care

It is also notable that some issues are more likely to affect primary care physicians early in their careers (e.g., work–life balance), whereas other issues are more relevant for primary care physicians later in their careers (e.g., administrative work, long hours).

Not surprisingly, there have been some attempts to find ways to reduce physician burnout. For example, one study found that providing a scribe to take notes for the physician was associated with a 27% decrease in burnout. In addition, a number of interventions have been tested with some success. These range from individual-level interventions for the individual doctor (e.g., mindfulness training, yoga) to those that attempt to address systemic issues with the health care system (e.g., reductions in workload). It is notable that experts believe there is no single intervention that always works and that different interventions may work better in different situations and for different doctors. In any case, the implications of burnout and quitting among primary care physicians are significant for doctors, patients, and society as a whole.[1]

CASE DISCUSSION QUESTIONS

1. It is understandable that physician burnout and turnover increased during the Covid-19 pandemic. Why do you think it is continuing?

2. How should health care systems design solutions to burnout that fit their organization? When thinking of this, be sure to include a strategy for assessing and addressing the root causes of physician burnout for a particular health care system.

3. Some physicians have argued that individual-level interventions place the responsibility on the burned-out physician to diagnose themselves and work on solutions to "fix themselves," rather than addressing the systemic causes of burnout (e.g., overwork, paperwork). Who do you think is responsible for addressing burnout, the physician or the organization, and why?

4. If you were working in a health care system, how would you go about convincing decision makers in your organization that reducing burnout among primary care physicians is important?

INTRODUCTION

In this chapter, we will discuss the strategic role that HRM plays in maintaining the safety, health, and well-being of employees. This includes how HRM can promote effective workplace safety programs along with promoting cybersecurity in organizations. In addition, we will discuss the outcomes of workplace stress and ways to manage it and the increasing role of workplace wellness programs, including the range of possible programs and their benefits. We conclude by describing an integrated organizational strategy, Total Worker Health`, that takes into account the safety, well-being, and wellness and that is gaining increased attention among today's employers. For each of these topics, we will discuss some of the key metrics that can help employers deploy programs that best fit their needs and evaluate program effectiveness.

THE ROLE OF HRM IN WORKER SAFETY AND HEALTH

LEARNING OBJECTIVE

15.1   Give reasons why workplace well-being is important for employers and regulatory agencies.

HRM plays a key role in attracting, hiring, developing, and rewarding employees to serve the strategic goals of the organization. Given this enormous investment in talent, organizations also have an interest in the safety, health, and well-being of their employees. This includes developing a culture of safety; providing a healthy, safe, and secure work environment; and actively supporting the health of employees through wellness programs—all with the goal of retaining the best talent, reducing health care costs, improving performance, and reducing legal liability. We begin by reviewing the importance of well-being and government regulatory agencies and resources.

The Case for Employee Well-Being

Organizations work to attract the best candidates, select those that are the best fit, and then work to develop and reward them as employees to help achieve organizations' goals. In addition, they invest a great deal in rewarding and training employees. Many organizations feel it is an ethical obligation to keep their workers safe, healthy, and happy. Taken together, these concepts of the safety, health, satisfaction, and engagement of employees are often referred to as worker well-being.[2] Organizations have a stake in worker well-being because it affects organizational productivity and effectiveness. For example, an unhealthy workforce can lead to high medical costs. High employee stress can lead to turnover and to distractions that cause accidents and injuries. Nonsecure systems that are open to cyberattacks can lead to the loss of both employee and customer privacy and pose serious risks to a company's reputation; they can be highly disruptive to its work processes as well. Workplace safety is an important goal in itself, and violating safety regulations can lead to fines and to legal liability.

On the positive side, an organization's reputation as a healthy and safe place to work is an excellent recruiting tool. Decreasing employee stress can lead to improved performance. And providing a safe, healthy environment can increase employee retention. It is not surprising, then, that many of the most successful organizations treat workplace safety and health as a key organizational goal and invest heavily in metrics to assess a range of safety and health indicators.

Yet maintaining workplace safety and health is an ongoing challenge. For example, there were more than 5,100 worker deaths in the United States in 2021 (see Figure 15.1). Further, a recent survey by the American Psychological Association said work stress has grown significantly and that employees experiencing stress were 3 times as likely to look for new jobs, illustrating that stress has significant costs to employers.[3]

FIGURE 15.1 ■ **Number of Workplace Fatalities by Event Type, 2021**

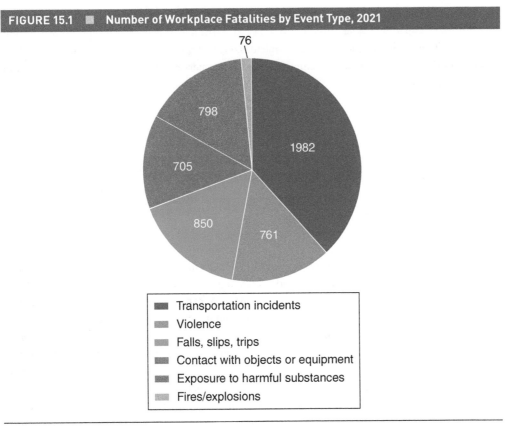

Sources: U.S. Bureau of Labor Statistics. (2022, December). *Economic news release: Census of fatal occupational injuries summary, 2021*, https://www.bls.gov/news.release/cfoi.nr0.htm; U.S. Bureau of Labor Statistics. (2022). *Fatal occupational injuries for selected events or exposures, 2017-2021*, https://www.bls.gov/news.release/cfoi.t02.htm.

It is clear that developing a safe and healthy workforce is complicated, with multiple causal variables. Accidents and injuries can be caused by the physical work environment, a factor that is not easy or inexpensive to address. Employee stress can be caused by a number of factors, such as a difficult supervisor or coworkers, poorly designed work, or work–life imbalance. Poor health can be caused by many factors outside of the workplace and seemingly outside of the employer's control, yet poor health can increase employer costs (e.g., medical costs, sick time) and even lead to accidents and injuries, as illustrated in the opening case.

Employers have a number of effective tools available to them to support the safety and health of their workers. For example, wellness programs can help workers manage their existing illnesses and decrease medical costs. Employers can train managers to be more supportive of employees not only to increase work–life balance but also to improve their sleep. Organizations can focus on ways to communicate with employees about safety not only to demonstrate its importance but also to gain input from workers about safety hazards and how to prevent them. These are all methods that have been tested as effective in improving measures of employee health.

The Legal Backdrop: Government Agencies and Resources

In the United States, there are a number of government agencies tasked with regulating the area of workplace well-being and also with providing a number of important resources to employers. The Occupational Safety and Health Administration (OSHA) was established through the Occupational Safety and Health Act of 1970. Under the U.S. Department of Labor, OSHA's purpose is to ensure safe and healthy working conditions for employees by setting and enforcing safety and health standards. It also provides training and outreach, education, and assistance to both employers and employees. For example, OSHA provides a range of materials to help employers monitor safety conditions in their organizations. In addition to OSHA, 26 states, Puerto Rico, and the Virgin Islands have their own equivalent to OSHA, which provides additional workplace safety oversight.[4] Further, the National Institute for Occupational Safety and Health (NIOSH) is the federal agency that supports research on workplace safety and health and makes recommendations to employers. As part of its mission, NIOSH also can provide recommendations to employers regarding interventions and other initiatives that can help improve worker well-being.[5]

WORKPLACE SAFETY

LEARNING OBJECTIVE
15.2   Describe the main workplace safety outcomes measured by organizations and what organizations can do to promote safety.

Workplace illness, injury, and mortality are important because of their human toll on workers and families. In addition, the costs associated with work-related injury were estimated at $163.9 billion in 2020, with medical expenses of $34.8 billion and administrative expenses of $61.0 billion.[6] Not surprisingly, reducing the numbers of work-related accidents and injuries is a major focus of most organizations. For example, electrical construction company Tri-City Electric, based in Davenport, Iowa, takes both a top-down and bottom-up approach: Management is responsible for employee safety, supervisors are accountable to their team members, and employees take account of their own safety and their coworkers.[7] As you might guess, HR takes a central role in implementing such safety-related programs. This section is concerned with the many antecedents of workplace accidents and injuries and how to address them, plus the regulatory environment for worker safety in the United States. Also highlighted is cybersecurity, a developing workplace safety issue.

Workplace Safety Outcomes and Their Antecedents

When tracking the issue of workplace safety, there are multiple types of safety and health outcomes that can be measured and analyzed by organizations. These include workplace accidents, such as spilling a hazardous chemical. More dramatic are workplace injuries, with the most extreme and rare being workplace fatalities; these might include workers being injured or killed by a chemical exposure.

However, in addition to these more dramatic safety outcomes, it is important for organizations to keep an eye on the more common issues that are antecedents of outright accidents and injuries. One safety measure frequently discussed in organizations is that of near misses, or when an accident could have occurred but did not. As an example of a near miss, an electrician working on wiring an office in a new building forgot to turn off the electrical current before proceeding to install a section of the heating system, but a coworker noticed the problem and turned off the power just in time. In this example, there was no accident or injury because the coworker acted in time, and in fact the workers and the employer might think that there was nothing to report or to discuss. If the coworker had not intervened, the electrician could have been seriously injured or killed. The point here is that analyzing near misses is important to understanding potential causes of accidents, and they should be given careful consideration and analysis in safety discussions. Near misses are typically measured by worker self-reports, or they are uncovered in discussions within the team, but they can provide an essential part of understanding situations in which accidents and injuries may occur and how to prevent them.[8]

One challenge for organizations trying to prevent serious and fatal injuries is knowing which data to collect in order to understand their causes. It is estimated that only a relatively small percentage of the standard "recordable events" required by OSHA reporting lead to fatalities. One way to uncover these important data is to speak with workers out in the field to better understand specific circumstances in which no one was injured but that might have led to a serious accident. For example, if an employee working on a tall building were to slip on a wet surface, it might not lead to an injury if they righted themselves in time. But understanding what led to that slip, which may otherwise have led to a fatal accident, is key to injury prevention.[9]

Another factor important to understanding the causes of safety outcomes is employees' safety behavior.[10] Safety behavior is the type of work behaviors that employees exhibit with regard to safety. The research has generally identified two different types of safety behavior. First, safety compliance behavior is the extent to which workers follow the safety rules and regulations, such as wearing personal protective equipment (PPE) to protect themselves from the specific hazards they are exposed to in their jobs. In the electrician's example, safety compliance behavior might include always following the rules about checking that a power source is turned off before performing electrical installations. Second, safety participation behavior refers to employees' willingness to support safety among their coworkers. This might include explaining the safety rules to new workers or mentioning a safety problem they have seen (e.g., broken safety equipment) to a supervisor so it can be taken care of. The electrician example shows the importance of safety participation behavior: A second employee noticed that her teammate had not turned off the power source and then did it herself before any injury could happen. In this sense, safety behaviors include both a worker's willingness to follow safety rules themselves and their willingness to support safety among colleagues and teammates.

Safety compliance and safety participation are often measured by self-ratings or supervisor and coworker observations and ratings. The *low-base-rate problem* presents challenges with measuring and thus preventing the most costly and catastrophic safety problems. That is, serious accidents and injuries are relatively rare, but when they do happen, they can take an enormous human and economic toll. One way to consider this problem is through a diagram referred to as Heinrich's triangle, shown in Figure 15.2, which illustrates that thousands of unsafe behaviors and near

On March 25, 1911, in New York City, 145 garment workers died in the Triangle Shirtwaist Factory fire. The factory was located on floors 8 through 10 of the building. Because the exit doors had been locked, the workers were trapped and died of smoke inhalation, the fire itself, or jumping or falling to their deaths. One of the deadliest industrial disasters in U.S. history, the fire served as an impetus for the development of early workplace safety regulations.[11]

Keystone/Getty Images

misses usually occur before a serious accident or injury occurs. Although there has been some debate over the exact nature of the triangle, such as the precise number of behaviors that occur before an accident, the triangle shows the value of examining the behaviors that lead up to accidents and injury before they occur. A key goal of HRM, particularly for those individuals who are focused on safety, is to uncover the factors that may lead to serious accidents, such as poor safety behaviors and near misses, so as to identify and prevent safety problems. In fact, larger employers might use data analytics to identify high-risk areas of the organization, such as those with large numbers of safety violations, near misses, or unsafe behaviors that can lead to injuries, health risks, and legal liability. And the use of sensors and wearable technology can be used to monitor hazardous conditions (e.g., combustible dust and gases, hazardous sound levels) and the safe use of equipment (e.g., ladders, motorized equipment) in real time.[12]

Figure 15.3 illustrates the idea of a number of factors leading to accidents and injuries and shows a model that has been developed and confirmed through a meta-analysis of the safety literature. The model illustrates a point that we have already made, namely, that accidents and injuries are a result of safety behaviors or performance on the part of workers. But there are additional antecedents as well, most of which can be addressed by the organization. First, safety knowledge, or workers' understanding of how to protect themselves and others on the job, is a key antecedent of accidents and injuries. In other words, organizations need to train workers regarding safety in general and about specific hazards that may be inherent in their jobs, such as how to handle dangerous equipment or specific chemicals and substances. For this reason OSHA requires employers to conduct safety training and even requires specific types of training for certain types of jobs and in certain industries.

FIGURE 15.2   ■   Heinrich's Triangle

A summary of Heinrich's triangle, which suggests that fatalities and catastrophes, though relatively rare, are a function of much more frequent problems like unsafe behaviors.

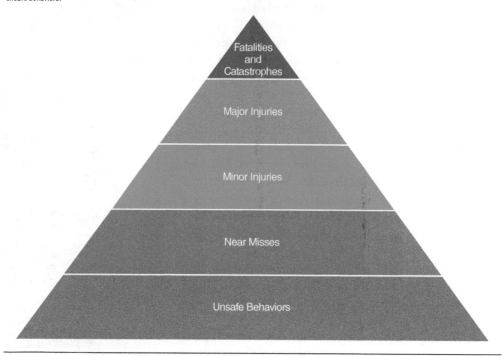

Sources: Based on information contained in Heinrich, H. W. (1931). *Industrial accident prevention: A scientific approach.* McGraw-Hill; Marshall, P., Hirmas, A., & Singer, M. (2018). Heinrich's pyramid and occupational safety: A statistical validation methodology. *Safety Science, 101,* 180–189; Martin, D. K., & Black, A. A. (2015, September). Preventing serious injuries and fatalities. *Professional Safety, 60,* 35–43.

FIGURE 15.3   ■   Safety Climate and Individual Characteristics

Both the safety climate and characteristics of the individual worker play critical roles in safety performance and workplace accidents.

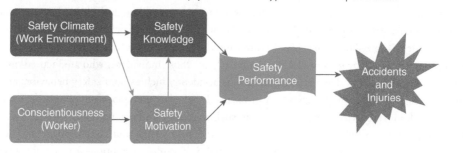

Source: Christian, M. S., Bradley, J. C., Wallace, J. C., & Burke, M. J. (2009). Workplace safety: A meta-analysis of the roles of person and situation factors. *Journal of Applied Psychology, 94,* 1103–1127.

Second, **safety motivation,** or the worker's value for safety and desire to perform safely on the job, is another key factor that has been shown repeatedly to be important for safe behaviors. The organization needs to reward safe behaviors (such as following safe procedures) and not reward unsafe behaviors (such as ignoring safe procedures due to pressure to work too quickly). The employer may also choose to hire workers that pose a lower safety risk, especially for particularly hazardous jobs, such as by evaluating applicants' levels of conscientiousness (see Chapter 7).

Third, the model also identifies the critical role of **safety climate,** or the shared understanding that workers have about the importance of safety, which is a key part of the workplace environment. Research has consistently shown that a strong safety climate, both within the team and in the organization overall, is one of the most important predictors of safe behavior at work. Thus, safety climate has become a central focus of most workplace safety programs.[13] Research has shown that management plays a central role in promoting and supporting the safety climate through showing they take safety seriously. This can take the form of modeling and rewarding safe behaviors, encouraging workers to identify any safety concerns that they observe, and training managers and workers on the importance of safety. For instance, one study of a heavy manufacturing company showed that improved supervisor–employee communications improved safety climate as well as safety behavior and safety audit scores.[14] A recent survey of electrical workers showed that 97.5% agreed that a strong safety culture is key to protecting worker health.[15]

Another employee safety and well-being concern is workplace aggression, including verbal abuse, harassment, intimidation, and physical assaults.[16] This is especially true for certain types of jobs. For example, there are nearly as many violent attacks among health care workers as in all other industries combined, even though health care workers make up only 9% of the workforce. And the rate of attacks against nurses has more than doubled in the past decade. OSHA recognizes the violence faced by health care workers and recommends that employers work with employees to identify hazards, carefully examine incidents to learn why a specific violent attack occurred, and train supervisors and managers to spot dangerous situations so workers are not placed into them.[17] Workplace aggression is a serious hindrance to effective workplace functioning, as research shows that aggression from supervisors, coworkers, and outsiders can affect job attitudes (e.g., job satisfaction), behavior (e.g., work performance), and health (e.g., depression).[18]

Hotel workers face the workplace hazard of sexual harassment and assault from hotel guests. This issue came to light most dramatically in the high-profile case of Dominique Strauss-Kahn, the head of the International Monetary Fund, who was accused of sexual assault by a hotel housekeeper in 2012 in New York City. As a result, some hotels now provide "panic buttons" and similar devices for their workers to alert security when they are concerned for their safety.[19]

©iStock.com/DragonImages

Other Antecedents of Workplace Safety

Although workers and supervisors play a role in maintaining safety, the physical environment obviously plays a role as well. One of the factors in some recent train accidents is that a device to warn the engineers about speeding was either not in place or not used.[20] This illustrates the importance of physical factors organizations can use to improve safety. One approach to this issue is shown in Figure 15.4, which illustrates the hierarchy of controls that an organization can use to reduce safety hazards. The hierarchy illustrates that although elimination of the safety hazard is most effective, there are other, less effective approaches that the organization can take.

FIGURE 15.4 ■ The Hierarchy of Controls

An organization can control workplace hazards in several ways, from most effective (elimination) to least effective (PPE: personal protective equipment).

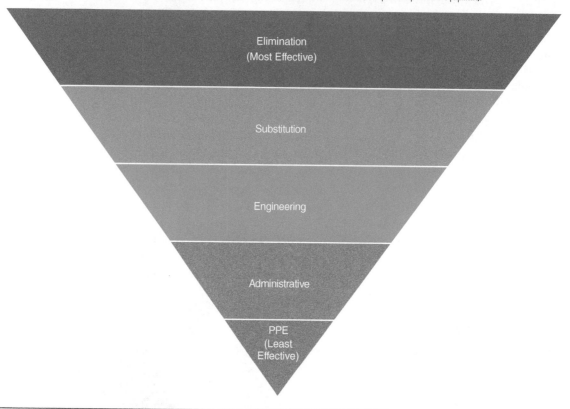

Elimination
(Most Effective)

Substitution

Engineering

Administrative

PPE
(Least
Effective)

Source: CDC/NIOSH. (2018). *Hierarchy of controls.* https://www.cdc.gov/niosh/topics/hierarchy/

As an example, a manufacturing company may be working to eliminate the noise hazards for workers that result from the use of noisy equipment. The most effective way for them to protect workers would be to completely eliminate the source of the hazardous noise. As a "second-best" alternative, they could find equipment that is quieter to replace the noisy equipment. Or if the equipment cannot be changed, the company could "engineer out" some of the noise by putting up noise barriers between the workers and the equipment. Less effective might be to take what is called an administrative approach that will reduce employees' exposure to the noise, such as by scheduling workers in such a way as to reduce their exposure, say, by only letting workers use the noisy equipment for a brief, set amount of time each day. If these options are not possible, the company might provide some sort of personal protective equipment (e.g., ear muffs) to employees to reduce their noise exposure. Although this last option would be the least effective in solving the noise problem, it is certainly better than nothing.[21]

Another factor that can affect workplace safety is worker health. For example, the health issue called sleep apnea (in which breathing stops and starts during sleep) has been cited as a possible cause of some recent train accidents that cause engineers to fall asleep.[22] Similar concerns about the role of sleep apnea in safety have been noted among long-haul truck drivers. For example, one study found that 28% of commercial truck drivers have mild to severe sleep apnea.[23] Work stressors, such as work–life balance issues, can lead to distractions and to errors and accidents as well.[24]

Given the range of factors that can affect safety—such as employee behaviors and near misses, the climate developed by managers and employees, the physical environment, health, and stress—measuring and analyzing these factors is an important function in organizations. Typically, there is a safety officer assigned to examine these and other workplace safety and health issues in the workplace, such as the promotion of safe practices and compliance with safety policies and rules. Or there may be a safety committee that provides employees with a voice and an opportunity to participate in safety-related decisions in the organization. In any case, HR plays a central role in analyzing the causes of potential safety and health issues and developing an effective safety program to address them (including for remote workers; see Table 15.1). This process can be enhanced by the measurement of safety-related variables and, where possible, the use of analytics to better understand how to prevent accidents and protect employee health. What is key is to view safety as a systemic issue with multiple antecedents such as leadership, the climate, employee individual differences, and the physical environment. Further, workplace safety should be incorporated into an organization's business strategy with support at all levels, including investment in workplace safety.

TABLE 15.1 ■ Workplace Safety Tips for Remote Workers
It may not occur to some employers that there are safety and security issues for the large number of workers working remotely. Here are a few tips for managing a remote workforce safely.
1. Be sure to have an at-home work policy, and be sure that employees are aware of it.
2. Require that the employee has a dedicated work area at home that is up to the employer's specifications.
3. Be sure that the employee has the correct insurance to cover any damage or liability.
4. Be sure that the employer's insurance covers issues like at-home workers and business travel.
5. Ensure computer security, including for workers who use their own equipment.
6. Be sure to have frequent contact with employees.

Source: Reprinted from "How to Manage Workplace Safety Issues for Remote Employees" (2017) with permission of the Society for Human Resource Management (SHRM). © SHRM. All rights reserved.

OSHA Regulations and Compliance

As noted earlier, OSHA was established to protect the safety and health of workers, and compliance with OSHA regulations is a serious matter for employers. Employers with more than 10 employees must maintain safety records of what OSHA calls "recordable events," such as work-related fatalities, injuries, and illnesses (including days away from work). Note that OSHA provides significant support to employers in terms of answering questions about workplace safety and health and how to comply with OSHA regulations for organizations of all sizes. In addition, OSHA provides guidelines and advice for organizations on how to develop emergency preparedness and response plans, such as to natural disasters, chemical spills, or even security threats (e.g., dangerous intruders).[25] Further, employers must provide training to employees so they can do their work safely. Note that OSHA may conduct workplace inspections, typically without advance notice to employers and when there is a specific reason. Figure 15.5 provides a sampling of the safety and health issues that are covered by OSHA regulations.[26]

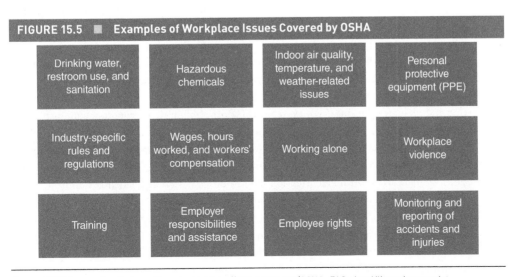

FIGURE 15.5 ■ Examples of Workplace Issues Covered by OSHA

Source: OSHA frequently asked questions. (n.d.). https://www.osha.gov/OSHA_FAQs.html#! employerassist

In addition, OSHA spells out the rights of workers, providing them with guidance and assistance if they are facing a workplace hazard. For example, OSHA will take complaints from workers who believe they are facing an unsafe or unhealthy workplace and will conduct an inspection if a worker believes there is a serious hazard or OSHA violation. They also provide protection for workers in situations in which an employer has retaliated against a worker. OSHA also can provide a worker with an inspection history of their employer if a worker is concerned that the employer has a history of violations.

SPOTLIGHT ON LEGAL ISSUES: SAFETY, HEALTH, AND OSHA COMPLIANCE

As discussed in this chapter, the Occupational Safety and Health Administration (OSHA) is charged with protecting the safety and health of workers in the United States. This includes setting and enforcing standards, as well as providing training, outreach, and assistance to employers and workers. Thus, OSHA provides a range of resources for organizations of all sizes and across industries with the goal of providing healthy and safe working conditions to employees. At a broad level, OSHA requirements ensure the following:

- Workers should feel free to report unsafe or hazardous working conditions to their employers without fear of retaliation. Retaliation on the part of employers is, in fact, illegal. For instance, a federal judge recently awarded over $1 million to two former employees that were fired for participating in an OSHA investigation. In addition, OSHA explicitly protects employees who raise concerns about Covid-19 in the workplace.
- Workers should receive training about job hazards, including training about hazardous substances on their jobs. This training should be provided to workers in language and at a level that they can understand.
- Workers can confidentially report any employer violations to OSHA.
- Employers must post the OSHA poster "Job Safety and Health: It's the Law" in a prominent place.

  What are the most typical types of OSHA violations? In 2020–2021, some of the most common violations had to do with failure to protect workers from falls, unsafe scaffolding, unsafe ladders, inadequate lockout-tagout procedures (e.g., being sure that equipment that is being serviced cannot accidentally be turned back on again), inadequate respiratory protection, having inadequate guards to protect workers from dangerous equipment, the use of industrial trucks, and inadequate hazard communication.[27]

Ergonomics and Office Design

In Chapter 5, we discussed job design in terms of designing the psychological characteristics of work—issues like making work less boring and giving workers more autonomy. In addition, an important workplace well-being issue is fitting the physical aspects of the job, often referred to as ergonomic design. The goal for most ergonomic approaches is to reduce musculoskeletal disorders such as muscle strain, back injury, or carpal tunnel syndrome. OSHA provides general guidance for specific industries such as nursing homes and food-processing work. In addition, OSHA recommends worker involvement to identify problems, provide training to workers and supervisors to avoid ergonomic problems, and develop and evaluate solutions.[28] For example, L.L.Bean, Maine's iconic outdoor equipment company, initiated a redesign of its warehouse, which included the use of machines rather than people for heavy lifting. Originally designed to protect the safety and health of its aging workforce, the redesign resulted in improved ergonomic conditions for workers of all ages.[29]

In addition, there has been much attention paid to office design and its effects on health. One issue is the effects of office natural lighting on worker health. One recent study found that workers working in windowless offices reported poorer sleep (i.e., shorter sleep duration, poorer sleep quality) and less physical activity than workers exposed to natural light.[31] Another recent trend in office design is the idea of open offices, where employees work in open spaces, without cubicles, with the idea that such work arrangements would lead to greater creativity and sharing of ideas. Thus far, however, the research on open offices has been less than encouraging, suggesting that these arrangements may lead

Sit-stand desks allow the user to alternate between sitting and standing while doing desk work. As an ergonomic solution, the use of sit-stand desks may benefit worker health and performance. Research has found that they lead to improvements in musculoskeletal pain, tension, and mental fatigue.[30]

©iStockphoto.com/Alvarez

to decreased satisfaction and greater stress due to less privacy and more chaotic work environments. Further, since the Covid-19 pandemic, many organizations and employees argue that an open plan may not be as safe.[32]

SPOTLIGHT ON GLOBAL ISSUES: SAFETY AND HEALTH STANDARDS AND NORMS WORLDWIDE

This chapter discusses issues associated with worker safety, health, and privacy primarily from a U.S. perspective. However, it is important to keep in mind that laws and norms around these issues can vary from country to country and in different cultures.

Regarding safety and health, U.S. employers focus mainly on compliance with worker safety regulations established by OSHA or specific U.S. states. However, individual countries where the company operates may have different rules and standards for safety. As one example, many European countries require that office workers have natural light in their offices, typically via a window, because of the positive effects of natural light on worker health, something that is often disregarded in the design of offices in the United States. In addition, the International Labor Organizations (ILO), an agency of the United Nations, can provide significant guidance to employers regarding labor standards, safety and health, and worker protection. The ILO also provides a number of publications to help guide employers. Although some of these are broad health and safety guidelines, others focus on specific industries such as construction, agriculture, and mining, or on specific hazards such as asbestos and chemical exposures.

There are also differences in privacy standards afforded to workers in the United States compared to workers in other countries. European privacy standards are more stringent. As one illustration, in 2017, a European Union (EU) advisory panel advised against employers issuing Fitbits or other health tracking devices to employees, even if employees are told how their data will be used, who will have access to it, and that they can opt out of the health tracking program. This is because the power differences between employers and employees may be implicitly coercive. In fact, EU privacy rules that went into effect in 2018 stipulate that employers should carry out impact assessments before the implementation of any technology that might affect workers' privacy rights. One implication is that, at the very least, EU employers may need to have third parties process their employees' health data for them, providing it to the employer only in aggregate form.[33]

Cybersecurity

Within the topic of workplace safety, it is important to examine the issue of cybersecurity. Cybersecurity is an evolving issue but one that involves HRM for several reasons. Much of the private information used in organizations is stored, analyzed, and reported by HR personnel, including everything from Social Security numbers to health issues and even some day-to-day work activities. Thus, HR professionals are responsible for maintaining the security of other employees' data as well as that of clients, and employees can do considerable damage either by mistake or on purpose. For example, in a recent UK court case, a disgruntled employee of Morrisons Supermarket published the personal information of about 100,000 employees on the Internet. Morrisons was successfully sued by those affected, although the UK supreme court later overturned this costly ruling.[34] Besides technological solutions to data breaches, human error is considered one of the greatest organizational vulnerabilities, where, for example, an employee might fall for a phishing scam and thus threaten the security of the entire system. Employee training is seen as one of the most useful solutions to this vulnerability.

As we discussed in Chapter 9, another emerging issue is employee monitoring, especially in the context of ensuring employees are not mishandling personal or sensitive data, either intentionally or unintentionally. This is also an issue now that workers are more likely to work remotely post-pandemic. New solutions continue to develop to facilitate monitoring, such as badges that can indicate how closely employees are working together. However, organizations should consider such monitoring carefully before undertaking it for several reasons. First, employee monitoring can erode employee trust. Second, such monitoring involves a range of legal issues, such as laws around employee monitoring and data breaches. In addition, there may be state laws to consider (as employee monitoring laws may vary by state) and ensuring employees' legal consent to be monitored. There are other concerns as well. A meta-analysis of 94 studies showed that electronic performance monitoring was not related to employee performance, but it did seem to increase worker stress.[35] Another study found that monitoring employees may actually make them more likely to break rules.[36] Workers may also find workarounds like "mouse jigglers" that make it appear they are working when they are away. If monitoring is to be used, recommendations include clearly articulating the business case for monitoring employee data, encrypting data to restrict data access, and involving employees in such monitoring solutions to gain employee buy-in.[37] Finally, it is important to realize that employee privacy issues differ around the world, with European rules much more focused on protecting the workers' rights.

SPOTLIGHT ON ETHICS: PRIVACY, TECHNOLOGY, AND HUMAN ERROR

The vast amount of highly personal data available to employers provides huge opportunities to better understand employee behavior. Such safety and health data can help uncover ways to support employees' well-being. However, it also presents an array of ethical issues regarding employees' rights to privacy. In addition, large datasets of personal information present challenges to employers with maintaining the security of data that, if released, could be damaging to employees, job applicants, or customers.

Some security vulnerabilities can be addressed by technological solutions; that is, an organization could work to ensure that the data are protected from hacking by third parties. But other security vulnerabilities are the result of human error. It might take only a single employee to mistakenly give out their login credentials in a phishing attack to make the entire database of all employees and customers available. For example, one survey suggests that a majority of U.S. health care providers rank e-mail as a leading source of their security problems. Training workers to avoid cyberattacks generally includes the advice to change administrative passwords frequently, limit who has access to sensitive data, and include multilevel authentication for access to data.

The ethical issue of maintaining the security of private data is one that will continue to evolve with technological advances—advances on the side of those seeking data and on the side of organizations working to protect such data. What is clear, however, is that an organization is ethically responsible for maintaining the safety and security of its employees' and clients' personal information.[38]

Questions

1. Individuals working in HR have access to a great deal of private information about employees. If you had access to such data and someone approached you with an offer of money or other rewards in exchange for disclosing confidential employee information, what specific steps would you take to respond to the situation? What kind of training content should an employer provide for its employees so that employees know how to respond to such a scenario?
2. Describe some everyday situations in which an employee in HR or another area could accidentally compromise employees' private data. How can workers prevent or contain the damage of such a lapse?

WORKPLACE STRESS

LEARNING OBJECTIVE

15.3   Summarize issues around workplace stress and well-being.

Work stress is something we hear about on a regular basis. It is very common to hear a friend, family member, or coworker describe how stressful their work is. A Gallup poll found that 44% of employees experienced a lot of daily stress on their job.[39] Although the human cost of work stress is substantial, there are additional reasons why work stress is an important issue for organizations. For example, high stress may lead workers to be distracted and thus lead to workplace accidents. At the societal level, stress costs billions of dollars ($187 billion in the United States alone) from factors such as productivity losses and health care expenses.[40]

Stress also can affect the health of an organization's workforce, even to the point of being deadly. The results of a study on the mortality of more than 2,363 workers in their 60s in high-demand (stressful) jobs are striking, particularly taking into account the degree to which they had control over their work. The researchers found that workers who had low levels of control over their work had a 15% higher risk of death; on the other hand, those with high control had a 34% lower death risk. Among those workers in the study who didn't die, low control combined with high demands was associated with a higher body mass index (BMI). The researchers note that one solution is for organizations to provide employees with greater input into their work.[41]

In addition, stress can have negative effects on productivity and retention, with one study by the American Psychological Association showing that employees who experience stress are 3 times as likely to look for another job. Top stressors may include relationship with the boss or coworkers, work overload, and poor work–life balance.[42] In short, worker stress can have serious implications for organizational competitiveness. At the same time, HRM can play a significant strategic role in reducing stress at work.

In discussing stress issues, it is important to differentiate the terms *stressors* and *strain*, which are both integral to stress. Stressors are demands in the environment to which a person must respond. Workplace stressors might include dangerous work conditions, a difficult boss, ambiguity in a person's work role, or a heavy workload. Strain refers to a person's reaction to stressors, such as heart disease, burnout, or depression, or behavioral outcomes such as low performance and turnover. Workplace stress has also been shown to lead to expressions of anger, aggression, and violence by employees, as well as to excessive alcohol consumption.[43] These strains in turn can lead to lower organization productivity, increased employee onboarding and training costs, and increased health care costs. Thus, it is increasingly common for many organizations to monitor workplace stressors, strains, and strain outcomes among their employees. Table 15.2 shows some common work stressors as identified by employees.

In Chapter 5, we introduced the job demands-resources model (JDR) as a way to consider the design of work. In addition, the JDR provides a comprehensive view of sources of stress. As a recap, the JDR describes a number of work demands that can negatively impact work engagement and

TABLE 15.2 ■ Results of a Survey of the Leading Stressors at Work	
Issue	**Percentage of Workers Reporting This Type of Stress**
1. Workload	39%
2. Interpersonal challenges	31%
3. Balancing work and personal life	19%
4. Job security	6%

Source: American Institute of Stress. (n.d.). *Workplace stress.* https://www.stress.org/workplace-stress#:~:text=The%20 main%20causes%20of%20workplace,and%20job%20security%20(6%25)

performance. These demands include categories like the physical workload, time pressure, physical environment, and shift work. Job demands that can act as negative stressors include role conflict (having conflicting roles at work); role ambiguity (a lack of clarity about what your role and responsibilities are in the organization and how your job fits in with other jobs); interpersonal conflicts with a boss or coworkers; risks, hazards, and poor work conditions; work–life conflict; emotionally demanding work; job insecurity (worry that you may lose your job); and performance demands. On the other hand, the JDR also discusses resources that can support workers and thus mitigate stress such as supervisor support, control over your work, job security, participation, and feedback (see Figure 15.6).

FIGURE 15.6 ■ Some Common Sources of Workplace Stress and Factors That Mitigate Them

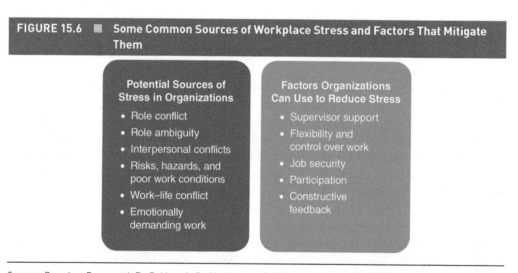

Sources: Based on Demerouti, E., Bakker, A. B., Nachreiner, F., & Schaufeli, W. B. (2001). The job demands-resources model of burnout. *Journal of Applied Psychology, 86*, 499–512; Schaufeli, W. B., & Taris, T. W. (2014). A critical review of the Job Demands-Resources model: Implications for improving work and health. In G. F. Bauer & O. Hämmig (Eds.), *Bridging occupational, organizational and public health* (pp. 43–68). Springer Netherlands.

From an organizational perspective, the more that employers can do to mitigate the stressful factors with improved resources, the better off the workers will be. For example, if employees are unsure about what their roles are, the organization can provide greater clarity through developing and updating job descriptions. Supervisors might also be trained to give workers support in dealing with emotionally demanding jobs. Or if employees are experiencing high work–life conflict due to lack of schedule control, the organization can provide greater control over work schedules to the extent possible. One analysis of the move to remote work during Covid-19 found that supervisors may themselves experience more stress in scheduling workers but that allowing workers greater control during remote work may increase productivity.[44] Not surprisingly, the best approach is for organizations to carefully analyze the particular sources of stress, including those that may be associated with certain types of work, so they can most effectively address the situation. For example, as noted in the opening case, physicians face a number of specific sources of stress, perhaps quite different from other workers.

Challenge and Hindrance Stressors

It would be a mistake, however, to assume that all stressors are bad. In fact, some work stress is good: Even the earliest models of stress emphasized that there is also what is called "eustress" (good stress), or that some level of stress is good to increase activation, motivation, and performance. More recently, this idea has been carried further with the concepts of challenge and hindrance stressors. Hindrance stressors include negative stressors like workplace hassles, organizational politics, poor resources, role overload, and constraints. These hindrance stressors are linked to lower engagement and lower performance among employees. In contrast, challenge stressors include factors like role demands and time urgency, and they are thought to be positively linked to factors like work engagement. They are also thought to be associated with the experience of growth and achievement for employees. A meta-analysis on challenge and hindrance stressors showed that although both types of stressors can have negative effects on workers, challenge stressors are more likely to improve worker outcomes (e.g., job satisfaction), and hindrance stressors are more likely to hurt worker outcomes. The point here is that some degree of stress, especially certain types of stress, may actually be positive for some employees.[45]

Work–Life Balance

For many workers these days, the quantity and pace of work are challenging. A 2022 Gallup poll found that the standard "40-hour workweek" is not a reality for many U.S. workers, who work on average 43 hours per week, which is almost a half workday beyond the "standard" 40 hours.[46] Other surveys suggest that many workers work over 9 hours extra per week.[47] In contrast, there may be benefits both for employees and the employer when such hours are reduced: One study in the United Kingdom showed that shortening to a 32-hour workweek led to increased employee well-being and that company revenue stayed the same.[48] In addition, expectations of long hours can be a source of stress for workers in terms of burnout and work–life balance problems, even for those who may seem to accept the "always on" situation. For example, before sending an e-mail, managers and coworkers may want to consider whether after-hours e-mails are appropriate and how they might affect both the employee and their family. And of course, the nature of the e-mails, such as how long they take to respond to and the tone of the e-mail, is important as well.[49]

This translates into less time for nonwork activities such as caring for children or aging parents, personal life, or outside interests. Further, always being connected by e-mail after work and on weekends is another challenge facing workers trying to balance their work and nonwork lives and is one that is particularly important with more people working remotely as a result of the pandemic. To address this issue, some countries have passed legislation to control e-mail. As a recent example, in 2022, a "right to disconnect" law went into effect in Belgium, allowing civil servants to turn off their work e-mail outside of office hours.[50] The issue of balancing work and nonwork time is usually thought of as work-to-family conflict, which is when work interferes with nonwork responsibilities, and family-to-work conflict, which is when nonwork responsibilities interfere with work responsibilities.[51]

Given the potential consequences associated with work–family conflict for both organizations and individuals (e.g., decreased job satisfaction and performance, increased turnover, and depression), it is not surprising that there is considerable interest in what organizations can do to support workers dealing with this imbalance between their work and nonwork lives. These include employer policies focused on providing increased flexibility and support for employees balancing work and nonwork demands. Examples of workplace policies include flexible work hours and compressed workweeks (e.g., fewer than 5 days per week as well as flexible work locations). Other examples include remote work (which is discussed in detail in Chapter 5, including that chapter's opening case), which has become increasingly common since the pandemic and can lead to either more or less work–family conflict depending on the worker and their circumstances. Other policies that employers can provide include caregiving (e.g., child care, elder care) control over work time and breaks, and sabbaticals and other types of employee leave. HRM plays a central role in implementing these types of workplace policies and programs, such as ensuring that the work gets done and defining the roles of both managers and employees in carrying out such policies.[52] In any case, providing this type of work–life support can have a big payoff in organizations. For example, SAS, a North Carolina–based business analytics software company, has had a reputation since it was founded in 1976 of supporting employees' work and non-work spheres, including a subsidized cafeteria and on-site medical care. This even includes a 35-hour workweek for many employees. Not surprisingly, SAS has one of the lowest turnover rates in the industry and a frequent spot on "best places to work" lists.[53] In addition, this type of visible and tangible support for employees can provide a definite advantage in terms of recruitment.

Ways for Organizations to Reduce Stress

In addition to helping employees with work–life balance, there are other ways for organizations to help reduce some of the more toxic types of stress faced by employees.

Determine the Sources of Employee Stress

As we have emphasized throughout this book, there is rarely a one-size-fits-all solution to organizational challenges. Of course, organizations should evaluate the levels of outcomes such as sick leave use, turnover, and performance issues. But the most successful organizations will also dig deeper to find the sources of these negative outcomes. This might include surveys and interviews with individual employees and managers. For example, Hackensack University Medical Center regularly surveys its staff and benchmarks their results against a national database.[54] In any case, because many employers do not really understand their employees' level of stress or do not understand what is causing it, they may approach the problem in the wrong way.

Eliminate the Root Causes of Employee Stress Before Looking for Fixes

Stress management programs intended for individual employees can be effective, but organizations should first see whether the primary sources of stress can be addressed.[55] For example, workplace bullying, either by supervisors or by coworkers, as well as an employee culture or climate that supports bullying, is a serious source of employee stress and dissatisfaction with work.[56] If employees perceive that there is a problem with difficult supervisors, removing or training those supervisors would be in order rather than training employees how to deal with it. Or if there is a technical aspect of the job that is disruptive to employees, address that first. For example, when a Starbucks employee work-scheduling algorithm was found to be disrupting employees' personal lives with constant last-minute changes, the company revamped it.[57]

Training Programs

A range of training programs can be used to support employees, such as training supervisors or employees on how to reduce stress.

Encourage and Allow for Employee Recovery Experiences

Detaching from work can be essential for employees trying to recover from stress. In fact, studies have shown that good detachment experiences can lead to higher energy levels at work. Not only can workers be trained about how to detach and have the most successful recovery experiences, but organizations can also provide greater experiences for employee recovery.[58] Depending on the nature of the work or the types of employee stress, this might mean setting up e-mail policies that protect employees' nonwork time or allowing for short "sabbaticals" in which employees can recover. For example, FedEx offers employees paid sabbaticals. Now some companies are also using sabbaticals to counteract the "great resignation" post-pandemic.[59]

In addition, employers can encourage workers to take vacation days, as many employees, especially in the United States, might let their vacation days, and thus an opportunity for recovery, go to waste. Some organizations may encourage employees to take short naps at work, as naps can increase performance, and the value of naps during the workday is recognized by companies such as Nike, Proctor & Gamble, Facebook, Ben and Jerry's, and Zappos.[60] Providing personal days, either paid or unpaid, can allow employees to take care of personal needs off the job and to manage their work–life balance.

Consider How to Redesign Work and Work Areas to Fit Employee Needs

This includes quiet areas where employees might be able to take a break. Or it could be more extensive, such as BMW's overhaul of some of its manufacturing facilities to address its aging workforce, introducing features like wood floors (that are easier on joints), seated assembly work, and easier grips. BMW found a 7% increase in productivity with the introduction of these changes.[61]

With the aging of the industrialized workforce, organizations have become interested in ways to support their older workers and keep them productive. BMW pioneered a model work redesign program among aging factory line workers.[62]

©iStock.com/vesilvio

Support the "Corporate Athlete"

Remaining in the stressful corporate world requires that employees take care of themselves in the same way that athletes would in terms of healthy behaviors, such as exercise and recovery. Organizations can play a role in supporting their "corporate athletes" to build and sustain their physical, emotional, mental, and spiritual capacities.[63]

In short, there are a number of ways that HRM professionals can work with organizational leaders to get a handle on employee stress and its negative impact on the employees and on the bottom line. In the next section, we discuss the role of wellness programs to support the safety, health, and well-being of workers.

EMPLOYEE WELLNESS PROGRAMS

LEARNING OBJECTIVE
15.4   Identify the characteristics of the variety of workplace wellness programs that are offered by employers.

As you can see, there are considerable benefits to organizations that consider the stress, health, and well-being of their employees—benefits to both the employees and the organization. One challenge, then, is what organizations can do to actively promote employee health and well-being to provide a competitive edge. **Employee wellness programs** are organizational initiatives that promote the health, fitness, and well-being of workers.[64] About 85% of large employers offer at least some sort of wellness program such as weight management or smoking cessation.[65] Because of their potential benefits both to organizations and to workers, wellness programs have taken center stage in HRM of late, and HRM practitioners are centrally involved in the most effective, strategic implementation of wellness programs.

As we will see, wellness programs can take many forms, given the needs and resources of organizations, employees, and the particular industry. They include everything from helping employees manage illnesses (e.g., diabetes), increase exercise, or quit smoking to providing onsite medical screenings and care or improving their financial knowledge. The key is to offer the program that is the best fit for the employee and their situation.

Benefits of Wellness Programs

Francis deSouza is the CEO of biotechnogy company, Illumina. deSouza argues that employee wellness is an essential issue today, affecting whether people choose to work for a company and whether they decide to remain there.[66]

Kevin Dietsch / Getty Images

The increased interest in employer wellness programs is a sign that organizational decision makers think that these programs matter. A recent review of the research on organizational wellness programs has shown that these programs matter in terms of several health outcomes such as dietary habits and cardiovascular risk factors.[67] There is the belief that a good wellness program is part of a progressive HR strategy that benefits the employer in other ways, such as attracting the best talent. Employees indicated that among the factors that would get them to participate in these programs would be to allocate some hours during the workday to wellness activities and provide on-site wellness facilities. One of the challenges of getting a good payoff from a wellness program is getting employees to participate in it. Both executives and employees identified two leading factors that could reduce employee participation: Employees do not have the time to participate, and employees worry that their information may not remain confidential. These findings are consistent with other studies that show that most employers use wellness programs to improve well-being and to attract and retain the best talent, and only a small number of employers use wellness as a way to reduce tangible costs such as medical costs.[68]

That said, there are data that suggest the dollar value of wellness programs, at least for certain types of programs. This includes taking into account short-term versus long-term return on investment (ROI). A Rand study showed that disease management programs that focus on helping workers with certain specific illnesses do seem to have the greatest short-term benefit in terms of saving money on health care costs, generating as much as $136 in savings per person and a 30% reduction in hospital admissions.[69] For example, a program that supports workers with heart disease could lead to a reduction in heart attacks; a program that supports workers with diabetes might lead to fewer amputations. On the other hand, "lifestyle management" programs that focus on issues like exercise and better eating habits might lead to long-term benefits like reduced rates of cancer or hypertension. Other reviews of the payoff from wellness programs cite lower medical costs and decreased absenteeism and presenteeism (working while having health problems).[70]

One of the challenges of evaluating the ROI for wellness programs is that there is a lot of variability in wellness programs, meaning, programs can vary considerably across organizations, including everything from smoking cessation, to disease management, to mindfulness training.[71] To further complicate things, another important issue is whether employees engage with the wellness program; that is, an excellent wellness program will have little benefit if employees do not use it because they do not think it matters, do not trust the company, or are concerned about their privacy.[72] Nevertheless, many would argue that given the value of worker well-being to increased engagement, performance, morale, and retention, an overly strong focus on ROI alone misses the point.[73]

Types of Wellness Programs

Wellness programs can include a range of elements (see Figure 15.7). We discuss only some of the more common examples in what follows. Note that most organizations would not include all these elements but would instead select the types of wellness products that best fit their employees.[74] Some broad categories include the following:

- *Fitness club memberships and centers.* These can involve providing an on-site gym or special rates, discounts, or reimbursements at local fitness centers.

FIGURE 15.7 ■ Workplace Wellness Programs

Such programs have expanded in their popularity and breadth, and they can take many different forms. Here are examples of just some of the many possible elements of a workplace wellness program.

- *Nutrition education and healthy eating.* These types of programs provide instructions for employees on eating well. Some include making healthful food and snacks available on site or even an on-site farmers market.

- *Disease management.* Disease management programs, which have existed since the early 2000s, are better researched than some other types of wellness programs, and they appear to be good at reducing medical costs and employee mortality. These include providing help, support, and guidance for employees who know that they have chronic conditions, such as heart disease or diabetes, so that they can better manage their diseases.

- *Emotional well-being.* With a focus on things like yoga instruction, mindfulness, and other ways to control employee stress, these programs have become more popular since the days of early wellness programs, which had a greater focus on physical health. As an example, Vancouver-based Mobify offers twice-weekly yoga classes to its employees.

- *Health incentives.* An organization may choose to reward any number of health behaviors such as smoking cessation, weight loss, or steps. Implementing health incentives should take into account the type of employee. The key is for workers to feel engaged, not coerced.

- *Sleep.* These programs may focus on anything from sleep hygiene education (explaining the value of sleep and how to develop good sleep habits) to workplace naps. For example, Asana offers its employees "nap rooms" where they can take a quick nap during work hours. And at LinkedIn, a recent focus of its wellness program was sleep health, including a "sleep fair."[75]

- *Financial health programs.* A number of surveys have shown that employees are not financially healthy (in terms of their personal finances), and the stress from this could affect their workplace behavior. Employer-sponsored financial programs can take any number of forms, ranging from financial education and advice to paying student loans. Nearly half of all companies offer such financial advice, according to a SHRM survey.

- *Smoking cessation.* Smoking cessation programs support people trying to quit. These are used at many organizations such as Microsoft.

- *Weight loss.* Weight-loss programs are often included as part of healthy eating and exercise programs and may also include Weight Watchers meetings and weight-loss competitions.

- *Health screening and assessment.* Sometimes employees are unaware that they have health risks. Simply offering employees the chance to get some basic health screening might uncover if they have particular medical needs (the privacy of which would also need to be protected).

- *On-site medical care.* This is not something that all companies can offer. In fact, only about 8% of companies have such a program, according to a SHRM survey. But given that employees are sometimes pressed for time and do not get around to taking care of their personal health needs, some companies such as Cisco are offering these on-site medical services to employees.

Employee Assistance Programs (EAPs)

Employee assistance programs (EAPs) are in some ways the predecessors of wellness programs but with a decidedly different approach. Rather than taking an active role in promoting employee health and well-being and preventing illness, EAPs are focused on identifying employees' personal issues that may be affecting their work and helping them with these existing problems. The issues they address include a range of issues such as alcohol and substance abuse, emotional challenges, and financial problems. The services offered by EAPs can take different forms depending on the type of problems, like providing basic legal assistance, counseling, advice on child care or elder care services, and/or nursing advice by telephone. Typically paid for by the employer, EAP services generally support not only the employee but the employee's family as well.[76] And although more research is needed, EAPs generally seem to work: One review found that EAPs improved employee functioning and decreased presenteeism (e.g., working while unwell.)[77] One classic example is the EAP offered to federal employees by Federal Occupational Health, which provides counseling and referrals to employees and help with financial issues, critical incident response, and management consultation.[78]

What began in the 1940s and 1950s with a primary focus on alcohol abuse has expanded through the years to become a program that is standard in most organizations, with many outside entities providing services (e.g., counseling) paid for by the employer. It is important to note that, like wellness programs, EAPs vary considerably from one organization to the next in what types of specific services they offer. Most medium- and large-sized organizations provide some type of EAP services to their employees. Many EAPs also require

- the development of consistent EAP rules and guidelines with input from employees and, in unionized organizations, from unions;

- legal guidance on the appropriateness of EAP rules and procedures;

- procedures for maintaining employee confidentiality;

- training for supervisors on appropriate methods for identifying employee performance problems that might be appropriate for referral to EAP;

- consultation services for supervisors dealing with a possible employee EAP issue; and

- a system for monitoring and follow-up.[79]

In relation to EAPs, there has recently been a growing awareness of mental health issues at work. This interest has increased as a result of stress associated with the pandemic and isolation due to remote work. Poor mental health may manifest at work as absenteeism, presenteeism (e.g., working while ill), turnover, disability, interpersonal conflict, and sickness. Researchers have identified five workplace warning signs of mental health issues: emotional distress (e.g., complaining), withdrawal, attendance changes, lower performance, and extreme behaviors (e.g., substance use at work, expressing a desire to hurt others or oneself). Notably, many EAP services may help with such mental health issues. In addition, the American Psychological Association recommends that organizations create a culture to support mental health by training leaders to promote well-being and developing policies that explicitly include mental health. Other researchers note the importance of increasing mental health literacy, accommodating those who need support (e.g., time off, schedule changes), and reducing the stigma around mental health through training.[80]

What is the role of HRM in EAPs? One issue is to ensure employee privacy and security of employee information, including which EAP services are used by individual employees. In addition, most employers, except for very large organizations, outsource EAP services given the highly specialized nature of the work in such matters, such as counseling and substance abuse treatment. Thus, HR personnel are heavily involved in selecting EAP vendors, developing EAP policies, and explaining to employees which EAP services are available.[81] This last issue may be particularly important, as it has been argued that employees tend to underuse EAP services either due to issues such as privacy concerns or not really being aware of which EAP services are offered.[82]

Best Practices for Implementing Wellness Programs and the Role of HRM

Given the costs of wellness programs, their careful implementation is essential to providing value to the organization. It is here that HRM plays a central role by ensuring the program fits employees' needs as well as those of the organization.[83]

- *Needs assessment.* As with all other HR functions, the wellness program should be designed to fit what employees want and to address organizational concerns. For example, if a key goal of the organization is to be seen as a healthy place to work, the wellness program might focus on nutrition and exercise. Or if medical claims are seen as a particular financial drain, the focus might be on disease management. Further, a program that does not fit a need felt on the part of employees is of little value. In other words, the program should also be tailored to the needs of the employees.

- *Engagement of leadership.* Research has shown that like so many other organizational initiatives, buy-in at all levels is necessary to ensure support and the success of the program.

- *Communication.* Another central role for HR is to ensure that employees know about the wellness services available to them. This means clear, consistent, and frequent messaging.

- *Ensure that the program is easy for employees to use.* Examples might include the decision to provide on-site child care or on-site health care services so that employees are more likely to use these services.

- *Evaluation.* We have noted that the payoff on wellness programs may not be as tangible as return on investment (ROI), although sometimes it is. In any case, whether it is reduced health costs, absenteeism, employee satisfaction and morale, or better retention, some evaluation of the program should be included to illustrate its value. For example, measurement and evaluation are a standard part of Johnson & Johnson's wellness program. The use of metrics, such as physical activity and biometric screening (e.g., blood pressure, BMI), is becoming part of the natural landscape in evaluating wellness programs.

- *Ensure integrity of private employee data.* Part of having rich data to evaluate wellness programs is the ethical responsibility to protect these data. Ensuring the safety and security of employee data as well as regulatory compliance can best assure employee buy-in.

- *Consider the use of incentives.* A wellness program that is never used by employees is a waste of money. In fact, the measurement of employee adoption of various wellness offerings may be one of the most important metrics of the program's value. But there are many ways to encourage adoption. One method is to provide financial incentives for employee participation in wellness programs. Such incentives generally seem to work, at least for certain types of wellness programs, although they may work better for certain types of health behaviors (e.g., eating more fruits and vegetables) than others (e.g., stopping smoking). Other ways to incent employees into participating in wellness programs is to introduce employee competitions for those who wish to participate in this way. Incentives should be seen as fair by employees and not coercive. The *Manager's Toolbox* presents a number of suggestions for ensuring the success of a wellness program in organizations.

Manager's Toolbox: Tips for Implementing an Effective Wellness Program

Wellness programs come in a wide range of shapes and sizes, with varying costs and payoffs. These can vary by organization and by individual employees. Plus, starting a wellness program that isn't a good fit (e.g., one that makes employees feel like they are being coerced into participating) may make matters worse. Here are some ideas to keep in mind when implementing a wellness program.

1. *Find out what employees actually want and need.* Whereas some employees may want assistance with financial planning, others may want gym memberships. The point is that an assessment of employee needs and interests—in other words, a program that employees will actually use—should guide the adoption of a new program.

2. *To the extent possible, make the program flexible to address individual employees' needs.* Focus not only on what most employees want but also on what different groups of employees want. A program that allows some flexibility to address the different needs of different workers should be well received.

3. *Think about how to encourage participation.* Some employees may be motivated to join a wellness program after some feedback about their current health. Others may be motivated by some sort of health competition among employees, although this could be a definite turnoff for other workers. Keep in mind what would work best for different employees in your organization.

4. *Consider the marketing angle.* This might be as simple as providing sufficient knowledge of the program. It might also mean carefully choosing names for the program elements so that employees aren't "turned off."

5. *Make participation convenient for employees.* An unused program is an unwise investment, so make it easy for employees to use. For example, if the focus is on greater exercise, consider whether employees might be more likely to participate in a gym program that is located on site or near the worksite. When it is easier for employees to use a program, it is easier for them to adopt it.

6. *Leverage technology.* Technology can help with wellness programs in numerous ways, such as apps that help employees with meeting their health goals, attending webinars, or scheduling medical appointments.[84]

SPOTLIGHT ON DATA AND ANALYTICS: WEARABLE TECHNOLOGY IN THE WORKPLACE

One of the biggest sources of data workplace safety and health analytics is wearable technology ("wearables") worn by employees. This can take a number of forms, such as fitness trackers or employee badges that monitor employee movements and their proximity to each other. For example, during the pandemic, some Ford employees wore wristbands that buzzed when they were within 6 feet of another employee.

Perhaps one of the most commonly cited uses of such wearables is for wellness programs. For example, a wearable allows employees to see not only their own steps in a day but how much their coworkers are walking as well. Wearables may allow employees to become aware of dysfunctional behaviors they are not aware of or to see where they might make simple changes to improve their health. Similarly, wearables can allow employers to set up incentives for employees to increase their activity or allow them to tailor health programs to fit the needs of an individual employee.

Wearables can be used in the realm of employee safety as well. For example, some wearable solutions alert employees operating heavy equipment when they are too close to other employees. Wearable technology has even been cited as a way for organizations to track worker well-being in terms of their happiness at work, with the hopes of improving worker happiness.

Workplace wearables are not without their challenges. First, wearables may provide far more data than most organizations are equipped to analyze or interpret. Relatedly, collecting such data about employees raises the issue of privacy and who will have access to the data. In addition, monitoring employees in personal ways may increase worker stress and resentment. In fact, an employer that wants to improve employee health and well-being may do better to reduce hours and let employees detach from work rather than introducing competitions or monitoring health behavior. Further, the collection of such personal data by employers has been challenged within the European Union, which has far more stringent privacy laws than the United States. Wearables can lead to serious security issues, such as when the wearables used by U.S. soldiers gave away their locations (which were not supposed to be revealed).

In short, workplace wearables can provide a tremendous opportunity to both employers and workers. However, they should be implemented with care, that is, employee input and participation and good communication.[85]

WORKPLACE INTERVENTIONS: SOLUTIONS TO ADDRESS SPECIFIC WELL-BEING ISSUES

LEARNING OBJECTIVE
15.5 Identify examples of focused workplace well-being interventions.

This chapter describes the role of HRM in employee safety and well-being and a variety of approaches employers use to support workplace safety and well-being. Sometimes, rather than implementing an entire program, employers uncover the need to focus on a very specific outcome (e.g., employee stress) or problematic issue (e.g., poor safety climate), or they may want to focus on the needs of their employee population (e.g., truckers). In these cases, they may choose to apply a more narrowly focused workplace intervention as a solution to address their needs. For example, workplace interventions have been found to improve stress-related outcomes.[86] In this section, we describe a few examples of workplace interventions that have been rigorously evaluated for their effectiveness.

Improving Work–Life Balance

As described earlier, work–life balance issues are a growing challenge for many organizations, with factors such as intrusion of e-mail outside of work playing a role. One intervention called STAR (Support, Transform, Achieve, Results), developed by Leslie Hammer and colleagues to support work–life balance, included training supervisors to support work–life balance among employees and helping supervisors apply these skills on the job through software and workshops. When applied to 30 health care facilities, the researchers found that in groups that went through the STAR intervention, there were improvements in safety behavior and organizational citizenship behavior compared with groups that did not get the intervention. In other studies, STAR was found to reduce smoking and improve workers' sleep.[87]

Enhancing Safety Through Improved Leadership and Communication

Given the importance of safety climate to other safety outcomes, there have been calls for interventions to improve safety climate and culture. Dov Zohar and colleagues examined ways to enhance the communication between leaders and employees to improve climate and other safety outcomes. These interventions focused on the effects of giving supervisors feedback about the quality of the safety-focused conversations with their team members and whether leaders discussed safety with team members on a daily basis. The effects on safety outcomes were compelling. Teams where the leader received the intervention showed significant improvements in safety climate, safety behavior, and safety audit scores.[88]

Addressing the Needs of Specific Occupations

Some interventions are developed to address the health and safety challenges of specific professions. For example, long-haul truck driving is a sedentary job that often requires extended periods away from home and involves a number of health and safety risks. In addition to the risk of accidents, long-haul truckers have rates of obesity, diabetes, and smoking that are double the rates of other workers. Many also report limited physical activity and poor sleep.[89] Therefore, some safety and health interventions are specifically focused on long-haul truckers, taking into consideration the specific nature of their work. The Safety and Health Involvement for Truckers (SHIFT) intervention was designed to address the sedentary nature of long-haul trucking with training, employees monitoring their own behaviors, and a weight-loss competition. An evaluation of SHIFT with a sample of 452 drivers showed that drivers who received the intervention had lower BMI and increased fruit and vegetable consumption those who did not receive the intervention.[90]

TOTAL WORKER HEALTH®: AN INTEGRATED APPROACH TO WORKER WELL-BEING

LEARNING OBJECTIVE

15.6   Explain what is meant by an integrated Total Worker Health® approach.

Throughout this chapter, we have discussed the issues of workplace safety, worker stress and well-being, and wellness programs as separate issues. In reality, however, these are all linked, because an employer concerned with worker safety will also be concerned with worker well-being and will develop wellness programs to address these issues. Consider the reported causes of some railway accidents: The causes of these accidents included worker health issues (e.g., sleep apnea) that could have been addressed by means of a health and well-being program across the organization. Specifically, such a program could have identified the underlying medical problems (e.g., sleep apnea tied to obesity) and perhaps even reduced it through treatment, weight loss, and exercise. The railway accidents, however, were also the result of a physical work environment that did not include safeguards (e.g., speed monitoring systems) to prevent accidents and perhaps a weak safety climate in the organization. The result was that workers with health problems were involved in accidents that caused injury to themselves and to the public.[91]

Thus, there is a growing recognition of the value of integrating wellness programs with traditional workplace safety and health programs because such integration can bring about systemic change within the organization. The National Institute for Occupational Safety and Health (NIOSH) refers to these integrated safety, well-being, and wellness programs as Total Worker Health' (TWH') programs (see Figure 15.8).[92] As one example, Novelis, a multinational aluminum manufacturing company, piloted a TWH' program in Italy. The program included involvement from a wide range of employees at all levels; safety management across multiple issues such as ergonomics, respiratory protection, first aid, and noise reduction; and health promotion activities (e.g., improving physical health, strength).[93]

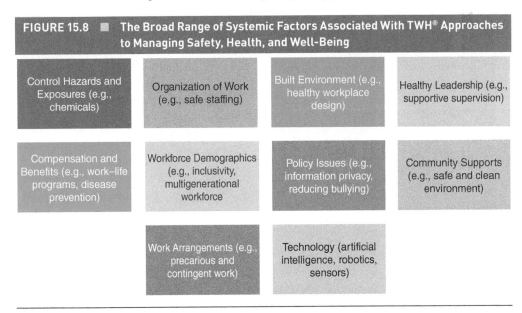

FIGURE 15.8 ■ The Broad Range of Systemic Factors Associated With TWH® Approaches to Managing Safety, Health, and Well-Being

Control Hazards and Exposures (e.g., chemicals)

Organization of Work (e.g., safe staffing)

Built Environment (e.g., healthy workplace design)

Healthy Leadership (e.g., supportive supervision)

Compensation and Benefits (e.g., work–life programs, disease prevention)

Workforce Demographics (e.g., inclusivity, multigenerational workforce)

Policy Issues (e.g., information privacy, reducing bullying)

Community Supports (e.g., safe and clean environment)

Work Arrangements (e.g., precarious and contingent work)

Technology (artificial intelligence, robotics, sensors)

Source: Based on recommendations from NIOSH. (2020). *Issues relevant to advancing well-being using* Total Worker Health® *approaches.* https://www.cdc.gov/niosh/twh/pdfs/Issues-Graphic-2020_508.pdf

Although the research on these integrated programs is still in the early stages, an initial review of 17 TWH' interventions found that they may have more long-term impact on worker safety and health than narrower, piecemeal approaches.[94] Further, seeing worker safety, health, and well-being through this integrated lens can help organizations identify underlying causes of safety and health issues. For example, through the use of data analytics, a company may be able to identify the relationship between costly outcomes (e.g., employee medical costs; accidents) that are associated with an underlying cause (e.g., safety climate) that could be addressed by specific management practices (e.g., top management support, supervisor training).

CHAPTER SUMMARY

HRM plays a central role in workplace safety, well-being, and wellness. HR professionals need to know the government agencies and resources devoted to safety and the safety regulations with which employers must comply. Proactive HRM will work to uncover workers' safety and health issues and their causes. HRM will also take steps to identify and implement appropriate solutions, including employee wellness programs and more specific interventions and integrated Total Worker Health' approaches. Organizations with a culture of safety communicate the importance of safety and health to both managers and employees. Looking at the big picture of safety and health across the organization is a key strategy in supporting employee health and well-being and organizational success.

KEY TERMS

Challenge stressors	Safety committee
Employee wellness programs	Safety compliance behavior
Ergonomic design	Safety knowledge
Family-to-work conflict	Safety motivation
Hierarchy of controls	Safety officer
Hindrance stressors	Safety participation behavior
National Institute for Occupational Safety and Health (NIOSH)	Strain
	Stressors
Natural lighting	Total Worker Health® (TWH®)
Near misses	Well-being
Occupational Safety and Health Administration (OSHA)	Workplace accidents
	Workplace bullying
Open offices	Workplace fatalities
Physical environment	Workplace injuries
Safety behavior	Workplace intervention
Safety climate	Work-to-family conflict

HR REASONING AND DECISION-MAKING EXERCISES

Mini-Case Analysis Exercise: Safety for All

You are working for a small construction company specializing in interior and exterior painting of newly built homes. You are the sole safety officer in this small company of 50 employees. The company is fairly young—5 years old—but it is growing rapidly with the high rate of construction in your metropolitan area. So far, things are going well from a safety perspective, with no severe accidents or injuries yet reported.

The company handles a number of safety issues well. It posts the required OSHA publications regarding employee rights and employer responsibilities. In addition, you have been able to use the checklists that OSHA publishes to improve safety standards and to demonstrate the need to provide safety training to employees on the hazards that are characteristic of this type of work.

However, you notice that the owner and the three lead supervisors in the company see safety as an issue that is addressed primarily through your role, not theirs. For example, the owner of the company rarely follows the company's own rules regarding safety, especially with regard to the handling of chemicals (e.g., solvents) that are used in painting work. Similarly, he and the three supervisors are very much on company growth and encourage workers to work quickly; in your view, this is sometimes at the expense of safety. In addition, you have noticed that when employees do voice a concern or suggestion regarding a safety problem, the suggestion is not welcomed by your supervisors, at least not in terms of their body language. You are trying to decide on your next steps in managing the safety function in the company.

1. What concerns do you have with the safety climate of this company? In what ways might these issues have a negative impact on worker safety?

2. What steps could you take in your role as safety officer to better illustrate to management the safety issues that you are observing in this company?

3. What arguments could you make to these top managers about the importance of safety climate and the role they play in it? What suggestions would you make to them as to how they might foster a positive safety climate?

HR Decision Analysis Exercise: The Wellness Competition

Tabular Communications runs a group of four call centers across the United States, with locations in Vermont, Iowa, Arizona, and California. Several retailers use Tabular's services. Specifically, Tabular's call center employees assist customers of these retailers with making purchases, also providing customers with product information.

These customer service jobs are highly sedentary. In addition, because these call centers are not located near restaurants, in the past employees could not easily purchase healthy food for lunch and for breaks, relying either on food they bring from home or on vending machines. In recognition of this issue, the HR team has persuaded Tabular's management to include some healthy options in the vending machines and even to provide on-site employee cafés with a range of food options. These innovations appear to be quite popular with employees.

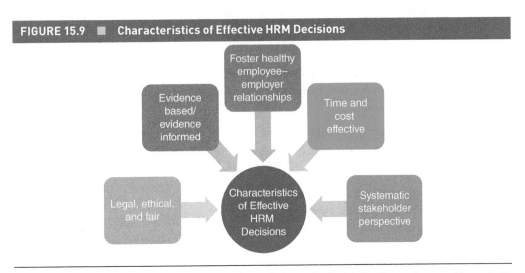

FIGURE 15.9 ■ Characteristics of Effective HRM Decisions

Source: Reprinted from *SHRM Competency Model* with permission of the Society for Human Resource Management. © SHRM. All rights reserved.

To go a step further, the HR director has recently proposed that management initiate an employee wellness program that incorporates competition among employees. Specifically, the director would like to provide health-tracking devices to employees. These would allow employees not only to track their own steps but also to compete with other employees, with the company awarding prizes to those with the most steps. The program would also include a competition between the different call center locations. The director points out that getting up and moving around more would be especially beneficial to employees in these types of sedentary jobs. Furthermore, data collected from the health tracking devices might help the company figure out ways to cut its health care costs.

Please provide the rationale for your answer to each of the questions below.

Does this wellness program seem legal, ethical, and fair?

Is it evidence based/evidence informed?

Does it foster healthy employee–employer relationships?

Is it time- and cost-effective?

Does it take a systematic stakeholder perspective?

Considering your analysis above, overall, do you think that undertaking this aspect of the wellness program would be an effective decision? Why or why not?

What, if anything, do you think should be done differently or considered to help make this decision more effective?

HR Decision-Making Exercise: Assessing the Value of a Wellness Program

A manufacturing company is preparing to implement a company wellness program within its East Coast, southeastern, and West Coast locations, which employ approximately 1,800 workers in total.

The proposed wellness program would involve five possible components:
- on-site exercise equipment,
- smoking cessation program,
- mindfulness training,
- free mental health counseling, and
- financial education.

The company's CEO is very supportive of a wellness program, having seen the benefits where she worked previously. But she is also concerned about justifying the program in terms of its costs and benefits. Thus, she would like to know which of these proposed components of the program, or which combination of components, the company should consider undertaking.

1. How would you investigate the potential value of each of these components prior to implementation? Aside from company data, what specific sources would you use to the possible value of each component?

2. What types of company data would you use to determine if each of these components is needed? Be specific in describing both (a) the type of data you would want to review and (b) what data patterns would suggest a need for the specific component.

3. Should you roll out the entire program at once, or should each component be rolled out separately? What would be the advantages and disadvantages of each approach? In crafting your response, consider whether the three company locations might be used differently for the rollout.

4. In the event that the program was implemented by the company, describe what types of data (e.g., objective data, employee attitudes, etc.) the company should collect to evaluate whether each component is effective.

5. Are there any "intangible" outcomes that might be considered in assessing the value of the wellness program?

DATA AND ANALYTICS EXERCISE: INVESTIGATING EMPLOYEE STRESS

Recall that employee stress can lead to workplace accidents, as well as to lower productivity and higher turnover. Stress can be conceptualized as a process involving stressors and strain, where stressors are demands in the environment to which a person must respond and strain refers to a person's reaction to stressors. Employees' perceptions of stressors and strain can be measured using surveys, and the data from such surveys can be used to understand which organizational units perceive the highest levels of stressors and strain and whether stressors and strain are associated with important outcomes, such as employee attitudes (e.g., job satisfaction, turnover intentions) and performance. Regression analysis can be used to understand whether the relationship between a stressor or strain variable and an outcome variable is statistically significant and, if so, the direction of the association (positive or negative). For example, consider the following dataset. It contains employees' perceptions of a common workplace stressor called interpersonal conflict and their turnover intentions. Each row represents a unique employee's set of responses to the different survey questions, and the numeric scores associated with each variable represent the employee's average response to items/questions associated with that particular variable.

Survey Number	Interpersonal Conflict	Turnover Intentions
1	4.6	4.1
2	4.7	3.4
3	3.7	4.0
4	3.9	3.1
5	3.6	3.7
6	2.0	3.9
7	3.3	2.9
8	2.9	3.4
9	3.2	3.7
10	2.9	4.0
11	2.9	3.4
12	3.1	3.4
13	3.3	3.8
14	2.0	2.9
15	2.5	3.4
16	2.3	2.5
17	2.5	2.7
18	3.5	2.3
19	2.6	2.1
20	1.4	1.5

If you were to plug these variables into a linear regression analysis, wherein interpersonal conflict is entered as a predictor variable and turnover intentions is entered as an outcome variable, you would find that the association between the two variables is statistically significant because the p value equals .03, which is less than the conventional cutoff of .05. Further, the unstandardized regression coefficient for interpersonal conflict is .58, which means that the association is positive and that for every 1.0-point increase in interpersonal conflict scores, turnover intentions scores tend to increase by .58 points. An excerpt from the regression analysis output is provided.

	Coefficients	Standard Error	t Stat	p Value	Lower 95%	Upper 95%
Intercept	1.20	.80	1.50	.15	–.48	2.88
Interpersonal Conflict	.58	.24	2.37	.03	.06	1.09

If the regression coefficient for interpersonal conflict were nonsignificant (i.e., the p value were equal to or greater than .05), then we would conclude that there is no association between the two variables.

Excel Extension: Now You Try!

- On **edge.sagepub.com/bauer2e**, you will find an Excel exercise on investigating employee stress.

- First, you will learn how to run a regression analysis in Excel.

- Second, you will run several regression analyses in which you investigate the associations between different stressor and strain variables and different outcome variables.

- Third, you will practice interpreting and communicating the results of the analyses.

©iStockphoto.com/metamorworks

16 OPPORTUNITIES AND CHALLENGES IN INTERNATIONAL HRM

MANAGING A REMOTE WORKFORCE AROUND THE GLOBE: THE CASE OF REMOTE.COM

©iStockphoto.com/fulltimetraveller

The Covid-19 pandemic greatly accelerated the trend toward remote work. Many employees left the big cities they were living and working in, in favor of more affordable cities that provided other perks such as proximity to one's family or access to outdoors. Some employees took this opportunity to move abroad, leaving their home country in favor of a different country, to try out a new lifestyle. In turn, companies started realizing that not having physical offices and having the ability to hire anyone from anywhere allowed them to hire applicants from different countries. Employees are increasingly demanding the ability to work from anywhere, and businesses are realizing the advantages of offering such flexibility means taking advantage of a bigger pool of talent.

Despite all its advantages, allowing employees to work across the borders or pursuing a global hiring strategy introduces an important set of complications for businesses, including but not limited to immigration law, taxation, benefits and compensation administration, and compliance with local laws. Many countries are aware of the increasing number of foreign nationals working within their boundaries, and while some are adjusting their laws around remote workers from foreign countries, they are also tightening enforcement around visa and tax compliance.

To deal with this complexity, an increasing number of companies are using the services of an employer of record (EOR) firm. EORs essentially hire employees from different countries and contract them to the organization. This way, they assume the costs, complications, and legal liabilities of managing global employees. Remote.com is one such EOR provider that offers international payroll, benefits, and compliance services.

Remote.com was founded in 2019 by Job van der Voort, who was one of the early employees of GitLab. GitLab was the world's largest all-remote company prior to the pandemic, employing over 1,000 employees in 65 countries. While working there, van der Voort witnessed firsthand the difficulties of managing a workforce remotely scattered around the world. How do you pay these employees and ensure legal compliance? How do you administer benefits? These questions typically become easier for a business that employs a lot of employees from a single country, but figuring out how to manage an employee from a specific country where there are no prior employees is a unique challenge. Essentially, the employer would need to have expertise in local laws and regulations in each country, which would be difficult for any large business, let alone small- and medium-sized organizations.

Seeing a business opportunity in solving this problem, van der Voort left GitLab in 2019 and co-founded Remote.com, where he currently serves as the CEO. The timing was fortuitous for the company with the start of the pandemic in 2020 and the resulting boom in remote work. The company raised $496 million in funding as of 2022 and used the funds raised to expand the business. Currently the firm operates in over 60 countries.

Here is how this works: Imagine that a company decides to hire an applicant from Indonesia. Or, the company may have an employee who wants to relocate to Indonesia. While they are excited about hiring the new person or keeping their existing employee, they have no local expertise in Indonesia. This is where Remote.com would come in. Remote.com owns local entities around the world, including in Indonesia. This means that the hiring company would work with Remote.com, so that the applicant would be hired by Remote and become an employee of Remote on paper. Remote.com would manage the end-to-end employment process, including onboarding, compensation including benefits, taxes, stock options, compliance, and other details of employment. Businesses would hire the employee using a localized employment contract and pay them in the local currency. This way, the company would work with the talent, without worrying about figuring out how to operate as an employer in Indonesia.

Remote.com is working toward seamlessly integrating employee data with other aspects of the HR information systems. For example, the company announced integrations with HiBob and BambooHR, which are HR technology firms also offering workforce analytics components. With the integration, data entered into HiBob and BambooHR will be automatically updated in the Remote platform, which should minimize duplication of data entry efforts, minimize errors, and result in a more streamlined process for managing employees around the globe. The connectedness of the data across multiple systems will make it easier to collect, manage, and analyze the data for HR analytics purposes.[1]

CASE DISCUSSION QUESTIONS

1. What are the benefits and challenges of working in a global fully remote company?

2. For businesses, what are the main advantages and challenges of employing workers from around the world and employing them remotely?

3. How should a company decide whether they should invest in an EOR service?

4. Do you see any downsides for a company that uses EOR services?

INTRODUCTION

For businesses, national boundaries have been losing their relevance. Many iconic "all-American" brands established in the United States, such as Budweiser, 7-Eleven, and IBM, now have non-U.S.-based owners. Companies such as Intel, Nike, GE, and McDonald's receive more than half their revenue from their overseas sales and operations. HR professionals are increasingly operating in a world in which they need to go outside of the local talent pool for recruitment, learn how to train and manage a global workforce, and ensure they create HR systems that explicitly consider the context in which they are operating. This chapter discusses international influences on the theory and practice of HRM.

Global markets often represent an important growth opportunity for businesses, providing the chance to reach previously untapped markets. Having access to a global talent pool may make companies more competitive and innovative. Moving production to a different country where labor, land, or raw materials are cheaper may provide advantages from a cost perspective. Regardless of its reasons, doing business globally is fast becoming the norm rather than the exception. Most multinationals have been headquartered in developed countries such as the United States, Europe, and Japan. However, this situation is changing, as exemplified by China-based Sinopec and PetroChina joining the list of largest multinational corporations in the world in terms of revenue.[2]

GLOBAL TRANSFER OF HR PRACTICES

LEARNING OBJECTIVE
16.1   Describe the advantages and disadvantages to standardizing HR practices in different locations of a business and barriers to standardization.

Organizations vary in their degree of internationalization. For example, international companies export and import, but their investments are within one home country. Most large firms these days are international given that they source at least some materials from overseas. Multinational companies operate in multiple countries but with clearly designated headquarters in their home country. The headquarters typically set the standards for how host-country or subsidiary operations will function. Examples include Ikea (based in Sweden) and Amazon (based in the United States). Transnational companies have operations in multiple countries. However, they act like a borderless company and do not consider any one country as the center of operations. These businesses are more decentralized and adapt their operations following the best practices that may emerge from different operations. Transnationals are a type of multinational organization. Examples include Nestlé and Unilever. Internationalization is not only occurring in private-sector and for-profit organizations. In fact, even universities are becoming multinational: Georgia Institute of Technology has a campus in Lorraine, France, and Carnegie Mellon University has a campus in Rwanda, Africa.[3]

An important trend resulting in internationalization of businesses is offshoring. Companies often find that producing physical goods or performing some of their operations overseas has cost advantages. As a result, they may move some of their operations to an overseas location. Offshoring may help companies to deal with talent shortages in local markets as well, such as the shortage in engineering and sciences graduates in the United States. Offshoring is more likely to occur when decision makers believe the infrastructure will be supportive and that they will have access to high-quality and affordable human resources. Note that offshoring is different from and may not involve outsourcing. Outsourcing refers to moving some operations of the company to a different company. For example, a company may decide to stop handling its own payroll operations and instead contract another company to provide this service. Outsourcing does not necessarily involve an international operation: A firm may outsource to another company in the same country or region. Offshoring may be combined with outsourcing, such as Apple's use of Taiwanese manufacturer Foxconn to produce its iPhones and iPads.

In a global organization, a key decision that needs to be made with respect to HR practices is striking a balance between global integration and local differentiation: Should the organization standardize its HR practices around the world? Or should it vary its practices in consideration of the local environment? There are clear advantages to having all units use the same selection, onboarding, training, performance management, and reward systems so that operations are more consistent and coherent. Having standardized HR practices around the world will prevent efforts to "reinvent the wheel" and helps to ensure consistency in operations. Global integration ensures that the company establishes a common corporate culture and common ways of doing business, which could be helpful in achieving fairness across different operations. In fact, the desire to transmit headquarter practices to subsidiaries will be strong, because HR practices that are in use at the country of origin will often be perceived as the "right way" of doing business.

Figure 16.1 summarizes different types of methods companies use to transfer HR practices from headquarters to subsidiaries. Companies may transfer their practices across units through the use of people, information technology, standardized procedures and rules, and centralizing particular decisions in one location. For example, an organization interested in globally integrating its diversity management practices might utilize people-, information-, formalization-, or centralization-based practices. People-based integration could involve ensuring that diversity managers around the globe have regular meetings and coordinate their activities. Information-based integration might entail including similar types of information in the corporate website in different localities. Formalization-based integration could take the form of using diversity-related metrics in performance evaluations around the globe. Finally, centralization-based integration might include drawing up a corporate-level diversity strategy in the headquarters.[4]

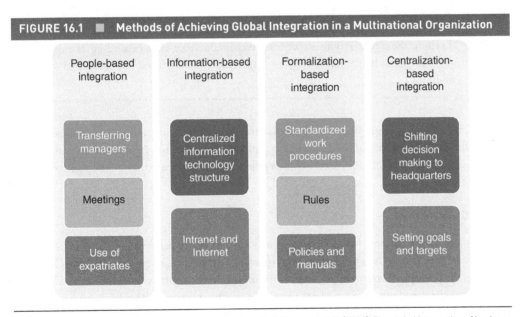

FIGURE 16.1 ■ Methods of Achieving Global Integration in a Multinational Organization

People-based integration	Information-based integration	Formalization-based integration	Centralization-based integration
Transferring managers	Centralized information technology structure	Standardized work procedures	Shifting decision making to headquarters
Meetings		Rules	
Use of expatriates	Intranet and Internet	Policies and manuals	Setting goals and targets

Source: Based on information contained in Kim, K., Park, J. H., & Prescott, J. E. (2003). The global integration of business functions: A study of multinational businesses in integrated global industries. *Journal of International Business Studies, 34,* 327–344.

At the same time, there are good reasons not to transfer all or even some HR practices and instead follow a local differentiation strategy. For example, headquarter HR practices might not fit with the regulatory or cultural context of subsidiaries in other countries. These practices from headquarters could make it more difficult to attract or retain employees in other countries. In fact, subsidiaries may sometimes develop their own HR practices that the company could be interested in disseminating to other overseas operations or to headquarters. Trying to centralize HR operations might prevent these opportunities from taking place.

There are occasions when headquarters will not try to transfer its policies to other locations. For example, a company that uses unlimited vacation days and remote work for headquarters employees may decide not to transfer these practices to overseas operations with the belief (correct or not) that such policies may be too expensive, not fit with the business context, and may be abused given lack of precedence in a particular location. There are instances in which overseas employees may prefer that the company uses headquarters' policies. As a case in point, in countries where informal business practices based on personal relationships dominate the business landscape, multinational firms may be attractive to employers because they will have policies and practices ensuring systematic and procedurally fair decisions in hiring, promotions, and pay. In other words, subsidiary employees may prefer that the firm transfer HR practices from headquarters rather than allow each locality to develop its own. As can be seen, the decision to transfer some or all HR practices to overseas operations is not a simple one.[5]

When considering the question of global integration versus local differentiation of HR practices, it is important to remember that this is not an "all or nothing" proposition; it is a matter of degree. Companies may choose to standardize some HR practices, whereas other practices may be subject to localization. Further, it is important to distinguish between HR philosophy and HR practices. The company may have HR practices that are adapted to each locality but may also have a centralized HR philosophy guiding HR-related decisions. As long as there is shared understanding about the company's fundamental values with respect to workforce management, the company may differentiate its HR practices yet manage to coordinate effectively across business units.

IMPORTANT CONSIDERATIONS WHEN TRANSFERRING HR PRACTICES ACROSS BORDERS

LEARNING OBJECTIVE
16.2   Examine the considerations an organization should make when expanding its business practices across borders such as cultural differences, unionization rates, and legal context.

When a multinational organization is interested in transferring particular HR practices across borders, it may run into difficulties. Cultural differences, unionization rates, and legal context are three of the many reasons businesses may find that their best practices in one country may not be possible or desirable in other countries.

Legal Context

Even though the discussions of HR-related laws may have led you to believe the contrary, businesses in the United States actually have a lot of freedom regarding talent management. For example, Chapter 10 discusses the principle of employment at will as the norm in most organizations, although its influence has been eroding over time due to several exceptions that have emerged. As a reminder, employment at will is the assumption that employees have the freedom to join and leave organizations any time they like, and businesses have the freedom to hire and terminate employees as they see fit. In contrast, in Europe, the commonly held assumption is that businesses need to be monitored, controlled, and constrained so that they do not harm employees. There are simply more protections for employees that constrain the autonomy of European businesses. For example, terminating an employee in Europe for any reason requires following specific procedures, giving employees advance notice, and providing generous severance pay. Most other countries around the world mandate paid time off for employees and new parents. The employee–organization relationship in the United States is often based on terms set by the company in negotiation with the employee, which is not necessarily the case in many other countries.

Differences in the legal environment may be as fundamental as whether a specific worker is an employee. Whether someone is an employee or not is an important distinction, as employee status usually confers specific rights. Someone who is considered a contractor or a freelancer in one context may have to be recognized as an employee in a different national context, requiring the organization to modify its HR practices. For example, in 2021 a Dutch court ruled that Uber drivers are employees, and not contractors, making them eligible for benefits and rights aligned with those provided to taxi drivers in the country.[6] Portugal passed a "right to disconnect" legislation similar to those that already exist in France, Belgium, and Spain, preventing companies from contacting their employees outside of work hours. Companies that violate this law face penalties up to €9,690.[7]

Unionization Rates

Chapter 14 discusses the decline of union membership in the United States, with labor union membership among the lowest in the world as a percentage of the workforce (see Figure 14.6). Further, European Union law requires most companies to establish employee representation committees. This means that having an adversarial relationship with the union will make it very difficult to conduct business. Instead, when operating in countries with a strong tradition of unions, businesses need to involve union representatives in their decision-making process and follow more participatory approaches to management.

Cultural Differences

HR practices that work well in one context may be difficult to transfer to other contexts because of differences in culture. A Dutch researcher, Geert Hofstede, conceptualized national culture as consisting of four dimensions (later versions added more dimensions), as shown in Table 16.1. Note that countries are not homogeneous with respect to cultural values: Some cities, regions, or different segments of the population will show variability. Still, the differences across countries with respect to average cultural values are important to consider.

TABLE 16.1 ■ Dimensions of Culture Based on Hofstede's Framework		
Dimension	**Definition**	**Example of countries high and low on this dimension**
Individualism versus collectivism	The degree to which individuals define themselves as individuals as opposed to through their relationships. Collectivists emphasize loyalty to the group, face saving, and cooperation within the in-group.	Highly individualistic: Australia, United States, United Kingdom Highly collectivistic: Ecuador, Guatemala, West Africa
Power distance	The degree to which the society accepts power in the society is distributed unequally and hierarchy is naturally accepted.	High power distance: Guatemala, Panama, Philippines, Romania, Slovakia Low power distance: Austria, Denmark, Israel
Uncertainty avoidance	The degree to which the society feels uncomfortable with uncertainty and risk and emphasizes procedures or traditions to deal with it.	High uncertainty avoidance: Australia, Greece, Guatemala, Portugal, Uruguay Low uncertainty avoidance: Denmark, Jamaica, Singapore
Masculinity versus femininity	Masculine cultures are those that embrace values such as achievement and materialism. Feminine cultures emphasize modesty, caring for the weak, and quality of life.	Highly masculine cultures: Japan, Slovakia Highly feminine cultures: Costa Rica, Netherlands, Norway, Sweden

Sources: https://www.hofstede-insights.com/models/national-culture/; https://harzing.com/download/hgindices.xls

When transferring HR practices that are regarded as highly successful in one location to cultures that are different from the country of origin, cultural differences may serve as a barrier. For example, overall, the United States is a highly individualistic, relatively highly masculine culture, with moderately low values in power distance and uncertainty avoidance. (Definitions of these values are in Table 16.1.) Let's say that a U.S.-based multinational is doing business in Colombia. Colombian culture is collectivistic and has higher power distance and uncertainty avoidance relative to the United States. The two countries are about the same in terms of masculinity, which suggests that both cultures are similarly materialistic. As a result, motivating individual employees through material awards is not very different between the two countries. However, the high level of collectivism in Colombia makes it more of a challenge to transfer reward systems that pit individuals against each other such as in individual sales competitions.

Some countries have specific traditions and norms around particular HR practices, necessitating that multinational companies adopt local practices. For example, in many countries in Asia, structured annual recruitment of new college graduates is widely practiced. Major companies hire a cohort of new graduates and subject them to specific and preplanned developmental experiences, preparing them for future managerial roles. Job applicants will expect major firms to follow this practice, and failing to adopt this practice may serve as a disadvantage in hiring. As a result, companies headquartered in a specific country may adopt certain selection practices regardless of their country of origin when they operate within a particular geography.[8]

Management practices may also be interpreted differently in different cultural contexts. For example, a flat organizational structure, absence of managerial supervision, and having a lot of autonomy over one's work may be regarded as empowering in cultures that emphasize low power distance. However, in cultures that emphasize high power distance such as India, the same practices may be disappointing to workers because they afford fewer opportunities for promotions and career growth. In Japan, remote work remained unpopular even during the pandemic, due to factors such as traditional management styles adopted at higher organizational levels and a culture that emphasizes face-to-face communication.[9] Organizations interested in transferring HR practices may benefit from considering the suggestions in Figure 16.2.

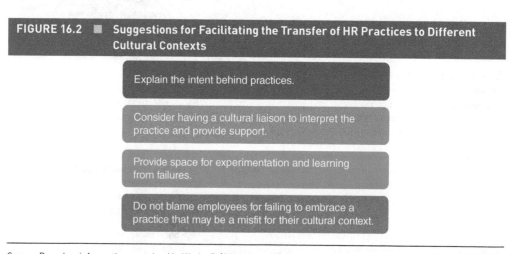

FIGURE 16.2 ■ Suggestions for Facilitating the Transfer of HR Practices to Different Cultural Contexts

Explain the intent behind practices.

Consider having a cultural liaison to interpret the practice and provide support.

Provide space for experimentation and learning from failures.

Do not blame employees for failing to embrace a practice that may be a misfit for their cultural context.

Source: Based on information contained in Hinds, P. (2016, June 27). Research: Why best practices don't translate across cultures. *Harvard Business Review.* https://hbr.org/2016/06/research-why-best-practices-dont-translate-across-cultures

SPOTLIGHT ON ETHICS: MANAGING ETHICS GLOBALLY IN MULTINATIONALS

What do Goldman Sachs, Deutsche Bank, and Ericsson have in common? These companies and others have faced investigations of corruption and bribing government officials to help win government contracts, get permits, or obtain licenses. A challenge all multinationals face is to uphold global ethical standards in diverse regions, including locations where anticorruption laws are loosely enforced or nonexistent and bribing government officials is considered a normal way of doing business. How can global businesses ensure they uphold global principles of ethics in their operations around the world while conducting business effectively?

Global organizations will benefit from enforcing a culture of ethics and integrity throughout their operations. This seems like common sense, given that allowing bribery and corruption in some parts of their operations threatens the culture and reputation of the entire operation. It is also important to remember that even though local businesses may in fact be using bribes to speed the process of approvals or facilitate their operations, multinationals are often held to a different and higher standard in other countries, making their ethics violations all the more damaging. A few steps multinationals can take and HR can facilitate are as follows:

- *Commit to a culture of integrity.* Multinationals should have top management who value and embrace ethics in global operations. This means a strong commitment to doing the right thing, dealing with unethical actions quickly, and holding people accountable.
- *Eliminate undue performance pressures.* Often, unethical actions are a symptom of pressures for short-term results. When headquarters evaluate performance of subsidiaries using short-term results such as how quickly a store was opened, pressure increases on local employees to get things done at all costs. It also signals to third parties that the company is in a hurry, giving them leverage to pressure the company.
- *Provide training and policies.* It is important to provide training not only about defining acceptable and unacceptable behaviors but also teaching employees what to do when confronted with questionable requests. Monitoring compliance via committees and audits can also help.
- *Eliminate a culture of silence.* It is important to encourage people to speak up about questionable ethical behaviors. Giving employees anonymous ways of reporting unethical behaviors and ensuring that reports are followed by action will help create a culture of ethics.[10]

Questions

1. As an HR professional, suppose you are assigned to arrange for your company's international employees to receive ethics training to define acceptable and unacceptable behaviors and to know what to do when confronted with questionable requests. How would you develop a set of training objectives? Would you hire an outside training vendor, and if so, how would you select the vendor?
2. Find an example in the news or in the HR literature of a global company that was accused of corruption. How was the case resolved? What did the individuals involved do right, and what could they have done better?

Causes and Forms of Internationalization

The reason a company chooses to internationalize is a key consideration in whether the organization chooses global integration in favor of local adaptations.[11] In some organizations, subsidiaries require close coordination with the parent company. Examples of this are Ford and General Motors, which offshore manufacturing in order to take advantage of lower labor costs overseas. Because the cars are manufactured for the global market, ensuring that subsidiaries around the world are closely coordinated with headquarters is important. In other cases, the reason subsidiaries exist is to reach overseas markets, as in the case of global food and beverage companies like Kellogg's and Kraft. Because local responsiveness in product design and marketing is important, the companies may give greater autonomy to subsidiaries and make greater efforts to ensure that HR practices fit the needs of each locality.

When the company is deciding how to approach its HR functions, the amount of autonomy the company has will also depend on the structure of its internationalization efforts. A company may have wholly owned subsidiaries overseas, giving the parent company full control over its overseas operations. Alternatively, the company may have less control over its overseas operations if it has a joint venture or a strategic alliance. A joint venture involves two companies coming together and investing to create a new company, whereas a strategic alliance is a partnership with other companies. Joint ventures and strategic alliances have the advantage of allowing the company to access local resources and expertise but will also prevent the organization from exercising complete control over overseas operations.[12]

MANAGING HR GLOBALLY

LEARNING OBJECTIVE
16.3   Identify HRM practices that would benefit from local adjustments and those that would benefit from standardization across borders.

Organizations need to design their HR practices to leverage the advantages of operating in multiple geographies; these advantages include access to a wider talent pool and the ability to transfer expertise across locations. They must also face challenges such as understanding the fundamental cultural, legal, and economic differences and adapting practices accordingly. It is important to note that there are also some best practices that companies could benefit from replicating. For example, researchers contend that giving newcomers an orientation, arriving at pay decisions using systematic analyses, and utilizing salary surveys are among the best practices that may be standardized across operations.[13] In this section, we discuss individual HR practices and important adaptations that often take place when operating globally.

Recruitment and Selection

Operating overseas necessitates hiring employees in diverse national contexts, which could be a major challenge. A key decision that needs to be made is to determine the proper mix of parent-country nationals, host-country nationals, and third-country nationals to be employed in a specific overseas operation. The degree to which the local labor market meets the multinational company's needs will vary by industry and geography, and there are costs and benefits associated with different mixes.

Multinational firms often find they have to compete with other multinational and local firms for the best talent. A well-known multinational company with positive brand recognition overseas may have a built-in advantage in recruiting local employees, but it also needs to provide a work environment and inducements that are competitive in order to attract talent. As IBM's loss of talent to local firms such as Infosys in India shows, companies should not assume that being well known globally will be sufficient for recruiting the best talent. Alternatively, a firm well known in its country of origin may have little name recognition in the subsidiary location, which may limit the ability to attract talent. Sometimes, the country of origin may serve as a barrier to recruitment. For example, some Indian multinationals operating in industrialized country contexts report experiencing difficulties attracting managerial employees and having to rely on sending expatriates instead of localizing their management team due to negative perceptions of Indian firms as employers with respect to their global image and concerns regarding some corporate policies being a poor fit to the local environments.[14] Organizations will need to invest in developing their brand as an employer and building a good reputation in the markets in which they operate.

Finding the necessary talent is also made difficult in markets in which demand for skilled talent exceeds local availability. Organizations may need to provide in-house training to employees to make them employment ready in localities where educational institutions fall short of meeting the training needs of organizations. At the same time, providing training introduces the problem of poaching by other organizations.[15]

In Europe, Asia, the Middle East, and South America, a company car is often a critical recruitment and retention tool and is intended to meet business and status needs. Determining who is eligible, whether to provide a car or a car allowance, and what make and model to allocate to different job levels requires careful consideration of each local market.[16]

©iStock.com/Tramino

SPOTLIGHT ON GLOBAL ISSUES: CULTURAL INFLUENCES ON HIGH-PERFORMANCE WORK SYSTEMS

HR practices designed to improve organizational performance are referred to as *high-performance work systems* (HPWS). These systems include selectivity in hiring decisions, investing in training, linking pay with performance, and involving employees in decision making. To what extent should these practices be adapted to the cultural context?

A meta-analysis conducted in 29 countries examined whether these practices had to fit with national culture in order to influence organizational performance. Researchers have shown that there was an overall positive correlation between HPWS and organizational performance. Further, researchers found no support for the argument that when these practices were a good fit with national culture, their effects were more positive. In fact, the results showed that in highly collectivistic and highly power-distant cultures, presumably contexts in which these practices should not be a very good fit, the effects of HPWS were even more positive.

These findings suggest there are actually best practices in HRM. The practices covered thus far as "best practices" seem to work regardless of the cultural context in which they are implemented. It appears that investing in people is good practice regardless of context or country.[17]

Motivating, Rewarding, and Managing Employees

Multinational companies often differentiate their reward systems and benefits around the world in order to fit the national context. To begin with, businesses need to be aware of differences in legal requirements that affect compensation practices. In many parts of the world, companies are mandated to provide 13th- (and 14th-month) bonuses (e.g., Brazil, Costa Rica, and Ecuador). In other countries, providing these bonuses is customary (e.g., Austria and Japan). Typically, these amount to 1/12 of the employee's pay. Different countries will have different requirements relating to who is eligible for 13th- and 14th-month bonuses, and payment schedules vary.[18]

Having extrinsic rewards that fit a given context is essential for attracting and retaining talent. In addition to cultural differences, workforce demographics may necessitate regional adaptation. For example, some countries have aging populations: Japan has a population with a median age of 49, whereas India, Ecuador, and Algeria have a median age of 29.[19] Such differences will inevitably affect benefits packages and workplace conditions employees find desirable.

At the same time, some benefits that are popular in the United States are finding positive reception in other contexts as well. As a case in point, historically, global firms relied on Social Security provided by local governments and avoided providing retirement benefits, but this is changing. According to the Willis Towers Watson 2022 International Pension Plan Survey, 13% of the 951 multinational firms surveyed reported that they cover local employees in their retirement plans.[20] Multinational firms are finding that by establishing defined-contribution plans similar to 401(k) plans (see Chapter 13), multinational firms may experience recruitment and retention advantages. Companies may need to make adaptations to the local context, such as investing the funds overseas if permissible and determining if the local financial system is unstable.[21]

SPOTLIGHT ON LEGAL ISSUES: THE LEGAL SIDE OF WORKING INTERNATIONALLY

When managing an international workforce, legal compliance is complicated due to the need to reconcile multiple legal frameworks. Here are a few important considerations[22]:

- When moving an employee overseas either as an expatriate or in short-term operations, the employee will likely need to acquire a work permit or visa.
- When an employee is staying in a different country for 6 months or more, the stay may trigger tax implications for the employer. This means that monitoring short-term assignments is important. U.S. citizens generally pay taxes to the United States regardless of where they work, so this may introduce a double taxation case. Further, many domestic insurance policies cover health care overseas for 6 months, and a different health care policy may be needed for longer assignments.
- EEOC laws discussed in Chapter 4 cover all employees of a U.S. employer working in the United States. For example, a Chinese citizen working in a U.S. firm is covered by EEOC laws. Some non-U.S. employers operating in the United States may be exempt. Foreign organizations operating in the United States based on a mutual treaty may be permitted to show preference to their own nationals for some positions. Host-country employees of U.S. firms are not subject to EEOC laws (e.g., Japanese employees of a U.S.-based multinational in Japan are not covered), but a U.S. citizen expatriate sent to work in the Japanese operations of a U.S.-based multinational is covered.
- When two laws clash, companies are required to follow the laws of the countries they operate in, even if this means violating the U.S. law.
- Educating employees on local laws is important to protect employees. Toyota found this out the hard way: An American executive moving to Japan was arrested and imprisoned for 20 days on suspicion of illegally importing a prescription painkiller.
- Organizations have a "duty of care," or a moral and legal obligation, to act in ways that will avoid preventable and foreseeable injuries and risks to their employees. Although the legal framework around duty of care varies around the world, taking care of employees proactively will help establish trust and prevent costly legal battles.

Employee Separations

Organizations that operate in multiple countries need to be aware of differences in how separations are handled, given the differences in labor law. For example, in Europe, employment is regarded as a fundamental right, and taking away that right may not be done in an arbitrary fashion. Given the high levels of unionization and prevalence of works councils (similar to unions) in Europe, organizations need to work with labor representatives in setting up procedures for terminating employees. Approaching the termination process systematically and respectfully, creating strong employment contracts, specifying how performance and absenteeism are to be handled, and ensuring that notice periods and severance pay follow the national legal requirements in each locality are essential for success.[23]

Handling of Personal Data

Recall from Chapter 3 that European Union countries have implemented the General Data Protection Regulation (GDPR), which overhauls how businesses store, safeguard, and use personal data. This law gives more power to individuals and has clear implications for HR functions that routinely retain, access, and use data about current and former employees as well as job applicants. For example, according to the law, companies need to have consent to store unsuccessful job candidates' details. If they fail to secure consent, companies must remove the data from their records. Employees have the right to access their own personal data with a required maximum turnaround time of 1 month. Companies may be required to designate a data-protection officer depending on the scope of data they handle. Faced with steep penalties for failures in compliance, companies need to make structural changes in collecting, storing, and using employee data. For example, the Swedish multinational clothing company H&M received one of the biggest fines for violations of the GDPR due to the actions at its German customer service center. It was revealed that the service center supervisors were making notes and keeping track of personal details of employees' private lives, such as employee religious beliefs, medical problems, and family issues. Supervisors were gathering this information through private conversations and storing them at a place accessible by 50 other supervisors. This practice was brought to light when a data breach accidentally made this information visible to all employees. The company was required to pay around €35 million in fines. As can be seen, HR has a key role to play to educate employees and managers on the implications of the GDPR for their day-to-day work.[24]

MANAGEMENT OF EXPATRIATES

> ### LEARNING OBJECTIVE
>
> **16.4**   Summarize the forces affecting adjustment of expatriates to their overseas assignments, and identify ways in which organizations can prepare expatriates for successful assignments.

When doing business internationally, a critically important HR issue relates to the management of expatriates. An expatriate (or expat) is a person who is living and working in a different country than their country of origin. Expatriate assignments typically describe a move overseas that is longer than 6 months. Multinational enterprises have organizationally assigned expatriates, employees who are sent by the organization for a predetermined time to work in an overseas operation. Alternatively, a self-initiated expatriate is a skilled professional who moves to a different country for a specific period of time with the intention of gaining overseas work experience. Although much can be learned from self-initiated expatriates, note that this chapter primarily focuses on organizationally assigned expatriates, given the importance of HR functions in systematically facilitating the process of effective expatriation.

With the increasing prevalence of remote work, countries such as Thailand (pictured here) are offering perks such as long-term visas and lower tax rates to employees of foreign companies wanting to base themselves in a different country. Such programs can ease the way for greater international mobility.[25]

©iStockphoto.com/Preto_perola

Benefits and Downsides of Using Expatriates

Expatriate assignments provide a variety of benefits to organizations and individuals. By moving talented employees overseas, companies aim to meet specific business needs and close skill gaps. Moving employees overseas ensures they gain skills in global management. Completing an overseas assignment successfully may be a boon to the career of the expatriate, helping them develop unique skills and achieve visibility. Expatriate assignments play an important role in knowledge diffusion, such as transferring innovations across units. Expatriates can facilitate direct knowledge sharing across units and indirect knowledge sharing by linking home- and host-country operations and acting as "boundary spanners" that tie units to each other. Research has shown that expatriate assignments in which headquarters employees are assigned to overseas locations facilitate knowledge transfer from the headquarters to host-country operations, whereas host-country employees working in headquarter locations (sometimes referred to as inpatriates) facilitate knowledge transfer from local operations to headquarters.[26] International assignments also help build individual skills. For example, managers at McKinsey & Company who worked on international assignments noted that the assignment was helpful in expanding their network and provided more access to information and resources relative to staying in one place.[27]

At the same time, there are potential downsides to the use of expatriates, and it is important to consider these when deciding whether to deploy expatriates. First, from the organization's perspective, overreliance on expatriates or using expatriates for the wrong types of positions may backfire. For example, research has shown that using expatriates for transfer of knowledge that does not require cultural adaptations (e.g., technical knowledge) facilitates subsidiary performance, whereas using them for types of assignments in which location-specific knowledge is needed (such as marketing knowledge) actually impedes the ability of the subsidiary to benefit from parent company expertise.[28] As discussed earlier, the use of expatriates is a way of transferring home-country practices overseas, and using expatriates may make it difficult to utilize regional knowledge. In other words, the organization should carefully consider whether a local employee is not in fact a better candidate for a given position. Second, expatriate assignments run the risk of failure and necessitate careful planning. Moving to a different country and taking on a new role is stressful, and poor adjustment results in low job satisfaction, low effectiveness, and premature return from the assignment.[29] Finally, failed expatriate assignments are costly: It is estimated that direct costs of failed assignments can range from $250,000 to $1 million for multinational businesses.[30] Given high costs and risk, understanding factors that facilitate quick adjustment is important to design expatriate assignments effectively.

Expatriate Adjustment

Expatriate adjustment refers to the degree of comfort and lack of stress associated with being an expatriate. Research shows that three forms of adjustment matter for expatriates. Cultural adjustment refers to adjusting to the new culture one is now living in, including factors such as transportation, entertainment, health system, education, and general living conditions. Work adjustment involves feeling comfortable at work and with one's new tasks. Interactional adjustment is the comfort felt with interacting with local individuals inside or outside work. In other words, being successful as an expatriate relies not only on feeling comfortable at work but also on achieving comfort with interpersonal interactions and with general living conditions. Which of these do you think is most important to an expatriate's success? Although work adjustment has the strongest effect on expatriate job satisfaction, the desire to quit the expatriate assignment is most strongly affected by cultural adjustment; simply mastering one's job will not be sufficient for a successful expatriate assignment. Social support from diverse sources, including host-country nationals and fellow expatriates, is an important resource for expatriate adjustment.[31] Other key factors that affect the pace of adjustment and the degree of adjustment success, including characteristics of expatriates, organizational factors, and nonwork factors, are shown in Figure 16.3.[32]

FIGURE 16.3   ■   Factors Affecting Expatriate Adjustment

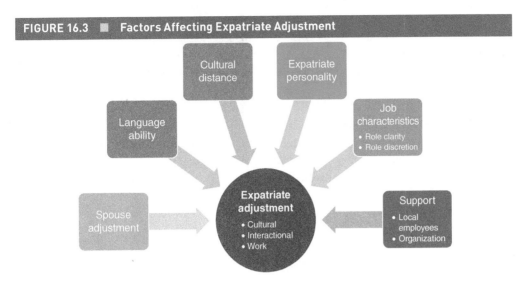

Spouse Adjustment

Research shows that the biggest influence over an expatriate's cultural adjustment is the adjustment of the spouse. When spouses have difficulty adjusting to the culture, the risk of a premature return increases, suggesting that preparing spouses for the assignment and ensuring they are ready and willing will have benefits for the success of the experience. In fact, one's family situation and relationships are key reasons mentioned for refusing to accept an expatriate assignment in the first place.[33] Experts suggest that before a family moves, it is important for them to be on the same page and discuss how the spouse will spend time, identify sources of social support, inquire into work and social activities for the spouse, and realistically examine the impact of the move for the whole family. If the expatriate is moving alone, then the risk is one of social isolation and loneliness, which necessitates identifying sources of social support prior to and early in the move. Realizing the importance of spouses for expatriate adjustment, many companies have programs that facilitate spouses' adjustment. For example, some companies provide support to spouses in getting a job in the local market as part of their relocation packages. This policy is valuable due to the rise in the number of dual-career couples. In cases in which the spouse is working in the same company, offering jobs for both may be another strategy in providing a type of support that will make a big difference in the adjustment of the expatriate.

Language Ability

Research shows a stronger effect for language ability on interactional and cultural adjustment and no effects on work adjustment. In fact, language ability seems to matter for work adjustment primarily when non-English speakers were sent to an English-speaking country, as opposed to vice versa.[34] It is likely that English emerges as the business language in workplaces around the world, so when an English speaker is sent to a non-English-speaking country, their work adjustment is not in serious jeopardy.

At the same time, not speaking the local language affects expatriates' ability to adjust to the culture and social interactions. Language not only facilitates interpersonal communication but also affects power and status relationships. For example, research has shown that adopting Swedish as the official language led to empowering some employees and disempowering others in a Nordic merger. Language proficiency is often used as a proxy for someone's overall competence, and it allows access to different social networks.[35]

Host-country employees often try to make sense of expatriates' behavior, attempting to understand how well-intentioned they are toward the local employees and how much respect they have toward their culture. One qualitative study in China found that when expatriates showed a willingness to learn the local language, local employees expressed more acceptance toward them. Such effort on the expatriates' part was interpreted as a sign of goodwill. Local employees also respected expatriates who allowed them to speak their native language in meetings, asking for a summary of the discussion at the end, instead of forcing everyone to speak English. Unfortunately, good intentions are not sufficient to build relationships over time. Trying but failing to speak the local language results in overreliance on a few people to interpret the work environment and in difficulties getting work done and building relationships. Not showing any interest results in social isolation and being segregated from the host-country nationals.[36]

Manager's Toolbox: Being Effective in Global Teams

In global organizations, there is often a need to work across borders. For example, a software development team may include employees from France, Australia, India, and the United States. With the increases in the prevalence of remote work, we are likely to see greater prevalence of global teams. Here are some tips on how to be more effective in these teams.[37]

1. *Do not confuse language fluency with job effectiveness.* It is likely that the team will include members with varying fluency in the language in which the team communicates. It is important for the team leader to understand that those who are the most articulate are not necessarily the best performers, and valuing their contributions more may affect team morale and sense of fairness.

2. *Be inclusive.* The team leader may create an inclusive climate by deliberately asking questions to the more silent members, giving members time to articulate their thoughts, and asking open-ended questions. The team leader may also frame a question as being within the expertise of some of the silent members of the group, putting them in positions of expertise, which may also encourage the participation of silent members.

3. *Provide cultural training.* Providing training on how culture affects assumptions and attributions may facilitate more effective communication with those from different cultural backgrounds.

4. *Learn how to adapt your behavior to fit the norms.* Understanding that different cultures have different norms is one thing. Learning how to adapt your behavior to fit the demands of the situation (such as giving more indirect feedback or being more authoritarian than you are used to) without feeling inauthentic is a learned skill. Remind yourself of the importance of understanding and practicing the norms of new contexts you enter. At the same time, be careful to calibrate the adaptation; it is easy to overdo, which will introduce problems of its own. For example, knowing that directness is valued in one culture may encourage someone to be overly aggressive and confrontational, potentially damaging relationships.

5. *Invest in relationship development.* When working with those from a different cultural upbringing, mistakes and misunderstandings are bound to happen. Forgiveness is easier to achieve if you have an existing relationship. Relating to your team members and bonding with them is not a waste of time: It is an investment that will pay off throughout the life of the project and beyond.

Cultural Distance

The cultural distance between one's own country of origin and the destination seems to have a negative effect on adjusting to a new culture.[38] This is perhaps not surprising, as a culture that emphasizes values that directly contradict one's own will pose more challenges. At the same time, it is important to note that cultural similarity may be a double-edged sword. A U.S. expatriate moving to South Korea will certainly encounter unfamiliar situations. At the same time, some potential expatriates will opt out of this move due to expectations of such difficulties, which means that those interested in moving will be the ones who are motivated to invest time and effort in preparing for the move. In contrast, a U.S. expatriate moving to Australia may assume that given the similarity in language, the move will be free of cultural challenges. However, despite speaking the same language, there are clear and important cultural differences between the two countries, and different leadership styles and ways of doing business, which may lead to misunderstandings and frustrations.

According to a survey by InterNations, the world's largest expatriate community representing 177 nationalities, the best destination for expatriates to live in 2022 was Mexico, with 91% of the expats expressing satisfaction with their life there.[39]

©iStockphoto.com/diegograndi

Expatriate Personality

The expatriate's social and relational skills affect all three forms of adjustment. Regardless of what their specific job description is, expatriates will need to be able to work with people who are different from themselves and influence them in ways that will facilitate their own adjustment. They will need to be accepted in order to get things done. This is no small feat and requires exceptional relational skills. Research has indicated that expatriate adjustment is most strongly affected by expatriates' levels of extraversion, emotional stability, and openness to new experiences.[40]

Job Characteristics

Research shows that the two job-related factors that matter the most to expatriate adjustment are role clarity and role discretion. In other words, there needs to be crystal-clear communication between management and the expatriate with respect to expectations, and expatriates should be given autonomy to perform their jobs effectively.[41]

Support

For successful adjustment of expatriates to their work, two sources of organizational support seem critical: support of the host-country employees and support from the organization itself. Support of local coworkers matters a great deal. Local employees are in a position to interact with the expatriate every day, share information, and give tips about how to get things done, facilitating all three forms of adjustment. One of the reasons local employees may choose not to cooperate with expatriates is that expatriates are likely to be classified as "out-group" members by local employees due to their dissimilarity to locals.[42] For example, host-country employees may be very polite to expatriates on the surface but classify expatriates as out-group members, resulting in expatriates feeling that achieving social integration will not be possible regardless of how hard they try. In order to prevent the new expatriate from being classified as an out-group member, organizations sometimes resort to sending an expatriate with ties to the local context (such as sending an employee who identifies as ethnic Chinese to their operations in China). However, this practice is not always successful and may sometimes create even more hostility, envy, or resentment among local employees.[43] Expatriates themselves also play a role in how much support they receive from local employees. Researchers proposed that expatriates who are motivated to seek support from the "right" coworkers who are capable and motivated to help them are likely to establish support networks, facilitating their own adjustment process.[44]

Organizational support is also critical to expatriate adjustment. Expatriates who feel that the organization cares about them, values them, and is invested in them report higher levels of adjustment in their assignments.[45] Organizations can also support expatriates by providing logistical support. This involves taking care of mundane but important details of the move, such as identifying appropriate housing, finding schools for children moving with the expatriate, opening bank accounts, and taking care of other daily details that are bound to create stress for the expatriates.

Preparing Expatriates for Assignments

Organizations may do a great deal to facilitate expatriates' adjustment to their new locale in the predeparture stage. Preparation may pay big dividends by facilitating quicker adjustment and preventing premature departures. Organizations will need to ensure that they (a) select the right person, (b) prepare them for the role, and (c) provide ongoing support.

Selecting Expatriates

Historically, companies selected expatriates based on their specific job knowledge and job-related skills. This approach was quickly revealed as misguided, as success in an expatriate assignment takes much more than being good at one's job. Just because someone is good at marketing products in the United States is no guarantee they will be equally good at doing so in Thailand. Therefore, experts recommend that the selection process also consider personality and social skills. Relational skills, or the ability to build effective relationships with key stakeholders, will be important. A **global mindset** is also important: Individuals who are open to learning about different cultures, have a sense of adventure, are comfortable dealing with ambiguity, and have a nonjudgmental attitude toward those from other cultures are more likely to be successful in complex environments.[46]

Many CEOs of Fortune 500 companies (including Satya Nadella, CEO of Microsoft) are immigrants, utilizing their experiences growing up in a different country and a global mindset in their influential roles.

Photo by Stephen Brashear/Getty Images

Cultural Training

An important barrier to effectiveness in a new location is lack of understanding of cultural differences. Expatriates may be frustrated because their normal ways of behaving at work may no longer be appropriate and in fact may generate very different reactions. The feeling of disorientation individuals experience when they enter a new culture is termed culture shock. For example, an expatriate who is used to relating to people and building quick relationships with others may realize that the idea of small talk is foreign in cultures such as Germany or Japan. In these cultures, relationships develop over a long period of time through mutually lived experiences and trust. Discussions of weather or traffic, or other lighthearted conversation that does not communicate anything real about the person, will not be useful for building relationships in these countries.[47] Understanding these and other cultural differences may facilitate the adjustment process by helping expatriates be attuned to instances in which they need to vary either their own behavior or interpretations of others' actions.

Relocation Assistance

The amount of assistance and the form of assistance provided will vary by the level of resources the company can afford, the specific location one is moving to, and the organizational level of the expatriate. For example, moving from one Western country to another will require different resources relative to moving to a big city in China such as Hong Kong, Shanghai, or Beijing. Conversely, different resources are necessary when moving from a large city to a less developed inland city in China such as Chengdu. Moving to a remote location may mean that the expatriate will need to deal with lack of adequate medical care, difficulty identifying international schools for kids, and lack of housing that matches what the expatriate is used to. The more declines expatriates are expected to experience in their quality of life relative to their home country, the more generous the expatriate relocation assistance and pay packages will need to be. Contracting a global relocation services provider may make this process easier and more professional, as HR professionals are rarely experts in employee mobility.

Organizations often cap the amount they will pay as relocation assistance. For example, only 42% of companies participating in a survey reported that they pay the entire cost of relocation. This means that relocation services firms had to reduce the types of services they offer to contain costs (e.g., moving hard-to-transport items). Further, companies are more likely to pay a lump-sum amount when expatriates are low-level employees, as opposed to covering the costs on an ongoing basis.[48] Working with a relocation company may help expatriates avoid numerous hassles they would not even expect to encounter during their initial move.

Compensation

Staffing overseas positions with expatriates is expensive. When determining pay packages, it is important to ensure that the expatriate does not suffer a serious financial penalty as a result of accepting the assignment. Key components of the pay package are summarized in Table 16.2. Additionally, benefits such as travel insurance; home, auto, and property insurance; and health insurance must be provided. Expatriate compensation packages have become subject to increased scrutiny over the years, and many organizations have reduced the types of benefits and allowances they provide. For example, in the past, Ford used to allow expatriates to sell their homes to the company at an assessed value. Ford abandoned this policy following the 2008 recession.[49]

As summarized in Table 16.2, companies make a choice regarding whether to make the home-country pay or the host-country pay the basis for expatriate pay. The approach chosen will depend on where the assignment is located. For example, assignments taking place in the Asia Pacific region, United Arab Emirates, and the United Kingdom are often on a "local-plus" package, given the high salaries, high quality of life, and high cost of living of these locations. The salary is localized, with a few additional expatriate benefits, such as housing and education allowances.[50]

When determining the pay and benefits packages, one size may not fit all, and it is important to consider the issues that are relevant for the expatriate and the family. For one family, educational opportunities for children may be the most important, whereas for another, finding employment for the spouse may be critical. Providing a compensation package that is consistent and fair while also

TABLE 16.2 ■ Components of an Expatriate's Compensation Package	
Component	**Explanation**
Base pay	Most companies use a *home-country-based approach* to determining expatriates' base pay. The expatriate's regular pay in the home country is divided into taxes, housing, savings, and spending components, and the organization makes adjustments so the employee does not lose money on the move. This approach protects the expatriate from cost differences in the new location. According to SHRM, 76% of all assignments use this approach. In a *host-country-based approach*, the expatriate is treated as a local employee for their salary. This approach is used in 14% of long-term assignments. The *headquarters-based approach* assumes that all expatriates are paid headquarters salaries regardless of location.
Performance-based pay	The expatriate may also be offered financial incentives in recognition of reaching performance targets or stock-based rewards.
Housing allowance	In some locations, the company may offer company-owned housing or pay for the differences between housing in home- and host-country locations. If the employee is moving with their family, this may be a larger allowance.
Cost-of-living adjustment	The employee's pay is adjusted for cost-of-living differences between home and host locations.
Hardship/hazard pay	When employees are assigned to a hazardous location, the pay package also includes hazard pay to compensate for the differences in living conditions and quality of life. This may be 10% to 50% of base pay.
Educational assistance	When local educational options are inadequate, the company may pay for the costs of dependents' educational expenses in a private school or offer a stipend to partly cover the costs.
Home leave	Companies usually cover travel expenses of the expatriate and their family to their home country once a year or more, and in long assignments, they may offer a period of leave to be spent in the home country. This policy will be more generous for expatriates in stressful locations.

Source: Based on information contained in Anonymous. (2017, April 3). *Designing global compensation systems*. SHRM. https://www.shrm.org/ResourcesAndTools/tools-and-samples/toolkits/Pages/designingglobalcompensation.aspx

considering the unique needs of each expatriate may increase the success of the assignment. For this purpose, one option is to use a **coreflex plan**, which provides some services (such as paying for movers and travel expenses) to all expatriates, with the remainder of benefits personalized to the unique situation of the expatriate (such as trips to look for a new house or assistance in identifying private schools). These plans are expected to become more popular as companies become more cost conscious.[51]

Risk Management

Organizations need to ensure the safety and security of their employees when sending them overseas. The world is increasingly unpredictable, and political turmoil, health risks (remote location, unsanitary conditions), individual high crime rates (murder, theft, break-ins), organized crime (terrorism, gang activities, kidnappings), and natural risks (earthquakes, extreme weather) pose serious threats and uncertainty to companies operating in some regions. Certain areas may pose a threat to expatriates in particular, such as the increasing frequency of kidnappings of expatriates in oil-producing Nigeria.[52] In Latin America and eastern Europe, someone who is dressed nicely may be subject to an "express kidnapping" in which they are forced to walk to an ATM and withdraw cash.[53] The Covid-19 pandemic resulted in significant changes in expatriates' lives. Many expatriates made emergency returns to their home countries when faced with extended lockdowns, a desire to be close to home and family, and the possibility of falling seriously ill in a foreign country.[54]

Organizations are responsible for ensuring the safety of all employees, and securing the services of professional security consultants may be advisable in some locations. It may be impossible for a company doing overseas business to eliminate all risks, as many of these are inherent in doing business everywhere and are often unpredictable, but these risks must be managed. Companies should decide whether expatriates need to be sent to a particular location or whether employing local employees is possible. Regardless of whether expatriates or locals are employed, the company will need to take steps to keep employees safe. According to one survey conducted on expatriates in hardship locations, the most commonly mentioned resources available to expatriates included emergency medical evaluation service, access to emergency 24/7 hotline, and e-mail alerts about health and security risks.[55]

Special Considerations Relating to Women and LGBTQ+ Employees as Expatriates

Women constitute 14% of the global expatriate population. These numbers depend on location (higher in Asia, lower in Europe and Africa) and industry (higher in consumer goods, lower in energy), but women as a group experience particular challenges as expatriates.[56] Stereotypes about women's unwillingness to serve as expatriates and potential inability to operate in other cultures have been debunked. At the same time, organizational decision makers' worries about sending women as expatriates have been identified as a reason for the lower representation of women among expatriates.[57] Still, in cultures where sexism has been institutionalized, female expatriates report greater problems, such as being excluded from social activities, being insulted, and experiencing physical violence.[58]

Research shows that organizational support and absence of family problems serve as buffers for female expatriates dealing with local employees' prejudices.[59] Despite challenges in some locations, organizations are advised against excluding female employees from expatriate opportunities. Instead, organizations may offer training to potential expatriates as well as work to introduce zero-tolerance policies in their subsidiaries regarding discrimination and harassment. By sending the signal that everyone is considered equally for expatriate positions and supported throughout the process, organizations benefit from the talent and skills of all their employees.

Similar concerns exist for LGBTQ+ employees. Research suggests that many LGBTQ+ employees are highly motivated to accept expatriate positions and have ways of facilitating their own adjustment such as via connections to the local LGBTQ+ community.[60] At the same time, serious concerns exist. More than 60 countries criminalize homosexuality, and 11 view it as punishable by death.[61] Thus, LGBTQ+ employees may also experience hurdles not experienced by other expatriates, such as difficulty obtaining visas for their spouses, lack of legal protection and presence of institutionalized harassment, and possibilities for social exclusion. Obtaining current information regarding legal and social climate in the target location is important. The organization should educate prospective expatriates regarding what to expect, provide resources that are inclusive in language and content (such as spousal-support policies inclusive of same-sex couples and their children), and provide information and support throughout the assignment.[62]

Repatriation

In many cases, the conclusion of the expatriate assignment means repatriation, or relocating the expatriate to their country of origin. The repatriation process presents challenges. Expatriates are valuable to their companies given the investments the company made in their career development. However, many companies have difficulty retaining expatriates. According to one estimate, 38% of expatriates leave their company within 1 year of their return.[63]

Sometimes, repatriation is a challenge because expatriates may not be interested in returning to their home country. This may be due to financial reasons: An employee who is relocated from India to the United Kingdom will likely have had their salary adjusted to the higher-cost location, which means they will experience a significant pay cut when they return to India. Further, expatriates may not have a desirable job waiting for them when they return home. In most cases, the company will have to find a new job for them, as their old job would have already been filled by someone else, and they may have outgrown their former job. Research has shown that perceptions of underemployment in the job they return to was a precursor to turnover intentions among expatriates.[64] Upon return, expatriates may also experience a **reverse culture shock**. Expatriates may find they have changed during the assignment and that their home country and company have also changed during their absence, resulting in the feeling that their country of origin does not feel like home anymore.

Unfortunately, despite the cost of an expatriate assignment to a company, organizations do not always approach repatriation of expatriates in a systematic way and often do not know what to do with expatriates once they return. Given that employees increasingly regard their careers as boundaryless (as opposed to specific to one organization), it is not surprising that when organizations are unable to absorb the additional experience and skills employees develop during an international assignment, those employees are likely to leave the organization.

ALTERNATIVES TO LONG-TERM RELOCATION ASSIGNMENTS

LEARNING OBJECTIVE
16.5   Identify alternatives to long-term relocation assignments.

Instead of sending expatriates on long-term assignments, organizations are increasingly designing short-term assignments to contain costs and reduce the disruptive effects of long-term stays on employees and their families. Instead of sending an employee as an expatriate for 3 years, the company may choose to send them for 3 months, extending the stay as needed or sending the employee multiple times. Extended business travel may be a useful way to meet short-term staffing needs.

Short-term assignments usually do not have much of the organizational support involved for expatriates: Typically there is no adjustment in pay or relocation allowances, and the company's investment may be limited to travel expenses for the expatriate to and from the location. Short-term assignments are also less burdensome for employees. In particular, employees with families may benefit from such assignments given the difficulty of moving an entire family overseas for several years. In short-term assignments, the employee's permanent job will usually not be given away, so repatriation will not be as challenging. The employee will typically retain their regular reporting relationships but most likely will also report to a local manager as well. As long as such arrangements meet business needs, there may be advantages for businesses (low cost) and employees (low risk while also carrying developmental benefits).[65]

Cross-border commuters represent another alternative to expatriate assignments. Employees may work in a different country during the week, returning home on weekends. These arrangements are popular in Europe. For example, it is not unusual for an employee to live in Italy and work in Switzerland. Such arrangements are often outside of formal mobility programs, but they still must be monitored. The company needs to comply with tax-withholding requirements in multiple countries, ensure that the employee has the appropriate work permit, and fulfill data privacy and legal requirements.[66] Companies often find that these programs are expensive, given the need to pay for a hotel or a serviced apartment and to pay for travel during peak travel periods.[67]

SPOTLIGHT ON DATA AND ANALYTICS: TRACKING EXPATRIATES AROUND THE WORLD

A volcano is erupting in Bali. Do you know where your employees are? This question may not have an easy answer for global firms that operate in multiple countries and those that have expatriates, frequent business travelers, and other employees who work remotely who do not even have a permanent place of assignment.

In addition to knowing where everyone is physically, companies need to ensure that their expatriate experience is managed smoothly. This means making sure that every paycheck is correct, preassignment experiences and requirements are checked off, visas are valid, and medical benefits are up-to-date.

Each expatriate assignment generates valuable data that companies can utilize to continuously improve the experience and manage the repatriation process. Expatriate satisfaction surveys, turnover data, and performance data may be analyzed to gain clues as to which systematic problems exist in each country of operations.

Tracking such data may be handled via Excel or other in-house products. For companies that employ hundreds of expatriates, investing in tracking technology is another option. Regardless of the method used, integrating data generated from expatriates with the remainder of HR information systems will provide benefits by making sense of how the company is managing the expatriate experience and what keeps expatriates committed to the company.[68]

Digital Nomads

So far in this chapter, we have focused on organizational expatriates and discussed the complications, advantages, and challenges of sending employees to a different country. We also mentioned the case of "self-initiated expatriates," or individuals who move overseas to look for work or to satisfy a desire for a different lifestyle. This category of expatriates does not have organizational support behind them, and they are largely outside the scope of this chapter, with the exception that their openness to new experiences, global mindset, and flexibility could make them attractive job candidates for organizations.

The Covid-19 pandemic helped speed up the rise of a new category of international workers. Digital nomads are individuals who work remotely, without being tied to a specific location, and they decide how long to stay in each location. When these employees are working across the borders, they are referred to as global nomads. This category was typically reserved for those who did freelance work in the past. However, with the quick rise in remote work and remote-friendly policies during the pandemic, now many organizations employ digital nomads. According to a study by MBO Partners, over 15 million American workers consider themselves to be digital nomads.[69] Some of these employees move to different countries and live overseas while retaining their jobs within a specific country. Even though they retain their jobs within an organization, they are not considered to be expatriates, as they were not sent on an international assignment. At the same time, their choice to live and work in a foreign country and the organization's flexibility to accommodate this decision introduces organizational obligations, as we illustrated in the opening case for this chapter.

When employees move to a different country, organizations will need to adjust employee withholding of taxes given the new location of the employee. Depending on the location and the employers' "duty of care," companies will also need to consider any safety risks the employees may encounter and whether health insurance would require adjustments. Employees need to be informed regarding whether they are violating any immigration-related rules. For example, some countries may not permit working within its boundaries for an extended period if the employee is on a tourist visa. There may be complications regarding coordination with the rest of the team as well, for example, whether the employee's time zone will make it more challenging to access and meet with that employee. Finally, the organization will need to consider cybersecurity and train the employee on various risks.[70] As we discussed in the opening case, some organizations are finding that benefiting from the services of employer of record companies may be an attractive solution in taking care of some of these organizational obligations. Employer of record refers to an organization that serves as the employer for an employee that performs work in a different country. This organization acts as a local employer for employees working overseas and ensures that HR functions remain compliant with local rules and regulations.

Despite its possible complications, accommodating employees interested in being global nomads provides important benefits, including employee retention and access to a greater pool of employees. To balance these interests, companies are advised to put in place a corporate mobility policy, outlining the employer and employee obligations and specifying the maximum length of stays and locations employees are allowed to work from. A long stay may introduce tax obligations on the part of the employer similar to opening up a branch in that country, and therefore companies are advised to seek legal counsel when drafting their policies.[71] Currently, different countries have a different legal framework in how they treat remote workers, with several countries, including Thailand and Iceland, introducing remote worker visas and tax breaks to accommodate these travelers. We expect that global nomads will grow in importance in the years to come.

In conclusion, increasing globalization of businesses introduces novel challenges for management of human resources. Managing a workforce that transcends local borders and managing employees who are mobile across borders are only two common challenges and ways in which HR can add value to businesses.

CHAPTER SUMMARY

HR faces many challenges when business goes global. One challenge is to determine the proper balance of global integration and local differentiation. There are advantages to standardizing HR practices, but local laws, differences in attitudes toward unions, national culture, and the reason the company chose to internationalize will influence how much standardization is appropriate. When operating in different countries, companies must consider local norms in their recruitment and selection, separations, compensation, and treatment of employees. An important HR challenge is to manage mobility of employees, either through short-term or longer-term expatriate assignments. There are both benefits and disadvantages to hiring expatriates. HR can add value by recognizing various kinds of adjustments expatriates and their families must make and by providing preparation and cultural training. Finally, organizations can be creative in devising alternatives to long-term relocation assignments.

KEY TERMS

Coreflex plan
Cultural adjustment
Culture shock
Digital nomads
Employer of record
Expatriate
Global integration
Global mindset
Global nomads
Joint venture
Inpatriates
Interactional adjustment

International companies
Local differentiation
Multinational companies
Offshoring
Organizationally assigned expatriate
Outsourcing
Reverse culture shock
Self-initiated expatriate
Strategic alliance
Transnational companies
Wholly owned subsidiaries
Work adjustment

HR REASONING AND DECISION-MAKING EXERCISES

Mini-Case Analysis Exercise: Developing a Global Mindset

Your company recently started marketing its products in different overseas markets, including China and France. Realizing that international expansion will drive the future of business, your CEO wants to make sure that managers over a certain organizational level all have "a global mindset." One idea the CEO has is to require all managers above a certain level to have at least 6 months of overseas experience to qualify for a promotion.

You are not really sure whether this is the right strategy. You worry that this will lead some high-potential individuals to quit or to feel resentment and a sense of unfairness. You agree that a global mindset is important to the future of business, but is requiring international experience for all managers the right way to go about ensuring it?

What would you advise your CEO that the company do? Develop a concrete proposal about how to develop a global mindset in the company and provide justification for your plan. Be sure to include a discussion of the resource requirements of your plan.

HR Decision Analysis Exercise: Exceptions to the Rule?

Your company is managing 100 expatriates located in 10 different countries. To approach the treatment and compensation of expatriates systematically, your company has strict rules around what the company will and will not pay for regardless of country. For example, the company specifically pays for housing of the immediate family and educational expenses of children. In addition, the company limits the number of trips back to the United States it will pay for. These rules are relatively specific and inflexible in order to achieve fairness among employees.

Requests for three exceptions to these rules have come across your desk for three expatriates based in Zurich. One employee would like to bring his mother from Egypt, as he is an only child and sole caretaker for his mother. This would mean moving the family to bigger housing and paying for the extra travel expenses. Another employee would like her child to attend nursing school during the relocation. A third expatriate wants to secure an extra trip to the United States to attend her grandmother's 100th birthday. However, the company directive is clear not to make exceptions. Analyze these company policies for expatriates in light of these requests

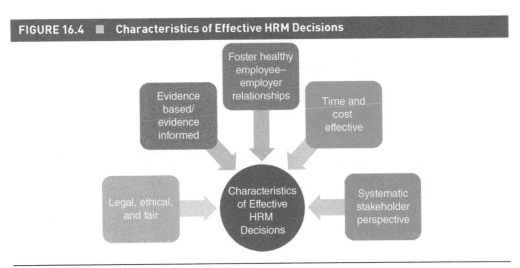

FIGURE 16.4 ■ Characteristics of Effective HRM Decisions

Please provide the rationale for your answer to each of the questions below.

Are the policies legal, ethical, and fair?

Are they evidence based/evidence informed?

Do they foster healthy employee–employer relationships?

Are they time- and cost-effective?

Do they take a systematic stakeholder perspective?

Considering your analysis above, overall, do you think refusing to make exceptions would be an effective decision? Why or why not?

What, if anything, do you think should be done differently or considered to help make this decision more effective?

HR Decision-Making Exercise: Assessing the Effectiveness of Expat Management

You are the HR director of Moore Markets, a grocery retailer that is in the process of overseas expansion. The company is U.S. based and just opened up several stores and branch offices in Mexico, Canada, China, and Germany. You currently have more than 50 expatriates working in these countries. These employees have been deployed as needed, working on assignments that will last anywhere from 1 to 3 years. Anecdotally, you know that a few expatriates who repatriated from these assignments will quit within 6 months. You also know that several expatriates cut their assignments short and asked to return early. Expatriates also voiced concerns that local employees often compare their pay and benefits with what they perceive as generous expatriate packages, expressing resentment. You realize that you are not really tracking the return on investment of expatriates. You do not really know whether your company is doing a good job managing expatriates and whether the company is having systematic problems with them.

1. How would you go about measuring the effectiveness of your expatriate program? What type of information would you collect, and how? Develop a plan to collect the information you need.

2. Would you assess whether you are sending the right employees for these assignments? Describe what steps you would follow.

3. Effectiveness of expatriates relies on their ability to cooperate with local employees, and perceived unfairness and resentment on the part of locals could hamper expatriate effectiveness. What can you do to prevent such resentment?

DATA AND ANALYTICS EXERCISE: MANAGING EXPATRIATES USING DATA

Ettinger Manufacturing currently has 30 expatriates working in three countries. They perform similar jobs, and they started their expatriate assignments at about the same time. A sample of the data collected from them is shown here. What would you do with such data to understand how best to manage expatriates at Ettinger Manufacturing?

Expatriate ID	Assignment Satisfaction	Family Satisfaction	Pay Satisfaction	Coworker Satisfaction	Received Predeparture training (1 = yes)	Location
1	4.57	3.55	2.70	2.85	1	Turkey
2	5.00	3.00	3.30	2.55	1	Turkey
3	4.14	3.19	3.00	3.19	1	Turkey
4	4.71	3.56	3.38	2.88	1	Turkey
5	4.57	4.13	3.13	3.25	1	Turkey
6	4.57	4.31	3.06	1.81	1	Turkey
7	4.14	3.00	2.58	1.50	0	Turkey
8	3.00	2.69	3.38	1.63	1	Turkey
9	1.57	1.38	1.50	1.13	0	Turkey
10	2.71	3.42	3.08	1.08	0	Turkey
11	3.14	2.50	3.31	1.31	1	Canada
12	3.86	2.88	3.00	1.88	1	Canada
13	3.86	2.83	2.67	1.17	0	Canada
14	2.71	1.95	2.05	1.40	0	Canada
15	3.86	3.25	2.25	1.80	1	Canada
16	3.57	2.82	2.57	1.57	1	Canada
17	4.71	4.00	2.42	1.17	0	Canada
18	4.86	3.50	1.69	1.13	0	Canada
19	4.00	3.15	2.05	1.55	1	Canada

Expatriate ID	Assignment Satisfaction	Family Satisfaction	Pay Satisfaction	Coworker Satisfaction	Received Predeparture training (1 = yes)	Location
20	2.71	2.63	2.13	1.63	0	Canada
21	4.00	2.78	2.84	1.84	0	Spain
22	3.00	1.38	2.13	1.50	0	Spain
23	3.50	1.90	2.70	1.20	1	Spain
24	3.57	2.50	1.38	1.00	1	Spain
25	3.29	2.75	2.63	2.38	1	Spain
26	3.00	2.75	2.63	1.63	1	Spain
27	4.86	4.06	2.75	2.19	1	Spain
28	4.43	3.19	3.00	1.94	1	Spain
29	4.57	3.69	3.44	2.38	0	Spain
30	4.00	3.50	2.94	2.44	0	Spain

Excel Extension: Now You Try!

- On **edge.sagepub.com/bauer2e**, you will find these same data in an Excel sheet. Analyze these data and consider what your recommendations would be to management. Consider using regression, *t* test, and one-way analysis of variance in your analyses. Questions you could consider by analyzing the data include the following:

- Does expatriate satisfaction depend on which country they are assigned to?

- What factors are significantly related to expatriate satisfaction?

- Do you find that training expatriates before departure is useful?

APPENDIX - 2022 SHRM BODY OF APPLIED SKILLS AND KNOWLEDGE (BASK)

Special thanks to **Nancy Woolover** (SHRM-SCP, Vice President, Certification) and **Alex Alonso** (SHRM-SCP, Chief Knowledge Officer) at SHRM for their help and support with this appendix and mapping of our content to the updated competencies.

HR Expertise and the 2022 Behavioral Competencies and Subcompetencies for Chapter 1 are found in this appendix. For a full mapping of our chapters onto the 2022 SHRM BASK, please go to edge.sagepub.com/bauer2e.

For more information on the updated SHRM BASK, go to https://www.shrm.org/certification/prepare/Pages/body-of-applied-skills-and-knowledge.aspx

HR EXPERTISE (HR KNOWLEDGE AREAS)

Required Content: Undergraduate Curriculum

People Knowledge Domain

HR Strategy

Chapter 2: *Strategic HRM, Data-Informed Decision Making, and HR Analytics*

Talent Acquisition

Chapter 6: *Workforce Planning and Recruitment*

Chapter 7: *Selection Processes and Procedures*

Employee Engagement & Retention

Chapter 10: *Managing Employee Separations and Retention*

Learning & Development

Chapter 8: *Training, Development, and Careers*

Total Rewards

Chapter 11: *Developing a Pay Structure*

Chapter 12: *Rewarding Performance*

Chapter 13: *Managing Benefits*

Organization Knowledge Domain

Structure of the HR Function

Chapter 1: *Introduction to Human Resource Management*

Chapter 2: *Strategic HRM, Data-Informed Decision Making, and HR Analytics*

Organizational Effectiveness & Development

Chapter 1: *Introduction to Human Resource Management*

Chapter 2: *Strategic HRM, Data-Informed Decision Making, and HR Analytics*

Workforce Management

Chapter 4: *Diversity, Equity, Inclusion (DEI), and Equal Employment Laws*

Chapter 5: *The Analysis and Design of Work*

Chapter 6: *Workforce Planning and Recruitment*

Chapter 9: *Performance Management*

Employee & Labor Relations

Chapter 14: *Employee and Labor Relations*

Technology Management

Chapter 1: *Introduction to Human Resource Management*

Chapter 2: *Strategic HRM, Data-Informed Decision Making, and HR Analytics*

Chapter 3: *Data Management and Human Resource Information Systems*

Workforce Knowledge Domain

Managing a Global Workforce

Chapter 16: *Opportunities and Challenges for International HRM*

Risk Management

Chapter 15: *Employee Safety, Well-Being, and Wellness*

Corporate Social Responsibility

Chapter 1: *Introduction to Human Resource Management*

Chapter 15: *Employee Safety, Well-Being, and Wellness*

U.S. Employment Law & Regulations

Chapter 1: *Introduction to Human Resource Management*

Chapter 4: *Diversity, Equity, Inclusion (DEI), and Equal Employment Laws*

Chapter 7: *Selection Processes and Procedures*

Chapter 11: *Developing a Pay Structure*

Chapter 12: *Rewarding Performance*

Chapter 13: *Managing Benefits*

Chapter 14: *Employee and Labor Relations*

Chapter 15: *Employee Safety, Well-Being, and Wellness*

CHAPTER 1: INTRODUCTION TO HUMAN RESOURCE MANAGEMENT

Behavioral Competencies and Subcompetencies

Leadership Cluster

Leadership & Navigation
Includes: *Navigating the Organization, Vision, Managing HR Initiatives, Influence*

Valuing Employees: The Case of Costco Wholesale [p. 4]

What Is Human Resource Management? [p. 6]

People Matter [p. 10]

Organizational Culture Matters [p. 11]

Types of Organizational Culture [p. 11]

How HRM Affects Organizational Culture [p. 11]

Who Is Involved in HRM? [p. 17]

Top Management Teams and HRM [p. 18]

HR Managers and HRM [p. 18]

Line Managers and HRM [p. 18]

HR Practitioners and HR Careers [p. 18]

Mini-Case Analysis Exercise: Information Seeking as a New Employee [p. 24]

HR Decision Analysis Exercise: Unlimited Vacation? [p. 24]

Ethical Practice
Includes: *Personal Integrity, Professional Integrity, Ethical Agent*

Valuing Employees: The Case of Costco Wholesale [p. 4]

What Is Human Resource Management? [p. 6]

People Matter [p. 10]

Ethical and Corporate Social Responsibility Challenges [p. 17]

Spotlight on Ethics: SHRM Code of Ethics [p. 20]

HR Decision Analysis Exercise: Unlimited Vacation? [p. 24]

Diversity, Equity, & Inclusion
Includes: *Creating a Diverse and Inclusive Culture, Ensuring Equity Effectiveness, Connecting DEI to Organizational Performance*

What Is Human Resource Management? [p. 6]

Organizational Culture Matters [p. 11]

Changing Demographics [p. 13]

Interpersonal Cluster

Relationship Management
Includes: *Networking, Relationship Building, Teamwork, Negotiation, Conflict Management*

Valuing Employees: The Case of Costco Wholesale [p. 4]

What Is Human Resource Management? [p. 6]

People Matter [p. 10]

Communication
Includes: *Delivering Messages, Exchanging Organizational Information, Listening*

Valuing Employees: The Case of Costco Wholesale [p. 4]

Global Mindset
Includes: *Operating in a Culturally Diverse Workplace, Operating in a Global Environment, Advocating for a Culturally Diverse and Inclusive Workplace*

Changing Demographics [p. 13]

Increasing Globalization [p. 14]

Spotlight on Global Issues: Labor Laws Diverge Globally [p. 14]

Spotlight on Legal Issues: U.S. Equal Employment Opportunity Commission [p. 23]

Mini-Case Analysis Exercise: Information Seeking as a New Employee [p. 24]

Business Cluster

Business Acumen
Includes: *Business and Competitive Awareness, Business Analysis, Strategic Alignment*

Pandemic Work Impacts [p. 14]

Gig Economy [p. 16]

Salary and Job Outlook [p. 20]

HR Practitioners and HR Careers [p. 18]

HR Competencies [p. 20]

HR Decision Analysis Exercise: Unlimited Vacation? [p. 24]

Mini-Case Analysis Exercise: Information Seeking as a New Employee [p. 24]

HR Decision-Making Exercise: The Changing Context of HRM [p. 12]

Consultation
Includes: *Evaluating Business Challenges, Designing HR Solutions, Advising on HR Solutions, Change Management, Service Excellence*

Why HRM Matters [p. 10]

HR Business Partners and HRM [p. 19]

Mini-Case Analysis Exercise: Information Seeking as a New Employee [p. 24]

Analytical Aptitude
Includes: *Data Advocate, Data Gathering, Data Analysis, Evidence-Based Decision Making*

What Is Human Resource Management? [p. 6]

HRM Decision Making in Action [p. 8]

How Do You Know If You Are Making a Good Decision? [p. 9]

Data and Processing [p. 15]

Spotlight on Data and Analytics: Descriptive, Predictive, and Prescriptive Analytics [p. 15]

Staying Up to Date: Evidence-Based Management [p. 21]

Mini-Case Analysis Exercise: Information Seeking as a New Employee [p. 24]

HR Decision Analysis Exercise: Unlimited Vacation? [p. 24]

Data and Analytics Exercise: Correlation Does Not Equal Causation [p. 25]

GLOSSARY

360-degree feedback: Multiple-rater systems, which present employees with feedback from different stakeholders and have the potential to provide useful, rich information

4/5ths (or 80%) rule: According to this rule, a protected group's selection ratio may not be less than 80% of the majority group's ratio

401(k) plan: A type of defined-contribution plan in which an employee (and in some cases the employer) makes contributions to an individual account in the form of deferred income

403(b) plan: Also known as a tax-sheltered annuity plan, a type of defined-contribution plan in which an employee (and in some cases the employer) makes contributions to an individual account in the form of deferred income; reserved for public schools and universities, religious organizations, and certain tax-exempt organizations such as charities

Ability-motivation-opportunity model: A model that proposes a system of HR practices that influences employee outcomes and, ultimately, operational and functional outcomes to the extent that the practices target three different elements: ability to perform, motivation to perform, and opportunity to perform

Absenteeism: Unscheduled absences from work

Adequate notice: The idea that employees should be evaluated using criteria and standards that were clearly communicated to them in advance

Adhocracy culture: Organizations with adhocracy cultures are creation-focused and emphasize entrepreneurship, flexibility, risk taking, and creativity

Administrative purposes: A performance review conducted to make decisions in the organization

Aging (of pay data): A process whereby previously collected market pay data are adjusted and updated based on market changes due to merit-based increases, cost-of-living adjustments, and other factors that affect pay

Alternative dispute resolution: Methods of resolving disputes that do not involve litigation

Anchoring bias: The tendency when making a judgment to rely on the first piece of information that one receives

Anniversary reviews: Performance reviews in which an employee is rated on the anniversary of their start date with the organization

Anonymous data: Pieces of information that cannot be linked to any information that might identify an individual, thereby disclosing the individual's identity

Applicant reactions: Job applicants' perspective regarding both the selection procedures they encounter and the employer that uses them

Applicant tracking system (ATS): An internal system that offers a centralized way to house applicant and employee data and to enable electronic business processes related to recruitment

Apprenticeship: A formal training program when a person enters and learns a trade or profession

Artificial intelligence (AI): Statistical or machine learning models that are highly complex

A-S-A framework: The process of attraction, selection, and attrition that defines an organization's culture

Assessment center: A specific type of work sample, often used for manager selection

Availability bias: The tendency to rely more on information that is more readily available than alternative information

Balanced scorecard: The evaluation of organizational performance based on the extent to which the organization satisfies different stakeholder needs, such as the needs of customers, investors, shareholders, employees, and the broader community

Behavior/behavior criteria: Actual behavior on the job that is an outcome of training

Behavioral interview: A type of structured selection interview that uses questions about how applicants handled a work-related situation in the past

Behavioral tracking: A process in which trainees keep track of their on-the-job behaviors and whether they are performing the behaviors they learned in training

Benchmarking: The measurement of the quality of an organization's practices in comparison with those of a peer organization

Benchmark jobs: Key jobs that are common across different organizations

Benefits: Employee rewards that are sometimes referred to as indirect pay and include health, life, and disability insurance; retirement programs; and work–life balance programs

Biases: A tendency, feeling, or opinion, especially one that is preconceived, unreasoned, and unsupported by evidence

Big data: Large amounts of unstructured, messy, or quickly streaming data, which can be described in terms of volume, variety, velocity, and veracity

Biographical data (biodata): Information about a job applicant based on their personal history that can be used to make selection decisions

Blockchain: A distributed incorruptible digital technology infrastructure that maintains a fully encoded database that serves as a ledger where all transactions are recorded and stored

Bona fide occupational qualification (BFOQ): A particular instance where a normally legally protected characteristic (such as age or gender) is an essential necessity of a job

Bonuses: A form of variable pay distributed as a one-time payout in recognition of performance after the fact, which may be attached to a performance rating or to a completed goal

Boomerang employees: Former employees who rejoin an organization

Bridge employment: Reducing one's hours or reducing job demands within the same or a different organization in preparation for full retirement

Broadbanding: The process of collapsing multiple pay grades into one large grade with a single minimum and maximum, resulting in fewer pay grades

Business ethics: A system of principles that govern how business operates, how decisions are made, and how people are treated

Bystander training: Teaches third parties to notice discriminatory and harassing behavior and offers them tools to stop inappropriate behavior before it rises to the level of unlawful actions

Calibration meeting: A meeting in which groups of managers come together and discuss the ratings they will give their employees before ratings are finalized

Candidate experience: A term for applicant reactions often used by employers

Career management: The continual process of setting career-related goals and planning a route to achieve those goals

Case studies: A managerial training method wherein participants analyze and discuss a difficult business case

Cash balance plan: Also known as a guaranteed account plan, a type of defined-benefit plan in which participants are provided with an account that is credited annually with a compensation credit and an interest credit

Central tendency error: The tendency to rate most employees in the middle category

Challenge stressors: Job factors like role demands and time urgency that are thought to be positively related to work engagement

Challenging (stretch) assignments: A task an employee is given that is outside their current KSAOs

Change: The second step in the model of change, this refers to enacting the change

Clan cultures: Organizations with clan cultures are collaboration and people oriented and value cohesion, employee empowerment, and team players

Class action lawsuit: When individuals who have similar claims sue as a group

Classification method: A job evaluation approach in which a written classification description is developed for each classification level, and based on its job description, each job is matched by subject matter experts to a classification level where the classification description is most similar

Cognitive ability test: A measure of the ability to perceive, process, evaluate, compare, create, understand, manipulate, or generally think about information and ideas

Cognitive task analysis: A type of job analysis that focuses on mental tasks that may not be observable by others but could be described by an SME

Collective bargaining: The process of negotiating in good faith toward agreed terms on wages, hours, and working conditions

Compa-ratio: A ratio that reflects how much employees are actually paid for a given job or pay grade as compared to the espoused pay structure and policies and thus can be used to assess whether systematic compression or inversion is occurring

Compensable factors: The common dimensions by which jobs vary in terms of their worth to the organization

Compensation: Employee reward that includes base pay and variable pay and is sometimes referred to as direct pay

Compensatory damages: Financial relief to the complainant for damages incurred, such as mental and emotional stress suffered as a result of discrimination

Compensatory time off (comp time): A program that allows nonexempt employees to receive paid time off (instead of earning time-and-a-half pay) in exchange for working overtime hours

Competency: A cluster of knowledge, skills, abilities, and other characteristics (KSAOs) necessary to be effective at one's job

Competency modeling: A type of job analysis with the goal of understanding what types of attributes and behaviors are required for a group of jobs, perhaps over an entire organization

Compliance training: Instruction focused on regulations, laws, and policies related to employees' daily work

Concept: A theoretical construct

Concurrent validity: Administering a selection procedure to current employees and showing that their scores are correlated with their current job performance in order to demonstrate criterion-related validity

Confidential data: Information for which individuals' identities are known by the researchers due to the linking of a name or code but are not generally disclosed or reported

Consolidated Omnibus Budget Reconciliation Act (COBRA): Introduced in 1985 to protect employees' and their beneficiaries' health care coverage for a designated amount of time in the event of job loss, work-hour reductions, or another major occurrence

Construct validity: The demonstration that a test actually measures a particular construct of interest through an accumulation of evidence about the test, including its pattern of relationships with other measures

Content validity: An approach to test development focused on sampling the domain

such as the job, usually shown through job analysis or SME judgment

Contingent employees: Individuals who are hired for a limited, fixed term such as a short-term contract or a project consulting contract

Coreflex plan: A plan that provides some services (such as paying for movers and travel expenses) to all expatriates, with the remainder of benefits personalized to the unique situation of the expatriate

Criterion-related validity: The demonstration of an empirical relationship between a predictor and measures of job performance

Critical incident method: A method through which managers identify examples of exceptionally high and low incidents of performance and document them in narrative form

Critical incidents technique: A technique that involves asking SMEs to describe important job situations that they frequently encounter on the job

Criticality survey: A more in-depth analysis of the criticality of tasks and KSAOs, in which larger groups of SMEs rate each task and KSAO in terms of how critical or essential it is

Cultural adjustment: Adjusting to the new culture one is now living in, including factors such as transportation, entertainment, health system, education, and general living conditions

Culture shock: The feeling of disorientation individuals experience when they enter a new culture

Cybersecurity: Data security applied to information accessible through the Internet

Database: An organized collection of data that is both stored and accessed electronically

Database management system (DBMS): The software used to manage and maintain a database or multiple databases

Data flow diagrams: Depict the logical design of how data move from one entity to the next and how data are processed within an information system

Data-informed decisions: Decisions that are made based on the analysis and interpretation of relevant, accurate, and timely data

Data lake: Stores a vast amount of raw data in its native (and often unstructured) format

Data privacy: Individual's control over the collection, storage, access, and reporting of their personal data

Data security: Protective measures taken to prevent unauthorized access to employee data and to preserve the confidentiality and integrity of the data; applied to information accessible through the Internet

Data visualizations: Pictorial and graphic representations of quantitative or qualitative data

Defined-benefit plan: Also known as a traditional pension plan, a type of retirement plan in which the employer provides plan participants with a pre-established benefit to be paid out over a fixed time period

Defined-contribution plan: A type of retirement plan in which the employee and/or employer contributes to an investment fund

Delayering: The process by which the hierarchy in an organizational structure is reduced

Descriptive analytics: Focuses on understanding what has already happened, which implies a focus on the past

Developmental purposes: A performance review conducted for the purpose of improving performance

Diary keeping: The practice of recording employee performance on a regular basis

Differential piecework plan: An individual-incentive program in which employees are paid one rate for units produced below a particular standard in a given time period and a higher rate for units produced above that standard

Digital nomads: Individuals who work remotely, without being tied to a specific location, and deciding for themselves how long to stay in each location

Dismissal: Employment termination because the worker fails to meet organizational expectations

Disparate (or adverse) impact: When employers use seemingly neutral criteria that have a discriminatory effect on a protected group

Disparate treatment: Treating different groups of applicants or employees differently because of their race, color, religion, sex, or national origin

Distributive justice: The perceived fairness or equity regarding the allocation of an outcome or resource, which can include rewards, punishments, or other organizational consequences

Diversity, equity, and inclusion (DEI): Policies and programs that promote representation and fair treatment of employees from different backgrounds

Diversity: Compositional differences among people within a work unit, which may lead them to perceive others as similar to them or different from them

Educational-assistance program: A program whereby the employer provides financial assistance for employee educational expenses

e-HRM: Internet-based information systems and technology that span across organizational levels

eLearning: Training that is delivered through an online platform via computers or mobile devices

Electronic monitoring: Using technology to observe, record, and analyze information that directly or indirectly relates to employees' job performance

Emotional intelligence (EI): One's ability to recognize and appraise emotions in oneself and others and behave accordingly

Employability: The degree to which an individual is able to gain initial employment and obtain new employment if required

Employee handbook: Manual created by an organization to outlines its guidelines and policies for employees to follow

Employee relations: The collective relationships between different employees as well as between employees and management in an organization

Employee Retirement Income Security Act (ERISA): Introduced in 1974 to establish minimum standards for many private employers' health care plans in order to protect employees

Employee stock ownership plan (ESOP): A type of pay-for-performance program and defined-contribution retirement plan that rewards employees when company stock shares increase in value and can only be used after a vesting period

Employee wellness programs: Organizational initiatives that promote the health, fitness, and well-being of workers

Employer of record: Organization that serves as the employer for an employee that performs work in a different country.

Employment at will: When organizations have the right to terminate the employment of anyone at any time, and employees have the right to quit at any time

Enterprise resource planning (ERP): Integrated business-management software intended to coordinate and integrate processes and data across different functional areas of a company, such as accounting, sales, human resource management, and finance

Equal Employment Opportunity Commission (EEOC): An independent federal agency that ensures compliance with the law and provides outreach activities designed to prevent discrimination

Equitable relief: Payments made to a plaintiff to bring them back to the position they would have had if they were not discriminated against

Equity: Ensuring that organizational policies and procedures are impartial and fair

Equity theory: Provides a way of understanding how an individual's sense of fairness is influenced by others with whom they compare themselves

Ergonomic design: Fitting the physical aspects of the job to the human body

Essential functions: Job tasks or goals that every incumbent needs to perform

Executive coaching: Individual advice and counseling to managers regarding their work and careers

Executive Order 11246: An executive order issued by President Lyndon B. Johnson that expanded the protections for different forms of employment discrimination (such as pay-based discrimination) to include employers with federal contracts or subcontracts in excess of $10,000

Executive orders: Presidential orders that carry the force of law

Exempt: A term that refers to those employees who do not fall under the purview of the minimum wage and overtime provisions

Expatriate: A person who is living and working in a different country than their country of origin

Expectancy: The extent to which an individual perceives that applying effort will lead to higher performance

Expectancy theory: A theory that suggests that if a person sees that their efforts will lead to greater performance, and if they believe that performance will lead to an outcome that they value, they will be more motivated

External equity: The extent to which the pay for a particular job is competitive and fair relative to the pay of the same or similar jobs at other organizations

External recruitment: An employer's actions that are intended to bring a job opening to the attention of potential job candidates outside of the organization and, in turn, influence their intention to pursue the opportunity

Extrinsic motivation: An external, environmental force that compels an individual to action

Fair hearing: A formal review meeting explaining to the employee why and how a particular rating was given

Fair Labor Standards Act (FLSA): Enacted in 1938, this act introduced major provisions aimed at regulating overtime pay, minimum wage, hours worked, and recordkeeping

Family and Medical Leave Act (FMLA): Introduced in 1993 to protect employees' job security when they need to take unpaid leave due to family or medical issues

Family-to-work conflict: When nonwork responsibilities interfere with work responsibilities

Federal Insurance Contributions Act (FICA): A federal payroll tax paid by both employees and employers that funds current Social Security beneficiaries

Feedback: Information provided to an employee regarding their performance

Feedback culture: A culture in which employees and managers feel comfortable giving and receiving feedback

Field (variable): A column in a table that represents a unique characteristic

Five Factor Model (FFM): A model of normal adult personality that includes the dimensions of Openness to Experience, Conscientiousness, Extraversion, Agreeableness, and Neuroticism

Flexible benefits plans: Offer employees some degree of choice for the employer-sponsored voluntary benefits they select and the benefits they are able to receive on a pretax basis

Flextime: A work arrangement in which workers can choose from a number of work schedules

Focal date reviews: Performance reviews that take place on the same date for all employees

Forced distribution: Also known as stack rankings; involves the rater placing a specific percentage of employees into categories such as exceptional, adequate, and poor

Forecasting: The act of determining estimates during workforce planning regarding what specific positions need to be filled and how to fill them

Form: A database object that provides a user interface with which to enter, edit, and/or display data in a database

Frame of reference (FOR) training: Training that involves raters observing specific instances of performance through videotapes or vignettes and then telling them the "true score" and why raters should rate in a particular way

Gainsharing: A type of group pay-for-performance program that rewards a group of employees for collectively achieving certain goals or objectives

Games and simulations: A type of managerial training in which teams challenge each other as if they were businesses in competition

Gamification: Training that is made into a game or competition among employees in terms of scores on their training performance

Gig economy: A type of contingent work that links up workers with organizations, often using a digital platform

Global integration: When a company standardizes its HR practices around the world

Global mindset: Refers to being open to learning about different cultures, having a sense of adventure, being comfortable dealing with ambiguity, and having a nonjudgmental attitude toward those from other cultures

Global nomads: Individuals who work remotely and across borders, without being tied to a specific location, and deciding for themselves how long to stay in each location

Goal-setting theory: The theory that setting specific, difficult yet achievable goals for people will lead to the highest performance

Halo error: Basing performance ratings on one or two performance dimensions, with one prominent dimension positively affecting how the employee is perceived on other dimensions

Harassment: Unwelcome behaviors based on sex, race, religion, national origin, and other protected characteristics

Health Insurance Portability and Accountability Act (HIPAA): Introduced in 1996 to add protections to the portability of employees' health care coverage and ensure the

privacy and security of employees' health care data

Hierarchy culture: Organizations with hierarchy cultures focus on control and value being efficient, timely, and consistent

Hierarchy of controls: Methods that an organization can use to reduce safety hazards, organized into a hierarchy based on their degree of effectiveness

High-performance work practices: Bundles of HR universal best practices, such as promoting within the organization and offering training

Hindrance stressors: Negative stressors, such as workplace hassles, organizational politics, poor resources, role overload, and constraints

Hiring manager: The person who asked for the role to be filled and/or to whom the new hire will be reporting as their manager

Holiday pay: A program that provides employees with compensation when taking time away from work for a recognized federal, state, or local holiday

Horns error: Ratings on one dimension negatively influencing how the employee is perceived on other dimensions

Hostile work environment: Behavior that contributes to an environment a reasonable person would find offensive

HR business partner: Someone who serves as a consultant to management on HR-related issues

HR generalist: A person who fulfills an HR generalist function attends to multiple HR functions

HR specialist: A person who fulfills an HR specialist function attends to all aspects of one specific HRM function

Human capital: The knowledge, skills, and abilities that people embody across an organization

Human resource (HR) analytics: The process of collecting, analyzing, interpreting, and reporting people-related data for the purpose of improving decision making, achieving strategic objectives, and sustaining a competitive advantage

Human resource information system (HRIS): System used to collect, store, manage, analyze, retrieve, and report HR data and allow for the automation of some HR management functions

Human resource management (HRM): The decisions and actions associated with managing individuals throughout the employee life cycle to maximize employee and organization effectiveness

Identical elements: The extent to which the training environment is the same as the actual work environment and thus enhances training transfer

Impasse: Possible outcome of a failure to reach an agreement

Incentive effects: The extent to which pay-for-performance programs motivate employees' on-the-job behavior and pursuit of goals

Inclusion: Treatment of individuals of all backgrounds with dignity and respect, including them in decision making and valuing them for who they are and what they bring to the group or organization

Individual equity: The fairness of how pay is administered and distributed to individual employees working similar jobs within the same organization

Individual incentives: The distribution of pay in response to the attainment of certain predetermined and objective levels of performance

Individual retirement plan :or individual retirement arrangement (IRA): A plan that allows an individual to make tax-deferred contributions to an investment fund and that does not need to be employer sponsored

Informal field-based learning (IFBL): When people decide to take part in learning on their jobs outside of a formal training context

Informational interview: The exchange of information between an individual and an organizational representative with the goal of learning more about the organization and its industry

Informing: Providing new employees with sources, materials, and training to help them learn what is expected of them

Inpatriates: Host-country employees working in headquarter locations

Instrumentality: The extent to which an individual perceives that achieving higher performance will lead to reward attainment

Integrity test: A test specifically developed to assess applicants' tendency toward counterproductive and antisocial behavior

Interactional adjustment: The comfort felt with interacting with local individuals inside or outside work

Interactional justice: The perceived fairness of an interpersonal or informational

interaction—for example, being treated with respect and consideration or receiving adequate explanation about a process

Internal equity: The fairness of pay rates across jobs within an organization

Internal Revenue Code: Stipulates income and payroll tax regulations

International companies: Companies that export or import, but their investments are within one home country

Intrinsic motivation: A force that originates inside an individual and compels the individual to action because they perceive the action as innately rewarding

Involuntary turnover: An employee terminated by the organization against their own wishes

Job (Job classification): A group of related duties within an organization

Job analysis: The analysis of work and the employee characteristics needed to perform the work successfully

Job characteristics model (JCM): The first complete model of job design, explaining which job characteristics are the most important to increasing worker motivation and productivity

Job crafting: Redesigning one's own job to fit one's needs (e.g., abilities, interests, personality)

Job demands-control model (JDC): This model emphasizes that employees experience stress when there are high job demands and little control over their job

Job demands-resources model (JDR): This model emphasizes that job demands, such as workload and time pressure, can be counteracted by characteristics such as job control, participation, and supervisor support

Job descriptions: Job descriptions provide the title and purpose of the job, as well as a general overview of the essential tasks, duties, and responsibilities (i.e., observable actions) associated with the job

Job design: The process of identifying how a job's characteristics are experienced from the employee's perspective in order to enhance well-being and performance

Job embeddedness model: A model that explains that employees stay because of their links to others and fit with the context at work and in their communities and how much they would have to sacrifice by leaving their work and communities

Job enlargement: The addition of more responsibilities to a job so that it is less boring and more motivating for workers

Job enrichment: Allowing workers to have greater decision-making power

Job evaluation: A systematic process used to determine the relative worth of jobs within an organization

Job rotation: Rotating employees from one job to another, allowing them to learn new skills

Job satisfaction: An employee's contentment with different facets of their work

Job specifications: Job specifications focus on the characteristics of an employee who does the job

Job structure: The ranking of jobs within an organization based on their respective worth

Joint venture: Two companies that come together and invest to create a new company

Judgment based on evidence: The principle that performance standards are administered consistently across all employees and that the ratings are, to the degree possible, free from personal biases and prejudice

Key performance indicators (KPIs): Measurable business metrics that are aligned with a company's strategy

Key variable: Provides the information necessary to construct the relationships between tables and to join (or merge) data from different tables

KSAOs: Knowledge, skills, abilities, and other characteristics employees need to have in order to do their work most effectively

Labor Management Relations Act (1947): Also known as the Taft-Hartley Act; amended the 1935 National Labor Act to restrict the activities and power of labor unions

Labor–Management Reporting and Disclosure Act (LMRDA) (1959): Prescribes how unions are internally regulated; requires labor organizations to report financial transactions and administrative practices of unions, employers, and labor consultants

Labor market: The availability of talent outside of an organization, which can be viewed through the lens of talent supply and demand

Labor market conditions: The number of jobs available compared to the number of individuals available with the required KSAOs to do those jobs

Labor relations: Managing in response to labor laws relating to unions and collective bargaining

Labor union: An organization of workers formed for the purpose of advancing its members' interests with respect to wages, benefits, and working conditions

Layoffs: Organizationally initiated termination of employment due to economic or strategic reasons

Leadership development: The formal and informal opportunities for employees to expand their KSAOs

Learning criteria: Measures of whether the trainee actually gained some sort of knowledge or skill while in training

Leniency error: The tendency of a rater to rate most employees highly

Life insurance program: Provides financial compensation for designated beneficiaries when the insured individual dies

Linkage survey: Where sample of SMEs are asked to indicate how important each of the KSAOs is to each job task

Little data: Structured data that are gathered in small volumes, usually for previously planned purposes

Local differentiation: When organizations vary their HR practices in consideration of the local environment

Local validation: Showing the test's validity for predicting job performance in a specific organization

Logical design: The translation of business requirements into improved business processes

Long-term disability insurance: A form of income protection for employees that is similar to short-term disability insurance, except it offers longer-term benefits activated once short-term disability insurance benefits expire

Magnitude: The size of a relationship

Managed-care plans: A medical plan designed to provide wide-ranging health care services to plan participants while managing the cost, quality, and use of services, where participants incur lower cost sharing when they use in-network (as opposed to out-of-network) providers and services

Management by objectives (MBO): A management strategy in which organizational goals are translated into department- and individual-level goals

Marginal functions: Job tasks or goals that can be assigned to others

Market culture: Organizations with market cultures are characterized by competition and as being aggressive, competitive, and customer oriented

Market pay line: The relationship between the internal job structure of the organization for benchmark jobs and the external pay practices of other organizations

Market pricing: When an organization bases its pay levels and pay structure directly on its competitors' pay levels and pay structures

Market review: The process of collecting pay data for benchmark jobs from other organizations

Massed learning: Training that occurs in one large chunk at one point in time

Measure: A tool used to assess the levels of a concept, such as a survey used to assess employee engagement

Merit pay: Pay distributed to employees and integrated into their base pay as a reward for the ratings and/or feedback they receive on a performance evaluation measure

Metacognitive skills: A person's ability to step back and assess their own skill, performance, or learning

Mindfulness training: Teaches a person to be present in the moment and to notice things around them in a nonjudgmental way

Mission: A core need that an organization strives to fulfill and thus represents the organization's overarching purpose

Money-purchase plan: A relatively straightforward defined-contribution plan in which employers contribute a specified amount to each plan participant's investment fund

Motivation: A psychological force that propels an individual (or a group of individuals) to enact certain behaviors or to strive for a goal

Multinational companies: Companies operating in multiple countries but with clearly designated headquarters in their home country

Multiple-hurdle approach: When a series of selection procedures is administered sequentially and applicants must pass each hurdle to move to the next one

National Institute for Occupational Safety and Health (NIOSH) The federal agency that supports research on workplace safety and health and makes recommendations to employers

National Labor Relations Act (NLRA): Enacted in 1935, this act stipulates that employees protected under the act have a right to discuss pay as part of activities related to collective bargaining and protection, thereby providing an avenue through which employees may uncover pay discrimination

National Labor Relations Board (NLRB): An independent U.S. government agency tasked with supervising union elections and empowered to investigate suspected unfair labor practices

Natural lighting: Lighting provided by sunlight

Near misses: Situations in which an accident almost occurred but did not

Needs assessment: A systematic evaluation of the organization, the jobs, and the employees to determine where training is most needed and what type of training is needed

Negotiation: Give-and-take process between two or more parties aimed toward reaching an agreement

Neurodivergent: Describes people whose cognitive functioning falls outside what is typical in the population

Neurodiversity: Differences in the ways in which the brain functions

Neurotypical: Describes people who process information in ways that are similar to the general population

Nonexempt: A term that refers to those employees who are directly affected by minimum wage and overtime provisions

Occupational Safety and Health Administration (OSHA) Under the U.S. Department of Labor, OSHA's purpose is to ensure safe and healthy working conditions for employees by setting and enforcing safety and health standards

Office of Federal Contract Compliance Programs (OFCCP): A division of the Department of Labor; monitors EEO compliance of federal contractors

Offshoring: When companies produce physical goods or perform some of their operations overseas

Onboarding (organizational socialization): The process of helping new employees adjust to their new organizations by imparting to them the knowledge, skills, behaviors, culture, and attitudes required to successfully function within the organization

One-on-one meetings: Meetings managers have with their direct reports on a regular basis, usually weekly, to discuss performance goals, progress, and related issues

On-the-job training (OJT): When a new employee works on the job in order to learn it, usually under the supervision of a more senior employee

Open offices: An office arrangement in which employees work in open spaces

Organizational culture: Assumptions shared by organization members, which affect their actions, thoughts, and perceptions

Organizational justice theory: A theory that focuses on perceptions of fairness in the workplace

Organizationally assigned expatriate: Expat who is sent by the organization for a predetermined time to work in an overseas operation

Orientation program: A specific type of training designed to help welcome, inform, and guide new employees

Outsourcing: Moving some operations of the organization to a different organization

Overconfidence bias: The tendency for an individual to be more confident in their own beliefs than reality would suggest

Overlearning: When trainees repeatedly practice a particular behavior in the training situation so that they can perform the behavior automatically without much cognitive effort

Paid time off (PTO): A program that provides employees with compensation when they take time away from work, subject to employer approval

Paired comparisons: Creating rankings by comparing two employees at the same time until every unique pair of employees has been compared and then compiling the results

Patient Protection and Affordable Care Act (ACA): Introduced in 2010 to provide rights and protections associated with access to health care coverage

Pay compression: Occurs when more recently hired employees with less experience earn nearly as much or the same as more experienced, longer tenured employees in the same job or when employees in a lower-level job earn nearly as much or the same as employees in a higher-level job

Pay-for-performance programs: Compensation programs that reward employees based on the behaviors they actually exhibit at work and the results or goals they actually achieve

Pay grade: A group of jobs with similar job evaluation point values that are then assigned common pay midpoint, minimum, and maximum values

Pay inversion: A more severe form of pay compression that occurs when a newer, less experienced employee in a given job earns more than another, more experienced employee in the same job or more than another employee in a higher-level job

Pay policy line: Portrays an organization's operationalization of its market pay line, thereby representing how an organization translates information about its internal job structure and external pay rates of competitors into actionable pay practices

Pay secrecy: The extent to which an organization has policies and practices aimed at suppressing the communication and exchange of pay information

Pay structure: The way in which an organization applies pay rates to different jobs, skills, or competencies

Pay transparency: The extent to which an organization communicates pay information and the extent to which employees are permitted to discuss pay with each other

Pension Benefit Guaranty Corporation (PBGC): A U.S. government agency that insures private-sector retirement plans

People data: Data associated with various groups of humans that are associated with an organization, such as employees and other stakeholders

Performance appraisal: An evaluation of employee performance

Performance improvement plan (PIP): Plan aimed at helping poor performers be accountable to meeting performance standards

Performance management: The process of measuring, communicating, and managing employee performance in the workplace so that performance is aligned with organizational strategy

Perquisites (perks): Nonmonetary services or benefits provided by an employer

Personality: An individual's dispositional and relatively stable pattern of cognition, behavior, and emotion

Personal leave: A benefit employers use to supplement vacation and sick-time offerings by allowing employees to take paid or unpaid time away from work

Personally identifiable data: Data readily linked to specific individuals

Person-based pay structures: A pay structure that emphasizes individuals' unique competencies or skills when determining pay, such that a person who possesses a particular competency or skill receives additional pay

Physical design: The actual software and hardware solutions used to translate business processes into an actual information system

Physical environment: The natural and human-made components of one's surroundings

Piecework plan: An individual-incentive program in which employees are compensated based on their respective production levels

Placement: A part of strategy development, which involves determining where talent needs to be placed and where the talent can be found

Point-factor method: A job evaluation approach in which a team of subject matter experts systematically identifies compensable factors and develops and applies scales and weights for compensable factors, ultimately resulting in points being assigned to different jobs to describe their relative worth

Position: Duties that can be carried out by one person

Predictive analytics: Focuses on what is likely to happen in the future based on what is already known and evaluating the accuracy of those predictions

Predictive validity: Administering a selection procedure to job applicants and showing that their scores are correlated with their later job performance scores in order to demonstrate criterion-related validity

Prescriptive analytics: Focuses on what actions should be taken based on what is already known and what is predicted to happen in the future

Pretext: An excuse given for a decision that is not the real reason

Prima facie evidence: At first glance, or preliminary evidence

Procedural justice: The perceived fairness of the process used to determine how an outcome or resource is determined and distributed

Product market: The final sale of products and services in the marketplace

Profit sharing: A pay-for-performance program in which employees share in their organization's profits

Profit-sharing program: A type of pay-for-performance program in which the employee earns rewards by sharing their organization's profits, and earned rewards can be placed in what can be considered a type of defined-contribution plan

Progressive discipline: The process of using increasingly severe steps to correct a performance problem

Psychometrics: A science used to estimate the quality of psychological measures such as those used in personnel selection

Pulse surveys: Short, frequent surveys

Punitive damages: Damages that are awarded if it is demonstrated that the company had engaged in reckless discrimination and failed to act in good faith

Qualitative data: Nonnumeric information that includes text or narrative data, such as interview transcripts

Quantitative data: Numeric data that can be counted or measured in some way

Query: A question that is posed to a database

Quid pro quo harassment: Involves making employment decisions contingent on sexual favors

Ranking method: A job evaluation approach in which subject matter experts evaluate the job descriptions and specifications for a selection of jobs and order them in terms of their relative contribution to the organization's strategic objectives and mission

Reactions criteria: The assessment of how trainees react to training such as whether they thought it was valuable

Realistic job preview (RJP): Offers potential applicants a realistic view of the actual job, including both positive and negative information

Reasonable accommodation: An accommodation provided to employees to help them perform their jobs that is reasonable given a firm's resources

Recency error: When a rater focuses on the most recent employee behaviors they have observed rather than focusing on the entire rating period

Record: A case in a database

Recruitment: The process of identifying a group of individuals (employees or potential applicants) who possess the KSAOs to fill a particular role

Recruitment funnel: A situation in which the number of applicants gets smaller as people move through the selection process

Recruitment needs: The results of the workforce planning process in terms of what KSAOs are needed within the organization as well as when they will be needed

Refreezing: The third and final step in the change model, this step refers to refreezing the new system in place so that it becomes the permanent replacement for the way things used to be done

Reinforcement theory: A motivational theory that provides a useful framework for understanding pay as an extrinsic motivator, particularly when pay is used for behavior modification

Relational database: A specific type of database in which different subsets or collections of data are integrated through pieces of information residing within the data themselves

Relational database management system (relational DBMS): The software used to manage and maintain a relational database

Relational returns: Nonmonetary incentives and rewards, such as new learning and developmental opportunities

Reliability: The consistency of measurement

Remote work: A work arrangement in which an employee is not physically at an office or other location but instead works a substantial amount of time away from the office

Replacement planning: The process of identifying a minimal plan of individuals to take over top leadership roles over time

Report: A database object that is used to organize, summarize, format, and present data residing in the database

Resource-based view: Proposes that a resource holds value to the extent that it is rare and inimitable, where example resources include physical, financial, organizational, and human resources

Results criteria: Whether the training actually translates into improved organizational outcomes

Retaliate: Taking adverse action against an employee who complains about discrimination or files a discrimination claim

Reverse culture shock: Situation in which expatriates return to their country of origin and find that their country of origin does not feel like home anymore

Reverse discrimination: Discriminating against majority or historically privileged groups such as white or male employees

Reward system: The policies, procedures, and practices used by an organization to determine the amount and types of returns individuals, teams, and the organization receive in exchange for their membership and contributions

Right-to-work laws: Vary from state to state but generally prohibit requiring employees to join a union or pay regular or fair-share union dues in order to obtain or keep a job

Role-plays: When trainees act in managerial situations such as counseling a difficult subordinate

Safety behavior: The type of work behaviors that employees exhibit with regard to safety

Safety climate: The shared understanding that workers have about the importance of safety

Safety committee: Provides employees with a voice and an opportunity to participate in safety-related decisions in the organization

Safety compliance behavior: The extent to which workers follow the safety rules and regulations

Safety knowledge: Workers' understanding of how to protect themselves and others on the job

Safety motivation: Workers' perceived value for safety and desire to perform safely on the job

Safety officer: An individual who is assigned to support safety and health issues in the workplace such as the promotion of safe practices and compliance with safety policies and rules

Safety participation behavior: Employees' willingness to support safety among their coworkers

Sales commissions: Pay-for-performance programs that reward the sale of a product or service as opposed to the production of a product or provision of a service

Schema: An outline or framework to help the learner organize the training material so that they will better retain the material

Scientific process: A method used for systematic and rigorous problem solving that is predicated on the assumption that knowledge requires evidence

Scraping and crawling tools: Programs designed to scour and pull data from websites and other electronic sources in a systematic manner

Selection interview: A conversation or discussion between a job applicant and an organizational representative used to screen job applicants

Self-efficacy: A person's belief that they can accomplish a task

Self-initiated expatriate: A skilled professional who moves to a different country for a specific period of time with the intention of gaining overseas work experience

Severance pay: Payments made to departing employees during organizationally initiated turnover

Severity error: The tendency to rate almost all ratees low

Sexual harassment: Unwanted advances and other harassment that is sexual in nature

Short-term disability insurance: A form of income protection for employees who temporarily become unable to work as a result of illness or injury

Sick time (sick leave): A program that permits employees to take time off from work due to a personal or immediate family member's health issue

Sign: The positive or negative direction of a relationship between variables

Similarity-attraction hypothesis: The theory that individuals prefer others who are similar to them

Site visit: When a job applicant physically agrees to go to the organization's location to meet with and to be interviewed by its representatives

Situational interview: A type of structured interview in which job applicants are asked what they would do in a hypothetical work-related situation

Situational judgment tests (SJTs): A test that captures some of the realism of work sample tests but in a format (e.g., multiple-choice) that can be used more easily with large numbers of applicants

SMART goals: Goals that are specific, measurable, aggressive, realistic, and time-bound

Social Security Act: Passed by the U.S. Congress in 1935 as part of the New Deal to help the United States recover from the Great Depression by providing economic security for old-age individuals and, later, additional programs for mothers and children in need, individuals with disabilities, the unemployed, and those whose family members have died

Society for Human Resource Management (SHRM): The world's largest professional society for human resource management with over 300,000 members in 165 countries

Software as a service (SaaS): Arrangements through which software and hardware associated with databases and applications are maintained and controlled by a third-party entity

Sorting effects: The associated processes of attraction, selection, and attrition that occur when employees gravitate toward jobs with reward systems that fit their disposition, goals, and performance capabilities

Spaced learning: Training that occurs through several sessions over time

Spot awards: A type of after-the-fact recognition that is often reserved for exceptional levels of performance on a project or for exceptionally high overall job performance

Spurious correlation: A correlation observed between two variables that are not actually related

Stakeholders: Different groups that an organization must appeal to, including customers and investors

Standard-hour plan: An individual-incentive program in which employee pay is based on the completion of a particular task within a predetermined time period

Stay interviews: Interviews of employees who are not leaving to understand what keeps them on their jobs and identify problems that may eventually result in turnover

Stereotypes: Overly simplified and generalized assumptions about a particular group that may not reflect reality

Stock options: A type of pay-for-performance program that makes employees partial owners of the organization by allowing employees to purchase a certain number of stock shares at a fixed price in a given time frame

Storytelling with data: Communicating data in a manner that brings it to life for the audience with a focus on simplicity and ease of interpretation and comprehension

Straight piecework plan: An individual-incentive program in which employee variable pay is based on the units they produce in a given time period, such that there is a direct correspondence between the amount of pay distributed and the number of units produced

Straight rankings: When a rater rank-orders all employees from best to worst

Strain: A person's reaction to stressors, such as heart disease, burnout, or depression; or behavioral outcomes such as low performance and turnover

Strategic alliance: A partnership with other companies

Strategic human resource management: The process of aligning HR policies and practices with the objectives of the organization, including employee, operational, stakeholder, and financial outcomes

Strategy: A well-devised and thoughtful plan for achieving an objective

Strategy formulation: The process of planning what to do to achieve organizational objectives

Strategy implementation: The enactment of a strategic plan

Strategy type: A general approach for how an organization will bring its mission, vision, and values to life

Stressors: Demands in the environment to which a person must respond

Strike: To stop work in order to force an employer to comply with demands

Structured interview: An interview in which all job applicants are asked the same, job-related questions

Subject matter experts (SMEs): People (e.g., employees, supervisors) who provide information about the job

Succession management: The process of identifying and developing successors at all levels of the organization

Succession planning: Taking stock of which employees are qualified to fill positions that are likely to be vacated soon

SWOT analysis: An analysis of the internal strengths and weaknesses of an organization and the external opportunities and threats to that organization

Systems perspective: The view of how all pieces of a system and its subsystems fit together

Table: A database object used to store data about cases and to add structure to the data

Talent analysis: The process of gathering data to determine potential talent gaps, or the difference between an organization's talent demand and the available talent supply

Talent pool: A group of individuals (employees or potential applicants) who possess the KSAOs to fill a particular role

Tardiness: Being late to work without giving advance notice

Tasks: The elements of a job analysis that are typically used to describe the job itself

Tax deferred: Taxable income that is not taxed until a later date, often when earnings are distributed

Team appraisals: A team evaluation in which goals and performance are evaluated at the team level

Total compensation: Package of compensation and benefits that employees receive

Total Worker Health® (TWH®): An integrated approach to safety, well-being, and wellness

Traditional-care plans: Also called conventional-indemnity plans, a medical plan that allows participants to select any provider of their choosing without affecting how they are reimbursed, and participants' expenses are reimbursed as they are incurred

Traditional-pay programs: Compensation programs that reward employees based on the content of their job description, title, and level

Trainee motivation: The sustained motivation of employees during the training process, which is a predictor of training success

Training relevance: The degree to which trainees see the training as important to their jobs

Training transfer: Whether the training results in changes in job performance

Training transfer climate: Support for training transfer in the work environment from supervisors and coworkers

Training utility reactions: Trainees' belief that the training was actually relevant and useful to their jobs

Transfer through principles: Teaching learners the principles underlying a training concept in order to enhance transfer

Transnational companies: Companies that have operations in multiple countries and do not view themselves as belonging to any one country

Two-step authentication (multifactor authentication): An extra layer of security that requires an additional piece of information that only the user would know

Unconscious (or implicit) bias: Stereotypes individuals hold that reside beyond their conscious awareness

Unemployment insurance: Payment made to unemployed individuals

Unfair labor practices: Defined in the United States as actions taken by either unions or employers that violate the National Labor Relations Act or other legislation. Such acts are investigated by the National Labor Relations Board.

Unfolding model of turnover: A model that recognizes that employees often leave without lining up a new job and that turnover is often a result of "shocks" to the system

Unfreezing: Step 1 in the model of change, which refers to the process of unfreezing the current system and checking to see that individuals are ready for change

Uniform Guidelines on Employee Selection Procedures: Guidelines adopted by EEOC, the Department of Labor, and the Department of Justice, which outline how selection systems can be designed to comply with EEO laws

Unstructured interview: When the interviewer has a conversation with a job applicant with no fixed protocol for each applicant

Utility: The degree to which an HR function (e.g., a selection procedure) is worth the time or money it requires

Vacation pay: A program that provides employees with compensation for taking time away from work for a planned reason

Valence: The extent to which individuals perceive a reward as being attractive or important

Validity: The accuracy of a measure, or the degree to which an assessment measures what it is supposed to measure

Validity coefficient: The correlation between a selection procedure (e.g., a test) and job performance

Validity generalization: The assumption that selection procedures that have been validated for similar jobs in similar organizations can be assumed to be valid for new situations

Values: Parameters and guidelines for decision making that help an organization realize its vision

Vision: An extension of an organization's mission that describes what the organization will look like or be at some point in the future

Voluntary turnover: A departure initiated by an employee

Welcoming: Activities that are intended to be friendly toward employees, such as giving them a personalized e-mail or call or having lunch with the new coworker

Well-being: A worker's well-being is composed of their safety, health, satisfaction, and engagement

Wholly owned subsidiaries: When an organization has subsidiaries overseas and gives the parent company full control over their overseas operations

Work adjustment: Feeling comfortable at work and with one's new tasks

Work analysis: A more recent term for job analysis, which is based on the idea that an employee may need to perform a variety of evolving jobs within an organization

Work engagement: Feelings of emotional connection to work and a state of being in which employees bring their personal selves to work

Workers' compensation: Program funded entirely by the employer in the form of payroll taxes that provides medical coverage and income replacement for an individual who is injured or becomes ill on the job due to an accident or hazard

Work flow analysis: A broad, organization-level focus on work within the organization and within organizational units and the input needed

Workforce labor shortages: Labor market conditions in which there are more jobs available than workers to fill them

Workforce labor surplus (or slack): Labor market conditions in which there is more available labor than organizations need

Workforce planning: The process of determining what work needs to be done in both the short and the long term and coming up with a strategy regarding how those positions will be filled

Workplace accidents: Accidents sustained while on duty in the workplace

Workplace bullying: Consistent mistreatment by others in the workplace

Workplace fatalities: Deaths that occur while on duty in the workplace

Workplace injuries: Injuries sustained while on duty in the workplace

Workplace intervention: A solution implemented within an organization that focuses on a very specific workplace well-being issue

Work sample: A sample or example of the work produced by a job applicant

Work-to-family conflict: When work interferes with nonwork responsibilities

Wrongful dismissal: A dismissal that violates the law

ENDNOTES

CHAPTER 1

1. Cascio, W. (2006). The high cost of low wages. *Harvard Business Review, 84*; Chu, J., & Rockwood, K. (2008). CEO interview: Costco's Jim Sinegal. *Fast Company*. https://www.fastcompany.com/1042487/ceo-interview-costcos-jim-sinegal; Costco. (2022). *About us*. https://www.costco.com/about.html; *Employee relations best practices: Costco's approach to HR*. Case IQ. https://www.caseiq.com/resources/employee-relations-best-practices-costco/; *Fortune*. (2022). Costco Wholesale. https://fortune.com/company/costco/; glassdoor.com (2022). *Costco Wholesale: Employee review*. https://www.glassdoor.com/Reviews/Employee-Review-Costco-Wholesale-RVW11951684.htm; La Monica, P. R. (2015). The best CEOs of the year are.... *CNN Money*. http://money.cnn.com/gallery/investing/2015/12/23/best-ceos-2015/; Market Watch. (n.d.). *Costco Wholesale Corp*. https://www.marketwatch.com/investing/stock/cost; Milligan, C. (2021). *How rich is the Costco CEO and what's the average pay of its employees?* https://www.mashed.com/361488/how-rich-is-the-costco-ceo-and-whats-the-average-pay-of-its-employees/; Porath, C. (2016). *SHRM Foundation's Effective Practice Guidelines.Creating a more human workplace where employees and business thrive*. SHRM Foundation. https://www.shrm.org/hr-today/trends-and-forecasting/special-reports-and-expert-views/Documents/Human-Workplace.pdf; Short, K. (2013). 11 reasons to love Costco that have nothing to do with shopping. *HuffPost*. http://www.huffingtonpost.com/2013/11/19/reasons-love-costco_n_4275774.html; Ton, Z. (2014). *The good jobs strategy: How the smartest companies invest in employees to lower costs and boost profits*. Houghton Mifflin Harcourt.

2. McKinsey & Company. (2019). *Decision making in the age of urgency*. https://www.mckinsey.com/business-functions/people-and-organizational-performance/our-insights/decision-making-in-the-age-of-urgency;

Nutt, P. C. (2002). *Why decisions fail*. Berrett-Koehler.

3. Virgin Air. (2015, January 26). *Why is looking after your employees so important?* https://www.virgin.com/entrepreneur/why-is-looking-after-your-employees-so-important

4. Pendell, R. (2022). *The world's $7.8 trillion workplace problem*. Gallup Workplace. https://www.gallup.com/workplace/393497/world-trillion-workplace-problem.aspx

5. *Fortune* 100 Best Companies to Work For 2021. (2021). https://www.greatplacetowork.com/best-workplaces/100-best/2021

6. Albrecht, S. L., Bakker, A. B., Gruman, J. A., Macey, W. H., & Saks, A. M. (2015). Employee engagement, human resource management practices and competitive advantage: An integrated approach. *Journal of Organizational Effectiveness: People and Performance, 2*, 7–35; Pfeffer, J. (1998). *The human equation: Building profits by putting people first*. Harvard Business School Press; Wright, P. M., Gardner, T. M., Moynihan, L. M., & Allen, M. R. (2005). The relationship between HR practices and firm performance: Examining causal order. *Personnel Psychology, 58*, 409–446.

7. Schein, E., & Schein, P. (2016). *Organizational culture and leadership* (5th ed.). Jossey-Bass.

8. Wiseman, P. (2022, January 4). *A record 4.5 million Americans quit their jobs in November*. AP News. https://apnews.com/article/coronavirus-pandemic-business-health-e4bfb475f3dd8858778d785a8e0a1149

9. Cameron, K. S., & Quinn, R. E. (2011). *Diagnosing and changing organizational culture: Based on the competing values framework*. Addison-Wesley.

10. Campiere, A. (2022, March 24). *Gamification of recruiting: Playing for your next job*. PCMA. https://www.pcma.org/gamification-recruiting-employees/; Zielinski, D. (2015, November). The gamification of recruitment. *HR Magazine*, 59–60.

11. Orlowski, A. (2021). Microsoft's extraordinary revival has proved the cool kids wrong. *The Telegraph*. https://www.telegraph.co.uk/business/2021/04/28/microsofts-extraordinary-revival-has-proved-cool-kids-wrong/

12. U.S. Census Bureau. (2019). *By 2030, all baby boomers will be age 65 or older*. https://www.census.gov/library/stories/2019/12/by-2030-all-baby-boomers-will-be-age-65-or-older.html; U.S. Department of Commerce, U.S. Census Bureau. (2014). *The baby boom cohort in the United States: 2012-2060*. https://www.census.gov/prod/2014pubs/p25-1141.pdf

13. Tanzi, A., & Sasso, M. (2021). Covid early retirees top 3 million in U.S., Fed research shows. *Bloomberg*. https://www.bloomberg.com/news/articles/2021-10-22/covid-early-retirees-top-3-million-in-u-s-fed-research-show#xj4y7vzkg

14. U.S. Bureau of Labor Statistics. (2022). *Usual weekly earnings of wage and salary workers*. https://www.bls.gov/news.release/wkyeng.t03.htm

15. McGlauflin, P. (2022). The number of Black Fortune 500 CEOs returns to record high—meet the 6 chief executives. *Fortune*. https://fortune.com/2022/05/23/meet-6-black-ceos-fortune-500-first-black-founder-to-ever-make-list/

16. World Health Organization. (2022). *WHO coronavirus (COVID-19) dashboard*. https://covid19.who.int/

17. Saad, L., & Wigert, B. (2021). *Remote work persisting and trending permanent*. Gallup. https://news.gallup.com/poll/355907/remote-work-persisting-trending-permanent.aspx

18. Nguyen, L. (2021). Wall Street grudgingly allows remote work as bankers dig in. *The New York Times*. https://www.nytimes.com/2021/11/24/business/wall-street-remote-work-banks.html

19. Meyer, Z. (2022). Here's an ever-growing list of companies that will let people work from home forever. *Fast Company*. https://www.fastcompany.

com/90508784/heres-an-ever-growing-list-of-companies-that-will-let-people-work-from-home-forever

20. SHRM. (2022). *Interactive chart: How historic has the Great Resignation been?* https://www.shrm.org/resourcesandtools/hr-topics/talent-acquisition/pages/interactive-quits-level-by-year.aspx

21. Statistica. (2022). Intel revenue worldwide 2011-2022, by region. https://www.statista.com/statistics/263560/net-revenue-of-intel-by-region-since-2006/

22. Frenkel, S. (2018). Tech giants brace for Europe's new data privacy rules. *The New York Times.* https://www.nytimes.com/2018/01/28/technology/europe-data-privacy-rules.html; Petroff, A., & Cornevin, O. (2017, January 2). France gives workers "right to disconnect" from office email. *CNN Money.* http://money.cnn.com/2017/01/02/technology/france-office-email-workers-law/index.html; Reed, B. (Ed.). (2017). Sweden rejects quotas for women on boards of listed companies. *The Guardian.* https://www.theguardian.com/world/2017/jan/12/sweden-rejects-quotas-women-boardroom-listed-companies; Wittenberg-Cox, A. (2021). France unanimously votes gender quotas for executive leadership. *Forbes.* https://www.forbes.com/sites/avivahwittenbergcox/2021/05/15/france-unanimously-votes-gender-quotas-for-executive-leadership/?sh=7f7dcabf2b8e

23. Data never sleeps. (n.d.). DOMO. https://www.domo.com/solution/data-never-sleeps-6

24. Internet live stats. (2022). https://www.internetlivestats.com/; Liberatore, S. (2016). What happens in an Internet second. *Daily Mail.* http://www.dailymail.co.uk/sciencetech/article-3662925/What-happens-Internet-second-54-907-Google-searches-7-252-tweets-125-406-YouTube-video-views-2-501-018-emails-sent.html; Pappas, S. (2016). How big is the Internet, really? *LiveScience.* http://www.livescience.com/54094-how-big-is-the-Internet.html

25. Wetherill, D. (2016). Broken links: Why analytics investments have yet to pay off. *The Economist.* https://www.zs.com/content/dam/pdfs/Broken_links_Why_analytics_investments_have_yet_to_pay_off.pdf

26. Deloitte. (2018). *Global Human Capital Trends Report 2018.*

27. SHRM Foundation. (2015). *What's next? Use of workforce analytics for competitive advantage.* https://www.shrm.org/about/foundation/ShapingtheFuture/Documents/EIU%20Theme%203%20Analytics%20Report-FINAL.pdf

28. Mercer. (2021). *The gig economy is booming as Americans search for non-traditional employment.* https://www.mercer.com/newsroom/the-gig-economy-is-booming-as-americans-search-for-non-traditional-employment-it-is-time-to-give-them-benefits.html; U.S. Bureau of Labor Statistics. (2016). *Employment situation summary Table A. Household data, seasonally adjusted.* http://www.bls.gov/news.release/empsit.a.htm

29. Torpey, E., & Hogan, A. (2016). *Working in a gig economy.* U.S. Department of Labor, Bureau of Labor Statistics. http://www.bls.gov/careeroutlook/2016/article/what-is-the-gig-economy.htm

30. Ethics & Compliance Initiative. (2018). *Business ethics and compliance timeline.* https://www.ethics.org/eci/research/free-toolkit/ethics-timeline

31. AACSB. (2022). *About us.* https://www.aacsb.edu/about-us

32. Hunter, S. T., Bedell, K. E., & Mumford, M. D. (2007). Climate for creativity: A quantitative review. *Creativity Research Journal, 19,* 69–90; Mayer, D. M., Kuenzi, M., & Greenbaum, R. L. (2010). Examining the link between ethical leadership and employee misconduct: The mediating role of ethical climate. *Journal of Business Ethics, 95,* 7–16; Zohar, D., & Luria, G. (2005). A multilevel model of safety climate: Cross-level relationships between organization and group-level climates. *Journal of Applied Psychology, 90,* 616–628.

33. Society for Human Resource Management. (2022). *About SHRM.* https://www.shrm.org/about-shrm

34. Glassdoor.com. (2022). *50 best jobs in America for 2022.* https://www.glassdoor.com/List/Best-Jobs-in-America-LST_KQ0,20.htm

35. Westfall, B. (2017). *Study: What employers are looking for in HR positions.* http://new-talent-times.softwareadvice.com/what-employers-look-for-hr-jobs-0514/

36. Campion, M. A., Fink, A. A., Ruggeberg, B. J., Carr, L., Phillips, G. M., & Odman, R. B. (2011). Doing competencies well: Best practices in competency modeling. *Personnel Psychology, 64,* 225–262; Shippman, J. S., Ash, R. A., Battista, M., Carr, L., Eyde, L. D., Hesketh, B., Kehoe, J., Pearlman, K., Prien, E. P., & Sanchez, J. I. (2000). The practice of competency modeling. *Personnel Psychology, 53,* 703–740; SHRM. (2022). *The SHRM competency model.* https://www.shrm.org/LearningAndCareer/competency-model/PublishingImages/pages/default/SHRM%20Competency%20Model_Detailed%20Report_Final_SECURED.pdf

37. Academy of Management. (2018). https://aom.org/; Society for Industrial-Organizational Psychology. (2018). *What is I-O?* www.siop.org

38. U.S. Equal Employment Opportunity Commission. (2022). *Charge statistics FYI 1997-2021.* https://www.eeoc.gov/data/charge-statistics-charges-filed-eeoc-fy-1997-through-fy-2021

CHAPTER 2

1. DeepHow. (n.d.). *Solution.* https://www.deephow.com/#solution; Fast Company. (2021). *100 Best workplaces for innovators.* https://www.fastcompany.com/90659148/best-workplaces-innovators-2021-not-for-profit; Fretty, P. (2020, December 10). *Stanley Black & Decker realizes AI is a powerful tool.* https://www.industryweek.com/technology-and-iiot/article/21150020/stanley-black-decker-realizes-ai-is-a-powerful-tool; HRTech News Desk. (2020, July 20). *Stanley Black & Decker partners with DeepHow to deploy AI-powered technology.* https://techrseries.com/artificial-intelligence/stanley-black-decker-partners-with-deephow-to-deploy-ai-powered-technology/; Meister, J. (2019, January 8). Ten HR trends in the age of artificial intelligence. *Forbes.* https://www.forbes.com/sites/jeannemeister/2019/01/08/ten-hr-trends-in-the-age-of-artificial-intelligence/?sh=fc38c763219d; Newcomb, A. (2021, November 8). Why Stanley Black & Decker's CEO initially had the chief A.I. officer report to human resources. *Fortune.* https://fortune.com/2021/11/08/stanley-black-decker-ceo-artificial-intelligence/; Stanley Black & Decker. (2021, August 4). *Stanley Black & Decker named to Fast Company's Best Workplaces for Innovators list for second year.* https://www.prnewswire.com/news-releases/s

tanley-black--decker-named-to-fas t-companys-best-workplaces-for-in novators-list-for-second-year-3013 48768.html

2. SAS Institute Inc. (n.d.). *Jim Goodnight, co-founder & CEO*. http://www.s as.com/en_us/company-information /leadership/jim-goodnight.html

3. Merriam-Webster. (n.d.). Strategy. In *Merriam-Webster online dictionary*. htt p://www.merriam-webster.com/dicti onary/strategy

4. Hambrick, D. C., & Fredrickson, J. W. (2001). Are you sure you have a strategy? *Academy of Management Executive, 15*, 48–59.

5. Fast Company. (2022). *The world's most innovative companies*. https://w ww.fastcompany.com/most-innova tive-companies/2022; Needham, K. (2022, February 23). *Musk's Starlink connects remote Tonga villages still cut off after tsunami*. Reuters. https://ww w.reuters.com/world/asia-pacific/m usks-starlink-connects-remote-ton ga-villages-still-cut-off-after-tsuna mi-2022-02-23/; SpaceX. (n.d.). *Mission*. https://www.spacex.com/miss ion/; SpaceX. (n.d.). *Starship*. https:// www.spacex.com/vehicles/starship/ ; Wall, M. (2022, February 25). *SpaceX launches 50 Starlink satellites, lands rocket on ship at sea*. https://www.spa ce.com/spacex-50-starlink-satellite s-launch-february-2022

6. Bender, B. (2022, February 12). Why Musk's biggest space gamble is freaking out his competitors. *Politico*. https://www.politico.com/news/20 22/02/12/elon-musk-space-freakin g-out-competitors-00008441; Mejia, Z. (2018, June 11). *Elon Musk wants employees with these 4 traits, according to a top HR exec at SpaceX*. CNBC. https://www.cnbc.com/2018/06/0 8/top-hr-exec-at-spacex-what-elo n-musk-looks-for-in-employees.h tml; Moore, E. (2017, December 14). *Inside SpaceX: What it's like working for a company on a mission to Mars*. Glassdoor. https://www.glassdoor.com/bl og/spacex-best-places-to-work/

7. Creswell, J. (2021, October 15). Plant-based food companies face critics: Environmental advocates. *The New York Times*. https://www.nytimes. com/2021/10/15/business/beyon d-meat-impossible-emissions.htm l; Impossible. (n.d.). *Welcome to the future of sustainable food*. https://imp ossiblefoods.com/sustainable-food ; Piper, K. (2019, October 7). Meatless

meat is becoming mainstream—and it's sparking a backlash. *Vox*. https:/ /www.vox.com/future-perfect/2019 /10/7/20880318/meatless-meat-m ainstream-backlash-impossible-b urger; Tepper, T. (2022, February 2). Impossible Foods IPO: What you need to know. *Forbes*. https://www.forbes .com/advisor/investing/impossible-f oods-ipo/

8. Learned, E. P., Christensen, C. R., Andrews, K. R., & Guth, W. D. (1969). *Business policy: Text and cases*. R. D. Irwin.

9. Dvorsky, G. (2023, March 27). *Is Rocket Lab the SpaceX competitor we've been waiting for?* Gizmodo. https ://gizmodo.com/rocket-lab-spacex-c ompetition-neutron-falcon-9-185026 8942

10. Barney, J. B. (1991). Firm resources and sustained competitive advantage. *Journal of Management, 17*, 99–120; Barney, J. B., Ketchen, D. J., Jr., & Wright, M. (2021). Resource-based theory and the value creation framework. *Journal of Management, 47*, 193–1955.

11. Porter, M. E. (1980). *Competitive strategy: Techniques for analyzing industries and competitors*. Free Press.

12. Fast Company. (2022). *The world's most innovative companies*. https://w ww.fastcompany.com/most-innovati ve-companies/2022; Ovide, S. (2021, February 18). Who wins the (online) corner store? *The New York Times*. htt ps://www.nytimes.com/2021/02/18/ technology/who-wins-the-online-co rner-store.html; Shopify. (2023, February 15). *Shopify announces fourth-quarter and full-year 2022 financial results*. https://news.shopify.com/sh opify-announces-fourth-quarter-an d-full-year-2022-financial-results

13. Eisenhardt, K. M. (1989). Agency theory: An assessment and review. *Academy of Management Review, 14*, 57–74; Guth, W. D., & MacMillan, I. C. (1986). Strategy implementation versus middle management self-interest. *Strategic Management Journal, 7*, 313–327.

14. When CEOs talk strategy, is anyone listening? (2013, June). *Harvard Business Review*. https://hbr.org/2013/0 6/when-ceos-talk-strategy-is-anyo ne-listening; Wright, P. M., Smart, D. L., & McMahan, G. C. (1995). Matches between human resources and strategy among NCAA basketball teams.

Academy of Management Journal, 38, 1052–1074.

15. Schuler, R. S., & Jackson, S. E. (1987). Linking competitive strategies with human resource management practices. *Academy of Management Executive* (1987–1989), 207–219.

16. Legge, K. (1995). What is human resource management? In *Human resource management: Management, work and organisations*. Palgrave.

17. Huselid, M. A., Becker, B. E., & Beatty, R. W. (2005). *The workforce scorecard: Managing human capital to execute strategy*. Harvard Business Review Press; Kaplan, R. S., & Norton, D. P. (1996). Using the balanced scorecard as a strategic management system. *Harvard Business Review*, 75–85.

18. Marler, J. H. (2012). Strategic human resource management in context: A historical and global perspective. *Academy of Management Perspectives, 26*, 6–11.

19. Huselid, M. A. (1995). The impact of human resource management practices on turnover, productivity, and corporate financial performance. *Academy of Management Journal, 38*, 635–672; Pfeffer, J. (1998). Seven practices of successful organizations. *California Management Review, 40*, 96–124.

20. Pfeffer, J. (1998). Seven practices of successful organizations. *California Management Review, 40*, 96–124.

21. Huselid, M. A. (1995). The impact of human resource management practices on turnover, productivity, and corporate financial performance. *Academy of Management Journal, 38*, 635–672.

22. Tzabbar, D., Tzafrir, S., & Baruch, Y. (2016). A bridge over troubled water: Replication, integration and extension of the relationship between HRM practices and organizational performance using moderating meta-analysis. *Human Resource Management Review, 27*, 134–148.

23. Boxall, P., & Huo, M. L. (2019). The theory of high-performance work systems. In K. Townsend, K. Cafferkey, A. M. McDermott, & T. Dundon (Eds.), *Elgar introduction to theories of human resources and employment relations* (pp. 97–111). Edward Elgar.

24. Huselid, M. A. (1995). The impact of human resource management

practices on turnover, productivity, and corporate financial performance. *Academy of Management Journal, 38,* 635–672.

25. Saridakis, G., Lai, Y., & Cooper, C. L. (2017). Exploring the relationship between HRM and firm performance: A meta-analysis of longitudinal studies. *Human Resource Management Review, 27*(1), 87–96.

26. Lepak, D. P., Liao, H., Chung, Y., & Harden, E. E. (2006). A conceptual review of human resource management systems in strategic human resource management research. *Research in Personnel and Human Resources Management, 25,* 217–271.

27. Milliman, J., Von Glinow, M. A., & Nathan, M. (1991). Organizational life cycles and strategic international human resource management in multinational companies: Implications for congruence theory. *Academy of Management Review, 16,* 318–339; Schuler, R. S., Dowling, P. J., & De Cieri, H. (1993). An integrative framework of strategic international human resource management. *Journal of Management, 19,* 419–459; Su, Z. X., Wright, P. M., & Ulrich, M. D. (2018). Going beyond the SHRM paradigm: Examining four approaches to governing employees. *Journal of Management, 44,* 1598–1619; Taylor, S., Beechler, S., & Napier, N. (1996). Toward an integrative model of strategic international human resource management. *Academy of Management Review, 21,* 959–985.

28. Ball, P. (2020, December 18). The lightning-fast quest for COVID vaccines—and what it means for other diseases. *Nature.* https://www.nature.com/articles/d41586-020-03626-1.

29. Pedersen, A. Y., & Caviglia, F. (2019). Data literacy as a compound competence. In T. Antipova & A. Rocha (Eds.), *Digital science* (Vol. 850, pp. 166–173). Springer International.

30. Collins, L., Fineman, D. R., & Tsuchida, A. (2017, February 28). *People analytics: Recalculating the route.* Deloitte. https://www2.deloitte.com/insights/us/en/focus/human-capital-trends/2017/people-analytics-in-hr.html#endnote-sup-16; Lewis, G. (2017, March 30). *3 ways data shapes the talent strategy at Tesla, Chevron, and LinkedIn.* LinkedIn. https://business.linkedin.com/talent-solutions/blog/talent-analytics/2017/3-ways-data-shapes-the-talent-strategy-at-te

sla-chevron-and-linkedin; McKeon, A. (2017). *How some companies reap rewards of people analytics tools.* TechTarget. http://searchhrsoftware.techtarget.com/feature/How-some-companies-reap-rewards-of-people-analytics-tools; Thibodeau, P. (2018, February 14). *HR is failing to use people analytics tools, new report says.* TechTarget. http://searchhrsoftware.techtarget.com/news/252435104/HR-is-failing-to-use-people-analytics-tools-new-report-says

31. Lohr, S. (2021, December 8). Group backed by top companies moves to combat AI bias in hiring. *The New York Times.* https://www.nytimes.com/2021/12/08/technology/data-trust-alliance-ai-hiring-bias.html

32. Andersen, M. K. (2017). Human capital analytics: The winding road. *Journal of Organizational Effectiveness: People and Performance, 4*(2), 133–136; Rasmussen, T., & Ulrich, D. (2015). Learning from practice: How HR analytics avoids being a management fad. *Organizational Dynamics, 44,* 236–242.

33. McCartney, S., & Fu, N. (2022). Bridging the gap: Why, how and when HR analytics can impact organizational performance. *Management Decision.* Samson, K., & Bhanugopan, R. (2022). Strategic human capital analytics and organisation performance: The mediating effects of managerial decision-making. *Journal of Business Research, 144,* 637–649.

34. Burrell, J. (2016). How the machine 'thinks': Understanding opacity in machine learning algorithms. *Big Data & Society, 3*(1), 1–12.

35. Anderson, D., Bjarnadottir, M. V., & Ross, D. G. (2022, January 27). Using people analytics to build an equitable workforce. *Harvard Business Review*; Burrell, J. (2016). How the machine "thinks": Understanding opacity in machine learning algorithms. *Big Data & Society, 3*(1), 2053951715622512; Charlwood, A., & Guenole, N. (2022). Can HR adapt to the paradoxes of artificial intelligence? *Human Resource Management Journal*; Deloitte. (2021). *Deloitte 2021 global human capital trends report.* https://www2.deloitte.com/ua/en/pages/about-deloitte/press-releases/gx-2021-global-human-capital-trends-report.html; Landers, R. N., & Behrend, T. S. (2022). Auditing the AI auditors: A framework for evaluating fairness and bias in high stakes

AI predictive models. *American Psychologist*; Lohr, S. (2021, December 8). Group backed by top companies moves to combat AI bias in hiring. *The New York Times.* https://www.nytimes.com/2021/12/08/technology/data-trust-alliance-ai-hiring-bias.html; PwC. (2017). *Workforce of the future: The views of 10,000 workers*; PwC. (2018). *Workforce of the future: The competing forces shaping 2030*; PwC. (2022). *PwC HR tech survey 2022.* https://www.pwc.com/us/en/tech-effect/cloud/hr-tech-survey.html; Society for Industrial & Organizational Psychology. (2022, January 29). *SIOP statement on the use of artificial intelligence (AI) for hiring*; Tippins, N. T., Oswald, F. L., & McPhail, S. M. (2021). Scientific, legal, and ethical concerns about AI-based personnel selection tools: A call to action. *Personnel Assessment and Decisions, 7*(2), 1; Zielinski, D. (2020, May 22). *Addressing artificial intelligence-based hiring concerns.* https://www.shrm.org/hr-today/news/hr-magazine/summer2020/pages/artificial-intelligence-based-hiring-concerns.aspx

36. van der Togt, J., & Rasmussen, T. H. (2017). Toward evidence-based HR. *Journal of Organizational Effectiveness: People and Performance, 4*(2), 127–132.

37. SHRM Foundation. (2016, May). *Use of workforce analytics for competitive advantage.* https://www.shrm.org/about/foundation/shapingthefuture/documents/eiu%20theme%203%20analytics%20report-final.pdf

38. SHRM Foundation. (2019). *The global skills shortage: Bridging the talent gap with education, training and sourcing.* https://www.shrm.org/hr-today/trends-and-forecasting/research-and-surveys/documents/shrm%20skills%20gap%202019.pdf

39. Deloitte. (2018). *Global human capital trends report 2018.* Deloitte University Press.

40. Davenport, T. (n.d.). In praise of "light quants" and "analytical translators." Deloitte. https://www2.deloitte.com/us/en/pages/deloitte-analytics/articles/in-praise-of-light-quants-and-analytical-translators.html

41. Prabhakar, K., Brodzik, C., Gest, D. M., & Nodi, N. (2022, January 13). *Build trust in diversity, equity, and inclusion commitments.* Deloitte Insights. https://www2.deloitte.com/uk/en/insights/topics/talent/buildi

ng-employee-trust-dei-programs.
html

42. SHRM Foundation. (2016, May). *Use of workforce analytics for competitive advantage.* https://www.shrm.org/about/foundation/shapingthefuture/documents/eiu%20theme%203%20analytics%20report-final.pdf

43. Allen, D. G., Bryant, P. C., & Vardaman, J. M. (2010). Retaining talent: Replacing misconceptions with evidence-based strategies. *Academy of Management Perspectives, 24,* 48–64.

44. Rubenstein, A. L., Eberly, M. B., Lee, T. W., & Mitchell, T. R. (2018). Surveying the forest: A meta-analysis, moderator investigation, and future-oriented discussion of the antecedents of voluntary employee turnover. *Personnel Psychology, 71*(1), 23–65.

45. Lee, T. W., & Mitchell, T. R. (1994). An alternative approach: The unfolding model of voluntary employee turnover. *Academy of Management Review, 19*(1), 51–89.

46. IBM Big Data & Analytics Hub. (n.d.). *The four V's of big data.* http://www.ibmbigdatahub.com/infographic/four-vs-big-data

47. Wilhelmy, A., & Köhler, T. (2021). Qualitative research in work and organizational psychology journals: Practices and future opportunities. *European Journal of Work and Organizational Psychology, 31*(2), 161–185.

48. Landers, R. N., & Behrend, T. S. (2022). Auditing the AI auditors: A framework for evaluating fairness and bias in high stakes AI predictive models. *American Psychologist.*

49. Dastin, J. (2018, October 9). *Amazon scraps secret AI recruiting tool that showed bias against women.* Reuters. https://www.reuters.com/article/uk-amazon-com-jobs-automation-insight/amazon-scraps-secret-ai-recruiting-tool-that-showed-bias-against-women-idUKKCN1MK08K?edition-redirect=uk; EEOC. (2021, October 28). EEOC launches initiative on artificial intelligence and algorithmic fairness. https://www.eeoc.gov/newsroom/eeoc-launches-initiative-artificial-intelligence-and-algorithmic-fairness; Lander, E., & Nelson, A. (2021, October 22). ICYMI: WIRED (Opinion): *Americans need a bill of rights for an AI-powered world.* White House Office of Science & Technology Policy. https://www.whitehouse.gov/ostp/news-updates/2021/10/22/icymi-wire d-opinion-americans-need-a-bill-of-rights-for-an-ai-powered-world/; Mauer, R. (2021, April 7). *Use of AI in the workplace raises legal concerns.* SHRM. https://www.shrm.org/resourcesandtools/hr-topics/technology/pages/use-of-ai-in-the-workplace-raises-legal-concerns.aspx; Meyer, D. (2018, October 10). Amazon reportedly killed an AI recruitment system because it couldn't stop the tool from discriminating against women. *Fortune.* https://fortune.com/2018/10/10/amazon-ai-recruitment-bias-women-sexist/; Mulvaney, E. (2021, December 29). Artificial intelligence hiring bias spurs scrutiny and new regs. *Bloomberg Law Daily Labor Report.* https://news.bloomberglaw.com/daily-labor-report/artificial-intelligence-hiring-bias-spurs-scrutiny-and-new-regs; Tambe, P., Capelli, P., & Yakubovich, V. (2019). Artificial intelligence in human resources management: Challenges and a path forward. *California Management Review, 61*(4), 15–42.

50. O'Neil, C. (2016). *Weapons of math destruction: How Big Data increases inequality and threatens democracy.* Crown.

51. Caughlin, D. E., & Bauer, T. N. (2019). Data visualizations and human resource management: The state of science and practice. In M. R. Buckley, A. R. Wheeler, J. E. Baur, & J. R. B. Halbesleben (Eds.), *Research in personnel and human resources management* (Vol. 37, pp. 89–131). Emerald Publishing.

52. Knaflic, C. N. (2015). *Storytelling with data: A data visualization guide for business professionals.* Wiley.

53. Denning, S. (2006). Effective storytelling: Strategic business narrative techniques. *Strategy & Leadership, 34*(1), 42–48.

54. Potts, R., & LaMarsh, J. (2004). *Managing change for success: Effecting change for optimum growth and maximum efficiency.* Duncan Baird.

55. Cohen, P. (2015, April 13). One company's new minimum wage: $70,000 a year. *The New York Times.* http://www.nytimes.com/2015/04/14/business/owner-of-gravity-payments-a-credit-card-processor-is-setting-a-new-minimum-wage-70000-a-year.html; Cohen, P. (2015, July 31). A company copes with backlash against the raise that roared. *The New York Times.* http://www.nytimes.com/2015/08/02/business/a-company-copes-with-backlash-against-the-raise-that-roared.html?smid=fb-nytimes&smtyp=cur&_r=1

56. CBS News. (2021, September 15). *CEO on why giving all employees minimum salary of $70,000 still "works" six years later: "Our turnover rate was cut in half."* https://www.cbsnews.com/news/dan-price-gravity-payments-ceo-70000-employee-minimum-wage/

CHAPTER 3

1. BusinessWire. (2021). *JetBlue named no. 1 domestic airline in the* Travel + Leisure *World's Best Awards 2021.* https://www.businesswire.com/news/home/20210908005885/en/JetBlue-Named-No.-1-Domestic-Airline-in-the-Travel-Leisure-Worlds-Best-Awards-2021; dbt Labs. (2022). *How JetBlue is eliminating the data engineering bottlenecks.* https://www.getdbt.com/success-stories/jetblue/; Hall, B. (2014). Learning analytics at JetBlue. *Chief Learning Officer.* https://www.chieflearningofficer.com/2014/11/03/learning-analytics-at-jetblue/; JetBlue. (2022). *About JetBlue Airways.* http://investor.jetblue.com/media-room/about-jetblue-airways; Solomon, M. (2019). How JetBlue topped its industry in customer service through company culture and a new breed of technology. *Forbes.* https://www.forbes.com/sites/micahsolomon/2019/08/26/jetblues-top-rated-customer-service-experience-blending-internal-customer-service-culture-and-new-technology/?sh=63f4fc672ddc/

2. Tannenbaum, S. I. (1990). Human resource information systems: User group implications. *Journal of Systems Management, 41,* 27–32.

3. Ruël, H., Bondarouk, T., & Looise, J. K. (2004). E-HRM: Innovation or irritation. An explorative empirical study in five large companies on web-based HRM. *Management Review, 15*(3), 364–380.

4. Kavanaugh, M. J., & Johnson, R. D. (2017). *Human resource information systems: Basics, applications, and future directions* (4th ed.). SAGE.

5. Quaosar, G. M. A. A., & Rahman, M. S. (2021). Human resource information systems (HRIS) of developing countries in 21st century: Review and prospects. *Journal of Human Resource and Sustainability Studies, 9,* 470–483.

6. Kavanaugh, M. J., Thite, M., & Johnson, R. D. (2015). *Human resource information systems: Basics, applications, and future directions* (p. 6, emphasis in original). SAGE.

7. Carlson, K. D., & Kavanaugh, M. J. (2015). HRIS in Action from HR metrics and workforce analytics chapter. Reprinted with permission from M. J. Kavanaugh, M. Thite, & R. D. Johnson (2015). *Human resource information systems: Basics, applications, and future directions*. SAGE; re:Work Editors. (2018). *Six HR metrics anyone can start tracking*. https://rework.withgoogle.com/blog/namely-hr-metrics-guide/

8. Iqbal, S., Hongyun, T., Akhtar, S., Ahman, U., & Ankomah, F. N. (2020). Impacts of supervisor support on turnover intentions: Mediating role of job satisfaction. *Asian Journal of Education and Social Studies, 6,* 1–9; Maier, C., Laumer, S., Eckhardt, A., & Weitzel, T. (2013). Analyzing the impact of HRIS implementations on HR personnel's job satisfaction and turnover intention. *Journal of Strategic Information Systems, 22,* 193–207.

9. Data Spotlight. (2022). *Data's role in driving employee success at a COVID test maker.* https://www.spotlightdata.co/datas-role-in-driving-employee-success-at-a-covid-test-maker/

10. Marler, J. H., & Floyd, B. D. (2015). Database concepts and applications in HRIS. In M. J. Kavanagh, M. Thite, & R. D. Johnson (Eds.), *Human resource information systems: Basics, applications, and future directions* (3rd ed.). SAGE.

11. SHRM. (2022). *Designing and managing a human resource information system.* https://www.shrm.org/resourcesandtools/tools-and-samples/toolkits/pages/managingahumanresourceinformationsystem.aspx

12. Kavanagh, M. J., & Carlson, K. D. (2018). *Human resource information systems: Basics, applications, and future directions* (p. 389). SAGE.

13. Cleveland, W. S., Diaconis, P., & McGill, R. (1982). Variables on scatterplots look more highly correlated when the scales are increased. *Science, 216,* 1138–1141.

14. Knaflic, C. N. (2022). *Storytelling with you: Plan, create, and deliver a stellar presentation.* Wiley.

15. Knaflic, C. N. (2015). *Storytelling with data: A data visualization guide for business professionals.* Wiley.

16. Vorhauser-Smith, S. (2014). The little word behind Big Data in HR. *Forbes.* https://www.forbes.com/sites/sylviavorhausersmith/2014/11/10/the-little-word-behind-big-data-in-hr-who/2/#590371fd4bd0

17. Quaosar, G. M. A. A., & Rhaman, M. S. (2022). Human resource information systems (HRIS) of developing countries in 21st century: Review and prospects. *Journal of Human Resource and Sustainability Studies, 9,* 470–483; Beadles, N., Lowery, C., & Johns, K. (2005). The impact of human resource information systems: An exploratory study in the public sector. *Communications of the IIMA, 5,* 39–46; Hussain, Z., Wallace, J., & Cornelius, N. E. (2007). The use and impact of human resource information systems on human resource management professionals. *Information & Management, 44,* 74–89.

18. Bidwell, L., Sendra, C., Bauer, T., & Truxillo, D. (2023). *Exploring the impact of intelligent technology on employee experience.* SAP/SuccessFactors White Paper Series.

19. Quaosar, G. M. A. A., & Rhaman, M. S. (2022). Human resource information systems (HRIS) of developing countries in 21st century: Review and prospects. *Journal of Human Resource and Sustainability Studies, 9,* 470–483; Teo, T. S. H., Lim, G. S., & Fedric, S. A. (2007). The adoption and diffusion of human resources information systems in Singapore. *Asia Pacific Journal of Human Resources, 45,* 44–62.

20. Bauer, T. N., Truxillo, D. M., Jones, M. P., & Brady, G. (2020). Privacy and cybersecurity challenges, opportunities, and recommendations: Personnel selection in an era of online application systems and big data. In S. E. Woo, R. Proctor, & L. Tay (Eds.), *Big data in psychological research* (pp. 393–409). American Psychological Association.

21. Lukaszewski, K. M., Stone, D. L., & Stone-Romero, E. F. (2008). The effects of the ability to choose the type of human resources system on perceptions of invasion of privacy and system satisfaction. *Journal of Business & Psychology, 23,* 73–86.

22. SHRM. (2016). *SHRM survey findings: Using social media for talent acquisition: Recruitment and screening.* https://www.shrm.org/hr-today/trends-and-forecasting/research-and-surveys/Documents/SHRM-Social-Media-Recruiting-Screening-2015.pdf

23. CareerArc. (2022). *2021 Future of Recruiting Study.* https://social.careerarc.com/2021-future-of-recruiting-study/

24. Rao, P. S., Frenkel, S., & Schreuer, M. (2018). Mark Zuckerberg to meet European Parliament members over Facebook's data use. *The New York Times.* https://www.nytimes.com/2018/05/16/technology/zuckerberg-europe-data-cambridge-analytica.html; Snell, J., & Care, D. (2013). *Use of online data in the Big Data era: Legal issues raised by the use of web crawling and scraping tools for analytics purposes.* Bloomberg Law. https://www.bna.com/legal-issues-raised-by-the-use-of-web-crawling-and-scraping-tools-for-analytics-purposes/

25. American Management Association. (2019). *The latest on workplace monitoring and surveillance.* https://www.amanet.org/articles/the-latest-on-workplace-monitoring-and-surveillance/; Raivd, D. N., White, J. C., Tomczak, D. L., Miles, A. F., & Behrend, T. S. (2023). A meta-analysis of the effects of electronic performance monitoring on work outcomes. *Personnel Psychology, 76*(1), 5–40. https://doi.org/10.1111/peps.12514; Virgin Pulse. (n.d.). *Personalized wellbeing.* https://www.virginpulse.com/our-products/; EEOC. (1997). *Enforcement guidance on the ADA and psychiatric disabilities.* https://www.eeoc.gov/policy/docs/psych.html

26. SHRM. (2022). *Record-keeping policy: Safeguarding Social Security numbers.* https://www.shrm.org/ResourcesAndTools/tools-and-samples/policies/Pages/cms_015266.aspx

27. Stallings, W., & Brown, L. (2018). *Computer security: Principles and practice* (4th ed.). Pearson.

28. Mathews, L. (2016). Mark Zuckerberg hacked for the third time this year. *Forbes.* https://www.forbes.com/sites/leemathews/2016/11/16/mark-zuckerberg-hacked-for-the-third-time-this-year/?sh=610e285bbd9a

29. Ibid.

30. Brown, G., & Smit, N. (2017). *Will blockchain disrupt the HR technology landscape?* Deloitte. https://www2.deloitte.com/nl/nl/pages/human-capit

al/articles/will-blockchain-disrupt-t he-hr-technology-landscape.html

31. Fowler, B. (2022). *Data breaches break record in 2021*. CNET. https://www.cn et.com/news/privacy/record-numbe r-of-data-breaches-reported-in-202 1-new-report-says/

32. Maurer, R. (2015). *Human error cited as top cause of data breaches*. SHRM. h ttps://www.shrm.org/ResourcesAn dTools/hr-topics/risk-management /Pages/Human-Error-Top-Cause-D ata-Breaches.aspx; Rayome, A. D. (2017). Negligent employees are no. 1 cause of cybersecurity breaches at SMBs. *TechRepublic*. https://www.tec hrepublic.com/article/report-neglig ent-employees-are-no-1-cause-of-c ybersecurity-breaches-at-smbs/; Ponemon Institute. (2017). *2017 state of cybersecurity in small & medium-sized businesses*. https://www.keeper security.com/assets/pdf/Keeper-201 7-Ponemon-Report.pdf

33. Fontana, J. (2016). *Tough new privacy laws in EU could signal global changes*. ZDNet. http://www.zdnet.com/articl e/tough-new-privacy-laws-in-eu-co uld-signal-global-changes/

34. PwC. (2017). *Pulse survey: US companies ramping up General Data Protection Regulation (GDPR) budgets*. https: //www.pwc.com/us/en/increasing-i t-effectiveness/publications/assets/ pwc-gdpr-series-pulse-survey.pdf

35. SHRM. (2021). *How to select an HRIS*. h ttps://www.shrm.org/resourcesand tools/tools-and-samples/how-to-gu ides/pages/howtoselectanhrissyste m.aspx

36. Valcik, N. A., Sabharwal, M., Bena-vides, T. J. (2021). The theory of how HRIS should work. In *Human resources information systems: Management for professionals* (pp. 99–113). Springer. https://doi.org/10 .1007/978-3-030-75111-1_7; Wilson-Evered, E., & Hartel, C. E. J. (2009). Measuring attitudes to HRIS implementation: A field study to inform implementation methodology. *Asia Pacific Journal of Human Resources, 47*, 374–384.

37. Kavanaugh, M. J., & Johnson, R. D. (2018). *Human resource information systems* (4th ed.). SAGE.

38. SHRM. (2021). *How to select an HRIS*. h ttps://www.shrm.org/resourcesand tools/tools-and-samples/how-to-gu ides/pages/howtoselectanhrissyste m.aspx

39. Dery, K., Hall, R., Wailes, N., & Wiblen, S. (2013). Lost in translation? An actor-network approach to HRIS implementation. *Journal of Strategic Information Systems, 22*, 225–237.

40. Sung, W., Woehler, M. L., Fagan, J. M., Grosser, T. J., Floyd, T. M., & Labiance, G. (2017). Employees' responses to an organizational merger: Intraindividual change in organizational identification, attachment, and turnover. *Journal of Applied Psychology, 102*, 910–934.

41. Change management: The HR strategic imperative as a business partner. (2007, December). *HR Magazine, 52*; SHRM. (2017). *Managing organizational change*. https://www.shrm.org/ resourcesandtools/tools-and-sampl es/toolkits/pages/managingorganiza tionalchange.aspx

42. Oreg, S., & Sverdlik, N. (2011). Ambivalence toward imposed change: The conflict between dispositional resistance to change and the orientation toward the change agent. *Journal of Applied Psychology, 96*, 337–349; Reinhardt, R., Hietschold, N., & Gurt-ner, S. (2019). Overcoming consumer resistance to innovations: An analysis of adoption triggers. *R&D Management, 49*, 139–154.

43. Baumann, B. (2022). *Lessons learned from the Avon ERP implementation failure*. Panorama Consulting Group. https://www.panorama-consulting.c om/avon-erp-implementation-failur e/; Kepes, B. (2013). Avon's failed SAP implementation a perfect example of the enterprise IT revolution. *Forbes*. h ttps://www.forbes.com/sites/benkep es/2013/12/17/avons-failed-sap-imp lementation-a-perfect-example-of-e nterprise-it-revolution/#6cb5dc4e31 a6

44. Bartlett, J. E., & Bartlett, M. E. (2022). *Introduction to human resource information systems*. SHRM. https://www. shrm.org/certification/educators/D ocuments/Bartlett%20HRIS%20PPT to%20Post%20Online.pptx; McGoon, C. (1995, March). Secrets of building influence. *Communication World, 12*(3), 16; Michelman, P. (2007, July). Overcoming resistance to change. *Harvard Management Update, 12*(7), 3–4; Stanley, T. L. (2002, January). Change: A common-sense approach. *Supervision, 63*(1), 7–10.

45. Dery, K., Hall, R., Wailes, N., & Wiblen, S. (2013). Lost in translation? An actor-network approach to HRIS implementation. *Journal of Strategic Information Systems, 22*, 225–237.

46. Bidwell, L., Sendra, C., Bauer, T., & Truxillo, D. (2023). *Exploring the impact of intelligent technology on employee experience*. SAP/Success-Factors White Paper Series.

47. Gargeya, V. B., & Brady, C. (2006). Success and failure factors of adopting SAP in ERP system implementation. *Business Process Management Journal, 11*, 501–516.

48. Kavanaugh, M. J., & Johnson, R. D. (2018). *Human resource information systems* (4th ed.). SAGE.

49. Oreg, S., Berson, Y. (2019). Leaders' impact on organizational change: Bridging theoretical and methodological chasms. *Academy of Management Annals, 13*, 272–307.

50. Zhao, H. H., Seibert, S. E., Taylor, S. M., Lee, C., & Lam, W. (2016). Not even the past: The joint influence of former leader and new leader during leader succession in the midst of organizational change. *Journal of Applied Psychology, 101*, 1730–1738.

CHAPTER 4

1. Accenture. (2022, August). *Company overview*. https://www.greatplaceto work.com/certified-company/1000 886; Accenture (2023). *Inclusion and diversity in the United States*. https://w ww.accenture.com/us-en/about/incl usion-diversity/us-workforce; Birch, K. (2022, May 10). How Accenture is leading the charge on diversity, inclusion. *Business Chief*. https://busines schief.com/sustainability/how-acce nture-is-leading-the-charge-on-di versity-inclusion; Hodgett, M. (2022, March 28). A commitment to advancing diversity, equity, and inclusion. *Los Angeles Business Journal*. https:/ /labusinessjournal.com/business-jo urnal-events/a-commitment-to-adv ancing-diversity-equity-and-inclusi on/; Reiss, R. (2022, November 23). I asked the world's top CEOs if they're taking diversity seriously. Here's why their answers could change your life. *Fortune*. https://fortune.com/2022/11 /23/world-top-ceos-diversity-seriou sly-careers-workplace-leadership-r obert-reiss/; Shook, E. (2021, June 25). How to set— and meet—your company's diversity goals. *Harvard Business Review*. https://hbr.org/202

1/06/how-to-set-and-meet-your-co
mpanys-diversity-goals.

2. Roberson, Q. M. (2019). Diversity in
the workplace: A review, synthesis,
and future research agenda. *Annual
Review of Organizational Psychology
and Organizational Behavior, 6*, 69–88.

3. U.S. Bureau of Labor Statistics.
(2022). *Labor force statistics from the
Current Population Survey.* https://ww
w.bls.gov/cps/cpsaat11.htm

4. Brown, J. (2022, July 27). Marvin
Ellison, Chairman and CEO, Lowe's
Companies, Inc. Drawing from his
pathway to success, a guide to help
others achieve the same. *Savoy.* http
://savoynetwork.com/marvin-elliso
n-chairman-and-ceo-lowes-compan
ies-inc-drawing-from-his-pathway-t
o-success-a-guide-to-help-others-a
chieve-the-same/

5. Roberson, Q. M. (2019). Diversity in
the workplace: A review, synthesis,
and future research agenda. *Annual
Review of Organizational Psychology
and Organizational Behavior, 6*, 69–88.

6. Holmes, O., Jiang, K., Avery, D. R.,
McKay, P. F., Oh, I. S., & Tillman, C.
J. (2021). A meta-analysis integrating 25 years of diversity climate
research. *Journal of Management, 47*,
1357–1382.

7. Georgeac, O. A. M., & Rattan, A.
(2023). The business case for diversity backfires: Detrimental effects of
organizations' instrumental diversity
rhetoric for underrepresented group
members' sense of belonging. *Journal of Personality and Social Psychology, 124*(1), 69–108. https://doi.org/10.
1037/pspi0000394

8. van Dijk, H., van Engen, M. L., & van
Knippenberg, D. (2012). Defying
conventional wisdom: A meta-analytical examination of the differences
between demographic and job-
related diversity relationships with
performance. *Organizational Behavior
and Human Decision Processes, 119*,
38–53.

9. Lieu, T. (2022, October 4). Opinion:
Facial recognition has a race problem. Can federal law help? *Los Angeles Times.* https://www.govtech.com/
opinion/opinion-facial-recognition-h
as-a-race-problem-can-federal-la
w-help

10. Kozlov, M. (2023, February 16). FDA to
require diversity plan for clinical trials. *Nature.* https://www.nature.com
/articles/d41586-023-00469-4

11. Smulowitz, S., Becerra, M., & Mayo,
M. (2019). Racial diversity and its
asymmetry within and across hierarchical levels: The effects on financial
performance. *Human Relations, 72*,
1671–1696.

12. Athul, C. K. (2022, April 4). *The rise of
South Asian CEOs.* Startup Talky. http
s://startuptalky.com/south-asian-c
eo/; Giacomazzo, B. (2022, May 30).
The Fortune 500 list has a "record
number" of Black CEOs—But there's
still only 6 of them. https://afrotech.c
om/fortune-500-black-ceos; Green,
J. (2022, March 22). *"Sea of white":
Latino leaders fight to reshape U.S.
boardrooms.* Bloomberg. https://w
ww.bloomberg.com/news/articles/
2022-03-22/-sea-of-white-latino-l
eaders-fight-to-reshape-u-s-boar
drooms?leadSource=uverify%20w
all; Hinchliffe, E. (2023, January 12).
Women CEOs run more than 10% of
Fortune 500 companies for the first
time in history. *Fortune.* https://fortu
ne.com/2023/01/12/fortune-500-co
mpanies-ceos-women-10-percent/

13. Roth, P. L., Thatcher, J. B., Bobko,
P., Matthews, K. D., Ellingson, J. E.,
& Goldberg, C. B. (2020). Political
affiliation and employment screening
decisions: The role of similarity and
identification processes. *Journal of
Applied Psychology, 105*, 472–486.

14. Zaniboni, S., Kmicinska, M., Truxillo,
D. M., Kahn, K., Paladino, M. P., &
Fraccaroli, F. (2019). Will you still hire
me when I am over 50? The effects of
implicit and explicit age stereotyp-
ing on résumé evaluations. *European
Journal of Work and Organizational
Psychology, 28*(4), 453–467.

15. Anonymous. (2022, October/Novem-
ber). Inspiring inclusion in the beauty
industry. *Fortune, 186*(2), Article
00158259; Anonymous. (2021). *The
racial bias in retail study.* https://www
.sephora.com/contentimages/belon
g/january2021/Sephora_RacialBias
_eBook_DES_12-23-20_V12%20(1).p
df; Gino, F., & Coffman, K. (2021, September 27). *Unconscious bias training
that works.* Harvard Business School.
https://tpmgphysicianed.org/sites/d
efault/files/Sec%20III%20Unconscio
us%20Bias%20Training%20That%20
Works.pdf

16. Johnson, S. K., & Kirk, J. F. (2020,
March 5). Research: To reduce gender bias, anonymize job applications.
Harvard Business Review. https://hbr.
org/2020/03/research-to-reduce-ge
nder-bias-anonymize-job-applicat
ions

17. Torres, M. B., Salles, A., & Cochran,
A. (2019). Recognizing and reacting
to microaggressions in medicine and
surgery. *JAMA Surgery, 154*, 868–872.

18. Williams, M. T. (2020). Psychology
cannot afford to ignore the many
harms caused by microaggressions.
*Perspectives on Psychological Science,
15*(1), 38–43.

19. U.S. Department of Labor. (2023).
Equal employment opportunity. https:/
/www.dol.gov/general/topic/discrimi
nation

20. Deschenaux, J. (2022, February 7).
*Ministerial exception bars principals'
bias lawsuit.* SHRM. https://www.shr
m.org/resourcesandtools/legal-an
d-compliance/state-and-local-upda
tes/pages/calif-ministerial-exceptio
n-bars-bias-lawsuit.aspx#:~:text=T
he%20Black%20principal%20of%20
a,Circuit%20Court%20of%20Appeal
s%20ruled

21. EEOC. (2016). *Coverage.* https://www.
eeoc.gov/employers/coverage.cfm

22. EEOC. (2023). *Filing a lawsuit.* https://
www.eeoc.gov/employees/lawsuit.cf
m

23. EEOC. (2023). *Employees and job applicants.* https://www.eeoc.gov/employ
ees/index.cfm

24. Nagele-Piazza, L. (2022, November
28). *How to avoid a workplace retaliation claim.* SHRM. https://www.shrm.
org/hr-today/news/hr-magazine/win
ter2022/pages/how-to-avoid-a-work
place-retaliation-claim.aspx

25. U.S. Census Bureau. (2022, March
15). *Equal pay day: March 15, 2022.* http
s://www.census.gov/newsroom/stori
es/equal-pay-day.html

26. EEOC. (2022, November 30). *Jerry's
Chevrolet and Jerry's Motor Cars will
pay $62,500 to settle EEOC equal pay
and retaliation suit.* https://www.eeoc
.gov/newsroom/jerrys-chevrolet-an
d-jerrys-motor-cars-will-pay-6250
0-settle-eeoc-equal-pay-and

27. EEOC. (2023). *Facts about equal pay
and compensation discrimination.* http
s://www.eeoc.gov/eeoc/publications
/fs-epa.cfm

28. EEOC. (2023). *Remedies for employment discrimination.* https://www.eeo
c.gov/employees/remedies.cfm

29. Bachman, E. (2022, March 21).
$70 million verdict against Texas

company in employment discrimination case. *Forbes.* https://www.forbes.com/sites/ericbachman/2022/03/21/70-million-verdict-against-texas-company-in-employment-discrimination-case/?sh=7eeb16a82ea8

30. EEOC. (2002). *Title VII: BFOQ.* https://www.eeoc.gov/eeoc/foia/letters/2002/titlevii_bfoq.html; Shorter, T. N., McLaughlin, C. L., & O'Day, T. (2007). *Can we use gender in our hiring decisions? The discrimination bona fide occupational qualification (BFOQ) applied to health care.* Godfrey Kahn. http://www.gklaw.com/news.cfm?action=pub_detail&publication_id=544

31. EEOC. (2018, June 13). *CSX Transportation to pay $3.2 million to settle EEOC disparate impact sex discrimination case* [Press release]. https://www.eeoc.gov/newsroom/csx-transportation-pay-32-million-settle-eeoc-disparate-impact-sex-discrimination-case

32. EEOC. (2023). *Harassment.* https://www.eeoc.gov/laws/types/harassment.cfm

33. Gonzales, M. (2022, October 17). *Five years of #MeToo: Sexual harassment still common in workplaces.* SHRM. https://www.shrm.org/resourcesandtools/hr-topics/behavioral-competencies/global-and-cultural-effectiveness/pages/five-years-of-metoo-sexual-harassment-still-common-in-workplaces.aspx

34. Kundro, T. G., Burke, V., Grandey, A. A., & Sayre, G. M. (2022). A perfect storm: Customer sexual harassment as a joint function of financial dependence and emotional labor. *Journal of Applied Psychology, 107*(8), 1385–1396.

35. Roehling, M. V., Wu, D., Choi, M. G., & Dulebohn, J. H. (2022). The effects of sexual harassment training on proximal and transfer training outcomes: A meta-analytic investigation. *Personnel Psychology, 75,* 3–31.

36. Ong, F. W. (2022, May 11). The EEOC speaks: Pay discrimination—The EPA v. Title VII. *Labor & Employment Report.* https://www.laboremploymentreport.com/2022/05/11/the-eeoc-speaks-pay-discrimination-the-epa-v-title-vii/

37. Gonzalez, M. (2022, December 14). *The damaging effects of workplace racism.* SHRM. https://www.shrm.org/resourcesandtools/hr-topics/behavioral-competencies/global-and-cultural-effectiveness/pages/the-damaging-effects-of-workplace-racism.aspx

38. Martin, J. (2021, March 25). *Edward Jones to settle race discrimination suit for $34 million.* AdvisorHub. https://www.advisorhub.com/edward-jones-to-settle-race-discrimination-suit-for-34-million/

39. Gonzalez, M. (2023, February 7). *CROWN Act: Does your state prohibit hair discrimination?* SHRM. https://www.shrm.org/resourcesandtools/hr-topics/behavioral-competencies/global-and-cultural-effectiveness/pages/crown-act-does-your-state-prohibit-hair-discrimination.aspx

40. SHRM. (n.d.). *Must employers allow employees to take religious holidays off?* https://www.shrm.org/resourcesandtools/tools-and-samples/hr-qa/pages/religiousholidaysoff.aspx; U.S. Department of Justice. (2023, February 15). *Justice Department secures settlement in religious discrimination suit against Lansing, Michigan.* https://www.justice.gov/opa/pr/justice-department-secures-settlement-religious-discrimination-suit-against-lansing-michigan

41. Shepherd, L. (2023, January 23). *Balancing anti-discrimination policies with religious protections.* SHRM. https://www.shrm.org/resourcesandtools/legal-and-compliance/employment-law/pages/religious-dialog-anti-discrimination-policy.aspx

42. Bhatt, K., & Kuo, F. (2023, January 30). Breaking out of the prison cycle. *Scot Scoop News.* https://scotscoop.com/breaking-out-of-the-prison-cycle/; Romeo, P. (2022, November 3). In their search for labor, restaurants turn to ex-offenders. *Restaurant Business.* https://www.restaurantbusinessonline.com/operations/their-search-labor-restaurants-turn-ex-offenders

43. EEOC. (2023). *Pregnancy discrimination.* https://www.eeoc.gov/eeoc/publications/fs-preg.cfm

44. Dunlap, N. B. (2015, November). Supreme Court "delivers" new life to pregnancy discrimination claims in *Young v. United Parcel Service, Inc. Florida Bar Journal,* 59–63.

45. Byrd, L. S., Halevy, A. K., & Bracewell, C. M. (2023, January 11). *New protections for pregnant and nursing workers in 2023.* SHRM. https://www.shrm.org/resourcesandtools/legal-and-compliance/employment-law/pages/pregnant-nursing-employee-protections-.aspx

46. Beier, M. E., Kanfer, R., Kooij, D. T. A. M., & Truxillo, D. M. (2022). What's age got to do with it? A primer and review of the workplace aging literature. *Personnel Psychology, 75,* 779–804.

47. EEOC. (2023). *Age discrimination.* https://www.eeoc.gov/laws/types/age.cfm

48. Gross v. FBL Financial Services, 557 U.S. ___ (2009). http://caselaw.findlaw.com/us-supreme-court/557/167.html

49. Babb v. Wilkie, 589 U.S. ___ (2020). https://www.supremecourt.gov/opinions/19pdf/18-882_3ebh.pdf

50. Majors, T. (2022, November 1). *Age discrimination in the workplace has increased post-pandemic, AARP survey finds.* KOMO News. https://komonews.com/news/local/age-discrimination-in-the-workplace-has-increased-post-pandemic-aarp-survey-finds

51. Sammer, J. (2022, February 5). *Employing older workers.* SHRM. https://www.shrm.org/hr-today/news/all-things-work/pages/employing-older-workers.aspx

52. Casey, L. (2023, February 20). Long Covid is a disability. Here's how to ask for workplace accommodations. *The Wall Street Journal.* https://www.wsj.com/articles/long-covid-is-a-disability-heres-how-to-ask-for-workplace-accommodations-9b63fd90

53. Gonzales, M. (2022, December 30). *Are employers required to accommodate employees with disabilities?* SHRM. https://www.shrm.org/resourcesandtools/hr-topics/behavioral-competencies/global-and-cultural-effectiveness/pages/are-employers-required-to-accommodate-employees-with-disabilities.aspx

54. U.S. Equal Employment Opportunity Commission. (2023). *The ADA: Your employment rights as an individual with a disability.* https://www.eeoc.gov/publications/ada-your-employment-rights-individual-disability

55. Rouvalis, C. (2020, June 12). *Neurodiverse employees may need accommodations for remote work.* SHRM. https://www.shrm.org/resourcesandtools/hr-topics/employee-relations/pages/neurodiverse-employees-may-need-accommodations-for-remote-work.aspx; Volpone, S. D., Avery, D. R., & Wayne, J. H. (2022). Shaping organizational climates to develop and leverage workforce neurodiversity.

In S. M. Bruyère & A. Colella (Eds.), *Neurodiversity in the workplace: Interests, issues, and opportunities* (pp. 16–59). Routledge.

56. Kaplan, D. A. (2020, July 20). *For people with a different way of thinking, a different approach to hiring.* Mastercard News. https://www.mastercard.com/news/perspectives/2022/supporting-neurodiversity-in-the-workforce/

57. EEOC. (2023). *The equal employment opportunity responsibilities of multinational employers.* https://www.eeoc.gov/facts/multi-employers.html

58. Berkowitz, P. M. (2015). *Gender, diversity, European quotas, and U.S. law.* Littler. https://www.littler.com/publication-press/press/gender-diversity-european-quotas-and-us-law; Liao, J. (2021). The quota system for employment of people with disabilities in China: Policy, practice, barriers, and ways forward. *Disability & Society, 36*(2), 326–331. https://doi.org/10.1080/09687599.2020.1833311.

59. U.S. Department of Labor. (2023). The Genetic Information Nondiscrimination Act of 2008: GINA. https://www.dol.gov/agencies/oasam/centers-offices/civil-rights-center/statutes/genetic-information-nondiscrimination-act-of-2008/guidance

60. Miller, S. (2015). United States District Court for the Northern District of Georgia finds employer liable for violation of Genetic Information Nondisclosure Act (GINA) in the case of the "devious defecator." *American Journal of Law & Medicine, 41,* 684–687.

61. Gigante, E., & Fant, L. (2022, July 7). EEOC sanctions employer for GINA violations relating to collection of employees' family members' Covid test results. *Law and the Workplace.* https://www.lawandtheworkplace.com/2022/07/eeoc-sanctions-employer-for-gina-violations-relating-to-collection-of-employees-family-members-covid-test-results/

62. EEOC. (2023). *Equal Pay Act of 1963 and Lilly Ledbetter Fair Pay Act of 2009.* https://www.eeoc.gov/eeoc/publications/brochure-equal_pay_and_ledbetter_act.cfm

63. EEOC. (2023). *Sexual orientation and gender identity (SOGI) discrimination.* https://www.eeoc.gov/sexual-orientation-and-gender-identity-sogi-discrimination

64. EEOC. (2023). *Sexual orientation and gender identity (SOGI) discrimination.* https://www.eeoc.gov/sexual-orientation-and-gender-identity-sogi-discrimination

65. Gigante, E., Fant, L., Kobetz, A. E., & Treece, D. D. (2022, October 7). Texas district court holds EEOC guidance on sexual orientation and gender identity discrimination unlawful. *Law and the Workplace.* https://www.lawandtheworkplace.com/2022/10/texas-district-court-holds-eeoc-guidance-on-sexual-orientation-and-gender-identity-discrimination-unlawful/

66. Mohr, J. J., Markell, H. M., King, E. B., Jones, K. P., Peddie, C. I., & Kendra, M. S. (2019). Affective antecedents and consequences of revealing and concealing a lesbian, gay, or bisexual identity. *Journal of Applied Psychology, 104*(10), 1266–1282. https://doi.org/10.1037/apl0000399

67. King, E. B., & Cortina, J. M. (2010). The social and economic imperative of lesbian, gay, bisexual, and transgendered supportive organizational policies. *Industrial and Organizational Psychology, 3,* 69–78.

68. INvolve People. (2023). *2022 top 100 LGBTQ+ executives.* https://outstanding.involverolemodels.org/poll/2022-top-100-lgbt-executives/

69. U.S. Department of Labor. (2023). *Know your rights: Protected veteran's rights.* https://www.dol.gov/sites/dolgov/files/ofccp/regs/compliance/factsheets/FACT_Veterans_Sept16_ENGESQA508c.pdf; U.S. Department of Labor (2023). *USERRA.* https://www.dol.gov/agencies/vets/programs/userra/USERRA-Pocket-Guide#ch1

70. SHRM. (2023). *Attracting veterans to your workplace.* https://www.shrm.org/resourcesandtools/tools-and-samples/hr-forms/pages/attracting_veterans.aspx

71. U.S. Department of Labor. (2022). *U.S. Department of Labor announces proposed rule on classifying employees, independent contractors; seeks to return to longstanding interpretation* [Press release]. https://www.dol.gov/newsroom/releases/WHD/WHD20221011-0

72. Benn, K. (2016, April 21). *Uber settles two class actions with drivers for up to $100 M.* LAW360. https://www.law360.com/articles/787770/uber-settles-2-class-actions-with-drivers-for-up-to-100m; Wood, R. (2015, June 16). W. FedEx settles independent contractor mislabeling case for $228 million. *Forbes.* http://www.forbes.com/sites/robertwood/2015/06/16/fedex-settles-driver-mislabeling-case-for-228-million/#199f59165f5a

73. SHRM. (2023). *Affirmative action: General: When would my company need to have an affirmative action program?* https://www.shrm.org/resourcesandtools/tools-and-samples/hr-qa/pages/whenisanaapneeded.aspx

74. Leslie, L. M., Mayer, D. M., & Kravitz, D. A. (2014). The stigma of affirmative action: A stereotyping-based theory and meta-analytic test of the consequences for performance. *Academy of Management Journal, 57,* 964–989.

75. SHRM. (2023). *Affirmative action: General: When would my company need to have an affirmative action program?* https://www.shrm.org/resourcesandtools/tools-and-samples/hr-qa/pages/whenisanaapneeded.aspx

76. EEOC. (2023). *Enforcement guidance on vicarious employer liability for unlawful harassment by supervisors.* https://www.eeoc.gov/policy/docs/harassment.html

77. Leslie, L. M. (2019). Diversity initiative effectiveness: A typological theory of unintended consequences. *Academy of Management Review, 44*(3), 538–563.

78. Shepherd, L. (2023, February 10). *Texas bans DE&I efforts in hiring state workers.* SHRM. https://www.shrm.org/resourcesandtools/legal-and-compliance/state-and-local-updates/pages/texas-bans-diversity-hiring.aspx

79. Yelp. (2023). *Diversity, inclusion, and belonging are part of our culture.* https://www.yelp.careers/us/en/culture-at-yelp

80. Gino, F., & Coffman, K. (2021, September 27). Unconscious bias training that works. *Harvard Business Review.* https://hbr.org/2021/09/unconscious-bias-training-that-works

81. Ibid.

82. Gurchiek, K. (2021, March 8). *Bystander intervention can disrupt the flow of bad behavior.* SHRM. https://www.shrm.org/resourcesandtools/hr-topics/behavioral-competencies/global-and-cultural-effectiveness/pages/bystander-intervention-can-disrupt-the-flow-of-bad-behavior.aspx

83. Bezrukova, K., Spell, C. S., Perry, J. L., & Jehn, K. A. (2016). A meta-analytical integration of over 40 years of research on diversity training evaluation. *Psychological Bulletin, 142*(11), 1227–1274.

84. Cox, J., & Musaddique, S. (2018, February 12). Lloyds banking group sets ethnic diversity target. *Independent.* http://www.independent.co.uk/news/business/news/lloyds-bank-ethnic-diversity-target-bame-increase-numbers-ftse-100-a8207046.html

85. Russ, H. (2021, February 18). *McDonald's ties executive bonuses to diversity, releases workforce data.* Reuters. https://www.reuters.com/business/mcdonalds-ties-executive-bonuses-diversity-releases-workforce-data-2021-02-18/

86. Shepherd, L. (2023, February 13). *EEO-1 reporting will begin in July.* SHRM. https://www.shrm.org/resourcesandtools/legal-and-compliance/employment-law/pages/eeo-1-reporting-deadline.aspx#:~:text=Employers%20need%20to%20understand,to%20begin%20in%20mid%2DJuly.

87. Morgan, W. B., Dunleavy, E., & DeVries, P. D. (2016). Using big data to create diversity and inclusion in organizations. In S. Tonidandel, E. King, & J. Cortina (Eds.), *Big data at work: The data science revolution and organizational psychology* (pp. 310–335). Routledge.

88. Feldmann, J. (2018, April 3). The benefits and shortcomings of blind hiring in the recruiting process. *Forbes.* https://www.forbes.com/sites/forbeshumanresourcescouncil/2018/04/03/the-benefits-and-shortcomings-of-blind-hiring-in-the-recruitment-process/?sh=54f0be4e38a3

89. Howson, C. (2021, May 21). To make real progress on D&I, move past vanity metrics. *Harvard Business Review.* https://hbr.org/2021/05/to-make-real-progress-on-di-move-past-vanity-metrics

90. Diversity First. (2023, February 2). *Diversity First announces 2023 top 50 companies for diversity* [Press release]. https://www.einnews.com/pr_news/613525162/diversity-first-announces-2023-top-50-companies-for-diversity; Murray, S. (2014, April 1). How one company put women in charge. *The Wall Street Journal.* http://blogs.wsj.com/atwork/2014/04/01/how-one-company-put-women-in-charge/; Petrilla, M. (2014, December

11). How analytics helped Kimberly-Clark solve its diversity problem. *Fortune.* http://fortune.com/2014/12/10/kimberly-clark-dodsworth-diversity/

91. Birch, K. (2022, January 28). How Salesforce is creating a more diverse, inclusive culture. *Business Chief.* https://businesschief.com/leadership-and-strategy/how-salesforce-is-creating-a-more-diverse-inclusive-culture; Orr, S. (February 3, 2023). Pay-transparency trend reaches Indiana as push for equity gains momentum. https://www.ibj.com/articles/pay-transparency-trend-reaches-indiana-as-push-for-equity-gains-momentum. Smith, A. (2016, July/August). Analyzing pay. *HR Magazine,* 69–72.

92. Peck, E. (2015, April 23). *Salesforce CEO takes radical step to pay men and women equally.* Huffington Post. http://www.huffingtonpost.com/2015/04/23/salesforce-pay-gap_n_7126892.html; Robbins, C. (2017, April 4). 2017 Salesforce equal pay assessment update. *The 360 Blog.* https://www.salesforce.com/blog/2017/04/salesforce-equal-pay-assessment-update.html; Zarya, V. (2016, July 12). Salesforce spent $3 million on equal pay—Here's how many employees got raises as a result. *Fortune.* http://fortune.com/2016/03/08/salesforce-equal-pay

93. Gonzales, M. (2022, August 22). *New LinkedIn features help recruiters improve DE&I efforts.* SHRM. https://www.shrm.org/resourcesandtools/hr-topics/behavioral-competencies/global-and-cultural-effectiveness/pages/new-linkedin-features-help-recruiters-improve-dei-efforts.aspx

94. Winsborough, D., & Chamorro-Premuzic, T. (2016, Spring). Talent identification in the digital world: New talent signals and the future of HR assessment. *People & Strategy, 39*(2), 28–31.

95. Bridgeford, L. C. (2015, September). Experts discuss big data's effect on hiring, bias claims. *HR Focus,* 4–6; Macheel, T. (2016, September 8). Women in banking: Is big data a weapon of mass discrimination? *American Banker.* https://www.americanbanker.com/opinion/women-in-banking-is-big-data-a-weapon-of-mass-discrimination

96. Maurer, R. (2021, April 7). *Use of AI in the workplace raises legal concerns.*

SHRM. https://www.shrm.org/resourcesandtools/hr-topics/technology/pages/use-of-ai-in-the-workplace-raises-legal-concerns.aspx

97. McGowan, K. (2016, July 27). *When is big data bad data? When it causes bias.* Bloomberg Law. https://news.bloomberglaw.com/daily-labor-report/when-is-big-data-bad-data-when-it-causes-bias

98. SHRM. (2015, September 14). *Avoiding adverse impact in employment practices.* https://www.shrm.org/resourcesandtools/tools-and-samples/toolkits/pages/avoidingadverseimpact.aspx

CHAPTER 5

1. Archambeau, S. (2022, September 7, 2022). Staying top of mind when working remotely. *Forbes.* https://www.forbes.com/sites/shellyearchambeau/2022/09/07/staying-top-of-mind-when-working-remotely/?sh=35494e6043c4; Brower, T. (2022, August 14). Power is shifting away from employees: Can remote work survive? *Forbes.* https://www.forbes.com/sites/tracybrower/2022/08/14/power-is-shifting-away-from-employees-can-remote-work-survive/?sh=2efe1573689e; Goldberg, E. (2022, June 9). A full return to the office: Does "never" work for you? *The New York Times.* https://www.nytimes.com/2022/06/09/business/return-to-work-office-plans.html; Goldberg, E. (2022, August 28). The office's last stand. *The New York Times.* https://www.nytimes.com/2022/08/28/business/the-offices-last-stand.html?searchResultPosition=8; Van Dam, A. (2022, August 19). The remote work revolution is already shaping America. *The Washington Post.* www.washingtonpost.com/business/2022/08/19/remote-work-hybrid-employment-revolution/

2. Cascio, W. F., & Aguinis, H. (2018). *Applied psychology in talent management* (8th ed.). Sage; Morgeson, F. P., Brannick, M. T., & Levine, E. L. (2019). *Job and work analysis: Methods, research, and applications for human resource management* (3rd ed.). Sage.

3. U.S. Office of Personnel Management. (2007). *Delegated examining operations handbook: A guide for federal agency examining offices.* https://www.opm.gov/policy-data-oversight

/hiring-information/competitive-hiring/deo_handbook.pdf

4. PDRI. (2014). *Validating the global competency model.* https://www.pdri.com/images/uploads/PDRI_EP_CM_IBM_FW.pdf

5. Cascio, W. F., & Aguinis, H. (2018). *Applied psychology in talent management* (8th ed.). Sage; Morgeson, F. P., Brannick, M. T., & Levine, E. L. (2019). *Job and work analysis: Methods, research, and applications for human resource management* (3rd ed.). Sage.

6. Sanchez, J. I., & Levine, E. L. (2012). The rise and fall of job analysis and the rise of work analysis. *Annual Review of Psychology,63,* 397–425.

7. Cascio, W. F., & Aguinis, H. (2018). *Applied psychology in talent management* (8th ed.). Sage; Morgeson, F. P., Brannick, M. T., & Levine, E. L. (2019). *Job and work analysis: Methods, research, and applications for human resource management* (3rd ed.). Sage.

8. Uniform Guidelines on Employee Selection Procedures. (1978). *Federal Register, 43,* 38290–38315.

9. Cascio, W. F., & Aguinis, H. (2018). *Applied psychology in talent management* (8th ed.). Sage; Morgeson, F. P., Brannick, M. T., & Levine, E. L. (2019). *Job and work analysis: Methods, research, and applications for human resource management* (3rd ed.). Sage.

10. Burroughs, A. (2017, January 3). The digitalization of retail means broad continuous change. *Smart Business.* http://www.sbnonline.com/article/digital-transformation-retail-broad-continuous-change/

11. Kerstetter, J. (2017, June 26). Daily report: Technology's effects on developing economies. *The New York Times.* https://www.nytimes.com/2017/06/26/technology/daily-report-automations-effect-on-developing-tech-economies.html; Lee, K. F. (2017, June 24). The real threat of artificial intelligence. *The New York Times.* https://www.nytimes.com/2017/06/24/opinion/Sunday/artificial-intelligence-economic-inequality.html

12. IBM Corporation. (2020). *The data science skills competency model: A blueprint for the growing data scientist profession.* https://www.ibm.com/downloads/cas/7109RLQM; McCartney, S., Murphy, C., & Mccarthy, J. (2021). 21st century HR: A competency model for the emerging role of HR Analysts. *Personnel Review, 50*(6), 1495–1513.

13. Putka, D. J., Oswald, F. L., Landers, R. N., Beatty, A. S., McCloy, R. A., & Yu, M. C. (2023). Evaluating a natural language processing approach to estimating KSA and interest job analysis ratings. *Journal of Business and Psychology, 38,* 385–410.

14. Morgeson, F. P., Brannick, M. T., & Levine, E. L. (2019). *Job and work analysis: Methods, research, and applications for human resource management* (3rd ed.). Sage; Gatewood, R., Feild, H., & Barrick, M. (2018). *Human resource selection* (9th ed.). Cengage Learning.

15. Leslie, C. (2016, June). *Engineering competency model.* Paper presented at the American Society for Engineering Education annual conference, New Orleans. https://peer.asee.org/engineering-competency-model

16. Strah, N., & Rupp, D. E. (2022). Are there cracks in our foundation? An integrative review of diversity issues in job analysis. *Journal of Applied Psychology, 107,* 1031–1051.

17. Morgeson, F. P., Brannick, M. T., & Levine, E. L. (2019). *Job and work analysis: Methods, research, and applications for human resource management* (3rd ed.). Sage.

18. Ibid.; Gatewood, R., Feild, H., & Barrick, M. (2018). *Human resource selection* (9th ed.). Cengage Learning.

19. Ibid.; Green, S. B., & Stutzman, T. (1986). An evaluation of methods to select respondents to structured job-analysis questionnaires. *Personnel Psychology, 39,* 543–564; Morgeson, F. P., Brannick, M. T., & Levine, E. L. (2019). *Job and work analysis: Methods, research, and applications for human resource management* (3rd ed.). Sage.

20. Flanagan, J. C. (1954). The critical incident technique. *Psychological Bulletin, 51,* 327–358.

21. McCormick, E. J., Jeanneret, P. R., & Mecham, R. C. (1972). A study of job characteristics and job dimensions as based on the position analysis questionnaire (PAQ). *Journal of Applied Psychology,56,* 347–368.

22. Gatewood, R., Feild, H., & Barrick, M. (2018). *Human resource selection* (9th ed.). Cengage Learning; Morgeson, F. P., Brannick, M. T., & Levine, E. L. (2019). *Job and work analysis: Methods, research, and applications for human resource management* (3rd ed.). Sage.

23. Peterson, N. G., Mumford, M. D., Borman, W. C., Jeanneret, P. R., Fleishman, E. A., Levin, K. Y., Campion, M., Mayfield, M. S., Morgeson, F. P., Pearlman, K., Gowing, M. K., Lancaster, A. R., Silver, M. B., & Dye, D. M. (2001). Understanding work using the Occupational Information Network (O*NET): Implications for practice and research. *Personnel Psychology, 54,* 451–492.

24. Campion, M. A., Fink, A. A., Ruggeberg, B. J., Carr, L., Phillips, G. M., & Odman, R. B. (2011). Doing competencies well: Best practices in competency modeling. *Personnel Psychology, 64,* 225–262.

25. Cappelli, P., & Keller, J. R. (2014). Talent management: Conceptual approaches and practical challenges. *Annual Review of Organizational Psychology and Organizational Behavior, 1,* 305–331; Stevens, G. W. (2013). A critical review of the science and practice of competency modeling. *Human Resource Development Review, 12*(1), 86–107.

26. Campion, M. C., Schepker, D. J., Campion, M. A., & Sanchez, J. I. (2020). Competency modeling: A theoretical and empirical examination of the strategy dissemination process. *Human Resource Management, 59,* 291–306.

27. O*NET database. https://www.onetcenter.org/dictionary/21.3/excel/work_styles.html; Society for Human Resource Management. (2022). SHRM body of applied skills and knowledge. https://www.shrm.org/certification/organizations/Documents/SHRM%20BASK%20HANDBOOK%202022.pdf; Tackett, S., Sugarman, J., Ng, C. J., Kamarulzaman, A., & Ali, J. (2022). Developing a competency framework for health research ethics education and training. *Journal of Medical Ethics, 48*(6), 391–396.

28. Campion, M. A., Fink, A. A., Ruggeberg, B. J., Carr, L., Phillips, G. M., & Odman, R. B. (2011). Doing competencies well: Best practices in competency modeling. *Personnel Psychology, 64,* 225–262; Sanchez, J. I., Levine, E. L. (2009). What is (or should be) the difference between competency modeling and traditional job analysis? *Human Resource Management Review,19,* 53–63; Shippmann, J. S., Ash, R. A., Battista, M., Carr, L., Eyde, L. D., Hesketh, B., Kehoe, J., Pearlman, K., Prien, E. P., & Sanchez, J. I. (2000). The practice

of competency modeling. *Personnel Psychology, 53,* 703–740.

29. World Health Organization. (2022). *Global competency and outcomes framework for universal health coverage.* https://www.who.int/publications/i/item/9789240034662

30. Parker, S. K. (2014). Beyond motivation: Job and work design for development, health, ambidexterity, and more. *Annual Review of Psychology, 65,* 661–691; Parker, S. K., Morgeson, F. P., & Johns, G. (2017). One hundred years of work design research: Looking back and looking forward. *Journal of Applied Psychology, 102,* 403–420.

31. Demerouti, E., Bakker, A. B., Nachreiner, F., & Schaufeli, W. B. (2001). The job demands–resources model of burnout. *Journal of Applied Psychology, 86,* 499–512; Hackman, J. R., & Oldham, G. R. (1975). Development of the job diagnostic survey. *Journal of Applied Psychology, 60,* 159–180; Karasek, R. A. (1979). Job demands, job decision latitude, and mental strain: Implications for job redesign. *Administrative Science Quarterly, 24,* 285–308.

32. Morgeson, F. P., & Humphrey, S. E. (2006). The Work Design Questionnaire (WDQ): Developing and validating a comprehensive measure for assessing job design and the nature of work. *Journal of Applied Psychology, 91,* 1321–1399.

33. Humphrey, S. E., Nahrgang, J. D., & Morgeson, F. P. (2007). Integrating motivational, social, and contextual work design features: A meta-analytic summary and theoretical extension of the work design literature. *Journal of Applied Psychology, 92,* 1332–1356.

34. Parker, S. K. (2014). Beyond motivation: Job and work design for development, health, ambidexterity, and more. *Annual Review of Psychology, 65,* 661–691.

35. Truxillo, D. M., Cadiz, D. A., Rineer, J. R., Zaniboni, S., & Fraccaroli, F. (2012). A lifespan perspective on job design: Fitting the job and the worker to promote job satisfaction, engagement, and performance. *Organizational Psychology Review, 2,* 340–360; Zaniboni, S., Truxillo, D. M., Rineer, J. R., Bodner, T. E., Hammer, L. B., & Krainer, M. (2016). Relating age, decision authority, job satisfaction, and mental health: A study of

construction workers. *Work, Aging, and Retirement, 2,* 428–435.

36. Rudolph, C. W., Katz, I. M., Lavigne, K. N., & Zacher, H. (2017). Job crafting: A meta-analysis of relationships with individual differences, job characteristics, and work outcomes. *Journal of Vocational Behavior, 102,* 112–138.

37. Lebowitz, S. (2015). A Yale professor explains how to turn a boring job into a meaningful career. *Business Insider.* http://www.businessinsider.com/turn-a-boring-job-into-a-meaningful-career-job-crafting-2015-12; Wrzesniewski, A., & Dutton, J. E. (2001). Crafting a job: Revisioning employees as active crafters of their work. *Academy of Management Review, 26,* 179–201.

38. Parker, S. K. (2014). Beyond motivation: Job and work design for development, health, ambidexterity, and more. *Annual Review of Psychology, 65,* 661–691.

39. Rudolph, C. W., Katz, I. M., Lavigne, K. N., & Zacher, H. (2017). Job crafting: A meta-analysis of relationships with individual differences, job characteristics, and work outcomes. *Journal of Vocational Behavior, 102,* 112–138.

40. Demerouti, E., Soyer, L. M., Vakola, M., & Xanthopoulou, D. (2021). The effects of a job crafting intervention on the success of an organizational change effort in a blue-collar work environment. *Journal of Occupational and Organizational Psychology, 94,* 374–399.

41. Tims, M., & Parker, S. K. (2020). How coworkers attribute, react to, and shape job crafting. *Organizational Psychology Review, 10,* 29–54.

42. Kooij, D. T., van Woerkom, M., Wilkenloh, J., Dorenbosch, L., & Denissen, J. J. (2017). Job crafting towards strengths and interests: The effects of a job crafting intervention on person-job fit and the role of age. *Journal of Applied Psychology, 102,* 971–981.

43. Kuijpers, E., Kooij, D. T., & van Woerkom, M. (2020). Align your job with yourself: The relationship between a job crafting intervention and work engagement, and the role of workload. *Journal of Occupational Health Psychology, 25,* 1–16.

44. Knight, C., Tims, M., Gawke, J., & Parker, S. K. (2021). When do job crafting interventions work? The moderating roles of workload,

intervention intensity, and participation. *Journal of Vocational Behavior, 124,* Article 103522.

45. Kniffin, K. M., Narayanan, J., Anseel, F., Antonakis, J., Ashford, S. P., Bakker, A. B., . . . & Vugt, M. V. (2021). COVID-19 and the workplace: Implications, issues, and insights for future research and action. *American Psychologist, 76,* 63–77.

46. Wang, B., Liu, Y., Qian, J., & Parker, S. K. (2021). Achieving effective remote working during the COVID-19 pandemic: A work design perspective. *Applied Psychology, 70,* 16–59.

47. Van Dam, A. (2022, August 19). The remote work revolution is already reshaping America. *The Washington Post.* https://www.washingtonpost.com/business/2022/08/19/remote-work-hybrid-employment-revolution/

48. Lufkin, B. (2022, July 25). *The companies doubling down on remote work.* BBC.com. https://www.bbc.com/worklife/article/20220722-the-companies-doubling-down-on-remote-work

49. Kane, J. (2022). Why employers that neglect the contingent worker experience risk losing the war for talent. *Forbes.* https://www.forbes.com/sites/forbeshumanresourcescouncil/2022/07/13/why-employers-that-neglect-the-contingent-worker-experience-risk-losing-the-war-for-talent/?sh=148eab8d10ad

50. Caza, B. B., Reid, E. M., Ashford, S. J., & Granger, S. (2021). Working on my own: Measuring the challenges of gig work. *Human Relations, 75*(11), 2122–2159; Cropanzano, R., Keplinger, K., Lambert, B. K., Caza, B., & Ashford, S. J. (2023). The organizational psychology of gig work: An integrative conceptual review. *Journal of Applied Psychology, 108*(3), 492–519; Fisher, S. L., & Connelly, C. E. (2017). Lower cost or just lower value? Modeling the organizational costs and benefits of contingent work. *Academy of Management Discoveries, 3,* 165–186; Tran, M., & Sokas, R. K. (2017). The gig economy and contingent work: An occupational health assessment. *Journal of Occupational and Environmental Medicine, 59,* e63–e66; Watson, G. P., Kistler, L. D., Graham, B. A., & Sinclair, R. R. (2021). Looking at the gig picture: Defining gig work and explaining profile differences in gig workers' job demands and resources. *Group & Organization Management, 46,* 327–361.

CHAPTER 6

1. Gittens, W., & Knorr-Evans, M. (2022). *What is the average student loan debt for a US graduate?* as.com https://en.as.com/latest_news/what-is-the-average-student-loan-debt-for-a-us-graduate-n/; Lee, M. (2022). How to prepare now that student loan forgiveness likely isn't coming anytime soon. *USAToday.* https://www.usatoday.com/story/money/personalfinance/2022/11/16/student-debt-relief-delayed-prepare/10705821002/; https://firsthand.co/best-internships-rankings-search/best-internships-by-industry/consulting; PwC. (2022). *Practice areas.* http://www.pwc.com/us/en/careers/campus/why-pwc/what-we-do.html; PwC. (2022). *Recruiting process.* http://www.pwc.com/us/en/careers/campus/recruiting.html

2. Boston, W. (2016). BMW loses core development team of its i3 and i8 electric vehicle line. *The Wall Street Journal.* https://www.wsj.com/articles/bmw-loses-core-development-team-of-its-i3-and-i8-electric-vehicle-line-1461086049

3. Bidwell, L., Sendra, C., Bauer, T., & Truxillo, D. (2023). *Exploring the impact of intelligent technology on employee experience.* SAP/SuccessFactors White Paper Series.

4. U.S. Bureau of Labor Statistics. (2023). *About BLS.* https://www.bls.gov/bls/infohome.htm

5. Cheryan, S., Master, A., & Meltzoff, A. (2022). There are two few women in computer science and engineering. *Scientific American.* https://www.scientificamerican.com/article/there-are-too-few-women-in-computer-science-and-engineering/; NACE. (2016). *Trends: Fewer women in computer sciences.* http://www.naceweb.org/talent-acquisition/trends-and-predictions/trends-fewer-women-in-computer-sciences/

6. American Association of Colleges of Nursing. (2022). *Nursing shortage.* https://www.aacnnursing.org/News-Information/Fact-Sheets/Nursing-Shortage; The Conference Board. (2014). *International comparisons of annual labor force statistics.* https://www.conference-board.org/ilcprogram/index.cfm?id=25444; U.S. Bureau of Labor Statistics. (2022). *Occupational outlook handbook: Water and wastewater treatment plant and system operators.* https://www.bls.gov/ooh/production/water-and-wastewater-treatment-plant-and-system-operators.htm; Yang, M. (2023). *America needs carpenters and plumbers: Gen Z doesn't seem interested.* NPR. https://www.npr.org/2023/01/05/1142817339/america-needs-carpenters-and-plumbers-try-telling-that-to-gen-z

7. Ferguson, S. (2022). *Understanding America's labor shortage: The most impacted industries.* U.S. Chamber of Commerce. https://www.uschamber.com/workforce/understanding-americas-labor-shortage-the-most-impacted-industries; Smith, M. (2022). As applications fall, police departments lure recruits with bonuses and attention. *The New York Times.* https://www.nytimes.com/2022/12/25/us/police-officer-recruits.html?searchResultPosition=1

8. Cote, C. (2021). *What is predictive analytics?* Harvard Business School Online.

9. U.S. Bureau of Labor Statistics. (2022). *Labor force characteristics of foreign-born workers summary.* https://www.bls.gov/news.release/forbrn.nr0.htm

10. Dineen, B. R., Yu, K. Y. T., & Stevenson-Street, J. (2023). Recruitment in personnel psychology and beyond: Where we've been working, and where we might work next. *Personnel Psychology, 76*(2), 617–650; Ployhart, R. E., Schmitt, N., & Tippins, N. T. (2017). Solving the Supreme Problem: 100 years of selection and recruitment at the *Journal of Applied Psychology. Journal of Applied Psychology, 102,* 291–304.

11. Ok, C., & Park, J. (2018). Change in newcomers' job satisfaction: Met-expectations effect as a moderator. *Social Behavior and Personality: An International Journal, 46,* 1513–1521.

12. Hilburn, J. (2022). The 50 best jobs in America for 2022, according to Glassdoor. *Forbes.* https://www.forbes.com/sites/jairhilburn/2022/02/02/the-50-best-jobs-in-america-for-2022-according-to-glassdoor/?sh=1180da82faee

13. Jobvite. (2016). *Jobvite recruiter national report: The annual social recruiting survey.* http://web.jobvite.com/Q316_Website_2016RecruiterNation_LP.html

14. Baert, S. (2017). Facebook profile picture appearance affects recruiters' first hiring decisions. *New Media & Society, 20,* 1220–1239.

15. Jobvite. (2016). *Jobvite recruiter national report: The annual social recruiting survey.* http://web.jobvite.com/Q316_Website_2016RecruiterNation_LP.html

16. Jones, B. I. (2011). *People management lessons from Disney.* https://cdns3.trainingindustry.com/media/3532077/disneypeoplemanagementlessons.pdf

17. Sekiguchi, T., Mitate, Y., & Yang, Y. (2022). Internship experience and organizational attractiveness: A realistic job fit perspective. *Journal of Career Development, 50*(2); Wilhelmy, A., Truxillo, D. M., & Funk, F. (2022). Reciprocity or backfiring? Examining the influence of realistic job previews on applicants' willingness to self-disclose and use image protection tactics. *International Journal of Selection and Assessment, 30*(3), 311–329.

18. Burkus, D. (2016). *Why Amazon bought into Zappos' "pay to quit" policy.* Inc. http://www.inc.com/david-burkus/why-amazon-bought-into-zappos-pay-to-quit-policy.html; Tedder, M. (2022). *Amazon won't pay (most) workers to quit anymore.* TheStreet. https://www.thestreet.com/investing/amazon-makes-changes-to-pay-to-quit-program-wont-cover-most-workers

19. SHRM. (2016). Talent acquisition: Selection. *HRToday.* https://www.shrm.org/hr-today/trends-and-forecasting/research-and-surveys/Documents/Talent-Acquisition-Selection.pdf

20. Kauflin, J. (2017). How to get the great jobs that are never advertised. *Forbes.* https://www.forbes.com/sites/jeffkauflin/2017/05/19/how-to-get-the-great-jobs-that-are-never-advertised/?sh=1cf421614abe; Weber, L., & Kwoh, L. (2013). Beware the phantom job listing. *The Wall Street Journal.* https://www.wsj.com/articles/SB10001424127887323706704578229661268628432

21. Gartner. (2022). *Gartner recommends organizations confront three internal labor market realities to retain talent* [Press release]. https://www.gartner.com/en/newsroom/2022-01-26-gartner-recommends-organizations-confront-three-internal-labor-market-inequities-to-retain-talent; Malinsky, G. (2022). *54% of jobseekers overlook openings at their company.* CNBC. https://www.cnbc.com/2022/05/26/duri

ng-your-job-search-look-at-internal-roles.html

22. Celanese. (2022, June 16). *Celanese named top noteworthy company by DiversityInc for second year.* https://sustainability.celanese.com/en/News/2022/top-noteworthy-company-by-diversityinc-for-second-year; iCIMS. (2023). *Customer success stories: Celanese.* https://www.icims.com/community/success-stories/celanese/

23. Thibodeau, P. (2022). *LinkedIn wants to make it easier to hire internal talent.* TechTarget. https://www.techtarget.com/searchhrsoftware/news/252526522/LinkedIn-wants-to-make-it-easier-to-hire-internal-talent

24. Rediff. (2014, July 15). *Hiring former employees is beneficial.* http://www.rediff.com/money/report/hiring-former-employees-is-beneficial/20140715.htm

25. Klotz, A. C., Derler, A., Kim, C., & Winlaw, M. (2023, March 15). The promise (and risk) of boomerang employees. *Harvard Business Review.*

26. Robinson, B. (2022). 5 reasons for "boomerang employees" and "the Great Regret" in employment. *Forbes.* forbes.com/sites/bryanrobinson/2022/12/01/5-reasons-for-boomerang-employees-and-the-great-regret-in-employment/?sh=3e16197f6092

27. Nitsch v. DreamWorks Animation SKG Inc., 100 F. Supp. 3d 851 (N.D. Cal. 2015); Rosenblatt, J. (2017). *Disney agrees to pay $100 million to end no-poaching lawsuit.* Bloomberg. https://www.bloomberg.com/news/articles/2017-02-01/disney-agrees-to-pay-100-million-to-end-no-poaching-lawsuit

28. Klotz, A. C., Derler, A., Kim, C., & Winlaw, M. (2023). The promise (and risk) of boomerang employees. *Harvard Business Review*; Microsoft Alumni Network. (2022). *About Microsoft alumni.* https://www.microsoftalumni.com/s/1769/19/home.aspx?gid=2&pgid=61

29. Bock, L. (2015). *Work rules! Insights from inside Google that will transform how you live and lead.* Twelve.

30. SHRM. (2016). *Designing and managing successful employee referral programs.* https://www.shrm.org/resourcesandtools/tools-and-samples/toolkits/pages/tk-designingandmanagingsuccessfulemployeereferralprograms.aspx

31. Gray, K. (2022). *Influential factor in tough hiring decisions.* NACE. https://www.naceweb.org/talent-acquisition/candidate-selection/internship-experience-the-most-influential-factor-in-tough-hiring-decisions/

32. Zhao, H., & Liden, R. C. (2011). Internship: A recruitment and selection perspective. *Journal of Applied Psychology, 96,* 221–229.

33. Jobboard Finder. (2018). *51job.* https://www.jobboardfinder.net/jobboard-51job-china

34. Bauer, T. N., Truxillo, D. M., Jones, M. P., & Brady, G. (2020). Privacy and cybersecurity challenges, opportunities, and recommendations: Personnel selection in an era of online application systems and big data. In S. E. Woo, R. Proctor, & L. Tay (Eds.), *Big data in psychological research* (pp. 393–409). American Psychological Association; Doyle, A. (2016, July 5). *How to avoid identity theft when you are job searching.* The Balance. https://www.thebalance.com/how-to-avoid-identity-theft-when-you-are-job-searching-2062151; Ryan, R. (2021). Job search scams to avoid. *Forbes.*

35. LinkedIn. (2022). *37 LinkedIn statistics you need to know in 2022.* https://www.linkedin.com/pulse/37-linkedin-statistics-you-need-know-2022-gaurav-sharma/

36. Sharma, P. (2016). *How Disney and 5 other top employers use Twitter to recruit.* Undercover Recruiter. http://theundercoverrecruiter.com/how-disney-and-5-other-top-employers-use-twitter-to-recruit/

37. Gibson Canner, M. (2023). *An inside look at our job application and hiring processes.* Marriott International. https://careers.marriott.com/blog/hiring-process/; Osawa, J., & Mozur, P. (2012). In China, recruiting gets social. *The Wall Street Journal.* https://www.wsj.com/articles/SB10000872396390444226904577561643928840040

38. Chorna, I. (2023). Examples of gamification in HR: A complete guide. *HR Forecast.*

39. Anderson, A. (2021). *DOJ focus on no-poach cases could have wide-ranging consequences for managers.* SHRM. https://www.shrm.org/resourcesandtools/hr-topics/people-managers/pages/no-poach-cases-.aspx; Nitsch v. DreamWorks Animation SKG Inc., 100 F. Supp. 3d 851 (N.D. Cal. 2015);

Rosenblatt, J. (2017). *Disney agrees to pay $100 million to end no-poaching lawsuit.* Bloomberg. https://www.bloomberg.com/news/articles/2017-02-01/disney-agrees-to-pay-100-million-to-end-no-poaching-lawsuit

40. McFarland, L. A., & Kim, Y. (2021). An examination of the relationship between applicant race and accrued recruitment source information: Implications for applicant withdrawal and test performance. *Personnel Psychology, 74,* 831–861.

41. Kelleher, K. (2017). Uber is facing a leadership crisis that could cause lasting damage. *Time.* http://time.com/4687491/uber-travis-kalanick-crisis-pr-brand-ipo-image-sexism-privacy/

42. Bock, L. (2015). *Work rules! Insights from inside Google that will transform how you live and lead.* Twelve; Lang, J., & Zapf, D. (2015). Quotas for women can improve recruitment procedures: Gender as a predictor of the frequency of use of passive job search behavior and the mediating roles of management aspirations, proactivity, and career level. *Journal of Personnel Psychology, 14,* 131–141.

43. ERE. (2017). *5 keys to recruiting women for your workforce.* www.eremedia.com

44. Wild, J. (2017, March 7). Wanted—A way with words in recruitment ads. *Financial Times.* https://www.ft.com/content/9974b0ce-e7bb-11e6-967b-c88452263daf

45. U.S. Bureau of Labor Statistics (2022). *Occupational outlook handbook.* https://www.bls.gov/ooh/healthcare/registered-nurses.htm

46. Avery, D. R., & McKay, P. F. (2006). Target practice: An organizational impression management approach to attracting minority and female job applicants. *Personnel Psychology, 59,* 157–187; Gibbs, J. C. (2019). Diversifying the police applicant pool: Motivations of women and minority candidates seeking police employment. *Criminal Justice Studies, 32,* 207–221.

47. Highhouse, S., Stierwalt, S. L., Bachiochi, P., Elder, A. E., & Slaughter, J. E. (1999). Effects of advertised human resource management practices on attraction of African American applicants. *Personnel Psychology, 52,* 425–442; Slaughter, J. E., Sinar, E., & Bachiochi, P. D. (2002). Black

applicants' reactions to affirmative action plans: Effects of plan content and previous experience with discrimination. *Journal of Applied Psychology, 87*, 333–344.

48. Avery, D. R., Hernandez, M., & Hebl, M. (2004). Who's watching the race? Racial salience in recruitment advertising. *Journal of Applied Social Psychology, 34*, 146–161; Walker, H. J., Feild, H. S., Bernerth, J. B., & Becton, J. B. (2012). Diversity cues on recruitment websites: Investigating the effects on job seekers' information processing. *Journal of Applied Psychology, 97*, 214–224.

49. Avery, D. R. (2003). Reactions to diversity in recruitment advertising— Are differences black and white? *Journal of Applied Psychology, 88*, 672–679.

50. Ng, T. W. H., & Feldman, D. C. (2008). The relationship of age to tend dimensions of job performance. *Journal of Applied Psychology, 93*, 392–423.

51. Karanika-Murray, M., Van Veldhoven, M., Michaelides, G., Baguley, T., Gkiontsi, D., & Harrison, N. (2022). Curvilinear relationships between age and job performance and the role of job complexity. *Work, Aging and Retirement.*

52. Bersin, J., & Chamorro-Premuzic, T. (2019). The case for hiring older workers. *Harvard Business Review.* https://hbr.org/2019/09/the-case-for-hiring-older-workers; Truxillo, D. M., Cadiz, D. M., & Rineer, J. R. (2014). The aging workforce: Implications for human resource management research and practice. *Oxford Handbooks Online: Business & Management.* https://www.researchgate.net/publication/282348874_The_Aging_Workforce_Implications_for_Human_Resource_Management_Research_and_Practice

53. Advisory Board. (2023). *"Age is an asset": Why companies are interested in older workers.* https://www.advisory.com/daily-briefing/2023/04/07/older-workers

54. Evans, M. (2017, February 24). *The stubborn problem of ageism in hiring.* Bloomberg. https://www.citylab.com/work/2017/02/ageism-in-hiring-is-rife-and-not-easy-to-fix/517323/; McGuireWoods. (2017, March 6). *Are college recruiting programs age discrimination?* http://www.lexology.com/library/detail.aspx?g=c08e77fc-9c83-4630-9344-b4d9e80136d4

55. Sammer, J. (February 5, 2022). *Employing older workers.* SHRM. https://www.shrm.org/hr-today/news/all-things-work/pages/employing-older-workers.aspx

56. U.S. Census Bureau. (2022). *Veterans.* https://www.census.gov/topics/population/veterans.html

57. SHRM. (2016). *Employing military personnel and recruiting veterans: What HR can do.* https://www.shrm.org/ResourcesAndTools/hr-topics/benefits/Documents/10-0531%20Military%20Program%20Report_FNL.pdf

58. Meinert, D. (2016). Why hiring veterans makes good business sense. *HR Magazine.* https://www.shrm.org/hr-today/news/hr-magazine/1116/pages/why-hiring-veterans-makes-good-business-sense.aspx

59. Vanden Brook, T. (2017). Army to spend $300 million on bonuses and ads to get 6,000 more recruits. *USA Today.* https://www.usatoday.com/story/news/politics/2017/02/12/army-spend-300-million-bonuses-and-ads-get-6000-more-recruits/97757094/

60. SERVe. (2018). *The SERVe project.* https://servestudy.org/about

61. Giannantonio, C. M., & Hurley-Hanson, A. E. (2022). Recruitment strategies: Generating a neurodiverse workforce. In S. M. Bruyère & A. Colella (Eds.), *Neurodiversity in the workplace* (pp. 60–97). Routledge.

62. NACE. (2015). *Measuring your organization's quality of hire.* http://www.naceweb.org/s10212015/measuring-quality-of-hire.aspx

63. Acikgoz, Y. (2019). Employee recruitment and job search: Towards a multi-level integration. *Human Resource Management Review, 29*, 1–13.

64. McCarthy, J. M., Bauer, T. N., Truxillo, D. M., Anderson, N. R., Costa, A. C., & Ahmed, S. M. (2017). Applicant perspectives during selection: A review addressing "So what?," "What's new?," and "Where to next?" *Journal of Management, 43*, 1661–1692.

65. Chapman, D. S., Uggerslev, K. L., Carroll, S. A., Piasentin, K. A., & Jones, D. A. (2005). Applicant attraction to organizations and job choice: A meta-analytic review of the correlates of recruiting outcomes. *Journal of Applied Psychology, 90*, 928–944.

66. Disney Programs (2023). *What is the status of my application?* https://support.disneyprograms.com/hc/en-us/articles/360004640732-What-is-the-status-of-my-application-

67. Boswell, W. R., Roehling, M. V., LePine, M. A., & Moynihan, L. M. (2003). Individual job-choice decisions and the impact of job attributes and recruitment practices: A longitudinal field study. *Human Resource Management, 42*, 23–37.

68. Bharadva, R. (2022, October). *EY recruits record 1,473 students this year—An increase of 35% on 2021* [Press release]. Ernst & Young. https://www.ey.com/en_uk/news/2022/10/ey-recruits-record-1473-students-this-year-an-increase-on-2021; Dipplinger, G., Tome, G. Straub, N. (2021). *Virtual reality personality assessment.* PwC. https://www.pwc.at/de/publikationen/2021_05_koia-report

69. Cable, D. M., & Yu, K. Y. T. (2006). Managing job seekers' organizational image beliefs: The role of media richness and media credibility. *Journal of Applied Psychology, 91*, 828–840.

70. Google. (2023). *How we review applications (and what happens next).* https://careers.google.com/how-we-hire/apply/

71. The Conference Board. (2017). *CEO challenge 2017: Meeting the customer relationships/corporate brand and reputation challenge.* https://www.conference-board.org/publications/publicationdetail.cfm?publicationid=7400&centerId=9

72. Murphy, B. (2018). *Wendy's can't stop trolling McDonald's on Twitter.* Inc. https://www.inc.com/bill-murphy-jr/wendys-cant-stop-trolling-mcdonalds-on-twitter-heres-latest-burn.html; Whitten, S. (2017). *A Wendy's tweet just went viral for all the wrong reasons.* CNBC. http://www.cnbc.com/2017/01/04/wendys-saucy-tweets-are-hit-and-miss-on-social-media.html

73. Stockman, S., van Hoye, G., Veiga, S. D. M. (2020). Negative word-of-mouth and applicant attraction: The role of employer brand equity. *Journal of Vocational Behavior, 118*, 103368.

74. Griepentrog, B. K., Harold, R. M., Holtz, B. C., Klimoski, R. J., & Marsh, S. M. (2012). Integrating social identity and the theory of planned behavior: Predicting withdrawal from an

organizational recruitment process. *Personnel Psychology, 65*, 723–753.

75. Dineen, B. R., Ash, S. R., & Noe, R. A. (2002). A web of applicant attraction: Person–organization fit in the context of web-based recruitment. *Journal of Applied Psychology, 87*, 723–734; Swider, B. W., Zimmerman, R. D., & Barrick, M. R. (2015). Searching for the right fit: Development of applicant person–organization fit during the recruitment process. *Journal of Applied Psychology, 100*, 880–893.

76. Wigert, B. (2022*). The top 6 things employees want in their next job.* Gallup.

CHAPTER 7

1. Data & Trust Alliance. (2022). *Algorithmic bias safeguards for workforce.* https://dataandtrustalliance.org/Algorithmic_Bias_Safeguards_for_Workforce_Overview.pdf; Lohr, S. (2021). Group backed by top companies moves to combat A.I. in hiring. *The New York Times,* Group Backed by Top Companies Moves to Combat A.I. Bias in Hiring - The New York Times (nytimes.com); Metz, R. (2022). *The White House releases an "AI Bill of Rights."* CNN Business. https://www.cnn.com/2022/10/04/tech/ai-bill-of-rights/index.html; Responsible Artificial Intelligence Institute. https://www.responsible.ai; U.S. Department of Justice, Civil Rights Division. (2022). *Algorithms, artificial intelligence, and disability discrimination in hiring.* https://beta.ada.gov/assets/_pdfs/ai-guidance.pdf; Wisenberg Brin, D. (2022). *EU: Proposed artificial intelligence law could affect employers globally.* SHRM. https://www.shrm.org/resourcesandtools/hr-topics/global-hr/pages/eu-proposed-artificial-intelligence-law.aspx#:~:text=Companies%20with%20employees%20in%20the,shape%20technology%20and%20standards%20worldwide

2. Millet, J. (2023). What will the hiring landscape look like in 2023? *Forbes,* https://www.forbes.com/sites/forbeshumanresourcescouncil/2023/01/13/what-will-the-hiring-landscape-look-like-in-2023/?sh=213ccb975522

3. Lievens, F., Sackett, P. R., & Zhang, C. (2021). Personnel selection: A longstanding story of impact at the individual, firm, and societal level. *European Journal of Work and Organizational Psychology, 30*(3), 444–455.

4. Society for Industrial and Organizational Psychology (SIOP). (2018). *Principles for the validation and use of personnel selection procedures* (5th ed.). Cambridge University Press; Uniform Guidelines on Employee Selection Procedures. (1978). *Federal Register, 43*, 38290–38315.

5. Gatewood, R., Feild, H., & Barrick, M. (2019). *Human resource selection* (9th ed.). Wessex Press.

6. Society for Industrial and Organizational Psychology (SIOP). (2018). *Principles for the validation and use of personnel selection procedures* (5th ed.). Cambridge University Press; Uniform Guidelines on Employee Selection Procedures. (1978). *Federal Register, 43*, 38290–38315.

7. Highhouse, S., & Brooks, M. E. (2023). Improving workplace judgments by reducing noise: Lessons learned from a century of selection research. *Annual Review of Organizational Psychology and Organizational Behavior, 10*, 519–523; Yu, M. C., & Kuncel, N. R. (2022). Testing the value of expert insight: Comparing local versus general expert judgment models. *International Journal of Selection and Assessment, 30*, 202–215.

8. Gatewood, R., Feild, H., & Barrick, M. (2019). *Human resource selection.* (9th ed.). Wessex Press.

9. Society for Industrial and Organizational Psychology (SIOP). (2018). *Principles for the validation and use of personnel selection procedures* (5th ed.). Cambridge University Press; Uniform Guidelines on Employee Selection Procedures. (1978). *Federal Register, 43*, 38290–38315.

10. Lawshe, C. H. (1975). A quantitative approach to content validity. *Personnel Psychology, 28*, 563–575.

11. Biddle Consulting Group. (2013). *Content-related and criterion-related validation study of CritiCall.* http://ww1.prweb.com/prfiles/2013/09/19/11143327/Florida%20Highway%20Patrol%20CritiCall%20Content%20and%20Criterion%20Validation%20Report%209-3-13.pdf; Biddle Consulting Group. (2022). *Dispatcher pre-employment testing.* https://critical911.com/

12. Ibid.

13. Sackett, P. R., Putka, D. J., & McCloy, R. A. (2012). The concept of validity and the process of validation. In N. Schmitt (Ed.), *The Oxford handbook of personnel assessment and selection*

(pp. 91–118). Oxford University Press; Schmitt, N., Gooding, R. Z., Noe, R. A., & Kirsch, M. (1984). Meta analyses of validity studies published between 1964 and 1982 and the investigation of study characteristics. *Personnel Psychology, 37*, 407–422.

14. Landy, F. J. (1986). Stamp collecting versus science: Validation as hypothesis testing. *American Psychologist, 41*, 1183–1192.

15. Sackett, P. R., Walmsley, P. T., Koch, A. J., Beatty, A. S., & Kuncel, N. R. (2016). Predictor content matters for knowledge testing: Evidence supporting content validation. *Human Performance, 29*, 54–71; Spitzmuller, M., Sin, H. P., Howe, M., & Fatimah, S. (2015). Investigating the uniqueness and usefulness of proactive personality in organizational research: A meta-analytic review. *Human Performance, 28*, 351–379.

16. Gatewood, R., Feild, H., & Barrick, M. (2019). *Human resource selection* (9th ed.). Wessex Press; Society for Industrial and Organizational Psychology (SIOP). (2018). *Principles for the validation and use of personnel selection procedures* (5th ed.). Cambridge University Press; Uniform Guidelines on Employee Selection Procedures. (1978). *Federal Register, 43*, 38290–38315.

17. Biddle Consulting Group. (2013). *Content-related and criterion-related validation study of CritiCall.*

18. Brislin, R. W. (1970). Back-translation for cross-cultural research. *Journal of Cross-Cultural Psychology, 1*, 185–216; Steiner, D. D. (2012). Personnel selection across the globe. In N. Schmitt (Ed.), *The Oxford handbook of personnel selection and assessment* (pp. 740–767). Oxford University Press; Tippins, N. T. (2010). Making global assessments work. *The Industrial-Organizational Psychologist, 48*, 59–64.

19. Anderson, N., Salgado, J. F., & Hülsheger, U. R. (2010). Applicant reactions in selection: Comprehensive meta-analysis into reaction generalization versus situational specificity. *International Journal of Selection and Assessment, 18*, 291–304.

20. McDaniel, M. A., Whetzel, D. L., Schmidt, F. L., & Maurer, S. D. (1994). The validity of employment interviews: A comprehensive review and meta-analysis. *Journal of Applied Psychology, 79*, 599–616; Sackett, P.

R., Zhang, C., Berry, C. M., & Lievens, F. (2022). Revisiting meta-analytic estimates of validity in personnel selection: Addressing systematic overcorrection for restriction of range. *Journal of Applied Psychology, 107*, 2040–2068; Schmidt, F. L., & Hunter, J. E. (1998). The validity and utility of selection methods in personnel psychology: Practical and theoretical implications of 85 years of research findings. *Psychological Bulletin, 124*, 262–274.

21. Levashina, J., Hartwell, C. J., Morgeson, F. P., & Campion, M. A. (2014). The structured employment interview: Narrative and quantitative review of the research literature. *Personnel Psychology, 67*, 241–293.

22. McDaniel, M. A., Whetzel, D. L., Schmidt, F. L., & Maurer, S. D. (1994). The validity of employment interviews: A comprehensive review and meta-analysis. *Journal of Applied Psychology, 79*, 599–616; Sackett, P. R., Zhang, C., Berry, C. M., & Lievens, F. (2022). Revisiting meta-analytic estimates of validity in personnel selection: Addressing systematic overcorrection for restriction of range. *Journal of Applied Psychology, 107*, 2040–2068; Schmidt, F. L., & Hunter, J. E. (1998). The validity and utility of selection methods in personnel psychology: Practical and theoretical implications of 85 years of research findings. *Psychological Bulletin, 124*, 262–274.

23. Sackett, P. R., Zhang, C., Berry, C. M., & Lievens, F. (2022). Revisiting meta-analytic estimates of validity in personnel selection: Addressing systematic overcorrection for restriction of range. *Journal of Applied Psychology, 107*, 2040–2068; Shaffer, J. A., & Postlethwaite, B. E. (2012). A matter of context: A meta-analytic investigation of the relative validity of contextualized and noncontextualized personality measures. *Personnel Psychology, 65*, 445–493.

24. Ones, D. S., Viswesvaran, C., & Schmidt, F. L. (1993). Comprehensive meta-analysis of integrity test validities: Findings and implications for personnel selection and theories of job performance. *Journal of Applied Psychology, 78*, 679–703; Sackett, P. R., Zhang, C., Berry, C. M., & Lievens, F. (2022). Revisiting meta-analytic estimates of validity in personnel selection: Addressing systematic overcorrection for restriction of

range. *Journal of Applied Psychology, 107*, 2040–2068; Van Iddekinge, C. H., Roth, P. L., Raymark, P. H., & Odle-Dusseau, H. N. (2012). The criterion-related validity of integrity tests: An updated meta-analysis. *Journal of Applied Psychology, 97*, 499–530.

25. Sackett, P. R., Zhang, C., Berry, C. M., & Lievens, F. (2022). Revisiting meta-analytic estimates of validity in personnel selection: Addressing systematic overcorrection for restriction of range. *Journal of Applied Psychology, 107*, 2040–2068; Schmidt, F. L., & Hunter, J. E. (1998). The validity and utility of selection methods in personnel psychology: Practical and theoretical implications of 85 years of research findings. *Psychological Bulletin, 124*, 262–274.

26. Hunter, J. E., & Hunter, R. F. (1984). Validity and utility of alternative predictors of job performance. *Psychological Bulletin, 96*, 72–98; Sackett, P. R., Zhang, C., Berry, C. M., & Lievens, F. (2022). Revisiting meta-analytic estimates of validity in personnel selection: Addressing systematic overcorrection for restriction of range. *Journal of Applied Psychology, 107*, 2040–2068; Schmidt, F. L., & Hunter, J. E. (1998). The validity and utility of selection methods in personnel psychology: Practical and theoretical implications of 85 years of research findings. *Psychological Bulletin, 124*, 262–274.

27. Christian, M. S., Edwards, B. D., & Bradley, J. C. (2010). Situational judgment tests: Constructs assessed and a meta-analysis of their criterion-related validities. *Personnel Psychology, 63*, 83–117; Sackett, P. R., Zhang, C., Berry, C. M., & Lievens, F. (2022). Revisiting meta-analytic estimates of validity in personnel selection: Addressing systematic overcorrection for restriction of range. *Journal of Applied Psychology, 107*, 2040–2068.

28. Arthur, W., Day, E. A., McNelly, T. L., & Edens, P. S. (2003). A meta-analysis of the criterion-related validity of assessment center dimensions. *Personnel Psychology, 56*, 125–153; Sackett, P. R., Shewach, O. R., & Keiser, H. N. (2017). Assessment centers versus cognitive ability tests: Challenging the conventional wisdom on criterion-related validity. *Journal of Applied Psychology, 102*(10), 1435–1447; Sackett, P. R., Zhang, C., Berry, C. M., & Lievens, F. (2022). Revisiting meta-analytic estimates of validity in

personnel selection: Addressing systematic overcorrection for restriction of range. *Journal of Applied Psychology, 107*, 2040–2068.

29. Hunter, J. E., & Hunter, R. F. (1984). Validity and utility of alternative predictors of job performance. *Psychological Bulletin, 96*, 72–98; Sackett, P. R., Zhang, C., Berry, C. M., & Lievens, F. (2022). Revisiting meta-analytic estimates of validity in personnel selection: Addressing systematic overcorrection for restriction of range. *Journal of Applied Psychology, 107*, 2040–2068. Vinchur, A. J., Schippmann, J. S., Switzer, F. S., III, & Roth, P. L. (1998). A meta-analytic review of predictors of job performance for salespeople. *Journal of Applied Psychology, 83*, 586–597.

30. Wilhelmy, A., Kleinmann, M., König, C., Melchers, K., & Truxillo, D. M. (2016). How and why do interviewers try to make impressions on applicants? A qualitative study. *Journal of Applied Psychology, 101*, 313–332.

31. Wilhelmy, A., Kleinmann, M., König, C., Melchers, K., & Truxillo, D. M. (2016). How and why do interviewers try to make impressions on applicants? A qualitative study. *Journal of Applied Psychology, 101*, 313–332.

32. Sackett, P. R., Zhang, C., Berry, C. M., & Lievens, F. (2022). Revisiting meta-analytic estimates of validity in personnel selection: Addressing systematic overcorrection for restriction of range. *Journal of Applied Psychology, 107*, 2040–2068.

33. Friedman, T. L. (2014). How to get a job at Google. *The New York Times.* https://www.nytimes.com/2014/02/23/opinion/sunday/friedman-how-to-get-a-job-at-google.html?_r=0

34. Arvey, R. D., & Campion, J. E. (1982). The employment interview: A summary and review of recent research. *Personnel Psychology, 35*, 281–322; Janz, T. (1982). Initial comparisons of patterned behavior description interviews versus unstructured interviews. *Journal of Applied Psychology, 67*, 577–580; Latham, G. P., Saari, L. M., Pursell, E. D., & Campion, M. A. (1980). The situational interview. *Journal of Applied Psychology, 65*, 422–427; Levashina, J., Hartwell, C. J., Morgeson, F. P., & Campion, M. A. (2014). The structured employment interview: Narrative and quantitative review of the research literature. *Personnel Psychology, 67*, 241–293.

35. Campion, M. A., Palmer, D. K., & Campion, J. E. (1997). A review of structure in the selection interview. *Personnel Psychology, 50,* 655–702; Chapman, D. S., & Zweig, D. I. (2005). Developing a nomological network for interview structure: Antecedents and consequences of the structured selection interview. *Personnel Psychology, 58,* 673–702; Hartwell, C. J., & Campion, M. A. (2016). Getting on the same page: The effect of normative feedback interventions on structured interview ratings. *Journal of Applied Psychology, 101,* 757–778.

36. Basch, J. M., Brenner, F., Melchers, K. G., Krumm, S., Dräger, L., Herzer, H., & Schuwerk, E. (2021). A good thing takes time: The role of preparation time in asynchronous video interviews. *International Journal of Selection and Assessment, 29*(3–4), 378–392; Basch, J. M., & Melchers, K. G. (2019). Fair and flexible?! Explanations can improve applicant reactions toward asynchronous video interviews. *Personnel Assessment and Decisions, 5,* 1–11; Lukacik, E. R., Bourdage, J. S., & Roulin, N. (2022). Into the void: A conceptual model and research agenda for the design and use of asynchronous video interviews. *Human Resource Management Review, 32*(1); McCarthy, J. M., Truxillo, D. M., Bauer, T. N., Erdogan, B., Shao, Y., Wang, M., . . . & Gardner, C. (2021). Distressed and distracted by COVID-19 during high-stakes virtual interviews: The role of job interview anxiety on performance and reactions. *Journal of Applied Psychology, 106,* 1103–1117.

37. Bye, H. H., & Sandal, G. M. (2016). Applicant personality and procedural justice perceptions of group selection interviews. *Journal of Business and Psychology, 31,* 569–582.

38. Barrick, M. R., & Mount, M. K. (1991). The Big Five personality dimensions and job performance: A meta-analysis. *Personnel Psychology, 44,* 1–26.

39. International Personality Item Pool: A Scientific Collaboratory for the Development of Advanced Measures of Personality Traits and Other Individual Differences. http://ipip.ori.org/

40. Goldberg, L. R. (1999). A broad-bandwidth, public domain, personality inventory measuring the lower-level facets of several five-factor models. *Personality Psychology in Europe, 7,* 7–28; International Personality Item Pool: A Scientific Collaboratory for the Development of Advanced Measures of Personality Traits and Other Individual Differences. http://ipip.ori.org/

41. Sackett, P. R., Zhang, C., Berry, C. M., & Lievens, F. (2022). Revisiting meta-analytic estimates of validity in personnel selection: Addressing systematic overcorrection for restriction of range. *Journal of Applied Psychology, 107,* 2040–2068.

42. Hogan, J., Barrett, P., & Hogan, R. (2007). Personality measurement, faking, and employment selection. *Journal of Applied Psychology, 92,* 1270–1285; Kleinmann, M., Ingold, P. V., Lievens, F., Jansen, A., Melchers, K. G., & König, C. J. (2011). A different look at why selection procedures work: The role of candidates' ability to identify criteria. *Organizational Psychology Review, 1,* 128–146. Marcus, B. (2009). Faking from the applicant's perspective: A theory of self-presentation in personnel selection settings. *International Journal of Selection and Assessment, 17,* 417–430; Van Hooft, E. A., & Born, M. P. (2012). Intentional response distortion on personality tests: Using eye-tracking to understand response processes when faking. *Journal of Applied Psychology, 97,* 301–316.

43. Crant, J. M. (1995). The Proactive Personality Scale and objective job performance among real estate agents. *Journal of Applied Psychology, 80,* 532–537; Spitzmuller, M., Sin, H. P., Howe, M., & Fatimah, S. (2015). Investigating the uniqueness and usefulness of proactive personality in organizational research: A meta-analytic review. *Human Performance, 28,* 351–379.

44. Cullen, K. L., Edwards, B. D., Casper, W. C., & Gue, K. R. (2014). Employees' adaptability and perceptions of change-related uncertainty: Implications for perceived organizational support, job satisfaction, and performance. *Journal of Business and Psychology, 29,* 269–280.

45. Lee, Y., Berry, C. M., & Gonzalez-Mulé, E. (2019). The importance of being humble: A meta-analysis and incremental validity analysis of the relationship between honesty-humility and job performance. *Journal of Applied Psychology, 104*(12), 1535–1546.

46. U.S. Department of Labor. (2009). *Other workplace standards: Lie detector tests.* https://www.dol.gov/compliance/guide/eppa.htm

47. Marcus, B., Lee, K., & Ashton, M. C. (2007). Personality dimensions explaining relationships between integrity tests and counterproductive behavior: Big Five, or one in addition? *Personnel Psychology, 60,* 1–34; Sackett, P. R., & Wanek, J. E. (1996). New developments in the use of measures of honesty, integrity, conscientiousness, dependability, trustworthiness, and reliability for personnel selection. *Personnel Psychology, 49,* 787–829.

48. Ones, D. S., Viswesvaran, C., & Schmidt, F. L. (1993). Comprehensive meta-analysis of integrity test validities: Findings and implications for personnel selection and theories of job performance. *Journal of Applied Psychology, 78,* 679–703.

49. Ones, D. S., Viswesvaran, C., & Schmidt, F. L. (2012). Integrity tests predict counterproductive work behaviors and job performance well: Comment on Van Iddekinge, Roth, Raymark, and Odle-Dusseau. *Journal of Applied Psychology, 97,* 537–542; Sackett, P. R., & Schmitt, N. (2012). On reconciling conflicting meta-analytic findings regarding integrity test validity. *Journal of Applied Psychology, 97,* 550–556; Van Iddekinge, C. H., Roth, P. L., Raymark, P. H., & Odle-Dusseau, H. N. (2012). The criterion-related validity of integrity tests: An updated meta-analysis. *Journal of Applied Psychology, 97,* 499–530.

50. Berry, C. M., Sackett, P. R., & Wiemann, S. (2007). A review of recent developments in integrity test research. *Personnel Psychology, 60,* 271–301; Marcus, B., Lee, K., & Ashton, M. C. (2007). Personality dimensions explaining relationships between integrity tests and counterproductive behavior: Big Five, or one in addition? *Personnel Psychology, 60,* 1–34.

51. Guion, R. M. (1998). *Assessment, measurement, and prediction for personnel decisions.* Erlbaum.

52. Schmidt, F. L., & Hunter, J. E. (1998). The validity and utility of selection methods in personnel psychology: Practical and theoretical implications of 85 years of research findings. *Psychological Bulletin, 124,* 262–274.

53. Sackett, P. R., Zhang, C., Berry, C. M., & Lievens, F. (2022). Revisiting meta-analytic estimates of validity in personnel selection: Addressing systematic overcorrection for restriction of range. *Journal of Applied Psychology, 107*, 2040–2068.

54. Ones, D. S., Dilchert, S., & Viswesvaran, C. (2012). Cognitive abilities. In N. Schmitt (Ed.), *The Oxford handbook of personnel assessment and selection* (pp. 179–224). Oxford University Press; Ryan, A. M., & Powers, C. (2012). Workplace diversity. In N. Schmitt (Ed.), *The Oxford handbook of personnel assessment and selection* (pp. 814–831). Oxford University Press.

55. Ones, D. S., Dilchert, S., & Viswesvaran, C. (2012). Cognitive abilities. In N. Schmitt (Ed.), *The Oxford handbook of personnel assessment and selection* (pp. 179–224). Oxford University Press; Schmidt, F. L., & Hunter, J. (2004). General mental ability in the world of work: occupational attainment and job performance. *Journal of Personality and Social Psychology, 86*, 162–173.

56. Guion, R. M. (1965). *Personnel testing.* McGraw-Hill.

57. Gatewood, R., Feild, H., & Barrick, M. (2019). *Human resource selection* (9th ed.). Wessex Press.

58. Salovey, P., & Mayer, J. D. (1990). Emotional intelligence. *Imagination, Cognition and Personality, 9*, 185–211.

59. Joseph, D. L., Jin, J., Newman, D. A., & O'Boyle, E. H. (2015). Why does self-reported emotional intelligence predict job performance? A meta-analytic investigation of mixed EI. *Journal of Applied Psychology, 100*, 298–342; Joseph, D. L., & Newman, D. A. (2010). Emotional intelligence: An integrative meta-analysis and cascading model. *Journal of Applied Psychology, 95*, 54–78.

60. Landers, R. N., Armstrong, M. B., Collmus, A. B., Mujcic, S., & Blaik, J. (2022). Theory-driven game-based assessment of general cognitive ability: Design theory, measurement, prediction of performance, and test fairness. *Journal of Applied Psychology, 107*, 1655–1677.

61. Georgiou, K., & Lievens, F. (2022). Gamifying an assessment method: what signals are organizations sending to applicants? *Journal of Managerial Psychology, 37*, 559–574; Gkorezis, P., Georgiou, K., Nikolaou, I., & Kyriazati, A. (2021). Gamified or traditional situational judgement test? A moderated mediation model of recommendation intentions via organizational attractiveness. *European Journal of Work and Organizational Psychology, 30*(2), 240–250; Landers, R. N., Armstrong, M. B., Collmus, A. B., Mujcic, S., & Blaik, J. (2022). Theory-driven game-based assessment of general cognitive ability: Design theory, measurement, prediction of performance, and test fairness. *Journal of Applied Psychology, 107*, 1655–1677.

Landers, R. N., & Sanchez, D. R. (2022). Game-based, gamified, and gamefully designed assessments for employee selection: Definitions, distinctions, design, and validation. *International Journal of Selection and Assessment, 30*, 1–13.; Tippins, N. T., Oswald, F. L., & McPhail, S. M. (2021). Scientific, legal, and ethical concerns about AI-based personnel selection tools: a call to action. *Personnel Assessment and Decisions, 7*(2), 1–22.

62. JetBlue. (n.d.). *JetBlue: Hiring crewmembers with the skills to thrive.* https://rework.withgoogle.com/case-studies/JetBlue-hiring-crewmembers-with-skills-to-thrive/

63. Anderson, N., Salgado, J. F., & Hülsheger, U. R. (2010). Applicant reactions in selection: Comprehensive meta-analysis into reaction generalization versus situational specificity. *International journal of selection and assessment, 18*(3), 291–304; Schmidt, F. L., & Hunter, J. E. (1998). The validity and utility of selection methods in personnel psychology: Practical and theoretical implications of 85 years of research findings. *Psychological Bulletin, 124*, 262–274.

64. Bauer, T. N., Truxillo, D. M., Mack, K., & Costa, A. B. (2011). Applicant reactions to technology-based selection: What we know so far. In N. T. Tippins & S. Adler (Eds.), *Technology-enhanced assessment* (pp. 190–223). Jossey-Bass.

65. Christian, M. S., Edwards, B. D., & Bradley, J. C. (2010). Situational judgment tests: Constructs assessed and a meta-analysis of their criterion-related validities. *Personnel Psychology, 63*, 83–117; Lievens, F., Sackett, P. R., & Zhang, C. (2021). Personnel selection: A longstanding story of impact at the individual, firm, and societal level. *European Journal of Work and Organizational Psychology, 30*, 444–455.

66. Arthur, W., Day, E. A., McNelly, T. L., & Edens, P. S. (2003). A meta-analysis of the criterion-related validity of assessment center dimensions. *Personnel Psychology, 56*, 125–153; Sackett, P. R., Shewach, O. R., & Keiser, H. N. (2017). Assessment centers versus cognitive ability tests: Challenging the conventional wisdom on criterion-related validity. *Journal of Applied Psychology, 102*, 1435–1447; Schmidt, F. L., & Hunter, J. E. (1998). The validity and utility of selection methods in personnel psychology: Practical and theoretical implications of 85 years of research findings. *Psychological Bulletin, 124*, 262–274.

67. Lievens, F., & De Soete, B. (2012). Simulations. In N. Schmitt (Ed.), *The Oxford handbook of personnel assessment and selection* (pp. 383–410). Oxford University Press.

68. Schmidt, F. L., & Hunter, J. E. (1998). The validity and utility of selection methods in personnel psychology: Practical and theoretical implications of 85 years of research findings. *Psychological Bulletin, 124*, 262–274.

69. Cucina, J. M., Caputo, P. M., Thibodeaux, H. F., & Maclane, C. N. (2012). Unlocking the key to biodata scoring: A comparison of empirical, rational, and hybrid approaches at different sample sizes. *Personnel Psychology, 65*, 385–428; Gatewood, R., Feild, H., & Barrick, M. (2019). *Human resource selection* (9th ed.). Wessex Press.

70. Schmidt, F. L., & Hunter, J. E. (1998). The validity and utility of selection methods in personnel psychology: Practical and theoretical implications of 85 years of research findings. *Psychological Bulletin, 124*, 262–274.

71. Ibid. Derous, E., & Ryan, A. M. (2019). When your resume is (not) turning you down: Modelling ethnic bias in resume screening. *Human Resource Management Journal, 29*, 113–130; Zaniboni, S., Kmicinska, M., Truxillo, D. M., Kahn, K., Paladino, M. P., & Fraccaroli, F. (2019). Will you still hire me when I am over 50? The effects of implicit and explicit age stereotyping on resume evaluations. *European Journal of Work and Organizational Psychology, 28*, 453–467.

72. Anderson, N., Salgado, J. F., & Hülsheger, U. R. (2010). Applicant reactions in selection: Comprehensive

meta-analysis into reaction generalization versus situational specificity. *International Journal of Selection and Assessment, 18*(3), 291–304.

73. Beltran, G. (2022). The pandemic changed everything about work, except the humble résumé. *The New York Times*, https://www.nytimes.com/2022/01/22/business/pandemic-work-resumes.html; Weed, J. (2021). Résumé-writing tips to help you get past the A.I. gatekeepers. *The New York Times*, https://www.nytimes.com/2021/03/19/business/resume-filter-articial-intelligence.html

74. Gatewood, R., Feild, H., & Barrick, M. (2019). *Human resource selection* (9th ed.). Wessex Press.

75. Ibid.

76. Griffith, J. N., & Harris, T. C. (2020). The relationship between criminal records and job performance: An examination of customer service representatives. *Personnel Assessment and Decisions, 6*(3), 13–17.

77. Mohan, P. (2022). Slack publishes playbook for hiring formerly incarcerated workers. *Fast Company*. https://www.fastcompany.com/90788078/slack-launhces-playbook-for-hiring-formerly-incarcerated-workers#:~:text=The%20playbook%2C%20a%20joint%20project,best%20to%20support%20those%20employees

78. Fair Chance to Compete for Jobs, 87 F. R. 24885 (proposed April 27, 2022). https://www.federalregister.gov/documents/2022/04/27/2022-08975/fair-chance-to-compete-for-jobs#:~:text=With%20some%20exceptions%2C%20the%20Fair,of%20employment%20to%20that%20applicant; "Ban the box" and background checks—Recent trends and movements. (2017, July 12). *Labor and Employment Law Blog*, SheppardMullins. https://www.laboremploymentlawblog.com/2017/07/articles/background-investigations/criminal-background-checks/

79. Chicago to pay $3.8 million as part of Fire Department gender bias case. (2016, December 9). *Chicago Tribune*. http://www.chicagotribune.com/news/local/politics/ct-chicago-fire-department-lawsuit-gender-bias-met-20161209-story.html

80. Gebhardt, D. L., & Baker, T. A. (2022). Designing criterion measures for physically demanding jobs. *Military Psychology*, 1–16; Courtright, S. H., McCormick, B. W., Postlethwaite, B. E., Reeves, C. J., & Mount, M. K. (2013). A meta-analysis of sex differences in physical ability: Revised estimates and strategies for reducing differences in selection contexts. *Journal of Applied Psychology, 98*, 623–641.

81. Van Iddekinge, C. H., Lanivich, S. E., Roth, P. L., & Junco, E. (2016). Social media for selection? Validity and adverse impact potential of a Facebook-based assessment. *Journal of Management, 42*, 1811–1835.

82. Zhang, L., Van Iddekinge, C. H., Arnold, J. D., Roth, P. L., Lievens, F., Lanivich, S. E., & Jordan, S. L. (2020). What's on job seekers' social media sites? A content analysis and effects of structure on recruiter judgments and predictive validity. *Journal of Applied Psychology, 105*, 1530–1546.

83. Hartwell, C. J., & Campion, M. A. (2020). Getting social in selection: How social networking website content is perceived and used in hiring. *International Journal of Selection and Assessment, 28*, 1–16.

84. Roulin, N., & Levashina, J. (2019). LinkedIn as a new selection method: Psychometric properties and assessment approach. *Personnel Psychology, 72*(2), 187–211.

85. Roulin, N., & Stronach, R. (2022). LinkedIn-based assessments of applicant personality, cognitive ability, and likelihood of organizational citizenship behaviors: Comparing self-, other-, and language-based automated ratings. *International Journal of Selection and Assessment, 30*(4), 503–525.

86. Marwan, S. (2022). Amazon, Hilton, Pepsi, and others commit to hiring thousands of refugees. *Fast Company*. https://www.fastcompany.com/90791056/amazon-hilton-pepsi-and-others-commit-to-hiring-thousands-of-refugees

87. EARN Employer Assistance and Resource Network on Disability Inclusion. (2022). *Neurodiversity hiring initiatives and partnerships*. https://askearn.org/page/neurodiversity-hiring-initiatives-and-partnerships

88. Bernerth, J. B., Taylor, S. G., Walker, H. J., & Whitman, D. S. (2012). An empirical investigation of dispositional antecedents and performance-related outcomes of credit scores. *Journal of Applied Psychology, 97*, 469–478.

89. Bernerth, J. B., Taylor, S. G., Walker, H. J., & Whitman, D. S. (2012). An empirical investigation of dispositional antecedents and performance-related outcomes of credit scores. *Journal of Applied Psychology, 97*, 469–478.

90. Bauer, T. N., Truxillo, D. M., Jones, M., & Brady, G. (2020). Privacy and cybersecurity challenges, opportunities, and recommendations: Personnel selection in an era of online application systems and big data. In S. E. Woo, L. Tay, & R. Proctor (Eds.), *Big data in psychological research*. APA Books; Brady, G. M., Truxillo, D. M., Bauer, T. N., & Jones, M. P. (2021). The development and validation of the Privacy and Data Security Concerns Scale (PDSCS). *International Journal of Selection and Assessment, 29*(1), 100–113; Kovacs, E. (2023). *Burger chain Five Guys discloses data breach impacting job applicants*. https://www.securityweek.com/burger-chain-five-guys-discloses-data-breach-impacting-job-applicants; Page, C. (2022). *Panasonic says hackers accessed personal data of job candidates*. TechCrunch. https://techcrunch.com/2022/01/10/panasonic-breach-data-stolen/#:~:text=Panasonic%20says%20hackers%20accessed%20personal%20data%20of%20job%20candidates,-Carly%20Page%40carlypage_&text=Japanese%20tech%20giant%20Panasonic%20has,interns%20during%20a%20November%20cyberattack; Pascu, L. (2018). *Third-party data breach exposes info of Alabama hospital job applicants*. Bitdefender. https://www.bitdefender.com/blog/hotforsecurity/third-party-data-breach-exposes-info-of-alabama-hospital-job-applicants/

91. Harold, C. M., Holtz, B. C., Griepentrog, B. K., Brewer, L. M., & Marsh, S. M. (2016). Investigating the effects of applicant justice perceptions on job offer acceptance. *Personnel Psychology, 69*, 199–227; McCarthy, J. M., Bauer, T. N., Truxillo, D. M., Anderson, N. R., Costa, A. C., & Ahmed, S. M. (2017). Applicant perspectives during selection: A review addressing "so what?," "what's new?," and "where to next?" *Journal of Management, 43*, 1693–1725.

92. Millet, J. (2023). What will the hiring landscape look like in 2023? *Forbes*. https://www.forbes.com/sites/forbes

humanresourcescouncil/2023/01/13/what-will-the-hiring-landscape-look-like-in-2023/?sh=213ccb975522

93. Steiner, K. (2017). Bad candidate experience cost Virgin Media $5M annually—and how they turned it around. *LinkedIn Talent Blog.* https://business.linkedin.com/talent-solutions/blog/candidate-experience/2017/bad-candidate-experience-cost-virgin-media-5m-annually-and-how-they-turned-that-around

94. McCarthy, J. M., Bauer, T. N., Truxillo, D. M., Anderson, N. R., Costa, A. C., & Ahmed, S. M. (2017). Applicant perspectives during selection: A review addressing "so what?," "what's new?," and "where to next?" *Journal of Management, 43,* 1693–1725.

95. Anderson, N., Salgado, J. F., & Hülsheger, U. R. (2010). Applicant reactions in selection: Comprehensive meta-analysis into reaction generalization versus situational specificity. *International Journal of Selection and Assessment, 18,* 291–304; Hoang, T. G., Truxillo, D. M., Erdogan, B., & Bauer, T. N. (2012). Cross-cultural examination of applicant reactions to selection methods: United States and Vietnam. *International Journal of Selection and Assessment, 20,* 209–219.

96. Bauer, T. N., McCarthy, J., Anderson, N., Truxillo, D. M., & Salgado, J. (2020) *What we know about the candidate experience: Research summary and best practices for applicant reactions.* SIOP White Paper series; Hausknecht, J. P., Day, D. V., & Thomas, S. C. (2004). Applicant reactions to selection procedures: An updated model and meta-analysis. *Personnel Psychology, 57,* 639–683.

97. Truxillo, D. M., Bauer, T. N., Campion, M. A., & Paronto, M. E. (2002). Selection fairness information and applicant reactions: A longitudinal field study. *Journal of Applied Psychology, 87,* 1020–1031; Truxillo, D. M., Bodner, T. E., Bertolino, M., Bauer, T. N., & Yonce, C. A. (2009). Effects of explanations on applicant reactions: A meta-analytic review. *International Journal of Selection and Assessment, 17,* 346–361.

98. Talent Board. (2022). *What are the CandE Awards?* https://www.thetalentboard.org/cande-awards/

99. Folger, N., Brosi, P., Stumpf-Wollersheim, J., & Welpe, I. M. (2022). Applicant reactions to digital selection methods: a signaling perspective on innovativeness and procedural justice. *Journal of Business and Psychology, 37*(4), 735–757; Köchling, A., & Wehner, M. C. (2023). Better explaining the benefits why AI? Analyzing the impact of explaining the benefits of AI-supported selection on applicant responses. *International Journal of Selection and Assessment, 31*(1), 45–62; Noble, S. M., Foster, L. L., & Craig, S. B. (2021). The procedural and interpersonal justice of automated application and résumé screening. *International Journal of Selection and Assessment, 29*(2), 139–153; Woods, S. A., Ahmed, S., Nikolaou, I., Costa, A. C., & Anderson, N. R. (2020). Personnel selection in the digital age: A review of validity and applicant reactions, and future research challenges. *European Journal of Work and Organizational Psychology, 29*(1), 64–77.

100. Gatewood, R., Feild, H., & Barrick, M. (2019). *Human resource selection* (9th ed.). Wessex Press.

CHAPTER 8

1. Johnson, J. (2022, February 22). Google launches career training initiative to help people secure higher-paying jobs. *Black Enterprise.* https://www.blackenterprise.com/google-launches-career-training-initiative-to-help-people-secure-higher-paying-jobs/; Lohr, S. (2022, February 17). Google creates $100 million fund for skills training program. *The New York Times.* https://www.nytimes.com/2022/02/17/business/google-training-program.html; Singman, B. (2022, February 17). *Google launching job training, placement initiative through $100 M career certificates fund.* Fox Business. https://www.foxbusiness.com/politics/google-job-training-placement-initiative-career-certificates-fund

2. Ho, M. (2021, December). What effect has the pandemic had on L&D? *TD: Talent Development, 75,* 24–29.

3. Ibid.

4. Aguinis, H., & Kraiger, K. (2009). Benefits of training and development for individuals and teams, organizations, and society. *Annual Review of Psychology, 60,* 451–474; Salas, E., Tannenbaum, S. I., Kraiger, K., & Smith-Jentsch, K. A. (2012). The science of training and development in organizations: What matters in practice. *Psychological Science in the Public Interest, 13,* 74–101.

5. Ford, J. K. (2020). *Learning in organizations: An evidence-based approach.* Routledge.

6. Oswald, F. L., Behrend, T. S., Putka, D. J., & Sinar, E. (2020). Big data in industrial-organizational psychology and human resource management: Forward progress for organizational research and practice. *Annual Review of Organizational Psychology and Organizational Behavior, 7,* 505–533.

7. Glenn, M. L., & Tellez, C. T. (2022, January). Nonclinical staff training adds more humanity to healthcare. *TD: Talent Development, 76,* 24–26.

8. Ho, M. (2021, December). What effect has the pandemic had on L&D? *TD: Talent Development, 75,* 24–29.

9. Donelson, M. (2021, August). Captivating compliance training is possible. *TD: Talent Development, 75,* 40–43; Uniform Guidelines on Employee Selection Procedures. (1978). *Federal Register, 43,* 38290–38315.

10. Ford, J. K. (2020). *Learning in organizations: An evidence-based approach.* Routledge.

11. Kraiger, K., & Ford, J. K. (2021). The science of workplace instruction: Learning and development applied to work. *Annual Review of Organizational Psychology and Organizational Behavior, 8,* 45–72.

12. Chung, S., Zhan, Y., Noe, R. A., & Jiang, K. (2022). Is it time to update and expand training motivation theory? A meta-analytic review of training motivation research in the 21st century. *Journal of Applied Psychology, 107*(7), 1150–1179; Ford, J. K. (2020). *Learning in organizations: An evidence-based approach.* Routledge.

13. Kruger, J., & Dunning, D. (1999). Unskilled and unaware of it: How difficulties in recognizing one's own incompetence lead to inflated self-assessments. *Journal of Personality and Social Psychology, 77,* 1121–1132.

14. Ford, J. K., Baldwin, T. T., & Prasad, J. (2018). Transfer of training: The known and the unknown. *Annual Review of Organizational Psychology and Organizational Behavior, 5,* 201–225.

15. Crain, T. L., Hammer, L. B., Bodner, T., Olson, R., Kossek, E. E., Moen, P.,

& Buxton, O. M. (2019). Sustaining sleep: Results from the randomized controlled work, family, and health study. *Journal of Occupational Health Psychology, 24*, 180–197; Hammer, L. B., Truxillo, D. M., Bodner, T., Rineer, J., Pytlovany, A. C., & Richman, A. (2015). Effects of a workplace intervention targeting psychosocial risk factors on safety and health outcomes. *BioMed Research International, 2015*.

16. Hammer, L. B., Truxillo, D. M., Bodner, T., Pytlovany, A. C., & Richman, A. (2019). Exploration of the impact of organisational context on a workplace safety and health intervention. *Work & Stress, 33*(2), 192–210.

17. Kraiger, K., & Ford, J. K. (2021). The science of workplace instruction: Learning and development applied to work. *Annual Review of Organizational Psychology and Organizational Behavior, 8*, 45–72.

18. Ford, J. K. (2020). *Learning in organizations: An evidence-based approach.* Routledge.

19. Ibid.

20. Wolfson, M. A., Mathieu, J. E., Tannenbaum, S. I., & Maynard, M. T. (2019). Informal field-based learning and work design. *Journal of Applied Psychology, 104*, 1283–1295; Wolfson, M. A., Tannenbaum, S. I., Mathieu, J. E., & Maynard, M. T. (2018). A cross-level investigation of informal field-based learning and performance improvements. *Journal of Applied Psychology, 103*, 14–36.

21. Arthur, W., Jr., Bennett, W., Jr., Edens, P. S., & Bell, S. T. (2003). Effectiveness of training in organizations: A meta-analysis of design and evaluation features. *Journal of Applied Psychology,88*, 234–245; Ford, J. K. (2020). *Learning in organizations: An evidence-based approach.* Routledge.

22. Delta Airlines. (n.d.). *Delta Atlanta Training Center: Let's take a tour of the facilities.* https://atpctp.delta.com/content/atp-ctp/en_US/datc/facilities.html

23. Ford, J. K. (2020). *Learning in organizations: An evidence-based approach.* Routledge.

24. Mao, R. Q., Lan, L., Kay, J., Lohre, R., Ayeni, O. R., & Goel, D. P. (2021). Immersive virtual reality for surgical training: A systematic review. *Journal of Surgical Research, 268*, 40–58.

25. Likens, S., & Mower, A. (2022, September 15). *What does virtual reality and the metaverse mean for training?* PwC. https://www.pwc.com/us/en/tech-effect/emerging-tech/virtual-reality-study.html

26. Feeney, R. (2017). Old tricks are the best tricks: Repurposing programmed instruction in the mobile, digital age. *Performance Improvement, 56*(5), 6–17; Goldstein, I. L., & Ford, J. K. (2002). *Training in organizations: Needs assessment, development, and evaluation* (4th ed.). Wadsworth Cengage Learning.

27. Ho, M. (2021, December). What effect has the pandemic had on L&D? *TD: Talent Development, 75*, 24–29.

28. Brown, K. G., Howardson, G., & Fisher, S. L. (2016). Learner control and e-learning: Taking stock and moving forward. *Annual Review of Organizational Psychology and Organizational Behavior, 3*, 267–291.

29. Bell, B. S., & Kozlowski, S. W. (2008). Active learning: Effects of core training design elements on self-regulatory processes, learning, and adaptability. *Journal of Applied Psychology, 93*, 296–316; Sitzmann, T., Kraiger, K., Stewart, D., & Wisher, R. (2006). The comparative effectiveness of web-based and classroom instruction: A meta-analysis. *Personnel Psychology, 59*, 623–664.

30. SAP Learning Hub. https://training.sap.com/shop/learninghub

31. Baldwin, T. T. (1992). Effects of alternative modeling strategies on outcomes of interpersonal-skills training. *Journal of Applied Psychology, 77*, 147–154; Bandura, A. (1977). *Social learning theory.* Prentice Hall; Taylor, P. J., Russ-Eft, D. F., & Chan, D. W. (2005); A meta-analytic review of behavior modeling training. *Journal of Applied Psychology, 90*, 692–709.

32. Alhejji, H., Garavan, T., Carbery, R., O'Brien, F., & McGuire, D. (2016). Diversity training programme outcomes: A systematic review. *Human Resource Development Quarterly, 27*, 95–149; Dobbin, F., & Kalev, A. (2016, July–August). Why diversity programs fail and what works better. *Harvard Business Review*, 52–60; Kalinoski, Z. T., Steele-Johnson, D., Peyton, E. J., Leas, K. A., Steinke, J., & Bowling, N. A. (2013). A meta-analytic evaluation of diversity training outcomes. *Journal of Organizational Behavior, 34*, 1076–1104; Lindsey, A., King, E., Hebl, M., & Levine, N. (2015). The impact of method, motivation, and empathy on diversity training effectiveness. *Journal of Business and Psychology, 30*, 605–617; Manjoo, F. (2014). Exposing hidden bias at Google. *The New York Times.* http://www.nytimes.com/2014/09/25/technology/exposing-hidden-biases-at-google-to-improve-diversity.html

33. Ragins, B. R., & Ehrhardt, K. (2021). Gaining perspective: The impact of close cross-race friendships on diversity training and education. *Journal of Applied Psychology, 106*, 856–881.

34. Devine, P. G., & Ash, T. L. (2022). Diversity training goals, limitations, and promise: a review of the multidisciplinary literature. *Annual Review of Psychology, 73*, 403–429.

35. Roberson, Q. M. (2019). Diversity in the workplace: A review, synthesis, and future research agenda. *Annual Review of Organizational Psychology and Organizational Behavior, 6*, 69–88.

36. Roehling, M. V., Wu, D., Choi, M. G., & Dulebohn, J. H. (2022). The effects of sexual harassment training on proximal and transfer training outcomes: A meta-analytic investigation. *Personnel Psychology, 75*, 3–31.

37. Hughes, A. M., Gregory, M. E., Joseph, D. L., Sonesh, S. C., Marlow, S. L., Lacerenza, C. N., . . . & Salas, E. (2016). Saving lives: A meta-analysis of team training in healthcare. *Journal of Applied Psychology, 101*, 1266–1304; Marks, M. A., Sabella, M. J., Burke, C. S., & Zaccaro, S. J. (2002). The impact of cross-training on team effectiveness. *Journal of Applied Psychology, 87*, 3–13; Salas, E., DiazGranados, D., Klein, C., Burke, C. S., Stagl, K. C., Goodwin, G. F., & Halpin, S. M. (2008). Does team training improve team performance? A meta-analysis. *Human Factors, 50*, 903–933.

38. Bono, J. E., Purvanova, R. K., Towler, A. J., & Peterson, D. B. (2009). A survey of executive coaching practices. *Personnel Psychology, 62*, 361–404; Ford, J. K. (2020). *Learning in organizations: An evidence-based approach.* Routledge.

39. Center for Creative Leadership. (n.d.). https://www.ccl.org/people/cindy-mccauley-2/; The long view: Cindy McCauley. (2017, February). *TD: Training and Development*, 62–63.

40. Byebierggaard, P., & Yoder, B. (2017, May). The sense-making loop. *TD: Training and Development*, 38–43; Ford, J. K. (2020). *Learning in organizations: An evidence-based approach.* Routledge.

41. Eby, L. T., Allen, T. D., Conley, K. M., Williamson, R. L., Henderson, T. G., & Mancini, V. S. (2019). Mindfulness-based training interventions for employees: A qualitative review of the literature. *Human Resource Management Review*, *29*, 156–178.

42. Hülsheger, U. R., Feinholdt, A., & Nübold, A. (2015). A low-dose mindfulness intervention and recovery from work: Effects on psychological detachment, sleep quality, and sleep duration. *Journal of Occupational and Organizational Psychology*, *88*, 464–489

43. Lau, Y. (2020). Increasing mindfulness in the workplace. *Forbes.* https://www.forbes.com/sites/forbeshumanresourcescouncil/2020/10/05/increasing-mindfulness-in-the-workplace/?sh=5907a4606956

44. Landers, R. N., & Armstrong, M. B. (2017). Enhancing instructional outcomes with gamification: An empirical test of the technology-enhanced training effectiveness model. *Computers in Human Behavior*, *71*, 499–507; Landers, R. N., Auer, E. M., Helms, A. B., Marin, S., & Armstrong, M. B. (2019). Gamification of adult learning: Gamifying employee training and development. In R. N. Landers (Ed.), *Cambridge handbook of technology and employee behavior* (pp. 271–295). Cambridge University Press.

45. Doak, K. (2021, December 30). Developing a microlearning strategy in an attention economy. *TD Magazine.* https://www.td.org/magazines/td-magazine/developing-a-microlearning-strategy-in-an-attention-economy

46. Bauer, T. N., Bodner, T., Erdogan, B., Truxillo, D. M., & Tucker, J. S. (2007). Newcomer adjustment during organizational socialization: A meta-analytic review of antecedents, outcomes, and methods. *Journal of Applied Psychology*, *92*, 707–721; Saks, A. M., Uggerslev, K. L., & Fassina, N. E. (2007). Socialization tactics and newcomer adjustment: A meta-analytic review and test of a model. *Journal of Vocational Behavior*, *70*, 413–446.

47. Smith, J. (2021, September 10). Online onboarding: How to master the new (virtual) reality. *Forbes* Technology Council post. https://www.forbes.com/sites/forbestechcouncil/2021/09/10/online-onboarding-how-to-master-the-new-virtual-reality/?sh=7d8ea2533770

48. Ellis, A. M., Nifadkar, S. S., Bauer, T. N., & Erdogan, B. (2017). Newcomer adjustment: Examining the role of managers' perception of newcomer proactive behavior during organizational socialization. *Journal of Applied Psychology*, *102*(6), 993–1001.

49. Klein, H. J., & Polin, B. (2012). Are organizations on board with best practices onboarding? In C. Wanberg (Ed.), *The Oxford handbook of organizational socialization* (pp. 267–287). Oxford University Press.

50. Bauer, T. N., Erdogan, B., Caughlin, D., Ellis, A. M., & Kurkoski, J. (2021). Jump-starting the socialization experience: The longitudinal role of day 1 newcomer resources on adjustment. *Journal of Management*, *47*(8), 2226–2261.

51. Bauer, T. N., & Erdogan, B. (2016). *Organizational behavior.* Flat World Knowledge; Durett, J. (2006, March 1). *Technology opens the door to success at Ritz-Carlton.* http://www.managesmarter.com/msg/search/article_display.jsp?vnu_content_id=1002157749; Elswick, J. (2000, February). Puttin' on the Ritz: Hotel chain touts training to benefit its recruiting and retention. *Employee Benefit News*, *14*, 9; The Ritz-Carlton Company: How it became a "legend" in service. (2001, January–February). *Corporate University Review*, *9*, 16.

52. Lerman, R., & Greene, J. (2020). Big tech was first to send workers home. Now it's in no hurry to bring them back. *The Washington Post.* https://www.washingtonpost.com/technology/2020/05/18/facebook-google-work-from-home/; Smith, J. (2021, September 10). Online onboarding: How to master the new (virtual) reality. *Forbes* Technology Council post. https://www.forbes.com/sites/forbestechcouncil/2021/09/10/online-onboarding-how-to-master-the-new-virtual-reality/?sh=7d8ea2533770

53. Bauer, T. N. (2015). *Onboarding: The critical role of hiring managers.* SuccessFactors white paper series. https://www.researchgate.net/publication/286447336_The_critical_role_of_the_hiring_manager_in_new_employee_onboarding

54. Information summarized based on research by Talya Bauer.

55. Ellis, A. M., Nifadkar, S. S., Bauer, T. N., & Erdogan, B. (2017). Newcomer adjustment: Examining the role of managers' perception of newcomer proactive behavior during organizational socialization. *Journal of Applied Psychology*, *102*(6), 993–1001.

56. Ellis, A. M., Nifadkar, S. S., Bauer, T. N., & Erdogan, B. (2017). Your new hires won't succeed unless you onboard them properly. *Harvard Business Review.* https://hbr.org/2017/06/your-new-hires-wont-succeed-unless-you-onboard-them-properly

57. National Institutes of Health NIH Ethics Program. (2022). *Welcome to annual ethics training.* https://ethics.od.nih.gov/aet; Raicu, I. (2017, May 26). Rethinking ethics training in Silicon Valley. *The Atlantic.* https://www.theatlantic.com/technology/archive/2017/05/rethinking-ethics-training-in-silicon-valley/525456/

58. Oswald, F. L., Behrend, T. S., Putka, D. J., & Sinar, E. (2020). Big data in industrial-organizational psychology and human resource management: Forward progress for organizational research and practice. *Annual Review of Organizational Psychology and Organizational Behavior*, *7*, 505–533.

59. Alliger, G. M., Tannenbaum, S. I., Bennett, W., Jr., Traver, H., & Shotland, A. (1997). A meta-analysis of the relations among training criteria. *Personnel Psychology*, *50*, 341–358.

60. McIntosh, C. (2017, June). Swapping training delivery for knowledge building. *TD: Talent Development*, 60–61.

61. Sitzmann, T., & Weinhardt, J. M. (2019). Approaching evaluation from a multilevel perspective: A comprehensive analysis of the indicators of training effectiveness. *Human Resource Management Review*, *29*, 253–269.

62. Bushée, D. (2017, March). Analyze this. *TD: Training and Development*, 28–29; Ketter, P. (2017, April). Artificial intelligence creeps into talent development. *TD: Talent Development*, 22–25; Oswald, F. L., Behrend, T. S., Putka, D. J., & Sinar, E. (2020). Big data in industrial-organizational psychology and human resource management: Forward progress for organizational research and practice. *Annual Review of Organizational*

Psychology and Organizational Behavior, 7, 505–533.

63. Ford, J. K. (2020). *Learning in organizations: An evidence-based approach.* Routledge.

64. Ibid.

65. Spurk, D., Hirschi, A., & Dries, N. (2019). Antecedents and outcomes of objective versus subjective career success: Competing perspectives and future directions. *Journal of Management, 45*(1), 35–69.

66. Raytheon Technologies. (n.d.). *Are you ready to take on a brand new challenge?* https://jobs.raytheon.com/college-jobs

67. Allen, T. D., Eby, L. T., Poteet, M. L., Lentz, E., & Lima, L. (2004). Career benefits associated with mentoring for protégés: A meta-analysis. *Journal of Applied Psychology, 89*, 127–136.

68. Dahling, J. J., Taylor, S. R., Chau, S. L., & Dwight, S. A. (2016). Does coaching matter? A multilevel model linking managerial coaching skill and frequency to sales goal attainment. *Personnel Psychology, 69*, 863–894.

69. Smith, M. (2022, February 15). *6 companies offering free tuition to employees from Dollywood to Starbucks.* CNBC. https://www.cnbc.com/2022/02/15/dolly-partons-dollywood-is-the-latest-company-to-offer-free-tuition.html

70. Gholston, I. S. (2021, October 1). Home Depot partnership seeks to address diversity deficiencies. *TD Magazine.* https://www.td.org/magazines/td-magazine/home-depot-partnership-seeks-to-combat-diversity-deficiencies

71. Blokker, R., Akkermans, J., Tims, M., Jansen, P., & Khapova, S. (2019). Building a sustainable start: The role of career competencies, career success, and career shocks in young professionals' employability. *Journal of Vocational Behavior, 112*, 172–184.

72. De Vos, A., Van der Heijden, B. I., & Akkermans, J. (2020). Sustainable careers: Towards a conceptual model. *Journal of Vocational Behavior, 117*, Article 103196.

CHAPTER 9

1. Kumar, A. K. (2022, March 15). *Data is the bedrock of an effective performance management system.* HumanCapital. https://humancapitalonline.com/Interviews/details/3120/Data+is+the+bedrock+of+an+effective+Performance+Management+System%3A+Amarpreet+Kaur+Ahuja; Webber, A. (2022, November 15). *Personnel Today* awards 2022: AstraZeneca takes performance management award. *Personnel Today.* https://www.personneltoday.com/hr/personnel-today-awards-2022-shortlist-performance-management-award/

2. Phillippi, M. (2022, December). The link between thriving workplaces and managers. *Leadership Excellence, 39*(12).

3. Kluger, A. N., & DeNisi, A. (1996). The effects of feedback interventions on performance: A historical review, a meta-analysis, and a preliminary feedback intervention theory. *Psychological Bulletin, 119*, 254–284.

4. Cram, W. A., & Wiener, M., Tarafdar, M., & Benlian, A. (2022). Examining the impact of algorithmic control on Uber drivers' technostress. *Journal of Management Information Systems, 39*(2), 426–453.

5. Guerin, L. (2022, September 27). *How to avoid legal trouble when conducting performance reviews.* Lawyers.com. https://www.lawyers.com/legal-info/labor-employment-law/human-resources-law/performance-reviews-and-employee-rights.html

6. Frier, S. (2020, March 17). *Facebook to pay workers $1000 bonus for expenses help.* Bloomberg. https://www.bloomberg.com/news/articles/2020-03-17/facebook-to-pay-employees-1-000-bonus-to-help-with-expenses

7. Bretz, R. D., Milkovich, G. T., & Read, W. (1992). The current state of performance appraisal research and practice: Concerns, directions, and implications. *Journal of Management, 18*, 321–352; DeNisi, A. S., & Murphy, K. R. (2017). Performance appraisal and performance management: 100 years of progress? *Journal of Applied Psychology, 102*, 421–433; Landy, F. J., & Farr, J. L. (1980). Performance rating. *Psychological Bulletin, 87*, 72–107.

8. Chen, R., & Ma, R. (2022, February 24). How ByteDance became the world's most valuable startup. *Harvard Business Review.* https://hbr.org/2022/02/how-bytedance-became-the-worlds-most-valuable-startup

9. Folger, R., Konovsky, M. A., & Cropanzano, R. (1992). A due process metaphor for performance appraisal. *Research in Organizational Behavior, 14*, 129–177.

10. Taylor, M. S., Tracy, K. B., Renard, M. K., Harrison, J. K., & Carroll, S. J. (1995). Due process in performance appraisal: A quasi-experiment in procedural justice. *Administrative Science Quarterly, 40*, 495–523.

11. Pichler, S. (2019). Performance appraisal reactions: A review and research agenda. In L. A. Steelman & J. R. Williams (Eds.), *Feedback at work* (pp. 75–96). Springer.

12. DeNisi, A., & Smith, C. E. (2014). Performance appraisal, performance management, and firm-level performance: A review, a proposed model, and new directions for future research. *Academy of Management Annals, 8*, 127–179.

13. Parker, S. K., Knight, C., & Keller, A. (2020, July 30). Remote managers are having trust issues. *Harvard Business Review.* https://hbr.org/2020/07/remote-managers-are-having-trust-issues

14. Tsipursky, G. (2022, September 8). Week-to-week management may be the solution to employers' distrust of remote work. *Fortune.* https://fortune.com/2022/09/07/week-management-solution-employers-distrust-remote-work-employee-monitoring-cognitive-science-gleb-tsipursky/

15. Wilke, D. (2016, February). Beyond the annual performance review, *HR Magazine, 7.*

16. Hassell, B. (2016, April). IBM's new checkpoint reflects employee preferences. *Workforce Magazine, 12.*

17. Heidemeier, H., & Moser, K. (2009). Self-other agreement in job performance ratings: A meta-analytic test of a process model. *Journal of Applied Psychology, 94*, 353–370.

18. He, W., Li, S. L., Feng, J., Zhang, G., & Sturman, M. C. (2021). When does pay for performance motivate employee helping behavior? The contextual influence of performance subjectivity. *Academy of Management Journal, 64*, 293–326.

19. Locke, E., & Latham, G. P. (1990). *A theory of goal setting & task performance.* Prentice Hall.

20. Park, T. Y., Park, S., & Barry, B. (2022). Incentive effects on ethics, *Academy of Management Annals, 16*, 297–333.

21. Ordoñez, L. D., Schweitzer, M. E., Galinsky, A. D., & Bazerman, M. H. (2009, February). Goals gone wild: The systematic side effects of over-prescribing goal setting. *Academy of Management Perspectives,23*(1), 6–14.

22. ExpressVPN. (2021, May 20). *ExpressVPN survey reveals the extent of surveillance on the remote workforce.* https://www.expressvpn.com/blog/expressvpn-survey-surveillance-on-the-remote-workforce/#firing&cjdata=MXxOfDB8WXww

23. Ravid, D. M., White, J. C., Tomczak, D. L., Miles, A. F., & Behrend, T. S. (2022). A meta-analysis of the effects of electronic performance monitoring on work outcomes. *Personnel Psychology.* Advance online publication. https://doi.org/10.1111/peps.12514

24. Egan, M. (2017, January 6). *Wells Fargo's notorious sales goals to get a makeover.* CNN Business. http://money.cnn.com/2017/01/06/investing/wells-fargo-replace-sales-goals-fake-accounts/index.html; Egan, M. (2016, September 9). *Workers tell Wells Fargo horror stories.* CNN Business. http://money.cnn.com/2016/09/09/investing/wells-fargo-phony-accounts-culture/index.html?iid=EL

25. Ghoshal, A. (2022, November 24). Changes to Google's employee appraisal system stir layoff fears. *Computerworld.* https://www.computerworld.com/article/3681109/changes-to-googles-employee-appraisal-system-stir-layoff-fears.html

26. O'Boyle, E., & Aguinis, H. (2012). The best and the rest: Revisiting the norm of normality of individual performance. *Personnel Psychology, 65,* 79–119.

27. Roepe, L. R. (2022, Summer). Continuous conversations. *HR Magazine, 67*(2), 81–83.

28. Speer, A. B. (2018). Quantifying with words: An investigation of the validity of narrative-derived performance scores. *Personnel Psychology, 71*(3), 299–333.

29. Ogrysko, N. (2020, June 2). *USDA to switch to "pass-fail" performance management system, new awards policy this fall.* Federal News Network. https://federalnewsnetwork.com/workforce/2020/06/usda-to-switch-to-pass-fail-performance-management-system-new-awards-policy-this-fall/

30. Mohan, P. (2017). Ready to scrap your annual performance reviews? Try these alternatives. *Fast Company.* https://www.fastcompany.com/40405106/ready-to-scrap-your-annual-performance-reviews-try-these-alternatives

31. Wiles, J. (2019, August 15). *The real impact on employees of removing performance ratings.* Gartner. https://www.gartner.com/smarterwithgartner/corporate-hr-removing-performance-ratings-is-unlikely-to-improve-performance

32. Viswesvaran, C., Ones, D. S., & Schmidt, F. L. (1996). Comparative analysis of the reliability of job performance ratings. *Journal of Applied Psychology, 81,* 557–574.

33. Sutton, A. W., Baldwin, S. P., Wood, L., & Hoffman, B. J. (2013). A meta-analysis of the relationship between rater liking and performance ratings. *Human Performance, 26,* 409–429.

34. Fleenor, J. W. (2019). Factors affecting the validity of strategic 360 feedback processes. In A. H. Church, D. Bracken, J. W. Fleenor, & D. S. Rose (Eds.), *The handbook of strategic 360 feedback* (pp. 237–255). Oxford University Press.

35. DiFiore, A., & Souza, M. (2021, January 12). Are peer reviews the future of performance evaluations? *Harvard Business Review.* https://hbr.org/2021/01/are-peer-reviews-the-future-of-performance-evaluations

36. Antonioni, D. (1994). The effects of feedback accountability on upward appraisal ratings. *Personnel Psychology, 47,* 349–356.

37. Hekman, D. R., Aquino, K., Owens, B. P., Mitchell, T. R., Schilpzand, P., & Leavitt, K. (2010). An examination of whether and how racial and gender biases influence customer satisfaction. *Academy of Management Journal, 53,* 238–264.

38. Farh, J. L., & Werbel, J. D. (1986). Effects of purpose of the appraisal and expectation of validation on self-appraisal leniency. *Journal of Applied Psychology, 71,* 527–529; Heidemeier, H., & Moser, K. (2009). Self–other agreement in job performance ratings: A meta-analytic test of a process model. *Journal of Applied Psychology, 94,* 353–370.

39. Zenger, J., & Folkman, J. (2020, December 23). What makes a 360-degree review successful? *Harvard Business Review.* https://hbr.org/2020/12/what-makes-a-360-degree-review-successful

40. Yahiaoui, D., Nakhle, S. F., & Farndale, E. (2021). Culture and performance appraisal in multinational enterprises: Implementing French headquarters' practices in Middle East and North Africa subsidiaries. *Human Resource Management, 60,* 771–785.

41. Cho, I., & Payne, S. C. (2016). Other important questions: When, how, and why do cultural values influence performance management? *Industrial and Organizational Psychology: Perspectives on Science and Practice, 9,* 343–350; Meyer, E. (2015, October). When culture doesn't translate. *Harvard Business Review.* https://hbr.org/2015/10/when-culture-doesnt-translate

42. Papp, F. (2017, March 14). *Avaloq: Employees evaluate team performance.* Finews.com. http://www.finews.com/news/english-news/26590-avaloq-where-employees-get-to-decide-about-bonuses

43. Nyberg, A. J., Pieper, J. R., & Trevor, C. O. (2016). Pay-for-performance's effect on future employee performance: Integrating psychological and economic principles toward a contingency perspective. *Journal of Management, 42,* 1753–1783.

44. Colquitt, J. A., Hill, E. T., & De Cremer, D. (2023). Forever focused on fairness: 75 years of organizational justice in *Personnel Psychology. Personnel Psychology, 76,* 413–435. https://doi.org/10.1111/peps.12556

45. Peck, J. A., & Levashina, J. (2017). Impression management and interview and job performance ratings: A meta-analysis of research design with tactics in mind. *Frontiers in Psychology, 8.* https://doi.org/10.3389/fpsyg.2017.00201

46. Ellis, J. (2022, October). Root out gender and ethnicity bias in performance reviews. *Talent Development, 76*(10).

47. Dorrian, P. (2022, November 16). *CBS TV station, part-time editor end age discrimination lawsuit.* Bloomberg Law. https://news.bloomberglaw.com/litigation/cbs-tv-station-part-time-editor-end-age-discrimination-lawsuit; Schneiner, M. J. (2022, May 3). *3 out of 4 age discrimination claims rejected, 1 survives.* SHRM. https://www.shrm.org/resourcesandtools/legal-and-compliance/employment-law/pages/co

urt-report-three-rejected-age-discr imination-claims.aspx

48. Robbins, R. L., & DeNisi, A. S. (1994). A closer look at interpersonal affect as a distinct influence on cognitive processing in performance appraisal. *Journal of Applied Psychology, 79*, 341–353.

49. Levy, P. E., & Williams, J. R. (2004). The social context of performance appraisal: A review and framework for the future. *Journal of Management, 30*, 881–905.

50. Cuadra, D. (2022, January/February). Technology: Breaking the "Zoom ceiling." *Employee Benefit News, 36*(1).

51. Levy, P. E., Cavanaugh, C. M., Frantz, N. B., Borden, L. A., & Roberts, A. (2018). Revisiting the social context of performance management: Performance appraisal effectiveness. In D. S. Ones & H. K. Sinangil (Eds.), *The Sage handbook of industrial, work, & organizational psychology* (chap. 9). Sage. https://doi.org/10.4135/978147 3914957

52. Gupta, S. (2022, July 20). Leaders, your employees think you lack self-awareness. *Fast Company.* https://w ww.fastcompany.com/90770313/lea ders-your-employees-think-you-lac k-self-awareness-consider-soft-skil ls-coaching-for-everyone

53. Tsai, M. H., Wee, S., & Koh, B. (2019). Restructured frame-of-reference training improves rating accuracy. *Journal of Organizational Behavior, 40*, 740–757.

54. Harari, M. B., & Rudolph, C. W. (2017). The effect of rater accountability on performance ratings: A meta-analytic review. *Human Resource Management Review, 27*, 121–133.

55. Lebowitz, S. (2015, June 15). Here's how performance reviews work at Google. *Business Insider.* http://www. businessinsider.com/how-google-pe rformance-reviews-work-2015-6

56. DeNisi, A. S., & Murphy, K. R. (2017). Performance appraisal and performance management: 100 years of progress? *Journal of Applied Psychology, 102*, 421–433.

57. Williams, J. C., Lloyd, D. L., Boginsky, M., & Armas-Edwards, F. (2021, April 21). How one company worked to root out bias from performance reviews. *Harvard Business Review.* https://hbr. org/2021/04/how-one-company-wor ked-to-root-out-bias-from-perform ance-reviews

58. Schleicher, D. J., Baumann, H. M., Sullivan, D. W., & Yim, J. (2019). Evaluating the effectiveness of performance management: A 30-year integrative conceptual review. *Journal of Applied Psychology, 104*, 851–887.

59. Pulakos, E. D., Hanson, R. M., Arad, S., & Moye, N. (2015). Performance management can be fixed: An on-the-job experiential learning approach for complex behavior change. *Industrial and Organizational Psychology, 8*, 51–76.

60. Meinecke, A. L., Klonek, F. E., & Kauffeld, S. (2017). Appraisal participation and perceived voice in annual appraisal interviews: Uncovering contextual factors. *Journal of Leadership & Organizational Studies, 24*, 230–245.

61. Cespedes, F. V., Aas, T., Hunt, A., & Newton-Hill, H. (2022, November 15). Using simulations to upskill employees. *Harvard Business Review.* https:// hbr.org/2022/11/using-simulations-t o-upskill-employees

62. Porath, C. (2016). Give your team more effective positive feedback. *Harvard Business Review.* https://hbr. org/2016/10/give-your-team-more-e ffective-positive-feedback

63. O'Connell, B. (2020, June 13). *Performance management evolves.* SHRM. h ttps://www.shrm.org/hr-today/news /all-things-work/pages/performanc e-management-evolves.aspx

64. SHRM. (2022, December 29). *How to establish a performance improvement plan.* https://www.shrm.org/Resour cesAndTools/tools-and-samples/ho w-to-guides/Pages/performanceimp rovementplan.aspx

65. Lally, R. (2021, June 23). *Agency must justify PIP when employee challenges removal.* SHRM. https://www.shrm.o rg/resourcesandtools/legal-and-co mpliance/employment-law/pages/c ourt-report-agency-must-justify-pi p-when-employee-challenges-remo val.aspx

CHAPTER 10

1. Bureau of Labor Statistics. (2022). *Table 4: Quits levels and rates by industry and region, seasonally adjusted* [Economic news release]. https://ww w.bls.gov/news.release/jolts.t04.ht m; Bureau of Labor Statistics. (2022, January 6). *Number of quits at all-time high in November 2021.* https://www .bls.gov/opub/ted/2022/number-o f-quits-at-all-time-high-in-novemb er-2021.htm; Candelon, F., Ha, S. M., & McDonald, C. (1/7/22). A.I. could make your company more productive—but not if it makes your people less happy. *Fortune.* https://fortune.c om/2022/01/07/artificial-intelligenc e-ai-productivity-challenges-human -element/; Data Privacy Group (2021, April 12). *Workplace surveillance: Being watched at work.* https://thedat aprivacygroup.com/us/blog/workpla ce-surveillance-being-watched-at-w ork/; Humanyze. (2017, February 7). *A U.S. bank improves call center productivity and employee retention.* https://h umanyze.com/case-studies-major-u s-bank/; Solon, O. (2015, August 12). *Wearable biosensors bring tracking tech into the workplace.* Bloomberg. com.

2. Rubenstein, A. L., Eberly, M. B., Lee, T. W., & Mitchell, T. R. (2018). Surveying the forest: A meta-analysis, moderator investigation, and future-oriented discussion of the antecedents of voluntary employee turnover. *Personnel Psychology, 71*, 23–65.

3. Maurer, R. (2017, March 21). *Data will show you why your employees leave or stay.* SHRM. https://www.shrm.org/r esourcesandtools/hr-topics/talent-a cquisition/pages/data-retention-turn over-hr.aspx

4. Navarra, K. (2022, April 11). *The real cost of recruitment.* SHRM. https://ww w.shrm.org/resourcesandtools/hr-t opics/talent-acquisition/pages/the-r eal-costs-of-recruitment.aspx

5. Park, T. Y., & Shaw, J. D. (2013). Turnover rates and organizational performance: A meta-analysis. *Journal of Applied Psychology, 98*, 268–309.

6. Kamal, R. (2022, January 4). Quitting is just half the story: The truth behind the "Great Resignation." *The Guardian.* https://www.theguardian.com/b usiness/2022/jan/04/great-resignati on-quitting-us-unemployment-econ omy

7. Porter, C. M., & Rigby, J. R. (2021). The turnover contagion process: An integrative review of theoretical and empirical research. *Journal of Organizational Behavior, 42*, 212–228.

8. Li, Q., Lourie, B., Nekrasov, A., & Shevlin, T. (2022). Employee turnover

and firm performance: Large-sample archival evidence. *Management Science, 68*, 5667–5683.

9. Based on Glebbeek, A. C., & Bax, E. H. (2004). Is high employee turnover really harmful? An empirical test using company records. *Academy of Management Journal, 47*, 277–286.

10. Muir, K. J. (2022, January 13). *The solution to the wave of nurse resignations? Cold, hard cash.* STAT. https://www.statnews.com/2022/01/13/nurse-resignations-solution-cold-hard-cash/

11. Rubenstein, A. L., Eberly, M. B., Lee, T. W., & Mitchell, T. R. (2018). Surveying the forest: A meta-analysis, moderator investigation, and future-oriented discussion of the antecedents of voluntary employee turnover. *Personnel Psychology, 71*, 23–65.

12. Parker, K., & Horowitz, J. M. (2022, March 9). *Majority of workers who quit a job in 2021 cite low pay, no opportunities for advancement, feeling disrespected.* Pew Research Center. https://www.pewresearch.org/fact-tank/2022/03/09/majority-of-workers-who-quit-a-job-in-2021-cite-low-pay-no-opportunities-for-advancement-feeling-disrespected/

13. Mitchell, T. R., & Lee, T. W. (2001). The unfolding model of voluntary turnover and job embeddedness: Foundations for a comprehensive theory of attachment. *Research in Organizational Behavior, 23*, 189–246.

14. Laulié, L., & Morgeson, F. P. (2021). The end is just the beginning: Turnover events and their impact on those who remain. *Personnel Psychology, 74*, 387–409.

15. Hom, P. W., Lee, T. W., Shaw, J. D., & Hausknecht, J. P. (2017). One hundred years of employee turnover theory and research. *Journal of Applied Psychology, 102*, 530–545.

16. Jiang, K., Liu, D., McKay, P. F., Lee, T. W., & Mitchell, T. R. (2012). When and how is job embeddedness predictive of turnover? A meta-analytic investigation. *Journal of Applied Psychology, 97*, 1077–1096.

17. Commendatore, C. (2020, October 21). *Fleets challenge the driver turnover status quo.* FleetOwner. https://www.fleetowner.com/operations/drivers/article/21145315/fleets-challenge-the-driver-turnover-status-quo

18. Kaplan, J., & Hoff, M. (2022, January 10). A White House economist says it's a "Great Upgrade" not a Great Resignation, as workers quit for higher pay. *Insider.* https://www.businessinsider.com/white-house-economist-great-upgrade-not-great-resignation-labor-shortage-2022-1; Morris, C. (2021, December 14). *Workers who don't quit this Orlando company could win a mortgage-free home.* Yahoo! https://www.yahoo.com/now/workers-don-t-quit-orlando-165710124.html

19. Allen, D. G., Weeks, K. P., & Moffitt, K. R. (2005). Turnover intentions and voluntary turnover: The moderating roles of self-monitoring, locus of control, proactive personality, and risk aversion. *Journal of Applied Psychology, 90*, 980–990.

20. Stohlmeyer Russell, M., & Lepler, L. M. (2017, May 19). How we closed the gap between men's and women's retention rates. *Harvard Business Review.* https://hbr.org/2017/05/how-we-closed-the-gap-between-mens-and-womens-retention-rates

21. Fedweek. (2022, January 11). *Survey: Supervisors more trusted than senior leaders on "reentry" issues.* https://www.fedweek.com/fedweek/survey-supervisors-more-trusted-than-senior-leaders-on-reentry-issues/

22. Sull, D., Sull, C., & Zweig, B. (2022, January 11). Toxic culture is driving the great resignation. *MIT Sloan Management Review.* https://sloanreview.mit.edu/article/toxic-culture-is-driving-the-great-resignation/

23. Huff, A. (2020, May). Trimble using "sentiment analysis" to predict driver turnover. *Commercial Carrier Journal*, p. 32; Waddell, K. (2016, September 29). The algorithms that tell bosses how employees are feeling. *The Atlantic.* https://www.theatlantic.com/technology/archive/2016/09/the-algorithms-that-tell-bosses-how-employees-feel/502064/; Zielinski, D. (2017, May 15). *Artificial intelligence and employee feedback.* SHRM. https://www.shrm.org/resourcesandtools/hr-topics/technology/pages/-artificial-intelligence-and-employee-feedback.aspx

24. Spain, E., & Groysberg, B. (2016, April). Making exit interviews count. *Harvard Business Review*, 88–95; Thier, J. (2021, December 16). Two HR experts debate the efficacy of the newly popular "stay interview." *Fortune.*

25. Maurer, R. (2017, March 31). *New hires skip out when the role doesn't meet expectations.* SHRM. https://www.shrm.org/resourcesandtools/hr-topics/talent-acquisition/pages/new-hires-retention-turnover.aspx

26. Gilbert, M. (2021, December 24). Onboarding new employees? Use this checklist. *Inc.* https://www.inc.com/mandy-gilbert/onboarding-new-hybrid-employees-use-this-checklist.html; Temkin, B. (2021, December 27). In 2022, get ready for the great onboarding. *Inc.* https://www.inc.com/bruce-temkin/in-2022-get-ready-for-great-onboarding.html

27. Ng, T. W. H., Yim, F. H. K., Chen, H., & Zou, Y. (2022). Employer sponsored career development practices and turnover: A meta-analysis. *Journal of Management.* https://doi.org/10.1177/01492063221125143

28. Nguyen, T. (2021, August 18). How free college became a perk for American workers. *Vox.* https://www.vox.com/the-goods/22627543/free-online-college-program-workers-target-walmart

29. Benson, G. S., Finegold, D., & Mohrman, S. A. (2004). You paid for the skills, now keep them: Tuition reimbursement and voluntary turnover. *Academy of Management Journal, 47*, 315–331.

30. Hamori, M., Koyuncu, B., Cao, J., & Graf, T. (2015, Fall). What high-potential young managers want. *MIT Sloan Management Review*, 61–68.

31. Rubenstein, A. L., Eberly, M. B., Lee, T. W., & Mitchell, T. R. (2018). Surveying the forest: A meta-analysis, moderator investigation, and future-oriented discussion of the antecedents of voluntary employee turnover. *Personnel Psychology, 71*, 23–65.

32. Vasel, K. (2021, April 3). *LinkedIn gives its entire company the week off to prevent burnout.* ABC News. https://abc7news.com/linkedin-giving-a-week-off-vacation-for-employees-burnout-of-time/10475793/

33. Hekman, D. R., Van Wagoner, H. P., Owens, B. P., Mitchell, T. R., Holtom, B. C., Lee, T. M., Dinger, J. (2022). An examination of whether and how prevention climate alters the influence of turnover on performance. *Journal of Management, 48*(3), 542–570. https://doi.org/10.1177/0149206320978451

34. Murnieks, C. Y., Allen, S. T., & Ferrante, C. J. (2011). Combating the effects of turnover: Military lessons learned from project teams rebuilding Iraq. *Business Horizons, 54,* 481–491.

35. Dachner, A. M., & Makarius, E. E. (2021, March/April). Turn departing employees into loyal alumni. *Harvard Business Review.* https://hbr.org/2021/03/turn-departing-employees-into-loyal-alumni

36. McMillan, A. (2022, September 26). *Alumni programs deepen brand ambassadorship and add company value: Just look at Accenture's alumni network.* Aluminati. https://www.aluminati.net/alumni-programs-deepen-brand-ambassadorship-and-add-company-value-just-look-at-accentures-alumni-network/

37. Vozza, S. (2022, February 9). *Why you should welcome back boomerang employees.* SHRM. https://www.shrm.org/resourcesandtools/hr-topics/people-managers/pages/boomerang-employees.aspx

38. Shipp, A., Furst-Holloway, S., Harris, T. B., & Rosen, B. (2014). Gone today but here tomorrow: Extending the unfolding model of turnover to consider boomerang employees. *Personnel Psychology, 67,* 421–462.

39. Swider, B. W., Liu, J. T., Harris, T. B., & Gardner, R. G. (2017). Employees on the rebound: Extending the careers literature to include boomerang employees. *Journal of Applied Psychology, 102,* 890–909.

40. Arnold, J. D., Van Iddekinge, C. H., Campion, M. C., Bauer, T. N., & Campion, M. A. (2021). Welcome back? Job performance and turnover of boomerang employees compared to internal and external hires. *Journal of Management, 47,* 2198–2225.

41. Grensing-Pophal, L. (2022, July 4). *The role of AI in retaining top talent.* SHRM. https://www.shrm.org/resourcesandtools/hr-topics/technology/pages/the-role-of-ai-in-retaining-top-talent.aspx; Miller, S. (2020, June 3). *Why counteroffers should address more than pay.* SHRM. https://www.shrm.org/resourcesandtools/hr-topics/compensation/pages/counteroffers-should-address-more-than-pay.aspx; Vozza, S. (2022, March 7). *What companies get wrong when conducting stay interviews.* SHRM. https://www.shrm.org/resourcesandtools/hr-topics/people-managers/pages/bad-stay-interviews.aspx

42. Tanzi, A. (2022, January 11). *"Great retirement" in the U.S. is driven by older female baby boomers.* Bloomberg.com; Wittenberg-Cox, A. (2021, November 16). Is the "Great resignation" actually a mass retirement? *Forbes.* https://www.forbes.com/sites/avivahwittenbergcox/2021/11/16/the-great-resignationactually-a-mass-retirement/?sh=4dc34b8118ba

43. Beier, M., Kanfer, R., Kooij, D. T. A. M., & Truxillo, D. M. (2022). What's age got to do with it? A primer and review of the workplace aging literature. *Personnel Psychology, 75*(4), 779–804. https://doi.org/10.1111/peps.12544

44. Rees, K. (2021, October 10). *U.K. pilot shortage threatens travel rebound, Telegraph reports.* Bloomberg.com.

45. Bove, T. (2022, January 13). 79% of baby boomers want to keep working, but with more flexibility. Is this the end of retirement? *Fortune.* https://fortune.com/2022/01/12/baby-boomers-retirement-flexible-hours-savings-covid/

46. Fisher, G. G., Chaffee, D. S., & Sonnega, A. (2016). Retirement timing: A review and recommendations for future research. *Work, Aging and Retirement, 2,* 230–261.

47. EEOC. (2000). *EEOC compliance manual.* https://www.eeoc.gov/policy/docs/benefits.html#VI.%20Early%20Retirement%20Incentives

48. Skarlicki, D. P., & Folger, R. (1997). Retaliation in the workplace: The roles of distributive, procedural, and interactional justice. *Journal of Applied Psychology, 82,* 434–443.

49. O'Connell, B. (2020, September 1). *Shock to the system: Dealing with toxic staffers at work.* SHRM. https://www.shrm.org/resourcesandtools/hr-topics/people-managers/pages/toxic-workers-cost-money-.aspx

50. Doyle, A. (2016, October 17). *Exceptions to employment at will.* The Balance. https://www.thebalance.com/exceptions-to-employment-at-will-2060484; Holzschu, M. (2017). *Just cause vs. employment-at-will.* Business Know-How. https://www.businessknowhow.com/manage/justcausevsfreewill.htm; National Conference of State Legislatures. (2017). *The at-will presumption and exceptions to the rule.* http://www.ncsl.org/research/labor-and-employment/at-will-employment-overview.aspx

51. Wood, M. S., & Karau, S. J. (2009). Preserving employee dignity during the termination interview: An empirical examination. *Journal of Business Ethics, 86,* 519–534.

52. Knight, R. (2016, February 5). The right way to fire someone. *Harvard Business Review.* https://hbr.org/2016/02/the-right-way-to-fire-someone

53. Smith, A. (2021, March 1). *Can an employer fire workers who are scared to return to the office?* SHRM. https://www.shrm.org/resourcesandtools/legal-and-compliance/employment-law/pages/coronavirus-workers-who-are-scared-to-return-to-the-office.aspx; Smith, A., Nagele-Piazza, L. (2021, December 9). *Employers react to workers who refuse a Covid-19 vaccination.* SHRM. https://www.shrm.org/resourcesandtools/legal-and-compliance/employment-law/pages/if-workers-refuse-a-covid-19-vaccination.aspx; Valderrama, C. (2021, May). Covid infections may be down but Covid lawsuits are up: What employers should consider. *Employee Benefit Plan Review,* 9–11; Vellequette, L. P. (2020, June 1). Virus complaints at issue in firing lawsuit. *Automotive News, 94*(6936).

54. Feng, R. (2022, January 10). Top Chinese tutoring company laid off 60,000 workers after crackdown. *Wall Street Journal.* https://www.wsj.com/articles/top-chinese-tutoring-company-laid-off-60-000-workers-after-crackdown-11641817724

55. Grunberg, L., Moore, S. Y., & Greenberg, E. S. (2006). Managers' reactions to implementing layoffs: Relationship to health problems and withdrawal behaviors. *Human Resource Management, 45,* 159–178; McKee-Ryan, F., Song, Z., Wanberg, C. R., & Kinicki, A. J. (2005). Psychological and physical well-being during unemployment: A meta-analytic study. *Journal of Applied Psychology, 90,* 53–76; Trevor, C. O., & Piyanontalee, R. (2020). Discharges, poor-performer quits, and layoffs as valued exits: Is it really addition by subtraction? *Annual Review of Organizational Psychology and Organizational Behavior, 7,* 181–211.

56. Datta, D. K., Guthrie, J. P., Basuil, D., & Pandey, A. (2010). Causes and effects of employee downsizing: A

review and synthesis. *Journal of Management, 36,* 281–348.

57. Asante, E. A., Oduro, F., Danquah, B., Mensah, R. D., Dartey-Baah, K., & Affum-Osei, E. (2023). From being sacked to being unwell: A conservation of resources view on the effects of psychological contract violation on layoff victims' wellbeing. *Human Resource Management Review, 33*(2), 362–383. https://doi.org/10.1111/1748-8583.12442

58. Davis, P. R., Trevor, C. O., & Feng, J. (2015). Creating a more quit-friendly national workforce? Individual layoff history and voluntary turnover. *Journal of Applied Psychology, 100,* 1434–1455.

59. Datta, D. K., Guthrie, J. P., Basuil, D., & Pandey, A. (2010). Causes and effects of employee downsizing: A review and synthesis. *Journal of Management, 36,* 281–348.

60. Doyle, A. (2017, July 3). *Can I collect unemployment if I am fired?* The Balance. https://www.thebalance.com/can-i-collect-unemployment-if-i-am-fired-2064150; Grossman, R. J. (2012, February). Hidden costs of layoffs. *HR Magazine,* 24–30.

61. Bennett, J. (2021, April 15). *Fewer jobs have been lost in the EU than in the U.S. during the COVID-19 downturn.* Pew Research Center. https://www.pewresearch.org/fact-tank/2021/04/15/fewer-jobs-have-been-lost-in-the-eu-than-in-the-u-s-during-the-covid-19-downturn/

62. Percivalle, U. (2022, January 20). *Italy: New measures may impact most employers planning layoffs.* SHRM. https://www.shrm.org/resourcesandtools/hr-topics/global-hr/pages/italy-layoffs.aspx

63. Skrzypinski, C. (2021, September 28). *Ontario court rules severance pay is based on global payroll.* SHRM. https://www.shrm.org/resourcesandtools/hr-topics/global-hr/pages/ontario-severance-global-payroll.aspx

64. Keim, A. C., Landis, R. S., Pierce, C. A., & Earnest, D. R. (2014). Why do employees worry about their jobs? A meta-analytic review of predictors of job insecurity. *Journal of Occupational Health Psychology, 19,* 269–290; Sverke, M., & Hellgren, J. (2002). The nature of job insecurity: Understanding employment uncertainty on the brink of a new millennium. *Applied Psychology: An International Review, 51,* 23–42.

65. Lincoln Electric. (2021, September 7). *Lincoln Electric announces up to $10k sign-on bonus for qualified, experienced new hires* [Press release]. https://www.lincolnelectric.com/en/Newsroom/Press-Releases/2021/09/Sign-On-Bonus-Promotion

66. BusinessWire. (2021, April 12). *NuStar once again recognized as one of the "100 Best Companies to Work For."* https://www.businesswire.com/news/home/20210412005903/en/NuStar-Once-Again-Recognized-as-One-of-the-%E2%80%9C100-Best-Companies-to-Work-For%E2%80%9D

67. Kalev, A. (2016, July 26). How "neutral" layoffs disproportionately affect women and minorities. *Harvard Business Review.* https://hbr.org/2016/07/how-neutral-layoffs-disproportionately-affect-women-and-minorities

68. Silvers, J. R. (2022, January 20). *Can discharging remote workers trigger the WARN act at a "single site of employment"?* Ogletree Deakins. https://ogletree.com/insights/can-discharging-remote-workers-trigger-the-warn-act-at-a-single-site-of-employment/

69. U.S. Department of Labor. (2009, February). *WARN advisor: Frequently asked questions about WARN.* https://webapps.dol.gov/elaws/eta/warn/faqs.asp

70. Anonymous. (2009, February). Know your layoff rules and procedures. *HR Focus, 86,* 2;*What is the California WARN Act and how does it differ from federal WARN?* (2012, December 27). SHRM. https://www.shrm.org/resourcesandtools/tools-and-samples/hr-qa/pages/californiawarnact.aspx

71. Anonymous. (2009, February). Know your layoff rules and procedures. *HR Focus, 86,* 2.

72. Richter, M., König, C. J., Koppermann, C., & Schilling, M. (2016). Displaying fairness while delivering bad news: Testing the effectiveness of organizational bad news training in the layoff context. *Journal of Applied Psychology, 101,* 779–792.

73. Vickers, M. H., & Parris, M. A. (2009). Layoffs: Australian executives speak of being disposed of. *Organizational Dynamics, 39,* 57–63.

74. Ibid.

75. Taylor, D. B., & Gross, J. (2021, December 8). The Better.com C.E.O. says he's "deeply sorry" for firing workers over Zoom. *The New York Times.* https://www.nytimes.com/2021/12/08/business/better-zoom-layoffs-vishal-garg.html

76. Kelly, J. (2022, February 8). Peloton CEO out, as 2,800 employees are laid off, but offered free Peloton memberships. *Forbes.* https://www.forbes.com/sites/jackkelly/2022/02/08/peloton-ceo-is-out-and-2800-employees-are-laid-off-but-offered-free-peloton-memberships/?sh=736215bf56cd

77. Nobel, C. (2015, January 7). *The quest for better layoffs.* Harvard Business School. http://hbswk.hbs.edu/item/the-quest-for-better-layoffs

78. Peralta, P. (2021, August 13). Severance packages might look a little different post-pandemic. *Employee Benefit News.* https://www.benefitnews.com/advisers/news/severance-pay-changes-happening-in-2021post-pandemic

79. EEOC. (2009). *Understanding waivers of discrimination claims in employee severance agreements.* https://www.eeoc.gov/policy/docs/qanda_severance-agreements.html#II

80. Miller, S. (2020, April 20). *Outplacement services are no longer a secondary perk.* SHRM. https://www.shrm.org/resourcesandtools/hr-topics/benefits/pages/outplacement-services-no-longer-a-secondary-perk-coronavirus.aspx

81. Trevor, C. O., & Nyberg, A. J. (2008). Keeping your headcount when all about you are losing theirs: Downsizing, voluntary turnover rates, and the moderating role of HR practices. *Academy of Management Journal, 51,* 259–276.

82. Kriz, T. D., Jolly, P. M., & Shoss, M. K. (2021). Coping with organizational layoffs: Managers' increased active listening reduces job insecurity via perceived situational control. *Journal of Occupational Health Psychology, 26,* 448–458.

CHAPTER 11

1. Barrero, J. M., Bloom, N., & Davis, S. J. (2022, September 9). *SWAA September 2022 updates.* WFH Research. https://wfhresearch.com/wp-con

tent/uploads/2022/09/WFHResea rch_updates_September2022.pdf ; Barrero, J. M., Bloom, N., Davis, S. J., Meyer, B. H., & Mihaylov, E. (2022). *The shift to remote work lessens wage-growth pressures* (NBER Working Paper No. 30197). National Bureau of Economic Research. https://www .nber.org/papers/w30197; Epstein, S. (2021, November 4). Google staff squirm as remote workers face pay cuts. *Wired*. https://www.wired.co m/story/google-remote-work-pa y-cuts-big-tech/; Golden, R. (2022, March 23). Report: Google employees increasingly dissatisfied with pay, return-to-office plans. *HR Dive*. http s://www.hrdive.com/news/report-g oogle-employees-increasingly-diss atisfied-with-pay-return-to-offi/62 0899/; Lee, D. (2022, August 23). You may soon be asked to take a pay cut to keep working from home. *Los Angeles Times*. https://www.latimes.com/po litics/story/2022-08-23/will-emplo yers-charge-employees-for-workin g-from-home-from-home; Miller, S. (2021, August 18). *Google's salary cuts for remote workers renew location-based pay debate*. SHRM. https://www .shrm.org/resourcesandtools/hr-to pics/compensation/pages/google-re news-location-based-pay-debate.as px; Payscale. (2021). *The 2021 state of remote work employer survey report*. h ttps://www.payscale.com/content/re port/2021-state-of-remote-work-em ployer-survey-report.pdf; Rosalasky, G. (2022, July 12). *Lean out: Employees are accepting lower pay in order to work remotely*. NPR. https://www.npr.or g/sections/money/2022/07/12/1110 510488/lean-out-employees-are-a ccepting-lower-pay-in-order-to-w ork-remotely; Zetlin, M. (2021, June 26). *Parents want to work from home. Here's why they shouldn't, a Stanford professor says.* Inc. https://www.inc .com/minda-zetlin/work-from-hom e-wfh-remote-work-parents-promo tions-career-nicholas-bloom-stanfo rd.html; Zetlin, M. (2021, August 29). *Why Google's plan to cut remote worker pay is a bad idea.* Inc. https://www.inc. com/minda-zetlin/google-remote-pa y-cut-calculator-facebook-twitter-e mployees-policy.html

2. U.S. Bureau of Labor Statistics. (2023, March 17). *Economic news release: Employer costs for employee compensation* (USDL-23-0488). https: //www.bls.gov/news.release/ecec.nr 0.htm

3. Parker, K., Horowitz, J. M. (2022). *Majority of workers who quit a job in 2021 cite low pay, not opportunities for advancement, feeling disrespected.* Pew Research Center. https://www.p ewresearch.org/fact-tank/2022/03/ 09/majority-of-workers-who-quit-a- job-in-2021-cite-low-pay-no-opport unities-for-advancement-feeling-dis respected/

4. Judge, T. A., Piccolo, R. F., Podsakoff, N. P., Shaw, J. C., & Rich, B. L. (2010). The relationship between pay and job satisfaction: A meta-analysis of the literature. *Journal of Vocational Behavior, 77*, 157–167.

5. Hoff, K. A., Song, Q. C., Wee, C. J., Phan, W. M. J., & Rounds, J. (2020). Interest fit and job satisfaction: A systematic review and meta-analysis. *Journal of Vocational Behavior, 123*, 103503; Humphrey, S. E., Nahr-gang, J. D., & Morgeson, F. P. (2007). Integrating motivational, social, and contextual work design features: A meta-analytic summary and theoretical extension of the work design literature. *Journal of Applied Psychology, 92*, 1332–1356; Judge, T. A., Heller, D., & Mount, M. K. (2002). Five-factor model of personality and job satisfaction: A meta-analysis. *Journal of Applied Psychology, 87*, 530–541; Kaplan, S., Bradley, J. C., Luchman, J. N., & Haynes, D. (2009). On the role of positive and negative affectivity in job performance: A meta-analytic investigation. *Journal of Applied Psychology, 94*, 162–176; Kinicki, A. J., McKee-Ryan, F. M., Schriesheim, C. A., & Carson, K. P. (2002). Assessing the construct validity of the job descriptive index: A review and meta-analysis. *Journal of Applied Psychology, 87*, 14–32; Kooij, D. T., Jansen, P. G., Dikkers, J. S., & De Lange, A. H. (2010). The influence of age on the associations between HR practices and both affective commitment and job satisfaction: A meta-analysis. *Journal of Organizational Behavior, 31*, 1111–1136; Paruzel, A., Klug, H. J., & Maier, G. W. (2021). The relationship between perceived corporate social responsibility and employee-related outcomes: A meta-analysis. *Frontiers in Psychology, 12*, Article 607108.

6. Gerhart, B. (2023). *Compensation* (14th ed.). McGraw Hill.

7. Clark, D. (2021, December 16). *Google's "20% rule" shows exactly how much time you should spend learning new skills—and why it works.* CNBC. h

ttps://www.cnbc.com/2021/12/16/go ogle-20-percent-rule-shows-exactl y-how-much-time-you-should-spen d-learning-new-skills.html; D'Onfro, J. (2015, April 17). The truth about Google's famous "20% time" policy. *Business Insider.* http://www.busines sinsider.com/google-20-percent-tim e-policy-2015-4

8. U.S. Bureau of Labor Statistics. (2023, March 17). *Economic news release: Employer costs for employee compensation* (USDL-23-0488). https: //www.bls.gov/news.release/ecec.nr 0.htm

9. Adams, J. S. (1963). Towards an understanding of inequity. *Journal of Abnormal and Social Psychology, 67*(5), 422–436.

10. Greenberg, J., & Cohen, R. L. (1982). The justice concept in social psychology. In J. Greenberg & R. L. Cohen (Eds.), *Equity and justice in social behavior* (pp. 1–47). Academic Press.

11. Carrell, M. R., & Dittrich, J. E. (1978). Equity theory: The recent literature, methodological considerations, and new directions. *Academy of Management Review, 3*, 202–210; Good-man, P. S., & Friedman, A. (1971). An examination of Adams' theory of inequity. *Administrative Science Quarterly, 16*, 271–288; Greenberg, J. (1990). Employee theft as a reaction to underpayment inequity: The hidden cost of pay cuts. *Journal of Applied Psychology, 75*, 561–568; Greenberg, J. (1993). Stealing in the name of justice: Informational and interpersonal moderators of theft reactions to underpayment inequity. *Organizational Behavior and Human Decision Processes, 54*, 81–103.

12. Austin, W., & Walster, E. (1974). Reactions to confirmations and discon-firmations of expectancies of equity and inequity. *Journal of Personality and Social Psychology, 30*, 208–216; Evan, W. M., & Simmons, R. G. (1969). Organizational effects of inequitable rewards: Two experiments in status inconsistency. *Administrative Science Quarterly, 14*, 224–237.

13. Huseman, R. C., Hatfield, J. D., & Miles, E. W. (1987). A new perspective on equity theory: The equity sensitivity construct. *Academy of Management Review, 12*, 222–234; King, W. C., Miles, E. W., & Day, D. D. (1993). A test and refinement of the equity sensitivity construct. *Journal of Organizational Behavior, 14*, 301–317.

14. Carrell, M. R., & Dittrich, J. E. (1978). Equity theory: The recent literature, methodological considerations, and new directions. *Academy of Management Review, 3*, 202–210.

15. Polk, D. M. (2022). Equity theory: Evaluating fairness. In D. Chadee (Ed.), *Theories in social psychology* (2nd ed., pp. 217–249). Wiley Blackwell; Schmitt, D. R., & Marwell, G. (1972). Withdrawal and reward reallocation as responses to inequity. *Journal of Experimental Social Psychology, 8*, 207–221.

16. Greenberg, J. (1987). A taxonomy of organizational justice theories. *Academy of Management Review, 12*, 9–22.

17. Robbins, J. M., Ford, M. T., & Tetrick, L. E. (2012). Perceived unfairness and employee health: A meta-analytic integration. *Journal of Applied Psychology, 97*, 235–272.

18. Homans, G. C. (1961). *Social behavior: Its elementary forms*. Harcourt Brace Jovanovich.

19. Colquitt, J. A., Conlon, D. E., Wesson, M. J., Porter, C. O., & Ng, K. Y. (2001). Justice at the millennium: A meta-analytic review of 25 years of organizational justice research. *Journal of Applied Psychology, 86*, 425–445; Colquitt, J. A., Scott, B. A., Rodell, J. B., Long, D. M., Zapata, C. P., Conlon, D. E., & Wesson, M. J. (2013). Justice at the millennium, a decade later: A meta-analytic test of social exchange and affect-based perspectives. *Journal of Applied Psychology, 98*, 199–236.

20. Leventhal, G. S. (1980). What should be done with equity theory? In K. J. Gergen, M. S. Greenberg, & R. H. Wills (Eds.), *Social exchange: Advances in theory and research* (pp. 27–55). Springer; Thibaut, J. W., & Walker, L. (1975). *Procedural justice: A psychological analysis*. Erlbaum.

21. Leventhal, G. S. (1980). What should be done with equity theory? In K. J. Gergen, M. S. Greenberg, & R. H. Wills (Eds.), *Social exchange: Advances in theory and research* (pp. 27–55). Springer; Leventhal, G. S., Karuza, J., & Fry, W. R. (1980). Beyond fairness: A theory of allocation preferences. *Justice and Social Interaction, 3*, 167–218.

22. Colquitt, J. A., Conlon, D. E., Wesson, M. J., Porter, C. O., & Ng, K. Y. (2001). Justice at the millennium: A meta-analytic review of 25 years of organizational justice research. *Journal of Applied Psychology, 86*, 425–445; Colquitt, J. A., Scott, B. A., Rodell, J. B., Long, D. M., Zapata, C. P., Conlon, D. E., & Wesson, M. J. (2013). Justice at the millennium, a decade later: A meta-analytic test of social exchange and affect-based perspectives. *Journal of Applied Psychology, 98*, 199–236.

23. Bies, R. J., & Moag, J. F. (1986). Interactional justice: Communication criteria for fairness. In R. J. Lewicki, B. H. Sheppard, & M. H. Bazerman (Eds.), *Research on negotiations in organizations* (Vol. 1, pp. 43–55). JAI Press.

24. Colquitt, J. A., Conlon, D. E., Wesson, M. J., Porter, C. O., & Ng, K. Y. (2001). Justice at the millennium: A meta-analytic re view of 25 years of organizational justice research. *Journal of Applied Psychology, 86*, 425–445; Colquitt, J. A., Scott, B. A., Rodell, J. B., Long, D. M., Zapata, C. P., Conlon, D. E., & Wesson, M. J. (2013). Justice at the millennium, a decade later: A meta-analytic test of social exchange and affect-based perspectives. *Journal of Applied Psychology, 98*, 199–236.

25. Brockner, J., & Wiesenfeld, B. M. (1996). An integrative framework for explaining reactions to decisions: Interactive effects of outcomes and procedures. *Psychological Bulletin, 120*, 189–208; Folger, R. (1977). Distributive and procedural justice: Combined impact of voice and improvement on experienced inequity. *Journal of Personality and Social Psychology, 35*, 108–119.

26. Gerhart, B. (2023). *Compensation* (14th ed.). McGraw Hill.

27. Heneman, R. L. (2003). Job and work evaluation: A literature review. *Public Personnel Management, 32*, 47–71.

28. Ibid.

29. Kilgour, J. G. (2008). Job evaluation revisited: The point factor method: The point factor method of job evaluation consists of a large number of discretionary decisions that result in something that appears to be entirely objective and, even, scientific. *Compensation & Benefits Review, 40*, 37–46; Society for Human Resource Management. (2016, October 27). *Performing job evaluations*. https://www.shrm.org/resourcesandtools/tools-and-samples/toolkits/pages/performingjobevaluations.aspx

30. WorldatWork. (2019). *Compensation programs & practices survey*. https:// worldatwork.org/media/CDN/dist/CDN2/documents/pdf/resources/research/Compensation%20Programs%20and%20Practices.pdf

31. Korn Ferry. (2017). *Job evaluation: Foundations and applications*. https://www.kornferry.com/content/dam/kornferry/docs/pdfs/job-evaluation.pdf; Korn Ferry. (2018). *Fact sheet: Job evaluation manager*. https://jem.haygroup.com/Public/JEM%20Brochure.pdf

32. Gates, D. (2022, September 23). Alaska Airlines reaches a milestone contract deal with its pilots union. *Seattle Times*. https://www.seattletimes.com/business/boeing-aerospace/alaska-airlines-reaches-a-milestone-contract-with-its-pilot-union/

33. Payscale. (n.d.). *How to perform compensation benchmarking & set salary ranges*. http://www.payscale.com/content/whitepaper/Perform-Compensation-Benchmarking.pdf

34. ADP. (n.d.). https://www.adp.com; Payscale. (n.d.) *Benchmark*. http://www.payscale.com/hr/product-benchmark; Smith, A. (2016, July 1). *HR's role in pay analyses*. SHRM. https://www.shrm.org/hr-today/news/hr-magazine/0716/pages/hrs-role-in-pay-analyses.aspx

35. CareerOneStop.org. (n.d.). *Salary Finder: Wages for licensed practical and licensed vocational nurses in Oregon*. https://www.careeronestop.org/toolkit/wages/find-salary.aspx?keyword=Licensed%20Practical%20and%20Licensed%20Vocational%20Nurses&soccode=292061&location=OREGON; Salary.com. (n.d.). *Licensed practical nurse*. http://swz.salary.com/salarywizard/Licensed-Practical-Nurse-Job-Description.aspx

36. Barcellos, D. (2005). The reality and promise of market-based pay. *Employment Relations Today, 32*, 1–10; Conroy, S. A. (2019). Setting base pay rates: Integrating compensation practice with human capital value creation and value capture. In A. J. Nyberg & T. P. Moliterno, *Handbook of research on strategic human capital resources* (pp. 15–33). Edward Elgar.

37. WorldatWork. (2019). *Compensation programs & practices survey*. https:// worldatwork.org/media/CDN/dist/CDN2/documents/pdf/resources/research/Compensation%20Programs%20and%20Practices.pdf

38. Society for Human Resource Management. (n.d.). *How to establish salary ranges.* https://www.shrm.org/resourcesandtools/tools-and-samples/how-to-guides/pages/howtoestablishsalaryranges.aspx#:~:text=%22Green%20circle%20rates%22%20are%20salaries,the%20minimum%20in%20the%20range

39. Bonache, J., Sanchez, J. I., & Zárraga-Oberty, C. (2009). The interaction of expatriate pay differential and expatriate inputs on host country nationals' pay unfairness. *International Journal of Human Resource Management, 20,* 2135–2149; Duarte, H., de Eccher, U., & Brewster, C. (2021). Expatriates' salary expectations, age, experience and country image. *Personnel Review, 50*(2), 731–750; Mahajan, A. (2011). Host country national's reactions to expatriate pay policies: Making a case for a cultural alignment pay model. *International Journal of Human Resource Management, 22,* 121–137; Shelton, T. (2008). Global compensation strategies: Managing and administering split pay for an expatriate workforce: Multinational companies need an effective and efficient solution to manage, track and calculate complex split-pay compensation arrangements. *Compensation & Benefits Review, 40,* 56–60; Toh, S. M., & Denisi, A. S. (2003). Host country national reactions to expatriate pay policies: A model and implications. *Academy of Management Review, 28,* 606–621.

40. U.S. Department of Labor. (n.d.). *Wage and hour division: Compliance assistance–wages and the Fair Labor Standards Act (FLSA).* https://www.dol.gov/whd/flsa/

41. U.S. Department of Labor. (2018). *Wage and hour division: Fact Sheet #17A: Exemption for executive, administrative, professional, computer & outside sales employees under the Fair Labor Standards Act (FLSA).* https://www.dol.gov/whd/overtime/fs17a_overview.pdf

42. U.S. Department of Labor. (n.d.). *Wage and hour division: Overtime pay.* https://www.dol.gov/whd/overtime_pay.htm

43. Schwartz, S. C. (2017). *Employment rules & regulations in the Trump administration.* LexisNexis. https://www.lexisnexis.com/communities/corporatecounselnewsletter/b/newsletter/archive/2017/05/18/employment-rules-amp-regulations-in-the-trump-administration.aspx

44. U.S. Department of Labor. (n.d.). *Wage and hour division: Minimum wage.* https://www.dol.gov/whd/minimumwage.htm

45. Minimum wage for federal contracts covered by Executive Order 14026, notice of rate change in effect as of January 1, 2023. (2022, September 30). *Federal Register.* https://www.federalregister.gov/documents/2022/09/30/2022-20905/minimum-wage-for-federal-contracts-covered-by-executive-order-13658-notice-of-rate-change-in-effect

46. District of Columbia Department of Employment Services. (n.d.). *Office of wage-hour compliance.* https://does.dc.gov/service/office-wage-hour-compliance-0#:~:text=Beginning%20July%201%2C%202023%2C%20the,%245.35%20per%20hour%20to%20%246.00.&text=Need%20to%20file%20a%20claim%3F

47. U.S. Department of Labor. (2008). *Wage and hour division: Fact Sheet #22: Hours worked under the Fair Labor Standards Act (FLSA).* https://www.dol.gov/whd/regs/compliance/whdfs22.pdf

48. U.S. Department of Labor. (2008). *Wage and hour division: Fact Sheet #21: Recordkeeping requirements under the Fair Labor Standards Act (FLSA).* https://www.dol.gov/whd/regs/compliance/whdfs21.pdf

49. U.S. Department of Labor, Office of Federal Contract Compliance Programs (OFCCP). (n.d.). Exec. Order No. 11246–Equal Employment Opportunity. https://www.dol.gov/ofccp/regs/compliance/ca_11246.htm; U.S. Equal Employment Opportunity Commission. (n.d.). *History of Executive Order No. 11246.* https://www.dol.gov/agencies/ofccp/about/executive-order-11246-history

50. U.S. Department of Labor, Office of Federal Contract Compliance Programs (OFCCP). (n.d.). *Pay transparency regulations.* https://www.dol.gov/agencies/ofccp/faqs/pay-transparency

51. U.S. National Labor Relations Board. (n.d.). *Employee rights.* https://www.nlrb.gov/rights-we-protect/employee-rights; U.S. National Labor Relations Board. (n.d.). *National Labor Relations Act.* https://www.nlrb.gov/resources/national-labor-relations-act

52. U.S. Government Publishing Office. (1954, August 16). Title 26–Internal Revenue Code. https://www.gpo.gov/fdsys/pkg/USCODE-2011-title26/pdf/USCODE-2011-title26.pdf

53. Cauterucci, C. (2017, April 5). The U.S. women's soccer team finally has a better contract, but not equal pay. *Slate.* http://www.slate.com/blogs/xx_factor/2017/04/05/the_u_s_women_s_soccer_team_finally_has_a_better_contract_but_not_equal.html; Das, A. (2016, April 21). Pay disparity in U.S. soccer? It's complicated. *The New York Times.* https://www.nytimes.com/2016/04/22/sports/soccer/usmnt-uswnt-soccer-equal-pay.html; Das, A. (2016, March 31). Top female players accuse U.S. soccer of wage discrimination. *The New York Times.* https://www.nytimes.com/2016/04/01/sports/soccer/uswnt-us-women-carli-lloyd-alex-morgan-hope-solo-complain.html; Das, A. (2017, April 5). Long days, Google Docs and anonymous surveys: How the U.S. soccer team forged a deal. *The New York Times.* https://www.nytimes.com/2017/04/05/sports/soccer/uswnt-us-soccer-labor-deal-contract.html; Doherty, E. (2022, September 7). *U.S. soccer teams officially sign equal pay agreements.* Axios. https://www.axios.com/2022/09/07/uswnt-equal-pay-agreement; O'Donnell, N. (2016, November 10). *Team USA members on historic fight for equal pay in women's soccer.* CBS News. http://www.cbsnews.com/news/60-minutes-women-soccer-team-usa-gender-discrimination-equal-pay; U.S. Soccer. (n.d.). *History: U.S. Soccer Team honors.* https://www.ussoccer.com/about/history/awards

54. Gupta, N., & Shaw, J. D. (2001). Successful skill-based pay plans. In C. H. Fay, M. A. Thompson, & D. Knight (Eds.), *The executive handbook of compensation.* Free Press; Lawler, E. E. (1994). From job-based to competency-based organizations. *Journal of Organizational Behavior, 15,* 3–15.

55. Dierdorff, E. C., & Surface, E. A. (2008). If you pay for skills, will they learn? Skill change and maintenance under a skill-based pay system. *Journal of Management, 34,* 721–743; Mitra, A., Gupta, N., & Shaw, J. D. (2011). A comparative examination of traditional and skill-based pay plans. *Journal of Managerial Psychology,*

26, 278–296; Murray, B., & Gerhart, B. (1998). An empirical analysis of a skill-based pay program and plant performance outcomes. *Academy of Management Journal, 41*, 68–78.

56. Connelly, B. L., Haynes, K. T., Tihanyi, L., Gamache, D. L., & Devers, C. E. (2016). Minding the gap: Antecedents and consequences of top management-to-worker pay dispersion. *Journal of Management, 42*, 862–885; Jaskiewicz, P., Block, J. H., Miller, D., & Combs, J. G. (2017). Founder versus family owners' impact on pay dispersion among non-CEO top managers: Implications for firm performance. *Journal of Management, 43*, 1524–1552.

57. Mishel, L., & Sabadish, N. (2012). *CEO pay and the top 1%: How executive compensation and financial-sector pay have fueled income inequality* (Issue Brief No. 331). Economic Policy Institute. h ttps://www.epi.org/publication/ib33 1-ceo-pay-top-1-percent/

58. Economic Policy Institute. (2022, October 4). *Aggregated CEO-to-worker compensation ratio for the 350 largest publicly owned companies in the United States from 1965 to 2021* [Graph]. Statista. Retrieved March 31, 2023, from https://www-statista-com.ezp roxy.lib.calpoly.edu/statistics/26146 3/ceo-to-worker-compensation-rati o-of-top-firms-in-the-us/?locale=e n

59. Blanes, F., de Fuentes, C., & Porcuna, R. (2020). Executive remuneration determinants: New evidence from meta-analysis. *Economic Research, 33*(1), 2844–2866; Tosi, H. L., Werner, S., Katz, J. P., & Gomez-Mejia, L. R. (2000). How much does performance matter? A meta-analysis of CEO pay studies. *Journal of Management, 26*, 301–339; Van Essen, M., Otten, J., & Carberry, E. J. (2015). Assessing managerial power theory: A meta-analytic approach to understanding the determinants of CEO compensation. *Journal of Management, 41*, 164–202.

60. Clifford, S. (2017, June 14). How companies actually decide what to pay CEOs. *The Atlantic*. https://www.thea tlantic.com/business/archive/2017/0 6/how-companies-decide-ceo-pay/5 30127/

61. Mishel, L., & Kandra, J. (2021, August 10). *CEO pay has skyrocketed 1,332% since 1978*. Economic Policy Institute.

https://www.epi.org/publication/ce o-pay-in-2020/

62. Johnson, Y. S., & Lewis, J. (2021, August 18). *San Francisco will tax employers based on CEO pay ratio*. SHRM. https://www.shrm.org/resou rcesandtools/legal-and-compliance /state-and-local-updates/pages/sa n-francisco-will-tax-employers-bas ed-on-ceo-pay-ratio.aspx

63. Gerhart, B. (2023). *Compensation* (14th ed.). McGraw-Hill.

64. Ibid.

65. Marasi, S., & Bennett, R. J. (2016). Pay communication: Where do we go from here? *Human Resource Management Review, 26*, 50–58.

66. Brown, M., Nyberg, A. J., Weller, I., & Strizver, S. D. (2022). Pay information disclosure: Review and recommendations for research spanning the pay secrecy-pay transparency continuum. *Journal of Management, 48*(6), 1661–1694.

67. Pew Research Center. (2023, March 1). *Gender pay gap in U.S. hasn't changed much in two decades*. https:// www.pewresearch.org/fact-tank/20 23/03/01/gender-pay-gap-facts/

68. U.S. Bureau of Labor Statistics. (2023, January 19). Median usual weekly earnings of full-time wage and salary workers by age, race, Hispanic or Latino ethnicity, and sex, fourth quarter 2022 averages, not seasonally adjusted [News release]. https://www.bls.gov/news.release/ wkyeng.t03.htm

69. Card, D., Mas, A., Moretti, E., & Saez, E. (2012). Inequality at work: The effect of peer salaries on job satisfaction. *American Economic Review, 102*, 2981–3003; Obloj, T., & Zenger, T. (2015). *Incentives, social comparison costs, and the proximity of envy's object* (HEC Paris Research Paper No. SPE-2015–1085). Social Science Research Network; Zenger, T. (2016, September 30). The case against pay transparency. *Harvard Business Review*. htt ps://hbr.org/2016/09/the-case-again st-pay-transparency

70. U.S. National Labor Relations Board. (n.d.). *Employee rights*. https://ww w.nlrb.gov/rights-we-protect/em ployee-rights; U.S. National Labor Relations Board. (n.d.). *The NLRB and social media*. https://www.nlrb.gov/ news-outreach/fact-sheets/nlrb-an d-social-media

71. Tate, D., Okamoto, W. T., Ebbink, B. M. (2022, September 30). *California requires pay range in job postings*. SHRM. https://www.shrm.org/resou rcesandtools/legal-and-compliance/ state-and-local-updates/pages/calif ornia-pay-transparency-new-law.as px

72. Griswold, A. (2014, March 3). Here's why Whole Foods lets employees look up each other's salaries. *Business Insider*. http://www.businessinsi der.com/whole-foods-employees-ha ve-open-salaries-2014-3

73. Grant, N. (2022, June 12). Google agrees to pay $118 million to settle pay discrimination case. *The New York Times*. https://www.nytimes.com/20 22/06/12/business/google-discrimin ation-settlement-women.html

74. Bamberger, P., & Belogolovsky, E. (2010). The impact of pay secrecy on individual task performance. *Personnel Psychology, 63*, 965–996; Belogolovsky, E., & Bamberger, P. A. (2014). Signaling in secret: Pay for performance and the incentive and sorting effects of pay secrecy. *Academy of Management Journal, 57*, 1706–1733; Brown, M., Nyberg, A. J., Weller, I., & Strizver, S. D. (2022). Pay information disclosure: Review and recommendations for research spanning the pay secrecy-pay transparency continuum. *Journal of Management, 48*(6), 1661–1694; Cullen, Z. B., & Pakzad-Hurson, B. (2019). *Equilibrium effects of pay transparency in a simple labor market*. Harvard Business School. ht tps://www.hbs.edu/faculty/Pages/it em.aspx?num=52648; Futrell, C. M., & Jenkins, O. C. (1978). Pay secrecy versus pay disclosure for salesmen: A longitudinal study. *Journal of Marketing Research*, 214–219.

75. Bjorke, C. (2022, January 4). *Portland restaurant Kachka replaces tipping with a service fee for customers*. KGW8. https://www.kgw.com/articl e/news/local/kachka-no-tipping/28 3-6f74c92b-484f-4f14-9de8-a07baa ad78c1; Burton, M. (2018, November 28). The definitive guide to tipping at any restaurant in America. *Eater*. http s://www.eater.com/2018/11/28/1811 2819/tipping-in-america-guide-rest aurants-how-much; Dixon, V. (2016). The case against tipping in America. *Eater*. https://www.eater.com/a/ca se-against-tipping?_gl=1*17e7ifp*; Jackson-Glidden, B. (2022, January 3). In 2022, Kachka wants to create a more equitable pay structure for its

employees. *Eater: Portland, OR.* https://pdx.eater.com/2022/1/3/22865367/kachka-eliminates-tipping-free-insurance-profit-sharing

CHAPTER 12

1. Arnade, C. (2013, February 27). Why it's smart to be reckless on Wall Street. *Scientific American.* https://blogs.scientificamerican.com/guest-blog/why-its-smart-to-be-reckless-on-wall-street/; Barlyn, S. (2016, April 11). *Goldman Sachs to pay $5 billion in U.S. Justice Dept mortgage bond pact.* Reuters. https://www.reuters.com/article/us-goldman-sachs-mbs-settlement/goldman-sachs-to-pay-5-billion-in-u-s-justice-dept-mortgage-bond-pact-idUSKCN0X81TI; Bautzer, T. (2023, March 30). *Wall Street bonuses dropped 26% in 2022 after record 2021.* Reuters. https://www.reuters.com/markets/us/wall-street-bonuses-dropped-26-2022-after-record-2021-2023-03-30/; Glode, V., & Lowery, R. (2016). Compensating financial experts. *Journal of Finance, 71*(6), 2781–2808; Herszenhorn, D. M. (2008, October 3). Bailout plan wins approval; Democrats vow tighter rules. *The New York Times.* https://www.nytimes.com/2008/10/04/business/economy/04bailout.html; Keoun, B. (2011, April 22). *Morgan Stanley at brink of collapse got $107 billion from fed.* Bloomberg. https://www.bloomberg.com/news/articles/2011-08-22/morgan-stanley-at-brink-of-collapse-got-107b-from-fed?leadSource=uverify%20wall; Nguyen, L., & Azhar, S. (2022, November 15). *Wall Street bonuses to plunge as much as 45% for bankers–study.* Reuters. https://www.reuters.com/business/finance/wall-street-bonuses-plunge-much-45-bankers-study-2022-11-15/; Story, L., & Dash, E. (2009, July 30). Bankers reaped lavish bonuses during bailouts. *The New York Times.* https://www.nytimes.com/2009/07/31/business/31pay.html; U.S. Department of Justice. (2016, April 11). *Goldman Sachs agrees to pay more than $5 billion in connection with its sale of residential mortgage backed securities.* https://www.justice.gov/opa/pr/goldman-sachs-agrees-pay-more-5-billion-connection-its-sale-residential-mortgage-backed

2. March, J. G., & Simon, H. A. (1958). *Organizations.* Wiley.

3. Carrell, M. R., & Dittrich, J. E. (1976). Employee perceptions of fair treatment. *Personnel Journal, 55*, 523–524.

4. Amabile, T. M. (1993). Motivational synergy: Toward new conceptualizations of intrinsic and extrinsic motivation in the workplace. *Human Resource Management Review, 3*, 185–201; Herzberg, F. (1966). *Work and the nature of man.* World.

5. Amabile, T. M. (1993). Motivational synergy: Toward new conceptualizations of intrinsic and extrinsic motivation in the workplace. *Human Resource Management Review, 3*, 185–201; Deci, E. L., & Ryan, R. M. (2000). The "what" and "why" of goal pursuits: Human needs and the self-determination behavior. *Psychological Inquiry, 11*, 227–268.

6. Cerasoli, C. P., Nicklin, J. M., & Ford, M. T. (2014). Intrinsic motivation and extrinsic incentives jointly predict performance: A 40-year meta-analysis. *Psychological Bulletin, 140*, 980–1008.

7. Skinner, B. F. (1953). *Science and human behavior.* Macmillan; Steers, R. M., Mowday, R. T., & Shapiro, D. L. (2004). Introduction to special topic forum: The future of work motivation theory. *Academy of Management Review, 29*, 379–387; Thorndike, E. L. (1911). *Animal intelligence.* Macmillan.

8. Porter, L. W., & Lawler, E. E. (1968). *Managerial attitudes and performance.* Irwin; Vroom, V. H. (1964). *Work and motivation.* Wiley.

9. Wright, P. M. (1989). Test of the mediating role of goals in the incentive–performance relationship. *Journal of Applied Psychology, 74*, 699–705; Wright, P. M. (1992). An examination of the relationships among monetary incentives, goal level, goal commitment, and performance. *Journal of Management, 18*, 677–693.

10. Locke, E. A., & Latham, G. P. (1984). *Goal setting: A motivational technique that works!* Prentice Hall.

11. Seijts, G. H., Latham, G. P., & Whyte, G. (2000). Effect of self-and group efficacy on group performance in a mixed-motive situation. *Human Performance, 13*, 279–298.

12. Payscale. (2022). *Refocusing compensation's role in the Great Reevaluation: 2022 compensation best practices report.*

13. March, J. G., & Simon, H. A. (1958). *Organizations.* Wiley.

14. Payscale. (2022). *Refocusing compensation's role in the Great Reevaluation: 2022 compensation best practices report.*

15. Heneman R. L. (1992). *Merit pay: Linking pay increases to performance ratings.* Addison-Wesley.

16. Pham, L. D., Nguyen, T. D., & Springer, M. G. (2021). Teacher merit pay: A meta-analysis. *American Educational Research Journal, 58*(3), 527–566.

17. Carey, K. (2017). The little-known statistician who taught us to measure teachers. *The New York Times.* https://www.nytimes.com/2017/05/19/upshot/the-little-known-statistician- who-transformed-education.html?_r=0; Chetty, R., Friedman, J. N., & Rockoff, J. E. (2014). Measuring the impacts of teachers II: Teacher value-added and student outcomes in adulthood. *American Economic Review, 104*, 2633–2679; Dee, T. S., & Keys, B. J. (2004). Does merit pay reward good teachers? Evidence from a randomized experiment. *Journal of Policy Analysis and Management, 23*, 471–488; Hanushek, E. A. (2011). The economic value of higher teacher quality. *Economics of Education Review, 30*, 466–479; Johnson, S. M. (2012). Having it both ways: Building the capacity of individual teachers and their schools. *Harvard Educational Review, 82*, 107–122; Murnane, R., & Cohen, D. (1986). Merit pay and the evaluation problem: Why most merit pay plans fail and a few survive. *Harvard Educational Review, 56*, 1–18; Woessmann, L. (2011). Cross-country evidence on teacher performance pay. *Economics of Education Review, 30*, 404–418; Yuan, K., Le, V. N., McCaffrey, D. F., Marsh, J. A., Hamilton, L. S., Stecher, B. M., & Springer, M. G. (2013). Incentive pay programs do not affect teacher motivation or reported practices: Results from three randomized studies. *Educational Evaluation and Policy Analysis, 35*, 3–22.

18. Gerhart, B. (2023). *Compensation* (14th ed.). McGraw-Hill.

19. Payscale. (2022). *Refocusing compensation's role in the Great Reevaluation: 2022 compensation best practices report.*

20. Ibid.

21. Berkeley Human Resources. (n.d.). *Spot awards*. https://hr.berkeley.edu/compensation-benefits/compensation/recognition/spot-awards

22. SAP SuccessFactors Compensation. (n.d.). *Attract, motivate, and retain top performers*. https://www.sap.com/mena/products/hcm/compensation-management.html

23. Rynes, S. L., Gerhart, B., & Parks, L. (2005). Personnel psychology: Performance evaluation and pay for performance. *Annual Review of Psychology, 56*, 571–600.

24. O'Connell, B. (1996). Dead solid perfect: Achieving sales compensation alignment. *Compensation & Benefits Review, 28*(2), 41–48.

25. Misra, S., & Nair, H. S. (2011). A structural model of sales-force compensation dynamics: Estimation and field implementation. *Quantitative Marketing and Economics, 9*, 211–257.

26. Deming, W. E. (1986). *Out of the crisis*. MIT Center for Advanced Engineering Study; Pfeffer J. (1998). *The human equation*. Harvard Business School Press.

27. Nyberg, A. J., Maltarich, M. A., Abdulsalam, D., Essman, S. M., Cragun, O. (2018). Collective pay for performance: A cross-disciplinary review and meta-analysis. *Journal of Management, 44*(6), 2433–2472; Rynes, S. L., Gerhart, B., & Parks, L. (2005). Personnel psychology: Performance evaluation and pay for performance. *Annual Review of Psychology, 56*, 571–600.

28. Payscale. (2022). *Refocusing compensation's role in the Great Reevaluation: 2022 compensation best practices report*.

29. Garbers, Y., & Konradt, U. (2014). The effect of financial incentives on performance: A quantitative review of individual and team-based financial incentives. *Journal of Occupational and Organizational Psychology, 87*, 102–137; Nyberg, A. J., Maltarich, M. A., Abdulsalam, D., Essman, S. M., Cragun, O. (2018). Collective pay for performance: A cross-disciplinary review and meta-analysis. *Journal of Management, 44*(6), 2433–2472.

30. Hu, Q., Adam, H., & Desai, S. (2019). Turning a blind eye to team members' unethical behavior: The role of incentive structures. *Academy of Management Proceedings, 2019*(1).

31. Major League Baseball. (n.d.). *Postseason share*. https://www.mlb.com/glossary/miscellaneous/postseason-share; Walsh, E. (2022, November 22). *Astros players receive record $516k playoff bonuses after 2022 World Series title*. Bleacher Report. https://bleacherreport.com/articles/10056529-astros-players-receive-record-516k-playoff-bonuses-after-2022-world-series-title

32. Beersma, B., Hollenbeck, J. R., Humphrey, S. E., Moon, H., Conlon, D. E., & Ilgen, D. R. (2003). Cooperation, competition, and team performance: Toward a contingency approach. *Academy of Management Journal, 46*, 572–590; Johnson, M. D., Hollenbeck, J. R., Humphrey, S. E., Ilgen, D. R., Jundt, D., & Meyer, C. J. (2006). Cutthroat cooperation: Asymmetrical adaptation to changes in team reward structures. *Academy of Management Journal, 49*, 103–119.

33. Hafner, K. (2005, February 1). New incentives for Google employees: Awards worth millions. *The New York Times*. http://www.nytimes.com/2005/02/01/technology/new-incentive-for-google-employees-awards-worth-millions.html

34. WorldatWork. (2016). *Compensation programs and practices survey*. https://www.worldatwork.org/adimLink?id=80656

35. Gardner, A. C. (2011). Goal setting and gainsharing: The evidence on effectiveness. *Compensation & Benefits Review, 43*, 236–244.

36. Welbourne, T. M., & Gomez-Mejia, L. (1995). Gainsharing: A critical review and a future research agenda. *Journal of Management, 21*, 559–609.

37. Leitman, I. M., Levin, R., Lipp, M. J., Sivaprasad, L., Karalakulasingam, C. J., Bernard, D. S., Friedmann, P., & Shulkin, D. J. (2010). Quality and financial outcomes from gainsharing for inpatient admissions: A three-year experience. *Journal of Hospital Medicine, 5*, 501–507.

38. Rynes, S. L., Gerhart, B., & Parks, L. (2005). Personnel psychology: Performance evaluation and pay for performance. *Annual Review of Psychology, 56*, 571–600.

39. SHRM. (2018, January 12). *Designing and managing incentive compensation programs*. https://www.shrm.org/resourcesandtools/tools-and-samples/toolkits/pages/designingincentivecompensation.aspx

40. Doucouliagos, C. (1995). Worker participation and productivity in labor-managed and participatory capitalist firms: A meta-analysis. *Industrial Labor Relations Review, 49*, 58–77; Weitzman, M. L., & Kruse, D. L. (1990). Profit sharing and productivity. In A. S. Blinder (Ed.), *Paying for productivity* (pp. 95–140). Brookings Institute.

41. Han, J. H., Bartol, K. M., & Kim, S. (2015). Tightening up the performance–pay linkage: Roles of contingent reward leadership and profit-sharing in the cross-level influence of individual pay-for-performance. *Journal of Applied Psychology, 100*, 417–430.

42. de Cremer, D., & Tao, T. (2015, September 24). Huawei: A case study of when profit sharing works. *Harvard Business Review*. https://hbr.org/2015/09/huawei-a-case-study-of-when-profit-sharing-works; Reuters. (2022, April 4). *Huawei pays out $9.65 billion in dividends to current and retired staff*. https://www.reuters.com/technology/huawei-pays-out-965-bln-dividends-current-retired-staff-2022-04-05/

43. Fong, S., & Shaffer, M. (2003). The dimensionality and determinants of pay satisfaction: A cross-cultural investigation of a group incentive plan. *International Journal of Human Resource Management, 14*, 559–580; Hofstede, G. (1991). *Culture and organisations: Software of the mind*. McGraw-Hill; Ramamoorthy, N., & Carroll, S. J. (1998). Individualism/collectivism orientations and reactions toward alternative human resource management practices. *Human Relations, 51*, 571–588.

44. Gerhart, B., & Milkovich, G. T. (1990). Organizational differences in managerial compensation and financial performance. *Academy of Management Journal, 33*, 663–691.

45. Siddiqui, F. (2022, April 26). Tesla's value dropped Tuesday by more than double the cost of Twitter. *The Washington Post*. https://www.washingtonpost.com/technology/2022/04/26/elon-musk-tesla-twitter-stock/

46. Nyberg, A. J., Maltarich, M. A., Abdulsalam, D. D., Essman, S. M., & Cragun, O. (2018). Collective pay for performance: A cross-disciplinary review and meta-analysis. *Journal of Management, 44*(6), 2433–2472.

47. French, J. L. (1987). Employee perspectives on stock ownership: Financial investment or mechanism of control. *Academy of Management Review, 12*, 427–435.

48. Great Place to Work. (2022). *Publix Super Markets*. https://www.greatplacetowork.com/certified-company/1000405#:~:text=83%25%20of%20employees%20at%20Publix,a%20typical%20U.S.%2Dbased%20company; Jazmyn M. (2020, August 12). *Your guide to earning Publix stock*. Publix. https://blog.publix.com/publix/your-guide-to-earning-publix-stock/

49. Salgado, J. F., & Moscoso, S. (2019). Meta-analysis of interrater reliability of supervisory performance ratings: Effects of appraisal purpose, scale type, and range restriction. *Frontiers in Psychology, 10*, 2281; Viswesvaran, C., Ones, D. S., & Schmidt, F. L. (1996). Comparative analysis of the reliability of job performance ratings. *Journal of Applied Psychology, 81*, 557–574.

50. Longenecker, C. O., Sims, H. P., Jr., & Gioia, D. A. (1987). Behind the mask: The politics of employee appraisal. *Academy of Management Executive*, 183–193.

51. Masunaga, S., & Lien, T. (2016). Yahoo ex-employee sues, alleging manipulation of performance reviews and gender bias. *Los Angeles Times*. http://www.latimes.com/business/technology/la-fi-tn-yahoo-lawsuit-20160202-story.html

52. California Senate Bill No. 1162 (2021–2022). Employment: Salaries and wages. https://leginfo.legislature.ca.gov/faces/billNavClient.xhtml?bill_id=202120220SB1162; Cox, J. (2022, October 27). *The bonus blind spot in US pay transparency*. BBC. https://www.bbc.com/worklife/article/20221025-the-bonus-blind-spot-in-us-pay-transparency; Marasi, S., & Bennett, R. J. (2016). Pay communication: Where do we go from here? *Human Resource Management Review, 26*, 50–58; NYC Commission on Human Rights. (2022, May 12). *Salary transparency in job advertisements*. https://www.nyc.gov/assets/cchr/downloads/pdf/publications/Salary-Transparency-Factsheet.pdf; U.S. Equal Employment Opportunity Commission. (n.d.). *Equal pay/compensation discrimination*. https://www.eeoc.gov/equal-paycompensation-discrimination;mU.S. Equal Employment Opportunity Commission. (n.d.). Title VII of the Civil Rights Act of 1964. https://www.eeoc.gov/statutes/title-vii-civil-rights-act-1964#:~:text=Title%20VII%20prohibits%20employment%20discrimination,Pay%20Act%20of%202009%20(Pub.

53. Gerhart, B., & Rynes, S. L. (2003). *Compensation: Theory, evidence, and strategic implications*. Sage; Lazear, E. P. (1986). Salaries and piece rates. *Journal of Business, 59*, 405–431.

54. Nyberg, A. J., Maltarich, M. A., Abdulsalam, D., Essman, S. M., Cragun, O. (2018). Collective pay for performance: A cross-disciplinary review and meta-analysis. *Journal of Management, 44*(6), 2433–2472; Park, S., & Sturman, M. C. (2016). Evaluating form and functionality of pay-for-performance plans: The relative incentive and sorting effects of merit pay, bonuses, and long-term incentives. *Human Resource Management, 55*(4), 697–719.

55. Bretz, R. D., Ash, R. A., & Dreher, G. F. (1989). Do people make the place? An examination of the attraction-selection-attrition hypothesis. *Personnel Psychology, 42*, 561–581; Cable, D. M., & Judge, T. A. (1994). Pay preferences and job search decisions: A person–organization fit perspective. *Personnel Psychology, 47*, 317–348; Cadsby, C. B., Song, F., & Tapon, F. (2007). Sorting and incentive effects of pay for performance: An experimental investigation. *Academy of Management Journal, 50*, 387–405.

56. Schneider, B. (1987). The people make the place. *Personnel Psychology, 40*, 437–453.

57. Uggerslev, K. L., Fassina, N. E., & Kraichy, D. (2012). Recruiting through the stages: A meta-analytic test of predictors of applicant attraction at different stages of the recruiting process. *Personnel Psychology, 65*, 597–660.

58. U.S. Bureau of Labor Statistics. (2022, September 20). Economic news release (USDL-22-1892): *Employer costs for employee compensation summary*. https://www.bls.gov/news.release/ecec.nr0.htm

59. George, J. M., & Jones, G. R. (1997). Organizational spontaneity in context. *Human Performance, 10*, 153–170; Park, T.-Y., Park, S., & Barry, B. (2022). Incentive effects on ethics. *Academy of Management Annals, 16*, 297–333; Wright, P. M., George, J. M., Farnsworth, S. R., & McMahan, G. C. (1993). Productivity and extra-role behavior: The effects of goals and incentives on spontaneous helping. *Journal of Applied Psychology, 78*, 374–381.

60. He, W., Li, S. L., Feng, J., Zhang, G., & Sturman, M. C. (2021). When does pay for performance motivate employee helping behavior? The contextual influence of performance subjectivity. *Academy of Management Journal, 64*, 293–326.

61. Deckop, J. R., Mangel, R., & Cirka, C. C. (1999). Getting more than you pay for: Organizational citizenship behavior and pay-for-performance plans. *Academy of Management Journal, 42*, 420–428.

62. Hegarty, W. H., & Sims, H. P. (1978). Some determinants of unethical decision behavior: An experiment. *Journal of Applied Psychology, 63*, 451–457.

63. Barro, J. (2016). Wells Fargo's scandal is a cautionary tale about incentive pay. *Business Insider*. http://www.businessinsider.com/wells-fargos-scandal-is-a-cautionary-tale-about-incentive-pay-2016-9; Bomey, N., & McCoy, K. (2017). Wells Fargo clawing back $75.3 million more from former execs in fake accounts scandal. *USA Today*. https://www.usatoday.com/story/money/2017/04/10/wells-fargo-compensation-clawback/100276472/; Morcroft, G. (2022, December 21). *Wells Fargo paying $3.7 billion for cheating clients and trashing credit histories*. Nasdaq. https://www.nasdaq.com/articles/wells-fargo-paying-$3.7-billion-for-cheating-clients-and-trashing-credit-histories; Telford, T. (2022, November 28). Incentives can lead employees to cheat or lie at work. *The Washington Post*. https://www.washingtonpost.com/business/2022/11/28/work-incentives-ethics-study/

64. DeMatteo, J. S., Eby, L. T., & Sundstrom, E. (1998). Team-based rewards: Current empirical evidence. *Research in Organizational Behavior, 20*, 141–183.

65. Nalbantian, H. R., & Schotter, A. (1997). Productivity under group incentives: An experimental study. *American Economic Review*, 314–341.

66. Lawler, E. E., & Cohen, S. G. (1992). Designing pay systems for teams. *ACA Journal, 1*, 6–19; Mohrman, A. M., Mohrman, S. A., & Lawler, E. E. (1992). The performance management of teams. In W. J. Bruns Jr. (Ed.), *Performance measurement, evaluation, and incentives* (pp. 217–241).

Harvard Business School Press; Wageman, R. (1996). Interdependence and group effectiveness. *Administrative Science Quarterly, 40*, 145–180; Wageman, R., & Baker, G. (1997). Incentives and cooperation: The joint effects of task and reward interdependence on group performance. *Journal of Organizational Behavior, 18*, 139–158.

67. Latané, B., Williams, K., & Harkins, S. (1979). Many hands make light the work: The causes and consequences of social loafing. *Journal of Personality and Social Psychology, 37*, 822–832.

68. Milkovich, G. T., & Wigdor, A. K. (1991). *Pay for performance: Evaluating performance appraisal and merit pay.* National Academies Press.

CHAPTER 13

1. Bennett, A. A., Bakker, A. B., & Field, J. G. (2018). Recovery from work-related effort: A meta-analysis. *Journal of Organizational Behavior, 39*(3), 262–275; Ford, M. T., Cerasoli, C. P., Higgins, J. A., & Decesare, A. L. (2011). Relationships between psychological, physical, and behavioural health and work performance: A review and meta-analysis. *Work & Stress, 25*(3), 185–204; Ginger. (2023). Mental healthcare for every moment. https://www.ginger.com/; Karabinski, T., Haun, V. C., Nübold, A., Wendsche, J., & Wegge, J. (2021). Interventions for improving psychological detachment from work: A meta-analysis. *Journal of Occupational Health Psychology, 26*(3), 224–242; Lyra. (2023). *State of workforce mental health: By the numbers.* https://www.lyrahealth.com/2023-state-of-workforce-mental-health-report/; National Alliance of Healthcare Purchaser Coalitions. (2023). *Voice of the purchaser survey on behavioral health support: Spring 2023 survey results.* https://www.nationalalliancehealth.org/news/news-press-releases/voice-purchaser-survey; Pereira, D., & Elfering, A. (2014). Social stressors at work and sleep during weekends: The mediating role of psychological detachment. *Journal of Occupational Health Psychology, 19*(1), 85–95; Riadi, I., Kervin, L., Dhillon, S., Teo, K., Churchill, R., Card, K. G., ... & Cosco, T. D. (2022). Digital interventions for depression and anxiety in older adults: A systematic review of randomised controlled trials. *The Lancet Healthy Longevity, 3*(8), e558–e571; Sonnentag, S., Binnewies, C., & Mojza, E. J. (2010). Staying well and engaged when demands are high: The role of psychological detachment. *Journal of Applied Psychology, 95*(5), 965-976; Sonnentag, S., & Fritz, C. (2007). The Recovery Experience Questionnaire: Development and validation of a measure for assessing recuperation and unwinding from work. *Journal of Occupational Health Psychology, 12*(3), 204–221; Weiss, T. (2023, April 18). The companies that give everyone the day off when life gets stressful. *The Wall Street Journal.* https://www.wsj.com/articles/timeout-days-and-respite-rooms-the-new-trends-in-mental-health-at-the-office-70dcbb08; WTW. (2022, October 20). *Employers making employee mental health and wellbeing a top health priority, WTW survey finds* [Press release]. https://www.wtwco.com/en-US/News/2022/10/employers-making-employee-mental-health-and-wellbeing-a-top-health-priority-wtw-survey-finds

2. U.S. Bureau of Labor Statistics. (2023, March 17). *Economic news release: Employer costs for employee compensation* (USDL-23-0488). https://www.bls.gov/news.release/ecec.nr0.htm

3. Society for Human Resource Management. (2017). *2017 strategic benefits survey: Strategize with benefits.* SHRM. https://www.shrm.org/hr-today/trends-and-forecasting/research-and-surveys/pages/strategize-with-benefits.aspx

4. Beam, B. T., & McFadden, J. J. (2007). *Employee benefits* (8th ed.). Dearborn Financial Publishing; U.S. Bureau of Labor Statistics. (2023, March 17). *Economic news release: Employer costs for employee compensation* (USDL-23-0488). https://www.bls.gov/news.release/ecec.nr0.htm

5. U.S. Social Security Administration. (2023). *Fact sheet: Social security.* https://www.ssa.gov/news/press/factsheets/basicfact-alt.pdf

6. Napoletano, E. (January 22, 2023). What is FICA tax and how does it work? *The Wall Street Journal.* https://www.wsj.com/buyside/personal-finance/what-is-fica-tax-01674395539

7. U.S. Social Security Administration. (2023). *Social security credits.* https://www.ssa.gov/benefits/retirement/planner/credits.html#:~:text=The%20 amount%20of%20earnings%20it,4%20credits%20for%20the%20year

8. U.S. Social Security Administration. (2023). *Retirement benefits.* https://www.ssa.gov/pubs/EN-05-10035.pdf

9. U.S. Social Security Administration. (2023). *If you are the survivor.* https://www.ssa.gov/benefits/survivors/ifyou.html#:~:text=Do%20we%20pay%20death%20benefits,the%20lump%2Dsum%20death%20payment; U.S. Social Security Administration. (2023). *Survivors benefits.* https://www.ssa.gov/benefits/survivors/

10. U.S. Social Security Administration. (2023). *Disability benefits.* https://www.ssa.gov/benefits/disability/; U.S. Social Security Administration. (2023). *Types of beneficiaries.* https://www.ssa.gov/oact/ProgData/types.html

11. U.S. Social Security Administration. (2023). *Medicare benefits.* https://www.ssa.gov/benefits/medicare/

12. Posthuma, R. A. (2009). *Workers' compensation.* SHRM. https://www.shrm.org/academicinitiatives/universities/teachingresources/Documents/Workers%27%20Comp%20IM%20Final.pdf

13. U.S. Department of Labor. (2023). *Unemployment insurance.* https://www.dol.gov/general/topic/unemployment-insurance

14. U.S. Social Security Administration. (2023). *Social Security programs in the United States: Unemployment insurance.* https://www.ssa.gov/policy/docs/progdesc/sspus/unemploy.pdf

15. U.S. Department of Labor. (2023). *Unemployment insurance data.* https://oui.doleta.gov/unemploy/DataDashboard.asp

16. U.S. Department of Labor, Wage and Hour Division. (2023). *Family and Medical Leave Act.* https://www.dol.gov/whd/fmla/

17. Abraham, E., Hendler, T., Shapira-Lichter, I., Kanat-Maymon, Y., Zagoory-Sharon, O., & Feldman, R. (2014). Father's brain is sensitive to childcare experiences. *Proceedings of the National Academy of Sciences, 111*(27), 9792–9797; Belle, J. V. (2016). RAND Europe: *Paternity and parental leave policies across the European Union.* RAND Corporation. https://www.rand.org/pubs/research_repor

ts/RR1666.html; Dishman, L. (2016, February 16). How U.S. employee benefits compare to Europe's. *Fast Company*. https://www.fastcompany.com/3056830/how-the-us-employee-benefits-compare-to-europe; European Parliament. (2022, March). *Maternity and paternity leave in the EU*. https://www.europarl.europa.eu/RegData/etudes/ATAG/2022/698892/EPRS_ATA(2022)698892_EN.pdf; Kela. (2015). *Home and family: Benefits for families with children and housing benefits*. https://www.kela.fi/documents/10180/1978560/2015_Home_family.pdf; InfoFinland. (2022, October 25). *Benefits for a family after a child is born*. https://www.infofinland.fi/en/family/financial-support-for-families/benefits-for-a-family-after-a-child-is-born; Lorenzo, G. (2015, October 7). How does life for working parents in Finland compare to those in the U.S.? *Fast Company*. https://www.fastcompany.com/3051689/how-does-life-for-working-parents-in-finland-really-compare-to-the-us; Saldana, C. (2021, January 6). Something to celebrate for new fathers in Spain, as paternity leave extended to 16 weeks. *El País*. https://english.elpais.com/spanish_news/2021-01-06/something-to-celebrate-for-new-fathers-in-spain-as-paternity-leave-extended-to-16-weeks.html; U.S. Department of Labor. (2023). *Paid parental leave*. https://www.dol.gov/general/jobs/benefits/paid-parental-leave

18. U.S. Department of Labor. (2023). *Health plans & benefits: ERISA*. https://www.dol.gov/general/topic/health-plans/erisa

19. U.S. Department of Labor. (2023). *Health plans & benefits: Continuation of health coverage—COBRA*. https://www.dol.gov/general/topic/health-plans/cobra; U.S. Department of Labor. (2023). *History of EBSA and ERISA*. https://www.dol.gov/agencies/ebsa/about-ebsa/about-us/history-of-ebsa-and-erisa

20. U.S. Department of Labor. (2023). *Health plans & benefits: Portability of health coverage*. https://www.dol.gov/general/topic/health-plans/portability; U.S. Department of Labor. (2023). *History of EBSA and ERISA*. https://www.dol.gov/agencies/ebsa/about-ebsa/about-us/history-of-ebsa-and-erisa

21. HealthCare.gov. (2023). *Health coverage rights and protections*. https://www.healthcare.gov/health-care-law-protections/; U.S. Government

Publishing Office. (2010, March 23). Public Law 111-148—Mar. 23, 2010. https://www.gpo.gov/fdsys/pkg/PLAW-111publ148/pdf/PLAW-111publ148.pdf; U.S. Internal Revenue Service. (2023). *Affordable Care Act: Employers*. https://www.irs.gov/affordable-care-act/employers; U.S. Internal Revenue Service. (2023). *Employer shared responsibility provisions*. https://www.irs.gov/affordable-care-act/employers/employer-shared-responsibility-provisions;

22. Beam, B. T., & McFadden, J. J. (2007). *Employee benefits* (8th ed.). Dearborn Financial Publishing.

23. The Kaiser Family Foundation. (2023). 2022 *employer health benefits survey*. https://www.kff.org/health-costs/report/2022-employer-health-benefits-survey/

24. Business Wire. (2022, August 11). *Health benefit costs growth will accelerate to 5.6% in 2023, Mercer survey finds*. https://www.businesswire.com/news/home/20220811005163/en/Health-Benefit-Cost-Growth-Will-Accelerate-to-5.6-in-2023-Mercer-Survey-Finds; Carrns, A. (2022, November 4). Expect higher health insurance premiums, but not a lot higher. *The New York Times*. https://www.nytimes.com/2022/11/04/your-money/health-insurance-premiums-employer-plans.html;

25. Society for Human Resource Management. (2022). *Employee benefits survey: Executive summary*. https://shrm-res.cloudinary.com/image/upload/v1654193525/Membership%202022/Employee_Benefits_Survey_-_Executive_Summary_-_FINAL.pdf

26. U.S. Internal Revenue Service. (2022). *Health savings accounts and other tax-favored health plans* (Publication No. 969). https://www.irs.gov/publications/p969

27. Song, G. Y. (2010, October 25). *Consumer-driven health care: What is it, and what does it mean for employees and employers*. U.S. Bureau of Labor Statistics. https://www.bls.gov/opub/mlr/cwc/consumer-driven-health-care-what-is-it-and-what-does-it-mean-for-employees-and-employers.pdf

28. U.S. Internal Revenue Service. (2022). *Health savings accounts and other tax-favored health plans* (Publication No. 969). https://www.irs.gov/publications/p969

29. Ibid.

30. Richardson, C. M. (1998). Ethics and employee benefits. *Benefits Quarterly, 14*, 9–16.

31. Morley, T. (2018). *Temporary disability insurance requirements by state*. SHRM. https://www.shrm.org/resourcesandtools/legal-and-compliance/state-and-local-updates/xperthr/pages/temporary-disability-insurance-requirements-by-state.aspx

32. Society for Human Resource Management. (2014, December 11). *Disability benefits: What are short-term disability and long-term disability?* https://www.shrm.org/resourcesandtools/tools-and-samples/hr-qa/pages/stdandltd.aspx

33. Ibid.

34. Society for Human Resource Management. (2022). *Employee benefits survey: Executive summary*. https://shrm-res.cloudinary.com/image/upload/v1654193525/Membership%202022/Employee_Benefits_Survey_-_Executive_Summary_-_FINAL.pdf

35. U.S. Department of Labor. (2023). *Health plans & benefits: ERISA*. https://www.dol.gov/general/topic/health-plans/erisa

36. U.S. Department of Labor. (2023). *FAQs about retirement plans and ERISA*. https://www.dol.gov/sites/dolgov/files/ebsa/about-ebsa/our-activities/resource-center/faqs/retirement-plans-and-erisa-for-workers.pdf; U.S. Department of Labor. (2023). *Participant rights*. https://www.dol.gov/general/topic/retirement/participantrights;

37. Pension Benefit Guaranty Corporation. (2023). *PBGC pension insurance: We've got you covered*. https://www.pbgc.gov/wr/find-an-insured-pension-plan/pbgc-protects-pensions; Pension Benefit Guaranty Corporation. (2023). *Workers & retirees*. https://www.pbgc.gov/workers-retirees

38. Beam, B. T., & McFadden, J. J. (2007). *Employee benefits* (8th ed.). Dearborn Financial Publishing; Society for Human Resource Management. (2015, April 24). *Pension plan: Defined benefit: General: What is a defined benefit plan?* https://www.shrm.org/resourcesandtools/tools-and-samples/hr-qa/pages/whataredefinedbenefitplans.aspx

39. Capelli, P. (2023, January–February). How financial accounting screws up

HR. *Harvard Business Review.* https:/ /hbr.org/2023/01/how-financial-acc ounting-screws-up-hr; U.S. Internal Revenue Service. (2018). *Choosing a retirement plan: Defined benefit plan.* h ttps://www.irs.gov/retirement-plans /choosing-a-retirement-plan-define d-benefit-plan

40. Beam, B. T., & McFadden, J. J. (2007). *Employee benefits* (8th ed.). Dearborn Financial Publishing; U.S. Department of Labor. (2014, January). *Cash balance pension plans.* https://www.d ol.gov/sites/dolgov/files/ebsa/abou t-ebsa/our-activities/resource-cent er/faqs/cash-balance-pension-plan s-consumer.pdf

41. Beam, B. T., & McFadden, J. J. (2007). *Employee benefits* (8th ed.). Dearborn Financial Publishing; U.S. Department of Labor. (2018). *Types of retire- ment plans.* https://www.dol.gov/gen eral/topic/retirement/typesofplans

42. U.S. Internal Revenue Service. (2023). *Definitions.* https://www.irs.g ov/retirement-plans/plan-participan t-employee/definitions

43. Society for Human Resource Man- agement. (2022). *Employee benefits survey: Executive summary.* https://sh rm-res.cloudinary.com/image/uploa d/v1654193525/Membership%20202 2/Employee_Benefits_Survey_-_Exe cutive_Summary_-_FINAL.pdf

44. U.S. Internal Revenue Service. (2023). *401(k) plan overview.* https://w ww.irs.gov/retirement-plans/plan-s ponsor/401k-plan-overview

45. U.S. Internal Revenue Service. (2023). *401(k) plans.* https://www.irs. gov/retirement-plans/401k-plans

46. Society for Human Resource Man- agement. (2022). *Employee benefits survey: Executive summary.* https://sh rm-res.cloudinary.com/image/uploa d/v1654193525/Membership%20202 2/Employee_Benefits_Survey_-_Exe cutive_Summary_-_FINAL.pdf

47. U.S. Internal Revenue Service. (2023). *Choosing a retirement plan: 401(k) plan.* https://www.irs.gov/retir ement-plans/choosing-a-retiremen t-plan-401k-plan

48. Chang, A., & Kurkoski, J. (2017, August 22). *Nudge employees to save more for retirement.* Re:Work. https: //rework.withgoogle.com/blog/nud ge-to-save-for-retirement/; Choi, J. J., Haisley, E., Kurkoski, J., & Massey, C. (2017). Small cues change savings

choices. *Journal of Economic Behavior & Organization, 142,* 378–395.

49. U.S. Internal Revenue Service. (2023). *IRC 403(b) tax-sheltered annuity plans.* https://www.irs.gov/retirement-plan s/irc-403b-tax-sheltered-annuity-pl ans

50. U.S. Internal Revenue Service. (2023). *Definitions.* https://www.irs.g ov/retirement-plans/plan-participan t-employee/definitions

51. U.S. Internal Revenue Service. (2023). *Choosing a retirement plan: Profit-sharing plan.* https://www.irs.g ov/retirement-plans/choosing-a-reti rement-plan-profit-sharing-plan

52. U.S. Internal Revenue Service. (2023). *Definitions.* https://www.irs.g ov/retirement-plans/plan-participan t-employee/definitions; U.S. Internal Revenue Service. (2023). *Employee stock ownership plans (ESOPs).* https:/ /www.irs.gov/retirement-plans/emp loyee-stock-ownership-plans-esops

53. Sammer, J. (2016, February 4). *ESOPs turn workers into owners.* SHRM. https ://www.shrm.org/resourcesandtool s/hr-topics/benefits/pages/esops-w orkers-owners.aspx

54. Beam, B. T., & McFadden, J. J. (2007). *Employee benefits* (8th ed.). Dearborn Financial Publishing; U.S. Depart- ment of Labor. (2018). *Types of retire- ment plans.* https://www.dol.gov/gen eral/topic/retirement/typesofplans; U.S. Internal Revenue Service. (2018). *Choosing a retirement plan: Money- purchase plan.* https://www.irs.gov/r etirement-plans/choosing-a-retirem ent-plan-money-purchase-plan

55. Beam, B. T., & McFadden, J. J. (2007). *Employee benefits* (8th ed.). Dearborn Financial Publishing; U.S. Internal Revenue Service. (2023). *Traditional and Roth IRAs.* https://www.irs.gov/r etirement-plans/traditional-and-rot h-iras

56. Foster, A. C. (1997). *Employee ben- efits: Life insurance.* U.S. Bureau of Labor Statistics. https://www.bls.gov /opub/mlr/cwc/life-insurance.pdf

57. U.S. Bureau of Labor Statistics. (2022, March). *Life insurance benefits: Access, participation, and take-up rates* (Table 5). https://www.bls.gov/n ews.release/ebs2.t05.htm

58. Society for Human Resource Man- agement. (2022). *Employee benefits survey: Executive summary.* https://sh rm-res.cloudinary.com/image/uploa

d/v1654193525/Membership%20202 2/Employee_Benefits_Survey_-_Exe cutive_Summary_-_FINAL.pdf

59. Gebhardt, D. L., & Crump, C. E. (1990). Employee fitness and well- ness programs in the workplace. *American Psychologist, 45,* 262–272; Goetzel, R. Z., Henke, R. M., Tabrizi, M., Pelletier, K. R., Loeppke, R., Bal- lard, D. W., . . . & Serxner, S. (2014). Do workplace health promotion (wellness) programs work? *Journal of Occupational and Environmental Medicine, 56,* 927–934; Mattke, S., Liu, H., Caloyeras, J., Huang, C. Y., Van Busum, K. R., Khodyakov, D., & Shier, V. (2013). Workplace wellness pro- grams study. *Rand Health Quarterly, 3*(2), 7; Peñalvo, J. L., Sagastume, D., Mertens, E., Uzhova, I., Smith, J., Wu, J. H., . . . & Mozaffarian, D. (2021). Effectiveness of workplace wellness programmes for dietary habits, over- weight, and cardiometabolic health: A systematic review and meta-anal- ysis. *The Lancet Public Health, 6*(9), e648–e660; Parks, K. M., & Steel- man, L. A. (2008). Organizational wellness programs: A meta-analysis. *Journal of Occupational Health Psy- chology, 13,* 58–68.

60. Lambert, S. J. (2000). Added benefits: The link between work–life benefits and organizational citizenship behav- ior. *Academy of Management Journal, 43,* 801–815; Muse, L., Harris, S. G., Giles, W. F., & Feild, H. S. (2008). Work-life benefits and positive organizational behavior: is there a connection? *Journal of Organizational Behavior, 29*(2), 171–192.

61. U.S. Department of Labor. (2023). *Holiday pay.* https://www.dol.gov/gen eral/topic/wages/holiday

62. PayScale. (2023). *2023 compensation best practices report.* https://www.pa yscale.com/research-and-insights/c bpr/

63. Sammer, J. (2017, January 9). *Employ- ers are banking on paid time off.* SHRM. https://www.shrm.org/resourcesan dtools/hr-topics/benefits/pages/ban king-on-paid-time-off.aspx

64. Umoh, R. (2018, April 28). *5 companies with employee perks that rival Google's.* CNBC. https://www.cnbc.com/2018 /04/27/facebook-netflix-amazon-an d-others-offer-perks-that-rival-goo gle.html; Netflix. (2023). *Taking care of yourself.* https://jobs.netflix.com/w ork-life-philosophy

65. Capelli, P. (2023, January–February). How financial accounting screws up HR. *Harvard Business Review*. https://hbr.org/2023/01/how-financial-accounting-screws-up-hr

66. Sammer, J. (2014, December 15). *Unlimited paid time off: A good or bad idea?* SHRM. https://www.shrm.org/resourcesandtools/hr-topics/benefits/pages/unlimited-pto.aspx

67. Deschenaux, J. (2015, June 16). *Put vacation policies in writing*. SHRM. https://www.shrm.org/resourcesandtools/legal-and-compliance/state-and-local-updates/pages/put-vacation-policies-in-writing-.aspx

68. Society for Human Resource Management. (2022). *Employee benefits survey: Executive summary*. https://shrm-res.cloudinary.com/image/upload/v1654193525/Membership%202022/Employee_Benefits_Survey_-_Executive_Summary_-_FINAL.pdf

69. Brownlee, D. (2022, July 6). *82% of employed Gen Zers want mental health days, study finds*. SHRM. https://www.shrm.org/executive/resources/articles/pages/most-generation-z-workers-want-mental-health-days.aspx

70. Smith, A. (2017, April 6). *SHRM to Congress: Make comp time available to businesses*. SHRM. https://www.shrm.org/resourcesandtools/legal-and-compliance/employment-law/pages/shrm-congress-comp-time-businesses.aspx; Society for Human Resource Management. (2016, August 31). *Legal & regulatory: Compensatory time: Is compensatory time allowed in the private sector?* https://www.shrm.org/resourcesandtools/tools-and-samples/hr-qa/pages/iscompensatorytimeallowedintheprivatesector.aspx

71. U.S. Bureau of Labor Statistics. (2019). *Unpaid eldercare in the United States—2017-2018 summary* (USDL-19-2051). https://www.bls.gov/news.release/elcare.nr0.htm; U.S. Bureau of Labor Statistics. (2019). *Employment characteristics of families–2018* (USDL-19-0666). https://www.bls.gov/news.release/pdf/famee.pdf; U.S. Bureau of Labor Statistics. (2021, December 20). *Employment characteristics of families–2020* (USDL-21-0695). https://www.bls.gov/news.release/pdf/famee.pdf

72. Care.com Editorial Staff. (2022, June 15). *This is how much child care costs in 2022*. https://www.care.com/c/how-much-does-child-care-cost/

73. Modestino, A. S., Ladge, J. J., Swartz, A., & Lincoln, A. (2021, April 29). Childcare is a business issue. *Harvard Business Review*. https://hbr.org/2021/04/childcare-is-a-business-issue

74. Dalton, M. (2017, December 21). *Companies realize benefits of pitching in for child care*. WABE. https://www.wabe.org/companies-realize-benefits-pitching-child-care/

75. The Best Place for Working Parents. (2022). *National trends report*. https://bestplace4workingparents.com/wp-content/uploads/2022/12/national-trends-report-2022-digital-12_15-sm.pdf

76. The Best Places for Working Parents. (2022). *Child care toolkit*. https://bestplace4workingparents.com/wp-content/uploads/2022/10/child-care-toolkit_national_10-28-22_sm.pdf

77. Piszczek, M. M. (2020). Reciprocal relationships between workplace childcare initiatives and collective turnover rates of men and women. *Journal of Management, 46*(3), 470–494.

78. Burd, C., Burrows, M., & McKenzie, B. (2021, March 18). *Travel time to work in the United States: 2019*. U.S. Census Bureau. https://www.census.gov/library/publications/2021/acs/acs-47.html

79. Parker, K. (2023, March 30). *About a third of U.S. workers who can work from home now do so all the time*. Pew Research Center. https://www.pewresearch.org/short-reads/2023/03/30/about-a-third-of-us-workers-who-can-work-from-home-do-so-all-the-time/

80. Hsu, A. (2023, April 28). *Airbnb let its workers live and work anywhere. Spoiler: They're loving it*. NPR. https://www.npr.org/2023/04/28/1172213330/airbnb-hybrid-remote-work-from-home-office-digital-nomad; Torchinsky, R. (2022, April 30). *Airbnb will let its employees live and work anywhere*. NPR. https://www.npr.org/2022/04/30/1095756450/airbnb-will-let-its-employees-live-and-work-anywhere

81. Hopkins, J. (2016, September 15). Understanding the tax benefits of 529 plans. *Forbes*. https://www.forbes.com/sites/jamiehopkins/2016/09/15/understanding-the-tax-benefits-of-529-plans/#3a7cf53a19aa

82. Kenney, J., & Mason, L. (2012, February 17). *Strengthen employee loyalty with corporate 529 plans*. SHRM. https://www.shrm.org/resourcesandtools/hr-topics/benefits/pages/529plans.aspx; LearnVest. (2017, April 1). College savings plans: The next big employee benefit? *Forbes*. https://www.forbes.com/sites/learnvest/2017/04/01/college-savings-plans-the-next-big-employee-benefit/#46fcae6272ce; Ward, L. (2016, March 27). The latest corporate benefit: The 529 plan. *The Wall Street Journal*. https://www.wsj.com/articles/the-latest-corporate-benefit-the-529-plan-1459130786

83. Society for Human Resource Management. (2015, November 14). *Designing and managing educational assistance programs*. https://www.shrm.org/resourcesandtools/tools-and-samples/toolkits/pages/educationalassistanceprograms.aspx; U.S. Congress. (2013, January 2). H.R.8—American Taxpayer Relief Act of 2012. https://www.congress.gov/bill/112th-congress/house-bill/8/text?overview=closed

84. Starbucks. (2018). *Starbucks college achievement plan*. https://www.starbucks.com/careers/college-plan

85. Sammer, J. (2014, July 10). *The case for legal services and ID theft benefits*. SHRM. https://www.shrm.org/resourcesandtools/hr-topics/benefits/pages/legal-services.aspx

86. Federal Trade Commission. (2014, February). *Consumer Sentinel Network: Data book*. https://www.shrm.org/ResourcesAndTools/hr-topics/benefits/Documents/sentinel-cy2013.pdf

87. Stewart, J. B. (2013, March 15). Looking for a lesson in Google's perks. *The New York Times*. http://www.nytimes.com/2013/03/16/business/at-google-a-place-to-work-and-play.html

88. D'Onfro, J. (2015, April 7). Here are all of Google's employees, and how much they cost the company. *Business Insider*. http://www.businessinsider.com/cost-benefit-of-google-perks-2015-4

89. Gottsegen, W. (2023, April 26). Goodbye to the dried office mangoes. *The Atlantic*. https://www.theatlantic.com/technology/archive/2023/04/tech-company-perks-free-food-google/673855/

90. Ibid.

91. Barber, A. E., Dunham, R. B., & Formisano, R. A. (1992). The impact

of flexible benefits on employee satisfaction: A field study. *Personnel Psychology, 45*, 55–75.

92. U.S. Internal Revenue Service. (2018). Section 125: *Cafeteria plans: Modification of application of rule prohibiting deferred compensation under a cafeteria plan.* https://www.irs.gov/pub/irs-drop/n-05-42.pdf; U.S. Internal Revenue Service. (2023). Publication 15-B. (2023). *Employer's tax guide to fringe benefits.* https://www.irs.gov/publications/p15b#en_US_2017_publink1000193624

93. Bernard, T. S. (2015, August 20). Gay couple are eligible for Social Security benefits, U.S. decides. *The New York Times.* https://www.nytimes.com/2015/08/21/business/gay-couples-are-eligible-for-benefits-us-decides.html; Liptak, A. (2015, June 26). Supreme Court ruling makes same-sex marriage a right nationwide. *The New York Times.* https://www.nytimes.com/2015/06/27/us/supreme-court-same-sex-marriage.html; Scheiber, N. (2016, December 2). Walmart settles discrimination suit over benefits for same-sex spouses. *The New York Times.* https://www.nytimes.com/2016/12/02/business/walmart-same-sex-discrimination-lawsuit.html?_r=0; United States v. Windsor, 699 F. 3d 169, affirmed (2013). https://www.law.cornell.edu/supremecourt/text/12-307; U.S. Equal Employment Opportunity Commission. *What you should know about EEOC and the enforcement protections for LGBT workers.* https://www.eeoc.gov/eeoc/newsroom/wysk/enforcement_protections_lgbt_workers.cfm; Freur, A. (2017, July 27). Justice Department says rights law doesn't protect gays. *The New York Times.* https://www.nytimes.com/2017/07/27/nyregion/justice-department-gays-workplace.html

94. Society for Human Resource Management. (2016). *Strategic benefits survey: Assessment and communication of benefits.*

95. Kass, E. M. (2017, July 19). Moving the meter on benefits utilization. *Employee Benefit News.* https://www.benefitnews.com/news/moving-the-meter-on-benefits-utilization; MetLife. (n.d.). *Work redefined: A new age of benefits.* https://benefittrends.metlife.com/us-perspectives/work-redefined-a-new-age-of-benefits/

96. Hennessey, H. W., Perrewe, P. L., & Hochwarter, W. A. (1992). Impact of benefit awareness on employee and

organizational outcomes: A longitudinal field examination. *Benefits Quarterly, 8*, 90–96.

97. Society for Human Resource Management. (2017). *2017 strategic benefits survey: Strategize with benefits.* https://www.shrm.org/hr-today/trends-and-forecasting/research-and-surveys/pages/strategize-with-benefits.aspx

98. Wilson, M., Northcraft, G. B., & Neale, M. A. (1985). The perceived value of fringe benefits. *Personnel Psychology, 38*(2), 309–320.

99. Freitag, A. R., & Picherit-Duthler, G. (2004). Employee benefits communication: Proposing a PR-HR cooperative approach. *Public Relations Review, 30*, 475–482.

CHAPTER 14

1. Amazon. (2023). *Working at Amazon.* https://www.amazon.jobs/en/landing_pages/working-at-amazon; *Amazon defeats historic Alabama union effort.* (2021). BBC News. https://www.bbc.com/news/business-56695667; Brier, E. (2022). The world's best employers 2022. *Forbes.* https://www.forbes.com/sites/elisabethbrier/2022/10/11/meet-the-worlds-best-employers-2022/?sh=75855f10c086; Gallup. (2022). *Labor unions.* https://news.gallup.com/poll/12751/labor-unions.aspx; Hsu, A. (2023). *Labor's labors lost? A year after stunning victory at Amazon, unions are stalled.* NPR. https://www.npr.org/2023/03/28/1165294695/labor-union-starbucks-amazon-howard-schultz-workers; Sherman, N., & Fleury, M. (2022, January 24). *Amazon union fight continues despite workers' win.* BBC News. https://www.bbc.com/news/business-64340884

2. Levin, M. (2023). *5 things companies should do now to avoid costly (and harmful) employee lawsuits.* Inc.

3. Buttigieg, D. M., Deery, S. J., & Iverson, R. D. (2007). An event history analysis of union joining and leaving. *Journal of Applied Psychology, 92*, 829–839; Colquitt, J. A., Scott, B. A., Rodell, J. B., Long, D. M., Zapata, C. P., Conlon, D. E., & Wesson, M. J. (2013). Justice at the millennium, a decade later: A meta-analytic test of social exchange and affect-based perspectives. *Journal of Applied Psychology, 98*, 199–236; Karam, E. P., Hu, J., Davison, R. B., Juravich, M.,

Nahrgang, J. D., Humphrey, S. E., & DeRue, D. S. (2019). Illuminating the "face" of justice: A meta-analytic examination of leadership and organizational justice. *Journal of Management Studies, 56*, 134–171.

4. Dhanani, L. Y., LaPalme, M. L., & Joseph, D. L. (2021). How prevalent is workplace mistreatment? A meta-analytic investigation. *Journal of Organizational Behavior, 42*, 1082–1098.

5. Corkery, M. (20121). Costco will raise its minimum wage to $16 an hour. *The New York Times*; Gabler, N. (2016). The magic in the warehouse. *Fortune.* http://fortune.com/costco-wholesale-shopping/; Trefis Team. (2020). Costco is a better bet than Walmart. *Forbes.* https://www.forbes.com/sites/greatspeculations/2020/08/14/costco-is-a-better-bet-than-walmart/?sh=59aa7ad819a6

6. Robinson, J. (2015). *6 inspiring employee handbook examples.* Nasdaq. http://www.nasdaq.com/article/6-inspiring-employee-handbook-examples-cm459464

7. Williams, G. (2022). 13 companies that offer unlimited vacation days. *US News & World Report.*

8. SHRM. (2011). *Dress & appearance: Body odor, what should HR do when an employee's body odor is affecting the workplace?* https://www.shrm.org/resourcesandtools/tools-and-samples/hr-qa/pages/bodyodoraffectingworkplace.aspx; Taylor, J. C. (2020). When your workplace literally stinks: Ask HR. *USA Today.*

9. Statista. (2023). *Americans with tattoos.* https://www.statista.com/statistics/719662/americans-with-tattoos/; Statista. (2023). *Share of Americans with one or more tattoos as of 2021, by generation.* https://www.statista.com/statistics/259601/share-of-americans-with-at-least-one-tattoo-by-age/;

10. Dunbar, P. (2018). *Workplace tattoo stigma fading away but potential employment law issues remain.* Lexology. https://www.lexology.com/library/detail.aspx?g=4c93a826-a85d-4c40-a4e7-18baff33fd79

11. Constantz, J. (2022). *Considering a tattoo? It may not be bad for your career after all.* Bloomberg. https://www.bloomberg.com/news/articles/2022-07-18/tattoos-in-the-workplace-changing-attitudes-on-how-ink-impacts-y

our-career?leadSource=uverify%
20wall

12. Thomas, I. (2022). *Why companies like UPS and Disney are allowing workers to show their tattoos.* CNBC.

13. Bromwich, J. E. (2019). Inside the Nordstrom dynasty. *The New York Times.* https://www.nytimes.com/2019/10/23/style/nordstrom-family-department-stores.html; Lucas, S. (2014). *Nordstrom's awesome employee handbook is a myth.* CBS News MoneyWatch. https://www.cbs news.com/news/nordstroms-aweso me-employee-handbook-is-a-myth0

14. Meisenzahl, M. (2021). Starbucks fired an employee over a TikTok video made at work as brands become increasingly wary of workers' social media. *Business Insider.* https://www.businessinsider.com/starbucks-em ployee-fired-for-filming-tiktok-video s-is-a-trend-2021-3?op = 1

15. Kis, D. (2022). New unionization, upskilling and the future of work. *Forbes.*

16. Cole, P. (2019). Beyond Labor Day: 3 ways unions have helped American workers. *Time.* https://time.com/566 3465/labor-day-union-history/

17. Knepper, M. (2020). From the fringe to the fore: Labor unions and employee compensation. *Review of Economics and Statistics, 102,* 98–112.

18. U.S. Bureau of Labor Statistics. (2023). *Median weekly earnings of full-time wage and salary workers by union affiliation and selected characteristics.* https://www.bls.gov/news.release/ union2.t02.htm

19. Pendell, R. (2023). Why so quiet? Breaking the workplace taboo of silence. *Gallup News Business Journal.* https://www.gallup.com/workpl ace/474236/why-quiet-breaking-wor kplace-taboo-silence.aspx

20. The World Bank. (2023). *Ease of doing business rank.* https://data.world bank.org/indicator/IC.BUS.EASE. XQ?view=

21. National Labor Relations Board. (2023). *Facilitate settlements.* https:/ /www.nlrb.gov/about-nlrb/what-w e-do/facilitate-settlements

22. Durham, C. (2017). *Court upholds T-Mobile's positive workplace environ- ment rules.* SHRM. https://www.shrm .org/resourcesandtools/legal-and-c ompliance/employment-law/pages/c

ourt-report-positive-workplace-rule s.aspx

23. U.S. Department of Labor. (2023). *Summary of the major laws of the Department of Labor.* https://www .dol.gov/general/aboutdol/majo rlaws; U.S. Department of Labor. (2023). *What is the Labor-Management Reporting and Disclosure Act?* https:// www.dol.gov/olms/regs/compliance /LMRDAQandA.htm#quest1

24. SHRM. (2016). *Norris LaGuardia Act.* h ttps://www.shrm.org/resourcesand tools/legal-and-compliance/employ ment-law/pages/norris-laguardia-a ct.aspx; U.S. Department of Bureau of Labor Statistics (2023). *Union members – 2022.* https://www.bls.gov /news.release/pdf/union2.pdf

25. Gallup. (2023). *Labor unions.* https:/ /news.gallup.com/poll/12751/labo r-unions.aspx; Hsu, A. (2023). *Labor's labors lost? A year after stunning vic- tory at Amazon, unions are stalled.* NPR.

26. European Commission. (2023). *Employee involvement.* http: //ec.europa.eu/social/main .jsp?catId=707&langId=en& intPageId=211

27. NHO. (2023). *Basics of Norwegian labour law.* https://www.nho.no/en/B usiness-in-Norway/Basic-Labour-L aw/

28. Reuters. (2022). *German union calls on Amazon workers to strike during sale.* https://www.reuters.com/business/ retail-consumer/german-union-call s-amazon-workers-strike-during-sa le-2022-10-11/; Wingfield, N., & Eddy, M. (2013). In Germany, union culture clashes with Amazon's labor prac- tices. *The New York Times.* http://ww w.nytimes.com/2013/08/05/business /workers-of-amazon-divergent.html

29. Calderone, M. (2017). *The Huffington Post ratifies union contract.* HuffPost. https://www.huffingtonpost.com/en try/huffington-post-union-contract_ us_588f7523e4b0c90efefed41a

30. UnionBase: https://unionbase.or g/; Wartzman, R. (2017). Meet the millennial who's trying to save the labor movement with a Facebook for unions. *Fast Company.* https://www.f astcompany.com/40461691/meet-th e-millennial-whos-trying-to-save-t he-labor-movement-with-a-faceboo k-for-unions

31. Abramson, J. (2023). Why BuzzFeed and Vice couldn't make news work.

Vanity Fair. https://www.vanityfair.co m/news/2023/05/why-buzzfeed-an d-vice-couldnt-make-news-work

32. National Labor Relations Board. (2023). *Your government conducts an election, For you—on the job. Informa- tion for voters in NLRB elections.* https: //www.nlrb.gov/sites/default/files/at tachments/basic-page/node-3024/el ection.pdf

33. Combs, R. (2021). *How long does it take unions to reach first contracts?* Bloom- berg. https://news.bloomberglaw.c om/bloomberg-law-analysis/analys is-how-long-does-it-take-unions-t o-reach-first-contracts; McNicholas, C., Poydock, M., & Schitt, J. (2023). *Working are winning union elections, but it can take years to get their first contract.* Economic Policy Institute. h ttps://www.epi.org/publication/unio n-first-contract-fact-sheet/

34. National Labor Relations Board. (2023). *About NLRB: Decertification election.* https://www.nlrb.gov/abou t-nlrb/rights-we-protect/the-law/e mployees/decertification-election

35. Caputo, A., Ayoko, O. B., Amoo, N., & Menke, C. (2019). The relationship between cultural values, cultural intelligence and negotiation styles. *Journal of Business Research, 99,* 23–36.

36. De Prins, P., Stuer, D., & Gielens, T. (2020). Revitalizing social dialogue in the workplace: The impact of a cooperative industrial relations cli- mate and sustainable HR practices on reducing employee harm. *Inter- national Journal of Human Resource Management, 31,* 1684–1704.

37. Harinck, F., De Dreau, C. K. W., & Van Vianen, A. E. M. (2000). The impact of conflict issues on fixed-pie perceptions, problem solving, and integrative outcomes in negotiation. *Organizational Behavior and Human Decision Processes, 81,* 329–358.

38. Bolkan, S., & Goodboy, A. K. (2021). Negotiating in distribution bargaining scenarios: The effect of sharing one's alternative. *Communication Studies, 72,* 720–733; Fisher, R., Ury, W. L., & Patton, B. (2011). *Getting to yes: Nego- tiating agreement without giving in.* Penguin Books.

39. Griffiths, J. (2016). *China on strike.* CNN. http://www.cnn.com/2016/03/ 28/asia/china-strike-worker-protes t-trade-union/index.html

40. U.S. Bureau of Labor Statistics. (2023). *Major work stoppages.* https://www.bls.gov/wsp/

41. U.S. Bureau of Labor Statistics. (2023). *Work stoppages: Questions and answers.* https://www.bls.gov/wsp/questions-and-answers.htm

42. Bellware, K., & Brasch, B. (2023). Why are Hollywood actors and writers on strike? Here are the issues. *The Washington Post.* https://www.washingtonpost.com/arts-entertainment/2023/07/13/why-actors-writers-strike-sag-wga-issues/; Chappell, B. (2023). *From mini rooms to streaming, things have changed since the last big writers' strike.* NPR. https://www.npr.org/2023/05/03/1173439467/writers-guild-strike-2023-comparison-2007; History.com. (2008). *Writers' strike ends after 100 days.* http://www.history.com/this-day-in-history/writers-strike-ends-after-100-days; Klowden, K., Chatterjee, A., & DeVol, R. (2008). The writers' strike of 2007–2008: The economic impact of digital distribution. *Milken Institute Review.* http://www.milkeninstitute.org/publications/view/347; Macaray, D. (2013). *The 2007–2008 writers strike.* HuffPost. https://www.huffingtonpost.com/david-macaray/the-200708-writers-strike_b_3840681.html; Ng, D., James, M., & Faughnder, R. (2017). They avoided a strike, but negotiations between writers and studios were a true Hollywood thriller. *Los Angeles Times.* http://www.latimes.com/business/hollywood/la-fi-ct-writers-guild-no-strike-20170501-story.html

43. Hastings, R. R. (2012). *Measure grievances to minimize costs.* SHRM. https://www.shrm.org/resourcesandtools/hr-topics/employee-relations/pages/measuregrievancestominimizecosts.aspx

CHAPTER 15

1. American Academy of Family Physicians. (2020). *Family physician burnout, well-being, and professional satisfaction* [Position paper]. https://www.aafp.org/about/policies/all/family-physician-burnout.html; Henry, T. A. (2023). *Scribes linked to 27% lower burnout rate in primary care.* American Medical Association. https://www.ama-assn.org/practice-management/physician-health/scribes-linked-27-lower-burnout-rate-primary-care; Hodkinson, A., Zhou, A., Johnson, J., Geraghty, K., Riley, R., Zhou, A., . . . & Panagioti, M. (2022). Associations of physician burnout with career engagement and quality of patient care: systematic review and meta-analysis. *BMJ, 378,* e070442; McAuliffe, M. (2023). *Fixing the health care worker shortage may be something Congress can agree on.* NPR. npr.org/sections/health-shots/2023/02/22/1158026497/fixing-the-health-care-worker-shortage-may-be-something-congress-can-agree-on; Melnikow, J., Padovani, A., & Miller, M. (2022). Frontline physician burnout during the COVID-19 pandemic: national survey findings. *BMC Health Services Research, 22*(1), 365; Patel, R. S., Sekhri, S., Bhimanadham, N. N., Imran, S., & Hossain, S. (2019). A review on strategies to manage physician burnout. *Cureus, 11*(6); Shrime, M. G. (2023). How physician wellness programs keep doctors captive. *STAT News.* https://www.statnews.com/2023/03/03/wellness-programs-keep-doctors-captive/; Sinsky, C. A., Shanafelt, T. D., Dyrbye, L. N., Sabety, A. H., Carlasare, L. E., & West, C. P. (2022, April). Health care expenditures attributable to primary care physician overall and burnout-related turnover: a cross-sectional analysis. *Mayo Clinic Proceedings, 97*(4), 693–702); Stephenson, J. (2022, November). Study highlights effects of Covid-19 burnout on primary care physicians in 10 high-income countries. *JAMA Health Forum, 3*(11), e225101–e225101.

2. International Labor Organization. (2018). *Workplace well-being.* http://www.ilo.org/safework/areasofwork/workplace-health-promotion-and-well-being/WCMS_118396/lang—en/index.htm

3. American Psychological Association. (2021). *The American workforce faces compounding pressure. APA's 2021 work and well-being survey.* https://www.apa.org/pubs/reports/work-well-being/compounding-pressure-2021

4. U.S. Department of Labor, OSHA. (n.d.) *State plans.* https://www.osha.gov/dcsp/osp/index.html

5. NIOSH. (2022). *About NIOSH.* http://www.cdc.gov/niosh/about/default.html

6. National Safety Council. (2023). *Work injury costs.* https://injuryfacts.nsc.org/work/costs/work-injury-costs/

7. Blanchard, D., Selko, A., & Stempak, N. (2022). America's safest companies of 2022. *EHS Today.* https://www.ehstoday.com/americas-safest-companies-awards/article/21252763/americas-safest-companies-of-2022

8. OSHA. (2021). *Near miss reporting policy.* https://www.osha.gov/sites/default/files/2021-07/Template%20for%20Near%20Miss%20Reporting%20Policy.pdf

9. Ibid.

10. Hofmann, D. A., Burke, M. J., & Zohar, D. (2017). 100 years of occupational safety research: From basic protections and work analysis to a multilevel view of workplace safety and risk. *Journal of Applied Psychology, 102*(3), 375–388.

11. History.com Editors. (2009). *Triangle Shirtwaist Factory fire.* http://www.history.com/topics/triangle-shirtwaist-fire

12. National Institute for Occupational Safety and Health. (2020). *Direct reading and sensor technology.* https://www.cdc.gov/niosh/topics/drst/default.html

13. Griffin, M. A., & Curcuruto, M. (2016). Safety climate in organizations. *Annual Review of Organizational Psychology and Organizational Behavior, 3,* 191–212.

14. Zohar, D., & Polachek, T. (2014). Discourse-based intervention for modifying supervisory communication as leverage for safety climate and performance improvement: A randomized field study. *Journal of Applied Psychology, 99,* 113–124.

15. Survey asks electrical workers about safety culture, responsibility and more. (2022). *Safety and Health Magazine.* https://www.safetyandhealthmagazine.com/articles/22781-survey-asks-electrical-workers-about-safety-culture-responsibility-and-more

16. Occupational Safety and Health Administration. (n.d.). *Workplace violence.* https://www.osha.gov/SLTC/workplaceviolence/

17. Byon, H. D., Sagherian, K., Kim, Y., Lipscomb, J., Crandall, M., & Steege, L. (2022). Nurses' experience with type II workplace violence and underreporting during the COVID-19 pandemic. *Workplace Health & Safety, 70*(9), 412–420; OSHA. (2016). *Guidelines for preventing workplace violence for healthcare and social service*

workers. https://www.osha.gov/Publications/osha3148.pdf

18. Han, S., Harold, C. M., Oh, I. S., Kim, J. K., & Agolli, A. (2022). A meta-analysis integrating 20 years of workplace incivility research: Antecedents, consequences, and boundary conditions. *Journal of Organizational Behavior*, *43*(3), 497–523; Hershcovis, M. S. (2011). "Incivility, social undermining, bullying . . . oh my!": A call to reconcile constructs within workplace aggression research. *Journal of Organizational Behavior*, *32*, 499–519.

19. Edelson, J. (2017). *Hotels add panic buttons to protect housekeepers from guests.* Bloomberg. https://www.bloomberg.com/news/articles/2017-12-13/hotels-add-panic-buttons-to-protect-housekeepers-from-guests; Shaw, E., Hegewisch, A., & Hess, C. (2018) *Sexual harassment and assault at work: Understanding the costs.* Institute for Women's Policy Research, https://iwpr.org/wp-content/uploads/2020/09/IWPR-sexual-harassment-brief_FINAL.pdf.

20. McGeehan, P., Mazzei, P., & Johnson, K. (December 20, 2017). Law requires life-saving braking device. Most trains don't have it. *The New York Times.* https://www.nytimes.com/2017/12/20/us/amtrak-train-safety.html

21. CDC/NIOSH. (2018). *Noise and hearing loss prevention.* https://www.cdc.gov/niosh/topics/noise/reducenoiseexposure/noisecontrols.html

22. Shepardson, D. (2017, September 21). U.S. Safety Board says train-crash engineers had undiagnosed sleep disorders. *Scientific American.* https://www.scientificamerican.com/article/u-s-safety-board-says-train-crash-engineers-had-undiagnosed-sleep-disorders/.

23. Huhta, R., Hirvonen, K., & Partinen, M. (2021). Prevalence of sleep apnea and daytime sleepiness in professional truck drivers. *Sleep Medicine*, *81*, 136–143.

24. Brossoit, R. M., Crain, T. L., Leslie, J. J., Hammer, L. B., Truxillo, D. M., & Bodner, T. E. (2019). The effects of sleep on workplace cognitive failure and safety. *Journal of Occupational Health Psychology*, *24*(4), 411–422; Kakemam, E., Kalhor, R., Khakdel, Z., Khezri, A., West, S., Visentin, D., & Cleary, M. (2019). Occupational stress and cognitive failure of nurses and associations with self-reported adverse events: A national cross-sectional survey. *Journal of Advanced Nursing*, *75*(12), 3609–3618.

25. OSHA. (2018). *Emergency preparedness and response.* https://www.osha.gov/SLTC/emergencypreparedness/index.html

26. OSHA. (2016). *OSHA inspections.* https://www.osha.gov/OshDoc/data_General_Facts/factsheet-inspections.pdf; OSHA. (2018). *OSHA frequently asked questions.* https://www.osha.gov/OSHA_FAQs.html#!employerassist

27. OSHA. (2015). *Job safety and health: It's the law.* https://www.osha.gov/Publications/poster.html; OSHA. (2019). *Federal judge orders Lloyd Industries and company owner to pay $1.04 million to employees terminated for assisting safety investigation* [Press release]. https://www.osha.gov/news/newsreleases/region3/08232019; OSHA. (2021). Fact sheet: Filing whistleblower complaints related to COVID-19; OSHA. (2021). *Top 10 most frequently cited standards.* https://www.osha.gov/top10citedstandards; OSHA. (2021). Fact sheet: Filing whistleblower complaints related to COVID-19.

28. OSHA. (2018). *Ergonomics.* https://www.osha.gov/SLTC/ergonomics/

29. National Institute for Occupational Safety and Health (NIOSH). (2016, August). *Total Worker Health in Action*, *5*(3). https://www.cdc.gov/niosh/twh/newsletter/twhnewsv5n3.html

30. Konradt, U., Heblich, F., Krys, S., Garbers, Y., & Otte, K. P. (2020). Beneficial, adverse, and spiraling health-promotion effects: Evidence from a longitudinal randomized controlled trial of working at sit–stand desks. *Journal of Occupational Health Psychology*, *25*(1), 68–81.

31. Boubekri, M., Cheung, I. N., Reid, K. J., Wang, C. H., & Zee, P. C. (2014). Impact of windows and daylight exposure on overall health and sleep quality of office workers: A case-control pilot study. *Journal of Clinical Sleep Medicine*, *10*, 603–611.

32. Evans, G. W., & Johnson, D. (2000). Stress and open-office noise. *Journal of Applied Psychology*, *85*, 779–783; Sarkis, S. (2021). Post-pandemic: Fight for an end to the open-plan office. *Forbes.* https://www.forbes.com/sites/stephaniesarkis/2021/01/17/post-pandemic-fight-for-an-end-to-the-open-plan-office/?sh=6d615 3506527; Wertz, J. (2019). Open-plan work spaces lower productivity and employee morale. *Forbes.* https://www.forbes.com/sites/jiawertz/2019/06/30/open-plan-work-spaces-lower-productivity-employee-morale/#46528a461cda

33. ECHY. (2018). *Natural light and Europe lighting regulations.* http://www.echy.fr/natural-light-and-europe-lighting-regulations/?lang=en; International Labour Organization. (2019). *Rules of the game: An introduction to the standards-related work of the International Labour Organization.* https://www.ilo.org/wcmsp5/groups/public/---ed_norm/---normes/documents/publication/wcms_672549.pdf; International Labour Organization. (2023). *Safety and health at work.* https://www.ilo.org/global/topics/safety-and-health-at-work/lang--en/index.htm; Kahn, J. (2017) *Fitness tracking startups are sweating due to EU privacy regulators.* Bloomberg. https://www.bloomberg.com/news/articles/2017-09-11/fitness-tracking-startups-are-sweating-due-to-eu-privacy-regulators

34. Morrisons not liable for massive staff data leak, court rules. (2020). *The Guardian.* https://www.theguardian.com/business/2020/apr/01/morrisons-is-not-liable-for-massive-staff-data-leak-court-rules

35. Ravid, D. M., White, J. C., Tomczak, D. L., Miles, A. F., & Behrend, T. S. (2022). A meta-analysis of the effects of electronic performance monitoring on work outcomes. *Personnel Psychology*, 76, 5–40.

36. Thiel, C., Bonner, J., Bush, J., Welsh, D., & Garud, N. (2022). Monitoring employees makes them more likely to break rules. *Harvard Business Review.* https://hbr.org/2022/06/monitoring-employees-makes-them-more-likely-to-break-rules

37. Shartonn, B. R., & Neuman, K. L. (2017). The legal risks of monitoring employees online. *Harvard Business Review.* https://hbr.org/2017/12/the-legal-risks-of-monitoring-employees-online

38. Alder, S. (2017, December 12). Email top attack vector in healthcare cyber-attacks. *HIPAA Journal.* https://www.hipaajournal.com/email-top-attack-vector-healthcare-cyberattacks/; Chowdhury, N., & Gkioulos, V. (2021). Cyber security training for critical infrastructure protection: A literature review. *Computer Science*

Review, *40*, 100361; Isaac, M., Benner, K., & Frenkel, S. (2017). Uber hid 2016 breach, paying hackers to delete stolen data. *The New York Times*. https://www.nytimes.com/2017/11/21/technology/uber-hack.html

39. Gallup. (2022). *State of the global workplace: 2022 report*. https://www.gallup.com/workplace/349484/state-of-the-global-workplace-2022-report.aspx

40. Hassard, J., Teoh, K. R., Visockaite, G., Dewe, P., & Cox, T. (2018). The cost of work-related stress to society: A systematic review. *Journal of Occupational Health Psychology*, *23*(1), 1–17; Wallace, J. C., & Chen, G. (2005). Development and validation of a work-specific measure of cognitive failure: Implications for occupational safety. *Journal of Occupational and Organizational Psychology*, *78*, 615–632.

41. Gonzalez-Mulé, E., & Cockburn, B. (2017). Worked to death: The relationships of job demands and job control with mortality. *Personnel Psychology*, *70*, 73–112; Workers in stressful, low-control jobs have higher risk of early death: Study. (2016, November 2). *Safety + Health Magazine*. http://www.safetyandhealthmagazine.com/articles/14913-workers-in-stressful-low-control-jobs-have-higher-risk-of-early-death-study

42. American Psychological Association. (2021). *The American workforce faces compounding pressure*. https://www.apa.org/pubs/reports/work-well-being/compounding-pressure-2021

43. Liu, S., Wang, M., Zhan, Y., & Shi, J. (2009). Daily work stress and alcohol use: Testing the cross-level moderation effects of neuroticism and job involvement. *Personnel Psychology*, *62*, 575–597.

44. Demerouti, E., Bakker, A. B., Nachreiner, F., & Schaufeli, W. B. (2001). The job demands-resources model of burnout. *Journal of Applied Psychology*, *86*, 499–512; George, T. J., Atwater, L. E., Maneethai, D., & Madera, J. M. (2022). Supporting the productivity and wellbeing of remote workers: Lessons from COVID-19. *Organizational Dynamics*, *51*(2), 100869; Schaufeli, W. B., & Taris, T. W. (2014). A critical review of the job demands-resources model: Implications for improving work and health. In G. F. Bauer & O. Hämmig (Eds.), *Bridging occupational, organizational and public health* (pp. 43–68). Springer.

45. Podsakoff, N. P., Freiburger, K. J., Podsakoff, P. M., & Rosen, C. C. (2023). Laying the foundation for the Challenge–Hindrance Stressor Framework 2.0. *Annual Review of Organizational Psychology and Organizational Behavior*, *10*, 165–199.

46. Gallup. (2022). *Work and workplace*. https://news.gallup.com/poll/1720/work-work-place.aspx

47. Richardson, N., & Klein, S. (2021). *People at work 2021: A global workforce view*. ADP. https://www.adpri.org/wp-content/uploads/2021/04/Updated_WFV-Global_2021_US_Screen_697691_162389_FV.pdf

48. Lewis, K., Stronge, W., Kellam, J., & Kikuchi, L. (2023). *The results are in: The UK's four-day week pilot*. Autonomy. https://static1.squarespace.com/static/60b956cbe7bf6f2efd86b04e/t/63f3df56276b3e6d7870207e/1676926845047/UK-4-Day-Week-Pilot-Results-Report-2023.pdf; Timsit, A. (2023). A four-day workweek pilot was so successful most firms say they won't go back. *The Washington Post*. https://www.washingtonpost.com/wellness/2023/02/21/four-day-work-week-results-uk/

49. "Always on" email culture contributes to worker stress: Researchers. (2016, August 8). *Safety + Health Magazine*. http://www.safetyandhealthmagazine.com/articles/14481-always-on-email-culture-contributes-to-worker-stress-research; Boswell, W. R., Olson-Buchanan, J. B., Butts, M. M., & Becker, W. J. (2016). Managing "after-hours" electronic work communication. *Organizational Dynamics*, *45*, 291–297; Butts, M., Becker, W. J., & Boswell, W. R. (2015). Hot buttons and time sinks: The effects of electronic communication during nonwork time on emotions and work–nonwork conflict. *Academy of Management Journal*, *58*, 763–788.

50. Wood, J., & Shine, I. (2023). *Right to disconnect: The countries passing laws to stop employees working out of hours*. World Economic Forum. https://www.weforum.org/agenda/2023/02/belgium-right-to-disconnect-from-work/

51. Allen, T. D., Johnson, R. C., Saboe, K. N., Cho, E., Dumani, S., & Evans, S. (2012). Dispositional variables and work–family conflict: A meta-analysis. *Journal of Vocational Behavior*, *80*, 17–26.

52. Kossek, E. E., Hammer, L. B., Thompson, R. J., & Buxbaum, L. B. (2014). *Leveraging workplace flexibility for engagement and productivity*. SHRM Foundation's Effective Practice Guidelines Series.

53. 100 best companies to work for: SAS Institute. (2023). *Fortune*. https://fortune.com/company/sas-institute/best-companies/

54. Masterson, L. (2017). *Nurses are burnt out. Here's how hospitals can help*. Health Care Dive. https://www.healthcaredive.com/news/nurses-are-burnt-out-heres-how-hospitals-can-help/442640/

55. Wellness Council of America. (WELCOA). (2018). *The benefits of stress management for employees*. https://www.welcoa.org/blog/benefits-stress-management-employees/

56. Tepper, B. J., Simon, L., & Park, H. M. (2017). Abusive supervision. *Annual Review of Organizational Psychology and Organizational Behavior*, *4*, 123–152; Yang, L. Q., Caughlin, D. E., Gazica, M. W., Truxillo, D. M., & Spector, P. E. (2014). Workplace mistreatment climate and potential employee and organizational outcomes: A meta-analytic review from the target's perspective. *Journal of Occupational Health Psychology*, *19*, 315–335.

57. Kantor, J. (2014, August 13). Working anything but 9 to 5. *The New York Times*. http://www.nytimes.com/interactive/2014/08/13/us/starbucks-workers-scheduling-hours.html

58. Sonnentag, S., Cheng, B. H., & Parker, S. L. (2022). Recovery from work: Advancing the field toward the future. *Annual Review of Organizational Psychology and Organizational Behavior*, *9*, 33–60.

59. *Fortune* 100 best companies to work for. (2021). *CNN Money*. https://money.cnn.com/magazines/fortune/best-companies/best_benefits/sabbaticals.html; Kadet, A. (2022). Sabbaticals are companies' latest weapon against the great resignation. *Fortune*. https://fortune.com/2022/03/15/sabbaticals-great-resignation-employee-benefit-perk/

60. Brody, B. (2022). Why napping at work can make you better at your job. *Fortune*. https://fastcompany.com/90725033/the-business-case-for-napping-at-work#:~:text=Nike%2C%20Proctor%20%26%20Gamble%2C%20Facebook,and%20built-in%20sound%2

0systems; Johnson, L. A. (2022). The case for taking naps (even at work). *Harvard Business Review.* https://hbr.org/2022/03/the-case-for-taking-naps-even-at-work

61. Druley, K. (2016). Keeping aging workers safe. *Safety + Health Magazine.* http://www.safetyandhealthmagazine.com/articles/15023-aging-workers; Loch, C. H., Sting, F. J., Bauer, N., & Mauermann, H. (2010). How BMW is defusing the demographic time bomb. *Harvard Business Review, 88*, 99–102.

62. Ibid.

63. Loehr, J., & Schwartz, T. (2001). The making of a corporate athlete. *Harvard Business Review.* https://hbr.org/2001/01/the-making-of-a-corporate-athlete

64. What is a wellness program? (2015). SHRM. https://www.shrm.org/resourcesandtools/tools-and-samples/hr-qa/pages/whatarewellnessbenefits.aspx

65. Kaiser Family Foundation. (2022). *2022 employer health benefits survey.* https://www.kff.org/report-section/ehbs-2022-summary-of-findings/#figureg

66. Payton, L. T. (2022). Employees care about their workplace well-being just as much as salary when it comes to finding a new job. *Fortune Well*, https://fortune.com/well/2022/11/11/work-life-wellness-gympass-survey/; Putnam, L. (2022). 5 workplace wellness trends to look out for in 2023: Employees will no longer settle for check-the-box wellness solutions. *HR.com*, https://www.hr.com/en/magazines/all_articles/5-workplace-wellness-trends-to-look-out-for-in-202_lbz0eqn6.html.

67. Peñalvo, J. L., Sagastume, D., Mertens, E., Uzhova, I., Smith, J., Wu, J. H., . . . & Mozaffarian, D. (2021). Effectiveness of workplace wellness programmes for dietary habits, overweight, and cardiometabolic health: A systematic review and meta-analysis. *The Lancet Public Health, 6*(9), e648–e660.

68. Milligan, S. (2017). *Employers take wellness to a higher level.* SHRM. https://www.shrm.org/hr-today/news/hr-magazine/0917/pages/employers-take-wellness-to-a-higher-level.aspx

69. Do wellness programs save employers money? (2014). Rand Corporation. https://www.rand.org/content/d am/rand/pubs/research_briefs/RB9 700/RB9744/RAND_RB9744.pdf

70. Ibid.; Harris, M. M. (2016). *The business case for employee health and wellness programs.* Society for Industrial and Organizational Psychology. http://www.siop.org/WhitePapers/c asehealth.pdf

71. Peñalvo, J. L., Sagastume, D., Mertens, E., Uzhova, I., Smith, J., Wu, J. H., . . . & Mozaffarian, D. (2021). Effectiveness of workplace wellness programmes for dietary habits, overweight, and cardiometabolic health: a systematic review and meta-analysis. *The Lancet Public Health, 6*(9), e648–e660.

72. Ott-Holland, C. J., Shepherd, W. J., & Ryan, A. M. (2019). Examining wellness programs over time: Predicting participation and workplace outcomes. *Journal of Occupational Health Psychology, 24*(1), 163–179; Perrault, E. K., Hildenbrand, G. M., & Rnoh, R. H. (2020). Employees' refusals to participate in an employer-sponsored wellness program: Barriers and benefits to engagement. *Compensation & Benefits Review, 52*(1), 8–18.

73. Payton, L. T. (2022). Employees care about their workplace well-being just as much as salary when it comes to finding a new job. *Fortune Well.* https://fortune.com/well/2022/11/11/work-life-wellness-gympass-survey/; Purcell, J. (2016). Meet the wellness programs that save companies money. *Harvard Business Review.* https://hbr.org/2016/04/meet-the-wellness-programs-that-save-companies-money

74. Designing and managing wellness programs. (2016). SHRM. https://www.shrm.org/resourcesandtools/tools-and-samples/toolkits/page s/designingandmanagingwellness programs.aspx; Kaiser Family Foundation. (2022). *2022 employer health benefits survey.* https://www.kff.org/report-section/ehbs-2022-summary-of-findings/#figureg; Mattke, S., Liu, H., Caloyeras, J. P., Huang, C. Y., Van Busum, K. R., Khodyakov, D., & Shier, V. (2013). *Workplace wellness programs study.* Rand Corporation. https://www.rand.org/pubs/research_reports/RR254.html; 10 great examples of workplace wellness programs. (2018). https://risepeople.com/blog/workplace-wellness-programs/; Thompson, D. (2021). *Making the leap from wellness to well-being.* ATD. https://www.td.org/magazines/td-magazine/making-the-leap-from-wellness-to-well-being

75. Milligan, S. (2017). Employers take wellness to a higher level. *HR Magazine.* https://www.shrm.org/hr-today/news/hr-magazine/0917/pages/employers-take-wellness-to-a-higher-level.aspx

76. SHRM. (2014, August 12). *Employee assistance program (EAP): General. What is an employee assistance program?* https://www.shrm.org/resourcesandtools/tools-and-samples/hr-qa/pages/whatisaneap.aspx

77. Joseph, B., Walker, A., & Fuller-Tyszkiewicz, M. (2018). Evaluating the effectiveness of employee assistance programmes: A systematic review. *European Journal of Work and Organizational Psychology, 27*(1), 1–15.

78. U.S. Department of Health and Human Services. (2023). *Employee assistance program.* https://www.hhs.gov/about/agencies/asa/foh/bhs/employee-assistant-program/index.html#:~:text=The%20Employee%20Assistance%20Program%20(EAP,day%2C%20365%20days%20a%20year.&text=Personal%20problems%20can%20affect%20the,at%20home%20and%20at%20work

79. International Employee Assistance Association. (October 2011). *Definitions of an employee assistance program (EAP) and EAP core technology.* http://www.eapassn.org/about/about-employee-assistance/eap-definitions-and-core-technology; SHRM. (2015). *Managing employee assistance programs.* https://www.shrm.org/resourcesandtools/tools-and-samples/toolkits/pages/managingemployeea ssistance programs.aspx

80. American Psychological Association. (2022). *Striving for mental health excellence in the workplace.* American Psychological Association. https://www.apa.org/topics/workplace/mental-health; Dimoff, J. K., & Kelloway, E. K. (2019). Signs of struggle (SOS): The development and validation of a behavioural mental health checklist for the workplace. *Work & Stress, 33*(3), 295–313; Kelloway, E. K., Dimoff, J. K., & Gilbert, S. (2023). Mental health in the workplace. *Annual Review of Organizational Psychology and Organizational Behavior, 10*, 363–387.

81. SHRM. (2015). *Managing employee assistance programs*. https://www.shrm.org/resourcesandtools/tools-and-samples/toolkits/pages/managing employeeassistance programs.aspx

82. Kinney, J. (2022). Why most employee assistance programs don't work. *Forbes*. https://www.forbes.com/sites/forbeshumanresourcescouncil/2022/07/26/why-most-employee-assistance-programs-dont-work/; Miller, S. (2019). *Underused EAPs are a missed opportunity to help workers*. SHRM. https://www.shrm.org/resourcesandtools/hr-topics/benefits/pages/under-used-eaps-are-a-missed-opportunity.aspx

83. Harris, M. M. (2016). *The business case for employee health and wellness programs* [White paper]. Society for Industrial and Organizational Psychology. http://www.siop.org/WhitePapers/casehealth.pdf; Mattke, S., Liu, H., Caloyeras, J. P., Huang, C. Y., Van Busum, K. R., Khodyakov, D., & Shier, V. (2013). *Workplace wellness programs study*. Rand Corporation. https://www.rand.org/pubs/research_reports/RR254.html; Milligan, S. (2017, August 21). Employers take wellness to a higher level. *HR Magazine*. https://www.shrm.org/hr-today/news/hr-magazine/0917/pages/employers-take-wellness-to-a-higher-level.aspx; SHRM. (2016). *Designing and managing wellness programs*. https://www.shrm.org/resourcesandtools/tools-and-samples/toolkits/pages/designingandmanagingwellness programs.aspx

84. Milligan, S. (2017, August 21). Employers take wellness to a higher level. *HR Magazine*. https://www.shrm.org/hr-today/news/hr-magazine/0917/pages/employers-take-wellness-to-a-higher-level.aspx

85. Kahn, J. (2017). *Fitness tracking start-ups are sweating due to EU privacy regulators*. Bloomberg. https://www.bloomberg.com/news/articles/2017-09-11/fitness-tracking-startups-are-sweating-due-to-eu-privacy-regulators; Navarra, K. (2022). *New uses for wearable devices in the workplace*. SHRM. https://www.shrm.org/resourcesandtools/hr-topics/technology/pages/new-uses-wearable-devices-in-the-workplace.aspx#:~:text=Outfitting%20workers%20with%20devices%20that,too%20close%20to%20a%20hazard; Sly, L. (2018). US soldiers are revealing sensitive and dangerous information by jogging. *The Washington Post*. https://www.washingtonpost.com/world/a-map-showing-the-users-of-fitness-devices-lets-the-world-see-where-us-soldiers-are-and-what-they-are-doing/2018/01/28/86915662-0441-11e8-aa61-f3391373867e_story.html?utm_term=.11e2967e71a4; Vanderkam, L. (2015, June 8). The dark side of corporate wellness programs. *Fast Company*. https://www.fastcompany.com/3047115/the-dark-side-of-corporate-wellness-programs

86. Estevez Cores, S., Sayed, A. A., Tracy, D. K., & Kempton, M. J. (2021). Individual-focused occupational health interventions: A meta-analysis of randomized controlled trials. *Journal of Occupational Health Psychology, 26*(3), 189–203.

87. Hammer, L. B., Johnson, R. C., Crain, T. L., Bodner, T., Kossek, E. E., Davis, K. D., Kelly, E. L., Buxton, O. M., Karuntzos, G., Chosewood, L. C., & Berkman, L. (2016). Intervention effects on the safety compliance and citizenship behaviors: Evidence from the Work, Family, and Health study. *Journal of Applied Psychology, 101*, 190–208; Hurtado, D. A., Okechukwu, C. A., Buxton, O. M., Hammer, L., Hanson, G. C., Moen, P. Klein, L. C., & Berkman, L. F. (2016). Effects on cigarette consumption of a work–family supportive organizational intervention: 6-month results from the work, family and health network. *Journal of Epidemiology and Community Health, 70*, 1155–1161; Olson, R., Crain, T. L., Bodner, T. E., King, R., Hammer. L. B., Klein, L. C., Erickson, L., Moen, P., Berkman, L. F., & Buxton, O. M. (2015). A workplace intervention improves sleep: Results from the randomized controlled Work, Family, and Health study. *Sleep Health, 1*, 55–65.

88. Aburumman, M., Newnam, S., & Fildes, B. (2019). Evaluating the effectiveness of workplace interventions in improving safety culture: A systematic review. *Safety Science, 115*, 376–392; Zohar, D., & Polachek, T. (2014). Discourse-based intervention for modifying supervisory communication as leverage for safety climate and performance improvement: A randomized field study. *Journal of Applied Psychology, 99*, 113–124.

89. Guest, A. J., Chen, Y. L., Pearson, N., King, J. A., Paine, N. J., & Clemes, S. A. (2020). Cardiometabolic risk factors and mental health status among truck drivers: a systematic review. *BMJ Open, 10*(10), e038993.

90. Olson, R., Wipfli, B., Thompson, S. V., Elliot, D. L., Anger, W. K., Bodner, T., Hammer, L. B., & Perrin, N. (2016). Weight control intervention for truck drivers: The SHIFT randomized controlled trial, United States. *American Journal of Public Health, 106*, 1698–1706.

91. McGeehan, P., Mazzei, P., & Johnson, K. (2017, December 20). Law requires life-saving braking device. Most trains don't have it. *The New York Times*. https://www.nytimes.com/2017/12/20/us/amtrak-train-safety.html; Shepardson, D. (2017, September 21). U.S. Safety Board says train-crash engineers had undiagnosed sleep disorders. *Scientific American*. https://www.scientificamerican.com/article/u-s-safety-board-says-train-crash-engineers-had-undiagnosed-sleep-disorders/

92. CDC. (2015). *What is Total Worker Health®?* https://www.cdc.gov/niosh/twh/totalhealth.html

93. CDC. (2023). Promising practice: Implementing an integrated worker health model. *Total Worker Health® in Action! 12*(1). https://www.cdc.gov/niosh/twh/newsletter/twhnewsv12n1.html#practice

94. Anger, W. K., Elliot, D. L., Bodner, T., Olson, R., Rohlman, D. S., Truxillo, D. M., . . . & Montgomery, D. (2015). Effectiveness of total worker health interventions. *Journal of Occupational Health Psychology, 20*, 226–247.

CHAPTER 16

1. Crunchbase. (2022, September 7). *About Remote*. https://www.crunchbase.com/organization/remote-d596; Farshchi, S. (2021, August 26). Ready to "just say no" to remote work? Here's how to say "yes" instead. *Forbes*. https://www.forbes.com/sites/forbeshumanresourcescouncil/2021/08/26/ready-to-just-say-no-to-remote-work-heres-how-to-say-yes-instead/?sh=3694d27d7e51; McDougall, M. (2022, August 30). UK probes tax status of remote workers. *Financial Times*. https://www.ft.com/content/9127a574-6e89-4f51-9105-1885303819d2; Remote announces exponential growth in 2021 following investment last year. (2021, June 9).

Business Wire. https://www.busin esswire.com/news/home/2021060 8006090/en/Remote-Announces-E xponential-Growth-in-2021-Follow ing-Investment-Last-Year; Remote announces integration with HiBob to streamline global HR processes. (2022, August 24). GlobeNewswire. h ttps://www.globenewswire.com/new s-release/2022/08/24/2503733/0/en /Remote-announces-integration-wit h-HiBob-to-streamline-global-HR-p rocesses.html; Russell, C. (2020, May 18). *Remote.com empowers employers to onboard global remote workers.* Rec Tech Media. https://www.rectechme dia.com/blog/2020/5/18/remotecom -empowers-employer-to-onboard-g lobal-remote-workers;

2. Multinational corporation: MNC. (2018). *Investopedia.* https://www.inv estopedia.com/terms/m/multination alcorporation.asp

3. Lane, J., & Kinser, K. (2015, June 5). *Is today's university the new multinational corporation?* The Conversation. https: //theconversation.com/is-todays-uni versity-the-new-multinational-corpo ration-40681

4. Sippola, A., & Smale, A. (2007). The global integration of diversity management: A longitudinal case study. *International Journal of Human Resource Management, 18*, 1895–1916.

5. Almond, P. (2011). Re-visiting country of origin effects on HRM in multinational corporations. *Human Resource Management Journal, 21*, 258–271.

6. Deutsch, A., & Sterling, T. (2021, September 13). *Uber drivers are employees, not contractors, says Dutch court.* Reuters. https://www.reuters.com/w orld/europe/dutch-court-rules-ube r-drivers-are-employees-not-contra ctors-newspaper-2021-09-13/

7. Flament, M. (August 15, 2022). How to manage the challenges and opportunities of a decentralized workforce. *Forbes.* https://www.forbes.com/site s/forbestechcouncil/2022/08/15/ho w-to-manage-the-challenges-and-o pportunities-of-a-decentralized-wor kforce/?sh=52e89a6a3702.

8. Farndale, E., & Paauwe, J. (2007). Uncovering competitive and institutional drivers of HRM practices in multinational corporations. *Human Resource Management Journal, 17*, 355–375.

9. Martin, A. K. T. (September 19, 2021). COVID-19 was expected to spur a remote-work revolution in Japan. What happened? *The Japan Times.* ht tps://www.japantimes.co.jp/news/2 021/09/19/business/pandemic-japa n-remote-work-failure/

10. U.S. Department of Justice. (2021, January 8). *Deutsche Bank agrees to pay over $130 million to resolve foreign corrupt practices act and fraud case.* ht tps://www.justice.gov/opa/pr/deutsc he-bank-agrees-pay-over-130-milli on-resolve-foreign-corrupt-practice s-act-and-fraud; U.S. Department of Justice. (2021, September 8). *Former Ericsson employee charged for role in foreign bribery scheme.* https://www.j ustice.gov/usao-sdny/pr/former-eric sson-employee-charged-role-foreig n-bribery-scheme; U.S. Department of Justice. (2022, April 8). *Former Goldman Sachs investment banker convicted in massive bribery and money laundering scheme.* https://www.justi ce.gov/opa/pr/former-goldman-sach s-investment-banker-convicted-ma ssive-bribery-and-money-launderin g-scheme

11. Brewster, C., Sparrow, P., & Harris, H. (2005). Towards a new model of globalizing HR. *International Journal of Human Resource Management, 16*, 949–970.

12. Jin, J. L., & Wang, L. (2021). Resource complementarity, partner differences, and international joint venture performance. *Journal of Business Research, 130*, 232–246.

13. Morris, S. S., Wright, P. M., Trevor, J., Stiles, P., Stahl, G., et al. (2009). Global challenges to replicating HR: The role of people, processes, and systems. *Human Resource Management, 48*, 973–995.

14. Thite, M., Wilkinson, A., & Shah, D. (2012). Internationalization and HRM strategies across subsidiaries in multinational corporations from emerging economies: A conceptual framework. *Journal of World Business, 47*, 251–258.

15. Budhwar, P. S., Varma, A., & Patel, C. (2016). Convergence-divergence of HRM in the Asia-Pacific: Context-specific analysis and future research agenda. *Human Resource Management Review, 26*, 311–326.

16. WillisTowersWatson. (2017, September 18). *A global approach to company car benefits policy.* https://www.willis towerswatson.com/en-LB/insights/2 017/09/A-global-approach-to-compa ny-car-benefits-policy

17. Rabl, T., Jayasinghe, M., Gerhart, B., & Kühlmann, T. M. (2014). A meta-analysis of country differences in the high performance work system–business performance relationship: The roles of national culture and managerial discretion. *Journal of Applied Psychology, 99*, 1011–1041.

18. Global Expansion. (2021, May 20). *The A-Z list of "13th month pay" countries.* h ttps://www.globalexpansion.com/bl og/the-a-z-list-of-13th-month-pay-c ountries

19. World Data. (2022). *The average age in global comparison.* https://www.worl ddata.info/average-age.php

20. Brough, M. (2022, March 22). *International pension survey 2022.* WTW. http s://www.wtwco.com/en-US/Insights /2022/03/2022-international-pensio n-plan

21. Tobenkin, D. (2011, June). Attention to pensions. *HR Magazine.* 93–98.

22. Claus, L. (2010, February). International assignees at risk. *HR Magazine*, 73–75; EEOC. (2003). *Employee rights when working for multinational employers.* https://www.eeoc.gov/f acts/multi-employees.html; Maurer, R. (2014, November). The rise of the accidental expat. *HR Magazine*, 12; Simms, J. (2017, February 21). The tricky logistics of global mobility—and HR's crucial role in getting it right. *People Management*, 46–48.

23. Onley, D. S. (2014, January). Terminating overseas employees. *HR Magazine*, 33–36.

24. Burgess, M. (2018, January 2). What is GDPR? WIRED explains what you need to know. *Wired.* http://www.wire d.co.uk/article/what-is-gdpr-uk-eu-legislation-compliance-summary-fi nes-2018; Ikeda, S. (2020, October 9). H&M hit with €35 million GDPR fine for profiling private lives of employees. *CPO Magazine.* https://www.cp omagazine.com/data-protection/h m-hit-with-e35-million-gdpr-fine-fo r-profiling-private-lives-of-employe es/

25. Gordon, N. (2022, August 6). Thailand lures digital nomads for the long term, with 10-year "work from Thailand" visas and ultra low tax rate. *Fortune.* https://fortune.com/2022/ 08/05/thailand-ten-year-visa-foreig n-workers-remote-work-digital-no mad-phuket/.

26. Harzing, A. W., Pudelko, M., & Reiche, S. (2016). The bridging role

of expatriates and inpatriates in knowledge transfer in multinational corporations. *Human Resource Management, 55*, 679–695.

27. Choudhury, P. (2020, July/August). Make the most of your relocation. *Harvard Business Review.*

28. Fang, Y., Jiang, G. L. F., Makino, S., & Beamish, P. W. (2010). Multinational firm knowledge, use of expatriates, and foreign subsidiary performance. *Journal of Management Studies, 47*, 27–54.

29. Chew, E. Y. T., Ghurburn, A., Terspstra-Tong, J. L. Y., & Perera, H. K. (2021). Multiple intelligence and expatriate effectiveness: The mediating roles of cross-cultural adjustment. *International Journal of Human Resource Management, 32*, 2856–2888.

30. Burgess, T. (2016, August 20). *Intenational assignment failure and tracking methods*. Forum for Expatriate Management. https://www.forum-expat-management.com/posts/11414-international-assignment-failure-and-tracking-methods

31. Bayraktar, S. (2019). A diary study of expatriate adjustment: Collaborative mechanisms of social support. *International Journal of Cross Cultural Management, 19*, 47–70.

32. Bhaskar-Shrinivas, P., Harrison, D. A., Shaffer, M. A., & Luk, D. M. (2005). Input-based and time-based models of international adjustment: Meta-analytic evidence and theoretical extensions. *Academy of Management Journal, 48*, 257–281.

33. Everson, K. (2014, July). Relocation sector keeps moving right along. *Workforce, 93*.

34. Bhaskar-Shrinivas, P., Harrison, D. A., Shaffer, M. A., & Luk, D. M. (2005). Input-based and time-based models of international adjustment: Meta-analytic evidence and theoretical extensions. *Academy of Management Journal, 48*, 257–281.

35. Primecz, H., Mahadevan, J., & Romani, L. (2016). Why is cross-cultural management scholarship blind to power relations? Investigating ethnicity, language, gender and religion in power-laden contexts. *International Journal of Cross Cultural Management, 16*, 127–126.

36. Zhang, L. E., & Harzing, A. W. (2016). From dilemmatic struggle to legitimized indifference: Expatriates' host country language learning and its impact on the expatriate–HCE relationship. *Journal of World Business, 51*, 774–786.

37. Molinsky, A. L. (2012, January/February). Code switching between cultures. *Harvard Business Review*, 140–141; Molinsky, A. L. (2014, January 30). Encourage foreign-born employees to participate more in meetings. *Harvard Business Review*. https://hbr.org/2014/01/encourage-foreign-born-employees-to-participate-more-in-meetings; Molinsky, A. L. (2014, July 15). Adapt to a new culture—but don't go too far. *Harvard Business Review*. https://hbr.org/2014/07/adapt-to-a-new-culture-but-dont-go-too-far; Neeley, T., & Kaplan, R. S. (2014, September). What's your language strategy? *Harvard Business Review*, 70–76.

38. Wang, C. H., & Varma, A. (2019). Cultural distance and expatriate failure rates: The moderating role of expatriate management practices. *International Journal of Human Resource Management, 30*, 2211–2230.

39. Bloom, L. B. (2022, July 12). Leave the US: Best places for expats to live. *Forbes*. https://www.forbes.com/sites/laurabegleybloom/2022/07/12/how-to-move-out-of-the-us-best-places-for-expats-to-live/?sh=2205de15703c

40. Harari, M. B., Reaves, A. C., Beane, D. A., Laginess, A. J., & Viswesvaran, C. (2018). Personality and expatriate adjustment: A meta-analysis. *Journal of Occupational and Organizational Psychology, 91*, 486–517.

41. Stoermer, S., Lauring, J., & Selmer, J. (2022). Job characteristics and perceived cultural novelty: Exploring the consequences for expatriate academics' job satisfaction. *International Journal of Human Resource Management, 33*, 417–443.

42. Shen, J., Wajeeh-ul-Husnain, S., Kang, H., & Jin, Q. (2021). Effect of outgroup social categorization by host-country nationals on expatriate premature return intention and buffering effect of mentoring. *Journal of International Management, 27*, 100855.

43. Fan, S. X., Cregan, C., Harzing, A. W., & Köhler, T. (2018). The benefits of being understood: The role of ethnic identity confirmation in knowledge acquisition by expatriates. *Human Resource Management, 57*, 327–339.

44. Farh, C. I. C., Bartol, K. M., Shapiro, D. L., & Shin, J. (2010). Networking abroad: A process model of how expatriates form support ties to facilitate adjustment. *Academy of Management Review, 35*, 434–454.

45. Sokro, E., Pillay, S., & Bednall, T. (2021). The effects of perceived organisational support on expatriate adjustment, assignment completion and job satisfaction. *International Journal of Cross Cultural Management, 21*, 452–473.

46. Andresen, M., & Bergdolt, F. (2017). A systematic literature review on the definitions of global mindset and cultural intelligence—merging two different research streams. *International Journal of Human Resource Management, 28*, 170–195.

47. Molinsky, A., & Hahn, M. (2015, April 8). Building relationships in cultures that don't do small talk. *Harvard Business Review*. https://hbr.org/2015/04/building-relationships-in-cultures-that-dont-do-small-talk

48. Everson, K. (2014, July). Relocation sector keeps moving right along. *Workforce, 93*.

49. Clemetson, L. (2010, December 15). The globe-trotters. *Workforce Management, 89*. http://www.workforce.com/2010/12/15/special-report-on-globalization-the-globe-trotters

50. Herod, R. (2017, May 15). *"Local plus" expatriate policies are on the rise*. SHRM. https://www.shrm.org/resourcesandtools/hr-topics/global-hr/pages/local-plus-expatriate-policies-are-on-the-rise.aspx

51. Gale, S. F. (2017, November/December). Finding agility in employee mobility. *Workforce*, 58–59.

52. Omonobi, K. (2022, August 12). *Troops arrest 2 pirates who kidnap expatriates in Niger Delta*. Vanguard Media. https://www.vanguardngr.com/2022/08/troops-arrest-2-pirates-who-kidnap-expatriates-in-niger-delta/

53. Bureau of National Affairs. (2011, January). Kidnappings remain a concern for firms doing business abroad. *HR Focus*, 6–8.

54. Nicholas, K., Cadman, E., Kwan, S., & Chang, R. (2020, June 8). Covid-19 chills the allure of expat life. *Bloomberg Businessweek, 4659*, 14–15.

55. Mercer. (2017). *Expatriates in hardship locations: Dealing with emergencies*. https://mobilityexchange.mercer.com/

Insights/article/Expatriates-in-Har
dship-Locations-Dealing-with-Eme
rgencies

56. Bravery, K., Baker, R., & Roche, S. (2022). *Expatriate management: Women in the workforce*. Mercer. https ://mobilityexchange.mercer.com/ins ights/article/expatriate-managemen t-women-in-the-workforce

57. Varma, A., & Russell, L. (2016). Women and expatriate assignments: Exploring the role of perceived organizational support. *Employee Relations, 38*, 200–223.

58. Bader, B. (2018, February 6). Do female expats experience a greater level of discrimination? *People Management*. https://www.peoplemanag ement.co.uk/voices/comment/femal e-expats-greater-discrimination

59. Shen, J., & Jiang, F. (2015). Factors influencing Chinese female expatriates' performance in international assignments. *International Journal of Human Resource Management, 26*, 299–315.

60. McPhail, R., McNulty, Y., & Hutchings, K. (2016). Lesbian and gay expatriation: Opportunities, barriers, and challenges for global mobility. *International Journal of Human Resource Management, 27*, 382–406.

61. Human Dignity Trust. (2022). *Map of countries that criminalize LGBT people*. https://www.humandignitytrust.org/ lgbt-the-law/map-of-criminalisation/

62. Florian, J. (2018, April 2). *Sending LGBTQ employees abroad poses challenges, requires planning*. Bloomberg. https://www.bna.com/sending-lgbt q-employees-b57982090600/

63. Bolino, M. C., Klotz, A. C., & Turnley, W. H. (2017, April 18). Will refusing an international assignment derail your career? *Harvard Business Review*. htt ps://hbr.org/2017/04/will-refusing-a n-international-assignment-derail-y our-career

64. Kraimer, M. L., Shaffer, M. A., & Bolino, M. C. (2009). The influence of expatriate and repatriate experiences on career advancement and repatriate intentions. *Human Resource Management, 48*, 27–47.

65. Krell, E. (2011, December). Taking care of business abroad. *HR Magazine*, 44–48.

66. Maurer, R. (2014, November). The rise of the accidental expat. *HR Magazine*, 12.

67. Simms, J. (2017, February 21). The tricky logistics of global mobility—and HR's crucial role in getting it right. *People Management*, 46–48.

68. Hannibal, E., Traber, Y., & Jelinek, P. (2015, April). Tracking your expatriate software. *HR Magazine*, 63–65.

69. MBO Partners. (2021, December). *The great realization*. https://info.mbo partners.com/rs/mbo/images/MBO_ 2021_State_of_Independence_Rese arch_Report.pdf

70. Meyer, C. (2022, July 26). *Weighing the risks of allowing digital nomad employees*. SHRM. https://www.shrm.org/r esourcesandtools/hr-topics/risk-ma nagement/pages/weighing-the-risk s-of-allowing-digital-nomad-employ ees.aspx

71. Umstadter, C. (2022, June 30). *Do you need a corporate mobility policy for your digital nomad workers?* EBN. http s://www.benefitnews.com/opinion/ how-to-create-a-corporate-mobilit y-policy

INDEX

360-degree feedback, 253, 286, 288, 297–98

AAPs (Affirmative action plans), 120–21
ability, physical, 168, 221
absolute ratings, 282–84
ACA (Affordable Care Act), 113, 401, 405, 410, 424
access to information, 80, 504
access to training, 185, 249
accidents, 257, 403, 463–66, 468–69, 484–86
accidents and injuries, 462–65, 469
accommodations, 108, 112–13, 115–16, 186, 200, 322, 448
action verb, 135, 143
ADA (Americans with Disabilities Act), 74, 102, 113, 115–16, 118, 138, 184, 186, 200–201, 320, 421
ADEA (Age Discrimination in Employment Act), 102, 113–14, 118, 184–85, 318, 421
adjustment, 124, 200–201, 252, 504–5, 507–8, 510–13
adverse impact, 106, 199, 208–9, 216, 219, 221–22
affirmative action, 101, 120–21
Affirmative action plans. See AAPs
affirmative action programs, 119, 121
Affordable Care Act. See ACA
Age Discrimination in Employment Act. See ADEA
aging factor, 348, 350–51
agreement, 49, 159, 183, 251, 279, 357, 432–33, 442, 448, 450–51, 453–54
algorithms, 29, 41–42, 48–50, 63, 124–25, 191, 196–97, 213, 220, 274, 378
alternatives to layoffs, 323–25
alumni employees, 177–79
alumni network, 233, 315
Amazon, 11, 39, 48, 50, 176, 180, 190, 432–33, 435, 444, 452
Americans with Disabilities Act. See ADA
analysts, 16, 19, 42–44, 47–50, 61–63, 68, 87, 348, 350–51
analytics, 15–16, 21, 23, 25, 27–57, 60–62, 64–68, 89–90, 123, 139, 255, 257–58, 283, 422, 453
analytics function, 28, 44, 52
analytics team, 40, 42–43, 52, 54, 123
anonymous data, 73, 89
applicant interest and participation, 175, 189, 191
applicant pool, 172, 179, 185, 199, 220, 225
applicant reactions, 196, 209, 213, 223–27

applicants, 41, 44, 50, 100, 104–8, 117, 119–20, 123–28, 166–70, 173–78, 183–92, 198–201, 204, 206, 209–15, 217–27, 388, 492–93
  best, 173–74, 191, 223
  female, 108, 121, 222
  potential, 17, 91, 169, 171, 175–76
  qualified, 169, 173–74, 186, 221
applicants and employees, 119–20, 186
applicant tracking system, 87, 178, 192
Applicant tracking system (ATS), 83, 87, 178, 192
appraisals, 270, 275, 277–79, 285, 288, 291, 293
artificial intelligence, 28, 30, 40–41, 44, 49–50, 53, 90, 124, 196, 258
assessment centers, 209, 217–19, 224, 226, 251
assignments, 118, 251, 261, 263, 312, 354, 502, 504–5, 508–12, 515–17
association, 17, 22, 121, 428, 488–90
asynchronous video interviews. See AVIs
ATS. See Applicant tracking system
attraction, 16, 217, 388
audience, 68–71, 81, 123
audits, 42, 50, 123–24, 294, 499
available information, 79, 124–25
AVIs (asynchronous video interviews), 213, 225

background research, 46, 207
balanced scorecard, 37, 53
base, 348, 357, 362, 369–70, 377–79, 381–82, 386–88, 393, 411–12, 503, 510
BATNA, 448–49
behavioral appraisals, 279–80, 292
behavioral interviews, 209–12, 227
behavioral modeling training. See BMT
behaviors, 83, 100–101, 122, 212, 215, 219–20, 223–24, 245, 249–52, 256–58, 276–77, 279–80, 284, 370–73, 375–76, 378, 389–90, 438–39, 465, 505–6
  ethical, 18, 149–50, 499
  reckless, 368–69
  safe, 18, 466–67
  unacceptable, 437, 499
  unsafe, 465–66
benchmark jobs, 344–52, 362, 365
beneficiaries, 121, 403, 405
benefits, 111–13, 154–55, 190–91, 282, 293, 312–13, 315–17, 322–24, 326–27, 337–39, 399–406, 409–17, 419–27, 435, 477–79, 492–93, 497–502, 504–5, 509–10, 512–14

available, 399, 423–24
benefits employees, 422, 425
benefits information session, 426–28
benefits of diversity, 96, 98, 126
benefits offerings, 387, 421, 423, 425–28
benefits programs, 184, 398, 420, 423
  voluntary, 420–21, 423
benefits satisfaction, 426–28
benefits satisfaction and turnover intentions, 426–27
benefits to employees, 406, 424, 446
BFOQ (Bona fide occupational qualification), 105–7, 110, 126
biases, 8–9, 23, 41–42, 49–50, 99–100, 102, 123, 126, 196–97, 274–75, 286–87, 289, 291, 294, 385–86
big data, 15, 30, 48–49, 53, 73, 90, 123, 125–26, 139
biodata, 219, 224, 226
biographical data, 209, 219
Black employees, 97, 110, 122
BMT (Behavioral modeling training), 249–50
Bona fide occupational qualification. See BFOQ
bonuses, 186, 188, 270, 273, 278–79, 289, 324, 368–69, 373–75, 377, 379, 387, 391, 393, 501
boomerang employees, 179, 315–16, 330
burnout, 9, 460–61, 473–75
businesses, 14, 22–24, 34, 42–44, 52–54, 61–63, 101–5, 109–10, 112–17, 119–21, 123, 306–7, 309–10, 315, 322–23, 326, 454–56, 492–99, 503–4, 514
business ethics, 5, 17, 23
business necessity, 106–8, 112, 187
business partner, 19–20, 23, 36
bystander training, 122, 126

candidate experience, 167, 188, 223–24, 226
candidates, 8–9, 30, 32, 50, 112, 138–39, 167–68, 174–76, 179, 199, 209, 211–13, 218–19, 222–23, 225
career management, 261–63
careeronestop.org, 347, 349, 365
categorical variables, 55, 92
CEO, 5, 17–18, 30, 32, 96, 98–99, 226–28, 298, 358, 363, 435–36, 508, 514
change management, 52, 82
changes, 5–6, 11, 13–14, 21–22, 35–36, 80–83, 122–23, 125–26, 139, 155, 258–60, 262, 271, 285–86, 294–95, 311–13, 329–30, 411, 452–53, 476–77
changing context, 4, 12–13, 23, 25

changing demographics, 13, 23, 25
characteristics, 10, 20, 25, 54, 135, 152–53, 158, 193, 197–98, 223–24, 227, 240–42, 245–46, 275–76, 279, 295, 298, 392, 408–9, 455
demographic, 100, 423
Charge Nurse (CN), 350, 352–53
classification method, 344, 362
COBRA (Consolidated Omnibus Budget Reconciliation Act), 401, 405, 424
cognitive ability, 209, 212, 216–18, 222, 227, 242–43
cognitive ability tests, 209, 214, 216–18, 226
collective bargaining process, 432–33, 447, 454
companies, 11–15, 24, 28–34, 96–100, 108–14, 122–26, 223–28, 234–38, 270–76, 291–94, 296–99, 305–7, 309–16, 318–31, 384–86, 392–94, 425–28, 485–88, 492–505, 508–16
company culture, 11, 50, 100, 313
compensable factors, 344–45, 362
compensatory time, 418, 424
competencies, 19–23, 43, 52, 54, 135, 140, 142, 149–51, 236, 238, 240, 342–43, 358
competency modeling, 132, 134–35, 141, 149–51, 156, 238
competency models, 20, 132, 134–35, 139–42, 149–51, 212
competitive advantage, 21, 28–30, 33, 35, 42–43, 52, 65, 187, 204, 226, 232
competitors, 30, 33, 169, 177, 183, 346–47, 349, 351–52, 363, 392–93, 420
comp time, 418, 424
conduct job analyses, 106, 134
conflict management approaches, 448, 454
conscientiousness, 202–3, 207, 213–15, 228–29, 243, 466
Consolidated Omnibus Budget Reconciliation Act. See COBRA
construction workers, 26, 235
content validity, 202–3, 226, 229
contingent employees, 155–56
contingent work, 156, 485
continuous variables, 49, 55, 57
contributions, 22, 24, 286, 289, 295, 297, 338–41, 351, 413–15, 419, 421
individual, 383–84, 392
control group, 47, 259, 263, 266–67
core information system concepts, 60, 83, 89
correlations, 25–26, 49, 125, 202–3, 209, 216, 218–19, 228–29, 288, 386
Costco, 4–5, 11, 23, 191, 435
countries, 14, 96, 117, 178–79, 208, 321, 323, 354, 404, 419, 441, 444–45, 471, 492–99, 501–4, 508–9, 512–17
host, 354–55
multiple, 323, 494, 502, 512
court cases, 199, 438
coverage period, 409–10
criterion-related validity, 202–4, 226, 228–29
cultural adjustment, 504–5, 514

cultural contexts, 39, 288, 495, 498, 501
multiple, 151, 251
cultural differences, 14, 151, 208, 384, 492, 496–97, 502, 509
cultural training, 506, 509, 514
cultures, 10–12, 38–39, 52, 81, 236–37, 251–53, 277–78, 281, 384, 434, 437, 497–99, 505–6, 508–9, 511
inclusive, 96–97, 122–23
individualistic, 251, 384
current employees, 65, 135, 138, 177–79, 202–4, 207, 228, 237, 246–47, 423, 425–26
customer problems, 144–46
customers, 11–12, 29–30, 34, 37, 60, 108–9, 143–47, 212, 218–19, 226–27, 239–40, 244–45, 279–80, 282, 286–87, 295–96, 361–62, 381, 390, 472
customer satisfaction, 12, 26, 37, 60, 244–45, 281–82, 381
customer service, 62, 91, 146–47, 207, 229, 279, 347, 382, 438
customer service jobs, 144, 206, 224, 487
customer service specialists, 6, 143–46

data, 15, 40–53, 61–69, 71–76, 78, 83–89, 91–93, 123, 178, 196–98, 304–5, 311–12, 347–51, 365, 422–24, 456–58, 471–73, 482–83, 487–88, 516–17
applicant, 83, 85, 178, 223
high-quality, 67–68, 273
raw, 67, 194
sensitive, 76–77, 472
data analysis, 40, 43–44, 48, 52, 54–55, 300, 422
data analysts, 44, 62
data analytics, 28–30, 44, 66–67, 123, 139, 191, 233, 272–73, 423, 485
data availability, 64, 66, 89
database object, 84–86
databases, 67, 78, 83, 85–86, 88–89, 148, 181, 472
data breach, 223, 503
data flow diagrams, 78, 89
data-informed decision making, 29–57
data-informed decisions, 28, 30, 40, 42, 45, 52–53, 61–62, 89
data lakes, 67, 89
data management, 43, 52, 54, 59–64, 71–72
data management and human resource information systems, 61–93
data privacy, 64, 72–74, 87, 89, 512
data scientist, 44, 48, 50, 139–40, 148
data security, 64, 74–76, 88–89
dataset, 73, 197, 229, 300, 302
data visualizations, 51, 53, 55–57, 68–71, 349, 423
effective, 68–69, 89
data warehouses, 61, 67
decision makers, 20, 61–62, 104, 173, 182, 191, 255, 258, 260, 312, 411

organizational, 63, 153, 156, 184, 234, 236, 255, 258, 272, 411, 422
decision-making process, 6, 9, 50, 81, 123, 173, 308, 363, 383, 497
decisions, 6–12, 16–17, 45–46, 49–50, 52–54, 100–101, 113–15, 157–59, 172–73, 192–93, 196–97, 226–28, 272–74, 285–86, 298, 319–21, 331–32, 364, 425–26, 455–56
good, 5, 9, 21, 43, 219, 222
layoff, 322, 325–26, 328
termination, 319, 321–22
defined-benefit plans, 413, 424
defined-contribution plans, 412–15, 424
delivery of training, 235, 240, 242, 264
departures, 6, 121, 305–6, 309, 312, 315–16, 332, 517
descriptive analytics, 15–16, 44–45, 53, 55, 57, 72, 266
designing jobs, 6, 64, 138, 151–52, 314
development programs, 79, 138
differential piecework plans, 380, 391
dimensions, behavioral, 280, 386, 392
dimensions of performance, 281, 284, 286, 290, 293
disabilities, 74, 97, 99, 102, 108, 115–20, 186, 197, 200, 349, 355, 401, 403
disability income, 401, 403
disadvantages, 122, 156, 193, 196–97, 208, 232, 246–47, 488, 492, 494, 498
discrimination, 23, 100–106, 108, 110–11, 115, 117–19, 121–22, 184, 186, 196–97, 328, 357, 387, 421, 437
discrimination and harassment, 121, 511
dismissals, 305, 318–20, 322–23, 328–30
disparate impact, 105–8, 125, 128–29, 187, 216, 238
disparate treatment, 104–8, 126
diversity, 19, 21–22, 95–129, 175, 178, 184–85, 189, 191, 198–99, 222–23, 226, 250, 325
diversity goals, 97, 122
diversity initiatives, 122–23
diversity management, 97, 101, 121, 126, 185
diversity training, 122, 250, 254, 257
drivers, 65, 181, 249, 274, 311–12, 484

EAPs (employee assistance program), 319, 480–81
EAP services, 480–81
educational-assistance programs, 419, 424
EEOC (Equal Employment Opportunity Commission), 23, 101–3, 106, 108, 110, 117–18, 121, 123, 126, 197, 199, 274, 355, 357, 387
EEOC laws, 326, 502
EEO laws, 23, 101–3, 106, 114, 116–17, 120, 123, 125
effectiveness
organizational, 6, 64, 98, 172–73
program's, 233, 255
effectiveness of training programs, 122, 255

EI (Emotional intelligence), 29, 216, 226, 229–30
EI tests, 216
eLearning, 237, 246, 249, 252, 263–64
eLearning platforms, 248–49, 255
elements, 39, 69, 110, 135, 148, 173, 326–27, 479
emotional intelligence. *See* EI
employee age, 47, 55–56
employee assistance program. *See* EAPs
employee attitudes, 83, 488
employee behaviors, 257, 274, 282, 468, 472
employee benefits, 5, 400, 414, 423
employee compensation, 104, 138, 273
employee data, 73–74, 77, 482, 493, 503
employee dismissals, 304, 318, 330
employee dismissals and layoffs, 304, 318, 330
employee experience, 14, 47, 133, 454
employee groups, 155, 179, 326, 366
employee handbooks, 121, 328, 355, 434, 436–38, 454
employee health, 462–63, 469, 477, 480, 483, 486
employee ID, 48, 91
employee knowledge, 235, 257, 260
employee life cycle, 6–9, 17, 64, 172
employee life cycle to maximize employee, 6, 64, 172
employee life cycle to maximize employee and organizational effectiveness, 6, 64, 172
employee monitoring, 74, 472, 483–84
employee motivation, 132, 151–52, 370, 374, 388
employee outcomes, 39, 52, 418
employee participation, 294, 478, 482
employee performance, 10, 29, 272–73, 279, 282, 284–86, 289, 293, 296, 383, 389
employee population, 423, 484
employee referrals, 177, 179
employee relations, 21, 432–37, 453–54
employee resource groups, 97, 122
employee retention, 63, 304–5, 308, 310, 314, 329, 462, 513
Employee Retirement Income Security Act. *See* ERISA
employee rights, 112, 274, 433, 469, 486
employees
    average, 56, 266, 358
    compensating, 6, 358, 387
    departing, 22, 306, 315, 326–29
    dismissed, 318, 321, 323
    experienced, 53, 280, 354, 359
    full-time, 326, 405
    hiring, 10, 65, 100, 148, 156, 168, 210, 227–28, 313, 500
    host-country, 502, 504–5, 507
    measuring, 272, 279, 422
    motivating, 329, 376, 393, 400
    organization's, 87, 149, 414
    rate, 277, 285–86, 386
    retail, 174–75, 279, 435
    reward, 7, 338, 370, 384, 414
employee safety, 461–89

employees and management, 19, 81, 434
employees and managers, 7, 35, 74, 119, 277, 290, 295, 436, 503
employee satisfaction, 304, 314, 482
employee selection, 124, 126–27, 198, 273, 294
employee selection procedures, 106–7, 126, 138, 199, 202, 238
employee separations, 305, 323, 502
employee stock ownership plan. *See* ESOPs
employee stock ownership plans, 384–85, 391, 414
employee stress, 463, 476–77, 484, 488, 490
employee surveys, 35, 240, 311, 329, 422–23, 426
employee turnover, 29, 40, 65, 305, 308, 329
employee wellness programs, 477, 486–87
employer contributions, 412–15, 423, 425
employer relationships, 24, 54, 90, 127, 159, 193, 228, 265, 298, 331, 364
employers, 103–7, 109–20, 133–34, 182–84, 196–201, 213–17, 219–27, 249–50, 320–21, 346–48, 356–57, 387, 399–407, 409–26, 442, 446–48, 462–66, 469–78, 483–85, 513–15
    surveyed, 406, 414, 416
employment decisions, 23, 74, 96, 101, 104–5, 107, 109–12, 117–18, 125, 183
employment laws, 43, 52, 54, 138, 183, 208, 323, 434, 436, 438, 443
employment practices, 107–8, 110, 357
employment relationship, 103, 318, 436, 444
Enterprise resource planning. *See* ERP
Equal Employment Opportunity Commission. *See* EEOC
equipment, 135, 139–40, 143, 157, 227, 235, 240–41, 310, 463, 465, 468–70
equitable relief, 104, 106, 126
equity, 21–22, 37, 44, 95–129, 339–43, 349, 361
equity theory, 339–42, 362
ERISA (Employee Retirement Income Security Act), 405, 412, 424
ERP (Enterprise resource planning), 62–63, 82, 89, 348
ESOPs (employee stock ownership plan), 384–85, 391, 414
essential functions, 115, 126, 138
ethical issues, 182, 199, 254, 472
ethics, 10, 13, 17, 20, 23, 43, 52, 54, 74, 76, 149–50, 254–55, 361–62, 498–99
ethics training, 254, 499
evaluating training programs, 256, 263, 267
evidence, 8–10, 25, 39–40, 102–3, 105–6, 113–14, 116, 127–29, 193, 202–3, 205–6, 227–28, 291–92, 297–98, 364–66, 378, 382–83, 425, 428, 455
executive order, 101, 120, 126, 355–57, 362
exit interviews, 73, 180, 312, 392, 424
expatriate adjustment, 492, 503–5, 507–8
expatriate assignments, 503–5, 508, 511–12, 516
expatriates, 354–55, 492, 495, 502–17
expectancy theory, 243, 372–74, 383, 391, 393

external environments, 31, 33–34, 39, 236, 238, 371, 389
external equity, 343, 346, 351–52, 358, 362, 377
extraversion, 44, 135, 204, 213–15, 224, 243, 299–300, 302, 507
extrinsic motivation, 371–72, 391

Fair Labor Standards Act. *See* FLSA
Family and Medical Leave Act. *See* FMLA
FAODs, 157
Federal Insurance Contributions Act (FICA), 402, 424
feedback, 152–53, 223, 225–26, 242–43, 245, 247–50, 271–73, 275, 277–79, 286–88, 291, 294–96, 298, 311, 474
feedback culture, 295–97
feedback delivery, 278, 294–95
FICA (Federal Insurance Contributions Act), 402, 424
financial rewards, 342, 368–70, 382, 391–92
Five Factor Model (FFM), 213, 226
flexible benefits plans, 420–21, 424
flexible work arrangements, 155–56, 400, 418
flextime, 155–56, 418
FLSA (Fair Labor Standards Act), 72, 355–56, 362, 416, 418, 440
FMLA (Family and Medical Leave Act), 113, 332, 404, 417, 424
formats, 86, 135, 200, 202, 218, 272
former employees, 5, 167, 179, 315, 326, 386, 424, 470, 503
framework, competing values, 11, 53
frequency table, 92–93
functional areas, 62, 84, 354, 423
functionality, 64, 66, 89

gainsharing programs, 382–83
gamified training, 167, 252
GDPR (General Data Protection Regulation), 15, 76–77, 503
gender identity, 55–56, 97, 111, 118–19
General Data Protection Regulation. *See* GDPR
generating applicants, 175, 188, 191
Genetic Information Nondiscrimination Act. *See* GINA
gig workers, 16, 120, 156, 183, 274
GINA (Genetic Information Nondiscrimination Act), 102, 113, 117, 421
giving employees feedback, 272, 274
Global organizations, 149, 251, 495, 499, 506
goals, 37, 49–50, 64, 66, 69, 71, 77–78, 169, 172–75, 187–89, 236, 241, 243, 275–76, 281–82, 370–72, 374–77, 382–83, 387–88, 390–92
    individual, 251, 376, 391
goal setting, 97, 122, 178, 241, 243, 271, 281–82, 368, 372, 391, 495
grievance procedures, 433, 453

group pay-for-performance programs, 368, 374, 376, 382, 384, 389–91
group performance, 315, 382, 390

harassment, 99, 104, 108–10, 112, 114, 118–19, 121–22, 126, 467, 511
HDHP (High-Deductible Health Plan), 408
headcount data, 70–71
health, 151–52, 317, 339, 399, 408, 462–64, 467–71, 473–74, 477, 479, 483–86
   personal, 144–45, 147, 480
health benefits, mental, 399, 417
health care plans, 405, 412
health care programs, 401, 405–6, 409
Health Insurance Portability and Account-ability Act. See HIPAA
health issues, 222, 404, 468–69, 472, 485
health maintenance organization. See HMO
health reimbursement arrangement. See HRA
health savings account. See HSAs
healthy employee, 54, 90, 127, 159, 193, 228, 265, 298, 331, 364, 393
helping behaviors, 280, 342, 390–91, 416
High-Deductible Health Plan. See HDHP
higher levels of performance, 281, 369, 375
high-performance work practices, 38, 53
HIPAA (Health Insurance Portability and Accountability Act), 401, 405, 424
hiring decisions, 100, 113, 138, 197–98, 204–5, 210–11, 222, 228, 501
hiring manager, 100, 105, 126, 173, 192, 201, 205, 210–11, 217, 219
hiring process, 108, 112, 116, 173, 189, 191, 200, 209, 213, 217, 223
HMO (health maintenance organization), 408, 411, 425
home, 14, 46, 74, 132–33, 155, 309, 321, 418–19, 484, 486–87, 509–11
home country, 354, 492, 494, 509–11
hostile work environment, 108–9, 114, 118, 126
hours, 5, 14–15, 20–21, 177, 179, 324, 326, 339–40, 355–56, 380–81, 417–18, 444, 447–48, 450, 475
HRA (health reimbursement arrangement), 408–9
HRIS (human resource information system), 60–93, 348
HRIS, new, 77–78, 80, 82–83, 91
HRM (human resource management), 4–160, 168, 192–93, 210, 253, 425, 454–55, 462, 465, 469, 472–73, 475, 481, 485–87, 515
HRM decisions, 9, 17, 24
HSAs (health savings account), 408–9, 421
human resource information system. See HRIS
human resource information systems, 61–93, 348
human resources, 33–34, 37, 41–42, 53, 61, 63, 65, 97, 159, 494, 514
hypothesis, 6, 46–47, 49, 51, 267, 428

ID, 66, 459–90, 516–17
identifiable data, 73, 89
IFBL (Informal field-based learning), 247, 263
implicit biases, 100, 122
impression management tactics, 290–91
inclusion, 19, 21–22, 44, 95–129, 168, 222, 286
income protection benefits, 411–12
individual employees, 17, 235–36, 240, 354, 357, 360, 362, 365, 370, 476, 481–83
individual equity, 104, 343, 354–55, 362
individual incentives, 375, 377, 379, 391
individual pay-for-performance programs, 377, 383, 391
individual retirement plans, 412, 415, 424
individuals, 10–11, 71–74, 80–82, 98–100, 104, 110–12, 114–21, 170–72, 183–85, 250–52, 261–62, 338–42, 356–58, 372–78, 382–84, 388–90, 405, 411–12, 415, 419–24
   reward, 370, 376–77
   talented, 37, 198, 346, 359
inequity, under-reward, 340–41
informal field-based learning. See IFBL
information, genetic, 117, 126, 421
informational interview, 189, 192
information systems, 43, 62–63, 75, 83, 88–89, 178, 356, 379, 420, 423, 493
injuries, 238, 257, 403, 405, 411, 417, 462–66, 469–70, 485–86, 502
in-network, 407–8
insiders, organizational, 189, 252, 254
instrumentality, 373–74, 383, 390–91, 393
integrity, 74, 91, 135, 149–50, 225, 482, 499
integrity tests, 198, 209, 215–16, 224–26
interactional justice, 341–42, 363
internal equity, 343, 346, 351, 358, 362, 377
internal equity and external equity, 351, 362
International Labor Organizations (ILO), 471
internship programs, 167, 178, 180
interpersonal conflicts, 474, 481, 489
interpersonal skills, 136, 144, 211, 239, 241, 244, 247
interventions, 65, 290, 311, 316, 399, 460–61, 464, 483–86
interviewers, 105, 210–13
interviews, 7–8, 140, 142–43, 154, 156, 167, 173–74, 189, 198, 200, 210–13, 216–17, 224–27, 312, 329–31
intrinsic motivation, 371–72, 375, 391
involuntary turnover, 7, 305–6, 318, 322, 329
items, 55–56, 145, 148, 208, 213, 216, 218–19, 393, 422, 426, 450

JCM (Job characteristics model), 152–53, 157
JDR, 152–53, 157, 473–74
job analysis, 132, 134–35, 137–43, 145, 148–51, 156–59, 196, 198, 202–3, 206–7, 217, 219–21, 235–36, 238, 343–44
   traditional, 149–50
job analysis and competency modeling, 132, 135, 141, 151, 238

job analysis data, 140, 142, 148, 156
job analysis information, 132, 140–41, 171
job analysis materials, 140, 142–43
job analysis methods, 141–42, 147–49, 151
job analysis process, 140–41, 148
job analyst, 140, 142–43, 148
job applicants, 100, 102, 107, 135–37, 181–83, 189–91, 196–97, 201–4, 206–7, 210–12, 215–17, 219, 221–24
Job characteristics model. See JCM
job demands-resources model, 152–53, 157, 473–74
job descriptions, 135–38, 140, 149, 154, 156–58, 343–44, 347, 349, 358, 365, 370
job design, 132, 137, 151–53, 157, 470
job dissatisfaction, 46, 439, 454
job evaluation, 137–38, 343–44, 351, 362
job interviews, 112, 126, 189, 198, 200, 223–24
job levels, 91–92, 142, 149–50, 172, 501
job performance, 49, 106, 196, 201–9, 213–16, 218–19, 221–22, 225, 227–28, 320, 322
   predicting, 202, 209–11, 215, 217, 219, 228
Job Performance Measure, 205, 207
job performance scores, 49, 203–4
jobs, 18–21, 102–8, 112–16, 133–43, 145–59, 167–77, 183–94, 202–6, 210–25, 235–41, 243–48, 256–60, 304–10, 312–19, 321–25, 342–54, 361–66, 369–70, 386–88, 473–74
   changing, 29, 309, 313
   new, 21, 245, 308–9, 313, 323, 329, 380, 405, 436, 462, 511
   redesigning, 151–52
job satisfaction, 26, 46–47, 66, 98, 154, 308, 314, 330, 338, 467, 475
job specifications, 135–36, 138, 156–57, 344
job structure, 343–44, 352, 363
job title of Research Scientist, 193–94
job titles, 18–19, 67, 104, 148, 159, 185, 193–94, 349–50, 353
justice, 20, 106, 199, 342, 434–35

Key Performance Indicator. See KPIs
Kky variables, 84, 89
Kirkpatrick framework, 256–57
knowledge of company procedures, 260–61
knowledge of results, 152–53
KPIs (Key Performance Indicator), 188, 281, 297, 378
KSAO analysis, 142, 145, 148, 159
KSAOs, 10, 20, 22, 135, 138–49, 157, 159, 168, 170–71, 173, 198, 236, 238–41, 343–44, 388
   required, 135, 170, 388

labor costs, 169, 323, 370, 385, 388–89
Labor Management Relations Act, 442, 447, 454

labor market conditions, 170–71, 191–92
labor relations, 431–57
labor unions, 23, 102, 433, 436, 438, 440, 442, 445, 454
laws, 23, 43, 101–5, 110–15, 117–19, 183–84, 187, 199, 238, 320–21, 326, 387, 421–22, 434, 436–38, 441, 443–45, 470–72, 502–3
    state, 108, 126, 320–21, 323, 326, 443, 472
lawsuit, 102–3, 105, 110, 117–18, 319–20, 329, 386, 419
layoffs, 105, 273, 283, 304–5, 318, 322–30, 389
leaders, organizational, 40, 477
leadership development, 170, 191–92
learners, 243, 245–50, 252, 258
lectures, 244–48, 250
legal context, 441, 492, 496
legal issues, 23, 43, 50, 187, 196, 198–200, 222, 226, 238, 416, 422, 470, 472
levels of HR analytics, 28, 40, 44
LGBTQ+ employees, 118–19, 511
licensed practical nurse, 349–50
Licensed Practical Nurse. See LPN
Life insurance program, 401, 415, 424
life programs, 401, 406, 416, 424, 485
line managers, 10, 17–18, 277, 305, 330
list of tasks and KSAOs, 142–43, 159
local employees, 499–500, 502, 504–5, 507–8, 510–11, 516
logical design, 78–79, 89
long-term disability insurance, 412, 424
LPN (Licensed Practical Nurse), 349–50, 352–54

maintaining applicant interest, 175, 189–90
maintaining applicant interest and partici-pation, 175, 189–90
managed-care plans, 401, 407–8, 424
management, upper, 35, 275, 391–92, 433
management reporting, 442, 454
manager ratings, 288, 392
managers, 17–18, 20–21, 35, 37, 39–40, 44–45, 86–87, 235–37, 251–52, 254–55, 271–73, 275–79, 281–99, 307–9, 314–15, 320–22, 326–27, 341–42, 374–75, 435–37
    effective, 81, 293, 315, 326
managers and employees, 109, 236–37, 271, 275, 288, 294, 296, 337, 436–37, 468, 475
managing benefits, 397–427
managing diversity, 6, 64, 98
managing employees, 493, 501, 514
managing employee separations, 303, 329–30
managing individuals, 6–7, 17, 64, 172
manufacturing workers, 391–92
market, 12, 53, 316, 322, 343, 347–48, 350–52, 359–60, 363, 494, 500
market cultures, 11–12, 23, 82
market pay, 343, 353
market pricing, 351, 363–64

market review data, 347–48, 350–51, 353, 363, 424
market reviews, 347–49, 351–52, 362–64, 422
market review sources, 348–49, 351, 365
market review surveys, 349–50
measurement tools, 275, 375
measures, 37, 47, 49–50, 138–39, 187–88, 200–204, 211–12, 228, 233, 235, 255–56, 258–59, 263–64, 276, 385–86
mechanical ability, 157, 203–4, 209, 216
median, 20, 55, 348–51, 358, 440
medical plans, 406–7, 409–10, 425
membership, organizational, 309, 370
mental health, 154, 398–400, 417, 481
    poor, 398–400, 481
mental health challenges, 398–99
midpoint, 353–54, 359–60, 365–66
mindfulness training, 251–52, 263, 461, 479, 488
mission, 30–34, 40, 53, 96, 170, 344, 464
model, statistical, 16, 44, 47, 389
money-purchase plan, 414–15, 424
monthly base pay, 349, 352
motivation, 39, 87, 151, 153, 156, 242–43, 274, 277, 287, 290, 293, 368, 370–74, 376–77, 391–93
multinational companies, 39, 77, 208, 251, 355, 494, 498, 500–501, 514

NACE (National Association of Colleges and Employers), 180, 190
National Association of Colleges and Employers (NACE), 180, 190
National Institute for Occupational Safety and Health. See NIOSH
National Labor Relations Act. See NLRA
National Labor Relations Board. See NLRB
negative effects of layoffs, 323, 329
negotiation process, 448–50
negotiations, 446, 448–50, 454, 496
net database, 148, 159, 226
NET framework, 148–49
network, 167, 253, 408, 425, 504
newcomers, 5, 252–54, 313, 315
new employees, 38, 46–47, 54, 166–67, 173, 175–76, 178, 183, 247, 252–54, 436–37
new system, 81–83, 271
NIOSH (National Institute for Occupational Safety and Health), 464, 485–86
NLRA (National Labor Relations Act), 357, 361, 363, 442, 450
NLRB (National Labor Relations Board), 438, 442, 444, 446–47, 454
nonbenchmark jobs, 345, 347, 351–52
nondiscriminatory reason, 105, 107, 114
nonexempt employees, 324, 355–56
nonwork, 155, 416, 419, 475
NP (Nurse Practitioner), 350–54
Nurse Practitioner. See NP
nurses, 115, 140, 158, 184, 235, 353, 467

Occupational Safety and Health Administra-tion. See OSHA
OFCCP (Office of Federal Contract Compli-ance Programs), 102, 119, 121, 126, 355, 357
office, physical, 133, 492
Office of Federal Contract Compliance Pro-grams. See OFCCP
office work, 132, 155, 311
OJT, 247–48, 263
older workers, 114, 125, 185, 291, 317, 477
onboarding process, 253–54, 436
on-the-job training, 246–47, 252, 263
opportunities for data management and HRIS, 60, 64, 72
organizational analysis, 235–36, 238
organizational behavior, 82, 309, 434
organizational changes, 82–83, 321, 456
organizational citizenship behaviors, 185, 389–90, 484
organizational commitment, 98, 308, 314, 342
organizational context, 203, 232, 241–42, 244
organizational culture, 7, 11–12, 23, 53, 60, 81, 172, 179, 191, 235–36, 282
organizational decisions, 8, 12, 31, 100, 197, 258, 276, 385
organizational goals, 133–34, 142, 150–51, 236, 255, 276, 279–81, 329, 462
organizational justice theory, 339, 341, 363
organizational levels, 13, 34, 63, 134, 139, 150, 234, 262, 509, 514
organizational members, 62–63, 80, 190, 262, 436, 453
organizational outcomes, 16, 38–40, 152–53, 257–58, 384, 423
organizational performance, 36–38, 98, 258, 289, 323, 379, 384, 501
    higher, 38, 40, 400
organizational policies, 98, 236, 313, 432–33, 436–37, 454
organizational resources, 139, 237, 255
organizational strategy, 31, 37–38, 43, 45, 52, 272, 275, 279, 282, 398, 400
organizations
    civilian, 185–86
    surveyed, 73, 344, 351
organizations and employees, 133, 149, 313, 471
organization's culture, 38, 184, 208, 236, 390
organization's strategy, 31, 34–35, 38, 53, 198, 352, 354
orientation program, 252–53, 263
OSHA (Occupational Safety and Health Administration), 463–64, 467, 469–71, 486
overlearning, 242, 245, 263
overtime, 355–56, 435
overtime provisions, 355, 418

paid time off. See PTO
PAQ (Position Analysis Questionnaire), 142, 148

parents, 122, 309, 403–5, 418
pay-for-performance, 273, 372, 388–89
pay-for-performance expense factor, 394–95
pay-for-performance programs, 368–70, 372, 374–78, 383–95, 414
new, 391–93
pay-for-performance revenue factor, 394–95
PBGC (Pension Benefit Guaranty Corporation), 412, 424
PDA (Pregnancy Discrimination Act), 113–14, 421
Pension Benefit Guaranty Corporation. *See* PBGC
perceived fairness, 223, 275–76, 286, 341–42
performance, 37–39, 106–8, 125, 151–54, 204–7, 217–19, 243–45, 249–51, 255, 257–59, 263–64, 271–91, 293–96, 299, 316, 319, 369–79, 385–86, 388–93, 474–76
actual, 283–85, 289
employee's, 274, 280, 282–83, 286, 290, 296, 318
individual, 38, 289, 379, 382–83, 391
poor, 206, 274, 291, 296, 319
teacher, 377–78
performance appraisals, 212, 240, 270–72, 274–78, 280, 286, 289–93, 296–97
performance appraisal system, 275–76, 288, 290
performance assessments, 282, 285–86, 288, 290–92
performance bonuses, 298, 368–69
performance data, 55, 78, 274, 512
performance evaluation measure, 377, 386
performance evaluations, 125, 291, 377, 386, 495
performance feedback, 271–72, 286, 294
performance goals, 272, 374–75, 400
performance improvement plans, 273, 296–97, 319
Performance Improvement Plans. *See* PIP
performance information, 275, 277, 286, 293, 296
performance levels, 138, 271, 292, 316, 369, 386
performance management, 63, 72, 134, 149, 156, 178, 269–301, 319, 374, 378, 495
performance management systems, 78–79, 138, 271–73, 276–78, 285, 293, 296, 299, 375
performance measurement, 271, 275, 280, 287, 385
performance measures, 282, 385–87
performance metrics, 273–74, 280–81, 288–89
performance ratings, 48, 187, 273, 275–77, 283, 286, 289–93, 296, 299–302
performance reviews, 273–74, 278, 285–86, 289–91, 293–94, 296–97, 316, 330
performance review system, 12, 275, 288, 298

personal data, 72–75, 77, 84, 87, 223, 363, 472, 483, 503
personal information, 87, 181, 223, 419, 472
personality, 154, 213, 216–17, 222, 225, 227, 242–43, 295, 299, 505, 508
proactive, 214–15, 243
personality and cognitive ability, 216, 222
personality tests, 127, 198, 201, 207, 209–10, 213–14, 216, 224–26, 273
personality variables, 214–16
personal protective equipment. *See* PPE
person analysis data, 240–41
personnel management, 35–36, 134
personnel selection, 196, 198, 201, 216, 219, 222
personnel selection procedures, 203–4, 208, 217, 226
perspective, employee's, 140–41, 156
physical ability tests, 106, 221
physical design, 78, 89
physicians, 158, 383, 408, 410, 460–61, 474
piecework plans, 380, 391
PIP (Performance Improvement Plans), 273, 296–97, 319
plaintiff, 104–7, 109–10, 114, 117, 291
plan participants, 407–8, 410–11, 413
plans, 30, 79, 81, 296, 380–82, 384, 400–401, 405, 407–9, 411–15, 419, 421, 424–26, 514, 516
dental, 409–10
point-factor method, 344–45, 351, 363
policies, 34–35, 107–8, 113, 122, 338, 342–43, 353–55, 359–60, 404, 406, 417–19, 433–38, 475, 495–96, 509–10, 513
Position Analysis Questionnaire. *See* PAQ
power, processing, 13, 15
PPE (personal protective equipment), 465, 468–69
PPO (preferred provider organization), 408, 411, 425
practices, 5, 10–12, 22, 34–40, 137, 149–50, 245–47, 249–50, 312–13, 328–29, 338–39, 342–43, 347–49, 351–52, 355–56, 359–63, 387, 436, 494–98, 500–501
predictive analytics, 15–16, 44–45, 53, 66, 124–25, 299, 310
predictor of job performance, 209, 216, 219
predictors, 202, 205, 207–8, 216, 219, 273, 300–302, 311
preferred provider organization. *See* PPO
Pregnancy Discrimination Act. *See* PDA
Pregnant Workers Fairness Act (PWFA), 113
prescriptive analytics, 15–16, 44–45, 49, 53, 72
prima facie evidence, 105–7, 110, 126, 128
procedural justice, 341–42, 363
procedures, emergency, 245, 260
process, application, 186, 188, 200, 204, 221, 224
process stops, 447, 453
product knowledge, 144, 260, 263–64, 279, 299
product markets, 346–47, 363

professional organizations, 19, 140, 347, 421
profit-sharing programs, 383, 414, 424
programmers, 156, 225, 305
programs, 73, 98, 186–87, 233, 254–55, 262–64, 313, 318, 370, 373–74, 377–79, 383–84, 388–93, 399–403, 412, 414–18, 455–56, 475–76, 478–85, 487–88
protections for employees, 412, 496
PTO (paid time off), 111, 324–25, 337, 399–400, 406, 411, 417–18, 424, 496
PWFA (Pregnant Workers Fairness Act), 113

qualitative data, 47, 49, 51, 53
quantitative data, 47–49, 53, 86
questions, job-related, 210–12, 223

ranking method, 344, 363
rating errors, 212, 277, 290, 293
rating scales, 212–13, 283
ratio of rewards to contributions, 339–40
raw numbers, 193–94
realistic job preview. *See* RJP
realistic timelines, 81–82
reasonable accommodations, 111–13, 115–16, 119, 126, 186, 200–201
recruiters, 19, 42, 170, 173–74, 185, 187–89, 192, 219–20, 222
recruiting process, 172–74, 189
recruitment, 50, 54, 134, 136–38, 149, 156, 165–93, 196, 198–200, 494, 500
effective, 168, 172–73, 191, 338
recruitment activities, 166, 173, 186
recruitment funnel, 174–75, 178, 192
recruitment process, 78, 168–69, 172–73, 175–77, 180, 187, 189–91, 222, 264
recruitment sources, 176, 178, 182–83, 186
recruitment strategies, 170, 173, 176, 180
redesign, 61, 133, 154, 470
Registered Nurse. *See* RNs
regression analysis, 300, 302, 488, 490
relational database, 83–84, 89, 91–92
relationships, personal, 133, 261–62, 339, 496
reliability, 43, 196, 201–2, 205, 226, 277, 296, 385
reliability and validity, 43, 201, 205, 277, 385
religion, 97, 102, 104–6, 108, 111–12, 126, 168, 274, 387, 421
remote work, 14, 116, 132–33, 155–57, 311, 313, 336–37, 418–19, 474–75, 492–93, 495, 498, 503, 506
remote workers, 14, 109, 253, 277, 292, 326, 336–37, 469, 493, 513
request, 72, 79, 89–91, 116, 201, 404
required benefits, 398, 400–401, 406, 424
required information, 25, 437
research designs, 40, 49
research findings, 21–23, 39, 375
research scientists, 193–94
responsibilities, nonwork, 418, 475
results criteria, 257, 263

résumés, 50, 87, 127, 167, 181–82, 191, 196, 198, 219–20, 224, 226
   structured, 219–20
retaliation, 102–4, 319, 327, 470
retention rate, 66, 179, 306
retirement, 30, 114, 118, 185, 305, 316–18, 346, 400, 406, 412–15
retirement plans, 318, 405, 412, 414, 421, 435, 502
retirement programs, 339, 400–401, 412–14
rewarding performance, 369–95
rewards, 134, 137, 242–43, 338–42, 368–70, 372–79, 381–84, 386, 389–92, 398, 400, 414, 433, 435, 466
rewards and contributions, 339, 341
right-to-work laws, 443, 454
RJP (Realistic job preview), 175–76, 185, 192, 211, 313
RNs (Registered Nurse), 348–50, 352–53, 424

safety, 8, 14, 112, 265–66, 437, 439, 460, 462–72, 477, 482, 484–86, 510
safety and health, 463, 470–71, 486
safety and health issues, 469, 485
safety behavior, 154, 465, 467, 484
safety climate, 466–67, 484–87
safety issues, 444, 486
safety outcomes, 464–65, 484
safety practices, 256, 265
safety rules, 256, 465
safety training, 238, 257, 486
safety training program, 266–67
sales commission program, 381–82, 392
sales numbers, 263–64, 279
salespeople, 49, 227, 240–41, 263, 392
sales performance, 44, 262, 272, 381–82
sales performance incentive fund. See SPIFs
salespersons, 86, 381–82
sample, 68, 202–4, 217, 219, 225, 263, 265, 348, 350–51, 423, 427
satisfaction, 66, 153, 156, 314, 421–22, 426–28, 453, 460, 462, 516–17
scientific process, 23, 40, 45–47, 49–50, 52–53
selection criterion, 106–7, 121
selection decisions, 124–25, 204, 216, 238
   making, 203, 216
selection interviews, 63, 189–90, 210, 212, 226
selection methods, 198, 210–11, 223
selection procedures, 134, 138, 143, 148, 196, 198–99, 201–11, 214, 216–17, 220–21, 223–27, 229, 238
selection processes, 12, 77, 127, 137, 173–75, 190, 192, 195–229, 338, 508
selection ratio, 106, 206
selection tests, 107, 214
self-initiated expatriates, 503, 513–14
sentiment analysis, 285, 311
service providers, 65, 408–9
severance, 318, 321, 323, 326–30, 503
sex discrimination, 102–3, 108, 118, 123

sexual harassment, 108–9, 126, 184, 250, 437, 467
Sexual harassment (SH), 108–9, 126, 184, 238, 250, 437, 467
SH. See Sexual harassment
short-term disability insurance, 411–12, 424
SHRM (Society for Human Resource Management), 19–20, 22–23, 25, 42, 54, 66, 90, 127, 149, 158, 179, 193, 210, 227, 265, 331, 425, 469, 510, 515
sick time, 399, 417, 424, 463
situational interview, 209, 211–12, 226–27
situational judgment test. See SJTs
situational judgment tests, 206–8, 217–18, 226
SJTs (situational judgment test), 206–9, 217–18, 226, 229–30
skill sets, 64, 72, 89, 251
skill variety, 152–53
SMART goals, 281, 296–97, 375
SMEs (subject matter experts), 135, 140–45, 147–48, 157, 159–60, 202–3, 213, 217, 219, 237, 343–44
Social Security benefits, 402–3, 424
Social Security numbers, 72–74, 181, 223, 472
Society for Human Resource Management. See SHRM
sorting effects, 385, 387–88, 391
specialists, 17–19, 21, 23, 408, 410
SPIFs (sales performance incentive fund), 393
standard deviation, 55–56, 144–45, 157, 159, 266
standard-hour plans, 379–81, 391
steps organizations, 296, 304, 310
stereotypes, 98, 100, 110, 114, 126, 291, 511
straight piecework plan, 380, 391
strategic HRM, 28–57, 63
strategic human resource management, 30, 39, 53
strategic objectives, 29–30, 34–36, 39, 42, 45, 51–52, 72, 198, 343–44, 369–70, 400
strategy, 28–31, 33–35, 37–38, 52–53, 168–70, 173, 184, 186, 191–92, 203–4, 236–37, 276, 353, 376
strategy formulation, 30–32, 53
strategy implementation, 31, 34, 53
strategy type, 31, 33–34, 53
stress, 74, 308, 314, 462, 468, 471, 473–77, 480–81, 488, 504, 508
stressors, 315, 468, 473, 475, 486, 488
strike, 220, 281, 327, 422, 441–42, 444, 446, 449–52, 454
structure, 48–49, 83–84, 211–12, 327, 336–37, 339, 342–43, 346–48, 350–52, 354–55, 357–64, 368, 387
structured interviews, 202, 209–12, 214, 225–26
students, 9, 44, 82, 166–67, 180, 204, 222, 233, 243, 288, 377–78
subject matter experts. See SMEs
success

group's, 374, 383
   organizational, 5–6, 30, 133, 172, 486
   organization's, 30, 62, 188, 369, 383
succession management, 138, 170, 192
succession planning, 98, 134, 138, 170, 175, 177, 191–92
supervisor and coworkers, 144–46
support
   organizational, 507–8, 511–13
   social, 153, 155, 314, 504–5
   supervisor, 152–53, 474
support employees, 133, 155, 262, 313, 472, 476
support for training, 237, 242, 244
survivor benefits, 401, 403
SWOT analysis, 33, 53
systems, 10, 12, 38–39, 42, 61–63, 66, 72, 77–79, 87–88, 136–39, 146, 271–72, 274–79, 282–85, 287–90, 293–94, 296, 298, 312, 319
systems perspective, 38, 52–53, 62, 393
system users, 87–88

talent analysis, 171, 191–92
tasks, 120, 134–35, 139–48, 153, 157–59, 161, 236, 238–40, 242, 245, 248, 250, 313–14, 317, 380–81
tasks and KSAOs, 142–44, 148, 159
team rewards, 382, 392
technology, wearable, 304–5, 465, 483
tenure, 124, 325, 360, 365, 386, 414
tests, 47, 49, 51, 105–7, 128, 199–207, 209, 213, 215–16, 221, 224–30, 256, 265, 273, 428
   new, 228–29
tests and measures, 202–3, 228
test scores, 124, 202–4, 207, 252, 259–60, 265, 273, 378
tests of mechanical ability, 204, 216
time period, 193–94, 290, 351, 358
time pressure, 152–53, 220, 474
Title VII, 96, 102, 104–8, 110–13, 118, 120–21, 123, 184, 199, 357, 387
tools, 28–29, 50, 52, 61–62, 67, 69, 93, 122–24, 126, 167–68, 271–73, 276, 295–96, 298, 440
   decision-support, 44–45, 423
total compensation, 338–40, 358, 362–63, 380–81, 387, 394
total compensation expense factor, 394–95
total compensation revenue factor, 394–95
total employees, 365, 445
total worker health, 462, 485
traditional-care plans, 401, 407, 424
traditional-pay programs, 370, 391
trainees, 167, 233–34, 241–49, 255–56, 258, 263, 267
train employees, 38, 223, 235, 240, 245–46, 248
trainers, 237, 241, 245–46, 248, 256, 260
training, 6–8, 16, 47, 63, 65, 75–76, 109–10, 137–38, 140–41, 149–51, 170, 185–86, 219, 231–67, 293, 327, 456, 469–70, 481, 499–501

training and development, 8, 134, 137, 172, 261–62, 264

training approach, 240, 244, 249–50

training content, 29, 41, 239, 245, 248, 473

training context, 233, 242–43, 266

training data, 50, 258

training effectiveness, 232, 241–42, 245, 255–56, 258

training efforts, 235–37, 258

training employees, 62, 64, 76, 237, 244, 250, 260, 273, 462, 472, 476

training evaluation, 255, 258, 260, 263, 266

training function, 41, 235, 238, 255, 258

training goals, 232, 235, 241–43

training managers, 75, 112, 251, 293, 295, 399, 467

training material, 245–46, 248

training methods, 234, 240, 246–49, 251

training outcomes, 242, 256–61, 264, 266

training performance, 242–43, 245, 252

training programs, 16, 76, 101, 122, 232–45, 250, 255–58, 260, 263–64, 266, 399
    effective, 234–36, 238, 240, 242
    new, 10, 62, 456

training success, 235, 243

training supervisors, 103, 476, 484–85

training system, 242–43, 249

training transfer, 244, 263

training workers, 154, 232, 472

transfer, 237, 242–47, 250, 256–57, 262–63, 296, 404, 446, 495–98, 504

transparency, 17, 32, 50, 274, 276, 282, 357, 359–61, 363, 378, 386–87

Trident Health System, 424–25

turnover, 40, 45–46, 65–66, 180, 187, 304–11, 313–16, 329–32, 338, 461–62, 473, 476, 481
    actual, 306, 310–11

turnover intentions, 310, 426–28, 488–89, 511

turnover rates, 5, 44–45, 53, 55, 66, 192, 306–7, 310–11, 313, 315–16, 332

TV, 452

unconscious biases, 100–101, 122, 184, 275, 277

unconscious bias training, 100, 122

unemployment insurance, 323, 330, 401, 403

unethical behavior, 255, 382, 389–90, 499

unfair labor practices, 442, 454

Uniformed Services Employment and Reemployment Rights Act (USERRA), 119, 417

Uniform Guidelines on Employee Selection Procedures, 106–7, 138, 199, 202, 238

union activities, 435, 442–43, 446

unionization, 433, 436, 439–40, 445, 502

unionization rates, 492, 496–97

unionize, 432, 439, 454

union members, 440–43, 445

union membership, 439–40, 443–45, 497

union organizers, 445–46

unions, 320, 323, 410, 432–36, 439–49, 453–54, 481, 497, 502, 514

United States, 13–14, 16–17, 98, 117–19, 170–73, 183–85, 323, 377–78, 387–88, 400–402, 404, 432–33, 438–40, 442–45, 451–52, 461–64, 470–71, 494, 496–98, 502

units, organizational, 87, 139, 488

unpaid time, 111, 325

unstructured interviews, 209–11, 226–27

USERRA (Uniformed Services Employment and Reemployment Rights Act), 119, 417

users, 61, 68–69, 75, 79, 83–89, 91, 182, 260, 277, 287, 296

utility, 201, 206, 208, 223–24, 226–27, 444

vacation, 416–17, 424, 437, 444, 476

vacation time, unused, 321, 417

validity, 107, 196, 201–6, 208–14, 216–17, 219, 224, 226–28, 277, 291, 296

validity of selection procedures, 138, 199, 202, 223

values
    compa-ratio, 359–60, 365
    dollar, 201, 206, 478
    maximum, 353–54

variable pay, 51, 69

vendors, 41, 50, 63, 77, 79, 87, 89, 136, 197, 235, 248

vice president. See VP

victim, 100, 104, 108–10, 121, 322, 327

virtual reality (VR), 190, 248

vision, 31–35, 53, 401, 406, 424

voluntary benefits, 398, 400–401, 405–6, 411, 419–20, 422, 424

voluntary turnover, 45–47, 304–10, 313, 316, 322, 329–30

VP (vice president), 29–30, 66, 89–90, 158–59, 192, 227–28, 363

VR (virtual reality), 190, 248

VRB training, 248

weights, 185, 229–30, 289, 319, 344–45, 350–51

wellness programs, 117, 401, 406, 416, 462–63, 477–83, 485–88

WHO (World Health Organization), 14, 151, 399

women, 13, 15, 55–56, 97–99, 103–6, 108, 121–24, 128, 170, 184, 221, 291, 357, 361, 511
    trans, 55–56

work, 10–11, 13–14, 131–61, 183–88, 214–19, 261–62, 305–6, 308–9, 313–17, 336–41, 398–401, 403–6, 416–20, 439–42, 460–63, 466–70, 472–78, 480–86, 501–7, 511–13

work activities, 148, 472

work adjustment, 504–5, 514

work analysis, 135, 157, 159, 198

work arrangements, 155–56, 470

work context, 153, 314

work councils, 323, 444

work engagement, 98, 314, 330, 399, 475

work environment, 14, 30, 244, 399, 462, 466, 500, 506

worker health, 468, 470–71, 484, 486
    integrated Total, 460, 484, 486

workers, 14–16, 44, 120, 133–34, 138–42, 148, 151–57, 328–29, 336, 355–56, 361–62, 398–401, 403, 405–6, 417–19, 441, 443–45, 451–52, 462–80, 482–86
    average, 358, 362
    individual, 134, 139, 249, 466
    pregnant, 102, 113

worker safety, 151, 462, 464, 471, 485–86

worker stress, 472–73, 483, 485

work experience, 21, 138, 148, 156, 212, 219

work flow analysis, 139, 157–58

workflows, 29, 61

workforce, 97–98, 179, 183, 188, 197, 199, 305, 308–9, 314, 317, 403, 493, 497
    diverse, 97–100, 184, 251
    organization's, 29, 326, 436, 441, 473

workforce labor shortages, 170, 192

workforce labor surplus, 171, 192

workforce planning, 40, 165–66, 168–70, 174, 177, 187, 192

workforce planning and recruitment, 167–93

work group, 18, 239, 262, 282, 284

work hours, 325, 438, 480, 497

working conditions, 170, 310, 314, 434–35, 438–39, 442, 444, 448, 450, 454, 470

work performance, 152, 217, 219, 222, 467

workplace, 13–14, 96, 98, 116, 120, 122, 221, 272, 437–39, 454, 460, 462–64, 468–70, 483, 486
    inclusive, 97, 122

workplace accidents, 464, 466, 473, 488

workplace policies, 105, 475

workplace safety, 462, 464, 466–69, 472, 485

workplace safety and health, 462, 464, 469

workplace stress, 460, 462, 473–74

workplace wellness programs, 460, 462, 477, 479

work processes, 133–34, 137, 139, 462

work samples, 209, 217–19, 224, 226

work schedules, 111, 155, 305, 419, 474
    flexible, 155, 375, 418

work stoppages, 451–52

work stress, 462, 473, 475

work unit, 98, 136, 198

workweek, 14–15, 440, 475–76

World at Work report, 344, 351

World Health Organization (WHO), 14, 151, 399